Railway Machinery: A Treatise On The Mechanical Engineering Of Railways: Embracing The Principles And Construction Of Rolling And Fixed Plant

Daniel Kinnear Clark

RAILWAY MACHINERY:

A TREATISE ON THE

MECHANICAL ENGINEERING OF RAILWAYS:

EMBRACING

THE PRINCIPLES AND CONSTRUCTION

OF

ROLLING AND FIXED PLANT;

ILLUSTRATED BY

A SERIES OF PLATES ON A LARGE SCALE, AND BY NUMEROUS ENGRAVINGS ON WOOD.

BY

DANIEL KINNEAR CLARK, C.E.

VOLUME FIRST——TEXT.

BLACKIE AND SON:
GLASGOW, EDINBURGH, LONDON, AND NEW YORK.
MDCCCLV.

GLASGOW:
W. G. BLACKIE AND CO., PRINTERS,
VILLAFIELD.

TO

ROBERT STEPHENSON, Esq., M.P., C.E.,

𝔗𝔥𝔦𝔰 𝔚𝔬𝔯𝔨 𝔬𝔫 ℜ𝔞𝔦𝔩𝔴𝔞𝔶 𝔐𝔞𝔠𝔥𝔦𝔫𝔢𝔯𝔶

IS

DEDICATED BY ESPECIAL PERMISSION:

A TRIBUTE TO HIS EMINENT CLAIMS AS AN ENGINEER,

AND AS THE WORTHY REPRESENTATIVE OF HIS FATHER,

[THE PRACTICAL ORIGINATOR OF THE PRESENT SYSTEM OF RAILWAYS;]

AS A KIND FRIEND, AND AS AN ENGLISH GENTLEMAN,

BY HIS OBLIGED SERVANT,

THE AUTHOR.

INTRODUCTORY PREFACE.

This Work was commenced in 1849, shortly after the season of the Railway-mania, as a means, partly, of filling up the interval of leisure in which most engineers engaged in railway business participated, during the lull that succeeded; and, principally, because I was impressed with the great variety of the working plant in use upon railways, and the desirability of introducing fixed principles of design and construction. Making allowance for the various nature of the traffic to be conducted, and of the lines of railway upon which it had to be carried, I found that from the highest to the lowest class of working plant, there existed exceeding contrariety in the design and detail; and I was puzzled to account for differences, not merely circumstantial, but functional also; not merely diverse, but antagonistic also. I applied to the authorities in railway mechanical questions, for explanations, and found that, naturally enough, they held opinions of which many were as various and as contradictory as the works which were the productions of their talents.

Feeling dissatisfied with the state of public professional opinion, knowing that much remained undone towards the establishment of fixed and recognized principles, being naturally averse to speculation, as an excuse for indolence or inaptitude, where facts can be had for the labour of observing them, and being aware that positive experimental data and practical observation, constitute the only basis on which a sound practical system of Railway Machinery can be constructed,—I devoted myself unreservedly to the prosecution of Railway Mechanical Engineering as a study, and entered upon a rather extensive course of observation and research. I visited nearly all the great railway stations in this country, and acquired a knowledge of their respective working plants:—the principles of construction, the style of detail, and the system of working. I was much assisted in my inquiries by the officers of departments, and acquired valuable information from them, conversationally, as well as in the form of documents,—the results of their own experiments. I frequented, also, many of the private manufactories of

railway plant, where I saw and acquired much that was good and useful.

The Locomotive, naturally, was my chief object of study; and to the investigation of that admirable machine, its construction, its working, and its performance, my attention principally was directed. I may add that the peculiar union of beauties, mechanical and æsthetical, to be found in the locomotive:—the association of compact, concentrated, mechanical action, with freedom and elegance of form, and with the most graceful of movements,—made me conscious that there was not alone a theorem to investigate, or a problem to solve, but an object, besides, of enduring admiration. Whatever the absolute magnitude, whatever the form into which it was moulded by eccentricity of genius, quaintness of originality, depravity of taste, or lack of the mechanical faculty, the essence at least was there, embodied in the admired combination of the multitubular boiler, the blastpipe, and, in later times, the link-motion.

On the subject of the modern locomotive, we have had, in the English language, three regular works of importance:—Wood's *Treatise* (1838), Pambour's *Treatise* (1840), and, more recently, the locomotive division of a new edition of *Tredgold on the Steam-Engine* (1850). The work of Pambour has been, for many years, the chief authority on locomotives; and, though it bears evidence of a mind imbued with the spirit of philosophical research, it would require to be entirely re-written to meet the present necessities of engineers. Pambour, it is true, established some principles, which later experience has confirmed, but his conclusions, it must be owned, were, in some respects, drawn from but meagre premises,—in some cases necessarily so; and it may be judged how far they would require modification, to meet the practice of the present day, when experiments of a more recent date shall have been brought forward. Valves and valve-mechanism have been revolutionized since 1836, and they have yielded results of the action of steam very superior to those which were to be had twenty years since. The application of the indicator to the cylinder of the locomotive,

—an instrument unknown to Pambour, or, at all events, not employed by him,—has aided essentially in giving precision to our knowledge of the behaviour of steam in the cylinder, and of the internal sources of resistance in the locomotive. Mr. Gooch was the first, so far as I am aware, who applied the indicator to locomotives; and he is the only engineer who systematically employs that instrument, as a sort of stethoscope for testing their physiological condition. With regard to the other work referred to, the new edition of Tredgold, it is remarkable rather for the general excellence of its illustrations, than for the originality of its letter-press, the more useful portions of which had previously been published. On the other hand, there is Mr. Gooch's able and original exposition of the principles of the modern locomotive, published with the Report of the Gauge Commissioners on Railway Communication between London and Birmingham (1848); which, though not avowedly a regular discussion, contains, in conjunction with Mr. Gooch's investigation, previously published with the Gauge Commissioners' Report (1846), some important and suggestive results. Touching the latter Report, with its appendices, they contain, scattered over their pages, numerous fragments of useful experience, given in evidence by leading authorities of the day.

In France, several works upon the locomotive have appeared. The first important work was written by MM. Armengaud, and published in 1839, under the auspices of Government.[*] It contains fully-detailed drawings and descriptions of the locomotives of the day, and is indebted to Pambour's treatise for its doctrinal matter. Another work of especial merit, the joint production of MM. Flachat and Petiet, was published in 1840, and was the first in which the various practice of locomotive-makers was classified and compared.[†] It comprises numerous dissertations on the power of locomotives, founded, like those of its predecessor, on the investigations of Pambour. A third practical work requiring notice, was written by Felix Matthias, and published in 1844.[‡] In this work, the example of MM. Flachat and Petiet was ably followed out, the locomotive built by Sharp and Roberts being adopted as a model, with which the engines of other makers were compared, with reference partly to structural characteristics, though chiefly with regard to proportions. It contains, also, some discussions of the theory of the expansive action of steam, and is a model of the conscientious care and perspicuity with which French writers generally arrange their materials. The fourth work, of general importance, is a treatise on locomotives, by MM. Le Chatelier, Flachat, Petiet, and Polonceau, published in 1851, founded partly on the work written by two of these writers in 1840; but, in the main, a new work.[§] It is a work of very great merit, and carries forward the investigation of the locomotive, constructively and physiologically, through several important stages. That work was issued at the same time that the publication of this Work was commenced.

With respect to my own investigations, having had ample occasion to observe the diversity of opinions about the locomotive, I resolved to accept nothing for granted, but to see, observe, or subject to experiment, everything not susceptible of direct demonstration, so far as my opportunities would permit. It was thought, for example, that steam was electrically active in its movements, so nimble as to render special facilities for its admission and release in the engine unnecessary; and that, moreover, the question of the condensation of steam by exposure in unprotected cylinders, was frivolous, the distribution of the steam proceeding so rapidly, as to reduce the condensation to an immaterial quantity. It was thought, by some, that firebox-surface had heating virtues peculiar to itself, not possessed by tube-flues; and, by others, that the fire-grate could never be too large. Troublesome questions were raised as to the completeness of the combustion of fuel in the locomotive. The link-motion had been received and adopted with a respectful deference, due to its undeniable convenience, but doubtingly and vaguely as to its superiority to the gabs, for the expansive working of steam; leading, in consequence, to numerous schemes for superseding the link. But, the question of inside *versus* outside cylinders has, perhaps, more than any other, vexed the mechanical world, involving, as it no doubt does, the stability of the locomotive as a carriage, the stiffness of the frame, and, in some degree, the action of the steam in the cylinders.

To the solution of these and other questions I directed my attention. In this Work, an analysis of the unrivalled link-motion, brought out by Mr. Stephenson, is attempted: with respect to its action geometrically in regulating the motion of the slide-valve, and physiologically on the behaviour of the steam in the cylinder. It is shown, too, that much of the steam is condensed in the cylinders of locomotives, when not well protected; and the conditions of success in expansive-working having been educed, the conditions of perfect combustion, and the true relations of

---

[*] *L'Industrie des Chemins de Fer,* 1839.
[†] *Guide du Mechanicien Conducteur de Machines Locomotives,* 1840.
[‡] *Etudes sur les Machines Locomotives,* 1844.

[§] *Guide du Mechanicien Constructeur et Conducteur de Machines Locomotives,* 1851.

firebox and tubesurface, and of these to the grate-area, have been expiscated:—demonstrating the fallacies of combustion-chambers, unlimited firegrates, air-holes, midfeathers, densely packed flue-tubes; and showing that the modern locomotive-boiler was truly typified in the Rocket, by Mr. Stephenson, in 1829, and received its most perfect development from the same source, in the long-boiler of 1843. The position of the cylinders, inside or outside, has also been shown to be a matter of indifference, so far as the stability of the locomotive is necessarily affected by it; as also, the position of the driving wheels and axle, before or behind the firebox,—a question that has been much agitated by engineers, but has been rendered of less importance since the superior method of equilibration suggested by Mr. Stephenson, propounded by Mr. Fernihough, investigated by Nollau and others, and developed in this Work, has been brought within our knowledge. Already, counterweights adjusted on this principle have been applied with complete success, in the outside-cylinder locomotives of the Great North of Scotland Railway, designed by me:—these engines run with perfect steadiness at the highest speeds attainable on that line.

Other important subjects of inquiry relating to the internal economy of the locomotive,—the preparation and management of the fuel and the water, the production and application of the steam,—as well as to the constructive principles and details, have been treated at length. In the department of internal economy, the field is not yet fully explored, and much remains to be accomplished, in balancing the slide-valves, by removing the steam-pressure from the backs of them, superheating the steam, heating the feed-water, and other steps of improvement.

While on this subject, the important results recently obtained by Mr. C. William Siemens, from his Patent Regenerative Steam Engines, must be remarked. These engines consist of three cylinders, and the principle of their action is, that a given volume of steam is alternately expanded and compressed, and is, simultaneously with these changes, superheated and reduced to its normal state of saturation. Thus, the duty of the fuel consumed, is only to replace the heat directly absorbed in expansion behind the working pistons:—the latent heat of the steam, which constitutes by far the greater proportion of heat expended in ordinary steam engines, is preserved, and a corresponding economy is effected, amounting practically, it is said, to more than two-thirds of the fuel consumed by the best engines at present in use. Some years since, Mr. Siemens invented the Regenerative Condenser, by which the condensing water of condensing engines was heated to the boiling point, at the same time effecting a vacuum; by the employment of this heated water to supply the boiler, a notable saving of fuel was effected. The portion of water so used, was necessarily but a small part of the whole quantity heated; and the Regenerative Engine may be considered as an extension of the idea of returning the heat to the boiler, because not only a portion, but the entire latent heat of the steam is returned to the engine.

In the constructive department of Locomotives, engineers have been, and are, widely at variance, as any one may judge from the variety of stock now made; and, whilst it has obtained much consideration in this Work, there doubtless remains something more to be done, in order to establish a complete system of models and proportions, towards the attainment of uniformity, in the design and detail of locomotives for different classes of traffic. Probably, five distinct classes of locomotive would afford a variety sufficiently accommodating to suit the most varied traffic of railways: whereas, I suppose the varieties of locomotives in actual operation in this country and elsewhere, are more nearly five hundred in number. Every one cannot be right, and most of them must be wrong; and it would be for the best interests of railways if the proper authorities could be unanimous in the selection of a given number of classes to uniform patterns, to be adopted in future practice. It is doubtful if such an arrangement could be worked out, unless there were an entire amalgamation of railway interests, in the hands of government or otherwise. But it is extremely desirable, and is certainly practicable, under each of the several railway-managements: it has been acted on for many years by some railway companies, and the principle of uniformity is likely to be adopted and acted on by others.

Meantime, the chief questions of interest affecting the internal proportions and economy of the locomotive, are, it is hoped, sufficiently elucidated to enable any one to select for himself the style of locomotive appropriate for a particular duty, and to work out a correct and satisfactory design and system of detail. The rule of routine is, in all cases, subordinated to the rule of scientific experience. To economize calculation, and to promote convenience of reference, tables of data are freely introduced, in connection with the rules interspersed with the text.

Railway Carriages and Waggons have occupied much of my attention. The practice of carriage-builders is pervaded by a spirit of routine, which obstructs the course of improvement; and yet, in their essential details, carriages are referable to very simple mechanical combinations.

The same may be said, in some degree, of waggons. In all rolling stock, simplicity, lightness, and strength, should be combined; whereas, some waggon-builders, to insure mere brute strength, throw in materials with an entire disregard to the dead weight of the vehicles, unmindful of the aphorism, that, though a vehicle cannot be too strong, it may be too heavy.

The interesting subject of Train-Resistance is treated at considerable length in these pages. There is no doubt that the most complete experiments on that subject, are those of Mr. Daniel Gooch, detailed in the Report of the Gauge Commissioners, 1848. The results of these experiments are worked out and tabulated at length; in many of the experiments, the observed speeds were accelerated or retarded, and the necessity for applying a correction in such as deviated from uniformity, has hitherto proved an obstacle in the way of their useful employment. I have, however, deduced a simple rule for finding the equivalent resistance for a uniform speed, when the rate of acceleration or retardation is relatively small, by the application of which all the observations made by Mr. Gooch are brought to bear upon each other, and turned them to their proper use for the development of the laws of Train-Resistance.

On the department of Fixed or Stationary Plant, there is little to be said. Perhaps there is no one who has done more for the perfecting of stationary plant, than Mr. C. H. Wild, whose improvements are worthy of commendation, not simply as instalments of progress, but also because they have stimulated others in the path of improvement:—they have illustrated the value of a few mechanical principles judiciously applied.

Permanent Way has obtained some share of my attention, though it was not originally designed to notice that subject, as it appeared scarcely to fall within the province of mechanical engineering,—technically at least; at the same time, there is no doubt, Permanent Way, by which is meant the system of rails, chairs, and sleepers,—is of vital importance, and its excellence is closely associated with that of the rolling stock, in governing the efficiency of the locomotive. The Permanent Way is, in fact, the platform upon which the duties of the locomotive and the train are discharged; and it is hoped that the contribution on that subject may be useful as a historical memorandum, and as a reflex of the opinions of the leading authorities on the various forms of rails and their fixtures. It may be added, further, that the solution of the different questions of Permanent Way, would be occasionally facilitated by a more liberal infusion of simple mechanical principles into the discussion.

This Work has consumed four years in publication, and it seems desirable that a brief chronological notice of its contents should be given. The first part was issued in June, 1851; and the whole of the historical account of the Locomotive, the geometrical investigation of the movements of the Slide-valve, and of the Link-motion, the chapters on the properties of Steam, and on the Indicator-diagram, and the first portion of the investigation of the Behaviour of Steam in the cylinder of the locomotive, were published during the remaining months of 1851. During the year 1852, the investigation of the Behaviour of Steam in the cylinder was completed, Blast-pressure and its relations discussed, also the Relation of the Steam-pressures in the Cylinder, the Valve-chest, and the Boiler; and the Work of Steam in the cylinder. The investigation of the Locomotive-boiler, physiologically, as well as of the Locomotive as a Carriage, appeared during the later months of the year:—comprising the results of my researches on Combustion of Fuel, Draft, Priming from the boiler, and Heating Surface; and on the Conditions of Stability, Internal Disturbing Forces, Balancing the Locomotive, and the Relations of the Centre of Gravity. In 1853, the investigation of the Anatomy or Construction of the Locomotive in all its details, was published:—comprising many examples of modern design, and developing the principles of correct construction. In 1854, the discussion of the Carriage and Waggon Stock appeared; also the articles on Permanent Way, Resistance of Trains, Proportioning Locomotives, and their Performances. The remainder of the Work, on Fixed or Stationary Plant, appeared in the present year, 1855.

A separate paper, in two parts, on the Expansive-working of Steam in Locomotives, was read by me before the Institution of Mechanical Engineers, in April and June, 1852.[*] It embraced the principal results of my investigations on the action of steam in the cylinder, given more at large in this Work. Another paper, on the Principles of the Locomotive Boiler, was read before the Institution of Civil Engineers, in March, 1853,[†] and it embraced, similarly, the results of my investigation on Locomotive-boilers, in this Work.

I shall now take the liberty, at the risk of making repetitions, of indicating precisely in what respects I have, as I believe, advanced the theory and practice of the Locomotive.

First, as to the Behaviour of Steam in the cylinder,

---

* Published in the *Proceedings of the Institution of Mechanical Engineers*, 1852.
† Published in the *Minutes of Proceedings of the Institution of Civil Engineers*, vol. xii., 1852-53.

and the conditions of successful and economical working. By the evidence of the steam-indicator, it is proved, on analyzing the indicator-diagram, that condensation of steam actually takes place in cylinders imperfectly protected; and, though the condensation of steam under unfavourable circumstances, had previously been supposed to exist, its existence is now, for the first time, demonstrated by direct evidence, and an absolute value assigned to it. Moreover, an approximate law of the rate of condensation has been developed, according to which it increases rapidly with the proportion of the expansion, throwing much light upon the apparent inefficiency of expansive-working in many classes of engines, and suggesting at once the remedy,—the perfect protection of the cylinders, and, further, perhaps, an application of heat externally to the cylinder, or internally in superheating the steam. An original investigation of the link-motion is introduced; its action on the slide-valve is shown to be identical in character with that of a single eccentric; it is proved to be practically perfect in action; its efficiency for expansive-working is demonstrated, and the law of that efficiency is defined.

Second, as to the Generation of Steam in the boiler, and the conditions of its economical production. The combustion of coke in the firebox is shown to be practically complete, and the relations of the grate-area and the heating surface, as well as the proper distribution of the latter, according to certain laws, are demonstrated. The conditions for obtaining dry steam, free of priming, are defined; the action of the blast is analyzed, and it is shown that, with all usefully proportioned boilers, the blastpipe may, with due attention to detail, be made abundantly wide enough to afford a free exhaust, with abundance of draft for the generation of steam:—proving that the antagonism hitherto supposed to prevail, as a necessary evil, between the boiler and the engine, in their respective demands for a sufficiently narrow and a sufficiently wide blast-orifice, does not necessarily exist.

Third, as to the Locomotive as a Carriage, and the Conditions of Stability. It is shown, that by judicious arrangements of the wheels and axles, and by the application of suitable counterweights in the wheels, according to certain given conditions, all useful forms of locomotives may be adopted with success. It is proved that, with respect to stability, the position of the cylinders, fore or aft, inside or outside, is of no moment. The principles of the design and arrangement of the frame, are discussed and exemplified at length, and the conditions of strength, durability, and simplicity, are fully detailed.

Fourth, as to the Resistance of Engines and Trains.

The resistances are analyzed on simple natural principles, and the laws of resistance deduced, from Mr. Gooch's experiments. These were made upon a straight and level line of rails; and the resistances thus deduced, are compared with the results of my experiments under diverse circumstances, as to curves, state of the way, and gradients; these results, for straight and for curved lines, are also compared between themselves. From which, the influence of certain circumstances on train-resistance, hitherto unappreciated, is subjected to measurement.

Fifth, as to Rules for Proportioning Locomotives. A system of Rules and Tables of Data is supplied, for the calculation of Locomotive power, sufficiently comprehensive to meet the necessities of practice. The formulas of which those rules are the expression, will be found much more simple and easier of application than Pambour's; and to embrace a greater variety of conditions with accuracy. Indeed, for useful purposes, it must be so, as the locomotive of 1855 is a more complex machine than that of 1830, and the diversity of conditions must be recognized in the general problem. There are materials sufficient for the development of a general theory of the locomotive, but the problem of their conversion must be deferred till some future opportunity.

With respect to the Carrying Stock, there is little of importance requiring mention in this place. I may only allude to the method of simplifying the framing of narrow-gauge waggons, by the lateral extension of the underframe, to admit of the direct application of the body-framing to it, without limiting the width of the body; to the incidental advantage of longer axles, larger journals, and greater room about the axleboxes; and to the application of iron side-plates and a system of tie-rods and continuous draw-rods in conjunction with the usual wooden underframing of Carriages and Waggons, by which greater strength and lightness are gained. In the matter of axleboxes, I have set forth what I believe to be the true doctrine of bearing surface of journals, and insisted on the necessity of providing distinct and independent counter surfaces, to meet separately the vertical and the horizontal wear in axleboxes.

It is now my pleasing duty to acknowledge the liberal and varied assistance I have received from valued friends and patrons. First of all, I have to mention the uniform kindness and liberality of Mr. Robert Sinclair, General Manager of the Caledonian Railway, who gave me every facility, favoured me with valuable statistical information, and otherwise promoted my views, while I was, in 1850, engaged, under his sanction, in an extensive course of experiments with the locomotive-stock of that railway. To Mr. William Paton, Locomotive Superintendent of the Edinburgh and Glasgow Railway, I am also deeply indebted for the liberal assistance and free choice of all the stock of that line, accorded to me in conducting my experiments there. To Mr. Peter Robertson, lately Locomotive Superintendent of the Glasgow and South-Western Railway, I have also to express my acknowledgments. To Mr. Daniel Gooch, Locomotive Superintendent of the Great Western Railway, I am laid under weighty obligations for the peculiar and valuable materials which he placed at my service, consisting of the results of extensive observations of the performance of locomotives, and two valuable series of indicator-diagrams; also to Mr. John V. Gooch, Locomotive Superintendent of the Eastern Counties Railway, for valuable experimental results of performance of locomotives, and other information; to Mr. Trevethick, Locomotive Superintendent of the London and North-Western Railway, Northern Division, for many important particulars respecting the Crewe Engines. I have also to record the substantial benefit I have derived from Mr. Alexander Allan, Locomotive Superintendent of the Scottish Central Railway, upon whose stores of valuable practical experience I have freely and frequently drawn, and who has at all times honoured the drafts. To the gentlemen whose names stand in connection with the illustrative engravings, several of whom I have already mentioned, I have to return my sincere thanks for their indispensable aid in supplying to me the materials for the drawings; and the invariable readiness with which they placed the fullest details at my command, in virtue of which I have been enabled to elaborate the drawings of the plates, and of the illustrative wood-cuts, and greatly to enhance their value.

In the other departments, I have to record the attentions of many manufacturers of Rolling Stock, who have allowed me the free range of their portfolios, and have, otherwise, materially advanced my views. To Messrs. Brown, Marshall, & Co., Birmingham, in particular, I have been deeply indebted for the uniform readiness with which they have met my views, and for the valued practical information derived from them. To Mr. Henry H. Henson, also, I am much indebted for the facilities he has at various times afforded me, and for much valuable information. To my intimate friend, Mr. W. M. Buchanan, of Glasgow, a gentleman of high scientific and sound practical attainments, I am indebted for some valuable suggestions in the preparation of this book; I may mention, in particular, the method of the base-line and curve, for graphically representing the co-relations of variable quantities, and extremely useful in investigating such relations. To the other gentlemen by whom I have, in various ways, been favoured, I beg to make my grateful acknowledgments.

I have made it my duty, while writing this Work, invariably to acknowledge the sources of my information, and to mention the authority for every statement made, not otherwise supported by my own experience or information; and in all cases to ascribe honour to whom honour was due. If I have erred in any of these respects, I have erred unwittingly, and I shall most readily submit to be corrected. I feel that this declaration is due to myself, as there are not wanting those who would detract from the just claims of the author. I can truly say that I have composed and written this Work single-handed, and that it is the result of almost unintermitted personal labour and superintendence during the last six or seven years, when I have not been otherwise engrossed by imperative duties.

To the periodical press, both in this country and in America, I return my best thanks for the consideration with which they have been pleased to notice my Work; I trust that their favourable expectations may have been realized.

I shall only now allude to the distinguished name which appears in the dedication of this Work. It is a compliment to which I turn with pleasure, and with a consciousness of the honour conferred by Mr. Stephenson in sanctioning the dedication.

D. K. CLARK.

LONDON, *June*, 1855.

ERRATA.

PAGE 11. Second table, top of fourth last column, for *miles*, read *minutes*.

„ „ Column 1, line 14 from bottom, for *Hecate*, read *Hecla*.

„ „ „ 2, line 11 from bottom, for *cwt.*, read *per cent.*

„ 15. „ 2, line 43, for *engine*, read *engines*.

„ 16. „ 2, line 31, for 1842, read 1843.

„ 18. „ 2, line 27, for 1847, read 1846.

„ 20. „ 2, line 15, for *Murdoch*, read *Murray*.

„ 24. „ 1, line 18, for *Jackon*, read *Jackson*.

„ „ „ 2, line 3, for *Murdoch*, read *Murray*.

„ 25. „ 1, line 10, for 25, read 21.

„ 80. „ 2, fig. 56, for 48°, read 84°.

„ 31. „ 1, line 2 from bottom, for *connectives*, read *connections*.

„ 32. „ 1, line 21, for *motion*, read *nature*.

„ „ „ 2, lines 8, 11, 13 from bottom, for *D F*, read *D E.*

„ 33. „ 1, line 20, for *D F*, read *D E.*

„ 45. „ 1, line 3, for *motion curves*, read *motion-curve.*

„ 48. „ 1, line 15, for *Then*, read *They.*

„ 52. „ 2, line 16, for 1, read 3.

„ 56. „ 1, line 12, for *lead*, read *travel.*

PAGE 62. Column 2, line 15, for —, read +.

„ 79. „ 2, line 12, for : read +.

„ 90. „ 2, lines 32 and 38, for *steam*, read *water.*

„ 106. „ 2, line 16, for 6th, read 1st.

„ 109. „ 2, line 12, for —, read =.

„ 131. „ 16 of table, line 7 from bottom, for 68, read 86.

„ 140. „ 2, line 19, for *firebox*, read *smokebox.*

„ 162. „ 1, line 20, for 72, read 172.

„ 170. „ 2, line 13, for *of*, read *for.*

„ 184. „ 2, line 15, for *crank*, read *tank.*

„ 198. „ 2, line 11 from bottom, for ⅜ inch, read ⅝ inch.

„ 224. „ 2, line 19, for 48 *times* 200 *lbs.*, read 24 *times* 200 *lbs.* on each side; lines 20, 23, for 9600, read 4800; line 23. for 25,600 *lbs.*, read 12,800 *lbs.*; line 24, after *approaches*, insert *half.*

„ 234. „ 2, line 8 from bottom, for *r*, read *n.*

„ 295. „ line 1, for *No.* XCIV., read *No.* XCV.

„ 298. „ 2, line 18, for *No.* 94, read *No.* 95.

CONTENTS.

DIVISION I.—WHEELED OR ROLLING PLANT.

PART SECOND.

CARRIAGES AND WAGGONS.

SECTION I.—PHYSIOLOGICAL PRINCIPLES.

c

DIVISION II.—FIXED OR STATIONARY PLANT.

LIST OF WOOD ENGRAVINGS.

LIST OF RULES.

LIST OF TABLES.

RAILWAY MACHINERY.

DIVISION I.—WHEELED OR ROLLING PLANT.

PART FIRST.—LOCOMOTIVES.

HISTORICAL PROGRESS OF THE LOCOMOTIVE.

CHAPTER I.

GENERAL HISTORY OF THE LOCOMOTIVE, FROM 1784 TILL 1830.

IT would probably be deemed an inconsistency, in a work professedly on the mechanism of railways, were nothing to be told of the doings of the 'fathers' of locomotion. The fathers are numerous, and the family have been innumerable; yet the whole matter is substantially of recent origin—being virtually comprised within the limits of half a century. Locomotives, though a recent, are already an honourable progeny; and their importance has imparted some vigour to the rivalry with which antagonistic claims have been supported, which renders the subject one of considerable confusion, and, we may add, of considerable delicacy. Altogether, the story of the locomotive wears an artificial aspect of antiquity, conferred equally by the scantiness of the published materials which have been handed down to us by the preceding generation, and by the difficulty of estimating relative merits where all have been indisputably of essential service, and many have remained unobtrusive, and their labours comparatively forgotten or unknown.

It is well understood that railways owe their origin to the necessities of the trade in coal, and that they were in operation in England as early as 1650. The rails, originally of timber simply, were, in 1760, shod with iron, for durability. In 1767, rails, entirely of cast-iron, were introduced at Coalbrookdale; and in 1805, rails formed of wrought-iron bars were laid down in the neighbourhood of Newcastle.

Solid wrought-iron, though employed so early as 1805, in the manufacture of rails, obtained but little consideration till 1820, when rails were formed in fifteen-feet lengths, of the 'fish-belly' form, which ultimately became extensively patronized. Soon after the introduction of the fish-belly rail, it was rivalled by the parallel rail, of uniform depth throughout, and was finally superseded by it.

The introduction and improvement of the locomotive followed gradually upon the improvements that had been made in the permanent way. The first suggestion of the locomotive is due to the illustrious Watt. So early as 1759, he suggested, to the late Dr. Robison, the application of the power of the steam-engine to the propulsion of wheeled carriages. The locomotive-carriage is also described in his patent of 1784. Watt, however, relinquished the idea, as he had no feeling for high-pressure steam; and the improvement of the steam-engine by condensation appears wholly to have engaged the mechanical genius of his time. Watt's sympathies were naturally in favour of his pet condenser; and though, centuries before he was born, it had been agreed that 'nature abhors vacuums,' it is certain that Watt loved nothing better.

Watt's friend and assistant, William Murdoch, took up the idea of the steam-carriage broached by his patron, and constructed a non-condensing steam locomotive of lilliputian dimensions, in the year 1784, the date of Watt's second patent. This locomotive, placed on three wheels, is shown in

Fig. 1.—Scale, One-sixth.

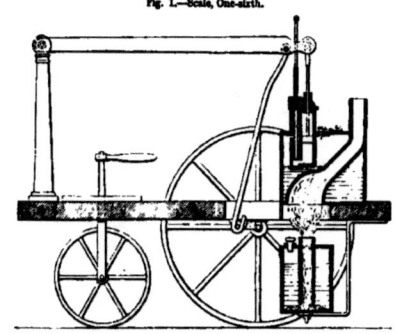

Murdoch's Locomotive, 1784.—Cylinder, ⅜ by 2 inches; Wheel, 9½ inches.

Fig. 1. The boiler is of copper; the flue passes obliquely through it, and is heated by a spirit lamp. The cylinder is ¼ inch diameter, and has 2 inches stroke; it is fixed on the top of the boiler, and the piston-rod is connected to one end of a vibrating beam, to which also is attached the connecting-rod for working the crank of the driving axle. The slide-valve is double-cylindrical, and worked directly by the beam, which strikes the shoulders of the valve-spindle; and the exhaust steam passes through the hollow of the spindle, going out near the top. One of the wheels only is fixed on the crank-axle, and a single wheel is placed in front, working in a swivel frame, to allow the carriage to run in a small circle. The driving-wheels are 9¼ inches diameter, and the leading-wheel 4¼ inches. Notwithstanding these diminutive dimensions, this little gentleman managed to outrun the inventor, on one occasion. 'One night, after returning from his duties at the mine,' in Redruth, Cornwall, where he resided for some time, in charge of the mining engines, 'he wished to put to the test the power of his engine; and, as railroads were then unknown, he had recourse to the walk leading to the church, situated about a mile from the town. This was rather narrow, but kept rolled like a garden-walk, and bounded on each side by high hedges. The night was dark, and he alone sallied out with his engine, lighted the fire or lamp under the boiler, and off started the locomotive, with the inventor in full chase after it. Shortly after, he heard distant, despair-like shouting; it was too dark to perceive objects, but he soon found that the cries for assistance proceeded from the worthy pastor, who, going into town on business, was met on this lonely road by the fiery monster, whom he subsequently declared he took to be the Evil One *in propria persona.*'[*]

It is to Richard Trevethick that the world is indebted for the introduction of the steam-engine on railways, acting solely by the expansive force of steam. In 1802, he, in conjunction with Vivian, patented the application of the non-condensing engine to propel carriages on railroads. It was obvious that lightness and portability were indispensable to any successful attempt at locomotion, and he, like Murdoch, at once adopted the high-pressure principle. The first steam-carriage made by Trevethick was tried on common roads. It resembled in form the ordinary stage coaches, having two small wheels in front, by which it was guided, and two larger ones behind, by which it was driven. It had but one cylinder, placed horizontal, and this, together with the boiler and fire, which were all enclosed in a cover, was situated low down in the rear of the hind axle. The motion of the piston was transmitted to a separate crank-axle, from which, through the medium of spur-gear, the axle of the driving-wheel derived its motion. The wheel-axle was mounted with a fly, to equalize the motion, and to offer brake surface down hill. The steam-cocks were worked off the crank-axle, as were also the force-pump, and the bellows for quickening combustion. In this engine may be recognized the horizontal inside cylinder, and the separate crank-axle, concerning which some discussion has arisen in later times.

In 1804, Mr. Trevethick patented and made a second engine in South Wales, to run upon the Merthyr-Tydvil Railway. It had a cylindrical boiler with flat ends, since called by his name. The furnace and flue were inside the boiler, the latter recurving and leaving the boiler at the fire-door end; the cylinder was 8 inches diameter, had 4½ feet stroke, and was immersed upright in the boiler. The waste steam was thrown into the chimney. The wheels were plain, and found to have ample adhesion. The engine drew 10 tons of bar iron, besides the waggons, at 5 miles per hour, for a distance of 9 miles, carrying with it sufficient water and fuel for the trip. The variable nature of the adhesion between the driving-wheels and the rails, which, no doubt, occasionally manifested itself, led Mr. Trevethick to suggest auxiliary means of propulsion. Following up the presumed necessity, Mr. Blenkinsop, of Middleton Colliery, Leeds, patented, in 1811, the application of a rack laid alongside the railway, which was geared into by suitable spur-wheels driven by the engine, and which would thereby effectually insure a regular progressive motion. This patent was at work for some years, and in the engine adapted with the gearing, two cylinders were employed, let into the boiler vertically, working, by suitable cross-heads and connecting-rods, separate shafts under the boiler. The cranks of the one shaft moved at right angles with those of the other. Each shaft carried a spur-wheel, which geared with an intermediate wheel on the shaft of the driving spur-wheel. The engine ran on four plain flanged wheels, unconnected with the propelling apparatus. By the use of this rack-rail, the engine ascended gradients inaccessible to Trevethick's engine.

The weight of Blenkinsop's engine was said to be five tons, its evaporation 8 cubic feet of water per hour, with a consumption of 75 lbs. of coal; it conveyed 94 tons on a level, at 3¼ miles per hour, or 15 tons up a gradient of 1 in 15; maximum speed, 10 miles per hour.

The rack-rail was not discontinued until, by an improved distribution of the load on the wheels, it was proved by Blackett that the simple adhesion was sufficient. The most important feature of originality in Blenkinsop's engine is the employment of two cylinders, working alternately into the same shaft. Certainty of starting, and uniformity of motion, were thereby obtained, and to this day equivalent means for that purpose are employed.

The next in the list of devices for procuring a fulcrum is a scheme—patented, of course—by the brothers Chapman, in the end of 1812. These worthies applied a chain extending the entire length of the rails, coiled once round a grooved wheel carried and driven by the locomotive. The wheel being turned, it found its way along the chain, which was firmly fixed at the extremities, and progressive motion was so obtained. An engine of this kind was tried on the Hetton Railway, near Newcastle.

But invention was busy with locomotives. Brunton, of Butterly Works, if he could not produce a better thing, at least brought out something original in 1813. He applied automaton legs to the hinder part of the engine, which were worked by a species of parallel motion, off the cylinders, of which there was a pair, placed horizontally on the end of the boiler. These legs, 'imitations of nature,' were to be the means of propulsion.

The current of invention in search of an independent fulcrum was arrested by the good sense and perseverance of Mr. Blackett, of the Wylam Railway. He had, about

---

[*] From a Biographical Notice of William Murdoch, by Mr. Buckle of Soho.—*Proceedings of the Institute of Mechanical Engineers.* Oct. 1850.

this time, considerably improved his engines, and, by experiments, had ascertained the amount of adhesion of wheels on the rails. He found that the weight of the engine, duly distributed on the wheels, was sufficient to drag, with ordinary certainty, a requisite number of loaded waggons. The sufficiency of the superficial adhesion or bite having been established, general attention was re-directed to the means of applying the steam power to the wheels. Double-cylinder engines were now exclusively employed, as the cylinders, working alternately, afforded, in all positions of the engine, available power for starting, and for maintaining a uniform motion.

Early in 1814, an engine was constructed at Killingworth Colliery by George Stephenson, and, in the middle of the year, was set to work. This engine had a cylindrical boiler, 34 inches diameter and 8 feet long, with an internal flue-tube, 20 inches diameter, passing through the boiler. It had two vertical cylinders, let into the boiler, 8 inches diameter and 2 feet stroke, working, with cross-heads and connecting-rods, the propelling gear. The peculiarity of this engine was the mode of turning the wheels—a modification of Blenkinsop's gear. The engine was carried on four wheels of equal diameter; the two axles were mounted each with a 24-inch spur-wheel; three 12-inch spur-wheels were disposed on the horizontal centre line of the axles,

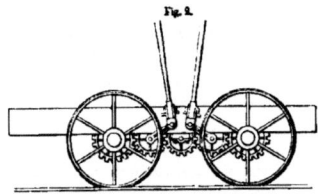

Fig. 2.

Stephenson's Locomotive—Driving Gear, 1814.

gearing into each other, and into those on the axles, forming a series of five working together. The connecting-rods were attached to cranks on the axles of the outer 12-inch wheels, from which the power was transmitted to the driving-wheels. The middle wheel operated as a regulator in preserving the two cranks at right angles, and in equalizing the propelling power. It is obvious, too, that the cranks made two revolutions for one of the wheels. This engine was tried on an incline of 1 in 450; it dragged 8 loaded carriages, about 30 tons gross weight, at 4 miles per hour; and continued regularly at work. The spur-wheel motion caused considerable noise and jarring, which increased with the wear. To remedy this, Mr. Stephenson, in conjunction with Mr. Dodds, patented, in 1815, a mode of driving the wheels directly by crank-pins, fixed in the arms of the wheels, one pair of wheels to each cylinder; the crank-pins were caused to work square with each other, by means of an endless chain, working round wheels fitted with cogs to receive the links. It had a third pair of wheels, between the two extreme pairs, which also was moved by the chain. This contrivance superseded the use of spur-gear, and worked well.

Expedients for stimulating the draught of the furnaces were not wanting, great height of chimney being of course

inadmissible. Trevethick employed bellows for that purpose, in his first engine; in his second, made in 1804, he turned the waste steam into the chimney. Many years afterwards, in 1815, he proposed two modes of aiding the draught mechanically; first, by fanners, which were to operate by blowing the fire; secondly, by a screw or set of vanes placed in the flue. The first proposal of fanners employed in this way is, however, due to the Chapmans, who embraced it in their patent of 1812. None of these modes of obtaining artificial draught appear to have been at all generally employed. The truth is, that until 1825 nothing but slow speeds were ever contemplated by those engaged in the manufacture of engines; and the unassisted evaporative power of the boiler of the old engines was, in general, competent to the production of at least as much steam as could do the work of seven or eight horses. This was, of itself, considered an achievement; and it seems to have contented mechanical men interested with railways, for a quarter of a century.

The locomotive remained, for many years, very much in the condition to which it was brought by Stephenson in 1814. In matters of detail, outside coupling-rods were substituted by Stephenson for chains, to connect the driving-wheels on the engines of the Killingworth Railway; and steel bearing-springs were interposed over the axle-boxes. Mr. Nicholas Wood, also, added wrought-iron tyres to the driving-wheels. On the Wylam Railway, the engines employed in 1825 were, in consequence of their extreme weight, placed on eight wheels, disposed in two groups of four, each of which was arranged under a distinct frame or 'bogie.' The total load being so placed on two frames connected by swivelling joints to the principal frame, not only was the load widely distributed upon the rails, the wheels were also enabled, notwithstanding the extended base which they presented, to pass round sharp curves with freedom. This was the first application of the bogie-frame system, though it had been proposed long previously by the Chapmans, who described it in their patent of 1812. In 1827, Mr. Timothy Hackworth, manager of the Stockton and Darlington Railway, applied the blast-pipe in the chimney to an engine, the Royal George, constructed for that line, and re-arranged by him. This is said to have been the first efficient application of the blast-pipe as a promoter of combustion. This engine, designed for coal traffic, had 6 wheels, of 4 feet diameter, four of them being mounted with bearing-springs, and was the earliest of the six-coupled wheel class. The cylinders, 11 inches by 20 inches stroke, were placed vertically over the leading-wheels, and fixed to the smoke-box. The boiler was cylindrical, 4 feet 4 inches in diameter, and 13 feet long. It contained an internal tube, which carried the fire-grate, bent double into a horse-shoe form, 26 and 18 inches diameter, at the furnace and chimney ends respectively. Thus the chimney, a mere continuation of the flue, was situated at the furnace end of the boiler; and the return of the tube yielded twice the ordinary heating surface of the locomotives of this period; as in these the tube passed but once through the boiler. In this locomotive, a cistern was attached to the smoke-box, into which the waste steam could be turned, for heating the feed-water; here also the short-stroke pump was first employed, being driven by the eccentrics, and spring balances for the safety-valves, in place of weights. This engine was capable of conveying 24 waggons of coal—100 tons gross weight—at a regular speed of 5 miles per hour, and it frequently travelled with its load at 9 miles per hour. The useful loads were, on this line, conveyed in the descending direction, from the pits. In ascending, on the return trips, the locomotive usually conveyed 30 empty waggons, each 30 cwt., making a total load of 45 tons, on gradients varying from 1 in 100 to 1 in 500.*

The general arrangement of the old Killingworth locomotive, as it existed previously to 1829, is represented by the annexed figure. The boiler was of wrought iron, cylindrical,

Fig. 8.—Scale, One forty-eighth.

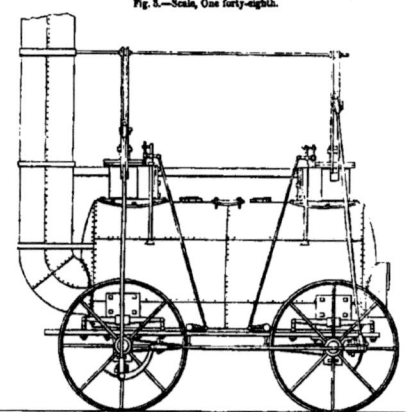

Killingworth Railway Locomotive, previous to 1829.

with flat round ends, 9 feet long, 4 feet diameter; a cylindrical tube, 22 inches diameter, passed through the boiler, two inches clear of the bottom. The fire-grate was placed in one end of the tube, 4 feet long. The other end terminated in the chimney. The boiler rested on a timber frame, with springs interposed. The wheels were 4 feet diameter, coupled. There were two cylinders let vertically into the boiler, each working its own pair of wheels, alternately with the other. The exhaust steam was thrown into the chimney, in compliance with a suggestion of the elder Stephenson's, previous to 1825, though the blast was not considered to be an essential feature. Indeed, Mr. Wood, writing in 1825, regarded the blast as 'an accidental circumstance,' and though it promoted evaporation, it wasted fuel, and he superseded it by an enlargement of the flue-tubes, and consequently of their heating surface. The engine was provided with a tender, carrying fuel and water. The maximum performance of this engine, weighing 6½ tons, and with tender, fuel, and water, 10 tons, was equal to 50 tons gross load, including engine and tender, on a level, at 6 miles per hour; the evaporation being 15 cubic feet of water per hour. This was the average performance of the engines on several other railways about the same time, as we find from the report of Messrs. Walker

and Rastrick to the Liverpool and Manchester Railway Company, published in 1829, that an engine weighing, with tender, 10½ tons, was capable of conveying a load of 19½ tons, or, including engine and tender, 30 tons, at 10 miles per hour on a level, equivalent to 300 tons conveyed 1 mile per hour, which is also the duty of the Killingworth engine, as 50 × 6 = 300 tons, 1 mile per hour.†

The opening of the Stockton and Darlington, in 1825, as a passenger railway, and the improvements effected in the locomotives by Mr. Hackworth, created a taste for high speeds. This feeling rendered it imperative to have light, solid, and powerful engines. So much did the feeling prevail about the time of the opening of the Liverpool and Manchester Railway, in 1829, that the directors, for want of locomotives possessed of the necessary qualities, seriously contemplated the employment of stationary engines to work the traffic of their 30-mile railway.

It was reserved for our French neighbours to work out the problem. The introduction into France of the imperfect locomotive of the time—imperfect so far as high speeds were desirable—led to the solution of the question of light and powerful engines. 'The first locomotives, two in number, that were sent to France,' says M. Lobet, 'were made by George Stephenson, and arrived there in 1829, for the Lyons and St. Etienne Railway, of which M. Seguin was the engineer. On trial, their mean velocity did not exceed 4 miles per hour. To increase the efficiency of his engines, M. Seguin felt the necessity of increasing their evaporating power, and resolved to apply a scheme of his own to the engines he was about to construct (on the model of Stephenson's)—a scheme which he had cherished since 1827 (and had patented in February 1828), and which consisted in multiplying the heating surface, by subdividing the current of hot air into streamlets, which flowed through a series of tubes immersed in the water of the boiler. The method of the tubes increased amazingly the heating surface, and with it the evaporative power, and it is precisely to this evaporation that we are indebted for speeds which before were thought impossible. But another difficulty presented itself; the height of the chimney, necessarily limited, was incompetent to maintain the draft, the resistance of which was so much increased by the increase of surface in the new boiler. M. Seguin, therefore, added a circular fan for promoting the draft, and it was partially successful. M. Pelletan, however, completed the solution of the problem, by suggesting the steam jet in the chimney; and, as usual, England appropriated the invention of the two French engineers.'‡

The suggestion and application of the subdivided tube surface is, by common consent, ascribed to M. Seguin. The steam-jet in the chimney, though no doubt invented independently by Pelletan, had been, as we have seen, previously applied by Stephenson and Hackworth. It was, however, at the same time, but partially employed in this country, as we may infer from the absence of the jet in the sample engines sent to France. The method of the multi-tubular flue and the steam-jet are parts of one system; they co-exist as naturally as the condenser and air-pump of Watt's engine. The locomotive was not ripe for the application of the blast pipe; the large and vacuous cavity of the flue-tube, while it presented a very restricted area of heating surface, permitted great freedom of circulation, and the greater length and surface of Hackworth's doubled flue, enabled him, on this account probably, to employ the blast with greater success than had been done by his predecessors. Again, the tubes of M. Seguin, while they increased the heating surface, increased the friction surface of the flue way simultaneously; and here it was that the aid of mechanical expedients became more than ever necessary, to uphold the requisite rate of combustion. The method of the steam blast, therefore, of spontaneous invention at home, was in France the child of necessity. The tubes formed the link between the fire-box and the jet, and thus the problem of producing a light and powerful locomotive was solved.

It was determined by the directors of the Liverpool and Manchester Railway, irrespective of what had been doing in France, of which probably they were unaware, to offer a premium for the best locomotive engine, which should draw, on a level plane, three times its own weight, at 10 miles per hour. The trial was to take place on a 1¾ mile stage, with one-eighth of a mile extra at each end for starting and stopping, and to consist of twenty double trips. The engine was to consume its own smoke, the whole weight of the engine and boiler to be carried upon springs, and should the weight have exceeded 4½ tons, the engine was to have six wheels. From this time, 1829, may be dated the era of modern locomotives in England.

Three locomotives were put in for competition, viz. :—

Engine.	Maker.
Rocket	Robert Stephenson, of Newcastle.
Sanspareil	Timothy Hackworth, of Shildon.
Novelty	Braithwaite and Ericson, of London.

The Rocket was the first locomotive made in England

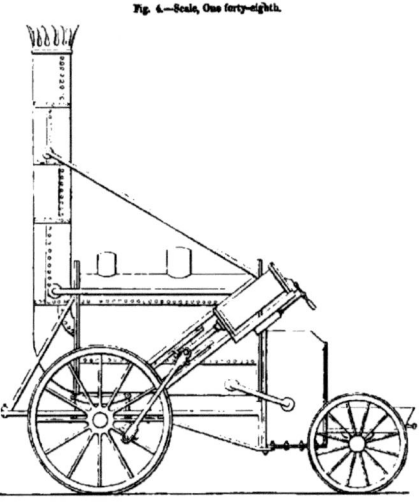

Fig. 4.—Scale, One forty-eighth.

R. Stephenson's Locomotive.—The Rocket, 1829.

with multitubular flues. The tubes were adopted at the suggestion of Mr. Booth of the Liverpool and Manchester

Railway, to whom the merit of their invention in this country is commonly ascribed. The boiler was cylindrical, with flat ends, 6 feet long, and 3 feet 4 inches diameter; the fire-box, in the rear of the engine, was 2 feet long, 3 feet broad, and 3 feet deep, inside measure, and was surrounded on the two sides, the front, and the top, by an external case, affording a 3 inch water-space. The flue consisted

Fig. 5.

Rocket.—Section of Boiler.

of 25 tubes, 3 inches diameter; the cylinders, two in number, placed obliquely next the fire-box, and working the fore-wheels, were 8 by 16½ inches stroke; driving-wheels 4 feet 8½ inches diameter; the exhaust pipes were originally arranged to deliver the steam directly from the cylinders into the atmosphere, under the impression, no doubt, that the abundance of heating surface, unaided, would have commanded an abundance of steam. After some preliminary trials, however, previous to the commencement of the competition, during which the superior evaporating power of the Sanspareil, with a sharp blast from the exhaust directed upwards into its chimney, became apparent, it was resolved to discharge the exhaust steam of the Rocket into the chimney; and on the eve of the first day of the trial, the exhaust pipes were diverted into the chimney with an upward termination. The fire-grate surface was 6 feet; fire-box surface, 20 feet; tube surface, 117·75 feet.

The Sanspareil had a cylindrical boiler 4 feet 2 inches diameter, and 6 feet long. The grate and chimney were

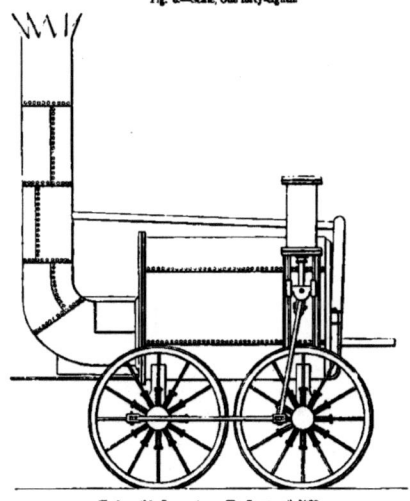

Fig. 6.—Scale, One forty-eighth.

Hackworth's Locomotive.—The Sanspareil, 1829.

situated at one end of the boiler, and connected by a single flue-tube, with one bend, 24 inches diameter at the grate, and 15 inches at the chimney. The grate was 5 feet long by 2 feet broad, and was overhung by the boiler, by the addition of semicircular water-chambers. The steam was thrown into the chimney to stimulate the draft, by means of the blast pipe already applied to the Royal George. The violence of the draft so produced, became very evident during the experiments. The two cylinders, 7 by 18 inches stroke,

Fig. 7.

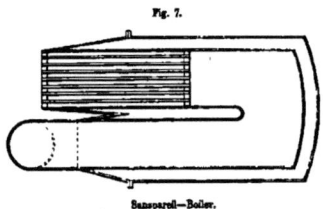

Sanspareil—Boiler.

were placed vertically over one pair of wheels, and the four wheels were 4½ feet diameter, coupled. The grate surface was 10 feet; fire-box surface, 15·7 feet; and tube surface, 74·6 feet.

The Novelty was peculiarly constructed; the fire-box was, like that of the Rocket, placed at one end, enveloped in the

Fig. 8.—Scale, One forty-eighth.

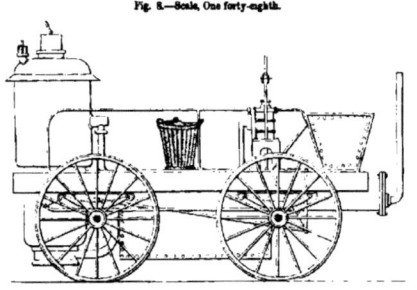

Braithwaite's Locomotive.—Novelty, 1829.

water of the boiler; it was 18 inches diameter, close at the bottom, and fed through an air-tight hopper. The flue was a single tube, 4 inches diameter at the fire-box, 3 inches at

Fig. 9.

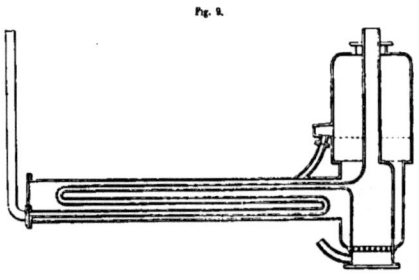

Novelty.—Boiler.

the chimney, and 36 feet long, traversing the boiler three times. The fire was urged by bellows, situated near the chimney. The engine had but one cylinder, 6 by 12 inches stroke, placed vertically, and driving one pair of wheels 4½

feet diameter, by means of bell-cranks; the steam was exhausted directly into the atmosphere. Grate surface, 1·8 feet; fire-box surface, 9·5 feet; tube surface, 33 feet.

The respective weights of the three engines and their loads in working order were as follows:—

	tons	cwt	qrs	lbs.
Rocket—Engine weight	4	5	0	0
Tender ... 3 4 0 2				
Two loaded carriages.... 9 10 3 26				
Drawn weight........	12	15	0	0
Total weight of Train..............	17	0	0	0
Sanspareil—Engine weight	4	15	2	0
Tender ... 3 6 3 0				
Three loaded carriages...10 19 3 0				
Drawn weight........	14	6	2	0
Total weight of Train..............	19	2	0	0
Novelty—Engine weight, exclusive of tank	3	1	0	0
Tank, loaded............... 0 16 0 14				
Two loaded carriages..... 6 17 0 0				
Drawn weight........	7	13	0	14
Total weight of Train..............	10	14	0	14

The drawn weights attached to the Rocket and the Sanspareil were the regulation loads, three times the weight of the engine. As the Novelty had no tender, the same carrying-weight was assigned to it, in proportion to the exclusive weight of the engine, that existed in the experiment with the Rocket.

The Rocket was the only engine that accomplished the stipulated distance of 70 miles. Its average speed on the stage was 13·8 miles per hour; the greatest velocity, in any trip, was 29 miles per hour; the consumption of coke per mile, per ton of total load of train, was 0·91 lbs., and per cubic foot of water evaporated, 11·7 lbs.; the evaporation, 18·24 cubic feet of water per hour.

The Sanspareil ran a distance of 27·5 miles; average speed, 14 miles; greatest speed, 22·6 miles; consumption of coke per mile, per ton of total load, 2·41 lbs., and per foot of water evaporated, 28·8 lbs.; evaporation, 24 feet of water per hour.

The Novelty, by a series of unfortunate accidents, failed twice in the midst of the experiments. The engine, with its load, traversed the stage at 15 miles per hour.

After these trials, the orifice of the exhaust tube of the Rocket was contracted, to sharpen the blast, and promote the evaporation. On trial, the engine evaporated 29·6 feet of water, and conveyed an average load of 40 tons at 13·3 miles per hour, with steam at 50 lbs. No notes of the consumption of fuel were taken.

The Novelty also underwent considerable alterations; amongst others, a separate cylinder was applied for working the bellows. At a subsequent trial on the experimental stage, the engine conveyed a total average load, its own weight included, of 28·5 tons, at an average speed, on the stage, of 8 miles per hour. The coke consumed per hour was 84 lbs., during 6¼ hours, the bellows being at work during the whole of that time. The consumption was, therefore, equivalent to 0·36 lbs. per ton per mile.

The advantage of extended flue surface having been established, the boiler of one of the old Killingworth engines was altered by Mr. Nicholas Wood, and fitted with tubular flues to the following dimensions:—boiler, 9 feet 2 inches long, and 4 feet in diameter; elliptical tube, within which the fire was placed, 28 by 24 inches high, and 4 feet 8 inches long; grate surface, 10·9 feet; fire-box surface, 22·56 feet; forty-three tubes, 2 inches diameter, and 4½ feet long; 101·5 feet of surface; sectional area of tubes, 135 inches. With a total load of 70·5 tons, including engine and tender, the speed attained on a level was 9 miles; the evaporation was 47·8 feet of water per hour, with a consumption of 14·7 lbs. of coal per foot of water. By another experiment, with a total load of 40 tons, at a speed of 9 miles, the evaporation was 40 feet of water per hour, with 13·2 lbs. of coal per foot. In both of these experiments, the steam was blowing off at the valve.

Experiments were made by Mr. Stephenson on two new engines constructed on the principles of the Rocket, namely, the Phœnix and the Arrow, with a much more extended flue surface. These engines had, respectively, 90 and 92 tubes, 2 inches diameter; their boilers were 3 feet diameter, and, respectively, 6½ and 6 feet long; grate surface of both, 6 feet; fire-box surface, 20 feet; tube surfaces, 306·0 and 283·8 feet respectively.* The average results of the trials are placed in the following Table, in which the experiments previously detailed are reduced, and classified for comparison:—

TABLE—SHOWING THE PROPORTIONS, EVAPORATIONS, AND PERFORMANCES, OF DIFFERENT ENGINES, 1829-30.

Name of Engine.	Surfaces.				Consumption.			Average speed of Train per hour.	Weights.	
	Fire-grate.	Fire-box.	Tubes.	Total sectional area of Tubes.	Water per hour.	Coke per foot of water.	Coke per ton per mile.		Total load of Train.	Engine and Tender.
	Feet.	Feet.	Feet.	Inches.	Cubic Feet.	Lbs. coal.	Lbs. coal.	Miles.	Tons.	Tons.
Killingworth (old)	7·0	11·5	29·75	380·0	16·0	18·34	0·98	6·0	50·0	10·0
Rocket	6·0	20·0	117·8	136·3	18·24	11·7	0·91	13·8	17·0	7·45
Rocket (altered)	6·0	20·0	117·8	136·3	29·6	...	...	13·3	47·45	7·45
Sanspareil	10·0	15·7	74·6	176·7	24·0	28·8	2·41	14·0	19·1	8·11
Novelty	1·8	9·5	33·0	7·1	...	...	...	15·0	10·7	3·85
Novelty (altered)	1·8	9·5	33·0	7·1	...	... coal.	0·36	8·0	28·5	3·85
Killingworth (improved)	10·9	22·56	101·5	135·0	{ 47·8 / 40·0	14·7 / 13·2	1·105 / 1·16	9·0 / 9·0	70·5 } / 50·5 }	10·5
Phœnix	6·0	20·0	306·0	282·7	34·4	9·4	0·78	10·0	41·5	7·0
Arrow	6·0	20·0	283·8	289·0	44·0	6·5	0·67	12·0	35·5	7·0
No. of column....................	1	2	3	4	5	6	7	8	9	10

In the Table it appears that while the old Killingworth engine moved a total load, including itself, of 50 tons, at 6 miles per hour, the Rocket, when altered, moved 47·45 tons at 13·3 miles per hour; subtracting the weights of engine and tender, the work done was 40 tons at 6 miles, and 40 tons at 13·3 miles. Thus the Rocket, which was 25 per cent. lighter than the old Killingworth, did more than double work. The evaporation of the Rocket, moreover, was nearly double that of the old engine, being as 29·6 to 16 feet of water per hour—a superiority owing jointly to the greater heating surface, and to the sharper blast of the Rocket, notwithstanding its smaller grate surface. How much depended on the blast, may be found from the relative evaporations of the Rocket before and after the alteration, which were 18·24 and 29·6 feet of water per hour. In comparing the Rocket, as first tried, with the old engine, though their relative evaporations were 18·24 and 16 feet of water, the performance of the former was the inferior, being equivalent to 133 tons at 1 mile per hour, while that of the other was 150 tons at 1 mile—a difference attributable, partially to the absorption of a portion of power in the exhausting action of the blast of the Rocket, and partially to the escape of a greater amount of unemployed heat by the chimney. It is remarkable that the two evaporations should be so nearly the same, when the heating surfaces are, in slump, so various as 41 and 138 feet. This is explained by the deficient energy of the blast, in the Rocket, to maintain the draft against the extensive fric-

tional tube-surface, and through a sectional area of flue little more than one-third that of the old engine. With the easy blast, nevertheless, the heat of the fuel was permitted to be more thoroughly extracted, in the ratio of 11·7 lbs. of coke per foot of water evaporated by the Rocket, to 18·34 lbs. of coal by the old engine.

The consumption of fuel by the Sanspareil was extravagant. This was due to a special imperfection in one of the cylinders which had been imperfectly cast, and had been reduced at one place by boring to 1⁄16 inch thick. The engine had no sooner commenced working than one cylinder burst, when the race had to be run with one perfect cylinder only; whilst the fracture of the other one opened at every stroke a direct communication between the boiler and the blast-pipe. The fuel was thus dragged from the fire-box in solid pieces, and was blown unconsumed through the chimney—a result which sufficiently explained the inferior economy of fuel per foot of water evaporated, compared even with the old engine; the consumptions being, respectively, 28·8 and 18·34 lbs.; though the proportions of the boiler surface of the Sanspareil are superior.

In the Killingworth new engine, with a heating surface three times that of the old engine, and a grate surface fully one-half greater, there is in one experiment three times the

* The Phœnix had two cylinders, 11 inches diameter, by 16 inches stroke; and was carried on four wheels, of which the driving-wheels were 5 feet in diameter, and the carrying-wheels 2 feet 8 inches diameter. The Arrow's cylinders were 10 by 16 inches; driving-wheels 5 feet diameter, and carrying-wheels 2 feet 8 inches diameter.

evaporation, with less consumption of fuel per foot of water, though the consumption per mile per ton is greater. This proves the efficiency of extended heating surface for purposes of evaporation; it proves too that superior evaporation was obtained at the cost of steam power in the blast, which resulted in a greater consumption of fuel per ton per mile. But this increased consumption was due not merely to increase of frictional surface, in the ratio of 1 to 3¼, but also to a diminution of sectional area of flue, in the ratio of 3 to 1, nearly.

The experiments with the Novelty are remarkable. This engine was proved, when fairly tried, to have consumed less than half the fuel per ton per mile required by the Rocket, notwithstanding the closeness and contracted sectional area of the flue of the Novelty, which was but one twenty-fifth of that of either of the other competing engines. The mode of stimulating combustion by compression, adopted in the Novelty, was, no doubt, the source of the economy, in conjunction with the very much greater proportion of heating surface to the area of grate, especially when intensity of action was essential.

We need not longer dwell over these rudimentary experiments. They have suited the purpose of exemplifying generally the nature of the considerations to be regarded in the composition of the locomotive engine. The experiments indicated plainly in what directions improvement was to be hoped for. The steam-blast permitted the use of coke as fuel, with excellent effect; and from the time of the trials of 1829, may be dated the general use of coke as fuel, in preference to raw coal, as it showed less flame, threw off less smoke, and imparted quite as much heat per unit of weight. While the Rocket had twenty-four tubes of 3 inches diameter, the Meteor had eighty tubes of 2 inches diameter; and the Comet, the Dart, and the Arrow, ninety 2-inch tubes. The boilers of these four last engines, which were made, soon after the Rocket, for the Liverpool and Manchester Railway, were not greater in lineal dimensions, being 3 feet diameter by 6 feet long; the cylinders, however, in virtue of the greater evaporation, were made 10 inches in diameter, 16-inch stroke, with 5-feet wheels. In the Northumbrian, and other succeeding engines, 1¼ inch tubes were introduced, the boiler was lengthened 6 inches, and the cylinders were made 11 inches in diameter.

The first eight engines made by Mr. R. Stephenson for the Liverpool and Manchester Railway, including those just noticed, were made on one general plan: 4-wheel engines, tall and square, with outside cylinders in an inclined position, and working on crank pins fixed to the driving-wheel. These engines, from their shortness, and from the extreme transverse distance of the cylinders, were susceptible at high speeds of a violent oscillatory motion, which eventually led to their abandonment.

While Mr. Stephenson was carrying out the perfections in the detail of his locomotive-boilers, Hackworth was equally busy on the Stockton Railway. He designed a locomotive, the 'Globe,' built by Messrs. Stephenson & Co., previous to 1830, comprising the following modifications. The wheels were four in number, and coupled, 5 feet in diameter, being the largest then in use. A single straight flue passed through the boiler, containing the fire-grate at one end. A series of small water-tubes were inserted as heating surface diametrically across the flue, in a spiral order, through which the water of the boiler circulated. A copper dome was placed on the top of the boiler, as a steam chamber, whence the name of the locomotive. The cylinders were placed beneath the boiler, and inside the wheels, alongside of each other; and worked the driving-axle direct, which was for that purpose fitted with two inside cranks at right angles. The valve-gear was reversed by a single lever, two drivers being placed on the axle, one on each side of the pair of eccentrics. The water-tubes, borrowed from Perkins's boiler, though they increased the heating surface, were speedily destroyed by the accumulation of mud in them, particularly those which lay horizontally. The Globe, nevertheless, frequently attained, it is said, a speed of 50 miles per hour.

In 1830, Mr. Hackworth designed two new classes of locomotives, to meet the increase of traffic on the Stockton line. In these he introduced two varieties of compound flue, the first of which comprised an arrangement the same as that already described for the new Killingworth locomotive, and from which probably Mr. Wood derived the idea. The second form of boiler contained the 'return multitubular fire-tube;' a single flue was passed right through the boiler, and discharged its contents into an intermediate smoke-box, whence a number of small tubes, returning through the boiler, conveyed the smoke to the fire-box end into the terminal smoke-box, whence it was discharged into the chimney. The second plan of boiler proved to be the best of its day for the general traffic of the line, both as to economy and durability; the flues have frequently been found to endure six years without removal. In the same locomotives, the cylinders were placed vertically at one end of the boiler, and the pistons were coupled to a separate crank-shaft, hung directly beneath, having two cranks on its extremities, at right angles to each other, and from which the whole set of wheels were driven by coupling rods. The slide-valves were driven each by a single eccentric; and the same eccentrics were employed to work the pumps.

The first engine made by Mr. Bury was the six-wheel engine Dreadnought, which was placed on the Liverpool and Manchester Railway on March 12, 1830. It was too heavy for the rails, and was on that account condemned. His next engine was the Liverpool, made for the same railway; it was made with inside horizontal cylinders, and double crank-axle; the cylinders were 12 by 18 inches; the wheels, four in number, were 6 feet diameter, coupled. This engine was placed on the rails on July 22, 1830. It was the first of a class which afterwards got extensively into use, and of which further notice is reserved for next chapter.

The Planet, which was the ninth engine built by Mr. Stephenson for the Liverpool and Manchester Railway, embraced some conspicuous improvements; it was the combination, in fact, of what had previously been known; the multitubular boiler, the blast pipe, the inside horizontal cylinders, which were placed inside the smoke-box, and the double crank-axle. This engine had 129 tubes, 1¼ inches diameter; and the boiler was 3 feet diameter, by 6¼ feet long, yielding a heating surface of 37·25 feet for the fire-box, and 370 for the tubes; the cylinders were 11 by 16 inches, and the four wheels 5 feet and 3 feet diameter; the weight of the engine, empty, was 8 tons; with coke and water, 9 tons; tender, with coke and water, 4 tons; making a total of 13 tons. The engine is said to have taken, on its first trial, on December 4, 1830, a train of 76 tons of goods and passengers from Liverpool to Man-

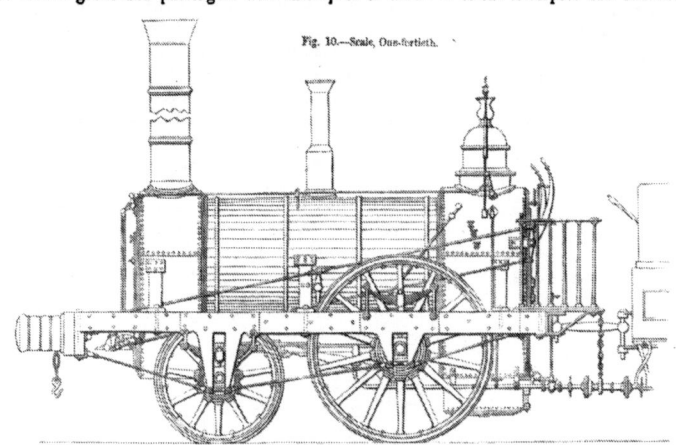

Fig. 10.—Scale, One-fortieth.

Four-wheeled Locomotive, with inside cylinders, on the model of the Planet, 1830.   By Fenton, Murray, and Jackson.
Cylinder 11 by 16 inches, Wheel 5 feet.

chester, in 2 hours 39 minutes, with a maximum velocity, on a level, of 15¼ miles per hour, under the disadvantage of an adverse wind, and new machinery.

The success of the arrangements combined in the Planet, formed a new starting point for improvement. New locomotives were from that time formed on the model of the inside-cylinder engine, and the pattern was early imitated on other railways.

From the foregoing notices, it appears that no single individual in this country had, up till the year 1830, done so much for the improvement of the locomotive, and for its establishment as a permanent railway motor, as Mr. Timothy Hackworth. He first employed six coupled-wheel locomotives; he first applied the waste steam to heat the feed-water; he first employed the eccentrics to work the feed-pumps, which, in many cases, is a matter of convenience; he substituted spring balances for weights to the safety valves; he schemed and first applied the steam-chamber in the boiler, a valuable auxiliary for obtaining dry steam; he first placed the cylinders beneath the boiler, and employed the double inside crank-axle, coupled directly to the pistons; and he also was the first to employ, in railway locomotives, a separate crank-shaft hung in bearings fixed to the frame. He claimed also the invention of the blast-pipe: though, taking his own dates, we have found that George Stephenson had applied it previously. But Trevethick appears to have the most unequivocal claim to the invention, if, indeed, it was not altogether a matter of accident; because he was at least the first who discharged the steam into the chimney, and it was at the time distinctly known that the blast improved the draft of his engine, as we find from some remarks by Gilbert, in the 12th volume of Nicholson's Journal, 1805.

CHAPTER II.

GENERAL HISTORY OF THE LOCOMOTIVE, FROM 1831 TO 1849.

THE increased weight and speed of the locomotives supplied to the Liverpool and Manchester Railway, gave rise to a new and unanticipated difficulty. The Rocket class of engine, in working order, did not weigh above 5 tons. This weight distributed amongst four wheels, did not afford above 30 cwt. to each driving-wheel, on a railway which was laid originally with 35 lb. rails. The additional weight of the engines of the Planet class, 9 tons charged, and loading the rails under the driving-wheels with 5¼ tons, or 2¼ tons to each rail, speedily disorganized the permanent way; the rails were, for the most part, broken or bent under the extra load moving at 30 miles per hour. The cause of the destruction was of a compound character. On the one hand, there was the unequal distribution of the weight, and the mal-arrangement of the wheels, made worse by the increased total load upon them; on the other hand, the radical defects in the mode of laying the rails had also much to do with it. It was impracticable more equally to divide the load over the four wheels; with inside cylinders, the crank-axle is necessarily placed in front of the fire-box; a large portion of the engine, therefore, overhangs that axle. The fore wheels, it is true, might have been placed so close to the drivers as to divide the weight equally with them; to secure sufficient base on the rails, however, they were necessarily placed forward, and were of course more remote from the centre of gravity of the suspended mass. Neither was the preponderating load on the driving-wheels required for purposes of adhesion, as their power of bite was more than ample. In Pambour's experiments on the velocity and load of locomotives on the Liverpool and Manchester Railway, there was not one in which the motion was stopped or slackened for want of adhesion, though there were loads amongst them equivalent to 300 tons on a level. Again, the wheels, fore and hind, did not exceed 5-feet apart centres, the axles being placed between the fire-box and the smoke-box, and thus with overhanging loads, and a total length of engine of 15 feet, depressions, and the other inequalities of the rails, gave rise to irregular motions, which were magnified seriously by the length of the machine.

It was proposed to replace the light rails with 66 lb. rails. Immediate measures, however, were imperative, and it was finally determined to add a pair of wheels to the engine *behind the fire-box*, constituting it a six-wheel engine, and extending the base to 9 feet. The object of the additional pair was not to relieve the driving-wheels of any fixed part of their load, but to check the pitching of the engine, by receiving a portion of the weight at the time of plunging. They were slightly loaded when the engine was empty, merely to bind the springs, and when the engine was charged, the springs had a burden of 5 cwt. each. The design was good, the hind wheels remedied the unsteadiness, both vertically and laterally, beyond all expectations; the speeds were maintained without involving any further destruction of the permanent way, and the engineer proceeded diligently to replace the light rails by heavier ones. Since that time, the rails have been increased successively to 50, 60, 70, and 75 lbs. per yard lineal.*

Besides deriving, from the addition, increased stability on the rails, the six-wheel engine kept firmly together for a longer time, the tubes leaked less, the frame was less disturbed at the bolts and stays, running off the rail became less frequent on the fracture of a crank-axle, this axle itself lasted longer, as it was saved from much of the straining to which, as hind axle, it was previously exposed. To preserve the crank-axle of the new engine from the lateral pressure on the wheel-flanges, on the passage of curves, the driving-wheels were deprived of their flanges, and formed straight on the rims, and were thus left free to suit themselves to the rails. The plain driving-wheel formed the subject of a patent in 1833.

Messrs. Sharp and Roberts of Manchester, conceiving that a crank-axle was objectionable, as essentially a weak form of axle, and being, moreover, impressed with the expediency of simplifying the locomotive generally, brought out a class of engine, of which one, the 'Experiment,' was put in operation on the Liverpool and Manchester Railway in 1833. The cylinders, 11 by 16 inches, were placed on the outside of the boiler, upright; they were fitted with the old radius-bar parallel motion in place of slides; the motion of the pistons was conveyed through bell-crank levers and side-rods to the driving-wheels; the driving axle was straight; the pistons were solid plugs, without spring packing; the slide-valves were similarly cylindrical and frictionless; the frame was entirely of wrought iron; the whole affair was carried on four wheels, 5¼ tons on the driving, and 3 tons on the leading; total weight, 8¼ tons; 108 tubes, 1¼ inch diameter, 6 feet long, 298 feet of surface; the fire-box held 13 cubic feet of coke, and had 45 feet of surface. This locomotive consumed ·67 lbs. of coke per ton per mile; whereas another of the ordinary class, of slightly smaller dimensions, consumed only ·47 lbs., showing an excess of 42 per cent. on the part of the 'Experiment.' It turned out no more than an experiment, and the class of engine was abandoned.

* E. Woods.—Trans. Inst. Civil Engineers, vol. ii.

Messrs. Forrester and Co. of Liverpool, with an equally laudable desire to improve the locomotive, and to simplify the machinery *under* the boiler—though at the risk of complicating it on the outside—designed a class of locomotive which found its way, in 1834, to the Dublin and Kingston Railway, to the Newcastle and Carlisle, and occasionally ran on the Grand Junction Railway. The engine (Fig. 11) had six wheels, and outside framing, with bearings for all the axles, the piston-rods being connected to cranks projecting beyond the outer bearings. The valve-gearing was likewise arranged on the outside above the frame. This was certainly an effective mode of banishing the machinery from the interior. The necessarily great lateral overhang of the cylinders, caused by the intervention of the outside frame, introduced, however, a formidable right and left sinuous motion at high speeds, which obtained for these engines the distinctive title of the 'Boxers.' This machine

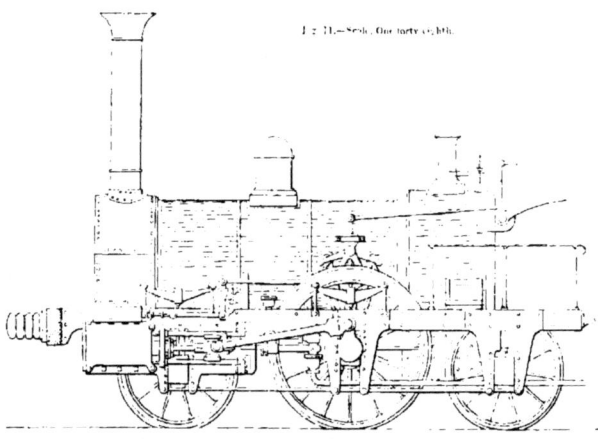

Forrester's Locomotive, 1834. Outside Cylinders and Valve-Gear.

of Forrester's can be regarded only as a transitionary class, in which a couple of outside cylinders were merely grafted upon the machine as it existed for inside cylinders; and though even at this time, 1834, the inconvenience of a crowded mass of machinery under the boiler was felt, it was certainly, in the new arrangement, balanced by the greater evil of widely spread lines of action.

The introduction of heavier rails in the permanent way, and of six wheels in the engines of the Liverpool and Manchester Railway, inspired the engineers with new confidence, and induced a still further increase in the power and weight of the locomotives. The following tabular statement by Pambour, exhibits the progressive state of the locomotive stock up till 1836. It is remarkable that in all these cases 5-feet driving-wheels were employed. It was considered unsafe to run at high speeds with larger wheels, though it is now well understood, that to obtain the greatest speeds high wheels are essential. Considering, then, that in the general practice of those days, a 5-feet driving-wheel was reckoned the practical maximum for high-speed engines, we are the better able to appreciate the adventurous spirit which prompted Brunel to adopt the Cyclopean dimensions of the Great Western stock :—

LOCOMOTIVES ON THE LIVERPOOL AND MANCHESTER RAILWAY (1836).

Number of Locomotives.	Diameter of Cylinder.	Length of Stroke	Diameter of Driving-wheel.	Weight of Locomotives.	Steam Pressure in Boiler.
	inches.	inches.	feet.	tons.	lbs.
2	8 to 10	17 to 18	5	7 to 8	50
9	11	16	5	8 ,, 9	50
6	11	18	5	10 ,, 12	50
2	11	20	5	11 ,, 12	50
2	12	16	5	11 ,, 12	50
2	12	18	5	12 ,, 12½	50
5	12½	16	5	10 ,, 11	50
1	14	12	5	11½	50
2	14	16	5	12	50
2	15	16	5	12½	50

Amongst these engines may be recognized the first of an order of ten short-stroked engines, for running at higher speeds, that was being delivered during 1836 and 1837, of which the cylinders were 14 inches diameter by 12 inches stroke. Thus, although to keep down the speed of piston, higher wheels were not tolerated, the alternative of a shorter stroke was adopted, with a diameter of piston even greater than the stroke. Some comparative experiments were made in 1837 and 1838, on the regular working engines of the line, to ascertain their consumptions of fuel while conveying the ordinary traffic of the railway, at the usual speeds. The following Table contains the results for various classes of engines, of which the leading data are prefixed. It was found generally, that the engines consumed as nearly as possible ¼ lb. of coke per ton per mile, with loads above 100 tons, or 20 loaded waggons, while the engines were actually working. The consumption for 17 hours in steam was of course greater, as the engines were not above half that time in motion, accomplishing four trips of 30 miles each.

LIVERPOOL AND MANCHESTER RAILWAY.—TABLE OF PERFORMANCE AND CONSUMPTION OF FUEL, WITH VARIOUS LOCOMOTIVES, AND THE ORDINARY TRAFFIC OF THE LINE, IN 1837 AND 1838.

Date of Experiment.	Name of Engine.	Cylinder.		Diameter of Driving-wheel.		Number of Tubes.	Heating Surface.		Nature and Weight of Load.				Time of Trip, not including Delays, 30 miles.		Delays.	Average Speed in miles per hour.	Consumption of Coke.	
		Diameter.	Length of Stroke.				Fire-box	Tubes.									Total for the whole Trip.	Per ton per mile.
				ft.	in.					tons.	cwt.	qrs.	h	m.	minutes.	miles.	lbs.	lbs.
April 26, 1837....	Planet........	11	16	5	0	89	35·5	225	20 waggs.,	96	4	0	1	30	0	20	808	0·280
June 23, 1837	Sun	14	12	5	0	109	42·3	320	25 ,,	128	8	0	1	42	9	17½	1200	0·340
March 20, 1838...	Lightning. ..	12½	16	5	0	95	43·0	285	25 ,,	133	0	0	1	43	15	17½	1248	0·313
April 3, 1838......	Phalaris......	12½	18	5	0	117	47·0	...	31 ,,	150	14	0	1	35	10	19	1350	0·300
June 5, 1838......	Firefly........	11	18	5	0	110	41·8	320	26 ,,	128	0	0	1	28	0	20½	997	0·260
July 5, 1838	Sirius.........	13	20	4	10	94	...	...	37 ,,	187	16	0	1	28	0	20½	1614	0·290
April 26, 1837....	Planet........	11	16	5	0	89	...	...	4 coaches,	20	0	0	1	1	3	29½	781	1·300
March 1, 1838....	Lightning....	12½	16	5	0	95	...	...	5 ,,	25	0	0	1	1	3	29½	664	0·885
March 2, 1838....	Lightning....	—	—	—		—	...	...	5 ,,	25	0	0	1	35	...	...	816	1·090
March 2, 1838....	Lightning....	—	—	—		—	...	...	8 waggs.,	40	0	0	{Including stoppages.} 1	10	26	25½	790	0·660
March 12, 1838..	Lightning....	—	—	—		—	...	...	4 coaches,	20	0	0	1	0	9	30	693	1·155
March 14, 1838...	Lightning....	—	—	—		—	...	..	5 ,,	25	0	0	0	58	2½	30	810	1·080

The locomotives of which the performances have been given in the foregoing table, are a fair sample of the locomotives of the time. They usually contrived to evaporate from 6 to 7·5 lbs. of water per pound of coke, according as the loads were light or heavy ; the less the load, the less was the draught on the fire, and the less the waste of heat through the chimney. Pambour found, as the average result of his experiments on the Liverpool and Manchester Railway, that 6 lbs. of water per pound of coke was the rate of evaporation.

On the Grand Junction Railway, a double trip was run with the Hecla, by Dr. Lardner and Mr. Woods, in July 1839, with one object of determining the ordinary performance of this, an ordinary passenger locomotive. Its cylinders were 12½ × 18 inches, wheel 5 feet, blast-orifice 2¼ inches, grate 8·33 square feet, heating surface 419 feet. With a train of 12 carriages, weighing 60 tons, and with engine and tender, 82 tons, this locomotive ran from Liverpool to Birmingham and back, 190 miles total, at a mean speed of 29·5 miles per hour, including four stoppages each way, with a mean consumption of 37·1 lbs. of coke per mile, or ·62 lbs. per mile per ton of load, and an evaporation of 5·7 lbs. of water per pound of coke, at a rate of 91 feet per hour in motion.* This may be reckoned as an ultimate performance, and it is manifest how unequal the boiler was to an economical evaporation at the rate above noted.

Some weak attempts were made in 1839, by Gray and Chanter, to introduce coal for fuel as a substitute for coke, subject to the legal condition of consuming its own smoke. The peculiarity lay in the fire-box, which was divided vertically, by a deep transverse water partition entering from the roof. Thus, two fire-grates were formed, on the nearest of which the fresh coal was subjected to a preliminary process of coking, after which it was passed to the second, in which it was intended to be thoroughly burnt by a due admixture of air. A locomotive, the Prince George of Cambridge, was fitted with this fire-box, with an unusually large allowance of tube surface, and tried in June 1839, on the Liverpool and Manchester. The engine weighed 15½ tons charged, and was found to consume 66⅔ per cent. more fuel than other engines of similar proportions; in short, it evaporated exactly 3·6 lbs. water per pound of fuel, at least 40 per cent. less than the others could do. Abundant smoke was emitted when standing; and even when moving, the incessant assiduity of the fireman was required to keep down the smoke. It is a pity that the whims of schemers should be patronized, on the grounds of such slight expectations as this fire-box held forth, to the neglect of worthier but less fortunate inventions.

Another scheme, of at least equal intelligence, was tried

* Trans. British Association, 1841.

on one of the locomotives of the Greenock Railway, about the year 1844. The ordinary fire-box was formed with rows of air-holes on the front and side, about the usual level of the fuel; the air was designed to mix with and more

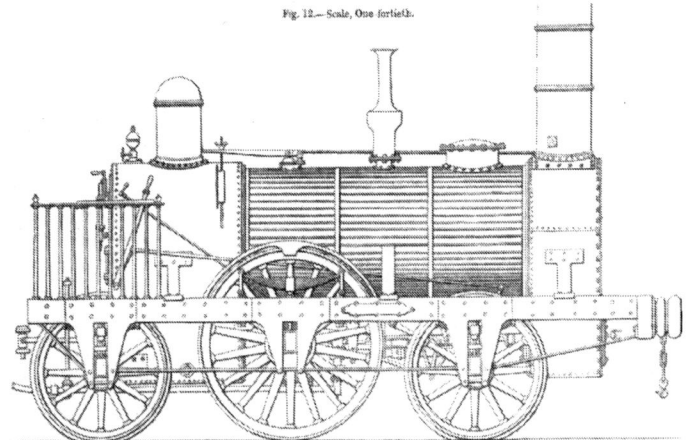

Fig. 12.—Scale, One-fortieth.

Stephenson's Six-wheel Locomotive, with inside cylinders, 1838.—General Type of the Six-wheeled Class.—Cylinder 12 by 18 inches, Wheel 6 feet.

thoroughly consume the gaseous elements formed in the fire-box, in the style of Williams's argand. It was of no use; the coke was apparently very well burned before it reached the argands, and the results showed a diminished rate of evaporation.

To return to our history. Until the opening of the Lon-

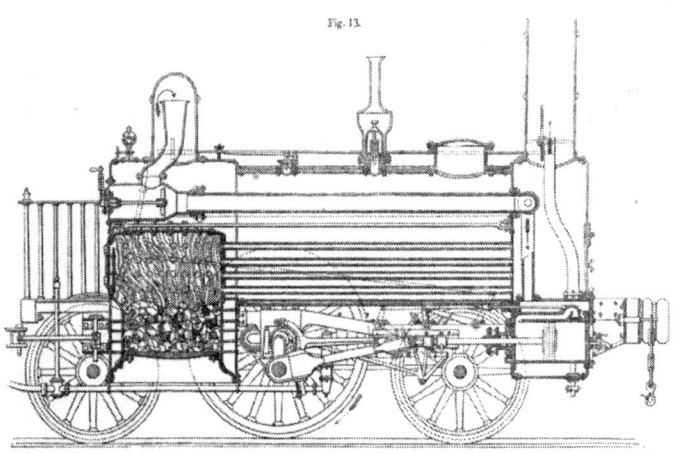

Fig. 13.

Six-wheel Locomotive, Longitudinal Section, showing the general disposition of the boiler and engine.

don and Birmingham Railway, in 1837, but little variation was observed in the general design and arrangement of locomotives; inside cylinders and crank-axles, gab-motions

for the valve, admirably intricate, square fire-boxes—facetiously described as tanks, when the battle of the fire-boxes was at its height—with a sprinkling of round ones, outside and inside frames combined, and six wheels under the whole—these were the prevailing characteristics, and the annexed illustrations will give precision to this enumeration.

A new and original class of engines had been advocated by Mr. Edward Bury of Liverpool since 1830, the date of the delivery of his first locomotive on the Liverpool and Manchester Railway. He was appointed Locomotive Superintendent of the London and Birmingham Railway, opened in 1837; and had opportunities of extensively introducing on that line his peculiar class of locomotives. Though the arguments then advanced by Mr. Bury were deemed irrefragable by a large section of the mechanical men of the time, and gave rise to animated discussion, they have, for the most part, sunk into unimportance, as the arts of construction have advanced. The peculiar features of Bury's engine were the circular fire-box, the arrangement of the tubes in circular arcs, the exclusive inside frame, compounded of forged iron bars, and the exclusive number of wheels, four, on which the engine was placed. Mr. Bury's ideas were all of a mathematical complexion. The fancied superiority of the circular fire-box, Fig. 15, and the arrangement of the tubes in circular lines, Fig. 16, for the promotion of equable combustion and the free circulation of the water in the boiler, is now estimated at nothing compared with the convenience of the square fire-box as a piece of manufacture, and its value as embodying greater area of grate and heating surface in proportion to its economic bulk. The superiority of the circular arrangement of the tubes, also, has proved a mere figment;

and when tube-surface is an object, above all, sectional area of tube, the arrangement of tubes in straight lines becomes imperative. Bury's inside frame, composed of bar-iron, imparted to his engine a peculiar *wiry* air of light-

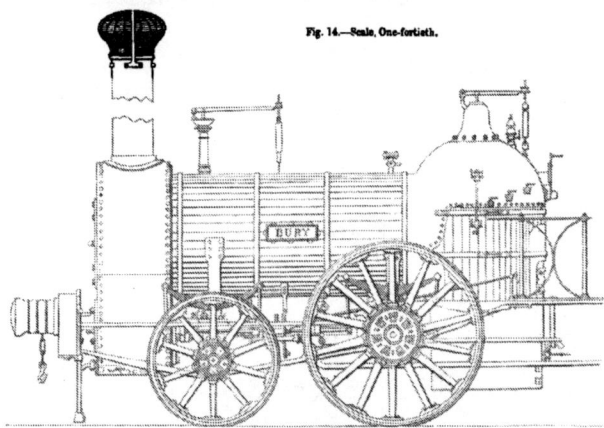

Fig. 14.—Scale, One-fortieth.

Bury's Locomotive. Originally introduced, 1830.

ness. Mr. Bury justly conceived that, next to a good boiler, 'the most important point in the construction of a locomotive was to connect all the parts firmly together by a strong and well-arranged framing, so that they shall retain their relative positions when the engine is in motion.' In this respect he considered the inside frame much superior

Fig. 15.—Scale, One-fortieth.   Fig. 16.—Scale, One-fortieth.

 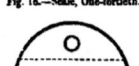

Bury's Fire-box.—Horizontal Section.   Bury's Boiler.—Vertical Section of Tubes.

to the outside frame, as the connection of the cylinder and crank-axle was more direct; and the boiler was considered to be relieved of much of the strain of the engine incidental to outside frames. Much of this is true, and has been followed up in the works of modern locomotive-builders. Mr. Bury appears, however, to have forgot that the smoke-box, which at least furnished a tube-plate to the boiler, was, except in his later engines, subjected, without any reserve, to the entire strain of the engine; the cylinders were bolted directly to the smoke-box—they had no direct connection with the frame, and consequently the strain operated through the boiler-stays, which rested over the axle-boxes. With regard to the position of the bearings inside the wheels, it was considered of great practical advantage, in case of the fracture of the crank-axles, as the weight on the bearings pressed the flanges of the wheels against the rail, and assisted the length of the journal in keeping the engine from being thrown off the rails. With reference to the number of bearings, five,

which were employed for crank-axles with outside bearings, Mr. Bury added that it was impossible to key so many bearings perfectly true, and to maintain them so while the engine was working.[*] This is a mere matter of manufacture; it is either possible or impossible—as the workmanship is good or bad. It may instruct us for a line or two to quote Mr. Edward Woods on the superiority of outside framing:—' The superior danger of the inside above the outside framed engine consists in the fact that, should the wheel of the former become loose, or the axle break, the engine would almost inevitably fall over on its side; whereas in the other form of engine, placed under similar circumstances, the wheel remains confined within the framing.' Safety is a very pliant sort of argument! In the case of axle-bearings, Mr. Woods has stated that no bearings can be made, or if made, could continue long in strict mathematical adjustment with the axis of motion; that the angle of vibration is as the distance of the bearings inversely, and that the play of the brasses becomes virtually greater with that angle.'[†] These quotations are sufficient to show how conveniently separate sets of facts may be enlisted in support of the special pleadings of interested or prejudiced minds. On the third characteristic of his engine, Mr. Bury thus sums up the advantages of four wheels—a specimen of conclusive reasoning, which has been quite as well met by Mr. Woods as the other branches of the discussion:—' The four-wheeled engine is less costly than that on six wheels; it can be got into less space; is much lighter, and, therefore, requires less power to take it up the inclines, and consequently leaves more available power to take up the train; is safer, as it adapts itself better to the rails, not being so likely to run off the lines at curves or crossings; is more economical in the working, there being fewer parts in motion, and consequently less friction; those parts of the machinery which are common to both plans are more easily got at in the four-wheeled engine; the buildings and turn-tables are not required to be on so large a scale, as there are fewer parts in the four-wheel engine; fewer tools, as lathes, drills, &c., are required; having fewer parts to be deranged, stoppages are not so likely to take place on the journey.'

The argument in favour of four wheels, for engines with inside cylinders in the smoke-box, is now obsolete. The addition of a couple of wheels to a four-wheel engine, for passenger trains requiring considerable speeds, had already been found conducive to stability on the rails; the simplicity of the engine was unimpaired, and the rails were subjected to very much less fatigue, as lateral elasticity was provided in the frames to suit the curves. The fewer the points of contact with the rail, and the shorter the wheel-base of the

* Trans. Inst. Civil Engineers, vol. iii. p. 311.   † Ibid. vol. i. p. 137.

engine, the more formidable does an inequality of level become. On a stiff and perfectly well-formed line of rails, four wheels may run as easily as six. But with the existing imperfections in construction, and relatively heavy engines, six wheels are necessary, at least as expedients, if not, according to Mr. Bury's idea, so perfect as four.

The original locomotive stock of the London and Birmingham Railway was composed exclusively of four-wheel engines, in compliance with the opinion of Mr. Bury; and from the opening of the line in 1837, till the middle of 1845, there was but one six-wheel engine employed. At the beginning of 1840, there were eighty-two engines on the line. The first passenger engines were made with 12-inch cylinders, 18-inch stroke, 5½ feet wheel, and weighed 8½ to 10 tons empty. The merchandise engines had cylinders 13 by 18 inches, and 5 feet coupled wheels. The average weight of thirty-two passenger trains, in 1839, was found, by Mr. Whishaw, to amount to 42 tons; the average speed was 25 miles per hour, the highest speed being 50 miles, with a train of 37½ tons. Mr. Bury states, that the original passenger engines evaporated 75 cubic feet of water per hour, at a mean speed of 30 miles, with a total heating surface of 420 feet. Mr. Nicholas Wood found by experiment, that, in one of Bury's engines, on the London and Birmingham Railway, having cylinders 12 by 18 inches, wheels 5½ feet, fire-grate 8·18 feet, fire-box surface 39 feet, tube surface 378 feet, the evaporation was 80 feet of water per hour, at a mean speed of 26 miles.

The engines of the London and Birmingham, like those of the Liverpool and Manchester Railway, were, in course of the development of the traffic, made somewhat heavier, and more powerful. The changes were confined principally to the length of the boiler, which was 8½ feet originally, and was increased to 11½ feet; the length of wheel-base was correspondingly increased, from 5 to 7½ feet; still, except in one case, the number of wheels was four, and the cylinders and framing inside. The following Table exhibits the locomotive stock as it existed in August 1845:*—

TABLE OF LOCOMOTIVE ENGINES ON THE LONDON AND BIRMINGHAM RAILWAY (1845).

Number of Engines.	Diameter of Cylinder.	Length of Stroke.	Diameter of Driving-wheel.	Average Weight when charged	Number of Wheels.
	inches.	inches.	ft. in.	tons.	
22	12	18	5 6	10½	4
28	13	18	5 6	12	4
5	13	18	5 9	12	4
1	13	18	6 0	12	4
3	14	18	5 9	12¼	4
30	13	18	5 0	11½	4
1	15	20	5 6	unknown.	6

* Gauge Commissioners' Report. 1846.

The largest passenger engine on four wheels, made by Mr. Bury, according to the authority just quoted, weighed 13 tons empty, and had 14-inch cylinders. For engines of greater power, he had recourse to six wheels, as the 65 and 75 lb. rails, then laid, could not safely be trusted with heavier loads.

Previous to the opening of the London and Birmingham Railway, in 1837, Dr. Church of Birmingham, a gentleman distinguished for the versatility of his genius, projected, and actually executed a locomotive on four wheels—the Eclipse, combining, within itself, all the functions of engine and tender. With a boiler of the usual arrangement, it was placed upon four wheels, arranged like those of the old Rocket—the driving-wheels in front of the others, and placed under the body of the boiler; the carrying-wheels were placed in the rear of the fire-box, under the foot-plate. The cylinders were outside, and lay horizontally, also under the foot-plate. They were fitted with piston-valves worked by a very light eccentric motion. By thus reversing the entire arrangement of the locomotive, Dr. Church had removed the objection to an overhung fire-box, complained of in other four-wheel engines. By disposing his water room amongst sundry tanks, distributed beneath the boiler, and within the frame of the engine, he also kept down the centre of gravity of the mass, a high wheel notwithstanding; and though there is a prodigious overhang at the front end, thus apparently converting the evil formerly complained of into one of a more dangerous character, it was partially neutralized by an overhung provender-box at the other extremity; and accordingly it was found that, of the total weight of 14 tons charged, 5 tons rested on the hind wheels, the remaining 9 tons on the drivers. Neither is it to be overlooked, that while the wheel-base of the ordinary four-wheel engine of the time did not commonly exceed 5 feet of length, that of the Eclipse amounted to 8 feet, a length of base which atoned for the sin of overhanging. To Dr. Church, at all events, is due the merit of devising and executing the first four-wheel tank-engines, with tubular boilers,

Fig. 17.—Scale, One forty-eighth.

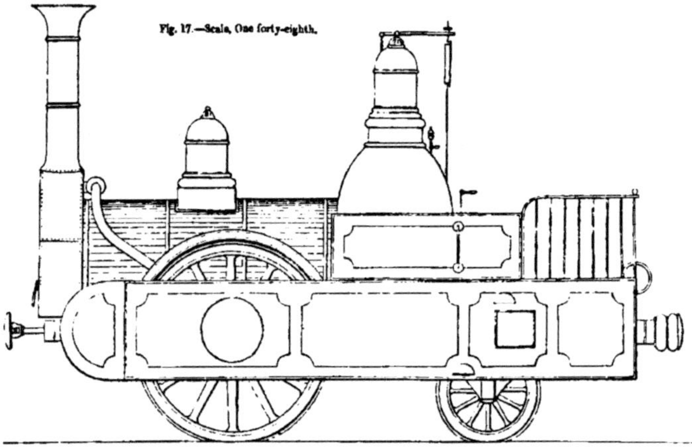

Church's Locomotive, 1838. Cylinder 11¼ by 24 inches, Wheel 6 feet 2½ inches diameter.

for railways, and of being amongst the first to carry out, and prove the advantage of a large driving-wheel. The cylinders of the Eclipse, as it now (1850) stands at Camphill station, Birmingham, are 11½ by 24-inch stroke; connecting-rod, 8 feet long; driving-wheel, 6 feet 2½ inches diameter; carrying-wheels, 3 feet, all with inside bearings; the framing is double, outside and inside the wheels, consisting of ½-inch plate, 3 feet deep, let into stiffening-rods on the upper and lower edges; the frame measures, externally, 18 by 7 feet. The fire-box is 3 feet by 2 feet 3 inches wide, and 3 feet high inside; 81 tubes, 2 inches diameter by 7½ feet long; blast orifice, 2½ inches diameter. This engine was employed, as a ballast engine, on the London and Birmingham Railway, in the spring of 1838, and conveyed, with ease, trains of 100 tons. On one occasion, it is said to have run, alone, 12 miles in 12 minutes—a speed unapproachable by contemporary engines, and due, there is no doubt, to the liberal diameter of the wheel. Nor must we overlook the voluminous dome which covers the fire-box, a rotundity which, though previously employed by Hackworth, was re-invented and enlarged by Dr. Church, and was a feature which aided in making Bury's engine famous. Though Dr. Church's engine has been neglected in its day, it is undeniable that the salient points of originality in that engine, the horizontal outside cylinder, the self-contained vehicle, with accommodation for provender, the generous height of driving-wheel, and the portly, blooming dome, as a reservoir of steam, are elements which have, at later periods, been special objects of solicitude to engineers.

In 1840, several bogie-engines were furnished by Norris of Philadelphia, for the Birmingham and Gloucester Railways, to work on the Lickey incline, of 1 in 37½, as an assistant engine. This class of locomotives (Fig. 18) had

Fig. 18.

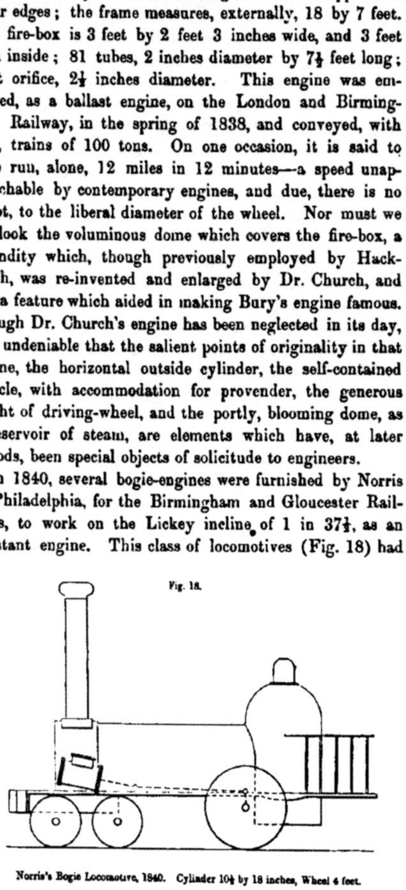

Norris's Bogie Locomotive, 1840. Cylinder 10½ by 18 inches, Wheel 4 feet.

six wheels, of which the front four, 30 inches diameter, were attached to a frame, or bogie, swivelling on a centre below the smoke-box, to ease the locomotive round curves; cylinders, 10½ by 18 inches; driving-wheels, 4 feet; seventy-eight tubes, 2 inches outside, 8 feet long; round fire-box; weight, 8 tons empty, 9½ tons charged; steam-pressure, 62 lbs. The locomotives were, however, converted into tank-engines; which increased the weight to about 14 tons. Their average performance was, to ascend with a maximum load of eight waggons, 53½ tons, at 8½ miles per hour; with six waggons, 39½ tons, at 10½ miles; with five waggons, 33 tons, at 12 to 15 miles, and assisting the ordinary passenger trains of seven carriages, at 13½ miles per hour. Captain Moorsom states, relative to the performance of these engines on the Grand Junction Railway, that they conveyed a load of 100 to 120 tons, on a plain 1 in 330, at 14 to 22½ miles per hour; and the same load on 1 in 177 at 10 to 14 miles. A mean of seven trips with goods trains of about 100 tons gross, from Birmingham to Liverpool, proved a consumption of 50 lbs. of coke per mile, and an evaporation of 4·27 lbs. of water per pound of coke.* With a modern Grand Junction locomotive, evaporating twice this quantity per pound of fuel, the fuel used would, on this account alone, fall to one-half of that consumed by the bogie-engines.

With the necessity, real or presumed, for larger locomotives, was increased the difficulty of packing the machinery of inside-cylinder engines, within the limits of the 4 feet 8½ inch gauge. We have seen that Sharp and Forrester made some attempts, if not to condense the machinery, at least to render it more accessible. The valve-gear sadly wanted condensation, it was in general excessively complicated; every engine-maker had his own mode, and such a riddle was made of it, that Mr. Braithwaite, in determining the gauge of the Eastern Counties Railway, opened in 1839, actually resolved upon a deviation from the common gauge of 4 feet 8½ inches, and adopted a 5-feet gauge for that line, with the sole object of gaining 3½ inches between the wheels! So minutely had he gone into his calculations on the subject, that he discovered that 3¼ inches was the exact extra width required. The wonder is that he threw in the additional quarter inch. To be sure he was going roundly to work at the time, making a rash innovation, insignificant in itself, and momentous in its ultimate consequences, and the additional quarter made a round number of the gauge.

In lieu of speculating upon the immediate conveniences of an increase of gauge—a plan which, in so far as it was simple, wore at least the semblance of originality, or of parting the machinery of his engine so extravagantly for the sake of outside connections, as had been done on some railways, Mr. Joseph Locke, engineer of the Grand Junction Railway, opened in 1837, and of the South-Western, opened in 1838, wisely determined to reduce the inconveniences that existed in the engines of the day, without sacrificing the merit of compactness, to which they were justly entitled. Mr. Allan, of the Crewe workshops of the Grand Junction Railway, suggested the removal of the cylinder to the outside of the smoke-box, the extension of the inside frame to the buffer-beam, the bolting of the cylinder immediately to that frame, the coupling of the piston-rod directly to a pin in the nave of the driving-wheel, and the entire dismissal of the inside cranks and the outside frame, leaving only the eccentrics and other valve-gear to be disposed of beneath the boiler, and entailing, of course, inside bearings for all the axles. Whilst the cylinder and wheels were, on that plan, almost directly opposed, and the strain between them received by the frame, to which the cylinder itself was firmly united, and which caught the axle by the neck, nothing on the score of direct action was sacri-

* Trans. Inst. Civil Engineers. 1843.

ficed, the machinery was simplified, and what remained was rendered easily accessible, leaving a clear way over the driving-axle, now made straight, sufficient to admit of a 6¼ feet wheel, where there was previously a 5½ feet wheel, without raising the mass of the boiler. An important suggestion was also made, which completed the design of the engine, according to which it was proposed to retain an outside frame, consisting of a single half-inch plate of wrought iron on each side, which could be bolted to, and would bestow additional firmness upon the cylinder, and would afford outside bearings for the carrying axles. The cylinders, moreover, were placed considerably above the horizontal centre line of the driving-wheel, inclining towards that centre, with the view of clearing the leading wheels, to admit of their being placed better forward, and partially under the cylinder, and the better to command their load. Thus the problem of producing a steady, compact, and durable engine, with outside cylinder, and a wide elastic base, was solved ; and to the re-introduction of the outside-cylinder engine, by Mr. Locke, after a period of abeyance, may be traced the origin of the most approved outside-cylinder engines of our own times. The original stock of locomotives on the Grand Junction, made in 1837, had inside cylinders and six wheels. They had cylinders of 12½, 13, and 14 by 18 inches stroke; wheels, 5 feet ; boiler, 8 feet long ; and they weighed from 9¼ to 15 tons charged. The cranks were found a frequent source of annoyance from breakage—an accident which occurred mostly on the ten-chain curves forming the junction of the line with the Liverpool and Manchester Railway, at Warrington.

In 1845, the stock of engines on the Grand Junction Railway, all made with six wheels, amounted to forty-six inside cylinder engines, of the proportions already noted, and twenty-seven engines with outside cylinders, 13 and 14½ by 20 inches, and wheels 5½ and 6 feet, weighing 15 and 16 tons charged. As the old engines wore out, they were progressively altered and fitted with outside cylinders and straight axles. The standard engine, now, in 1851, adopted on this railway, known as the Crewe engine, is not substantially different, in general arrangement, to that first adopted by Mr. Locke. Having found it to succeed to his satisfaction, on the Grand Junction Railway, he adopted the same class of engines for the South-western, the Paris and Rouen, and more lately, for the Caledonian, Scottish Central, and other lines.

On the South-western Railway, stocked originally with the older inside-cylinder engines, the first outside-cylinder engine, planned and executed by Mr. J. V. Gooch, commenced to run in November 1843 ; and was fitted with 6¼ feet driving-wheels. This was the first example of a driving-wheel, on the 4 feet 8½ inch gauge, of a diameter greater than 6 feet ; excepting, to be sure, Dr. Church's 6 feet 2½ inch wheel ; and there are now 64 outside-cylinder engines on the same railway, made identically to the pattern of the original engine, of which illustrations are to be found amongst the accompanying Plates. The numerous reproductions of the primary pattern, are a good evidence of the mechanical skill developed in the original engine, and Mr. Gooch has lately completed a locomotive, furnished with 7-feet wheels, for express trains.

The engineering—in other words, the gearing—difficulty was felt in common with others, by Mr. R. Stephenson. He wished, like Mr. Braithwaite, for an additional 3 or 4 inches of gauge. But with the Stephensons nothing is impossible. By improvements in the working gear, and the introduction of a direct communication between the eccentrics and the valves, in place of a series of levers, which previously occupied the width, he found, that even with inside cylinders, and four eccentrics, which require the most room under the boilers, there was 'ample space, and even space to spare.' Another difficulty existed, which had no reference to the machinery ; that of increasing the power or fire and heating surface of the boiler. As his boilers had generally been made as wide as the gauge would admit of, the fire-box and the boiler proper were considerably increased in length. The boiler was lengthened from 8 and 8½ feet, the common length, to 12, and, by degrees, to 13 and 14 feet; and to remove the extravagant spread of the wheels, to which those lengths of boilers would give rise, were they to be placed, according to the general practice, with the hind wheels behind the fire-box, all the three axles were confined to the space between the fire-box and smoke-box, at an extreme distance of 10, 11, 12, and 12¾ feet centres. Mr. Stephenson's opinion then was, that 12-feet centres was the utmost limit consistent with safety. The cylinders also were removed to the outside of the smoke-box, and placed precisely in the horizontal line of the centre of the driving-axle—a feature in which this engine was inferior to the inclined-cylinder engines of Locke, as it required the leading-wheels to be considerably underhung. The long-boiler engine, as it was denominated, was patented in April 1843 ; and in 1846, there were upwards of 150 of the patent engines in daily use, in this country, and on the Continent.

With an unexampled length of tube, and a large fire-box, it was anticipated that a very powerful and economical engine would be produced. It is generally believed, however, that the due proportion of length to diameter and total sectional area of tubes, has been much exceeded, with respect to the power of draught required. This is a question for future consideration. Meantime, it may be stated, the White Horse of Kent, a celebrated example of the long-boiler engine—cylinder, 15 × 22 inches; wheel, 5½ feet ; fire-grate, 9 feet ; fire-box surface, 48 feet ; tube-surface, 860 feet ; total length, 21 feet 10 inches ; extreme centres, 10 feet 3¼ inches—was found by Mr. D. Gooch to evaporate 93 feet of water per hour, with a 13½ feet flue-tube. On the contrary, the South-western new engine, with a tube of 10 feet in length, evaporated 141 feet per hour. A general feeling, nevertheless, has existed, that a long tube to the boiler, without reference to other circumstances, is as indifferent a matter as a long stroke to the cylinder, without any good foundation for the one excellence or the other ; and the general practice of engineers has been, to increase their length of tube, from the old 8-feet standard, to 10, 11, and 12 feet.

The first disposition of the wheels of the long-boiler engine, by which the drivers were placed between the fore and hind carrying-wheels, and therefore under the middle of the boiler, threw the cylinders forward to the outside of the smoke-box. This arrangement rendered the engine peculiarly susceptible of all sorts of unsteadiness at high speeds approaching 45 and 50 miles per hour; there was a combination of disturbing influences—the overhanging masses, at the ends, imperfectly controlled by the wheels; the position of the driving-wheels, in the middle, sustaining the greater part of the load, and carrying the engine as on a pivot; and the consequent situation of the cylinders, at the extreme front of the engine, aggravating the over-hung weight. To relieve the engine, the driving-wheels were, in a second design (1846), placed close in front of the fire-box, and were preceded by two pairs of small carrying-wheels. The alteration admitted of the removal of the cylinders to a position between the carrying axles. This form of engine (Fig. 19) has been long adhered to by Mr. Stephen-

son, though still possessing the elements of instability. The total length of the most modern engines of this class is 20 feet, and that of the wheel-base, 12 feet. The boiler is 13½ feet long between fire-box and smoke-box, and 3½ feet diameter; cylinders, 15 by 24 inches; driving-wheels, 6 feet; and carrying-wheels, 3 feet 9 inches. In this engine the outside frame is dispensed with, the axle bearings are placed, exclusively, inside the wheels; and the exclusive use of the inside frame, for this purpose, has simplified it into a mere rectangular bar, 8 inches deep by 1¼ inch thick.

Mr. I. K. Brunel, engineer of the Great Western Railway, which was opened in 1838, had, so early as 1833, conceived the desirableness of a decided extension of gauge, even to the width of 7 feet. He contemplated loads and

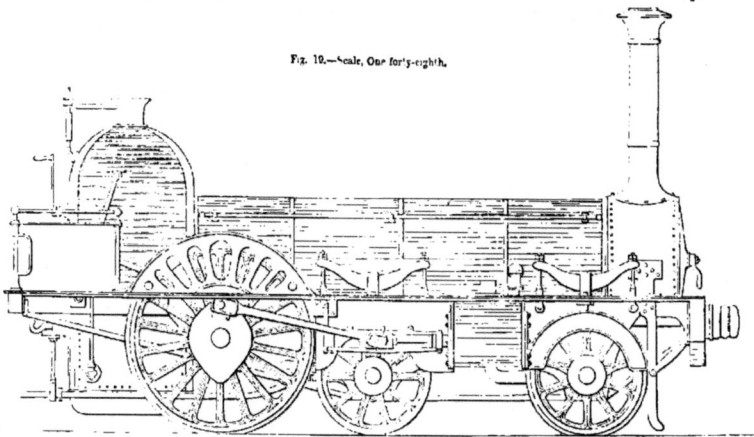

Fig. 19.—Scale, One forty-eighth.

Stephenson's Locomotive, 1846. Cylinder outside, 15 by 24 inches, Wheel 6 feet.

speeds much superior to those which then existed, as he very truly considered that the railway traffic of the country must be immensely increased. It is not our purpose, neither is it our inclination, to canvass the respective merits of the gauges. The Great Western gauge of 7 feet is now referred to only as it affects the mechanism of railways. All that was inconvenient and limiting, in the smaller gauge, as respects the engine, disappeared in the larger gauge; scope was afforded, without radically altering the design of the engine, for a liberal generation of steam, a spacious cylinder, an unlimited wheel, and a high velocity, with great loads. Mr. Brunel's original idea was to have 7 and 8 feet wheels for passenger engines, to take a load of 80 tons at about 45 miles per hour—a high speed in comparison with the existing speeds, of 25 and 30 miles, on other railways. The first of the Great Western stock comprehended engines with 6, 7, 8, and 10 feet wheels, of proportions varying with the ideas of the makers. The Ajax, which was made with 10-feet wheels, had but 474 feet of heating surface, and was found unequal to the duty required. The first engine, the North Star, was made for the company by Messrs. Stephenson and Co. It had six wheels, and inside cylinders. The cylinders were 16 by 16 inches; driving-wheel, 7 feet; carrying-wheels, 4 feet; fire-box

surface, 66⅓ feet; tubes, 9 feet long, 640 feet of surface. Its total weight was 16¼ tons empty, 18¼ tons full. On the 20th September, 1838, this engine conveyed a train of nine carriages and twelve waggons (gross weight, 184 tons, exclusive of engine and tender), from Maidenhead to London, a distance of 22¾ miles, at 32·5 miles per hour. In July 1839, Mr. Whishaw found the greatest speed attained with passenger trains was 50 miles per hour, and the average speed 25·43 miles. In 1844, Mr. Gooch states, the average speed of passenger trains was 27¼ miles, including stoppages, with an average load of 67 tons; on the London and Birmingham Railway, an average train of 42·4 tons was conveyed at 20 miles per hour; and on the South-western Railway, an average train of 36 tons was conveyed at a speed of 24 miles.* At this period, the efficiency of the locomotive stock of the Great Western Railway had been much improved; in the beginning of 1840, the delivery of the engines, made to the Great Western drawings, had commenced, and it was completed in the end of 1842; and it is only from results obtained posterior to this date, that a correct judgment can be formed of the merits of engines adapted to the 7-feet gauge. The engines referred to were

---

* Gauge Commissioners' Report, 1846, p. 152.

C

of the 'Ixion' class—inside cylinders, and six wheels. The Ixion had cylinders 15¼ by 18 inches; wheel, 7 feet; fire-grate, 13·4 feet; fire-box surface, 97 feet; 131 tubes, 2 inch diameter, surface, 732 feet; total heating surface, 829 feet. Weight, 22 tons empty; tender, 8 tons empty. According to the experiments of the Gauge Commissioners, in December 1845, with an average train of 76½ tons, a maximum speed of 59 miles was attained; and the average speed was 50 miles, on a total run of 53 miles; the total consumption of coke was 35·3 lbs. per mile, and of water, 201·5 feet per hour.

Of late, a still more powerful class of passenger engines has been designed by Mr. Brunel and Mr. Gooch, known as the 'Great Britain' class (Fig. 20). It has inside cylin-ders, and is carried on eight wheels. The cylinders are 18 by 24 inches; wheel, 8 feet; grate, 21 feet; fire-box surface, 153 feet; 305 tubes, 2 inches in diameter; surface, 1799 feet; total heating surface, 1952 square feet. Weight of engine, 31 tons empty; of tender, 8½ tons; total weight, 50 tons loaded. Mr. Gooch states, that this engine is capable of evaporating 300 feet of water per hour at a high velocity; that it is capable of conveying a load of 236 tons, at 40 miles per hour, and a load of 181 tons, at 60 miles per hour. This, then, is practically the *ne plus ultra* of the 'broad' gauge; though Mr. Gooch states that the evaporation could be still further increased to 360 feet of water, without inter-fering with the due proportions of the engine. In 1848, Mr. Stephenson considered that the best passenger engines on

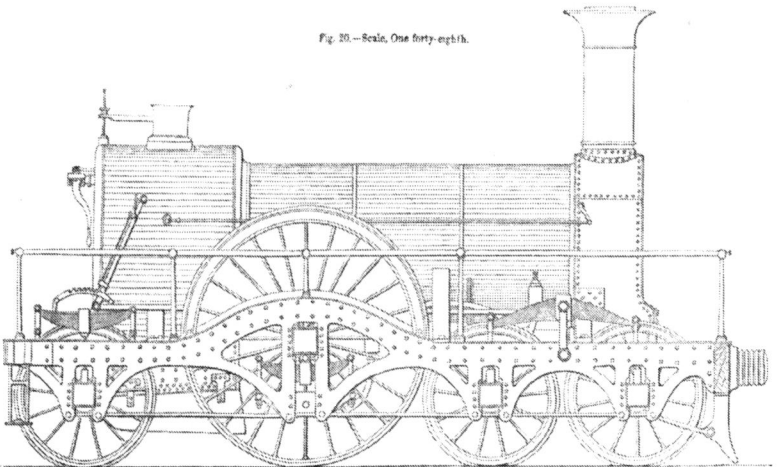

Fig. 20.—Scale, One forty-eighth.

Gooch's Locomotive, Great Western Railway, 1846. Cylinder, inside, 18 by 24 inches. Wheel 8 feet. Ultimatum for the 7-feet gauge.

the 4 feet 8½ inch gauge, were capable of conveying a train of 180 tons, including engine and tender, at 40 miles per hour, on a level; and a train of 110 tons, at 60 miles. Adding the weight of engine and tender, with coke and water, 50 tons, to the weight of train, on the Great Western, we find that, at 40 miles per hour, the total load conveyed on that line, 286 tons, is, to that conveyed on the common gauge, 180 tons, as 1·6 to 1.

After all that had been done by Stephenson and others, to turn out an engine to suit the common gauge, which should combine the three desiderata, power, speed, and stability, it was obvious that a low centre of gravity and a high driving-wheel were antagonistic elements, and they were assumed to be incompatible. The gauge could not be increased; engineers had, therefore, to find their additional power longitudinally, and upwards; to gain high speeds, they assumed a high wheel, and a high wheel required a high boiler. To exert power, they adopted large cylinders; and to obtain power, they applied long boilers. Mr. T. R. Crampton has the merit of having solved the problem, in all its fulness, of combining a low centre of gravity with a large wheel and a powerful boiler. He conceived the idea of an extreme driving-axle, removing it from under the boiler, and placing it in the rear of the fire-box. This stumbling-block being removed, he lowered the boiler to just clear the axles of the carrying-wheels, removed all the machinery to the outside, enlarged the fire-box, and rendered every part accessible. Great freedom in every respect was thus gained, and unwonted facilities were af-forded for properly proportioning the engine. The method of the outside driving-wheel, with some minor novelties, formed the subject of a patent by Mr. Crampton, granted in February 1843. The first engines constructed on Cramp-ton's patent, were two, made by Messrs. Tulk and Ley of Whitehaven, in 1847, for the Namur and Liege Railway. The first of these, a six-wheel engine, named the 'Namur,' was tried on the London and North-western Railway, with every variety of train, previously to being forwarded to its ultimate destination. It had cylinders 16 by 20 inches; driving-wheels, 7 feet; carrying-wheels, 3 feet 9 inches; extreme centres of axles, 13 feet; 182 tubes, 2 inches by 11 feet; fire-grate surface, 14½ feet; fire-box surface, 62 feet; tube surface, 927 feet. In the course of experiments, over a distance of 2300 miles, this engine conveyed a train of 80 tons, exclusive of engine and tender, at 51 miles per hour on a level; and a train of 50 tons at 62 miles per hour.

The first of Crampton's engines made for the London and North-western Railway, was a six-wheel engine, the 'London,' placed on the line, and working, in 1847. It has cylinders 18 by 20 inches; wheels, 8 feet, and 3 feet 9 inches; 229 tubes 2 inches outside diameter, and 12 feet long; grate surface, 21¼ feet; fire-box surface, 91 feet; tube surface, 1438 feet; total surface, 1529 feet; weight of engine, 24 tons empty; tender, 20 tons. By experiment, this engine was found to convey a train of 15 carriages, 75 tons weight, at 55·4 miles per hour for 3 miles; and a train of 11 carriages, 55 tons weight, at 53·4 miles per hour, in one run of 30 miles long.

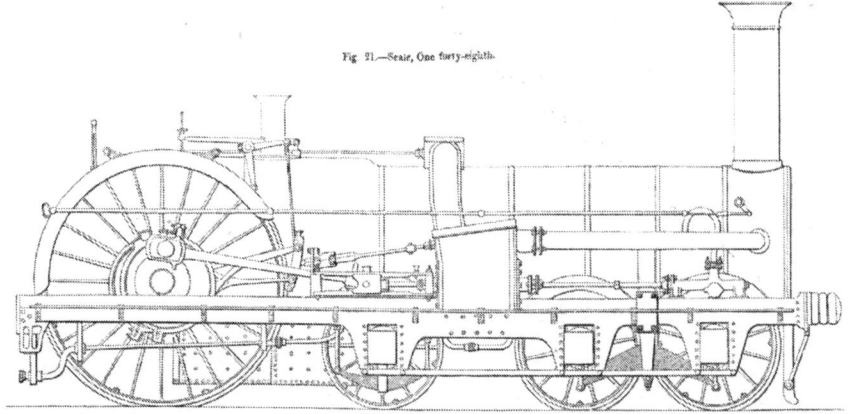

Fig 21.—Scale, One forty-eighth.

Crampton's Locomotive, London and North-western Railway, 1848. Outside cylinders, 18 by 24 inches, Wheel 8 feet. Ultimatum for the 4 feet 8½ inch gauge.

The facilities for adding to the power of the engines of the 4 feet 8½ inch gauge, consistently with stability, which are peculiar to Mr. Crampton's plan, pointed out his style as the most eligible for an engine capable of competing, in point of power and speed, with the Great Western, or 7-feet gauge engines. The unsoundness of the policy of getting up heavy engines, merely to show what can be done, is apparent; it may, nevertheless, be useful to state some particulars of Crampton's engine, the 'Liverpool,' with eight wheels (Fig. 21), made by Messrs. Bury, Curtis, and Kennedy, for the London and North-western Railway, and pompously announced as the most powerful locomotive in the world; cylinders, 18 by 24 inches; driving-wheel, 8 feet; carrying-wheels, 4 feet; centres of extreme wheels, 18½ feet apart; total length of engine, 27 feet; 300 tubes 2¹⁄₁₆ inch outside diameter, by 12½ feet long; fire-grate surface, 21¼ feet; fire-box surface, 154 feet; outside tube surface, 2136 feet; total heating surface, 2290 feet; weight of engine, 35 tons charged, of which load 12 tons are placed upon the driving-wheels, 17 tons on the four leading-wheels, and 6 tons on the intermediate wheels; tender, 21 tons; total, 56 tons. This splendid monster worked the express trains between London and Wolverton for some time, and on one occasion conveyed a train of 40 carriages within time, more than work for three ordinary engines; it was, however, laid aside, on account of its excessive weight, aggravated, no doubt, by the great distance of end centres, which quickly told upon the maintenance of the permanent way.

Numerous modifications of the locomotive, of various merit, besides those that have been referred to, have been introduced and patronized by divers manufacturers of cele- brity. As the most prominent of them are engines of the present day, a further notice of them is reserved for a future chapter.

Special mention has been made of particular lines of railway in the preceding historical sketch of locomotives, obviously for the purpose of general illustration. There are many other district railways now in operation, which have been open for traffic several years; but it is unneces- sary to extend our notices of individual lines further, as all the railways in the country have been engineered and officered by a few, and have consequently but few specialities of the working stock requiring notice. The history of one or two railways, is the history of all: the main features are identical. The leading facts are, that on the first introduc- tion of passenger railways, speeds of about 12 miles per hour only were anticipated; the rails thus employed weighed only 35 lbs. per yard, and the engines from 5 to 7 tons. When speeds of 20 and 24 miles were attempted, it was found necessary to have 50 lb. rails, and engines of 10 and 12 tons. The engines were thus divisible into two classes, four-wheel engines, and six-wheel engines, patronized re- spectively by Bury and by Stephenson, as the leading makers. As speed and power, convertible terms, increased, more accommodation was wanted; outside-cylinder engines, therefore, were constructed, weighing 15 and 16 tons; in- side cylinders continued in vogue, as by simplification of the machinery, accommodation was provided for them. In other quarters, the gauge of the railway having been in- creased 50 per cent. upon the previously existing gauge, the constraint incidental to the inside cylinder was very much relaxed, and still more powerful engines were made, weighing, from first to last, 15 to 35 tons charged. On the ordinary gauge, too, the boilers of the engines were lengthened, and the fire-box increased, and the long-boiler engine was the result, weighing from 20 to 22 tons. Finally, as some of the later engines on the common gauge had, owing to peculiarities of construction, acquired a character of unsteadiness at high speeds, and of increased cost of maintenance, Crampton's engine was introduced, in which the wheel-base was extended, and more solidly arranged, the driving-wheel being placed behind the fire-box, and the boiler lowered considerably. Meanwhile, the rails were increased progressively to 65, 75, and 85 pounds per yard.

The annexed Table, drawn from Captain Huish's *Reports on Railway Plant* (1849), exhibits, in contrast, the different circumstances at the time of being opened, and, finally, in the year 1848, of three principal lines, originally distinct, but now amalgamated, under the name of the London and North-western Railway, and under one general management :—

COMPARATIVE TABLE OF LOADS AND SPEEDS OF TRAINS, 1849.

Loads and Speeds.	Liverpool and Manchester.		Grand Junction.		London and Birmingham.	
	1831.	1848.	1837.	1848.	1837.	1848.
Number of Trains to and from principal terminus or station, in 24 hours	26*	90	14†	38	19‡	44
	tons. cwts.	tons. cwts.	tons. cwts.	tons. cwts.	tons. cwts.	tons. cwts.
Average weight of Engines	7 0	15 7	15 7	17 3	12 7	18 13
Greatest weight of Engines	7 0	17 3	15 5	26 5	12 7	37 0
Average weight of Carriages—						
First Class	3 10	4 10	4 0	4 18	3 13	4 6
Second Class	3 5	3 10	3 10	4 10	3 5	4 1
Third Class	3 0	3 2	3 2	3 17	2 10	3 18
Average weight of Passenger Trains, with engine and tender	18 0	70 0	60 0	70 0	58 0	70 0
Average weight of Goods Trains, with engine and tender	52 0	126 0	133 0	176 0	124 0	160 0
			Miles per hour.			
Average speed of Goods Trains	10	19	17	19½	16	20
Greatest speed of Goods Trains	12	30	20	30	21	32
Average speed of Passenger Trains	17	29	20	30	20	30
Greatest speed of Passenger Trains	24	40	28	50	28	50

* Manchester (Victoria).　　　† Stafford.　　　‡ Euston Square.

Goods engines have not, in this sketch, received or required special attention. The difficulties which led to improvements were, in general, encountered in the passenger engines; and what had been found good for the latter, was of course available for the former. It has been, of course, impracticable, without greatly involving the business of the chapter, to entertain questions of detail. It was sufficient to refer to such matters of internal arrangement, as affected the general dispositions of the machine; for the locomotive has been treated quite as much with reference to its qualifications as a carriage, as it has been with regard to its efficiency as an engine of power. And it must have been observed throughout the discussion, that the carriage-qualifications of the locomotive have had much greater influence upon the direction and rate of its progress from time to time, than any other single cause; and that one of the main distinctions betwixt one generation of locomotives and another, was to be found in their respective rolling abilities.

The considerations which affect the merits of a locomotive, as a steady-going vehicle, usually harmonize with those which concern its abilities, as a producer and dispenser of power. In the succeeding chapters, the mechanism of the locomotive will be historically considered more in detail, our business being to trace the course of alteration and improvement, from the time when intricacy and fancy appeared to regulate the tastes of engine-builders.

CHAPTER III.

MECHANISM OF THE VALVES.

THE main mechanical features of the non-condensing steam-engine were familiar to engineers, previously to Trevethick's experiments in 1804. The double-acting cylinder, the crank and connecting-rod motion, the slide-valve and eccentric of Murdoch—all of these had been matured at Soho, and were in common use before the end of last century. The pioneers of railway locomotion by steam were thus but a colony, not planted, certainly, but thrown off by the patriarchal Watt, whose fruitful patents contained the germs of the application of steam in all its variety.

Trevethick applied the elements of the steam-engine very much as he found them. He even contented himself with an ordinary cock for the distribution of the steam. A motion which should work the valves truly, during both fore and back gear, appears to have been a frequent study for locomotive builders. In the early Killingworth engines, the valves were moved by means of a 'square box or tumbler,' similar, no doubt, to the familiar cam-motion, with which it was found, that when the set was most favourable for fore-gear, it was inferior for back gear. Mr. Wood, the engineer, ultimately adopted a loose eccentric, fitting the

Fig. 22.

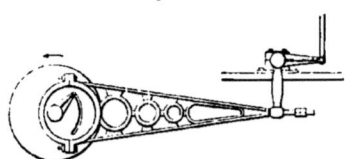

Killingworth Engine.—Valve Motion, 1820-30.

driving-axle, Fig. 22, a motion which exactly met the desideratum, and was employed permanently in the Killingworth engines, till the revolutionary year 1829. A lever was fixed upon, and revolved with, the driving-axle, formed with a stud, which entered and slid freely in a concentric groove cut in the body of the eccentric. The stud found its way to one end of the groove, and determined the position of the eccentric on the axle, for the fore or back gear. The small end of the eccentric rod was permitted some longitudinal play in the eye of the intermediate lever—adjustable by nuts. With an adjustable eccentric, of sufficient throw, and the adjustable limits of the travel of valve, the valve was quickly opened and closed, and its movement was equally good for both directions. The motion so derived, was obviously similar to that of the ancient tappet-frame, or the more modern cam; and we have seen that Murdoch applied the former with much success, in his unique Lilliputian.

The loose-eccentric gear was employed with modifications, by Hackworth, as we have already seen, and in the original inside-cylinder engines of the Liverpool and Manchester Railway. The two eccentrics were cast in two pieces, and bolted together into one mass, capable of sliding laterally on the axle between the cranks. No play was permitted between the eccentric-rods and the valve-levers—a necessary precaution in high-speed engines. The eccentrics were engaged in fore and back gear, by two snugs or catches fixed on the axle, one behind each crank, the locking of the eccentrics being accomplished by a forcible lateral movement. Separate mechanism was employed to control the small ends of the eccentric-rods, formed with gabs to disengage them when it was necessary to work the valves by 'hand-gear,' which was occasionally required at starting. In Fenton, Murray, and Jackson's first engines, Fig. 10, five handles and a foot-pedal were provided for working them—the regulator handle, two gab-handles, two for working the valves, and the pedal for shifting the eccentrics. Tayleur and Co. substituted a handle for the pedal, and had but one gab-handle, in all four handles besides that of the regulator. Bury, like Tayleur, also employed four handles, Fig. 23.

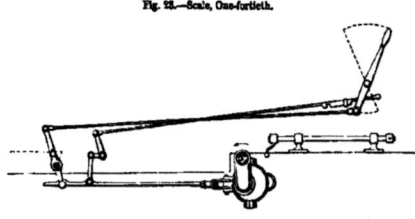

Fig. 23.—Scale, One-fortieth.

Bury's Locomotive,—Valve-gear, 1830-40.

The system of loose eccentrics was for locomotives, cumbrous, complicated, abrupt, and easily deranged. It was therefore readily abandoned for a simpler and firmer plan. Two fast eccentrics were substituted for the loose ones, one to each cylinder; this was partially a reversion to the primitive plan of the fixed cam, and the same difficulty of working equally well in fore and back gear was encountered. Mechanism suitable for working each valve with one fixed eccentric, affording the required lead both ways, was in-

vented by J. and C. Carmichael of Dundee in 1818, and has been variously applied by them. For locomotives, Fig. 24,

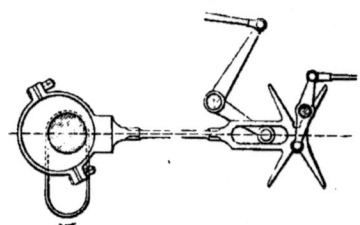

Fig. 24.—Scale, One-sixteenth.

Carmichael's Valve-gear, 1830-40.

the eccentric rod was finished with a double fork, to gear with the pivots of a double spanner on the traverse shaft of the valve, and was grooved to receive a roller on the end of the reversing lever, by which it was placed in fore or back gear, with the lower or upper spanner. The spread of the forks enabled them to engage the pivots of the spanner in all positions of the valve, and to bring them home to the gabs. This motion, duly proportioned, preserved the lead of the valve both ways—a matter of fact which for many years proved a *pons asinorum* for ingenious youths. It was a real advance upon the system of the loose eccentric, as one handle sufficed for working the gear, and all the parts were solidly put together. As definite proportions must subsist between the lengths of the rods and levers, to afford the necessary angle of the eccentric, due to the lead in fore and back gear, this meritorious piece of mechanism was found, in many cases, to be inconvenient in application; and though other plans were suggested and occasionally employed, it was not superseded in locomotives until the method of four eccentrics was introduced.[*]

A modification of Carmichael's gearing, Fig. 25, was em-

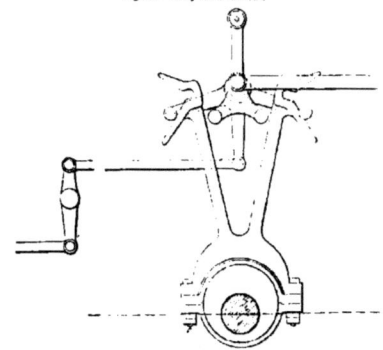

Fig. 25.—Scale, One-twentieth.

Forrester's Valve-gear, 1834.

ployed in Forrester's outside cylinder locomotive, already

* A discussion of the geometrical principle of Carmichael's valve-gear would, in this place, be inappropriate. A full explanation, with illustrations, is contained in the *Glasgow Engineer's Magazine*, vol. ii., 1843, p. 262.

described. The eccentric acted vertically; it had two diverging rods finished with gabs, and these were placed in gear with the double spanner, on the one side or the other, or held out of gear, by a double-ended pall hung betwixt them, and worked from the foot-plate. Though it is very possible that this was the most commodious plan of gearing for the engines in question, the confusion and clatter of so many pieces was notorious.

The inconvenience of combining in one eccentric the functions of two was removed by the adoption of four fixed eccentrics, of which the authorship is uncertain. Two were provided for each cylinder, for working respectively in fore and back gear. Each eccentric had its own fork; and though the plan entailed the use of four eccentrics, and additional bearings, the increased workmanship was compensated by precision and certainty of action. The first application of four eccentrics to locomotives, was made by the Hawthorns of Newcastle, in 1837. It has been ascertained, however, that some time previously, an ingenious mechanic, in private circumstances, residing at Newcastle, had contrived, and constructed, an efficient model of valvegear, for locomotives, in which four eccentrics were employed, in the manner afterwards wrought out in practice.

In all the forms of double-eccentric gear, it was necessary to effect simultaneously the disengagement of one pair of eccentrics, and the engagement of the other. Various plans of reversing were adopted. Stephenson employed two trans-

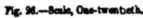
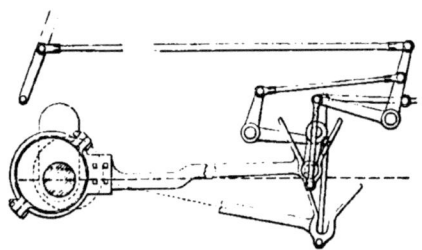

Fig. 26.—Scale, One-twentieth.

Stephenson's Valve-gear. 1838.

verse shafts, the principal of which was worked by the reversing handle, and commanded the fore gabs; the secondary shaft was linked to, and worked by, the principal shaft, and it had charge of the back gabs. All the forks geared from below, and one movement of the reversing handle elevated one pair, and lowered the other. Thus the manipulation was simple and easy, as the reciprocal action of the gear balanced the weight of one pair of rods with that of the other.

Sharp and Roberts' plan was less happy in its arrangement. With two transverse shafts, as in Stephenson's, the one for back gear was placed below the other, and worked by short back levers, and links—a modification by which all the gabs were raised or lowered at once. Thus the fore gabs engaged from above, and the back gabs from below. In this plan, it is obvious, the second shaft might have been dispensed with, as the first shaft could have discharged the

double function with great propriety. By placing the fore gab *above* the pivot, it was permitted to lie solidly in gear, while in action; though the gearing has not the self-balan-

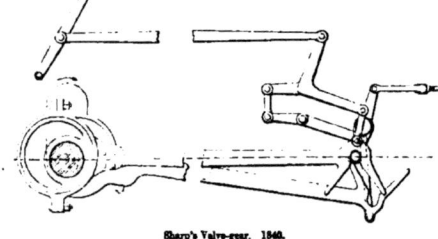

Fig. 27.—Scale, One-twentieth.

Sharp's Valve-gear. 1840.

cing character of Stephenson's; and, moreover, should the fore gab, by an accident, have fallen into gear, while the engine was placed in back gear, rupture was inevitable.

A common modification of the underhung gear, Fig. 28,

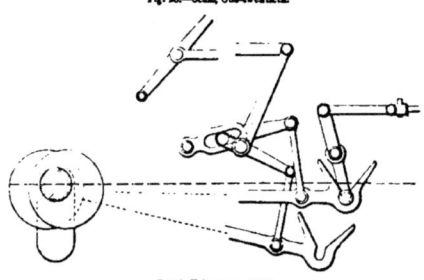

Fig. 28.—Scale, One-twentieth.

Bury's Valve-gear. 1840.

was in very general use by Bury and Co., and others. The second shaft, placed behind the first, was slotted, and worked by a short cranked part of the latter. Thus compactness was combined with the self-balanced method of Stephenson. A variety of this motion, Fig. 29, was employed by Haw-

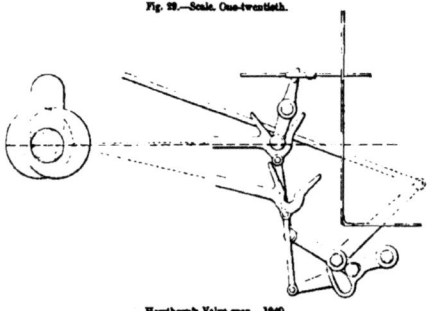

Fig. 29.—Scale, One-twentieth.

Hawthorn's Valve-gear. 1840.

thorn; he transferred the reversing shafts to a position below the forks, and had their bearings fixed to the smoke-box. This arrangement entirely cleared out the space below the boiler, and rendered the gearing more accessible than before. The fore gabs were worked by the first shaft—a duty which, in the previous example, devolved upon the second; and though the shortness of the levers employed in working the second shaft increased and concentrated strains in the working parts, and magnified the slackness arising from the wear of surfaces, Hawthorn's motion was more simple and solid than the other; and the repairs upon engines fitted with it, have been found to be remarkably slight. In Bury's motion, a peculiar source of wear existed, in the mode of suspending the eccentric rods by points apart from the notches, as the vertical motion of the eccentrics was transmitted to the notches through the points of suspension as fulcra: with a 3¼ inch throw, and a leverage of 8 to 1, the vertical motion of the forks was nearly half an inch.

To consolidate the gearing by dispensing with the second shaft, Buddicom employed a system, Fig. 30, for the outside-

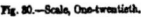

Fig. 30.—Scale, One-twentieth.

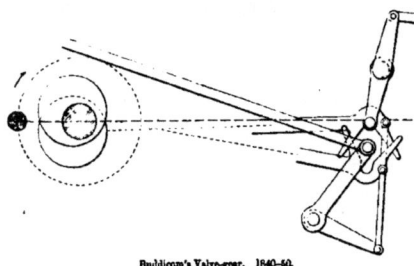

Buddicom's Valve-gear. 1840-50.

cylinder engines of the Paris and Rouen Railway, in which the forks were opposed, and worked by one lever on the reversing shaft. The position of this shaft below leaves clear head-room under the boiler. The same motion is employed on that railway at this day.

Jackson made an effort still further to simplify the gearing, by making the reversing shaft, Fig. 31, hollow, and con-

Fig. 31.—Scale, One-twentieth.

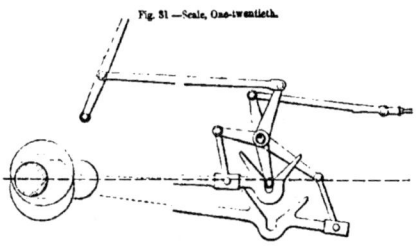

Jackson's Valve-gear. 1840.

centric with that which carried the valve lever. The suspending levers were necessarily placed on opposite sides of the shaft, and linked at some distance from the notches; which involved the objections already noted in Bury's gear, of the vertical play of the gabs.

Some attempts have been made to supersede the eccentric motion, by contrivances deriving their motion from the connecting-rod. Mr. Melling, formerly of the Liverpool and Manchester Railway, made a stud fast on the middle of the connecting-rod, which, by the nature of connecting-rod motion, described a species of elliptic curve, as represented in Fig. 32. The stud worked in a slot formed in a lever, of

Fig. 32.—Scale, One twenty-fourth.

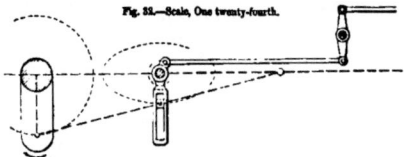

Melling's Valve-gear, without Eccentrics. 1830-40.

which the axis was placed in the centre of the oval. This arm the pin carried round with it, and on the same axis a small crank worked the valve-rod, like an ordinary eccentric. The angular motion of this crank was variable, and it was slowest when the crank turned the dead points, at the time when it ought to have opened the port with the greatest celerity. Melling, perceiving the objection, caused the valves to be worked by the connecting-rods of the alternate cylinders, which effected a marked improvement of the exhaust. Hawthorn's motion, for the same object, Fig. 33, is,

Fig. 33.—Scale, One-twentieth.

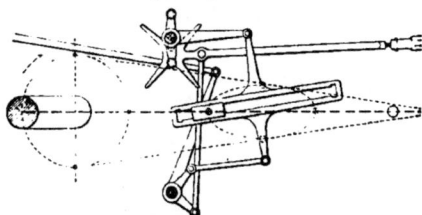

Hawthorn's Valve-gear, without Eccentrics. 1836.

like the other, actuated by a pin in the side of the connecting-rod, which works in a slotted link that transmits only the vertical motion of the pin to the valve-levers. The lead is regulated by the inclination of the parallelogram, adjustable upon the levers and links. This scheme is an example of what George Stephenson used to phrase 'the danger of too much ingenuity.' Though it yielded respectable results, the plan has not been received with much favour, for its motion really was no better than that of the eccentric.

In all of these plans, an intermediate traverse shaft was necessary to transmit the motion to the valves, as the valve-spindles could not, according to the prevailing arrangement of the steam chest over the cylinder, be in the same horizontal plane with the driving-axle. A modification introduced by Stephenson, however, by which the steam-chests were removed from the top and placed between the cylinders, uniting into one capacious chest with vertical valve-faces, enabled him to bring the valve-spindles to the level of the driving-axle, to dismiss the intermediate shaft, and to work the valves directly. The forks, Fig. 34, were transferred to the valve-rods, and the eccentric-rod ends formed with plain

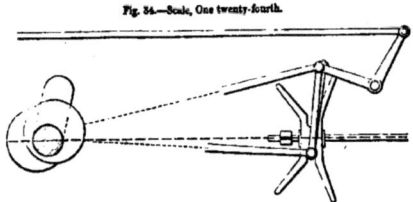

Fig. 34.—Scale, One twenty-fourth.

Stephenson's Valve-gear. 1840.

pins, and linked. This motion, as it was the most direct, and involved the fewest parts, was the best of all that had yet appeared.

Mr. Pauwels, in France, imitated the direct motion of Stephenson. He adopted the vertical valve-face, retained the forked rods, Fig. 35, placed them facing one another, and

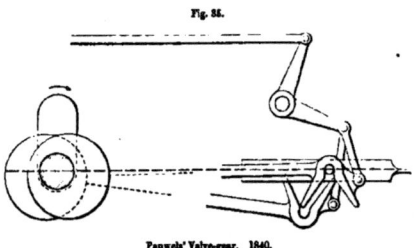

Fig. 35.

Pauwels' Valve-gear. 1840.

linked them to the reversing shaft above. In this machine, as in some of the others, the weight of the moving parts of the gearing is unbalanced. The application of the balance-weight for the purpose of establishing an equilibrium, is a refinement of later application.

Mr. Robertson, of the Glasgow and South-western Railway, following in the school of Buddicom (with outside cylinder and fixed valve-gear), has, in his most modern locomotives, retained the gab motion. The motion is, like Pauwels', direct and suspended from above; and, like Jackon's, it has one transverse shaft with two levers, one on each side, to carry the forks. This motion is direct and self-balancing, and is probably the best arrangement of gab motion.

A glance over the foregoing specimens of valve-mechanism, is sufficient to satisfy one of the difficulties encountered by engine-builders, in following out their respective designs. A fancy for intricacy and quaint originality, appears in some instances to have regulated their practice, though it is probable that professional jealousy had more to do with it than either. To imitate was dishonourable, and to alter was easier than to improve; yet there is a talent in selection, clearly distinguishable from imitation, which constitutes the staple of many a man's reputation. We have found that the gab motion maintained its position in locomotive valve-gear under various modifications, being competent for all the ordinary requirements of the engine-driver. It was finally superseded by the necessities of variable expansion.

CHAPTER IV.

Expansion Valves.

Murdoch's valve, which has been universally employed in the locomotive for distributing the steam, had, in its primitive form, Fig. 36, but a trifling amount of lap, only $\frac{1}{16}$ inch, merely nominal, and applied only as an assurance that the steam should not enter at both ends of the cylinder at the

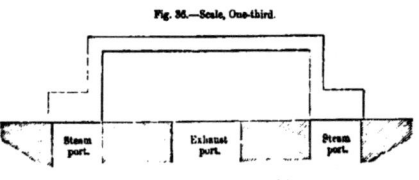

Fig. 36.—Scale, One-third.

Primitive Valve, One-sixteenth inch lap.

same time. Engineers were solicitous chiefly to insure a timely and free admission of steam, unaware of the much greater necessity for an early and liberal exhaustion. This valve was in common use until 1838. The steam passage was opened to the exhaust immediately after it was closed for admission, and both events took place at the termination of the stroke. Thus no time was allowed for exhaustion previously to the beginning of the succeeding stroke; and so little were the defects of this valve understood, according to Mr. Woods, that when, in 1836, short-stroke passenger locomotives were introduced on the Liverpool and Manchester Railway, to run at high speeds, their greater consumption of fuel was referred to the mechanical disadvantage of the short-stroke.

In 1838, on the Liverpool and Manchester Railway, it was determined that as, in some instances, $\frac{3}{8}$ and $\frac{1}{2}$ inch lead on the steam side was permitted, the effect of transferring the lead to the exhaust side of the valve should be tried. The valves of the Lightning, having originally $\frac{1}{4}$ inch outside lap, had it increased to $\frac{3}{8}$ inch; thus, being set to open the ports for steam just at the beginning of the stroke, the exhaust was necessarily, at the same time, open $\frac{1}{8}$ inch. The more efficient and timely exhaust so effected, reduced the consumption of coke 25 per cent., and improved the speeds, which with many locomotives of the day, did not previously exceed 30 miles per hour. In the beginning of 1840, $\frac{3}{4}$ inch of lap was given to the valves of the Rapid and the Arrow, the stroke of the valve, $3\frac{1}{2}$ inches, remaining unaltered; the consumption was thereby reduced from 40 to 32 lbs. per mile, or 20 per cent. with the same trains.

In 1839, Mr. John Gray's variable expansion-gear was applied to the Cyclops, on the same railway. This gearing, by varying the travel of the valve, varied the period of the admission of steam, between 82 and 46 per cent. of the stroke, the steam operating expansively, during the greater part of the remainder. The valves had $\frac{3}{4}$ inch of outside lap, and $\frac{1}{4}$ inch inside; the difference, $\frac{1}{2}$ inch, was therefore the excess of inside lead, and the lead was preserved constant for all variations of travel. The results of Gray's gearing showed an economy of 12 per cent. of fuel, as compared with the best working engines on the same line—an advantage which was, without doubt, attributable to the earlier exhaustion of the steam, and to the higher pressure that was employed, quite as much as to the use of expansion.

In 1840, Mr. Dewrance, on the same railway, conceiving that the passage to the exhaust ought to be nearly wide open at the end of the stroke, employed 1 inch of lap outside, and 4¼ inch travel. The results, with the Rapid, showed a

Fig. 37.—Scale, One-third.

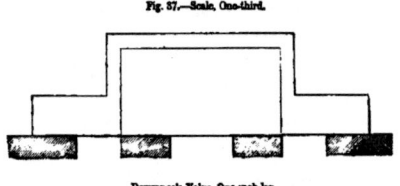

Dewrance's Valve, One inch lap.

fall of consumption from 36·3 lbs. to 28·6 lbs. per mile, 25 per cent. The steam was cut off at 79 per cent. of the stroke, and exhausted at 95 per cent.; and the valve was 1 inch opened for the exhaust at the end of the stroke. The waste steam previously choked up in the cylinder, and so causing ruinous back pressure, was freely released, less steam was thus employed, the blast orifice was enlarged, the blast was thereby softened, while it maintained a sufficiency of steam, the coke was no longer dragged from its bed by the violence of draft, and the fire-bars could be placed closer together to reduce the leakage of cinders.*

The following table, arranged by Mr. Woods, in 1844, exhibits the results in the consumption of coke, of the improvements successively applied to the locomotives of the Liverpool and Manchester Railway. The second result was the effect of a new mode of delivering the coke to the engines, by which the individual consumption of every engine was ascertained, and which induced a spirit of rivalry amongst the drivers.

Gross average consumption of Coke per mile.

49 lbs.	Old valve, ¹⁄₁₆ inch lap, 1830.
40 lbs.	Old valve, after the introduction of the new mode of delivery, 1830.
36 lbs.	Valves with ¼ inch lap.
32 lbs.	Valves with ½ inch lap
28 lbs.	Valves with 1 inch lap.
22 lbs.	Valves with 1 inch lap, with increased care in firing.
15 lbs.	Valves with 1 inch lap, applied to new engines with enlarged exhausting passages, larger tubes, closer fire-bars, and superior construction.

The necessity and advantage of lap was established by these experiments, both as to its facilities for affording a free exhaust, and for working steam expansively. Without lap there could be no expansion; and though it was introduced primarily for the purpose of an efficient release, its advantages as a means of working expansively, became likewise apparent; and it quickly found its way into common use on other lines of railway.

Variable Expansion Gear.—The engines having, by the application of lap, got relieved of the greater part of the overpowering resistance of back pressure, the refinements of variable-expansion gear were introduced. These are reducible to two classes—first, those mechanisms which operate upon single valves, by varying their travel; secondly, those with which two valves are employed, one of which is specially designed for varying the expansion. Increase of expansion, it must be observed, is obtained simply by causing the valve to cut the steam off earlier in the course of the stroke.

Variable Expansion Gear with a single valve.—In all the individuals of this class, the travel is varied by means of mechanism external to the valve-chest. Gray's gearing, Fig. 38, already referred to, as applied on the Liverpool

Fig. 38.—Scale, One twenty-fourth.

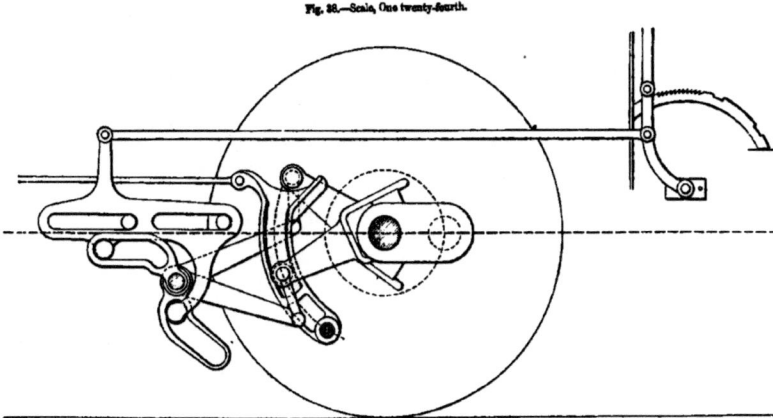

John Gray's Expansion gear. 1839.

and Manchester Railway, is the first that was in this country

applied to locomotives. The pin of the eccentric-rod works in a segmental lever, curved to the radius of the rod, the upper end of which is linked to the valve-spindle. Thus,

* On the Consumption of Fuel in the Locomotives of the Liverpool and Manchester Railway. By Edward Woods. *Glasgow Engineers' Magazine.* 1845.

D

the lever, being concentric with the fore-rod at the beginning of the stroke, the rod may be raised or lowered in the slot of the lever to any required distance from the fulcrum, which, of course, regulates the travel of the valve, while the lead remains unchanged. The reversing mechanism consists principally of a wrought-iron frame, which slides horizontally on two fixed pivots, and carries rollers, which, working in grooved levers linked to the eccentric-rods, place these rods in and out of gear, with the segmental lever, as required. The action of reversing is, in this mechanism, very suddenly performed in the quick bends of the grooved levers; and accordingly, in practice, very great manual power was demanded for the operation. To Mr. Gray is due the merit of the first application of the principle of varying expansion by variation of travel, whether in locomotive, land, or marine engines—a principle of primary importance at the present day, though originally embodied in a complicated and inconvenient piece of gear.

Mr. Cabrey, of the North Midland Railway, embodied the idea of the variation of travel in a simpler form, Fig. 39,

Fig. 39.—Scale, One-twentieth.

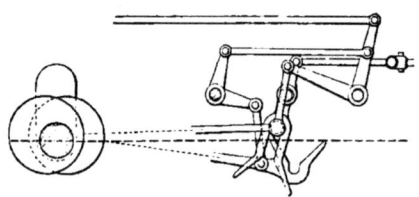

Cabrey's Expansion Valve-gear.

in which the pin of the fore-rod was adjustable in a slotted lever or 'sliding fork' on the valve-shaft. In this mechanism the lead increased rapidly as the travel was shortened.

The last and most perfect embodiment of Gray's principle of the variation of travel, for working expansively, is to be found in the 'Link-motion.' Nothing but an impulse of genius could have given birth to this exquisite motion; and though, in its first conception by Mr. Williams, at one time of Newcastle, it was rude, and even impracticable, the idea was there, and it had only to be cleverly worked out by Mr. Howe of the Forth Street Works, to render it, in conjunction with the lap of the valve, the most felicitous acquisition to the locomotive since the introduction of the

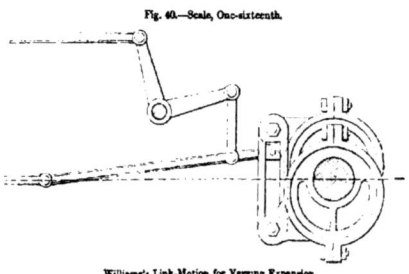

Fig. 40.—Scale, One-sixteenth.

Williams's Link-Motion for Varying Expansion.

blast-pipe and the multitubular flue. Williams's incipient 'link,' Fig. 40, was a slotted straight bar, which connected the straps of the fore and back eccentrics, formed with ears to secure the linking pins. In the slot of the link a slide-block, hung on the end of a radius link from the valve-spindle, was adjustable towards one end or the other, to receive the motion of the one or the other eccentric, for fore or back gear. While the link would partake jointly of the two motions of the eccentrics, its horizontal motion would be smallest at the centre of its length, and increase towards the extremities. Thus, by shifting the block towards the centre, the travel of valve would be reduced, and variable expansion thereby obtained. The objections to the special arrangement here proposed are obvious; the idea was, however, developed by Mr. Howe into the more practicable arrangement, Fig. 41, first applied to the engines of Robert

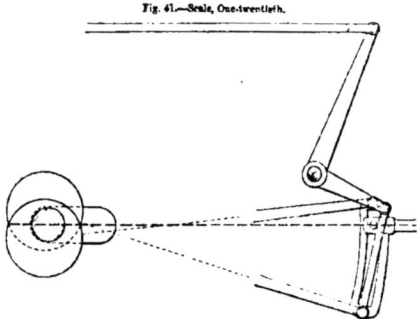

Fig. 41.—Scale, One-twentieth.

Howe's (or Stephenson's) Link-motion. 1843.

Stephenson and Co. in 1843, and from this time the link has been adopted generally by all other English manufacturers. The eccentric-rods, dismissed in the original conception, are here retained, and their extremities connected by a curved link, curved to the radius of the rods. The slide-block is placed directly on the end of the valve-spindle, and the eccentric-rods and link are shifted vertically, similarly to the ordinary gab-motion, and may be maintained at any elevation required. Thus a simple and direct connection is established between the eccentrics and the valve, and the more nearly the centre of the link is brought to the slide-block, the shorter becomes the travel of the valve, and the greater the degree of expansion. The lead of the valve increases with the degree of expansion; this variation the curvature of the link cannot annihilate, but it is reduced and made equal for the front and back strokes of the piston. Since the application of the link by Mr. Howe, but little has been done to improve its action. In many cases, Williams's original arrangement has been partially adhered to, by suspending the link directly from a stationary point, and employing a radius link for shifting the block. In this plan the curvature of the link is reversed, to face the radius link, and the lead is constant for all degrees of expansion. A minute analysis of the link-motion is reserved for succeeding chapters.

Substitutes for the 'link' have been proposed, with no very tangible object except the saving of an eccentric, and the regulation of the lead. In the first place, we have Fenton's mode, Figs. 42, 43, of modifying the angular

Figs. 42, 43.—Scale, One-twentieth.

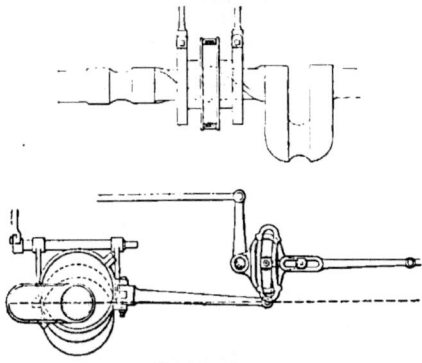

Fenton's Expansion-gear.

advance of the eccentrics, one to each cylinder, by adjusting them laterally on the axle between the crank, fitted with spiral feathers, which work in grooves in the eccentrics. Each eccentric is attached to a link, which vibrates on a fixed centre, and is slotted to receive the end of a radius-link from the valve-spindle; the elevation of the radius-link in the link proper, regulates the degree of expansion, and the lead is preserved constant by a simultaneous adjustment of the eccentrics. Again, Mr. Crampton's brochure, Fig. 44, is merely a development of Carmichael's gear, with a single fixed eccentric; in this

Fig. 44.—Scale, One twenty-fourth.

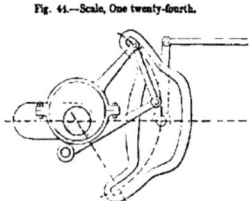

Crampton's Expansion Gear, 1845.

case the eccentric-rod is movable, and slides in a double link, placed on a traverse shaft as centre. A third design, Fig. 45, by Mr. Dodds of Newcastle, probably more used

Fig. 45.—Scale, One twenty-fourth.

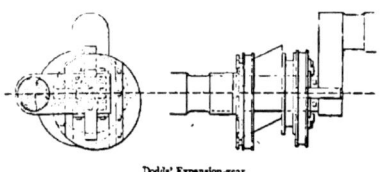

Dodds' Expansion-gear.

than either of the others, is the last fruit of labouring genius in pursuit of the *ignus fatuus*—good expansion-gear, with a single eccentric. He relapsed into the exploded practice of the loose eccentric, movable—not like Fenton's, laterally—but transversely on the axle. A sheave, with two pairs of wedges in one piece with it, and square with each other, is

movable along the axle; and by forcible lateral motion, the wedges, one pair to each eccentric, pass through and act upon corresponding slopes in the eccentrics, and shift them across the axle between the forward and the backward positions. At intermediate positions, of course, the eccentricity is shortened, and thus variable expansion is at command, though the lead increases with the expansion for one end of the cylinder, and decreases for the other end.

Variable Expansion Gear with Double or Superposed Valves.—These are of three classes—Tappet-valves, screw-set valves, and lever-set valves.

1. *Tappet-valves.* — Edwards' valve, originally schemed for stationary engines, was first applied, in 1840, to a loco-

Fig. 46.—Scale, One-sixteenth.

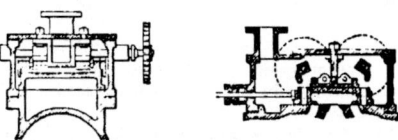

Edwards' Expansion-valve. Applied 1840.

motive on the St. Germains Railway in France. The valve proper contains the ordinary exhaust cavity, and two thorough passages for steam, and its travel is a fixed quantity. The second valve, a flat plate, is placed loose on the back of the valve, and moves with it; the extent of its travel being defined by a couple of cams, between which it vibrates, and of which the clear opening is regulated by toothed sectors and levers on the outside of the chest. At each reciprocation, the progress of the upper valve is checked by one of the cams, and the lower valve continuing to progress in the same direction towards the end of its travel, the steam passage closes under the upper valve, and the steam is suppressed. By drawing together the cams, the suppression takes place earlier, and thus variable expansion is obtained. This motion was too loose for the high speeds of locomotives, for the jarring of the plate and the cams was incessant and violent, and gave rise to frequent repair.

Edwards' valve was available for cutting off only during the first half of the stroke, because, as the crank and eccentric were nearly at right angles on the shaft, the travel of the valve, and consequently the action of the cams, terminated about the half stroke of the piston.

M. Farcot, a French engineer, devised, in 1836, a modification, Fig. 47, of Edwards' valve. He divided the upper plate into two, one to each steam way, and multiplied the entrances, to yield a speedier suppression. The plates were set right for the admission by studs, which

Fig. 47.—Scale, One-sixteenth.

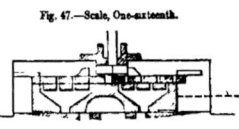

Farcot's Expansion Valve. Patented, 1836.

acted on the ends of the valve-chest; and their movement for the suppression was regulated by a double central cam fixed on a vertical spindle. The expansive function in this valve, is, as in Edwards', limited to the first half of the stroke.

MM. Lagavrian and Dequoy, of Lille, patented, in 1842, a mode of rendering Farcop's valve available for suppressing at all parts of the stroke. They interposed a third valve between those employed by Farcop, which was moved by a separate eccentric at right angles with the first, and coinciding therefore

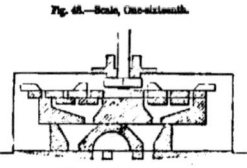

Fig. 48.—Scale, One-sixteenth.

Lagavrian's Expansion Valve. Patented, 1842.

with the crank. As the travel of the middle valve is consequently simultaneous with the stroke of the piston, it is obviously available, in conjunction with the paraphernalia of plates, cams, and tappets, for suppression at all parts of the stroke.

2. Screw-set Valves.—The abolition of tappet-valves, as impracticable pieces of mechanism for locomotives, gave rise to other expedients, in which the character of the motion was gradual and continuous.

Mr. Bodmer, formerly of Manchester, was the first to apply, in his double-piston locomotive, patented in 1841, the right and left hand screw for adjusting the expansion valve. Besides the ordinary slide-valve, he introduced a cylindrical valve for expansion, working steam tight in a cylindrical case without packing, and moved by a separate eccentric. The valve was in two pieces on one spindle, and it was the function of the double-acting screw to regulate their distance apart on the spindle. The steam, entering from within the expan-

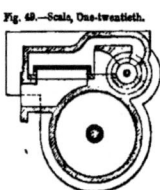

Fig. 49.—Scale, One-twentieth.

Bodmer's Expansion Valve. 1841.

sion valve, was admitted through openings in the case to the back of the ordinary slide, which were alternately closed and opened by the second valve; and the time of suppression was thus regulated by the distance apart of the two pieces of the valve.

Mr. Bodmer's expansion valve, placed at some distance from the ordinary valve, had no control over the body of steam that existed between the two of them. This imperfection was remedied by M. Meyer of Mulhausen, who patented, in 1842, a modification of Bodmer's valve, Fig. 50,

Fig. 50.—Scale, One-twentieth.

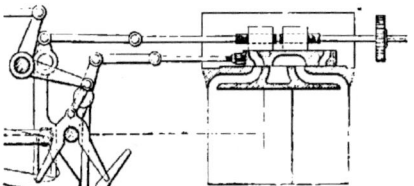

Meyer's Expansion Valve. 1842.

in which a pair of blocks, adjustable on right and left hand

screws, are planted on the back of the principal valve, and control the steam passages which pass through the latter, as in Edwards' valve. The spindle of the expansion blocks is moved by a slotted lever directly off the cross-head of the piston-rod, the motion of which is equivalent to that of an eccentric coinciding with the crank, as employed by Lagavrian. The main valve is moved by the ordinary gab-motion. The separation of the blocks is adjustable by means of spur gear on the outside of the chest, and the mechanism is equally well adapted for fore and back gear. This expansion gear has yielded good results in France, where chiefly it has been employed. It is obviously attended in its action with greater friction than Bodmer's, as the cylindrical valve is comparatively frictionless.

Naysmith, Gaskell, and Co. modified Meyer's valve by converting the blocks into appendages to the principal valve, and superposing a flat plate over all, Fig. 51, which received the motion of the cross-head. The double screw is collared to a snug on the back of the valve, which thereby carries the blocks with it,

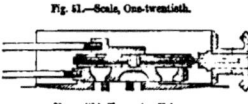

Fig. 51.—Scale, One-twentieth.

Naysmith's Expansion Valve.

and is virtually converted into a *variable-port valve*. The screw is finished with a square spindle, which slides in the nave of a mitre wheel, and by this means the blocks may be adjusted from the outside, for the degree of expansion required. The principle of the action of this gearing is essentially identical with that of Meyer's valve, and it possesses the economical advantage of reducing the fatigue on the screws.

3. Lever-set Valves.—This group comprises those valves which are adjusted from without the valve-chest; the valves themselves are invariable, and the adjustment is effected by varying the travel of valve, by the interposition of slotted levers. Naysmith, in a plan of this kind, Fig. 52, caused

Fig. 52.—Scale, One twenty-fourth.

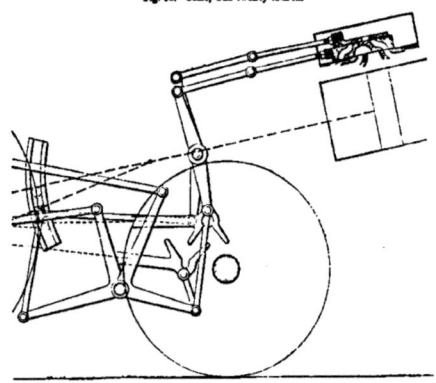

Naysmith's Expansion-Valve.

the steam to pass directly into the valve passage, through an aperture in the superposed plate; in place of a variable port as in the previous plan, Fig. 51, he employed variable travel for the upper valve, and moved it by a distinct eccentric, which actuated a segmental slotted lever, in which the end of a radius link from the expansion plate was adjustable for the required travel.

The Hawthorns of Newcastle employed, until lately, an elaborate expansion valve, Fig. 53, patented in 1843, which worked, like the principal valve, directly on the face of the cylinder, and also steam-tight on the back of the valve. When not in use, the valve was stationary, and therefore involved no frictional resistance except when actually working. The upper valve,

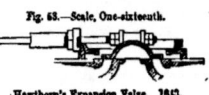

Fig. 53.—Scale, One-sixteenth.

Hawthorn's Expansion Valve. 1843.

it will be seen, suppresses the steam against the extreme edges of the lower; the spindles are concentric, and the lower valve is driven by a gab-motion, while the upper one is worked by the back eccentric, which moves a slotted lever, from which the motion is conveyed to the valve by a radius link, adjustable in the slot for the required travel. The experience of this valve on the North British Railway, where it has been extensively employed, has shown that the lower valve, always in motion, generally wore itself out of contact with the upper, to the extent of $\frac{1}{16}$ inch in the course of a year or two, which was certainly sufficient to neutralize any attempt at economical expansion working. In one locomotive on that railway, a 6-feet wheel express, under the care of a first-class driver, the valves remained in tolerably good order for three years, at the end of which period they had parted about $\frac{1}{32}$ inch.

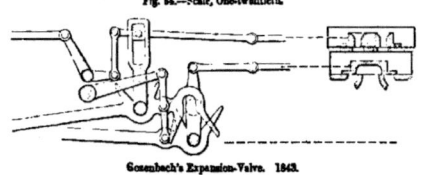

Fig. 54.—Scale, One-twentieth.

Gozenbach's Expansion-Valve. 1843.

M. Gozenbach, of the Strasburg and Basle Railway, patented, in 1843, an expansion-valve working in a separate chest over the ordinary one, the steam being passed through apertures in the interposed diaphragm. The upper valve was driven by the back eccentric, actuating a slotted lever in the usual manner, from which an adjustable radius link conveyed the motion to the valve. There is, of course, the objection of the intervening vacuity of the lower chest; this gearing has been found, however, to work well and economically.

We have been at some pains to illustrate the leading varieties of expansion valve-gear, because, though in England generally it is agreed that for locomotives nothing can surpass the link-motion for genuine simplicity and efficiency, it is not so thoroughly established abroad; and in America particularly, it is rather held in abeyance before the more popular system of the separate valve for expansion. As nothing has occurred within our own experience to damage the supremacy of the link-motion for locomotive engines, it is deemed unnecessary to bestow further attention upon other modes of expansive working. All *a priori* objections based upon premature exhaustion, premature compression, premature admission, illegitimate resistances, and so on, are good for nothing, except as they are founded on direct observation by the aid of the indicator; and this class of evidence we shall bring forward in good time. A link-substitute is about as reasonable a thing as a substitute for the crank. The clumsiness and complicacy of many of the schemes herein detailed, the liability to unequal and excessive wear, and the friction of surfaces incidental to all, indicate rather the efforts of men to meet speculative objections, than a clear perception of the obstacles to be removed. One brilliant exception to this general inference, exists in the case of the early improvements in the valves of the Liverpool and Manchester engines : a felicitous example of inductive reasoning; and it is further remarkable that the only two genuine 'improvements,' the fundamental elements of modern valve-gear—the lap of the valve, and the link-motion—are almost the only ones which were not monopolized under the protection of patents.

The substantial progress of the locomotive, with reference to the three elements—the boiler, the engine, and the carriage, has, in the foregoing chapters, been passed under review. Some minor matters which have not been particularly recognized, will be noticed on future occasions.

SECTION II.—PHYSIOLOGY OF THE LOCOMOTIVE.

THE locomotive may be regarded in two aspects—with reference to its functions, and to its construction; otherwise, by a slight license, its physiology, and its anatomy. The second of these, though it claims precedence in the order of nature, will be treated last, as a matter of convenience. There can be no practical objection to this arrangement, for those who are likely to consult this work are supposed to be perfectly aware of the general design and disposition of the locomotive. Again, the locomotive is composed of three distinct elements—the boiler, the engine, and the carriage. These shall be considered in succession, and first of the engine :—

SUB-SECTION I.

PHYSIOLOGY OF THE ENGINE.

IN the engine, there are two distinct and independent series of periodical movements. There is, first, the reciprocation of the piston under the alternate pressure of steam on its two surfaces, in conjunction with the simultaneous revolution of the crank and its axle; secondly, the revolution of the eccentrics, which are rigid on the crank axle, and the reciprocating movements communicated by them to the slide valve. The former motion, that of the piston in conjunction with the crank, is so simple and obvious, that what we have mostly to say of it will be found in the course of our discussion of the valve-motion. The functions of the valve are, in truth, the essence of the whole ; as on the valve is devolved the important business of distributing the steam, or prime mover, directing it on the piston, and providing an escape for it after it drives the piston home. According as this is efficiently or slovenly done, the engine must be either efficient or wanting in the discharge of its duty. In the course of the following chapters, therefore, the valve-motion will receive the consideration due to its paramount importance. First, the movements of valves will be considered geometrically, with reference to the timeing of the admission, suppression, and release of steam to and from the cylinder. Second, the effects of these movements on the motions of the steam will be considered with respect to the comparative facilities which they afford for the ingress and egress of the steam, ascertained from direct experiments, under various circumstances, on the action of steam in the cylinder.

First, as to the nature of valve-motion : —

CHAPTER I.

MOTION OF THE VALVE.—ITS FUNCTIONS.

THE motion of the valve, when driven directly by an eccentric, as in the ordinary gab-motions, is simply rectilineal and reciprocating, and is precisely on a smaller scale what the motion of the piston is on a larger. This is manifest in considering that the eccentric is but a crank of a very small radius, which has, like the greater crank, its own circle of revolution, its own throw, and its own dead points, which terminate the reciprocations of the valve in the one case, and those of the piston in the other.

The motion of the valve must, of course, be considered in its relation to that of the piston. The relation of these motions is founded upon the uniform circular motions of the crank and eccentric. These being rigidly fixed on one axle, have the same angular motion, and accomplish their revolutions in the same time. Their relations, therefore, and those of the piston and valve derived from them, may be established by following them through a complete revolution.

The motion of the piston is ruled by two circumstances : the varying angularity of the crank, and the varying angularity of the connecting-rod, but mainly the former. With an indefinitely long connecting-rod, of which the angularity is inconsiderable, the relation of the motion of the crank and the piston is represented by the annexed diagram, Fig. 55, in which $a c$ is the stroke of the piston, and $a b c$ the half revolution of the crank-pin, simultaneously described. Let the path of the crank-pin be divided into equal parts at the points 1, 2, 3, 4, and draw verticals from the points of division to the line $a c$; then as the angular speed of the crank is uniform, and the divisions of the circular path, $a b c$, are equal, the line

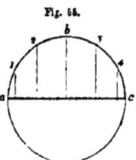

Fig. 55.

Motion of Crank and Piston.

$a c$ will be divided by the perpendiculars already drawn, into segments representing spaces described by the piston in equal times; and therefore also, the varying average velocity of the piston in the same spaces. Whence it is obvious, that the speed of the piston, during one stroke, begins and ends at nothing at the extreme or dead points a, c, that it accelerates towards b, the position, at half stroke, when it reaches a maximum, and that, beyond this point, it is retarded till it gains the end of its stroke. The two halves of the stroke are described in equal times; and in these halves, the variation of the velocity of the piston are exact counterparts.

The obliquity of the connecting rod destroys the symmetry here observed. In a stroke of the piston there are three cardinal points : the commencement, the middle, and the termination of the stroke. According to the preceding diagram, these three points are arrived at by the piston, simultaneously with the horizontal and vertical positions of the crank. But the angularity of the connecting rod, at half stroke of the piston, virtually shortens its length, and the crank-pin is by as much short of its midway position. As the crank is presumed to move with a uniform angular velocity, it follows that the piston describes the two halves of its stroke with different average velocities, and in unequal times. In Stephenson's engine, for example, with a stroke of 22 inches, and a connecting rod 5½ feet long, or six times the length of the crank, we find from the annexed diagram, Fig. 56, of the relative positions of the piston and the

Fig. 56.

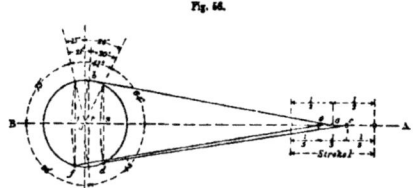

Diagram of the effect of the Connecting Rod.

crank, that at half stroke of the piston, the connecting rod $a b$ falls short of the vertical centre line of the crank by the amount $o r$, fully 1 inch. Dividing the stroke of the piston into three equal parts, the connecting-rod being in the relative positions, $c d$, $e f$, the distances of the points d, f, from the centre line are $o s$, $o t$, respectively 4½ and 2¾ inches. The corresponding angular positions of the crank are, for the half stroke of piston, 6° with the vertical, and for the one-thirds of the stroke, respectively 26° and 15°. The sum of 26° and 15°, or 41°, is the angular motion of the crank during the middle third of the stroke, and the complements of these, 75° and 64°, are the angular motions for the extreme thirds. The average speeds of the piston, therefore, in describing the successive thirds of its stroke in the direction A B, are inversely as 64, 41, 75, or directly as 6, 9, 5, nearly ; and the two halves of the whole stroke are described with average speeds inversely as 84 to 96, or directly as 8 to 7. The shorter the connecting rod, the greater is the irregularity so introduced into the motion of the piston. The general effect, therefore, of the connecting-rod on the motion of the piston, is that the piston anticipates its position due simply to the crank throughout the whole of the front stroke, which is described *towards* the crank; and that throughout the back stroke, the piston is in the same degree behind the position due to the crank alone.

The rectilineal motion of the valve, like that of the piston, is accelerated and retarded during the travel, and is affected likewise by the angularity of the eccentric-rod. The relative length of the rod is, however, so considerable as to render the perturbations, in the case of direct action, nearly inappreciable. The motion of the valve may therefore be deduced from that of the eccentric by the method of perpendiculars already applied to the crank and piston motion.

All that is imperatively required of a slide valve in governing the distribution is, that it be at least of sufficient extent to close both of the steam ports at the time of changing the admission of the steam, in order that the steam may not enter at both ends of the cylinder at one time; and that it release the steam from one end of the cylinder, at least as soon as it is admitted to the other end. The normal valve, Fig. 57, meets these conditions; in the position in which it is shown, its inner and outer edges coincide

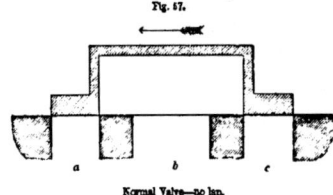

Fig. 57.

Normal Valve—no lap.

with those of the steam ports *a, c*; and the smallest motion of the valve either way, opens one of the steam ports to the steam, and the other to the exhaust port *b*. At this juncture, the valve is at half stroke and therefore at its greatest speed, while the piston is at the end of its stroke; and as, to move the piston, in the direction of the arrow, for example, the valve must move in the same direction, the eccentric must be set on the axle at right angles to the crank, and preceding it, in the order of the circular motion, by as much as one-fourth of a revolution.

From this account of the normal valve, it appears that one end of the cylinder is open to the steam from the boiler throughout the whole of the stroke, while the other end is open to the exhaust; and that the suppression, release, and admission of steam take place simultaneously at the end of each stroke of the piston.

The normal valve has inherent and incidental disadvantages. The process of exhaustion occupies some time, and while there is steam to be expelled, a prejudicial back pressure exists. The imperfections of the valve-gear in practice, when valves of this kind were in use, frequently delayed the opening of the ports for some space beyond the commencement of the stroke; the evil of imperfect exhaustion was thereby aggravated. Again, the free admission of the steam until the completion of the stroke was hurtful to the machinery, as it co-operated with the momentum of the piston and its connections in accumulating unbalanced strains on the working parts; the unchecked admission

also clogged the exhaust passages during the escape; it is well ascertained that a cylinder with even unusually large ports, will develop more work at high speed from steam cut off at some distance from the end of the stroke, than from steam admitted throughout the whole of the stroke. These evils are removed or palliated by causing the changes of distribution to take place *before* the completion of each stroke; and this is effected by shifting forward the eccentric round the axle. The motion of the valve is advanced to the same extent; the arrival of the piston at the end of its stroke is anticipated by the changes of distribution; and the steam has thereby gained some time to re-arrange itself for the next stroke. The advantage so obtained is obvious, on considering that the piston lingers in its motion, both in approaching and in receding from the end of the cylinder; and that if the space during which the business of releasing and fully admitting the steam is discharged, be equally divided on both sides of the dead point, the most time is afforded for these operations with the least motion of the piston, and a minimum retarding effect.

While, by these arrangements, a more efficient admission and exhaust are provided, nothing can be done with the same valve to employ the self-contained expansive force of the steam in the cylinder in propelling the piston. This implies the confinement of the steam within the cylinder during a portion of the stroke; whereas, we find that the suppression and the release take place simultaneously. "Expansion" is, however, attained by the simple expedient of adding to the length of the valve; its two outer edges are, by the addition, set so much the further apart than the extreme edges of the steam ports, and by as much does the suppression, and consequently the commencement of expansion, anticipate the exhaust during the travel of the valve. While the valve describes this fraction of its stroke, the piston is moving under the pressure developed by the expansion of the steam already in the cylinder.

Definitions.—The width of the opening of the steam ports for the admission or for the release of steam, at the beginning of the stroke, is known as *lead*; on the steam side, it is denominated *outside lead*, or lead for the admission; on the exhaust side, it is *inside lead*, or lead for the exhaust.

When the valve is placed at half stroke over the ports, the amount by which it overlaps each steam port either internally or externally, is known as *lap*. On the steam side, it is named *outside lap*; on the exhaust side, *inside lap*.

When the terms *lap* and *lead* are employed alone, they are understood to designate the outside lap and lead.

The *advance* of the eccentric and the valve, is a term used, in the first instance, to denote the angle which the eccentric forms with its position at its half stroke, when the piston is at the commencement of its stroke, and is then named *angular advance*; in the second case, it denotes the amount by which the valve has travelled beyond its middle position, when the piston is at the end of the stroke, and is known as *linear advance*. The linear advance is, then, equal to the sum of the outside lap and lead, and to the sum of the inside lap and lead.

When the valve is so formed that, at half stroke, the faces of the valve do not close the steam ports internally, the amount by which each face comes short of the inner edge of the port, is known as *inside clearance.*

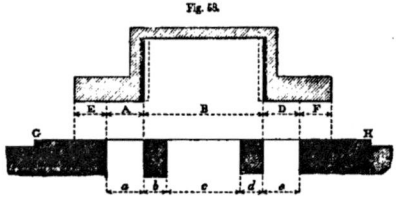

Fig. 53.

The valve-entrances to the steam-ways, usually three in number, are denominated *ports.* The extreme ports leading to the ends of the cylinder, are the *steam ports;* the middle port is the *exhaust port.* The partitions which separate the ports are named *bars* or *bridges.* The flat surface in which the ports terminate, and on which the valve works is the *valve-face.* The two working surfaces of the valve, we must distinguish as the *faces of the valve.* Referring to the annexed figure,

G H is the valve-face.	A E, D F, the faces of the valve.
a, e, are the steam-ports.	E, F, the outside lap.
b, d, the bars.	B, the exhaust cavity.
c, the exhaust port.	

In this figure, inside lap is not specified; were the faces of the valve extended inwardly to an extent, say, indicated by the dot-lines, the extensions would constitute inside laps. Were the faces shortened on the inside, as shown in dark shading, the difference would be inside clearance.

As the peculiarities of valve-motion are, from its nature, to be observed only from a consideration of its varying position during one double stroke, or one revolution of the crank, it is of course necessary either to construct working models of the valve-gear contemplated, or to represent by diagrams the progressive positions of the valve corresponding to the progress of the piston or the crank. The latter is, for our purpose the only available method, and is in some respects superior to that of the model.[*]

The method of the diagram, most commonly employed, does not seem to be generally known. It is, therefore, expedient that the method should be explained; and it shall be illustrated by an example derived from the old locomotive valve-motion. Fig. 1. Diagram-Plate I. comprises a series of twelve skeleton-views of the piston, crank, and valve, moving in conjunction; the motion of the valve is derived from the eccentric through an intermediate shaft, and the mechanism is supposed to be in fore gear. The arrows attached to the figures indicate the directions of the motions. The dimensions are as follow:—

OLD VALVE.—Travel	3 inches.
Outside lap	$\frac{7}{8}$ —
Inside lap	0 —
Outside lead	0 —
Inside lead	$\frac{7}{8}$ —
Cylinder 12 inch diameter, 18 in. stroke.	
Steam ports 1½ inch wide.	

[*] The principle of the polytechnic toy, consisting of a revolving disc combining a succession of attitudes into an equivalent for motion, might be usefully employed for developing the motions of the valve and piston.

The path of the crank is divided into twelve parts of 30 degrees each, and at each point of division, the attitude of the mechanism is represented. Nos. 1 to 6, illustrate the motion during the front stroke of the piston or half a revolution of the crank; Nos. 7 to 12 show the motion during the back stroke. The large dot-circle, (a, in No. 1 position) represents the path of the crank; the small circle b that of the eccentric; æ is the centre of the axle, o is the crank-pin, and e the centre of the eccentric; d the intermediate shaft, p the piston, v the valve, m the centre of the cross-head, n the centre of the valve-link. The connecting rod and other parts are readily distinguishable. In No. 1 position, the crank is at the dead point, next the cylinder, and the piston is at the top of the cylinder. The radius of the eccentric, æ e, is not just square with the crank; it rather inclines towards it, sufficiently to shift the valve $\frac{7}{8}$ inch from its middle position, and to have it therefore in readiness for the admission of steam with the smallest additional movement of the crank. The front steam-port is thus opened for the admission of steam throughout the entire motion of the piston represented by the first six positions; and is not closed till within ½ in. from the end of the front stroke, represented in the 7th position. This seventh position forms the commencement of the back stroke, and the succeeding positions sufficiently indicate the corresponding motions for the return of the piston, at equal intervals of 30 degrees of a revolution.

To combine these twelve positions in one diagram is the problem before us. Plate I. Draw A B, Fig. 2, equal to the length of the stroke of piston, and bisect it at c. From c as a centre with c A as a radius, describe a circle A B, to represent the path of the crank-pin; and from c as a centre, with the radius of the eccentric, describe a smaller circle, as the path of the centre of the eccentric. Draw a perpendicular line, D E, through the centre c; and construct a square F G H I upon the greater circle. Consider H I as the level of the valve-face; set off, equally on both sides of the centre line, A B, the width of the ports and bars, as shown on the figure; and parallel to A B, draw lines a, b, c, d, e, f across the figure from the edges of the ports, so determined. As the motion of the valve is the counterpart of the longitudinal movement of the eccentric, all that is necessary in determining the position of the valve at any part of the stroke, or angle of the crank—the angularity of the connecting and eccentric rods being neglected,—is to find the position of the centre of the eccentric in its circular path. Let the vertical movement of the eccentric be reckoned in the direction of the line D F, and the horizontal movement in the direction of the line A B; then it is obvious that when the centre of the eccentric lies in the line D F, either above or below the centre c, the eccentric is midway in its horizontal movement, and the valve must be simultaneously in its middle position. The vertical line D F is, then, a very convenient datum line from which the motion of the eccentric may be measured, either way, towards the right or the left. Similarly, the middle position of the valve is also convenient as a datum for the valve's motion on the face of the cylinder; it is defined by two dot-lines drawn across the figure parallel to A B. These lines represent the extreme length of the valve over its face, and therefore lie

$\frac{7}{8}$ inch clear of the outer lines a, and f, of the steam ports, thereby defining the lap.

While, then, the horizontal or effective movement of the eccentric is defined by its lateral motion parallel to the line A B, the motion of the valve along the valve-face is represented on the diagram by its transverse motion parallel to the line of the assumed valve-face H I. The diagram thus represents the direction of the motion of the eccentric as at right angles with that of the motion of the valve. This, though not a matter of fact, and therefore likely to confuse, does not affect the integrity of the method of illustration, as it is a mere matter of arrangement.

Let us now assume the crank to be in the position C A at the commencement of a revolution, being the first position represented under figure 1. The steam edge of the valve is then line and line with the edge a of the steam port for the admission, and the valve is, therefore, at the same time, removed $\frac{7}{8}$ inch (the lap) from its middle position, as shown in Fig. 2. This imports that the centre of the eccentric is removed also $\frac{7}{8}$ inch from the datum line D F, and lies at the point, 1, in the smaller circle. The radius, C 1, is then the position of the radius of the eccentric at the commencement of the stroke of the piston, and is the same as that of the eccentric in No. 1 of Fig. 1. Divide the large and small circles each into twelve equal parts, numbered in succession from the point 1, in the direction of the circular motion; and draw lines to the centre from the points of division; the lines so drawn represent the successive simultaneous positions of the crank and the eccentric; also, the transverse lines drawn through the points of division in the large circle, parallel to B D, represent the corresponding progressive positions of the crank during the front and back strokes, while the perpendiculars drawn to the datum line B D from the points of division in the smaller circle, measure the simultaneous lateral movements of the eccentric.

As the lateral movement of the eccentric measures directly the motion of the valve, set off, on the transverse line K L, the distance i 2′ equal to the perpendicular from the point 2, in the smaller circle; then 2′ is the position of the edge of the valve, when the crank-pin is at 2. Set off in the same way, the distances k 3′, l 4′, m 5′, and n 6′, for the succeeding positions of the valve relative to the crank during its first half-revolution; set off also the position 7′ for the commencement of the second half-revolution, and the succeeding positions, 8′, 9′, 10′, 11′, 12′. It is observable that these positions range in an elliptic curve. By drawing the curve complete, as shown in a heavy line on the diagram, we perceive not only the 12 positions of the valve already determined, but also every intermediate position. This valuable curve, which in the case before us, is a true ellipse, represents what could not possibly be obtained by models or other contrivances—it exhibits in one view, the whole routine of the valve-motion. But this is not all. The other edges of the faces of the valve describe the same form of curve as that we have now traced for one edge. The portions of the three other curves so described during the first stroke are drawn in faint lines on the diagram, and thus the motion of the valve with reference to all its functions, is mapped out in a succinct and intelligible manner.

A companion diagram may now be constructed for a valve

of more modern proportions. A valve, commonly employed by Stephenson, may be selected; and it will, for present purposes, be assumed to be driven by a single eccentric. instead of the link-motion, giving the same lead and travel. As, in direct-action motions, the valve is placed vertically against a vertical valve-face; we must conceive the cylinder turned on its axis, into a position at right angles to its literal position, that the sectional views of the valve and steam-passages may be represented in connection with the paths of the crank and the eccentric. The principal dimensions of Stephenson's valve are:—

Travel,	4½ inches.
Outside Lap,	1 "
Inside Lap,	0 "
Outside Lead,	$\frac{7}{8}$ "
Inside Lead,	1$\frac{7}{8}$ "
Linear Advance,	1$\frac{7}{8}$ "
Angular Advance,	37°

Cylinder, 15 inches by 22 inches stroke.
Steam Ports, 1¼ inch wide.

Fig. 1, Diagram-Plate 2, contains four positions of the modern valve, corresponding to the four quarters of a revolution of the crank-pin. In position No. 1, the piston is at the front end of its stroke; and the eccentric, instead of being at right angles, or even nearly so, with the crank, as it existed in the case of the old valve, is very considerably in advance of that position; its linear advance is the lap plus the lead, or 1$\frac{7}{8}$ inch from the vertical centre line. In position No. 4, accordingly, in which the crank has described only a quarter of a revolution, the eccentric has not only completed its throw, but is by as much as the angular advance, on its way on the return throw. The valve, therefore, has attained the end of its path, or has given 'full port' to the steam, some time before even the first half of the throw of the crank has been completed, and is already returning to close the port. In position No. 7, in which the crank is at the commencement of the return throw, the valve has not only closed the front steam-port, it has also admitted the steam for the back stroke, and released the steam employed in the front stroke of the piston—all this it has done some time before the end of the front stroke. When the position No. 10, is attained, the eccentric has completed its retrograde movement, and, consequently, that of the valve, and has recommenced its forward throw in the direction in which it set out from position No. 1.

To give precision to these considerations, to point out the peculiarities of the motion of the valve relatively to that of the piston, caused by the introduction of lap, and the consequent advance of the eccentric; and to define the points of the stroke at which the principal events of the distribution take place, we must have recourse to the general diagram, Fig. 2. The mode of construction is similar to that employed for the motion-diagram of the old valve. Twelve positions of the crank are chosen, as in the previous case; for the first position, the valve is placed at 1$\frac{7}{8}$ inch, the linear advance, from its middle position (1 inch of lap + $\frac{7}{8}$ inch of lead); the centre of the eccentric is, therefore, necessarily placed with a linear advance of 1$\frac{7}{8}$ inch, measured on the perpendicular drawn from No. 1, on the circular path of the eccentric, to the vertical centre line B D. If both circles be divided into 12 equal parts, in the direction of the revolution, reckoning forward from No. 1, the perpendiculars drawn to the datum line E D, from the points of the smaller circle, measure directly the transverse distances of the valve-edges above or below their middle positions, which are duly set off on the ordinate lines, and connected by elliptic curves. To render the action of the valve the more apparent, as regards the distribution of the steam, the motion of the steam side during the admission of steam for the front stroke, is defined by dark shading K, between the line a, and the elliptic curve; the motion of the valve for releasing the steam on the front side, which takes place towards the end of the stroke, is distinguished by lighter shading L. On the other side of the piston, during the front stroke, the cylinder is wide open to the exhaust, as indicated by shading M, and is only closed towards the end of the stroke, at the point where the elliptic curve crosses the line e. As the waste steam is, from this point, locked up in the cylinder, and is subjected to compression by the advancing piston, until the port is opened for admission, the triangular shaded space N represents the period of compression. Just before the completion of the front stroke, when the piston has about $\frac{1}{16}$ inch yet to describe, the opposite steam-side of the valve opens the port for the admission of steam for the commencement of the back stroke, at the intersection of the elliptic curve with the line f. The period of admission against the piston is distinguished by the very small triangular shaded space O, at the termination of which the port is open $\frac{1}{16}$ inch for the commencement of the back stroke. The same triangular allowance for the commencement of the front stroke is observable at the opposite corner of the diagram, P.

The operations of the old and new valves are clearly distinguished by the two general diagrams in Plates 1 and 2. The admission of the steam, which barely commences with the stroke in the old valve, anticipates the commencement of the stroke of the new valve, and secures a timely admission of steam; the suppression or cutting off, which is delayed till the end of the stroke with the old valve, is performed by the new valve before three-fourths of the stroke are completed, and provides room in the cylinder for working the steam expansively; the release or exhaust, which, by the old valve, does not occur till the piston has completed its stroke, takes place with the new valve, while the piston has yet above 2 inches of the stroke to describe. It plainly appears, then, that to lap of valve we are indebted for the united advantages of working expansively and exhausting early.

Another peculiarity induced by the introduction of lap is, that the valve reaches the end of its travel earlier in the course of the stroke; that is, the maximum opening for steam and exhaust is more quickly arrived at. This is a direct consequence of the necessarily greater linear advance of the valve with lap, for by as much does it anticipate the movements of the old valve.

The use of lap introduces compression of the waste steam; and it is obvious that, in the example before us, the compression of the exhaust steam behind the piston, occurs simultaneously with the liberation of the steam from the front of the piston; the two areas, L and N, are, in short, similar and equal. The reason of this coincidence may readily be gathered from an inspection of the diagram;

as it is apparent that when, as in the present instance, the inside edges of the valve, at half travel, are line and line with those of the steam ports, that is, when there is neither inside lap nor clearance, the valve cannot release steam on one side without, at the same instant, locking it in on the other side of the piston.

The last peculiarity that may be noted, is, that the use of lap insures a most liberal opening for release. The lead for the exhaust is by as much as the lap in excess of the lead for admission, the one being $1\frac{1}{16}$ inch, the other $\frac{1}{16}$ inch; and a capacious inside lead and early 'full port' inside, are of much more real importance than the same things for the admission. With the old valve, the inside lead is but $\frac{1}{16}$th inch, and even for this it is indebted to the lap.

Once more, it must be remarked, that while the elliptic figures are correct as representations of the motion of the valve in relation to that of the crank, they are but approximately so in respect of that of the piston. It has already been explained that the angularity of the connecting rod affects the motion of the piston, and that while, during the front stroke, the piston is in advance of the position it would occupy were there no obliquity of the connecting rod, it is behind its due position throughout the whole of the back stroke. This is illustrated by positions Nos. 4 and 10, Fig. 1, in both of the examples. The period of admission, therefore, indicated by the diagram of the new valve, is less than that which corresponds to the motion of the piston during the front stroke; and exceeds that which takes place for the back stroke. The points of release and compression are so near to the end of the stroke, where the angularity vanishes, that the variation in their case is unimportant. The diagram, however, yields correct mean positions for all the points of the distribution, as what it exceeds one way, it recedes the other way. It is, besides, correct for the motion of the crank, which, as a measure of time, is, at all events, a better measure of the quality of the exhaust than the motion of the piston.

While, therefore, it is impossible by means of a single eccentric and the ordinary slide-valve, with the same lap at both ends, to render the admission equal for the front and back strokes—a fact with which we are familiarized by the unequal beat or blast of the old gab-engines, and even of the more modern engines fitted with Hawthorn's valve-gear, already described—the evil may be removed by providing a difference of lap on the two ends of the valve. An excess of lap on the front end reduces, of course, the comparative value of the front admission, already too great, and makes it more nearly equal to the back. Of the efficiency of this mode of correction, we shall have an opportunity of judging in the sequel.

The elliptic curve, or development of the motion of the valve, may be termed the *motion-curve, or motion-diagram of the valve*, being understood to express the relation between the motion of the piston or the crank, and that of the valve; the horizontal line representing the middle position of the point chosen for tracing the curve, may be termed the *axis of the motion*.

From the nature of valve-motion, it follows that the distribution is controlled by the outer and inner edges of the extreme ports and of the valve. The mere width of exhaust-port, or thickness of bars, is immaterial to the timing of the distribution. The extreme edges of the steam ports, and those of the valve, regulate the admission and suppression; and the inner edges of the ports and the valve command the release and the compression. The distribution of the steam thus involves, for every stroke of the piston, four distinct events, which it is the duty of the valve to accomplish: the admission, the suppression, the release, and the compression.

Simplification of the Diagram.—As the motion-curves of the four edges of the valve are identical in form, one curve may be employed to represent them all, by assuming a common axis. Thus we may condense the diagram, and indicate the distribution equally well. For example, draw the datum line A B, Fig. 3, Diagram-Plate II., for the length of stroke; bisect it, and draw the vertical line D E through the centre; on this centre draw circles, as before, for the paths of the crank-pin and eccentric. Divide the crank-circle, as previously, into 12 equal segments, and draw transverse lines through the points of division, perpendicular to the datum line. As the motion of the valve is to be represented in the transverse direction, and is therefore measurable, as before, by perpendicular distances from the datum line, we shall, for simplicity, adopt the same datum line for the movements of the eccentric. Set off, on the smaller circle, the point 1, of which the perpendicular distance 1, 1″, from the datum line, is equal to the linear advance; starting from this point, so obtained, divide the circle into 12 equal parts, numbered in succession in the direction of the motion, and from the points of division severally, draw lines parallel to the datum line to meet the transverse lines from the crank-circle correspondingly numbered. The points of intersection, 1′, 2′, 3′, &c., so found, are points of the motion-curve, which may then be completed.

The curves for the four events of the distribution being referred to one axis, lines must be drawn upon the figure, parallel to the datum line, to represent the working edges of the steam-ports. The extreme edge of the port, that is, the position of the line for admission, or the *steam-line*, is, according to the previous diagram, Fig. 2, 1 inch, the lap, from the axis of the motion-curve associated with it; therefore, draw a steam line *a*, 1 inch apart, and parallel to the datum line. Again, the inner edge of the port, represented by the *exhaust-line b*, is line-and-line, or identical with the axis of the corresponding motion-curve; it is, therefore, identical with, and expressed by, the datum line. Thus, the period of admission during the front stroke is represented, as in Fig. 2, by the area K enclosed by the steam line, and the release of the steam so admitted is expressed by the area L, bounded by the datum line, towards the end of the stroke. We may likewise define the simultaneous operations on the other side of the piston, comprising the exhaust and the ultimate compression of the waste steam,—operations which, indeed, are supposed to be the same on both sides of the piston. The exhaust and compression line, *e*, Fig. 2, is, like its neighbour, *b*, identical with the axis of the relative motion-curve; the datum line, therefore, becomes the exhaust line for both the front and the back ends of the cylinder, and consequently the large-shaded area M, Fig. 3, indicates the period of exhaust for the back steam, and the

dark area N, commencing where the exhaust terminates, indicates the compression of that steam. The two areas N and L, are, in short, identical in the condensed diagram, as it has already been proved by Fig. 2, that they are described simultaneously. The position of the steam line, *f*, for the other end of the cylinder, would clearly be as much above the datum line as the line *a* is below it. It is omitted in Fig. 3, as it could define nothing more than the small period of pre-admission for the back stroke, similar to the area P for the front stroke.

CHAPTER II.

PROPORTIONS OF VALVES.

THE distribution of steam by the slide-valve is regulated by three elements—lap, lead, and travel of valve—and an alteration of any one of these affects, in a definable manner, all the events of the distribution. The influence of these elements is susceptible of exact calculation; it is, however, expedient, in the first place, to exhibit, by the method of the condensed diagram, the nature of the changes so effected. Stephenson's valve, already exemplified, will be retained as the subject of illustration for this purpose; the direct connection with a single eccentric being resumed. An acquaintance with the normal motion-curves thence derived, will facilitate the subsequent business of illustrating the compound motion derived from the joint operation of two eccentrics and the coupling link.

The annexed figure repeats, in the curve No. 1, the motion of Stephenson's valve, already represented on a larger scale, by Fig. 3 of Plate II. According to the scale of hundredth

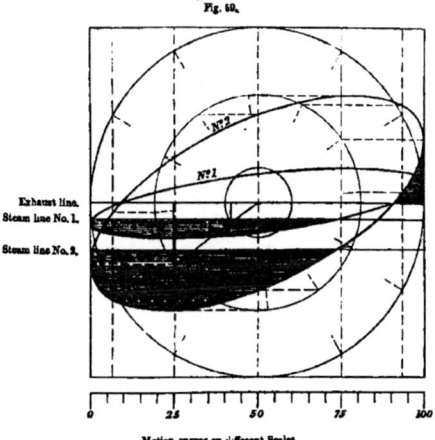

Fig. 49.

parts, appended to the figure, intended to facilitate measurements, the point of suppression occurs when the piston has described 73·5 per cent. of the stroke, and the release commences at 91 per cent. of the stroke. The travel of the valve is 4½ inches; lap, 1 inch; and the lead, 1/16 inch. If these values be increased in the same proportion, say trebled, the travel would be 13½ inches, the lap 3 inches, and the lead $\frac{15}{16}$ inch; with these data, let the curve No. 2, Fig. 59, be constructed. It appears that, notwithstanding the exaggerated dimensions adopted, the suppression and the exhaust take place at the same points of the stroke, 73·5 and 91 per cent., that were provided for them by the first valve. The positions of the points of admission and compression are also identical for the two valves; and it is, therefore, to be inferred, that *if the three elements, lap, lead, and travel of valve, be increased or diminished in conjunction, so as to preserve the same ratios with respect to one another, the events of the distribution are also constant, measured in percentages of the stroke.*

Besides confirming this general proposition, Fig. 59 answers the purpose of showing that an enlarged scale may, with propriety, be adopted for illustrating the valve-motion—enlarged with reference to the scale on which the stroke of the piston is represented. The general scale to which the figure is drawn is ⅛th of full size, applicable for the measurement of the motion of the valve, as it is for that of the piston. By this scale, it has just been seen that the larger curve is constructed for a travel of 13½ inches. If we suppose the scale to be trebled, in lieu of the travel, lap, and lead, the larger curve will measure, on a scale of ⅜ths, precisely what the smaller curve measures on a ⅛th scale—the original 4½ inches travel, 1 inch lap, and $\frac{5}{16}$ lead. The enlarged scale is, of course, only applicable vertically, and while it yields the points of the distribution with equal fidelity, the intersections are more obtuse, and are, therefore, much more clearly defined. The adoption of a separate scale for the valve-motion, condenses the whole diagram, and will be followed out in the subsequent illustrations.

The influence of travel, lap, and lead, may most readily be appreciated by means of distinct diagrams, to show what

Fig. 60

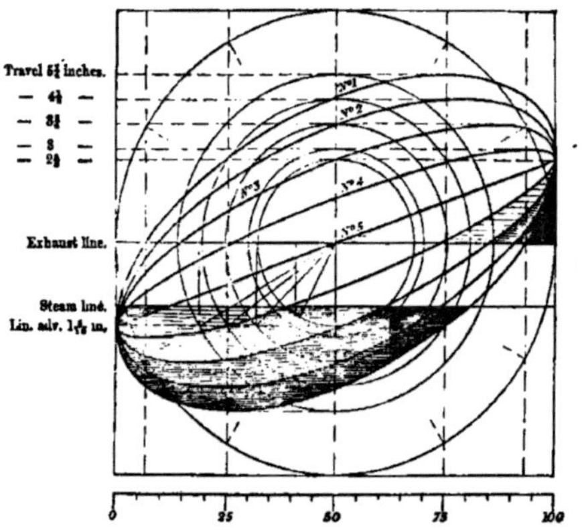
Travel 5¼ inches.
— 4½ —
— 3¾ —
— 3 —
— 2⅝ —
Exhaust line.
Steam line.
Lin. adv. 1 5/16 in.
0
25
50
75
100

Diagram of the Influence of Varying Travel.

each separately can do. The three following figures, 60, 61, 62, comprise, in each, a series of motion-curves formed from different travels, different laps, and different leads, respectively. The variation in each case, is made by equal differences; and not only is the general influence of the variation rendered very obvious, but also the influence of the same difference upon different periods of admission. The influence of a varying travel, within the limits of 5¼ and 2⅝ inches, with 1 inch lap, and $\frac{5}{16}$ lead, is represented by Fig. 60, annexed; the travel is reduced by equal differences of ¾ inch, excepting the last difference of ⅜ inch. The shortest possible travel is 2⅝ inches, consistently with the attainment of 1$\frac{5}{16}$ inch of linear advance, a constant quantity in the diagram. It is apparent that the effect of a reduction of travel is to collapse the motion-curve, and ultimately, in the case of No. 5, with 2⅝ inch travel, to reduce it to a straight line; with the diminution of travel the points of suppression and release are approximated to the beginning of the stroke, which reduces the period of admission, and increases that of release; with 2⅝ inch travel, the period of admission is but 12 per cent. of the stroke, while that of release is 50 per cent., or half of the stroke. The period of admission previous to the beginning of the stroke, also increases with the diminution of travel, until finally, with 2⅝ inch travel, it is 12 per cent., equal to the period of admission proper. And it is, in general, distinctly shown that ¾ inch difference of travel alters the period of admission much the more largely with the shorter travels. The elliptic form of the curve affords a ready explanation of this variable influence, for it is plain that, as the steam line is intersected by the curve at a more acute angle, as the travel is reduced, the point of intersection is also more susceptible of change.

The effect of a varying lap is illustrated by Fig. 61, in which the travel, 4½ inches, and the lead, $\frac{5}{16}$ inch, are constant. The lap is increased by progressive differences of

Fig. 61

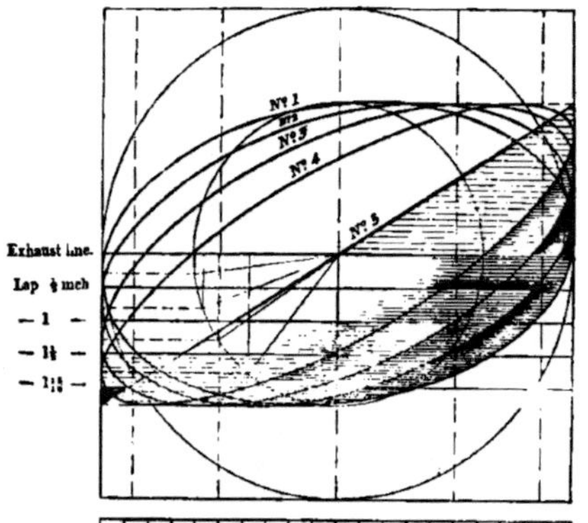
No. 1
No. 4
No. 5
Exhaust line.
Lap ½ inch
— 1 —
— 1½ —
— 1 15/16 —
0
25
50
75
100

Diagram of the Influence of Varying Lap.

½ inch; the last difference is $\frac{7}{16}$ inch, which yields a linear advance of 2¼ inches, the half travel, and reduces the curve to a straight line. The separate effect of increasing lap is, like that of shortening travel, to collapse the curve, shorten the period of admission, and lengthen the period of exhaust; and a given increase of lap, like a reduction of travel, reduces the shorter admissions more than the longer.

Varying lead is the least influential of the three elements. With a constant lap of 1 inch, and a 4½ inch travel, the lead is increased by intervals of $\frac{5}{16}$ inch, Fig. 62, till it

Fig. 62.

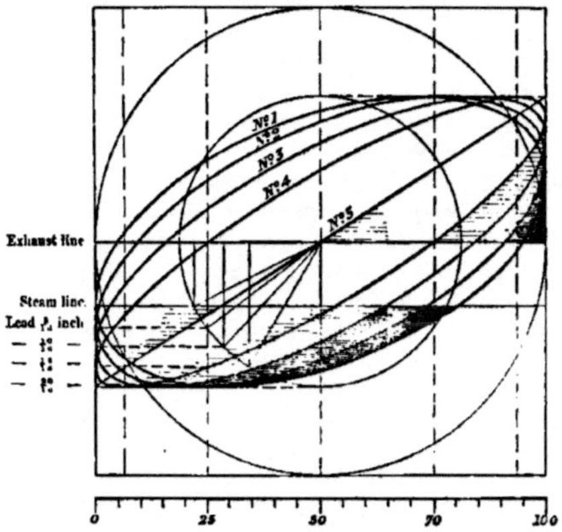

Diagram of the Influence of Varying Lead.

reaches the extravagant sum of 1¼ inch, and even then, when the curve becomes a straight line, the period of admission amounts to 28 per cent.

The following Table comprises the principal peculiarities of the foregoing illustrations, derived by direct measurement from the diagrams :—

TABLE No. V.—THE DISTRIBUTION OF STEAM, WITH VARYING TRAVEL, LAP, AND LEAD OF VALVE, IN PER CENTAGES OF THE STROKE OF PISTON.

	Position of points of suppression in per centage of stroke.	Position of points of release and compression.	Position of points of admission.	Linear advance.	Angular advance.
	FIRST SERIES.				
Travel.	Fig. 60.—Travel decreasing, Lap 1 inch, Lead five-sixteenths.				
No. 1......5¼ inch	81·5	93·5	·4	1 5/16 inch	30°
No. 2......4½ ,,	73 5	91 0	·62	1 5/16 ,,	35°
No. 3......3¾ ,,	60 0	86 0	1·1	1 5/16 ,,	44°
No. 4......3 ,,	39·0	73·5	2·6	1 5/16 ,,	62°
No. 5......2⅝ ,,	12·0	50·0	12 25	1 5/16 ,,	90°
	SECOND SERIES.				
Lap.	Fig. 61.—Lap increasing, Travel 4½ inches, Lead five-sixteenths.				
No. 1......0 inch	99 25	99·25	0·75	5/16 inch	7°
No. 2...... ½ ,,	91 5	97·0	0 9	13/16 ,,	20°
No. 3......1 ,,	73 5	91·0	0·62	1 5/16 ,,	35°
No. 4......1½ ,,	49 0	81·0	1 12	1 13/16 ,,	51°
No. 5......1 15/16 ,,	6·5	50·0	6·5	2¼ ,,	90°
	THIRD SERIES.				
Lead.	Fig. 62.—Lead increasing, Travel 4½ inch, Lap 1 inch.				
No. 1......0 inch	80 5	95	0	1 inch	26°
No. 2...... 5/16 ,,	73·5	91	·62	1 5/16 ,,	35°
No. 3...... 10/16 ,,	64 0	84	3·0	1⅝ ,,	46°
No. 4...... 15/16 ,,	53 5	75	8 5	1 15/16 ,,	60°
No. 5...... 20/16 ,,	28 0	50	28 0	2¼ ,,	90

Inasmuch as it is desirable, when shortening the period of admission, to employ the spare room in the cylinder for working the steam expansively, and for that object to delay the point of release, varying travel and varying lap appear to be most efficient of the three modes of causing an early suppression. Comparing No. 4 of the first series with No. 4 of the third, we find that while the period of admission is, in the first case, 39 per cent., and in the second case, 53·5 per cent. of the stroke, the point of release occurs in both cases at about 75 per cent. Thus, while in the second instance, one-third more steam is admitted, the period of expansion is shorter; and, accordingly, the steam in the first nearly doubles its volume during expansion previous to its release, whereas, in the second, it barely reaches 1⅓ times its initial volume. An early release, also, involves an equally early compression; and, moreover, in the third series, the period of pre-admission rapidly increases with the lead, much more so than with the shortening of the travel in the first.

To pursue the comparison farther, it is advisable to arrange the periods of expansion due to the periods of admission as ordinates to a base line representing the stroke. The periods of expansion, of course, are measures of the position of the points of release, as they are simply the distance between the positions of these points, and those of the points of suppression. The periods of expansion are selected for comparison, as they are understood to constitute the principal element in the efficiency of valve-motions. A larger expansion, also, implies a smaller compression.

First, with the varying travel, the periods of expansion are as follow :—

	Period of Admission.	Period of Expansion.
No. 1,	81·5 per cent.	12 0 per cent.
No. 2,	73·5 ,,	17·5 ,,
No. 3,	62 0 ,,	23·0 ,,
No. 4,	39·0 ,,	34·5 ,,

No. 5 is omitted in this series, as it is an irregular case. Lay down a base-line, A B, Fig. 63, to represent the length of the stroke. From A set off 81·5 per cent. on the base-line, as the period of admission for No. 1, and at this point draw a perpendicular equal in length to 12 per cent., the period of expansion. Set off, in the same way, from the same point A, the periods of admission for Nos. 2, 3, and 4, and draw perpendiculars to represent the respective expansions. The extremities of the four ordinates so obtained may be joined by a curve, which, if continued, passes through the point B; and this curve will represent, by means of ordinates, the periods of expansion due to all periods of admission, within the limits, at least, of those which have already been laid down. The same process may be applied to find curves of expansion for the remaining cases of varying lap and varying lead. The three expansion-curves

Fig. 63.

Periods of expansion in percentages of stroke.

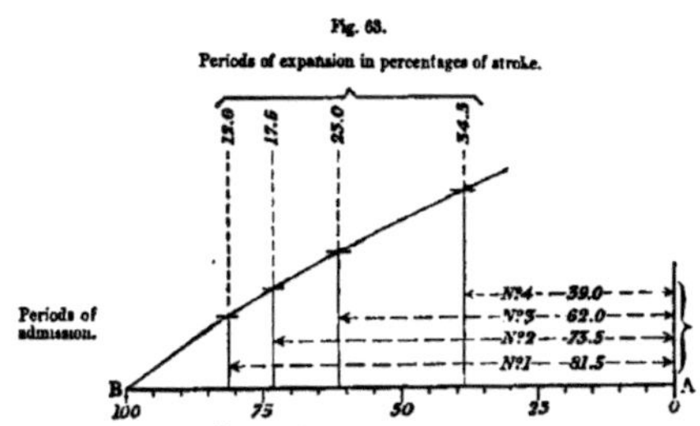

Expansion Curve for Varying Travel.

formed in this manner are placed in juxtaposition upon a common base-line, in Fig. 64; the ordinate due to an admis-

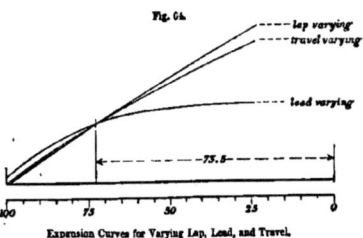

Fig. 64.

--- lap varying
--- travel varying

--- lead varying

— 73.5 — — — — — —

100   75   50   25   0

Expansion Curves for Varying Lap, Lead, and Travel.

sion of 73·5 per cent. is drawn on the figure, as it is common to the three curves. It is, in short, the starting line for them all, and corresponds to the special case of 4½ inch travel, 1 inch lap, and ₁⁄₁₆ inch lead, with which each series was commenced. It plainly appears, from the compound figure, that varying lap is the most efficient mode of working expansively. It is slightly superior to varying travel in this respect, and the periods of pre-admission are shorter with varying lap. With a diminished travel, however, an increased pre-admission is of the less importance, as the wire-drawing so caused retards the influx of steam. Variation by lead is obviously a poor mode of working; the expansion soon attains a maximum.

Of the two modes of varying expansion, by lap and travel, the latter involves mechanism of a simpler character than that which is required by the former. Variation by travel, with constant lap, appears, therefore, to be the most eligible means of varying expansion. The wire-drawing influence of reduced travel, already alluded to, must remain for the present a subject for speculation, till the evidence of diagrams is brought forward.

Inside lap and inside clearance modify the periods of expansion and compression. The addition of inside lap defers the point of release, and, consequently, like outside lap, prolongs the expansive action of the steam. But, while delaying the release, inside lap hastens the compression, and the delay in the one case is approximately equal to the anticipation in the other. Inside clearance operates re-

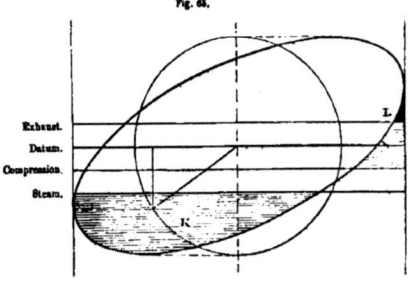

Fig. 65.

Exhaust.
Datum.
Compression.
Steam.

L

K

Diagram showing Effect of Inside Lap and Inside Clearance.

versely; it hastens the release, and, therefore, shortens the expansion, whilst it delays the compression. These con-

clusions are exemplified in the diagram, Fig. 65, for the valve of 4½ inch travel, 1 inch lap outside, ₁⁄₁₆ inch lead, with ¼ inch lap inside. The exhaust line is placed ⅓ inch above the datum line, for the same reason that the steam line is 1 inch below; and the compression line is placed ⅓ inch below the datum. The steam compartment, K, remains unaffected by inside lap; the exhaust compartment, L, is made shorter than in the original diagram, Fig. 59, that is, the point of release is removed towards the end of the stroke; the compression, N, is fully as much greater than before as the release is less; and it is pretty obvious that the effect of inside lap would be still more important for shorter travels. On the other hand, an inside clearance of ¼ inch would cause the exhaust and compression precisely to exchange positions—the compartment L would become the representative of compression, and N that of release—the compression would be delayed, the release hastened.

Inside lap and inside clearance appear to be unimportant variations from the common arrangement, as what is gained or lost in expansion is approximately lost or gained in compression. Of the two, inside clearance is probably the more innocent; as it, at all events, secures a free exhaust, which, at high speeds, may so keep down the back pressure as to be more than a match for the benefit of prolonged expansion.

It was stated, in the previous chapter, that an excess of lap on the front end of the valve tended to equalize the front and back admissions. To find the value of this correction: it has been found that, with our model valve, the uncorrected suppression takes place at 73·5 per cent. of the stroke; corrected for a connecting rod of six times the length of the crank, which is an ordinary proportion, the admissions for the front and back strokes are, respectively, 76·75 and 70·25 per cent., yielding a difference of 6·5 per cent. It is, then, required to add as much lap as will reduce the front admission to (73·5—6·5) 67 per cent. uncorrected. By the Table No. 5, showing the action of lap, we find that an addition of ⅛ inch lap reduces the admission to 49 per cent. An addition of ⅛ inch is therefore too great; and, in fact, it is found that ₁⁄₁₆ inch additional lap reduces the front admission to 66¾ per cent., and, correcting for the rod, the actual admission is 70·5 per cent., which is sensibly the same as that of the back stroke, namely, 70·25, resulting from the application of 1 inch lap. The points of release are similarly approximated by the same expedient of unequal lap.

CHAPTER III.

THE LINK-MOTION.—THE STATIONARY LINK.

IT has been explained that, to realize the benefit of expansive working by means of a single valve, lap is essential; and, in simple connection with an eccentric, the valve so made may be proportioned and set so as to yield any definite degree of expansive action. To vary the degree of expansion is the province of the link; and, though simple in construction, it is delicate in its motions, as these are affected materially by apparently slight modifications of design and arrangement. So sensitive is the link, that all the difference betwixt a very good and a very bad valve-motion may arise from the mode of suspending it, and from the arrangement of the joints or points of attachment. It is, therefore, necessary that the leading varieties of link mechanism should be considered, as well as the main circumstances by which the motion derived from the link is affected.

The first condition of a good link, common to all valve-motions, is, that it should command a free admission and a free release. The second is, that it should suppress and release the steam equally for the front and back strokes of the piston, under all degrees of expansion. And the third, that the period of expansion should be sufficiently extended to evolve the most, if not the whole, of the steam's force, excepting a deduction to meet the necessities of the blast. These conditions, of course, apply simply to the distribution of the steam. The second condition appears to have been the most difficult to attain, judging at least from the almost universal practice of unequal beating characteristic, generally, of locomotives fitted with link-motions. This inequality of action, according to which the period of admission is greater, generally, during the front strokes of the two pistons than during the back strokes, has been made the ground of one objection to the use of the link. The objection is, however, merely incidental, and may, by a proper disposition of the elements of the motion, be absolutely, or at least virtually, removed in practice.

Link-motions are all of two classes; in which, first, the link is suspended directly from a fixed point, as a stationary link; secondly, the link is moveable vertically, carrying with it, of course, the eccentric rods which are directly connected to it. In the first class, therefore, the variable expansion is accomplished by shifting the sliding blocks in the link; in the other class, the link is shifted upon the block. The link itself is employed under three general forms, distinguished as much by structural characteristics as by peculiarity of action,—the box-link, the open link joined to the eccentric-rods at the extremities, and the open link joined behind. The box-link (Fig. 66) is formed in two halves or sides, bolted together at the extremities, enclosing a rectangular recess for the reception of the block, as shown in section. The eccentric-rods are attached to the extreme stud-pins, forged on the outsides of the link, and thus a clear way is obtained for the blocks from one end of the link to the other; they may be shifted even to a position

concentric with the eccentric-rod ends. The two forms of open link are adopted with a view to simplify the parts. The one (Fig. 68) with the extreme connections, is the form first used by Stephenson; by its form, it does not

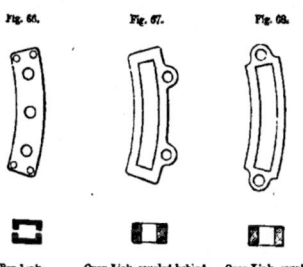

permit of the block being placed concentric with the eccentric-rod ends; the range being so limited, it is plain that the block never can receive and transmit the full throw of the eccentric to the valve, a feature in which the box-link has the advantage. With this link, the throw of the eccentrics, and therefore their diameters, must be greater than those required by the box-link for a given maximum travel of valve. The third form of link (Fig. 67), connected behind, permits of the same freedom for the block that is yielded by the box-link; the block may be shifted to a position level with the point of attachment, at which it may transmit the whole throw of the eccentric. The overhung nature of this knuckle-jointed sort of link, and its peculiarly irregular movements in consequence, render it a more ticklish variety than the others; as, however, it combines the advantage of the box-link, in respect of the transmission of the whole motion, with the simplicity of the other link, it is now most commonly employed, at least in locomotives where vertical clearance is limited. The nature of the motion of the link, the aberrations by which it is affected, and the mode of compensation, are now to be investigated; and, in doing so, the dimensions adopted in our previous illustrations of valve-motion will be retained.

Investigation of Link-motion.—Our normal or fundamental pattern of link-motion shall consist of a stationary box-link, sustained from below, with a pair of moveable sliding blocks,

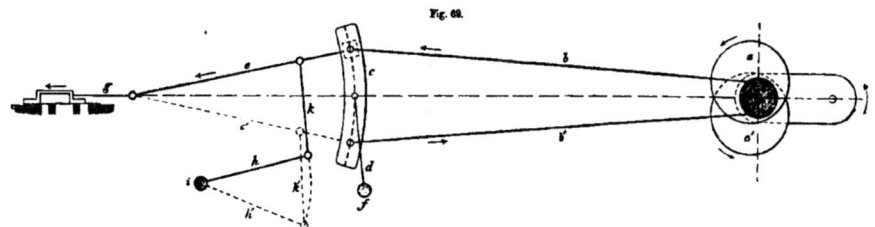

Stationary Link-motion, Normal. In full gear forward, for the beginning of the back-stroke.

which shall in the following discussion be considered as one. The block shall be hung on one end of the valve-rod link, and shall be shifted by means of the reversing lever, linked

to the body of the valve-rod link. With the aid of the annexed centre-line drawing of the motion now referred to, the following definitions may be premised. The valve and the valve-face are supposed to be so turned about the valve-rod as to be represented in section.

Definitions.—1. The forward and backward eccentrics *a, a'*, are known briefly as the *fore-eccentric, a,* and *back-eccentric. a'*. In the course of our illustrations, the eccentrics shall frequently be represented by their radii simply, as the motions of the radii of course represent all that is done by the eccentrics.

2. The eccentric-rods *b, b'*, are distinguished as the *fore-eccentric-rod, b,* and the *back-eccentric-rod. b'*.

3. The 'link' *c*, is known simply as the *link*, as it is the principal link in the mechanism. It will frequently be represented by its centre-line only.

4. The link *d*, which sustains the 'link' off the transverse shaft *f*, and is, in short, the only support for the link end of the eccentric-rods, is distinguished as the *sustaining link*. When the shaft *f* is above the 'link,' the link *d* is called the *suspending link*. The distinction is merely circumstantial.

5. The link *e*, proceeding from the valve-rod *g* to the 'link,' is the *radius link* or *valve-rod link*.

6. The *reversing lever, h*, is keyed on the *reversing shaft, i*.

7. The link *k* is the *reversing link;* connecting the valve-rod link with the reversing lever, its function is to shift and sustain in the required position the valve-rod link. In the figure, the valve-rod link is shown in full gear with the fore eccentric-rod. The dot lines *d', k', k'*, indicate the position of the reversing mechanism for full gear backwards.

8. The system of eccentrics, rods, and links, through which the valve receives motion from the axle, is known as the *link motion, valve-motion, or valve-gear.* The latter is the more comprehensive term, as it comprises, besides the items now enumerated as the valve-motion, the reversing mechanism generally. The *piston-motion,* though not a common phrase, may consistently be applied to the mechanism employed in conveying the motion from the piston to the crank.

9. The *front stroke* of the piston, is that which is described from the front end of the cylinder, towards the crank. The *back stroke* is that described from the back end of the cylinder towards the front.

The principal dimensions of the mechanism, or those which concern the distribution of the steam, are as follow:—

Lap of valve, 1 inch ; lead, $\frac{7}{16}$ inch.
Throw of each eccentric, 4½ inches.
Length of each eccentric-rod, 54 inches.
Length of the link, measured directly between the ends of the eccentric-rods, 12 inches.
Length of the sustaining link, 12 inches; attached to the link, at the middle of its length between the eccentric-rods, and on the centre line.
Length of valve-rod link, 30 inches betwixt end centres.
Length of reversing link, 12 inches ; attached to the valve-rod link at 7 inches from the centre of the block.
Length of reversing lever, 15 inches.
The length of the valve-rod is immaterial.

The mechanism of the link-motion before us is divisible into two distinct sections—the eccentrics, eccentric-rods, and the link with its subsidiary sustaining link, form one system, the motion of which is constant and unchangeable. On the other hand, the valve, valve-rod, and valve-rod link, derive their motion from the link, and the quality of this motion is dependent upon the position of the block in the link, a position assigned to it by the reversing-lever. The motion of the valve is, therefore, derived entirely from the link, and is controlled by the reversing-lever.

The obtainment of variable expansion is effected in the link-motion by varying the travel of the valve. This mode of varying the admission has already been exemplified in the motion of a single eccentric. The motion yielded by the link is apparently not of so simple a character ; throughout the whole length of the link, it is a compound of the motions imparted separately by the eccentrics, excepting only at the points where it joins the eccentric-rods. Though the motion of every other point of the link is so compounded, the motion of each eccentric, nevertheless, predominates in its own half of the link above and below the centre of sus-

pension, and results in a motion communicated to the valve, of which each reciprocation has a varying velocity, accelerated and retarded, like that yielded by the single eccentric. With respect to the variability of the travel of the valve, a condition which has just been alluded to as the means of working expansively, it is obtained by shifting the block towards the centre of the link—in this case, the centre of suspension. No point of the link, it is true, is permitted to remain stationary, as one or the other eccentric-rod is constantly on the move. The least horizontal range of the link, however, takes place at the centre, and the difference of the travel derivable from that point, and from the neighbourhood of the eccentric-rod, is considerable enough to give precision to the expansive functions of the link.

But while the practicability of variable expansion by means of the link is thus established, a condition necessary to its most successful operation, is the preservation of a constant lead for all degrees of expansion, implying, of course, that the valve should, at the commencement of the stroke, occupy the same position on the valve-face, and have the same opening of the port for steam, whatever may be the total travel assigned to it, through the reversing mechanism. This condition is simply met by forming the link, as a segment of a circle, to the radius of the valve-rod link. Referring to the foregoing figure, the eccentrics are set on the axle with the same linear advance, and it follows that when the crank is at the beginning of its throw, as in the figure, which is the critical period now contemplated, the centres of the eccentrics are in the same vertical line, and are equally distant from the horizontal line. Also, the eccentric-rods are of one length, and are attached to the link at equal distances from its centre, which is in the horizontal line. The ends of these rods must, therefore, like the other extremities, be in one vertical line ; and if the link be formed circularly to the radius of the valve-rod link, it follows that the block may sweep the entire link from end to end, while the valve and valve-rod remain perfectly at rest. It appears, then, that by the simple device of circling the link specially to the radius of the valve-rod link, the lead imposed upon the valve when the block is in full gear, is preserved unaltered when the block is shifted into any other position.

Again, supposing the crank to have accomplished a half revolution, it returns into the horizontal line diametrically opposed to its former position, as in Fig. 70, in readiness for the commencement of the front stroke. The eccentrics also have described a half-revolution, and their centres similarly are on the opposite sides of their paths. So inverted, with their linear advance situated on the opposite side of the vertical line, the link has been removed at both of its ends from its first position, by as much as at least twice this linear advance. Also, the removal at both ends is equal; for the angularity of the eccentric-rods, though they are now crossed, is the same. The removal is in fact a small quantity more than twice the linear advance of the eccentrics, due to the greater obliquity of the rods, their deviation from the first position being indicated by dot lines. Thus, the link occupies a new position parallel to its first, and the valve-rod link, which still vibrates on the horizontal line, is removed with it, and the block may sweep the link as before, while the valve remains stationary. The new position of the valve, is such as to yield the same lead for the front stroke that was found for the back stroke. The space through which it travels for this purpose is indicated by the figure, and is equal to that described by the link. It is, in short, twice the linear advance of the valve; and, as the horizontal removal of the link slightly exceeds the double of the linear advance of the eccentrics, the linear advance

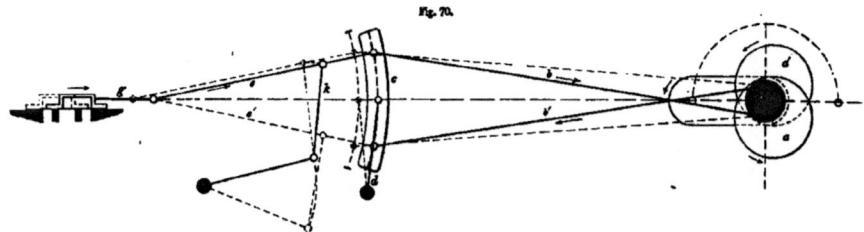

Fig. 70.

Stationary Link-Motion. In full gear forward, for the beginning of the front-stroke.

of the valve must also be something greater than that of the eccentrics.

Our next inquiry is to follow out the motion of the valve for the other cardinal points, those of suppression, release, and compression, due to different elevations of the block in the link; with this object, the consecutive positions of the link must be determined, corresponding to equal intervals of a revolution of the crank, and formed into motion-curves as already adopted for the single-eccentric motion. The movements of the link are maintained independently of the valve, and it is thus expedient that they should be treated distinctly. The method of setting out the link-motion shall be treated in conjunction with this investigation, as the one process conveniently explains the other.

To set the Eccentrics.—They must be so placed as to yield the necessary linear advance of the valve. This multiplied by two, or the sum of the advances for the front and back strokes, is, as we have seen, equal to the horizontal distance between the two positions of the link at the commencement of the front and back strokes. The condition is, therefore, to place the eccentrics with such an amount of linear advance as shall, in conjunction with the varying obliquity of the rods, create the necessary separation of the front and back positions of the link—twice the advance of the valve. Let A B, Fig. 71, be the horizontal or centre line of the motion,

Fig. 71.

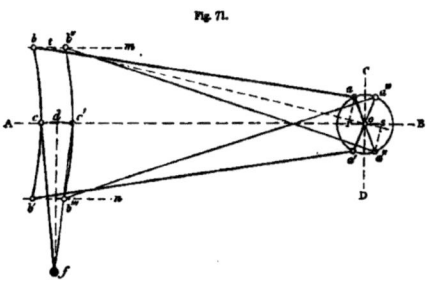

Link-Motion. Diagram for setting the Eccentrics.

and o the centre of the driving-axle. Through o draw the vertical o D, and describe the circle a a' for the path of the eccentrics, 4½ inches diameter; draw the lines m, n, 12 inches

apart, parallel to the centre line, and equally distant from it, to define the locality of the link vertically, the centres of the link being 12 inches distant. On the centre o, with the length of the eccentric-rod as radius, which in this case is assumed for convenience at 27 inches, or 6 times the throw of the eccentric, intersect the line m at t, and draw t o; set off o r and o s, each equal to the linear advance of the valve, 1⅟₁₆ inches, and draw the perpendiculars r a, s a'' to meet the circle; draw the diameter a a'. Then o a, and o a'' are the positions found for the fore-eccentric for the lead of the back and front strokes respectively; from a and a'', as centres, with the length of the eccentric-rod, find on the line m, the points b, b'; join a b, a' b'. These are the positions of the fore eccentric-rod for the back and front strokes, and the interval b b', which will be found equal to r s, represents twice the linear advance of the valve. This process is empirical, and can be viewed only as an approximate method; in ordinary cases it yields tolerably correct results, as in the example before us, which is, indeed, an extreme case with a short rod. The exact value of b b', so found, should, of course, in all cases, be checked by comparison with r s. Any difference of value is usually in favour of b b', and the excess is commonly so small, as to render at once obvious the correction required for the position of the diameter a a', by approximating it to the vertical line.

The position of the back eccentric may be assigned to it by drawing a line vertically from a, cutting the circle on the other side at a', and the diameter drawn from a' to a'' comprises the positions of the eccentric corresponding with those of the fore-eccentric; b' b''' on the line n, is the interval for the lower end of the link, found similarly to that for the upper end. Draw b c b' and b' c' b''' for the positions of the link; from c and c' as centres, with the length of the sustaining link as radius, find the point of intersection f. This is the position of the fulcrum, over which the link will vibrate equally on both sides of the vertical f d, and the centre of the link o, will find itself in the horizontal line at the end of each vibration. It is assumed, and will shortly be shown, that the oscillations of the centre of the link do not exceed the interval c c' now prescribed for them.

The diagram shows very plainly that the varying positions of the eccentric-rods have a marked effect upon the horizontal motion of the link. The linear advance of the

F

eccentrics, that is, their perpendicular distance from the vertical line, is found not to exceed $\frac{7}{8}$ inch. This advance is, nevertheless, sufficient, aided by the angle of the rods, to cause an advance of $1\frac{1}{16}$ inch at the link. The set of the eccentrics is thus obviously dependent, not only upon the advance of the valves, but on every dimension of the valve-motion.

Applying the foregoing method of finding the position of the eccentrics, it appears that for the 54-inch rods of the valve-motion already illustrated, the advance of the eccentric is exactly 1·075 inch, or, in common fractions, $1\frac{1}{13}$ inch, for an advance of the valve of $1\frac{1}{16}$ inch.

The open forms of link already described, require precisely the same process for the setting of the eccentrics. The intervention of a knuckle does not alter the conditions of the advance, on the supposition of the centres of connection being at the same distance apart. In the annexed figure 72, of one open link coupled at the extremity, we find the same radical lines that appear in the box-link yielding, of course, the same motion; and in fig. 73 of the link coupled

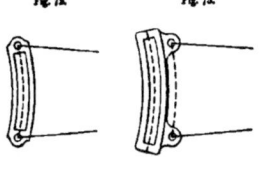

Fig. 72.   Fig. 73.

Centre Lines of Open Links.

behind, we may readily conceive two parallel radical curves, one of which appertains to the body of the link, and the other to the centres of connection. The interval for linear advance being regulated for one, is precisely the same for the other, and is identical with that required for the box-link.

Motion of the Link.—The next step is to lay down a succession of positions of the link corresponding to given positions of the crank. The dimensions of the normal link-motion shall be resumed; and with a 54-inch eccentric-rod, the linear advance of the eccentrics has been found to be $1\frac{1}{16}$ inch. Let A B (Diagram-Plate III., fig. 1) be the centre line of the motion, placed horizontally; o D the vertical through the centre of the axle o; o B the position of the crank; and $o\,a$ and $o\,a'$, the positions of the eccentrics with $1\frac{1}{13}$ inch of advance, at the commencement of the back stroke; and $b\,b'$ the corresponding position of the link with $1\frac{1}{16}$ inch of advance. Let f be the fulcrum of the sustaining link, its position being determined in the manner already described; the centre of the link then vibrates in the arc $c\,c'$. Divide the paths of the crank and of each eccentric into a number of equal parts—say 12 parts, a distinct series of divisions being made for each eccentric, and attach numbers to the divisions in the order of the circular motion, from 1 to 12. On the two 2d points of the paths of the eccentrics, as centres, with the eccentric-rod as radius, describe short circular arcs in the neighbourhood of the 1st position of the link, as indicated on the figure; then the three working centres of the link must be found somewhere in these two arcs, and in the arc $c\,c'$. This condition fixes the 2d position of the link, and it may be at once laid down with the aid of a templet. No doubt it may be laid down also by means of the compasses set to the

radius of the link. This is, however, a cumbrous process, and usually involves more than one trial before the precise position is ascertained. If a templet be made to the line $b\,b'$, it may readily be manœuvred into the true position, and the 2d position of the link marked 2, 2, may thus be defined. The same operation is performed with the succeeding positions of the eccentrics for those of the link, and it results in 12 positions of the link, numbered successively in the order of a revolution, simultaneous with those of the crank. The 1st and 7th positions of the link, in dark lines, correspond, as shown, to the 1st and 7th of the crank, at the commencement of the back and front strokes. If the two extreme centres and the ends of the link, in the congeries of positions, be run together into lines traced through them, as in the figure, these lines indicate precisely the movements of the points in question, and they are useful for illustrating the nature and extent of the vertical motion of the link at different points. The extremities of the link, it is obvious, have a greater vertical motion than points nearer the centre, and the centre itself has only a rise and fall due to the versed sine of the arc of vibration on the sustaining fulcrum. It also appears that the arc of vibration $c\,c'$ terminates in the leading positions 1 and 7. These positions crop out at the centre from amongst the others, and bound the motion of the link in that neighbourhood. It also appears that the back centre of the link is constantly in advance of the fore-centre. In shifting from the 1st position to the 2d, the fore and back centres, following the arrows, move to the left and right respectively, so that when the fore-centre has but attained the left extremity of its motion, in the 3d position, the back-centre is well on for the right end of its motion; in consequence, the position of the link is much inclined, and the upper end of the link, aided by its curvature, is considerably beyond the fore-centre. In the 4th position, the link is still farther inclined, and attains its maximum inclination during the back stroke, when the crank is at half throw on the upper centre, and the eccentrics have attained their maximum horizontal divergence from each other. In the 5th position, the link begins to recover from its obliquity as the back centre has arrived at the end of its course, in which neighbourhood, of course, it travels but slowly, while the fore-centre, moving towards the right, is approaching the middle of its course, where its greatest horizontal velocity is acquired. Finally, in the 7th position, the link becomes upright when the crank has reached the front end of its throw. Once again, in the 8th position, the link heels over, the back-centre going foremost, and a similar series of movements is described until it regains the 1st position. In brief, the link is upright in the 1st and 7th positions, when the crank is passing the end centres, and it attains its greatest inclination in the 4th and 10th positions, when the crank is on the upper and lower centres.

Position of the Valve.—To Set the Reversing Gear.—As the block of the radius link vibrates in a circular arc, while engaged with the link, we have only to project that arc upon the group of positions to find the consecutive positions of the block. To find the paths of the block it is necessary, as a preliminary step, to arrange the reversing gear.

The first condition is that the block should vibrate in a

horizontal line, when in full gear forward, or at its greatest elevation; and when in mid gear, or at the middle of the link on the horizontal centre line. These two extreme elevations are selected, because if the condition is made to hold with respect to them, it holds sensibly with intermediate elevations. The greatest elevation required for the block is regulated by the proposed maximum travel of the valve, which is, in the present example, 4½ inches, equal to the throw of the eccentrics. Find, by measurement, the place of the horizontal line *e e'*, to intersect the group of positions over a breadth of 4½ inches; on this line the block must vibrate. On *e*, as a centre, find, with the valve-rod link as radius, the point *g* in the horizontal line; draw *e g* for the extreme left position of the valve-rod link, and in the same way find *e' g'* for the parallel position on the extreme right. Set off the points of suspension *k, k'*, and join them; the line *k k'* is parallel and equal to *e e'*, and upon that line the point of suspension must vibrate; *g g'* is also equal and parallel, and represents the travel of the valve. On *k* and *k'*, as centres, with the sustaining link as radius, describe segments of circles, cutting at *h*; then *h* is the fulcrum of the sustaining link, or the position of the end of the reversing lever at its greatest elevation. Again, when out of gear, the block vibrates on the horizontal line *c c'* at the centre; setting off, as before from *c* and *c'* the points of suspension *k'', k'''*, this point must vibrate on the line *k'' k'''* equal to *c c'*. On the centres *k''* and *k'''*, with the sustaining link as radius, find as before the point *h'*; then *h'* must be the position of the fulcrum when the block is out of gear. On the two positions *h, h'*, so found, with the length of the reversing lever as radius, describe two circular arcs intersecting at *i*; then *i* is the position of the reversing shaft, and the circular arc *k k'*, described on that centre is the path of the fulcrum of the sustaining link betwixt the positions for full gear forward, and mid gear. To show that this arrangement is sensibly correct for intermediate elevations of the block draw the line *e'' e'''* for half gear forward, equally distant from the lines for full and mid gear. On *e', e'''*, as centres, cut the base line at *g'', g'''* and draw as before the two corresponding positions of the valve-rod link; set off on these two lines the points of suspension K, K'; and from K, with the sustaining link, cut the arc at *h''* for the fulcrum. The arc of vibration described on this fulcrum, passes sensibly through both points, K, K'. It so happens, from the dimensions adopted, that the position *i h'*, for mid gear, inclines below the horizontal line; this circumstance is of no importance, except as it may affect the operation of the link in back gear. It may, however, be removed by lengthening the reversing lever, for which the required length may be found as follows:—Through *h'* draw a horizontal line *h' i'*; draw *h h'* and bisect it, and at the point of bisection project a perpendicular, meeting the horizontal line at *i'*; the point *i'* is the situation of the new reversing shaft, and it would require a 21-inch reversing lever.

Having arranged the reversing gear, we are now in a position to define the path of the block in its progress with

the link. To make a separate example, let A B, fig. 74, be the horizontal line, *g e* the valve-rod link *g g'* the travel of the valve, the arc *k k'* the travel of the point of suspension

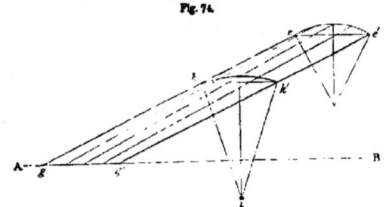

Fig. 74.

Motion of the Valve-rod Link.

on the fulcrum *h*. Divide this arc into four equal segments, and draw the positions of the valve-rod link passing through the points of division. Their upper extremities will be found sensibly to lie in a circular arc—*e* E *e'*, of a radius shorter than the sustaining link, and having therefore a greater rise than the arc *k k'*. From this it appears sufficient in all cases to find simply the elevation E of the block at half travel, and to describe a circular arc, *e* E *e''*, embracing this point, for the path of the block.

By this method we find, in the general figure, the arc *e e'* for the path of the block while driven by the link. The intersections of this arc with the positions of the link, are the precise positions of the block corresponding; and if, from these positions as centres, with the valve-rod link as radius, the interval *g g'*, or travel of the valve, be intersected, the points so found will be the simultaneous positions of the valve. In the same way the interval *g'' g'''* may be inter-

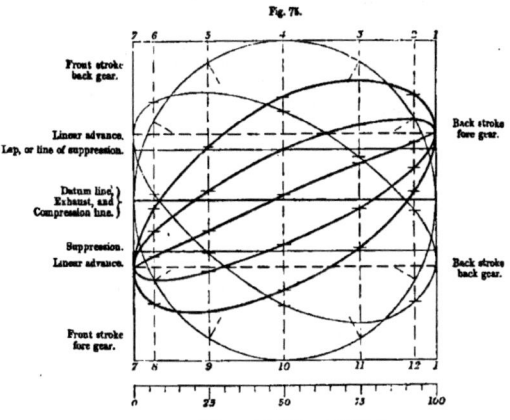

Fig. 75.

Front stroke back gear.

Linear advance. Lap, or line of suppression.

Datum line, Exhaust, and Compression line.

Suppression. Linear advance.

Front stroke fore gear.

Back stroke fore gear.

Back stroke back gear.

Motion-curves for Stationary Link, No. 1

sected for the positions of the valve in half gear forward, and G G' for mid gear. The vibration of the block in full gear backwards is also shown, from which we see that the arc of vibration falls slightly below the horizontal line. Four series of positions of the valve are appended on separate lines, for the sake of distinction; and they may be arranged in motion-curves, in the manner already adopted for the motion of a single eccentric. The foregoing figure, 75, comprises three motion-curves constructed from the positions found in forward gear, and for full gear backwards. They are not of the symmetrical form which results from the use of a single eccentric; and it is therefore necessary to lay down the lines for the advance and lap on both sides of the datum line, for the front and back strokes. From this we learn that, with all the three elevations of the block, the period of admission is greater for the back stroke than for the front, measured by the progress of the crank. No doubt, the corrections due to the play of the connecting rod might reverse the inequality here remarked. But, before considering the effects of the connecting rod, it is expedient to construct other motion-curves for modified arrangements of the link, for purposes of comparison.

Influence of the Mode of Suspension.—In our second example, Fig. 2, Plate 3, we have the link suspended by the middle, as previously, and coupled behind to the rods, at centres 12 inches apart, and 3 inches distant from the centre line of the link, measured horizontally, as indicated on the smaller scale figure attached to the diagram. The third example, Fig. 3, contains all the three centres of suspension in a curve line, behind the link, and parallel to its centre line, 3 inches apart horizontally. The fourth case, Fig. 4, has the link suspended at a point 1½ inches behind its centre line, the eccentric rods being coupled 3 inches behind; the point of suspension is, in this case, mid-way betwixt the two positions assigned for it in the second and third cases. In brief, the three last examples are composed of an open link connected behind, variation being made in the positions of the point of suspension. This difference is plainly indicated in the developments of the motion, where the arc of vibration of the link on the sustaining fulcrum, is defined. A general condition has been observed, that the arc of vibration should, in all cases, lie equally over the fulcrum. In these examples, two series of points have been defined; one series represents the movements of the centres to which the eccentric rods are attached; the other series shows the resulting motion of the corresponding points in the centre line of the link, to which the rods are attached in the case of the box link. We have thus a ready means of comparing some of the effects of the mode of suspending. It is clear that, in the first case, that of the box link, the motion of the centre is the simplest of all. It is direct from the eccentrics, and gives rise to a very limited quantity of vertical movement—less than ½ inch; and this is diminished, so far as concerns the play of the block in the link, to ₁⁄₁₆ inch. In the second case, also, the vertical movement of the link does not exceed ¼ inch. In this and the previous case, the link is suspended on its own centre line; whereas, in the remaining examples, where the point of suspension is situated behind the centre line, the vertical undulation amounts to 2¼ inches in the third case, and 1¼ inches in the fourth.

With respect to the general outline of these maps of motion, they are concave on both sides, though the concavity, externally, is so nearly balanced by the curvature of the link, as to render it nearly vertical, and less susceptible of modification than the other side. The removal of the centre of suspension from the centre line, has an obvious

tendency to quicken the inside curvature of the figure, as in the third case. This results from the link heeling forward, at both ends, to a greater extent, the more that the centre of suspension is removed backwards. The convex outline of the figure is but slightly affected by such alterations.

To construct motion curves for these figures, the reversing mechanism is to be arranged in the manner already pointed out; the same lineal dimensions being assumed, it is unnecessary, for the present purpose, to repeat the operation, as the path of the block will be the same as in the first case. Draw the lines *e* across the figures horizontally, and 4½ inches long, and upon them describe the circular arcs for

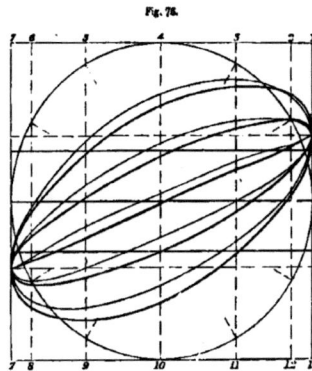

Fig. 76.

Motion-curves for Stationary Links, Nos. 2 and 3.

the path of the block; mid-way above the horizontal centre line, draw horizontals, with circular arcs, for the paths of the block in half gear. The motion curves, derived from the second and third examples, are placed together in Fig. 76, in dark and light lines respectively; the nature of the changes caused by the shifting of the centre of suspension is conspicuous—not only is the travel of the valve

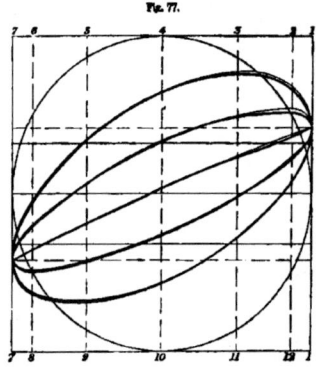

Fig. 77.

Motion-curves for Stationary Links, Nos. 4 and 5.

more unequally divided on the two sides of the datum line, being reduced for the front stroke, and increased for the back stroke, but the period of admission is also reduced for the front stroke and increased for the back stroke. Finally, the motion curves for the fourth example, Fig. 77, in dark lining, indicate periods of admission, ranging betwixt those for the second and third cases. From these precognitions, it appears that a case may be made out for establishing a link motion, which shall afford equal periods of admission for the front and back strokes; finding, as we have done, that these are controlled by the position of the suspended centre. By a scale of 100 parts, appended to Fig. 75, and applicable to the other figures, we find that the motion-curves yield the following periods of admission, measured by the horizontal progress of the crank, and expressed in hundredth parts of the stroke.—

TABLE No. VI.—OF LINK-MOTION ADMISSIONS.

Number of Link.	Full Gear Forward.		Half Gear Forward.		Mid Gear Forward.	
	Front Stroke.	Back Stroke.	Front Stroke.	Back Stroke.	Front Stroke.	Back Stroke.
No. 1	73½	76	45	50	10	12¼
No. 2	76	73½	50½	46	14	10½
No. 3	69½	77½	38	55	9½	13½
No. 4	72½	76	41½	52	10	12

Nos. 1 and 2, it is seen, operate reversely, as the back stroke, in the first case, and the front stroke, in the second, admit the greater quantity of steam. The periods of admission, in the two cases, are merely the same quantities simply exchanged. No. 3 contrasts with the previous cases, by the extreme inequality of the admission, the difference amounting, in half gear, to 17 per cent. of the stroke. Its differences, like those of the first case, preponderate in the back stroke; and this similarity of the two cases is due to their centres of suspension and connection ranging in one centre-line; notwithstanding that, in the third case, the link is overhung. The fourth case shows quantities ranging between those of the two preceding cases, suitably to the intermediate position of the sustaining centre.

Influence of the Connecting Rod.—The modifications due to the angularity of the connecting rod, must be ascertained before a practical comparison can be made of these motions. The following table of corrections is convenient for this purpose. The first two columns contain the distances of the piston from the commencement of the stroke, in percentages of the whole stroke. The three remaining columns contain the corrections, also in percentages of the stroke, due to the connecting rod, when four times, six times, and eight times the length of the crank; these corrections are additive for front strokes, and subtractive for back strokes.*

TABLE No. VII.—OF CORRECTIONS FOR THE POSITION OF THE PISTON, DUE TO THE ANGULARITY OF THE CONNECTING ROD.

Distance of Piston from commencement of stroke, measured by the progress of the Crank, in percentage of the whole stroke.		Corrections for positions of Piston due to Connecting rods of various lengths, in percentage of the whole stroke.		
		Four times the length of Crank.	Six times the length of Crank.	Eight times the length of Crank.
0	100	0	0	0
2	98	0½	0¼	0¼
4	96	1	0½	0½
6	94	1½	1	0¾
8	92	2	1¼	1
10	90	2¼	1½	1
12	88	2¾	1¾	1¼
14	86	3	2	1½
16	84	3½	2¼	1¾
18	82	3¾	2½	2
20	80	4	2¾	2
22	78	4½	3	2¼
24	76	4½	3	2¼
26	74	5	3¼	2½
28	72	5	3¼	2½
30	70	5¼	3½	2½
32	68	5½	3¾	2¾
34	66	5¾	3¾	3
36	64	6	4	3
38	62	6	4	3
40	60	6	4	3
42	58	6¼	4	3
44	56	6¼	4¼	3
46	54	6¼	4¼	3
48	52	6½	4¼	3¼
50	50	6½	4¼	3¼

Applying the corrections supplied in the foregoing table, we find the motions affected as follows:—

TABLE No. VIII.—OF LINK-MOTIONS.

Number of Link.	Periods of Admission, in percentages of the whole stroke.							
	Uncorrected or Normal Values.		Corrected for Connecting rods of the following lengths, the length of the Crank being 1.					
			4 length Rod.		6 length Rod.		8 length Rod.	
	Front	Back.	Front.	Back	Front.	Back.	Front.	Back.
No. 1, Full gear,............	73½	76	78½	71½	76¾	73	75½	73¾
Half gear,............	44	50	50¼	43½	48¼	45¾	47	46¾
Mid gear,............	10	12¼	12¼	9½	11½	10½	11	10¾
No. 2, Full gear,............	26	73½	80½	68½	79	70¼	78¼	71
Half gear,............	50½	46	57	39¼	54¾	41¾	53¾	43
Mid gear,............	14	10½	17	8	16	9	15½	9¼
No. 3, Full gear,............	69½	77½	74¾	73	73	74½	72	75¼
Half gear,............	38	55	44	48¾	42	50¾	41	52
Mid gear,............	9½	13½	11¾	10½	11	11½	10½	12
No. 4, Full gear,......	72½	76	77½	71½	75¾	73	75	73¾
Half gear,............	41½	52	47¾	45½	45½	47¾	44½	48¾
Mid gear,............	10	12	12¼	9¼	11½	10¼	11	10½
No. 5, Full gear,............	72½	76½	77½	72	75¾	73½	75	74¼
Half gear,............	42½	50½	48¾	44	46½	46¼	45½	47¼
Mid gear,............	10	14½	12¼	11½	11½	12½	11	13
No. 6, Full gear, ...	78	70	82½	64¾	81	66½	80¼	67½
Half gear,............	54	38¼	60¼	32¼	58¼	34¼	57	35¼
Mid gear,............	13	10	16	7¾	15	8½	14½	9
No. 7, Full gear,............	75	73	80	68	78	69¾	77½	70½
Half gear,............	47	43½	53½	37¼	51½	39¼	50¼	40½
Mid gear,............	11	13	13¼	10	12¾	11	12	11½
No. 8, Full gear,............	72	78	...	...	75	75	...	...
Half gear,............	43¾	52¼	...	...	48	48	...	...
Mid gear,............	10	12	...	...	11½	10½	...	...

It appears from this tabular statement, that, with reference to the first four cases, now under notice, the admission, for full and mid gear, is less liable to modification than

* This table is constructed by means of the formula—

$$s = ar - \sqrt{(a^2 - 1)\, r^2 + b^2},$$

in which a is the number of times that the connecting rod contains the length of the crank, b the distance of the piston from the *middle* of the stroke, measured by the horizontal progress of the crank, r the radius or length of crank, and s the correction. The formula is derived from the known properties of right-angled triangles.

for half gear; in full and mid gear, the horizontal motion of the crank and piston is comparatively slow about the points of suppression, as these points occur in both cases towards the end of the stroke. In half gear, the suppression occurs in the neighbourhood of the half-stroke, when the piston is about its maximum velocity, and consequently, the same causes affect the suppression to a greater extent. The suppression in mid gear, as it occurs most nearly to the end of the stroke, is the most stationary of all. With link No. 3, for instance, the difference of admission in full gear is 3½ per cent.; in half gear, 11 per cent.; and in mid gear only 1½ per cent. In other cases, the compensation yielded by the connecting rods, may render the admission practically equal. The operation of the rods is well shown with No. 1 link, where we find that, in the first place, a 4-length rod so entirely overshoots the mark of equality, as to do more than invert the difference. The 6-length rod also overshoots the mark of equality, but to a smaller extent. The 8-length rod still effects an inversion of the inequality, though so very slight as to reduce the difference in full gear to 1¾ per cent., in half gear, to ½ per cent., and in mid gear, to ½ per cent. This is an example of a practically correct link-motion,—correct as to the equality of the admissions. Again, with No. 2 link, the alterations caused by the rods, merely aggravate the differences already existing in the motion itself. It has already been remarked, that the inequalities due to this link, are merely simple inversions of those of the first link; and thus, while the back stroke, when unaffected, has already 2½ per cent. less admission, the difference is raised to 12 per cent., with a 4-length rod; and even in mid gear, the absolute difference is raised to 9 per cent., and in half gear, to 17½ per cent. Though these results of No. 2 link are unsatisfactory, this is nevertheless a standard plan of stationary link, much employed on account of its simplicity and convenience, in spite of its unequal action on the distribution. Link No. 3, like No. 1, admits an excess of steam for the back-stroke; so great is the irregularity in half gear, that even the corrections due to the 4-length rod do not reverse it.

It is obvious, from these considerations, that the term 'link-motion,' though technically it comprehends exclusively the valve-gear—yet virtually it includes all the mechanism that intervenes the piston and the valve, inasmuch as the motion of the valve derives its quality from its relation to that of the piston. It is, therefore, useless to speculate on the merits of a link-motion, without reference to the proportions of the piston-motion, and all diagrams of valve-motion related simply to the motion of the crank are subject to corrections for the effects of connecting rods on the movement of pistons. The standard link-motion, No. 2, gives a feasible distribution in half gear, being but 4½ per cent. in excess for the front stroke, irrespective of the connecting rod. A 6-length rod, however, upsets this promising motion, and trebles the excess. Referring these percentages to a 24-inch stroke, the excess is, in the first case, 1$\frac{1}{16}$ inch, while in the second it is 3¼ inches. It is apparent, also, that, as the influence of the connecting rod varies with its length, the link-motion must be specifically adapted to particular cases. For present purposes, the 6-length rod, an ordinary average proportion, will be adhered to in the course of the following illustrations. The state of the distribution for half gear will also, for the present, be alone considered, as when a motion is correct for half gear, it is commonly but a trifle wrong for other elevations of the block; and, besides, locomotives are much more frequently worked in half gear forward, or thereabouts, than in full-gear; and particularly so at high speeds. When the admission for the front-stroke is in excess of that for the back-stroke, the difference will be viewed as positive (+); when that for the back-stroke is the greater, the difference will be negative (—).

The Method of Three Trials.—On reviewing the admissions in half gear, for Nos. 2, 3, and 4 links, with 6-length rods, we find that the difference for No. 2 is positive, and for No. 3, negative. As this variation is due solely to the different positions assigned to the suspended centre, it is clear that the centre is too far forward in the first, and too far back in the second, and that there is, therefore, some intermediate position for the centre, on which the difference would become nothing, and the admissions equal. Accordingly, by placing the centre of suspension 1½ inches behind the centre line of the link, or half way between the extremes, as in No. 4 link, we find a reduced negative difference of 2½. The place of the centre in No. 4, is then plainly an approximation to the neutral position, and as the difference is negative, this neutral point must lie nearer to the centre line. To avoid the labour of making additional trials by way of approximation, the required place may be at once found by throwing the ascertained differences into a curve. Let A B, Fig. 78, be a datum line 3 inches long, to represent

Fig. 78.

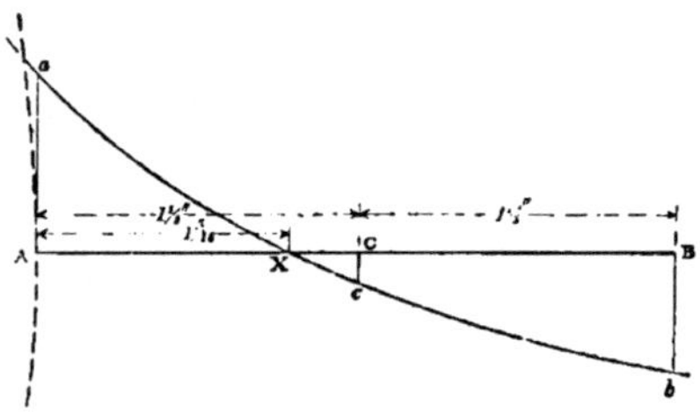

Application of the Method of Three Trials for Link No. 5.

the extreme distance of the centres selected for Nos. 2 and 3. Then A and B are the positions respectively of the centres in these two cases; and C, midway, is the place of the centre for No. 4. Draw perpendiculars from the points A, B, C, upwards in the first instance, and downwards in the other two, to represent the respective positive and negative differences, making Aa = 13, Bb = 8¾, and Cc = 2½, measured from any scale of equal parts. A curve line so described as to pass through the extreme points a, b, c, will intersect the datum line at the neutral point X, which is the required position of the centre, and measures 1$\frac{1}{16}$ inch from the centre line of the link at A. In drawing the curve it is of course very possible to find a different curve, which shall cut the datum line at another point; the relative positions of the points A, B, C, however, indicate beforehand the general form of the curve which ought to be adopted.

To prove the general accuracy of this mode of finding by three trials the neutral centre of suspension, construct the diagram of motion, Fig. 5, on the diagram-Plate III., with the link motion used for the other diagrams, and having the link suspended at 1⁷/₁₆ inch behind the centre-line, and develope the motion-curves in the usual way. These are shown, in light lines, on Fig. 77, which already contains the curves for No. 4, with which in many places they coincide. Tabulating the points of suppression, as done in the 8th table, and supplying the corrections for connecting rods, the duration of the admission derived by measurement from the curves, does not differ above ¼ per cent. in half gear, a difference due to small errors. The link so hung is thus practically correct in half gear; in full gear it yields only 2¼ per cent. of positive difference, and in mid gear 1 per cent. of negative difference. It is, therefore, sensibly correct, for every practical use, with a 6-length connecting rod.

This method of three trials is of course applicable for other lengths of rod, and other proportions of valve gear. It is not proposed for the purpose of superseding the use of the model, as doubtless the model, when once made with adjustable centres, is more convenient for investigating valve motion, at least with the object of fixing upon the centre of suspension. It has been shown that with given points of connection between the eccentric-rods and the link, a neutral position may be found for the sustaining centre. Conversely, we may find, for a given centre of suspension, the neutral centres of connection with the eccentric-rods. Nos. 1 and 2 links may be selected as examples for this purpose; and we find that No. 2, connected 3 inches behind the centre-line, yields a positive difference of 13 in half gear; and No. 1, connected upon the centre-line shows a positive difference of 2½ per cent. No. 1 is, thus, a more favourable arrangement than No. 2, but as the differences are both positive, the neutral centres of connection must be found in advance of the link. It is thus necessary to make a third trial with the centres shifted to some other positions to complete the number of three points upon which the curve is to be constructed.

The general Influence of the Link on the Distribution.— With respect to the other points of the distribution besides that of suppression, and first of the release, when the valves are right for the suppression they are never far amiss for the release; and it is really of small importance that the release should be strictly correct in time, which affects the regularity rather than the strength of the blast. Again, the points of release are identically the points of compression for the alternative strokes. The following table comprises the distribution for link No. 5; the positions being measured from the beginning of the stroke, off the motion-curves, and corrected for a 6-length rod:—

TABLE No. IX.—OF A PRACTICALLY CORRECT LINK-MOTION.
Lap, 1 inch; Lead, ¼ inch; Travel, 4½ inches.

Link No. 5.		Distribution from Motion-curve in percentages of Stroke.				Distribution corrected for a 6-length Rod, in percentages of Stroke.							
		Position of Points of				Position of Points of				Period of			
		Admission.	Suppression.	Release.	Compression.	Admission.	Suppression.	Release.	Compression.	Admission.	Expansion.	Exhaust.	Compression.
Full gear,	Front,	0¼	72½	91	8½	0¼	75½	92¼	9¼	75¼	16¼	7¼	9¼
	Back,	0¼	76¼	91½	9	0¼	73½	90¼	7½	73½	16¼	9¼	7¼
Half gear,	Front,	1½	42½	77½	20½	1½	46½	80½	23¼	46½	34	19½	23¼
	Back,	2	50½	79½	22½	1½	46½	76½	19½	46½	30½	23½	19½
Mid gear,	Front,	10	10	46½	46½	11½	11½	50¼	50½	11½	39½	49½	50½
	Back,	14½	14½	53½	53½	12½	12½	49¼	49½	12½	36½	50½	49½

From this table, the second part, it appears that as the period of admission is reduced, the periods of pre-admission, expansion, exhaust, and compression, are increased. To show by a curve how expansion varies with admission, take the mean periods of admission and expansion during the front and back strokes, as under :—

	Mean Admission.	Mean Expansion.	Ratio of Expansion to Admission.
Full gear, ...	74·5 per cent.	16·5 per cent.	½
Half gear, ...	46·25 ,,	32·0 ,,	¼
Mid gear, ...	12·0 ,,	38·0 ,,	3·17

Taking the base-line A B, Fig. 79, set off upon it the percentages of admission, and draw ordinates equal to the values of the expansions; the curve traced through the extremities of these ordinates, as already done for the case of a single-eccentric motion, shows how expansion increases as admission is diminished by the link. This curve is virtually

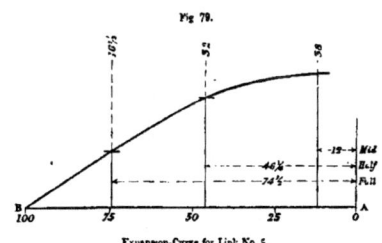

Fig 79.

Expansion-Curve for Link No. 5.

identical with that for the single-eccentric motion, Fig. 63, with the same lap, lead, and travel,—the travel having in the two cases, the maximum and minimum values, 4½ and 2¾ inches. Whence it appears that variation of travel by a single eccentric, and by the suspended link, yields the same general values of expansion. Compare the actual values as follow:—

TABLE No. X.

COMPARATIVE TABLE OF EXPANSION BY A SINGLE ECCENTRIC, AND BY THE LINK-MOTION No. 5.—LAP, 1 INCH, LEAD, $\frac{1}{16}$ INCH.

Travel.	Admission.		Expansion.	
	Single Eccentric.	Link.	Single Eccentric.	Link.
4½ inches.	73·5	74·5	17·5	16·5
2½ „	12 0	12 0	38·0	38·0

This table indicates so strikingly an identity of action in the two cases, as to prove that *the compounded motion of two eccentrics transmitted through a correct link-motion, is essentially the same as that of a single eccentric, having the same lap, lead, and variable travel.*

Variation in Mode of Suspension.—The influence of variation vertically is exhibited in links No. 6 and 7, figured in the Plate, and detailed in the table No. 8; they are each sustained by a point in the centre-line 3 inches above the eccentric-rod end, with links 21 inches long, and they yield the annexed motion curves, from which the data in the table are derived. Then strikingly illustrate the influence of the mode of suspension. No. 6 makes a positive differ-

Fig. 92.

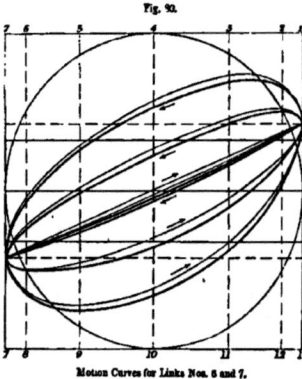

Motion Curves for Links Nos. 6 and 7.

ence in half-gear, of 24 per cent., which for a 24 inch stroke, is 5¾ inches; No. 7 has 12 per cent. of difference in half gear, good in comparison with No. 6, but as bad as the worst of the others. To apply the method of three trials, we find Nos. 7 and 1, both connected on the centre-line, yield respectively the positive differences 12 and 2½, indicating a neutral centre of suspension lower down. The link No. 8, with a 9-inch sustaining link connected lower on the centre-line, at 3 inches above the lower rod, yields the distribution in the following table.

As this third trial yields, when corrected, a perfectly true motion, there is no occasion for further investigation.

Again, comparing Nos. 2 and 6, their differences 13 and

24 indicate as in the previous case that the true centre is to be found lower, though at an extravagant distance.

TABLE No. XI.—DISTRIBUTION OF LINK No. 8.

Link No. 8.	From Curve.				Corrected for a 6-length Rod			
	Suppression.		Release.		Suppression.		Release.	
	Front.	Back.	Front.	Back.	Front.	Back.	Front.	Back.
Full gear, ...	72	78	90½	93	75	75	92	92
Half gear, ...	43½	52½	77	82½	48	48	80	96
Mid gear, ...	10	12	48	54	11½	10½	50	50

Finally, the open link, No. 9 (diagram-Plate 3), sustained at the upper end, 3 inches behind the centre-line, yields a difference in half gear of 17½ for a 6-length rod,— an improvement on its neighbour No. 6, though still so great as to render a neutral suspension unattainable in that quarter.

Influence of the positions of the Fulcrum and the Reversing Lever.—The fulcrum on which the link is sustained may be placed *above* the link; the reversing lever, in like manner, may be placed above the radius link. These modifications have their influence on the distribution, as we shall now show.

The developments of the movements of the stationary link in diagram-Plate 3, may for this purpose be again referred to, for if we conceive the system embracing the eccentrics, rods, and link, to be inverted, the link may then be viewed as suspended from above, and motion-curves obtained as previously. Also, the radius link and reversing lever may with ease be inverted; indeed the effect of inversion is at once produced by inverting the circular arc which represents the path of the block.

First, supposing the reversing lever hung below, as illustrated, and the link suspended from above; a' becomes the fore-eccentric, a, the back-eccentric, and the end of the link next the fulcrum, becomes the upper end for fore-gear. The crank, eccentrics, and link, also, pass into the positions 1, 12, 11, 10, &c., successively, in fore-gear. The circular arcs in dot-lines, applied separately to Fig. 3, for the sake of avoiding confusion, may be applied to all the figures in the same manner, for full, half, and mid gear; and from these motion-curves may be constructed.

Second, if the reversing lever be placed above the horizontal centre-line, while the link also, is suspended from above, the eccentrics still exchange their functions, and arcs as applied in dot lines to Fig. 4, will represent the paths of the block.

Third, the reversing lever being above the centre-line, and the link sustained from below, the eccentrics resume their original functions, and the dot curves in Fig. 5, will represent the paths of the block.

Applying the curves to all the figures in the manner now indicated, for the three cases here stated, and constructing motion-curves from them, we find the admissions in the following table as the result of these combinations, in half gear and with a 6-length rod.

From the table, the following general inferences may be established. It clearly shows, first, the influence of the position of the suspended centre Comparing Nos. 2, 5, 4, and 3, it is plain that under any arrangement of the other

TABLE No. XII.—OF LINK-MOTION.—ADMISSIONS AND DIFFERENCES, WITH VARIOUS ARRANGEMENTS OF MECHANISM. FOR HALF GEAR FORWARD, AND WITH A 6-LENGTH ROD.

Number of Link.	Lever Below.				Lever Above.			
	Fulcrum Below.		Fulcrum Above.		Fulcrum Above.		Fulcrum Below.	
	Front.	Back.	Front.	Back.	Front.	Back	Front.	Back.
No. 1	48¾	45¾	46½	47¾	45	46¾	45½	44¼
No. 2	54¾	41¾	53¼	44¾	52¼	42¼	54¼	39
No. 3	42	50¾	43	55	41½	53½	42	48¾
No. 4	45½	47¾	44	50¾	42½	47¼	44½	45¾
No. 5	46½	46¼	47	50¾	45½	48¼	45½	44¾
No. 6	58¼	34¼	56¾	41¾	55¼	38½	55¾	34
No. 7	51¼	39¼	51¼	46¾	49¾	45¾	48¼	38½
No. 8	48	48	50¼	48¼	48¼	45¼	45	46

WHENCE THE FOLLOWING DIFFERENCES, IN WHICH THE LINKS ARE RE-ARRANGED FOR COMPARISON:—

No. 1	+ 2½	− 1¼	− 1¾	+ 1¼
No. 8	0	+ 1½	+ 2½	− 1
No. 2	+ 13	+ 8¾	+ 10	+ 15¼
No. 5	+ 0¼	− 3¾	− 2½	+ 0¾
No. 4	− 2¼	− 6¾	− 4¾	− 1¼
No. 3	− 8¾	− 12	− 12	− 6¾
No. 7	+ 12	+ 5	+ 4	+ 9¾
No. 6	+ 24	+ 15	+ 16¾	+ 21¾

centres, the removal of the centre of suspension towards the axle, strikingly depreciates the value of the front admission with relation to the back. Thus, to quote from the first column of differences, we find—

No. of links,	2	5	4	3
Differences,	+ 13	+ ¼	− 2¼	− 8¾

Secondly, as the centre of suspension is shifted upwards in the centre line of the link, the fulcrum being below, the relative value of the front admission is raised. Thus, in the first column,

Box, No. 8,	No. 1,	No. 7.	Open, No. 2,	No. 6.
Diff. 0	+ 2½	+ 12	Diff. + 13,	+ 24.

Now, here we find that it has required the centre of suspension to be removed 3 inches, in No. 8, below its position in No. 1, to cause a difference of 2½ per cent.; whereas a removal of 3 inches horizontally, converting No. 2 into No. 3, causes a difference of from + 13, to − 8¾, or totally 21¾ per cent. From this it appears that the admission is much more sensitive to a variation of the centre of suspension horizontally, than to a vertical transposition.

Third, the removal of the centres for the eccentric-rod ends, horizontally towards the axle, raises the relative value of the front admission. Compare Nos. 1 and 2, 7 and 6.

Fourth, it follows from this, that the horizontal removal of the eccentric-rod centres tends to neutralize the effects of removing the centre of suspension in the same direction. The influence of the latter is, however, greater than that of the former, as we find on comparing Nos. 1 and 3. In No. 3, the centres of No. 1 are all equally removed towards the axle. Now we find the result as follows—

No. of Links,	1.	3.
Difference,	+ 2½	− 8¾

in which we find that the influence of the centre of suspension preponderates, in depreciating the relative value of the front admission.

Besides these general results of the influence of the link centres, which appears to over-rule all other minor influences, it may be observed of the local influence of the fulcrum and lever, that,

Fifth, when the link is hung from above, the relative value of the front admission is less than when the fulcrum is placed below. Compare the quantities in the 1st and 2d, and in the 3th and 4th columns.

Sixth, the influence of the position of the lever above or below the centre line is not so well marked, as it affects the relative values of the admissions differently; its total effect is but trifling, and may readily be over-ruled by other influences. It may be added that when placed above, the lever yields shorter admissions for both strokes than when placed below.

All of these conclusions may be explained by an examination of the diagrams of motion; the main influence, and that which has more to do with the relative admissions than any other circumstance, is the special vertical movement of the link that characterizes each mode of suspension. The study of these vertical movements is much facilitated by the curves showing the motion of the points in the centre line of the link opposed to the eccentric-rod ends, introduced in the figures.

The length of the eccentric-rods is another element which influences the distribution. In general, the shorter the rods the smaller are the admissions. Unequal laps on the front and back ends of the valve, with suitable linear advances for the eccentrics, are occasionally employed for equalizing the distribution.

A link motion (with suspended link) which yields perfectly equal admissions and expansions for all the notches, has been arranged by Mr. Gooch, for the Great Britain and other classes of locomotives running on the Great Western

Fig. 81.

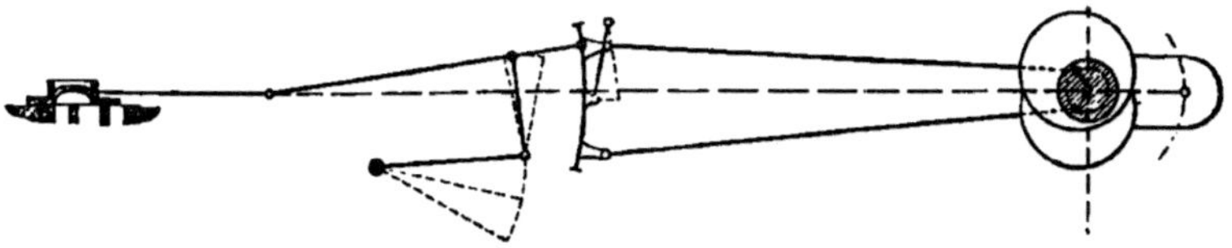

Eccentrics, 2½ in. radius.—Fore rod, 4' 9½".—Back rod, 4' 10".—Lin. advance of fore ecc., 1·19 in.—Do. back ecc., 1·15 in.—Lap outside, 1⅛ in.—Do. inside, $\frac{1}{16}$ in.—Lead, ⅜ in.—Travel in 1st notch, 4⅝ in.

Railway. The suspended link-motion, with the shifting radius-link, was, we believe, first matured and employed by Mr. Gooch, in 1843. In this motion, Fig. 81, complete and perfect accuracy with respect to the distribution, has, after some investigation, been accomplished. As specially arranged for the Great Britain, the back eccentric-rod is made ⅜ inch longer than the fore-rod, and the suspended centre of the link is dropped 1½ inch below the centre line of the motion; the cylinder is 18 by 24 inches, and the connecting rod 7 feet long, or 7 times the length of the crank. It is to be remarked, also, that the eccentric-rods are attached at 3 inches behind the centre line of the link, while the centre of suspension is placed at 1½ inches. The peculiar feature of the motion lies in the relative positions of these centres, a matter on which nothing further now requires to be explained. To Mr. Gooch belongs the merit of having originally apprehended the virtue of this method of adjustment, and of applying it in his locomotives; and by combining it with the other niceties already mentioned, he has succeeded in turning out a perfectly correct system of valve-motion, for all degrees of admission and expansion in fore-gear. The Great Britain engine was at first fitted with valves of 1 inch lap, ¼ inch lead, and 4¾ inches travel, in the first notch; it was with these proportions the engine was employed in the Experiments on Resistance for the Gauge Commissioners. Desirous of increasing the periods of expansion, by cutting off the steam earlier in the several notches, while the points of release were nearly unaltered, Mr. Gooch increased the lap to 1½ inch, and reduced the lead to ⅜ inch. By this alteration, the action of the engine has been greatly improved, as the diagrams taken from the cylinder (Diagram-plate 4) will show. The distribution effected by this valve-gear, under these two conditions, is exhibited in the following table:—

TABLE No. XIII.—THE DISTRIBUTION FOR THE GREAT BRITAIN LOCOMOTIVE, WITH VALVE-GEAR ARRANGED BY MR. DANIEL GOOCH.

Cylinder, 18 by 24 inches; Wheel, 8 feet; Steam Port, 13 by 2 inches; Exhaust Port, 13 by 3½ inches; Connecting rod, 7 feet.					
Notch.	Valve. Lap, 1 inch outside. — 1/16 inch inside. Lead, ¼ inch.		Distribution for Front and Back Strokes.		
	Travel.	Port opens.	Suppression	Release.	Compression
	inches.	inches.	inches.	inches.	inches.
1st............	4¾	1¼	17¾	21½	2⅝
3d............	3⅞	⅞	14¾	20	4¼
5th............	3¼	⅝	9⅝	17¼	7
	Lap, 1½ inch outside. — 1/16 inch inside. Lead, ⅜ inch.				
1st............	4¾	1 1/16	16	21¾	3
3d............	3 13/16	⅝ 1/16	11¾	19¾	5
5th............	3 7/16	⅜	7	17⅝	7½

Fig. 82.

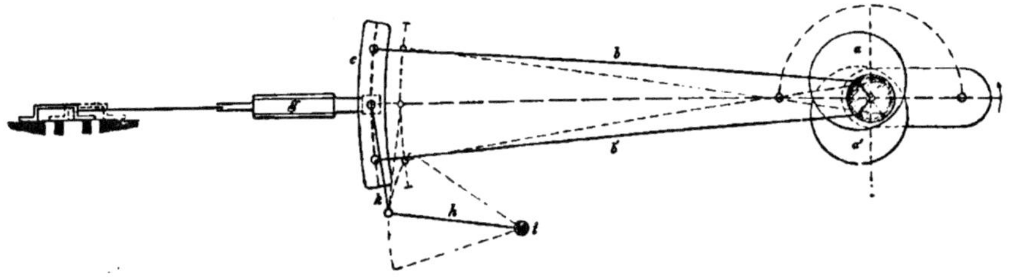

Shifting Link-Motion, normal. In mid gear, beginning of the back-stroke.

CHAPTER IV.

The Link-motion.—The Shifting-Link.

In the shifting-link motion, as the designation implies, the reversing gear operates on the link, by shifting it vertically upon the block, the latter being confined by guides to the centre-line of the valve-motion, as indicated generally by the annexed centre-line diagram. The use of fixed guides for the block is optional. The radius-link is employed in some engines (as Fairbairn's), not as a radius-link, but as a matter of arrangement, to permit of the block being suspended, by stationary links, from the boiler or other fixture.

All the dimensions and literal references of the stationary link-motion, discussed in last chapter, are retained in the motion before us.

Variation of Lead.—The vertical motion of the link, for the regulation of expansive working, takes place round the two distinct centres of the eccentrics; the upper end of the link turning on the fore eccentric, and the lower end on the back eccentric. Thus a compound radial movement is caused, the peculiarity of which is, as we shall presently see, that the lead necessarily varies with the degree of expansion: the greater the expansion, that is, the less the admission, the greater, also, is the lead. This is an injurious condition, but it is one which is inseparable from the motion of the shifting link, and the most that can be done to relieve the objection, is to equalize the variation for the front and back strokes. This palliation is most simply applied by curving the link to the radius of the eccentric-rod, concavely to the axle; as, with all proportions of valve-gear, and with the link so curved, it is found that the variation of lead is sensibly equal for the front and back strokes of the piston. Thus the curvature of the shifting link inclines towards the axle, while that of the suspended link finds its centre towards the valve.

To trace the action of the shifting link upon the lead, let A B, Fig. 83, be the centre-line of the link-motion; C D, a vertical through the centre of the axle; O B, the position of the crank for the beginning of the back stroke; $o\,a$, $o\,a'$, the radii of the eccentrics, each 2½ inches; $a\,b$, $a'\,b'$, the eccentric-rods, 18 inches long, or eight times the radius of the eccentric; and $b\,b'$, the link, 12-inch centres, and curved to an 18-inch radius. The heavy lining shows the position of the motion in mid gear, in which case the centre e of

the link coincides with the centre line A B. Lowering the link into full gear forward, in the position $o\,o'$, in which the upper centre o is brought into the centre line, the

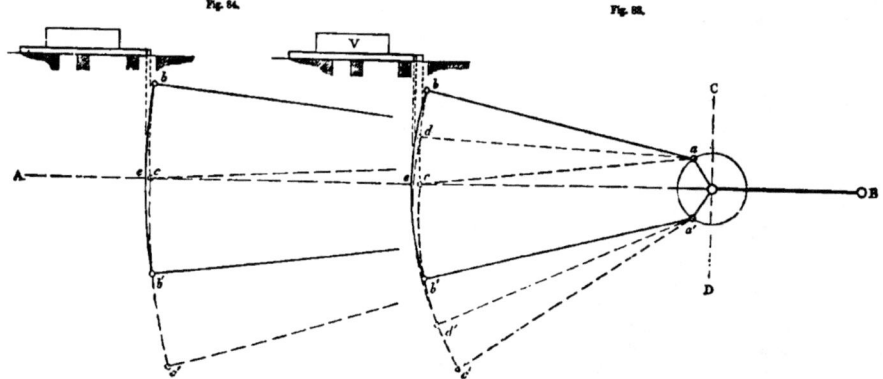

Shifting Link-motion. Diagrams illustrative of the Variation of Lead.

point o falls within the previous position of the link by the amount $o\,e$; and as the block engages with the points of the link e and o respectively, it follows that the lead in mid gear is greater than that in full gear by the amount $e\,o$. Again, when the link is placed in half gear, in the positions $d\,d'$, it still intersects the centre line at a point within the first position of the link, though at the same time beyond the point o for full gear. It, therefore, appears that by shifting the link progressively from mid into full gear, the lead is progressively reduced till in full gear it falls to its lowest value. This is further exhibited by means of the section V of the valve and the ports, connected with the successive removals of the valve.

With eccentric-rods of double the length, 3 feet, and a link of 3 feet radius, the valve-motion, Fig. 84, indicates a reduction of the difference $e\,o$, to about one-half of its previous value with the shorter rods. It, therefore, appears that the longer the eccentric-rods, the less is the absolute difference of the leads for full and mid gear.

With a link of half the length, or 6 inches between end centres, its radius of curvature being the same, we shall, similarly, find a reduction of the difference of lead to one-half of its primitive value. This is obvious on considering that the shorter the link, with the same curvature, the shorter is its versed sine, or its deviation from a straight line; and, in fact, the point d, Fig. 83, would be the upper centre of such a link in mid gear, and a curve drawn through that point would lie within the longer curve $b\,b'$, and would of course pass the centre line nearer to o. Therefore, the shorter the link, and the longer the eccentric-rods, the less is the variation of lead.

These remarks refer only to the lead for the back stroke. For the front stroke, $b''\,b'''$, Fig. 85, is the position of the link in mid gear, the eccentric-rods being crossed in the usual manner; and, in full gear, the upper centre of the link falls into the position o'', on the outside of the first

position of the link. Thus the lead at the other extremity of the valve, for the front stroke, is less in full gear than in mid gear, as already found for the back stroke, and the difference appears by the diagram to be practically the same. It therefore follows that for the front and back strokes, the lead increases as the admission is diminished, or as the link is approximated to its position for mid gear; and that the variation of the lead is the same for both ends of the cylinder.

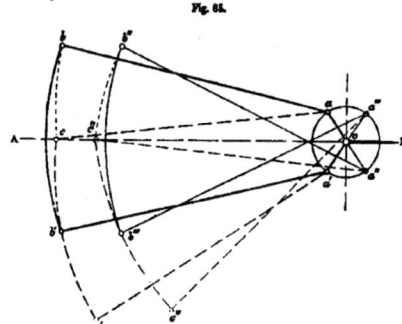

Shifting Link-motion. Diagram illustrative of the Variation of Lead, and of Linear Advance.

It appears further, that, in Fig. 85, as the positions a and a'' of the fore-eccentric for the back and front strokes respectively, are diametrically opposed, they are placed at the same distance from the centre line A B; the angularity of the lines $a\,c$, $a''\,o''$, with reference to this line, is therefore the same, and it follows that the interval $o\,o''$, which is, in short, twice the linear advance of the valve in full gear, is equal to the horizontal interval between the points a and a'', or to the direct interval $a\,a'''$, which is twice the linear advance of the eccentrics. As this equality is unaffected by the length of the rods; it follows generally that, for the shifting-link motion, the linear advance of the eccentrics is equal to that of the valve in full gear; that it is necessarily less for other positions of the gearing, and that the difference increases till it attains a maximum in mid gear, when indeed the circumstances become identified with those of the suspended link.

The general positions thus established for the shifting-link in fore-gear, are valid also for back-gear, as the character of the motion is essentially the same. The particular differences of lead due to the lengths of the rods in the examples before us, we find from measurement as follow :—

Length of Rods.	Lead in Full Gear.	Lead in Mid Gear.	Difference of Lead.
Inches.	Inchrs.	Inchos.	
Fig. 83...18	$\frac{7}{8}$	1	$\frac{1\frac{1}{8}}{}$
Fig. 84...36	$\frac{7}{8}$	$\frac{7}{8}$	$\frac{1}{8}$
Fig. 82...54	$\frac{7}{8}$	$\frac{7}{8}$	$\frac{7}{8}$

Here, as the rod is lengthened, the difference is reduced; though the reduction of this difference becomes less sensible as the rod is increased. For the 54 inch rod, the lead in mid gear is nearly double that in full gear.

To set the eccentrics.—As the linear advance of the eccentrics has been found to be in all cases equal to that of the valve in full gear, independently altogether of the throw of the eccentrics, or the lengths of the rods and links; it is plain that the linear advance of the valve being specified, that of the eccentrics is known directly, without the aid of any such diagram as was found necessary for the suspended link. It is customary on some railways to divide the evil of varying lead, by setting the valves to the most desirable lead, while in half gear. For example, if, with the 54 inch rods, the valves be set with $\frac{7}{8}$ inch lead in half gear, the total difference of lead, $\frac{7}{8}$ inch by the previous table, will be divided in such a way that the lead in mid gear, the worst position, does not exceed $\frac{1\frac{1}{8}}{}$ inch, while the lead in full gear is reduced to $\frac{1\frac{3}{8}}{}$ inch. Here it will be observed that the variation of lead is very slight towards the position of mid gear, and takes place most rapidly towards full gear; and an inspection of the diagram, Figure 83, clearly shows how slowly the variation takes place in the neighbourhood of mid gear. It is, therefore, with great propriety that the valves should be set right for half gear, about which position mostly the gearing is employed for the higher speeds.

To arrange the reversing mechanism.—The position of the reversing shaft is required to be such as shall, for all elevations of the link in fore gear, cause the suspended centre of the link to vibrate on a horizontal line. The horizontal motion of this centre when it is placed at the middle of the link, is in all cases equal to twice the linear advance of the valve in mid gear, as with the stationary link. Let a and b, fig. 86, be the positions of the link for the beginning of the front and back strokes, in mid gear, and a', b', the positions for full gear; these second positions are determined by the condition that the upper or fore centre of the link, should in both positions, be found in the centre-line A B, and in consequence the central points of suspension a', b', are sensibly in a horizontal line. With the length of the sustaining link as radius, and on the centres, a and b, draw

circular arcs intersecting at o; and with the same radius, on the centres a', b', find the centre o'. The points o, o', are the required extreme positions of the extremity of the reversing lever; on these centres, with the lever as radius,

Fig. 86.

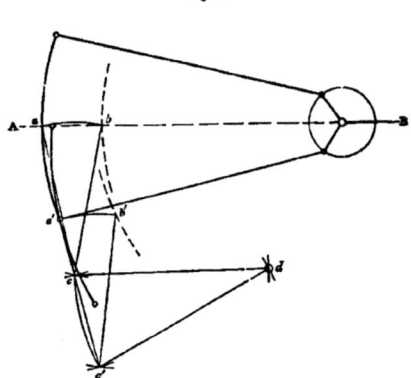

Shifting Link-motion. Diagram for placing the Reversing Shaft.

draw arcs cutting at d; then d is the required position of the reversing shaft, which will not only send the suspended centre of the link in a horizontal line, for the extreme positions, but will be sensibly correct for intermediate elevations.

Should the centre of suspension be placed at any other point of the link, as one of the extremities, the same mode of finding the centre is available.

Motion of the link.—As the link is shifted for each change of distribution, its total movement throughout a revolution is modified for each case. It is therefore necessary, in order to find the distribution for full, half, and mid gear, that three distinct series of positions should be projected. These have been executed for the case of the box link in diagram-plate 3, figs. 8, 9, 10, subject to the conditions already imposed, and with the dimensions already specified. The positions for other varieties of the link may in the same way be projected. Of these, a selection are inserted in the diagram-plate 3, figs. 11 to 17, containing the movements of the working half of the link, in half gear. The small figures annexed to these illustrations show the arrangements of link illustrated. By the method of motion-curves, the admissions for the front and back strokes are determined, as inserted in the table which follows.

The periods of admission so found being corrected for the obliquity of a six-length connecting rod, with a direct action valve-motion, the corrected quantities so obtained are also entered in the table. In this case, the corrections are additive for the front strokes and subtractive for the back strokes.

Again, the motion of the shifting link is, in some cases, transmitted to the valve-rod, through an intermediate lever, which carries the sliding block on the lower end. Here, the conditions are reversed, as the intervention of the lever causes the valve and the block to move in contrary directions. For this arrangement the eccentrics must be set on the axle in positions diametrically opposed to those due to direct action; from which it follows, in short, that the terms of the distribution for the front and back strokes as found from the motion-curves, for direct action, are necessarily exchanged in the case of intermediate action;—those for the front, in the former case, becoming those for the back stroke in the latter case, and *vice versa*. The normal values, therefore, entered in the table, as those of the front and back strokes, being those which are derived by direct action, become respectively those for the back and front strokes by intermediate action: as such they are assumed in the formation of the last two columns of the table, in which, as previously, the corrections for the front strokes are additive, and those for the back strokes subtractive. The extremity of the intermediate lever vibrates, of course, in a circular arc, which becomes the path of the block, instead of a straight line, as already assumed. This alteration further modifies the distribution, but so slightly, in comparison with the main circumstances, that, for simplicity, it is neglected in the composition of the last two columns.

TABLE No. XIV.—OF LINK MOTIONS.

DISTRIBUTION BY THE SHIFTING LINK, UNDER DIFFERENT ARRANGEMENTS, AND WITH DIRECT AND INTERMEDIATE ACTION.

Number and Nature of Link.	Periods of Admission in per centages of the whole stroke.					
	Direct Action.				Intermediate Action.	
	Uncorrected or Normal Values.		Corrected for a Six-length Rod.		Corrected for a Six-length Rod.	
	Front.	Back.	Front.	Back.	Front.	Back.
No. 1, Full gear	76	75	79	72	78	73
Half gear	47	49	51¼	44¾	53¼	42¾
Mid gear	15	18	17	15½	20½	13
No. 2, Full gear	75	69	78	65½	72½	72
Half gear	48½	41	52¾	37	45	44¼
Mid gear	20	14½	22¾	12½	16½	17¼
No. 3, Full gear	73	73	76¼	69¾	76¼	69¾
Half gear	48½	48	52¾	43¾	52¼	44¼
Mid gear	17	17	19¼	14¾	19¼	14¾
No. 4, Full gear	70½	76	74	73	79	67
Half gear	43	52	47	47¾	56¼	39
Mid gear	16	19	18¼	16½	21½	13¼
No. 5, Full gear	75	75	78	72	78	72
Half gear	44	50	48¼	45¾	54¼	39¾
Mid gear	15	18	17	15½	20½	13
No 6, Full gear	74	70	77¼	66½	73½	70¾
Half gear	50	43½	54¼	39½	47½	45¾
Mid gear	19	14	21½	12	16	16½
No. 7, Full gear	75	80	78	77¼	82¾	72
Half gear	48	56	52¼	52	60	43¾
Mid gear	17	23	19½	20	26	14½
No. 8, Full gear	78	75	81	72	78	75
Half gear	53	54	57¼	49¾	58¼	48¾
Mid gear	22	18	25	15½	20½	19

In looking over the uncorrected values, we find that in one case, No. 3, the admissions for the front and back strokes are identical, yielding precisely the regularity of a single eccentric. In No. 1, also, the admissions are very nearly the same. The corrected values show that the differences of the admissions for the front and back strokes are frequently as great in full and mid gear as in half gear, though it holds as a general result that when for half gear the admissions are sensibly equal, they are also about equal for the full and mid gear. Examples of this agreement are found in the cases of Nos. 4 and 7 direct action, and Nos. 2 and 6, intermediate action. We may therefore with propriety confine our remarks, by way of comparison, to the values for half gear, as was done in the discussion of the stationary link. The following is an abstract of these values, with two columns of differences annexed: the differences are distinguished as positive or negative quantities, according as they are in favour of the front or the back stroke.

TABLE No. XV.—OF LINK MOTIONS.

ADMISSIONS BY THE SHIFTING LINK, IN HALF GEAR, CORRECTED FOR A SIX-LENGTH ROD.

Number of Link.	Periods of Admission.				Differences of Admission.	
	Direct Action.		Intermediate Action.		Direct.	Intermediate.
	Front.	Back.	Front.	Back		
No. 1	51¼	44¾	53¼	42¾	+ 6½	+10½
No. 2	52¾	37	45	44¼	+15¾	+ ¾
No. 3	52¾	43¾	52¼	44¼	+ 9	+ 8
No. 4	47	47¾	56¼	39	— ¾	+17¼
No. 5	48¼	45¾	54¼	39¾	+ 2½	+14½
No. 6	54¼	39½	47½	45¾	+14¾	+ 1¾
No. 7	52¼	52	60	43¾	+ ¼	+16¼
No. 8	57¼	49¾	58¼	48¾	+ 7½	+ 9½

From this table it appears, first, that to shift the centre of suspension horizontally towards the axle, reduces the relative value of the front admission, with respect to the back admission, with direct action; and raises it, when the action is intermediate. Thus—

Nos. of Link	2.	3.	4.
Differences (direct action)	+15¾	+9	— ¾
Do. (intermediate)	+ ¾	+8	+17¼

in which we find that, of the three examples, No. 4 is the best arrangement of the open link for direct action; and No. 2, for intermediate action.

Secondly, to shift the centre of suspension upwards in the centre line of the link, keeping the fulcrum below, has a slight influence of the same kind, which is further carried out by shifting the centre to the lower end of the link and suspending from above. Thus—

	Box.			Open.		
Nos. of Link	1.	5.	7.	2.	6.	8.
Diff. (direct)	+ 6½	+ 2½	+ ¼	+ 15¾	+ 14¾	+ 7½
Do. (interm.)	+ 10½	+ 14½	+ 16¼	+ ¾	+ 1¾	+ 9½

Thirdly, to shift the centres of the eccentric-rod ends horizontally towards the axle, converting the box into the open link, raises the relative value of the front admission, with direct action, and reduces it with intermediate action. Compare Nos. 1 and 2, 5 and 6, 7 and 8.

Fourthly, it thus appears that the effects of a horizontal translation of the suspended centre of the link, are opposed to and tend to neutralize those which result from shifting the centres of connection in the same direction. Accordingly we find that, in the series of box-links, Nos. 1, 4, 5, 7, in all of which the centres are placed in vertical order, the differences do not materially vary, at least in the last three cases. The same neutralizing tendency is observable amongst the open links, Nos. 2 and 6, 3 and 8.

Fifthly, the practically correct motions are those of Nos. 4, 5, and 7 for direct action; and Nos. 2 and 6 for intermediate action. Nos. 2 and 4 contrast simply in the extreme positions of the suspended centre. Nos. 5, 6, and 7, examples of links hung by the extremity, show that however irregular may be the action of extreme hung links when stationary, they may operate very well for shifting links, whether directly or through an intermediate shaft.

CHAPTER V.

Recapitulation of the Preceding Four Chapters.

1. The relation of the motions of the piston and the valve are founded upon the uniform circular motion of the crank and eccentrics on one shaft.

2. The motion of the piston, throughout the stroke, when not affected by the angularity of the connecting-rod, is represented directly by the progressive motion of the crank-pin: the velocity being nothing at the beginning and end of the stroke, between which points it is accelerated and retarded, and reaches its maximum at half-stroke. Under the influence of a connecting-rod, the piston is placed in advance of its progress due to the crank alone, throughout the front stroke, and is behind its due position at all parts of the back stroke.

3. *Single valve and eccentric.*—The normal or primitive valve, with neither lap nor lead, operates in such a manner that one end of the cylinder is necessarily open to the steam in the valve-chest throughout the whole of each stroke, while the other end is open to the exhaust; and that the suppression, release, and admission of steam take place simultaneously at the end of each stroke. In this state of things, the eccentric is placed on the axle at right angles to the crank, in advance of it. By shifting forward the eccentric round the axle a little way, and fixing it there, the changes of the distribution take place *before* the end of the stroke. Thus, by the provision of lead, some time is allowed for the exhaust steam to escape, previously to the end of the stroke, and for the steam from the boiler to enter the cylinder for the succeeding stroke. "Expansion" of steam in the cylinder takes place during the interval between the suppression and the release of the steam admitted. Lap of valve provides expansive action of the steam, and is essential for this object, with the single valve. Without lap, as in the normal valve, there can be no expansion, properly so called; because then the suppression and release of the steam admitted to one end of the cylinder, occur at the same instant.

4. Lap operates jointly with lead in procuring an early and efficient release; because the lead of the exhaust, or the amount by which the valve is open to the exhaust, at the end of the stroke, is increased by as much as the addition of lap on the outside.

5. Lap causes the valve to reach the end of its travel, or the maximum opening for steam and exhaust, earlier in the course of the stroke. No great importance is to be attached

to this circumstance, as the steam and exhaust pressures arrange themselves very much independently of this event.

6. It is impossible, with the ordinary single valve with equal outside-laps, and worked directly by one eccentric, to admit equal quantities of steam for the front and back strokes, owing to the action of the connecting rod on the progress of the piston. The preponderance of steam is in favour of the front stroke.

7. For each stroke of the piston, there are four distinct events concerned in the distribution of the steam:—the admission, the suppression, the release, and the compression.

8. The distribution of steam is regulated by the working edges of the valve and the valve-face. The outer edges of the valve and the steam ports work together, and determine the admission and the suppression. The inner edges of the valve and of the steam ports, jointly, determine the points of release and compression. Thus the mere thickness of the bars or bridges, or the widths of the ports, have nothing to do with the distribution: this is governed exclusively by the lap, lead, and travel of valve.

9. The method of the motion-curve represents in one view the whole routine of the motion of the valve; and a single curve is competent to indicate the whole course of the distribution.

10. As the lap, lead, and travel of valve regulate the distribution, an alteration of any one of these affects it in a definable manner. If, however, these three elements be equally varied in conjunction, the distribution remains unaffected.

11. As the period of admission varies with the variation of any one of these elements, so also does that of expansion, which increases as the admission decreases; and a reduction of the period of admission may be the result of an increase of lap, an increase of lead, or a reduction of travel. Variation by lead is inadmissible, because it creates a formidable counterpressure by pre-admission, which rapidly augments with the lead, and it makes the period of expansion nearly a constant quantity for all admissions less than three-fourths of the stroke. Variation by lap and variation by travel, are, practically, the only legitimate modes, and are equally good; the latter is, however, more simply effected, and is therefore the most eligible.

The addition of inside lap, by deferring the point of release, prolongs the expansion. It likewise increases the period of compression to the same extent that the release is deferred. Inside clearance operates reversely: by hastening the release, it shortens the expansion; it shortens also the period of compression.

12. By adding an excess of lap on the front end of the valve, the unequal periods of admission due to the ordinary single eccentric and single valve-motion, may be equalized. For example, with $\frac{1}{16}$ inch lead, and $4\frac{1}{2}$ inch travel, 1 inch of back lap, and $1\frac{1}{16}$ inch of front lap, we secure an equal admission of 70·5 per cent. for the front and back strokes, with a connecting rod six times the length of the crank.

13. *Variable Expansion Gear.*—The first qualifications of expansion gear are to insure, for every variation of expansive action, a free admission and a free release for the steam; to render the periods of admission equal for the front and back strokes; and to promote the expansive action of

the steam sufficiently to extract the most, if not the whole, of its work, for propulsion, excepting a percentage required for the purposes of the blast.

14. Link-motions are reducible to two classes: first, those having a stationary link and a shifting block; second, those with a shifting link and a stationary block. The mechanism of the link is divisible into two sections: in the stationary link-motion, there are the eccentrics, the rods, and the link, which yield the motion; and the valve, rod, and reversing mechanism, which transmit and receive it. In the shifting link motion, the reversing mechanism operates upon the link.

15. *Lead.*—In the stationary link-motion a constant lead throughout the forward and backward gear, is obtained, by circling the link to the radius of the valve-rod link, and the same lead may be had for the front and back strokes. In the shifting link-motion, the lead essentially varies with the expansion. The greater the degree of expansion,—that is, the less the admission,—the greater also is the lead. The lead is thus least in full gear, and attains its maximum in mid gear. It may, however, always be made the same for the front and back strokes; and this equality is obtained by circling the link to the radius of the eccentric-rod.

Thus, the conditions of constant lead and varying admission, which are incompatible with the nature of the shifting link-motion, are obtainable by the stationary link, with a single valve.

16. The longer the eccentric-rod, and the shorter the link, the less is the variation of lead, in the shifting link-motion.

17. The shifting-link-motion may, with advantage, be set with the desired lead in half gear, which is the most ordinary working position of the mechanism. The evil of varying lead is thus divided and reduced.

18. *Linear Advance.* — With the stationary link, the linear advance of the eccentrics is in all cases less than that of the valve, and is a quantity affected by the length of the eccentric-rods: these rods by their varying obliquity, increase the advance while transmitting it to the link, and the shorter the rods the greater is the difference so caused.

With the shifting link, the linear advance of the valve is in all cases equal to that of the eccentrics in full gear, independently altogether of the length of the rods,—expressly meaning by full gear, that the fore-rod end is brought into the centre line of the valve-rod. In other positions, however, the linear advance of the valve varies precisely with the lead, as the lead, in fact, partly constitutes the advance.

19. *Motion of the Link.*—The motion of the link is composed of the distinct motions of the eccentrics, and every part of the link is subject to this compound influence. The motion of each eccentric prevails in that half of the link to which it is coupled; and at the centre, the motion of the link is equally composed of the two. The final result of this combined action is approximately the same as that available by the action of a single eccentric of variable throw. Thus the object which was proposed to be obtained by the spiral and wedge reversing motions of Fenton and Dodds—variable expansion with (if possible) constant lead—is realized in the simplest manner by the combined operation of two eccentrics, and with an efficiency and precision which probably the original promoters of the link-motion did not anticipate.

20. The horizontal motion communicated to the link by the joint action of the eccentrics, is a minimum at the centre of its length, where it is equal to twice the linear advance, and it increases towards the extremities. Various periods of admission are, thus, attainable by shifting the position of the block in the link, or of the link on the block: on the general principle that admission varies with the travel of valve.

21. The distribution derived from the link, is affected by the length of the connecting rod relative to that of the crank: the shorter the rod, the greater is the front admission, and the less is the admission for the back stroke. Therefore the term " link-motion," in so far as it involves the relation of the valve's motion to that of the piston, virtually includes the proportions of the piston-motion.

22. The quality of the motion derived from the link is modified by the positions of the working centres; and most especially of the centres of suspension and connection. The centre of suspension is the most influential of all in regulating the admission; and its transition horizontally is much more efficacious than a vertical change of place to the same extent.

23. The periods of admission in half gear are much more sensitive to variation by modes of suspension and connection, than those in full and mid gear. As locomotives are most frequently worked in half gear, it is expedient to set the motion right for this position, as regards the equality of the admissions; because the differences for other positions are then inconsiderable.

24. There are certain neutral positions of the centre of suspension, on which the link, in vibrating, yields equal admissions; and these may be found for any specific arrangement by the method of three trials.

25. These neutral positions may be located either in the centre-line of the link, vertically; or horizontally, in the neighbourhood of the middle of the link. As the vertical movement of the body of the link, with the consequent slip between the link and the block, is the least possible when the suspended centre lies in the centre line of the link, increasing as the centre is removed laterally,—the centre line of the link is in this respect the most favourable locality for the suspension, though not always practicable for equal admissions.

26. It has been found that the stationary and shifting links have not the same neutral centres of suspension; that, in general, the stationary link should be hung by a centre in the neighbourhood of the middle of its length; and the shifting link towards one of the extremities.

27. The periods of expansion and release increase as those of admission are diminished; and when the points of suppression are equally adjusted, those of release do not considerably differ. It has been found, in short, that the values of the admissions and the expansions, may be made absolutely identical, as in No. 8 stationary link, and the Great Western link. An admission of 75 per cent., or three-fourths of the stroke, is attended with a mean expansion of 16 per cent., the release taking place at 91 per cent.; 50 per cent. of admission, or one-half of the stroke, yields about 30 per cent. of expansion, exhausting at 80 per cent. The utmost period of expansion obtained by No. 5 stationary

link in mid gear is 38 per cent. for 12 per cent of admission, in which case the steam is cut off at less than one-eighth of the stroke, and expanded into a volume of 50 per cent., or one-half stroke, 4 times the initial volume, exclusive of clearance, after which it exhausts during the remaining half-stroke. With No. 8 stationary link, the shortest admission is 11 per cent., or one-ninth of the stroke, expanding into 50 per cent., or 4½ times the initial volume, before the release takes place. With the shifting link, the smallest attainable admission is about 17 per cent., or one-sixth of the stroke. This is about one-half more than what is obtained by the stationary link, the difference being due to the excess of travel yielded by the shifting link. As the release takes place at half-stroke, the shifting link cannot expand the steam above three times its initial volume, exclusive of clearance.

28. The average period of admission in full gear does not exceed 75 per cent., or three-fourths of the stroke, according to the examples before us. More than this should not be required, nor indeed could it be beneficially employed at regular speeds. The admission may, however, be increased by forcing the mechanism of the valve beyond full gear; that is, by causing the block to work in the extreme overhung parts of the link, which must be extended, for the purpose, beyond the centres of connection. By this expedient the throw of the valve is increased, and it is practicable with the box and back hung links, and may in many cases be usefully employed when a ready start with a heavy train is required.

29. The open link, connected by its extremities in its own centre line, is identical in its motions with the box link. In the use of that link it is imperative that the throw of the eccentric should be greater than that designed for the valve, as in full gear the block is of necessity placed nearer to the centre of the link than the rod-centres.

30. Though the deductions now recapitulated are based upon special examples, it is not difficult to perceive their general application. It were an endless task to follow out all the possible variations that may be imposed on the link-motion. The general influence of circumstances common to all links, has been pointed out with some minuteness, and enough has been done to show that correctly working link-motions may be applied in all situations,—so completely is the motion controlled by the location of the centre of suspension. Little has been said of the method of unequal laps on the ends of the valve for correcting unequal admissions, because in general it has been found unnecessary to adopt this expedient. It would be, however, a very effectual plan of equalizing the distribution.

CHAPTER VI.
RULES FOR VALVE-MOTION.

THE mean distribution derived from the link-motion, in any position from full to mid gear, has been found to be approximately the same as that derivable from the motion of a single eccentric, yielding the same travel, and with the same lap and lead. It is, to be sure, to some extent variable with different arrangements of link; the variation is

however but limited, and the near equivalence of the distributions founded on the two systems of driving the valve, enables us to apply to the link-motion, when the lap, lead, and travel are given, the rules which are founded directly on the motion of a single eccentric for determining the points of the distribution.

With a single-eccentric motion, the crank and the eccentric, as they revolve, describe equal angles in equal times; and the precedence of the crank by the eccentric, each from its own datum-line, is measured, in all parts of a revolution, by the angle of advance; or, referring to Fig. 2, Diagram-plate 2, by the angle formed by the 1st position of the eccentric with the datum-line D E. Again, overlooking the effect of the angularity of the connecting rod, the movements of the piston and the valve are measurable respectively by the cosine of the angle of the crank, and the sine of the angle of the eccentric, formed with their respective datum lines. On these two propositions the rules for valve-motion are founded. We take no account of the influence of the connecting rod, because the link-motion may be adjusted to neutralize that influence, while the *mean* distribution for the front and back strokes is not materially affected.

For the distribution derivable from a single eccentric:— Given the *lap*, *lead*, and *travel* of the valve. First of all, to find the angular advance of the eccentric,

$$\frac{\text{linear advance}}{\text{half travel}} = \text{sine of angle of advance};$$

from which the angle may be found by a table of natural sines.

1. To find the point of suppression. This point occurs when the steam side of the valve arrives at the outer edge of the steam-port, and a part of the half-travel equal to the lap remains to be described. Now,

$$\frac{\text{lap}}{\text{half-travel}} = \text{sine angle of eccentric}$$

at the instant of suppression. This angle, measured from the commencement of the throw, is obtuse; and selecting the greater value of the sine, given in the table of sines, the difference of the angle so found and the angle of advance, measures the angle of the crank at the point of suppression.

If the length of crank, or half-stroke, (50 per cent. of whole stroke) be taken equal to 1, the cosine of the angle of crank expresses the position of the piston, with reference to half-stroke; the cosine must be added to 1, if the angle be obtuse, or subtracted from 1, if acute; to give the position with reference to the beginning of the stroke. In brief,

angle of eccentric — angle of advance = angle of crank.

And

1 + *cosine angle of crank = position* of point of suppression in terms of half stroke.

2. To find the point of admission. This point occurs when the valve has passed its middle position by an amount equal to the lap. Then,

$$\frac{\text{lap}}{\text{half-travel}} = \text{sine angle of eccentric}.$$

This angle is acute, and

angle of advance — angle of eccentric = angle of crank.

And

1 — cosine angle of crank = position of point of admission.

3. To find the point of release. Should there be neither lap nor clearance inside, the release takes place when the valve is at half travel. The eccentric is then on the datum line, and the crank is by as much as the angle of advance from the end of the stroke; thus,

1 + cosine angle of advance = position of piston at point of release.

With inside lap or clearance,

$$\frac{\text{lap or clearance}}{\text{half-travel}} = \text{sine angle of eccentric, whence the angle.}$$

This angle is subtracted if due to lap, or added, if due to clearance, to the angle of advance; and the result is the angle of the crank; or,

$$\text{angle of } advance \pm \text{angle of } eccentric \begin{pmatrix}\text{for clearance}\\ \text{for lap}\end{pmatrix} = \text{angle of } crank.$$

And

1 + cosine angle of crank = position of piston.

4. To find the point of compression. With no inside lap or clearance, it occurs, like the release, when the valve is at half-travel: the eccentric is then on the datum line, and the crank is distant from the beginning of the stroke by as much as the angle of advance; thus,

1 — cosine angle of advance = position of piston.

Inside lap or clearance becomes the sine of the angle of the eccentric, and this angle is accordingly added to or subtracted from the advance, or,

$$\text{angle of advance} \pm \text{angle of eccentric} \begin{pmatrix}\text{for lap}\\ \text{for clearance}\end{pmatrix} = \text{angle of crank}$$

And

1 — cosine angle of crank = position of piston.

The general similarity of these four operations is apparent. In all cases, the lap or clearance divided by the half travel yields the sine of the angle of the eccentric due to the points of the distribution: outside lap being employed for the first two points, and inside lap or clearance for the last two. As inside lap and clearance are quite exceptional, and indeed not found in ordinary practice essential to the efficiency of the valve-motion, they will be overlooked in the following discussion. The second general process is to deduce the angle of the crank from the angle of the eccentric and the advance conjointly, taking the sum or difference as required.

To convert these operations into verbal rules.—Given the lap, lead, and travel.

Rule I.—For the *angular advance.* Divide the linear advance by the half-travel; the quotient is the natural sine of the angle of advance; whence the angle, which is always acute, may be found in a table of natural sines.

Rule II.—For the point of *suppression.* Divide the lap by the half-travel of valve, and the quotient is the natural sine of the angle of the eccentric; whence the angle, which is always obtuse, may be found from the table. From the angle of the eccentric so found, subtract the advance found by Rule I.; the difference is the angle of the crank. If this angle be obtuse, add 1 to its natural cosine; if acute, subtract the cosine from 1. The sum or difference so found multiplied by 50, expresses the position of the suppression, or the period of admission, in percentage of the whole stroke.

Rule III.—For the point of *admission.* Subtract the angle of the eccentric, as found by Rule II. (being in the present case acute), from the advance; subtract the cosine of the difference so found, from 1; the remainder multiplied by 50, expresses the position of the point of admission.

Rule IV.—For the *release.* Add 1 to the cosine of the angle of advance; and multiply the sum by 50, the product is the place of the release.

Rule V.—For the *compression.* Subtract the cosine of the angle of advance from 1; and multiply the remainder by 50. The product is the place of the compression. Or, subtract the release from 100; the remainder is the place or period of compression.

The following table comprises the periods of admission due to the lap varying from ½ inch to 1½ inch, and travel varying from 1⅝ inch to 6 inches, the lead being taken in all cases at $\frac{5}{16}$ inch, a very ordinary value. The table has been calculated by means of Rule II., with the assistance of Rule I.:—

TABLE No. XVI.—OF PERIODS OF ADMISSION FOR VARIOUS LAPS AND TRAVELS OF VALVE, IN PERCENTAGES OF THE STROKE.

Lead Constant, $\frac{5}{16}$ inch.

Travel	Lap.								
Inches.	½	⅝	¾	⅞	1	1⅛	1¼	1⅜	1½
1⅝	19								
1¾	39								
1⅞	47	17							
2	55	34							
2⅛	61	42	14						
2¼	65	50	30						
2⅜	68	55	38	13					
2½	71	59	45	27					
2⅝	74	63	49	36	12				
2¾	76	67	56	43	26				
2⅞	78	70	59	47	32	11			
3	80	73	62	50	38	23			
3⅛	81	74	65	55	44	30	10		
3¼	83	76	68	59	48	34	22		
3⅜	84	78	71	62	51	40	29	9	
3½	85	80	73	64	53	45	34	20	
3⅝	86	81	75	66	57	49	38	26	9
3¾	87	82	76	68	60	52	42	32	19
3⅞	87	83	78	70	63	55	46	36	25
4	88	84	79	72	66	58	49	40	29
4¼	89	86	81	76	70	63	56	47	37
4½	90	87	83	79	73	67	61	54	45
4¾	92	89	85	81	76	70	65	58	51
5	93	90	87	83	78	73	67	62	56
5½	94	92	89	86	82	78	73	68	63
6	95	93	91	88	85	82	78	74	69

The mode of calculation employed in forming the Table may be illustrated by an example. Take the case of a valve with 4½ inch travel, 1 inch lap, and $\frac{5}{16}$ inch lead, to find the period of admission. To find, first of all, the angle of advance by Rule I.

The linear advance $= 1 + \frac{5}{16} = \frac{21}{16}$ inch, and the half-travel $= \frac{36}{16}$ inches; then,

$\frac{21}{36} = 583 =$ sine angle of advance $= 36°$, by table of natural sines.

Again, by Rule II., as the lap $= \frac{4}{4}$ inch, and half-travel $= \frac{9}{4}$ inch,

$\frac{4}{9} = \cdot 444 =$ sine angle of eccentric at point of suppression

This corresponds in the Table to 26°, or its complement, 154°; and, as the angle of the eccentric is always obtuse, the greater value is selected. Then,

154° — 36° = 118° = angle of crank at the point of suppression.

The cosine of 118°, or its complement, 62°, is ·469; adding 1, it becomes 1·469, and

$1\cdot 469 \times 50 = 73\cdot 4$ per cent. of stroke.

which is the mean period of admission due to the action of a single eccentric.

The following abstract shows the coincidence between the motions derived from the link and a single eccentric, with the same lap, lead, and travel.

TABLE NO. XVII.—SHOWING THE CORRESPONDENCE OF THE MOTION DERIVED FROM THE LINK WITH THAT OF THE SINGLE ECCENTRIC.

Name of Link.	Particulars of Valve.			Period of Admission in percentage of Stroke.	
	Lap.	Lead.	Travel.	Derived from the Link.	Derived from a single Eccentric, calculated by Rules I. and II.
	inch.	inch.	inch.		
Stationary, No. 5	1	$\frac{1}{16}$	$4\frac{1}{2}$	74·5	73
	1	$\frac{1}{16}$	$3\frac{1}{4}$	46	44
	1	$\frac{1}{16}$	$2\frac{1}{4}$	12	12
Shifting Link, No. 2. Intermediate	1	$\frac{1}{16}$	$4\frac{1}{2}$	72	73
	1	$\frac{1}{16}$	$3\frac{1}{4}$	44	42
	1	$\frac{1}{16}$	$3\frac{1}{4}$	17	18
Shifting Link, No. 5. Direct	1	$\frac{1}{16}$	$4\frac{1}{2}$	75	75
	1	$\frac{1}{16}$	$3\frac{1}{4}$	47	45
	1	$\frac{1}{16}$	$3\frac{1}{4}$	16	18
Shifting Link, No. 7. Direct	1	$\frac{1}{16}$	$4\frac{1}{2}$	77·5	77
	1	$\frac{1}{16}$	$3\frac{1}{4}$	52	45
	1	$\frac{1}{16}$	$3\frac{1}{4}$	20	18
Great Western Link, No. 1	1	$\frac{1}{8}$	$4\frac{1}{2}$	74	72
	1	$\frac{1}{8}$	$3\frac{1}{4}$	59	55
	1	$\frac{1}{8}$	$3\frac{1}{4}$	40	37
Great Western Link, No. 2	$1\frac{1}{4}$	$\frac{1}{8}$	$4\frac{1}{2}$	66	63
	$1\frac{1}{4}$	$\frac{1}{8}$	$3\frac{1}{8}$	49	47
	$1\frac{1}{4}$	$\frac{1}{8}$	$3\frac{1}{16}$	29	26

The corresponding values in the last two columns, as found from the links directly, and by calculation from the given lap, lead, and travel, do not exhibit greater differences than are to be found among the links themselves. In no case do the values differ above 3 per cent. in full gear, and 2 per cent. in mid gear; and the positions of full and mid gear are indeed the only conditions of the link-motion which concern us in a preliminary trial, as, between these extremes any required admission may be obtained by placing a suitable notch in the sector.

An admission of 75 per cent. is the greatest that is desirable in full gear, though, of course, much greater admissions are practicable. For example, with 1 inch lap, and $\frac{1}{16}$ inch lead, a travel of 6 inches extends the admission to 85 per cent. But, for a practical maximum of 75 per cent., any of the following couples may be employed, with a constant lead of $\frac{1}{16}$ inch:—

TABLE NO. XVIII.—OF TRAVEL AND LAP REQUIRED FOR ABOUT 75 PER CENT. ADMISSION.

CONSTANT LEAD, $\frac{1}{16}$ INCH.

6 inches travel,	and $1\frac{1}{4}$ inch lap.
$5\frac{1}{2}$,, ,,	,, $1\frac{1}{8}$,, ,,
5 ,, ,,	,, $1\frac{1}{8}$,, ,,
$4\frac{1}{2}$,, ,,	,, 1 ,, ,,
4 ,, ,,	,, $\frac{7}{8}$,, ,,
$3\frac{1}{2}$,, ,,	,, $\frac{3}{4}$,, ,,
3 ,, ,,	,, $\frac{5}{8}$,, ,,
$2\frac{1}{2}$,, ,,	,, $\frac{1}{2}$,, ,,

It is rarely advisable to set the valve with less than $\frac{1}{16}$ inch lead, as allowance should be made for the straining and wear of the joints and other surfaces of the valve-gear which combine to reduce the lead when in actual work. As some engineers, however, rigidly proportion the lead to the travel and lap, the standard proportions of 1 inch lap, $\frac{1}{16}$ inch lead, and $4\frac{1}{2}$ inch travel, may be reduced to general terms. Assuming the travel as unity, and dividing it into 100 parts, the lap and lead may be expressed in percentages. Thus,

Travel, $4\frac{1}{2}$ inches = $\frac{72}{16}$ = 100 parts.
Lap, 1 inch = $\frac{16}{16}$ = 22·2 parts, say 22 per cent. of travel.
Lead, $\frac{1}{16}$ inch = $\frac{1}{16}$ = 6·94 parts, say 7 per cent. of travel.

Whence the general rule

RULE VI.—Given the travel of valve. To find the lap and lead necessary for a maximum admission of 75 per cent., or three-fourths of the stroke.

1st. For Lap.—Multiply the travel by 22, and divide by 100; the result is the required lap.

2d. For Lead.—Multiply the travel by 7, and divide by 100; the result is the required lead.

By this rule the following table has been constructed.

TABLE No. XIX.—OF RELATIVE TRAVEL, LAP, AND LEAD, FOR A MAXIMUM ADMISSION OF ABOUT 75 PER CENT. OF THE STROKE

Travel.	Lap.	Lead.	Travel.	Lap.	Lead.
Inches.	Inches.	Inches.	Inches.	Inches.	Inches.
$1\frac{1}{2}$	·33 or $\frac{5}{16}\frac{11}{32}$	·10 or $\frac{3}{32}$	$3\frac{1}{4}$	·71 or $\frac{11}{16}\frac{23}{32}$	·22 or $\frac{7}{32}\frac{15}{64}$
$1\frac{5}{8}$	·36 ,, $\frac{1}{3}\frac{3}{8}$	·11 ,, $\frac{1}{8}\frac{7}{64}$	$3\frac{1}{2}$	·77 = $\frac{3}{4}\frac{25}{32}$	·24 ,, $\frac{1}{4}\frac{15}{64}$
$1\frac{3}{4}$	·38 ,, $\frac{3}{8}$	·12 ,, $\frac{1}{8}$	$3\frac{3}{4}$	·82 ,, $\frac{13}{16}$	·26 ,, $\frac{1}{4}$
$1\frac{7}{8}$	·41 ,, $\frac{7}{16}\frac{13}{32}$	·13 ,, $\frac{1}{8}$	4	·88 ,, $\frac{7}{8}$	·28 ,, $\frac{1}{4}\frac{9}{32}$
2	·44 ,, $\frac{7}{16}$	·14 ,, $\frac{1}{8}\frac{9}{64}$	$4\frac{1}{4}$	·93 ,, $\frac{15}{16}$	·30 ,, $\frac{5}{16}$
$2\frac{1}{8}$	·47 ,, $\frac{7}{16}\frac{15}{32}$	·15 ,, $\frac{1}{8}\frac{5}{32}$	$4\frac{1}{2}$	·99 ,, 1	·31 ,, $\frac{5}{16}$
$2\frac{1}{4}$	·50 ,, $\frac{1}{2}$	·16 ,, $\frac{5}{32}\frac{11}{64}$	$4\frac{3}{4}$	1·04 ,, $1\frac{1}{16}$	·33 ,, $\frac{5}{16}\frac{11}{32}$
$2\frac{3}{8}$	·52 ,, $\frac{1}{2}\frac{17}{32}$	·17 ,, $\frac{5}{32}\frac{11}{64}$	5	1·10 ,, $1\frac{1}{8}$	·35 ,, $\frac{3}{8}$
$2\frac{1}{2}$	·55 ,, $\frac{9}{16}\frac{17}{32}$	·17 ,, $\frac{5}{32}\frac{11}{64}$	$5\frac{1}{4}$	1·15 ,, $1\frac{1}{8}\frac{5}{32}$	·37 ,, $\frac{3}{8}$
$2\frac{5}{8}$	·58 ,, $\frac{9}{16}\frac{19}{32}$	·18 ,, $\frac{3}{16}$	$5\frac{1}{2}$	1·21 ,, $1\frac{3}{16}\frac{7}{32}$	·38 ,, $\frac{3}{8}$
$2\frac{3}{4}$	·60 ,, $\frac{9}{16}\frac{19}{32}$	·19 ,, $\frac{3}{16}$	$5\frac{3}{4}$	1·26 ,, $1\frac{1}{4}$	·40 ,, $\frac{3}{8}\frac{13}{32}$
$2\frac{7}{8}$	·63 ,, $\frac{5}{8}\frac{19}{32}$	·20 ,, $\frac{3}{16}\frac{13}{64}$	6	1·32 ,, $1\frac{5}{16}$	·42 ,, $\frac{3}{8}\frac{13}{32}$
3	·66 ,, $\frac{5}{8}\frac{21}{32}$	·21 ,, $\frac{3}{16}\frac{7}{32}$	$6\frac{1}{2}$	1·5 ,, $1\frac{1}{2}$	·47 ,, $\frac{7}{16}\frac{15}{32}$

The contents of this and the preceding tables, are really all that is required for practical purposes, and supersede any further calculation, as the proportions of lap, lead, and travel therein followed out, are universally applicable in locomotives worked with a link-motion. The travels noted in these tables are competent for a maximum admission of about 75 per cent., and the shortening of the travel in the usual way by the link, affords in all cases the same facility for shortening the admission. The periods of admission are thus entirely under control; and with the certainty of regulating them with facility and accuracy, the other events of the distribution may safely be left to take care of themselves. We may conclude the chapter with the following table, No. XX., showing the relative distribution for a valve of the standard proportions, with admissions varied from 73·5 to 12 per cent., by reducing the travel to the values stated in the last two columns.

In this table, it is made obvious how unequally the travel is varied for nearly equal variations of admission; the variation is greatest about full gear, and is smallest at mid gear; as, while the first interval is $\frac{3}{4}$ inch, the last is but $\frac{1}{16}$ inch. The notches, of course, may be so placed in the sector, as to regulate the grades of expansion by equal intervals of admission, being for that object more closely placed towards mid gear; but it is clear that, as $\frac{1}{16}$ inch of travel makes all the difference between 12 and 20 per cent. of admission, the valve-gear, to be effective for high expansion, should at all times be maintained in the best order. The wear of the valve-gear, though of course it shortens the travel, nevertheless operates directly in delaying the events of the distribution, and is really equivalent to an increase of travel, as a greater admission is the result. The slackness incidental to worn valve-gear permits the valve to "slugger" or remain stationary for some time at each end of its travel, *while turning the centre;* thus the motion is assimilated to that derivable from cams—sudden, and abrupt.

TABLE No. XX.—OF THE DISTRIBUTION FROM FULL GEAR TO MID GEAR, WITH A VALVE OF THE STANDARD PROPORTIONS.

Points of the distribution in percentages of the whole stroke, measured from the beginning of the steam-stroke.				Corresponding travel of valve.	
Suppression.	Release.	Compression.	Admission.	Travel in full gear being 4½ inches.	In percentages of travel in full gear.
73·5	91	9	·62	4½ ins.	100
60	86	14	1·10	3¾ —	83
50	80	20	1·00	3¼ —	75
40	75	25	2·50	3$\frac{1}{16}$ —	67
30	68	32	4·35	2$\frac{1}{4}$ —	62
20	57	43	7·60	2$\frac{1}{4}$ —	60
12	50	50	12·25	2½ —	58·3

SUB-SECTION I.—(CONTINUED.)

OF THE MECHANICAL ACTION OF STEAM IN THE LOCOMOTIVE.

CHAPTER I.

PRELIMINARY CHAPTER ON THE PROPERTIES OF STEAM AND OTHER GASES.

PRESSURE, density, and temperature, are the important characteristics of steam; as they are those properties which regulate the economical production and application of steam power. Steam, as a gas, is amenable to the common laws of gaseous fluids; and according to these laws, the pressure, the density, and the temperature, bear fixed relations to one another. The influence of temperature on the expansion of gases under constant pressures, is nearly uniform for equal increments of temperature, and is nearly the same for different gases. For the special temperatures which concern the performance of locomotives, the rate of expansion is sensibly constant. We do not, of course, refer to the temperatures existing in the fire-box, but to those which occur in the boiler and the smoke-box, rarely exceeding 350° and 800° Fahrenheit. The rates of expansion of the different gases of combustion discharged from the locomotive furnace—the principal of which are air, nitrogen, carbonic oxide, and carbonic acid—do not vary above one five-hundredth between the maximum and minimum rate. The expansion of air

may therefore be assumed to represent that of other gases, and it is found by the latest experiments, that air expands $\frac{1}{490}$th of its volume at 32° for each degree of temperature communicated.

The relation betwixt pressure and volume, under constant temperatures is also sensibly uniform within ordinary limits. For an expansion of four times the initial volume, experiments on various gases show a corresponding diminution of pressure in the ratio of 1 to 3·99, or, sensibly, 1 to 4. The condition of constant temperature involved by this ratio, does not in all cases hold with the expansion of steam in the cylinder of the locomotive, as the maintenance of a constant temperature during an enlargement of volume, implies an accession of heat to the steam, which in many cases there is no sufficient means of supplying. It is true that, in inside cylinders, the temperature of the gases by which they are enveloped, when inclosed in the smoke-box, is usually higher than that of the steam contained in them, and it has been proved that under the most favourable circumstances, the steam is maintained at a sensibly constant temperature. With cylinders, however, which are dropped low in the smoke-box, as in the case of Bury's coupled engines, it is probable that their mean temperature is lower than that of the steam. It is, however, demonstrable that outside cylinders only partially protected, or not protected at all, condense to a certain extent the steam which passes through them, owing to their inferior temperature; and the insufficiency of temperature must be greater, in proportion as the steam is more expansively worked. It is, then, only under the most favourable conditions, when the smoke-box virtually discharges a portion of the duty of the other end of the boiler, that the temperature of the steam can be expected to remain tolerably constant during expansion.

The total or constituent heat of saturated steam,—or steam formed in contact with the water from which it is generated,—is at all temperatures separable into two parts, latent and sensible heat. The sensible heat is that indicated by the thermometer, and it varies with the pressure. The latent heat absorbed during the conversion of water into steam, constitutes by far the greater proportion of the total heat. The experiments of Regnault have superseded those of previous experimenters; and whereas it was formerly supposed that the sum of the latent and sensible heats was a constant quantity for all temperatures,—the one varying inversely with the other,—Regnault has proved that the total heat increases with the temperature. Thus, for saturated steam of 212° and 320°·2, we have the following values:

Pressure.	Temperature.	Latent Heat.	Total Heat.
14·7 lbs.	212°	966°·6	1178°·6
90 lbs.	320°·2	891°·4	1211°·6

The difference of total heat is, in this case, 33° in favour of the higher pressure. It appears, then, that by expansion, perfectly dry and well protected steam becomes slightly surcharged, in virtue of the excess of total heat due to higher pressures; and should it contain a portion of water in a state of suspension, as usually occurs in locomotives, a small part of this water must be evaporated during expansion, thereby reducing the dead weight of water in suspension, to be expelled through the exhaust passage.

For steam and for gases generally, the following ratios may, from what has been said, be adopted without error:—

With a *constant temperature*, the pressure varies simply as the density, and inversely as the volume. This is known as Boyle or Marriotte's law.

With a *constant pressure*, expansion is uniform under a uniform accession of heat, or rise of temperature, at the rate of $\frac{1}{490}$th of the volume at 32° for each degree of heat. If, then, we add (490° — 32°) or 458° to the indicated temperature, the sum is directly as the total volume by expansion, and inversely as the density. This is known as the law of Gay Lussac.

With a *constant volume*, or density, the increase of pressure is uniformly $\frac{1}{490}$th of that at 32°, for each degree of temperature acquired, and adding, as in the previous case, 458° to the indicated temperature, the sum is directly as the total pressure.

As applied to steam, these ratios have a general reference to it in a state of isolation. They likewise bear upon saturated steam as raised in the ordinary boiler, though the conditions under which steam in the boiler is generated are of a specific nature. With a constant temperature, the density and pressure are also constant; and whereas, with isolated steam, one of these three elements may remain constant, while the two others vary in proportion to each other, in the ratios already stated, with steam over water, the three elements must vary in common. And, as one density, one pressure, and one temperature, invariably occur in conjunction, should any one of the elements be changed, a definite corresponding alteration takes place in the remaining two. Steam produced over water, therefore, is necessarily, as saturated steam, 'at its maximum density and pressure for its temperature.'

It follows, that if a quantity of saturated steam be isolated, and a part of its heat be withdrawn, the density and pressure will fall, by the precipitation of a quantity of the steam as water.

An accession of heat to the same isolated volume, raises the temperature and pressure, the volume and density being constant. The state of saturation ceases, and the steam is distinguished as *surcharged* with heat, as it possesses a quantity of heat greater than that which is due to its density over water. And it would, were it placed in contact with water of the original temperature, evaporate a part of the water by the communication of the surcharge of heat, and resume its original state of saturation.

Though the law of the formation of saturated steam has been the subject of much and varied experimenting, it can as yet be reached only by the aid of empirical formulas. The weight of a cubic foot of steam at 212° raised from water under the ordinary atmospheric pressure, namely, 14·7 lbs. per square inch, is 0·03666 pounds, and this is an expression of the density of the steam, as weight is a direct measure of mass or quantity of matter. A cubic foot of pure water at 62° weighs 62·321 lbs.; and the ascertained *relative volume* of saturated steam produced under the atmospheric pressure, is 1700 times that of the water at 62° of which it is made; therefore $\frac{1}{1700}$th of the weight of a cubic foot of this water, expresses the weight of an equal bulk of the steam so formed; and it was in this way that

the weight of steam, already noted, was determined. From these data, with the aid of the ratios already established, the relations of pressure, volume, and temperature may be expressed. Thus,

Let p = the total pressure in pounds per square inch.
t = the temperature in degrees of Fahrenheit.
v = the relative volume, or the number of times that the volume of the steam contains the volume of the water from which it is converted.
w = the weight of one cubic foot, in pounds.

Then, to find the *relative volume* of steam of a given pressure p, and temperature t, we may employ the data found by experiment for saturated steam of atmospheric pressure, and throw them into the ratios according to which steam contracts or expands under pressure and heat. Thus,

$$v = 1700 \left(\frac{14·7}{p} \times \frac{(458 + t)}{(458 + 212)} \right)$$

or by simplification,

$$v = 37·3 \frac{(458 + t)}{p} \quad \ldots \quad (1.)$$

The *pressure* of steam per square inch, in terms of the relative volume and the temperature, is deducible directly from formula (1.)

$$p = 37·3 \frac{(458 + t)}{v} \quad \ldots \quad (2.)$$

The *temperature* of steam in terms of the relative volume and the pressure, is, from the same formula,

$$t = \frac{p\,v}{37·3} - 458 \quad \ldots \quad (3.)$$

The *weight* or density of steam is inversely as the relative volume. As a cubic foot of water at 62° weighs 62·321 lbs., divide this by the relative volume, and the quotient is the weight of the steam, thus

$$w = \frac{62·321}{v} \quad \ldots \quad (4.)$$

These formulæ may be expressed in words as follow:—

RULE I.—*To find the relative volume of steam.*—Add 458 to the temperature; divide the sum so found by the total pressure; and multiply by 37·3; the product is the relative volume.

RULE II.—*To find the total pressure of steam.* Add 458 to the temperature; divide the sum by the relative volume, and multiply by 37·3; the product is the total pressure.

RULE III.—*To find the temperature of steam.*—Multiply the total pressure by the relative volume, and divide by 37·3; from the quotient subtract 458; the remainder is the temperature.

RULE IV.—*To find the weight of steam.*—Divide 62·321 by the relative volume; the quotient is the weight per cubic foot.

From the irregular manner in which steam is formed in the locomotive boiler, and from other sources of error, these, the ordinary formulæ for steam, are applicable only under restrictions. It is, however, useful and necessary to know the most that can possibly be made of water converted into steam,—and the maximum is realized only when the latter is perfectly dry;—it is therefore expedient to adopt for our guidance an orthodox table (No. XXI.) of the corresponding pressures, temperatures, and volumes of saturated steam, within the limits employed in locomotives, and to furnish the necessary data for correction when the disposable power of the locomotive falls under discussion. The columns of

TABLE No. XXI.—THE PROPERTIES OF SATURATED STEAM.

Total pressure per square inch	Relative volume	Temperature	Total Heat	Weight of one cubic foot	Total pressure per square inch	Relative volume	Temperature	Total Heat	Weight of one cubic foot
lbs.		Fahr	Fahr lbs.	lbs.	lbs.		Fahr	Fahr	lbs.
15	1680	213.1	1178.0	.0373	81	355	312.8	1209.4	.1756
16	1572	216.3	1179.9	.0397	82	351	313.6	1209.7	.1776
17	1487	219.5	1180.9	.0419	83	348	314.5	1209.9	.1795
18	1410	222.5	1181.8	.0442	84	344	315.3	1210.1	.1814
19	1342	225.4	1182.7	.0465	85	340	316.1	1210.4	.1833
20	1280	228.0	1183.5	.0487	86	337	316.9	1210.7	.1852
21	1224	230.6	1184.3	.0510	87	333	317.8	1210.9	.1871
22	1172	233.1	1185.0	.0532	88	330	318.6	1211.1	.1891
23	1125	235.5	1185.7	.0554	89	326	319.4	1211.4	.1910
24	1082	237.9	1186.5	.0576	90	323	320.2	1211.6	.1929
25	1042	240.2	1187.2	.0598	91	320	321.0	1211.8	.1950
26	1005	242.3	1187.9	.0620	92	317	321.7	1212.0	.1970
27	971	244.4	1188.5	.0642	93	313	322.5	1212.3	.1990
28	939	246.4	1189.1	.0664	94	310	323.3	1212.5	.2010
29	909	248.4	1189.7	.0686	95	307	324.1	1212.8	.2030
30	881	250.4	1190.3	.0707	96	305	324.8	1213.0	.2050
31	855	252.2	1190.8	.0729	97	302	325.6	1213.3	.2070
32	830	254.1	1191.4	.0751	98	299	326.3	1213.5	.2089
33	807	255.9	1192.0	.0772	99	296	327.1	1213.7	.2108
34	785	257.6	1192.5	.0794	100	293	327.8	1213.9	.2127
35	765	259.3	1193.0	.0815	101	290	328.5	1214.2	.2149
36	745	260.9	1193.5	.0837	102	288	329.1	1214.4	.2167
37	727	262.6	1194.0	.0858	103	285	329.9	1214.6	.2184
38	709	264.2	1194.5	.0879	104	283	330.6	1214.8	.2201
39	693	265.8	1195.0	.0900	105	281	331.3	1215.0	.2218
40	677	267.3	1195.4	.0921	106	278	332.0	1215.2	.2230
41	661	268.7	1195.9	.0942	107	276	332.6	1215.4	.2258
42	647	270.2	1196.3	.0963	108	273	333.3	1215.6	.2278
43	634	271.6	1196.8	.0983	109	271	334.0	1215.8	.2298
44	621	273.0	1197.2	.1004	110	269	334.6	1216.0	.2317
45	608	274.4	1197.6	.1025	111	267	335.3	1216.2	.2334
46	595	275.8	1198.0	.1046	112	265	336.0	1216.4	.2351
47	584	277.1	1198.4	.1067	113	263	336.7	1216.6	.2370
48	573	278.4	1198.8	.1087	114	261	337.4	1216.8	.2388
49	562	279.7	1199.2	.1106	115	259	338.0	1217.0	.2406
50	552	281.0	1199.6	.1129	116	257	338.6	1217.2	.2426
51	542	282.3	1200.0	.1150	117	255	339.3	1217.4	.2446
52	532	283.5	1200.4	.1171	118	253	339.9	1217.6	.2465
53	523	284.7	1200.8	.1192	119	251	340.5	1217.8	.2484
54	514	285.9	1201.1	.1212	120	249	341.1	1218.0	.2503
55	506	287.1	1201.5	.1232	121	247	341.8	1218.2	.2524
56	498	288.2	1201.8	.1252	122	245	342.4	1218.4	.2545
57	490	289.3	1202.2	.1272	123	243	343.0	1218.6	.2566
58	482	290.4	1202.5	.1292	124	241	343.6	1218.7	.2587
59	474	291.6	1202.9	.1314	125	239	344.2	1218.9	.2608
60	467	292.7	1203.2	.1335	126	238	344.8	1219.1	.2626
61	460	293.8	1203.6	.1356	127	236	345.4	1219.3	.2644
62	453	294.8	1203.9	.1376	128	234	346.0	1219.4	.2662
63	447	295.9	1204.2	.1396	129	232	346.6	1219.6	.2680
64	440	296.9	1204.5	.1416	130	231	347.2	1219.8	.2698
65	434	298.0	1204.8	.1436	132	228	348.3	1220.2	.2735
66	428	299.0	1205.1	.1456	134	225	349.5	1220.6	.2771
67	422	300.0	1205.4	.1477	136	222	350.6	1220.9	.2807
68	417	300.9	1205.7	.1497	138	219	351.8	1221.2	.2846
69	411	301.9	1206.0	.1516	140	216	352.9	1221.5	.2885
70	406	302.9	1206.3	.1535	142	213	354.0	1221.9	.2922
71	401	303.9	1206.6	.1555	144	210	355.0	1222.2	.2959
72	396	304.8	1206.9	.1574	146	208	356.1	1222.5	.2996
73	391	305.7	1207.2	.1595	148	205	357.2	1222.9	.3033
74	386	306.6	1207.5	.1616	150	203	358.3	1223.2	.3070
75	381	307.5	1207.8	.1636	160	191	363.4	1224.8	.3263
76	377	308.4	1208.0	.1656	170	181	368.2	1226.1	.3443
77	372	309.3	1208.3	.1675	180	172	372.9	1227.7	.3621
78	368	310.2	1208.6	.1696	190	164	377.5	1229.1	.3800
79	364	311.1	1208.9	.1716	200	157	381.7	1230.3	.3970
80	359	312.0	1209.1	.1736					

pressure and temperature are the direct results of Mr. Regnault's experiments, the necessary interpolations being made from the data supplied by him by means of a simple formula constructed by himself. These results vary but slightly from those long since deduced by Pambour. Regnault has not yet published his observations on the relative volume of steam. The column under this heading has been composed in terms of the pressures and temperatures, by means of the ratios already announced as regulating the volumes of gases under varying pressures and temperatures separately. This mode of deducing the relative volumes is embodied in the first formula, and was employed by Pambour, as he very properly conceived that, in obedience to the general laws of gases in relation to heat and pressure, the relative volume of saturated steam should be deducible from the joint application of these laws:—knowing as we do that the pressure of steam over water does not rise without a corresponding elevation of temperature.

The fourth column contains the total heat of the steam at various pressures, being the results of direct experiment by Regnault.

The fifth column contains the weight of a cubic foot of dry saturated steam at the given pressures, determined by dividing 62·321 lbs., the weight of a cubic foot of water at 62°, by the relative volume.

Motion of Steam.—It is well understood that steam, *if unimpeded*, moves with unexampled velocity from one locality to another, under slight differences of pressure. Neither the movements nor the constitution of steam, are, however, in practice, so simple as we should like them; and partial rules applied without qualification to the former lead to results quite as diverse from the fact of the matter as when applied to the latter element. It is nevertheless important that the conditions of the free motion of steam should be exhibited, for they will remain as a standard to which we may usefully seek to adapt the actual conditions of locomotive mechanism.

Steam may flow into a vacuum, or it may deliver itself into the atmosphere; or, further, it may flow into steam of less density. The conditions of its flow in the first and in the other cases are different; as, in the second case, for example, 14·7 lbs., or approximately 15 lbs. of its total pressure go for nothing in counteracting the atmospheric resistance, before the slightest motion is possible. Thus, in the second case, at all pressures, the motion of the steam is due solely to the difference of its inherent pressure and that of the atmosphere. The ordinary method of estimating the velocity of the flow of gases or liquids under pressure, is founded on the laws of falling bodies; it is a very beautiful application of the law of gravitation, and it yields results simply and directly. A quantity of steam confined in a boiler, of a given pressure and known density, would flow into a vacuum through an opening from the boiler with a certain initial velocity, and this velocity would be the same as that which would be given to a liquid of the same weight as the steam, flowing out under the same pressure. The velocity of efflux referred to, when unretarded by physical obstructions, is precisely that which the liquid would acquire in falling through the height of a column of the same liquid, 1 inch square, equal in weight to the pressure of the steam per square inch. By the laws of falling bodies, it is known that the velocity, v, acquired in falling freely through any height h, is equal to eight times the square root of the height, or $v = 8\sqrt{h}$. Thus the velocity of efflux into a vacuum is determinable, and the following is the method of finding it.

Given, the total pressure of the steam, which we suppose to be saturated, as in all ordinary cases it is; divide the pressure per inch by the weight of a cubic foot of the steam, as found in the table, the quotient is the height of a uniform column of steam, 1 foot square, equal in weight to the pressure of the steam per square inch; multiply the quotient so found by 144, the number of square inches in a square foot of base, and the product is the height of a one-inch square column of the steam equal in weight to the given pressure of that steam on the square inch. The arithmetical process for finding this height is thus represented—

$$\frac{p}{w} \times 144 = h.$$

and the velocity of flow into a vacuum in terms of this height, is

$$v = 8 \sqrt{h}.$$

Substituting in this expression, the value of h previously found, we have

$$v = 8 \sqrt{\frac{p}{w} \times 144,}$$

or simplifying,

$$v = 96 \sqrt{\frac{p}{w}} \quad \cdots \quad (5.)$$

The following is the verbal expression of this formula:—

RULE V.—*To find the velocity with which saturated steam flows freely into a vacuum.*—Divide the total pressure per square inch, in pounds, by the weight of a cubic foot of the steam, in pounds, and find the square root of the quotient; multiply this result by 96, the product is the required velocity in feet per second.

Note.—Should the steam be surcharged, the weight may be found by means of the rules previously established.

Example 1.—Given, saturated steam of 15 lbs. total pressure; to find the velocity of efflux into a vacuum. A cubic foot of 15 lbs. steam weighs ·0373 lb., and 15 ÷ ·0373 = 401·7. Then, $\sqrt{401·7} \times 96 = 1924$ feet per second, is the velocity of efflux of 15 lbs. steam into a vacuum.

Example 2.—Given, saturated steam of 100 lbs. total pressure. A cubic foot weighs ·2127 lb., and 100 ÷ ·2127 = 470·1. And $\sqrt{(470·1)} \times 96 = 2081$ feet per second.

These two examples show that saturated steam of higher pressure flows into a vacuum with a trifle greater velocity than steam of lower pressure; and only a trifle greater, being in any case but a small fraction above or below 2000 feet per second. The reason of the near equality of speeds observable, is due to the density or weight of the mass of saturated steam to be moved, increasing nearly as rapidly as the pressure. If they increased at the same rate, the velocity would be also the same. The proportion of the pressure rather exceeds that of the density, and hence the slight preponderance of velocity at the higher pressures.

Again, a question which immediately concerns the locomotive, is to find the velocity of the free flow of steam into the atmosphere, or into steam of inferior density. In this case, the *difference* of pressures is the moving force, and the steam of greater density is the mass to be moved. Therefore, the velocity of free efflux is that due to the height of a column of the steam of greater density, one inch square, equal in weight to the difference of pressures per square inch. Thus, if p' be the pressure of the weaker medium (the atmosphere, or the steam of inferior pressure), and p and w as before, the pressure and weight of the stronger steam, then, by a modification of formula (5), we have

$$v = 96 \sqrt{\frac{p - p'}{w}} \quad \cdots \quad (8.)$$

expressed at length as follows:—

RULE VI.—*To find the velocity with which saturated steam flows freely into the atmosphere, or into steam of inferior pressure.*—Take the difference of pressures of the two steams for the effective pressure; divide the effective pressure in pounds per inch, by the weight of a cubic foot of the denser steam, in pounds; and multiply the square root of the quotient by 96. The product is the required velocity in feet per second.

Example 1.—Given, steam of 16 lbs. total pressure, to find the velocity of free efflux into the atmosphere.—Taking the counter-pressure of the atmosphere at 15 lbs., which we shall do in all cases, we have 16 — 15, or 1 lb., for the effective pressure. Then $1 \div ·397 = 25·19$; and $\sqrt{25·19} \times 96 = 481·8$ feet per second, the velocity required.

In the same way, the velocity of saturated steam of any other pressure, freely flowing into the atmosphere, may be obtained, and the following is a selection of the results so found:—

TABLE No. XXII.—OF THE VELOCITY OF FREE EFFLUX OF STEAM INTO THE ATMOSPHERE OF 15 LBS. PRESSURE.

Effective pressure of steam, or pressure above the atmosphere.	Velocity of free efflux, in feet per second.	Effective pressure.	Velocity.
lbs.	Feet.	lbs.	Feet.
1	482	50	1791
2	683	60	1838
3	791	70	1877
4	890	80	1919
5	973	90	1936
10	1241	100	1957
20	1504	110	1972
30	1643	120	1990
40	1729	130	2004

Here it is observable that, with only 1 lb. effective pressure, the velocity does not amount to 500 feet per second,—an inferiority in comparison with the velocity into a vacuum, owing to the comparatively small pressure available for moving a mass of steam of 16 lbs. total pressure. The difficulty is, however, got over as the pressure rises, for the proportional resistance of the atmosphere becomes less, and at 130 lbs. effective pressure the velocity reaches 2000 feet.

But, inferior though the velocity of 1 lb. steam may be, it is greater than what is due to higher pressures, when the same effective pressure exists. Thus, the velocity of the free flow of 101 lbs. steam, total pressure, into steam of 100 lbs., where the effective pressure is 1 lb., as in the previous case, amounts to only 207 feet per second. In this instance, while the moving pressure is the same as in the other, the density or mass of the steam to be moved is greatly superior.

The next and last question which requires consideration is relative to the determination of the inferior pressure, when the superior one and the velocity of efflux are given. We may readily suppose a case in which a solution of this question would be desirable. For example, to find what ought to be the pressure existing in the cylinder of the locomotive, were there no resistance by friction, bends, &c., when the piston moves at a given speed, and the pressure in the boiler and the opening of regulator are known. The formula (6.) for velocity merely requires to be inverted—thus, if

$$v = 96 \sqrt{\frac{p - p'}{w}}, \text{ then } \frac{v}{96} = \sqrt{\frac{p - p'}{w}}; \text{ and, squaring both sides,}$$

$$\frac{v^2}{9216} = \frac{p - p'}{w}, \text{ and } \frac{w v^2}{9216} = p - p'; \text{ wherefore,}$$

$$p' = p - \frac{w v^2}{9216} \quad \cdot \quad \cdot \quad \cdot \quad \cdot \quad (7.)$$

Whence the following rule:—

RULE VII.—*To find the pressure to which saturated steam is reduced, when it flows freely, with a given velocity, from one vessel into another.*—Multiply the square of the velocity in feet per second, by the weight in pounds of a cubic foot of steam of the initial total pressure, and divide the product by 9216. The quotient thus found expresses the difference of the initial and final pressures; subtract this quotient from the given initial pressure, and the remainder is the reduced total pressure sought.

Example.—Given, saturated steam of 101 lbs. total pressure, flowing at a speed of 207 feet per second, what is the reduced pressure? The weight of a cubic foot of 101 lbs. steam is ·2149 lbs. Then, ·2149 × 207² ÷ 9216 = 1 lb., the difference of pressure; therefore 100 lbs. is the reduced total pressure.

Of the loss of pressure generally which accompanies the movements of steam.—It has been seen that a reduction of pressure, great or small, necessarily accompanies even the free motion of steam, the difference being consumed in communicating that motion. By far the heaviest losses are, however, due to the resistances of bends and superficial friction of pipes, &c. These of course vary with every arrangement of steam-passages. M. Morin has found from experiment on stationary engines and boilers, that the losses, on various accounts, follow these general ratios:—

The difference of pressures in the boiler and the cylinder is, 1st, As the density of the steam, and as the square of the speed of piston.

2d, As the square of the ratio of area of piston to cross section of steam-pipe.

3d, As a factor dependent on bends and friction.

The permanent difference of pressure caused by passing through a stricture in a pipe, otherwise of uniform diameter before and behind the stricture, is as the density of the steam, and as the square of the difference of speeds through the larger and smaller parts of the pipe.

The friction of a fluid through a pipe is, 1st, As the length directly.

2d, As the diameter inversely.

3d, As the square of the velocity directly.

4th, As the density directly.

It is needless at present to attempt to affix absolute values to any of these ratios. Estimates of actual loss will be more readily formed when we have before us the results of special experiments of our own. The general arrangement of the boiler and steam-passages of locomotives is so much after one model, that we anticipate little difficulty in reducing the question of loss to a simple form.

CHAPTER II.

OF THE BEHAVIOUR OF STEAM IN THE CYLINDER; OF THE INDICATOR; AND OF THE STEAM-DIAGRAM.

As the steam is encumbered with diverse resistances in the course of its passage from the boiler, through the cylinder, into the atmosphere, its condition under such circumstances, to be understood, must be subjected to special observation. The general laws of steam may afford suggestions, but under actual circumstances, they are sufficient simply as guides; and the aid of the indicator is essential for a complete and systematic investigation of its action.

The steam-indicator is an instrument which is connected directly with the interior of the cylinder, and registers the variations of pressure which occur throughout the double stroke of the piston. Two forms of the instrument,—those of Mr. Gooch, and Mr. M'Naught,—have been, in this country, applied to locomotives. The more perfect instrument is that designed by Mr. Gooch, employed by him in conducting the Experiments on Train Resistances, upon the Bristol and Exeter Railway, and regularly applied to the locomotives of the Great Western Railway. The whole apparatus, shown generally by Figs. 87 and 88, is contained

Fig. 87.

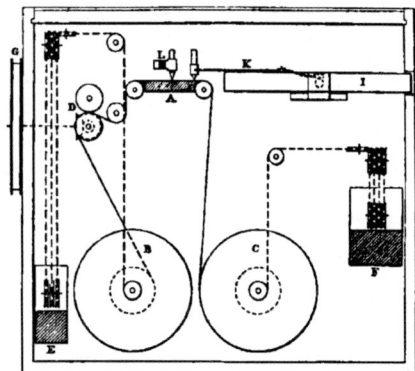

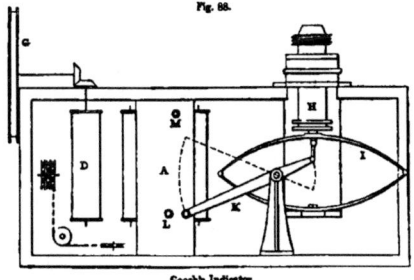
Gooch's Indicator.

in a chest, and comprises two motions; one for shifting the paper destined to receive the diagrams, the other for transmitting and registering the steam-pressure. The table A, fixed across the chamber, carries the paper-surface on which the diagrams are inscribed. The paper, prepared in stripe of considerable length, is passed regularly across the table, while the instrument is in operation, so that a continuous diagram may be obtained, to represent the periodical movements of the steam throughout several turns of the wheel, or double strokes of the piston. For this purpose, two deeply flanged rollers, B, C, are suspended near the bottom of the chest; on one of them, C, a roll of paper is coiled, the free end of which is passed over guiding rollers, across the table, between the driving rollers D, and terminates and is fixed on the empty roller B. The paper is kept taut on the table and rollers by means of weights E, F, opposed to each other and connected by lines which coil upon barrels on the axes of the paper-rollers, and coupled to them by ratchets and spring palls. The paper is pinched between the rollers D, to yield the necessary traction; and the upper roller is driven, through mitre-gear, by a band from the driving axle over the pulley G, which may be thrown out of gear when necessary.

The pressure-cylinder H, shown in detail, Fig. 89, is coupled directly to the engine-cylinder by an exterior coupling. The piston a is of steel, hollow, turned to fit the cylinder, without packing, so closely as *just* to permit steam to pass. It is thus made at once frictionless and practically tight. A small hole is drilled in the corner of the cylinder, to maintain atmospheric pressure on the outer face of the piston. The piston is secured directly by its rod to the double elliptic spring I. This again is linked to one end of the lever K, the other end of which carries the pencil; and under the action of steam-pressure, the pencil moves over the paper in the circular arc shown in dot lines. The pencil L, is adjustable on a transverse slide (not shown in plan) to stand opposite the indicator pencil when at rest. In this condition, when the paper is drawn across the table, both pencils describe the atmospheric line; and the pencil L, continues to do so while the other is employed in describing the diagram. A third pencil M is actuated by the cross head of the engine-piston, and its function is to notify the arrival of the piston at every half stroke. The cylinder-casting, Fig. 89, is of brass, bored out; b is the coupling, c, the sluice valve to open or close the communication between the cylinders; and the waste passage d, admits of blowing through to clear out water, &c. The piston has 1 square inch of area; the spring is formed of two plates of steel, 1¼ inch broad, ⅛ inch thick at middle, 1/16 inch at ends, and 12 inches span unloaded, with 4½ inches total inside compass. The arms of the lever are 2½ and 6¼ inches long, in the ratio of 1 to 2·43. Thus a large scale of diagram is obtained, with a small range of piston,—a matter of importance at high speeds, when the disturbing influence of the momentum of the reciprocating parts come into play.

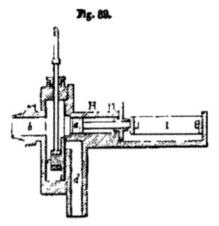

Fig. 89.

Gooch's Indicator.—Detail.

M'Naught's indicator, Fig. 90, is simpler and lighter than Gooch's; and for ordinary purposes it is tolerably efficient. The whole of the instrument is of brass, except the springs and their spindles, which are of steel. This indicator, like the other, consists of two motions: one for carrying and shifting the paper to receive the diagram, and the other for registering the steam pressure. The paper is simply lapped once round the cylinder A, and held by spring clamps. The cylinder rotates on its axis, carried by the bracket, b, and is connected to it by a flat spiral spring; thus, when the cylinder is drawn round by a cord actuated by the cross-head of the piston, through one revolution, it is withdrawn by the action of the spring when the cord is relaxed; and thus its alternate motion is made to coincide with the reciprocations of the piston. The piston c, on the spindle d, works nearly tight and frictionless in the cylinder; when raised by the steam pressure it distends the spring B, to which it is connected; and the pencil which fits into a socket carried by the spindle, when turned into contact with the paper, traces a diagram showing the steam pressure in one end of the cylinder during the double stroke. The piston is fully ½ inch diameter, having ⅛ inch area; the tension of the spring increases at the rate of 40 lbs. per square inch, to the inch of rise.

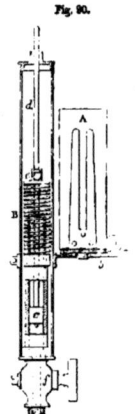

Fig. 90.

M'Naught's Indicator.

Account of the Steam-diagram.—We have seen that while Gooch's instrument yields a continuous web of diagrams, M'Naught's is capable only of repeating the diagram on the same paper surface. We have remarked, however,—what Mr. Gooch has well established,—that the recurring curves of a consecutive series are very close repetitions; and M'Naught's indicator, as it may in general be made to register with distinctness during three or four revolutions, on the same paper, usually turns out a satisfactory diagram. Fig. 91 is a portion of a diagram taken by Mr. Gooch, with his indicator, from the cylinder of the 'Great Britain'

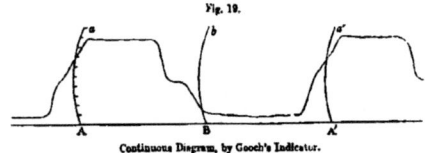

Fig. 19.

Continuous Diagram, by Gooch's Indicator.

locomotive on the Great Western Railway. The atmospheric line A A', or line of no-pressure, was described by the stationary pencil L, already named; and the curve line was traced by the pencil K, showing the variation of steam pressure in the cylinder. The points A, B, A', being successively the beginning, end, and recommencement of the front stroke, then the segmental lines A a, &c., drawn through these points to the radius of the longer arm of the lever carrying the pencil K, will cut the diagram at the points simultaneously arrived at by that pencil, showing thereby the pressures at the beginning and end of the stroke. At every other point in the base-line, if similar curved ordinates be raised to meet the diagrams, the lengths of the ordinates, measured by scale, are the simultaneous steam pressures.

As the paper is drawn over the table at a uniform speed, while the speed of piston varies during the stroke, the intervals of the base-line due to one inch of stroke are greatest about the points A, B, A', when the motion of the piston is slowest. Setting out the divisions, for each inch of stroke, and allowing for the angularity of the connecting rod, the diagram will be divided as in the annexed fig. 92, in which the pressure on one end of the piston for each inch of stroke is clearly set forth.

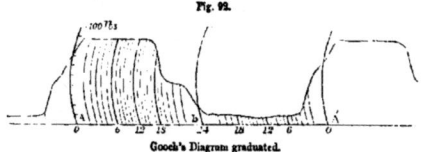

Fig. 92.

Gooch's Diagram graduated.

The diagrams from M'Naught's indicator, more directly represent the action of the steam, for the pencil moves vertically in a straight line; and the reciprocations of the paper transversely, as they are derived from the piston-rod directly through a simple lever, are *bona fide* those of the piston on a reduced scale. The atmospheric line may then be adopted for the length of stroke, each inch of which is represented by an aliquot part of the base-line. Perpendiculars raised on this line will also cut the diagram at points indicating the corresponding pressures. Thus, in the annexed diagram, taken by this instrument, the atmospheric line A B, described by the pencil without steam, is equivalent to

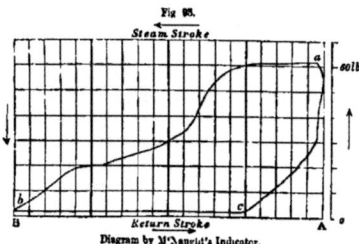

Fig. 93.

Steam Stroke

Return Stroke

Diagram by M'Naught's Indicator.

the stroke of piston; the curve-line *a b*, traced by the pencil, exhibits the varying pressure of the steam during the steam stroke in the direction A B; and during the return stroke, B A, the continuation, *b c a*, represents similarly the back pressure due to incomplete exhaust. The curve is thus arranged to begin and end in itself, and it plainly represents the pressure of the steam on one side of the piston during a double-stroke. Divide the base-line into inches of stroke, of which in this case there are 20, and at each inch draw vertical lines. Similarly, draw a series of parallels to the base, at equal intervals of, say, 10 lbs. pressure, by the scale of the indicator. Thus, the force of the steam at all

points of the stroke is made obvious; and a diagram so divided may be reduced or enlarged, by the ordinary method of rectangles, to other required scales of inches and pounds.

Into the general form here described, Mr. Gooch reduces all the diagrams taken by himself. In doing so, he selects from each roll, for reduction, the best average curve for one double-stroke. To reduce the curve, Fig. 92, draw the atmospheric line, A B, Fig.

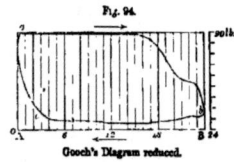

Fig. 94.

Gooch's Diagram reduced.

94, of a convenient length; divide it into 24 equal parts, as inches of stroke; through the points of division draw verticals; set off on the verticals, in order from A towards B, by a convenient pressure-scale, the positive pressures measured from the base-line A B, Fig. 92, for each inch of stroke; similarly, from B towards A, Fig. 94, set off the back pressures in order from B to A', Fig. 92. Through the points so found, trace a curve line as shown. The curve terminates in itself, and it assumes a form convenient for direct reference. By this method, Mr. Gooch has prepared, from their originals, two valuable series of diagrams, fifty in number, obtained by himself from the cylinder of the Great Britain, which the writer has been enabled, through the kindness of that able investigator, to exhibit in one view, in diagram-Plate 4; and only those who have undergone the fatigue and the risk of a sojournment on the buffer-beam, at 60 miles an hour, with occasionally a brisk side wind to make them conscious of how short a distance there is between time and eternity,—those only can fully appreciate their value. The diagrams are ranged in two series; for the second of these, greater initial pressures in general were employed; and, as specified on the margin of the plate, the lap of the valve was increased, and the lead slightly reduced, with the view of prolonging the periods of expansion, and of reducing the back pressure. They are arranged in the order of the notches and the speeds; and on the body of each diagram are inscribed the positive, exhaust, and effective mean pressures indicated by it.

The locomotives which have been made the subjects of experiment by the author, are chiefly those of the Glasgow and South Western, Caledonian, and Edinburgh and Glasgow Railways. The passenger-engines of the Caledonian Railway are similar in general arrangement to those of the London and South Western,—for example, the 'Snake,' published in our plates—cylinders outside, partially embraced by the plates of the smoke-box; valve-chest inside, with vertical valves. The goods-engines have the cylinders outside, horizontal, and hung from the outside of the frame, entirely clear of the smoke-box, protected by felt and plated on the outside and on the front cover; valve-chest inside the smoke-box, with vertical face. On the Edinburgh and Glasgow Railway, all the passenger-engines have the cylinders inside the smoke-box.

The following table comprises the necessary dimensions of the locomotives with which experiments have been made on the action of steam in the cylinder; the actual states of the valves at the time of experiment, have been noted in the table:—

I

TABLE No. XXIII.—DIMENSIONS OF LOCOMOTIVE ENGINES, RELATIVE TO THE ACTION OF STEAM IN THE CYLINDER. 1850.

Name of Railway.	Name and Designation of Engine.	Diameter and Stroke of Cylinder.	Diameter of Driving Wheel.	Dimensions of Ports. Steam. Wide.	Steam. Long.	Exhaust. Wide.	Exhaust. Long.	Diameter of Blast Orifice.	Dimensions of Valve. Lap.	Lead in full gear.	Travel in full gear.	Name of Maker.	Remarks.
		inches.	feet.	ins.	ins.	ins.	ins.	inches.	inches.	inches.	inches.		
Great Western,	Great Britain, Pass	18 × 24	8	13	2	13	3½	4½, 5, 5½	1, 1¼	⅛, ⅜	4½	G. W. R. Co.	Cylinder inside of smoke-Box. Stationary Link-Motion.
Caledonian, ..	No. 13, Do...	15 × 20	6	10	1 3/16	10	3	4⅛	1 3/16	1/16	4½	Tayleur & Co.	Cylinders outside. Shifting Link, intermediate.
Do.	No. 14, Goods,.......	15 × 20	6	10	1 3/16	10	3	3½	1 3/16	0	4½	Do.	Do. Do. Gearing much worn.
Do.	No. 33, Pass.. ...	15 × 20	6	10	1¼	10	3	4	1¼	1/16	4½	C. R. Co........	Do. Stationary Link,—worn.
Do.	Nos. 41, 42, Do ...	15 × 20	6	10	1¼	10	3	No. 41, 4 1/16; No. 42, 4	1¼	⅛	4½	Do.	Do. Shifting Link. Newly repaired.
Do.	No. 51, Do. with old and new valves,.......	15 × 20	6	10	1¼	10	3	4, old; 4 1/16, new	1¼; 1⅛	1/16; ⅛	4½; 5½	Do.	Do. Do. Old gearing worn.
Do.	No. 73, Do...........	13 × 18	5	8⅝	1	8⅝	3½	3½, 3⅝	1	1/16, 1/16	4	Sharp & Roberts	Cylinder inside. Gab-motion.
Do.	Nos. 124, 125, Goods,	17 × 24	4′ 7″ coupled	12	1¼	13	2⅞	No. 124, 3⅞; No. 125, 3¾	1¼	1/16	5	C. R. Co........	Cylinders outside, clear of smoke-box. Stationary Link.
Do. .. .	No. 127, Do...	17 × 24	4′ 7″ Do.	12	1¼	12	2⅞	4	1¼	⅛	5	Do.	Do. Do. Do.
Do.	No. 109, Do ..	16 × 18	4½ Do.	11½	1¼	11½	2 1/16	4 1/16	1	0	4	Do.	Do. Stationary Link,—Gearing worn.
Edin. and Glas.	Orion, Pass.......	15 × 20	6	10	1 3/16	10	2¼	4 1/16	1	⅛	4	E. & G. R. Co.	Cylinders inside of smoke-box. Stationary Link.
Do.	Hebe, Do	15 × 20	5½	9½	1¼	9½	2⅜	3½	¾	0	3½	Sharp, Brothers	Do. Do. Shifting Link, worn.
Do.	Nile, Do..... ..	16 × 18	6	11½	1¼	11½	2⅜	4½	1	1/16	3¾	Hawthorne. .	Do. Do. Gab motion.
Do.	Pallas, Do.........	15 × 20	6	10	1¼	10	2½	4½	¾	⅛	4	Neilson & Co.	Do. Do. Link, intermediate.
Do.	Brindley, Do.........	14 × 18	5½	6½	1¼	6½	2	3½	1	⅛	4	Bury & Co. ..	Do Do. Shifting Link.
Do.	England Do	9 × 12	4½	7	⅞	7	—	2⅜	½	⅛	—	England & Co.	Cylinder inside of frame. Shifting Link.

The diagrams, Figs. 93 and 94, it is plain, reach the maximum pressure at the commencement of the stroke, *a*. In the course of the stroke, the pressure falls, and the figure tapers towards the atmospheric line, as it approaches the end of the stroke. Conversely, during the return of the piston,—the observations being confined always to one end of the cylinder,—the back pressure at *b* is at or near a minimum, and as the piston finds its way towards the end of the return, the pressure rises towards *a*, in preparation for the beginning of the next steam stroke. But while this reciprocation of extreme pressures is rendered obvious generally by the diagrams, the figure fails for want of angularity to indicate precisely at what points of the stroke such changes occur. The roundness of figure is characteristic of all diagrams taken at any ordinary speed, and is to be attributed partially to the momentum of the spring of the indicator, and partially to that of the steam. Be that as it may, the desired precision of outline may be obtained at very slow speeds, as with these the disturbing influence of momentum has no existence. The dark-line diagram, Fig. 95, was obtained from the cylinder of a locomotive,

Fig. 95.

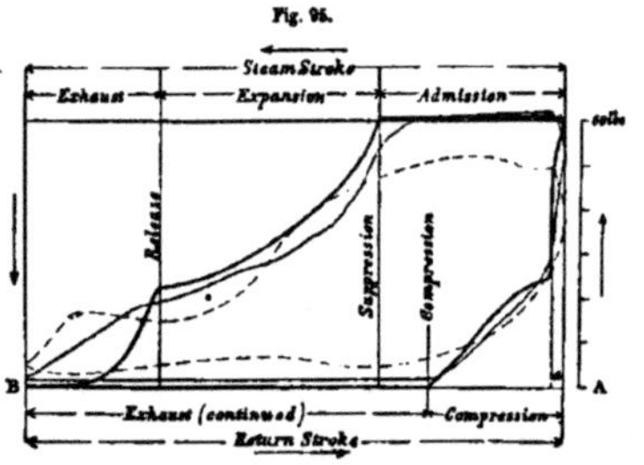

General Illustration of the Behaviour of Steam in the Cylinder, relative to the successive periods of the Distribution.

20 inch stroke, while moving at 2½ miles per hour. It indicates distinctly the nature of the distribution in the special case, and graphically displays the behaviour of the steam under the influence of the valve. In the first place, the piston is represented as starting from the upper right hand corner under a uniform pressure of steam of 61 lbs., till it reaches the point of suppression. The admission being terminated, the expansion of the steam that has been admitted, and is now locked up, commences, and is plainly indicated by a sudden fall of the curve, intimating a rapid reduction of pressure as the piston moves on,—the natural result of the forced attenuation of the steam. The progressive reduction of the pressure throughout the whole period of expansion is demonstrated by the continual depression of the curve, which falls steadily until the piston reaches the point of release. At this point a second change takes place, and the piston enters upon the third and last stage of its progress towards the termination of the steam stroke. The period of exhaust commences while yet the piston is considerably short of the end of the stroke: the curve breaks away almost vertically towards the point B, and shows that at the instant of release, the steam, which was primarily admitted at 61 lbs. pressure, and attenuated to 23 lbs. pressure previously to its being released, quickly discharges itself in virtue of its remaining elasticity, and is entirely evacuated even before the piston has finished the stroke. The complete evacuation of the steam is proved by the merging of the curve into the datum line, and its coinciding with it, finishing in a mere point of no-pressure at the end of the steam stroke. But though the indicated pressure of the steam at this point, is nothing, it intimates simply that the elastic force of the steam is reduced to an equality with that of the atmosphere. The evacuation is, therefore, only relative; it is not absolute, as there is left a necessary residue of latent or insensible steam of one atmosphere or 15 lbs. absolute pressure, and there exists a complete cylinder-full of this steam behind the piston at the end of the steam stroke. On this account, it is clear that the business of the exhaust is by no means completed, even when the pressure has been reduced to nothing: the exhaust port ought to be kept continuously open to the face of the piston which we have been following, throughout the whole of the return stroke; and the benefit of this provision is proved by the diagram, in which it appears that during the continuation of the exhaust the steam of latent pressure remains at the zero point, insensible to the indicator. At the instant of closing or compression, however, when there is no longer an exit for the exhaust steam before the advancing piston, the diagram-line starts upwards towards the right hand; the steam, hitherto insensible, and finding no way of escape, is compressed against the end of the cylinder into a space which continually grows less as the piston advances. While the volume of the confined steam is being thus forcibly reduced, its density is increased, its pressure is

raised in proportion, and the accumulation of back pressure so induced is promoted till near the end of the return stroke, when it becomes lost in the superior pressure of the steam admitted by anticipation for the business of the next steam stroke. The critical point at which this interruption of the gradual compression occurs, is indicated by the small compartment *a*, in the figure, representing the period of pre-admission. The curve starts vertically upwards at the instant at which the valve opens the steam port for the admission of steam from the valve-chest, and reaches the initial pressure of 61 lbs. for the commencement of the next steam stroke.

The phenomena so clearly illustrated by the diagram, point out the relative importance of the functions of the valve, and we may readily observe the analogy betwixt the general formation of this diagram and the motion-curve of the valve-motion : all the points of the distribution are conspicuously defined, and the method of the slow diagram affords a ready means of determining the state of the valves and the distribution, fully more exact than by ocular inspection of the valve-gear, as it includes all the allowances for the elasticity and wear of the gearing. The period of admission, it appears, is about one-third of the whole stroke; that of expansion is something more, and a simple inspection of the diagram is sufficient to prove that in this instance, one-half of the work of the steam is performed while shut up in the cylinder. Even the period of exhaust supplies its quota of effect, inasmuch as the evacuation is a work of time, and the extra positive pressure so yielded is represented by the small triangular space between the point of release and the end of the stroke. The force developed by compression, as it opposes the motion of the piston, is properly denominated resistance, and must be classed with the slight opposition also made by the entering steam during its pre-admission for the steam stroke.

General Influence of Speed on the Steam Diagram.—We are now in a position to appreciate the character of ordinary high-speed diagrams; and the following remarks apply only to the diagrams thrown off by M'Naught's Indicator:—The two diagrams in light and dotted lining, Fig. 95, were taken at speeds of 20 and 44 miles per hour respectively, from the engine with which the slow diagram was made, the points of the distribution being in all the cases identical. There is therefore nothing to observe but the effect of speed; and, in the first place, the steam though admitted with an initial pressure of 62 lbs., in the case of the slower speed, slightly loses its force as the piston recedes before it,—a circumstance which may at once be attributed to the accelerating speed of the piston in the cylinder, and the consequently greater difficulty of following it. The difficulty is however but small, and it is only when the piston nears the point of suppression, and the opening of the port for steam approaches to nothing, that the pressure rapidly falls in the diagram towards the suppression-line. This is a case of simple wire-drawing, as the opening of the port, previously large enough to admit all the steam that could find its way through, against the frictional resistance of the passage,—now arrives at the minimum width consistent with this condition, and a further contraction and final closing necessarily occasions an accelerated fall of the pressure.

The pressure at the instant of suppression, under these circumstances, is 54 lbs. The curve descends during the period of expansion and cuts the line of release at a pressure of 19 lbs., and on reaching the end of the stroke it attains a minimum of 2 lbs. pressure. The curve of expansion, it appears, runs into those of the admission and the exhaust without any of the abruptness which distinguishes the slow diagram. The truth is that before the steam was nominally suppressed, expansion had begun,—a result necessarily implied in the idea of wire-drawing,—and there was therefore not the same liability to sudden change of direction. The curve nevertheless rapidly alters its course after crossing the suppression line. At the other end of the expansion the curve crosses the exhaust line, nearly at right angles, and barely reaches the minimum pressure at the termination of the stroke. The comparative delay so evinced in the accomplishment of the exhaust, is plainly a consequence of the shorter time allowed for this purpose by the greater speed of the piston ; and accordingly we find a considerable accession to the useful effect of the steam in the very circumstance that it exhausts less freely. On the other hand, a drawback on this effect exists in the continued back pressure of 2 lbs. per inch during the return stroke, referrible to the same imperfect exhaust. The curve of the exhaust during the return stroke joins the compression curve with a slight bend, and it is observable that before the pre-admission takes place, the compressed steam attains a final pressure higher than that found by the slow diagram,—a circumstance referrible to the greater condensation of steam in the cylinder which accompanies very slow speeds, and which is consequent on a reduced mean temperature. But though the curve of high speed is in advance of that of the slow diagram at the point of admission, it falls behind at the commencement of the stroke, as at this point the pressure does not get beyond 51 lbs., and only attains the maximum, 62 lbs., when the piston has described half an inch of the steam stroke. This delay is chiefly attributable to the insufficiency of the time allowed for the re-establishment of the working pressure, by the speedy motion of the piston, and by insufficient lead.

The diagram, Fig. 95, shown in dotted lining, affords another example of the irregularities that occur from high speeds. In this case the speed is 44 miles per hour, more than twice that which existed in the previous instance ; and the diagram nowhere appears to be a straight line. We observe that the maximum pressure during admission (52 lbs.) is not attained till the piston has described 4 inches of the stroke. From the same point it falls towards the suppression-line, which it crosses at a pressure of 47 lbs.; and describing an ogee wave-line during the expansion, it crosses the release-line, at a pressure of 15 lbs., and terminates the stroke with 5 lbs. of pressure, after rebounding to a height indicating 17 lbs. With all these irregularities, there is no doubt that the inertia of the reciprocating parts of the indicator has much to do. The first disturbance takes place at the point of suppression, and it may be granted that the wire-drawing which precedes the suppression is not fully indicated; that, in short, the indicator barely follows the pressure of the steam with sufficient celerity. As, therefore, the indicated pressure at the suppression-line is certainly not less than the real pressure, and as moreover the pressure falls at that place with great rapidity, the indicator piston sinks under the disposable power of the spring with accelerated speed, by which it not only ultimately reaches the pressure of the steam, but is driven below the level due to the existing pressure. A rebound is the natural result, and, stimulated by the superior pressure of the steam, the piston ascends even in crossing the release-line, and continues to ascend in obedience to the upward impulse until within 2 inches from the end of the stroke, whence it finally falls. Something of the irregularity is of course attributable to the natural agitation of the steam. It is inconceivable, however, that even at the highest possible speed, the true expansion-curve should be otherwise than regular and similar to that developed by the indicator at the low speeds. During the period of expansion, the steam virtually remains in one place and simply follows up the piston,—an operation which involves no effort at any speed. In respect of the exhaust, we have already found that speed very materially detains the fall of the curve towards the end of the stroke, and judging by the evidence of the diagram at 20 miles per hour, it is probable that even at the most eccentric point of the curve beyond the line of release, it varies in the case before us not more than 3 lbs. from the veritable pressure. During the return stroke, the exhaust falls to a minimum of 3 lbs., rises to 7 lbs. at the middle of the stroke, falls to 5 lbs. at a little distance from the compression line, and finally rises as the valve goes to close the passage for exhaust, and crosses the compression line at 6¼ lbs. The curve proceeds regularly round, in place of angularly upwards, as in the previous cases, and it attains a pressure of 40 lbs. at the end of the stroke. As in the previous example, the piston travels ½ inch of the steam stroke before the indicator becomes stationary. This it does at 50 lbs., and it rises only to 52 lbs. at a more advanced stage, as already described. The increase of the back pressure, observed about the middle of the stroke, is referrible generally to two circumstances,—the accelerated speed of the piston in the cylinder towards that point, which, of course, hastens the expulsion of the exhaust steam and creates an increase of back pressure; the reaction of exhaust steam from the neighbouring cylinder tends also to swell the resistance. This last circumstance, is much dependent upon the peculiar conformation of the exhaust passages, and it is sufficient at present only to allude to it. The final increase of back pressure previously to the closing of the exhaust is a case precisely the converse of what was found to occur before the suppression in the steam stroke—in the latter case expansion commenced previously to the closing of the port for steam, and was indicated by a falling of the pressure; in the former case, compression commences previously to the closing of the port for the exhaust, and is accompanied by a rise of pressure. That the pressure for the steam stroke should increase upon the piston, so far forward as 4 inches of the stroke, seems rather irreconcileable with the reverse phenomenon exhibited on the second diagram, in which, though the speed is less, the pressure slightly falls from the commencement forward. The contrariety is to be explained by the relative pressures which exist in the valve-chest. A sudden withdrawal of steam from the chest for the com-

mencement of the stroke, though it does but transiently affect the supply at a low speed, as it may be timely replaced by steam from the boiler, and a uniform pressure maintained in the chest,—is more sensibly felt at a higher speed; and accordingly the first rush of steam brings down the pressure so materially as only to be replaced when the piston has considerably advanced. That much depends on the varying pressure in the valve-chest in explanation of this circumstance is proved by diagrams taken from the chest, which in some instances show a variation of 5 lbs. pressure.

Character of M'Naught's Indicator.—From what has been explained of the operation of M'Naught's indicator, by means of which the foregoing illustrations have been obtained, and by which many of the writer's inquiries have been conducted, it is obvious that the indications of that instrument cannot be implicitly relied upon at very high speeds, with respect to the conformation of the diagrams afforded. Of its integrity as an indicator of total power, it is highly probable that, notwithstanding the deviations due to undulations, the total area of the diagram, which is the measure of power, should be correct in amount, at least approximately so, on the general principle that action and reaction are equal, and that an excess at one part should be compensated by a deficiency at another part of the diagram. In the third example before us, if we assume the pressures at the point of suppression and the end of the stroke to be literally correct, and construct an expansion and exhaust curve similar to that actually described in the 2d example, the interpolated curves will be found to take a mean path with respect to the line traced by the indicator, and will enclose the same slump area of diagram. A reference to some other examples in which the steam has itself provided a confirmation of the general integrity of the indicator, will make this point still more satisfactory. The dark-line diagram, Fig. 96, was described by a locomotive (Caledonian, No. 42) running at 38 miles per hour. The light-line diagram was caused to be described by suddenly opening the stop-cock communicating with the steam-cylinder. The steam, by an instantaneous blow, had surprised the piston of the indicator into the extreme oscillations shown in light lining, throughout a complete double stroke, after which the diagram subsided into the constant figure in heavy lining. It is clear there is a method even in the preliminary vibra-

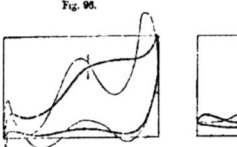 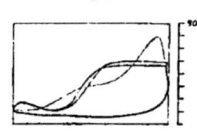

Fig. 96.   Fig. 97.

C. R. No. 42—4th notch—38 mph.   E. and G. R. Pallas—10th notch—42 mph.

tions; their sinuosity is referrible exactly to the more regular curve as a centre line, during both the steam and the return strokes; and the areas of the two figures are approximately the same. Fig. 97 is a quieter example from another engine (cylinder 15″ by 20″; wheel 6 feet), running at 42 miles per hour; in this case, the diagrams were described in immediate succession, and the same general equality is observable. Fig. 98 comprises two series of diagrams taken from a long-stroked cylinder (17″ × 24″, wheel 4½ feet), the

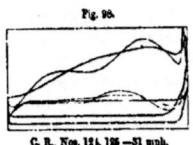

Fig. 98.

C. R., Nos. 124, 125.—31 mph.

engine moving at 31 miles per hour; in the larger of which the steam is cut off at 13 inches of the stroke, and the smaller at 18 inches. These examples are sufficient to prove the general integrity of M'- Naught's indicator as a meter of power, and that for all speeds, and all proportions of expansive working, the diagrams may be relied on, in this respect, whatever may be the cause of the variations of the pencil.

To reduce the diagram to its radical form.—As the fundamental figure of the diagram is a mean of the irregularities with which it is affected, we may, by the knowledge of this principle, and by the aid of the points of suppression and release, approximate with ease and certainty to the radical form of the curve. The diagram, Fig. 99, was obtained from the

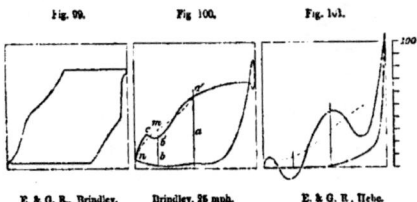

Fig. 99.   Fig. 100.   Fig. 101.

E. & G. R., Brindley.   Brindley, 25 mph.   E. & G. R., Hebe.

Brindley, E. & G. R., under the 4th notch, at a slow speed, from which it appears that the steam is suppressed and released at 9·34 and 15 inches out of 18 inches stroke. The diagram, Fig. 100, in which every deviation of the curve is rounded, was taken under the same notch, at 25 miles per hour. Draw perpendiculars, a, b, to the base line at distances from the beginning of the stroke, of 9·34 and 15 inches respectively. As the curve is formed regularly during the admission, it is clear that the indicated pressure at a', where it meets the vertical, is the real pressure of the steam. It is plain, however, that the segment a' b', does not literally represent the pressure during expansion; it shows a pressure too high at the beginning, and too low at the end, which is proved by the rebound of the pencil to the point o, during the release. We have, therefore, to interpose the expansion and exhaust curve a' m n, subject to the conditions that the segment a' m should fall regularly, like that literally described in the slow diagram, that the segment m n, should show a regular fall of pressure during release, and that the whole interposed curve should enclose the same superficial area as that actually described. Again, Fig. 101, obtained from the Hebe, E. & G. R., at 48 miles per hour, and under the 5th notch, suppressing and releasing at 9 and 15½ inches, is readily reducible on the same principle of equal mean areas, and with the assistance of the suppression and release lines, to the regular steam line in dotting. By the assistance of this mode of removing the apparent irregularities of high-speed diagrams, we are enabled to turn them to some account in the investigation of the action of steam in the cylinder.

CHAPTER III.

Of the Behaviour of Steam in the Cylinder during Admission.

In discussing the distribution, we found that for each face of the piston there were four periods of importance during one revolution of the wheel, or a double-stroke of the piston, namely, those of admission, expansion, release, and compression. Our object shall now be to point out the characteristic varieties of the action of steam in the cylinder, exemplified in the course of our experiments, during the successive periods of the distribution. We have, first, to investigate the action of steam during its admission to the cylinder.

Of the Action of Wiredrawing.—At ordinary speeds, the steam-line of admission in the diagram is sensibly a straight line, parallel to the atmospheric line—for periods of admission greater than 50 per cent.; that is, the steam pressure in the cylinder is sensibly constant during admission. This regularity disappears at the higher speeds, as there is commonly a considerable fall of pressure towards the suppression, attributable to the joint influence of the local acceleration of the speed of piston towards half-stroke, and the wire-drawing action of the valve as it closes the port for admission.

The motion of steam through a passage of some length, such as the steam or exhaust passage of the cylinder, is, like that of other gases, regulated by several circumstances—amongst others, the cross sectional area of the passage, which we suppose the same at all parts of the length, and the frictional resistance of its sides to the motion of the steam. The motion of steam from one chamber into another is the result of a difference of pressure in the two places; and between a locomotive-cylinder and its valve-chest, the pressure in the valve-chest is necessarily the greater of the two, while the engine is in motion. Were the steam-passage of no appreciable length, or were its sides frictionless and straight, the quantity of steam that would pass into the cylinder under a given pressure, would be directly as the area of the opening of the port. As matters are, by the bends and lateral friction of the passage, this ratio is very far from being realized, inasmuch as deductions of speed take place in practice, chargeable to those sources of resistance; and thus the practical charge of steam transmitted through the passage falls in all cases short of what the sectional area of the port is of itself capable of admitting. It therefore frequently happens that the opening of the port allowed by the valve, though it may be much inferior to the total area of the port itself, is sufficiently large to admit all the steam that can force its way along the passage. Indeed, this fact is constantly exemplified in practice, for we know that the opening of the port beyond a specific amount, in all cases less than the area of the port itself, ceases to facilitate the passage of the steam into the cylinder. As, however, the maximum opening of port is at least an index to the relative freedom for admission and absence of wiredrawing towards the closing of the port, it will be so employed in the following discussions.

We find in the diagrams from the Great Britain (Diagram-plate 4), that at the lower speeds, the steam-line is perfectly constant till within an inch or so of the suppression; and that, as the speeds rise, the fall of pressure commences earlier, and even, in extreme cases, at the beginning of the stroke.

The following table comprises the lowest speeds at which wire-drawing exists in the cylinders of the locomotives therein specified, to any extent greater than one inch before the point of suppression, and also the reduction of pressure due to wire-drawing at the highest observed speeds. The mean speeds of piston are deduced from the observed speeds of the engine in terms of the stroke and the diameter of wheel. The sixth column contains the ratios of the maximum openings of steam-port to the areas of the pistons, expressed as ordinary fractions. These ratios vary in general as the lineal opening of port simply, owing to the width of the ports across the cylinder being in all the cases about the same fraction of the diameter. We shall, therefore, in the following remarks, refer merely to the lineal values of the openings.

TABLE No. XXIV.—SHOWING THE WIRE-DRAWING OF STEAM DURING ADMISSION, IN THE CYLINDERS OF THE GREAT BRITAIN, AND OTHER ENGINES.

Name of Engine.	Notch.	Period of Admission.	Travel of valve.	Port opening.	Ratio of opening of port to area of piston.	Wire-drawing commences at speeds of Engine.	Wire-drawing commences at speeds of Piston.	Wire-drawing at the highest attained speed. Speed of Engine.	Speed of Piston.	Observed pressures during admission. Initial.	Final.	Difference.
	1st Series.	per cent.	inches.	inches.		m.ph.	f.p.m.	m.ph.	f.p.m.	lbs.	lbs.	lbs.
Great Britain.												
Port 26 inches........	No. 1	74	4⅞	1⅛	1/23	42	588	55	770	64	57	7, or 11 per cent.
Piston 255 inches......	No. 3	59	3⅞	⅞	1/33	35	490	63	882	53	40	12, or 23 ..
Ratio 1/10..................	No. 5	40	3¼	⅝	1/46	30	420	56	784	86	62	24, or 28 ..
	2d Series.											
	No. 1	66	4⅞	1 1/16	1/19	49	606	54	756	89	86	3, or 3.5 ..
	No. 3	49	3·⅝	⅞ 1/16	1/26	40	560	55	770	84	72	12, or 14 ..
	No. 5	29	3 1/16	⅝	1/39	31	434	56	784	90	65	25, or 28 ..
C. R. No. 33.												
Port 12.5 inches......	No. 4	61	3¼	½	1/27	36	558	40	620	36	34	2, or 6 ..
Piston 176.7 inches..	No. 5	55	3⅛	⅜	1/24	30	465	41	635	62	59	3, or 5 ..
Ratio 1/14..................	No. 7	35	2·⅞	5/16	1/40	20	310	44	682	52	47	5, or 10 ..
C. R. No. 125.												
Port 15 inches	No. 2	71	4 1/16	⅞	1/14	22	340	29	711	27	25	2, or 7 ..
Piston 227 inches......	No. 3	55	3⅞	⅝	1/18	14.5	355	30	735	64	53	11, or 17 ..
Ratio 1/15..................	No. 4	35	3⅛	⅝	1/26	15.5	380	26	637	54	40	14, or 26 ..
EXTRA EXAMPLES OF WIRE-DRAWING, DEDUCED FROM STEAM-DIAGRAMS, PAGE 71.												
		per cent.	inches.	inches.		m.ph.	f.p.m.	m.ph.	f.p.m.	lbs.	lbs.	lbs.
E. & G. R.												
Hebe..........	2d	75	3	⅞	1/21	33	561	40	630	34	25	9, or 26 per cent.
,, ...	4th	58	...	...	...	13	221	41	697	50	26	24, or 48 ..
,, ...	5th	45	...	...	...	...	...	30	510	72	48	24, or 33 ..
,, ...	6th	45	...	...	...	...	...	45	745	52	23	29, or 57 ..
Orion....................	5th	57	3	1/16	1/21	20	310	30	465	58	48	10, or 17 ..
,, ...	6th	50	2⅞	1/8	1/36	18	279	40	620	56	39	17, or 30 ..
[illegible]..................	gab	68	3⅞	⅞	1/16	30	465	40	590	55	45	10, or 18 ..
C. R.												
No. 42	4th	45	3·⅜	1/8	1/21	...	...	38	539	70	56	14, or 20 ..
,, ...	5th	18	3⅛	1/4	1/60	...	...	36	558	63	46	17, or 27 ..
No. 13	1st	62	4⅛	1 1/16	1/17	...	...	54	837	58	49	9, or 15 ..
No. 61 [illegible] valve,......	4th	41	3·⅛	⅝	1/18	...	...	32	496	48	41	7, or 15 ..
,, ...	5th	28	3 1/16	⅝	1/31	...	...	31	480	62	55	7, or 11 ..
Do. (new valve)........	3d	46	4⅞	1⅛	1/13	20	310	40	620	55	40	15, or 27 ..
,, ...	4th	30	4⅞	1⅛	1/15	20	310	49	760	45	35	10, or 22 ..

NOTE.—The ratio of the port to the piston is, in all of these extra examples, about 1/14.

In each series, of the first part of this table, it is plain that the shorter the admission, the lower is the speed at which wire-drawing becomes sensible, and the greater is the fall of pressure due to this influence at the higher speeds. This is explained by the reduction of travel and maximum opening required for a smaller admission, and the consequent more sluggish movement of the valve at the critical point of suppression. In the Great Britain, an admission of above two-thirds of the stroke is unattended by wire-drawing of any importance under 60 miles per hour, or about 800 feet of piston per minute; at the same speed, an admission of one-half reduces the pressure one-fourth; and an admission of one-third brings down the pressure nearly one-third. As the steam-line in the diagrams from the Great Britain, is in general, straight from the beginning until it nears the suppression, it is clear that beyond a certain opening of the port, in all cases much less than its total width, any extra opening does not further facilitate the ingress of steam. The uniformity thus maintained with a very variable and inferior opening, up to the speeds at which wire-drawing prevails, even while the pressure in the valve-chest may be much superior to that in the cylinder, is explained by the frictional resistance to the movements of the steam chargeable to the steam-ways, which practically renders insensible at lower speeds the throttling action of the valve. As the speed increases, the opening of valve becomes insufficient to maintain a constant pressure, because, as we have seen, wire-drawing or fall of pressure is created by speed and increases with it. This is attributable both to the greater flow of steam through the port, by which a throttling action comes into play, and to the greater local acceleration of the speed of piston towards half stroke, due to a higher speed, which increases the difficulty experienced by the steam in following up the piston.

The following diagrams to illustrate wire-drawing under various conditions and proportions of valve, have been selected as average examples from amongst a numerous collection obtained from the Hebe, the Orion, and the Nile, on the Edinburgh and Glasgow Railway, and from Nos. 42, 13, and 51, on the Caledonian Railway.

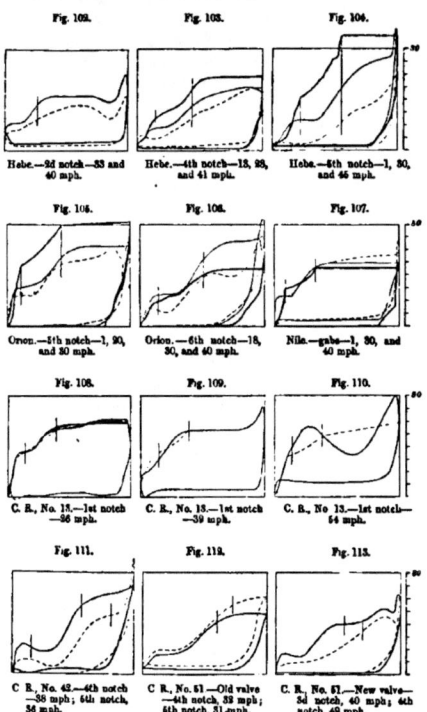

Fig. 102.   Fig. 103.   Fig. 104.

Hebe.—2d notch—33 and 40 mph.   Hebe.—4th notch—13, 23, and 41 mph.   Hebe.—5th notch—1, 30, and 46 mph.

Fig. 105.   Fig. 106.   Fig. 107.

Orion.—5th notch—1, 30, and 30 mph.   Orion.—6th notch—13, 30, and 60 mph.   Nile.—gabe—1, 30, and 40 mph.

Fig. 108.   Fig. 109.   Fig. 110.

C. R., No. 13.—1st notch—36 mph.   C. R., No. 13.—1st notch—39 mph.   C. R., No. 13.—1st notch—54 mph.

Fig. 111.   Fig. 112.   Fig. 113.

C. R., No. 42.—4th notch—38 mph; 6th notch, 56 mph.   C. R., No. 51.—Old valve—4th notch, 33 mph; 6th notch, 51 mph.   C. R., No. 51.—New valve—3d notch, 40 mph; 4th notch, 49 mph.

DIAGRAMS TO ILLUSTRATE WIRE-DRAWING.

The extra examples in the foregoing table comprise the results of wire-drawing indicated in these diagrams, deduced from *mean lines* of admission, applied to the diagrams on the principle described in the foregoing chapter.

In these cases, we observe, generally, as in the previous cases, that the shorter the admission, the greater is the wire-drawing in each cylinder, and that the wire-drawing also increases with the speed.

Of the outside cylinders, those which have nearly or entirely lost their lead, show less wire-drawing than the others. Thus, in No. 33 and No. 42, the lead in the former being nearly extinguished, No. 33 shows, with a shorter admission and a higher speed, a reduction of 10 per cent., which is but half of that shown by No. 42. This will be made obvious on referring to the diagrams from those

engines introduced in the previous chapter. Again, No. 51 with the old worn valve-gear, exhibits only one-half of the fall of pressure created by No. 51 with the new valve, though the speed in the latter case was but one-third greater. Thirdly, Nos. 33 and 13, cutting off at about the same point, 61 and 62 per cent. respectively, and at the same speed, show practically no reduction, though No. 13 is slightly superior, while it has most lead. No. 13, however, also has the longest travel, as it opens the port $1\frac{1}{16}$ inch, while No. 33 opens only $\frac{1}{2}$ inch. Thus it appears that No. 13 required double the opening of port, to reduce the wire-drawing due to its superior lead, to an equality with that incidental to No. 33.

The influence of lap and travel in promoting a free passage of steam is not very marked beyond certain limits. Thus, with No. 42, and No. 51 (new valve), having about equal admissions and equal openings, in the 4th and 3d notches, and equal speeds, the fall of pressure is least with No. 42; in which apparently the engine with the smaller lap, $1\frac{1}{4}$ inch, passes the steam most unreservedly. Secondly, with the inside-cylinder engines, comparing, at the same speed, the 2d notch of the Hebe and the Nile, the latter of which has the shorter admission, we find that the Nile with 1 inch lap shows but two-thirds of the wire-drawing due to the Hebe with $\frac{3}{4}$ inch of lap. Now the opening of the port is the same for the two engines, and the superiority of the Nile's valve is thus apparent. Again, in the 4th notch of the Hebe, and the 5th of the Orion with 1 inch lap, with equal openings, and suppressing about equally, though the speed of piston of the first is but one-half greater than that of the second, the wire-drawing is three times as great. Again, comparing the Hebe and the Great Britain with 1 inch lap, in the 4th and 3d notches respectively, yielding equal admissions, while the speeds of piston are about 700 and 900 feet, the wire-drawing with the Hebe, at the less speed, is double that of the Great Britain; and, taking the 5th notch of both engines, at nearly equal speeds, the throttling in the Hebe, is again double that in the Great Britain. Lastly, comparing the two series of the Great Britain itself, the $1\frac{1}{4}$ inch lap is manifestly superior to the lap of 1 inch.

To compare inside and outside cylinders. Taking the Great Britain, the Orion, and the Nile, on the one hand, with the Caledonian engines, on the other, a slight inspection suffices to show that the outside cylinders apparently wire-draw the steam to an extent much less than the insides, even with the advantage of the greater lap. This fact may at first sight be taken for a mark of superiority. It is, however, to be ascribed to the greater quantity of water habitually present in the outside cylinder, as a partial condensation of steam due to imperfect protection. The presence of water in the cylinder in a state of suspension, levels the steam line, because it clogs the movements of the steam. This argument we shall afterwards have an opportunity of clenching, in discussing the existence of water in the cylinder.

With regard to the influence of size of port on the steam-line, we find that in the larger ports of the Great Britain, the steam is least wire-drawn. Thus, with the Nile and the 1st notch of the Great Britain, second series, having equal admissions, the former draws down the steam five times as much as the latter, while the speed in the case of the latter is much the greater. Again, the 3d notch of the Great Britain, second series, reduces the steam only half as much as the 6th of the Orion, with the same admission, and at a much greater speed of piston. Lastly, the Great Britain, by means of its wider ports, is nearly on a par with the outside cylinders, notwithstanding the *advantage* of situation possessed by the latter; this is particularly obvious in comparing the second series of the Great Britain with C. R. No. 125.

*Of the Undulations of the Steam-Diagram.—Influence of Lead.—Initial Percussion.—*As to the cause of the regular irregularities of the pencil, we are entitled, *a priori*, to presume that the vibratory movements of the steam, have at least as much to do with them as those of the Indicator. Steam, indeed, is a more perfect spring than steel, and it is easily understood that as every change in the distribution, is a source of new motions of the steam, simultaneous irruptions or interruptions of pressure should ensue. That some of the more frequent irregularities are due directly to the steam's own elasticity, is indubitable. One of the most common is the initial excess of pressure with which the steam stroke is frequently commenced, exemplified in many of the figures immediately preceding, and still more strikingly developed upon the diagrams, Figs. 114, 115, 116, all taken

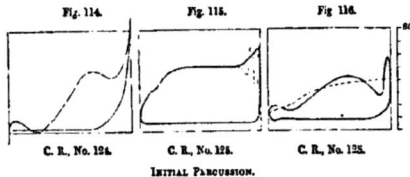

Fig. 114.   Fig. 115.   Fig. 116.

C. R., No. 124.   C. R., No. 124.   C. R., No. 125.

INITIAL PERCUSSION.

from the same class of engines. Figures 113 and 115 were both described at a speed of 25 miles per hour. In the former case, as the period of admission is considerably less than in the latter case, the point of pre-admission, by the nature of the link-motion, takes place earlier. It therefore happens that whereas, in the latter case, there is little more than time for the steam to find its maximum pressure in the cylinder for the commencement of the steam stroke,—in the former case, the entrance is premature,—the steam fills the clearance while the piston has yet to complete a small part of the return stroke, a collision takes place, a partial expulsion of the newly admitted steam follows, and there is in consequence a great and sudden exaltation of pressure. It is, however, only momentary, or at least covers but a small part of the diagram, as the pressure recovers its due intensity before the piston describes 2 inches of the stroke. In figure 115, as the period of pre-admission is less than in the previous figure, the piston attains the end of the stroke in time to meet the entering steam, without repelling it. The exaltation is, therefore, less great, and the restoration of the ordinary pressure more gradual, at the same speed. The extra compression naturally shows itself less on the diagram at slower speeds, as there is the more time allowed for adjustment to the average pressure; and accordingly, the disturbance at 15 miles per hour in the same cylinder frequently assumes the appearance of the dot line on figure 115. At still

slower speeds, the vertical disturbance assumes the form of a single line, the adjustment being effected before the piston starts on the steam stroke. Fig. 116 was taken with a period of pre-admission intermediate betwixt those of the two preceding examples, and at a speed of 41 miles. The nipple of compression appears as a mean betwixt those of the others. It is more obtuse than the first, because the admission takes place later, and the speed is higher; and it is sharper than the second, notwithstanding the greater speed, because the admission occurs earlier. Thus it is clear that the constant lead characteristic of the stationary link, (which is employed in the engines before us), if adjusted for full gear, is abundantly sufficient for the timely entrance of steam, under all degrees of expansion, and at all speeds.

The sufficiency of a constant lead is further illustrated by examples figs. 117 and 118, from the Orion, E. and G. B.,

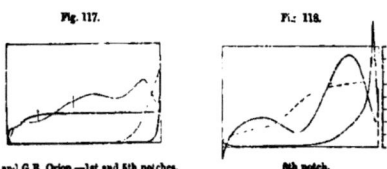

Fig. 117.   Fig. 118.

E. and G.B. Orion.—1st and 5th notches.   6th notch.

SUFFICIENCY OF A CONSTANT LEAD.

which is fitted with a stationary link, yielding a constant lead of ¼ inch. The periods of admission and speeds are as follow :—

Fig. 117.	Heavy line.	1st notch.	16 inches.	27 mph.
Fig. 117.	Light line.	5th do.	11½ ,,	27 mph.
Fig. 118.		6th do.	10 ,,	40 mph.

These diagrams show that the same lead, when sufficient for full gear, or the 1st notch, is amply sufficient, and indeed rather excessive, for the shorter admissions, as the reaction due to compression is completed before the commencement of the steam stroke; and its sufficiency is very much independent of speed. Indeed, with short admissions we have long compressions, and thus a sufficiency of " waste " steam is intercepted and stored up, so as to secure nearly a full initial pressure, even were there no lead or pre-admission at all; and this is a serviceable provision, as it is commonly at the higher speeds that the shorter admissions are employed.

It follows, that if even constant lead be rather excessive for the shorter admissions, an increasing lead, such as is provided by the shifting link, if competent to the necessities of full gear, must be quite superfluous, if not prejudicial, for the shorter travels of the valve.

The originals of the diagrams from the Great Britain show remarkably steady steam-lines even at the highest speeds and under the greatest expansion, the only disturbance being a very small initial excess of pressure of 2 to 5 lbs., which does not in any case extend beyond ¼ inch of the stroke, after which the steam line is perfectly straight till it nears the suppression. We are persuaded that this superior action of Gooch's instrument is due jointly to the lightness and reduced speed of the moving parts which describe the steam line, and to the perfect proportions of the cylinder and valve-gear.

The saltatory movements of the indicator may be and have frequently been checked by the addition of extra clearance between the piston and the cylinder-cover, in cases of stationary engines affected with reacting compression. The addition of clearance operates like the addition of an air vessel or reservoir, in subduing violent extremes, and the equalizing effect of clearance, as exhibited by the indicator, proves that the saltations are, in good faith, expressions of agitation inside the cylinder. What is thus established by inference may be confirmed more directly, if the spindle of the indicator be forcibly sustained by the hand at a level just above the position due to the regular steam pressure in the cylinder; the indicator receiving as freely as when at liberty, the initial impulse of the steam, and performing precisely the complement of the saltatory movement due to its free action. In this case, it is clear that no momentum is accumulated in the indicator-piston previously to the saltation, as it is started from a state of rest, and that to the steam's elasticity, exalted for an instant, the phenomenon is attributable.

A further proof of the correctness of this position is to be found in the experience with Cornwall engines. In these engines, which work the steam at high pressure and very expansively, the cylinder-covers are observed, as remarked many years ago by Mr. Parkes, to yield sensibly outwards, by as much as ¾ inch of convexity at the centre, at the instant of the admission of steam. The resilience certainly is but momentary; it however proves the existence of an extraordinary pressure at the instant, and this is correspondingly demonstrated by the diagram of the indicator. The elasticity of the cylinder-cover, on the immense scale of the Cornish engines, is so severely tried by this instantaneous pressure that it has been found advisable to discontinue the application of stiffening flanges in the hollow of the cover, as they injure the ready elasticity of the whole casting. All such irruptions of pressure are simply forms of percussive action, and though the deductions of Mr. Parkes on this topic are of less value than his facts, he has brought together a quantity of curious matter for speculation.[*]

Pulsations of Steam.—Satisfied that at least one violent vibratory movement is attributable directly to the steam, there is reason to believe that much of the subsequent oscillation, observable on some diagrams, is developed by the steam's elasticity. This assumption is so far probable that the same indicator placed upon different cylinders, behaves differently; and even so on the same cylinder under different circumstances. Were the undulations, in all cases, due merely to the mass of the indicator-piston and appendages, they ought to be independent of the speed of engine, and of the reciprocations of the piston; whereas we find, in all cases, that their periodicity coincides with the double stroke of the piston, and accordingly the diagrams of a consecutive series coincide, in general, very closely. The indicator has been found to vibrate freely at the rate of about 22 pulsations per minute. Now in Fig. 119, described at 16½ miles per hour, with a 2 feet stroke and 4½ feet wheel, we find that 3·2 single strokes were made per second; at the same time, during

* Trans. Inst. C. E., 1842.

the return stroke, 3½ pulsations are indicated, and must have been delivered at the rate of (3·5 × 3·2) or 11·2 per second, which is only one half the rate of free vibration of the instrument alone. It follows that the indicated pulsations are, to some extent at least, due to the exhaust steam.

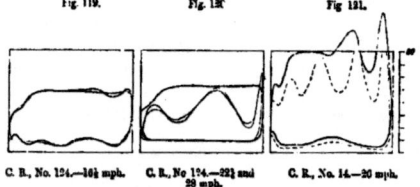

Fig. 119.　　　Fig. 120.　　　Fig. 121.

C. R., No. 124.—16½ mph.　　C. R., No 124.—22½ and 28 mph.　　C. R., No. 14.—26 mph.

Fig. 120 is a compound diagram, of which the undulating figure was described at the higher speed, and it is remarkable that the undulations very closely coincide. Also, the rate and extent of pulsation is decidedly greater during the steam-stroke than in that of the exhaust, regulated apparently by the respective mean pressures in the cylinder,— and this is a difference which would not occur, were the undulations in all cases a mere affection of the instrument.

Influence of the absence of Lead on the Steam-diagram.— The diagram, figure 121, was obtained from a locomotive (C.R., No. 14,) moving at a speed of 26 miles per hour, the valve gearing of which had so worn as to banish the lead, a fact which was plainly proved by the evidence of a slow diagram. The maximum pressure is not attained till nearly 2 inches of the stroke is described, the steam being admitted precisely at the commencement. While lateness of the admission tends commonly to neutralize the pulsation, this engine never worked under high pressure on the piston, without a constant pulsatory action like that illustrated, and which occasionally extended throughout the whole stroke, as figured in dot-lines. The extent of pulsation reached 50 lbs., according to the diagram, on a mean pressure of 80 lbs., which is proportionally the same as in the case previously noticed, where the undulation amounted to 21 lbs. upon 35 lbs. of mean pressure. The extravagance of the pulsations appears further, by comparing the speeds of the larger and smaller pistons in their cylinders, which, from the data, were respectively about 700 and 400 feet per minute. If again, we compare this engine with another, C. R., No. 13, of the same class, of which the valves had the customary lead of ¹⁄₁₆ inch, we find that at all equivalent speeds, the diagrams are square and solid. Figure 108 is an average sample of the diagram described by No. 13, at 26 miles per hour, in the 1st notch, and the slow diagram proves that the piston had nearly ¼ inch to go at the instant the valve opened for admission. The pressure of the steam during admission was 60 lbs., and yet we find not one trace of agitation. Again, the diagram, Fig. 109, was described at a speed of 39 miles. Here the preliminary nipple makes its appearance; the steam line, however, becomes perfectly straight, and the exhaust is as regular. The diagram, Fig. 110, was taken at 54 miles per hour, when we may observe at last that the undulations just match those of No. 14 at one-third of the speed. These facts appear to show that the want of lead is as prejudicial to the regular working of steam as too much of it. Pulsation cannot be viewed as a matter of indifference, for it is very possible that the point of suppression may occur at the summit of an undulation, when of course the dense body of steam enclosed at the same instant is ultimately blown away, after describing a deeply indented and inferior steam line; on the other hand, it is as conceivable that the suppression may occur at the lowest point of an undulation, in which case we obtain a few hillocks of power for nothing. The influence of the want of lead on the form of the diagram is likewise shown in the case of No. 102, C. R. (cylinder 16″ × 18″, wheel 4½ feet), illustrated by Figs. 122, 123, 124.

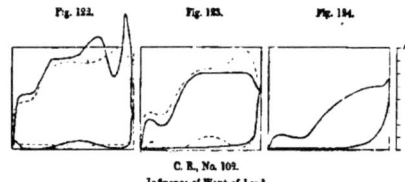

Fig. 122.   Fig. 123.   Fig. 124.

C. R., No. 102.
Influence of Want of Lead.

At the time of experimenting with this engine, her valves had entirely lost their lead in the first notch or full gear, though in mid gear it still remained to the extent of $\frac{1}{17}$ inch. For intermediate notches, of course, the lead was proportionally less. The circumstances are as follow:

Fig. 122 { Dark line diagram, 2d notch, 17½ miles per hour.
         { Dot line   do...... 3d notch, 23½ miles.
Fig. 123 { Dark line do......4th notch, 21½ miles.
         { Dot line   do.......4th notch, 26 miles.
Fig. 124 ....5th notch, 29 miles.

It is apparent that at the slowest speed of all, the 2d notch, with no sensible lead, exhibits the heaviest pulsations. The 3d notch, at a higher speed, shows but a single pulsation, and of smaller extent, than those of the 2d notch. With the 4th notch, at a mean speed between the others, the steam line is perfectly flat; and at a greater speed, shows an undulation less than that of the 3d notch. The 5th notch at the highest of all the speeds turns out a very common form of diagram, in which the nipple is merely rudimentary. It is to be observed, also, that every diagram shows an incipient pulsation, where the return stroke terminates, preparatory to the more obvious undulation which commences the steam-line,—an appearance similar to what takes place in the diagram from No. 14, and which indicates the shortness of the pre-admission, due to insufficiency of lead. These incipient pulsations find their way upwards as the lead is increased, till with the 5th notch they merge into the first and only perceptible oscillation that occurs on the steam-line.

Influence of Clearance on the Steam-diagram.—The influence of clearance has already been alluded to as modifying the force of the initial percussion. Its use is, however, mostly apparent for stationary and marine engines, in which the piston moves at comparatively moderate speeds, as the character of diagram from those classes of engine is usually quiet and regular. In locomotives, on the contrary, the effect of clearance in reducing the percussive action of steam is apparently of small efficacy, at high speeds. The movements of the steam are at all events, as we have seen, readily controlled by the disposition of the valve, in a manner that cannot be claimed for mere clearance. In the locomotive (C. R. No. 102), from which the diagrams Figs 122, 123, 124 have been taken, the clearance at the experimental end of the cylinder was equal to 1$\frac{1}{17}$ inches measured betwixt the faces of the piston and the cover, and the total clearance, including steam passage and occasional recesses, amounted to an equivalent of 2 inches of the length of the cylinder; yet we do not find that it has been of any appreciable use in keeping down irregularities. At the slowest speeds, we found that the mere absence of lead created very heavy undulations, in spite of clearance, and at the highest speeds, an addition of lead, though small, was competent to remove the initial nipple, independent of clearance. In C. R. No. 13, also, already quoted, the clearance was equal to $\frac{9}{17}$ inch betwixt the piston and cover, and the total clearance was 1½ inches; notwithstanding this advantage, we have not found that the diagram was on this account any thing superior to those from other engines of the same class, in which the piston is commonly but ¼ inch clear of the cover. The diagrams taken from C. R. No. 51, Passenger Locomotive, of the same class, may be referred to as being entirely free of undulations at all speeds; in this engine the direct clearance did not exceed $\frac{1}{17}$ inch, and with the lead nearly gone, the average samples of diagrams already given, prove the general regularity of the movements of the steam. The same remark may be applied to other engines equally limited as to clearance; with respect, for example, to the goods Locomotives C. R. Nos. 124, 125, before adverted to, the direct clearance in their cylinders is ⅜ inch, and the lead $\frac{1}{17}$ inch, and their average form of diagram may fairly be represented by Figs. 114, 119, 120.

Influence of water in the cylinder on the Steam-diagram.—It is well understood by engine-drivers that the efficiency of their engines is considerably dependent upon the state of their boilers, so far as it affects the purity of the water from which steam is generated. Mechanical, not chemical, impurities are now referred to; greasy or muddy water, primes into the cylinder with greater alacrity than perfectly clean water, and it is very troublesome to discharge from the cylinder when it gets there. The influence of the presence of water in the cylinder upon the diagram, is what we have at present before us, and this, as we shall find, is very considerable. Water appears in the cylinder under two conditions: it primes over from the boiler, and it arises by condensation from the steam after its admission into the cylinder even in a dry state. The direct result of priming is to raise the exhaust line of the diagram; in short, it increases the back pressure, and imposes a duty upon the steam, of pumping the water out of the cylinder at an enormous sacrifice of power. A difference of 5 lbs. of back pressure, for example, in an ordinary passenger locomotive, may readily amount to 12 horse power expended on ejecting a comparative trifle of water. Two series of diagrams were obtained from the Orion immediately previous and subsequent to blowing off the boiler, when the water had been unusually impure; of these, the figure 125 represents fair average examples taken in both cases at 38 miles per hour. The heavy line was described before the boiler was blown off, and the dot line shows the improved diagram. In both cases the steam was cut off at 11 inches of the stroke, under pressures of 51 and 46 lbs. respectively. The back pressure of exhaust was by the substitution of clean water

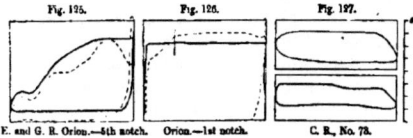

Fig. 125. Fig. 126. Fig. 127.

E. and G. R. Orion.—4th notch. Orion.—1st notch. C. R., No. 73.

Influence of Water in the Cylinder.

reduced in these instances from 9 lbs. to about $1\frac{1}{4}$ lbs. per inch; and in the majority of the other diagrams taken on the same trips, when the speeds did not exceed 30 miles, the back pressure was reduced from an average of 6 lbs. to nothing with clean water. It is also to be remarked that the compression line rises in general much more easily in the second series of diagrams than in the first; in the latter it is dull and square—no objection of course in itself—but it indicates plainly that the steam is damp, and the indicator water-logged, as the lead appears to have been no more than sufficient to provide a timely entrance for the steam stroke, which is proceeded with in a straight steam line. In the other case, the steam becomes lively and mercurial; the lead is evidently superfluously much, as the steam has performed a complete somersault before the commencement of the stroke. The whole character of the superior diagram proves the extreme susceptibility of steam, and shows how seriously it may be retarded by the water from which it has been formed.

There can be no hesitation in ascribing the difference of the diagrams to the priming of water in the first instance, as it is consistent with all experience that foul water is peculiarly liable to pass into the cylinder. Moreover, an incidental proof that aggravated priming existed on the first day was the fictitious evaporation of 9 lbs. of water per pound of coke on that day; while on the second day, when pure steam was made, the evaporation proceeded at the rate of only 8 lbs. per pound of fuel. Another couple of diagrams, fig. 126, taken from the same engine on the same consecutive days, shows in a striking manner how the indicator may be affected by the presence of water and impurities in the steam. In both cases, the engine was in full gear, starting from a road-station; and whereas on the second day, with clean water, all the changes of the distribution, shown in dot-lining, are clearly defined, the diagram in dark lining, formed by impure steam, turns out nearly a mathematical parallelogram, in which all distinctions are merged in two vertical lines of ascent and descent.

Another example selected for illustration is the case of C. R. No. 73, Passenger Locomotive, on the Greenock Railway, figure 127. This engine, in average working order, was always affected by a heavy back pressure, due mostly to priming, partially to the lateness of the release, and partially to a peculiar cubical chamber situated betwixt the cylinders, into which the steam was exhausted before its final expulsion by the blast pipe. The chamber was designed as an *air*-vessel, to equalize the blast. The heavy line,

figure 127, represents an average diagram taken from the cylinder, while the water in the boiler was muddy. The boiler having been blown off, and refilled with clean water, the engine turned out a diagram of the superior kind shown in light lining. Both of the diagrams were taken at a speed of 36 miles per hour; and the maximum pressure in the cylinder was, in both cases, 28 lbs., and the back pressure fell from 12 to 6 lbs. The maximum steam pressure in the cylinder is also, in the second case, earlier attained, and the same comparative alacrity is observable on the exhaust line. The diagrams appear inverted end for end, with respect to those of fig. 125; the commencement of the steam stroke, however, lies on the right hand side. These illustrations prove the benefit of frequent blowing off, in respect of the available effect of the steam, and the direct experience of the engine-driver of No. 73—a locomotive of ancient proportions, in the special case before us, proved how sensibly easier it is to keep up the steam with a boiler free of mechanical impurities. Yet, superior though the second diagram may appear to the first, they are both unrivalled as specimens of the action of water-logged steam, for even during the admission, about which there is commonly the least difficulty in setting the steam right at the commencement, the maximum pressure is not reached till from 3 to 6 inches of the stroke are described, and with the rare advantage of $\frac{1}{16}$ inch of lead.

The drawback on the effect of steam in the cylinder of the locomotive, on account of the foulness of the boiler, has been dwelt upon only now, because it affected the configuration of the steam-diagram. The subject of priming shall be afterwards treated in detail. That the exaggerated back pressure due to the foulness of the boiler, is attributable simply to the greater quantity of water carried over by the steam, is placed beyond doubt by the occurrence of the same drawback in the case of an over-full boiler. An example of this kind occurs in the course of experiments conducted by Mr. D. Gooch, upon the resistance of trains, on the Bristol and Exeter Railway.[*] The locomotive (Great Britain) was in ordinary working order, running at 45 miles per hour,

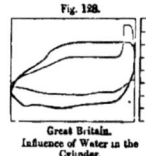

Fig. 128.

Great Britain.
Influence of Water in the Cylinder.

while the first diagram, shown in heavy lining, fig. 128, was taken from the cylinder; in the second case, in light lining, the boiler primed heavily, a phenomenon which when excessive is always discernible at the top of the chimney, and the diagram shows not only a reduction of the steam-line from 63 to 51 lbs., due solely to priming, but also an increase of back pressure from a mean of 15 lbs. to 24 lbs.

The ominous tardiness of the compression line which was apparent on the priming diagram taken from the Orion, is visible also in the case before us. The saltation of the pressure in the present instance, is without doubt referrible to the obstruction offered by the body of water in the cylinder to the progress of the piston towards the termination of the return stroke.

* Report of the Commissioners of Railways on Railway Communication between London and Birmingham, 1848.

Another question arises as to the influence of condensed steam in the cylinder occasioned subsequently to the arrival of the steam. It has been abundantly proved that water of condensation is, equally with water of priming, productive of back pressure. This will receive further consideration in a following chapter. Meantime, it may be stated that in general, and indeed in all the observed cases, particularly with outside cylinders, the less the period of admission relative to the whole stroke, the greater is the quantity of free water existing in the cylinder. This is familiarly proved by the experience of the indicator; it is usually flooded with water, which passes the piston of the instrument and escapes as spray from the slot in the upper part, when the steam is worked expansively; and the discharge of water increases with the proportion which the period of expansion bears to that of admission.

These remarks are particularly applicable to outside cylinders—and the diagrams obtained from the locomotives on the Caledonian Railway, confirm the general conclusion that water in the cylinder, however it may get there, smooths and levels the steam-line. This railway, composed of alternate gradients, is peculiarly adapted for illustrating extremes. With the Goods Locomotives, it generally happened that of two diagrams, taken consecutively on the ascending and descending sides of a double gradient, under the same notch, the first and heavier one possessed a steady, regular steam-line, with little or no undulation; while the second, taken shortly after doubling the summit, had a violently undulating steam-line. The diagrams, Fig. 120, taken from C. R., No. 124, are an example of this class; the valves were maintained in full gear over a summit of 1 in 330, while the speeds were successively $22\frac{1}{4}$ and 28 miles. The agitation of the steam-line of the second diagram may be explained by the liveliness of the steam of low pressure and temperature working dry in a cylinder which had just before been heated to a higher temperature—with a speed of piston of nearly 700 feet per minute. Many low pressure diagrams taken in full gear, possessed, on the contrary, a perfectly straight steam-line; for example, the smaller diagram in Fig. 98. Diagrams of this character were, however, commonly taken on light runs, or when the cylinder had not been previously heated under a heavier pressure.

RECAPITULATION.—1. The pressure of steam in the cylinder, during admission, at the lower speeds, and when the valve-gear is in good order, is sensibly constant. In full gear, there is no material wiredrawing under a speed of piston of about 600 feet per minute.

2. The shorter the admission in the same cylinder, that is, the shorter the travel, the lower is the speed of piston at which wiredrawing takes place; and the greater is the fall of pressure at the higher speeds.

3. The resistance to the progress of steam through the passage to the cylinder is considerable, and increases with the speed. And, there is a certain amount of opening of the port,—in all cases much less than its total width,—beyond which any extra opening does not further facilitate the ingress of the steam. This is proved by the straightness of the steam-line during admission, at the lower speeds, indicating that while the opening of port increases from the lead at the beginning of the stroke, there is no consequent increase of pressure.

4. The smaller the lead, the less is the apparent wiredrawing or fall of pressure.

5. Increase of lap with the same opening, up to certain limits, operates in reducing wiredrawing. With the outside 15-inch cylinder, $1\frac{1}{4}$ inch appears to be the greatest useful lap for this object. With the outside 17-inch cylinder, $1\frac{1}{4}$ inch wiredraws more than with the 15-inch one; and it is probable that for the larger cylinder, $1\frac{1}{2}$ inch lap would be preferable.

For the 15-inch inside cylinder, at least 1 inch lap is beneficial; and for the 18-inch inside, at least $1\frac{1}{4}$ inch. It is probable that an additional $\frac{1}{4}$ inch would, in both cases, further reduce the wiredrawing.

6. Beyond the useful limits of lap, in promoting the free action of steam, additional facility is to be had only by enlarging the cross section of the steam-passage. Thus, we find that with the same lap, 1 inch, the sectional area of port of the Great Britain, $\frac{1}{13}$th of that of the cylinder, permits of less wiredrawing than the relatively smaller ports of the other inside cylinders.

It follows that long lap, in conjunction with wide ports, reduces the wiredrawing to a minimum.

7. The more dry the steam, which it is in inside cylinders, the more susceptible is it of apparent wiredrawing, because it enters the cylinder more freely, and attains a higher initial pressure.

8. For the 15-inch cylinder, ports $10 \times 1\frac{1}{4}$ inch; $\frac{1}{4}$ inch lead for insides, and $\frac{1}{5}$ inch for outsides, or one-fifth and one-fourth of port respectively, are sufficient for securing timely admission, at all speeds, in full gear; and about $\frac{1}{16}$ inch in mid gear. In the latter case, less lead is needed, as the pressure is already brought up by compression. For the 18-inch cylinder of the Great Britain, $\frac{1}{4}$ inch lead, or barely one-fifth port, is amply sufficient.

9. When the lead is redundant, which is commonly the case, the steam is admitted so easily as to be momentarily compressed, and to exhibit on the diagram an exalted pressure, due jointly to percussion and compression. The greater the lead, or the higher the speed, the more intense is this initial pressure.

10. The initial action of the steam, when considerable, causes, in some cases, a pulsatory action during admission, which is likely to be, to some extent, an affection of the steam's motion, exaggerated on the diagram by the interference of the indicator-spring, as the vibratory motion occasionally extends to the end of the stroke.

11. The absence of lead promotes vibratory action during admission. Thus, too much lead, and no lead at all, are equally prejudicial to the uniform action of the steam; the reason being, in both circumstances, that the piston is some distance from the end or the beginning of the stroke, at the instant the port is opened.

12. As smaller lead is required for shorter admissions than for full gear, the distribution yielded by the stationary link, which provides the same lead for all admissions, is more favourable for the regular action of the steam than that yielded by the shifting-link, as in the latter case the lead increases as the admission is shortened,—the reverse of what is really required.

13. The amount of clearance, in respect of its total volume, permitted between the valve and the piston, has no sensible influence on the steam line.

14. The presence of water in the cylinder, whether it arises from priming or from condensation, brakes the steam; as it lowers and straightens the steam-line, thereby apparently reducing wiredrawing, though this is actually increased, between the valve-chest and the cylinder, by as much as the line is lowered.

CHAPTER IV.

Of the Behaviour of Steam in the Cylinder during Expansion.

In treating the subject of expansion by the assistance of diagrams, the irregularities of these will be reduced to a mean path where necessary, in the manner already explained; the majority of the diagrams referred to in this discussion are very steady, and in most cases the literally indicated pressures have been adhered to.

General principle.—During the expansion of a body of steam, the pressure falls as the volume increases. With a constant temperature, the reduction of total pressure is proportional to the increase of volume according to Boyle's law; so that, if the volume be increased to two or three times the initial volume, the total pressure simultaneously falls to one-half or one-third of the initial pressure.

Expansion of steam in the cylinder at very slow speeds.—To resume our example, Fig. 95, page 66, let A B, in the annexed figure 129, be the atmospheric line, or stroke of piston; A b, the period of admission of steam; and the height, A a, the uniform indicated pressure of 61 lbs. maintained during admission. Then, the rectangle, A c, is the area of effective pressure due to the period of admission, under the steam-line $a\,c$. The expansion-curve $c\,e$, in dark

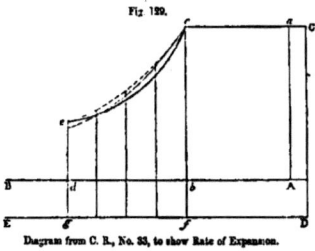

Fig. 129.

Diagram from C. R., No. 33, to show Rate of Expansion.

lining, expresses the progressive fall of pressure to 23 lbs. indicated, during an increase of volume when the face of the piston has passed from b to the release-line $d\,e$. The total clearance between the valve and the piston amounts to 1·1 inch of the length of the cylinder, and this must be added to the volume described by the piston, to find the total volume of the steam. The stroke of the piston is 20 inches, and the points of suppression and release are, by measurement from the diagram, 6·9 and 15 inches from the beginning. Add to each of these, the clearance, 1·1 inch,

and the sums, 8 and 16·1, are the inches of stroke occupied by the *initial* and *final* volumes of steam, at the beginning and the end of the expansion. Add the rectangular space A C, 1·1 inch wide, to represent the clearance, and draw the zero line of pressure, D E, 15 lbs. below the line A B, as the true base-line for the expansion-curve. Then the total initial and final pressures of the steam during expansion, represented by $c f$ and $e g$, are 76 and 38 lbs. Thus, while the total volume was raised from 8 to 16 inches, or doubled, the total pressure fell from 76 to 38 lbs., or to one half. Here we find a coincidence with Boyle's law, at the extremities of the curve; but, if we divide the period of expansion, $f g$, into four equal parts, and draw vertical ordinates from the points of division to the expansion-curve, the ordinates measure successively 56, 47, and 41 lbs. of total pressure, for which the total volumes are 10, 12, and 14 inches. By Boyle, these pressures would be,

For 10 inches, $76 \times \frac{8}{10} = 60·8$ lbs.
   12 ,, $76 \times \frac{8}{12} = 50·6$ lbs.
   14 ,, $76 \times \frac{8}{14} = 43·4$ lbs.

all in excess of those indicated; and they would belong to the curve in dot-lining, which properly represents the operation of Boyle's law, and which touches the actual curve only at the extreme points.

Again, had the steam neither lost nor gained heat during expansion, it would have expanded sensibly according to the laws of simply saturated steam. It is in the state of saturation during admission, and we can readily find the due curve of expansion. The relative volume of saturated steam of 76 lbs., is 377; as the volume in the cylinder is doubled by expansion, it becomes 754, and this is due to saturated steam of 35½ lbs., which is 2½ lbs. less than the indicated pressure. For the three intermediate volumes, the saturated pressures are—

For 10 inches, $377 \times \frac{8}{10} = 471·2$, rel. vol. for 59½ lbs.
  12 inches, $377 \times \frac{8}{12} = 565·5$, rel. vol. for 48½ lbs.
  14 inches, $377 \times \frac{8}{14} = 659·7$, rel. vol. for 41 lbs.

The four pressures so found, are represented by the curve of saturation, in light lining, which for the greater part of the expansion lies above the actual curve and only crosses and passes below it near the extremity. It is hence to be inferred that partial condensation took place during the early part of the expansion, and was succeeded by a slight re-

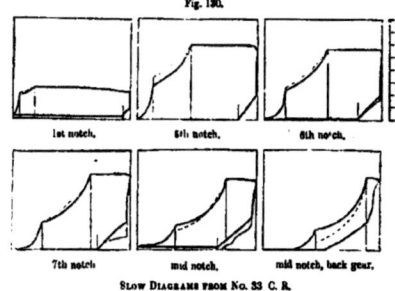

Fig. 130.

1st notch.   4th notch.   6th notch.

7th notch.   mid notch.   mid notch, back gear.

Slow Diagrams from No. 33 C. R.

evaporation, when the temperature of the steam, which falls with the pressure, got lower than that of the cylinder.

The example before us is one of a series of slow diagrams, Fig. 130, taken consecutively from No. 33, C. R., with different periods of admission and expansion, as regulated by the notches of the valve-gear. The following table contains the positions of the points of suppression and release in inches of stroke, measured from the diagrams, with clearance, 1·1 inch included; and also the ratio of the initial and final volumes so expressed. It contains also the total initial and final pressures, for the expansion-curve, measured from the diagrams; and an extra column of the total final pressures which would have resulted from the single operation of Boyle's law:—

TABLE No. XXV.—OF EXPANSION OF STEAM IN THE CYLINDER OF C. R. No. 33, AT SLOW SPEEDS.

Notch.	Suppression, clearance included.	Release, clearance included.	Ratio of initial and final volumes.	Total initial and final pressures for expansion curve as measured		Final pressure by Boyle's law.	
	inches.	inches.		lbs.	lbs.	lbs.	lbs.
1	17·4	19·8	1 to 1·14	40	33	35	or +2
5	12·0	18·3	1 to 1·52	75	42	49	or +7
6	10·1	17·5	1 to 1·73	71	39	41	or +2
7	8·0	16·1	1 to 2·01	76	38	37·7	or —0·3
Mid.	6·0	14·6	1 to 2·43	72	34	29·6	or —4·4
Do. Back.	3·5	12·1	1 to 3·5	73	31	21·1	or —9·9

In this table it appears that for the shorter periods of expansion the pressure falls below what is due to Boyle's law; and that for the longer expansions, it rises considerably above. Referring to the diagrams, on which the expansion-curves due to Boyle, are projected in dot-lines, it is plain that, generally, in the first stages of expansion, the actual curve sinks below the dot-curve; and that, if the expansion be continued materially beyond double the initial volume, it rises above the dot-curve. The conclusion is, that as the mean temperature of the cylinder is not greater, and must indeed be less than that of the steam which passes through it, the temperature of the cylinder is lower than that of the steam during admission; at this time, therefore, partial condensation takes place, attended with two results: the formation of water, and the raising of the temperature of the cylinder. Expansion begins, and condensation proceeds, and accelerates the fall of pressure, until the sensible heat of the steam becomes equal to that of the cylinder. As expansion continues, the temperature of the steam necessarily falls below that of the cylinder; then the steam previously precipitated as water, is re-evaporated wholly or partially, and thus a final pressure results even higher than what is due to the indicated initial pressure. The mass of the cylinder is, in short, an equalizer of temperature and pressure: it alternately abstracts and restores these elements; though the restoration is only partial, as heat is constantly dissipated through the cylinder into the atmosphere.

The foregoing diagrams from No. 33, C. R., were taken under extreme circumstances, after a repose of some hours, during which the cylinder had cooled. The cylinder, if on the outside is, in general, more or less a condenser of steam, and its action as such is the more sensible, the greater the degree of expansive working. Indeed, a diagram, Fig. 131, taken from C. R. No. 125, Goods, immediately at starting, after two hours of inactivity, exhibits all the symptoms of condensation: a water-logged indicator, a corrugated and precipitous steam-line,—which, had the cylinder been quite hot, would have followed the dotted curve,—an indefinite suppression, with nothing well marked but the point of release.

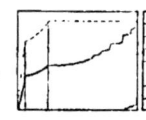

Fig. 131.

Diagram from C. R., No. 125, to show condensation of steam.

That the mean temperature of the cylinder very much affects the action of the steam, is confirmed by a number of slow diagrams, Fig. 132, taken from No. 13, C. R., immediately after an express trip of 27½ miles, while yet the cylinder was hot. The diagrams, we find, are sharp and square, and exhibit nothing of the indecision traceable on those from No. 33.

The following table, constructed like that for No. 33, shows the relation of the total initial and final volumes and pressures during expansion, taken from the diagrams; the clearance for No. 13 being 1·52 inches of the length of the cylinder:—

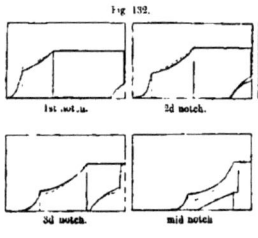

Fig. 132.

1st and 2d.   2d notch.

3d notch.   mid notch.

SLOW DIAGRAMS FROM C. R., No. 13.

TABLE No. XXVI.—EXPANSION OF STEAM IN THE CYLINDER OF No. 13 C. R., AT SLOW SPEEDS.

Notch.	Suppression, clearance included.	Release, clearance included.	Ratio.	Total initial and final pressures.		Final pressure by Boyle.	
	inches.	inches.		lbs.	lbs.	lbs.	lbs.
1	14·0	18·8	1 to 1·34	53	37	39·5	or +2·5
2	11·25	17·8	1 to 1·53	56	34	33·5	or —0·5
3	8·1	15·8	1 to 1·95	53	31	27·2	or —3·8
Mid.	4·6	12·2	1 to 2·66	54	28	20·3	or —7·7

In the hotter cylinder of No. 13, an expansion into 1½ times the initial volume, brings up the pressure to an equality with that available by Boyle's law, as illustrated by the dot-curves; this could be done in No. 33 only by an expansion of double the volume.

Of the expansion of steam in the cylinder during regular work.—Though it is impracticable, with the link-motion, to promote the expansion of steam by confinement, materially farther than 3¼ times the initial volume, we may note that experiments on the ultimate expansion of steam in the cylinders of stationary engines have been made in France by M. Morin. He found that with a ratio of 1 to 6, the mean error, reckoned on the area of the diagram, did not exceed one-thirtieth by excess when computed by the Boylean law. As these experiments were conducted with inferior pressures and under other circumstances than those which attend the locomotive, it is necessary to inquire specially into the expansive action of steam in locomotive cylinders, under actual circumstances. It has been seen that the curve of expansion affords a clue to one condition of the steam; and it will assist us in estimating the amount of condensation that prevails in cylinders under imperfect protection; and this is, in truth, the only subject of practical interest associated with the quality of the expansion-curve.

The two classes of cylinders under experiment, the results from which may be expected to contrast most obviously, are the inside and outside classes,—or generally, the fully protected, and the partially protected; and if it be true that protection is of any moment in the economical consumption of steam, the benefit ought to be made obvious on the expansion-curves, in so far as their final pressures are regulated by temperature.

Of the inside cylinders which have been subjected to experiment, it may be explained, that all of them are in the usual way placed inside the smoke-box, and, in general, totally enveloped in its atmosphere of hot smoke, or in a non-conducting bed of cinders, as the case may be. All the outside cylinders are those of the locomotives on the Caledonian Railway. In general arrangement, the passenger-engines are much alike, and as already explained, they are similar to the South Western Railway class of passenger-locomotives: cylinders bolted between the outer and inner frame-plates, and embraced partially by the plates of the smoke-box. On the outer and under sides, the cylinders are practically beyond the benefit of the positive heat that may exist in the smoke-box, and there is no felting about them, except what may be packed into the hollows of the front covers. The cylinders of the goods-engines, placed entirely clear of the smoke-box, are hung from the outside of the frame-plate, deriving no benefit whatever from its warm atmosphere, and protected only by a sheathing of felt and sheet-iron. The style of diagrams described by the greater number of these engines, has already been illustrated, and it is unnecessary now to multiply their number. They have been carefully reduced, where necessary, by the method already described.

The following table, No. XXVII., page 80, founded on the diagrams from the Great Britain (diagram-plate 4), is introduced, as it exhibits the manner in which each of the diagrams has been analyzed, and the mode of deriving the mean results for each cylinder and each degree of expansion. The indicated pressures of the steam at the commencement and termination of the allotted periods of expansion, are in the first place measured from the diagram; their disagreement with the law of Boyle, is then ascertained; the quantities of water in the condition of steam, are next deduced from the measured pressures and the known volumes at the points of suppression and release; and finally the differences are expressed in percentages of the initial equivalents of water. In particular, the first column of the table contains the positions of the points of suppression and release, measured from the beginning of the *steam*-stroke, in which the clearance is included, for the respective sets of diagrams. The ratio of these values expresses also that of the initial and final volumes of the steam for the period of expansion. The fourth and fifth columns comprise the nett pressures of the steam above the atmospheric pressure, as indicated. The sixth column contains the final pressures deduced exclusively by Boyle's law from the initial pressures; and the differences of the final pressures so calculated and as indicated

are contained in the seventh column. The two succeeding columns of water-equivalents were composed in the following manner by means of the table of Properties of Steam, already given. Example: No. 1 diagram.—To find the volume of steam admitted, or the initial volume: The cross area of the cylinder, 18 inches diameter, is 254·47 square inches; the total volume of steam admitted occupies 19·55 inches of the length of the cylinder, and is equal to 254·47 × 19·55 = 4975 cubic inches of steam at 66 lbs. sensible pressure. Now, 66 + 15 = 81 lbs. is the total pressure of the steam, and the relative volume for this pressure is 355; the volume of water, as steam, is therefore 4975 ÷ 355 = 14·01 cubic inches, as set down in the eighth column. The final equivalent is determined in the same way.

It appears, plainly, from the table that the influence of speed on the relation of the initial and final quantities is appreciably nothing. In each group of diagrams taken under one notch, the differences appear, in general, to be equally great throughout, from the lowest to the highest speed. The means of each group may, therefore, be legitimately adopted for comparison without reference to speed, which considerably simplifies the inquiry. On the contrary, the results from one notch differ very sensibly from those derived from the others; it is therefore necessary to distinguish these results in the abstract table which follows. This table, No. XXVIII., is a summary of the mean results derived from detail tables compiled for the engines named, similar to the 27th table, for each cylinder and notch experimented with, and comprises the substance of numerous diagrams for each case.

In the first columns, the dimensions and ratios employed in the formation of the succeeding columns, are inserted. The tenth and fourteenth columns contain the percentages of the differences of pressures and equivalents, in terms of the initial quantities. The total averages of the ratios of expansion, and of the differences of final pressure and water-equivalents, are added for the inside and outside cylinders separately.

Of the Final Pressure.—The contents of this table show, what was found in the case of slow diagrams, that, in each cylinder, as the proportion of the final to the initial volume is raised, the differences of the final pressures, positive at first, become less, and in some cases negative, when the pressure by Boyle, falls below the observed pressure. But this inferiority of pressure occurs only in the outside cylinders, and after the total volume reaches one and a half times the initial volume admitted. For example, in C. R. No. 13, when the steam has expanded to 1·6 times the initial volume, the difference of pressure is negative, and amounts to 2·2 per cent.; and in No. 125, after an expansion of 1·54 times, the difference is —0·7 per cent. With an expanded volume of double, we find that while, in the inside cylinders, the difference remains positive, it falls to —10 per cent. in No. 51, and to —11 per cent. in No. 125.

Variation of Water-Equivalents.—In each cylinder, for the smaller expansions, the final is less than the initial equivalent of water, and the greater the proportion of expansion, the more nearly do the equivalents reach equality, until ultimately in some of the cylinders the final becomes greater than the initial. In the first series of the Great

TABLE No. XXVII.—OF THE EXPANSION AND WATER-EQUIVALENTS OF STEAM, MEASURED FROM DIAGRAMS TAKEN FROM THE "GREAT BRITAIN" LOCOMOTIVE.

CYLINDER, 18″ × 24″; TOTAL CLEARANCE, 1·6″.

Positions of the Points of Suppression and Release, Clearance in all cases included, indicating the Initial and Final volumes by Expansion.	No. of Diagram.	Speed of Engine.	Nett pressures during expansion.		Nett final pressures, by Boyle's law.		Equivalents of Water.		
			Initial.	Final.	Pressure.	Difference.	Initial.	Final.	Difference.
		Miles per hour.	lbs.	lbs.	lbs.	lbs.	cub. in.	cub. in.	cub. in.
FIRST SERIES. First Notch. Suppression, 19·55 ins. Release, 23·3 ins. Ratio, 1 to 1·2.	1	11	66	50	52	+ 2	14·01	13·66	− ·35
	2	16¼	61·5	47	49	+ 2	13·27	13·09	− ·18
	3	20	48	37	37	0	11·13	11·14	+ ·01
	4	30	83	62	66	+ 4	16·64	16·62	− ·02
	5	35	50	39	39	0	11·46	11·54	+ ·08
	6	42	47	36·5	37	+ ·5	10·98	11·04	+ ·06
	7	52·3	58	43	46	+ 3	12·72	12·30	− ·42
	8	53·6	61	45	48	+ 3	13·2	12·7	− ·50
	9	55	57	44	45	+ 1	12·5	12·51	+ ·01
	Means.		59	44·83	46·55	+ 1·72	12·68	12·73	− ·15
Third Notch. Suppression, 16·05 ins. Release, 21·8 ins. Ratio, 1 to 1·36.	10	11	62	43	42	− 1	10·98	11·48	+ ·50
	11	16¼	63	40	42	+ 2	11·10	10·94	− ·16
	12	20	49	32	32	0	9·28	9·48	+ ·20
	13	30	83	50	57	+ 7	13·66	12·75	− ·91
	14	35	52	34	34	0	9·68	9·85	+ ·17
	15	46	62	42	42	0	10·98	11·30	+ ·32
	16	52·3	61	37·5	41	+ 3·5	10·83	10·48	− ·35
	17	57	92	56	65	+ 9	14·80	13·80	− 1·00
	18	63·	40	25·5	25	− 0·5	8·07	8·26	+ ·19
	Means.		63	40	42·2	+ 2·2	11·05	10·93	− ·12
Fifth Notch. Suppression, 11·4 ins. Release, 19·05 ins. Ratio, 1 to 1·7.	19	11	62	33	30	− 3	7·90	8·66	+ ·96
	20	20	65	31	34	+ 3	8·09	8·15	+ ·06
	21	30	85	39	45	+ 6	9·90	9·43	− ·47
	22	35	58	28	28	0	7·40	8·10	+ ·70
	23	39	43	18	10	− 8	6·02	6·37	+ ·35
	24	50·2	62	26	30	+ 4	7·70	7·78	+ ·08
	Means.		62·5	29·17	29·5	+ ·33	7·82	8·08	+ ·26
SECOND SERIES. First Notch. Suppression, 17·8 ins. *Release, 22·8 ins. Ratio, 1 to 1·3. * Release measured at 21 inches.	25	15	70	* 50	50	0	13·32	13·37	+ ·05
	26	17	88	65	65	0	15·89	16·16	+ ·27
	27	21	94	65	69	+ 4	16·71	16·16	− ·55
	28	24	84	57	61	+ 4	15·30	14·65	− ·65
	29	27	74	49	53	+ 4	13·89	13·19	− ·70
	30	31	86	55	65	+ 10	15·62	14·29	− 1·33
	31	31	90	56	58	+ 2	14·76	14·47	− ·29
	32	49	52	34	36	+ 2	10·73	10·32	− ·41
	33	54	86	60	65	+ 5	15·62	15·23	− ·39
	Means.		79	54·6	58	+ 3·44	14·65	14·21	− ·44
Third Notch. *Suppression, 13·8 ins. *Release, 20·8 ins. Ratio, 1 to 1·5. * The points of suppression and release are assumed at 13 and 19 inches, for even numbers.	34	17	87	48	55	+ 7	12·19	11·84	− ·35
	35	18	70	37	42	+ 5	10·33	9·95	− ·38
	36	21	90	48	55	+ 7	12·50	11·84	− ·66
	37	26	72	38	43	+ 5	10·55	10·12	− ·43
	38	31	75	38	45	+ 5	10·87	10·12	− ·75
	39	32	79	38	48	+ 10	11·33	10·12	− 1·21
	40	40	65	33	38	+ 5	9·78	9·24	− ·54
	41	51	55	28	32	+ 4	8·65	8·35	− ·30
	42	55	72	37	43	+ 6	10·54	9·95	− ·59
	Means.		74	38·4	44·4	+ 6	10·75	10·17	− ·58
Fifth Notch. Suppression, 8·8 ins. *Release, 18·8 ins. Ratio, 1 to 2·14. * Measured at 17 inches.	43	17	80	33	34	+ 1	7·90	8·30	+ ·40
	44	18	70	24	25	+ 1	6·59	6·90	+ ·37
	45	21	93	33	35	+ 2	8·20	8·35	+ ·15
	46	28	74	21	26	+ 5	6·87	6·42	− ·45
	47	31	80	22	29	+ 7	7·29	6·58	− ·71
	48	36	63	17	21	+ 4	6·08	5·76	− ·32
	49	50	55	15	18	+ 3	5·52	5·43	− ·09
	50	56	65	16	22	+ 6	6·24	5·60	− ·64
	Means.		74	26·25	22·62	+ 3·62	6·83	6·67	− ·16

Britain, a greater expansion converts the difference from —1·2 per cent. into + 3·3 per cent.; in No. 33, it converts —9 into + 8·3 per cent.; and in No. 125, —3·7 into + 24 per cent. of excess.

Further, for long expansions, the difference exists as a deficiency only in the inside cylinders; in the exposed cylinders, we have seen it to be greatly in excess; and with No. 42, which, in the 5th notch, expands the steam into 3·33 times the initial volume, the difference actually amounts to an excess of 67 per cent. of the initial equivalent. Thus

TABLE No. XXVIII.—OF THE EXPANSION AND WATER EQUIVALENTS OF STEAM, IN THE CYLINDERS OF LOCOMOTIVES, ABSTRACTED FROM THE RESULTS OF ABOVE 200 INDICATOR DIAGRAMS.

Name of Engine.	Diameter and stroke of Cylinder.	No. of M.leb.	Initial and Final Volumes of Steam during Expansion, deep-ance Incl led, in inches of Stroke.	Ratio of Initial and Final Volume=1 bsg as 1.	Mean Pressures during Expansion.					Equivalents of Water as Steam.				Date of Observations.	Remarks.
					Initial (actual).	Final (actual).	Final (theor.)	Difference of the last two Columns.	Ratio of Difference to Initial Pressure.	Initial.	Final.	Difference.	Ratio of Difference to Initial Equivalent.		
					INSIDE CYLINDERS.										
	in.		lbs.		lbs.	lbs.	lbs.	lbs.		cub. in.	cub. in.	cub. in.		Year.	
Great Britain (1st Series)...	18 24	1	19·55 23·3	1·20	49	44·63	46·55	+ 1·72	+ 3 per cent.	12·88	12·73	− ·15	− 1·2 per cent	1849	The diagrams from which these results are deduced, were obtained by Mr. Gooch with Experimental Trains.
Do.	„	3	16·05	21·8	1·36	68	40	42·20	+ 2·20	+ 3·6	11·05	10·96	− ·19	− 1·1	1847–49	
Do.	„	5	11·40	19·06	1·70	63·5	29·17	29·50	0·33	+ 0·5	7·69	8·06	+ ·36	+ 3·2	1849	
Great Britain (3d Series)...	„	1	17·8	22·9	1·30	79	54·60	44·40	+ 3·40	+ 4·3	14·65	14·21	− ·44	− 3·0	1850	
Do.	„	3	13·8	20·2	1·40	74	39·40	44·40	+ 6	+ 8	10·75	10·17	− ·53	− 5·4	„	
Do.	„	5	8·8	18·6	2·16	74	26·25	22·62	+ 3·63	+ 6	6·85	6·67	− ·16	− 3·2	„	These diagrams were taken during a single Express trip.
E. & G. R. Nile.	16 × 18	gab.	19·4	17·35	1·30	48	24	29	+ 5	+ 12	5·50	5·04	− ·46	− 8·4	„	Taken with an ordinary stopping train.
E. & G. R. Orion	15 × 20	3	13·6	19·1	1·40	53	29	30	+ 1	+ 2	5·85	5·49	− ·36	− 6·2	„	Taken with an Express train.
E. & G. R. Hebe	15 × 20	5	10·1	16·6	1·64	48	19	22	+ 3	+ 6·5	3·24	3·18	− ·06	− 1·6	„	
Means.				1·42				+ 5	per cent				− 3·3 per cent.		
					OUTSIDE CYLINDERS.										
	ins.		ins.	ins.	lbs.	lbs.	lbs.	lbs.		cub. in.	cub. in.	cub. in.			
C. R. No 13 ...	16 × 20	1	14·02	18·62	1·38	53	54	55	+ 1	+ 2 per cent	5·93	5·92	− ·01	− 0·2 per cent.	1850	Taken with an Express train.
Do.	„	2	11·27	17·3	1·40	48	24	23	− 1	− 2·2	4·36	4·51	+ ·25	+ 1·2	„	Taken with a stopping train.
C. R. No. 33...	15 × 20	3	14·55	18·75	1·40	46	22	28	+ 6	+ 15·6	5·02	4·97	− ·44	− 9·0	„	Taken with Express, Mail, and Parliamentary trains.
Do.	„	3	12·0	18·3	1·62	44	27	31·5	+ 4·5	+ 8	4·99	5·38	− ·39	+ 8·2	„	
Do.	„	4	8·6	16·1	2·01	45	16·5	14·5	− 1	− 6	3·13	3·33	+ ·20	+ 6·1	„	
C. R. No. 41...	15 × 20	1	13·5	18·6	1·38	36	24	26	+ 4	+ 11	5·07	5·00	− ·07	− 1·4	„	Taken over a friction-brake at Greenock workshops.
Do.	„	2	14·2	18·6	1·31	26	16	20	+ 4	+ 16	3·84	3·82	− ·02	− 0·5	„	
C. R. No. 42...	15 × 20	3	11·1	18·35	1·33	25	30	31	+ 1	+ 1·6	4·57	4·54	+ ·07	+ 1·3	„	
Do.	„	4	10·1	17·1	1·70	49	22	21	+ 1	+ 2	4·06	4·18	− ·10	+ 2·4	„	
C. R. No 51 (old valve)	15 × 20	5	4·5	16·1	3·33	68	22	10	− 12	− 18	2·29	3·68	+ 1·39	+ 67·0	„	Taken with Express and Mail trains.
C. R. No 51 (new valve)	„		10·36	17·7	1·72	59	29	28	− 1	− 1·7	4·56	4·94	+ ·38	+ 8·3	„	
Do. (new valve)	„		7·1	15·4	2·20	50	30	15	− 5	− 10	2·91	3·63	+ ·72	+ 25·0	„	
C. R. No. 135...	17 × 24	1	16·8	21·85	1·27	53	20	23	+ 3	+ 9	7·48	7·20	− ·28	− 3·7	„	Taken with Goods trains.
Do.	„	3	14·9	23·0	1·54	48	26·48	26·13	− 0·33	− 0·7	7·47	7·96	+ ·41	+ 5·4	„	
Do.	„	4	10·2	23·1	2·16	37	13·43	9·29	− 4·13	− 11	4·36	5·39	+ 1·03	+ 34·0	„	
C. R. No. 197...	17 × 24	5	5·7	16·3	2·84	47	20	10	− 10	− 17·5	3·36	4·77	+ 1·41	+ 46·3	„	Taken with engine and tender running alone.
Means				1·795					− 0·12 per cent				+ 10·6 per cent		
1	2	3	4	5	6	7	8	9	10	11	12	13	14	15	16

it appears that the differences are more affected by increase of expansion, the greater the exposure of the cylinder.

That the differences due to greater expansions are much more considerable in the outside cylinders, is rendered further apparent by contrasting the total averages contained in the table. These indicate that, generally, in the inside cylinders, during an expansion from a volume of 1 to 1·52, the equivalent falls 3·3 per cent; while, in the outside cylinder, an expansion of 1 to 1·79, raises the equivalent 10·6 per cent. As it is clear that, generally, the greater the degree of expansion, the greater also is the excess of the final quantity of water in the condition of steam, it is desirable to ascertain at what average rate this excess increases. This may be found graphically by the method of the curve, already employed in a previous chapter in the discussion of the valve-motion. Thus, let the base-line A B, Fig. 133, be assumed to represent, by equal divisions, the proportional volumes of expansion, measured from A towards B—not the total volumes, but simply the increments of volume due to expansion. The division from Q to 1 will then represent a volume due to expansion equal to the initial volume, and though marked 1, signifies a total volume of double the initial. Similarly, assume the vertical scale A C, as a measure of the percentages of difference. Draw vertical ordinates from the line A B, through the points corresponding to the amounts of expansion given in the table, set off, on these ordinates, the relative percentages in terms of the vertical scale, and designate by stars the points so found. For example, No. 127, with an expanded volume of 2·84, yields a percentage of 46·3; from the point in A B, representing

an increment of 1·84, draw a vertical line equal in length to the percentage, 46·3, measured by the vertical scale; and terminate the line with the cross d. A line, curved or

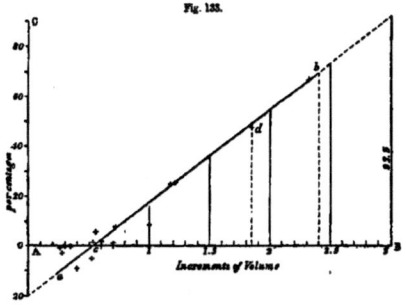

Fig. 133.

Diagram of the differences of Water-equivalents that occur during expansion in Outside Cylinders.

straight, traced through this series of stars, taking a mean path amongst them, will represent, by its direction and form, the mean rate of variation of the percentage in question. Minus percentages are placed below the base-line, and positive percentages above. The operation being so performed, for the outside cylinders, as shown on the figure, we find that the mean percentage line a b is straight, and if produced would cut the vertical A C at 20 per cent. below the base-line; it also cuts the base-line at a, which represents a total volume of 1·53, and its upper end, b,

L

reaches a percentage of 70, at the extremity of an ordinate indicating a total expanded volume of 3·4. The straightness of the line implies that equal increments of expansion relative to the initial volume, are accompanied by equal additions to the percentage. Thus, according to the diagram, the following final volumes by expansion, incur the annexed percentages, the initial volume being 1,

Final Volumes.	Percentages of Difference of Water Equivalents.	Relative periods of Admission.
1·50	— 1·25	52·5 per cent.
1·53	0	50·0 ,,
2·00	+ 17·50	32·5 ,,
2·50	+ 36·25	19·0 ,,
3·00	+ 55·00	13·0 ,,
3·50	+ 73·75	
4·00	+ 92·50	

the difference for each increment of expansion of half the initial volume, being 18·75 per cent. A test of the faithfulness of this method of averaging, is supplied by the circumstance that, for a final volume of 1·795, which was the average for the outside cylinders, the mean path shows a percentage of 9·8, which is a near approximation to the actual average percentage by the table, namely, 10·6.

If the same course be adopted for the inside cylinders, though the data in this case are more restricted, we find the following mean expansions and percentages—

Final Volumes.	Percentages.
1·50	— 3·0
2·00	0
2·50	+ 3·0
3·00	+ 6·0

Here the percentage becomes nothing, or the initial and final equivalents become equal, when the initial volume is doubled, and for each half volume extra, there results 3 per cent. of difference in excess. Thus the difference is merely nominal in cylinders which are well protected.

In general, it is to be concluded that, first, when the cylinder is thoroughly immersed in the hot-bath of the smoke-box, the temperature of which is commonly much higher than that of the steam, the quantity of water existing as steam during expansion is virtually constant. Secondly, when the cylinder is placed nearly or entirely beyond the influence of the heat of the smoke-box, or protected only in the usual manner by felting and plating, the quantity of water as steam varies very considerably during expansion; it suffers a rapid and transient diminution during the first stages of expansion, and remounts to an excess over the initial quantity, which increases uniformly as expansion is promoted, till, for a final volume of three times the initial, the excess reaches 55 per cent. of the weight of steam cut off at the point of suppression.

Throughout this discussion we have been careful to name the magnitude of the expanded volume always in terms of the initial volume; for, with the link-motion, the initial volume varies for every degree of expansion, its absolute magnitude being reduced as the ratio of expansion rises, as shown in the column of admissions attached to the foregoing

statement for outside cylinders. These admissions were found by means of the data contained in the table No. XX., of link-motion, in the following manner. To find the ratio of the total initial and final volumes due to a given admission, for example, of 73·5 per cent.,—as we have found that for a 20 inch stroke, 1·1 inch of clearance, or 5·5 per cent. of the stroke was required, the total initial and final volumes are (73·5 + 5·5) and (91 + 5·5), or 79 and 96·5 per cent., of which the ratio is 1 to 1·22. In the same way, the ratios for the other admissions are found, 5·5 per cent. being in all cases added for clearance; and thus we obtain the quantities in the second column of the following table—

TABLE No. XXIX.—OF THE INDICATED DIFFERENCES OF WATER EQUIVALENTS, SHOWING INITIAL CONDENSATION OF STEAM, FOR VARIOUS PERIODS OF ADMISSION, IN OUTSIDE CYLINDERS.

Periods of Admission in percentages of Stroke.	Final volumes by Expansion, clearance included, the Initial Volumes being taken as 1.	Differences of Initial and Final Equivalents, in percentages of Initial Equivalents.
73·5 per cent.	1·22	— 12·0
60 ,,	1·40	— 5·2
50 ,,	1·54	0·0
40 ,,	1·78	9·4
30 ,,	2·07	19·9
20 ,,	2·45	34·1
12 ,,	3·17	61·1

Arranging these final volumes in a curve, of which the baseline represents the admissions in percentages of the stroke, we obtain by simple interpolation the percentages of admission due to the final volumes, contained in the statement already made for outside cylinders.

The 3d column of the accompanying table is filled up by direct measurement from the diagram, Fig. 133, from which we find that while the indicated differences of water-equivalents for an admission of 50 per cent. or half stroke, is nothing at all, it rises rapidly for shorter admissions, amounting to above 60 per cent. of excess, for an admission of 12 per cent.

The foregoing results are directly contrary to what might have been anticipated, as, at first sight, they appear to show that the less protected the cylinders, the more work is done with a given initial quantity of steam. In the inside cylinder so far from any apparent evaporation, or accession to the total weight of the steam, during expansion, the quantity is at least not more than constant, and is in fact slightly reduced during expansion. The outside cylinders, on the contrary, show, by the great excess of steam at the end of expansion, very significant amounts of factitious evaporation. In this case, as in that of the slow diagrams, the difference is referrible to a primary condensation of the steam, during admission, by which water is formed, and the heat of the cylinder is raised. After suppression, and when the steam's temperature falls by expansion below the newly acquired temperature of the cylinder, the hot water flashes into steam in virtue of its own heat and that of the cylinder, according to the law of the maximum density and pressure for the temperature; and what appears at first sight to have been positively one advantage of an exposed cylinder, in the auxiliary evaporation during the later stages of expansion, is nothing more than a partial resuscitation of the precipitated steam, and a compromise for lost initial action. The greater the proportion of expansion, the greater is the final excess of steam, as the extreme temperatures become more widely different; and, moreover, for higher degrees of expansion, smaller absolute volumes of steam are admitted, for which there is always the same cooling superficies of cylinder; and this is relatively greater, of course, as the period of admission is reduced. In the enclosed inside cylinder, on the other hand, bathed in hot air or coke-cinders, usually as hot or hotter than the steam that passes through them, the initial pressure of the steam as it enters the cylinder is maintained in all its integrity; as even for the greatest expansions, there appear no symptoms of a resurrection of steam. The evidence goes rather to show that the steam is slightly surcharged during its passage through the steam-pipes previous to admission.

An elegant confirmation of these conclusions on the condensation of steam by imperfect protection is derivable even from inside cylinders themselves. It is known by observation that whatever be the temperature in the smoke-box during the action of the blast, it falls very rapidly to about 200° when the steam is shut off. On starting from a station, therefore, the atmosphere of the smoke-box requires re-heating, which involves a little time to accomplish. During this interval, the cylinder is colder than the steam, and is becoming gradually hotter,—a process which is plainly traceable on a succession of diagrams taken at short intervals after starting. Thus, on the occasion of the express trip from Edinburgh to Glasgow with the Nile, E. and G. R., referred to in the 28th table, we started from Linlithgow station and passed the mile-posts at the intervals and speeds expressed in the following table, in the last column of which are contained the successive differences of the water-equivalents.

Mile posts.	Time of passing mile-posts.			Speed of passing mile-posts.	Difference of Water equivalents.
	h.	m. start.	s.	Miles per hour.	percentages.
Linlithgow, 16½ m.p...	11	8	40	...	...
17 —	„	11	10	15·0	+ 55·3
17½ —	„	12	35	22·5	— 0·5
18 —	„	13	50	24·0	+ 1·0
19 —	„	16	12	27·0	— 3·2
20 —	„	18	17	30·0	— 5·0
21 —	„	20	12	32·0	— 9·8
22 —	„	22	0	34·0	— 9·1

From this it would appear that the train had run one mile before the difference, previously positive, had been reduced to nothing; and that when it reached the 21st mile-post, after a run of 5½ miles, during an interval of 11½ minutes, the negative differences attained their maximum, by a process due to the gradual rise of the temperature in the smoke-box, about the cylinders.

From these investigations, it would appear that the loss by condensation in the outside cylinder, is not constant, but varies with the proportion of expansion directly. We have already seen that the greater the ratio of expansion, the less is the volume of steam admitted. Therefore, generally, the loss by condensation increases, and that in a very high ratio,

as the period of admission is shortened, amounting, as we have seen, to a loss equal to 60 per cent. of the sensible steam admitted, for an expansion into three times the initial volume, which by the nature of the link motion is due to an admission of about 12 or 15 per cent. of the stroke. This loss, great as it appears to be, is after all only the obvious loss discoverable on the diagram, which is certainly less than the actual loss, for we cannot assume that the final equivalent, even for long expansions, represents the total quantity of steam that enters the cylinder. There must necessarily be an extra constant percentage of loss by condensation, which never appears on the diagram, and is dissipated through the sides of the cylinder, setting out, as we do, with the proposition, now established, that the outside or imperfectly protected cylinder is a partial condenser. The heat so dissipated leaves in the cylinder a constant quantity of unseen water, which is exhausted with the steam, and only makes itself felt on the diagram by an exaggeration of the back pressure.

Though it has been found, therefore, that an expansion into a volume of 1·53, in the outside cylinder, indicates equal initial and final equivalents, it by no means proves the absence of condensation, any more than an expansion of 1·5, indicating a final reduction of — 1·25 per cent, proves a case of initial surcharge, such as was fairly inferred for inside cylinders. The equality of the equivalents in the first case simply shows that the condensation continues until the expansion is partially accomplished, and is succeeded by re-evaporation during the remainder of that period. For the shorter expansion of 1·5, and of course for still smaller expansions, the amount of re-evaporation being insufficient to restore the equality, an inferior final equivalent is the result. And although, in these cases, the condensation, less obvious on the expansion-curve, is not the less a reality, it is probable that the permanent condensation is less in amount than for greater expansions, and also that for higher mean pressures, there is a smaller percentage of loss than for lower pressures, as we know that the sensible temperature of steam, and the corresponding liability to external radiation of heat, increases much more slowly than the pressure and density. Seeing then that the indicated expansion-curve leaves us in a state of uncertainty as to the total loss by condensation, though we know that what we do discern by an examination of the curve, is certainly much less than the actual loss, especially for admissions above 40 per cent., we can at present only regard the ordinary loss by condensation in outside cylinders, working with 35 per cent. of admission—a common practice on ordinary lines,—as, at least (9·4 × 4·7), or 14 per cent. of the sensible steam that exists during admission. It is certainly more; and the real excess is a matter for future consideration. To cause initial condensation it is not even necessary to permit of any external dissipation of heat; for however well a cylinder may be protected, it must operate as an equalizer of heat, by in the first place condensing a part of the steam as it enters, causing a certain irrecoverable loss, and secondly, restoring the heat only when the pressure has fallen. It is, therefore, necessary for the perfect application of steam in the cylinder, to maintain the temperature of the latter at least equal to the initial temperature of the steam, by independent means applied *without* the cylinder, in place of ruinously drawing upon the constituent heat of the steam *within*.

Another question suggests itself as to the loss of *pressure* in the outside cylinder during admission, that occurs by condensation. We do not at present refer to the total loss of effect, as this point will more properly be considered in treating of the relation of the steam visibly used to the water consumed from the tender. Suppose we find 60 lbs. steam in the cylinder during an admission of 30 per cent.; then, as a quantity equal to 20 per cent. of this steam has entered the cylinder with it and has been condensed, we might deduct 20 per cent. or one-fifth of its relative volume to find that of the steam originally introduced, if the loss be represented by fall of pressure. The relative volume of 60 lbs. steam is 381; and ⅘ (381) = 305, is the relative volume of 81 lbs. steam, and this would be the original pressure of the steam flowing into the cylinder, 21 lbs. of it being lost by condensation. Thus we find that for 20 per cent. of condensation, 35 per cent. of pressure would be sunk; and in general the percentage of lost initial pressure would be greater than that of condensation. This view of the question, however, is only partially correct, as it is obvious that much condensation may go on, especially at low speeds, without any material fall of the pressure. At the higher speeds, the fall of pressure due to condensation must become more sensible, as the difficulty of following up the loss increases with the speed.

These results sufficiently explain how it happens that expansive working, especially in outside cylinders, is in practice carried out to such a limited extent. We have rarely found on the Caledonian Railway,—a line stocked with outside cylinder locomotives,—that a suppression materially above 30 per cent. of the stroke is voluntarily adopted by the engine-drivers. In their own words, "they lose as much as they get," if they endeavour to work with a suppression much less than 30 per cent., and yet it is not easy to conceive a line better adapted than the Caledonian, composed of long and steep double gradients, for the practice of highly expansive working. The balance of loss and gain, above described, is abundantly explained by the extra condensation which attends the earlier suppression, and is not at all referrible to the very popular notion that there is something wrong in the nature of the link-motion. We may refer to an example in point; in the case of two locomotives on this railway, Nos. 25 and 51, with the same train, as much water was consumed from the tender of No. 51, of which the driver was one of the most economical consumers on the line, and which was worked by variable expansion, within the limits already stated—as was withdrawn from the tender of No. 25, an engine worked mostly by the regulator. Whereas, according to the ordinary tabular data, the relative volume of steam being approximately in the inverse ratio of the pressure at which it is employed, steam of a higher pressure worked expansively should consume a less quantity of water than wiredrawn steam, in the discharge of the same duty. There is no doubt that much of the economy of fuel effected with No. 51 was due to the judicious system of firing practised by the driver, and to his unceasing care in preventing waste of steam by the safety valve,—matters to which little attention was paid with No. 25. Nothing is more common

than a rush of water when the outside cylinder is tapped while the steam is under considerable expansion; and with the goods engine No. 125, C. R., of which the cylinders are still more exposed than those of No. 51, the cylinders were during our experiments never free of water even in the course of long-continued runs; and, during temporary stoppages, large accumulations of water were usually formed, which could never be entirely dissipated, even through the open cylinder-cocks.

In the condensation of steam in imperfectly protected cylinders, we have an explanation of the assertion repeatedly made by experienced men, that a fixed gab-motion for working the valves, may yield results as economical, with reference to the consumption of coke, as any variable expansion-gear. This is certainly not true of the better class of inside-cylinder engines, as our experience on the Edinburgh and Glasgow Railway abundantly testifies. Still, it may to a considerable extent hold true with outside cylinders as usually disposed of, running on lines of easy gradients. Mr. Peter Robertson, locomotive superintendent of the Glasgow and South-Western Railway, and a staunch advocate of the outside-cylinder system, has adopted a fixed gab-motion for the engines designed by him, —cutting off at half stroke,—no doubt aware by experience of the limits to useful expansive working in outside cylinders, though probably not conscious of the rationale of the matter. Indeed, so much has he considered the protection of the cylinders to be a matter of indifference, that he has placed them on the outside of the frame, with three-fourths of their circumference bare cast-iron, finished with ornamental beads, without sheathing or covering, and directly exposed to the atmosphere.

With respect to Mr. Samuel's mode, lately patented, of working steam expansively to a degree contemplated at four to six times the initial volume, by exhausting from one cylinder into the other, it is plain that the necessary conditions for the economical employment of such an extent of expansion, demand a much better provision for the preservation of the steam than is to be found in the ordinary arrangements of outside cylinders. According to Mr. Samuel's designs, the cylinders are placed outside in the usual manner, without any expedient for preserving the temperature of the steam, and it is easy to understand that special means must be adopted for this object, to secure an economical promotion of expansive action to the extent peculiarly available by his system.

RECAPITULATION.—1. When steam is admitted to the cylinder, while the latter is comparatively cold, a very sensible condensation of the steam takes place during admission, which continues to a certain extent during expansion. The heat thereby separated is absorbed by the material of the cylinders, and raises its temperature. A portion of this heat passes off, and is irrecoverably lost; the remainder is retained, and is re-absorbed by the precipitated steam during the expansion of the existing steam, if it be long enough continued,—that is, until the temperature of the latter has fallen below that of the cylinder. This is proved by diagrams taken at very slow speeds, on which occasions the cylinder is cold enough to exhibit these operations in high relief.

2. The consequence is, under these circumstances, that

the weight of steam existing in the cylinder at the instant of suppression is less than that which exists at the instant of release, when the degree of expansion is considerable.

3. Thus the curve of expansion, as described on the diagram, may be made available for testing the condition of the steam in the cylinder.

4. When an engine is engaged in the actual performance of its duty, the inequality of the weights of steam here referred to, does not appear to be influenced by speed.

5. In the course of ordinary duty, the final pressures, or those existing at the point of release, do not, in inside cylinders, materially differ from the pressures deducible by the law of Boyle from the initial pressures, or those at the point of suppression. That is, the initial and final total pressures of the steam during the period of expansion, are approximately in the inverse ratio of the total initial and final volumes of the steam expanded, though in general the final pressures are slightly inferior to the pressures by Boyle. In outside cylinders, the pressures by Boyle would fall below the observed pressures when the expanded volume exceeds one and a half times the initial.

6. In the inside cylinder, the weight of steam, in other words, its water-equivalent, is virtually constant during expansion. In the outside cylinder, it falls during the first stages of expansion; as expansion proceeds, it remounts to the initial value when the volume reaches above one and a half times the initial volume; beyond this point the equivalent exceeds the initial, and the excess increases uniformly at the rate of 18·75 per cent. of the initial for each half volume of expansion, till for a final volume of three times, it amounts to 55 per cent. of the actual weight of steam suppressed.

7. The excesses of final equivalents shown by outside cylinders are due, as in the case of the slow diagrams, to condensation of steam during admission: the heat so disengaged being reserved and employed during the later stages of expansion, in partially resuscitating the condensed steam. Thus, the excess is, in other words, the quantity of steam reduced to water during admission.

8. The indicated initial condensation is certainly not all that really takes place, for the resuscitation of the steam, from which the condensation is estimated, is confessedly only partial. The actual condensation, then, is plainly, in all cases, greater than that indicated.

9. To prevent entirely the condensation of steam worked expansively, the cylinder must not only be simply protected by a non-conductor; it must be *maintained* by independent external means at the initial temperature of the steam.

10. The percentage of loss of the steam power during admission, is always at least as great as the percentage of condensation; it is generally greater, inasmuch as if there be any positive fall of pressure due to condensation, which generally takes place to some extent, the fall of pressure is, as we have found, greater than the relative condensation.

11. The important losses by condensation in outside cylinders, which accompany great expansions, account for the inability to work these engines expansively and economically, with admissions materially less than 30 per cent. of the stroke.

CHAPTER V.

OF THE BEHAVIOUR OF STEAM IN THE CYLINDER, DURING EXHAUST.

IT remains to examine the circumstances which regulate the exhaust of steam from the point of release in the steam stroke to the end of the return stroke. The resistance of compression is, of course, superadded to that of exhaust, towards the termination of the return of the piston; it will, however, be considered separately, and in averaging the amount of back pressure due simply to the exhaust, the back pressure existing at the point of compression will be extended to the end of the stroke. For example, in the diagram Fig. 93, the back pressure in the return stroke during the period of exhaust, is 2 lbs. up to the point of compression. The area of resistance, called compression, has therefore a constant fraction of 2 lbs. introduced as an initial pressure, chargeable directly to the imperfection of the exhaust, and represented by a prolongation of the 2 lbs. exhaust line to the end of the return stroke.

In no part of the engine is the advantage of time for the performance of the evolutions of steam more apparent than in the cylinder during the period of exhaust. Recurring to Fig. 95, in which the diagrams in heavy and light lining were described at speeds of 2½ and 20 miles per hour, it is proved that the steam does not discharge itself instantaneously at the point of release, as the piston has in both cases visibly to go some distance before the pressure falls to a minimum. In the first case, the movement of the piston from the release line to the point at which the exhaust pressure becomes nothing, amounts to 3¼ inches, which at this locality is equivalent to an angular motion of the crank through about 23°; at the given speed, the crank makes one revolution or 360° in 5 seconds, and it therefore describes 23° in about 3-10ths of a second, which is the time occupied by the steam in fully discharging itself. In the second example, the steam only reaches a minimum of 2 lbs. pressure when the piston has attained the end of the stroke through 5 inches of exhaust, or when the crank has described an angle of 63° in one-ninth of a second. The times, though small, are of course perfectly appreciable, and the comparatively full exhaust line exhibited at the higher speed with the 2 lbs. of back pressure entailed in consequence, is a good elementary proof of the benefit of time for securing a perfect exhaust.

Of the General Law of Exhaustion.—In the course of our remarks on the motion of steam (chapter I.) it appeared that the velocity of steam flowing or escaping into the atmosphere was, to a considerable extent, dependent upon its pressure, being less as the pressure falls. Thus the disengagement of exhaust steam, extremely rapid at first, becomes more gradual as the exhaustion continues, and the differences of pressure for equal intervals of time, become regularly less. It is plain, also, that the final pressure of the exhausting steam at the end of a given interval of time, should be very much in the ratio of the pressure of the steam at the instant of release, because a greater density accompanies a greater pressure, and the work to be done is proportionally increased.

The question for the solution of which we are really

interested in applying the laws of the free motion of steam, is to find whether, within the highest speeds of piston which exist in practice, dry steam could clear itself out of the cylinder with celerity sufficient, were there no obstruction from bends or friction, to render the back pressure practically null. The maximum mean speed of piston in any case may be stated at 1000 feet per minute, and the minimum ratio of the sectional area of the blast orifice, to the area of the piston, at $\frac{1}{10}$. As the blast orifice is, or ought to be, the narrowest part of the passage from the cylinder, the maximum speed of the steam through the passage required to fly before the piston without back resistance, is 20,000 feet per minute. Steam of 1 lb., we find from the table of Velocities of Efflux, flows freely into the atmosphere at a speed of 482 feet per second, or about 30,000 feet per minute. Thus 1 lb. steam would freely move one-half faster than could in practice ever be required; and steam of higher pressure would move with still greater celerity. But we find in practice, that at speeds very much inferior, and with blast orifices very much wider, important back pressures do occur, evenly sustained throughout the whole of the return stroke. We may therefore justly infer that all back pressure of exhaust is due to the circumstantial hindrance of mixed water, strictures, crooks, and superficial friction.

The efficiency of time for the absolute reduction of exhaust pressure, decreases, we have said, for each successive interval, and thus it is that the course of the exhaust line, at slow speeds, becomes more nearly parallel to that of the horizontal line, as it approaches the end of the steam stroke. If the speed of the piston be increased, the exhaustion of the steam is thrown forward upon the end of the stroke, the exhaust line descends almost vertically where the motion of the piston is between something and nothing; and at the highest speeds of the engine, precipitate though the descent may be, the fall of the exhaust line to its permanent level runs in some cases into the return stroke.

But, even while the speed of the piston may remain unchanged, the time for exhaust may be affected singly by the position of the point of release: the later the release, the shorter is the time devoted to it at the same speed, and the more completely is the exhaust line thrown forward on the end of the stroke, in a manner similar to that which results from increased speed singly. The retardation of the exhaust experienced in these ways, is the direct cause of the back pressure of diagrams. During the steam-stroke, while yet the piston moves before the steam, the release, or at least the fall of the steam line, is assisted by the recession of the piston, which enlarges the volume of the cylinder, and eases off the pressure till the end of the stroke. At this point, however, the piston reciprocates: it turns upon the exhaust steam, and drives it before it into the atmosphere, should the remaining elasticity of the steam prove insufficient for the purpose. Under these circumstances, it is apparent that, to secure a perfect exhaust line, or according to M'Naught's idea, a "pure" exhaust, the steam must be conclusively cleared out by the commencement of the return stroke. The resistance on the piston due to the business of pumping out the back steam, should vary as the square of the speed of the engine, or of the piston, according to the received law of fluid motion, which expresses that the

frictional resistance of a passage to the motion of steam, is as the square of the velocity through the passage. Again, the frictional resistance to the motion of gaseous fluids through passages, varies with the density or pressure simply; as, in general, and in the case of steam in particular, these vary very much in the same ratio. It is accordingly found in practice that an increase of pressure has much less influence in raising the back pressure than a similar increase of speed

The back pressure may be considered either in relation to the mean positive pressure throughout the steam stroke, or to the special pressure of the steam at the point of suppression or that of release. These three elements have no doubt a close dependence on each other, and a reference of the back pressure to either one of these should yield tolerably consistent results. At high speeds, it is true, wire-drawing of the steam during admission occasionally exists, the consequence of which is to exaggerate the mean pressure due to the actual quantity of steam admitted; and in outside cylinders, on the other hand, the quantities of steam admitted are on account of condensation, inadequately represented by the mean pressures. To establish a ratio of back pressure, therefore, it is preferable to select for comparison the final pressures at the release points, which are preferable even to the pressures at the suppression, as those alone afford a true measure of the discharge to be accomplished. The back resistance of exhaust follows in many instances a somewhat fluctuating line; the mean exhaust shall therefore in all cases be adopted for our purpose, exclusive of the triangular space above the level of the exhaust line, already dedicated to compression.

Of the Ratio of Steam Pressure to Back Pressure.—And, first, a preliminary series of double observations made with low and high pressures consecutively, on No. 73, C. R., already alluded to, shows that back pressure varies virtually with the sensible pressure of the steam admitted. In this case, the steam is cut off at $12\frac{1}{4}$ out of 18 inches of stroke, and as the exhaust lines on the diagrams were particularly indefinite, the pressures at the point of suppression are tabulated.

TABLE No. XXX.—C. R. No. 73.—BACK PRESSURE.

No. of Observation.	Speed.	Steam Pressure	Mean exhaust pressure.	Ratio of Exhaust to steam pressure.	
	mph	lbs.	lbs.		
1	17	18	3	1 to 6	1 to 4
		28	7	...	
2	29	12	5·5	1 to 2·2	1 to 2·4
		22	9	...	
3	32	16	6	1 to 2·6	1 to 2·6
		32	12	...	
4	34	29	10	1 to 2·9	1 to 2·6
		36	14	...	
5	39	23	9	1 to 2·5	1 to 2·5
		35	14	...	
			Mean Ratios.	1 to 3·2	1 to 2·8

These ratios intimate that the proportion of the back pressure of exhaust slightly rises with the steam pressures at the slower speeds, and becomes constant at the higher speeds. Examples selected from the performance of other cylinders prove the same law of the back pressure. Thus, the following couples were described consecutively, while the circumstances were the same.

C. R. No. 33......	{ 33½ mph.	28 lbs. at release,	10 lbs. Exht.,	1 to 2·8 ratio.
	{ 36 mph.	19 lbs. do.	6·5 lbs. do.	1 to 2·9 „
C. R. No. 125,	{ 8 lbs.	do.	3·5 lbs. do.	1 to 2·3 „
29 mph........	{ 28 lbs.	do.	12·0 lbs. do.	1 to 2·3 „
Do.	{ 10 lbs.	do.	3·5 lbs. do.	1 to 2·9 „
28 mph........	{ 30 lbs.	do.	10 lbs. do.	1 to 3 „
E. & G. R. Nile,	{ 38 lbs.	do,	5 lbs. do.	1 to 7·6 „
41 mph........	{ 53 lbs.	do.	7 lbs. do.	1 to 7·6 „
Do.	{ 39 lbs.	do.	5 lbs. do.	1 to 7·8 „
42 mph........	{ 52 lbs.	do.	7 lbs. do.	1 to 7·4 „

These instances are sufficient to prove that the back pressure follows generally the simple ratio of the sensible steam pressure; each couplet of observations was made at the same time, and therefore under circumstances virtually identical.

Of the Variation of Back Exhaust Pressure with Speed.— The same condition of identity of circumstances being carried out, enables us to confirm the presumed law of the variation of the back pressure in the ratio of the square of the speed. During an express trip with the Nile, alluded to in the foregoing chapter, diagrams were taken at every mile-post, in starting from stations and at full speed, and the speeds were noted. Forty of these diagrams, of which examples have already been given in the third chapter, have been selected and arranged according to the speeds; and in cases where the speeds did not differ above 2 miles per hour, or 3 miles at the higher speeds, upon several diagrams, these have been classed together at the mean speed, and the means of the steam and back pressures of exhaust adopted for comparison. The steam pressures at the point of suppression have been in the first place selected, as they were better defined on the diagrams. The speeds, pressures, and back pressures, so classified form the first three columns of the following table :—

TABLE No. XXXI—OF THE BACK PRESSURES OF EXHAUST, IN RELATION TO SPEED, IN THE NILE, E. & G. R.

STROKE, 18 INCHES; SUPPRESSION, 12·3 INCHES; RELEASE, 16·25 INCHES; DURING 97 PER CENT. OF STROKE.

Speed of Engine.	Observed Pressures.		Exhaust Back Pressure.	
	At Suppression.	Of Exhaust.	Reduced for a common pressure of 40 lbs at Suppression.	Measured from mean curve.
mph.	lbs.	lbs.	lbs	lbs.
16	33	0	0	0·9
20	25	1·0	1·6	1·5
24	26	1·5	2·3	2·1
28	38	3·0	3·2	2·4
34	39	4·1	4·2	4·2
36	35	4·25	4·9	4·7
39	45	6·2	5·5	5·5
41	43	6·0	5·6	6·0
44	52	9·0	7·0	7·0

The fourth column contains the values of the back pressures in the third column, reduced for common steam pressures of 40 lbs. The reduction has been made on the principle, now established, that the exhaust pressure varies directly as the steam pressure ; thus, for a speed of 44 miles per hour, and 52 lbs. observed pressure, the back pressure is 9 lbs.; and reducing this in the ratio of 52 to 40, we have $\frac{40}{52} \times 9 = 7$ lbs., as the back pressure of exhaust due to 40 lbs. steam pressure. The reduction of the observed

exhausts for a common pressure is necessary, that we may separate the distinct influence of speed, and 40 lbs. has been selected, as it lies within the range of the observed pressures.

To represent the exhaust pressures graphically, let A B, Fig. 134, be assumed as a base-line on which the speeds are to be laid down: proceeding from left to right, set off divisions at equal intervals, to represent speeds of 10, 20, 30, &c.

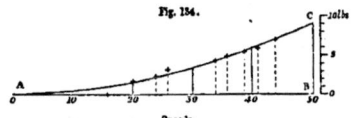

Fig. 134.

E. and G. R. Nile—Curve showing relation of back exhaust pressure to speed.

miles per hour, measured from the extreme left, and subdivide these divisions into intervals of 1 mile per hour, a process which is omitted in the figure, for simplicity. From the point in the base-line representing each speed in the foregoing table, draw a vertical ordinate, measuring by its length, according to any convenient scale, the tabulated back pressure for 40 lbs. of suppression, due to the speed. Having raised these verticals, and defined their extremities by stars, the curve A C, traced and taking a mean path through the constellation so formed, will represent by its ordinates the average back pressure due to any speed measured on the base line, for 40 lbs. steam suppressed. When there is no speed, there can be no back pressure; the apex of the curve is therefore started from the point A, which indicates no pressure; and the curve assumes a parabolic form, evolving the important principle that the back pressure of exhaust varies as the square of the speed. The pressures lie very closely about the curve, and this gives us additional confidence in its verity. The extreme ordinate BC measures, by the scale, 9 lbs. of back pressure at 50 miles per hour. At 25 miles, or one half speed, the back pressure falls to one fourth, or 2·25 lbs.

But this curve has been constructed for a pressure at the point of suppression. To convert this into the pressure at the release, we find from the distribution, that the ratio of the initial to the final volume including clearance, is ·77 to 1, and by the expansion-table, No. 28, the final pressures amount to but 86 per cent. of those due by Boyle's law. We have, therefore, $·77 \times \frac{100}{100} = ·66$ for the actual ratio of the initial and final pressures. Then, $40 \times ·66 = 26·4$ lbs. is the pressure at the release for the curve of back pressure above found. It is desirable, however, to re-construct the curve for a release-pressure of 40 lbs.; and its ordinates must for that purpose be multiplied by $\frac{100}{66}$, and the following are the back pressures due to the notified speeds :—

NILE—BACK PRESSURES.

Speeds in Miles per hour	Back Pressure for 40 lbs. at suppression.	Back Pressure for 40 lbs. final.
0	0 lbs.	0·lbs.
10	0·30	0·55
20	1·44	2·18
30	3·24	4·91
40	5·75	8·71
50	9·00	13·64
60	13·00	19·70

As the general disposition of locomotive engines is much of one kind, it is probable that the law of back pressure

TABLE No. XXXII.—OF FINAL AND EXHAUST BACK PRESSURES OF STEAM IN THE CYLINDER OF THE GREAT BRITAIN. 1847-50.
STROKE, 24 INCHES.

Notch	No. of Diagram	Speed	Nett Pressures during Exhaust.		Back Pressures reduced for a common final pressure for each Notch.
			Final, at po.nt of Re'ease.	Mean Back Pressure.	
		mph.	lbs.	lbs.	lbs.
FIRST SERIES.	1	11	50	0·08	for 45 lbs final. 0·07
	2	16·5	47	1·0	0·96
First Notch.	3	20	37	0·08	0·1
	4	30	62	6·9	5·0
	5	35	39	2·9	3·4
	6	42	36·5	9·0	12·2
Release 21½ ins.	7	52·3	43	15·6	16·3
	8	53·6	45	19·7	19·7
	9	55	44	18·1	18·5
		Mean final pressure 45 lbs.			
	10	11	43	0·0	for 40 lbs. final. 0·0
	11	16·5	40	0·8	0·8
	12	20	32	0·0	0·0
Third Notch.	13	30	50	4·8	3·8
	14	35	34	2·6	3·06
	15	40	42	9·6	9·14
Release 20 ins.	16	52·3	37·5	11·4	12·2
	17	57	56	18·8	13·4
	18	63	25·5	8·0	12·5
		Mean final pressure 40 lbs.			
	19	11	33	0·0	for 30 lbs. final. 0·0
Fifth Notch.	20	20	31	0·0	0·0
	21	30	39	3·5	2·7
	22	35	28	1·0	1·1
Release 17½ ins.	23	39	18	1·0	1·7
	24	56·2	26	8·7	10·0
		Mean final pressure 30 lbs.			
	25	15	48	2·2	for 50 lbs. final. 2·3
SECOND SERIES.	26	17	63	0·6	0·5
	27	21	62	1·3	1·05
First Notch.	28	24	54	1·0	0·93
	29	27	47·5	1·9	2·0
	30	31	52	2·2	2·1
Release 21½ ins.	31	31	54	3·3	3·05
	32	49	32·5	4·6	7·1
	33	54	57	8·7	7·63
		Mean final pressure 50 lbs.			
	34	17	46	0·0	for 40 lbs. final. 0·0
	35	18	34	1·3	1·5
	36	21	46	0·0	0·0
Third Notch.	37	26	36	0·0	0·0
	38	31	35	1·6	1·8
	39	32	35	1·3	1·5
Release 19½ ins.	40	40	31	0·7	0·9
	41	51	27	3·1	4·0
	42	55	34	5·2	6·1
		Mean final pressure 40 lbs.			
	43	17	32	0	for 20 lbs. final. 0
	44	18	23	1·1	0·95
	45	21	32·5	0	0
Fifth Notch.	46	28	20	1·1	1·1
	47	31	21	0	0
	48	36	15·5	0	0
Release 17½ ins.	49	50	14·5	1·0	1·4
	50	56	15·5	0	0
		Mean final pressure 20 lbs.			

now determined for the Nile is the same for other inside cylinders. To compare the results from the Great Britain, supplied in the diagrams, (diagram-plate IV.) the necessary data are arranged in the table No. 32, first five columns.

As the indicated final pressures vary considerably, the observed back pressures are reduced for one common final pressure, for each notch, in the ratio of the pressures simply, as already done for the Nile, to develope the influence of speed alone. The mean final pressure under each notch is selected, as that for which the back pressures are reduced. These pressures are represented graphically in the Fig. 135,

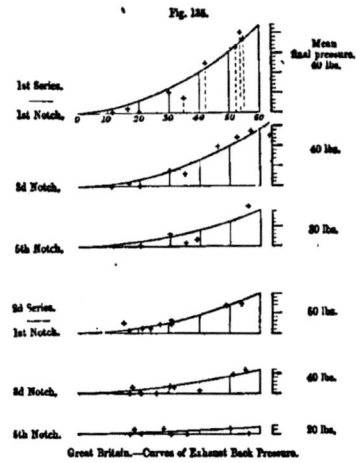

Great Britain.—Curves of Exhaust Back Pressure.

for the six different cases contained in the table, and reduced to curves of mean value, constructed upon ordinates varying as the square of the speed. Some of the pressures lie rather widely, yet the curves are good averages. In the last curve, the pressures are merely nominal, practically nothing; we have assumed for it a resistance of 1½ lbs, for 20 lbs. final, at 60 miles per hour.

Lastly, a third example from the Hebe, E. and G. R., in the 4th notch, 11½ inches suppression, 17 inches release, stroke 20 inches. The following table contains the results from two different trips; in the 4th column are the reduced back pressures for 30 lbs. at release.

TABLE, No. XXXIII.—HEBE, E. & G. R. BACK PRESSURE. RELEASE 15 PER CENT.

Speed of Engine.	Observed Pressures.		Exhaust Back Pressure.	
	At Release.	Of Exhaust.	Reduced for 30 lbs common pressure at release.	Measured from mean curve.
mph.	lbs.	lbs.	lbs.	lbs.
19	33	1·0	0·91	1·7
20	38	2·5	2·00	1·88
22	28	3·5	3·75	2·27
29	27	1·5	1·67	3·94
30	18	2·5	4·10	4·23
32	20	3·0	4·50	4·80
34	21	4·0	5·71	5·42
36	19	4·0	6·30	6·07
40	16	4·0	7·50	7·50
44	16	4·0	7·50	9·07

The annexed Fig. 136, contains the curve founded on the contents of the fourth column, and formed according to the law of the squares of the speeds. At 40 miles per hour, it

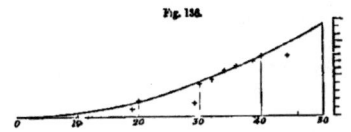

Fig. 136.

E and G R. Hobs.—4th notch.—Exhaust back pressure for 15 per cent. release, and 30 lbs. final.

exhibits a back pressure of 7·5 lbs. for 30 lbs. final. The correspondence of the back pressures with the proposed law is satisfactory.

The three cylinders in which we have now been considering the variation of back pressure, are all of them inside, and heated in the smoke-box. In this case, the steam may be reckoned to be under favourable conditions of dryness; and it may be considered as an established law that, in inside cylinders generally, where the steam is well protected, and under the ordinary conditions of the boiler, as to steam-room and cleanliness, the back pressure of exhaust varies directly as the pressure of the steam at the point of release, and directly as the square of the speed. The speed may be reckoned either in miles per hour on the rail, or in feet per minute of the piston in the cylinder.

Outside cylinders in general exhibit the operation of the same law of back pressure. The annexed curves are illus-

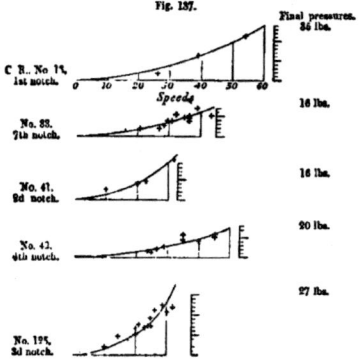

Fig. 137.

Final pressures. 36 lbs.

C R. No 19, 1st notch. Speed

No. 33. 7th notch. 16 lbs.

No. 41. 3d notch. 16 lbs.

No. 42. 4th notch. 20 lbs.

No. 19, 3d notch. 27 lbs.

trations in point, constructed according to that law. It is unnecessary at present to particularize; but No. 13, must be noted as affording a remarkably direct proof of the influence of speed. The three diagrams, Figs. 108, 109, 110, chap. 3, already selected for another purpose, were taken in succession from No. 13 under the first notch, and in exactly the same circumstances, during an express trip, at speeds successively of 26, 39, and 54 miles per hour, and yielding the results shown in the following table.

The general coincidence of the values in the last two columns, emphatically confirms the law of the square of the speeds as one measure of back pressure, in outside cylinders under ordinary circumstances.

TABLE, NO. XXXIV.—C. R. No. 13. BACK PRESSURE. PERIOD OF RELEASE 13·5 PER CENT.

Speed of Engine.	Observed Pressures.		Exhaust Back Pressures.	
	At Release.	Of Exhaust.	For 35 lbs final.	Measured from curve.
mph.	lbs.	lbs.	lbs	lbs
26	35	1·75	1·75	2·5
39	35	6·00	6·00	5·7
54	32	10 00	10·94	11·0

Exceptions to the Law of Back Pressure of Exhaust.—Influence of Water in the Cylinder.—Under special circumstances, exceptions to this law are to be found, as in the cases of C. R. No. 73, No. 124, and No. 127. During the three days, in April 1850, on which No. 73 was submitted to experiment, the engine was under the following conditions:

First day.—State of valves: Suppression 14⁷⁄₁₆ inches, release 16¾ ins., lap 1 inch, lead ₁⁄₁₆ in., travel 4 ins. Cylinder inside, 13 in. × 18 in. stroke. Blast-orifice 3¼ in. diameter. Boiler foul, water muddy.

Second day.—Valves altered: Suppression 12¹¹⁄₁₆ inch, release 15¼ inch, lead ₇⁄₁₆ in. Blast-orifice 3¾ inch diameter. Boiler foul, as on previous day.

Third day.—Valves and blast-orifice as on second day. Boiler run off, fresh water supplied.

The dark-line diagram, Fig. 138, is one of a number taken from the cylinder during the first day, the beginning of the steam-stroke being towards the right hand. Though liberally supplied with lead, the steam was incapable of reaching its maximum pressure, 24 lbs., till about one-third of the stroke was described. This proves a case of extreme priming, and accordingly at 41 miles per hour a back-pressure of 11 lbs. is the result, or nearly one-half of the acting pressure. Again, at 15 miles per hour, a speed at which most ordinary engines, with the same size of wheel, can manage to clear off the back pressure,—this engine is afflicted with 13 lbs. of back resistance, for only 30 lbs. of acting pressure, as shown by the light-line diagram. Thus, at the widely different speeds of 15 and 41 miles, the percentage of back pressure is virtually the same; and even at a starting speed of 5 miles, the dot-line diagram' proves a back resistance of 5 to 10 lbs.

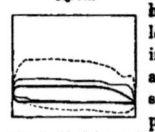

Fig. 138.

C. R. No. 73.—Influence of Water in the Cylinder on Back Pressure.

That this engine was, at the time of the experiment, subjected to heavy priming, is proved by a careful estimate of the consumption of water as steam. This was founded upon the pressures indicated at regular intervals throughout the trip from Greenock to Glasgow, and the priming of water was proved to amount to 31 per cent. of the water which passed through the cylinder as steam. The inference, then, is that the existence of bodies of water in the cylinder of No. 73, brings up the back pressure rapidly at first as the speeds rise; but that above 15 miles per hour, the ratio increases slowly—much more slowly than the speed, though in all cases greater than what is due to a clean boiler and pure water. This last conclusion is confirmed by the diagrams from No. 73 already given, fig. 127, showing that the back pressure fell to one-half by changing the water in the boiler; and it must be added that, agreeably with this fall of

M

pressure, the priming on that occasion, estimated as before, fell in about the same ratio to 13 per cent. of the weight of steam.

Referring to the table, page 86, of back pressures for No. 73, the contents of which are derived from the third day's performance, with comparatively clean, though still impure water, and with 13 per cent. of priming, we find that the back pressure varies directly as the speed simply, as well as directly as the acting pressure. Such is no doubt the influence of water in the cylinder, in aggravating to a greater degree the back pressures for the lower speeds, for the addition of the same extra resistance makes a greater apparent difference on a smaller pressure. A special example of the effects of priming in the cylinder of the Great Britain, was quoted in the first chapter, fig. 128, containing a direct proof of the consequent rise of back pressure—in that case from 15 to 24 lbs.—and it is within the experience of Mr. Gooch that in similar cases the exhaust line has been raised to a level with the steam line! when of course the back pressure amounted to 100 per cent. of the positive pressure.

In the diagrams from the Orion, fig. 125, a supply of clean in place of muddy water, reduced the back pressure from 9lbs. to 1¼ lbs., or practically nothing.

Our next illustration shall be drawn from the performance of C. R. No. 124, goods-engine, under the first notch, exhausting at 23 inches, during 4·2 per cent. of the stroke. The annexed curve is the result of 32 diagrams reduced in the usual manner for 30 lbs. final pressure. The curve is peculiarly flat, indeed nearly straight, and is symptomatic of a considerable amount of priming or condensation, probably both—indicating a more serious proportional obstruction to the exhausting of the steam at lower than at higher speeds.

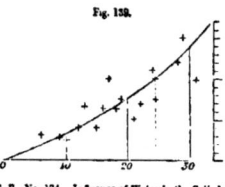

Fig. 139.

C. R. No. 124.—Influence of Water in the Cylinder on curve of Exhaust Pressure.

In the course of some experiments on the resistance of trains, with No. 127, C. R., a goods-locomotive, of the class of No. 125, the incidental back pressure of exhaust was strikingly contrasted for low and high pressures, and for extreme expansive working. During a preliminary run of 20 miles alone, under the fifth notch, or mid gear, cutting off at 4 inches, and exhausting at 14½ inches of the stroke, the diagrams in heavy and light lining, Fig. 140, were taken at 17 and 29 miles per hour respectively, and after 9 miles of the trip had been performed, when consequently the cylinder had got into its regular working condition for that

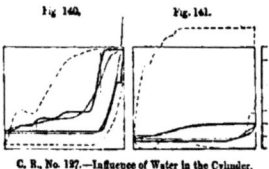

Fig. 140.   Fig. 141.

C. R. No. 127.—Influence of Water in the Cylinder.

notch. With final pressures of 24 and 21 lbs., the back pressures amounted to 14 and 12 lbs., about two-thirds, without any distinction being made for speed. This formidable resistance, due to a case in which the steam was cut off at one-sixth, and expansion carried to nearly three times the admission, including clearance, is a conspicuous

proof of the influence of condensation in the cylinder in aggravating back pressure,—a condensation which in the second case, with 56 lbs. pressure at suppression, amounts to at least 53 per cent. of the weight of steam suppressed. When the engine was attached to its load, the back pressure to a great extent disappeared under larger admissions and therefore smaller degrees of condensation, as exemplified in the dot-line diagram, fig. 140, at 23 miles per hour, taken after doubling a summit, when the cylinder had been previously well heated by hard work. Again, when the locomotive with its tender ascended Beattock incline alone, and at speeds of 15 and 23 miles, the heavy and light line diagrams, fig. 141, were the result, in which, while the pressures of admission were in both cases, 20 lbs., the exhausts were 6 and 8 lbs. But when, on the same incline, the engine with its load, ascended at 13 miles per hour, in full gear, suppressing at 16⅝ inches, and with 95 lbs. steam during admission, the back pressure as shown in the dot-line diagram was nothing at all. There is, to be sure, the impression of a gust of steam from the neighbouring cylinder. This resistance is, however, an extra, due to the peculiar formation of the blast-pipe, and is not recognizable as regular back pressure. That there is at least abundant scope for condensation, in the disposal of the water consumed from the tender, is evidenced by the relative consumptions of water as steam. In the second case, on the Beattock incline, the engine and tender alone, suppressing at 12 inches, with an average of 18¼ lbs. steam during admission, consumed on a 10 mile run 18·83 cubic feet of water indicated as steam; the measured consumption from the tender amounted to 23 feet, showing a condensation equal to 18 per cent. of the steam used. Further, when the locomotive ascended the incline with the train attached, it was found that 127 feet of water passed through the cylinders as steam, measuring the pressures from the admission-line, and that 170 feet was the total consumption, or 17 feet per mile; the difference, 43 feet, indicates a condensation and priming together equal to 25·3 per cent. of the steam. But these quantities, which will be fully discussed in treating of the boiler, are quoted now only to follow up the argument for the reality and importance of condensation in exposed outside cylinders, and to show how productive is water in the cylinder of back pressure.

In inside cylinders, partially heated, extra back pressure due to condensation, is occasionally apparent immediately after starting a train from a terminus. Thus, on the Edinburgh and Glasgow Railway, during the ascent of the Cowlairs incline, starting immediately from Glasgow, the locomotives, assisted by the stationary engine at the summit, and working under an easy pressure, usually exhibit an extra proportion of back pressure which is only removed after a run of some miles with full steam on. With the Brindley, on this railway, of which the cylinders, though inside, are, to be sure, but imperfectly protected, 7 to 10 pounds of back pressure commonly exists for the first one or two miles' run, and the resistance ultimately falls to about 2 lbs. regular.

Having directed attention to the circumstances by which mainly exhaust pressure is regulated, in certain cylinders, it is expedient now to classify the results from these and other cylinders. The table, No. 35, contains, in the fifth and sixth columns, the mean release and exhaust pressures actually observed, at the speeds named in the third and fourth columns, for the given engine and notch,—the means being deduced by the method of the curve, in the way already described. These pressures, then, are in no way hypothetical: they are, in connection with the speeds, the expressions of actual average results. It is, however, desirable to reduce the exhaust pressures for a common mean speed of piston, and one common pressure at release, as on these conditions alone, can the exhausting abilities of different cylinders be compared. The seventh column contains the back pressures so reduced for a common speed of piston of 600 feet per minute, and a common release-pressure of 30 lbs., which are about the means of the observed quantities. The reduction has been made generally according to the general law of back pressure already established, except in the cases of C. R. Nos. 73, 124, and 127, in which we have found that the variation proceeded as the speed and release-pressure simply. The reduced pressures in the seventh column, though calculated, are all very safely derived, for most of them indeed fall within the scope of actual observation, and the others but a trifle beyond.

TABLE, NO. XXXV.—OF EXHAUST BACK PRESSURES.

Name of Engine.	No of Notch.	Mean Observed Results, averaged by the method of the curve.				Back pressure of Exhaust, reduced from the foregoing data, for a common speed of piston of 600 feet per minute, and a common pressure at release of 30 lbs.	Speed of Engine.
		Speed of Engine.	Speed of Piston.	Steam pressure at Release.	Steam pressure of Exhaust.	Back pressure of Exhaust.	
INSIDE CYLINDERS	No.	mph.	fpm.	lbs.	lbs.	lbs.	mph.
Great Britain, 1st Series.	1	60	840	45	22	7 5	43
Do.	3	60	840	40	14	5 36	43
Do.	5	60	840	30	9	4 85	43
Great Britain, 2d Series.	1	60	840	50	10	3 06	43
Do.	3	60	840	40	6	2 3	43
Do.	5	60	840	20	1 5	1 15	43
E. and G. R. Nile......	gab.	50	700	26 5	9	7 5	43
E. and G. R. Orion....	5	40	620	21	5 5	7 06	39
Do.	6	40	620	20	2 75	3 86	39
E. and G. R. Hebe...	4	40	680	30	7 5	5 84	35
C. R. No. 73, 3d day...	gab.	40	608	30	8	8	40
Do. 2d day...	,,	40	608	30	13	13	40
Do. 1st day...	,,	40	608	30	16	16	40
OUTSIDE CYLINDERS.	No.	mph.	fpm.	lbs.	lbs.	lbs.	mph.
C. R. No. 13............	1	50	775	35	9 5	4 88	39
C. R. No. 14............	1	30	465	40	7	8 74	39
C. R. No. 33............	4	40	620	22	11	14 05	39
Do.	5	40	620	27	9	9 89	39
Do.	7	40	620	16	6	10 53	39
C. R. No. 41............	1	30	465	24	14	29 14	39
Do.	2	30	465	16	9	28 1	39
C. R. No. 42............	3	40	620	30	5 3	4 96	39
Do.	4	50	775	20	7 75	6 97	39
Do.	5	40	620	30	4	3 75	39
C.R. No. 51 (New valve)	1	20	310	30	2	7 49	39
Do.	3	40	620	30	3 5	3 28	39
Do.	4	40	620	30	2 5	2 34	39
C. R. No. 124............	1	24 5	600	30	10	10	24 5
C. R. No. 125............	2	20	490	30	7	10 5	24 5
Do.	3	30	735	27	13	9 63	24 5
Do.	4	30	735	14	7	10	24 5
C. R. No. 127............	5 or mid.	24 5	600	20	10 6	16	24 5

The back pressures of exhaust due to one speed of piston and one final pressure, having thus been worked out, they are now on one footing with respect to two of the most influential causes of their existence. We have yet to find how they are modified by the period of release, by the cross sectional areas of the steam-ports and blast-orifices, and by inside lead and travel of valve; and to promote this inquiry, the table, No. 37, page 92, has been prepared, containing the data necessary for following out the comparison, and it is the foundation of the following discussions. The first part of the table contains lineal values; the second, areas and their ratios; and the last two columns, the percentages of the periods of release, in terms of the whole stroke, and the back pressures of exhaust due to one speed of piston and one final pressure, transferred from the foregoing table.

Influence of the Period of Release on Back Pressure.—In all the inside cylinders, the greater the period of release, the less is the exhaust back-pressure. This is best exemplified in the Great Britain, and may be further elucidated thus.

TABLE, NO. XXXVI.—GREAT BRITAIN. EXHAUST PRESSURES.

Notch.	Exhaust Pressure at 600 ft of Piston per minute, for 30 lbs. final pressure.	Relative times of release, during the steam stroke, measured by angle to be described by crank.	Periods of release, in percentages of stroke.
	lbs.	degrees.	per centage.
1ST SERIES.			
1st Notch......	7 5	35°	10 4
3d do.	5 4	45	17 0
5th do.	4 8	60	28 0
2D SERIES.			
1st Notch......	3 1	33°	9 4
3d do.	2 3	46	17 7
5th do.	1 15	59	27 5

The third column contains the angles remaining to be described by the crank during the release in the steam-stroke, which, as the crank revolves uniformly, express the relative times for release before the end of the stroke. We thus distinguish the *times* and the *periods* of release. The back pressures appear generally to be inversely as the times of exhaust during the steam-stroke. Thus, comparing the 1st and 5th notches of the first series, while the times are as 7 to 12, the pressures are inversely as 7 to 11; and for the 1st and 3d notches of the second series, while the times are as 3 to 4·2, the pressures are inversely as 3 to 4. The fifth notch, to be sure, shows a smaller pressure than the time would indicate; the evidence of the diagrams, however, was not very decided as to the usual amount of that pressure. The periods of release, in lineal inches of stroke, become obviously of less value as they increase, in reducing the back pressure, because the times of release, by the nature of crank-motion, increase much less rapidly than the lineal values of the release. On this ground it is that an early exhaust,—early, as measured in inches of the stroke,—is practically a very harmless thing as a dissipator of steam-pressure. We say *practically*, because the earlier suppression, which is accompanied by the earlier release, in the use of the link-motion, is employed only at high speeds, when of course the steam is much the better of a few extra inches of the stroke to help it out of the way. We find it so in the diagrams of the Great Britain. At the higher speeds, and even at the lower, we do not observe that the 5th notch discharges the steam unnecessarily early. Indeed, at the higher speeds of the first series it appears to have been rather late. The

TABLE, NO. XXXVII.—OF EXHAUST BACK PRESSURES REDUCED TO ONE STANDARD OF COMPARISON, WITH THE PERCENTAGES OF RELEASE, AND OTHER DATA. 1850.

Name of Engine.	No. of Notch.	Dimensions relative to Exhaust Back Pressure.						Transverse Sectional Areas.							Pressure sum of the Periods of Release, &c.	Exhaust Back Pressures.	
		Of Valve.				Release.		Actual Values.				Relative values, that of Piston being = 1.						
		Lap.	Lead.	Travel.	Inside Lead.	Position.	Period.	Piston.	Steam Port.	Waste Orifice.	Inside Lead.	Steam Port.	Waste Orifice.	Inside Lead.	Release.	Value in Pounds.	Percentages of Real Back Pressure.
INSIDE CYLINDERS.	No.	ins.	ins.	ins.	ins.	ins.	ins.	sq. ins.	sq. ins.	sq. ins.	sq. ins.				percent-ages.	lbs.	percent-ages.
Great Britain, 1st Series.....	1	1	⅜	4½	1 7/16	21½	2¼	255	26	15·9	18·7				10·4	7·4	25
Do. do.	3	"	"	5¼	"	20	5	"	"	"	"				17·0	6·4	18
Do. do.	5	"	"	5½	"	17½	6¼	"	"	"	"				29·0	4·6	14
Great Britain, 2d Series.....	1	1¼	⅜	4½	1 7/16	21½	2¼	255	26	25·76	20·3				9·4	3·1	10
Do. do.	3	"	"	5 11/16	"	19½	4½	"	"	"	"				17·7	2·3	8
Do. do.	5	"	"	5 7/16	"	17½	6½	"	"	"	"				27·5	1·15	4
E. & G. R. Nile...........	gab.	1 ½ inside	1/16	5½	1 7/16	16½	1½	201	14½	16	13·4				9·7	7·5	26
Do. Orion.........	6	1	⅜	3	1½	18	2	176·7	18	14·6	11·25				10·0	7·4	25
Do. Do........	8	"	"	2½	"	17	3	"	"	"	"				15·0	3·9	13
Do. Hebe........	4	½	⅜	—	⅜	17	3	176·7	15	11·8	7·1				16·0	5·8	19
C. R. No. 73, 1st day..........	gab.	1	1/16	4	1 7/16	16½	1½	132·7	8·9	9·09	11·4				7·9	16·0	53
Do. 2d day..........	"	"	1/16	"	1 7/16	16	2	"	"	11	12·75				11·0	13·0	43
Do. 3d day..........	"	"	"	"	"	"	"	"	"	"	"				11·0	8·0	27
							Means, exclusive of C. R. No. 73.								16	4·9	16·5
OUTSIDE CYLINDERS.	ins.	ins.	ins.	ins.	ins.	ins.	sq. ins.	sq. ins.	sq. ins.	sq. ins.				percent-ages.	lbs.	percent-ages.
C. R. No. 13..................	1	1½	1/16	4 1/16	1 7/16	17·30	2·70	176·7	19·0	13·16	15·6				15·5	4·9	16
C. R. No. 14..................	1	1 7/16	inns 1/16	3½	1 7/16	19·25	0·75	176·7	19·0	10·48	12·0				4·0	8·75	29
C. R. No. 33..................	4	1¼	0	5⅛	1⅜	17·65	2·35	176·7	19·6	13·37	13·5				11·7	14·1	47
Do.	5	"	0	5 7/16	1¼	17·20	2·80	"	"	"	13·5				14·0	9·3	33
Do.	7	"	1/16	3½	1 7/16	13·00	6·00	"	"	"	13·1				22·0	10·5	35
C. R. No. 41..................	1	1½	⅜	4½	1½	18·50	1·50	176·7	12·5	12·7	15·0				7·5	29·1	97
Do.	3	"	⅜	4	1½	17·40	2·50	"	"	"	15·0				12·5	29·1	94
C. R. No. 43..................	3	1¼	1/16	5⅝ 1/16	1 7/16	17·25	2·75	176·7	12·5	12·47	15·6				14·0	5·0	17
Do.	4	"	⅜	5 7/16	1¾	16·00	6·00	"	"	"	16·25				20·0	7·0	23
Do.	5	"	1/16	3½	1 11/16	14·00	6·00	"	"	"	16·65				30·0	3·75	12
C. R. No. 51 (New Valve).	3	1⅜	⅜	5½	1⅜	17·75	2·25	176·7	13·6	13·77	16·75				11·0	7·5	25
Do.	4	"	1/16	4⅛	1 11/16	16·60	3·40	"	"	"	20·0				17·0	3·3	11
Do.	5	"	1/16	4 1/16 1/16	1 11/16	14·40	5·60	"	"	"	20·6				23·0	2·3	8
C. R. No. 124..................	1	1¾	¼	4½	1½ 1/16	23·00	1·00	227	15·0	10·6	17·0				4·2	11·0	40
C. R. No. 125..................	2	1¼	1/16	4 1/16	1½ 1/16	22·15	1·85	227	15·0	11·0	17·0				7·7	10·5	35
Do.	3	"	"	3½	"	21·30	2·70	"	"	"	"				11·2	9·4	33
Do.	4	"	"	3½	"	20·40	3·60	"	"	"	"				15·0	10·0	33
C. R. No. 127..................	6 or mid.	1¼	⅜	3	1¼	14·50	9·50	227	15·0	14·5	18·0				32·6	16·0	53
							Means, exclusive of C. R. No. 41.								16·6	8·6	28
1	2	3	4	5	6	7	8	9	10	11	12	13	14	15	16	17	18

great object should not be to cram in the power upon the steam-line, so much as to remove the resistance upon the exhaust-line, inasmuch as this resistance, if it operate at all, endures throughout the entire return-stroke. Hence the greatest doctrinal objection to Hawthorn's double-valve expansive gear; indeed, to most of the variable expansive gears with double valves: by means of the principal valve, which is worked by a fixed gab-motion, and is intrusted exclusively with the duty of releasing the steam, the release takes place at one invariable point of the stroke, for all expansions and of course for all speeds, and therefore a percentage of release that may suffice for the lower speeds, becomes injuriously small for the higher, as in the latter cases the unquestionable advantage of a thorough exhaust is bartered for an obscure trifle of extra expansion.

Still more decidedly does the folly appear of deferring the point of release in all cases to the latest inch of the stroke, on examining the results from the outside cylinders. With No. 33, between the fourth and fifth notches, the back pressure certainly falls one-third, but for the seventh notch, notwithstanding its high percentage of release, the resistance rises. In No. 42, the fourth notch has shown more resistance than the third, and the fifth is but a trifle lower than

the third. In No. 51, the disadvantage of exposure is met by the advantage of a spacious inside lead, and the highest notch shows least resistance. On the other hand, if we take the results from Nos. 124, 125, and 127, as one series from one class of engine, embracing the performances of all the notches from full to mid gear, the back pressure slightly falls towards the third notch, and rises towards mid gear, for which the resistance is indeed the greatest of all,—even with ten times the percentage of release that belongs to the first notch.

Influence of Inside Lead on Back Pressure.—As inside lead is equal to the sum of the lap and the outside lead, affected of course by inside lap or clearance, it is in all cases considerable; and in the inside cylinders before us, it does not appear to have had any appreciable influence on the exhaust, as may appear from the following re-statement of the results from the Great Britain, the Orion, and the Hebe.

TABLE, No. XXXVIII.—INSIDE LEAD AND BACK PRESSURE, IN INSIDE CYLINDERS

Great Britain (first series).	1 7/16	lead,	17	release,	5·4 lbs.	back pressure.
Orion,	1 7/16	"	15	"	3·9	"
Hebe,	1 7/16	"	15	"	5·8	"

With little more than half the inside lead, the Hebe exhausts as freely as the Great Britain, though it has less release and a smaller port ; with the same release, however, the Hebe has a greater exhaust than the Orion, but this is well explained by the much smaller blast-orifice of the former.

In the outside cylinders, on the contrary, inside lead is very influential in reducing back pressure, as the following classification will show: the engines being of one general plan, and the ports and blast-orifices nearly identical.

TABLE, No. XXXIX.—INSIDE LEAD AND BACK PRESSURE, IN
OUTSIDE CYLINDERS.

No. 33,	......................$\frac{7}{16}$ lead,	11·7 release,	14·1 lbs. back pressure.
No. 51,	......................$\frac{5}{16}$,,	11·0 ,,	7·5 lbs. ,,
No. 33,	..............$\frac{7}{16}$,,	14 0 ,,	9·9 lbs. ,,
No. 13,	..............$\frac{7}{16}$,,	13 5 ,,	4·9 lbs. ,,
No. 42,	..............$\frac{7}{16}$,,	14·0 ,,	5·0 lbs. ,,
No. 33,	...........$\frac{1}{2}$,,	25 0 .,	10 5 lbs. ,,
No. 42, mean of 4th and 5th notches,	$\frac{7}{16}$,,	25·0 ,	5·375 lbs. ,,
No. 51, mean of 3d and 4th notches,	$\frac{5}{16}$,,	25 0 ,,	2 7 lbs. ,,

In these cases, the superiority of No. 51, with the most liberal inside lead, is conspicuous. No. 33, with the smallest lead, is obviously the worst. This engine, when the valve-gearing was in new order, was set to have the same lead as No. 42; but as the gearing had worn, the inside lead was reduced, and the back pressure was accordingly increased. There is, therefore, a decided distinction between outside and inside cylinders, in respect of the necessity for inside lead; and this is further exemplified by the following contrasts :—

TABLE, No. XL.—INSIDE LEAD AND BACK PRESSURE, OUTSIDE
AND INSIDE CYLINDERS CONTRASTED.

No. 42 (outside)	.......$\frac{7}{16}$ lead,	14·0 release,	5·0 lbs. back pressure.
Hebe (inside)	..........$\frac{5}{16}$,,	15·0 ,,	5·8 lbs. ,,
No. 51 (outside)	.....$\frac{5}{16}$,,	11·0 ,,	7 5 lbs. ,,
Orion, (inside)	$\frac{3}{16}$,,	10 0 ,,	7 4 lbs. ,,
Nile,	$\frac{3}{16}$,,	9·7 ,,	7·5 lbs. ,,
No. 51 (outside)	......$\frac{5}{16}$,,	28 0 ,,	2·3 lbs. ,,
Great Britain (inside)	......$\frac{1}{4}$,,	27·5 ,,	1·15 lbs. ,,

In the first case, the smaller blast-orifice of the Hebe accounts for the excess of back pressure, while the lead is not half that of No. 42. In the second and third cases, the inside cylinders exhaust as well as the outside, though they have not two-thirds of the lead. In the third case, indeed, the inside cylinder is much superior to the outside, showing only half the back pressure, though to be sure its blast-orifice is slightly greater. These comparisons prove the propriety of an adjustment of inside lead to the necessities of an engine, by providing a sufficiency of outside lap; and they furnish an explanation of the various practice of locomotive engineers in the use of lap and travel. For we have seen that $\frac{1}{8}$ inch lap in Sharp's inside-cylinder engines exhausts as well as the 1¼ and 1½ inch of lap, which Mr. Sinclair has found necessary in his outside-cylinder engines on the Caledonian Railway. Thus it is that we may reconcile the practices of the leading makers, apparently contradictory, and yet necessary for the attainment of the great object, a free exhaust.

Influence of the Blast-Orifice on Back Pressure.—A wide blast-orifice is the ultimatum of all real improvement in the locomotive; whatever tends to economize steam, relieves the functions of the blast-pipe, and permits, therefore, of a wider orifice; and the wider the orifice, the lower, as we shall see, is the back pressure. In so far as back exhaust pressure is dependent on the facility with which the steam may pass through the orifice, which is in all ordinary cases the narrowest part of the exhaust-passage, it is clear that the greater the area of orifice, the more easily the steam escapes, and the less is the back pressure. The effort of pumping the steam through the orifice, as measured in back pressure, ought to be that due to creating a speed of exit inversely as the area; but the pressure so required varies as the square of the speed, therefore, finally, this part of the back pressure should vary inversely as the square of area of orifice, or, lastly, inversely as the square of the square, or the fourth power of the diameter of orifice.

The most direct method of testing the influence of the orifice, is to operate upon the same engine with an orifice capable of being varied in area. This we have not done. There is much in the table, however, worthy of notice; and, first, of the Great Britain. During the two series of observations, the areas of the orifice were relatively as 2 and 3, for the first and the second series, other circumstances being materially the same. For these cases, the back pressures and their ratios were as follow:—

	FIRST SERIES. (Orifice, $\frac{7}{16}$th.)	SECOND SERIES. (Orifice, $\frac{11}{16}$th.)	
1st notch,	7·5 lbs.	3·1 lbs.	ratio, 2·42 to 1
3rd do.,	5·4 lbs.	2·3 lbs.	do., 2·35 to 1
5th do.,	4·8 lbs.	1·15 lbs.	do., 4·17 to 1

As the back pressure for the fifth notch of the second series has been remarked as rather an uncertain quantity, and as so small a difference as even 1 lb. would materially affect the ratio, our attention will be confined to the ratios from the first and third notches. These ratios are nearly the same, and the mean of the two is 2·38 to 1. Now the areas of orifice are as 2 to 3 nearly, and their squares inversely are as 9 to 4, or as 2·25 to 1, which is nearly the ratio of the back pressures. Again, the diameters of orifice are 4½ and 5¼ inches, and their fourth powers are 410 and 915, which inversely are as 2·23 to 1; which is synonymous with the ratio of the squares of the orifices, and is nearly that of the back pressures. These ratios it will be observed err in defect, as the back pressures vary in a still higher ratio; we are therefore safe in concluding that, in the Great Britain, the back pressure varies inversely as the square of the area of blast-orifice; in other words, inversely as the fourth power of the diameter.

With No. 73, O. R., it is not so. The areas on the first and second days are 8 and 11 inches, or inversely as 1·37 to 1; the pressures are 16 and 13 lbs., or as 1·23 to 1. Thus, the pressures hardly even vary so rapidly as the areas inversely. These remarks are made on the performance of two days while the boiler was in the same condition; and they show that the back pressure of water-laden steam varies simply as the area of blast-orifice inversely, just as it varies in the peculiar ratio of the speed simply. Nor must it be overlooked that on the second day an extra percentage of release was granted.

The data yielded by the outside cylinders are insufficient for any general conclusion. We may only remark that No. 14 and No. 124, with equal percentages of release, exhibit back pressures which are simply in the inverse ratio of the areas of orifices; and we know that in each engine the back pressure varied as the velocity simply.

Influence of Area of Steam-port on Back Pressure.—This point is not very clearly illustrated in the table. But there is no doubt that the port should be at least as wide as the blast-orifice. Even in the cylinder, we have seen that the area of blast-orifice makes itself known, on the back of the piston; so also must that of the steam-port, should it be inferior to the orifice. In short, the smallest sectional area of the passage for exhaust steam, largely determines the back pressure. So long, therefore, as the steam-port exceeds the orifice, the useful limit of area of port appears to be obtained with respect to back pressure. For example, the Great Britain, in the 3d notch of the 1st series, and the Hebe, with nearly equal orifices, and percentages of release, show nearly equal back pressures, though the latter has a much smaller port, and much less inside lead than the former; and it is only when the blast-orifice of the Great Britain is enlarged, and approximated to the size of port, that the back pressure falls. From this it should follow inversely that little advantage by way of removing back pressure—in cylinders in good order—would accrue from an orifice wider than the steam-port. In some of the examples before us, the orifice slightly exceeds the port; but there is no doubt that the full advantage of the unrivalled blast-orifice of the Great Britain, second series, would not have been developed but for the equally spacious ports with which the engine has been constructed.

Influence of General Magnitude of parts on Back Pressure.—So far as the contents of the table would indicate, the movements of the steam are independent of the mere size of the cylinder. Some experiments with the England, E. and G. R., an engine of very small dimensions, support this conclusion. The areas and proportions of the engine, derived from Table XXIII, are as follow:—

Piston,   63·6 square inches area = 1
Steam-port, 5·25   do.   do.   = $\frac{1}{12}$th of piston.
Blast-orifice, 5·94 do.   do.   = $\frac{1}{10}$th do.
Inside lead, 4·8   do.   do.   = $\frac{1}{13}$th do.
    4th Notch, suppression 7·8 inches out of 12 inches stroke.
    Release, 10·5 ins.
    Period of release, 1·5 ins. = 12·5 per cent. of stroke.

With an express train, on the 15th July, 1851, diagrams were obtained from the cylinder, of which the annexed, fig. 142, is a favourable example, in ordinary working order, with the following particulars:—

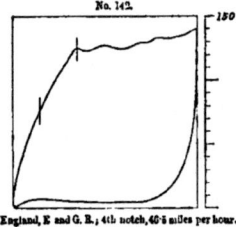

No. 142.

England, E and G. R.; 4th notch, 46·5 miles per hour.

Maximum pressure,   140 lbs.
Pressure at suppression 125 lbs.
Do. at release   75 lbs.
Do. of back exhaust   6 lbs.
  = 8 per cent. of release-pressure
Speed 46·5 miles per hour, or 579 feet of piston per minute.

To raise the percentage of back pressure for 600 feet of piston per minute, in the ratio of the square of the speed, we have $8 \times 600^2 \div 579^2 = 8·6$ per cent., with 12·5 per cent. of release. With a cylinder entirely clear of the smoke-box, though well clad, and with an orifice of the same relative area as that of the Great Britain, second series, though the port and inside lead are rather less, we find the England exhausting as perfectly as this engine, allowing for the difference of release; thus,—

England, 65 p.c. admis. $\frac{1}{10}$, orifice, 12·5 release, 8·6 p.c. back press.
Gt. Brit., 66·0   „ $\frac{1}{10}$ „   0·4   „   10   „   „

From this it appears that a small engine, of the same proportions as a large one, discharges the steam as freely, and yields as perfect an exhaust.

Influence of Water in the Cylinder on Back Pressure.—This subject has already been generally treated. The table, however, shows us that, whereas in inside cylinders, the back pressure falls as the release increases; in outside cylinders, generally, the reverse to some extent takes place. This is most conspicuously illustrated by Nos. 124, 125, and 127; and in general is to be ascribed to the presence of water of condensation in the cylinder, the amount of which, as we have already found, increases with the release and the degree of expansion simultaneously. It is remarkable that towards full gear, the Great Britain, in the first series, should appear so slightly superior to these engines, with all their condensation,—a superiority which is referrible simply to the wider orifice. It is possible that in the former, the great heat of the cylinder tends to raise the back pressure, while in the latter the inferior temperature may condense even the exhaust steam. However this may be, it is clear that the Great Britain, with a longer release, gains by a large difference on the others, for with 27·5 and 39·6 percentages respectively, the former is affected by a nominal resistance of 1·15 lbs., while the latter is burdened with 16 lbs., or fifteen times that amount. Even the passenger-class of outside cylinders contrast favourably with the goods-engines, for they in most cases show a fall of back pressure as the release increases. The heavy resistance of No. 41, in the first and second notches, were incurred under peculiar circumstances, during a course of experiments, already alluded to, conducted within the engine-shed at Greenock, over a pair of ground-wheels, fitted with a brake. The engine was maintained in motion, at intervals, during only five to ten minutes at one time; thus, with frequent intervals of rest, the cylinders never had acquired their ordinary working temperature, and hence increased condensation and its consequence, increased back pressure. Comparing No. 41 with No. 13, we find that with equal releases of 12·5 and 13·5 per cent., and equal inside leads, while the exhaust pressure of the former is 94 per cent. that of the latter is but 16 per cent. of the release pressure, or about one-sixth of the other. The very great difference in favour of No. 13, is due entirely to the circumstance of this engine having been well heated during a hard and constant run, when the diagrams were taken; whereas No. 41 was worked only for short periods.

The diagram, fig. 97, from the Pallas, E. and G.R., affords incidentally a proof of the action of water on the back pressure. In that case, the indicator had been connected to the cylinder by a ⅜ inch copper tube about 2 feet long, quite bare and exposed to the current. The consequence was that condensation in the tube interrupted the movements of the steam, and a back pressure on the indicator-piston was occasioned, which had virtually no existence in the cylinder; and, accordingly, in the Orion, which has the same proportions of engine, the indicated back pressure, more truly registered, was practically nothing.

General Conclusions.—Of the three elements under discussion,—port, orifice, and lead, it is clear that, in protected cylinders, the proportion of orifice is that which mainly regulates the back exhaust pressure, so long as the port is greater than the orifice, as it ought in all cases to be; inside lead, within practical limits, appears not to affect the exhaust, and therefore the amount of outside lead, or of outside lap, which mainly constitutes inside lead, makes no difference on the amount of the exhaust pressure. In partially protected cylinders, on the contrary, the back pressure is regulated by the blast-orifice and the inside lead jointly, and the influence of the latter in reducing it, is apparent, even though much wider than the orifice. Hence the great advantage of long lap and long travel for exposed cylinders,—a peculiar advantage which Mr. Sinclair was the first to appreciate and follow up;—which makes it practicable to exhaust a half enclosed cylinder as perfectly as a cylinder enclosed and heated, and to provide for a free exhaust against the wear of the valve-gear.

The common practice of giving greater lead to the valves of quick passenger engines, with the object of improving the exhaust, though it answers this purpose, is not to be recommended. It operates, no doubt, in reducing the exhaust precisely like an equal addition of lap,—by adding as much to the inside lead; but it also occasions an injuriously early pre-admission of steam, as we have found in discussing the action of steam in the cylinder during admission. The more elegant and direct, and certainly the more comprehensive remedy for insufficient exhaustion, is the extension of the lap and the travel, or even lap singly, which has been found so beneficial in the engines of the Caledonian railway.

The mean results, contained in the table, of the performance of inside and outside cylinders, exclusive of the exceptional cases of Nos. 41 and 73, C. R., are simply the arithmetical means of the contents of the columns. As the mean ratio of the orifice is in both cases less than that of the port, the latter may, for purposes of comparison, be left out of consideration. To simplify the matter further, the mean of the ratios of blast-orifice and inside lead may be adopted, to represent the mean facility for the escape of steam; and the following abstract is the result.

Here we observe that the joint mean ratios and the average periods of release, are about the same; and as the latter are due to admissions of about 50 per cent. of the stroke, which are very commonly practised, the average drawback by back exhaust-pressure at the ordinary speed of 600 feet of piston per minute, or about 40 miles an hour, is for the

Cylinder.	Joint mean ratios of blast orifice and inside lead.	Mean period of release in percentage of stroke.	Mean Back-pressure in percentage of final pressure—speed of piston, 600 feet per minute.
Inside..........	₁⁰₁	16	16·3
Outside........	₁⁷₈	16·6	28

inside cylinders 16·3 per cent. of the final steam pressure; and, for the outside cylinders, 28 per cent. Lastly, taking the ratio of these percentages, we conclude that the relative loss by back pressure, for equal final pressures, and at a speed of 600 feet of piston, is as 1 in the inside or well protected cylinder, to 1·72 in the outside or partially protected.

These general results are of course founded on the average working condition of the engines. Great variations may take place in practice, independent altogether of the state of the valves, or the position of the cylinder, and arising directly from the state of the water in the boiler. In the Orion, E. and G. R., we have seen that by blowing off foul water, and introducing fresh clean water, the back pressure was practically banished, even at 30 and 40 miles per hour, in the 5th and 6th notches, suppressing at 57 and 50 per cent. of the stroke. The tabulated percentages of back pressure, therefore, awarded to the Orion and other engines, must be viewed, not as the lowest attainable averages, but rather as the averages due under ordinary management. And these considerations prove the advantage of a more frequent cleansing of the boiler, and change of water, where the latter is affected with impurities.

Again, the adoption of a release-pressure of 30 lbs., for all grades of expansion, must be viewed as a matter of expediency, to simplify the comparison. By this assumption of equal release-pressures, the shorter admissions contrast unfavourably with the longer, in respect of their contingent back pressure, for equal release-pressures imply very unequal pressures during admission; the shorter the admission, the greater must be the initial pressure of steam to yield the same final pressure, in virtue of the greater expansion to which it is subjected; whereas, practically, the pressure in the boiler is the same for all the notches, and the pressure in the cylinder during admission may likewise be made practically the same. This is the true footing on which actual cases are to be compared; and for equal admission-pressures, the shortest admissions, with the longest expansions, yield the lowest release-pressures, and by as much as these are proportionally lower, the tabulated pressures ought also to be reduced, to show what are the actual conditions for comparison. For example, the averages of the second series of diagrams from the Great Britain, show, according to the table, page 81, nearly equal admission-pressures of 79 to 74 lbs., while the final and release-pressures are so various as 55, 38, and 26 lbs. successively for the 1st, 3d, and 5th notches, the last of which, for the largest expansion, is only *one-half* of the first.

The disadvantage here pointed out, is removed in the last column of the table of exhaust-pressures, page 92, as there the back pressures are expressed in percentages of the pressures at release.

Formulas for back pressure may readily be deduced from these data. They would, however, be of little use singly. To this subject we shall return in treating of the work of steam.

Influence of the Form of the Exhaust Passage on Back Pressure.—Nothing is better established than the propriety of equalizing, smoothing, and regularly forming the channels in which fluids are conveyed. Strictures, or alternations of wide and narrow cross sections ought to be prevented; so also should variations of the form of section, though these are much less under control. Smoothness of the interior surface also is desirable, as roughness or excrescence gives rise to eddies. But above all, the general direction of the channel should be attended to. Continuity should be studied—freedom from avoidable angles or bends. We are not at present in a position to separate the effects of these influences as they operate in the blast-pipe; but this we do know, that their combined effect is to create much of the back pressure that we have been discussing, seeing that, under even very unfavourable proportions, the orifice of the blast-pipe is of itself wide enough to give vent to all the steam, when perfectly dry, that can be supplied to it, without any unfavourable demand on its elastic force.

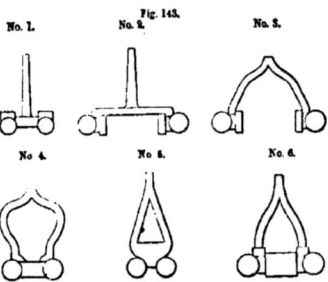

Fig. 143.

No. 1.   No. 2.   No. 3.

No. 4.   No. 5.   No. 6.

Influence of Form of Blast-pipe on Back Pressure.

And, first, of our little friend on the Greenock Railway, C. R. No. 73. According to the arrangement of the exhaust passage, No. 1, in the annexed figure, the steam exhausts from both cylinders into a cubical chamber, from which it finds its way up the blast-pipe,—a single tube springing directly from the chamber. The objection in this case is, that the two exhaust passages from the cylinders are directly opposed, and are not above 18 inches clear of each other. During the motion of the engine, therefore, these ports keep up a continuous cross fire, discharging the steam from one into the other, instead of being conducted directly into the chimney, to the detriment of the exhaust in the cylinder, and the draught in the smoke-box. We have already seen enough of the exhaust to settle that point. The supposed advantage of this intermediate reservoir of exhaust steam is that it equalizes the blast,—a modification which was expected to improve the draft in the smoke-box. This we shall afterwards consider; but it is plain that it could operate only by obstructing the steam, and that to whatever extent the steam is so detained, the pistons must work against an atmosphere artificially increased by the detention.

The expedient of the intermediate reservoir was tried on an English railway, several years ago, but without success, the previous arrangement having been resumed.

No. 2 exhibits the exhaust passage originally adopted for the passenger-engines on the Glasgow and South-Western Railway. Here, the vital error, already noticed in No. 1, has been repeated in a more obvious form, for the exhaust steam is at once projected from the one into the neighbouring cylinder, through the horizontal passage; and if it gains admission at all, it must increase the back pressure there, before it flows out by the blast-pipe. This objection appears ultimately to have been suspected, from the difficulty of "getting steam;" for, more lately, the rectangular bend at the base of the blast-pipe has been replaced by a double curved breech-pipe, in some of the engines, and with marked advantage, as now they run with their orifices half an inch wider than before. It may be added that these engines are found to work best with an allowance of inside clearance to the valves, which are made with $1\frac{1}{16}$ inch of lap, $\frac{1}{4}$ inch lead, and 4 inches travel. It has already been mentioned that the cylinders are outside, and entirely exposed, and that they precipitate much of the steam as water; it is therefore with great propriety that the clearance is provided, as it increases by so much the inside lead, which we have already found to be so beneficial in aiding the escape of steam partially disabled by condensation. The advantage derived from the clearance in this case has been erroneously ascribed to the saving of a portion of steam by exhaustion from one end of the cylinder to the other, while the two ends are open to the inside of the valves, as a small contribution for the succeeding stroke. But steam introduced thus prematurely raises back pressure in proportion to its amount, and though it may do a little more work before leaving the cylinder, it barely pays the expense of retaining it.

The standard form of blast-pipe, No. 3, for the engines of the Grand Junction and Caledonian Railways, and similar to the one applied to the Snake on the South-Western Railway, is not entirely free from the defects of the others just noticed. The branches meet rather abruptly just below the orifice, and the consequence is that under heavy pressures the initial violence of the exhaust from one cylinder is distinctly experienced in the other. The dot-line diagram from No. 127. C. R. fig. 141, is an example in proof of this, as the exhaust line exhibits a sudden exaltation and gradual decline for which there is no other reason. Similar impressions are traceable in the diagrams from C. R. Nos. 14 and 102, figured in previous chapters, and in many others. They become less distinct as the speed rises, and though the general effect may remain, the peculiarity vanishes at high speeds. Partitions have been in some cases inserted at abrupt junctions like that in No. 3, and with good results.

The very common form, No. 4, adopted in the engines of Fairbairn and other makers, is superior to No. 3, in the finish of its orifice. But No. 5, by Bury, Curtis, and Kennedy, and No. 6, by Mr. Gooch, adopted in the Great Britain, and other Great Western engines, are, for purposes of free release, the best of the forms now detailed.

The exhaust-pipes which must be provided for outside cylinders removed from the smoke-box towards the middle of the boiler, labour under the considerable disadvantages of great length, exposure, and numerous bends. The length and the twisted course of these pipes, together with the condensation of exhaust steam within them by exposure, are aggravations of the causes of resistance which nothing but sheer necessity should enforce. Stephenson's long-boiler locomotive, already figured in a previous page, and Crampton's locomotive fall under this objection, and it is no doubt one reason why the blast-orifice of the former is so injuriously small.

The transverse sectional area of the exhaust pipe ought certainly to be at all points, short of the orifice, as wide as that of the exhaust port, to induce a uniform velocity of the exit of the steam. The exhaust port has not hitherto been noticed, because it is invariably made wider than the steam port; its sectional dimensions are, therefore of little moment, especially as the passage is short from the port to the blast pipe. Beyond the port, the dimensions should be liberal, as the steam should exhaust with as moderate a velocity as convenient.

RECAPITULATION.—1. It is found that dry steam of any pressure above 1 lb. per square inch might, by its own free motion, exhaust itself from a cylinder at a speed much greater than is ever in practice required, so as to render the back pressure practically null. The back exhaust pressures actually experienced are due chiefly to the presence of mixed water in the steam, and to the strictures, bends, and lateral friction of the exhaust passages.

2. In inside and outside cylinders generally, and under ordinary circumstances, the back exhaust pressure varies directly as the pressure of the steam at the point of release, and directly as the square of the speed.

Note.—The distinction here made as between *inside* and *outside* cylinders, refers to the incidental conditions of *well-protected* and *partially protected*, which usually characterize these situations of the cylinder; and it is not to be accepted as implying any essential disadvantage of the outsides, as these may be as well protected as the insides.

3. In cylinders, inside or outside, which are subjected to priming water from the boilers, or in which the steam is condensed by an inferior temperature (which occurs in outside cylinders), the back exhaust pressure is to a very large extent greater than is due to the exhaustion of the steam in a dry state; and it varies directly or approximately as the speed simply and the positive pressure simply, the proportion of excess due to the presence of water being greater for the lower speeds.

4. In inside cylinders, the greater the period of release, the less is the exhaust back pressure due to a given final pressure of release, and measuring the *time* of release by the angle of the crank at the release-point of the stroke, the back pressure varies inversely as the time of release.

5. An early exhaust,—early, as measured by the period of release,—is comparatively harmless as a dissipator of steam-pressure, because the times of exhaust increase much less rapidly than the periods of exhaust.

6. In outside cylinders, as the periods of release increase, —involving greater degrees of expansion, and greater condensation,—the back exhaust pressure due to a given release-pressure, does not fall so rapidly as in inside cylinders; and in many cases, it rises with the periods of release.

Though this is true, the conclusion hardly meets the actual circumstances of engines, as in fact the same maximum pressure in the cylinder should be contemplated for all grades of expansion; the release-pressure is, then, in all cases considerably less for the higher grades, and there is usually in practice a decided fall of back pressure as expansion is increased.

7. In inside cylinders, within practical limits, the amount of inside lead does not appear to have any appreciable influence on the value of back pressure. In outside cylinders, on the contrary, inside lead is very influential in reducing back pressure, and to increase the inside lead, clearance on the inside of the valves appears beneficial for the better exhaust of the steam.

8. In inside cylinders, the back pressure varies inversely as the square of the area of blast-orifice; or inversely as the fourth power of the diameter. It is probable that this ratio is applicable also to outside cylinders in good order; though in cases of priming or extra condensation, the variation appears to take place more nearly as the area of orifice simply,—this lower ratio resulting from the aggravation of the pressures at the lower speeds, by the presence of water, and their smaller comparative rise for the higher speeds.

9. The sectional area of the steam-port should, in all cases, be at least as great as that of the blast-orifice.

10. The mean facility for the exhaust of steam in well protected cylinders, is regulated entirely by the area of blast-orifice, so long as the port is larger. In partially protected cylinders, the mean facility is regulated by the orifice and the inside lead jointly; and may be represented by the mean of their two values, or by their mean ratio to the area of piston.

11. With a mean of 16 per cent. of release, due to an admission of half stroke, and at a speed of 600 feet of piston per minute, or about 40 miles per hour for ordinary passenger-engines, and 20 to 30 miles for goods-engines, the mean back pressure of exhaust in the engines subjected to observation, is 16·3 per cent. of the final pressure, for inside protected cylinders, and 28 per cent. for outside cylinders partially protected. The ratio of these percentages is 1 to 1·72. Expressed in percents of the mean pressure during the steam-stroke, they would be still less than we have now stated; but of this we shall judge in treating of the work of steam.

12. With the same proportions for exhausting, the magnitude of the engine makes no difference on the quality of the exhaust.

13. With pure water in the boiler, and an orifice $\frac{1}{117}$th of the cylinder, with the other proportions equally favourable, the greatest exhaust back-pressure, at speeds of 600 feet of piston per minute, or 40 to 50 miles per hour on the rail, is within 10 per cent. of the release-pressure, for admissions of about 66 per cent., or two thirds of the stroke. As the admission is shortened, back pressure falls, until for 30 percent. admission it becomes nothing.

14. As the inside lead varies with the state of the valve-gear, being reduced by as much as the slugger of the valve increases, it is necessary, in order to maintain the best exhaust in exposed cylinders, that the gearing be maintained in the highest order; in well-protected cylinders, this is of secondary importance, as the exhaust is very much independent of inside lead.

N

15. The form of the blast-pipe materially affects the exhaust pressure. Strictures, and rectangular bends increase it. Length and exposure also increase it,—the latter by condensing the exhaust steam. An abrupt junction of the two branches from the cylinder increases it, by facilitating the entrance of back steam from one cylinder to the other. Shortness, continuity of form, a liberal and uniform cross section, and few and gradual changes of direction, constitute the good points of a well-made blast pipe.

CHAPTER VI.

Of the Behaviour of Steam in the Cylinder during Compression.

The resistance of compression, as represented on the diagram, was found to be measured by the triangular area described by the pencil towards the end of the return stroke, subject to a deduction charged to exhaust pressure, represented by an extension of the exhaust-line parallel to the atmospheric. The compression-line is to the exhaust, conversely what the expansion-line is to the admission; and as compression is simply the converse of expansion, it is regulated by the same law. If the cylinder be maintained at a high and sensibly uniform temperature, the compression of a given quantity of locked-up steam, would indicate a total pressure varying inversely as the volume by compression; and, in general, as the piston approaches the end of the return stroke, the compression-line rises and joins the admission for the next steam-stroke.

A curve of compression is produced equally whether steam or air be the resisting element. Thus, when the steam is off, and the piston works in the ordinary atmosphere of the cylinder, the diagram, fig. 144, taken under such circumstances, shows that, during the return stroke, when the

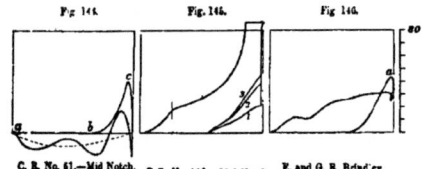

Fig. 144.   Fig. 145.   Fig 146.

C. R. No. 61.—Mid Notch.   C. R. No. 125.—Mid Notch.   E. and G. R. Brind'cy.
87 mph.   Steam off.   26 mph.
Illustrations of Compression in the Cylinder.

curve $a\,b\,c$ is described, the air in the cylinder is exhausted in advance of the piston, till the point b is reached; here the valve closes the exhaust, and the enclosed air rises in pressure, raising the pencil till the steam-port is opened for "admission" at c. Instead of the usual saltation, a descent of the pencil takes place, because the compressed air in the cylinder, now placed in communication with the valve-chest and the steam-pipes, hastens to relieve the partial vacuum in these localities created by the recession of the piston in the cylinder. The undulating curve of negative pressure, from c towards a, is thus described during the "steam" stroke; and, taking the dot-line for the mean path, it is clear that a vacuum is created behind the piston, and that the atmospheric line is not reached till after the exhaust opens to the blast-pipe, when equili-

brium is restored. In passing, it may be observed that this simply explains the peculiar trumpet-like sound emitted by the blast-pipe of an engine in good order when running without steam, obviously caused by the circulation of air due to the action of the piston; it also explains the clatter of valves supported by springs, that may be heard under the same circumstances, as the force of the compressed air moves them off the valve-face at the end of every stroke.

The rate of the variation of pressure by compression, is, as in the case of expansion, affected by the temperature of the cylinder. As the temperature is then, after a period of exhaustion, at a minimum, partial condensation ensues, particularly in outside cylinders, as the pressure and temperature of steam rise together. This is very observable in some of the slow diagrams already figured, where we find in the same diagram, successive compression-lines of different elevation, indicating different degrees of condensation. The diagram fig. 145, from C. R. No. 125, furnishes a striking illustration in point. Taken at a slow speed, the compression lines, 1, 2, 3, were described successively during three revolutions of the wheel, showing regularly less condensation, though all of them very far below what would have been due to a constant high temperature of cylinder. The diagrams, fig. 106, from the Orion, show a quicker ascent of the compression-line at the higher speeds, of 30 and 40 miles, than at 18 miles per hour. In the same way, in the Nile, fig. 107, and in the Brindley, figs. 99 and 100, the line rises much less at the lowest speed than at the higher speeds. In these cases, the more rapid ascent of the line of compression at the higher speeds, is doubtless the result of a hotter cylinder, by which less steam is condensed.

As compression is independent of the steam-pressure during admission, it occasionally happens, as in fig. 146, that the compression raises the pressure above the level of the steam-line. The culminating point a is obviously reached at the time of admission, when the pressure, thus artificially raised, is restored to an equilibrium by the communication opened with the steam-chest, and the pencil falls to the steam-line.

Compression is regulated in amount by the total pressure of the exhaust steam at the point of closing the exhaust, as it is only the steam so locked up that experiences compression. It is also, like expansion, in general independent of speed, except as this affects the amount of back pressure of exhaust. The variation of compression, however, as it depends on the total exhaust pressure, is of course much less than that of the indicated exhaust. For example, with 3 lbs. and 6 lbs. of exhaust pressure, the one twice the other, the compression operates upon steams of the total pressures, 18 lbs. and 21 lbs., the second of which is only one-sixth more than the first. It follows then that in general the resistance of compression is nearly the same for all speeds, though it rather increases as the speed rises; and for this increase it is indebted mainly to increase of back exhaust pressure; and partially also to the better preservation of the steam in cylinders to some extent hotter. An inspection of the diagrams from the Great Britain, will explain the near uniformity here observed.

Finally, the indicated compression depends much on the total clearance in the cylinder and steam-port. With smaller clearance, the compression-line rises more rapidly, as the volume by compression is more quickly reduced by the reaction of the piston.

The period of pre-admission has been, in the foregoing remarks, classed with that of compression, because it is comparatively short; and, besides, the action of compression lodges a body of high-pressure steam in the ports, which, in well-ordered engines, with small clearance, goes far to supersede the pre-admission and render it a practical nullity, particularly in cases of greater expansion, when the compression commences earlier. The action of steam on its entry into the cylinder at the beginning of the stroke, has already been considered in the third chapter preceding, in which the function of pre-admission is identified with that of lead. A further consideration of the use of pre-admission is therefore superfluous.

CHAPTER VII.
BLAST-PRESSURE.

MANY erroneous impressions prevail on the subject of the pressure in the blast-pipe, its causes and consequences. Mr. Parkes, about 1836, concluded from a few limited experiments on a stationary engine, that the blast-pressure varied simply with the pressure in the cylinder, and was independent of velocity. M. Pambour, in 1836, concluded from observations of the pressure existing at the base of the blast-pipe, that this pressure varied directly as the speed of the piston, directly as the total vaporisation per hour, and inversely as the area of the blast-orifice. This conclusion was more rational than that of Mr. Parkes, though based on experiments of very limited range; and besides, the assumption by Pambour that the pressures so indicated were exclusively and entirely the measures of the back pressures on the piston, was incorrect, insomuch as, in the first place, some proportion at least of blast-pressure is due to the initial pressure of the exhaust steam, released during the steam-stroke, and secondly, it could be no gauge of the back pressure on the piston, as even were it due solely to the back pressure it did not include the resistance to the motion of the steam through the passages. MM. Gouin and Lechatelier were the first to point out, in their Experimental Researches on Locomotives (1847), the distinction that is to be made between the back pressure on the piston, as expressed by the indicator, and the pressure in the blast-pipe. Mr. Bourne, in his Catechism, 1848, has apparently fallen into the opposite error, of supposing the back pressure on the piston due entirely to blast-pipe resistance, when he states, that at high speeds, half the engine-power is dissipated upon the blast-pipe. This is an exaggerated allowance, even as back pressure, and it is probable that he had seen only the general table of moving and resisting pressures contained in the French work above noted. Mr. Bourne is not, however, alone in this mode of estimating blast-pressure, as we find Mr. Sewell, at a later period, in his paper on train-resistance (Tredgold, 1850), while constructing his formula for the resistance of the blast-pipe, assumes the total back pressure on the piston as blast-pipe resistance, slumping together exhaust pressure, properly so called, and

compression-resistance; of which the latter has clearly nothing to do with the blast-pipe. With such misapprehensions of the circumstances of the blast-pipe, from which irrelevant reflections have been made on the costliness of that important functionary as a promoter of combustion, it is only necessary to gauge the pressure directly at the blast-orifice, to show that much of the resistance in the cylinder is referrible to the contracted dimensions of the steam-ways, the friction of the steam on the surfaces of these passages, and the resistance offered by water and condensed steam.

Fig. 147.—1-12th.

Blast-Pressure Gauge.

The instrument employed by the author for this purpose, was an ordinary mercurial gauge, A, fig. 147, secured to the side of the smoke-box. It consisted of a glass syphon, $\frac{1}{6}$ inch bore, open at both ends and fitted with a stop-cock and a $\frac{1}{4}$ inch brass tube led through the side of the chimney and dipping one inch into the blast-orifice, as at a. The orifice of the tube was bevelled off on the outside to a knife-edge, as at fig. 148, to receive the pressure as fairly as possible, and to reduce the obstruction to the blast. The blast-pressure was thus gauged and read off on a scale graduated to measure quarter inches of the mercurial column. The tube invariably got filled with condensed steam from the blast, the weight of which acting on the mercury affected its level in the gauge.

Fig. 148.—Full size.

Orifice of Gauge-Tube.

The amount of disturbance, a constant quantity for each case, was noted and deducted as a constant quantity from the indications, to yield the true pressure of the blast. Though the impulse of the blast agitated the mercury with considerable undulations, at very slow speeds, yet, at all ordinary speeds, the indications were perfectly readable, as the agitation subsided into a mere tremor at the surface. In special cases, when it was desirable to observe the mean pressure at very slow speeds, the undulations could be reduced by throttling the passage by the stop-cock, without affecting the mean value of the indications.

By observing the blast-pressure simultaneously with diagrams taken from the cylinder, we obtain by a few single observations the data for finding in a direct manner the relation of blast-pressure and evaporation,—a question which by Pambour's indirect mode of observation, unaided by the indicator, could only be solved, and that approximately, by continued observation over long runs. The indicated blast-pressure, it must not be overlooked, is the mean result of two continuous discharges of steam from the cylinders alternately.

Of the Influence of Exhaust Pressure on Blast-Pressure. —The exhaust pressure at the point of release, as it is a measure of the quantity and force of steam discharged, is the most proper datum for comparison with blast-pressure. It has been found that the back exhaust pressure in the cylinder varies simply as the pressure at the release-point. It is thus probable that the blast-pressure (at a greater distance) should vary in the same ratio. The mean results of numerous observations confirm this inference, and as a sample of the evidence, we may quote the following from C. B. No. 124, all taken in the course of a single trip.

TABLE No. XLI.—RELATION OF BLAST-PRESSURE TO RELEASE-PRESSURE. C. R. No. 124.—1st Notch.

Speeds.	Exhaust Pressure at release.	Blast-Pressure in inches of mercury.
mph.	lbs.	ins.
20	15	5½
19	23½	8¼
18	28	9
19	37	12¼

Each of these is a mean of two observations at nearly equal speeds and exhaust pressures, and it is plain that the blast-pressure varies virtually as the pressure of exhaust at the release-point.

Of the Influence of Speed on Blast-Pressure.—In so far as the elevation of the mercury is due to the intermittent impulses of the blast, it may be conceived to be directly as the frequency of these impulses, or as the speed simply. Much of it is dependent also on the continuous expulsion of residuary steam, and in so far it must vary as the square of the speed. The superior influence of the latter appears from the following observations selected to illustrate the influence of speed. The last column contains the blast-pressures reduced for a mean uniform exhaust pressure at release, the reductions being made according to the law that the blast-pressure is directly as the release-pressure.

TABLE No. XLII.—RELATION OF BLAST-PRESSURE TO SPEED.

Nos. of Observations.	Mean speeds of Engine.	Mean Release Pressures.	Mean Blast Pressures.	Reduced Blast-Pressures	
	mph.	lbs.	ins.	ins.	
	E. & G. R. Hebe.—4th Notch.				
1	13	11	¼	½	for 20 lbs. release.
2—5	17	20	¾	¾	
6—13	21	29	1¼	⅞	
14—17	30	21	1¾	1¾	
18	40	11	2	3⅝	
	C. R. No. 124.—1st Notch.				
1	6	23	¾	1	for 30 lbs. release.
2—3	11	38	5¾	4½	
4—6	16	39	11	8½	
7—14	20	25	8½	10	
15—19	24	30	11	11	
20—23	30	17	9¼	16¼	
	C. R. No. 125.—2d Notch.				
1—2	12	20	2	1¾	for 18 lbs. release.
3—5	16	19	2	2⅛	
6—9	20	19	4	4	
10—11	25	15	4¾	5¾	
	Do. 3d Notch.				
1	11	13	½	⅝	for 17 lbs. release.
2—4	20	21	3¼	2⅝	
5—11	24	15	4	4½	
12—14	30	19	7	6¼	
	Do. 4th Notch.				
1	16	12	1	1⅛	for 14 lbs. release.
2—3	20	16	1¼	1	
4—6	27	13	1½	1⅝	
7	33	13	1	1	

In each series of pressures in the last column, it is clear that, except in the last case, the blast-pressures rise very rapidly with the speeds. Throwing them into curves in the usual way, we obtain the following results, fig. 149, for the respective examples noted. The last case, of No. 125,

Fig. 149.

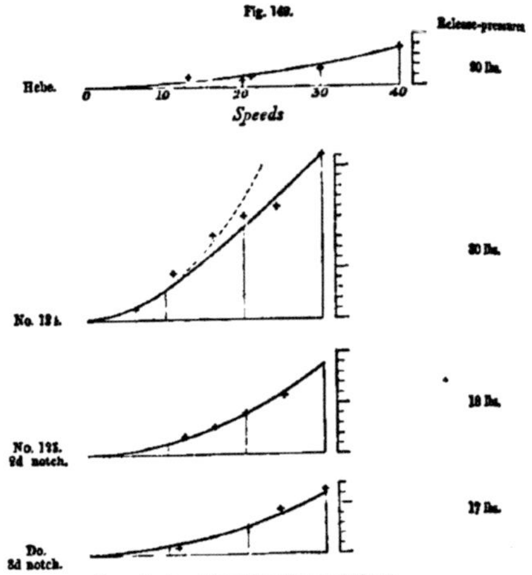

Curves showing relation of Blast-Pressure to Speed.

4th notch, has been omitted, as the data are insufficiently distinct. The base-lines contain the speeds in miles per hour, and the perpendiculars express the blast-pressures in inches of mercury. All the curves, but the second, follow the law of the variation of blast-pressure as the square of the speed; the dot-curve in the second case is constructed on this law, but it is plain that the true curve is flatter, and indicates a law of variation inferior to the square of the speed, but superior to the speed simply. The other cases so distinctly harmonize with the law, that it may be inferred generally that the mean pressure at the blast-orifice varies as the square of the speed; though occasionally (in exposed cylinders) the variation does not proceed so rapidly; but, in all cases, in a much higher ratio than the speed simply.

Comparative Values of Blast-Pressure and the Pressure of Exhaust.—To compare these pressures directly, the former, indicated in inches of mercury, must be reduced to pounds; and, as 30 inches of mercury balance 14·7 lbs. pressure per inch, we shall adopt 1 lb. of pressure as an equivalent for 2 inches of mercury.

The mean blast-pressure, as measured by the gauge, results from the average indicated pressure of exhaust in the cylinders, exerted from the release-point onwards to the point of compression. In each cylinder, usually, there is a perpetual exhaust, as the valve no sooner closes the exhaust for one end of the cylinder than it opens it for the other. There are, therefore, two constant exhausts in operation, yielding jointly the blast-pressure observed. Each exhaust is derived from a series of explosions, and is therefore variable in intensity. The variation in the cylinder is indicated directly on the diagram, ranging from the pressure at release to the lowest back pressure, and this may be otherwise represented as follows: Let the line A B be the centre line of the engine, and the circle A B, the path of the crank. This circle may be adopted for an ideal atmospheric line, upon which the exhaust pressure that exists throughout one revolution may be represented. To select No. 15 diagram from the Great Britain, for illustration, divide A B, fig. 150, into 24 parts, as inches of stroke, and draw ordinates to meet the circumference. Assuming the crank-pin to move in the direction of the arrow; then, as the exhaust opens at the 20th inch of the stroke, the point a, where the 20th ordinate meets the circle, is the position of the crank-pin at the time of release for the back stroke; and b, diametrically opposite, is the position for the front stroke. From these points draw radial lines to c and d, representing the release-pressure, 42 lbs., on the diagram. Similarly, from the ends of the other ordinates for each successive inch of stroke, occurring within the semicircle a A b, draw radii equal to the successive exhaust pressures set forth on the diagram, terminating with b e, the back pressure of 11 lbs., at the point of compression. The curve traced through the extremities of these radii, will represent the exhaust pressure for half a revolution due to the back end of the cylinder. The termination of this curve at e, coincides with the commencement of the duplicate curve of exhaust pressure, d f, for the front stroke; and it is clear that the pressure of exhaust, though perpetual, is abrupt and variable.

To represent this pressure on a straight atmospheric line, we may conceive the circular line A B to be unrolled flat with

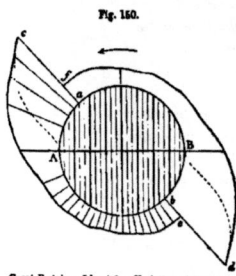

Fig. 150.

Great Britain.—3d notch.—Variation of Exhaust Pressure in one Cylinder, during one revolution.

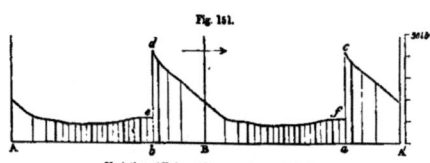

Fig. 151.

Variation of Exhaust Pressure, for one Cylinder.

its ordinates attached. The diagram then assumes the appearance of fig. 151, in which the base line A B A' is equal to the circumference of the circle A B in the previous figure, and represents the path of the crank-pin through one revolution. The ordinates being drawn from the points already found for them, and connected by a curve, the curve so enclosed shews the exhaust pressure on a straight base line, for one cylinder as before. The curve of exhaust pressure for the neighbouring cylinder, is of course precisely of the same form; and the two may be shown conjointly on opposite sides of the base. As the cranks are set at right angles on the axle, the release-points represented at d and c from one cylinder, must occur at equal intervals between those from the other; and therefore, the four explosions that occur during one revolution should be placed at equal intervals on the base-line, as in fig. 152. To simplify the diagram,

the whole area of pressure may be thrown to one side of the base line, as in fig. 153, in which the ordinates from the second

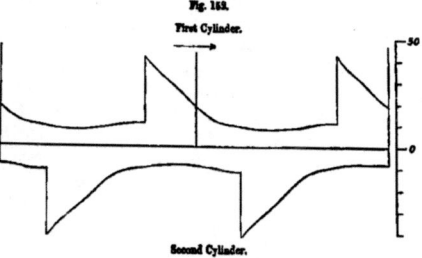

Fig. 153.
First Cylinder.

Second Cylinder.

Variation of total Exhaust Pressure.—Compound Diagram for one revolution.

cylinder are superposed on the first series, and a heavy-lined curve is traced over all to show the slump pressure of the exhaust steam from the two cylinders during one revolu-

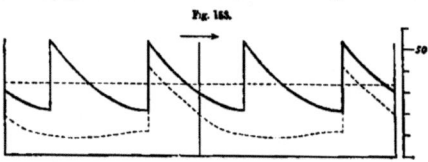

Fig. 153.

Great Britain, 3d notch, 46 mph.—Previous Diagram simplified.

tion,—deduced from the diagram No. 15 from the Great Britain. This figure clearly shows how far the joint pressures of exhaust may be reduced to a uniform force at high

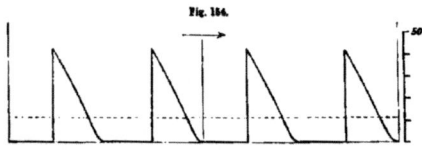

Fig. 154.

Great Britain, 3d notch, 11 mph.—Variation of Exhaust Pressure for two Cylinders, 11 mph.

speeds, approximating the action of the blast to that of a steady jet of steam. The joint pressure in this case never falls below 21 lbs. in the cylinder; whereas, in figure 154, showing the joint exhaust pressure in the same cylinders, at 11 miles per hour, drawn from No. 10 diagram, and projected in dot-lining on fig. 150,—we find the pressure developed in four distinct jets, each of which is isolated from its neighbours, and is thoroughly exhausted before the succeeding release takes place. The following figure 155, showing

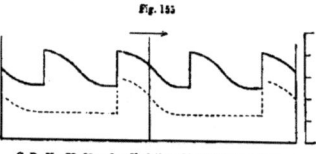

Fig. 155.

C. R., No 73, 80 mph.—Variation of total Exhaust Pressure.

in the same way the ordinary blast of No. 73, C. R., at 30 miles per hour, still more obviously declares the approximation of the joint exhaust to a uniform pressure at high speeds. These illustrations explain, on the one hand, the clear "spit" of a well-made engine with large ports and an easy orifice, proclaiming a rapid and efficient exhaust; and on the other hand, the throttled shouts of overloaded steam-ways, distressed by deficient dimensions.

The dot lines drawn in figs. 153 and 154, parallel to the base-lines, indicate the mean exhaust pressures in the two cases, and measure respectively 33 lbs. and 11 lbs. Thus, we perceive, in the latter case, a strong power of exhaust, capable of creating a blast without back pressure. A few examples of the proportional values of exhaust and blast pressures, are contained in the following table:—

TABLE No. XLIII.—COMPARISON OF BLAST-PRESSURE AND THE WHOLE PRESSURE OF EXHAUST IN THE CYLINDERS.

No. of Diagram.	Speed of Engine.	Release Pressure.	Mean total Exhaust Pressure for one Cylinder.	Mean Back Pressure of Exhaust for one Cylinder	Mean Blast-Pressure for two Cylinders.	
	mph.	lbs.	lbs.	lbs.	inches of mercury.	lbs.
		C. R. No. 73.—2d day.				
1	25	41	16	10	4¾	2 4
2	32	29	11	6	4¾	2·4
3	32	35	16 5	13	5¼	2 6
		Do. 3d day.				
1	24	38	20	12	2½	1·25
2	30	30	15	12	1¾	1·4
3	34	21	9	7	1¼	0·6
4	30	28	12	10	2¾	1 4
		C. R. No. 124.—1st Notch.				
1	6	23	3	2	¾	0 4
2	12	38	7 5	5	7½	3 75
3	16	34	9	7	11½	5 75
4	18	30	12	10	9	4 5
5	22	34	12	10	18	9
6	24	28	12	10	12½	6 25
7	27	12	8	7 5	6½	3·25
8	28	20	11	10	13	6 5

In the case of No. 73, the insignificance of the blast-pressure in respect of the mean exhaust, is striking. For example, on the second day, a mean exhaust-pressure of 16 lbs. for one cylinder, does not raise above 2½ lbs. of blast-pressure for two; on the third day, still less. No. 124, yields higher values, as, with 12 lbs. mean pressure, in each cylinder, it yields for the same speed of piston from 4½ to 9 lbs. of joint blast-pressure.

Again, a comparison of the blast-pressure with the simple back pressure of exhaust, will abundantly prove how unlike the "resistance of the blast-pipe" may be to the back pressure of the diagram. While No. 73 shows back pressures of 12 and 13 lbs. the blast does not in any case rise above 2·6 lbs., and is commonly but ¼th to 1/13th of the other, reckoning even for one cylinder only. On the other hand, the blast of No. 124 is much more formidable, in some cases, as in No. 5 diagram; being nearly equal to the back pressure for one cylinder, and in general fully one-half.

It was observed, also, that during the experiments with the Orion, E. and G. R., the blast-pressure remained almost unaltered at about ¾ lb., while the back pressure ranged from about 8 lbs. with foul water, to nothing with clean water in the boiler. These remarks are sufficient to show that the resistance at the blast-orifice constitutes but a part, and in many cases a very small part of the total back pressure on the piston. For this conclusion, now verified by actual experiment, we should be quite prepared by the investigations on back exhaust-pressure in the fifth chapter, where the influence of various circumstances was set forth. It was there inferred that the influence of the blast-area on back pressure is sensibly nothing when it exceeds the area of steam-way, and only operates when it is smaller than any other part of the exhausting passage. This conclusion also is verified by the blast-gauge; for we shall find that it is generally in the cases of the smallest orifice in proportion to the steam-port, that the importance of blast-pressure is greatest. Thus, in the following table containing the mean results of above a hundred observations, it appears that in the Hebe and No. 124, in which the blast-orifice is decidedly smaller than the steam-port, the total blast-pressure is about one-half of the back pressure in each cylinder; whereas in the Orion and No. 73, with wider orifices, the proportion of blast is sensibly small.

TABLE No. XLIV.—MEAN RATIOS OF BLAST TO BACK EXHAUST PRESSURE.

Name of Engine.	Ratios, that of Piston being 1.		Mean observed Pressures.		Ratio of blast to back Pressure in one Cylinder.
	Steam port.	Blast orifice.	Back Pressure for one Cylinder.	Blast for two Cylinders.	
			lbs.	lbs.	
E. & G. R. Hebe, 4th Notch..................	1/18	1/13	2	¾	⅜
E. & G. R. Orion, 5th Notch, foul water....	1/17	1/13	8	¾	1/11
Do. do. clean water.	"	"	0	¾	—
C. R. No. 73, foul water.	1/13.3	1/17	10	2½	¼
Do. clean water.	"	"	10	1⅓	⅛
C. R. No. 124, 1st Notch	1/17	1/27	8	5	⅝

It is unnecessary to pursue this comparison further. We are only concerned in showing by direct experiment the fallacy of charging blast-pipe resistance, without limitation, with all the back pressure that occurs in the cylinder.

RECAPITULATION.—1. The pressure of the blast, gauged at the orifice, is developed in pulsations, due to the alternate discharges of steam from the cylinders; sharp and isolated at the slower speeds, and sensibly uniform at the higher.

2. Blast-pressure varies directly as the exhaust-pressure in the cylinder, at the point of release.

3. Blast-pressure varies, generally, directly as the square of the speed.

4. Blast-pressure, gauged for two cylinders, is in all cases much smaller than the mean exhaust-pressure even for one cylinder. Also, it is in all cases smaller than even the back pressure of exhaust alone; and in many cases it forms but an insignificant fraction of the back pressure. It has been observed to vary from 1/11th to ⅝ths of the back pressure in each cylinder. Blast-pipe resistance, therefore, constitutes but a part, and commonly but a very small part, of the observed back pressure in the cylinder.

5. The observation of blast-pressure shows that the influence of the area of blast-orifice on back pressure is sensibly nothing when it exceeds the area of the steam-port; and only operates as a cause of back pressure when it is less than any other part of the exhausting passage.

CHAPTER VIII.

RELATIVE PRESSURES OF STEAM IN THE BOILER, THE VALVE-CHEST, AND THE CYLINDER.

THE question of relative pressures is of importance chiefly as it affects the facility for running with heavy loads at high speeds, and for working at the same time with high expansion. Whatever be the steaming power of the boiler, the limit to speed may be imposed by a deficiency in the proportions of the steam-passages for transmitting the steam to the cylinders with the necessary celerity; and this would imply the necessity of working the engine with a large percentage of admission to yield the required power of traction.

The following are dimensions of the engines which have, to our knowledge, been subjected to observations of relative pressures:—

TABLE, NO. XLV.—DIMENSIONS OF ENGINES WITH RESPECT TO THE RELATIVE PRESSURES IN BOILER, VALVE-CHEST, AND CYLINDER.

Name of Railway.	Name of Engine.	Name of Observer.	Date.	Area of greatest opening of Regulator.	Steam-pipe in Boiler. Section.	Steam-pipe in Boiler. Length.	Steam-pipe in Smoke-box. Section.	Steam-pipe in Smoke-box. Length.	Steam-port. Section.	Steam-port. Length of Passage.	Cylinder. Diameter.	Cylinder. Stroke.	Diameter of Wheel.	Capacity of Boiler. Water space.	Capacity of Boiler. Steam space.
			Year.	sq. ins.	sq. ins.	feet.	sq. ins.	feet.	sq. ins.	ins.	ins.	ins.	feet.	cub. ft.	cub. ft.
Versailles	Gironde	Gouin and Le Chatelier	1844	14·2	18·6	3	8·95	4' 4"	13		15	18	5½	42	38
Greenock	No. 73. C. R.	Clark	1850	—	—	3' 6"	14	4	9	10	13	18	5	—	—
Do.	No. 41. C. R.	Do.	1850	10	16	15' 6"	16	3' 6"	12·5	12	15	20	6	74	39
Great Western	Great Britain	D. Gooch	1850	13	19·6	8	19·6	4' 6"	26	14	18	24	8	151	54
Orleans	No. 154 Goods, by Polonceau	Bertera	1850	16·3	12·1	5	16	2	18·76	14	17·3	24	4' 11"	—	—
Do.	No. 62 Pass., by Stephenson.	Do.	1850	19·4	12·1	5	19	3	17·4	12·6	15·75	22	5' 6"	—	—

Results from the Gironde.—MM. Gouin and Le Chatelier, in 1844, were the first who made observations on the relative pressures. In the Gironde the cylinders were inside the smoke-box, and the regulator was placed in a small dome close behind the chimney. The observers directed their attention first, to the simultaneous pressures in the boiler and cylinder during admission, and the influence of the regulator; secondly, to the pressures in the boiler and valve-chest; thirdly, to the pressures in the cylinder and valve-chest; fourthly, to the influence of priming on these pressures. The following table contains an abstract of the observations.

The first part of the table shows that the pressure in the cylinder is in all cases less than that in the boiler. When the regulator was just open, the steam found its way into the cylinder, and at 22 miles reached a pressure one-third of that in the boiler. An increase of opening raised the pressure in the cylinder, until when it amounted to 5·58 inches area, at the ordinary speed of 28 miles, the cylinder-pressure rose to a maximum of 60 lbs., 8 lbs. less than the boiler-pressure. Additional opening did not further facilitate the flow of steam.

Secondly, at 29 miles, in the second part of the table, the pressure in the chest attained its maximum relative to the boiler-pressure, with an opening of 8·52 inches, when it was 42 lbs., only 3 lbs. less than the boiler-pressure. In this series, the water-level was maintained higher than usual.

Thirdly, the cylinder-pressure, at 29 miles, was 6 lbs. lower than the pressure in the chest.

Fourthly, with an extremely high water-level, above the top of the glass-gauge, and the regulator wide open, the means of the quantities in the last part of the table are as follow:—

31 miles | 29 lbs. cyldr | 45 lbs. chest | 16 lbs. difference.

From this we find that the difference increases from 6 lbs. with ordinary steam, to 16 lbs. with heavy priming, between

TABLE, No. XLVI.—RELATIVE PRESSURES IN THE GIRONDE, 1844.
ADMISSION 13½ INCHES. STROKE 18 INCHES.

Area of Opening of Regulator	Speed.	Indicated Steam Pressures.		Differences of these Pressures.	Remarks.
square inches.	miles.	lbs.	lbs.	lbs.	
		Cylinder.	Boiler.		
Just open	22	22	68	46	
1·39	32	34	66	32	
2·79	29	39	66	27	
3·62	31	44	68	24	
4·59	28	47	56	9	
5·58	27	60	68	8	
11·31	26	60	68	8	
6·82	28	53	60	7	
7·28	25	63	70	7	
11·31	24	62	67	5	
8·37	17	64	68	4	
		Valve-chest.	Boiler.		
2·32	Ordinary speed 29 miles.	19	37	18	Means of 67 observations.
3·97		34	47	13	
5·52		48	55	7	
8·52		42	45	3	
14·10		45	48	3	
		Cylinder.	Valve-chest.		
	29	42	48	6	Mean of 22 observations.
EXTREME PRIMING.					
		Cylinder.	Valve-chest.		
	30·6	32	48	16	
	31·8	20	31	11	
	29·5	36	54	18	
Full open	29·5	30	47	17	
	33·0	27	45	18	
			Boiler.		
	23·5	26	51	25	

the cylinder and the chest; and from 8 lbs. to 25 lbs. between the cylinder and the boiler. These greater differences are plainly due to the greater resistance of passages to the motion of steam when charged with water than when dry; and this conclusion is amply supported by analogical cases.

Fifthly, it having been found that the lowest differences, at ordinary speeds, are as follow:—

	Cylinder and Boiler.	Cylinder and Chest.
Steam in ordinary condition, ...	8 lbs.	6 lbs.
Steam charged with water	25 lbs.	16 lbs.

the differences between cylinder and chest are from three-fourths to two-thirds of the other; and in general it was concluded that one-third of the total resistance to the motion of the steam, was due to the passage from the boiler to the chest, and the remaining two-thirds to the steam-passages into the cylinders. It also appears that heavily charged steam requires about three times the pressure absorbed by ordinary steam.

Results from No. 73, C. R.—This engine is of the same general dimensions and arrangement as the Gironde. The following are the mean results of 50 observations made during the second and third days of our engagement with this engine, as already explained, *ante,* page 89.

TABLE, No. XLVII.—RELATIVE PRESSURES IN C. R., No. 73.
ADMISSION 12½ INCHES. STROKE 18 INCHES.

Speed of Engine.	Pressures indicated in		Difference of Pressures.
	Cylinder during Admission.	Valve-chest.	
mph.	lbs.	lbs.	lbs.
Starting	46	50	4
7	38	54	16
18	45	60	15
19	23	39	16
25	23	32	9
29	33	44	11
31	25	35	10
36	28	38	10
38	30	40	10
39	30	43	13
41	18	30	12
42	32	47	15
43	30	45	15

Great differences of pressure are here shown to be required at ordinary speeds in sending the steam through the passages. The results for 36 and 38 miles are the most numerously supported by observation, and in these cases we have a difference of 10 lbs., or one-fourth of the indicated pressure in the chest. At 43 miles per hour, we observe a difference of 15 lbs., or one-third of the sensible pressure in the chest. Even a starting pace, 2 or 3 miles per hour, creates a difference of 4 lbs. Such decided differences are owing for the most part to the dampness of the steam, and it was found, as already remarked in the chapter on exhaust pressure, that with foul water, a mass of water, equal in weight to 32 per cent. of the sensible steam, passed through the cylinders.

As the openings of the regulator of No. 73 were not found, the boiler-pressures are not given in the table. They were, however, at all times as much superior to those of the chest, as these were to the cylinder-pressures.

Results from the regular Engines of the Caledonian Railway.—The only one of these submitted to detailed experiment, was No. 41 Passenger Engine, on the Greenock

Railway. The regulator is placed over the fire-box; and the steam is drawn from a dome placed directly above. The following table contains the average results of above 70 observations made during three trips with ordinary passenger trains.

TABLE, No. XLVIII.—RELATIVE PRESSURES IN C. R., No. 41.
ADMISSION 9½ INCHES. STROKE 20 INCHES.

Speed of Engine.	Pressures indicated in		Difference of Pressures.
	Cylinder.	Valve-chest.	
mph.	lbs.	lbs.	lbs.
20	30·5	43	3·5
26	44	49·25	5·25
28	38	43	5
32	39	49	10
33	38	47	9
34	44	54	10
35	46	56	10
36	35	42·5	7·5
37	50	60	10
38	49	61	12
40	50	63	13
42	48	60	12

The differences at the slower speeds are much smaller than were found with No. 73, but for the higher speeds they are much more nearly the same. The differences at 20 and 40 miles were very regularly about 3½ lbs. and 13 lbs., and were amply confirmed by observation.

During the experiments with No. 41 over the brake at Greenock, the following results were obtained:—

TABLE, No. XLIX.—RELATIVE PRESSURES IN C. R., No. 41.
INFLUENCE OF THE REGULATOR.

Speed of Engine.	Pressures indicated			Opening of Regulator.
	in Cylinder.	in Valve-chest.	in Boiler.	
mph.	lbs.	lbs.	lbs.	sq. ins.
	1st Notch.	Admission 14·4 ins.		
11	—	16	54	·62
11	27	34	70	·62
11	45	57	80	·62
17	45	57	78	1·25
19	18	26	76	·62
24½	14	18	74	·62
18	43	57	57	9·37
18	50	57	58	9·37
26	40	—	82	1·87
	2d Notch.	Admission 13·1 ins.		
10	15	17	76	·31
23	14	19	76	·31
32	16	21	76	·02
10	27	36	64	1·25
20	26	30	56	1·87
23	36	46	52	1·87
	3d Notch.	Admission 11 ins.		
16	14	17	76	·31
32	56	77	90	1·87
38	58	63	—	—
	4th Notch.	Admission 7·3 ins.		
13	55	67	84	·62
19	65	80	82	2·5
26	61	70	90	·62
38	28	36	94	·31

It appears, that the smallest opening recorded, less than one-third of a square inch, passes steam sufficient to keep the engine going at 23 miles per hour, with a pressure in the cylinder about one-fifth of that in the boiler, under the 2d notch. It is obvious too that, in general, the difference of pressures in the boiler and cylinder increases with the speed.

Again, it appears that the shorter the admission, the smaller is the opening of regulator required for a given pressure in the cylinder. This we infer from the fact, that with the same opening and speeds, the shorter admissions give the smaller percentages of differences. Thus with an opening of 1·87 inches in the 1st, 2d, and 3d notches, we find the pressures as follow:—

```
                mph.   cyl.    boiler.   differences.
1st Notch 26 mph. 40 lbs. 82 lbs. 42 lbs. or 51 per cent.
2d    „   23 „   36 lbs. 52 lbs. 16 lbs. or 31   „
3d    „   33 „   56 lbs. 90 lbs. 34 lbs. or 38   „
```

The reduction of pressure is much greater in the 1st notch than in the two others, and the greater percentage for the 3d than for the 2d is explained by the higher speed.

Greater differences of pressures in the cylinder and valve-chest are shown in this than in the previous table. We find, for example, 25 lbs. of difference under the 3d notch, at 38 miles per hour, which is double what is found in the table No. 48. This, we consider, is due to the desultory mode in which the engine was worked over the brake, when the cylinder remained in a lukewarm condition, and greater condensation took place than under the ordinary work of trains.

It is well understood among the engine-drivers of the Caledonian railway, that at the ordinary speeds of trains, the cylinder receives its maximum quantity of steam, when the regulator-handle is "straight up," or half open, yielding an opening of 4 square inches, only one-fourth of the sectional area of the steam-pipe. This we have frequently verified; in one case, with No. 33, C. R., at 20 miles per hour, in the 6th notch, cutting off at 9 inches, it was found that with 4 inches of opening, the pressure in the boiler being 85 lbs., that in the cylinder was 65 lbs.; and that any extra opening of the regulator did not appreciably raise this pressure. And the highest pressure was obtained in the cylinder with about 5 inches of opening, in the 2d notch, suppressing at 14⅖ inches, at 31 miles per hour; it amounted to 67 lbs., while the steam was blowing off at 90 lbs. Indeed, for all admissions under 12 inches of the stroke, 4 inches is the greatest useful opening; and on no occasion is more than 5 inches necessary. Again, with No. 124, C. R., having pipes of the same dimensions, at 16 miles per hour, in the 1st notch, cutting off at 20¼ inches, we have found that, with 4 inches, the pressure in the cylinder was 62 lbs., that in the boiler being above 100 lbs., and that a greater opening did not raise the pressure. Thus in the goods-engine, as in the passenger, 4 to 5 inches of area is about the maximum useful opening.

Relative Steam Pressures in the Great Britain.—Mr. Gooch's observations on this point are very remarkable. Simultaneously with the second series of diagrams from this engine, the pressures in the steam-chest and boiler were observed. The steam-pipe is 16 feet long in the boiler; but, as the steam is admitted to the pipe by small openings formed along its whole length in the boiler, the mean effective length for the passage of steam is but one-half, or 8 feet, in the boiler. The following table contains the observed relative pressures:—

TABLE, No. L.—RELATIVE PRESSURES IN THE GREAT BRITAIN.
SECOND SERIES.

No. of Diagram.	Speed of Engine.	Pressures indicated		
		in Cylinder.	in Valve-chest.	in Boiler.
	mph.	lbs.	lbs.	lbs.
	1st Notch. Admission 16 inches.			
25	15	70	77	78
26	17	83	93	97
27	21	95	98	105
28	24	85	95	90
29	27	80	85	75
30	31	90	100	97
31	31	80	88	82
32	49	60	73	76
33	54	89	100	98
	3d Notch. Admission 11½ inches.			
34	17	88	95	100
35	18	70	77	77½
36	21	92	98	105
37	26	72	93	87
38	31	79	90	83
39	32	86	101	98
40	40	76	87	75
41	51	70	77	74
42	55	84	100	98
	5th Notch. Admission 7 inches.			
43	17	89	97	105
44	18	70	77	77½
45	21	93	100	105
46	28	74	85	80
47	31	83	90	90
48	36	80	90	75
49	50	77	78	72
50	56	90	105	98
Means of the above.	1st Notch,	82 lbs.	90 lbs.	89 lbs.
	3d Notch,	81 lbs.	91 lbs.	89 lbs.
	5th Notch,	82 lbs.	90 lbs.	88 lbs.

At the lower speeds, the pressure in the valve-chest is, as usual, lower than that in the boiler; but, as the speed increases, the former rises superior to the latter, under all the notches. This is contrary to all ordinary experience, though very accurate indicators were employed. Assuming the genuineness of the indications, which it is as difficult to doubt as to believe, the only apparent cause of the superior pressure in the valve-chest, is the high temperature in the smoke-box, which, operating on the steam as it passes through the pipe, close in front of the tubes, in the manner shown in the G. W. R. Tank-Engine, figured in our plates, may evaporate any water associated with the steam, and even surcharge the latter, and raise its elasticity before it enters the valve-chest. We have had abundant evidence, at least, to show that perfectly dry steam moves through passages with much less effort than steam charged with water; and the Great Britain, with its capacious boiler and easy evaporation, has been found by Mr. Gooch, after repeated experiments, not to be sensibly affected with priming. The steam, therefore, before it leaves the boiler, is comparatively dry, and is further heated on its way to the chest; and we may warrantably conceive that the pressure in the chest may be at least sensibly equal to that in the boiler. Still the difficulty remains of conceiving that steam of lower pressure should flow towards higher-pressure steam; this, however, consistently enough, takes place only under the higher temperatures which accompany higher speeds.

The pressures in the cylinder are in all cases lower than those in the valve-chest: there the acquisition of extra heat

o

is trifling. At the same time the steam is maintained so thoroughly dry that the differences are comparatively small. Accordingly, in the observations Nos. 29, 40, 48, 49, at the highest speeds, the pressures in the cylinder actually exceed those in the boiler.

The total means of the three pressures for each notch, at the end of the table, show that, upon the whole, the chest-pressure is about 2 lbs. higher than the boiler-pressure; this intimates that the increase of pressure due to surcharge in the smoke-box, does more than balance the obvious wire-drawing at the slower speeds. The mean cylinder-pressures are all about 8 lbs. less than those of the chest.

Results from the Orleans Railway Engines.—For the materials of the following table we are indebted to the late French work of Le Chatelier, &c., already named:—

TABLE, No. LI.—RELATIVE PRESSURES IN THE ORLEANS ENGINES.

Name of Engine.	No. of Notch.	Period of Admission.	Mean Speed	Indicated Pressures in			Difference of pressures in valve-chest and cylinder
				Boiler.	Valve-chest.	Cylinder.	
	No.	percentage.	mph.	lbs.	lbs.	lbs.	lbs.
No 154	7	50	19·5	69	61	41	20
,,	8	38	15·5	70	59	33	26
,,	9	28	16·5	73	68	31	37
No. 62	7	77	26·3	83	68	30	38
,,	8	61	25·2	82	72	33	39

The differences of pressure, in the last column, are so great as to lead us to doubt whether M. Bertera, the observer, has registered the maximum, or only the mean pressures in the cylinder during admission. That he has selected the latter, is most probable from the circumstance that the cylinder-pressures fall as the period of admission is shortened; whereas, as we shall find, the maximum pressure in the cylinder generally rises as the admission is shortened. The great inferiority of pressure in the cylinder, being in such cases but one-half of that in the valve-chest, is no doubt owing very much to condensation of steam by the exposure of the cylinders.

Of the Influence of Speed on the Relative Pressures.—First, between the cylinder and the valve-chest. In No. 73, C. R., the following differences of pressure were well established for the annexed speeds:—

36 miles per hour, 10 lbs. difference.
43   do.   15 lbs.   do.

The squares of 36 and 43 are 1296 and 1849, which are as 2 to 3 nearly; the pressures, 10 and 15, are also as 2 to 3; and it follows that at speeds above 30 miles, the difference of pressure varies as the square of the speed nearly. For all speeds lower than 36 miles, and above 7 miles, the difference is nearly constant, uninfluenced by speed. This is analogous to the condition of the back exhaust pressure of this engine, already discussed.

In No. 41, C. R., in the ordinary course of its work, the differences of pressure rise quickly with the speed; at 20

and 40 miles, which were the best observed speeds, the differences were as follow:—

20 miles per hour, 3·5 lbs. difference.
40   do.   13 lbs.   do.

The speeds are as 1 to 2, and the differences as 1 to 4; it follows that in No. 41, the difference of pressure varies as the square of the speed.

In No. 41, over the brake, the difference is exceedingly various, even with the same speeds; and the great variation so observed is due to the varying temperature of the steam-passages under the circumstances, causing as much impediment from water by condensation, as was found in No. 73 by priming.

In the Great Britain, the differences do not rise rapidly; the case is somewhat exceptional, as the condition of the steam varies with the speed, in the manner already described: the higher the speed, the better dried and the more volatile is the steam, and therefore the more easily does it flow. So great is the advantage so derived, that the differences of pressure rise more slowly than even the speeds simply.

Secondly, between the valve-chest and the boiler. The difference of pressure ought to vary, like the other, as the square of the speed; but the ratio may be easily upset by peculiar circumstances, as in the Great Britain, where we find that the difference *falls* as the speed rises.

Influence of the Period of Admission on the Pressure in the Cylinder.—This influence has already been alluded to in No. 41, where we have seen that with the same opening, the pressure in the cylinder rises as the period of admission is shortened. This variation is simply proved by double diagrams taken from the cylinder immediately before and after a change of notch. Thus, in No. 48, C. R., (cylinder 15 × 20 in., wheel 6 feet) at 20 miles, with the regulator unaltered, the valve-gear was shifted from the 3d to the 1st notch, increasing the admission from 11¾ to 15¼ inches; the pressure in the cylinder fell simultaneously from 70 to 56 lbs. as shown by the diagrams fig. 156. Similarly, in No. 51,

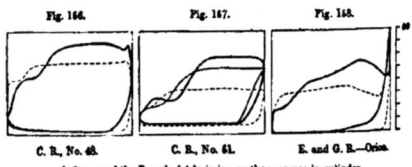

Fig. 156.   Fig. 157.   Fig. 158.

C. R., No. 48.   C. R., No. 51.   E. and G. R.—Orion.

Influence of the Period of Admission on the pressure in cylinder.

C. R., with admissions of 11¾, 12¼, and 14½ inches successively, the pressure fell from 60 lbs. to 52 lbs. and 35 lbs. in succession, fig. 157. A diagram, fig. 158, from the Orion, E. and G. R., shows a fall from 50 to 33 lbs., with successive admissions of 11 and 16 inches. The Jupiter, E. and G. R., (the same as the Hebe) indicates pressures of 45 and 37 lbs., fig. 159, for 11 and 15 inches admission, at 36 miles; and 65 and 44 lbs., fig. 160, for 5 and 15 inches, at 30 miles. In all these instances, the steam-pipes in the smoke-box were conducted round the sides clear of the tubes, and out of direct contact with the smoke. In the first case, the steam-pipe was 19 feet long to the valve-chest; in the second and third, it was only from 8 to 10 feet long. Whether, then, the steam-pipe be long or short, the influence of the period

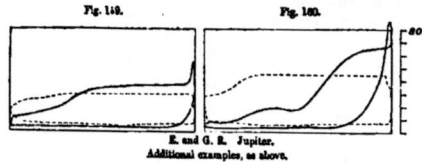

Fig. 149.   Fig. 150.

E. and G. R. Jupiter.
Additional examples, as above.

of admission on the pressure in the cylinder is in these engines very decided.

In the Great Britain, the period of admission appears not sensibly to affect the relative pressure in the cylinder, as appears from the means in the table of pressures. This remarkable exception is doubtless due to the highly volatile condition of the steam, due to desiccation in the steam-pipe, so favourably situated for the purpose, and exposing only ⅛ inch thickness of copper between the hot smoke and the steam.

Of the Variation of Pressure in the Valve-chest.—We have already remarked that this pressure is not in all cases constant, and it may be added that in our own enquiries, we have noted the *mean* indications for comparison with the other pressures. The intermittent flow of steam into the cylinder is the cause of the variation, the pressure being lowest during admission. The amount of this variation sometimes reaches 8 lbs., as diagrams obtained from the valve-chest of No. 41, C. R., will show. Figs. 161 and 162 exhibit diagrams under the 3d notch, from the cylinder and the valve-chest taken simultaneously, at speeds of 32 and

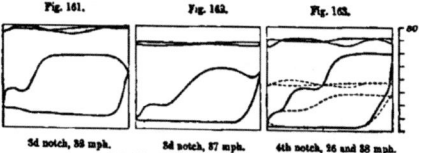

Fig. 161.   Fig. 162.   Fig. 163.

3d notch, 32 mph.   3d notch, 37 mph.   4th notch, 26 and 38 mph.
C. R., No. 41.—Pressures in the Valve-chest.

37 miles; the upper figure in each diagram shows the variation of pressure in the valve-chest and its correspondence with that in the cylinder. Fig. 163 also shows the pressures for the 4th notch at 26 and 38 miles. Under the first notch, the chest-pressure appeared more nearly constant, as the admission was nearly continuous. In the Great Britain, all the pressures in the valve-chest were observed to be sensibly constant, which indeed they ought to be, consistently with the observed fact that the period of admission does not affect the ratio of these pressures to those in the cylinder.

General Results.—The following well-authenticated relative pressures have been found for the prefixed speeds:—

	mph.	cylinder.	chest.	difference.	
Gironde,	29	42 lbs.	48 lbs.	6 lbs.	
Do.	31	29 ,,	45 ,,	16 ,,	(heavy priming)
No. 73,	36	28 ,,	38 ,,	10 ,,	
No. 41,	40	50 ,,	63 ,,	13 ,,	
Gt. Britain,	30 (mean)	82 ,,	90 ,,	8 ,,	

Converting the speeds into feet of piston per minute, and the differences into percentages of the pressures in the chest; we have,

	fpm.	differences.		ratio of port to piston.
Gironde,	504	13·3 per cent.		$\frac{1}{1\frac{3}{4}}$
Do.	521	35·5 ,,	(priming)	,,
No. 73,	605	26 ,,		$\frac{1}{1\frac{4}{7}}$
No. 41,	622	21 ,,		$\frac{1}{1\frac{1}{4}}$
Gt. Britain,	420	9 ,,		$\frac{1}{1\frac{1}{5}}$

Though the speed of piston selected for the Great Britain is lower than the others, it may be considered the same, as the difference is little affected by speed. Of the first three engines, with about the same port, the Gironde, in ordinary condition, has the smallest difference, which, though partly owing to smaller speed, is owing also to cleaner water, with respect to No. 73; and to better protection of cylinders, with respect to No. 41. The differences of the Gironde, if raised for 600 feet of piston, in the ratio of the speeds, would be 16 and 43 per cent. for clean and impure water respectively. In No. 41, we have seen that a desultory mode of working the engine doubled the difference of pressures, owing merely to the insufficiently heated state of the cylinders. In the Great Britain, at the same speeds, the percentage is least of all, owing to the larger port, and the better condition of the cylinders and steam-pipes.

As to the resistance of the steam-pipes, the fall of pressure on this account is, in the Gironde, about one-third of the total reduction, the smallest area of pipe being $\frac{1}{10}$th of the piston. In No. 41, with a pipe $\frac{1}{11}$th of piston, the fall due to the pipe is very small. In the second table for this engine, 1st notch, at 18 miles, while the cylinder-pressure is 14 lbs. less than that of the chest, the pressures in the chest and boiler are the same, 57 lbs. In the 4th notch, at 19 miles, with only 2½ inch opening, the cylinder is 15 lbs. below the chest, and the latter only 2 lbs. below the boiler. It follows that nearly all the fall of pressure in the C. R. passenger-engines, takes place in the cylinder-passages, at least at speeds under 20 miles, with openings above 2½ inches.

Again, in the diagram from No. 13, C. R., fig. 110, at 54 miles, with 62 per cent. admission and 95 lbs. steam in the boiler, the initial pressure was 58 lbs., showing a fall of 37 lbs. or 40 per cent. Now, in the C. R. engines, the fall increases as the square of the speed, and we therefore infer from the stated result for No. 41, in which the fall in the cylinder-passages is 21 per cent. at 40 miles, that at 54 miles the fall would amount to $(21 \times 54^2 \div 40^2)$ or 40 per cent., equal to the entire observed fall in No. 13. It follows, therefore, that as the influence of the cylinder-passages, sufficiently accounts for the total reduction, there is practically but a very small resistance to the motion of steam through the pipes of the C. R. passenger-engines even at 54 or 60 miles per hour; and that virtually the whole of the resistance, measured by a fall of pressure, takes place between the chest and the cylinder.

The following is a re-statement of the examples quoted of Nos. 33 and 124, C. R.

No. 33.

opening.	admission.	speed.	cylinder.	boiler.	difference.
4 ins.	45 per cent.	20 miles	65 lbs.	85 lbs.	20 lbs., or 24 per cent.
5 ins.	75 do.	31 do.	67 lbs.	90 lbs.	23 lbs., or 26 per cent.

No. 124.

4 ins.	84	do.	16 do.	62 lbs.	100 lbs.	38 lbs., or 38 per cent.

The differences in No. 33 harmonize with those of No. 41, and doubtless take place in the cylinder-passages.

In No. 124, with a steam-pipe only $\frac{1}{17}$th of piston, one-fourth of the difference, probably, is due to the pipes; and the remainder, or about 30 per cent., to the cylinder-passages.

In the Orleans engines, with steam-pipes respectively $\frac{1}{11}$th and $\frac{1}{15}$th, the resistance of the pipes was, for the first, one-third to one-eighth of the total difference; and for the second, about one-fourth.

Thus, finally, with clean water, and a port about $\frac{1}{11}$th of the piston, the fall of pressure between the chest and cylinder, at speeds of about 40 miles, or 600 feet of piston, is about 16 per cent. of the sensible pressure in the chest, when the cylinder is well protected; and that for speeds of 20 to 60 miles, it varies from 20 to 40 per cent., in cylinders partially protected; and that by excessive priming, or even by a desultory mode of working with partially protected cylinders, the reduction may in many cases be trebled. With a port of $\frac{1}{11}$th, dry steam, and well protected cylinders, the reduction is not greater than 9 per cent. of the pressure even at the highest speeds. The effect of wiredrawing on the pressure during admission is not here taken into account, for wiredrawing, as we have already had occasion to remark, is merely equivalent to an earlier suppression, as it introduces partial expansion in the cylinder during admission; and may be provided for by placing the valves more nearly into full gear.

Again, it follows that with a steam-pipe $\frac{1}{30}$th to $\frac{1}{17}$th of the piston, the fall of pressure in the steam-pipe is from one-third to one-fourth of the total; and that with pipes not less in section than $\frac{1}{11}$th of the piston there is practically no reduction of pressure between the boiler and the chest, when the regulator is sufficiently open, and the steam in good condition. And when the pipe is led down to the chest directly through the smoke-box, in front of the tubes, and exposed to the current of hot smoke from the tubes, the pressure in the chest at the lowest speeds, is sensibly the same as that in the boiler, except as it may be reduced by the regulator; as the speeds increase above 20 miles, with the regulator well open, the pressure in the chest exceeds that in the boiler, until at 50 and 60 miles, it frequently reaches an excess of 10 per cent. of the boiler-pressure, with a pipe $\frac{1}{30}$th of the piston.

The greatest useful opening of regulator has been observed to vary from 4 to 9 square inches for a 15-inch cylinder, or about $\frac{1}{17}$th to $\frac{1}{30}$th of the piston. In the Great Britain it cannot exceed $\frac{1}{30}$th, as this is the whole area of the entrance.

In the foregoing discussions it has been shown how seriously the working pressure in the cylinder may be reduced below that of the boiler, at ordinary speeds, and what an effectual limit may thus be imposed upon the tractive power of the engine at high speeds. It has also been seen how, by wide pipes and ports, by well protected cylinders, and especially by well dried steam, this reduction of pressure may be extinguished, and the tractive power of the engine fully maintained at all speeds. This separate heating of the steam, in the smoke-box, introduces us into a new field of inquiry, as to which we shall now only say that if means can be devised for

economically surcharging the steam after it leaves the boiler, converting it into what has been called " anhydrous steam," or " stame," much benefit may be anticipated from such a course.

RECAPITULATION.—1. During the ordinary working of locomotives, the pressure in the cylinder, while the steam is admitted, is, in general, considerably less than that in the boiler.

2. This fall of pressure is caused by the wiredrawing action of the regulator, and by the resistance of lateral friction, bends, and strictures in the steam-passages.

3. The fall of pressure is greatly increased by the existence of water in the steam, whether due to priming or to condensation.

4. The fall of pressure increases as the square of the speed, under ordinary circumstances,—the steam-pipes being led clear of the direct action of the draught in the smoke-box, and the steam in good condition.

5. When the steam is specially subjected to desiccation in the smoke-box, by direct exposure to the draft, the fall of pressure in the steam-pipes, between the boiler and the chest, becomes less as the speed rises; and it ultimately, at the highest speeds, disappears, when the chest-pressure becomes equal to, if it does not exceed, the boiler-pressure. The fall of pressure in the cylinder-passages, rises very slowly with the speed, at a rate even less than the speed simply.

6. The shorter the period of admission, the greater is the pressure in the cylinder, and the less is the fall of pressure from the boiler, under ordinary conditions. With highly dried steam, the fall of pressure is not sensibly affected by the period of admission.

7. The pressure in the valve-chest, with ordinary steam, fluctuates during the stroke of piston, from 5 to 8 lbs., with ports $\frac{1}{11}$th of the piston. With highly dried steam, and a port $\frac{1}{11}$th of the piston, the pressures in the chest are sensibly constant.

8. The greatest useful opening of the regulator does not in any case exceed $\frac{1}{30}$th of the area of piston.

9. In well protected cylinders, with ordinary steam, a port $\frac{1}{11}$th of piston, and a speed of 40 miles or about 600 feet of piston per minute, the fall of pressure in the cylinder-passages is about 16 per cent. of the pressure in the chest; and in partially protected cylinders, for speeds of 20 to 60 miles, it varies from 20 to 40 per cent. Excessive priming by foul water or otherwise, or extra condensation, has been found to treble the fall of pressure.

In well protected cylinders, with highly dried or surcharged steam, and a port of $\frac{1}{11}$th, the fall in the cylinder-passages does not exceed 9 per cent., even at the highest speeds.

10. The fall of pressure in steam-pipes less than $\frac{1}{11}$th of the piston, is from one-third to one-fourth of the total fall, at all speeds, with the regulator wide open. With pipes not less than $\frac{1}{11}$th, and ordinary steam, the fall is practically nothing. With pipes at least $\frac{1}{11}$th, and highly dried steam, the fall is nothing; on the contrary, the chest-pressure exceeds that in the boiler at the higher speeds.

11. The total fall between boiler and cylinder, under ordinary circumstances, may reach from 30 to 60 per cent. at the highest speeds.

12. By removing the causes of these heavy falls of pressure, the tractive capabilities of engines subject to such reductions may be greatly increased at high speeds, and in some cases more than doubled.

CHAPTER IX.

OF THE WORK DONE BY STEAM IN THE CYLINDER OF THE LOCOMOTIVE.

Definition of Work.—Work is " an exertion of pressure through space." The *unit* by which quantities of work is measurable is " the labour necessary to raise one pound through the height of one foot." The *rate* at which work is done is expressed in *horse-power*, and one horse-power is equivalent to work done by continuous exertion at the rate of 33,000 pounds raised through one foot in one minute; that is, to the performance of 33,000 units of work per minute.

Measurement of Work from the Steam-diagram.—The diagram represents the active pressure and back pressure per square inch exerted by the steam on one face of the piston. During one stroke of the piston, therefore, if we suppose the steam-pressure to be exerted uniformly throughout the stroke, and that there is no back pressure, the work done would be simply expressed by the product of the whole pressure on the piston in pounds into the stroke in feet. The diagram expressing such an exertion of force would necessarily be rectangular, and the product of its length in feet by its height in pounds, measured by scale, would be an expression of its area, and would express the work done for one stroke per square inch of piston. Should a uniform back pressure be indicated, it forms a deduction from the 'useful pressure; and the difference of heights representing power and resistance on the diagram, is the effective pressure, which multiplied by the length, expresses, as before, the useful area of diagram, or the useful *work done* per inch of piston.

In practice, the positive or steam and back-pressure lines of the diagram are not straight, but curved. These conditions involve a preliminary process of reduction before the area of the diagram can be estimated, and the work for one stroke found: take the mean positive pressures during the successive inches of stroke, add together these pressures, and divide the sum by the length of the stroke in inches. The quotient is the mean positive pressure per inch of piston, for the whole of the stroke, equivalent to the variable pressure actually indicated. Similarly, add together the back pressures for every inch of stroke, and divide the sum by the stroke, for the mean back pressure. The difference of the mean positive and back pressures expresses the effective mean pressure per inch, and this multiplied by the stroke in feet, expresses the area of the diagram, and the work done per inch of piston for one stroke. Finally, the whole work done upon the whole surface of the piston, is equal to the effective mean pressure per inch of piston multiplied by the area in inches, and by the stroke.

For example, to find the work indicated by the diagram, fig. 93, page 65. The diameter of piston is 15 inches, and the stroke is 20 inches, and the indicated pressures for the successive inches of stroke are as follow :—

Inches of Stroke.	Positive pressures during the steam-stroke.	Back pressures during the return-stroke.
1	61 lbs. per inch.	35 lbs. per inch.
2	62	21
3	62	14
4	62	9
5	61	4
6	60	2
7	56	2
8	49	2
9	38	2
10	32	2
11	29	2
12	26	2
13	24	2
14	22	2
15	20	2
16	19	2
17	17	2
18	13	2
19	7	2
20	4	2
Sums of the pressures,	724	113
Dividing by 20 for the mean pressures,	36·2 lbs.	5·6 lbs.

The difference of the mean pressures, equal to (36·2 — 5·6) or 30·6 lbs. per inch, is the effective mean pressure. The area of piston is 176·7 inches, and the whole effective mean pressure on the piston is (176·7 × 30·6) or 5407 lbs. The work of the steam on one side of the piston during one double stroke, or one turn of the wheel, is therefore (5407 × $\frac{20}{12}$) or 9011·6 units of work, or pounds raised through 1 foot.

The work so determined for one face of the piston, being taken four times, the product is the total work done by the engine during one revolution, assuming for the present that the steam operates alike on the four faces of the two pistons. Then (9011·6 × 4) or 36046·4 units is the total work for one turn of the driving wheel.

Measurement of Horse-power from the Steam-diagram.—Rules for Calculation.—The diagram just examined was described at a speed of 20 miles per hour, and from this we shall find the speed of piston. The driving wheel is 6 feet diameter = 18·85 feet circumference; one mile = 5280 feet, and 5280 ÷ 18·85 = 280 turns of wheel in one mile; therefore 280 × 20 = 5600 turns per hour. and 5600 ÷ 60 = 93⅓ turns per minute. For one turn, each piston describes two steam-strokes, equal to 40 inches or 3⅓ feet under the effective mean pressure; then 3⅓ × 93⅓ = 311 feet per minute, the mean speed of piston. Now 311 × 5407 (the whole effective mean pressure) = 1681577 units of work per hour; and this divided by 33000 — 51 horse-power for one cylinder, or, for two cylinders, (51 × 2) or 102 horse-power; and this is the whole power developed in the engine, measured from the diagram.

This operation for finding the horse power may be expressed symbolically as follows :—

Let P = the effective mean pressure in pounds per square inch of piston.

v = the speed of engine in miles per hour.

d = the diameter of piston in inches.

s = the stroke of piston in inches.

d' = the diameter of driving wheel in feet.

Then $d^2 \times \cdot7854 =$ area of the piston.

$\text{P} \times d^2 \times \cdot7854 =$ whole effective mean pressure on the piston, in pounds.

$d \times 3\cdot1416 =$ circumference of the wheel.

$\dfrac{5280}{d \times 3\cdot1416} =$ number of turns per mile.

Turns per mile $\times \dfrac{\text{v}}{60} =$ number of turns per minute.

Turns per minute $\times \dfrac{2s}{12} =$ speed of piston in feet per minute.

Speed of piston $\times \cdot7854\,\text{P}\,d^2 =$ units of work done per minute for one cylinder.

$\dfrac{\text{Work per minute for one cylr.} \times 2}{33000} =$ effective horse-power for two cylinders.

All of these elementary expressions may be converted into useful formulas and rules. Thus,

$\cdot7854\,d^2\,\text{P} =$ the whole effective mean pressure on the piston in pounds. (1.)

$\dfrac{5280}{3\cdot1416\,d} = \dfrac{1680}{d} =$ number of turns per mile. (2.)

$\dfrac{1680}{d} \times \dfrac{\text{v}}{60} = 28\,\dfrac{\text{v}}{d} =$ number of turns per minute. (3.)

$28\,\dfrac{\text{v}}{d} \times \dfrac{2s}{12} = 4\tfrac{2}{3}\,\dfrac{\text{v}\,s}{d} =$ speed of piston in feet per minute. (4.)

$4\tfrac{2}{3}\,\dfrac{\text{v}\,s}{d} \times \cdot7854\,d^2\,\text{P} = 3\tfrac{2}{3}\,\dfrac{\text{v}\,s\,d^2\,\text{P}}{d} =$ units of work per minute for one cylinder. (5.)

$3\tfrac{2}{3}\,\dfrac{\text{v}\,s\,\text{P}\,d^2}{d} \times \dfrac{2}{33000} = \dfrac{\text{v}\,s\,d^2\,\text{P}}{4500\,d} =$ the effective horse-power for two cylinders. (6.)

or verbally :—

Rule I.—*For the whole Effective Mean Pressure on the Piston.* Multiply the square of the diameter of piston in inches, by $\cdot7854$,—and by the effective mean pressure in pounds per square inch. The product is the number required.

Rule II.—*For the number of Turns of the Driving Wheel per mile.* Divide 1680 by the diameter of the driving wheel in feet.

Rule III.—*For the number of Turns of the Driving Wheel per minute.* Multiply the speed in miles per hour by 28,—and divide by the diameter of the wheel.

Rule IV.—*For the Speed of Piston in feet per minute.* Multiply the speed in miles per hour by the stroke of piston in inches,—and by $4\tfrac{2}{3}$,—and divide by the diameter of the wheel in feet.

Rule V.—*For the Work done in one Cylinder per minute.* Multiply the speed in miles per hour by the square of the diameter of piston in inches,—by the stroke in inches,—by the effective mean pressure in pounds per inch on the piston,—and by $3\tfrac{2}{3}$;—and divide by the diameter of the wheel in feet.

Rule VI.—*For the Horse-power of a Locomotive.* Multiply the speed in miles per hour by the square of the diameter of the piston in inches,—by the stroke in inches,—and by the effective mean pressure on the piston in pounds per inch ;—divide the product by the diameter of the driving wheel in feet,—and by 4500.

Example for Rule 6. In connection with the foregoing example,

the speed is 20 miles per hour,
the piston has 15 inches diameter and 20 inches stroke,
the effective mean pressure on the piston is 30·6 lbs. per inch.

Then, by rule, $\dfrac{20 \times 15^2 \times 20 \times 30\cdot6}{6 \times 4500} = 102$ horse-power,

which is the result we have already worked out in detail.

As the atmospheric resistance, 15 lbs. per inch, forms a constant deduction in all cases, from the total steam pressure in the cylinder, it follows that the deduction or loss so experienced, is proportionally less as the total pressure is greater. For example, with a total pressure of 30 lbs., the deduction amounts to one-half of the whole pressure; and with 90 lbs. of total pressure, the deduction is only one-sixth; with 180 lbs. it is only one-twelfth, and, on the other hand, with but 15 lbs. total pressure, it would be entirely met by atmospheric resistance, leaving no useful pressure at all. The advantage of high pressure is thus manifest, because, as we have found, steam of all pressures may be formed from a given weight of water, at the same cost of heat, or coke; and the atmospheric resistance, formidable for the lower pressures, diminishes in importance as the pressures rise.

Work of Steam specially developed by "Expansion."—We have found that steam in the cylinder, under favourable circumstances, follows nearly the law of Boyle during expansion: that is, that the total volume by expansion varies inversely as the total pressure. Though the pressure falls thus rapidly by expansion, the work done during this period may be considerable, and in short constitutes, in conjunction with the fragment of power appended by exhaust-pressure, all the difference on the score of efficiency per pound of steam used, between a full and a partial admission to the cylinder. To recur to our initiatory diagram, page 66, in heavy lining, the steam is cut off at about one-third of the stroke, leaving the remaining two-thirds to be described under expansive action only,—the expansive action of the steam previously admitted. Now, without going into figures, it is obvious that the area of that part of the diagram due to the period of " expansion," is about equal to that of the first part of the diagram, described during " admission," at least if we add the fragment of area due to the " exhaust;" and, as area is the measure of work done, it follows that the extra work done by the separate expansion of the steam is, in this instance, as much as the work regularly done by it during admission; and that the work of the steam admitted to the cylinder has been thus doubled by the expedient of confining it and employing its expansive force throughout a large remainder of the stroke. The sooner the steam is cut off, the greater is the part of the stroke left for expansion; and therefore the economical action of the steam should also be greater in some proportion to the shortness of the admission. Our business is now to find at what rate this holds good in practice.

Means of estimating the Work of steam under Expansion. —According to the Boylean law of the expansion of steam, the area of diagram due to expansion may be computed by known rules, which assume that there is no atmospheric resistance, and that the release takes place at the end of the stroke.

As the condition of a vacuum on the exhaust side of the piston, does not in present practice exist in locomotives, such results show rather what is the ultimate possible performance of steam under expansion, than what it can do in the locomotive. Allowance is also to be made for the steam employed in filling the clearance, the loss of expansive force due to an early exhaust, the loss by back exhaust-pressure, and the reserve of steam by compression. We shall, then, in the first place, show generally, with the aid of a few examples, how the power developed during the different periods of the steam-stroke may be varied by the period of admission ; and shall afterwards deduce from the diagrams of the Great Britain, the rate at which, in practice, the efficiency of steam in the locomotive-cylinder is increased by expansive working.

Work of Steam during the individual periods of the Distribution.—Select, for example, Nos. 26, 34, and 43 diagrams from the second series of the Great Britain, (Diagram-Plate 4,) all of them taken at 17 miles per hour under the 1st, 3d, and 5th notches respectively. Divide the diagrams, as

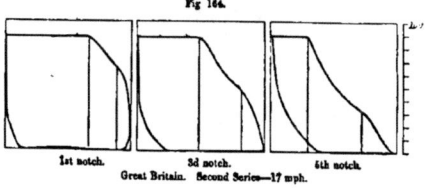

Fig 164.

1st notch.   3d notch.   5th notch.

Great Britain. Second Series—17 mph.

ILLUSTRATIONS OF THE WORK OF STEAM.

in the fig. 164, by vertical lines through the points of suppression and release ; the areas so set off represent the amounts of work done during the admission, the expansion, and the exhaust, independent of the drawback by compression. To reduce them to a common standard, the mean pressures exerted during each period may be converted into equivalent mean-pressures for the whole stroke,—or such as should enclose equal areas. The following table contains, in the 3d, 4th, and 5th columns, the results of this reduction.

TABLE, No. LII.—DETAILED PRESSURES OF STEAM IN THE CYLINDER OF THE GREAT BRITAIN, FROM DIAGRAMS, Nos. 26, 34, 43.

Notch.	Initial Pressures.	Mean Pressures reduced for the whole stroke, during			Sum of Expansion and Exhaust mean pressures	
		Admission.	Expansion.	Exhaust.	Whole stroke.	Sum.	Percentage of whole mean press
No.	lbs	lbs.	lbs.	lbs.	lbs.	lbs.	per cent.
1	88	58·66	16 33	5	80	21·33	27
3	88	44	21·4	4·5	69·9	25·9	37
5	89	26	22·8	4·4	53·2	27·2	51
1	2	3	4	5	6	7	8

While the initial pressure is sensibly the same in all the diagrams, 88 to 89 lbs., the whole mean pressures (col. 6,) fall from 80 lbs. in the 1st notch, to 53·2 lbs. in the 5th, which of course signifies a reduction of the whole work done, by shortening the admission. And while the mean reduced admission-pressures (col. 3,) fall rapidly as the admission is shortened, it is remarkable that those of expansion (col. 4,) absolutely rise ; that is, the smaller the quantity of steam admitted to the same cylinder, at a given initial pressure, the greater absolutely is the work which the charge of steam has an opportunity of doing by expansion alone. Also, for the different notches, the work done by exhaust pressures (col. 5,) is sensibly constant. Taking, then, the sums of the expansion and exhaust mean-pressures (col. 7,) they increase as the admission is reduced ; which implies that, within the limits of the 1st and 5th notches, the work

done by steam in the cylinder subsequently to suppression, increases as the admission is shortened ; and that the same work, as expressed in percentages (col. 8,) of the whole mean pressures (col. 6,) rises from one-fourth to one-half of the whole work done.

The near equality of the mean reduced pressures of exhaust under different notches, prevails even at high speeds, as we find that, for Nos. 33, 42, and 47, high-speed diagrams, these pressures are respectively 5½, 5¼, and 4 lbs., reduced for the whole stroke, for nearly equal initial pressures. The useful pressure of exhaust, during the steam-stroke, though usually considered to be nothing, is really not to be overlooked ; and indeed the course of the steam-line is in general so little affected by an early release, particularly at high speeds, as to show that the loss of expansive force by a " premature" release is a mere trifle, and is at least compensated by the prevention of back exhaust-pressure. To clench this argument, select diagrams Nos. 45 and 50 from the Great Britain, repeated in fig. 165, and extend their expansion-lines to the end of the stroke, as shown in dot-lining. This is done as follows :—the total volume at the release-

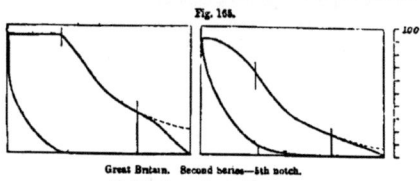

Fig. 165.

Great Britain. Second Series—5th notch.

WORK OF STEAM DURING EXHAUST.

point, taken at 17 inches, as defined by vertical lines, is 18·8 inches of the stroke ; at the end of the stroke it is (24+1·8) or 25·8 inches. The ratio of these total volumes is 1 to 1·37, and the release-pressures on the two diagrams are 33 and 16 lbs., or, adding 15 lbs., the totals are 48 and 31 lbs. The pressures falling during expansion as the volumes increase, the final pressures at the end of the stroke would be,

for No. 45, 48 × $\frac{1}{1·37}$ = 35 lbs. total, or 20 lbs. sensible.

for No. 50, 31 × $\frac{1}{1·37}$ = 23 lbs. total, or 8 lbs. sensible.

The expansion-curves thus produced ought to terminate upon 20 lbs. and 8 lbs. respectively, according to the dot lines, and the extra areas so enclosed, when averaged for the whole stroke, are equivalent to the following mean pressures per inch :—

No. 45. 21 miles per hour, 2·25 lbs. extra mean pressure.

No. 50. 56   do.   0·44 lbs.   do.

These are all the gains that would be had by deferring the release till the end of the stroke. At the higher speed, the gain is merely nominal, less than half a pound per inch, or about 1½ per cent. of the effective mean pressure ; and as highly expansive working is employed only at considerable speeds, it is clear that, even overlooking the creation of back pressure, a period of expansion protracted beyond what is available for given periods of admission by ordinary link-motions and valves without inside lap, is not worth providing for.

We have now to find at what rate, in practice, the efficiency of steam is increased by expansive working with the link-motion, under the combined existing conditions of back exhaust-pressure, compression, clearance, wire-drawing, and so forth.

Practical Efficiency of Steam under the Variable Expansion yielded by the Link-motion.—To facilitate the investigation of this question, as well as for general reference, the table of results, No. 54, founded on the diagrams of the Great Britain, is introduced at pp. 114, 115.

The materials of this table are derived partly from the smaller tables in preceding chapters; and the table, for the most part, explains itself. In estimating the back pressures, cols. 10 and 12, the exhaust pressure has been reckoned only up to the point of compression, and the total area of back pressure beyond this point is separated as compression. In this we have departed from the distinction hitherto made, of extending the exhaust-line up to the end of the stroke, because our present object is to separate the real loss by imperfect exhaust from the neutral back pressure of compression,—neutral, in so far as the steam so retained and compressed reciprocates the exchangeable pressure during the succeeding steam-stroke; just as the power absorbed in the compression of an ordinary spring is given forth in the recoil. And, not even should the whole of the back pressure of exhaust, up to the compression-line, be reckoned as *loss,* for the throttling of the exhaust at high speeds, indicated by a rise of the exhaust-line towards the ostensible point of compression, is due to premature compression, or reservation of steam, which we have already found to be strictly neutral in its relation to the steam's efficiency.

The effective mean pressures, col. 16, are the differences of cols. 9 and 14.

The five columns, 17 to 21, of horse-power are estimated by means of rule 6, page 110.

The column of water-equivalents for the admission, col. 22, is extracted from table No. 27, page 80, and shows the total volume of water admitted as steam, clearance included. For the quantity of water reserved as steam, col. 23, the pressure indicated at the point of compression has been adopted, and the volume has been deduced from the period of compression plus the clearance, in the way already explained at page 79. The differences of the cols. 22 and 23, given in col. 24, show the actual expenditure of water as steam, for each steam-stroke. This multiplied by 4 gives the whole consumption for one turn of the wheel, and multiplied by the number of turns per mile, which is 210, and by the speed, the final result is the consumption of water per hour, in col. 25, expressed in cubic feet. Dividing the contents of col. 25 by the effective horse-powers in col. 21, we have the actual consumption of water for effective horse-power per hour, col. 26, expressed in cubic inches; or in pounds in col. 27.

The relative consumption of coke, allowing 8 lbs. of water to be evaporated per pound of coke, is entered in the last column, as the running consumption of coke per horse-power per hour.

Assuming for present purposes, until superior results can be obtained, that the performances deduced from the 2d series of diagrams from the Great Britain, are practically perfect, we shall adopt them as standard results, actually achieved in practice, under the most favourable circumstances; from which useful practical rules may be constructed, for the real performance of steam in locomotives of the most favourable existing proportions and disposition of cylinders, and worked by the link-motion. In a future section, the application of these rules to practical cases will be considered.

Of the Loss of Efficiency by Back Exhaust Pressure.—The percentages of loss in terms of the positive mean pressures are contained in col. 11; and are reduced to curves for each notch, fig. 166, where the base-lines measure the speeds in miles per hour,

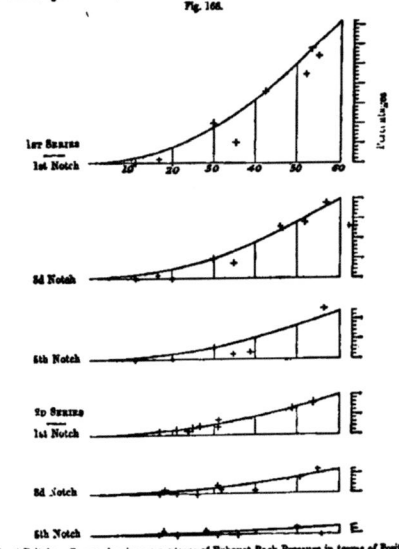

Fig. 166.

Great Britain.—Curves showing percentages of Exhaust Back-Pressure in terms of Positive Mean Pressure, at different Speeds.

and the vertical heights of the stars above the base-line are the percentages measured by the vertical scale. These curves show that the loss in each case varies as the square of the speed; and from them we have composed the following table:—

TABLE, No. LIII.—OF THE LOSS OF EFFICIENCY OF STEAM IN THE CYLINDER OF THE GREAT BRITAIN, BY BACK EXHAUST PRESSURE.

Notch.	Losses by Back Exhaust Pressure, in per cents. of the positive mean pressures, at the following speeds in miles per hour.					
	20 Miles.	30 Miles.	40 Miles.	50 Miles.	60 Miles.	
	per cent.	per cent.	per cent.	per cent.	per cent.	
1st Series.						Blast-orifice $\frac{1}{7}$th area of piston.
1st Notch....	4	9	16	25	36	
3d Do......	2·25	5	9	14	20	
5th Do......	1·3	3	5·3	8·3	12	
2d Series.						Blast-orifice $\frac{1}{10}$th area of piston.
1st Notch....	1·1	2·5	4·5	7	10	
3d Do......	·7	1·5	2·7	4·2	6	
5th Do......	·25	·5	1·0	1·4	2	

The smaller losses in the 2d series we have seen to be due to the wider blast-orifice; and it appears, generally, that, at 60 miles, or 840 feet of piston per minute,

When the orifice is enlarged from $\frac{1}{7}$th to $\frac{1}{12.7}$th of piston,
The loss in full gear falls from $\frac{1}{3}$d to $\frac{1}{10}$th of whole power,
And the loss in 5th notch falls from $\frac{1}{8}$th to $\frac{1}{50}$th of do.

Here the fine effect of enlarging the orifice is decided: while the enlargement is as 2 to 3, the loss in full gear falls from 36 to 10 per cent., at 60 miles, or as 3·6 to 1; and, even allowing for the difference of admission in full gear, for the two series, it is plain that the loss by back pressure diminishes quite as fast as the square of the blast-area increases, and that in short, as already proved in another way, the back exhaust-pressure varies inversely as the fourth power of the diameter of orifice.

Of the Resistance by Compression.—In col. 12, the actual values of compression in general rise slowly with the speed. This gradual rise is due partially to the increased pressure of exhaust-steam as the speeds rise, and chiefly to the increased temperature of the cylinder. At the highest speeds, it varies,

In 1st Series, from 4 lbs. in 1st notch, to 11·7 lbs. in 5th notch.
2d do. from 6 lbs. in 1st notch, to 11·5 lbs. in 5th notch.

In the 1st series, as the period of compression is less, the resistance should also have been less; whereas it is the same as in the 2d series, and this is owing to the greater back pressure of exhaust in the first case.

The reductions of power by compression, in the 2d series, vary from about 8 per cent. in full gear to 28 per cent. in the 5th notch. Thus, with great expansion, fully one-fourth of the power exerted is neutralized by compression-resistance.

It follows that at the highest speeds, the total drawback by back pressure is nearly the same for all the notches, as what is reduced in exhaust pressure is increased in compression. For example, the following diagrams, from the 2d series, show the annexed drawbacks (col. 14) in pounds per inch:—

No. 33, 1st notch, 54 mph. 12·8 lbs.
No. 44, 3d do., 55 ,, 11·2 lbs.
No. 50, 5th do., 56 ,, 11·5 lbs.

Therefore it is that the percentages of drawback (col. 15) rise as the whole mean pressure falls. Thus,

No. 33, 1st notch, 15·8 per cent. of drawback.
No. 44, 3d do., 18·0 do.
No. 50, 5th do., 28·1 do.

Of the Effective Mean Pressure in the Cylinder.—The drawback on useful power occasioned by back pressure is in practice a matter of common experience with ordinary engines; for with an admission of about two-thirds of the stroke or even less, as much work, or more, may be done at high speeds, than with longer admissions. This effect is, to be sure, owing partially also to the fall of pressure in the cylinder which usually follows an increase of admission. "In this and similarly constructed engines," says Mr. Gooch, in 1848, alluding to the Great Britain with the original valves, "the variation of the power is effected by the amount of expansion used, and the practice is at present to use No. 1 notch (18 inches) when starting a heavy train; and if the full power of the engine is required at a high speed of from 40 to 50 miles per hour, the 2d notch (17 inches) is used; for higher speeds than this the best result is obtained from the 3d notch (14½ inches); if more than this quantity of steam is admitted, the increase in back pressure arising therefrom more than absorbs the additional power on the steam-side." *

* *Report of Guage Commissioners*, 1848.

Again, on the Caledonian Railway, the passenger-engines running at speeds of 30 to 50 miles on the heavy inclines of the Edinburgh branch, perform their maximum work with an admission of 50 to 60 per cent., and full steam on.

In the Great Britain, 2d series, it appears, on the contrary, that even at the highest speeds, the admission for full gear is available for maximum work. For the three notches, we find the following pressures in the cylinder, the boiler-pressure being 98 lbs. :—

1st notch, 54 mph. 67·6 lbs. effective mean pressure.
3d do. 55 ,, 50·8 lbs. do.
5th do. 56 ,, 29·4 lbs. do.

The superiority of the mean pressure in the 1st notch, 66 per cent. admission, is so decided, that we may fairly place the maximum beneficial admission at not less than 75 per cent. of the stroke.

Again, as to the *rate* at which the effective mean pressure increases with the admission, for given maximum pressures in the cylinder; it has been seen that in the 2d series, the back pressures do not seriously increase with the speeds. The means of the maximum and effective mean pressures may therefore, without prejudice, be taken for each notch, as follow :—

2d Series.	Average Maximum Pressure in Cylinder.	Average Effective Mean Pressure in Cylinder.	
		Pressure.	Percentage of Average Maximum Pressure.
Notch.	lbs.	lbs.	per cent.
1	82	68·2	83
3	80	54·5	68
5	82	36·1	44

The last column contains the values of the average effective mean pressures in percentages of the maximum pressures during admission. Arrange these percentages in a curve, fig. 167, of which the base-line A B represents the

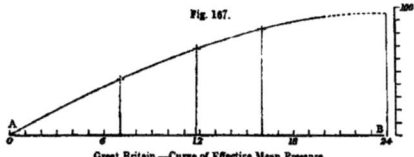

Fig. 167.

Great Britain.—Curve of Effective Mean Pressure.

stroke of the piston divided into inches; the three ordinates terminated by stars, are equal to the percentages as measured by the vertical scale, and erected at intervals on the base-line equal to the periods of admission for the three notches. Besides the three points thus defined by the stars, the point A must be a fourth, as the ordinate at A must be about nothing; and the other end of the curve above B, for an admission equal to the whole stroke, must terminate somewhere *below* 100 per cent., as something must come off for back pressure. Thus guided with points, the curve shows with accuracy the rate of increase up to about 75 per cent. of admission, beyond which the curve is of no moment.

If the periods of admission be expressed in percentages of the stroke, we derive from the curve the following formula for the effective mean pressure due to a given admission, in percent. of the maximum pressure during admission; *a*

P

TABLE No. LIV. (FIRST PART.)—OF THE GENERAL RESULTS FROM FIFTY INDICATOR-DIAGRAMS, TAKEN FROM THE CYLINDER OF THE GREAT BRITAIN LOCOMOTIVE BY MR. D. GOOCH, AND EXHIBITED IN DIAGRAM-PLATE IV. 1851.

CYLINDER, 18 x 24 INCHES STROKE; WHEEL, 8 FEET DIAMETER; STEAM-PORT, 13 x 2 INCHES; EXHAUST-PORT, 13 x 3½ INCHES; STEAM-PIPE, 4½ INCHES DIAMETER.

Date of Experiment.	No. of Experiment.	Speeds. Of Engine in miles per hour.	Speeds. Of Piston in feet per minute.	Period of Admission in inches of stroke.	Positive Steam Pressures, in pounds per square inch. In Boiler.	In Valve-chest.	Maximum in cylinder.	Mean pressure in cylinder.	Mean Back Pressures, in pounds per square inch. Of Exhaust. Pressure.	Of Exhaust. Percent of Steam Pressure.	Of Compression. Pressure.	Of Compression. Percent of Steam Pressure.	Whole Back Pressure. Pressure.	Whole Back Pressure. Percent of Steam Pressure.	Effective Mean Pressure per square inch.
	1st. Series.	miles.	feet.	ins.	lbs.	lbs.	lbs.	lbs.	lbs.	percent.	lbs.	percent.	lbs.	percent.	lbs.
	1st Notch.														
27th June, 1849...	1	11	154		...	...	67	62·5	0·08	0·01	0·5	0·8	0·58	0·81	61·9
,, ...	2	16½	231		...	...	62	58·1	0·90	1·40	1·6	2·6	2·5	4·3	55·6
5th April, ,, ...	3	20	280		...	...	50	46·5	0 0	0·0	1·4	3·0	1·4	3·0	45·1
,, ...	4	30	420		...	...	86	79 8	6·9	9·9	2·0	2·5	8·9	12·4	70·9
,, ...	5	35	490	17½	...	...	50	47·4	2·5	5·2	1·8	3·8	4·3	9·0	43·1
27th June, ,, ...	6	42	588		...	...	54	48·7	9 0	18·2	2·1	4 3	11·1	23·0	37·6
,, ...	7	52·3	732		...	...	65	59·4	13·3	22·4	3·9	6·5	17·2	28·9	42·2
,, ...	8	53 6	750		...	...	66	60·0	17·2	28·6	4·0	6·6	21·2	35·2	38·8
,, ...	9	55	770		...	...	64	58·0	15·9	27·4	3·6	6·2	19·5	33·6	38·5
Means							63								48·2
	3rd Notch.														
,, ...	10	11	154		...	...	62	54·1	0·0	0·0	2·5	4·6	2·5	4·6	51·6
,, ...	11	16½	231		...	...	63	54·3	0·64	1·10	2·8	5·1	3·44	6·2	50·9
5th April, ,, ...	12	20	280		...	...	55	45·5	0 0	0·0	2·9	6·3	2·9	6·3	42·6
,, ...	13	30	420		...	...	88	73·4	3·7	5·0	5·2	7·1	8·9	12·1	64·5
,, ...	14	35	490	14¼	...	...	58	48·8	1·8	3·6	3·6	7·4	5·4	11·0	43·3
Sept. 1847...	15	46	644		...	...	74	59·3	7·8	13·1	4·0	6·7	11·8	19·8	47·5
27th June, 1849...	16	52·3	732		...	...	74	58·3	8·2	14 0	7·4	12·6	15·6	26·6	42 7
Sept. 1847...	17	57	798		...	...	96	81·6	15·3	18 7	6·0	7·3	21·3	26·0	60·3
,, ...	18	63	882		...	...	53	40·9	5·3	13·2	6·5	15·8	12·0	29·0	28·9
Means							69								48·0
	5th Notch.														
27th June, 1849...	19	11	154		...	...	62	44·3	0·0	0·0	6·4	14·5	6·4	14·5	37·9
5th April, ,, ...	20	20	280		...	...	68	46·2	0·0	0·0	5·7	12·3	5·7	12·3	40·5
,, ...	21	30	420	9¾	...	...	96	63·1	1·5	2·3	9·0	14·2	10·5	16·5	52·6
,, ...	22	35	490		...	...	73	46·4	0·7	1·4	7·4	15·9	8·1	17·3	38·3
27th June, 1849...	23	39	546		...	...	58	34 0	0·7	2·0	7·3	21·4	8·0	24·0	26·0
,, ...	24	56·2	787		...	...	86	47·4	6·0	12·6	11·7	24·8	17·7	37·4	29·7
Means							74								37·5
	2d Series.	miles.	feet.	ins.	lbs.	lbs.	lbs.	lbs.	lbs.	percent.	lbs.	percent.	lbs.	percent.	lbs.
	1st Notch.														
13th Feb., 1850...	25	15	210		78	77	70	63·8	1·6	2·4	2·4	3·7	4 0	6·1	59·8
20th ,, ,, ...	26	17	238		97	93	88	80·0	0 6	0·7	1·9	2·3	2 5	3 0	77·5
,, ,, ,, ...	27	21	294		105	98	95	86·2	1·2	1·3	3·0	3·4	4·2	4·7	82·0
13th ,, ,, ...	28	24	336		90	95	85	76·7	0·9	1·1	1·6	2·0	2 5	3·1	74·2
,, ,, ,, ...	29	27	378	16	75	85	80	70·6	1·5	2·2	2·2	3·1	3·7	5 3	66·9
20th ,, ,, ...	30	31	434		97	100	90	79 6	1·7	2·1	3·7	4·6	5·4	6·7	74·2
,, ,, ,, ...	31	31	434		82	88	80	73·2	2·9	3 9	2·2	3·0	5·1	6·9	68·1
13th ,, ,, ...	32	49	686		76	73	60	51·4	3·6	7·0	4·4	8·5	8·0	15·5	43·4
20th ,, ,, ...	33	54	756		98	100	89	80·4	6 8	8·4	6·0	7·4	12·8	15·8	67.6
Means							82								68·2
	3rd Notch.														
,, ,, ,, ...	34	17	238		100	95	88	69·9	0·0	0·0	3·8	5·4	3·8	5·4	66·1
13th ,, ,, ...	35	18	252		77½	77	70	55·3	0·8	1·4	4·5	8·0	5·3	9·4	50·0
20th ,, ,, ...	36	21	294		105	98	92	72·3	0·0	0·0	4·2	5·7	4·2	5·7	68·1
13th ,, ,, ...	37	26	364		87	93	72	57·1	0·0	0·0	4·9	8·5	4·9	8·5	52·2
20th ,, ,, ...	38	31	434	11¾	83	90	79	60·3	1·2	1·9	6·0	10·0	7·2	11 9	53·1
,, ,, ,, ...	39	32	448		98	101	86	64·4	0·8	1·2	4·9	7·2	5·7	8·4	58·7
13th ,, ,, ...	40	40	560		75	87	76	55·7	0 4	0·7	4·7	8·4	5·1	9·1	50·6
,, ,, ,, ...	41	51	714		74	77	70	49·1	2·0	4·0	6·2	12·6	8·2	16·6	40·9
20th ,, ,, ...	42	55	770		98	100	84	62·0	3·6	5·8	7·6	12·2	11·2	18·0	50·8
Means							80								54·5
	5th Notch.														
,, ,, ,, ...	43	17	238		105	97	89	53 2	0 0	0·0	9·6	18·0	9·6	18·0	43·5
13th ,, ,, ...	44	18	252		77½	77	70	42·1	0·5	1·1	6·6	15·6	7·1	16·7	35·0
20th ,, ,, ...	45	21	294		105	100	93	56·5	0 0	0·0	6·3	11·1	6·3	11·1	50·2
13th ,, ,, ...	46	28	392	7	80	85	74	41·8	0·4	0·9	6·2	14·8	6·[illegible]	15·7	35·2
20th ,, ,, ...	47	31	434		90	90	83	46·5	0·0	0·0	7·4	15·5	7·4	15·5	39·1
13th ,, ,, ...	48	36	504		75	90	80	39 0	0·0	0·0	8·5	21·1	8·5	21·1	30·5
,, ,, ,, ...	49	50	700		72	78	77	34 7	0·5	1·4	8·0	23·0	8·5	24·4	26·2
20th ,, ,, ...	50	56	784		98	105	90	40 9	0·0	0·0	11·5	28·1	11·5	28·1	29·4
Means							82								30·1
1	2	3	4	5	6	7	8	9	10	11	12	13	14	15	16

TABLE No. LIV.—(SECOND PART)

FIRST SERIES.—Lap, 1 inch outside, ₁₀ inch inside; Blast-orifice, 4¼ inch diameter, except for Nos. 15, 17, 18, 4¾ inches.
SECOND SERIES.—Lap, 1¼ inch outside, ₁₀ inch inside; Blast-orifice, 5¼ inches diameter.

Whole Power during Steam-Stroke.	Horse Power.			Effective Power.	Water-Equivalents.					Coke consumed, per effective horse-power, allowing 1 lb. for 8 lbs. of water evaporated.
	Back Pressure.				Total admitted for one stroke, measured from diagram.	Reserved by Compression.	Actually expended during one Steam-Stroke.	Actually expended per hour.	Actually expended per effective horse-power per hour.	
	Of Exhaust.	Of Compression.	Whole back Pressure.							
H. P.	H. P.	H. P.	H. P.	H. P.	cub. ins.	cub. ins.	cub. ins.	cub. feet.	cub. ins.	lbs.	lbs.
148	0·19	1·2	1·39	147	14·01	0·68	13·33	71·24	822	30·3	3·79
207	3·10	5·5	8·6	199	13·27	0·73	12·54	100·60	873	31·6	3·95
200	0·0	5·4	5·4	195	11·13	0·68	10·45	101·60	900	32·5	4·06
516	38·8	18·6	57·4	459	16·64	1·00	15·64	223·10	859	30·1	3·76
458	18·8	13·6	32·4	326	11·46	0·84	10·62	180·70	958	34·6	4·32
447	82·6	19·3	101·9	345	10·98	1·12	9·86	201·30	1008	36·5	4·56
670	150·0	43·9	193·9	476	12·72	1·32	11·40	289·83	1052	38·0	4·75
694	198·9	46·2	245·1	449	13·20	1·47	11·73	305·63	1176	42·5	5·31
688	188·6	42·6	231·2	457	12·50	1·39	11·11	297·05	1123	40·6	5·07
Means										35·2	4·40
128	0·00	5·0	5·0	122	10·98	0·02	10·06	53·79	762	27·5	3·44
193	2·29	10·0	12·20	181	11·10	1·00	10·10	81·01	773	28·0	3·50
197	0·0	12·0	12·0	185	9·28	1·04	7·24	70·39	657	23·8	2·97
473	23·9	33·7	37·6	415	13·66	1·23	12·43	181·33	755	27·3	3·42
368	13·5	27·1	40·6	327	9·68	1·26	8·42	143·26	757	27·4	3·82
558	77·3	39·6	116·9	441	10·98	1·53	9·45	211·32	828	29·9	3·74
658	92·5	83·4	175·9	482	10·83	1·80	9·03	229·57	823	29·7	3·71
1005	188·4	73·8	262·2	743	14·80	2·07	12·73	352·72	820	29·6	3·70
557	74·7	88·5	163·2	394	8·07	1·69	6·38	195·37	857	31·0	3·87
Means										28·2	3·57
105	0·0	15·2	15·2	90	7·80	1·42	6·38	34·11	655	23·7	2·96
200	0·0	25·0	25·0	175	8·09	1·42	6·67	64·84	640	23·2	2·90
408	9·7	58·1	67·8	340	9·90	1·91	7·99	116·52	592	21·4	2·67
350	5·2	35·8	61·0	289	7·40	1·83	5·57	94·77	593	21·4	2·67
286	5·8	61·4	67·2	219	6·02	1·67	4·35	82·47	651	23·5	2·94
575	72·0	141·9	213·9	361	7·70	2·31	5·39	147·26	705	25·5	3·19
Means										23·1	2·89
H. P.	H. P.	H. P.	H. P.	H. P.	cub. ins.	cub. ins.	cub. ins.	cub. feet.	cub. ins.	lbs.	lbs.
203	5·09	7·63	12·7	190	13·32	1·00	12·32	89·83	817	29·5	3·69
293	2·1	6·9	9·0	284	15·89	0·82	15·07	124·53	758	27·4	3·42
391	5·4	13·6	19·0	372	16·71	1·09	15·62	159·45	741	26·8	3·35
397	4·6	8·2	12·8	384	15·30	0·82	14·48	168·95	760	27·5	3·44
411	8·7	12·8	21·5	389	13·89	0·91	12·98	170·37	757	27·4	3·42
533	11·3	24·7	36·0	497	15·62	1·13	14·49	218·35	759	27·4	3·42
490	19·4	14·7	34·1	456	14·76	1·00	13·76	207·35	796	28·4	3·55
543	33·0	66·4	84·4	439	10·73	1·34	9·39	223·60	842	30·4	3·80
907	76·7	67·6	144·3	763	15·62	1·56	14·06	369·07	836	30·2	3·77
Means										28·3	3·54
256	0·0	13·9	13·9	242	12·19	1·10	11·09	91·65	654	23·7	2·96
215	3·1	17·5	20·6	194	10·33	1·35	8·98	78·57	700	25·3	3·16
328	0·0	19·0	19·0	309	12·50	1·16	11·34	115·78	647	23·4	2·92
320	0·0	27·4	27·4	293	10·55	1·41	9·14	115·52	681	24·6	3·07
404	8·0	42·2	48·2	356	10·87	1·48	9·39	141·50	687	24·8	3·10
445	5·5	32·3	37·8	407	11·33	1·29	10·04	156·20	663	24·0	3·00
481	3·4	40·5	43·9	437	9·78	1·35	8·43	163·87	648	23·4	2·92
540	22·0	68·1	90·1	450	8·65	1·54	7·11	176·30	677	24·5	3·06
736	42·7	90·2	132·9	603	10·54	1·66	8·88	237·42	680	24·6	3·07
Means										24·3	3·03
194	0·0	35·1	35·1	159	7·90	1·85	6·05	50·00	543	19·6	2·45
163	1·9	25·5	27·4	136	6·59	1·76	4·83	42·26	537	19·4	2·42
256	0·0	28·5	28·5	228	8·20	1·42	6·78	69·21	525	18·9	2·36
253	2·4	37·5	39·9	213	6·87	1·68	5·19	70·64	537	20·7	2·50
311	0·0	49·4	49·4	262	7·29	1·59	5·70	85·89	566	20·5	2·56
303	0·0	66·0	66·0	237	6·08	1·85	4·23	74·02	540	19·5	2·44
374	5·3	86·2	91·5	263	5·52	1·76	3·76	91·39	600	21·7	2·71
491	0·0	138·0	138·0	353	6·24	2·10	4·14	113·20	554	20·1	2·51
Means										20·1	2·51
17	18	19	20	21	22	23	24	25	26	27	28

denotes the percentage of admission, and P, the effective mean pressure:—

$$\text{P} = 13.5 \sqrt{a} - 28 \qquad (7.)$$

Whence the following rule,

RULE VII.—*To find the Effective Mean Pressure in the Cylinder, the Maximum Pressure being given, and the Period of Admission.* Find the square root of the period of admission expressed in percent. of the stroke;—multiply by 13.5,—and subtract 28 from the product. The remainder is the effective mean pressure in percent. of the maximum pressure of the steam admitted.

Note.—This rule applies to any dimensions of cylinder, with proportions like those of the Great Britain.

Example.—Given, the maximum pressure in the cylinder equal to 90 lbs.; the period of admission equal to 9 inches out of 18 inches stroke. Required, the effective mean pressure.

The admission is $\dfrac{9 \times 100}{18} = 50$ per cent. of the stroke. The square root of 50 is 7.07, and $7.07 \times 13.5 = 95.5$; then $95.5 - 28 = 67.5$ per cent., is the effective mean pressure in per cent. of the maximum, and $90 \times \dfrac{67.5}{100} = 60.75$ lbs., is the pressure in pounds.

This rule being based upon the average results of very various speeds, the conclusions it yields will be slightly too small for the lowest speeds, and slightly too great for the highest; but these deviations we have considered of no practical moment, especially as the small error is thus divided. At 40 miles, or 560 feet of piston per minute in the Great Britain, the deviation is nothing; and this is an ordinary speed of piston in both passenger and goods-engines. The rule also applies without material error to periods of admission from 10 to 75 per cent., and to maximum pressures ranging from 60 to 100 lbs., or even 150 lbs., for the elements which regulate the effective mean pressure, vary very much in the same ratio.

By rule 7 we have the following table of effective mean pressures for admissions advancing by twentieths, or intervals of 5 per cent. of the stroke; most of these are also expressed in common fractions in the last two columns.

TABLE, No. LV.—OF EFFECTIVE MEAN PRESSURES IN THE CYLINDER, FOR VARIOUS ADMISSIONS, AND FOR MAXIMUM PRESSURES OF 60 LBS TO 150 LBS.

Period of Admission, in per cent. of the stroke.	Effective Mean Pressure, in per cent. of maximum pressure.	Period of Admission, in fractions of the stroke.	Effective Mean Pressure, in parts of maximum pressure.
per cent.	per cent.		
10	15	1–10th	1–7th fully
12.5	20	1–8th	1–5th
15	24	1–6th	1–4th
17.5	28		
20	32	1–5th	1–3d
25	40	1–4th	1–2.5th
30	46		
35	52	1–3d	1–2d
40	57		
45	62		
50	67	1–2d	2–3ds
55	72		
60	77		
65	81	2–3ds	4–5ths
70	85		
75	89	3–4ths	9–10ths

Of the Horse-power developed in the Cylinder.—The power stated in col. 21, of the table 54, is that which is left *in the cylinder*, after allowance for drawbacks. The greatest total power exerted is 1005 H. P. (horse-power) in No. 17, at 57 miles, in the 3d notch, 1st series; the drawback, chiefly in back pressure, amounts to 262 H. P., or 26 per cent., leaving a balance in the cylinder, of 743 H. P. In the 2d series, the drawbacks are much less, and accordingly, in No. 33, 1st notch, while the total power is 907 H. P., or about 100 H. P. less than in No. 17, the available power in the cylinder is 763 H. P., or 20 H. P. more.

As, upon the whole, the effective mean pressure is found to vary with the period of admission, the effective horse-power, which is founded on that pressure, must also vary with the admission, in the same ratio as the effective pressure.

Of the Consumption of Water and Coke.—Under each notch of the 1st series the consumption of water and coke per effective horse-power per hour (last three cols.), rises very obviously with the speed, owing to the greater losses by back pressure at the higher speeds. In the 2d series, as the losses are much less, the rate of consumption is much less variable, indeed nearly constant; and in the 5th notch, it is virtually nothing. If we take the mean consumption for each notch, the variation from the mean will be but trifling. We have, then, from col. 27, the following mean consumptions of water:—

2D SERIES.
1st notch, 28.3 lbs. of water per horse-power per hour.
3d do. 24.3 lbs. do. do.
5th do. 20.1 lbs. do. do.

Arrange these quantities in a curve to find their rate of variation. Thus, fig. 168, let A B be the stroke of piston divided into inches; for the periods of admission, 16, 11¼,

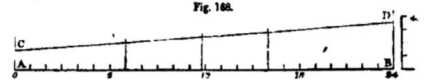

Fig. 168.

Diagram to show Consumption of Water as Steam, per H. P. per hour, for various Admissions.

and 7 inches respectively, draw ordinates equal to the weights of water above given. The upper extremities of these ordinates are found to range in a straight line, C D, which meets the vertical A C at 14 lbs., and B D at 36 lbs. The curve is, in fact, a straight line, showing that the consumption per H.P. per hour increases uniformly with the period of admission, commencing with a constant quantity of 14 lbs. The total increase is $36 - 14$ or 22 lbs.; therefore, for each extra inch of admission, the increase is $\frac{2}{9}$ lbs. of water. In general, it follows that if we multiply 22 by the period of admission, expressed as a fraction of the whole stroke, and add 14 to the product, the sum expresses the consumption. Thus, let $a = $ the period of admission in percentage of the stroke, then $\frac{a}{100}$ expresses the same as a common fraction, and

$$\text{the consumption of water per H.P. per hour} = 22 \left(\frac{a}{100} \right) + 14$$
$$= 0.22\,a + 14 \qquad (8.)$$

or, verbally,

RULE VIII.—*To find the Consumption of Water as Steam, in pounds per horse-power per hour, for a given period of admission.* Multiply the period of admission, expressed as a percent. of the stroke, by 0·22,—and add 14 to the product. The sum is the required consumption.

For the consumption of coke, allowing 1 lb. of coke for the evaporation of 8 lbs. of water, we have only to divide by 8 the water as above found; or, dividing the terms of the above formula by 8, we have

the consumption of coke per H.P. per hour $= \dfrac{0 \cdot 22\, a + 14}{8}$

$$= \cdot 0275\, a + 1 \cdot 75 \quad (0.)$$

or, verbally,

RULE IX.—*To find the Consumption of Coke in pounds per horse-power per hour, for a given period of admission.* Multiply the period of admission expressed in percent. of the stroke, by ·0275,—and add 1·75 to the product. The sum is the required consumption.

These rules may be employed without sensible error for admissions varying between 10 and 75 per cent. of the stroke; and though based upon results from steam of the maximum pressures of 80 lbs. to 84 lbs. in the cylinder, they apply with practical accuracy to pressures ranging from 60 lbs. to 120 lbs. For pressures considerably different from 80 lbs., there are slight deviations by the rule from the real quantities, the results being slightly too small for the lower pressures, and too great for the higher. The deviation is due to the constant deduction of 15 lbs. for atmospheric resistance, from the total pressure of steam. It is, however, but small; for example, for 60 lbs. steam, of 75 lbs. total pressure, the atmosphere deducts $\frac{1}{5}$th of the total pressure, and for 80 lbs. steam, $\frac{1}{6 \cdot 3 3}$d, then $(\frac{1}{5} - \frac{1}{6 \cdot 3 3})$ or $\frac{1}{7 5}$th is the deviation by defect of the results by rule for 60 lbs. steam. For 100 lbs. steam, the deviation is $\frac{1}{7 5}$th by excess; for 120 lbs. it is $\frac{1}{5 1}$th by excess; and even for 150 lbs. steam, it is only $\frac{1}{3 1}$th by excess. For the higher pressures, then, which will be universally used in future, the rules for coke and water, may safely be employed, as their results err on the safe side; and these considerations show that the relative advantage of high pressure steam, in reducing the opposition of the atmosphere to a smaller fraction of the total pressure, progresses but slowly for pressures above 80 lbs. The chief advantage is to be sought for in the liberty of working more expansively, while the same power is developed.

Table of the Efficiency of Steam by Expansion.—As the practical efficiency of steam by expansion is measured ultimately by the consumption of steam, or water as steam, for the same work done, we can, by the foregoing rules for finding this, determine directly the comparative economy of steam cut off at various parts of the stroke, by the link-motion.

The following table presents in contrast, the relative efficiency of steam worked expansively in the locomotive, as found in actual practice, and the maximum relative efficiency by Boyle's law, acting against a vacuum, without clearance, back pressure, or compression, and fully expanding until the end of the stroke. The 2d column, of water-consumption, is found by rule 8; the inverse ratios of these quantities of water are contained in the 3d column, the consumption for 100 per cent. being expressed by 1, or unity; thus the actual relative efficiency of steam is found for various admissions. The 4th column contains the maximum relative

efficiency with a vacuum on the exhaust side, as above explained.

In the 5th column are given the relative amounts of work done by steam under various admissions. These are of course directly in proportion to the effective mean pressures found by rule 7, and are simply transcribed from the 2d column of table No. 55.

TABLE NO. LVI.—EFFICIENCY OF STEAM BY EXPANSION IN THE CYLINDER OF THE LOCOMOTIVE, IN ACTUAL PRACTICE. FOR MAXIMUM PRESSURES DURING ADMISSION OF 60 LBS. TO 120 LBS.

Periods of admission, in per cent. of stroke.	Water as steam consumed per H.P. per hour	Relative efficiency of steam in actual practice.	Possible maximum relative efficiency.	Relative Work done by steam of the same maximum pressure in the cylinder.
10 per cent.	16·2 lbs.	2·22	3·30	15
12·5	16·7	2 15	3·08	20
15	17·3	2·08	2·90	24
17·5	17·8	2·02	2·73	28
20	18·4	1·96	2 60	32
25	19·5	1·85	2·39	40
30	20·6	1·75	2·20	46
35	21·7	1·66	2·05	52
40	22·8	1·58	1·92	57
45	23·9	1·50	1·90	62
50	25·0	1·44	1·69	67
55	26·1	1·38	1·60	72
60	27·2	1·32	1·51	77
65	28·3	1·27	1·43	81
70	29·4	1·23	1·35	85
75	30·5	1·18	1·28	89
100	36·0	1·00	1·00	100
1	2	3	4	5

Here we see that the actual efficiency of steam increases with expansive working at a much slower rate than would be possible if every drawback were removed. For example, in practice, an admission of $\frac{1}{5}$th, or 20 per cent., yields, by this table, just about double the efficiency due to a full admission,—an increase which, without any drawback, would be accomplished with $\frac{1}{3}$d admission. Atmospheric resistance cannot as yet be removed by known means; but it is plain that if the clearance in the cylinder and the ports could be reduced to nothing, the relative efficiency would be materially increased.

A period of 75 per cent. being in practice the greatest useful admission yielded by the link-motion; having found also, when discussing the link-motion, that about 10 per cent. is the smallest possible admission, if we compare the relative efficiencies of these extremes, namely 1·18 and 2·22, col. 3, they are in the ratio of 1 to 1·9, or nearly 1 to 2. Thus it follows finally, that *under the most favourable existing circumstances the utmost possible efficiency of steam worked expansively in locomotive engines by the link-motion, is about twice that of the steam when worked under full gear; that is, the same quantity of steam does twice the quantity of work.*

Now, as an example of what would be saved by annihilating the clearance: if this were done in the Great Britain, we would save 1·8 inches of steam, in parts of the stroke, which would amount to (254·47 × 1·8) or 458 cubic inches of steam, equivalent to 1·55 inches of water, reckoning for 84 lbs. steam. In the 5th notch, 5·08 inches of water are expended in one stroke, for steam of that pressure; the proportion of saving would therefore be $\frac{1 \cdot 5 5}{5 \cdot 0 8} = 30$ per cent. in this notch, and the relative efficiency with respect to full gear, 75 per cent. admission, would be raised from 1·5 to 2·13; that is, with an admission of 29 per cent., or a little less than one-third of the stroke, the efficiency would be fully double of what is due to full gear, which is more than what is attainable under present arrangements with the smallest admission, 10 per cent., or one-tenth of the stroke.

General Application of the foregoing Rules.—In all well-protected cylinders, with blast-orifices not greater than $\frac{1}{14}$th, these rules apply to the action of steam, under link-motion, at all speeds under 30 to 40 miles, as the proportional total clearance is much the same in all cases, and the back exhaust pressure when the engine and boiler are in good working condition, is a comparative trifle. In the 1st series of the Great Britain, for example, the mean consumption of water per horse-power per hour for speeds under 30 and 40 miles, are, by table 54, as follow:—

Admission.				Means.
1st notch,	74 per cent.,	experiments 1 to 4,	31·1 lbs. water.
3d do.,	59 do.,	do.	10 to 13,	27·0 lbs.
5th do.,	40 do.,	do.	19 to 23,	22·6 lbs.

Now, by the contents of column 2 of the table 56, the water used would be 30·3, 27·0, and 22·8 lbs. respectively, which are virtually the same as those just found in actual practice. For the highest speeds of 55 to 63 miles, the actual consumptions are decidedly in excess, as they amount to 40·6, 31·0, and 25·5 lbs. respectively, or from 33 to 12 per cent. of excess, or loss by imperfect exhaust.

For engines like the Orion, the Nile, and the Hebe, with ports of about $\frac{1}{12}$th, and orifices $\frac{1}{17}$th to $\frac{1}{14}$th of the cylinder, the rule also applies for the lower speeds; because, the back exhaust pressure in these engines is sensibly the same as in the 1st series of the Great Britain, as we find on reference to table 37, page 92. When the Orion ran with good clean water in the boiler, the back exhaust pressure was sensibly nothing, at the observed speeds; and we may infer that with engines proportioned and arranged like the Orion, when the boilers are perfectly clean and the water pure, the rules founded on the *average* practice of the Great Britain, 2d series, may be adopted, as worked out in table 56.

Sharp's engine, the Hebe, E. and G. R., as we have seen, wiredraws the steam very considerably during admission, owing to the small lap and short travel of valve. Wiredrawing is synonymous with partial expansion, and is equivalent to an earlier suppression. Mr. Bourne was the first to point out this characteristic of wiredrawing. "An engine," he says, "with lap enough upon the valve to cut off the steam at two-thirds of the stroke, may, by the aid of wiredrawing, be virtually rendered capable of cutting off the steam at one-third of the stroke."[*] The benefit of wiredrawing is, however, merely incidental to a less perfect action of the valve; as, were the valves of the Hebe so proportioned as to extinguish wiredrawing, we would be enabled to cut off earlier, *and to do the same work with less steam*. But, as expansive-working reduces the effective mean pressure, and consequently the work done, the maximum expansion is regulated both by the work to be done and by the greatest

[*] *Catechism of the Steam Engine,* 1848. Also noticed in the *Artisan Journal,* 1844, under the Editorship of Mr. Bourne.

initial pressure available in the cylinder, or by the pressure in the boiler.

In partially protected (outside) cylinders, the greater back pressure causes a greater expenditure of water as steam for the same work done, independently of the excess by condensation. The excess by back pressure is, as we have seen, very variable; but the best results for outside-cylinders, in table 37, founded on release-pressures under 40 lbs.,—generally about 20 to 30 lbs.,—or 40 to 60 lbs. during admission, show that with an orifice of $\frac{1}{15}$th to $\frac{1}{14}$th and inside lead of $\frac{1}{8}$th to $\frac{1}{14}$ (Nos. 13, 42, and 51) the loss, in regular work, is about the same as for the 1st series of the Great Britain, and the consumptions of steam, *as indicated*, will therefore be the same per horse-power. When the steam is worked under full gear, and exhausted at pressures above 60 or 70 lbs., with steam of 90 to 150 lbs. in the cylinder during admission, the back pressure is proportionally much less, as we have already had occasion to show (figs. 140, 141, 142), and, indeed, in the last case, with the England, page 94, having an orifice of $\frac{1}{107}$th, with 140 lbs. steam, and 65 per cent. admission, the exhaust was found to be as good as that of the Great Britain, with the same orifice. It follows that, as exposed cylinders exhaust as freely as well protected ones, with steam above 90 lbs. and an admission of above 65 per cent., the consumption of water indicated as steam under these conditions, will also be the same. It would be premature to attempt any modification of the formula, to suit exposed cylinders, under all circumstances, till we shall have approximated more exactly than has yet been done, to the real amount of condensation.

Concluding Remarks. — We have seen how much the mechanical efficiency of steam is opposed by atmospheric resistance, and impaired by clearance and back pressure. It is known, also, how severely steam suffers by condensation in the cylinder under certain circumstances. These are all impediments to the complete success of expansive gear. Another, but less obvious impediment is the adoption of a low standard of boiler-pressure; because the lower the head of pressure, the greater is the relative loss by the atmosphere, but principally because the expansive functions of the valve-gear are less available. On level railways, like the Edinburgh and Glasgow, this objection exists with greater force than even on railways with steep gradients, like the Caledonian; because, on the former, the pull is nearly uniform throughout, and therefore a constant high pressure in the boiler would be the more necessary for carrying out great expansion; whereas, on the latter class of lines, a lower boiler-pressure may suffice for purposes of great expansion, on descending gradients where but little steam is required. Moreover, the evil of low pressure is, as we have found in last chapter, greatly aggravated by the resistance of the passages to the flow of steam from the boiler, at high speeds, which reduces the available pressure in the cylinder, precisely at the time it is most wanted. It is clear, that, in general practice, cutting off at half stroke is reckoned good work for expansion; and very rarely indeed is the admission reduced below 30 per cent. of the stroke. There is no sufficient reason why the ultimate expansion of steam enforced in certain classes of stationary engines, should not be more thoroughly followed out in the practice of locomotives, seeing that by the link-motion a minimum suppression of 10 to 20 per cent. of the stroke is available. We have already shown that in exposed cylinders, the economical use of expansion-gear is limited by the formidable condensation that attends great expansion. In all locomotive engines, it is essential to the entire success of expansive working, that the cylinders be well protected and well heated; that all the steam-passages be wide and free; that the valve-gear be maintained in firstrate order, so that early suppressions may be effected, because the wear of the valve-gear delays the movements of the valve, and lengthens the admission, especially towards mid-gear; that by improved arrangements, the clearance at each end of the cylinder should be reduced to the lowest possible fraction; and that a high pressure in the boiler, of 100 lbs. to 150 lbs. should be constantly maintained.

RECAPITULATION.—1. WORK is an exertion of pressure through space; and the unit of work is the labour necessary to raise one pound through the height of one foot. Horse-power expresses the rate of work done, and one horse-power is equivalent to work done at the rate of 33,000 pounds raised through one foot in one minute.

2. The effective mean pressure on the piston under the action of steam, is equal to the difference of the mean positive and back pressures, as indicated on the diagram, and the area of the diagram is a measure of the work done during one stroke of the piston.

3. The horse-power of a locomotive, developed in the cylinder, is estimated from the diagram in terms of the speed, the diameter and stroke of piston, the diameter of the driving wheel, and the effective mean pressure on the piston.

4. The resistance of the atmosphere on the piston is virtually constant under all conditions, being about 15 pounds per square inch. The greater the steam-pressure, therefore, the less is that resistance in proportion; and hence, partly, the advantage, in point of efficiency, of employing steam of higher pressure in the cylinder.

5. The superior efficiency of steam worked expansively is due to the work done by the steam during the period of expansion, and up to the end of the steam-stroke; and also to the reduction of back exhaust-pressure by an earlier release.

6. If steam be admitted to the cylinder at the same pressure, the work done during expansion is actually *increased* as the period of admission is reduced, notwithstanding there is a smaller body of steam to be expanded; and during the exhaust, till the end of the steam-stroke, the work done is sensibly *constant* for all admissions. Thus, the whole useful work done by the steam subsequently to the period of its admission, is absolutely increased as the admission is reduced.

7. The loss of useful expansive force by a "premature" release of the steam worked expansively by a link-motion, is a mere trifle, practically nothing; and is much more than compensated by the prevention of back pressure.

8. The results from the Great Britain,—with well protected cylinders, port about $\frac{1}{10}$th, orifice $\frac{1}{12}$th to $\frac{1}{11}$th, and inside lead about $\frac{1}{11}$th of the area of piston,—having been found upon the whole superior to those derived from the other locomotives subjected to experiment, they are

assumed, for present purposes, to be standard practical results of the action of steam in locomotives, worked by link-motions; and they form the basis of the following observations.

9. The loss of efficiency by back exhaust pressure varies as the square of the speed, and inversely as the square of the area of blast-orifice. At 60 miles, or 840 feet of piston, the loss in full gear amounts to from $\frac{1}{4}$th to $\frac{1}{10}$th of the whole power, when the orifice is enlarged within the practical limits of $\frac{1}{17}$th to $\frac{1}{11}$th of the piston; in the 5th notch, suppressing at 30 to 40 per cent., the loss at the same speed, and within the same limits of orifice, is from $\frac{1}{5}$th to $\frac{1}{11}$th of the whole power. At 30 miles, the loss is from $\frac{1}{11}$th to $\frac{1}{40}$th in full gear.

10. The resistance by compression rises very slowly with the speed; it increases also with the degree of expansion, from about 8 per cent. in full gear to 28 per cent. in the 5th notch,—by which in the latter case above one-fourth of the power is neutralized by compression.

11. At the highest speeds the *whole* drawback by back pressure is nearly the same for all degrees of expansion, as what is reduced in exhaust pressure is made up by compression.

12. At the higher speeds of 30 to 60 miles, and with heavy loads, the greatest work done by engines generally, having ports about $\frac{1}{11}$th, and blast-orifices $\frac{1}{11}$th to $\frac{1}{10}$th of the piston, is effected with admissions not greater than 66 per cent.; showing that the greatest effective pressure is obtained with this admission.

13. In the Great Britain, with the wider port and wider orifice, the greatest useful admission at high speeds with heavy loads is at least 75 per cent. of the stroke.

14. The effective mean pressure in the cylinder varies with the period of admission. For an admission of three-fourths of the stroke, it is about 90 per cent. of the maximum pressure; for half stroke, it is 67 per cent.; for one-fourth stroke, it is 40 per cent.

15. The consumption of water *as steam* under the same notch, per horse-power per hour, is practically constant for all the speeds observed.

16. The efficiency of steam worked expansively, increases uniformly as the admission is shortened, until for 10 per cent. admission it is just about double the efficiency of steam under ordinary full gear, or 75 per cent. admission. That is, the steam, when urged to the utmost degree of expansion by the link-motion, does about twice as much work per pound weight as when under full gear.

17. Accordingly, the steam consumed per horse-power per hour, varies from about 30½ lbs. in full gear to 16 lbs. with 10 per cent. admission. The consumption of coke, allowing 1 lb. for 8 lbs. of water, varies in the same way from 3·8 lbs. to 2 lbs. per horse-power per hour.

18. The clearance between the piston and the valve should be reduced to the smallest practicable amount, as the removal of clearance adds to the efficiency of the steam.

19. The preceding conclusions hold good, at speeds under 30 to 40 miles, or about 500 feet of piston per minute, for all cylinders, in good order, with ports at least $\frac{1}{11}$th, and orifice $\frac{1}{17}$th to $\frac{1}{15}$th of the piston, and having, if but par-

tially protected, ⅓th to ₁⁄₁₁th of inside lead. At the highest speeds, of 55 to 65 miles, for passenger engines, or about 800 feet of piston, engines of the above proportions consume by back pressure an excess of 33 to 12 per cent. of water above what is given by the rule, the excess being less as the admission is shortened.

In partially protected cylinders, additional allowance must be made for condensation, particularly when the maximum pressures are under 60 lbs. When the maximum pressures are 90 lbs. and upwards, and with above 60 per cent. admission, there is less condensation comparatively, and the exhaust is practically as good as in well protected cylinders. But, for highly expansive working, no pressure of steam, however great, can prevent the great evils of condensation.

20. Wiredrawing by the valve is really a partial "expansion," and is equivalent, in its action, to an earlier suppression than that with which the valve is ostensibly working.

21. In all locomotives, the thorough efficiency of steam by expansion can be developed only by well protecting and well heating the cylinders and steam-passages; by providing wide and free steam-passages; by maintaining the valve-gear in the best order; by reducing the clearance at each end of the cylinder to the lowest possible amount; and by the adoption of a sufficiently high pressure in the boiler.

SUB-SECTION II.

PHYSIOLOGY OF THE BOILER.

CHAPTER I.

OF FUEL, AND THE GENERAL PRINCIPLES OF COMBUSTION.

Chemical Elements of Combustion.—Coke and coal are the combustibles employed in the fire-box of the locomotive. Combustion is effected by the combination of atmospheric air with the coal or coke, in certain proportions, and is regulated by the chemical relations of their elements. Of the gases chiefly concerned in combustion, either as inflammables, supporters, or products of combustion, the chemical equivalents are expressed in the following table, derived from Reid's *Practical Chemistry.*

Combustion of Coke.—Coke, when pure, consists exclusively of solid carbon. It usually contains a small percentage of earthy matter, which is discharged as ashes during combustion, and varies in amount from 1·5 to 10 per cent. of the total weight of the coke. Sulphur, also, exists in minute quantities, usually less than 1 per cent., and seldom above 3 per cent. The following is the composition of Ramsay's Garesfield coke, a coke of great purity, analysed by Dr. Richardson of Newcastle:—In 100 parts there are

Of Carbon.....................97·6 parts.
Of Sulphur .... 0·85 ,,
Of Ashes....................... 1·55 ,,

                              100·00

In the combustion of carbon, we find by the table that 8 parts by weight of oxygen combined with 6 parts by weight

---

TABLE, No. LVII.—OF CHEMICAL EQUIVALENTS CONCERNED IN THE COMBUSTION OF COKE AND COAL.

Gases.	Elements of the Gases.	Chemical Equivalents. By Weight.	Chemical Equivalents. By Measure. □ = one volume.
Oxygen	Oxygen, 1 part	8	□
Hydrogen	Hydrogen, 1 part	1	□
Carbon	Carbon, 1 part	6	□
Nitrogen	Nitrogen, 1 part	14	□
Sulphur	Sulphur, 1 part	16	□
Atmospheric air	Oxygen, 1 part; Nitrogen, 2 parts	8 } 28 } = 36	□ □ } = □
Carbonic oxide	Oxygen, 1 part; Carbon, 1 part	8 } 6 } = 14	□ □ } = □
Carbonic acid	Oxygen, 2 parts; Carbon, 1 part	16 } 6 } = 22	□ □ } = □
Aqueous vapour	Oxygen, 1 part; Hydrogen, 1 part	8 } 1 } = 9	□ □ } = □
Sulphurous acid	Oxygen, 2 parts; Sulphur, 1 part	16 } 16 } = 32	□ □ } = □

NOTE.—In this table, the indicated volumes of the elements are their combining volumes as gases, though carbon and sulphur, uncombined, exist exclusively in the solid form. It is only at the instant of combination that they can be supposed to exist as gases.

The equivalent volumes of the compound gases, entered in the last column of the table, indicate a condensation of the elementary gases at the time of combustion. Atmospheric air forms an exception; the oxygen and nitrogen are only mechanically combined.

In this table, oxygen is the only supporter of combustion; the other elementary gases are inflammables or combustibles.

of carbon, form carbonic oxide; and that 16 parts of oxygen combined with 6 of carbon produce carbonic acid. The conversion of carbon into carbonic acid is thus necessary to complete combustion; and to meet this condition the respective weights of the elements, oxygen and carbon, must be as 16 to 6, that is, for a given weight of carbon, 2⅔ times that weight of oxygen must be supplied. As the oxygen of atmospheric air, with which the coke is burned, is associated with nitrogen in the proportion of 8 to 28, or 1 to 3½ by weight, we find, in the first place, that for the complete combustion of 1 pound of carbon, 2⅔ pounds of pure oxygen are required; and this is accompanied by 3½ times 2⅔, or 9⅓ pounds of nitrogen, making a total of 12 pounds of atmospheric air. The annexed diagram exhibits the process of combustion, in which the elements are expressed with their chemical equivalents. The nitrogen, which takes no part in combustion, is set free and passes, as a neutral gas, with the carbonic acid into the chimney.

1 pound coke,	Carbon, 6	——— 22 Carbonic acid, 3⅔ pounds
	Oxygen, 8	
	Oxygen, 8	
12 pounds air,	Nitrogen, 14	
	Nitrogen, 14	56 Nitrogen, ... 9⅓ pounds
	Nitrogen, 14	
	Nitrogen, 14	

13 pounds   13 pounds

As 1 cubic foot of air at the ordinary temperature, 60°, weighs ·0766 pounds, about 160 feet of air weigh 12 pounds. For the total combustion of 1 pound of carbon, therefore, 160 cubic feet of air at 60° are consumed. Practically, the presence of carbonic acid and nitrogen, the results of combustion, interferes so materially with the conversion of the air, that in ordinary furnaces double the amount of air chemically necessary must be provided to meet mechanical obstructions. This allowance is a minimum in practice, as even in the most perfectly managed fire-places attached to the boilers of Cornwall, an analysis of the gaseous contents of the chimney, by Mr. Hunt, indicates the presence of as much free oxygen as was consumed in promoting combustion; and according to the later and more elaborate experiments of the Royal Commission on Coals suited to the Steam Navy, the quantity of free oxygen in the chimney varied from one-fourth to one-half of that which combined with the fuel. It is true that where coal is employed as fuel, a more complicated process of combustion is involved, with a larger effusion of gaseous products, than takes place in the coke-fire. It is true, also, that in locomotive fire-boxes the coke is commonly laid in comparatively deep beds through which the air must penetrate, and is likely to be well drained of its oxygen. The probability of a very full consumption of the oxygen is established by the frequent production of carbonic oxide in even a moderately filled fire-box, indicating a super-abundance of carbon gas, when there is green coke present; the blue flame which is then to be observed on opening the fire-door, indicates the conversion of the oxide into acid by the appropriation of an additional equivalent of oxygen from the air that enters by the door. In the absence of more direct data, a mean surplus of 25 per cent. of air shall be assumed, or a total of 200 feet of air at 60°, as the amount which, with ordinary fires, passes through the grate for 1 pound of carbon or pure coke consumed; and this estimate is confirmed by the conclusions of practical chemists.

The temperature in the fire-box must reach some thousand degrees of Fahrenheit in the body of the fuel, under an active blast, as we know that blasts of the same power acting upon coke in the founder's cupola are sufficient to melt pig iron and raise it to a white heat, about 3000° Fahrenheit. Assuming, as we justly may, that the combustion of the coke is in general very complete, then, as the bulk or volume of carbonic acid gas is equal to that of the oxygen, in a free state, which is one of its elements; and as, also, the volume of nitrogen separated by combustion is equal to that which it occupies as an element of air; it follows that the gaseous products of the complete combustion of coke occupy, at the same temperature, the same volume as the air consumed in the operation. Therefore, to obtain the total volume of the gases in the fire-box after combustion, we have simply to find the expansion of the whole volume of air admitted, due to the temperature there. This may be done by means of the ratio already announced, page 60, connecting the volume and temperature of gases under a constant pressure, from which the following formula for the expanded volume is readily derived :—

$$v = \frac{t + 458}{518} \quad \dots\dots\dots\dots\dots (1.)$$

in which v is the enlarged volume of the gases at the temperature $t°$ in the fire-box, relative to the volume at 60°, which is taken as one, or unity. Whence the following rule :—

RULE I.—*To find the relative volume of a gas by expansion due to a given temperature, and under a constant pressure, the volume of the gas at 60° being = 1. To the given tem-*

perature add 458,—and divide the sum by 518. The quotient is the relative volume required.

By this rule, the volume of air due to 3000°, the heat of combustion, is 6·7 times the volume at 60°, for (3000 + 458) ÷ 518 = 6·7. In the complete combustion of 1 lb. of coke, then, 6·7 times 200, or 1340 feet of heated gases are generated over the bars. This volume is speedily reduced by contraction due to the abstraction of heat in the fire-box and flues, as in liberally proportioned boilers, the gases enter the smoke-box at reduced temperatures of 400° to 800°. For an average temperature of 600°, the reduced volume of gases for 1 lb. of coke is, by the rule, 408 feet, and of this $\frac{4}{20}$ths are air, $\frac{4}{20}$ths carbonic acid, and $\frac{12}{20}$ths nitrogen,—these proportions being such as result from the complete combustion of the fuel. To find how these conclusions tally with experience, we shall compare the heat-properties of the elements.

The total heating power of 1 pound of carbon, due to its complete combustion, by conversion into carbonic acid, has been determined by experiment to be approximately 14,000 units, adopting for the unit of heat that which raises through 1 degree of Fahrenheit, 1 pound of water; that is, 1 pound of carbon is capable by combustion of raising 14,000 pounds of water through 1 degree of temperature. Now, the total heat of steam at 320°, or 90 lbs. total pressure, is 1211°·54, and one pound of carbon should convert

$$\frac{14,000}{1211·54 - 60} = 12·16 \text{ pounds of water at } 60°$$

into steam of 90 lbs.; and the result is sensibly the same for steam of other temperatures. This is the utmost possible evaporation, and supposes all the heat to be utilised. The utmost practical performance of 1 pound of coke in locomotive boilers is equal to the evaporation of about 9·5 pounds of water, or 78 per cent. of the possible maximum, having 22 per cent. of heat to pass off not usefully employed. This drawback is due to the heat lost in the hot gases which pass into the smoke-box; possibly also to the loss of heating power by the imperfect combustion of a part of the coke in the formation of carbonic oxide; due, moreover, to a percentage of incombustible matter in the coke; and lastly to the abstraction of small pieces of unburnt coke from the fire-box, by the force of the draft.

The volume of the gases in the smoke-box, due to the complete combustion of 1 pound of coke, being 200 feet, reduced to a temperature of 60°, which is in fact the volume of air per pound of coke found to be necessary for its combustion, if we divide 200 in the proportions already assigned for air, carbonic acid, and nitrogen, we have

$$\frac{4}{20}\text{ths, or} \quad 40 \text{ feet of air}$$
$$\frac{4}{20}\text{ths, or} \quad 32 \text{ feet of carbonic acid}$$
$$\frac{12}{20}\text{ths, or} \quad 128 \text{ feet of nitrogen}$$
$$\overline{200 \text{ feet.}}$$

The heat required to raise the temperature of these gases to 600°, through 540°, is regulated by their specific heats. The specific heats of equal weights of water and air, are as 1·0000 to 0·2669; and as a unit of heat raises 1 lb. of water through 1 degree, the number of degrees through which 1 lb. of air is raised by a unit of heat, is inversely as the specific heats of air and water. Thus, $1° \times \frac{1·0000}{·2669} = 3°·75$,

Q

the number of degrees. The volume of 1 lb. of air at 60° is 13 cubic feet; then 1 unit of heat raises 13 feet of air, measured at 60°, through 3°·75, or 1 foot of air through (3·75 × 13) or 48°·75. The relative number of degrees for 1 foot of other gases may be found similarly, in terms of their specific heats, and their volumes per pound weight, the latter being deducible directly from their specific gravities. The following is a tabular statement of data for water and various gases :—

TABLE, No. LVIII.—OF THE SPECIFIC HEAT, AND OTHER PROPERTIES OF WATER AND GASES.

Name.	Specific Heat by Weight.	Increase of Temperature of one pound by one unit of heat.	Specific Gravity at 60°.	Cubic feet in one pound at 60°.	Increase of Temperature of one cubic foot of gas, measured at 60°, per unit of heat.
		degrees.		cub. feet.	degrees.
Water	1·0000	1	816·000	0·016	48·75
Air	0·2669	3·75	1·000	13·0	38·50
Carbonic Acid..	0·2210	4·52	1·527	8·5	46·90
Carbonic Oxide	0·2884	3·47	0·960	13·5	48·50
Nitrogen.	0·2754	3·63	0·969	13·4	49·50
Oxygen..........	0·2361	4·23	1·111	11·7	55·90
Hydrogen.......	3·2936	0·30	0·070	186·0	
Steam............	0·8470				

To find the extra heat contained in the escaping gases at 600°, for 540° elevation of temperature above 60°, we have, for 1 lb. of coke,

40 feet of air (at 60°) × 540° = 1 foot raised through 21600°
32 ,,   carbonic acid × 540° = 1 foot   ,,   17280°
128 ,,   nitrogen   × 540° = 1 foot   ,,   69120°
200

The quantity of heat so consumed is by the preceding table, last column,

for the air, 21600° ÷ 48°·75 = 443 units of heat
the acid, 17280° ÷ 38°·50 = 448   do.
the nitrogen, 69120° ÷ 48°·50 = 1425   do.
            loss   2316 units.

This loss amounts to 16·5 per cent. of 14000 units, the possible maximum performance of 1 pound of coke; and as the total loss amounts to 22 per cent., or 3080 units, the excess of the latter, 5·5 per cent., or 764 units is all that remains due to imperfect combustion, impurities and waste. Thus, the whole heat of combustion of 1 pound of coke is disposed of as follows :—

10920 units, = 78   percent in the formation of steam
2316   do. = 16·5   do.   loss by the heat of the gases in the smoke-box.
764   do. = 5·5   do.   drawback by ashes and waste.
14000 units   100 parts.

These results show that the combustion of coke in the locomotive-furnace is practically perfect, as the total deficit by imperfect combustion must be less than 5¼ per cent. of the whole duty of pure coke, in cases where it is burned at a sufficiently moderate rate to permit of a full transmission of heat to the water. Further appropriation of the heat of coke, therefore, is to be looked for, not by expedients for improving combustion, but by means for using up the waste heat of the gases in the smoke-box; and if the heat of the smoke at 600° were utilised, it would be equivalent to an extra evaporation of (2316 ÷ 1211 = 1·91) or nearly 2 lbs. of water per pound of coke, making in all 11·5 lbs. water per pound of coke. The ordinary duty of 1 pound of coke

in modern locomotive boilers is the evaporation of about 8 lbs. of water, or two-thirds of the possible maximum,—an inferiority due mostly to the usually rapid rate of combustion, and a deficiency of surface to absorb the heat, as well as to other causes already named.

Though little is to be feared from the partial combustion of coke by the formation of carbonic oxide, it may be useful to know what is the loss of heat by it. One pound of carbonic oxide is found to evolve 4376 units of heat, during its conversion into carbonic acid; as the oxide contains $\frac{4}{7}$ths of its weight, of carbon, this is the duty of $\frac{4}{7}$ lb. of carbon as an oxide, and (4376 × $\frac{14}{8}$) or 10211 units is the duty of one pound of carbon as an oxide when converted into carbonic acid, and amounts to 73 per cent. of the total heat of conversion. The remaining 27 per cent. is then all that is obtained by the partial combustion of carbon, and the 73 per cent. goes for nothing, as loss.

Combustion of Coal.—The combustion of coal is a more complicated process than that of coke, and implies more careful preparation for insuring complete success. Six items go to the composition of coal, of which numerous analyses have been published in the late Report on Coals suited to the Steam Navy, by De la Beche and Playfair. The following examples are selected from that Report :—

TABLE, No. LIX.—COMPOSITION OF COALS.

Locality, or Name of Coal.	Specific Gravity.	Carbon.	Hydrogen.	Nitrogen.	Sulphur.	Oxygen.	Ash.	Percentage of Coke left by such Coal.
		per cent.	per cent.	p. cent.	p. cent.	p. cent.	p. cent.	p. cent.
Anthracite	1·375	91·44	3·46	0·21	0·79	2·58	1·52	92·9
Graigola..........	1·300	84·87	3·84	0·41	0·45	7·19	3·24	85·5
Oldcastle's Fiery Vein.........	1·289	87·68	4·89	1·31	0·09	3·39	2·64	79·8
Dalkeith Jewel Seam	1·277	74·55	5·14	0·10	0·33	15·51	4·37	49·8
Grangemouth	1·200	79·85	5·28	1·35	1·42	8·58	3·52	56·6
Broomhill..........	1·260	81·70	6·17	1·84	2·85	4·37	3·07	59·2
Park End, Lydney	1·283	73·52	5·69	2·04	2·27	6·48	10·00	57·8
Means.............	1·283	81·94	4·92	1·04	1·17	6·87	4·05	68·8

Of these elements there are but two of importance in the present question,—carbon and hydrogen. These, when the coal is burnt, mostly combine with each other, and ultimately with atmospheric oxygen; forming, when the combustion is perfect, carbonic acid and water, the latter of which is a compound of 1 part of hydrogen and 8 parts of oxygen. It was proved, in fact, by repeated analyses of the gases in the chimney during the experiments of the Royal Commissioners, that the products of combustion consisted exclusively of carbonic acid, sulphurous acid, oxygen, and nitrogen—besides a proportion of the vapour of water precipitated by condensation. These results indicated a very perfect combustion of the elements, as they proved the total absence of any unburnt inflammable gases in the chimney; at the same time the quantity of free oxygen in the chimney varied from one-fourth to one-half of that which combined with the fuel, showing that though, on the one hand, all the carbon may be converted into carbonic acid, and its heat of combination exhausted, a surplus of oxygen, to the amount of 50 per cent. of that which is necessary for actual combustion, may pass into the chimney. With such practically perfect results of combustion, the economic evaporation of water from 212°, under atmospheric pressure, measured in pounds per pound of fuel, were found to be, for the coals already selected, as expressed in the following table. The contents of the last column were calculated by the experimenters from the heating powers of carbon and hydrogen :—

TABLE, No. LX.—OF THE ECONOMIC VALUE OF COAL.

Name.	Constituent Carbon of Coal.	Constituent Hydrogen of Coal.	Coke yielded by destructive distillation.	Water actually evaporated from 212° by 1 lb. of Coal.	Theoretical Maximum of Water evaporated from 212° by 1 lb. of Coal.
	per cent.	per cent.	per cent.	lbs.	lbs.
Anthracite	91·44	3·46	92·9	9·46	14·59
Graigola	84·87	3·84	85·5	9·35	13·56
Oldcastle's Fiery Vein...	87·68	4·89	79·8	8·94	14·94
Dalkeith Jewel Seam	74·55	5·14	49·8	7·08	12·31
Grangemouth ..	79·85	5·28	56·6	7·40	13·69
Broomhill	81·70	6·17	59·2	7·30	14·86
Park-End, Lydney	73·52	5·69	57·8	8·52	13·26
1	2	3	4	5	6

Here we find, generally, that the greatest practical evaporation of water, col. 5, is very much in proportion to the percentage of carbon in the coal, col. 2, and, taking the means of the quantities, in these columns, we have an average evaporation of 8·29 lbs. with an average percentage of 81·94 of carbon. If the coal had been wholly carbon, equivalent to pure coke, and the evaporation increased in proportion, we should have had

$$8·29 \times \frac{100}{81·94} = 10·1 \text{ lbs. of water}$$

evaporated per pound of fuel, which is little above what we have found good coke capable of doing, even with a greater waste of heat. It would appear from this that the evaporative power of coal is closely related to the quantity of carbon or coke-particles it contains, and is in short chiefly dependent upon the carbon.

Consistently with these deductions, Mr. Josiah Parkes invariably found that coal to be the strongest which contained the least gas,—that is, which contained the most carbon, and showed least flame. He found also that 75 pounds of coke produced from 100 pounds of coal evaporated as much water as 100 pounds of the same coal. Mr. Apsley Pellatt likewise found that London gas coke exceeds coal 25 per cent. in the development of heat for melting glass.* In the locomotive-boiler the writer has found that, in general, coal is capable of about two-thirds, or 66 per cent. of the duty of an equal weight of coke. These observations confirm the conclusion that the evaporative efficiency of coal and its preparations is dependent on, and arises from the quantity of carbon they contain. Nor is this conclusion affected by the very superior heating power of hydrogen gas when burnt with oxygen, amounting to above 60,000 units per pound, or above four times that of carbon, and the consequent apparent value of an excess of hydrogen in coal. It may be observed from the last table that the coals which contain the most hydrogen are the lowest in evaporating power. The preparatory distillation

of the combustible gases of coal before combustion involves an outlay of heat for their conversion into the gaseous form which may go some length to balance the heat arising from their combustion. Oxygen combines with twice its volume of hydrogen to form aqueous vapour, of which the volume is equal to that of the elementary hydrogen as a gas ; the product of combustion is then of double the volume of the oxygen employed, and it is this excess of volume for the conversion of the hydrogen into gas to which the absorption of heat is due. Carbonic acid, on the contrary, possesses the volume simply of its constituent oxygen : there is no extension of volume for the conversion of carbon into the gaseous form, and there is no absorption of heat thereby. The distinction here made appears to explain the practical neutrality of solid hydrogen as a dispenser of heat by combustion, as it is supposed to absorb as much heat in assuming the gaseous form as it subsequently discharges in combining with oxygen. Further, carbonic oxide, like aqueous vapour, assumes double the volume of oxygen of which it is formed ; hence, similarly, the very inferior heating power of carbon when converted into the oxide.

The inferiority, above-noted, of coal to coke per pound weight, as a source of heat in the locomotive-boiler, is due not wholly to its composition but also to the unfavourable conditions under which it is burnt. The combustion of coke proceeds at a uniform rate, while that of coal is much less regular. In the first stages of its combustion, large volumes of heavy hydro-carbon gases are discharged, which must be rapidly taken up by the oxygen that they may be perfectly burnt. Hence the sanguine blaze and rapid disengagement of heat soon after coal is thrown on the grate ; and it is only after the hydrogen, oxygen, and a portion of the carbon are thus driven off and consumed, that the staple of the fuel, coke, is left as a residue to burn off at a slower rate. The locomotive-boiler is designed to combine lightness and efficiency, and the uniform rate of combustion to which coke is predisposed, admits of near approximations to the minimum areas of grate and heating surface, and fire and smoke-room, consistent with efficiency. The sanguine and impulsive combustion of coal, on the contrary, during the discharge of its gaseous compounds under a strong draft, demand a more liberal allowance of surface for its economical employment than is convenient within the limits of the locomotive ; and though we believe, contrary to much authority, that a rapid draft is decidedly that which is most favourable for the complete combustion of coal as well as of coke, it is precisely that which reduces its mechanical evaporative value in the locomotive.*

Combustion of Wood.—Though wood is unknown in this country as fuel for locomotives,—except indeed in the case of stray railway-sleepers, of which engine-drivers understand the value,—we may add the following particulars of its performance in America.

In the engines of the Baltimore Railroad it is found that 1 ton of Cumberland coal, best quality, is equal to 1·25 tons

---

* *Trans. Inst. C.E.*

* Those who wish to understand thoroughly the combustion of coal in furnaces, the author begs to refer to *Notes on the Smoke Nuisance Question,* by W. M. Buchanan of Glasgow,—the most original and valuable discussion of the subject that has come under his observation.

of anthracite coal, or to 2·12 cords of pine-wood.[*] One cord of dry pine is equal in bulk to 128 cubic feet, and weighs about 2700 lbs. or 1·205 tons; 2·12 cords, therefore, weigh 2·55 tons, and it follows that 1 lb. of coal is equal to 2·55 lbs. of pine, or pine has but two-fifths of the evaporative power of coal, equal to about 2¼ lbs. of water converted into steam per pound of pine.

Other experiments on the Reading Railroad have shown that 1 lb. of coal is equal to 3 lbs. of pine.[†] This indicates an evaporative power of only 2 lbs. of water per pound of fuel, in the locomotive. Mr. Haswell states that 2¼ to 2¾ lbs. of pine are equal to 1 lb. of best coal; and allowing 6 lbs. water per pound of coal, we have (6 ÷ 2¼) or nearly 2½ lbs. water per pound of pine, as already found. Now, Professor W. R. Johnson found, in 1844, that 1 lb. of dry pine would, by careful management, evaporate 4·69 lbs. of water. It seems then that, as fuel, wood, like coal, is unfavourably treated in the locomotive, as in practice it does not evaporate above 2¼ lbs. per pound weight. In both cases, the extreme facility of combustion, and the rapid evolution of heat, in the first stages, have something to do with the inferiority of effect.

The low evaporative power of wood strengthens our conclusion that the efficiency of fuel is regulated very much by the percentage of carbon it contains. According to Haswell, the following are the mean compositions of various woods:—

	Oak.	Ash.	Maple.	Chestnut.	Norway Pine.
Charcoal (carbon)	22·7	17·9	20·0	23·3	19·2
Volatile matter	76·9	81·3	79·3	76·3	80·4
Ashes	0·4	0·7	0·7	0·7	0·4
	100·0	100·0	100·0	100·0	100·0

Here we find that the proportion of carbon is but one-fifth of the whole mass of the fuel, or about 20 per cent. by weight.

Physical Characteristics of Coke.—Thoroughly converted coke is clean, crystalline, and porous in structure, and exists in columnar masses. It has a steel gray colour, possesses a metallic lustre, and is so hard as to be successfully employed for cutting glass. In these respects coke has a mechanical advantage over coal; by its hardness and tenacity when well made it resists the violence of the draft in the fire-box, and though it is lighter than coal, yet the thorough draft facilitated by the openness of the fuel, prevents a concentrated action of the blast, and promotes an intimate mixture with air, and thorough combustion.

Coke, however, varies considerably in physical condition, and, even when of equal purity, its evaporative power is various. Mr. Woods states that in Lancashire, the Hulton and Worsley cokes rank highest, that the cokes from other mines varied in efficiency from 76 to 90 per cent. of those just named. In several of these cases the inferiority was due mostly to the tenderness of the coke, which was broken up and dispersed by the violence of the draft, and to a great extent shaken through the bars.[‡] These are common sources of waste,—the tubes are occasionally choked with small coke unburnt, in the smoke-box mounds of carbon-

* Haswell's *Engineers' Pocket-Book.* New York, 1850.
† *Practical Mechanics' Journal*, 1851.
‡ Tredgold on the *Steam Engine*, vol. i., 1850.

dust are collected, and in the more violent cases large pieces are projected by the blast from the chimney. Accordingly, we have known 25 cwt. of firm coke go as far as 30 cwt. of fragile stuff, of a less specific gravity, showing that the latter coke had but 83 per cent. of the efficiency of the former,—an inferiority mainly owing to its inferior physical condition.

Coal loses about one-third of its weight in the process of coking, while the bulk increases about one-tenth. Thus, in the conversion of coal from Andrew's House Colliery, as described in the Report on Coals, the weight of coke was 65 per cent. of the coal, and the increase of bulk was 11 per cent. Bristol coke is from 60 to 63·5 per cent. of the coal. Kilsyth coal yields 60 per cent. of its weight of coke.

At Newcastle, 50 hours is the usual period assigned for the conversion of coal into coke. Though this period is deemed sufficient for conversion, the physical quality of the coke is improved by confining it in the ovens for 40 hours longer, or a total of 90 hours. This gives time for consolidation, and turns out a firmer, brighter, and more crystalline mass. Mr. Gooch made experiments on the relative power of Bristol coke confined in the oven for different periods, and he had the following results for one class of engines:—

	In the Oven.	Yield per ton of Coals.	Water evaporated per pound of Coke.
No. 1,	48 hours,	12·71 cwt.	7·1 lbs.
No. 2,	72 „	12·00 „	7·7 „
No. 3,	48 „	11·74 „	7·2 „

No. 2 evaporated 8½ per cent. more water than the others, showing the superiority of coke confined for long periods and slowly matured.

Coke frequently absorbs, according to Mr. Woods, as much as 8 per cent. of its weight of water in its passage from the oven to the place of consumption, in uncovered waggons. A quantity of damp coke, on being exposed for a few days to a drying wind, was reduced from 388 cwt. to 360 cwt., showing an accession of 8 per cent. of water under exposure to rain. Hence the advantage of keeping coke dry for use. In some experiments made to find the maximum capacity of coke for water, three specimens of Mickley coke were selected, weighing, when dry, 31, 21, and 52 ounces respectively. No. 1 was columnar, close-grained, and of good quality; No. 2 was very ordinary, clumpy, and porous; No. 3 was very close-grained, and of average good quality. The three specimens were immersed in water, the first two for 2½ hours, and the third for 4 hours; and they absorbed the following quantities of water:—

No. 1, 4½ oz., having imbibed 14½ per cent. of water.
No. 2, 3½ „ „ 17 „ „
No. 3, 10 „ „ 20 „ „

No. 2, it appears, in virtue of its opener body, absorbed more water than No. 1. No. 3, immersed nearly double the time, acquired more water than either of the others; and it is probable that 20 per cent. of the weight of average coke is the greatest practical absorption. Should this water have to be evaporated in the fire-box, it would monopolise 2½ per cent. of the coke, allowing 1 lb. of coke to 8 lbs. of water.

Storage of Fuel.—The absolute weight or bulk of fuel is

distinguishable from its economic weight or bulk, by the latter of which is meant the weight of heaped coal, for example, per cubic foot of total bulk, or the number of cubic feet required to stow a ton. If the fuel could be disposed of in one solid mass, this mass would represent its absolute weight and bulk; but, as the fuel occupies more room when broken in pieces and heaped, it is clear that its absolute weight is greater and its bulk less, than its economic weight and bulk. The average weight of solid coal is 80 lbs. per cubic foot; and of heaped coal 51 lbs. per foot. Thus the economic weight is but five-eighths of the absolute weight; and the average economic bulk of coal is 44 cubic feet per ton.

The absolute weight of coke varies. The bulks of the three specimens of Mickley coke already noted, were found, from the displacement of water by immersion, to be respectively 52·5, 39·4, and 83 cubic inches. The respective solid weights were therefore, 63·8, 57·5, and 67·7 pounds per cubic foot, and the mean of these is 63 lbs. The weight of water is 62½ lbs. per foot; and here we have a very fair test of the density of coke suitable for the furnace of the locomotive. Should a piece of dry coke float in water, it is too light, or at least below the average density; should it sink, we may safely conclude that it is sufficiently weighty to withstand the ordinary action of the draft.

In the experiments on the formation of Tanfield coke, it was found that the stowage-rooms, or economic bulks of 1 ton of the coal and its coke, were respectively 42·92 and 74·66 feet, in the ratio of 1 to 1·74. Therefore, the usual weight of heaped coke is $\frac{51}{1·74} = 29·3$ pounds per cubic foot.

We have frequently checked this result by measurement of the waggon-loads of coke for railways. Mickley coke, for example, of good quality, and measured in the waggon, weighs about 28 lbs. per foot, which agrees very nearly with the result from Tanfield coke; and we may in general reckon the economic bulk of coke of good quality at 4 cubic feet per cwt., or 80 cubic feet per ton.

One cord of pine-wood weighing 2700 lbs. occupies 128 feet of stowage-room. The economic weight of pine-wood for fuel is, thus, 21 lbs. per cubic foot; and its economic bulk is 107 cubic feet per ton.

As the evaporative powers of coal, coke, and pine, in the locomotive, are various, it is plain that, to find the *equivalent* economic bulks of the three fuels, in point of efficiency, their economic bulks as above found, must be divided by their evaporative powers per pound weight. Thus,

For Coal, 44 ÷ 6 = 7·3 } Relative or Equivalent Economic
„ Coke, 80 ÷ 8½ = 9·4 } Bulks, to evaporate the same
„ Pine, 107 ÷ 2½ = 43·0 } weight of water.

To express these figures in simpler terms, assume that, for coal, the equivalent economic bulk is unity or 1. Then for coke it is $\frac{9·4}{7·3}$ or 1·3; and for pine, it is $\frac{43·0}{7·3}$ or 6·0. That is, about one-third more coke than coal, by bulk, is required to evaporate, in the locomotive, equal weights of water; and for the same evaporation, a mass of pine-wood six times the bulk of coal is required.

The following table, No. LXI., comprises these results in a form convenient for reference :—

TABLE, No. LXI.—WEIGHT AND STOWAGE OF FUELS.

Name of Fuel.	Absolute Weight per cubic foot.	Economic, or Stowage Weight per cubic foot.	Economic Bulk or Space required to stow 1 ton.	Weight of water evaporated per pound of fuel, in ordinary practice.	Equivalent Economic Bulk, to evaporate the same weight of water.
	lbs.	lbs.	cubic feet.	lbs.	ratio.
Coal ...	80	51	44	6	1·0
Coke ...	63	28	80	8½	1·3
Pine ...		21	107	2½	6·0

RECAPITULATION.—1. Combustion is effected by the chemical combination of atmospheric air with the elements of the fuel employed.

2. Coke consists almost entirely of solid carbon. Coal consists mainly of carbon, hydrogen, and oxygen, in average proportions of about 80, 5, and 7 per cent. of the whole weight of the fuel. The remaining 8 per cent. is composed of the neutral substances, nitrogen, sulphur, and ash.

3. The useful heat of combustion is derived, entirely, in the case of coke, and chiefly, in the case of coal, from the complete union of the constituent carbon with the oxygen gas of the atmosphere, forming carbonic acid gas.

4. One pound of pure coke, which is carbon, requires for its complete combustion, 12 pounds of air, by weight, or 160 cubic feet by measure, at the temperature 60°. In practice, a surplus of 25 per cent., making a total of 200 feet at 60°, for each pound of coke, is necessary, to allow for leakage of air unconsumed through the furnace.

5. The temperature in the fire-box reaches 3000° in the body of the coke. The temperature in the smoke-box varies usually from 400° to 800°.

6. The heating power of one pound of carbon, when completely burnt, is equal to 14,000 units of heat, and is capable of converting above 12 pounds of water at 60° into steam. The ordinary duty of good coke is the evaporation of 8 to 8½ pounds of water per pound of coke. Under the most favourable conditions, the evaporation of 9½ lbs. of water is about the greatest practical performance of 1 lb. of coke; or 78 per cent. of the possible maximum.

7. Under the most favourable conditions, the evaporative power of coal is at least equal to that of the carbon it contains. But in the ordinary locomotive-boiler, the practical evaporative power of coal is only about two-thirds of that of good, pure coke, or from 5 to 6 pounds of water per pound of coal.

8. The evaporative power of American pine-wood in the locomotive, varies from two-fifths to one-third of that of the best coal, or about 2½ pounds of water per pound of pine.

9. The combustion of coke in the locomotive-boiler is, under ordinary conditions, practically perfect. The inferior performance of coal and wood as fuels, is due in some degree to the irregularity of combustion ; and with coal, it is due also to imperfect combustion.

10. It results, generally, that the power of fuel for evaporation is regulated mainly by the proportion of carbon in its composition.

11. The quality of coke is various. It is affected by its composition chiefly as it may contain ash, which may vary from 1½ to 10 per cent. of its weight. Its physical qualities also affect its usefulness: if light and fragile it may be dissipated through the tubes and the grate unconsumed, and in extreme cases 17 to 20 per cent. may be so wasted. It will

absorb, under ordinary exposure to wet weather, 8 per cent. of moisture, and it is capable of imbibing 20 per cent. In its best condition, coke is dry, hard, dense, columnar, crystalline, and free of cinder.

12. In the stowage of fuels, the equivalent economic bulks of coal, coke, and pine-wood, or such as evaporate equal weights of water in the locomotive-boiler, are as 1, 1·3, and 6; or nearly one-third more bulk of coke than of coal, and six times as much pine.

CHAPTER II.

MECHANICAL PRINCIPLES OF THE LOCOMOTIVE-BOILER.

"IN the fire-box and boiler," says Pambour, "resides the real source of the effects of the engine;" and we have now to develope the mechanical principles on which the action of this admirable steam-generator is based.

Of Heating Surface.—In the fire-box and the tubes the heat is generated and conducted, which is destined for the generation of steam; and this is effected by the passage of the heat through the material of the fire-box and tubes, and its absorption by the water with which these are everywhere surrounded. The surface thus presented for the transmission of heat is known as *heating surface.* The efficiency of this surface depends much on its situation. Mr. Armstrong found that a cubical metallic box submerged in water and heated from within, generated steam from its upper surface more than twice as fast, per unit of area, as it did from the sides when vertical, and that the bottom yielded none at all. These remarkable differences are owing to the difficulty with which steam separates from a vertical surface, to give place to fresh charges of water, and to the impossibility of leaving the inverted surface at all. By slightly inclining the box, the elevated side much more easily parted with the steam, and the rate of evaporation was increased; while on the depressed side the steam hung so sluggishly as to lead to an overheating of the metal.[*] It is, therefore, clearly of importance to incline inwardly the sides of the fire-box, and the rather as they are closely hedged in by the outer shell, which leaves but a thin wall of water in contact with them, and thus restricts the circulation of both water and steam; whereas, in modern practice, the sides of the fire-box are mostly vertical, with but 2½ to 3 inch water-spaces. In older practice, with smaller fire-boxes, 4 to 5 inch spaces were allowed, and we think wisely; it is bad policy to eke out the grate-surface at the cost of the water-spaces. In a number of Bury's circular fire-boxes, of which the outer shells were flattened externally to make room for the frame-bars, the prevailing water-space of 2½ inches was reduced to 2 inches at those places. "Nature" rebelled: the steam got entangled, the fire-boxes were bulged inwards about half an inch by the pressure on the overheated plate, just opposite the flattened outer part, and restored the narrowed water space to the regular 2½ inch width. In some engines the sides of the fire-box are inclined at a slope of about 1 in 50; and of late, Mr. Sinclair has employed an advantageous slope of 1 in 10, in his tank-engine, figured in our plates.

As fire-boxes are much alike in form and arrangement of surface, their heating surface will be estimated in the usual way in terms of the slump superficies exposed to the fire, without dealing in distinctions. Fire-box surface is no doubt very efficient for making steam; but this is merely because it gets the first of the fire, and, as Mr. W. Fernihough has observed, with great scientific discernment, "the object of the fire-box is more to generate heat than to absorb it, and the absorption takes place principally in the tubes." [*]

In the same way, we shall slump the tube-surface without making distinctions, though there is reason to believe that in the upper semicircular part of each tube the efficiency principally resides. The winding progressive motion of flame observable in tubes of considerable diameter, confirms this conclusion, as it is with much probability due to the cooling of the upper portions of the gases of combustion, which as they cool also become heavier, and descend laterally to make room for the hotter smoke next the bottom of the flue; the general result of which is the revolving motion of the current in its progress forward.

The efficiency of tube-surface depends of course on the work it has to do. Its function is to take up the heat which passes from the fire-box, and which no doubt is the greater part of the heat of combustion. As its real value is variable, influenced as it is by the extent of fire-box surface, strength of blast, and other obvious causes, it is impracticable to establish any fixed ratio of efficiency for it in terms of the surface of the fire-box. It has nevertheless been a common practice, in France, to adopt a fixed fraction of one-third of the tube-surface as its equivalent value in terms of the fire-box area, making what they call the "reduced" surface of the tubes. We shall not attempt such artificial distinctions, for in different tubes, and even in the different parts of the same tube, and still more under different states of the fire, the intensity of the heat in the tubes is very various.

The conducting power of the metal composing the fire-box and tubes is one condition which limits the rate of evaporation, when the heat is abundant on the one side, and circulation free on the other, as the water certainly carries off the heat as fast as it arrives at the outer surface. The interior superficies of the fire-box and tubes is, therefore, properly the "heating surface" of the boiler, and this interpretation of the phrase shall be adhered to in the discussions which follow.

The desirable ratio of tube-surface to the surface of the fire-box has been variously estimated, from 6 to 18 times the latter. It depends on the area of grate-surface and the rate of combustion, and on other elements, which in a following chapter will be duly considered.

Capacity of the Fire-Box.—The available capacity for fuel is measured jointly by the area of the grate and the depth of the grate below the tubes and the fire-door. The fuel cannot usefully be heaped above these levels, as if so it closes the tubes and obstructs the draft. Where the grate-area is small, a deeper bed of coke and a sharper blast are required, to pass the necessary quantity of air, and to develope the same amount of heat. Thus, within limits to be

---

[*] Tredgold on the *Steam Engine*, vol. i., 1850.

[*] *Report of the Gauge Commissioners*, 1846.

afterwards defined, a smaller grate and a deeper fire-box may be capable of generating as much steam as a larger grate and a shallower fire-box: the coke room being the same. With the same depth of coke-room, the rate of combustion in the fire-box may be simply in proportion to the area of grate. Thus Mr. Stephenson has with propriety stated that "the power of the engine, supposing the power to be absorbed, may be taken to be directly as the area of the fire-grate or the quantity of fuel contained in the fire-box."[*]

The Mechanical Action of the Blast.—Rapid combustion is imperative in the locomotive-boiler, where everything must be as light and compact as possible, whereas the natural draft of the very limited chimneys which locomotives must carry is quite insufficient for the purpose. Hence the use of the blast-pipe: it directs the exhaust steam from the engine right up the chimney, with which its orifice is placed concentrically; each discharge of steam expands as it leaves the orifice, and, filling the chimney like a plunger, it drives off the smoke which precedes it, and also drags with it an additional quantity of smoke from the smoke-box by the mere frictional force of contact. That the combined action of the exhaust steam as a forcing and as a sucking agent is necessary for its most successful action, will be afterwards proved. The partial vacancy made in the smoke-box by the expulsion and withdrawal of the smoke by the blast, must be supplied from the tubes, the tubes from the fire-box, and the fire-box from the external air. The current thereby created, though it changes its character on its passage into the fire-box, by combustion, nevertheless finds its way regularly and rapidly into the chimney under the direct action of the blast, and a practically steady, active draft is the result.

The action of the blast may be made more obvious by means of the skeleton-view, fig. 169, in which *a* is the

Fig. 169

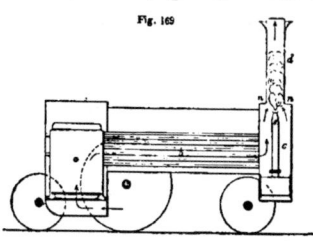

Diagram to show the Mechanical action of the Blast.

fire-box, *b*, the tubes, *c*, the smoke-box, and *d*, the chimney. The blast-orifice *e*, terminating below the crown of the smoke-box, and concentric with the chimney, is shown discharging a cylinder-full of steam. The steam expanding laterally as it ascends, strikes the walls of the chimney at *n, n*, some distance above the orifice, as found by observation, the suction surfaces *en* forming an acute angle, about 30°, with the centre line of the chimney. Thus the chimney becomes a species of syringe from which the contents are projected by the blast in successive charges, renewed from the tubes and the fire-box as indicated by the arrows. The circulation of air is thus established in virtue of the

* *Report of the Gauge Commissioners*, 1846.

reduced pressure of the gases in the smoke-box, maintained by the action of the blast, as the difference of pressure within the smoke-box and that of the atmosphere,—in other words, the vacuum in the smoke-box,—is the force which generates the current. This force is measureable by a vacuum-gauge, and in our experiments on the draft, the gauge employed consisted of a glass syphon, ⅜-inch bore, fixed against a scale of inches and parts, like the blast-gauge already described; it was filled to the zero level with tinted water, and one of the limbs being in communication with the interior of the smoke-box, by a small brass tube, while the other was open to the atmosphere, any difference of pressure, or vacuum, was indicated on the gauge, by the descent of the water in the open limb, in obedience to the excess of atmospheric pressure, and an equivalent ascent in the other limb. The difference of water-levels so exhibited was an exact measure of the vacuum in the smoke-box. At very slow speeds, the water-levels oscillated considerably, in pulsations exactly like those of the blast-gauge, and simultaneous with them; and it was thus proved that the vacuum varied directly, or nearly so, with the blast-pressure at every instant. As the speed rose, the pulsations subsided into a slight undulary motion, in precisely the manner already described for the blast-gauge; and even at the highest speeds, the sympathy that subsisted between the blast and the vacuum was made very apparent, showing the immediate dependence of the one upon the other.

Vacuum-gauges have been in some cases applied simultaneously to the smoke-box and the fire-box, to determine the proportions of the total vacuum in the smoke-box due to the resistance of the tubes and the contents of the fire-box separately.

The indications of the gauge, in inches of water, are convertible into pressure, on the principle that the atmospheric pressure of 15 lbs. per inch balances a column of water 34⅓ feet high; 1 lb. of pressure, therefore, balances $\frac{1}{15}$th of 34⅓, or 2·3 feet of water; or, further dividing by 16, 1 ounce balances 1·7 inches of water. A pressure represented by inches of water may thus be converted into ounces per square inch, by dividing the number of inches indicated, by 1·7; the quotient is the equivalent pressure in ounces per square inch.

As the blast operates by exhaustion, it rather *solicits* than forces a current; and the same vacuum in the smoke-box may, under different conditions of the boiler, indicate drafts of very various strength. For example, the vacuum indicated with an ash-pan damper wide open, and when there is a maximum draft, would be at once increased while the draft would be reduced, by merely closing the damper. The increase of vacuum in this case naturally accompanies the suppression of the draft, as it merely indicates a more thorough exhaustion of the closed fire-box and flues, while there is less work done. Again, the greater the number of tubes, the more easily a given quantity of air flows through, and the less is the indicated vacuum, even while the same rate of combustion is maintained. It is necessary, then, in estimating the draft from the vacuum, to take account of such varieties of circumstances.

Conclusion.—From what has been said, it appears that the steam-generating power of the boiler is regulated jointly by grate-surface, coke-room, and heating surface. In the disposal of the heating surface regard should be had rather to its slump numerical value than to the individual fire-box and tube-quantities, the ratio of which we consider practically a matter of indifference. But, in the arrangement of a given area of tube-surface, the leading principle should be to obtain a large sectional area of flue-way. Heating surface is also friction-surface, and the wider the flue-way the easier is the circulation of the gases of combustion, and the milder is the necessary blast. The elements which go to form tube-surface and flue-way, are the number, the inside diameter, and the length of the tubes. The larger the grate, also, the easier is the passage of air into the fire-box. It follows, finally, that the larger the grate, the greater the number and diameter of the tubes, and the shorter their length, the milder is the draft, and the softer the blast required to produce it. The useful limits within which this principle may be observed will be afterwards considered.

CHAPTER III.

MECHANICAL PRINCIPLES (CONTINUED).—CIRCUMSTANCES WHICH REGULATE THE ACTION OF THE BLAST AND THE DRAFT.

Relation of the Blast-Pressure and the Vacuum in the Smoke-Box.—It has been observed that, in general, in the same boiler, the vacuum in the smoke-box varies simply with the blast-pressure; that is, that equal increments of blast-pressure are accompanied by sensibly equal increments of vacuum. With C. R., No. 25, the following pressures and vacuums were observed in close succession, at a uniform speed, with the same state of fire, and nothing to vary but the pressure of the steam in the cylinder, and the blast-pressure as noted.—

TABLE, No. LXII.—BLAST AND VACUUM, IN C. R., No. 25.

1st Notch. Uniform speed 35 miles per hour.		2d Notch. Uniform speed 37 miles per hour.	
Blast. ins. of merc.	Vacuum. ins. of water.	Blast. ins.	Vacuum. ins.
3	2¼	2	1¾
5	3¼	2½	2¼
5½	4	2¾	2½
6½	4½	3½	3
7½	5	4½	3½
8½	5½	5	3¾
		5½	4
		5¾	4¼

Under the 1st notch, and under the 2d also, for the most part, we find that for every inch of blast the vacuum rises regularly half an inch. It appears also that the same blast produces the same vacuum under either notch.

In two other boilers of one class, differing materially from C. R., No. 25, we find the same simple relations of the blast and the vacuum, shown in the following table. With the Hebe we find that the vacuum rises inch for inch with the blast; in the Jupiter, the former rises about ¾ inch per inch of the latter. In all cases, we have found that the vacuum increases simply and directly with

TABLE, No. LXIII.—BLAST AND VACUUM, IN E. & G. R., HEBE AND JUPITER.

HEBE. 40 miles per hour.		JUPITER. Speed accelerating.		
Blast. ins.	Vacuum. ins.	Speed. m.p.h.	Blast. ins.	Vacuum. ins.
1½	3½	11	1⅝	—
2	4	16	2¼	1⅞
2½	4½	18	2½	2¼
3	5	20	3⅜	2½
3½	5½	24	4¼	3¼
4½	6½	30	5⅝	4¼
		31	6⅜	5

the blast. Moreover, in the example of the Jupiter, the rise of the blast-pressure is caused by increase of speed alone, accompanied no doubt by a certain fall of pressure in the cylinder due to wire-drawing, as the speed rises. Thus it follows, generally, that whether the variation of the blast is due to the pressure of the steam in the cylinder, or to an increase of speed, the vacuum varies in a simple ratio with the blast. Again, the vacuum due to a given blast does not appear sensibly affected by the period of admission: the following results from the Jupiter, observed in succession, show that for three successive notches, the value of the vacuum is the same for equal blasts:—

notch.	blast.	vacuum.
2d	3½	2¼
3d	3½	3
"	6	5½
"	7¼	6⅜
4th	6¾	6
"	7	6¼

The same agreement has already been remarked for the 1st and 2d notches of C. R., No. 25; and we may conclude in general that the relation of the vacuum to the blast is not affected by the point at which the steam is cut off in the cylinder. Indeed, within ordinary working limits, there is some reason why it should not be so, for the position of the point of release, which regulates the volume discharged, is much less variable than that of suppression, for different admissions.

Though the vacuum in the same boiler varies in a simple ratio with the blast-pressure, it is affected by other circumstances, the influence of which is readily perceived in the course of a journey. A deeper bed of coke on the grate raises the vacuum due to a given blast, by increasing the difficulty of the passage of air into the fire-box; the closing of the damper has the same effect, by narrowing the passage for air into the ash-pan. On the other hand, the opening of the fire-door reduces the vacuum, as it admits a current of air directly into the fire-box, and proportionally relieves the draft through the coke. An opening into the smoke-box, either by leakage or otherwise, has the same effect in reducing the draft through the grate and the tubes.

The relations of vacuum and draft may be graphically shown by the method of curves drawn to a straight base-line, adopted in previous chapters. For example, to place in a curve the values of the vacuum for the 1st notch of C. R. No. 25, in table No. 62, draw a base-line A B, and divide it into equal spaces, as numbered, to represent inches of mercury, or blast-pressure; divide the vertical scale C into equal parts, for inches of water, as a measure of vacuum. Then, for 3 inches of blast, we have in the table 2¼ inches of vacuum; from the 3d division, or 3 inches, of the base-line, draw an upright equal in length to 2¾ divisions of the vertical scale, and finish it with a star, *a*; similarly, from the

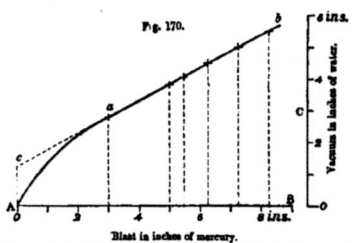

Fig. 170.

Diagram to show Relation of Blast and Vacuum in C. R., No. 25, 1st notch.

5th and other divisions of the base-line, for the successive blast-pressures tabulated, draw verticals equal in numerical value to the relative vacuums, and finish them with stars, as in the figure. It appears that they range precisely in a straight line, *a b*, which when produced meets the vertical scale at *c*, a height of 1¼ inches. But, when there is no blast, there can be no vacuum except what is due to the unaided draft of the chimney; and this is not usually above ⅟₁₀ inch. The line *b a* must therefore be deflected to pass through the point A, to show the true relation of blast and vacuum, as drawn in the figure, forming the line A *a b*.

To arrange in the same way, the tabulated vacuums for the 2d notch of No. 25, and drawing a mean curve line, we

find the curve, fig. 171, passing very closely through them; and it appears practically the same as the curve for the 1st notch, showing graphically, what we have already remarked, that, under the same circumstances, the same vacuum accompanies the same blast, under either notch.

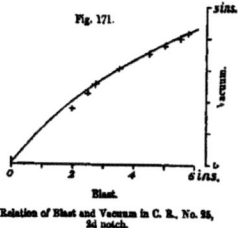

Fig. 171.

Relation of Blast and Vacuum in C. R., No. 25, 2d notch.

By projecting in the same way a whole series of vacuums observed throughout an entire trip, their variable values, due to one or more of the causes already noted, are clearly shown. During a run from Glasgow to Carlisle, with No. 25, the blast and vacuum were observed at regular intervals; and

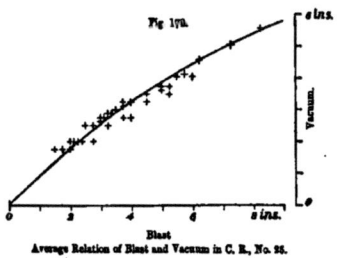

Fig 172.

Average Relation of Blast and Vacuum in C. R., No. 25.

the results so obtained are projected together in fig. 172. The damper was in general kept freely open, and a deep bed of coke, from 12 to 16 inches thick, was maintained in the fire-box. Here, it appears that the greatest variation of the vacuum for any one blast-pressure is ¾ inch, between 2¾ and 3½ inches, due to a blast of 4½ inches. In general, the variation is much less than this, and indicates, what was really the case, a steady depth of fire. Drawing a mean line for the average vacuum, the curve so produced turns out to be identical with those already found from the isolated series of observations in table, No. 63; and it shows that the vacuum rises more rapidly in proportion to the blast during the first inch or two of the latter, and that ultimately it rises uniformly at the rate of about ½ inch per inch of blast, as previously found.

In No. 51, C. R., the variation of vacuum was much greater than in No. 25, as we find on projecting in fig. 173, the results from one or two long runs. Here, for example,

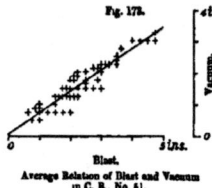

Fig. 173.

Average Relation of Blast and Vacuum in C. R., No. 51.

a variation of 1 inch takes place on very low vacuums not exceeding altogether 2 inches. The mean line turns out perfectly straight, and ascends uniformly at the rate of ⅓ inch per inch of blast. This engine was at all times worked with the lowest possible fire, commonly about 4 to 6 inches thick; though occasionally, in preparing for a heavy pull, the coke was laid on considerably thicker. Thus, altogether, the thickness of coke over the bars of No. 51, though generally much less than in No. 25, was less uniformly maintained. This explains the greater fluctuation of vacuum in No. 51. Further, No. 51 maintains a lower mean vacuum than No. 25 does, for blast-pressures under 5 inches, and this is a direct result of the much thinner bed of fuel carried by the former.

The table, No. 64, next page, contains the dimensions of the boilers subjected to observation by the author, relative to the production of the vacuum and the generation of steam. Between the vacuum and the formation of steam there is a necessary relation, as the vacuum measures the strength of the draft, which regulates the combustion, and consequently also the formation of steam. In the table, there are also included the dimensions of the Snake (London and South Western Railway), the Sphynx and the Atlas (Manchester, Sheffield and Lincolnshire Railway), and No. 30 (Manchester and Birmingham Railway), of which the last three are goods-engines, made by Sharp Brothers and Co., and the Snake and the Sphynx form subjects of our plates. Also, the dimensions of Kitson and Co.'s passenger-engine (Leeds Northern Railway), for the detail of which see our plates; Wilson and Co.'s passenger-engine on the same railway, and Stephenson's early six-wheel engine, figured at page 12.

The variations of vacuum which take place in other engines are the same in character as those already illustrated. Mean vacuum-lines have been found for most of the boilers specified in the table No. 64, by the method already explained; and they are grouped together for comparison on diagram-plate V (upper part), on graduated surfaces, representing inches of blast horizontally, and inches of vacuum ver-

TABLE NO. LXIV.—OF DIMENSIONS OF LOCOMOTIVES, RELATIVE TO THE GENERATION OF STEAM.

Name of Engine.	Engine.			Fire-box.					Tubes.					Chimney.			Blast-orifice.	
	Cylinder.		Diameter of Wheel.	Inside Dimensions.			Fire-bars.		Number.	Outside Diameter.	Length between Plates.	Clearance between neighbouring tubes.	Inside Diameter of Ferules.	Diameter inside, at			Diameter.	Level as to crown of Smoke-box, a, above, b, below.
	Diameter.	Stroke.		Length.	Width.	Height of Bars.	Number.	Thickness.						Entrance in crown of Smoke-box.	Bottom of Shaft or straight part.	Top.		
	ins.	ins.	feet.	ins.	ins.	ins.	no.	ins.	no.	inches.	feet. ins.	ins.	inches.	inches.	inches.	ins.	inches.	inches.
G.W.R. Gt. Britain	18	24	8	53	63	63	29	⅞	305	2	11 3	½	1 5/16	18	17	...	5½	2 b.
C. R. No. 13......	15	20	6	36	42	41½	19	1	158	1¾	10 2½	...	1¼ full	18½	14⅝	...	4 3/16	1½ a.
No. 14......	15	20	6	36	42	41½	18	1⅛	158	1¾	10 2½	...	1¼ "	20	14⅝	14	3 11/16	1 a.
No. 25......	15	20	6	36	42	40	19	1	158	1¾	10 2	...	1 5/16	15	14½	...	3½	flush.
No. 33......	15	20	6	36	42	41½	19	1	156	1⅞	10 2	⅝	1⅜	...	15	...	4	do.
No. 41......	15	20	6	36	42	41½	18	1⅛	158	1¾	10 2	...	1¼ full	...	15¾	15¾	4 1/16	do.
No. 42......	15	20	6	36	42	41½	19	1	158	1¾	10 2	...	1¼ "	...	...	...	4	do.
No. 51 (old valve) ...	15	20	6	36	42	41½	19	1	158	1¾	10 2	9/16	1½	15	15	15	4	do.
No. 73......	13	18	5	33½	40½	43¾	15	1⅛	115	1¾	8 0	...	1 5/16	...	14	...	3½, 3¾	1½ a., ½ b.
No. 102......	16	18	4½	42½	40½	43½	19	1	178	1⅞	10 6	½	1⅜ / none s.b.	...	14	13⅜	4 1/16	1 a.
No. 124 / No. 125 ...	17	24	4′ 7″	42	30	50½	15	1	193	1⅞	10 5	⅝	1 5/16	...	17½ / 15¾	18¾ / 15¾	3 9/16 / 3¾	½ a. / flush.
No. 127......	17	24	4′ 7″	...	...	...	...	...	...	...	...	...	...	...	...	...	4	
G. & S.W.R. Orion	14	18	5½	35	38	47½	...	1	88	2⅛	9 0	...	1⅝	14½	13¼	...	3⅝	5½ b.
Queen	15	22	6	38½	39½	54	16	1	107	2⅛	10 6	9/16	1⅝	17¼	14¼	...	4	2 b.
No. 46	16	24	5	48	40½	52	20	1⅛	157	2⅛	12 0	1	1⅝	21	15¼	...	4½	2 b.
E. & G.R. Pallas...	15	20	6	55	42	52	9 bars / 1 blind	1¼ / 12	134	2	10 6	¾	1½	18½	15	...	4⅝	flush.
Orion	15	20	6	43⅝	40½	53½	14	1¼	125	2	10 6	1	1½	18	14½	...	4 5/16	do.
Hebe / Jupiter	15	20	5½	37	42½	48	16	⅞	148	1¾	10 3	...	1 1/16 full / none s.b.	13¾	12½	...	3⅞	do.
America / Nile	16	18	6	38	42	51	16	1¼	110	2	11 8	1	1½ / none s.b.	19	14½	...	4½	
Brindley...	14	18	5½	35	44½	49	...	1	115	2½	11 10	11/16	1⅝ / 1⅛ s.b.	10½	14½	...	3½	3¼ a.
England...	9	12	4½	26	33	38	18	¾	90	1½	11 4	...	1 3/16	8¾	8¾	...	2¾	7 b.
L & S.W.R. Snake	14¾	21	6½	41½	43¾	48½	32	⅞	181	1¾ / 1⅞	10 3½	½	1 5/16	13	13	12½	4¼	1½ b.
M.S.&L.R. Sphynx	18	24	5	44	30½	55½	16	1	142	2⅛	14 3¼	...	1⅝	18	15½	14¼	4¾	18 b.
Atlas...	16	24	4′ 6″	36	42	48	16	1	175	1⅝	13 10	⅝	none.	18	15½	...	3⅞	18 b.
M. & B. R. No. 30	18	24	4′ 6″	36	42	48	16	1	147	1⅝	13 10	⅝	1⅜ / 1¼ s.b.	18	15½	...	3½	flush.
L. N. R. No. 7...	16	22	6	51	43	57½	24	1	147	1⅞	11 0	¾	1 7/16	21	13¾	...	4⅝	8 b.
No. 10...	16	22	6	40½	43	64½	24	1	185	2	10 10½	⅝	1 5/16	17½	13⅜	...	5	level.
Stephenson's original 6-wheel engine.........	12	18	5	34½	39½	38	15	1	124	1⅝	7 10	¾	1½	15	15	...	2½	7 a.

NOTE.—Thickness of Tubes 3/32 inch, except in Stephenson's Locomotive, 5/32 inch.
The Blast-orifice of the America, originally 4⅞ inches with gab-motion, was reduced to 4½ inches, when fitted with the link-motion.

tically. For many of the engines, curves in dot-lining are added, showing the influence of an open fire-door and other circumstances on the observed vacuum. To show the dependence of the vacuum-line on the proportions and arrangement of the boiler and the conditions of its successful action, table No. 65 has been prepared, containing the necessary data, derived from the preceding table of dimensions. The first eight columns contain the sectional areas of the flue-ways or passages by which the air and smoke are drawn through the boiler, the friction-surface of the tubes, and the area of cylinder. The sectional areas are deduced from ascertained dimensions. The area of grate is, in all cases, calculated from the inside horizontal dimensions of the fire-box at the bottom, as these give the really available area; and the area of air-space of grate is found by deducting the collective area of grate-bars and bar-frame from the grate-area. The interior sectional area of tubes is had by multiplying the area of one tube, due to its interior diameter, by the number of tubes; the area of ferule in like manner; the sectional area at the bottom of shaft of chimney is taken just where the base meets the body or shaft; the friction-surface of the tubes is found by multiplying the interior circumference of one tube by the length between plates, and by the number of tubes, and it is in fact identical with their heating surface. Cols. 9 to 15 contain the relative values of the flue-areas in terms of the grate-area, which for this purpose is taken equal to 1; and cols. 16, 17, 18 contain the values of some of these areas in terms of the blast-orifice. The grate and the blast-area are the principal elements concerned in the production of steam, and it is thus expedient that they should be adopted as units for comparison.

Constancy of the Exhausting Power of the Blast.—It has in all cases been remarked that an increase of vacuum accompanies an increase of blast-pressure, whether this may arise from an increase of speed or of exhaust pressure at release. Even at the highest observed speeds, the vacuum rises steadily with the blast; and this unfailing sympathy of action proves that the blast retains its property of exhaustion within all practical limits of speed and steam-pressure. The vacuum-diagrams afford abundant evidence of

TABLE, No. LXV.—FLUE AREAS AND PROPORTIONS OF BOILERS, RELATIVE TO DRAUGHT AND EVAPORATION.

Name of Engine.	Total Sectional Areas of Flue-ways, &c.						Friction-surface of Tubes.	Sectional Area of Cylinder.	Ratios of Areas, Grate-area = 1, or Unity.							Ratios of Areas, Blast-orifice = 1.		
	Grate.	Air-space of Grate.	Tubes.	Ferrules.	Chimney at bottom of shaft.	Blast-orifice.			Air-space of Grate.	Tubes.	Ferrules.	Chimney.	Blast-orifice.	Tube-surface.	Cylinder.	Grate.	Chimney.	Cylinder.
	sq. feet.	sq. feet.	sq. feet.	sq. feet.	sq. feet.	sq. ins.	sq. feet.	sq. ins.										
G.W.R. Gt. Britain	21	11·4	5·46	4·0	1·77	23·76	1627	254·5	·54	·26	·20	·084	1/127	77·5	1/12	127	10·7	10·7
C. R. No. 13......	10·5	4·77	2·104	1·41	1·13	13·16	646·2	176·7	·45	·20	·13	·11	1/115	61·5	1/8·6	115	12	13·4
No. 14......	10·5	3·2	2·104	1·41	1·13	10·48	646·2	176·7	·30	·20	·13	·11	1/144	61·5	1/8·6	144	19	16·9
No. 25......	10·5	4·77	2·104	1·48	1·14	11·8	646·2	176·7	·45	·20	·14	·11	1/128	61·5	1/8·6	128	14	15·8
No. 33......	10·5	4·77	2·42	1·61	...	12·57	702	176·7	·45	·23	·15	...	1/120	67·0	1/8·6	120		14·3
No. 41......	10·5	4·4	2·104	1·41	1·35	12·7	646·2	176·7	·42	·20	·13	·13	1/119	61·5	1/8·6	119	15	14
No. 42......	10·5	4·77	2·104	1·41	...	12·57	646·2	176·7	·45	·20	·13	...	1/120	61·5	1/8·6	120		14·3
No. 51......	10·5	4·77	2·104	1·346	1·23	12·57	646·2	176·7	·45	·20	·13	·12	1/120	61·5	1/8·6	120	14	14·3
No. 73......	9·35	4·41	1·84	1·08	1·07	{8·09 / 11·0}	376·3	132·7	·47	·107	·12	·11	{1/164 / 1/121}	40·2	1/10	{164 / 121}	19 / 14	16·4 / 12·1
No. 102......	11·8	4·6	2·8	2·13	1·07	13·0	818·8	201	·40	·24	·18	·09	1/131	69·4	1/8·5	131	12	15·5
No. 124......	11·37	5·06	3·0	2·30	{1·67 / 1·27}	10·0	888	227	·44	·26	·20	{·15 / ·11}	1/164	78·1	1/7·2	164	{24 / 18}	22·7
No. 125......	11·37	5·28	3·0	2·30	{1·27 / 1·67}	11·0	888	227	·46	·26	·20	·11	1/149	78·1	1/7·2	149	{16 / 22}	20·6
No. 127......	11·37	5·28	3·0	2·30	1·27	12·57	888	227	·46	·26	·20	...	1/130	78·1	1/7·2	130	14·5	18
G. & S.W.R. Orion	9·24	4·81	1·8	1·27	0·96	10·3	401·7	154	·52	·195	·14	·10	1/129	43·5	1/8·6	129	13	15
Queen	10·5	5·5	2·2	1·54	1·11	12·57	570	176·7	·52	·21	·14	·11	1/120	54·3	1/8·6	120	13	14·3
No. 46	13·4	5·2	3·22	2·62	1·27	16·0	956	201	·39	·24	·20	·09	1/121	71·3	1/10	121	11·4	12·6
E. & G. R. Pallas...	16·04	4·08	2·40	1·64	1·23	16·8	668·7	176·7	·25	·15	·10	·08	1/137	41·7	1/13	137	10·5	10·5
Orion	12·23	5·29	2·24	1·53	1·14	14·5	623·7	176·7	·43	·18	·125	·09	1/121	51·0	1/10	121	11	12·2
Hebe / Jupiter	10·92	6·7	2·06	{0·95 / 2·06 s.b}	0·85	11·8	619·4	176·7	·61	·19	·09	·075	1/133	56·7	1/9	133	10	15
America / Nile	11·10	3·50	1·97	{1·35 / 1·58}	1·14	16·0	595·1	201	·31	·18	·12	·10	1/100	53·6	1/8	100	10·2	12·0
Brindley...	9·15	3·44	2·36	1·66	1·15	9·6	690·6	154	·38	·26	·18	·13	1/137	75·5	1/8·6	137	17	16
England...	5·03	2·26	1·01	0·69	0·42	5·04	382·5	63·6	·45	·20	·14	·083	1/122	76·0	1/11·4	122	10	10·7
L. & S.W.R. Snake	12·4	5·54	{2·40 / 2·80}	1·7 / 2·0	·852 top / ·921 bot.	14·18	823·5	159·5	·45	{·20 / ·23}	·14 / ·16	·074	1/126	66·4	1/11·2	126	{8·6 top / 9·4 bot.	11·2
M.S. & L.R. Sphynx	10·56	5·0	2·92	2·04	1·31	17·7	864·8	254·5	·47	·28	·20	·12	1/86	82	1/6	86	10·6	14·4
Atlas	9·5	4·5	1·97	1·97	1·31	11·8	908	201	·47	·207	·207	·14	1/116	95·5	1/6·8	116	16	17·9
M. & B. R. No. 30	9·5	4·5	1·94	1·0	1·31	8·3	830	254·5	·47	·204	·105	·14	1/164	87	1/5·4	164	22.5	30·6
L. N. R. No. 7	15·23	6·5	2·28	1·65	1·03	16·8	714·2	201	·43	·15	·11	·068	1/130	47	1/10·9	130	8.8	12
No. 10	14·71	6·0	3·31	2·45	0·97	19·6	955·4	201	·41	·22	·17	·066	1/108	65	1/10·5	108	7·2	10·3
Stephenson's	9·46	4·6	1·46	1·06	1·23	4·0	432	113	·49	·15	·11	·13	1/278	45·6	1/12·1	278	36	23
	1	2	3	4	5	6	7	8	9	10	11	12	13	14	15	16	17	18

the correctness of this conclusion, as they, all of them, rise to the last without any material change of direction, in a steady ratio with the blast. Particular proofs in point occur when an engine slips its driving wheels; on such an occasion, the speed of piston may suddenly be raised to a degree much above what ever occurs in practice; the blast-pressure and the vacuums have been observed to mount equally and simultaneously even to the highest limits of the gauges, and to subside as sympathetically when the steam is shut off or reduced.

It is observed also that, though the vacuum rises with the blast at rates considerably different for different engines, yet, as a general result, the vacuum in the smoke-box, expressed in inches of water, is about equal to the blast-pressure which creates it, measured in inches of mercury.

Relation of the Form and Size of Chimney to the Area of Blast-orifice; Evidence of the Vacuum-line.—The diameter of chimney is a matter of essential importance in the design of a locomotive. Ordinary stationary-engine chimneys can hardly be made too large in horizontal area, as ease of exit improves the draft. The known advantage of sectional area in these cases is sometimes attempted to be transferred to locomotive-chimneys, and this has been the vice of the system. It is apparently overlooked that the draft of the locomotive-boiler is mainly due, not to the superior levity of a column of hot air in the chimney, as in stationary and marine examples, but to the exhaustion effected by the mechanical action of the blast. The chimney, therefore, assumes a new character, and is, in conjunction with the blast-pipe, an exhausting machine; and its efficiency is dependent on entirely different considerations. To these we shall now direct attention, with the aid of the group of chimneys and blast-pipes pertaining to the engines under review, shown in diagram-plate V.

First, as to the Influence of the Diameter of Chimney.—That a chimney may be too large is easily proved. For example, C. R. Nos. 124 and 125, identical in all other respects, had chimneys respectively 17½ and 15¼ inches diameter. It was attempted to find steam by employing a reduced orifice of 3 3/16 inches for the wider chimney, 1/24th of its area; that for the smaller chimney of No. 125, being 3¼ inches, or 1/16th of the area of chimney; and even with the smaller orifice of No. 124, the engine was known to steam badly. The inferior steaming power here alluded to is confirmed by the vacuum-lines for the respective engines, diagram-plate 5, in which we find that to obtain 4 inches of vacuum, No. 125 required 4½ inches of blast; whereas No. 124 required double this pressure, or 9 inches of blast. To prove that the inferior vacuum of No. 124 was due to the excess of chimney, the chimneys of the two engines were exchanged. With the smaller chimney the vacuum-line of No. 124 was much improved, as shown by the vacuum-diagram, and the necessary blast for 4 inches of vacuum fell from 9 to $6\frac{1}{2}$ inches; that is, $6\frac{1}{2}$ inches of blast in the latter case yielded as good a draft as 9 inches in the former. Further, to refer to No. 102, with a $13\frac{5}{8}$ inch chimney, and an orifice of $4\frac{1}{16}$ inches, a 4 inch vacuum was producible by a $5\frac{1}{2}$ inch blast, the proportions of boiler being much like those of the other engines named. These results may be thus placed together:—To yield a 4 inch vacuum,

	orifice.	chimney.	ratio of areas.	blast.
No. 124.	$3\frac{9}{16}$ ins.	$17\frac{1}{2}$ ins.	1 to 24	requires 9 ins.
Do.	do.	$15\frac{1}{2}$ ins.	1 to 18	requires $6\frac{1}{2}$ ins.
No. 125.	$3\frac{3}{4}$ ins.	$15\frac{1}{2}$ ins.	1 to 16	requires $4\frac{1}{2}$ ins.
Do.	do.	do.	(door open)	requires $5\frac{3}{4}$ ins.
No. 102.	$4\frac{1}{16}$ ins.	$13\frac{5}{8}$ ins.	1 to 12	requires $5\frac{1}{2}$ ins.

Here it is clear that the smaller the chimney the larger is the orifice, while the vacuum also is improved. No. 102 indeed requires a slightly greater blast to give the same vacuum; but this difference is due to the blocking up of the base of the chimney by the blast pipe, which is more prejudicial as the diameter of chimney is reduced. Thus, in these cases, the best result has been obtained by reducing the chimney and enlarging the orifice, till the area of the former becomes only 12 times that of the latter. With the $15\frac{1}{2}$ inch chimney, it is found that No. 127 steams as well with a 4 inch orifice, $\frac{1}{15}$th of the chimney-area, as No. 125 with a smaller orifice.

Another example of the inefficiency of a reduction of orifice under certain conditions is afforded by the results from Nos. 13 and 14, C. R.; with precisely the same chimneys, they have orifices of $4\frac{3}{32}$ and $3\frac{11}{16}$ inches, respectively $\frac{1}{13}$th and $\frac{1}{15}$th of the chimney; whereas the vacuum-line of No. 13 is much the superior. Thus, to yield 4 inches of vacuum,

No. 13 requires	4 inches	of blast.
No. 14, with clinkered grate,	$5\frac{1}{2}$	do.
Do., with clear grate,	$6\frac{1}{2}$	do.

No. 14 being employed in goods traffic, with heavy loads at moderate speeds, when an engine works to most advantage, the air-space of grate was reduced to less than that of No. 13, as shown in the table, with the view of checking the draft, and the driver was in the habit of further checking the passage of air by a layer of clinkers on the grate. Though these circumstances operated towards increasing the vacuum, we find that No. 13, with an open grate and no clinker, shows the best vacuum.

Again, with No. 73, the enlargement of the orifice from $3\frac{1}{4}$ to $3\frac{3}{4}$ inches, from $\frac{1}{19}$th to $\frac{1}{14}$th of the chimney's area, had a beneficial effect upon the draft, as we find from the vacuum-lines that for 4 inches of vacuum,

an orifice $3\frac{1}{4}$ inches, to chimney as 1 to 19, requires $5\frac{1}{2}$ ins. of blast,
and do. $3\frac{3}{4}$ do., do. as 1 to 14, do. 3 do.

The vacuum-lines of the Hebe and the Orion (E. & G. R.) are remarkable for being the quickest on the diagram, and they appear to be about equally quick, while their orifices are 11·8 and 14·5 square inches. These boilers differ mostly in the flue-areas through the ferules, which are 0·95 and 1·53 square feet respectively, or as 2 to 3 nearly. The extremely contracted flue-way of the Hebe accounts for the smaller orifice of that engine; and the sagacious designer has *adapted the chimney to the blast-orifice*, by making it suitably small, only $12\frac{1}{4}$ inches diameter, or 10 times the area of orifice. But, vacuum-lines cannot be implicitly trusted as indices to the steaming qualities of the engines, where the proportions are materially different. We find that the Pallas yields a very low vacuum-line, which apparently indicates a want of draught; whereas this engine had on all occasions a superabundance of steam, which required the door to be kept mostly open; and the moderate vacuum which it exhibits, is the result of its extensive grate-surface. Irrespective of the vacuum-line, we find in the Pallas, as in the two others, that the area of chimney, 15 inches diameter, is relatively small, being only $10\frac{1}{2}$ times the blast-orifice.

The proportions of the Snake afford further proof of the efficiency of a small diameter of chimney. To compare the Snake, and the Orion, E. & G. R., while their boilers have about the same flue-areas, the former has 200 feet more tube-surface; and though altogether its boiler is larger, its chimney is but 13 inches, while that of the Orion is $14\frac{1}{2}$ inches, and their respective orifices are $4\frac{1}{4}$ and $4\frac{5}{16}$ inches. Thus, with sensibly the same orifice, the Snake works a much larger boiler by the aid of a smaller chimney, the area of which is but 9·4 times the blast-orifice; notwithstanding the incidental disadvantage of an indirect exhaust passage. Again, the Queen, G. & S. W. R., with nearly the same flue-areas, has not much above two-thirds of the tube-surface; and yet this engine requires a 4 inch orifice, for a $14\frac{1}{2}$ inch chimney, $1\frac{1}{2}$ inch larger than the Snake's; in this case, the chimney has an area of 13 times the orifice.

From what has just been said, it is sufficiently clear that for a given boiler, there is but one diameter of chimney of greatest efficiency,—that is, which permits of the greatest blast-orifice. Should the chimney be increased the orifice must be reduced; and of the necessity of this we have found several examples; though even the effect of a reduction of orifice beyond a limited proportion of area, ceases to be perceptible.

Secondly, of the Influence of the Form of the Blast-pipe.—A crooked exhaust passage, especially towards the orifice, is unfavourable for efficiency of exhaustion. The oblique direction impressed on the exhaust steam by the inclined jet of engines like No. 51, is conspicuous even to the eye, when engines of this class are working under high steam at a slow pace. The steam is observed to shoot right and left alternately from the top of the chimney, according as it leaves the left or right hand cylinder; and follows the direction of the dot lines, fig. 174. So decided is this bias laterally, in practice, that the material of the chimney on the two sides, about 26 inches above the crown, wears away by the lateral impingement of the blast, insomuch that occasional patches are required to cover the failures of the original metal, for about 18 inches above and below that level. Engines of the variety of No. 13, fitted with an adjutage 4 inches long and nearly cylindrical, show a much better action of the blast, the lateral deviation being nearly imperceptible.

Fig. 174.

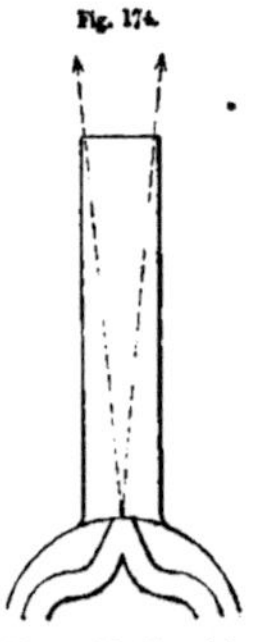

Influence of the Form of the Blast-pipe.

Accordingly, we find that No. 13 has a quicker vacuum-line than No. 51, though this is doubtless referrible also to other causes. A very marked contrast is, however, to be found between No. 51 and the Orion; in the former, all the sectional areas of flue-way are less than in the latter, and the tube or friction-surface is greater, and therefore we should look for a quicker vacuum-line in No. 51; whereas in this engine 2 inches of vacuum require 3 inches of blast, while for the Orion only $\frac{3}{4}$ inch of blast is necessary. With the same cylinder and wheel, and nearly the same chimney, this difference is conspicuous, and is due mainly to the inferior mode of delivering the blast of No. 51—obliquely from the orifice, while from the Orion it is discharged vertically from a straight pipe. On the same ground, the vacuum-line of No. 46, G. & S. W. R., with a wide orifice, is as good as that of No. 125, C. R., with a much smaller orifice.

But even though the blast-pipe may be formed to project the steam vertically upwards, it must also be placed precisely concentric with the chimney. A half inch of divergence has been known to spoil the draft of an engine, and yet such want of adjustment is frequent enough. Even the finish of the orifice is of importance; and it has been found that superior results are obtained from an orifice finished to an angle on the outside, as here sketched, leaving an edge of $\frac{1}{16}$ inch thick, and slightly turned over from the inside, as at *a*. The benefit of the exterior bevil appears to consist in the facility it offers for the approach of the surrounding smoke into contact with the steam-jet as it leaves the orifice.

Fig. 178.

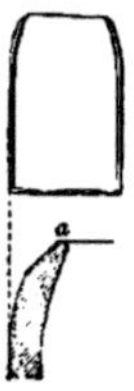

Form of Blast-orifice.

An easy exhaust passage from the cylinder to the orifice is of importance; the blast-pipe should taper only slightly from the base upwards, and should be gathered in chiefly at the extremity. A wide passage up to the nozzle places the blast much more under the control of the area of orifice.

Thirdly, of the Advantage of ready access to the Chimney.—In this respect great differences are observed. Comparing No. 13 and No. 51, C.R., of which the chimney of the former is gradually gathered in from an 18$\frac{1}{2}$ inch opening in the smoke-box, permitting some freedom round the blast-pipe, while that of No. 51 is planted abruptly on an opening of 15 inches, with which the orifice is flush, we find that for a 4-inch vacuum,

No. 13, with orifice 4$\frac{3}{16}$ inches, requires 4 inches of blast.
No. 51, with do. 4 inches, requires 6 inches do.

The extra blast required for No. 51, though partially due to its larger chimney, is no doubt owing also to the inferior entrance it provides, and the contraction is aggravated by the spreading form of its blast-pipe, which plainly offers a greater obstruction than that of No. 13. Accordingly, it has been found that the engines of the variety of No. 13, make steam more readily than those like No. 51,—a difference which is due to the relative conformation of the chimney and the blast-pipe.

For the capacious orifice of the America, the engine is no doubt much indebted to the easy entrance of its chimney; the body of the chimney being only nine times the area of the blast-orifice. But of all the engines before us, the Orion, G. & S. W. R., No. 7, L. N. R., the England, and the Sphynx, have the best disposition of blast-pipe; in these the orifice is placed considerably below the crown of the smoke-box,—in the Orion 5$\frac{1}{8}$ inches, in No. 7, 8 inches, in the England 7 inches (below bottom of chimney), and in the Sphynx 18 inches. In the arrangements of the England, the makers have studied the obtainment of the greatest efficiency in every part of the engine, and with much success; and they have found the best level, consistent with the largest orifice, for keeping up the steam, to be as now stated,—7 inches, which is but a little less than 8$\frac{3}{4}$ inches, the diameter of the chimney; and this is but 10 times the area of blast-orifice.

The remarkably low level adopted in the Sphynx as that which permitted of the widest orifice, was the result of some successfully conducted experiments by Mr. Peacock, locomotive superintendent of the Manchester, Sheffield, and Lincolnshire Railway, made with a view to ascertain the most favourable conditions of draft. The table No. 66, drawn up by Mr. Peacock, contains the successive results obtained by him on this subject; from which he has perfectly established that in the Sphynx class of engines, the lower the level of the orifice, within 18 inches of the crown, the greater may be its diameter. To such an extent is the diameter affected that a 4$\frac{1}{8}$ inch orifice, $\frac{1}{8}$ inch below the crown, is not so efficient as a 4$\frac{3}{4}$ inch orifice at 18 inches below, and the areas of these are as 3 to 4. At 6 inches below the crown, a 4$\frac{5}{8}$ inch orifice was as good as 4$\frac{1}{8}$ inches at $\frac{1}{8}$ inch below. At 11$\frac{1}{2}$ inches below, a 4$\frac{5}{8}$ inch orifice made abundance of steam, and was as good as a 4$\frac{1}{2}$ inch orifice at 9 inches. Though it has been agreed that an orifice at least as low as the base of the chimney, is favourable for draft, the advantage of passing the blast *through* and not *above* the smoke has been but partially recognized. By the use of the low orifice, Mr. Peacock brings up the blast-area to the desirable ratio of $\frac{1}{106}$th of the lower part of the chimney; and he has adopted the same arrangement, as far as practicable, in all the other engines under his charge,—and with such advantage in the passenger-engines, as in all cases to permit of orifices equal in area to the steam-ports,—some of them even larger.

The orifice of the England, we have seen, is at a distance from the entrance to the chimney a little less than the diameter of the latter, or 80 per cent.; in the Sphynx, we have found it something more, or 120 per cent. The mean of these, 100 per cent., indicates a level of blast-orifice below the entrance equal to the diameter of chimney, to be in general a safe and efficient rule of practice.

The benefit of small chimneys and free access to them, is fully acknowledged in the engines of Kitson and Co., and Wilson and Co., specimens of which are tabulated. Of these we shall have more to say in following paragraphs.

Of the Relative Vacuums in the Smoke-box and the Fire-box.—Mr. Ramsbottom of Manchester made some observations on this subject in 1847, on the Manchester and Birmingham Railway; and he found that in one of Sharp's goods-engines, No. 30, M. B. R., quoted in the table, having 147 tubes, 1$\frac{3}{4}$ inches outside diameter, and 13 feet 10 inches long, grate-area 9·5 feet, the vacuum in the smoke-box was, at all speeds, three times that indicated in the

TABLE, No. LXVI.—RESULTS OF EXPERIMENTS WITH THE SPHYNX LOCOMOTIVE, ON THE MANCHESTER, SHEFFIELD, AND LINCOLNSHIRE RAILWAY, TO ASCERTAIN THE BEST LEVEL OF BLAST-ORIFICE CONSISTENT WITH THE WIDEST AREA.

Date.	From Manchester.		From Sheffield.		Position of Blast-Orifice in Smoke-Box.	Diameter of Blast-Orifice.	Coke consumed in cwts.	Number of miles run.	Consumption per mile in lbs.	Time from Manchester to Woodhead.	Time from Sheffield to Dunford.	No. of observations.	Remarks on the Performance of the Engine with various Diameters and Levels of Blast-Orifice.
	Loaded Waggons.	Empty Waggons.	Loaded Waggons.	Empty Waggons.									
1850.	No.	No.	No.	No.	inches.	ins.	cwts	miles.	lbs.	H. M.	H. M.		
July 28th ...					(Above roof of box) 1 inch.	$4\frac{1}{2}$						1	Could not make steam without having two large hooks in blast-pipe.
Augt. 1st ...					(Below roof of box) $\frac{7}{8}$	$4\frac{1}{8}$						2	Made steam much better, but not well.
Augt. 3rd ...					$2\frac{1}{4}$	$4\frac{3}{8}$						3	Much better for steam than the $4\frac{1}{2}$, but not so well as with $4\frac{3}{8}$ blast-pipe.
Augt. 8th ...		60			6	$4\frac{3}{8}$						4	Made steam equally as well as with $4\frac{1}{8}$ blast-pipe.
Augt. 8th Alteration at Sheffield.			25	15	$11\frac{1}{2}$	$4\frac{3}{8}$						5	Found it to be better in this position than anywhere where we have tried it. Steam plenty, and blowing off about one-half time.
Augt. 10th...	24		24		$11\frac{1}{2}$	$4\frac{3}{8}$						6	Steam plenty both ways, but load light.
Augt. 12th...		12	27		$11\frac{1}{2}$	$4\frac{3}{8}$	33	90	$41\frac{1}{12}$			7	Hot water in tank one way, and steam plenty.
Augt. 13th...		6	30		$11\frac{1}{2}$	$4\frac{3}{8}$	30	90	$37\frac{1}{3}$			8	Hot water in tender both ways.
Augt. 15th...		55	18		9	$4\frac{1}{4}$	31	90	$38\frac{1}{3}$			9	The $4\frac{3}{8}$ pipe made steam quite as well in the lower position as the $4\frac{1}{4}$ did in the higher.
Augt. 17th...	26		28		9	$4\frac{1}{4}$	33	90	$41\frac{1}{12}$			10	Steam sufficient, but none to spare.
Augt. 18th...			3rd class Coaches. 34		9	$4\frac{1}{4}$	23	90	$28\frac{1}{3}$			11	Required the pilot engine from Sheffield, on account of the rain and a very heavy side wind. We could not have got up without assistance.
Augt. 19th...	20		30		9	$4\frac{1}{4}$	43	115	$41\frac{7}{8}$			12	Commenced with Eckington goods, and reduced the capacity of the smoke-box $\frac{1}{3}$rd; found the engine to make steam decidedly better with the alteration. Steam blowing off both ways, and the damper closed about one-half time.
Augt. 20th...	29		27		9	$4\frac{1}{3}$	44	115	$42\frac{7}{8}$	1 30	1 25	13	Smoke-box the same as August 19th. We did not make steam so well as on the 19th, but it was partly owing to the flue-area being too contracted from the tube-ends to chimney.
Augt. 21st...	31		29		9	$4\frac{1}{3}$	45	115	$43\frac{5}{8}$	1 20	1 27	14	Made steam much better than on the 20th, but not so well as on the 19th.
Augt. 22nd...	24		22		9	$4\frac{1}{3}$		115		1 32	1 27	15	Smoke-box enlarged to its full size. Made steam very badly. Either the capacity of the smoke-box must be reduced, or the area of the blast-pipe about 2 square inches before the engine will make steam for a load.
Sept. 11th...	31		28		$9\frac{3}{8}$	$4\frac{5}{16}$	40	90	$49\frac{3}{4}$	1 23	1 26	16	Commenced with Hull goods, and the telescope blast-pipe. Made steam well both ways.
Sept. 12th...	28		21		18	$4\frac{4}{16}$	32	90	$39\frac{5}{8}$	1 15	1 10	17	Made steam decidedly better in this place than it did in the higher one. It is now as low as we can put it. Steam blowing off, both ways; both dampers closed, and fire-door open about half time.
Sept. 13th...	30	7	20		18	$4\frac{3}{16}$	35	90	$43\frac{1}{3}$	1 15	0 58	18	Made steam ample, blowing off nearly all the way. No pilot through the Woodhead tunnel. I think the blast-pipe would do a little larger.
Sept. 14th...	34		22		18	$4\frac{3}{8}$	41	90	51	1 43	1 2	19	Blast-pipe too large for such a load as this. Could not make steam, and obliged to put one hook in. This is the greatest load we have yet taken. The waggons were very heavily laden, and most of the springs down. Water evaporated from Manchester to Dunford, 2500 gallons. We have taken before 33 loaded waggons, with 1400 gallons; but I should think they would not be as heavily laden by one-fourth as those above mentioned.
Sept. 16th...	10		33		18	$4\frac{3}{8}$	35	100	$39\frac{1}{3}$		1 35	20	Commenced with the Pick-up train. Made steam very badly; the blast-pipe too large for such a load as this, but will make steam for about 26 waggons.
Sept. 17th...	23	24	33		18	$4\frac{3}{8}$	50	100	56		1 15	21	The coke that we got from Gorton of bad quality—the worst we have ever had from there; could only just make steam with it. It went all to puddle, and the grate-bars were made up before we got to Woodhead. We had the North Country coke on our return, and then we had plenty of steam, and consumed less coke by 9 or 10 cwt.
Sept. 18th...	28	9	34		18	$4\frac{3}{8}$	58	100	$51\frac{1}{3}$		1 10	22	Got on more coke at Sheffield, the Gorton coke being so very bad. The quantity used from Manchester to Sheffield, 30 cwt.; returning, 16 cwt. = 46 cwt.: or $51\frac{1}{3}$ per mile.
Sept. 19th...	33		27		$9\frac{3}{8}$	$4\frac{3}{8}$	46	100	$51\frac{1}{3}$		1 6	23	Coke from Gorton to-day very good; made steam plenty up to Woodhead; and from Sheffield to Dunford, with the North coke, we had the greatest difficulty in making steam for the lighter load with the blast-pipe in the higher position. If the Gorton coke were always of the same quality as this we have had to-day, the blast-pipe would work very well $\frac{1}{4}$ of an inch larger.

fire-box. In ordinary circumstances, the vacuums in the smoke and fire-boxes were respectively about 12 and 4 inches of water, showing that 4 inches of vacuum was required to draw the air through the grate and the fuel, and (12—4), or 8 inches, for drawing the smoke through the tubes.* He found also that the quantity of air which could be forced

* *Proc. Inst. Mech. Engineers*, July, 1849.

through one of these tubes, having a ferule 1¼ inch inside diameter, at the fire-box end only, was 10 per cent. more than could be passed through the same tube with ferules at both ends; and that, under the same pressure, 25 per cent. more than in the latter case, could be sent through the same tube without a ferule at either end.[*]

In September 1848, Mr. J. V. Gooch made experiments, with the same object, on the Snake, running on the London and South-Western Railway, from which we find a very different ratio. The following series of relative vacuums observed at close intervals is selected from his communications on the subject, with which we have been favoured. The steam was cut off at 8¾ inches out of 21 inches of stroke; and the speed varied from 55 to 63 miles per hour.

TABLE, No. LXVII.—OF RELATIVE VACUUMS.—SNAKE, 1848.

Smoke-box.	Fire-box.	Difference, due to the Tubes.	Remarks.
inches.	inches.	inches.	The total mean vacuums observed during the experiments were
2½	1	1½	
3	1	2	
4	1½	2½	Smoke-box, 5 9 ins.
4½	1½	2¾	Fire-box, 2 6 „ or 44 per cent.
5	2	3	
6	2½	3½	difference, 3 3 „ or 56 do.
7	3½	3½	
8	4	4	
9	4	5	
5·44	2·36	3·08	Means.

Here we observe the difference due to the tubes rises very much with the vacuum in the fire-box; and that whereas, in Mr. Ramsbottom's experiments, the tubes employed two-thirds of the total vacuum, in this case, they require little more than one-half.

In 1850, M. Polonceau, in France, made observations on one of the Orleans Railway passenger-engines. The engine, made by Stephenson, was of the following dimensions:—Grate-area, 9·16 feet; 160 tubes, 1¾ inch inside diameter, 12 feet long. The speed varied from 25 to 30 miles per hour, with a light train. The blast-orifice was of variable area, and the observations were made with it under three conditions,—entirely open, half open, closed (fermé); and under eight notches of the sector. The following were the results obtained as tabulated by M. Polonceau, translated into English measures:[†]

TABLE, No. LXVIII.—OF RELATIVE VACUUMS. No. 132, PARIS AND ORLEANS RAILWAY, 1850.

No. of Notch.	Entirely open.		Half open.		Closed.		Remarks.
	Smoke-box.	Fire-box.	Smoke-box.	Fire-box.	Smoke-box.	Fire-box.	
	ins.	ins.	ins.	ins.	ins.	ins.	The vacuum in either the smoke-box or the fire-box varies sensibly as the following numbers:—
1	2·1	1·3	4·3	2·3	8·3	4·1	
2	2·0	1·1	3·4	1·7	6·7	3·3	
3	1·7	0·9	3·2	1·6	5·6	2·8	
4	2·3	1·3	3·5	1·8	5·3	2·9	
5	1·8	1·1	2·6	1·5	4·9	2·6	Orifice open.........1·0
6	1·4	0·8	2·2	1·2	3·8	2·0	Do. half open ......1·5
7	1·3	0·8	1·5	0·9	3·2	1·7	Do. closed (fermé) 3·0
8	0·6	0·4	1·2	0·7	1·9	1·0	
Mean ratios.	fire-box 59 per cent. of smoke-box.		fire-box 53 per cent. of smoke-box.		fire-box 52 per cent. of smoke-box.		General mean ratio 55 per cent.

* Tredgold on the *Steam Engine*, vol. i., 1850.
† *Guide du Mécanicien Constructeur et Conducteur de Machines Locomotives*, Paris, 1851.

In this case we perceive that the vacuum in the fire-box is above one half of that in the smoke-box. Numerous experiments of the same kind were made upon the Northern Railway of France, of which M. Polonceau furnishes some of the mean results in the following table:—separately for each engine, with three different areas of blast-orifice in ordinary use on the line.

TABLE, No. LXIX.—OF RELATIVE VACUUMS. NORTHERN RAILWAY OF FRANCE, 1850.

No. and Designation of Engine.	Speed.	Number of Carriages in Train.	Blast-Area.					
			17 to 16 square inches.		14 to 11 square inches.		11 to 8 square inches.	
			Smoke-box.	Fire-box.	Smoke-box.	Fire-box.	Smoke-box.	Fire-box.
	miles.	No.	ins.	ins.	ins.	ins.	ins.	ins.
No. 166 Passr. Engine (Stephenson's)	34	11	3·2	2·0	3·5	2·5	...	...
		12	...	...	...	...	6·0	3·9
No. 18 Passr. (Clapeyron)	34	10	4·5	2·5	6·4	4·1	...	...
		16	...	...	...	...	7·3	4·7
No. 260 Goods ...	13½	33	3·8	2·7	4·0	2·8	4·9	3·4
			32·6 to 22 sq. inches		22 to 15·5 sq. inches			
No. 133 Passr. (Crampton)	37	12	2·5	1·7	2·6	1·7	...	...
Mean ratio of Fire-box to Smoke-box varies from 60 to 70 per cent.								

Here the vacuum in the fire-box constitutes the greater part of the total vacuum, being 60 to 70 per cent., and leaving only 30 to 40 per cent. due to the tubes. M. Polonceau has not, however, favoured his readers with the relative dimensions of these engines. To compare the vacuums of the engines of which the particulars have already been given, the following are the data concerned:—

TABLE, No. LXX.—RELATIVE VACUUMS OF DIFFERENTLY PROPORTIONED BOILERS.

Engine.	Observer.	Area of Grate.	Flue-way of Tubes.		Heating or Friction-surface of Tubes.	Percentage of Total Vacuum due to	
			Ferules at Fire-box.	Body of Tubes.		Grate.	Tubes.
		sq. ft.	sq. ft.	sq. ft.	sq. ft.	per cent.	per cent.
Sharp's Goods	Ramsbottom	9·5	1·0	1·94	830	33·3	66·6
Snake......	J. V. Gooch	12·4	1·7	2·80	824	56	44
Orleans No. 132	Polonceau	9·16	1·30	1·96	784	55	45

Of the first and second, the tubes of the latter required much the smaller percentage of vacuum, only two-thirds of that monopolized by the other. This is clearly owing to its having a much wider flue-way of tube than the other, *while the friction-surface is sensibly the same*. Hence the advantage of the shorter and more numerous tubes of the Snake, which becomes still more conspicuous on observing that it has a larger grate, which requires a smaller percentage of vacuum.

Of the second and third everything is varied in proportion,—grate, flue-way, and friction-surface; consequently the percentages of vacuum are the same.

Of the first and third, which differ as much as the first and second, though they have the same grate and the same flue-way in the body of the tubes, the smaller percentage of vacuum devoted to the tubes of the third, is due to the wider flue-way of its ferules, and to the smaller friction-surface, but principally to the former.

These deductions prove the advantage of short and numerous tubes, yielding an easy flue-way in the body; they show also the very material opposition to free circulation offered by the ferules at the fire-box ends; and the latter conclusion is confirmed by the experiments made by Mr. Ramsbottom, on the resistance of ferules. A ferule at the fire-box is doubtless a much more formidable obstruction to circulation than one of the same diameter at the smoke-box; as in the former case smoke passes through the ferule at a much higher temperature, and therefore also at a much higher speed than in the latter case, by as much as the volume of the gases is greater.

Apart from the considerations to be derived from the indicated vacuums of boilers, it is expedient to institute some more general inquiries into the circumstances which affect their action. The area of blast-orifice, as it is undoubtedly the most critical item in the composition of the locomotive, is also the most important. In the following discussions, therefore, the blast-area will be appealed to, as the final test of the merits of boilers variously proportioned.

Relation of the Blast-Area to the Dimensions and Proportions of the Boiler.—The question resolves itself practically into a comparison of the three elements,—grate-area, tube-surface, and blast-area. It has to do with the first, as this is the principal measure of the rate of combustion; and with the second, as the principal measure of the evaporating and resisting surface. To these we shall add the chimney-area, as, though a very simple element, it is a most influential one, and has perhaps as much to do with the blast-area as any other element. Our concern is to find the essential difference between boilers equally well proportioned, but of different sizes; and between boilers of different proportions.

As to the influence of difference of size, comparing the Great Britain, the Snake, and the England, and assuming the grate-area as unity, we have the following quantities by the table:—

	grate-area	tube-surface	chimney-area	blast-area
Great Britain	1 (21 feet)	77	·084	1/147
Snake	1 (12·4 feet)	66·4	·074	1/146
England	1 (5·03 feet)	76	·083	1/132

Here we find that with the same proportions of boiler, in which indeed the Great Britain has the advantage of a proportionally wider flue-way, extremely various dimensions make no difference on the ratio of the blast-area to the grate-area. That of the England is, indeed, rather wider than the others, but this is sufficiently accounted for by the superior arrangement of its blast-pipe.

The influence of the diameter of chimney on the blast-area, which has already been discussed in another way, is well developed in the following series, of which the proportions otherwise are very much the same:—

	grate	tubes	chimney	orifice
L. N. R. No. 10	1	65	·066	1/105
G. & S. W. R. No. 46	1	71·3	·09	1/118
C. R. No. 102	1	69·4	·09	1/121
C. R. No. 127	1	78·1	·11	1/128
Brindley	1	75·5	·13	1/147
C. R. No. 124	1	78·1	·15	1/145

The orifice in this series plainly becomes smaller in proportion to the grate as the chimney is enlarged from a relative value of ·066 to ·15, or, in common fractions, from 1/15th to 1/6·6th of the grate.

The influence of the length of the chimney on the blast-area is not perceptible in the examples before us. The chimney of the Great Britain is the shortest of all, its length being 5 feet, or 3·33 times its diameter, yet the orifice of this engine is as liberal as that of any of the others, similarly arranged. A greater length of chimney than is necessary for the best action of the blast is more likely to operate injuriously than otherwise, and it can be useful only in getting up the steam, when it has to depend on its natural draft, unaided by the blast.

A length of four times the diameter of chimney is probably the greatest length necessary for the complete action of the blast.

The influence of tube-surface on the blast-area appears to be of little importance, as may be inferred from the examples following, the flue-areas being much the same:—

	grate	tubes	chimney	orifice
C. R. No. 73	1	40·2	·11	1/171
G. & S. W. R. Orion	1	43·5	·10	1/158
E. & G. R. Orion	1	51	·09	1/171
C. R. No. 13	1	61·5	·11	1/171
C. R. No. 51	1	61·5	·12	1/168
England	1	76	·063	1/132
Sphynx,	1	82	·12	1/88
Do.	(4¼ ins. orifice, 9 ins. below crown)			1/171
Do.	(4 ins. orifice level with crown)			1/171

In these examples we find a remarkable indifference to proportion of tube-surface in the proportion of orifice required, as this appears nearly constant. In the case of the Sphynx, the 4 inch orifice level with the crown, and therefore situated similarly to the others, has the same fractional value as these, though it has by far the greatest tube-surface. It has, however, the advantage of a much greater relative ferule and flue-area, which we shall find, shortly, to be a considerable benefit. The unrivalled orifice of the same engine, 1/88th of the grate, when placed at 18 inches below the crown, proves indubitably the advantage of a thorough blast in the smoke-box.

The influence of the flue-area of tubes and ferules is very material. Take the following series:—

	grate	tubes	tube-area	ferule-area	chimney	orifice
Brindley	1	75·5	·26	·18	·13	1/147
Hebe	1	56·7	·19	·09	·075	1/147
Pallas	1	41·7	·15	·10	·08	1/147
America	1	53·6	·18	·12	·10	1/168
Sphynx	1	82	·28	·20	·12	1/88
Do.		(4 inch orifice, flush)				1/171
Atlas	1	95·5	·207	·207	·14	1/171 { 18 ins. below }
M. B. R. No. 30	1	87	·20	·10	·14	1/147 (flush)
L. N. R. No. 10	1	65	·22	·17	·066	1/105
Do., No. 7	1	47	·15	·11	·068	1/105
Stephenson's	1	45·6	·15	·11	·13	1/172

Comparing the Brindley and the Hebe, the Hebe has much the smaller chimney of the two, less tube-surface, and nearly twice the air-space of grate, yet it has nearly as small an orifice, which is clearly due to its inferior flue-areas. For the same reason, the Pallas, though it has also the benefit of a small chimney, and very limited tube-surface, has the same fractional orifice as the Brindley. The case of the America is apparently contradictory, as it has a wide orifice; but for this it is indebted, in company with the Brindley, to its smaller chimney and easier entrance; and in company with the Hebe and the Pallas to its wider ferule and tube-areas respectively. Reductions of the ferule-area in the Brindley, to one-half, in the Hebe, and of tube-area to two-thirds, are, as we have seen, fully balanced in their effect on the orifice, by a reduction of the chimney to three-fifths. The mean of the two ratios, ½ and ⅔, being also three-fifths, it follows that a reduction of the chimney-area in the proportion of the flue-areas of tubes and ferules preserves the blast-area constant. Thus, chimney-area is as influential on the blast-orifice as flue-area.

Again, the Sphynx with the flush orifice has twice the ferule-area of No. 30, M. B. R., and also greater tube-area, and agreeably to this it has one-third more blast-area. Lastly, the Atlas, with the same ferule-area, but only about two-thirds of the tube-area, has only three-fourths of the orifice of the Sphynx, the orifice being in both cases 18 inches below the crown. This evidence harmonizes with that of the observed relative vacuums previously discussed.

It may also be noted that the Jupiter, on the M. S. & L. Railway, a goods engine of the Atlas class, having 116 tubes, 2 inches outside, a ferule-area of 1·42 feet, and a tube-area of 3 feet, steams as well with a 4 inch orifice as the Atlas with one of 3¼ inches, and a uniform flue-area of 1·97 feet. The advantage here is in the tube-area of the Jupiter, which is one-half more than that of the Atlas, and gives greater facility of draft than even the absence of ferules in the latter boiler.

Of Nos. 10 and 7, L. N. R., and of the Brindley and Stephenson's, each couple having the same relative chimney, the furnace in each case has considerably greater flue-area, and in consequence a wider orifice. The very small orifice of Stephenson's is remarkable, and had the chimney been of but half the area, and the blast-pipe kept within the smoke-box, it might have been of double the area, and reduced to one-twelfth of the cylinder.

The Influence of the Capacity of the Smoke-Box was sensibly manifested in the course of the experiments with the Sphynx. With a 4¼ inch orifice, at 9 inches below the crown, a reduction of the capacity of the smoke-box by lining with brick, made steam in abundance, of which there was previously none to spare, and the damper was closed above half the time. With the orifice at 4¼ inches, same level, the engine steamed fully as well as with a 4¼ inch orifice, and full size smoke-box; thus, a ¼ inch of diameter, yielding 1·8 inches extra area, was the equivalent for the reduction of the smoke-box.

The superior efficiency of the smaller smoke-box, shows that this appendage operates in the manner of an "air-vessel," absorbing part of the exhausting action of each discharge before the tubes get the benefit of it. The tubes themselves are air-vessels with respect to the fire-box; and it is well known that in short boilers, the action of the blast on the fire is more impulsive than in long boilers; hence the advocates of long tubes are accustomed to object to short tubes that "the blast is too near the fire," that is, that the inequality of its action on the coke is excessive and injurious, and that the coke is liable to be dragged through the tubes. Mr. Peacock has found it beneficial to reduce by one-fourth the capacity of smoke-box of all such engines as the Sphynx, on his line. The smoke-box of this engine

has about 40 cubic feet of capacity above the cylinders; deducting one-fourth, we have 30 feet for the most favourable capacity; or, as a general result, numerically about three times the area of grate.

The Influence of air-space of grate upon the blast-area is not very sensible. We find it at least over-ruled by other circumstances; referring to the last selection of examples, the America has a half less air-space than the Hebe, and only one-third more ferule-area, and while it has also a slightly wider chimney, it has nevertheless a wider orifice, clearly due to its superior ferule-area.

The influence of clinkers on the grate, which reduce the air-spaces, is exhibited in the vacuum-lines of No. 14, from which it appears that 4 inches of vacuum require 6¼ inches of blast with the clean grate, and only 5½ inches with clinkers; that is, the clinkering so far obstructs the entrance of air, for it increases the vacuum artificially. The difference, though apparently inconsiderable, commanded the attention of the engine-driver, who found he had more than usual steam blowing off, with the clean grate.

The Influence of the Damper at the mouth of the Ash-pan is well-known. It is observable on the gauge by an increase of vacuum when the damper is closed. Thus, with No. 33, C. R., at 31 miles per hour, in full gear, and at a hard pull, the ordinary vacuum was 7 inches, and it was raised to 9 inches by closing the damper. It is observed that the damper is far from gradual in its action, as it affects the vacuum materially only within a range of 4 or 5 inches of opening; and accordingly a damper to be efficient must fit the opening tightly, and be kept in good order,—a matter very well understood by intelligent drivers.

The Influence of the Fire-door is abundantly manifested in the vacuum-lines of different boilers, in the diagram-plate; and in No. 33, C. R., on the occasion just noted, the vacuum fell from 7 to 4 inches on opening the door, showing plainly that air passes through the fire-door more easily than through the grate. In the same boiler, a vacuum of 1¾ inch fell to ¼ inch on opening the door. The door is thus a very efficient damper, and as such it is much more frequently used by the drivers than the ash-pan damper: it is quicker in action, and equally or more efficient.

Of the Effects of Strong Side and Head Wind on the Draft; and of the Form of the Chimney-top.—This is shown to a slight degree in the vacuum-lines of the Queen, G. & S. W. R.; the strong head wind there named having raised the vacuum in the smoke-box. It is found that in the teeth of heavy winds, engines do not steam with the same facility as in calm weather,—particularly such as are, like the Queen, unfurnished with an ash-pan and damper. This, though deemed mysterious by engine-drivers, is referrible simply to the counter-draft of wind externally across the lower side of the fire-grate, which as it passes exerts an exhaustive action on the fire. Thus it is only the difference of the two exhaustive actions,—that of the wind externally across the bottom of the fire-box, and that of the steam in the chimney, that is available for through draft. It must be added that a certain degree of aid to the draft in the smoke-box is supplied by the draft across the chimney-top, but this is inferior to the counter-draft at the fire-box. To pass from small things to great, we may refer to experi-

.ments on the draft of the great chimney of the Edinburgh Gas Works, made by Mr. George Buchanan, the consulting engineer of the gas-works. He found that, in calm weather, the draft was measured by 2¼ inches of water; in windy weather it rose to 3½ inches, and with high winds it amounted to 6 or 7 inches.[*] The increase here observed is clearly due to the stimulating action of the cross draft at the top of the chimney, and proves the influence of wind whether at the chimney-top or at the grate of the locomotive-boiler. It also shows how little is to be feared from down-draughts, or obstruction to the exit of smoke and steam, from the usually abrupt and square termination of the chimney. In the England, the chimney-top is bevelled off behind, as shown in fig. 176, to facilitate the escape and increase the draft by the action of the atmosphere in the direction of the arrow, due to the motion of the train. There may be some good in this, but it is subject to the objection that when the engine runs foot-plate foremost, an injurious down-draught is created, and there is difficulty in keeping up the steam. The rolling collars with which chimney-tops are commonly finished, ought always to be placed some inches below the top, as in the England here shown, though perhaps hardly so picturesque as the flush collars of Sharp's engine and others; for the action of a "bluff" chimney-top is to throw off the wind, clear the chimney-top, and increase the draft, while the collar acts as a "cutwater," and allows the current to skim the chimney. On this ground, Fairbairn's chimney-top, though perhaps the most elegant, is the most unsuitable, and Sinclair's, though the plainest we have seen, is, we think, the best. Their effects on the draft are shown in figs. 177 and 178, in which the upward diversion of the wind by the bluff chimney is shown to aid the draft. That the wind is thrown aside is consistent with all experience of similar cases,—and, as a gigantic example in point, the experience of thousands on the top of the Britannia Bridge has proved that in the strongest gales blowing at right-angles to the bridge, a man could with security walk along the top, as the wind falling on the flat side of the bridge was thrown off above and below, and cleared the great tube by several feet. More accessible evidence may be had standing behind the parapet of a bridge during a stiff gale.

Influence of the Proportions of the Boiler on the relation of the blast-area to the area of cylinder.—The intimate dependence of the blast-area on the proportions of the boiler, lead us to infer that the ratio of the orifice to the cylinder-area is altogether arbitrary. If large cylinders be associated with small boilers, we must be content to have small orifices relatively to the cylinder, and with larger boilers, we shall have absolutely larger orifices, whether we increase the cylinder or not; and the question appears to resolve itself into the general proposition, that all the steam generated in the boiler, must find its way through the blast-orifice; and this must be of such an area as will, by the force of the issuing steam, create the draft required for the rate of combustion necessary to generate steam as fast as it flows off. It passes through the cylinders, to be sure, and is measured off in successive discharges; but this is merely incidental, as regards the boiler, and the capacity of cylinder is a matter of detail, which does not materially affect the question. Accordingly, though different diameters of cylinder have been adopted for the same boiler, it has not at the same time followed that different orifices were required. There are in the table numerous illustrations of the independence of the orifice upon the cylinder; and it may only be remarked further that the Atlas engine had originally an 18 inch cylinder, which was reduced to 16 inches diameter, and that the alteration made no sensible difference on the desirable area of blast-orifice.

Conclusions.—It appears from all that has been said, that in the proportions of boilers the elements which practically regulate the area of blast-orifice, are the grate-area, the flue-areas of the tubes and the ferules, and the sectional area of the chimney; and, in general, the wider the flue-areas in proportion to the grate, and the smaller the chimney, within the limits that have come under our inquiry, the wider is the relative blast-area competent to the generation of steam.

Of the air-space of grate, and the flue-ways, the ferule-area at fire-box ranks first in importance, the tube-area next, and the air-space last. Within practical limits, tube-surface is of no moment, nor is ferule-area at smoke-box, so far as they are found to affect the blast-area. These conclusions by direct experiment, are in harmony with our general ideas on the motion of gases. The air, on entering the grate, is fresh from the atmosphere and of the same temperature. Its volume is therefore of the smallest, and it enters with ease; above the bars, it at once expands by contact and combustion with the fuel, and while its volume is thus greatly enlarged, it at the same time meets with extensive superficial resistance from the coke. The enlargement of volume implies a corresponding increase of velocity through the fuel, and as the resistance to the motion of gases along friction-surfaces is as the square of the velocity, it is altogether probable, apart from the evidence of direct experience, that the greater part of the grate or fire-box resistance takes place above the bars, and is mainly independent of their number and thickness. The atmosphere of the fire-box, on its departure through the ferules, carries with it at least two-thirds of the heat of combustion, even on the rudest estimate, and its volume must be several times as great as that of the air which passes through the grate. Taking it at only 4 times, then it must pass through the ferules, had they even an area equal to the air-space, at 4 times the speed; but the ferule-area is from ⅓d to ¼th of the air-space, take a mean of ¼th; then, as the speed must be increased as the flue-area is reduced, the gases of the

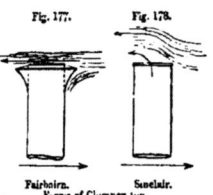

Fig. 176.

E. and G. R. England.
Form of Chimney-top.

Fig. 177.　　　Fig. 178.

Fairbairn.　　　Sinclair.
Forms of Chimney-top.

* The Edinburgh Gas-work's Chimney was designed by Mr. Taylor, engineer to the gas company. It has 341½ feet of total height, 20 feet inside diameter at the bottom, and 11 feet 4 inches at the top; it receives the smoke and vapours of 68 furnaces, heating 178 retorts; and, by making one or more openings at the bottom, it creates powerful currents of air in all directions, and thoroughly ventilates the works.

fire-box must move 4 times 4, or 16 times as fast through the ferules as through the grate. This abundantly explains the very marked influence of the ferule-area on the facility of the draft. As the smoke passes along the tubes, it cools to a temperature of 300° to 600° or thereabouts, and contracts, and therefore passes with a constantly reduced speed till it is discharged into the smoke-box; and the very inferior velocity of its exit there freely explains the inferior value of the absence of smoke-box ferules in relieving the draft. The virtue of liberal flue-way is inapplicable to the chimney, as the smoke is here *forced* as well as *drawn;* and whereas all the other air-passages may with advantage be made of easy section, the chimney-area must, fully to develope the exhausting action of the blast, be specially reduced to a small fraction of the flue-room.

These conclusions weaken the force of the ordinary objection to long tubes, that their great friction-surface is the cause of the small blast-orifice with which long boilers have been worked. It is rather the restricted grate-area and flue-ways, than the mere tube-surface; for it has so happened, unfortunately, that where long tubes were adopted, the fire-box was overhung, for the sake of confining the wheel-base; and the conditions of stability demanded the smallest possible back-weight, and therefore the minimum area of grate.

The question of the desirable proportions of boilers has been rather complicated by variety of circumstances,—of the form of the chimney-entrance, the form and level of the blast-orifice, and so forth. But, in similar circumstances, the widest orifice in relation to the grate, has been obtained with the narrowest chimney on record,—that of No. 10, L. N. R., of which the area is a little less than one-fifteenth of the grate-area. There is probably no limit to the advantage of width of flue-area; it has at least been found of sensible benefit in easing the blast-orifice, up to the widest observed limits. The level of the blast-orifice, in conjunction with a suitable diameter of chimney, are together more influential than any other single circumstance in easing the orifice, and fortunately these are just the most accommodating elements; for whatever proportions may be imposed upon the boiler in compliance with certain conditions of stability, weight, or arrangement, there can be nothing to interfere with the adoption of the most efficient chimney and blast-pipe. To illustrate what can be effected in this way, the Sphynx furnishes a good illustration in point: with a tube-area of ·28, a ferule-area of ·20, and a chimney-area of ·12, the orifice at the most efficient level, is $\frac{1}{14}$th of the grate. Were the chimney of this engine reduced to the most efficient proportion, or ·066, almost one half the actual area, the orifice, judging by analogous cases already noted, might be further enlarged to $\frac{1}{7}$th of the grate. Again, the Hebe, with an ordinary tube-area, and the smallest of ferule-areas, ·09, or $\frac{1}{11}$th of the grate, and a chimney of ·075, has an orifice of $\frac{1}{13}$d; were the orifice to be sufficiently lowered, it ought to be capable of enlargement to as great an extent as that of the Sphynx, or nearly one-half wider, making an orifice of $\frac{1}{7}$th of the grate; and a reduction of the chimney would widen the orifice to at least $\frac{1}{6}$th. As these boilers are of extreme proportions, rivalling even the celebrated "long-boiler," in length of tube and limited ferule-area, we feel justified in concluding that even with the most unfavourable propor-

tion of boiler of the most various dimensions, the blast-area need never be less than $\frac{1}{10}$th of the area of the grate; and in boilers of ordinary ferule-areas equal to ·20, or $\frac{1}{5}$th of the grate, the orifice may be as wide as $\frac{1}{6}$th of the grate. These are conclusions of some importance, for they put an end to those loose speculations on the consumption of steam-power in back pressure to provide the necessary force of blast for long-tube boilers, in which even men of experience have indulged; as it plainly appears that injuriously small orifices are, in almost every case, chargeable to mal-arrangement of smoke-box details. In discussing the subject of back pressure, it was found that, in well arranged and well proportioned cylinders, like those of the Great Britain, with a blast-orifice $\frac{1}{10\cdot7}$th of the area of cylinder, the back pressure of exhaust was practically nothing. The question thus resolves itself into the practicability of using a blast-area not less than $\frac{1}{10\cdot7}$th of the cylinder, for one great object of an easy boiler and a wide blast-pipe is to secure a practically perfect exhaust. This question properly belongs to another chapter, in which the relative proportions of the boiler and the engine are to be discussed. Meantime, if we take even the engine No. 30, M. B. R., the grate of which is confessedly too small, or conversely the cylinder is too large, being $\frac{1}{4}$th of the grate, the orifice, which was at the time of observation, $\frac{1}{30\cdot6}$th of the cylinder, may be enlarged to $\frac{5\cdot4}{50}$ or $\frac{1}{11}$th. This case, we must confess, is beyond our remedy, on account of the extremely small ferule-area at the fire-box in conjunction with the limited grate; and it must be noted that the tubes of this engine are reduced from $1\frac{3}{4}$ to $1\frac{1}{2}$ inch outside diameter in the fire-box tube-plate. If, however, we take the Sphynx, with a more liberal flue, and of which the cylinder is $\frac{1}{6}$th of the grate, much above the average practice, the orifice may be widened to $\frac{1}{9}$ or $\frac{1}{11}$th of the cylinder, which would be practically perfect. With No. 124, C. R., having an orifice at present equal to $\frac{1}{22\cdot7}$th of the cylinder, a reduction of chimney and a re-adjustment of the blast-pipe, would permit of an orifice $\frac{1}{9}$ or $\frac{1}{8}$th of the cylinder. With No. 51, C. R., the orifice, now $\frac{1}{14\cdot5}$, might be $\frac{5\cdot8}{50}$ or $\frac{1}{10\cdot6}$th of the cylinder; and with the Great Britain, the orifice might be $\frac{1}{9}$ or $\frac{1}{8}$th, though for this there would not be any necessity.

In short, though it would be premature in this place to consider the fitting proportions of cylinder and boiler conjointly, it may safely be concluded that, in all cases, even with the most contracted flue-ways, the blast-orifice may, by a proper adjustment of chimney and blast-pipe, be made wide enough, to permit of a practically perfect exhaust, where there is a properly protected cylinder, properly proportioned to the boiler.

RECAPITULATION.—1. In the same boiler, the vacuum in the smoke-box varies directly with the blast-pressure. For different boilers, the vacuum due to a given blast-pressure varies considerably, but as a general result, the vacuum in inches of water is about equal to the blast-pressure in inches of mercury.

2. The relation of the vacuum to the blast is not materially affected by the point at which the steam is cut off.

3. The blast retains its property of exhaustion within all observed limits of speed and steam-pressure,—such that even at the highest speeds, the vacuum rises steadily with the blast.

4. The exhausting power of the blast, or its efficiency in creating a draft, is largely dependent on the form and size of the chimney, and the form of the blast-pipe; and that is reckoned to be the most efficient chimney which admits of the widest blast-orifice.

5. For a given boiler, there is but one diameter of chimney of greatest efficiency. For greater or less diameters, the orifice must be reduced

6. The best form of blast-pipe is that which projects the steam straight up the chimney. The orifice must also be truly concentric with the chimney, and it should be bevelled up to the edge on the outside. The body of the blast-pipe should be very wide, and should be gathered in chiefly at the nozzle.

7. The smoke must have free access to the chimney, either by widening the entrance, with a bell-form base, and cutting out the crown of the smoke-box; or, what is as good, by keeping down the blast-orifice to a level below the crown of the smoke-box, equal to the diameter of the chimney or thereby, and giving the chimney a square entrance; or by a combination of both expedients. In short, the blast should be projected *through* the smoke, and not above it. Thus a straight, vertical blast-pipe is to be preferred to the double, bridge-pipe in common use, both on account of the superior discharge of the steam, and because it affords much less obstruction to the passage of smoke.

8. Of the relative vacuums in the smoke-box and the fire-box, the latter varies from one-third to above one-half of the former; in other words, the resistance of the grate and the fuel to the passage of air and smoke, varies from one-half to more than equal the resistance offered by the tubes. In the boilers having the widest flue-way through the tubes and the ferules, the resistance of the tubes is proportionally the lowest.

9. The question of the internal proportions of boilers, without reference to the demands of the cylinders, resolves itself practically into a comparison of grate-area, tube-surface, and blast-area.

10. With the same proportions of boiler, the actual dimensions, within the widest observed limits, make no difference on the ratio of the blast-area to the grate-area. It follows that the smallest of locomotives may be as favourably proportioned as the largest.

11. The elements which regulate the area of blast-orifice, are the grate-area, the flue-areas of the tubes and the ferules, the sectional area of the chimney, and the capacity of the smoke-box. The larger the grate-area, the wider the flue-areas, the smaller the chimney, and the less the capacity of the smoke-box, within observed limits, the wider also may be the blast-area.

12. The grate-area being assumed as a standard for comparison, the elements of the boiler proper, which affect the blast-area, are, in order of importance, as follow:—1st, The ferule-area at fire-box; 2d, the tube-area; 3d, the air-space of grate; 4th, the ferule-area at smoke-box; 5th, the tube-surface. The influence of the last two, within practical limits, is very slight.

13. Of the appendages to the boiler,—the smoke-box and the chimney,—the latter has as much or more influence on the area of blast-orifice, than any other single circumstance.

For, it was found that a proportionally smaller chimney operated as efficiently for easing the orifice, as a smaller ferule-area did in narrowing it.

14. The area of the smallest observed chimney is about one-fifteenth of the grate-area; and this proportional area yields a wider orifice, under the same circumstances, than any greater chimney-area. The ratio of *one-fifteenth* is therefore the best, so far as observation leads us. A length of chimney of about four times the diameter is probably the greatest length necessary for developing the best action of the blast.

15. The capacity of the smoke-box also affects the action of the blast. The most suitable capacity has been found to be three times, in cubic measure, the area of grate in square measure; or three cubic feet per foot of grate.

16. In boilers of ordinary proportions, of which the ferule-area at fire-box is one-fifth of the grate-area, or thereabouts, and the tube-area about one-fourth, the orifice may, by the best adjustment of the smoke-box, blast-pipe, and chimney, be made as wide as *one-sixty-sixth* of the grate-area. And in even the most unfavourably proportioned boilers, where the ferule-area may not be above one-tenth of the grate, the orifice may be as wide as *one-ninetieth* of the grate.

17. The amount of blast-area being regulated mainly, if not entirely, by the boiler, it is practically independent of the dimensions of the cylinder.

18. Advantage being taken of the known means of perfecting the action of the blast, the orifice may in all cases be made wide enough to permit of a practically perfect exhaust, when the cylinder is proportioned to the boiler. And, even with extravagantly large cylinders, all the useful area of orifice may be obtained, except in boilers having very small ferule-areas, one-tenth of the grate or thereby.

19. It follows, generally, that, as the orifice depends so directly on the grate and the tubes, the essential advantages of a large grate and a wide tube-area, consists mainly in the facilities they afford for supplying a sufficiency of steam, with an easy blast, a liberal orifice, heavy loads, and high velocities.

CHAPTER IV.

OF THE RELATION OF THE VACUUM IN THE SMOKE-BOX TO THE RATE OF EVAPORATION.

As the vacuum in the smoke-box measures the unbalanced pressure of the atmosphere, or that in virtue of which it forces its way through the grate and the tubes, a certain relation subsists between this unbalanced pressure and the quantity of air which so circulates through the boiler in a given time. To measure this force with complete accuracy, the open end of the vacuum-gauge should be in communication with the atmosphere of the ash-pan; as the pressure in the ash-pan is no doubt, at high speeds, greater than that of the external air, when the pan is directly open to the current due to the speed of the engine; and, on the other hand, it is less, when the door is nearly or entirely closed. The variable element thus introduced may sensibly affect the deductions from the observed vacuums in the smoke-box. The indications will, however, be sufficiently decided to yield an approximation to the law in question.

Relation of Evaporation to the Vacuum, in the same boiler.—The quantity of air which passes through the grate in a given time is a direct measure of the rate of combustion, assuming, as we may, that the air is equally well burned, whether it is forced by a strong draft through a small grate and a deep bed of coke, or by a weak draft through a large grate and a thin bed. The rate of combustion, also, is, within wide limits, nearly a direct measure of the rate of evaporation. Therefore, also, the velocity or the rate at which the air passes through the grate measures approximately the rate of evaporation. Now, the velocity of an elastic fluid is as the square root of the impelling pressure, and the pressure is, in the present case, measured by the vacuum; consequently, the velocity of the air through the grate, or finally, the rate of evaporation, is as the square root of the vacuum.

From this conclusion it would follow that to procure twice the rate of evaporation, we should require not merely twice, but at least four times the vacuum in the smoke-box; probably more, as there is likely to be a greater leakage of air through the grate at higher rates of evaporation, and a higher temperature and loss of heat in the smoke-box. To verify this doctrine, we may compare the results from the same boiler under the same circumstances, as to depth of coke over the grate, &c., with different loads and speeds, and therefore different rates of evaporation. No. 14, C. R., for example, running between Glasgow and Greenock, evaporated the following quantities of water during three different trips:—

(1.) 15th April, 1850. Goods train, Green. to Glas. 127 cubic feet.
(2.) 17th do. do. Green. to Glas. 93 do.
(3.) 18th do. Pass. train, Glas. to Green. 65 do.

The total time of each trip, and the times during which the steam was on, or the blast was on the fire, were noted; the vacuum in the smoke-box was also noted at intervals of one minute, and occasionally at shorter intervals. The following are the total times for each trip, and the sums separately of the times the steam was on and off:—

	No. of stops.	Time of steam on.	Time of steam off.	Total time of trip.
(1)	5	56 min.	34 min.	90 min.
(2.)	6	50 ,,	36½ ,,	86½ ,,
(3.)	3	46 ,,	13 ,,	59 ,,

For each of these trips, the successive values of the vacuum, and the intervals during which the steam was shut off, are shown graphically in the upper right hand figures, diagram-plate V., in each of which the base-line represents the time of the trip, divided into minutes by vertical lines, set off from left to right, as marked. Parallel to the base-line, a number of lines are drawn from the divisions of the vertical scale, representing successive half-inches of vacuum. From the point of time in the base-line at which each observation was made, a vertical height is set off, and defined by a star, equal, by the vertical scale, to the vacuum in inches; and through the successive series of stars so found, curve lines are traced, and form continuous vacuum-lines. During the intervals of rest, at the stations, as the fire was in a lively condition, an allowance of ½ inch of vacuum is made, as shown in the diagrams, and this is indeed a sufficient allowance, according to the gauge. It is however, not recog-

nized in the following statement of the mean vacuums for every minute, observed during the first trip on the 15th April. In this table, No. 71, the intervals during which the steam was on and off, are tabulated, and the vacuums (2d column), taken from the diagram for the first trip, are expressed in eighths of an inch, to avoid fractions. The 3d column contains the square roots of the numerical values of the vacuums; and agreeably to our presumed law that the rate of evaporation is as the square root of the vacuum, the contents of the 3d column should express the comparative efficiency for evaporation of the vacuums named in the 2d column. The total mean of those roots is 5·55, and this is the square root of 31 eighths, or 3⅞ inches, which is the vacuum of average efficiency, or that which would have evaporated the same quantity of water in 56 minutes.

TABLE, No. LXXI.—OF OBSERVED VACUUMS IN No. 14, C. R., DURING ONE TRIP. 15TH APRIL, 1850.

Progressive intervals by the minute.	Mean observed vacuums for each minute, in eighths of an inch.	Square roots of the values in the preceding column.	Progressive intervals by the minute.	Mean observed vacuums for each minute, in eighths of an inch.	Square roots of the values in the preceding column.
minutes.	eighths inch.		minutes.	eighths inch.	
Green. start.			50	38	6·16
1, steam on.	6	2·45	51	41	6·40
2	12	3·46	52	48	6·93
3	20	4·47	53	49	7·00
4	23	4·79	54	50	7 07
5	26	5 10	55	52	7 21
6	30	5·48	56	52	7·21
7	12	3 46	57	44	6·63
8–11, steam off. Ladybank.			58	28	5·29
12	12	3·46	59	12	3·46
13–19, steam off. Port-Glasgow.			60	9	3 0
20, steam on.	9	3 0	61–74, steam off. Paisley.		
21	24	4·9	75, steam on.	4	2·0
22	32	5 66	76	7	2·65
23	35	5 92	77	16	4·0
24	40	6·32	78	25	5·0
25	42	6 48	79	32	5·66
26	48	6 93	80	40	6 32
27	50	7 07	81	44	6·63
28	48	6 93	82	52	7 21
29	48	6 93	83	60	7·75
30	38	6 16	84	60	7·75
31	46	6 63	85	57	7·55
32	44	6 63	86	57	7·55
33	36	6 0	87	54	7·35
34	36	6 0	88	54	7·35
35	32	5·66	89–97, steam off. Junction.		
36	25	5·0	98, steam on.	12	3·46
37	16	4 0	99	25	5·0
38	5	2 24	100–102, steam off. Glasgow.		
39–47, steam off. Bishopton.					
48, steam on.	6	2·45	Mean of all the values in the last column }		5 55
49	24	4·00			

The observed vacuums for the two remaining trips being tabulated in the same way, we find for the 2d trip, the mean square root, 4·77, which is the root of 23 eighths, or 2⅞ inches of vacuum; and for the 3d trip, the mean root, 3, for 9 eighths, or 1⅛ inch of vacuum. The results for the three trips stand as in the following table, first five columns.

The last three columns contain the actual and estimated evaporations per hour, from which it appears that the evaporation estimated by the mean square root of the observed vacuums, and taking the lowest, No. 3, as the datum, considerably exceeds the actual performance,—by 21 per cent.

TABLE, No. LXXII.—TO SHOW RELATION OF EVAPORATION TO THE VACUUM IN THE SMOKE-BOX, IN No. 14, C. R.

No. of Trip.	Mean square root of vacuums.	Vacuums of average efficiency.	Total time of steam on.	Total water actually evaporated.	Rate of actual evaporation per hour.	Evaporation per hour, estimated in the ratio of the mean square roots of vacuums, from No. 3 trip.	Difference of the last two columns.
		inches.	minutes.	cubic feet.	cubic feet.	cubic feet.	cubic feet.
1	5·55	3½	56	127	136	157	+ 21
2	4·77	2¾	50	93	111·5	135	+ 23·5
3	3	1½	46	65	85	85	0

in the 2d trip, and about 16 per cent. in the 1st. The inference is that the evaporating efficiency of the vacuum does not vary even so rapidly as the square root of the vacuum,—that is, for example, to obtain twice the rate of evaporation, we must have something *more* than four times the vacuum. This is a remarkable conclusion, and it clenches the argument with which we set out, that though the influx of air may and ought to be as the square root of the vacuum, the rate of evaporation may not be even so rapid, owing to leakage of air and to loss of heat.

Another example in point may be obtained from the working of two goods engines, C. R. Nos. 124 and 125, in making the ascent of the Beattock Incline, 10 miles long. The boilers are of the same dimensions. No. 124, with its wide chimney, ascended with difficulty, in one hour, with a low vacuum, which did not greatly vary, averaging 2·7 inches. No. 125, ran at double the speed, and with an average vacuum of 5·4 inches, or double the other. The engines in performing the ascent, evaporated 125 and 81·5 feet of water, in one hour and half an hour respectively; the evaporations per hour were, then, 125 and 163 feet, with 2·7 and 5·4 inches of vacuum. The square roots of the vacuums are 1·64 and 2·32, or as 1 to 1·4; and estimating the evaporation in this ratio, we should have 125 × ¹·⁴⁄₁ = 175 feet per hour for No. 125, which is 12 feet per hour, or 7·4 per cent. more than was actually evaporated. It follows, as in the case of No. 14, that in the same class of boiler, the evaporation is not as the square root of the vacuum, but proceeds in a sensibly less ratio.

Relation of Evaporation to the Vacuum, in boilers of different proportions.—This relation is obviously affected by the proportions of the boilers, as we have found how very various the vacuum may be in different boilers doing the same work. It is a question of some importance, as the greater wear of the tubes near the fire-box is due mostly to the attacks of small coke carried with the draft; and therefore, the milder the draft the less is the damage so done.

With ordinary passenger-trains, the usual vacuums in the engines named in the following table, are stated in connection with the mean evaporations per mile. In evaporating the same water, the Hebe uses three times the vacuum

TABLE, No. LXXIII.—OF EVAPORATIONS AND VACUUMS.

Name of Engine.	Water evaporated per mile.	Ordinary vacuum in the smoke-box.	Date of Experiment.	Observer.
	cubic feet.	inches.		
Pallas........	4	1¼	16th Aug. 1850	Clark.
Orion........	2·91	1½	6th Sep. 1850	Do.
Hebe........	2·91	4½	19th Oct. 1850	Do.
Snake........	3·6	6	9th Sep. 1848	J. V. Gooch.

of the Orion; and the Pallas uses the least vacuum of all, for the greatest rate of evaporation. The Snake has the highest vacuum; this is due partially to the unusually high rate of speed, with express trains.

It is unnecessary to follow out the discussion of variations of this class. In extreme cases, it is known, 12 and 13 inches of vacuum have been found necessary to work some boilers. As intense currents must accompany such high vacuums, it is plainly worth while, if not for the sake of insuring a free exhaust, at least for the sake of mild draft, to ease out the proportions of boilers, consistently with other circumstances.

RECAPITULATION.—1. The rate of evaporation in the same boiler or class of boilers, varies nearly with the square root of the vacuum in the smoke-box;—we say *nearly*, as it varies in a sensibly less ratio than this, yielding as much as from 7 to 21 per cent. *less* evaporation than is due to the square root of the vacuum.

2. The deficiency here noted is caused by the passage of a greater proportion of free air through the grate, under greater vacuums, but mostly by the greater loss of heat in the escape of smoke at a higher temperature.

3. In boilers of small size or unfavourable proportions, greater vacuums are required for given rates of evaporation, than in easier boilers. As a mild draft is conducive to economy and durability, boilers should be of liberal dimensions and proportions.

CHAPTER V.

OF THE LOSS OF WATER AND STEAM BY PRIMING AND CONDENSATION.

PRIMING is the issue of water from the boiler, in mechanical combination with the steam which passes over to the cylinders, either as mere spray or water-drops, or in a more finely divided state, suspended in the steam like clouds in the atmosphere. Of these, the first is but an aggravated form of the second, and their effect is the same,—the abstraction of liquid water from the boiler, in a passive state, inelastic, and therefore doing no useful work on the piston; thus passive, the water becomes a drag on the steam, in the passages, and while at work in the cylinder, as we have had abundant evidence to show.

The condensation of steam in the cylinder is of still greater moment, for, besides operating like priming as a drag on the steam, it creates a much greater loss of heat, as the constituent heat of steam, lost by condensation, is four to five times that of water of the same temperature.

Mode of Experiment.—To find the amount of priming and condensation, the writer, in his experiments on the subject, obtained indicator-diagrams from one of the cylinders of the engine under experiment, at regular intervals generally of one mile on the trip. The number of the notch under which the valve-gear was placed was noted, and thus the suppression and other points were accurately known for each diagram, having been previously found for every notch by slow diagrams. The volume of steam admitted to the cylinder for each stroke was deduced from the diagrams, and the equivalent volume of water consumed as steam was inferred from the pressure at the point of suppression in the manner already shown at page 79. From the averages of the observations so made, an estimate was formed of the quantity of water consumed as steam, on the trip.

The total consumption of water during the trip, was found by gauging the tender at the beginning and end of the trip, and also at intermediate stations where it was refilled. The differences of level so obtained, multiplied into the horizontal area of the tank, yielded the volume of water withdrawn from the tender into the boiler. The water-levels in the boilers were also noted at the beginning and end of the trip, and the volume due to the difference of these levels, was added to that withdrawn from the tender, when the final level was lower than the first, and subtracted when higher. The result so found was taken as the actual consumption of water *from the boiler*. When the levels were measured while standing on inclines, proper allowance was made for the deviations of level so caused.

The temperature of the water in the tender was also in general observed. The relative volume of steam is referred to water at 62°; but even though the mean temperature in the tender were 100°, which it rarely reaches in long journeys, the expansion of water for 100° would not exceed $\frac{1}{2}$ per cent. of the volume at 62°, and we have not, in general, made any allowance for so small a deviation.

Causes of Priming.—Priming is caused generally by impurities in the water evaporated, and by deficiency or improper arrangement of steam-room in the boilers. The design of the locomotive-boiler, formed to evaporate the greatest quantity of water in a given time within the smallest practicable space, is rather unfavourable to efficient evaporation. The steam, emerging in numerous streams from a multitude of thick-set tubes and from the limited water-spaces round the fire-box, lifts the water at the surface, and throws it about as spray, which in the limited space assigned to the steam, is sometimes carried with the current towards the orifice of the steam-pipe, and much of it passes over as priming. With steam-room so limited at ordinary water-levels, the effect of a rise of level, or an overfull boiler, is greatly to increase the priming, by reducing the steam-room, or the available space for separating the steam and water.

With very limited steam-room, the position of the entrance to the steam-pipe sensibly affects the amount of priming, for towards this point all the steam that is generated over the whole length of the boiler must find its way. Independently of partial causes, there is a general rise of level due to ebullition when the boiler is at work; for the steam which rises from and is mixed with it, of course swells the volume which it occupies in a state of rest. When the entrance is placed in a dome over the fire-box, there is the greatest liability to prime, for not only is the ebullition at this place the most violent and concentrated, but the steam from the tubes flows towards the same locality, and drives the loose impurities of the boiler into the water-spaces round the fire-box. It is known, too, that in boilers, the water in the neighbourhood of the steam-orifice is raised above the general level, which further increases the liability to prime; and the false level thus maintained while the steam is flowing off, is prejudicial to the safety of the boiler, because it suddenly falls to the level of " solid" water when the regulator is shut and the evaporation checked, and may lay bare the crown of the fire-box. The extra depth of water so caused, and indicated in the glass gauge, is known to enginemen as " false-water," and it varies from $\frac{1}{4}$ inch to 4 and 5 inches, as measured by the glass gauge, at the fire-box, according to the design of the boiler. In the smaller boilers of former days, with the steam-dome placed over the fire-box, the false-water amounted usually to 5 and 6 inches in the glass,—particularly in Bury's older engines, which not only have the steam-dome placed over the fire-box, but also have the available steam-room reduced by the spherical form of the outer shell. These engines were, in consequence, ticklish to feed, as the variation of the water-level was confined to very narrow limits, with the risk of an overfull boiler, excessive priming, and a break-down, on the one hand; or a low water-level, a bare crown, and a burnt fire-box on the other.

When the dome is placed on the body of the boiler, at the middle or towards the front, the steam is drafted from a point where the ebullition is little or nothing; and as the water is quiet the steam is less liable to be burdened with spray, than when taken from the fire-box. Also, the impurities in the boiler are deposited rather towards the front, where they are comparatively harmless; and the water-level over the fire-box remains more nearly constant, as the accumulation of water under the dome reduces the false water, by partially withdrawing it from the fire-box. In some boilers, however, the space devoted to tubes is so great as to leave but a shallow steam-space above them; this is another cause of priming, as the current which sets into the fire-box towards the dome, drags the water with it. In this case, it is better to divide the steam into two currents by the adoption of two domes and orifices, one over the fire-box and the other forward on the boiler.

Impurities are at least as injurious as deficiency of steam-room. Those which commonly exist in locomotive-boilers, and occasion priming, are soap, oil, grease of all kinds, and earthy and vegetable matters suspended in the water received into the tender; and it is well established that the economy of combustibles is greatly promoted by the maintenance of pure water in the boiler.

Experiments of M. Pambour, 1834.—Pambour concluded that an average of at least 24 per cent., or one-fourth of the water consumed from the boiler, passed off in the liquid state, with the steam through the cylinder. As Pambour assumed a pressure in the cylinder equal to that in the boiler,—an assumption which was far from the truth, the quantity of priming in the boilers with which he experimented was doubtless above 30 per cent. of the total consumption.

Experiments of M. Le Chatelier, 1843-44.*—The engine Mulhouse, made by M. Meyer, was tried on the Versailles railway, at 30 to 40 miles per hour; it was found that from 38 to 50 per cent. of the water consumed passed through the cylinders as water, due jointly to priming and condensation; and that the shorter the admission the greater was

---

* *Guide du Méchanicien Constructeur et Conducteur de Machines Locomotives,* Paris, 1851.

the percentage of water passed. We have already found, by an examination of the expansion-curves of indicator-diagrams, that greater condensation attends longer expansions, and we have no doubt that on this principle the varying percentages above noted are to be accounted for. In this opinion we are confirmed by M. Le Chatelier.

Experiments of MM. Gouin and Le Chatelier, 1844.—In the experiments with the Gironde, on the Versailles railway, the loss of water was found to be 18 per cent. of the whole consumption. With very little expansion, and cylinders well protected, and with a very small steam-chamber in the boiler, it is probable that this percentage is due entirely to priming.

Experiments of M. Bertora, 1850.[*]—With the engines, Nos. 62 and 154, Orleans railway, he found as follows:—

	Usual period of admission.	Water evaporated per pound of coke.	Priming and condensation.
No. 62.	35 per cent.	9·17 lbs.	42 per cent. of total.
No. 154.	25 do.	10·05 lbs.	52 do.

Here we find a very large surplus, and that the engine worked with shorter admissions yields the greater surplus of water in the cylinder. There is also in the second engine, a greater apparent evaporation per pound of coke; this the authors of the work from which we quote explain by the greater heating surface and lower speed of the second engine, and by the numerous perforations of the steam-receiving pipe within the boiler, just over the fire-box, there being no separate steam-chamber: the greater apparent efficiency being therefore due both to evaporation and priming.

Experiments on the Caledonian, Greenock, and Edinburgh and Glasgow railways, 1850.—The engines on which observations were made by the author, for the determination of the water-surplus as priming and condensation, are named in the table No. 74, with dimensions relative to the inquiry. Sections of the boilers are appended to the table, with their general dimensions.

TABLE, No. LXXIV.—DIMENSIONS OF LOCOMOTIVES, RELATIVE TO PRIMING AND CONDENSATION.

Name.	Engine.			Boiler, (Form and Size, as in the annexed Figures).							
	Cylinder.		Wheel, Diameter.	Capacity.					Height of steam-room in barrel of boiler.	Orifice of Steam-pipe.	
	Diameter.	Stroke.		Total.	Ordinary Water-room.	Steam-room.				Position.	Height above water-level.
						Ordinary.	Above top of Gauge-glass.				
	inches.	inches.	feet.	cubic feet.	cubic feet.	cubic feet.	cubic feet.	inches.		inches.
C. R.										
No. 73...............	13	18	5	74	48	26	...	8	barrel	36
Nos. 42, 48..........	15	20	6	113	74	39	20	11	fire-box	42
No. 127..............	17	24	4′ 7″	117	82	35	18½	8½	fire-box	42
E. & G. R.										
Orion...............	15	20	6	137	88	49	...	11	barrel	40
Nile {	16	18	6	138	92	46	...	12	barrel	43
America {										
Brindley............	14	18	5½	116	91	25	...	6	fire-box	30

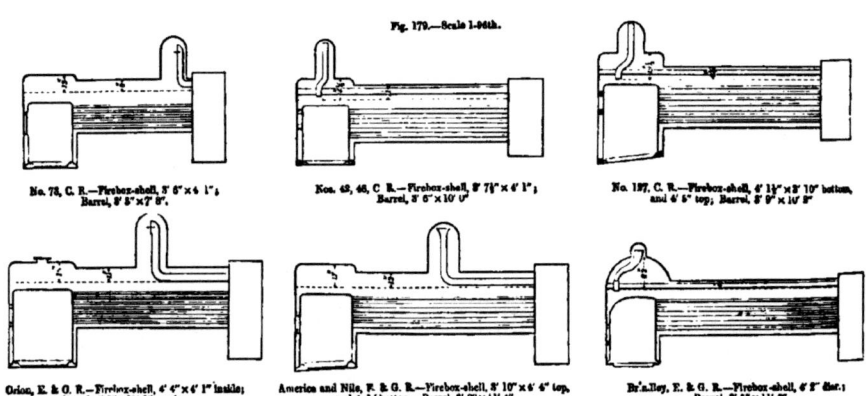

Fig. 179.—Scale 1-96th.

No. 73, C. R.—Firebox-shell, 3′ 6″×4′ 1″; Barrel, 3′ 5″×7′ 8″.   Nos. 42, 48, C. R.—Firebox-shell, 3′ 7½″×4′ 1″; Barrel, 3′ 5″×10′ 0″.   No. 127, C. R.—Firebox-shell, 4′ 1½″×2′ 10″ bottom, and 4′ 5″ top; Barrel, 3′ 9″×10′ 8″.

Orion, E. & G. R.—Firebox-shell, 4′ 4″×4′ 1″ inside; Barrel, 3′ 9″×10′ 2″ inside.   America and Nile, E. & G. R.—Firebox-shell, 3′ 10″×6′ 4″ top, and 4′ 1′ bottom; Barrel, 3′ 9″×11′ 6″.   Br'n.lley, E. & G. R.—Firebox-shell, 4′ 3″ dia.; Barrel, 3′ 5″×11′ 6″.

SECTIONS OF LOCOMOTIVE BOILERS, RELATIVE TO THE PRODUCTION OF STEAM.

Preliminary Estimate of Condensation in Exposed Cylinders.—Before going into the experiments, we must reconsider the internal evidence of indicator-diagrams, on the condensation of steam, discussed in a previous chapter, and

the results of which are embodied in table 29, page 82. It was concluded that the stated losses by condensation, there noted, were only what were deducible from the expansion-curves; and that the total condensation must be much greater. In that table, 3d column, we find that for 73·5 per cent. admission, there was less steam by 12 per cent., at the end of the expansion than when the steam was cut off; that is, there

---

* *Guide du Mécanicien Constructeur et Conducteur de Machines Locomotives,* Paris, 1851.

was a loss of 12 per cent. by condensation during expansion. Now, as this loss was caused near the end of the stroke, the loss must have been at least as great during the admission, when the cylinder was at least as cold; and if there be 12 per cent. of condensation for full gear, there must be at least as much for admissions of 50 per cent., knowing as we do that shorter admissions cause greater percentages of condensation. We shall, therefore, adopt a general loss of 12 per cent. by condensation in exposed cylinders, for all admissions between full gear and half stroke. The *indicated* loss for an admission of half stroke, or 50 per cent., is, by the table, nothing; but this signifies simply that the steam lost during the first part of expansion is restored in the last part, and it gives no indication of what is lost during admission. The same considerations go to show that the losses during shorter admissions, indicated by the excess of steam at the end of expansion, col. 3, are certainly less than the total losses; and, therefore, to afford approximations to the total losses by condensation, we shall add a uniform extra loss, 12 per cent., to all the indicated losses in the 3d column, for the shorter admissions. Making these additions, and adopting 12 per cent. of loss for all admissions above half stroke, we have the percentages of total loss by condensation, in the 2d column of the annexed table:—

TABLE, No. LXXV.—OF THE CONDENSATION OF STEAM IN PARTIALLY PROTECTED CYLINDERS, FOR VARIOUS PERIODS OF ADMISSION, DEDUCED FROM THE EVIDENCE OF THE INDICATOR.

Period of Admission, in parts of stroke.	Proportion of Steam Condensed.	
	In parts of the INDICATED Steam consumed.	In parts of the WHOLE Steam consumed, (*including* the condensed steam).
percentage.	percentage.	percentage.
73·5	12	11
60	12	11
50	12	11
40	21	17
30	32	24
20	46	32
12	73	42

To reduce the contents of the 2d column to more ordinary terms for comparison, we have, in the 3d column, repeated the percentages of condensation, expressed in terms of the *whole* steam consumed from the boiler, including what is condensed. These were thus found:—For example, the steam *lost* in full gear, being, as stated in col. 2, 12 per cent. of the steam *used* in the cylinder, that is, 12 parts lost for every 100 parts used; then, the *whole* steam admitted is (100+12) or 112 parts for every 12 parts lost; and the loss is 12×100÷112=11 per cent. of the whole steam, as entered in col. 3. The other results are found in the same way.

The contents of this table express the losses, of course, only in average figures, as these must vary, with every degree of protection for the cylinder; and to some extent with the pressure during admission. For ordinary outside cylinders, and for pressures under 60 lbs., they are substantially right; when the pressure amounts to 90 lbs. and upwards, the proportional loss is probably much reduced for admissions above 60 per cent., but for materially shorter admissions, no amount of pressure (in other words, density) materially reduces the loss.

Experiments with No. 42, *C. R.*, 29*th August*, 1850.—This engine was run with the 10.30 A.M. express train, averaging 6·7 carriages, from Glasgow to Carlisle, a distance of 105 miles, on the Caledonian Railway, and it performed the trip in 3 hours, 22 minutes, five stoppages included. Indicator-diagrams were taken from the cylinder at intervals of one or two miles, with the number of the notch under which the engine was worked. The points at which the steam was put on and shut off, and at which the changes of notch were made, were also noted; and these supplied the means of estimating the volumes of steam passed through the cylinders. Table No. LXXVI. contains these data; the last two columns contain the miles run under each notch, and the average pressures at which the steam was suppressed.

TABLE, No. LXXVI.—CONSUMPTION OF STEAM.—WORKING OF THE ENGINE, No. 42, C.R., WITH EXPRESS TRAIN. AUGUST, 1850.

Stations, and Distances from Carlisle.	Notch under which the engine was worked.	Indicated steam-pressure at point of suppression.	Miles run under each notch, with steam on.	Average indicated pressures at suppression under each notch.
miles.	notch.	lbs.	miles.	lbs.
Glasgow, Buchanan St. Station, 105 miles. Start 10 h. 9 m. A.M.	4	72	3	72
102	4	25		
101	,,	49		
100	,,	35		
99	,,	37	5½	36
98	,,	35		
97	,,	36		
96½ shut off at 10 h. 26 m.				
Gartsherrie Station, 96 miles. Start 10 h. 30 m.	2	47	½	47
95½, change.	4	55		
92	,,	45	5½	50
90, shut off at 10 h. 43 m.	,,	50		
Motherwell. 89 Start, 10 h. 58 m.				
88¾	3	77		
88	,,	75		
87	,,	75		
86	,,	68		
85	,,	62		
84	,,	65	10	69
83	,,	70		
82	,,	63		
81	,,	65		
80	,,	72		
79, change.	4	57		
78	,,	42	2	50
77, shut off at	,,			
76, set on.	3	41		
75	,,	36	2½	38
74½, shut off at 11 h. 27½ m.	,,			
Carstairs, 73½ Start, 11 h. 35½ m.	4			
73	,,	55		
71	,,	70		
69	,,	52		
67	,,	50	11	50
65	,,	35		
63	,,	40		
62½, change.	3			
61	,,	57		
59	,,	51		
57	,,	46	9½	50
55	,,	44		
53	,,	51		
Change at 53	4			
51	,,	63	3¾	58
50	,,	53		
49½, shut off at 12 h. 13¾ m. P.M.	,,			

TABLE, No. LXXVI.—(*Continued.*)

Stations, and Distances from Carlisle.	Notch under which the engine was worked.	Indicated steam-pressure at point of suppression.	Miles run under each notch, with steam on.	Average indicated pressures at suppression under each notch.
miles.	notch.	lbs.	miles.	lbs.
Beattock, 39½ Start, 12 h. 31½ m.	4			
39	,,	40		
37	,,	36		
35	,,	35	12¾	38
33	,,	43		
31	,,	31		
29	,,	38		
27	,,	41		
26¾, shut off at 12 h. 50 m.	,,			
Lockerbie, 26 Start, 12 h. 53½ m.	3		3	60
25	,,	60		
23, change.	4	56	4	50
21	,,	45		
21, change.	5		3½	30
19	,,	30		
17½, change.	4		1¾	33
17	,,	33		
15¾, change.	3		1¼	30
15	,,	30		
14½, change.	5			
13	,,	56	6½	56
11	,,	55		
8, change.	4	40		
6	,,	57	7½	52
4	,,	60		
2	,,	50		
½, change.	2	60	½	60
Carlisle. 0, shut off at 1 h. 31 m. P.M.				
ABSTRACT OF CONTENTS.				
Glasgow to Motherwell.	2		½	47
16 miles.	4		5½	36
Steam on 30 min.	,,		5⅓	50
	,,		3	72
			14⅓	
Motherwell to Carstairs.	3		10	69
15½ miles.	,,		2¼	38
Steam on 29½ min.	4		2	50
			14¼	
Carstairs to Beattock.	3		9½	50
34 miles.	4		11	50
Steam on 38¼ min.	,,		3	58
			23½	
Beattock to Carlisle.	2		½	60
39½ miles.	3		3	60
Steam on 56¼ min.	,,		1¼	30
	4		12¾	38
	,,		2	50
	,,		1¾	33
	,,		7½	52
	5		3½	30
	,,		6½	56
			38¾	

GENERAL ABSTRACT.

2d notch	1	mile run.
3d ,,	26	do.
4th ,,	54	,,
5th ,,	10	,,
Steam on,	91	miles.
Do. off,	14	
Whole distance,	105	miles.

We have now to find the volumes of steam passed through the cylinders per mile run, for each notch. By means of slow diagrams, No. 42 was found to suppress the steam for the front stroke, as follows:—

1st Notch, suppression at	14·5	inches of stroke.	
2d ,,	do.	13	,,
3d ,,	do.	11	,,
4th ,,	do.	9	,,
5th or mid.,	do.	3·4	,,

And by a previous examination of the valves, the admission for the back stroke was found to be 1 inch shorter than for the front, under the 1st notch, and the difference became smaller for the higher notches, until in the 5th notch, or mid-gear, the admissions were perfectly equal. The mean admission for the 1st notch is thus only 14 inches; and, adding the clearance, 1·1 inch, 15·1 inches is the mean total admission. The periods of compression were also found by the slow diagram, and 1·1 inch must be added to each of them, to give the total volumes retained. In this way, we find the mean total admissions and compressions, as follow:—

	Total admissions.	Total compressions.
2d Notch	13·6 inches.	4·1 inches.
3d ,,	11·7 ,,	4·5 ,,
4th ,,	9·85 ,,	5·3 ,,
5th ,,	4·5 ,,	8·1 ,,

The piston, 15 inches diameter, is 176·7 inches area; then the volume admitted for the 2d notch is $176·7 \times 13·6 \div 1728 = 1·391$ cubic feet, which taken 4 times is 5·564 feet for one turn of wheel. A 6 feet wheel makes 280 turns per mile; and $5·564 \times 280 = 1558$ cubic feet, is the total volume admitted per mile, for the 2d notch. The volume retained by compression is found by the same process, and for the different notches we have the following volumes admitted and compressed:—

	Admitted per mile.	Compressed per mile.
2d Notch	1558 feet.	469 feet.
3d ,,	1340 ,,	515 ,,
4th ,,	1128 ,,	607 ,,
5th ,,	515 ,,	916 ,,

The abstract of contents appended to the foregoing table, is drawn up in four parts, for four successive sections of the railway, and to find the quantities of water received into the cylinder as sensible steam, that is, the water-equivalents of the indicated steam, estimated from the pressures at suppression, the volumes of steam expended for each notch, must be divided by the relative volumes due to the pressures. For example, in the first section, we find that 47 lbs. steam has been admitted for ½ mile, under the 2d notch, which admits 1558 feet per mile. For ½ mile, the volume admitted is one-half, or 779 feet; and the relative volume of 47 lbs. steam being 453, then $779 \div 453 = 1·72$ cubic feet, is the volume of water admitted as steam. Steam of 4 lbs. is retained by compression, the total volume of which for ½ mile is 235 feet; its relative volume is 1342, and $235 \div 1342 = ·17$ cubic foot, is the volume as water. Thus $1·72 - ·17 = 1·55$ cubic feet, is the volume of water as steam expended under the 2d notch. To take the next example, 36 lbs. steam is admitted for 5½ miles under the 4th notch; this notch admits 1128 feet of steam per mile, and the relative volume of 36 lbs. steam is 542; then $1128 \div 542 = 2·08$ feet of water as steam admitted per mile, and $2·08 \times 5½ = 11·44$ feet for the whole distance

Similarly, for the next charge of 50 lbs. for 5½ miles, the water-equivalent is 14·30 feet, and for 72 lbs. steam over 3 miles, it is 10·05 feet. The sum of these three quantities for the 4th notch is 35·79 feet for 14 miles. The compression-pressure of the exhaust steam averages about 5 lbs. for the 4th notch, at the observed speeds; the relative volume of this steam is 1280, and the volume per mile compressed, is 607 feet; then 607 ÷ 1280 = ·47 feet, is the water-equivalent per mile, and ·47 × 14 = 6·58 feet, is the total volume retained; finally, 35·79 — 6·58 = 29·21 cubic feet, is the water-equivalent of sensible steam expended under the 4th notch. Adding 1·55 feet for the 2d notch, we have a total of 30·76 feet of water, used as steam sensible to the indicator, on the first section of railway from Glasgow to Motherwell. The total water consumed from the boiler was found by measurement equal to 35·82 cubic feet, exceeding the indicated consumption by 5·06 feet. This excess is due to priming or condensation, or to both, and amounts to 14 per cent. of the total water used.

The operations just detailed are now more briefly repeated:—

Glasgow to Motherwell.			Steam pressure.	Water-equivalents admitted.		Do. compressed.		Water expended.
2d Notch,	⅓ mile,		47 lbs.	1·72 feet.	—	·17 feet	=	1·55 feet.
4th ,,	5½	,,	36 ,,	11·44 ,,				
,,	5½	,,	50 ,,	14·30 ,,				
,,	3	,,	72 ,,	10·05 ,,				
				35·79 feet	—	6·58 feet	=	29·21 feet.

Water-equivalent of steam used, ... 30·76 feet.
Total water used, as measured, . . . 35·82

Excess, in priming and condensation, . . 5·06 feet,
or 14 per cent. of total.

The same style of reduction being applied to the diagrams taken on the other sections of the line, we obtain the following general results:—

	Water used as sensible steam.	Water consumed, as measured.	Excess.	
1. Glasgow to Motherwell,	30·76ft.	35·82ft.	5·06ft.,	or 14 p.ct. of total.
2. Motherwell to Carstairs,	43·91	48·85	4 94	or 10 ,,
3. Carstairs to Beattock,	57·28	67 74	10·46	or 15·4 ,,
4. Beattock to Carlisle,	62·42	79·50	17 06	or 21·5 ,,
Total, Glasgow to Carlisle,	194·37	231·91	37·52	or 16·2 per cent.

Having thus found that a considerable excess of water has passed into the cylinder, the question remains, How much is due to condensation, and how much to priming? To answer this, we must find the average period of admission for each section of the trip. The following is an abstract of the miles run under each notch, in each section; and the average admissions are added:—

(1.)	2d Notch,	13 inches.	⅓ mile.	9 inches average admission, or 45 per cent. of stroke.
	4th ,,	9 ,,	14 ,,	
(2.)	3d ,,	11 ,,	12¼ ,,	10¾ inches, or 54 per cent.
	4th ,,	9 ,,	2 ,,	
(3.)	3d ,,	11 ,,	9½ ,,	10½ inches, or 50 per cent.
	4th ,,	9 ,,	14 ,,	
(4.)	2d ,,	13 ,,	½ ,,	8 inches, or 40 per cent.
	3d ,,	11 ,,	4¼ ,,	
	4th ,,	9 ,,	24 ,,	
	5th ,,	3·4 ,,	10 ,,	

Total average, Glasgow to Carlisle, 9 inches, or 45 per cent.

These averages are obtained, in each case, by multiplying the admissions by their respective mileages, and dividing the sum of the products by the sum of the mileages. The following table shows, in the third column, the loss by condensation, in parts of the indicated steam consumed, due to these average admissions, derived from Table LXXV., and in the fourth column these losses are converted by simple proportion into parts of the whole water consumed. The fifth column contains the total observed loss.

TABLE, No. LXXVII.—LOSSES OF STEAM AND WATER IN THE WORKING OF No. 42, C.R., WITH EXPRESS TRAIN. AUGUST, 1850.

Section of Trip.	Average Periods of Admission.	Steam Lost by Condensation. In parts of *indicated steam* consumed, by Table, No. LXXV.	Steam Lost by Condensation. In parts of the *whole water* consumed.	Whole loss by condensation and priming, in parts of the *whole water* consumed.	Consumption of water per hour of steam on.
	per cent. of stroke.	per cent.	per cent.	per cent.	cubic feet.
(1.)	45	16·5	14	14	71·6
(2.)	54	12	11	10	99·4
(3.)	50	12	10	15·4	106·2
(4.)	40	21	16·5	21·5	84·8
Whole trip...	45	16 5	13	16·2	93 6
1	2	3	4	5	6

The contents of col. 5 show that the shorter the average admission the greater is the actual loss of steam and water. Thus, comparing sections (2) and (4), a reduction of admission from 54 to 40 per cent. fully doubles the loss. Again, the 4th column shows that nearly all the actual loss is by condensation; for, in sections (1) and (2), the known losses by condensation are equal to the whole losses, leaving nothing to be accounted for by priming; in (3) and (4) the condensation is from two-thirds to three-fourths of the total loss, leaving 5½ per cent. of the whole water used, as a percentage of priming. Further, the average for the whole trip shows that, out of 16·2 percentage of actual loss, 13 per cent. is certainly condensation, and the difference is so small as to show that there is substantially no priming. The rates of consumption per hour while the steam was on the piston, which are added in the last column, are deduced from the observed intervals of time between the opening and the closing of the regulator, stated in the abstract of the table. These show that the rate of evaporation had nothing to do with the observed losses of water, as the smallest loss, (section 2), has taken place with a comparatively high rate of evaporation, and the greatest loss (section 4) with a much lower evaporation.

Experiments with Passenger-Engine, No. 48, C. R., 27th March, 1850.—This engine was run with a coke-train up Beattock Incline, C. R., nearly 10 miles long, and of a gradient varying from 1 in 88 to 1 in 75. The ascent was performed in 29¼ minutes, or at a mean speed of 20 miles per hour; and 42·7 feet of water was consumed from the boiler. The engine was worked in the 1st and 3d notches, as follows:—

		Mean admission.	Mean compression.
For 3 miles,	1st notch,	15 7 inches,	1·15 inches.
For 6¾ ,,	3d ,,	11·25 ,,	3 01 ,,
9¾ miles steam on.			

and adding the total clearance, 1·1 inch, the volumes of steam admitted and retained per mile run, are:—

	Admitted per mile.	Compressed per mile.
1st Notch,	1809 feet.	258 feet.
3d ,,	1415 ,,	471 ,,

The mean pressure of steam suppressed was, for the 1st notch, 50 lbs., and for the 3d, 66 lbs.; the pressure compressed was, in both cases, 3 lbs. From these data we find that 36·95 feet of sensible steam was passed through the cylinders; and the following are the general results:—

Water consumed from the boiler,	42·70 feet, or 87 feet per hour.	
Do. do. as sensible steam,	36·95 ,,	
Loss, 13·47 per cent, or	5·75 feet.	

As the average admission on the trip was above half-stroke, a part of this loss, equal to 12 per cent. of the indicated steam is by table LXXV., due to condensation, and is consequently 10·4 per cent. of the whole consumption, leaving only a loss of 3·07 per cent. for priming.

Experiments with Goods-Engine, No. 127, C. R., July, 1850.—The engine was, on the 3d July, run alone from St. Rollox Station, Glasgow, to Gariongill, whence it picked up a train of loaded coal-waggons; and this train it conveyed to Beattock. On the 4th, it ascended Beattock Incline, with the train; and finally, having left the train at Beattock, it returned alone from Beattock to Glasgow.

3d July, the engine and tender alone, ran from St. Rollox to Gariongill, 20 miles, in the 5th notch, or mid gear; with its load it worked from Gariongill to Beattock, 44¼ miles, in the 1st, 2d, and 3d notches, according to the gradients. The following are the mean values for these notches, and the lengths of line over which they were worked:—

		Mean admission.	Mean compression.
For 14 miles,	1st notch,	16·62 inches.	3·25 inches.
6 ,,	2d ,,	14·0 ,,	4·0 ,,
15½ ,,	3d ,,	12·0 ,,	6·0 ,,
20 ,,	5th ,,	4·0 ,,	7·0 ,,
55½ miles steam on.			

From this it appears the average admission for the whole trip is 10·5 inches, or 43 per cent. The total clearance, 1·4 inch, being added, the volumes per mile are as follow:—

	Admitted per mile.	Compressed per mile.
1st Notch,	3538 feet.	911 feet.
2d ,,	3018 ,,	1058 ,,
3d ,,	2627 ,,	1450 ,,
5th ,,	1117 ,,	1704 ,,

The pressures of the steam suppressed were averaged for each notch, and allowing for the steam compressed, the pressure of which averaged 12 lbs. for the 5th notch, and practically nothing for the other notches, we have the following general results:—

	Suppression.		Water used as sensible steam.
1st Notch,	94 lbs.	for 9 miles,	156·71 cubic feet.
	61 lbs.	,, 5 ,,	
2d ,,	73 lbs.	,, 6 ,,	51·10 ,,
3d ,,	69 lbs.	,, 5½ ,,	81·31 ,,
	43 lbs.	,, 10 ,,	
5th ,,	61 lbs.	,, 20 ,,	25·40 ,,
Total water consumed as sensible steam,			314·52 ,,
Do. consumed from the boiler,			392·50 ,
Loss, 19·87 per cent., or			77·98 cubic feet.

As the average admission was 43 per cent. of the stroke, we have to deduct for condensation, by table LXXV., 18 per cent. of the indicated steam, or 14·42 per cent. of the whole water, leaving 5·45 per cent. for priming. The total time the steam was on, was 2¾ hours, at a mean speed of 20 miles per hour; and the water was consumed from the boiler at the rate of 143 feet per hour steam on.

4th July, 1st Experiment. The engine ascended Beattock Incline with its load, under the 1st notch, 10 miles in 72½ minutes with full steam on, the diagrams being all of the form in dot-lining, fig. 141, page 90; it also ran 1½ miles extra, alone, after reaching the summit, to feed itself with water, the time of which, as of little moment, was not observed. Averaging the observed pressures, we have the following:—

	Pressures at suppression.	Water used as sensible steam.
1st Notch,	104 lbs. for 1 mile,	120·91 cubic feet.
	95 lbs. ,, 4½ ,,	
	85 lbs. ,, 4½ ,,	
	20 lbs. ,, 1 ,,	
	15 lbs. ,, ½ ,,	
Water consumed from the boiler,		170·0 ,,
Loss, 25·3 per cent., or		43·09 feet.

The admission being 69 per cent., 12 per cent. of the sensible steam, or 9 per cent. of the whole water, comes off for condensation, and 16·3 per cent. remains as priming. The mean speed on the incline was 8·3 miles per hour; the consumption of water, 141 feet per hour.

2d Experiment. The engine and tender alone, ascended Beattock Incline, under the 3d notch, 10 miles in 25 minutes, the diagrams being of the forms in full lining, fig. 141. The mean pressure at suppression was 18·5 lbs., back pressure 8 lbs., yielding the following results:—

Water consumed from the boiler,	23·0 feet, or 55 feet per hour.	
Do. do. as sensible steam,	18·83 ,,	
Loss, 18·1 per cent., or	4·17 feet.	

By the table, the loss for the 3d notch suppressing at half-stroke, is 12 per cent. of the sensible steam, or 9·8 per cent. of the whole water, for condensation, leaving 8·3 per cent. as priming. It is most likely, however, considering the low rate of evaporation, the low pressure in the cylinder, and the great back pressure, that the loss is all by condensation.

29th July. The engine, No. 127, conveyed a train of loaded coal waggons from Gariongill to Edinburgh, via Carstairs. Indicator-diagrams were taken from the cylinder, during the ascent of the Wishaw Incline from Gariongill: and, separately, in the ascent from Carstairs to Cobbenshaw, the summit level on the Edinburgh branch.

1st Experiment, Wishaw Incline. Diagrams were taken over a distance of 7⅝ miles, at ¼ mile intervals, under the 1st and 2d notches, which was run over in 36 minutes, with the following mean pressures:—

	Suppression.	Water used as sensible steam.
1st Notch,	74 lbs. for 6¼ miles,	66·98 feet.
2d ,,	37 lbs. ,, 1⅜ ,,	5·67 ,,
Total water consumed as sensible steam,		72·65 ,,
Do. do. from the boiler,		106·00
Loss, 31·4 per cent., or		33·35 feet.

Twelve per cent. of the sensible steam, or 8·2 per cent. of the whole water goes as condensation, and 23·2 per cent. as priming. Mean speed, 13 miles per hour; consumption of water, 177 feet per hour.

2d Experiment, Carstairs Incline. Diagrams were taken over 8½ miles under the 1st notch, in 39 minutes, with the following results:—

	Suppression.		Water used as sensible steam.
1st Notch,	70 lbs.	for 5½ miles,	74·26 feet.
	42 lbs.	„ 3 „	
Water consumed from the boiler,			88·36 „
Loss, 16 per cent., or			14·10 feet.

Setting aside 12 per cent. of the sensible steam, or 10 per cent. of the whole water, for condensation, we have 6 per cent. over for priming. Mean speed, 13 miles per hour; consumption of water, 136 feet per hour.

In this trip, we find 20 per cent. of priming in the first experiment; and only 4 per cent. in the second. The difference is due to the relative purity of the water employed; for, whereas St. Rollox water, used in the first instance, is muddy and otherwise impure, the water at Carstairs, with which the tender was refilled, previous to the second trial, is clean, and is indeed ackowledged by the enginemen to be the best on the line. Thus, it is clearly proved how impurities in the water increase the priming; thus, also, the preference of the enginemen is to be accounted for.

In the experiments, previously discussed, with Nos. 127 and 42, the water was an average of the supplies obtained from different parts of the railway; and with the passenger-engines it is studied to depend as little as practicable upon the St. Rollox tank for supply. A more uniform quality of water is thus obtained, and this explains the more favourable results on the first sections of the line, with No. 42.

Experiments with No. 73, *C. R., April*, 1850.—The conditions under which this engine was tested, have been noted at page 89, *ante*.

10th April, first day. Greenock to Glasgow, 22½ miles. Admission 14$\frac{3}{16}$ inches, compression 1½ inch. Boiler foul, water muddy. Time on the trip, 1 hour, including 3 stoppages; mean speed 22½ miles per hour, running speed 30 miles.

Ten indicator-diagrams were taken on the trip, like those at page 89; the steam-pressure is averaged from the diagrams for the whole length of each gradient. No allowance has been made for the spaces run over while the steam was shut off coming up to stations, as we have assumed roughly that the extra pressure and density of steam at starting from stations is an equivalent for the steam so shut off. The pressure of steam suppressed varied from 16 lbs. to 26 lbs., and the mean compression-pressure was 12 lbs. The consumption of water was as follows:—

Water used as sensible steam,	42·24	feet.
Do. consumed from the boiler,	62·60	„
Loss, 32·5 per cent., or	20·36	feet.

12th April, third day, Greenock to Glasgow. Admission 12$\frac{11}{16}$ inches. Boiler run off, fresh water supplied.

Water used as sensible steam,	46·97	feet.
Do. consumed from boiler,	58·60	„
Loss, 19·9 per cent., or	11·63	feet.

These results show a reduction of priming fully one-third, by using cleaner water. In the second case the water was still impure; and, as the cylinders of No. 73 are well placed inside the smoke-box, it is probable that the loss of water is nearly all by priming.

We turn now to the experiments with the engines of the Edinburgh and Glasgow railway. The main line is 48 miles long, and is nearly level for about 46½ miles, on which the steepest gradient is 1 in 880, from Edinburgh to Cowlairs station, whence it descends to Glasgow by an incline of 1 in 43. The engines leave the trains towards Glasgow, at Cowlairs; and they descend to Glasgow station for outgoing trains, being assisted on the incline by a stationary engine at the summit. Thus, the lengths of trip for the engines are, E. to G., 46⅝ miles, and G. to E., 48 miles.

Experiments with the Orion, E. & G. R., September, 1850. —This engine was subjected to observation on two days successively, in the performance of its ordinary work; and indicator-diagrams were taken at one-mile intervals during three successive trips, as follows:—

6th Sep.	1st trip.	Just before blowing off the boiler.
7th Sep.	2d do.	Just after blowing off.
„	3d do.	Second trip after blowing off.

1st Experiment, 11 A.M. ordinary train, Glasgow to Edinburgh, 48 miles; 12 stoppages. Total time of trip 2 h. 1 m. 30 s.; steam on, 1 h. 31 m. 5 s., over a distance of 39¾ miles. Total water consumed, 135 feet, or 89 feet per hour of steam on. The engine was worked under the 5th and 6th notches, except a few paces in the 2d at starting; and the valve-gear was so hung as to give under these notches, about 3 inches shorter admission for the back stroke than for the front. The admission was as follows:—

	Front stroke.	Back stroke.
2d Notch.	15 inches.	13 inches.
5th „	11½ „	8½ „
6th „	10 „	7 „

Forty-one diagrams were taken on the trip; 20 were under the 5th, and 21 under the 6th notch,—nearly equal numbers, and showing an average admission of 10¾ inches, front stroke, and 7¾ inches back stroke. The average indicated pressure at suppression was, 50 lbs. for the front stroke; for the back stroke, it must be higher, as the admission is shorter, and we have seen that shorter admissions give higher pressures in the cylinder, the regulator remaining the same. For example, in fig. 117, page 72, the two diagrams, taken consecutively from the Orion, in the 2d and 5th notches, show a suppression-pressure in the 5th notch, higher by 10 lbs. than in the 2d, and the excess is due to a shorter admission. We are, then, safe in adopting an excess of 10 lbs. pressure for the back stroke in the case before us; and the suppression-pressure will be 60 lbs. Finally, the mean average admission is (10¾ + 7¾) ÷ 2, or 9¼ inches, and the compression is 4 inches; the mean suppression-pressure is (50 + 60) ÷ 2, or 55 lbs., and the compression-pressure was 4 lbs. Allowing 1·1 inch of clearance, we have

Water used as sensible steam,	102 feet.
Total water consumed, ...	135 „
Loss, 24·5 per cent., or	33 feet.

2d Experiment, 6·30 A.M. ordinary train, Edinburgh to Glasgow, 46⅝ miles; 12 stoppages. Total time of trip with engine, 2 h. 22 m. ; steam on, 1 h. 44 m. 15 s., over a distance of 37¼ miles. Total water consumed, 126 feet, or 72·7 feet per hour, steam on. The engine was started in the 2d notch, and worked regularly in the 5th, with the exception of 4 miles in the 6th notch. The mean pressure of steam suppressed, deduced from sixty diagrams, was 55 lbs. for the front strokes ; and, adding 10 lbs., we have 65 lbs. for the back strokes. Estimating, accordingly, the steam admitted, and deducting for a compression of 3 inches, and exhaust steam at atmospheric pressure, we find as follows:—

Water used as sensible steam,	111·3 feet.
Total water consumed, ...	126 ,,

Loss, 11·6 per cent., or 14·7 feet.

3d Experiment, 10·30 A.M. express, Glasgow to Edinburgh, 48 miles; 3 stoppages. Total time of trip, 1 h. 27 m. 40 s.; steam on, 1 h. 18 m. 20 s., over a distance of 44 miles. Total water consumed, 78·33 feet, or 60 feet per hour steam on. Started in the 2d notch, and worked all the way in the 5th. From forty-six diagrams, the mean pressure at suppression was 40 lbs. for the front stroke ; and, adding 10 lbs., it is 50 lbs. for the back stroke. With atmospheric steam compressed at 5 inches, the water is estimated as follows :—

Water used as sensible steam,	75·83 feet.
Total water consumed, ...	78·33 ,,

Loss, 3·2 per cent., or 2·50 feet.

On the three occasions just detailed, it appears that the losses were successively 24·5, 11·6, and 3·2 per cent. These we believe to be almost entirely by the priming of foul water, as we shall afterwards discuss at length.

Experiment with the Nile, E. and G. R., 10th October, 1850. —10·30 A.M. express, Edinburgh to Glasgow, 46¼ miles ; 3 stoppages. Total time, 1 h. 34 m. 45 s.; steam on, 1 h. 21 m. 45 s., for 43¼ miles. Water consumed, 143 feet, or 104·6 feet per hour steam on. Forty-seven diagrams were taken on the trip, showing suppression-pressures from 25 lbs. to 61 lbs. To insure correctness, with such various pressures, they have been averaged into nine different pressures, for which the equivalents of water due to their respective mileages have been estimated separately. The compression-pressure averaged 7 lbs. With 12·3 inches front admission, 11·3 back admission, and 3·1 inches compression, we have as follows :—

Water used as sensible steam,	135·5 feet.
Total consumption, ...	143·0 ,,

Loss, 5·24 per cent., or 7·5 feet.

Experiments with the America, E. and. G. R., September, 1850.—The consumption of steam in this engine was observed for three trips. On the first and second trips, the spring-balance of the safety-valve was weak, and could not bear above 75 lbs. without blowing off, which caused a loss of steam at the safety-valve, in the first trip ; in the second, the balance was frequently held down to reduce the loss. On the third trip, a 95 lbs. balance was substituted, which prevented further waste in that direction.

1st Experiment, 2d Sep. 1·30 P.M. E. to G.; 11 stoppages. Total time, 2 h. 39 m. 30 s., steam on 2 h. 1 m. 35 s., over 42½ miles. Water consumed, 193 feet, or 95 feet per

hour steam on. In forty-four diagrams, the suppression-pressure varied from 36 lbs. to 66 lbs. ; and averaging into several mean pressures, with 4 lbs. back pressure, for 12¼ inches front, and 11¼ inches back admission, and 2·1 inches compression, we have

Water used as sensible steam,	158·55 feet.
Total consumption, ...	193·00 ,,

Loss, 17·8 per cent., or 34·45 feet.

2d Experiment, 3d Sep., 8 A.M., E. to G. ; 9 stops. Total time, 1 h. 52 m. ; steam on, 1 h. 27 m. 25 s., over 42 miles. Water consumed, 141 feet, or 97·2 feet per hour steam on. Fifty-three observations of the maximum pressures in the cylinder were made by a simple inspection of the indicator, no diagrams having been taken on this trip. The mean of these observed pressures, which varied but little, was 53 lbs., and, the average wiredrawing on the diagrams taken in the other trips being 8 lbs., we have (53 — 8) or 45 lbs. for the average pressure at which the steam was cut off. Accordingly, we find as follows :—

Water used as sensible steam,	141 feet.
Total consumption, ...	141 ,,

Loss, nothing, 0

3d Experiment, 3d Sep., 5·30 P.M. G. to E., 46 miles to Haymarket (west-end station) ; 9 stops, whole time, 2 h. 8 m. 30 s. ; steam on, 1 h. 33 m. 10 s., over 40¾ miles. Water used, 148 feet, or 95¼ feet per hour steam on. Thirty-four diagrams showed from 40 lbs. to 60 lbs. at suppression; averaging into groups, with 4 lbs. back pressure, we have

Water used as sensible steam,	143 feet.
Total consumption, ...	148 ,,

Loss, 3·4 per cent., or 5 feet.

Experiment with the Brindley, E. and G. R., 21st November, 1850.—10·30 A.M. express, G. to E., 3 stops. Whole time, 1 h. 25 m. ; steam on 1 h. 17 m. 35 s., over 45 miles. Water used, 88 feet, or 68·7 feet per hour steam on. Forty diagrams show from 30 lbs. to 47 lbs. at suppression ; and they have been reduced to six average pressures. The engine was worked four miles in the 1st notch, and the remainder in the 4th, with the following admissions :—

	Front stroke.	Back stroke.
1st Notch.	13·8 inches.	12·8 inches.
4th do.	9·34 ,,	6·34 ,,

We must allow, as before, 10 lbs. extra pressure for the back stroke. Add 1·1 inch for clearance, and allow 2·14 inches compression in the 1st notch, and 5·8 inches in the 4th. Then, with 4 lbs. pressure average for compression, we have

Water used as sensible steam,	65·21 feet.
Total consumption, ...	88·0 ,,

Loss, 26 per cent., or 22·79 feet.

This large percentage of loss is, there is little doubt, almost entirely by priming :—the steam-room is small, the steam is withdrawn at the firebox, and the indicator-diagrams taken from the engine, while they have all the characteristics due to water in the cylinder, give no indication of condensation.

Deductions from the foregoing experiments.—To afford a ready means of comparison, the results just detailed are arranged in Table No. LXXVIII., with some additional columns connected with the rate of evaporation:—

TABLE, No. LXXVIII.—DIGEST OF EXPERIMENTS ON CONDENSATION AND PRIMING OF STEAM IN LOCOMOTIVES.

Date of Experiment.	Name of Engine.	Locality of Trial.	Condition of Cylinder.	Average period of Admission during Experiment.	Steam Room.			Consumption of Water per hour steam on.		Loss of Water in percent. of Total Consumption.			No. of Experiment.	Remarks.
					In firebox shell.	In barrel.	Total.	Total.	Per cubic foot of steam-room.	Loss by Condensation.	Loss by Priming.	Total.		
				per cent. of stroke.	cub. ft.	cub. ft.	cub. ft.	cub. feet.	cub feet	per cent.	per cent.	per cent.		
1850. 29th Aug.	C.R. No. 42	C.R. Glasgow to Carlisle 1st Section	Outside, and partially protected.	45	20	19	39	71·6	1·84	14	0	14	1	
		2d Section		54	...	...	...	99·4	2·55	11	0	10	2	
		3d Section		50	...	...	...	106·2	2·72	10	5·4	15·4	3	
		4th Section		40	...	...	...	84·8	2·17	16·5	5	21·5	4	
		Whole trip		45	...	...	...	93·6	2·4	13	3·2	16·2	5	
27th March	No. 48	Beat. Incline	Do. do.	63	20	19	39	87	2·23	10·4	3·07	13·47	6	The loss is here placed all to condensation, as the evaporation was slow, and the pressure in the cylinder low.
3d July	No. 127	Glas. to Beat.	Do. do.	43	20	15	35	143	4·1	14·42	5·45	19·87	7	
4th July	Do.	Beat. Incline	,,	69	...	...	...	141	4·0	11	14·3	25·3	8	
,,	Do.	Do.	,,	50	...	...	...	55	1·57	18·1	0	18·1	9	
29th July	Do.	Wish. Incline	,,	68	...	...	...	177	5·06	8·2	23·2	31·4	10	Water foul.
,,	Do.	Cars. Incline	,,	69	...	...	...	136	3·9	10	6	16	11	Water good.
10th April	No. 73	Green. Rail.	,,	80	117	14·3	26·0	62·6	2·41	0	32·5	32·5	12	Water foul.
12th ,, E.&G.R.	Do.	Do.	,,	71	...	...	...	58·6	2·25	0	19·9	19·9	13	Water better than on previous day.
6th Sep.	Orion	Glas. to Edin.	Inside.	46	19	30	49	89	1·81	0	24·5	24·5	14	Water foul.
7th ,,	Do.	Edin. to Glas.	,,	48	...	...	...	72·7	1·48	0	11·6	11·6	15	Water blown off, fresh water.
,, ,,	Do.	Glas. to Edin.	,,	43	...	...	...	60	1·22	0	3·2	3·2	16	3d trip after blowing off.
10th Oct.	Nile	Edin. to Glas.	,,	66	16	30	46	104·6	2·28	0	5·24	5·24	17	
2d Sep.	America	Edin. to Glas.	,,	67	16	30	46	95	2·06	0	uncertain	17·8	18	Considerable loss by blowing off.
3d ,,	Do.	Edin. to Glas.	,,	67	...	...	...	97·2	2·11	0	0	0	19	
,, ,,	Do.	Glas. to Edin.	,,	67	...	...	...	95·5	2·08	0	3·4	3·4	20	
21st Nov.	Brindley	Glas. to Edin.	,,	46	16·5	8·5	25	63·7	2·75	0	26	26	21	
1	2	3	4	5	6	7	8	9	10	11	12	13	14	15

It is in the first place established that the condensation of steam in imperfectly protected cylinders, increases with the degree of expansion. The most direct proof in point is supplied by the observations on No. 42, C. R., from which it appears that

with 54, 50, 45, 40 per cent. of admission, the total loss is 10, 15·4, 14, . 21·5 per cent. of the whole water, with an evaporation of } 99·4, 106·2, 71·6, 84·8 feet per hour.

That the loss is mainly by condensation, is made more obvious by the circumstance that the greater losses have attended the lower rates of evaporation, when there was less liability to loss by priming. The probability is indeed that in the 3d and 4th sections, the loss is entirely by condensation, as it certainly is in the 1st and 2d, for in the former case, on the southern parts of the line, there was a better chance of pure water.

The liability to prime is regulated very much by the quality of the water, and so great is the influence of mechanical impurities, that foul water primes under any arrangement of boiler that can be adopted. For example, in experiments 10 and 11 with No. 127 C. R., made with inferior and superior water respectively, the loss of water, even with the same admission, fell from 31·4 to 16 per cent., or one-half, certainly owing to a reduction of priming. With No. 73, similarly, there was effected a great reduction of priming by a change of water; and with the Orion it fell from 24·5 to 3·2 per cent., or nearly nothing. In the latter case, the smallest loss occurred with the shortest admission, and obviously condensation had nothing to do with it. It is further curiously remarkable that on the *first* trip after blowing off, exp. 15, the priming, though less than before, was greater than on the succeeding trip, exp. 16, consistently with the experience of drivers, that an engine *improves* in working condition during the second and third trip after blowing off; —this improvement is due to the gradual settlement of the remains of the mud in the boiler, which may have been agitated by the process of cleansing, but has not been carried off.

Though it has been shown by the results of experiments 10, 12, 14, and 21, that with foul water no arrangement of boiler or capacity of steam-room can prevent priming, or even seriously mitigate it, there is much to be done for its prevention by suitable provisions, with the use of clean water; first, there should be a sufficiency of steam-room; second, it should be freely distributed over the length of the boiler; third, the steam should be so collected and drawn off as not injuriously to concentrate its movements towards the orifice of the steam-pipe, in rising from the water.

First, the advantage of steam-room is proved by ordinary experience, as, with an over-full boiler, when of course the steam-room is reduced, there is a much greater tendency to prime. Further, comparing the results from the Brindley, and Nos. 42 and 127, C. R., with the same arrangement of steam-room, and with ordinary water, we have,

(5.) No. 42, 30 feet of steam-room, 3·2 per cent. priming.
(7. and 8.) No. 127, 35 do. do. 6 to 14 do. do.
(21.) Brindley, 25 do. do. 26 do. do.

Here the evidence goes to show that the smaller the steam-room the greater is the priming. The general excellence of the results from the capacious boilers of the Orion, Nile, and America, with good water, confirms the advantage of steam-room.

Second, the steam-room must be well arranged. Here again the Brindley contrasts unfavourably with Nos. 42 and 127, for while in the former the firebox-shell monopolizes two-thirds of the whole steam-room, in the latter it is little more than a half. It is plain, that the limited steam-room in the barrel of the Brindley, only 6 inch deep, and from which more than half the steam that is generated must be discharged, will tend materially to the disturbance of the water-surface and the priming of water. In the Orion and the Nile, the barrel yields about two-thirds of the whole steam-room, and the space is 11 and 12 inches deep.

Third, as to the position of the orifice of the steam-pipe, it should be such as to equalize so far as practicable the currents of steam from different parts of the water-surface. It certainly ought not to be over the firebox, unless there be abundance of steam-room, as it not only increases the agitation of the water in that quarter, already greater than anywhere else, but it also drags to it all the steam generated in the barrel, which forms the greater part of the whole supply. As all this steam must find its way through the junction of the barrel with the firebox-shell, a strong accumulated current sets in at that point, which drifts the water towards the orifice, and manifestly tends to aggravate the priming. But, when the orifice is placed over the barrel in a dome at the middle of its length, or towards the front, the force of the current from the firebox through the junction above noted, is much less than in the previous case, and though it increases as it approaches the dome, it collects in a much quieter neighbourhood, and causes less disturbance. General experience points so distinctly to this conclusion that there is perhaps but one modern type of engine, the Crewe engine (see plates) and its derivatives, in which the dome is placed over the firebox; and even in the Crewe engines, the single dome over the firebox is being replaced in the later designs (August, 1852) by two smaller steam-chambers, one over the firebox and one over the middle of the barrel, like the smaller one shown in section in Plate XXII. From both of these the steam is conducted by 3 inch branch-pipes to the regulator, and the steam is equally withdrawn from the two compartments of the boiler. This is a revival of the practice of two domes for increasing the steam-room and dividing the draught of steam, which was formerly much in vogue. The roofs of the chambers are probably too low, as they do not admit of more than 15 and 20 inches for the height of the steampipe orifices above the water-level.

The *height* of the orifice of the steam-pipe above the water-surface, is a matter of consequence, as the freeer it is from the atmosphere of spray which floats over the water, the less likely is it to receive priming. Hence, chiefly, the value of the high domes in the Orion and the Nile, at the summits of which the steam makes an exit, and their efficiency is on the same ground enhanced by the position judiciously allotted to them. In one variety of the C. R. passenger-engines, having the dome and the orifice of steam-pipe 6 inches lower than in the ordinary boilers, shown in fig. 179, it is found necessary to work with a usually lower water-level to prevent priming,—in other words, "they carry

less water." On the contrary, engines like the Nile have been known to carry 6 inches more water than their usual complement, which would reduce their steam-room to nearly one-half, without anything like priming. For this immunity they are indebted to their high, capacious, and well-placed dome. It is likely also that something of the imperfect action of the Brindley is due to its low orifice.

By the use of Hawthorn's plan, shown in our plates of the Snake and the Corsair, of carrying the steam-pipe all the length of the boiler and perforating it with numerous small holes or longitudinal slits on the upper side, the dome is dispensed with, as the steam on rising from the water enters the tube directly over it, and thus partial currents are avoided, and with them the contingent tendency to prime. This plan is not successfully available when the steam-space in the barrel is much less than 11 or 12 inches deep, as at less depths the water is liable to prime over. It has been found to work well in the Great Britain class of engines, to which it has been permanently applied, in an 11 inch steam space, with a total capacity of 54 cubic feet; in these engines 200 to 300 feet of water may be evaporated per hour, as Mr. Gooch has frequently proved, without any sensible priming, being at the rate of $5\frac{1}{2}$ feet of water per hour per foot of steam-room.

An efficacious mode of separating the water of priming was several years ago applied in France by Mr. Edwards, to the celebrated "Victorieuse." The top of the steam-

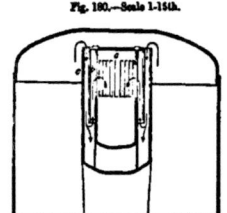
Fig. 180.—Scale 1-15th.

Edwards' Separator, for disengaging Priming.

pipe *a*, fig. 180, was pierced with vertical slits, and finished with a cap *b*, close at top, and quite open below; and the whole was surrounded by a pipe *c*, open at top, but closed round the steam-pipe at the bottom. The mixture of steam and water entered the outer pipe, round the cap *b*, and descended; the force of the descent carried the water to the bottom of the outer pipe, from which it was conducted by a small tube, while the steam parted from it on doubling the edge of the cap, whence it made its way into the steam-pipe, as shown by arrows. This method of turning to account the inertia of the water, operates, there is no doubt, very well, and it has been revived more lately under various modifications, one of which is employed in the C. R. Tank-locomotive (see Plates). It may be very usefully applied in domes which are placed over the fire-box, and in all cases where clean water is difficult to be had.

Concluding Results.—Whether the dome and steampipe-orifice be placed over the firebox or over the barrel, there should be plenty of steam-room in the barrel. Dividing the diameter of barrel by the depth of steam-space given in a previous table, we have, for

No. 73,	39 ÷ 8 inches	= $4\frac{7}{8}$
Nos. 42, 48,	42 ÷ 11	= $3\frac{9}{11}$
No. 127,	45 ÷ 8·5	= $5\frac{2}{6}$
Orion,	45 ÷ 11	= $4\frac{1}{11}$
Nile,	} 45 ÷ 12	= $3\frac{3}{4}$
America,		
Brindley,	41 ÷ 6	= $6\frac{5}{6}$

From this it is plain that the boilers least given to prime under ordinary conditions,—Nos. 42, 48, Orion, Nile, America,—are those which have the greatest depth of steam-room relative to the diameter of barrel; in two of these, Nos. 42, 48, the dome is placed over the firebox, and from the table of priming, it appears, for example, that

No. 42, (3.) using 2·72 feet of water per foot of steam-room, primes 5·4 per cent.

No. 48,	(6.)	„	2·23	do.	„	3·07	„
Orion,	(16)	„	1·22	do.	„	3·2	„
Nile,	(17.)	„	2·28	do.	„	5·24	„

It thus appears that when the depth of steam-space in the barrel is at least one-fourth of its diameter, the position of the dome does not materially affect the priming, when the rate of consumption is under 3 feet per foot of steam-room per hour. There are indeed one or two cases with No. 127, having only $\frac{1}{11}$d of the diameter for steam-room, where the priming is not above 6 per cent., with a consumption of 4 feet per foot of space per hour; but in general, the priming is much greater, as it is also with the Brindley, which has a space of little above $\frac{1}{4}$th.

Again, deducting, as an extra, the capacity of the dome in each boiler, we have the steam-spaces as follows:—

No. 73,	firebox-shell 11·7 feet,	barrel,	9	feet.
Nos. 42, 48,	do.	17·3 „	do.	19	„
No. 127,	do.	16 „	do.	15	„
Orion,	do.	19 „	do.	20	„
Nile,	do.	16 „	do.	20	„
Brindley,	do.	15·5 „	do.	8·5	„

Here, the boilers which prime least have at least as much steam-room in the barrel as in the firebox shell, independently of the dome; and, it may be concluded generally that, for satisfactory action, the steam-space of the firebox-shell should be equal to that of the barrel, the capacity of the dome being considered an extra.

As to the height of the orifice of steam-pipe above the water-surface, it ought to have some relation to the diameter of barrel, and in the best examples before us, it is nearly equal to the diameter; otherwise, it stands three-fourths of a diameter above the barrel.

In fine, though there is no example in the table of the better arranged boilers evaporating more than 2¼ feet of water per foot of steam-room per hour, yet No. 127 has been found to consume 4 feet of water, with but 5 to 6 per cent. of priming. Further, the perforated steam-pipe, while it is certainly not superior to a well-arranged dome and plain pipe, has been found to work without priming in a steam-space one-fifth of the diameter of barrel, with an evaporation of 5¼ feet of water. It may then with safety be concluded that, first, when the depth of steam-space in the barrel is at least one-fourth of the diameter; second, when the steam-room in the firebox-shell is equal to that in the barrel; third, when the steam is withdrawn through a plain pipe placed upon and above the barrel, at an elevation of at least three-fourths of its diameter, or through a perforated tube the whole length of boiler; and, fourth, *when the water is clean*, an evaporation of 5 feet of water per foot of the total steam-room per hour, may be effected without any priming of importance. These are the conditions most conducive to efficiency of evaporation; though they may be deviated from, singly or jointly, to some extent, when slower rates of evaporation, under 3 feet per foot of steam-room per hour,

are contemplated. For example, the dome may be placed over the firebox; or the steam-space may be less than one-fourth of the diameter of the barrel; and if much less, two domes and receiving orifices may be placed apart on the boiler. It may be added that, if good water is not to be had for the service of the engines, a couple of domes and receiving orifices should always be employed; and that the boiler should be frequently cleaned out or blown off, and supplied with fresh water, and the worse the quality of the water, the more frequently this should be done.

RECAPITULATION.—1. Priming is the issue of water from the boiler, mechanically mixed with and carried over by the steam, while the engine is at work.

2. Priming is caused by impurities in the water evaporated, and by deficiency or improper arrangement of steam-room.

3. "False water" is the extra bulk of water in the boiler due to a state of ebullition, by the mixture of the steam with the water through which it ascends. False water varies from ½ inch to 4 and 5 inches, as gauged at the firebox; it reduces the steam-room, properly so called, and thereby increases the tendency to prime.

4. If the water be foul, or muddy, it is certain to prime, and no practical amount of steam-room can prevent its doing so.

5. For the prevention of priming, the water must be clean, and there should be a sufficiency of steam-room, which should be freely distributed over the length of the boiler, from which the steam should be drawn off so as not injuriously to concentrate its movements towards the orifice of the steam-pipe.

6. These demands are met in practice, first, by allotting an average depth of steam-space in the barrel, equal to one-fourth of its diameter; second, by so arranging the boiler that the steam-space in the firebox-shell should be equal to that in the barrel; third, by withdrawing the steam through a plain pipe of which the entrance is placed over the barrel, at an elevation above the crown, of at least three-fourths of the diameter, or through Hawthorn's perforated tube placed the whole length of the boiler; fourth, by frequently cleaning out or blowing off the boiler.

7. Under these conditions, an evaporation of as much as 5 cubic feet of water per cubic foot of steam-space per hour, may be effected without any priming of importance.

8. Though those conditions are the most conducive to free evaporation, they may be deviated from to some extent, singly or jointly, without impairing the production of steam, when slower rates of evaporation, under 3 feet per foot of steam-room per hour, are practised.

9. Edwards' separating pipes, and others on the same principle, for disengaging the steam from the priming which may enter with it, by giving the current sudden changes of direction, are useful for preventing priming.

10. It is estimated from experiments, that with ordinary admission-pressures, of 60 lbs. and less, the loss of steam by condensation in exposed cylinders, commonly outside, averages from 11 per cent. of the whole consumption, in full gear, to 30 and 40 per cent. in mid gear. For 90 lbs. pressures and upwards, the losses for 60 per cent. of admission and upwards are considerably less.

U

CHAPTER VI.

OF THE EVAPORATIVE POWER OF LOCOMOTIVE-BOILERS.

THOUGH the steam-generating power of a boiler is regulated generally by its amount of grate-surface, coke-room, and heating surface, it is plain that the ultimate limit of power is defined by the greatest rate of combustion which it is practicable to enforce by the use of the blast. The evaporating power is commonly referred to the heating surface of a boiler, but it is regulated quite as much by the grate-area, and this is at least the most natural datum for comparison. The production of steam, it is true, has been shown by Mr. Gooch to have some relation to the firebox-surface, but this is probably because, by the similarity of fireboxes to one normal form, their heating surface bears a nearly constant ratio to the area of grate.

Experiments of Mr. D. Gooch, 1845.[*]—These experiments, made upon locomotives of very various proportions, were adduced to show that the evaporative power of the boiler intimately depended upon the extent of firebox-surface. The following table comprises a selection of cases referred to by Mr. Gooch:—

TABLE, No. LXXIX.—EXPERIMENTS TO SHOW RELATION OF EVAPORATIVE POWER TO FIREBOX-SURFACE.[†]

Name of Engine.	Name of Observer, or Authority.	Areas of Surface.			Rate of Evaporation.	
		Grate.	Firebox.	Tubes.	Greatest observed	Calculated at the rate of 2 feet per foot of firebox surface.
		sq. feet.	sq. feet.	square feet.	cub. feet.	cubic feet.
G.W.R., Passr. Engine	D. Gooch	13·4	94	602 steam-chamber 130	196	188
White Horse of Kent	Do.	9	48	860	93	93
So. West. New Engine	Do.	9·4	74	693	141	148
N. & E. Old Engine	Do.	12·6	64	654	175	128
Lon. & Birm. Old Engine, 4 wheels	Bidder	9·2	51	405	100	102
N. & E. New Engine	Fernihough, Stephenson	11·0	65	822	{115 130}	130

Here it appears that the observed evaporation follows nearly the rate of 2 feet per foot of firebox per hour, according to the last column; and, what appears to show its independence of the tube-surface, this rate is followed under extreme proportions of tube and firebox. Thus, in the Ixion and the White Horse, with tube-surfaces respectively 7¼ and 18 times the firebox-surfaces, the evaporations are 2·1 and 1·94 feet respectively per foot of firebox, which are nearly the same; per foot of grate, they are 15 and 10·33 feet, which are very different. In this case, the flue-way

[*] *Gauge Commissioners' Report, 1846. Observations on the Report, by the Great Western Railway Company, 1846.*
[†] The heating surface is measured from the *outside* of the firebox and tubes.

of the Ixion is much more liberal than that of the White Horse, and the combustion in the former might therefore be easily made to exceed that of the latter, per foot of grate, independently of the firebox-surface. A wider range of examples will assist us in discussing the argument.

Preliminary Discussion of the Influence of the temperature of the water introduced into the Boiler.—The estimates of evaporative power usually assume an initial temperature of 62° from which the water is heated and converted into steam. It is occasionally employed at much higher temperatures, and it is desirable to show the effect of this change of temperature on the estimate.

First, as to the *influence of a change of temperature* on the performance of coke, reckoned in pounds of water per pound of fuel. It is clear that the hotter the water delivered to the boiler, the greater is the weight which a pound of fuel can evaporate, and the greater is the available rate of evaporation. Not that the evaporative power of the fuel is increased, for it matters not to the total evaporation per pound of the whole fuel, at what temperature the water may be pumped into the boiler, when the water of the tender is indebted for its extra heat to steam blown back from the boiler. It is only in cases where the water is heated by other means, that an allowance is to be made in the observed consumption of water per pound of fuel.

Let T = the total heat of steam of a given pressure.
  t = the temperature of the water in the tender.
  W = the measured weight of water evaporated from the temperature t, by one pound of fuel.
  w = the equivalent weight of water which would be evaporated from 62°, by one pound of fuel.

Then $t - 62 =$ the extra heat of the water; and $T - (t - 62) =$ the reduced total heat required for evaporation from temperature t°. The weight of water evaporable from 62° by the same weight of fuel, must be less than that which can be converted from t°, in the ratio of T to $T - (t - 62)$; that is,

$$T : T - (t - 62) :: W : w$$
$$\text{and } w = W \times \frac{T - t + 62}{T}.$$

As the total heat of steam varies but slightly with the pressure, the heat for the ordinary pressure of 100 lbs., or 1217°, will be selected, and substituted in the above formula, thus,

$$w = W \times \frac{1217 - t + 62}{1217} = W \times \frac{1279 - t}{1217}.$$

If 100 be substituted for W, the formula will express the value of w as the percentage of water at 62°, evaporable by the same weight of fuel, and

$$w = 100 \times \frac{1279 - t}{1217} = \frac{127900 - 100\,t}{1217} \qquad (1.)$$

Working out the results for temperatures up to 212°, the 2d column of Table LXXX. contains the equivalent percentages of water evaporable from 62°, in terms of the weight evaporated from the temperature in the 1st column.

Second, as to the *change of volume of water by temperature*, water expands as the temperature rises, though in a somewhat irregular ratio. From the ordinary tables of the expansion of water by heat, we have, by an easy process of inversion, the contents of the 3d column, Table LXXX., which are the percentages of weight of equal volumes of water at the temperatures in col. 1, in terms of the weight at 62°.

To find the equivalent *volumes* of water evaporable from 62°, in terms of the volumes at the temperatures, col. 1, the contents of col. 2 must be increased in the ratio in which those of col. 3 fall; or, each quantity in col. 2 should be multiplied by 100, and divided by the relative number in col. 3; the results so obtained are entered in col. 4.

TABLE, No. LXXX.—OF THE EVAPORATION OF WATER AT DIFFERENT TEMPERATURES.

Temperatures.	Equivalent weights of water evaporable from 62°, in parts of the weights of water at the temperatures in col. 1, evaporated by one pound of fuel.	Weights of equal volumes of water, in parts of the weight of water at 62°.	Equivalent volumes of water evaporable from 62°, in parts of the volume of water at the temperatures in col. 1, evaporated by one pound of fuel.
degrees.	percentages of weight.	percentages of weight.	percentages of volume.
42	102	100·1	101·9
62	100	100	100
72	99	99·9	99
82	98	99·75	98·25
92	97	99·6	97·4
102	96	99·45	96·5
112	95	99·21	95·76
122	94	99	95
132	93	98·72	94·2
142	92	98·48	93·4
152	91	98·24	92·6
162	90	97·91	92
172	89	97·56	91·2
182	88	97·28	90·5
192	87	97	89·7
202	86	96·5	89
212	85	96·25	88·3
1	2	3	4

NOTE.—By col. 2, it appears that the equivalent weights fall 1 per cent. for every 10° rise of temperature.

Table of Experiments on Rates of Evaporation.—The Table No. LXXXI., page 156, contains the results derived from various sources, showing the performance of locomotive-boilers of the earliest and the latest construction, and of widely-different proportions. Experiments Nos. 1 to 5 are derived from a previous table, page 7, and are amongst the earliest recorded performances of engines. Obs. 6 is reported by Mr. N. Wood, in his work on railways, and is inserted as an example of what boilers on the plan of the Novelty's, page 6, with a single winding flue, and worked by a fan-blast, are capable of doing. Obs. 7, 8, 9, are derived from Pambour's work; and Obs. 10, 11, 12, from private sources. Obs. 13 is from the Report of the British Association, 1841; and Obs. 14, 15, from the Transactions of the Institution of Civil Engineers. Obs. 16 is from the report of the Gauge Commissioners, 1846; Obs. 17–20 are from the same source, being some of the results of the "Gauge Experiments." The total consumptions of water per hour, col. 15, have been, by means of Table LXXX., reduced for a temperature of 62° from the quantities originally observed, of which the temperatures in the tender were much higher; this operation was necessary to show the equivalent rate of evaporation with ordinary cold water. Obs. 21 to 29 are communicated by Mr. D. Gooch; and Obs. 30 by Mr. J. V. Gooch. Obs. 31 is deduced from the 19th experiment by Mr. Peacock, Table LXVI., as follows:—2500 gallons, or 400 feet of water were consumed between Manchester and Dunford, a distance of 21¼ miles, on an average gradient of about 1 in 140 in 103 minutes, at a

speed of 12·2 miles per hour, and at the rate of 233 feet per hour. The whole consumption of coke in the double trip was 41 cwt. over 40¾ miles each way; and, as the railway ascends from the two termini towards the summit at about half-way, the consumption of coke takes place almost entirely during the first half of each trip, and should be in the two directions as the respective slump weights of the trains, or as 34 waggons from Manchester to 22 waggons from Sheffield, plus the engine and tender in both cases. Taking the gross weight of the waggons, which were heavy-loaded, at 7 tons each, and that of the engine and tender at 40 tons; and dividing the coke in the ratio of the slump weights of the trains, we have 25¼ cwt. consumed in the ascent from Manchester, over 21¼ miles, equal to 133 pounds per mile, and evaporating 8·75 pounds of water per pound of coke. For Obs. 32 to 61, the author is responsible, with the exception of the results of four trips with No. 51, C. R., communicated by Mr. Sinclair. In Obs. 51 and 53, the water of the tender was at about 110° at starting; and of the observed *rate* of evaporation of 128 and 123 feet per hour respectively, only 95 per cent. should, by Table LXXX., be accepted, for water at 62°; or 122 and 117 feet, as entered in column 18.*

The contents of the Table LXXXI. fully illustrate the influence of the form and proportions of boilers on the rate of evaporation per hour and per pound of fuel, and the worth of extended heating surface for increasing the evaporative efficiency of the fuel.

Of the General Influence of the Heating Surface on the rate of evaporation per pound of fuel.—To begin at the beginning, the Killingworth engine, Obs. 1 and 2, shows a decided increase from 3·4 to 4·5 pounds of water per pound of coal by an increase of surface from 6 to 11·4 times the grate, even while the rate of evaporation per foot of grate is much higher. Again, in Obs. 3 and 4, with surfaces of 23 and 55 times the grate, the evaporation is raised from 5·3 to 6·65 pounds. In Obs. 7, 8, 9, under the same circumstances, Pambour found that

with surfaces, 27·6, 42·3, and 49 times the grate, the evaporations were, 5·37, 5·52, and 6·8 pounds, and were also, ·186, ·193, and ·20 feet per hour per foot of total surface;

showing that, even while the rapidity of evaporation per foot of surface was greater, the efficiency of the fuel was raised by an increase of surface to 49 times the grate. Nor had the firebox-surface to do with this increase of duty, for the most efficient boiler has the smallest box-surface both absolutely and with respect to the grate. Bury, also, found his goods-engines, with a surface 50 times the grate, evaporated more per pound of coke, than the passenger-engines with a surface of only 42 times, in the ratio of 5·2 to 4·17 pounds.

* The author declines making use of many of the later published experiments on the performance of locomotive-boilers, and rests his arguments principally on the facts observed and collected by himself. He has adopted this course from necessity, as the accounts are, many of them, so inconsistent as to be unworthy of confidence. As an example, he may refer to the account of experiments with Hawthorn's express engine on the North British Railway, published in the last edition of Tredgold (1850); in which it is stated that 2640 gallons of water was evaporated by 1625 pounds of coke, or at the rate of 16¼ pounds of water per pound of coke! "The results," we are told, "may be relied upon as correct."!!

TABLE, No. LXXXI.—OF DATA RELATIVE TO THE EVAPORATIVE POWERS OF LOCOMOTIVE-BOILERS. 1852.

To come to more modern instances, the gauge-experiments, Obs. 17–20, show that a total surface still greater than 50 times the grate is beneficial. Omitting Obs. 19, as the engine visibly primed a good deal, we find that for—

Obs.	17,	20,	18
with heating surfaces,	52,	86,	94 times the grate,
and hourly consumptions of	15,	14·2,	17 feet per foot of grate,
the water used was	7,	8·96,	8·8 lbs. per pound of coke.

It is plain that the greater surfaces in Obs. 20 and 18,

averaging 90 times the grate, with a mean hourly consumption per foot of grate in excess of that in Obs. 17, are much more efficient at high rates of evaporation, than the surface in Obs. 17, which is but 52 times the grate. In these experiments the best coke was employed; and though the Welsh coke used in Obs. 17, was softer than the north country coke used for the others, the physical difference affected rather the diameter of the blast-orifice than the evaporative efficiency.

Observations 21–30 were made on the locomotive stock of the Great Western Railway, of very various proportions, all in the course of regular traffic. In Obs. 21–27 the heating surfaces are stated in the table as communicated by Mr. Gooch, and are measured from the exterior; the others are from the interior. Omitting meantime the case of the Hesperus, as exceptional, the boiler having been fitted with Hawthorn's return-tubes, it is shown by Obs. 21–27, in which the hourly consumption does not materially vary from 10 to 11 feet per foot of grate, that the increase of total surface from 41 to 78 times the grate, raises the efficiency of the coke from 6·87 to 8·28 pounds of water. In Obs. 29, 30, with interior surfaces of 84 and 73 times the grate, the water used per pound of coke was 7·67 and 7·19 pounds, even while in the second case the rate per foot of grate was much the lower. On another occasion, the same class of engines used in Obs. 29, was found, Obs. 28, to use 8·32 pounds of water. Upon the whole, it is fairly deducible from these remarks, founded on about 200 distinct trips with 27 engines on the Great Western Railway, that an increase of heating surface from 40 to 84 times the grate-area, with a rate of evaporation of about 11 feet per hour per foot of grate, was attended with a substantial increase of the evaporative efficiency of coke, represented by a rise from about 6¼ to 8¼ pounds of water per pound of coke, a difference of 1½ pounds.

Obs. 31 and 32 confirm the utility of extensive surfaces, as they both show a high efficiency, notwithstanding that, in Obs. 32, the evaporation reaches the unprecedented rate of 22 feet per hour per foot of grate. Nor is it likely that any material part of this consumption is due to priming, as the train was observed to be unusually heavy; besides, the steam-dome is placed in the most favourable position, close behind the chimney, and, moreover, the water used per pound of coke, 8·75 lbs., is at least not above what might be expected from the very large amount of heating surface.

In the succeeding observations, Nos. 33–62, made by the author, he has in all cases reduced the allowance of coal served out to the engine, usually a small fraction of the whole fuel, into its equivalent value of coke, by adopting two-thirds of its weight, the proportion assigned in a previous chapter, and slumping the whole together; except in Obs. 59 and 62, where coal almost entirely was used. Comparing the means of Obs. 33–42, and Obs. 43–45, made with goods engines, C. R., we see that

with heating surfaces, 83 and 74 times the grate,
and hourly evaporations of 8·66 and 10·3 feet per foot of grate,
there were consumed 8·17 and 6·85 lbs. water per pound of coke.

Showing as before that an extension of surface to even as much as 83 times the grate is of sensible benefit. The C. R. passenger-engines, in Nos. 46–53, with a surface about 66 times the grate, and a mean hourly rate of 8 feet of water per foot of grate, evaporate 8·43 pounds per pound of coke; thus, at nearly the same hourly rate of feet of grate, and with a *less* surface-ratio, these engines evaporate *more* water per pound of fuel than the goods-engines on the same line and with the same kind of coke. This superior result is due partly to the superior management of the former engines:—the judicious use of the damper (with which the goods-engines are not supplied, nor even with an ash-pan), and the system of low firing usually practised; but mostly, we believe, to the smaller clearance and greater number of the tubes of the goods-engines. (See Table LXIV., page 130). The economy of low firing is, however, shown to be considerable by a comparison of the means of Obs. 46, 51, 52, with full fires, and Obs. 47–50, and 53, with low fires; for we find that

with the fire *full*, and *low* worked,
and hourly evaporations of 8·2 and 8·0 feet per foot of grate,
there were consumed 6·9 and 9·35 lbs. water per pound of coke.

Finally, of the passenger-engines, one, C. R., No. 33, has more surface than the others, in the ratio of 71 to 66·4; and it is in virtue of this excess, no doubt, that that engine evaporates 10·47 lbs. per pound of coke (Obs. 47), which is more than any of the others can show.

The results on the Edinburgh and Glasgow Railway, Obs. 55–57, show as before that with judicious management, a favourable evaporation may be obtained per pound of coke, —in this case 8·56 lbs.,—at a moderate rate of consumption, a mean of 7 feet per hour per foot of grate, even with a mean heating-surface ratio as low as 54 times the grate. For some reason not very obvious, the Brindley, Obs. 58, though it has a surface-ratio of 80 times the grate, does not raise above 8·35 lbs. of water per pound of coke. Passing to the Orion and Queen, G. & S. W. R., with 49 and 60 times the heating surface, the water raised is successively 6·92 and 7·2 lbs. per pound of coke, for nearly equal rates of consumption per foot of grate.

The rate of evaporation per hour per foot of grate is found also to affect the poundage of water per pound of coke: the greater the former, the less is the latter. Thus, in the C. R. engines, taking a mean of Obs. 46–51, and 53, and comparing these with Obs. 52, having all a heating surface of about 66 times the grate, we have

for consumptions of 7·4 and 11·6 feet per hour per foot,
evaporations of 8·66 and 6·8 pounds per pound of coke,

showing a decrease per pound of coke as the consumption per hour is increased above 7 feet per foot of grate.

To sum up the general argument, the rate of evaporation per pound of fuel is materially influenced both by the extent of heating surface, and by the rate of consumption per hour. The greater the heating surface and the less the rate of consumption per hour, the greater within certain limits is the poundage of water evaporated. And, therefore, the greater the rate of evaporation contemplated per foot of grate, the greater also should be the heating surface, to secure an equally economical use of the fuel.

Further, with reference to the more modern results, Obs. 17–62, we observe considerable differences even in the same circumstances as to proportion of surfaces and evaporation, which point to other causes affecting the economy of the boiler, arising, we believe, out of the proximity of the tubes to each other, and the depth of the whole pile of the tubes, or number of rows. Comparing the C. R. goods-engines with the passenger-engines, we almost uniformly find the former inferior to the latter in economy of evaporation, at the same rates per foot of grate, notwithstanding the much greater surface of the goods-engines. Though this inferiority is due partly to circumstances already explained, it is doubtless due also to the smaller clearance between the tubes of the goods-engines, being only ⅜ and ½ inch, while that of the passenger-engines is ⅜ and ⁷⁄₁₆ inch, and gives freer scope for the circulation of water and the disengagement of steam.

Comparing, again, the results from the G. W. R. engines of the Great Britain and Courier class, Obs. 28, 29, 30, with those from the C. R., and E. & G. R. engines, Obs. 46–58, the former are inferior in economic evaporation to the latter, though they have a greater relative heating surface. As the Welsh coke used on the Great Western Railway, has been found at least equal in quality to that employed in the North of England and in Scotland,* the inferior results of the G. W. R. boilers, are, we believe, caused by the much greater mass of tubes brought together in the larger engines, being 305 in number, or more than twice as many as are in some of the other boilers : and though their number is much greater, they are only ½ inch clear, while in the other boilers the clearance is from ⅝ to 1 inch ; neither is there any greater free space for water between the tubes and the sides of the boiler, though from the larger diameter of barrel, there are 17 rows of tubes, and 22 tubes in the longest rows, whereas in the C. R. passenger-engines, there are only 12 rows, and 16 tubes in the longest row. The number and distribution of the tubes in the barrel is shown in fig. 181 for different boilers, from which it is plain that,

Fig. 181.—Scale 1-64th.

Sphynx—142 tubes.　　C. R. passenger Engine—　　Great Britain—305 tubes.
　　　　　　　　　　　158 tubes.

SECTIONS OF BOILERS TO ILLUSTRATE FREEDOM FOR CIRCULATION.

with the larger mass of tubes, the facilities for the circulation of water and the removal of the steam are less in the Great Britain than in the other boilers ; and it ought to follow, from the greater entanglement of the steam among the tubes, that, as we find in fact, the evaporative efficiency of the heating surface of the Great Britain, measured by economy of evaporation, is inferior to that of the other engines.

It is further to be noted, as a circumstance in favour of the Great Britain, that, by Table LXV., the sectional area of flue-way through the tubes is much greater in proportion to the area of grate, than in most of the other engines, and that therefore the smoke will by so much pass less rapidly through them, and remain longer in contact. We have therefore the more confidence in attributing the inferiority of the larger boiler to the want of clearance among the tubes.

* Sewell on *Locomotion*, vol. i., 1852.

These results show that the clearance between the tubes should have some proportion to the total number of tubes employed. It may be added that some makers, amongst whom we may instance the Hawthorns, Kitson & Co., and Mr. Paton (E. & G. R.), appear from their practice to be aware of the necessity of a greater clearance than is usually admitted, as they allow from ¾ to 1 inch in their own engines.

Confining our attention, for the present, to the cases which yield the most economical evaporation, by which we mean an evaporation of about 9 lbs. of water per pound of coke, it appears that, in the Orion, the Sirius, and the Pallas, E. & G. R., with a mean heating surface of about 50 times the grate, a mean of 8·9 lbs. of water is evaporated per pound of coke, at a rate of about 6 feet per hour per foot of grate. Again in the C. R. passenger-engines, when judiciously worked, as in Obs. 48–50, and 53, with a surface of 66 times the grate, we have a poundage of water equal to 9·1 lbs., at a mean rate of 8 feet per foot of grate. The Snake, Obs. 31, with a surface 72 times the grate, and an hourly consumption of 12·26, or, say, 12 feet per foot of grate, evaporated 8·9 pounds. Lastly, the Sphynx, Obs. 32, with a surface of 90 times, and an hourly consumption of 22·1 feet per foot, evaporated 8·75 lbs. Indeed, as the estimated coke used includes what was burnt in the descent of the incline towards Sheffield, though a very small quantity, while the stated water was exclusively what was used during the ascent from Manchester, the coke must have evaporated a little more than we have given it credit for, or, as a round number, 9 lbs. per pound of coke. Associating with this engine, the A and Hercules, Obs. 18, 20, the total means of the three show that with a surface of 90 times, and an hourly consumption of 17·8, or, say 18 feet per foot of grate, 8·92 pounds per pound of coke was evaporated. In all these cases, the heating surface has been very fairly proportioned to the evaporation, as, in all of them, as much as 9 lbs. of water has been evaporated per pound of coke. In these cases, also, the number of tubes ranges between 125 and 158, disposed in from 10 to 12 rows, with from ⁷⁄₁₆ to 1 inch clearance ; except the Snake, which has 181 tubes, in 13 rows, with ½ inch clearance. With reference, then, to boilers which range within these limits, or are under equally favourable conditions, some useful rules may be deduced from the results just referred to, and which are assembled in the following table :—

TABLE, No. LXXXII.—OF RELATIVE HEATING SURFACES AND
RATES OF CONSUMPTION.

Classified Group of Engines.	Ratio of Heating Surface to Grate-area.	Consumption of Water per hour per square foot of		Water evaporated per pound of Coke.	Number of sample trips from which these results are deduced.
		Grate.	Heating surface.		
	ratio.	cub. feet.	cub. feet.	lbs.	trips.
Orion, &c.	52	6·15	·12	9	13
C.R., passr.	66	8	·13	9·1	17
Snake	72	12	·17	8·9	2
Sphynx, &c.	90	18	·20	8·92	8*
1	2	3	4	5	6

The table shows that the consumption per hour per foot

* Namely, 1 trip with Sphynx, 5 with "York" A, and 2 with "York" Hercules.

of grate, col. 3, may be increased in a much greater ratio per foot of grate, consistent with economical evaporation, than the heating surface, col. 2; for, whereas in the fourth group, the surface is not double that of the first, the consumption per foot of grate is thrice that of the other; indeed the latter increases virtually as the square of the former, as may at once be shown by throwing the contents of col. 3 into a curve, fig. 182, of which the base-line A B

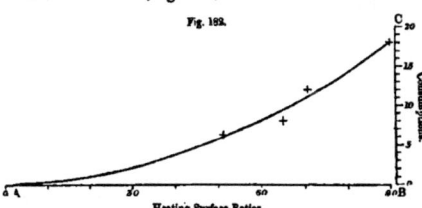

Fig. 182.

Heating Surface-Ratios.
DIAGRAM TO SHOW RATE OF ECONOMICAL CONSUMPTION OF WATER PER HOUR PER FOOT OF GRATE, FOR GIVEN SURFACE-RATIOS.

measures the ratios of heating surface, col. 2, set off at points 52, 66, 72, and 90 graduations from A; verticals being drawn from these points equal by the vertical scale C to the respective contents of col. 3, and terminated by stars, the mean curve traced closely through these stars, has the verticals varying as the squares of the surface-ratios in the base-line. At B, or 90 in the base-line, the curve starts exactly from the 18 feet star; and from this a formula may be found for the feet due to any other surface-ratio.

Practical Rules and Tables for the Proportions of Locomotive-Boilers.—Let $f =$ the feet required for any other ratio, r; then, as the feet vary as the square of the ratio,

$$90^2 : r^2 :: 18 : f$$

or $f = \dfrac{18 \, r^2}{90^2}$, and, by reducing, $f = \cdot00222 \, r^2$.

As r is equal to the heating surface divided by the grate-area, which may be symbolised by h and g respectively,

then $r = \dfrac{h}{g}$, and substituting in the above equation,

$$f = \cdot00222 \left(\frac{h}{g} \right)^2 \qquad . \quad . \quad . \quad . \quad . \quad . \quad . \quad (1.)$$

The quantities in the 4th column of the foregoing table are obviously deducible from the contents of col. 3 by dividing these by the respective surface-ratios in col. 2; and it is remarkable that the efficiency per square foot of total surface, as shown in col. 4, consistent with economical evaporation, *increases* as the relative heating surface, col. 2, increases; in other words, the more heating surface that is given to a boiler with the same grate-area, the greater is the economical evaporative power per foot of surface. In fact, by the table, when the surface is but 52 times the grate, each square foot can evaporate but ·12 feet of water per hour with economy, but when the surface is increased to 90 times the grate, each foot of surface may economically evaporate ·20 foot per hour.

The formula (1.) above found may be modified to suit the contents of col. 4. Let $f' =$ the economical consumption per hour per foot of heating surface, for a given surface-ratio, r. Now, as above stated,

$f' = \dfrac{f}{r}$, and, therefore $f' r = f$.

Substituting this value of f in the equation $f = \cdot00222 \, r^2$, we have

$f' r = \cdot00222 \, r^2$, and, dividing by r, $f' = \cdot00222 \, r$.

Substituting $\dfrac{h}{g}$ for r in this equation, we have

$$f' = \cdot00222 \, \frac{h}{g} \qquad . \quad . \quad . \quad . \quad . \quad . \quad . \quad . \quad (2.)$$

Lastly, to find the consumption in terms of the whole grate-area and heating surface, in fact, the total consumption (which make = c), we may either multiply the second term of (1.) by g, or the second term of (2.) by h. Either way we have

$$c = \cdot00222 \, \frac{h^2}{g} \qquad . \quad . \quad . \quad . \quad . \quad . \quad . \quad (3.)$$

To find the heating surface in terms of the grate-area and the consumption, we have, by inverting formula (3.),

$c \, g = \cdot00222 \, h^2$, whence $h^2 = \dfrac{c \, g}{\cdot00222} \quad 450 \, c \, g$;

and, taking the square root of both sides,

$$h = 21 \cdot 2 \, \sqrt{c \, g} \qquad . \quad . \quad . \quad . \quad . \quad . \quad . \quad . \quad (4.)$$

To find the grate-area in terms of the heating surface and the consumption, we have, from (3.), as before,

$c \, g = \cdot00222 \, h^2$, and dividing both sides by c,

$$g = \cdot00222 \, \frac{h^2}{c} \qquad . \quad . \quad . \quad . \quad . \quad . \quad . \quad (5.)$$

The last three formulas enable us to find any one of the three terms,—grate-area, heating surface, and consumption, when the two other terms are given; and all the five formulas are convertible into the following rules, which are expected to apply with correctness only to locomotive-boilers of the prevailing form,—with horizontal tubes,—and having the tubes arranged as favourably for free evaporation as in the engines from which the rules have been deduced.

RULES I., II., III.—*To find the greatest Rate of Consumption of Water consistent with its economical evaporation, for a given heating surface and grate-area.*

1st. The rate of consumption *per square foot of grate-area.* Divide the heating surface by the grate-area, both in superficial feet,—square the quotient,—and multiply by ·00222. The product is the consumption in cubic feet per hour per square foot of grate.

2d. The rate of consumption *per square foot of heating surface.* Divide the heating surface by the grate-area, both in square feet,—and multiply by ·00222. The product is the consumption in cubic feet per hour per square foot of heating surface.

3d. The rate of *total consumption.* Divide the square of the heating surface by the grate-area, both in feet,—and multiply by ·00222. The product is the total consumption in cubic feet per hour.

RULE IV.—*To find the Heating Surface necessary to maintain a given hourly Consumption of Water economically, with a given area of grate.*—Multiply the grate-area in square feet, by the consumption of water in cubic feet per hour,—find the square root of the product;—and multiply the root so found by 21·2. The final product is the area of heating surface in square feet.

RULE V.—*To find the Grate-area suitable for maintaining a given hourly Consumption of Water economically, with a given heating surface.*—Divide the square of the heating surface in feet, by the consumption of water in cubic feet per hour,—and multiply by ·00222. The product is the area of grate in square feet.

By the aid of the first and second rules, the 2d and 3d columns of the following table are calculated,—the surface-ratios in the 1st column being taken as the quotients obtained by dividing the heating surface by the grate-area, according to the first step of the rules. The last column, of the consumption of coke per foot of grate, is estimated from the contents of the second column, allowing 1 lb. coke to 9 lbs. water.

TABLE, No. LXXXIII.—OF THE GREATEST RATES OF CONSUMPTION OF WATER CONSISTENT WITH ITS ECONOMICAL EVAPORATION, AT THE RATE OF 9 LBS. PER POUND OF COKE, FOR GIVEN PROPORTIONS OF HEATING SURFACE AND GRATE-AREA.

Ratio of Heating surface to Area of Grate, found by dividing the former by the latter.	Economical Consumption of Water per hour		Economical Consumption of Coke per hour, per square foot of Grate.
	Per square foot of Grate.	Per square foot of Heating Surface.	
Ratio, Grate = 1.	cubic feet.	cubic feet.	lbs.
30	2·0	·07	14
35	2·7	·08	18·75
40	3·55	·09	24·6
45	4·5	·10	31·25
50	5·5	·11	38·2
55	6·7	·12	46·5
60	8·0	·13	55·6
65	9·4	·14	65·3
70	10·9	·155	75·7
75	12·5	·166	86·8
80	14·1	·18	97·9
85	15·9	·19	110·4
90	18·0	·20	125
95	20·0	·21	139
100	22·0	·22	153

For intermediate surface-ratios not named in this table, the intermediate values of the consumption may readily be deduced from the contents of the second and third columns; conversely, for a given rate of consumption the necessary surface-ratio may be found.

Though the foregoing table is useful so far as it goes, it is still desirable to construct a table which should afford the means of at once determining either the grate-area, the heating surface, or the consumption, when the other two quantities are given. The Table, No. LXXXIV., is constructed for this object, by means of Rule IV.; it shows all the combinations of grate-area, heating surface, and water-consumption, consistent with economical evaporation. Along the top of the table are ranged the grate-areas, advancing by 1 foot intervals from 4 to 30 square feet; in the margins the total consumptions of water are placed, from 20 to 400 cubic feet per hour. In the body of the table are placed the heating surfaces due to the respective grate-areas and consumptions, below and opposite to which they are placed, the rate of evaporation being assumed at a minimum of 2 feet, and a maximum of 22 feet per foot of grate per hour. The table is equally serviceable for finding the consumption due to a given grate-area and heating surface, or the grate-area due to a given consumption and heating surface. For fractional quantities not found in the table, proportional values may be allowed, and may be easily estimated from the nearest values recorded.

To secure the same conditions for evaporation in boilers proportioned from this table, equally favourable with those on the results of which the table is founded, it is necessary that the clearance of the tubes should bear some ratio to the number of tubes employed. As, in all boilers, the tubes, few or many, are disposed much in the same way, in the lower part of the barrel (Fig. 181), it is sufficient, in estimating the necessary clearance, to refer simply to the number and diameter of the tubes. The quantity of steam raised from the tubes, and the water required to replace the steam, are presumed to increase in proportion to their number: the facilities for the circulation of the water, and for the ascent of the steam through the mass of tubes, should therefore be increased in the same proportion. In other words, the clearance between the tubes themselves, and between them and the boiler, should be in proportion to their number. The circumstances of the tubes in some of the engines on which the table is founded are as follow:—

		Diameter.	Clearance.
Orion, Sirius,	125 tubes,	2 ins.	1 in.
Pallas,	134 do.	2 ins.	¾ in.
C.R. Pass. Engine,	158 do.	1¾ ins.	11/16 in.
Snake,	181 do.	1⅝ ins.	½ in.
Sphynx,	142 do.	2⅛ ins.	9/16 in. nearly.

The data for the York engines, A and Hercules, are uncertain, but the usual clearance in Stephenson's long boilers, of which these are examples, is fully ½ inch for 1⅝ and 2 inch tubes, 125 to 140 in number. The diameter of the tubes need not be taken into the question, as the diameters employed in modern practice vary very little from 2 inches outside, being regulated, not by the size of boiler, but by the necessity of being large enough to pass the cinders which are occasionally dragged from the firebox; and also small enough to multiply and increase the surface as required.

Passing over the Snake, as her observed performance was limited to two trips, we find that the Sphynx and the other long boilers, with about 142 tubes, have nearly 9/16 inch clearance, and the C. R. passenger engines with 158 tubes have 11/16 inch; the mean of these gives, for 150 tubes, ⅝ inch clearance. This allowance having been found to work well, we should infer that in the Orion and the Pallas the clearance is more than sufficient, and we shall adopt the result just found as a standard. A clearance of ⅝ inch for 150 tubes, is at the rate of ⅛ inch for every thirty tubes, as 150 ÷ 5 = 30. We have, then, only to divide the total number of tubes in a given boiler by 30, to find the suitable clearance in eighths of an inch; whence the following rule:—

RULE VI.—*To find the clearance between the tubes, suitable for economical evaporation, for a given number of tubes.*—Divide the number of tubes by 30. The quotient is the required clearance in eighths of an inch.

By this rule the following Table, No. LXXXV., is constructed.

As clearance between the tubes is most essential about the centre of the mass, from which most of the steam rises, the tubes may with propriety be placed closer together at the bottom than is named in the table, particularly where it is de-

TABLE, No. LXXXIV.—OF RELATIVE GRATE-AREAS, HEATING SURFACES, AND MAXIMUM CONSUMPTIONS OF WATER CONSISTENT WITH ECONOMICAL EVAPORATION, AT THE RATE OF 9 LBS. OF WATER PER POUND OF COKE.

Total consumptions of water per hour, in cubic feet	Areas of Grate, in square feet.																											Total consumptions of water per hour, in cubic feet
	4	5	6	7	8	9	10	11	12	13	14	15	16	17	18	19	20	21	22	23	24	25	26	27	28	29	30	
	Total Heating Surfaces, in square feet, relative to the above Grate-areas, and the annexed Consumptions.																											
20	190	212	232	251	268	284	300	..	..	..	..	..	..	..	..	..	..	..	..	..	..	..	..	..	..	..	..	20
25	212	237	260	280	300	318	335	352	367	382	..	..	..	..	..	..	..	..	..	..	..	..	..	..	..	..	..	25
30	232	260	285	307	328	348	367	385	402	419	434	450	..	..	..	..	..	..	..	..	..	..	..	..	..	..	..	30
35	251	280	307	332	355	376	396	416	434	452	469	486	502	517	532	..	..	..	..	..	..	..	..	..	..	..	..	35
40	268	300	328	355	379	402	424	444	464	483	501	519	536	553	569	585	600	..	..	..	..	..	..	..	..	..	..	40
45	284	318	348	376	402	427	450	473	492	513	532	551	569	587	603	620	636	653	670	682	..	..	..	..	..	..	..	45
50	300	335	367	396	424	450	474	497	519	541	561	580	599	618	636	653	670	687	703	719	734	750	..	..	..	..	..	50
55	315	342	385	416	445	472	497	521	545	567	588	608	628	647	667	685	702	720	737	754	770	786	802	817	..	..	..	55
60	328	367	402	435	464	493	519	545	569	593	614	636	657	676	697	716	734	752	770	788	805	821	837	853	869	885	900	60
65	342	382	419	452	484	512	541	569	593	616	639	661	683	703	725	742	764	780	801	819	837	854	871	887	904	920	936	65
70	355	396	435	469	502	530	562	590	614	639	663	686	709	730	752	773	793	812	831	850	869	887	904	921	938	955	972	70
75	367	410	450	485	519	550	581	610	636	661	686	710	734	756	779	800	821	841	860	879	900	917	935	952	971	984	1006	75
80	379	424	464	501	546	569	600	629	657	683	709	734	758	782	805	827	848	869	889	908	927	947	966	985	1004	1012	1039	80
85	391	437	479	517	553	586	618	651	676	704	731	757	782	806	829	852	874	896	916	936	957	977	996	1016	1034	1048	1071	85
90	402	450	493	532	569	603	636	670	697	725	752	779	805	829	853	877	900	922	943	964	985	1006	1025	1045	1064	1083	1102	90
95	..	463	506	547	584	620	653	687	716	745	773	800	827	852	877	901	924	947	969	991	1013	1033	1053	1074	1093	1113	1132	95
100	..	474	519	561	599	636	670	703	734	764	793	821	848	874	900	924	948	972	995	1017	1039	1060	1081	1102	1122	1142	1161	100
110	..	..	545	588	628	667	702	737	770	802	831	861	888	916	943	969	994	1018	1042	1066	1089	1111	1133	1155	1176	1197	1217	110
120	..	..	569	614	657	697	734	770	805	837	869	900	927	957	985	1013	1039	1064	1089	1114	1138	1162	1184	1207	1229	1251	1272	120
130	..	..	593	639	683	725	764	801	837	871	904	936	965	996	1025	1053	1081	1107	1133	1159	1184	1208	1232	1255	1278	1300	1323	130
140	..	..	..	663	709	752	793	831	869	904	938	972	1003	1034	1064	1093	1122	1150	1177	1203	1229	1254	1279	1303	1327	1351	1374	140
150	..	..	..	686	734	779	821	860	900	935	971	1006	1038	1070	1101	1131	1161	1190	1218	1245	1272	1298	1323	1350	1373	1398	1422	150
160	..	..	..	..	758	805	848	889	927	966	1004	1039	1073	1106	1138	1169	1199	1229	1258	1286	1314	1341	1367	1393	1419	1444	1469	160
170	..	..	..	..	782	829	874	916	957	996	1034	1071	1106	1140	1173	1205	1236	1266	1296	1325	1354	1382	1409	1436	1463	1488	1514	170
180	..	..	..	..	805	853	900	943	985	1025	1064	1102	1138	1173	1207	1240	1272	1303	1334	1364	1393	1422	1450	1478	1505	1532	1558	180
190	..	..	..	..	..	877	924	969	1013	1053	1093	1132	1169	1205	1240	1274	1307	1339	1370	1401	1431	1461	1490	1518	1546	1573	1600	190
200	..	..	..	..	..	900	948	995	1039	1081	1122	1161	1199	1236	1272	1307	1341	1374	1406	1437	1468	1499	1529	1558	1586	1614	1642	200
210	..	..	..	..	..	928	974	1019	1064	1107	1149	1189	1229	1264	1298	1336	1374	1408	1441	1473	1505	1536	1566	1596	1625	1654	1683	210
220	..	..	..	..	..	..	1000	1042	1089	1133	1176	1217	1258	1291	1324	1365	1406	1441	1475	1508	1541	1572	1603	1634	1664	1693	1722	220
230	..	..	..	..	..	..	1019	1067	1114	1159	1203	1245	1286	1323	1359	1398	1437	1473	1508	1542	1575	1607	1639	1663	1701	1724	1761	230
240	..	..	..	..	..	..	..	1091	1138	1184	1229	1272	1314	1354	1393	1431	1468	1505	1541	1575	1609	1642	1675	1692	1738	1754	1799	240
250	..	..	..	..	..	..	..	1111	1162	1208	1254	1298	1341	1380	1422	1458	1499	1533	1572	1606	1642	1675	1709	1733	1774	1797	1836	250
260	..	..	..	..	..	..	..	..	1184	1232	1278	1323	1367	1406	1450	1484	1529	1560	1603	1636	1675	1708	1743	1774	1809	1840	1872	260
270	..	..	..	..	..	..	..	..	1207	1256	1303	1349	1401	1433	1478	1515	1557	1592	1634	1668	1692	1741	1776	1808	1843	1875	1908	270
280	..	..	..	..	..	..	..	..	..	1279	1327	1374	1435	1460	1505	1546	1586	1624	1664	1700	1738	1774	1809	1842	1877	1910	1948	280
290	..	..	..	..	..	..	..	..	..	1302	1351	1400	1452	1486	1532	1573	1614	1653	1693	1729	1754	1804	1841	1873	1910	1939	1977	290
300	..	..	..	..	..	..	..	..	..	..	1374	1425	1469	1512	1558	1600	1642	1682	1723	1758	1799	1834	1872	1904	1943	1968	2011	300
320	..	..	..	..	..	..	..	..	..	..	..	1469	1516	1564	1610	1654	1696	1738	1778	1816	1859	1894	1932	1970	2008	2024	2078	320
340	..	..	..	..	..	..	..	..	..	..	..	..	1564	1612	1658	1704	1748	1792	1833	1872	1915	1954	1993	2032	2069	2096	2141	340
360	..	..	..	..	..	..	..	..	..	..	..	..	..	1658	1706	1754	1800	1844	1886	1928	1971	2012	2050	2090	2128	2166	2204	360
380	..	..	..	..	..	..	..	..	..	..	..	..	..	..	1753	1802	1848	1894	1938	1982	2025	2066	2107	2148	2187	2226	2264	380
400	..	..	..	..	..	..	..	..	..	..	..	..	..	..	1800	1848	1900	1944	1990	2034	2077	2120	2162	2204	2244	2284	2322	400

NOTE 1.—For values intermediate between those in this table, the quantities relative to the nearest expressed value may be adopted. Or, if great accuracy be demanded, proportional allowances may be made for the observed differences from the nearest expressed values.

2.—The proportions in this table should be selected for maximum evaporations not exceeding 16 cubic feet per hour per foot of grate, due to the combustion of 112 lbs. of good coke per hour per foot. This allows for inferior qualities of coke, and moderates the intensity of combustion.

3.—Still lower maximum rates of evaporation should be adopted for grates less than 8 feet, to meet the practical difficulties of working with very small grates, as follow:—

Areas of grate, ...	4,	5,	6,	7,	8 square feet.	
Suitable Maximum Rates of Evaporation,	11,	12,	13,	14,	16 cubic feet of water per hour per foot of grate.	
Relative Consumptions of Coke, .	76,	83,	90,	97,	112 pounds per hour per foot of grate.	

TABLE, No LXXXV.—OF THE CLEARANCE BETWEEN THE TUBES SUITABLE FOR ECONOMICAL EVAPORATION, AT THE RATE OF 9 LBS. WATER PER POUND OF COKE.

Number of Tubes.	Clearance between Tubes.	Number of Tubes.	Clearance between Tubes
	inch.		inch.
below 90	$\frac{3}{8}$	195 to 210	$\frac{7}{8}$
90 to 105	$\frac{7}{16}$	210 to 225	$\frac{15}{16}$
105 to 120	$\frac{1}{2}$	225 to 240	1
120 to 135	$\frac{9}{16}$	240 to 255	$1\frac{1}{16}$
135 to 150	$\frac{5}{8}$	255 to 270	$1\frac{1}{8}$
150 to 165	$\frac{11}{16}$	270 to 285	$1\frac{3}{16}$
165 to 180	$\frac{3}{4}$	285 to 300	$1\frac{1}{4}$
180 to 195	$\frac{13}{16}$		

NOTE.—The lateral clearance between the upper rows of tubes and the barrel, should be at least $\frac{1}{16}$th of the diameter of barrel, at each side.

sirable to increase their number, and opening out gradually towards the upper rows. If, also, the number be unduly restricted by the demand for clearance, the remedy, for obtaining a sufficiency of surface, is to increase their length.

General Deductions.—From the equations established between grate-area, heating surface, and maximum economical consumption, it follows that

1st. The economical hourly consumption *decreases* directly as the grate-area is increased; that is, the larger the grate, the smaller is the economical consumption, *even with the same heating surface*, showing that the economic value of heating surface is reduced by increasing the grate.

2d. The economical hourly consumption *increases* directly as the square of the heating surface; that is, the greater the heating surface, the greater also is the economical consumption, and at such a rate that twice the heating surface would yield four times the consumption, with the same grate-area; thus, the economic evaporative power increases at a higher rate than the surface; and therefore an increase of surface increases the economic value of each square foot of that surface.

3d. The necessary heating surface *increases* directly as the square root of the consumption; that is, for four times the consumption, twice the surface only would be required.

4th. The necessary heating surface *increases* directly as the square root of the grate; that is, for four times the grate, twice the surface would be required, to meet the same economical consumption.

Thus, practically, there can never be too much heating surface, as regards economical evaporation, but there may be too little; on the other hand, there may be too much grate-area for economical evaporation but there cannot be too little, so long as the required rate of combustion does not exceed the limits to be afterwards defined.

Examples of the Application of the foregoing Rules.—Though the foregoing discussion is based upon conditions of economical evaporation, these conditions are in practice very commonly overlooked, in so far as the rate of evaporation per pound of fuel is often much below the economical pitch. For example, with No. 13, C. R., while it evaporates comfortably 86 feet of water per hour at 9 lbs. per pound of coke, yet, with a forced evaporation of 122 feet per hour, and a relative deficiency of surface, it raises only 6·8 lbs. per pound of coke: the poundage of water indeed is reduced nearly at the same rate that the total evaporation is increased. The Hecla, by the table, would not evaporate above 45 feet of water economically: the observed evaporation was 94 feet, fully double, and the poundage of water was 5·63 lbs., or less than two-thirds of the economical standard, 9 lbs.,—no allowance off that poundage being made for priming. To meet those demands economically, No. 13 should by the table have had 760 feet of heating surface, or an addition of 63 feet, and the Hecla should have had 590 feet of surface, or 172 feet more. These examples show that an increase of evaporation per hour above that economically due to the grate and the surface, is attended by a reduction of the poundage of water raised per pound of fuel, in nearly the ratio of the increase; so that if the evaporation be doubled, the poundage is reduced to nearly one-half, and the extra evaporation is thus obtained at a much greater extra rate of combustion, and a very great sacrifice of fuel. The examples also illustrate the virtue of heating surface, as the additional surfaces necessary to restore economical evaporation, represented by 12 or 18 extra tubes, are a very small fraction of the existing surfaces, compared with the extra economical advantages.

As the economic value of the heating surface is materially affected by the grate-area, being less as the area is greater, it is clearly of advantage to have as small a grate as is consistent with the demands for steam, in order that it should at least come within the economic limits; and, on the other hand, there can be no economical objection to any amount of heating surface which can be got into a boiler, consistently with the conditions of clearance: extra heating surface not only by so much adds to the economical evaporative capacity of the boiler, but the felicity is that it increases that of the previously existing surface. If No. 13, C. R., instead of having an addition of heating surface, as before suggested, had a grate of 9 square feet, or 1½ feet less than it actually has, it would with the same heating surface have evaporated 122 feet per hour, or 13·55 feet per foot of grate, with economy of coke in the ratio of 6·8 to 9 lbs. of water. Moreover, the economy would have been so great as to have reduced the rate of combustion *per foot of grate*, notwithstanding the smaller area of the latter. Similarly, had the grate of the Hecla been of but half the size, it would have evaporated the same water with much less coke, and with very little increase in the rate of combustion per foot of grate.

There are, in short, two ways of remedying defective proportions,—defective so far as economical evaporation is required,—by increasing the heating surface, or by reducing the grate-area, either of which increases the economic value of the heating surface. Table LXXXIV. furnishes some striking contrasts of this kind: to show what may be done by increasing the surface, the following economical consumptions with a 10 feet grate, are due to the heating surfaces annexed:—

Consumptions,   20, 40, 80. 160, 220 cubic feet;
Heating surfaces, 300, 424, 600, 848, 1000 square feet,

showing that, with the same grate, an increase of surface, from 300 to 1000 feet, or 3⅓ times, raises the capacity for economic evaporation at a much higher rate,—as the square of the surface,—from 20 to 220 feet, or 11 times. Again, with a given surface of 500 feet, the following are the maximum economical consumptions effected with the annexed grate-areas:—

Consumptions, 35, 40, 47, 55, 70, 93 cubic feet,
Grate-areas, 16, 14, 12, 10, 8, 6 square feet,

showing that the same heating surface is actually raised in economic value, and will economically evaporate larger quantities of water per hour, by reducing the grate-area:—the consumption is thus doubled from 35 to 70 feet, by reducing the grate-area one-half, from 16 to 8 feet.

The increased economic value of heating surface when associated with a reduced grate-area, is strikingly exemplified in the performance of the Great Britain and Iron Duke, Obs. 28, Table LXXXI., contrasted with that of the Sphynx, Obs. 32. As these engines have about equal proportions of heating surface per foot of grate, we must attribute the inferior poundage of water per pound of coke in the former case, to the incidental deficiency of clearance between the tubes. The striking fact is, that the Sphynx, with a 10½ feet grate, evaporates 233 feet per hour as economically as the Great Britain with a 21 feet grate; that is, that by making a liberal and sufficient allowance of heating surface, or,—taking another view of it,—by making a sufficiently small grate, the small grate may, by increasing the intensity of the combustion, and at the same time increasing the value of the surface, evaporate great quantities of water as economically as a larger grate. It is true, the capabilities of the boiler of the Sphynx were probably strained to the utmost in doing what the Great Britain did with ease; it is true, also, that the Great Britain would, by Table LXXXIV., evaporate 330 feet of water with equal economy, supposing the tubes set with sufficient clearance; still the performance of the Sphynx shows what can be done with a moderate grate, when there is plenty of heating surface to back it out, and, further, it vindicates, in conjunction with the A and Hercules engines, Obs. 18 and 20, the adoption of the "long boiler" plan,—of which these engines are examples,—so far as concerns the evaporating function.

In the Great Britain, with 305 tubes, there is, as we have seen, only ½ inch clearance, which has been shown to be injuriously small: the tubes should have been 1¼ inch apart. But, by the Table of relative proportions, No. LXXXIV., a total surface of 1473 feet, or 296 feet less than the actual, with the tubes suitably apart, would have evaporated 230 feet of water with economy; now one tube gives 5·3 feet of surface, and 296 ÷ 5·3 = 56, the number of tubes that might be removed with advantage, leaving 305 − 56 = 249 tubes remaining. By Table LXXXV., these ought to be 1 1/16 inch apart, and though this interval could not be maintained throughout, even with a reduced number of 249 tubes, yet by keeping the lower tubes closer, the same result would be had; and consequently the Great Britain could be made a more economical engine by withdrawing 20 per cent. of the tube-surface.*

Of the Maximum Rates of Combustion and Evaporation to be adopted in practice.—To define the limits within which the conclusions to which we have come may be followed out in practice, it is necessary to find the maximum rate at which the combustion of coke may be properly effected, as this is the ultimate limit to the rate of evaporation. In contemplating maximum rates, it is presumed that the coke employed be of good quality,—well converted, round, solid, and weighty. The results from the Sphynx show probably the greatest rate of efficient combustion on record,—157 lbs. of coke per square foot of grate per hour. That this was a case of real and thorough combustion, is confirmed by the consistent proportion of water evaporated; and from the position of the steam-dome, there was little likelihood of priming. In this conclusion we are confirmed by Mr. Peacock, who states that there is no material difference in the action of the boilers of the Sphynx class from that of larger boilers, as regards the condition of the fuel or the behaviour of the water, and, as a test of the efficiency of the combustion, he adds that he finds no difference as to the length of time in clearing the tubes and cleaning out the smoke-boxes.

It was concluded that 9 lbs. of water were evaporated by 1 lb. of fuel, in the experiment with the Sphynx; at this rate, the combustion would have been, for the observed evaporation, exactly equal to 153⅓ lbs. of coke per hour per foot of grate. This rate is approached in the experiments with the Hecla and other engines, in which 120 to 140 pounds per hour per foot of grate were consumed. The feasibility of such high rates is thus confirmed; indeed, it is rather to the earlier practice with very short boilers and deficient heating surface, that we have to look for cases of rapid combustion. Some of the earlier passenger-engines of the Grand Junction Railway have been found to consume 50 lbs. of best coke per mile, with 9 feet grates. At 30 miles per hour, this would amount to 50 × 30 ÷ 9 = 167 lbs. per hour per foot of grate, when it was well known that the coke was shaken and broken in the firebox by the violence of the draft. The rate of consumption was clearly extravagant, and, therefore, in general it may be concluded that the maximum rate of efficient combustion of good coke in the firebox of the locomotive has been found in practice to be about 150 pounds per hour per foot of grate.

The minimum rate of economical combustion is a matter which has not been definitely ascertained, nor is it of importance in the locomotive. In the Table of proportions, No. LXXXIV., 2 feet of water per hour per foot of grate is assumed to be the lowest rate worth providing for in practice; and is equivalent to a combustion of 14 lbs. of coke. It is proved by daily experience that an engine, with 10½ feet of grate carefully damped up, so as to retard as much as possible the waste of fuel, while at rest, may burn off above 50 lbs.

* It follows, also, that the Liverpool, the much lauded rival of the Great Britain, described at page 19, inasmuch as she had 300 tubes, only 1/16 inch clear—was *less* powerful than this engine, though she had *more* surface.

of coke per hour, without any apparent loss of steam at the safety-valve. This is equal to a combustion of about 5 lbs. per hour per foot of grate, without any sensible generation of steam; and it is probable that about 14 lbs. of coke per hour per foot of grate is the lowest useful rate in practice.

From our own experience we have found, that in well-managed boilers, good coke may be properly consumed at a rate of 100 lbs. to 112 lbs. at least, per hour per foot of grate, without involving any objectionable consequences to the boiler. Higher rates are attainable; but the higher the rate, the more intense is the combustion, and as a general rule for practice, as well as to allow for inferior qualities of coke, a rate of combustion equal to 112 lbs., or 1 cwt., of coke per hour per foot of grate, is recommended as the maximum rate at which locomotive-boilers should be designed to work.

Agreeably to this conclusion, 16 cubic feet of water per hour per foot of grate, allowing 9 lbs. per pound of coke, should be adopted as the maximum rate of evaporation for locomotive-boilers.

The proportion of heating surface required for meeting these rates of consumption, by Table LXXXIII., is 85 feet per foot of grate; and this is recommended as the lowest proportion of heating surface that should be adopted for locomotive-boilers.

Though it has been shown that much may be done by adjusting the grate to the heating surface, there is a limit below which the grate-area should not be reduced, and for trespassing which indeed there can be no physical necessity. Coke is most efficiently burnt in masses, and the grate should be at least large enough to meet this condition. An area of 4 square feet is as small as for railway purposes can be required; and a smaller would probably impair the efficiency of combustion, or at least demand an inconvenient degree of attention in firing. Even in the working of the England, E. & G. R., with a small boiler and a 5 feet grate, this inconvenience is found to be very considerable, as the fire is much more liable to variation, and requires more delicate treatment, than in larger grates doing even the same work per foot of grate. Allowing that engine to burn 10 lbs. of coke per mile, with an express train, at 40 miles per hour, the consumption per foot of grate is 10 × 40 : 5 = 80 lbs. per hour per foot of grate. Now, with ordinary 10 or 11 feet grates, this rate of consumption is maintained without difficulty, because the coke is in greater mass, and may be used in larger pieces. The smallest useful area of grate has, for reasons of this nature, been fixed at 4 square feet, in the table of relative proportions; and though in the compilation of this table, 4 feet grates are supposed capable of evaporating 22 feet of water per foot per hour, they should not be trusted with more than half that duty, with a combustion of about 76 lbs. of coke per foot per hour. Larger grates may be trusted with higher duties, and for grates of 8 feet and upwards our standard duty of 16 feet of water, and 112 lbs. of coke per foot per hour, may be adopted. For grates between 4 and 8 feet, the greatest desirable duties are appended in a note to Table LXXXIV.

Influence of Speed on the Evaporative Capacity of Boilers.—Steam may be generated quite as rapidly at low as at high speeds. Indeed, the Sphynx, at 12 miles per hour, does more, per foot of grate, than the other long boilers A and Hercules (Obs. 18, 20) at 48 and 20 miles. No. 127, C. R., at 20 and 8·3 miles (Obs. 34, 35) doing good work in both cases, evaporates equal quantities per hour; in the case of the lower speed, indeed, even more water could have been raised, as the fire-door was kept mostly open to prevent the steam blowing off. It is a matter of common observation that an engine works to the best advantage at a low speed with heavy loads, the meaning of which is, that she "gets steam" with the least trouble to the driver, and plenty of it; as the same engine which would blow off readily at low speeds, proving a redundancy of steam, may require every inch of it at high velocities, and more careful firing to keep up the supply. It may, then, be inferred that, practically, whether the steam be sent through the engine in larger quantities at wider intervals, or in smaller quantities at more frequent intervals; in other words, whether it be worked at lower or at higher speeds, it is capable of evaporating, by the action of the blast, the same quantity of water per hour.

Of the Combustion of Coal.—In a previous chapter, it has been stated that, in the locomotive-boiler, coal has about two-thirds of the evaporative value of coke, per pound weight. The experiments with Goods Engines (Obs. 59, 62) give a mean of 5·375 lbs. water raised per pound of coal; increasing this as 2 to 3, we should have 8 lbs. of water in proportion raised with coke; now, 8 lbs. is probably as much as would have actually been done with coke, seeing that in No. 61, E. & G. R., the steam was raised at a rate much above the economical limit due to the grate and heating surface. In both of these cases, we were convinced at the time of the experiment, the coal might have been, with a little extra care, still more efficiently burnt, and would have done extra duty; and we have confidence in re-stating that, in good practice, a duty of two-thirds of that obtainable from coke, may be had from coal. But, after all, we feel very careless about special provisions for economically burning coal. *Coal, at least of the ordinary bituminous kinds, ought not to be used as a staple fuel at all.* It is the mere raw material of fuel,—the ore from which coke is extracted; and contains some valuable compounds which, on the one hand, ought never to be thrown into the furnace, and, on the other, ought not to be wasted by the prevailing system of coking. "At some time hence," says Mr. Buchanan, in his able pamphlet on Smoke-nuisance, "it will be difficult to believe that those hydro-carbons, some of which are in themselves so valuable, and which yet constitute the whole difficulty we have been considering [smoke-nuisance], are actually burned off and entirely lost in the process of coking. The more difficultly manageable of those compounds are obtainable from the coal at temperatures so low, and so easily, and are yet so valuable, from the oil alone, that the fact cannot fail much longer to attract spare capital, and open up a new manufacture, of which we cannot meantime guess the extent."[*] These very just observations point out the true course of improvement; and confirm our impressions that ultimately green bituminous coal will be entirely abandoned as the staple fuel for either locomotive or any other class

of boilers, however useful it may continue to be as an auxiliary.

RECAPITULATION.—1. The quantity, or weight, of water evaporable per hour, at a given rate of combustion, increases with the temperature at which the water is pumped into the boiler.

2. Consequently, the equivalent *weight* of water evaporable from the standard temperature, 62°, decreases as the initial temperature of the water actually evaporated, rises; at such a rate that the equivalent weights fall 1 per cent. for every 10° rise of initial temperature. At this rate, only 85 per cent. of water evaporated from 212°, would be evaporable from 62°.

3. The equivalent *volumes* of water evaporable from 62°, also decrease as the initial temperature rises; but rather more slowly than the equivalent weights, inasmuch as water expands by heat; 88 per cent. of water evaporated at 212°, would be evaporable from 62°.

4. The evaporative efficiency of locomotives depends very much on the management of the fire. Low fires, in general, evaporate more water than deep fires, as there is less coke exposed to waste; the proper use of the ash-pan damper also promotes the economy of combustion, by regulating the draught to the requirements of the time.

5. A poundage of water equal to 9 lbs. per pound of coke, is adopted as the standard of economical consumption, in practice.

6. The rate of evaporation per pound of fuel, or the *poundage* of water, is regulated by the area of the fire-grate, the extent of heating surface, and the rate of consumption per hour. In general, the smaller the fire-grate, the greater the heating surface, and the less the consumption per hour, within certain limits, the greater is the poundage of water. Conversely, the poundage of water falls nearly as the rate of evaporation is increased above the economic limit, involving a reduced efficiency and a heavy sacrifice of fuel.

7. The maximum economical hourly consumption increases directly as the grate-area is reduced, even with the same heating surface; showing that the economic value of heating surface is increased by reducing the grate, and that by this simple expedient, the same heating surface can economically evaporate larger quantities of water per hour.

8. The economical hourly consumption increases directly as the square of the heating surface, with the same grate: so that twice the surface would yield four times the consumption; showing that the economic value of each foot of surface is increased *by merely increasing the surface.*

9. The necessary heating surface increases only as the square root of the consumption, the grate being the same.

10. The necessary heating surface increases as the square root of the grate, the consumption being the same.

11. As the economic value of heating surface depends so much on the grate-area, being less as the area is greater, the grate should be kept as small as is consistent with the demands for steam, and the practicable rate of combustion. On the other hand, there can be no economical objection to any amount of heating surface which can be got into a boiler, even though greater than the economic limits. Thus there are two ways of meeting defective proportions,—by increasing the heating surface, or by reducing the grate, either of

---

[*] *Notes on the Smoke-Nuisance Question*, 1852.

which increases the economic value of the heating surface,—in other words, the economic evaporative power of the boiler.

12. The relations of grate-area, heating surface, and economical consumption are such that

with heating surfaces, 30, 60, 90, 100 times the grate, the maximum economical consumptions are { 2, 8, 18, 22 } cubic feet of water per hour per foot of grate, and 14, 55·6, 125, 153 pounds of coke.

13. The amount of clearance between the tubes affects the evaporative efficiency of the tube-surface; and it ought to be greater, the greater the number of tubes. For ordinary good practice, on which the foregoing conclusions are founded, clearance at the rate of ⅜ inch for every 30 tubes is sufficient; for example, ½ inch for 120 tubes, ⅝ inch for 150 tubes, and ⅜ inch for 180 tubes.

14. The maximum rate of efficient combustion of good coke in the firebox has been found in practice to be about 150 lbs. per hour per foot of grate; and of evaporation, about 22 cubic feet of water per hour per foot.

15. The minimum rate of combustion worth anything for evaporation is probably about 14 lbs. per hour per foot of grate.

16. The maximum rate of combustion recommended for locomotive-boilers is 112 lbs. or 1 cwt. of coke per hour per foot of grate, when the grate has at least 8 feet of surface; and of evaporation, 16 cubic feet of water per hour per foot.

17. These rates of consumption require a heating surface of 85 feet per foot of grate; and this is the lowest proportion that should be adopted for locomotive-boilers.

18. A grate-area of 4 feet is probably the smallest that should be adopted for railway purposes; and as the smallest grates require the greatest attention in firing, a consumption of about 76 lbs. of coke, and 11 feet of water, per hour per foot of grate is the highest duty for which 4 feet grates should be designed; for larger grates the duty may be increased up to the standard for 8 feet grates.

19. The evaporative capacity of locomotive-boilers appears, so far as experience goes, to be the same at all speeds.[*]

20. The economic evaporative value of coal is, according to ordinary practice, about two-thirds of that of coke. But, as coal is not likely to come into more general use as fuel, and will continue to be used only as an auxiliary with coke, it is not necessary to reconsider the proportions of the locomotive-boiler with any view to the increased employment of that fuel.[†]

---

[*] Assuming the efficiency of combustion to be the same, it might be deduced from previous discussions of the relations of evaporative power, blast-pressure, vacuum in the smoke-box, and speed, that the maximum rate of evaporation should be the same for all speeds. This question will be duly considered, when we have to construct a general theory of the locomotive, from the materials supplied by experiment.

[†] The author is gratified to find from the later writings of Mr. Fairbairn of Manchester, and Mr. Buchanan of Glasgow, that his views of the economy of combustion and evaporation harmonize with those of these authorities. Mr. Fairbairn has, in his paper "On the Consumption of Fuel and Prevention of Smoke," (1851), repeatedly recognized and set forth the value of a "large heating surface as opposed to a small grate," and the author is not sure but his formulas for economic proportions might apply to ordinary land and marine boilers. He feels certain that at least the principles on which the formulas are based will be found to apply to other classes of boilers.

SUB-SECTION III.

PHYSIOLOGY OF THE LOCOMOTIVE, AS A CARRIAGE: FRAME, AND WHEELS.

The objects to be aimed at in the arrangement of the locomotive as a carriage, are, that it shall be just heavy enough to secure, by its weight, sufficient adhesion for purposes of traction, that the loads on the wheels be properly distributed to effect this object, and that it shall run steadily on the rails at all practicable speeds. By steadiness or stability is meant the property of moving along the rail without any inclination from the centre-line of progression,—in fact without oscillation or other incidental and erratic movements. Of course, the perfect stability of a slide-lathe or a planing machine is not to be looked for in the motion of a locomotive, as it is affected by small and unavoidable irregularities; but in practice these minor deviations are not considered to bear upon the main question, and, in the language of M. Le Chatelier, "a locomotive is allowed to be steady, or stable, when it has only a very small degree of instability."

The main causes of instability are of three kinds:—The internal disturbing forces generated by the motion of the machinery; those due to the arrangement and the state of repair of the vehicle; and the imperfections of the permanent way.

CHAPTER I.

OF THE INTERNAL DISTURBING FORCES GENERATED BY THE MOTION OF THE MACHINERY.

Historical Summary.—Since 1810, Mr. George Heaton, of Birmingham, has paid great attention to the balancing of machines in motion, with a view both to their stability and their durability. In 1838, he experimented with a model of a railway-carriage wheels and axle, and showed that by loading the wheels on one side, to represent full-size wheels with tyres ⅓-inch unequally thick, instability of various kinds would be developed, when they were rolled along the table. He classed the driving wheels and axles of locomotives, with their revolving appendages, as unbalanced wheels; and proposed to apply counterweights to the wheels, between the spokes, to balance the revolving masses, an idea which was carried out by Mr. M'Connell, in 1842, on the Birmingham and Gloucester Railway. On the Eastern Counties Railway, Mr. E. A. Cowper states, Messrs. Braithwaite and Milner had balanced wheels in the same way, in 1837.[*] About the same time, Messrs. Sharp and Roberts of Manchester, applied balance-weights in their driving wheels for the revolving masses, and they were, we believe, the first among English makers who did so.

To meet not only the revolving unbalanced weights, but also the reciprocating masses of the piston and appendages, as well as for other objects, Mr. J. G. Bodmer patented in 1841, the application of two pistons, of the same stroke, to work in each cylinder, operating upon a double crank on

---

[*] *Proceedings of the Institution of Mechanical Engineers*, June, 1848.

the axle, in opposite directions. Thus the disturbing action of one piston, with its crank and connecting rod, neutralised that of the other, and perfect equilibrium was gained.*

It is needless to add that Mr. Bodmer's plan was too complicated for general use. Mr. Heaton simplified the idea by applying duplicate reciprocating masses, of equal weight with the piston and appendages, placed alongside the fire-box, and worked by a reverse crank from the axle,—a plan which he patented in 1847. Still too complicated.

Mr. W. Fernihough, in October, 1845, conceived that if a revolving balance-weight be applied to the wheel sufficiently heavy to balance not only the crank, but also the connecting rod, piston, and appendages, the objects of Mr. Heaton's apparatus would be gained, while the irregularities of vertical pressure on the rail due to the excess of centrifugal force of the balance-weight, would not materially affect the stability of the engine. This conception was well borne out in practice, as he found that outside-cylinder engines so balanced were made "infinitely steadier;"† and the truth is, that centrifugal disturbance vertically, however potently it may affect the motion of carriages and other lighter vehicles, is by far the least important element of instability in locomotives. But, though the means of obtaining the material objects of a complete balance were thus early pointed out by Mr. Fernihough, English engineers generally have not appreciated the importance of extending the balance beyond the revolving parts; and they have endeavoured to increase the stability rather by such means as extending the wheel-base, lowering the centre of gravity, and coupling taut to the tender.

Three years after Fernihough, in October, 1848, M. Nollau, of the Holstein Railway, published his researches on the balancing of locomotives.‡ He analysed the causes of instability, and recognised the advantage of balancing, by counter weights applied to the wheels, the alternate action of the piston, as well as the centrifugal force of the revolving parts.

In 1849, M. Le Chatelier published his important investigations on the stability of locomotives,‖ in which he works out the whole theory of the subject, embracing all that had been done by previous engineers, and supplies rules for practice, confirmed by actual experiment. To this work we are indebted for much of what follows, on the balancing of the engine.

Nature of the Internal disturbing forces caused by the inertia of the mechanism.—A locomotive in motion may be affected by angular or pendulous movements horizontally and vertically, and by a longitudinal fore-and-aft movement, coinciding in their oscillations with, and arising from the internal reciprocations of the mechanism. The pendulous movements are of three kinds, and take place round the horizontal and vertical axes of the machine, passing through its centre of gravity or nearly so:—1st, horizontal vibration round the imaginary axis of motion, A B, fig. 183, giving rise to a *sinuous* or serpentine motion, right and left, which would be visible in plan and end elevation; 2d, vertical vibration on the axis C D, or a *pitching* or plunging motion,

* *Transactions of the British Association,* 1846.
† *Report of the Gauge Commissioners,* 1846.
‡ *Journal des Chemins de Fer Allemands,* Oct., 1848.
‖ *Etudes sur la Stabilité des Machines Locomotives en Mouvement.* Paris, 1849.

visible in side elevation; 3d, vertical vibration on the axis E F, or a rocking or *rolling* motion laterally, visible in

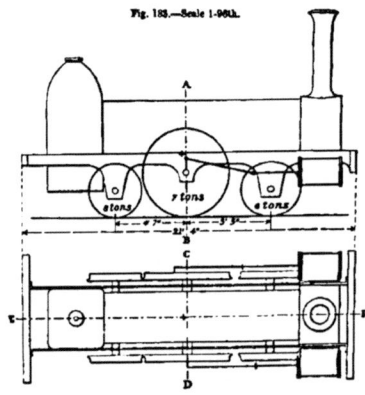

Fig. 183.—Scale 1-96th.

Long-Boiler Locomotive—to illustrate the Action of Internal Disturbing Force.
Cyl., 15 x 22 ins. Wheel, 5½ feet.

end elevation; there is, 4th, a longitudinal reciprocating, or fore-and-aft movement, rectilineal and parallel to the rails, causing a jolting movement visible in side elevation and plan. These erratic movements, though originating in the mechanism, are materially affected by the general arrangements of the machine, as to disposition of weight, placing of axles, design of springs, and so forth.

The operation of the reciprocating parts of the mechanism as disturbing causes is readily explained: they are, during each stroke, moved from a state of rest and accelerated in motion throughout the first half of each stroke, and retarded in motion and finally reduced to a state of rest throughout the last half of the stroke. The steam-pressure required to move them is exerted also upon the cylinder-end, and ultimately upon the body of the machine,—the steam operating as a screw-jack between the cylinder-cover and the piston,—and the whole machine in consequence sways to one side. During the last half stroke, the momentum acquired by the moving parts is delivered to the crank-pin and axle, and thence to the engine, causing it to swerve to the opposite side. This process is repeated during the return stroke; and thus, during one revolution of the crank, or one double-stroke of the piston, four changes of disturbing force are called into action. The operation of these forces may be illustrated by diagram, fig. 184; A B represents the cylinder

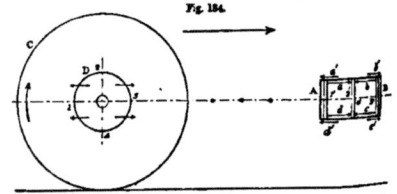

Fig. 184.

Cylinder and Driving-Wheel. Illustration of Internal Disturbing Forces due to the Reciprocating Parts.

with the piston inside, shown at the two ends and at the middle of the stroke, in the positions 1', 2', 3'; C is the driving wheel with the axle, and the circle D the path of the crank-pin, in which the pin is supposed to arrive at the positions 1, 2, 3, 4, simultaneously with the positions 1′, 2′, 3′, 4′, of the piston. The piston, in moving from 1′ to 2′ is impelled by the force of the steam in the same direction, as shown by the arrow a, to produce which an equal and opposite force is exerted on the end A of the cylinder, shown by the arrow a′ and transmitted to the whole machine; moving from 2′ to 3′, the piston is retarded by a force b, resulting from an equal and opposite strain, b′, on the machine; from 3′ to 4′, in the return stroke, the piston is moved by the force c, derived from the force c′ on the cylinder-end; and from 4′ to 1′, it is opposed by the force d, due to the force d′.

The horizontal forces, a′, b′, c′, d′, spent upon the machine during each double-stroke, act each of them simultaneously at the axle, through the framing and the connections of the piston, as shown by arrows inscribed on each quarter of the circle D, from which it is plain that while the crank passes from the upper to the lower centre of its throw, from 2 to 4, the disturbing forces successively act ahead; and from 4 to 2, they act aback. The circumstances under which the accelerated motion of the piston is acquired, are altered when the engine runs without steam. In this case, the labour of directly moving the piston, discharged when the steam is on, by the steam itself in the cylinder, necessarily devolves upon the crank on the driving axle; that is, the immediate strain thus incurred is transferred from the *end* of the machine, where the cylinder is placed, to the *middle*. This circumstance, though it does not affect the longitudinal reciprocating movement, increases the lateral oscillation, because the disturbing force has, in the latter case, a greater control over the mass of the machine. This distinction is verified in practice, for engines are known to run steadier with the steam on.

The four disturbing forces described for one cylinder, exist likewise for the other; and for the two cylinders there are eight forces brought into operation during one turn of the wheel, which may be further represented as follow:—Let the circles A, B, fig. 185, be the paths of the two crank-pins of the engine, of which A is that of the leading or right-hand crank. The four quarters of a revolution simultaneously described by them, are figured 1, 2, 3, 4. By arranging them in pairs described consecutively, as in the annexed Table, the nature of the disturbance is at once apparent,

In the 1st and the 3d quarters, the forces pull together, backward and forward alternately, and give rise to the horizontal reciprocating movement; in the 2d and 4th quarters, they are opposed, but at different points of the axle, in the centre-lines of the cylinders, and pull the machine alternately to the left and the right for one revolution of the driving wheel, giving rise to the sinuous motion on the rails. The centrifugal force of the revolving parts affects the stability of the machine, only as it gives rise to the horizontal disturbances which have just been pointed out. Its vertical action is insignificant in practice, considering that it has to contend, upwardly, with the whole weight of the machine,

Fig. 185.

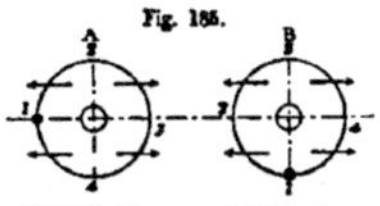

Right Crank. Left Crank.
HORIZONTAL DISTURBING FORCES.

TABLE, No. LXXXVI.—SHOWING THE HORIZONTAL DISTURBANCE OF A LOCOMOTIVE IN MOTION, DUE TO THE INERTIA OF THE MECHANISM.

	Direction of the Disturbing Forces, that of the Progressive Motion of the Engine being thus ——→ During the successive parts of a Revolution.			
	1st Quarter.	2d Quarter.	3d Quarter.	4th Quarter.
Crank A	←	→	→	←
Crank B	←	←	→	→
A and B combined	⇐	↜	⇒	↝
Nature of the compound disturbance produced.	Direct Backward Impulse to the whole Machine.	Horizontal Oscillation, swaying head of engine to the left.	Direct Forward Impulse to the whole Machine.	Horizontal Oscillation, swaying head of engine to the right.

and without any sensible advantage, seeing that the centre of gravity is commonly so nearly over the driving axle; and, downwardly, it is met and balanced by the rigidity of the rails.

Disturbances caused by the Action of the Steam on the pistons.—When the cylinder is horizontal, the steam-pressure on either end of the cylinder would be transmitted through the piston to the axle in a direction at right angles to the guides of the axle-box, and would be fairly and fully received by these guides, if the connecting rod were so long as not, at any part of the stroke, to form any sensible angle with the centre line of the cylinder. An indefinitely long rod is of course impracticable; and as the pressure of the steam through the connecting rod, and may be conceived to act in its centre line, the obliquity of the rod, or the angle which it forms with the centre line of the cylinder everywhere but at the ends of the stroke, operates to produce irregularities by the upward strain which it throws on the crosshead, which it is the function of the guide-bars to receive as the angularity varies; this irregular pressure varies also, from being nothing at the end of the stroke, to its maximum at half stroke, when the angle of the rod is also greatest, and when the pressure is received upon the middle of the guide-bar. The tendency of this variable pressure, which is constantly exerted on the upper guide-bar, when the engine is going ahead, is to lift the machine off its leading springs at half stroke, and to ease it down at the dead points. The alternate heaving and sinking so caused, gives rise to the *pitching* of the machine; and, further, as the variations of upward pressure are not simultaneous for the two cylinders, inasmuch as the half stroke of one cylinder is arrived at simultaneously with the dead point of the other, the heaving of the engine must take place alternately on the two sides, and will cause a *rocking*, or lateral rolling motion on the springs. Pitching and rocking are at least the tendencies of the oblique action of the connecting rod; and they become more sensible, the shorter the rod and the more susceptible the springs.

If, instead of being horizontal, the cylinders be placed vertically over the driving axle, it is clear that the alternate thrust and pull on the axle caused directly by the steam pressure, would give rise to some vertical play on the springs; this would work alternately on the two sides of the machine, and would create the rocking motion in all its simplicity, as has actually been found in practice with the earlier engines with upright cylinders; and, further, if the driving axle be placed either before or behind the centre of gravity of the machine, the vertical action of the strain would superinduce a pitching of the engines which in conjunction with the rocking, produces an *elbowing* or *shouldering* motion.*

This compound motion takes place, in a modified degree, in all inclined-cylinder locomotives. The incline of the cylinder, in fact, aggravates the irregularities due to the angle of the connecting rod, and becomes more formidable in its effects, not only by increasing the incline, but also by increasing the pressure on the piston with the same angle of cylinder. These disturbances are quite obvious in outside-cylinder engines working under full pressure, when the angle of the cylinder amounts to 1 in 10.

There is another source of unsteadiness in the unequal periods of admission which attend the use of certain arrangements of valve-gear, by which a greater quantity of steam is admitted to the cylinder, and a greater mean pressure is reached, during the front stroke of the piston, than during the back stroke. As the two front strokes for the two cylinders occur consecutively, and in due rotation with the two back strokes, it follows that the machine cannot be uniformly impelled, and that while the mean speed must be that due to the average mean pressure on both sides of the piston, the machine will advance and recede during each turn of the driving wheel, alternately straining and relaxing the connection with the tender; and that, in short, a longitudinal reciprocating movement results, combining with and complicating the movements already described as due to the inertia of the mechanism.

There are, then, three principal internal disturbing causes which affect the stability of the locomotive. 1st, The inertia of the reciprocating masses of machinery which tend to produce a lateral *sinuous* movement, and a longitudinal *reciprocal* movement. 2d, The oblique action of the steam through the connecting rod, and in inclined cylinders, which tends to produce vertical *pitching* and *rolling* movements. 3d, The unequal propelling action of the steam when unequally admitted to the two ends of the cylinders, inducing a longitudinal reciprocating movement, of the same kind as that caused by the inertia of the mechanism.

The unbalanced inertia of the valve-gear has not required notice, as its influence on the stability of the machine is insignificant.

——————

CHAPTER II.

INTERNAL DISTURBING FORCES (Continued)—NUMERICAL VALUES.

Central Forces.—*Centrifugal force* is excited by the constrained circular motion of a heavy body, and is the force with which the revolving body tends to fly from the centre round which it revolves. It acts on the centre, and must be met by an equal and opposite strain, known as *centripetal force*, and the two forces so opposed are classed as *central forces:*—they are mere cases of action and reaction, and necessarily co-exist; and it is customary to allude to the disturbing action so induced as, simply, central or centrifugal force.

Central force depends upon the weight of the revolving body, its velocity in the circle or orbit of motion, and the radius of the circle, or the distance of the body from the centre of motion. The intensity of the force in pounds is found by the following rule:—

RULE I.—*To find the Centrifugal Force of a Revolving Body.* Multiply the weight in pounds by the square of the velocity in the circular path, in feet per second,—divide by the radius of the circle in feet,—and by 32. The quotient is the central force in pounds.

Applying the laws of central force to the circumstances of locomotive machinery, it appears that,

1st. When the diameter of the wheel, and the speed on the rails are the same, the central force increases directly with the length of crank, or with the length of stroke; it also increases directly with the weight of the revolving masses of the crank and the connecting rod.

2d. When the diameter of wheel, and other matters are the same, the centrifugal force of the crank and connecting rod, increases as the square of the speed on the rails; that is, for twice the speed, there is four times the disturbing force.

3d. When the speed on the rails, and other matters, are the same, the centrifugal force of the crank and connecting rod, increases as the square of the diameter of wheel inversely; that is, for half the diameter, with the same speed, the disturbance is not merely doubled, but increased four times; on the contrary, with double the wheel, there is only one-fourth of the disturbing force.

These conclusions show, not only the great influence of speed in increasing centrifugal force, but also the equally great influence of the diameter of wheel in reducing it; so that if the diameter of wheel be increased in proportion with the speed, other matters being the same, the centrifugal force of the crank and connecting rod would remain unaltered. They explain also the great increase of disturbance from unbalanced masses, arising from a relatively small reduction of the wheel; for example, a reduction of the wheel from 6 feet to 4½ feet, or in the ratio of 4 to 3, would increase the disturbing force, at the same speed, in the ratio of 3^2 to 4^2, or as 9 to 16, to nearly double.

Analysis of Disturbing Forces in the Locomotive.—It has already been stated that the centrifugal force of the crank and connecting rod is of more consequence to the stability of the locomotive by its horizontal action, parallel to the rail, than by its vertical action. These two actions may be separated by diagram, thus:—Let A B be the centre line of the engine, and *a b*, the right-hand crank revolving in the circle C D, with its load on the pin at *b*; the centrifugal force at *b* acts in the direction *a b*, and may be represented in intensity by *a b*. Draw *b c* and *a d* perpendicular, and *b d* parallel, to A B; then *a c* represents the horizontal strain

——————

* Known in French by the phrase, *mouvement déhanché*, literally, a motion like that of one *whose hips are out of joint.*

on the axle at *a* towards B, and *a d* the vertical strain downwards, caused by the central force *a b*. Similarly, for any

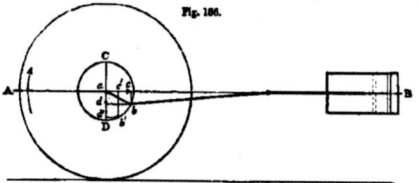

Cylinder and Wheel.—Diagram of the Vertical and Horizontal Actions of Central Forces.

other position of the crank, *a' b'*, the horizontal and vertical forces, *a c', a d'*, are developed. In the position *a* D, at half throw, the force is entirely vertical, and the horizontal element vanishes; the same may be said of the position *a* C, on the opposite side. At the dead points A, B, on the contrary, the force is entirely horizontal, and the vertical element becomes nothing. Thus, though the central force be constant, its horizontal and vertical actions are variable, and alternate in such a manner that the horizontal action is greatest at the dead points, and vanishes at half throw, while the vertical action is greatest at half throw, and vanishes at the dead points.

The horizontal forces developed in the successive acceleration and retardation of the piston and its appendages vary in the same manner and at the same rate as the horizontal element of central force; they are greatest at the dead points, where the piston is to be started and stopped, and vanish at half stroke. The horizontal action due to the piston is, in brief, *centrifugal force, wanting the vertical element.* This is the coincidence to which Mr. Fernihough alluded in his evidence, referred to in last chapter.

The disturbing forces for the left hand cylinder act in the same way, and they unite with those of the other cylinder in unsettling the progressive motion of the engine on the rail. In tracing the joint action of these forces, it is necessary to separate the revolving masses from those which merely reciprocate. The connecting rod partakes of the two motions, as it works between the crank and the crosshead; one-half of its weight will therefore be classed with the revolving mass, and the remainder with the piston and appendages.

As central force varies with the distance of the centre of gravity of the revolving body from the centre of motion, a fixed radius, the length of crank, is that for which, as a matter of convenience, the central forces of all the revolving masses may be estimated. While the crank-pin and the half connecting rod work on this radius, the crank itself, inasmuch as its centre of gravity is nearer the axle, works on a shorter radius, and it requires to be reduced in the same ratio, *to refer it to the crank-pin,* that is, to find the equivalent weight, centred at the pin, which would produce the same central force. This is done by the following rule:—

RULE II.—*To refer a given revolving weight to the crank-pin.*—Multiply the weight in pounds by the distance of its centre of gravity from the centre of the axle, in inches,—and divide by the length of crank, in inches. The quotient is the equivalent weight in pounds at the crank-pin.

Let A B, fig. 187, be one cheek of an inside crank, B the axle, A the pin, and c the circle described by the centre of

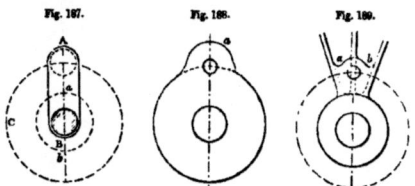

Diagrams to find the Centre of Gravity of the Crank, inside or outside.

the pin. The centre of gravity of the cheek is at *a*, midway of the crank, and moves in the circle *a b*, with half the radius of the crank-pin. If the crank be 10 inches long, and weigh 96 lbs., the radius B *a* will be 5 inches, and by the rule

$$\frac{96 \times 5}{10} = 48 \text{ lbs.,}$$

the equivalent weight of the crank, referred to the pin; or exactly one-half of its actual weight.

For outside wheel-cranks of cast iron, as in fig. 188, the metal, *a*, extra to the nave, formed round the pin may, without material error, be estimated as a semi-cylinder, of which the centre of gravity is at the centre of the pin. When the wheel-cranks are malleable, and wrought into the spokes, as in fig. 189, the extra metal consists of the wedges *a*, *b*, defined by dotting, at the length of the crank from the centre.

Fig. 190.

Outside Crank. Centre of Gravity.

For independent outside cranks, as in fig. 190, the centre of gravity of the entire crank may be found directly by balancing it horizontally over a pivot; or, overlooking the boss, *a*, which is not a part of the disturbing weight, the socket *c* may be taken as weight at the crank-pin, and half the weight of the part, *b*, may be taken as equivalent weight at the pin.

Numerical Values of the Disturbing Forces.—Le Chatelier's results for the sample engine, fig. 183, are here quoted,

in English measures; they are estimated at intervals of 45° of a revolution of the right hand crank, commencing with 0° at the dead point, as set off in fig. 191; and are taken separately for the two cranks, the simultaneous forces for the left hand crank being estimated for positions at right angles to the

Fig 191.

Diagram of the Principal Positions of the Crank.

others, or 90° behind it in the direction of motion.

For the engine in question,

Diameter of cylinder is 15 inches; stroke, 22 inches.
Crank, 11 inches; connecting rod, 54 inches;
Wheel, 66 inches.
Cylinders, 6 ft. 2 ins. apart centres.
Wheels, 4 ft. 7 ins. apart centres, transversely.
Fore and hind axles, 9 ft. 10 in. apart.
Centre of gravity, 3 in. behind vertical centre line of driving axle.

Y

Weight on rails at fore-wheels	...	6 tons.
Do. do. driving do.	...	7 ,,
Do. do. hind do.	...	8 ,,
Total, in working order	...	21 tons.

Weight of piston and rod	...	178 lbs.
Crosshead	...	56
Connecting rod	...	172
Crank, referred to pin	...	100
Crank-pin	...	34
Total	...	540 lbs.

Weight of crank, referred to pin	...	100 lbs.
Crank-pin	...	34
Half connecting rod	...	86
Total revolving weight	...	220 lbs.

1st. *Of the tendency to Pitching and Rolling.*—This is caused by the upward pressure on the guide-bars due to the oblique action of the connecting rod. With 40 lbs. steam in the cylinder, under full gear it varies from 0 at the end of the stroke, to about 1560 lbs., or 14 cwt. at half stroke, for each cylinder; by the combined action of the two rods, the total upward pressure fluctuates between 14 and 21 cwt., inducing vertical play on the springs, or pitching; and the difference of pressures, right and left, varies from 1 to 14 cwt., four times during a revolution, inducing a rolling motion. The wider apart the cylinders, the greater is the effect from this cause, because the greater is the leverage laterally of the fluctuating forces on the machine.

2d. *Vertical Action of Centrifugal Force.*—Calculated for 220 lbs., or about 2 cwt., the weight of the revolving mass referred to the crank-pin, the following are the vertical pressures for speeds of 25 and 50 miles per hour, reckoned positive (+) when acting downwards, and negative (—) upwards.

TABLE, No. LXXXVII.—VERTICAL ACTION BY CENTRIFUGAL FORCE, OF A REVOLVING MASS OF 2 CWT. AT THE CRANK-PIN.

Angle of Right hand Crank.	Right hand Cylinder.		Left hand Cylinder.		Sum of the two Cylinders.	
	25 m.p.h.	50 m p.h.	25 m.p.h.	50 m p.h.	25 m.p.h.	50 m p h.
	cwt.	cwt.	cwt.	cwt.	cwt.	cwt.
0°	0	0	— 8¾	— 35	— 8¾	— 35
45°	+ 6¼	+ 25	— 6¼	— 25	0	0
90°	+ 8¾	+ 35	0	0	+ 8¾	+ 35
135°	+ 6¼	+ 25	+ 6¼	+ 25	+ 12½	+ 50
180°	0	0	+ 8¾	+ 35	+ 8¾	+ 35
225°	— 6¼	— 25	+ 6¼	+ 25	0	0
270°	— 8¾	— 35	0	0	— 8¾	— 35
315°	— 6¼	— 25	— 6¼	— 25	— 12½	— 50

By this Table, it appears, the centrifugal action of about 2 cwt. on the driving axle, alternately adds and subtracts

Fig. 192.

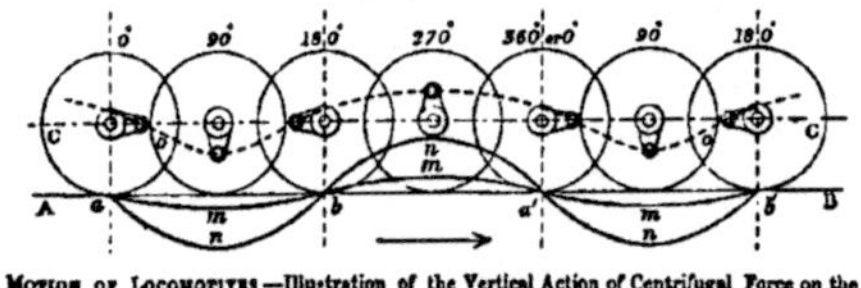

MOTION OF LOCOMOTIVES.—Illustration of the Vertical Action of Centrifugal Force on the Driving Wheel, at 25 and 50 miles per hour.

about 9 cwt. from the pressure on the rails, on one side, at 25 miles per hour; and the variation amounts to 35 cwt. at 50 miles. This is illustrated in fig. 192, where the wheel and crank are shown at intervals of one-fourth of a turn. Over the distance *a a'*, a whole turn is made, and an extra half turn to *b'*; *c c* is the path of the centre of the axle, and the wave-line *o o* is that of the crank-pin. The wave-lines *m*, *n*, are constructed by a scale of parts, from the contents of the 2d and 3d columns of the table, and indicate the variations of vertical action for 25 and 50 miles per hour, their depression below the rail-line showing extra downward action, and their elevation above, upward action. They show not only how the action is increased by extra speed, but also that the upward and downward actions coincide with the upward and downward movements of the crank-pin.

The joint vertical action for the two cylinders never exceeds 12½ cwt. up or down, at 25 miles; at 50 miles, it reaches 50 cwt. The downward pressure is met by the rails, and the stability can be affected only by the upward pressure, when it exceeds the weight of the wheels and axles and the mounting, for otherwise the springs cannot be affected. As the wheels and axle alone weigh 2 tons, and with mounting, 2½ tons, their dead weight alone balances the combined upward pressure at 50 miles. The vertical action at each wheel singly is more powerful, as it reaches 35 cwt. at 50 miles; and, operating at the end of the axle, it has a leverage of 2 to 1 upon the whole dead weight, and would balance it with a force of 25 cwt., leaving 10 cwt. to act on the springs and the load. But this could not affect the compass of the spring materially above ⅛ inch; still less can the vertical action affect the stability of inside-cylinder locomotives, where it has less leverage upon the load; and, in fact, it is not found in practice that the vertical action of central force in the locomotive operates as a cause of instability.

3d. *Longitudinal Fore-and-aft Movement.*—The horizontal action of the whole reciprocating mass may be calculated by the rules employed for the vertical action of centrifugal force; and in proportion as the whole moving weight exceeds that of the revolving weight, the horizontal will be found to exceed the vertical actions. The combined horizontal forces are as follow, calculated for a reciprocating weight of 540 lbs. to each cylinder, or a total of 1080 lbs., about 10 cwt. for the whole machine.

TABLE, No. LXXXVIII.—COMBINED FORE-AND-AFT HORIZONTAL ACTION OF THE WHOLE REVOLVING AND RECIPROCATING WEIGHT, ABOUT 5 CWT. TO EACH CYLINDER.

Angle of Right hand Crank.	Horizontal Force, — Forward. + Backward.	
	25 m.p h.	50 m p h.
	cwt.	cwt.
0°	— 21¾	— 87
45°	— 30¾	— 123
90°	— 21¾	— 87
135°	0	0
180°	+ 21¾	+ 87
225°	+ 30¾	+ 123
270°	+ 21¾	+ 87
315°	0	0

The Table shows that the combined horizontal force varies from 0 to 1½ tons at 25 miles; and to above 6 tons at 50 miles, or 3 tons to each crank due to the mere inertia of the mechanism! These are most formidable pressures, and they contribute seriously to the tear and wear of the machinery.

At 45° and 225°, where the action is greatest, the cranks are in the positions shown in fig. 193; R and L being the

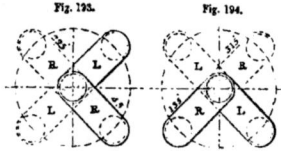

Fig. 193.   Fig. 194.

right and left hand cranks, the action vanishes at the positions shown in fig. 194.

4th. *Horizontal Sinuous Movement.*—This arises from the same causes which create longitudinal fore-and-aft movement, and in practice the two results are combined; the distinction being that the forces causing sinuous movement predominate *alternately* with those causing longitudinal movement, as exhibited by the arrows in Table LXXXVI., last chapter, and further shown in the following Table LXXXIX, in contrast

TABLE, No. LXXXIX.—COMBINED SINUOUS ACTION OF THE WHOLE REVOLVING AND RECIPROCATING WEIGHT.

Angle of Right hand Crank.	Sinuous Forces.	
	25 m.p.h.	50 m p.h.
0°	— 21¾	— 87
45°	0	0
90°	+ 21¾	+ 87
135°	+ 30¾	+ 123
180°	+ 21¾	+ 87
225°	0	0
270°	— 21¾	— 87
315°	— 30¾	— 123

with the contents of Table LXXXVIII. preceding. In these tables it is shown that the sinuous forces are the same in intensity and rate of variation as the fore-and-aft forces just given. The leverage with which they act on the whole mass is equal to half the distance of the centres of cylinders, as the axis round which the pendulous action takes place must be at the middle of the driving axle. The action is greatest at 135° and 315°, when the cranks are in the positions, fig. 194, and reduced to nothing in the positions, fig. 193. Sinuous motion is still more detrimental to the durability of the engine than fore-and-aft motion.

CHAPTER III.

INTERNAL DISTURBING FORCES (*continued*)—CIRCUMSTANCES WHICH AFFECT THEIR ACTION, RESULTS OF THEIR ACTION, AND THE ORDINARY REMEDIES.

Of the Pitching Movement.—The resistance to pitching, and thereby the stability, is promoted by shifting the driving axle backwards, towards the firebox, principally because it increases the mass of the machine in advance of the axle, or that which is submitted to the oblique action of the connecting rod; the removal of the axle also, in so far as it lengthens the connecting rod, reduces the obliquity which is the source of the disturbance. In Crampton's engine, having the axle behind the firebox, the whole mass lies forward; while, at the same time, the guide-bars, where the action takes place, are in the neighbourhood of the centre of

gravity; thus, the oblique action is entirely controlled, and the pitching is extinguished.

Above all, the number and position of the points of support, mostly control the pitching. The springs, also, particularly the fore and hind springs, should be as stiff as is consistent with the preservation of the frame and mechanism, to neutralise the oscillations which may arise from imperfections of the permanent way,—such as loose sleepers, open joints, or want of correct gauge; for if these oscillations should coincide with the action on the guide-bars, they increase the straining of the machine, and the liability of the leading wheels to mount the rails. Susceptible springs also, for the same reason, increase the danger from accidental obstructions.

Vertical Action by the Centrifugal force of the Revolving Weight.—This action may be entirely neutralised by the application of suitable counterweights. This question, however, belongs to the more general question of balancing all the revolving and reciprocating masses.

The reduction of adhesion, by vertical action, explains the occasional slipping of the driving wheels at high speeds. It explains also the extra wear of driving wheel-tyres, when very much out of balance, next the crank-pin, where the pressure on the rail is greatest,—producing "flat places," and in consequence a vertical jolting of the engine while in motion.

Longitudinal Fore-and-Aft Motion.—It was found that in the sample engine, fig. 183, a joint longitudinal action on the driving axle of above six tons, or three tons for each cylinder, was incurred at certain points of the stroke, at a speed of fifty miles, by the crank and the other moving masses. Now, the whole pressure of 100 lbs. steam on a fifteen-inch piston does not exceed eight tons; thus, the inertia of the mechanism alternately adds and subtracts three-eighths, or 40 per cent. of this pressure, reducing the useful pressure to five tons, or 60 per cent., when the crank is at 45° during the first half-stroke; and raising it to eleven tons, or 140 per cent., at 135° in the second half-stroke. This example shows how very greatly the inertia of the machinery may affect the useful work of the engine. And so long as the whole effective pressure in the cylinder exceeds this inertia, the coupling bars between engine and tender remain taut on their pins, though subject to oscillation with the coupling spring. But when the steam-pressure is less, or altogether removed,—with a small train, or going down an incline,—they play fast and loose, owing to the fore-and-aft action, by which the machine is alternately thrown forward, and backward on the tender. This explains the extra racket and jarring which takes place between an unbalanced engine and its tender immediately after shutting off the steam, in approaching stations, particularly where the nature of the coupling gear permits of some play. The shocks arising from these fore-and-aft vibrations are destructive to the coupling links and bolts, to the framing which carries them, and to the general connection of the whole machine, especially at the axleboxes and guardplates. And the greater the play of the parts of the engine, the more injurious is this action.

To neutralise or soften the longitudinal action, it is usual to employ a traction-spring under the foot-plate of the engine or tender, to receive the shocks; it is either coupled to a draw-bar of a fixed length, under permanent tension between the draw-bolts, or adjustable by a double screw, right and left hand; in either case, buffing blocks of wood are fixed at some distance apart laterally, upon the front beam of the tender-frame, to bear upon the engine-frame, as fulcrums for the action of the spring. With the object of softening the action still further, the buffing blocks are in some cases made elastic within a limited compass, by the use of india-rubber springs. Counterweights, also, are applied to the wheels, and are efficient so far as they go; but they are, for the most part, much too light, as they are estimated for the revolving weight only.

Of the Sinuous Movement.—As this affection of the motion of the engine implies the lateral play of the fore and hind wheels upon the rails, the friction of the tyres upon the rails, due to this lateral displacement, is opposed to the motion, and its tendency is therefore to steady the engine. Accordingly, in practice, at the lower speeds, and when the intensity of the disturbing forces is low, the machine, though unbalanced, runs sufficiently steady in respect of sinuous motion. At speeds above thirty miles, the greater disturbing forces overcome the resistance to their development, and the sinuous motion becomes more violent, the higher the speed. Even in Crampton's ordinary engines, sinuous action becomes sensible when the speed reaches sixty miles.

Many things go to increase the sinuous motion to which engines may be predisposed by want of balance: such as a want of parallelism of the axles, unequal diameters of the wheels, the wear of ruts or hollows in the tyres, the wear of the axleboxes and bushes, which gives rise to longitudinal and transverse play at the axle-guards and on the journals, the outline of the rails, and sometimes a want of accuracy in the adjustment of the draw-bars. When the axles are not parallel, but incline towards each other on one side of the engine, their disposition is to roll the engine forward in a curved path, and always towards the same side, causing perpetual collisions between the flanges and the rail. This oblique tendency is injurious enough on the straight parts of the line, but it is much worse on curves which diverge towards the other side, and increases the liability to get off the rails. The same tendency is caused by wheels of unequal diameter on the same axle. Again, when the tyre wears hollow, the outer part, originally less, is left larger in diameter than the middle of the breadth of tyre. This state of wear reverses the action intended in coning the tyres, as the greatest diameter, instead of being next the flange, is shifted to the outside; and, whereas a properly coned tyre constantly seeks to maintain the wheels in the centre of the track, a hollow tyre leads the engine continually astray, and subjects it to constant concussions against the rail. Play of the axles and axleboxes, by giving scope for irregular action, converts what without play would be a simple strain or flexure of the guards, into shocks upon the journals and wheels laterally. And it must be noted that though some degree of flexibility in the frame may be beneficial for the easy working and adjustment of the machine to the rails, when in good order, it is a very dangerous accompaniment for a slack and unsteady engine. That these varieties of tear and wear are all productive of unstea-

diness, is proved by the superior stability of a new engine, with all its parts well up to their gauges, and all its bearings taut.

The means employed to reduce the fore-and-aft movement, operate also in reducing sinuous movement. A great extension of the wheel-base has also been employed with benefit, because it reduces the angular play of the wheels between the rails, and increases the command of the leading wheels in controlling erratic movements, by their frictional resistance transversely on the rails. In Crampton's engines, which carry out this principle to its limits, and impose the greatest loads upon the extreme wheels, the mass of matter in advance of the driving axle, still further promotes the stability; and these engines, though they may not be balanced artificially, are practically steady at sixty miles per hour. But the great spread of wheels, though beneficial on straight lines, is prejudicial on the curves, and particularly in passing into sidings; for it is plain, that the farther apart the extreme axles, the greater is the angle at which the leading wheel-flange meets the outer rail on curves, and the more severe is the labour of guiding the engine.

The springs between engine and tender, though useful for reducing the fore-and-aft motion, have been introduced chiefly to meet the horizontal oscillation. But, it is clear that, in so far as they, and all similar appliances, reduce this movement, they tend to consolidate the engine and tender, and injuriously to increase the length of fixed wheel-base. A draw-spring between engine and tender is no doubt a good thing; but it should be employed rather as a mere carriage-spring, to soften the irregular motions of the tender itself. The wheel-bases of locomotives are abundantly long enough for the fair purposes of a carriage, and it is mechanically unsound in principle, and inexpedient in practice, to divert them from their legitimate function; for, as M. Le Chatelier most justly observes, "it is only in a direct manner—by attacking and destroying the cause itself, —that we should seek to extinguish the lateral oscillation of locomotives."

CHAPTER IV.

Internal Disturbing Forces (*continued*)—Method of Balancing by Counterweights.

From what has been stated, the longitudinal and lateral, or horizontal action of the internal forces, are those alone which materially affect the stability of the engine, and it is to the correct balancing of these forces that we have now to direct attention. The action of the reciprocating masses was found to be identical with the horizontal action of the revolving masses, wanting the vertical action of the latter; therefore, happily, the same means may be employed to balance the whole revolving and reciprocating weights,—namely, Fernihough's method of counterweights attached to the wheels, and opposed to the cranks, and *weighty enough to balance not merely the crank, pin, and one-half the connecting rod, but also the other half, with the piston and appendages.* That part of the counterweight which balances the piston, developes, of course, a superfluous vertical action in virtue of its centrifugal force; but vertical action, we have seen, is harmless to the stability.

Were the balance to be applied at the same part of the axle as the centre of the crank-pin and cylinder, the same counterweight would exactly destroy both the erratic movements, longitudinally and laterally, caused by the mechanism. In practice, however, while the weight works in the centre line of the cylinder, the counterweight is, for convenience, applied to the wheel, between the spokes; and as sinuous motion is caused by and increases with the leverage of the swinging masses, which is measured by the distance of their line of action from the middle of the axle, it follows that, to have perfect equilibrium laterally, the counterweight for outside cylinders must be greater, and for inside cylinders less than the moving weights referred to the crank-pin. Whereas, to neutralise exactly the longitudinal action, which is independent of leverage, an equal counterweight, referred to the crank-pin, must be applied in all cases. It will be shown that some latitude may be admitted in practice, for the mutual adjustment of these claims, after investigating the conditions of lateral equilibrium for different classes of engines.

Conditions of Lateral Equilibrium in Outside-Cylinder Single Engines.—Let A, B, fig. 195, be the cylinders of our sample engine, fig. 183, c, D, the wheels, and E F, the centre line of the axle; let w be the weight of the piston and appendages, connecting rod, and half the crank-pin, which act in the centre line of the cylin-

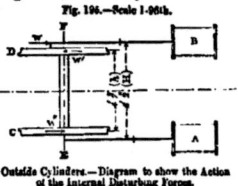
Fig. 196.—Scale 1·96th.

Outside Cylinders.—Diagram to show the Action of the Internal Disturbing Forces.

der B; and e the weight of the inner half of crank-pin, and the crank referred to the pin, acting in the body of the wheel D. Then, w, overhanging the wheel D, acts partly on the wheel c, and for perfect balance, must be met by suitable counterweights, w', w'', on opposite sides of the two wheels, as illustrated in fig. 196. The arrows w, w', w'', fig. 195, show the action of the axle in resisting the three centrifugal forces developed by these counterweights in motion, and which also balance at all speeds. The counterweight w', fig. 196, referred to the crank-pin, is greater than the weight w, by as much as w'', referred to the crank-pin; that is

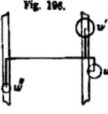
Fig. 195.

Outside Cylinders.—Internal Disturbing Forces and Counterweights.

$$w' = w + w'', \text{ and therefore } w'' = w' - w.$$

Also, the product of the weight w', by its distance along the axle-line from w, is equal to that of w'' into its distance from w; or, putting the width apart of the cylinder-centres $= \text{H}$, and that of the wheel-centres $= h$, we have

$$\tfrac{1}{2} (\text{H} + h) w'' = \tfrac{1}{2} (\text{H} - h) w';$$

doubling both sides, and putting for w'' its value as above, we have

$$(\text{H} + h) (w' - w) = (\text{H} - h) w';$$

therefore

$$w' = \frac{\text{H} + h}{2 h} w, \text{ and } w'' = \frac{\text{H} - h}{2 h} w;$$

that is, the weight w', referred to the crank-pin, is equal to w multiplied by the sum of the widths of the cylinders and wheels, and divided by twice the width of the wheels; w'', likewise, is equal to w multiplied by the difference of widths, and divided by twice the width of wheels. It may be noted, also, that the two weights w', w'', on the near and off wheels, are to each other as the sum and the difference of the widths of cylinders and wheels. Adding the weight of the crank and half the pin, e, as above, we have $w' + e$, for the whole counterweight on the wheel D.

Reasoning in the same way for the cylinder, A, we should find for each wheel two counterweights, the greater $= w' + e$, to meet the action from the near cylinder, and the less $= w''$, at right angles to it, to meet the action from the off cylinder, referring everything to the crank-pin. Thus, in

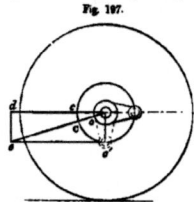
Fig. 197.

Outside Cylinders.—Diagram to find the Counterweight in the Wheel.

fig. 197 showing the right hand wheel D, from the inside, the larger weight would be located at c, opposed to the crank, and the smaller at d, at right angles to it, and coinciding in end view with the left hand crank. These two weights may be replaced by a single weight at c, of which the magnitude and position are given by the diagonal $o e$ of the rectangle formed on the two sides $o d$, $o d'$, proportioned by any convenient scale, to represent by their lengths the respective weights c, d.

Applying this process to the engine before us, the total weight is 540 lbs., of which $w = 423$ lbs., and $e = 117$ lbs. Then

$$w' = \frac{(74+55)}{2 \times 55} 423 = 496 \text{ lbs.}; w' + e = 613 \text{ lbs.}; \& w'' = \frac{(74-55)}{2 \times 55} 423 = 73 \text{ lbs.}$$

Thus we have 613 lbs. and 73 lbs. for the elementary counterweights in each wheel, for which the single equivalent counterweight is found by the process of the rectangle to be 617 lbs., referred to the crank-pin, placed at an inclination of 7° with the line $o c$, nearly opposite the near crank, and *towards* the off crank.

In practice, as shall afterwards be found, it is not necessary, for outside cylinders, coupled close to the wheel, to take account of the greater width apart of the cylinders with respect to the wheels; nor of the small angle of divergence of the counterweight from the centre line of the crank produced across the wheel-centre. It is sufficient to apply to the wheel directly opposite the crank, a weight to balance the sum of the reciprocating weights, at the crank-pin, which is, in the example before us, 540 lbs. It is only in cases of extreme difference of widths, that the foregoing method of investigation need be employed.

Outside-Cylinder Coupled Engines.—These machines, with coupled wheels, are the most unstable of all, when unbalanced, as the coupling rods increase the usual revolving and reciprocating mass for a single engine, to double the amount; and the cylinders, are farther apart than in single engines, to admit the coupling rods inside the connecting rods. Moreover, the wheels are of smaller diameter, and demand more rapid reciprocations of the piston for given speeds. The counterweights are consequently enormous.

In the goods engines made by Gouin & Co. for the Lyons Railway, fig. 198, with four wheels coupled, the masses to

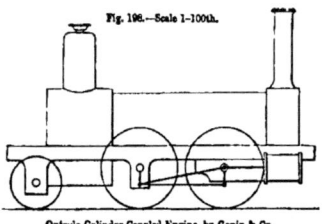

Fig. 198.—Scale 1–100th.

Outside-Cylinder Coupled Engine, by Gouin & Co.

be balanced, referred to the crank-pin, were for the respective wheels on each side, as follow :—

	Driving Wheels.	Leading Wheels.
Crank,...	66 lbs.	88 lbs.
Pin, ...	73	22
Connecting rod, ...	238	...
Piston, ...	401	...
Coupling rod, 209 lbs., distributed between the two wheels,	121	88
	899 lbs.	198 lbs.
Total for each side of engine,	... ...	1097 lbs., or fully 9¾ cwts.

With wheels only 5 feet 3 inches, and large naves, more than three spaces between the arms are required to contain the balance necessary to meet the load on the driving wheel; it is better to relieve the wheel by transferring one-half of the counterweight for the reciprocating masses, to the leading wheel. The reciprocating weight is as follow :—

Piston and appendages, ...	401 lbs.
Half the connecting rod, ...	119 lbs.
Total, ...	520 lbs.

One-half of this, or 260 lbs., is to be balanced at the fore-wheels; and the modified loads for the respective wheels, are

Driving wheel (899 — 260), ...	639 lbs.
Leading wheel (198 + 260), ...	458 lbs.
Total, as before, ...	1097 lbs.

This transfer of duty only increases the labour of the coupling rod to a small extent; and it has the advantage of distributing the vertical action of the counterweight between the two wheels, and reducing the local wear of the wheel-tyres.

The outside-cylinder goods-engine, Crewe, (plate 21), with four coupled wheels, contrasts very favourably with the engine now discussed, as the total weight of the disturbing masses is 546 lbs., or 4 cwt. 98 lbs.,—only one-half of the other. This shows what can be done by a careful study of proportions, and attention to the real necessities for strength of parts.

Six-coupled-wheel engines involve still greater disturbing masses than those with four wheels coupled. In the goods-engines of the Northern Railway of France, fig. 199, with 4 feet wheels, by Derosne & Cail, the weights were, for each side of the engine, as follow :—

Driving, ...	695 lbs.
Leading, ...	165
Trailing, ...	176
Total, ...	1036 lbs., or 9¼ cwt.

In this, as in Gouin's engine, the balance for the reciprocating mass must be distributed equally between the three wheels, to secure the most favourable action.

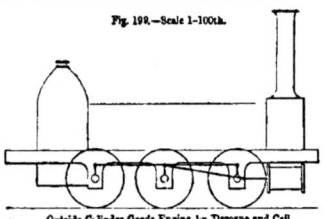

Fig. 199.—Scale 1–100th.

Outside Cylinder Goods Engine, by Derosne and Cail.

In the goods-engine of the Caledonian Railway, with cylinders 17×24 inches, and six 4½ feet coupled wheels, with the hind wheels behind the firebox, and arranged otherwise like Derosne and Cail's engine, the disturbing masses are even greater than in this, and amount in some of the engines to 10¼ cwt. for each cylinder. These engines are already partially balanced by counterweights amounting to 5½ cwt. on each side of the engine, and equivalent to about 6¼ cwt. at the crank-pin; but they are very unsteady laterally, and it would be difficult to place them in complete equilibrium.

Inside-Cylinder Single Engines. — Let A B, fig. 200, be

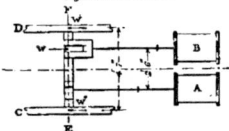

Fig. 200.—Scale 1–96th.

Inside Cylinders.—Diagram to show the Action of the Internal Disturbing Forces.

the cylinders, C, D the wheels, and E F, the centre line of the axle; if w be the disturbing weight for one cylinder, B, referred to the crank-pin, it must be opposed by two weights, w' w'', in the wheels D, C, as shown in fig. 201, on the same side of the axle, and together equal to the weight w. Then $w = w' + w''$; and making H and h, the distances apart of the cylinders and the wheels, as before, we have

$$\tfrac{1}{2}(h - H)\,w' = \tfrac{1}{2}(h + H)\,w'',$$

Fig. 201.

Inside Cylinders.—Internal Disturbing Forces and Counter-weights.

whence, reasoning as before,

$$w' = \frac{h + H}{2\,h}\,w, \text{ and } w'' = \frac{h - H}{2\,h}\,w;$$

that is, as before, the near weight w', is equal to the disturbing weight w, multiplied by the sum of the widths of the cylinders and wheels, and divided by twice the width of the wheels; and the off weight, w'', is equal to w multiplied by the difference of the widths, and divided by twice the width of wheels. Also, as before, the balance-weights, w', w'', on the near and off wheels, are to each other as the sum and the difference of widths of the cylinders and the wheels.

Finding, in the same way, the balance-weights for the other cylinder, we have in each wheel two weights equal to w' and w'' of which the greater is opposed to the near crank, and the less is at right angles to it, and *opposed* to the off crank, or just the reverse of its position for outside cylinders: as in fig. 202, showing the weights for the right hand wheel.

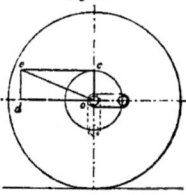

Fig. 202.

Inside Cylinders.—Diagram to find the Counterweight in the Wheel.

Here *o d*, *o c*, represent the elementary weights for the right hand crank; and the diagonal, *o e*, the magnitude and direction of the resulting counterweight, *diverging from* the off crank.

For example, let the total weight of the disturbing masses referred to the crank-pin, be assumed at 540 lbs., the same as in the outside-cylinder single engine already analyzed; the weights at each wheel are 407 lbs. and 133 lbs., and their resultant is 428 lbs. at an angle of $18\frac{1}{4}°$ with the centre line of the near crank.

The equivalent counterweight may be found arithmetically by extracting the square root of the sum of the squares of the elementary ones: thus $\sqrt{407^2 + 133^2} = 428$ lbs. Its direction also is found by setting off the line *o e*, at the inclination indicated by the ratio of the two weights: thus $407 \div 133 = 3$; and the counterweight is placed in a direction diverging from the centre line of the near crank, at the rate of 1 in 3.

To show the relative positions of the counterweights in one view, let A, B, fig. 203, be the right and left hand cranks, in side elevation, respectively in horizontal and vertical positions; then the counterweight A′, for the right hand wheel lies in the direction *o a*, at $18\frac{1}{4}°$ from the centre line O A, diverging from the crank B; and the counterweight B′, for the left hand wheel lies in the line o *b*, $18\frac{1}{4}°$ from the centre line C B. Thus the two counterweights,

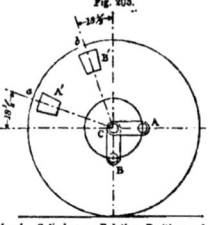

Fig. 203.

Inside Cylinders. — Relative Positions of Counterweights in Wheels.

on the opposite sides of the engine, *incline* towards each other when seen in side elevation, and their directions o *a*, o *b*, form an angle of 53°, or *less* than a right angle by as much as twice $18\frac{1}{4}°$, or 37°.

The angle of divergence of the counterweight from the centre line of the crank, as found in the foregoing examples, is shown to be much greater, nearly three times, for inside cylinders than for outsides: obviously on account of the more nearly equal action of the reciprocating weights of each cylinder upon the wheels, in the former case; and though inside-cylinder engines are more stable laterally than outsides, it is still of importance to apply counterweights, both to remove the fore and aft motions, and to reduce the internal wear of the mechanism.

Inside Cylinder Goods-Locomotives, with Coupled Wheels.— Inside-cylinder engines, with coupled wheels, have always been remarkable for steadiness, as the cranks and coupling rods outside balance approximately the pistons and connecting rods. The dimensions and relative positions of the inside and outside pieces, ought to be so combined as to

balance correctly. As already pointed out for inside cylinders, the true direction of the counterweight from the centre, is not directly opposed to that of the crank, but at a considerable angle with its centre line, dependent upon the relative widths apart of the wheels and cylinders, and such that, in side elevation, the two counterweights incline together; the outside cranks should, then, be set at the necessary angle to form a correct balance, and there is every freedom for doing so, whether the crank be formed within the wheel, or separately, as the wheel or the crank may be set in any position on the axle.

When the outside cranks are longer than the insides, the weight of the coupling rods, as well as of the cranks, must be referred to the inside crank-pin, to find their equivalent balancing weight.

When the bearings are inside, the coupling rods lie close to the wheels, and may be supposed to move in the same plane with them. With outside bearings, the overhung cranks and rods are so much wider than the wheels, that their extra leverage must be allowed for; and their equivalent weight, at the wheels, is found by multiplying their whole weight, for one side, referred to the inside crank-pin, by the width apart of the outside rods, and dividing by the width apart of the wheels.

When only four wheels are coupled, the balance requires to be helped with a little extra counterweight in the wheels; it may also be raised by making the outside cranks longer. When six wheels are coupled, there is an excess of balance, which may be neutralised by a back-counterweight to each wheel.

In the four coupled-wheel engines, fig. 204, made by Gouin for the Orleans Railway, the total moving weight

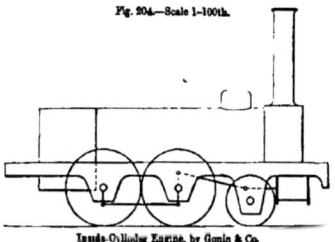

Fig. 204.—Scale 1–100th.

Inside-Cylinder Engine, by Gouin & Co.

on each inside crank is 597 lbs., the wheels are 4 feet 7 inches apart centres, and the cylinders 2 feet 6 inches apart. The moving weight to be balanced is found, in the way already described, to be divided into 441 lbs., and 156 lbs. for each wheel on the driving axle, the resultant of which is 467 lbs. requiring to be balanced at an angle of $19\frac{1}{4}°$ with the centre line of the inside crank. To make a perfect balance, it thus appears that the outside cranks, which are equal in length to the inside ones, should be keyed at an angle of 20° with the direction of the inside cranks, and that the weight of the outside cranks referred to the crank-pin, and the coupling rod, should be 467 lbs., supposing, as we may, that they act in the plane of the wheel. In reality their slump weight is but 353 lbs., or 114 lbs. short, and it is exactly opposed to the inside cranks; nevertheless, as the disturbing action is so materially reduced, these engines run with remarkable steadiness even at 45 miles per hour, with 5 feet wheels.

Crampton's Locomotives.—These engines are distinguished by the great length of their wheel-base, which has in some examples, as in annexed figure, 205, been made 16 feet

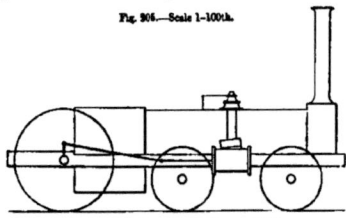

Fig. 205.—Scale 1–100th.

Crampton's Locomotive, by Derosne & Cail.

long, and in the Liverpool (page 19, *ante*) 18 feet; also, by the position of the driving axle behind the firebox, and by the great diameter of driving wheel, 7 to 8 feet. They are peculiarly steady at all speeds,—a result which is due jointly to their weight, the great distance apart of the axles—the leading and driving—which carry the greatest part of the weight, and by the reduced working velocity of the mechanism at given speeds on the rail.

In Crampton's engines, the whole of the working gear is placed close under the eye of the driver. The centre of gravity of the machine, also, is placed very low; and this is a condition on which great stress has been laid, and to which much of the stability of the engine is attributed. The height of the centre of gravity we regard as practically a matter of indifference, for we have found high-pitched engines, in point of stability, a match for any that have come under our notice. The position of the driving wheels in the rear is, we believe, the only tangible cause of the superior stability of those engines, as the unbalanced action of the reciprocating weights, operating at the extremity of the machine, is completely controlled by the mass in front of the axle. This is, however, in our view, a very questionable mode of doing what can be done as directly, and certainly more rationally, by the method of counterweights; for the great length of wheel-base, *well loaded at each end*, acts severely on the permanent way, in the passage along curves. Everything that has been gained by this over ordinary engines, in point of stability, can be met by the means of placing them in balance; and it should not be forgotten, that every engine, Crampton's included, should be fitted with counterweights, not merely because external stability is desirable, but also because the internal forces which tend to wear down any engine at work, should be as completely neutralised as possible. We are not sure but that, had the "long-boiler" engine been fitted with suitable counterweights, it would have remained in favour till this day, for it had much to recommend it, in the moderated wheel-base for the easy passage of curves, and in the facilities for extending the heating surface, and increasing its evaporating value per foot of area, even with the same size of firebox.

Of the Distribution and Calculation of Counterweights.—Counterweights, like the other revolving masses in the engine, are referred to the crank-pin, to find their equiva-

lent balancing weight. As they are necessarily irregular in form, the following methods of finding the centre of gravity are given:—

To find the Centre of Gravity of a Counterweight in one Segment.—Let A B, fig. 206,

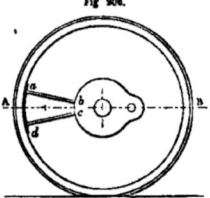

Fig. 206.

Driving Wheel and Counterweight in one Segment.

be the centre line through the crank, of the driving wheel to be balanced, and a b c d the space to be filled, between two spokes, opposed to the crank, and reaching from the nave to the rim. This space, done to a larger scale, fig. 207, is bisected by the centre line A B. Draw a c,

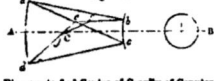

Fig. 207.

Diagram to find Centre of Gravity of Counterweight.

and bisect it at *e*; draw *d e* and *e b*, and set off on these lines, one-third of their lengths respectively, *e f* and *e g*; and draw *f g*. The point of intersection, c, of this line with the centre line A B, is the centre of gravity of the surface. So much for the geometrical process.

The centre of gravity may be found also by cutting a templet of uniform thickness to

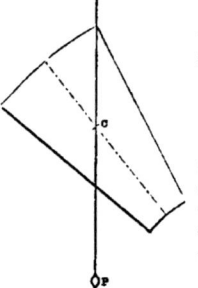

Fig. 208.

Mode of finding the Centre of Gravity by Templet.

the form of the surface, and freely suspending it by one of the corners, a, as in fig. 208; a plummet-line, P, dropped from the same point of suspension in front of the templet, will intersect the centre line at the centre of gravity, c. Reverting to fig. 206, and setting off the centre of gravity of the space *a c*, thus found, it stands at twenty-two inches from the centre of the wheel.

2d. *In three Segments, fig. 209.*—Find the centre of gravity c of one of the counterweights, as

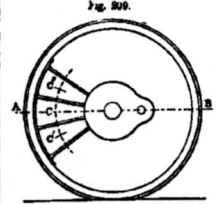

Fig. 209.

Driving Wheel and Counterweight in three Segments.

above, through c strike an arc from the centre of the wheel, and crossing the centre lines of the other segments at their centres c′, c″, as shown more distinctly in fig. 210; draw c′ c″ meeting A B at D, and set off D E, one-third of the interval D c. Then E is the common centre of gravity of the three segments, and is 20·82, or 20⅘ inches from the centre of the wheel.

3d. *In two Segments, fig. 211.*—This is required when the crank is opposed to a spoke, as in the figure. Find the centre of gravity, c, of one segment as before, and by an arc find the other centre c′; draw c c′ cutting A B at D, the common centre of gravity.

4th, *In four Segments, fig. 212.* — Find, as before, the centres c, c′, c″, c‴, of the segments; draw c″ c′ and c‴ c, cutting the line A B; bisect the interval so enclosed at E, for the common centre of gravity.

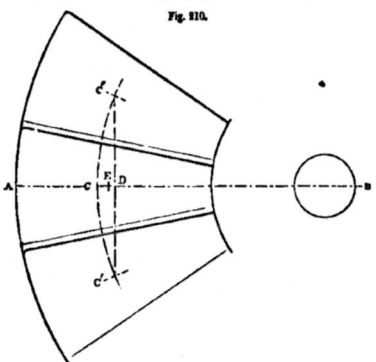

Fig. 210.

Method of finding the Common Centre of Gravity of three Segments.

When the counterweight occupies only a part of the space between the arms, the centre of gravity may either be

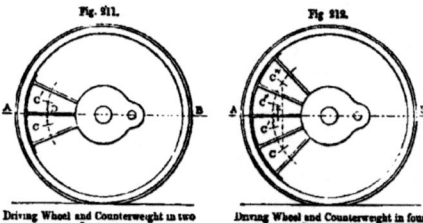

Fig. 211.   *Fig. 212.*

Driving Wheel and Counterweight in two Segments.   Driving Wheel and Counterweight in four Segments.

found as above, or approximated to by bisecting its radial centre line.

Calculation of the required Counterweight.—Having found the weight to be balanced in the wheel, referred to the crank-pin, it may be thence referred to the centre of gravity of the counterweight, by multiplying it by the length of crank, and dividing by the distance of the centre of gravity from the centre of the wheel. In the sample engine, fig. 183, the weight to be balanced was found to be 540 lbs., referred to the crank-pin; and if the counterweight be in one segment to fill one space, its centre of gravity is, by the method just given, at 22 inches radius, and

$$\frac{540 \times 11}{22} = 270 \text{ lbs.,}$$

the required counterweight,—in this case exactly one-half of the weight at the pin. To find the proper thickness, if it be of cast-iron, and formed exactly to fit the space *a c*, fig. 206, this space has 191·5 square inches area, and as cast iron weighs ·26 lb. per cubic inch, it requires 270 ÷ ·26 = 1038 cubic inches of metal. Now 1038 ÷ 191·5 = 5·4 inches, the requisite thickness of the counterweight.

If it be of lead, which is weightier than cast iron in the ratio of 1 to 1·6, the thickness will be 5·4 ÷ 1·6 = 3·4 ins.

Again, if, in the same engine, the weight is to be equally distributed in three segments, over three entire spaces, fig. 209, the common centre of gravity would be at

20·82, or 20¾ inches radius, and the whole counterweight would be

$$\frac{540 \times 11}{20\cdot82} = 285 \text{ lbs.}$$

The united area of surface would be 191·5 × 3 = 574·5 inches, and 285 ÷ ·26 = 1096 cubic inches of cast-iron required; therefore 1096 ÷ 574·5 = 1·9 inches, the necessary uniform thickness of metal.

Our next business is to show by experiment to what extent a compromise may be effected between the respective claims of longitudinal and lateral disturbances on the rails, in the adjustment of the counterweight, and to give a number of rules for practice.

CHAPTER V.

EXPERIMENTS ON THE BALANCING OF LOCOMOTIVES. RULES FOR PRACTICE.

Experiments of M. Nollau, 1848.[*]—One of these experiments was made with an inside-cylinder engine of the following dimensions:—Cylinders 15 inches by 20 inch stroke, 26 inches apart centres; driving wheels, 6 feet diameter, leading and trailing, 3½ feet, and 11 feet apart. Weight of crank, referred to the pin, and the half of connecting rod, 152 lbs.; crank, connecting rod, piston, and appendages, 400 lbs.

Counterweights were applied at 30 inches radius, between the spokes of each driving wheel; and to balance 152 lbs., the revolving weight, on a 10-inch crank, 152 × 1⁰⁄₃₀ = 51 lbs. was applied, and the engine suspended from the roof clear of the rails, free to vibrate any way; the centrifugal action was perfectly balanced, as there was not the slightest vertical action, even at 250 turns per minute. The fore-and-aft motion was, however, decided; but it was entirely destroyed by a weight of 400 × 1⁰⁄₃₀ = 133 lbs., balancing the entire moving weight. In this case, again, the excess of centrifugal force caused a vertical action of the machine; and there was also considerable sinuous movement, owing to the greater leverage of the balance-weights, being double that of the pistons, &c., measured from the centre of the axle.

As 51 lbs. was too light, and 133 lbs. too heavy, a mean of them was applied, (133 + 51) ÷ 2 = 92 lbs.; and the engine was set to work on the rails with this counterweight on each wheel. Such was the improved action of the engine, that, after a twelvemonth's work, there did not appear the slightest tear or wear of the draw-gear; while, formerly, even with buffing and draw springs, the bolts wore rapidly, and even the foot-plate was occasionally buckled or otherwise strained.[†]

Experiments of M. Le Chatelier.[‡]—In the workshops of

---

[*] Quoted in Le Chatelier's work on Stability.

[†] Though the details of this experiment show that M. Nollau was in the right direction, it is plain that he did not recognise the divided action of each crank and its appendages in the two wheels, nor the necessity, for perfect equilibrium, of placing the balance-weights at an angle with the centre lines of the cranks. This was reserved for Le Chatelier to work out.

[‡] The author has converted the results from French into English measures.

the Orleans Railway, an outside-cylinder long-boiler loco-motive, like fig. 183, was freely suspended from the roof of the building, 8 inches clear of the rails, by ropes about 12 feet long.

The following were the weights of the moving parts :—

Crank, referred to the pin,	...	...	93 lbs.
Connecting rod, ...	...	...	188
Piston and rod,	...	...	174
Crosshead,	...	...	64
	Total,	...	519 lbs.

Three counterweights were applied : 1st, a block of lead, which filled nearly the whole space opposed to the crank, and weighed 141 lbs. Its centre of gravity was 26 inches from the centre of the axle, and as the length of crank was 11 inches, it would balance a weight of 333 lbs. at the crank-pin, for

$$\frac{141 \times 26}{11} = 333 \text{ lbs.}$$

2d, two extra weights, together equal to 88 lbs., were placed, one on each side of the first weight, the centre of gravity of each being $28\frac{3}{4}$ inches from the centre, and their common centre of gravity $26\frac{1}{2}$ inches from the centre of the axle ; they would therefore balance 212 lbs. at the crank-pin, for $88 \times 26\frac{1}{2} \div 11 = 212$ lbs. The total counterweight was thus equivalent to $333 + 212 = 545$ lbs. at the crank-pin, which is somewhat in excess of 519 lbs., the weight of the moving parts.

To register the horizontal oscillations, a pencil was fixed to the buffer-beam, which traced the movement on a sheet of paper placed below it, the paper being so disposed as to yield to the vertical movements of the pencil.

Observations were made at various speeds of the engine on its driving axle, up to three turns per second, or an equiva-lent of 35 miles per hour on the rail, under three conditions, —1st, without any counterweight ; 2d, with the partial balance of 333 lbs. referred to the crank-pin ; 3d, with the total balance of 545 lbs. Though the speed was limited as above, it was established that, in the same state of balance, the extent of free oscillation was not affected by speed, as the diagrams described by the pencil were the same for all observed speeds,—an experimental result which was plainly predicable from the nature of moving forces, for, though, at higher speeds, the intensity of the disturbing force was increased, the time for each oscil-lation was also shorter. Fig. 213 contains full-size copies of the oscillation - diagrams obtained. No. 1 was described during the free action of the machine, without counterweight ; it is elliptical in form, and indicates the combined action of the two varying forces, which cause fore-and-aft motion and sinuous motion, in the directions of the dot-lines $a\,b$, $a\,c$, respectively, and showing a range of action both ways of about $\frac{1}{4}$d inch. No. 2 was described under the influence of a partial balance of 333 lbs., which, though much below the equilibrium-load, reduced the range of action either way to about ·08 or $\frac{1}{12}$ inch. When the full coun-terweight of 545 lbs. at the crank-pin was applied, the hori-zontal oscillation was effectually extinguished, and the dia-gram, No. 3, dwindled into a simple point.

Fig. 213.—Full size.

No 1.   No. 2.   No. 3.

Oscillation-Diagrams from Passenger-Engine.

These results show not only the nature and extent of the disturbing action, but the efficacy of counterweights in ex-tinguishing it. When the engine was placed on the rails, with its counterweights attached, it ran with steadiness at 50 to 60 miles per hour, subject only to shocks from the imperfections of the way. The balances being removed, the engine resumed its customary oscillatory motions, violently concussing the draw-gear, and working the spring even at much lower speeds.

The experiment was repeated with the same results, on a six coupled wheel goods-engine, with outside inclined cylin-ders, and 4 feet 3 inch wheels. This class of engine had been found very unsteady on the rails, and required frequent repair. Counterweights equivalent to 1100 lbs. at the crank-pin, were equally distributed between the three wheels on each side of the engine, well worn by long service; they were placed exactly opposite the cranks, the total weight being less than would exactly have balanced the engine. With a train of 44 waggons, at 30 miles per hour, the engine ran with steadiness, though the wheels had already been well-worn by long service, and the axle-boxes had considerable play. The counterweights being removed, the engine was again set to work with the same train ; it was then found impossible to exceed a speed of 25 miles, as the engine ran so unsteadily, and was affected with very violent oscillation and fore-and-aft motion.

Similar experiments were made, on the Northern Railway of France, upon a six-coupled wheel goods-engine, with out-side horizontal cylinders, by suspending it in the workshops. When unbalanced, and put in motion, it described the curve, fig. 214, at the buffer-beam, showing a compound lateral and fore-and-aft vibration equal to about $\frac{5}{8}$-inch. A counterweight equi-valent to 882 lbs., or about seven-eighths of the whole weight was applied on each side of the engine. The engine had just been turned in for repair, on account of the play at the bearings and other parts, and was thus under very unfavourable conditions for the trial. It was disconnected from the tender, and, with 4 feet wheels, ran alone at a speed of 40 miles per hour, with satisfactory steadiness : there was no fore-and-aft motion at all, and only a slight degree of sinuous movement. Four of the five blocks for balancing being then removed, leaving only an equivalent balance of 176 lbs., or 17 per cent. of the whole weight, the engine alone could not get above 31 miles per hour, and at this speed the unsteadiness was "fearful." When the tender was screwed up to the engine, the fore-and-aft move-ment was partially destroyed, but the lateral was as violent as before.

Conclusions.—It is clear that, with inside cylinders, though the weight required to balance exactly the sinuous action is much less than that for fore-and-aft action, yet the general stability of the engine is well secured by the exact adaptation of the counterweight to the sinuous action. In the first experiment, by Nollau, a counterweight only 69 per cent. of the whole disturbing weight yielded very good results, and it was less than would have been found by cal-culation to meet the sinuous action. In Gouin's inside-cylinder engine, referred to in last chapter, which worked

Fig. 214.—Full size.

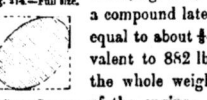

Oscillation-Diagram, from Goods-Engine.

steadily, the balance weight was but 60 per cent. of the whole disturbing weight, while 78 per cent. would have been required to meet the sinuous action exactly. In outside-cylinder engines, particularly with coupled wheels, complete stability cannot be effected with less than an equivalent of seven-eighths of the whole disturbing weight.

In general, for inside cylinders, a counterweight in the wheels equivalent to three-fourths of the gross disturbing weight on each side of the engine, is practically sufficient to secure the external stability of the engine on the rails. For outside cylinders it ought to be equivalent to the whole, or, in single engines, not less than seven-eighths of the weight.

Secondly, The application of suitable balance-weights is attended by a sensible reduction of resistance on the rails at high speeds; as, in the experiments of Le Chatelier, the engine unbalanced could not reach the same speed as when balanced. This is corroborated by the writer's observations on the single and coupled passenger-engines of the Caledonian Railway. Also by some results obtained by Le Chatelier, from the Orleans goods-engine. This engine was continued at work with the counterweights attached, after the experiment already described, without having anything done to it, in the way of repairs. In the hands of the same driver, at the same kind of work, the following are the mean consumptions of coke during three months:—

	Coke per Mile.	
1848, December,	49·5 lbs.	} Without counterweights.
1849, January,	50·3 lbs.	
,, February,	42·3 lbs.	} Mean of 12 trips, of which 10 only were made with counterweights.

Of course, a single result like this can hardly be considered a clencher; but it affords a strong presumption of the material economy of combustible effected by a suitable use of counterweights.

Thirdly, The balance-weight should in all cases be distributed over at least two or three spaces, to distribute and reduce the unequal wear of the tyres by vertical action, and the tendency to slip at high speeds.

Fourthly, The experiments of Le Chatelier show the limited extent of even free oscillation in a single engine, and how much greater it is in a coupled engine with outside cylinders. This difference explains the greater liability of the latter engines to violent concussions laterally against the rails.

Fifthly, To reduce so far as practicable the reciprocating weights, and the severe and unavoidable strains they throw on the crank-pins at high speeds, the pistons should be of wrought iron, the crossheads and slides should be hollowed out,[*] and the connecting rods as simple and light as possible.

Sixthly, The more nearly the width of the cylinders is equal to that of the wheels, the more exactly may both the longitudinal and lateral actions be balanced by a given counterweight in the wheel. Thus, outside cylinders are susceptible of a more perfect balance than insides, and the closer that inside cylinders are placed, the less perfectly can they be balanced in the wheels.

---

* Mr. M'Connell has lately patented a light form of wrought iron piston, and the formation of piston-rods and connecting rods from wrought iron tubes: the object being to combine lightness with strength. This, we apprehend, would be a serviceable idea for outside-cylinder coupled engines.

From all that has been said we derive the following practical rules for the application of counterweights:—

RULE I.—*To find the Counterweight for Outside-Cylinder Single Engines.* Find the total weight, in pounds, of the revolving and reciprocating masses for one side, namely, the piston and appendages, connecting rod, crank, and crank-pin, (the crank being referred to the pin)—multiply by the length of crank in inches,—and divide by the radial distance, in inches, of the centre of gravity of the space to be occupied by the counterweight. The result is the counterweight in pounds, to be placed exactly opposite to the crank.

RULE II.—*To find the Counterweights for Outside-Cylinder Coupled Engines.* Find the separate revolving weights, in pounds, of crank-pin, coupling rods and connecting rod, for each wheel,—also the reciprocating weight of the piston and appendages, and half the connecting rod; divide the reciprocating weight equally between the coupled wheels, and add the aliquot part, so allotted, to the revolving weight on each wheel. The sums so obtained are the weights to be balanced at the several wheels, for which the necessary counterweight may be found by Rule I.

RULE III.—*To find the Counterweight for Inside-Cylinder Single Engines.* 1st, To find its value. Find the total weight, in pounds, to be balanced on each side, as in Rule I.;—multiply it by the sum of the widths apart centres of the cylinders and the wheels, in inches,—and divide by twice the width apart of the cylinders;—subtract the quotient (A) from the total weight, leaving a remainder (B),—square the quantities A and B, add the squares, and find the square root of the sum. This root is the resulting weight in pounds, to be balanced at the crank-pin, for which the counterweight may be found by Rule I.

2d. To find its direction. Divide the greater weight (A) by the less (B). The quotient is the denominator of the fraction of which the numerator is 1, which expresses the inclination of the direction sought, with the centre line of the near crank, diverging *from* the off crank.

RULE IV.—*To find the Counterweights for Inside-Cylinder Coupled Engines.* Find the value and direction of the counterweights for the inside revolving and reciprocating masses to be balanced, as in Rule III.; and key the driving wheels on the axle in such positions as to place the outside cranks in the direction so found, or key on the cranks themselves as required, if independent of the wheels;—find the total weight of the outside cranks and coupling rods, referred to the inside crank-pin,—and, if less than the inside weight, subtract the outside weight from it, and distribute the difference between the coupled wheels, to be balanced according to Rule I.;—or, if greater, balance the difference by counterweights *opposed* to the outside cranks.

Note 1. The counterweight for inside cylinders may be found approximately by assuming three-fourths of the whole disturbing weight as the weight to be balanced in the wheel.

2. Inside-cylinder coupled engines as they stand, usually fall within the requirements of *Note* 1.

3. Though *Note* 1 contains a good general rule, for general stability, the other rules should be employed where exact equilibrium is required, so as to balance as well as possible every internal strain.

4. For the method of referring the weight to the crank-pin, see page 169.

5. For the method of finding the centre of gravity of the counterweight, see page 176.

6. In the use of Rule 4, the outside weight for four coupled wheels is usually found to be less than what is required ; and, for six coupled wheels, greater.

7. To substitute lead for cast iron counterweights, divide the volume found for the latter by 1·6, to find the equivalent volume of lead.

8. Examples of the application of the rules are given in previous chapters.

CHAPTER VI.

OF THE CAUSES OF INSTABILITY DUE TO THE PERMANENT WAY.

The Form of the Rails.—The tyres of the wheels are formed conically, with the object of promoting stability, as shown exaggerated in fig. 215, where A, B, are the apices of the cones of which the tyres form parts. The ordinary

Fig. 215.

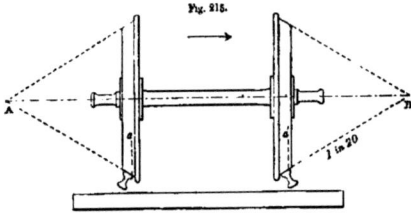

Diagram to show Conical Form of Wheel Tyres, and their action.

slope of the surface of the tyre, referred to the centre line of the axle, is 1 in 20, as marked, which upon a tyre 5 inches broad would amount to ¼ inch. To suit the rails to the tyres, they are inclined inwards, to the same slope, which, upon a width of 2½ inches, would amount to ⅛ inch, off the horizontal. Now, as the rails may not be set with perfect uniformity to the slope, or if set so at first, they may not continue so, from a deviation or subsidence of the chair, or the seating of the rail, or the sleeper, or the ballast ; and as the conicity of the tyre does not remain uniform, and is indeed destroyed by wear, it is clear that, supposing the rail to be flat on the upper surface, there are many causes why the surfaces of the tyre and the rail, at the point of contact, should not coincide across the whole width of the latter. On this account it may, and often does happen that the wheels roll on the inner edge of one rail and the outer edge of the other ; and that they roll on different diameters, as at a, a′, fig. 215, possibly ⅛ inch difference on each side, or ¼ inch total on the diameter, equal to ¾ inch on the circumference. Thus, in one turn of the axle, one wheel a would be ¾ inch in advance of the other, a′, and would tend to sway the engine over to the short side, as indicated by the arrow, when the inequality would be reversed, and the engine thrown back towards the other side. Thus a sinuous motion would be created, which would vanish after a few vibrations, were it not that each successive length of

rail presents some new state of matters, giving rise to a succession of irregularities.

Much of the irregularity due to the flat-headed rail, of which fig. 216 is an example, is removed by rounding the head with a curve of 10 or 12 inch radius, added in dot-lining ; as thereby the point of contact with the wheel is usually very near the summit of the curve, and is less susceptible of change laterally ; the rail also suits itself more freely to the change of form of the tyre, by friction and wear.

Fig. 216.—1-4th.

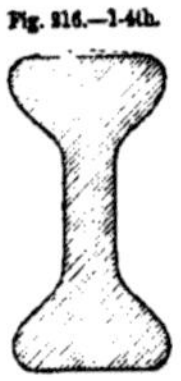

Section of Flat-headed Rail.

Clearance of the Rails.—Clearance between the wheel-flanges and the rails is necessary both for the passage of the engine along curves, and to give liberty for unavoidable oscillation within certain limits, without incurring perpetual collisions between the wheels and the rails. On the earlier railways, where the clearance was small, lateral concussion was much more active and injurious than it has been found to be with extra clearance. Half an inch is the usual lateral play with which new wheels are adjusted, between the rails.

Maintenance of the Way.—Subsidence of the rails, on one or both sides, equally or unequally, and lateral deviations from the gauge, are obvious causes of instability. A low rail on one side, below the general level, brings down the engine on that side, causes it to swerve from the right line, and to commence a course of oscillation ; and this may be aggravated by a succession of unequal levels, particularly if they coincide in their action, and both sinuous and rolling movements may be produced. But independently of vertical deflection, the rails may be bent, or otherwise caused to deviate laterally, and assume a horizontally undulating course ; when the leading wheels advance upon the deformed rail, they immediately shift their point of contact towards the outside of the tyre, and roll on a smaller circumference, in virtue of their conical form ; the engine deviates towards the wide rail and oscillates accordingly, and this erratic movement may readily be incurred to so dangerous an extent, should the lateral deflections of the rail coincide with the oscillations of the engine, that on bad or on newly made parts of the line, the driver is obliged to shut off the steam wholly or partially, to reduce the speed.

If the state of the way be such that both rails sink at once under the engine, at successive intervals, while at the other parts they remain firm, as in the case of weak joints, or elastic longitudinal timbers propped at intervals on piles, or of weak or imperfectly trussed timber bridges, between the piers,—the engine readily acquires a plunging motion, which is all the greater, the more flexible the springs.

All the effects just sketched of the imperfections of the way, are notoriously familiar to those who have been in the habit of riding on locomotives at high speeds. Every means should be employed to bring up the character of the way to that of a lathe-bed. We are sensible that, in many points, the prevailing system of permanent way is objectionable, and open to improvement ; and only trust that, amongst the numerous specifics now afloat for improving the system, something may be found to produce, in the words of Mr. W. B. Adams, a "*really* permanent way," as a well-made way is quite as important as a well-balanced engine.

CHAPTER VII.

OF THE CAUSES OF INSTABILITY DUE TO THE TEAR AND WEAR OF THE MACHINE.

TEAR and wear affects the parallelism of the axles, the diameter of the wheels, the wear of the tyres, the play of the axle-boxes, &c.

Want of Parallelism of the Axles.—When the axles are inclined together, or nearer on one side of the engine than on the other, the result is the same as that caused by unequal diameters of wheel, already noticed, in causing the engine to swerve from its course towards the side at which the axles incline; and the nearer the axles are placed together, the stronger is the tendency to diverge. This tendency is constant, and if it do not produce sinuous movements, it at least harasses the engine by withdrawing it from the direct course. The result is a constant friction and extra wear of the wheel-flanges on the near side.

Unequal Diameters of the Wheels on the same Axles.—This arises from unequal wear of the tyres, due to difference of quality and other causes. The result is, like want of parallelism of the axle, to drag the engine to one side, toward the smaller wheel. The action is constant, and, like that arising from want of parallelism, it wears down the flanges. Cases of unequal wear of flanges, more or less, are very frequent.

Wear of the Tyres.—The originally straight contour of the tyres wears generally into a hollow, deepest about the middle of the breadth of the tyre; of which several examples are given in the following figures. The effect of this wear is to increase the conicity of the wheels, next the flanges, and consequently the liability to sinuous motion from other causes.

Examples of Worn Tyres. — *The Atlas Goods-Engine, M. S. & L. R.*—Fig. 217 contains sections of the tyres of

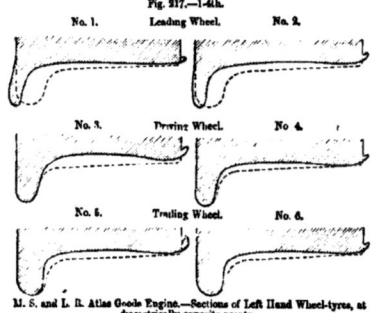

Fig. 217.—1-4th.

No. 1.   Leading Wheel.   No. 2.

No. 3.   Driving Wheel.   No. 4.

No. 5.   Trailing Wheel.   No. 6.

M. S. and L. R. Atlas Goods Engine.—Sections of Left Hand Wheel-tyres, at diametrically opposite points.

this engine, which was put to work in May 1846, and had run 40,222 miles, up to the end of October 1847; at the end of this time the sections of the tyres, of Lowmoor iron, were taken; and the wear is shown by contrast with the original sections in dot-lining.* The Atlas had cylinders 18 inches by 2 feet stroke, and six 4½ feet wheels coupled; extreme centres, about 11¼ feet apart; weight, in working

* *Trans. Inst. Mech. Engineers*, 1848.

order, 24 tons, about equally distributed on the wheels, and in general design and arrangement the same as the Sphynx (Plate 18, and No. 17 diagram-plate 6). The front wheels have shown most wear at the flanges, the hind wheels the next, and the middle or driving wheels least; indeed, the whole wear and labour of guiding the machine may be said to have come on the front and hind wheel-flanges, and on the former chiefly, those of the driving wheels being turned originally ½ inch thinner than the others, as per sections. On the tread of the tyres, or rolling part, the middle wheels, upon the whole, have worn most, the front next, and the hind least. The greater wear of the leading flanges, proves a greater lateral movement of the front wheels on the rails, which has been increased by the extra lateral wear; this explains why the leading tyres are more equally worn breadthwise than the others, and have become in fact nearly cylindrical.

Looking more in detail, each wheel is found to be worn unequally,—to have "most worn" and "least worn" parts; these are, in each wheel, opposed to each other, and are certainly owing to the unbalanced centrifugal action of the coupling rods,—vertically, on the treads of the middle and hind wheels; and horizontally, on the flange of the leading wheel. On the middle wheel there is most vertical action, as it carries half the whole weight of the coupling rods; and accordingly it shows a greater excess of wear on the tread (No. 3 section), which must have taken place next the outside crank-pin, than either of the other wheels. The unequal wear of the leading flange is attributable to the sinuous motion caused by the unbalanced excess of the outside rods, whereby the flange is driven against the rail at a particular time during each revolution. This explanation is confirmed by the circumstance that the flange is *most* worn where the tread is *least* worn (section 1), and *vice versa* (section 2), as the left hand flange is supposed to be thrown to the rail by the right hand coupling rod when it is at the front end of its throw, and when the left hand coupling rod is on the upper centre, and where consequently the wear of the tread ought to be smallest. On the same grounds, the most worn parts of the flange and tread of the hind wheel ought to wear *together*; and this in fact they do, (sections 5 and 6).

This irregular wear of the tyres operates injuriously not merely by overstraining the coupling rods, but also by exciting a wriggling motion of the engine, as the wheels with constantly varying radii, are like wheels with different diameters on the same axle, the twisting action of which has already been explained.

C. R. No. 51, Passenger-Engine.—Fig. 218 contains sections of the Lowmoor wheel-tyres of this engine and its tender, after 10 months running without repair, over above 28,000 miles. The dotted lines show the original sections from which the wheels had worn during that time. The weight of an engine of the same build, after the Crewe model, (No. 30, diagram-plate 6) was found, by one of Pooley's machines to be 19 tons in working order, as follows :—

Leading wheels,	...	...	5¾	tons.
Driving do.,	...	...	9½	
Trailing do.,	...	...	3¾	
	Total,	...	19	tons.

In this engine, as in the Atlas, the leading tyres are the most worn at the flange, and the other wheels very little, the greater wear of the former being due to oscillation and the fatigue of leading the engine along the curves.

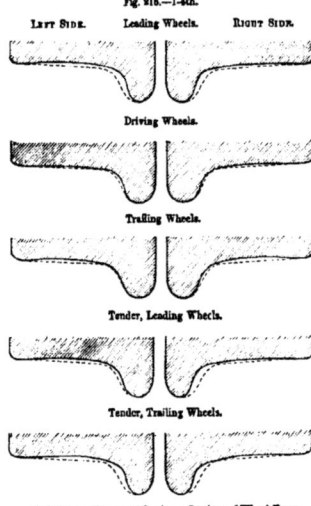

Fig. 218.—1-4th.

LEFT SIDE.　　Leading Wheels.　　RIGHT SIDE.

Driving Wheels.

Trailing Wheels.

Tender, Leading Wheels.

Tender, Trailing Wheels.

C. R. No. 51, Passenger-Engine.—Sections of Wheel-Tyres.

The driving tyres wore uniformly, as the counterweight just balanced the revolving parts, and the sections, taken from points at right angles to the crank, show very little wear of the tread. The fore and the hind tyres show more wear, and, as in the Atlas, the wear of the hind tyres is more confined to one part. Moreover, the flanges of each pair of wheels are unequally worn. Thus, the left hand leading and driving wheels, and the right hand trailing wheels, have thinner flanges than their neighbours at the other ends of the axles. This must have been by an extra bias of the front of the engine towards the left hand, due likely to the greater wear of the tread of the left hand leading wheel, which would reduce this wheel to a smaller diameter than its neighbour. This would throw the hinder part towards the right ; the hinder part would lead the fore-end of the tender with it towards the same side, and would swing the back part to the left ; accordingly, in fact, the right hand fore wheel, and the left hand trailing wheel of the tender, show a greater wear of the flange than the alternate wheels.

No. 46, C. R. Coupled Passenger-Engine.—This engine has 6 feet driving wheels, with the hind wheels coupled, arranged like No. 42, diagram-plate 6. In working trim, the weight is 19¼ tons, as follows :—

Leading wheels,	...	...	6¼ tons.
Driving do.,	...	...	8¼
Trailing do.,	...	...	4¾
	Total,	...	19½ tons.

Fig. 219 contains worn sections of the Lowmoor tyres, after running upwards of 60,000 miles since being turned up. The treads of the right hand leading and driving

wheels, and the left hand trailing wheels, are decidedly more worn than their opposite neighbours ; and consequently also their flanges, as the head of the engine must have been strongly biassed towards the right, and the other end

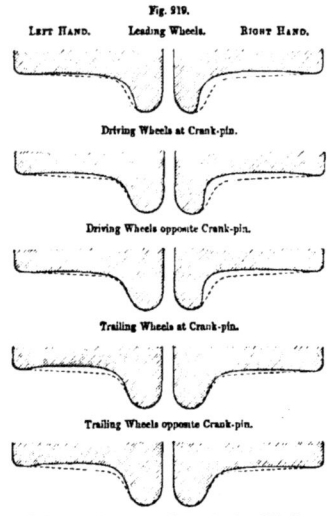

Fig. 219.

LEFT HAND.　　Leading Wheels.　　RIGHT HAND.

Driving Wheels at Crank-pin.

Driving Wheels opposite Crank-pin.

Trailing Wheels at Crank-pin.

Trailing Wheels opposite Crank-pin.

C. R. No. 46, Coupled Passenger-Engine.—Sections of Wheel-tyres.

towards the left. This is an illustration of the value of a full turned driving flange in assisting the leader, for had the middle flanges of No. 46 been turned originally thinner than the others, the right hand leading flange would have been ground to a shred like that of the Atlas. On each of the driving and hind wheels, the sections taken *at* and *opposite* the crank-pin show nearly equal amounts of wear, and prove the revolving parts to have been well balanced.

No. 49, C. R. Passenger-Engine.—Fig. 220 contains sections of the leading and driving tyres of this engine, which is like No. 51. The left hand leading flange is much more worn than the right hand one, owing likely to the

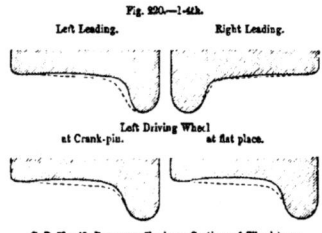

Fig. 220.—1-4th.

Left Leading.　　　　Right Leading.

Left Driving Wheel
at Crank-pin.　　　　at flat place.

C. R. No. 49, Passenger Engine.—Sections of Wheel-tyres.

greater wear of the tread, as in No. 51. The sections of the driving tyre were both taken from the left hand wheel, at less than 9 inches apart, showing the ordinary wear, and the excessive wear at a faulty place ; and though the latter is but $\frac{1}{16}$ inch greater, the difference was sufficient to bring down the wheel with violence on the rail, at high speeds.

No. 107, C. R. Goods-Engine.—This is an outside-cylinder

six-wheel engine, with the leading wheels coupled, arranged like No. 15 of diagram-plate 6, with single hind wheels ; cylinder 16 by 20 inches, driving wheels 4½ feet, trailing do. 3½ feet. The left-hand leading and driving tyres, fig. 221, are

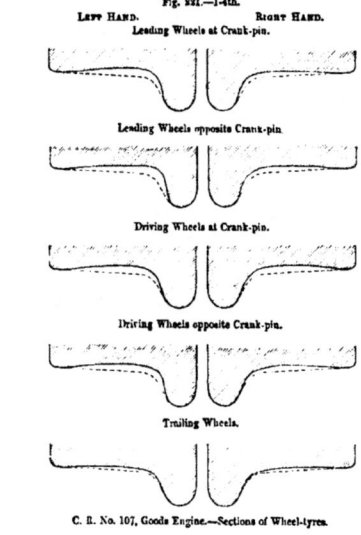

Fig. 221.—1-4th.
LEFT HAND. RIGHT HAND.
Leading Wheels at Crank-pin.

Leading Wheels opposite Crank-pin.

Driving Wheels at Crank-pin.

Driving Wheels opposite Crank-pin.

Trailing Wheels.

C. R. No. 107, Goods Engine.—Sections of Wheel-tyres.

more worn on the tread than the right hand ones, and in consequence their flanges also are more worn. On the sides of the leading flanges, too, opposite the crank-pin, the wear is greater than next the pin, as the head of the engine sways from side to side, and strains the flanges at these particular places.

Tender of No. 13, C. R. Passenger-Engine.—This tender is on the model usually employed for the C. R. passenger-engines. The wheels are 3½ feet in diameter, with Lowmoor tyres. Fig. 222 shows the wear upon them after running

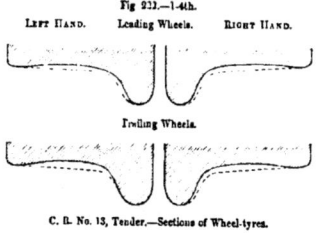

Fig 222.—1-4th.
LEFT HAND. Leading Wheels. RIGHT HAND.

Trailing Wheels.

C. R. No. 13, Tender.—Sections of Wheel-tyres.

for 14 months, over 30,000 miles. The tyres are all well hollowed, and, as before, the leading flanges are most worn.

These instances show the importance of the disturbing causes at work in the engine, affecting the stability and ease of its motion.

Play of the Journals and Axleboxes.—Two kinds of play may arise : lateral play of the journal in its bearing when the latter wears endwise, and longitudinal play of the axlebox between the guides on the guardplates. The lateral

play of the journal increases the movement due to lateral action on the engine, and if also the guardplates be flexible, and there be any play in the boiler-stays, the lateral movements of the engine are by so much increased, and may be much greater than the mere play of the wheels. If, also, the axleboxes have fore-and-aft play, the evil is increased by the want of parallelism of the axles, which is certain, under the circumstances, to be induced by the unequal wear of the tyres.

That the agencies referred to in this and the preceding chapters are real causes of instability, is proved by the direct experience that stability is more and more improved by the successive removal of these causes :—play of the axle-boxes, play of the journals, deformed tyres, want of parallelism of the axles, disrepair of the way, flatness of the rails ; having, instead, an engine well brought up to its bearings, with well-formed tyres, a firm and even railway, and rails with a properly rounded rolling surface.

CHAPTER VIII.

CONDITIONS OF THE GENERAL ARRANGEMENT, AND THE DISPOSITION OF THE WEIGHT, CONSISTENT WITH THE STABILITY OF LOCOMOTIVES.—EXPERIMENTAL EVIDENCE.

THOUGH the machinery of an engine be well balanced, and in such good order as to remove every internal cause of instability, it must also be well placed on its wheels, and well suspended, to provide against the instability due to the nature and imperfections of the way. The wheels ought to command the load,—the leading wheels being well forward, and the trailing wheels well backward : the former, chiefly to prevent or reduce injurious oscillation horizontally ; the latter to prevent the pitching of the engine. This arrangement is necessary, not merely on general grounds, but specially also, because, in the locomotive, the heaviest parts of the suspended or pendulous mass are placed usually at the extremities, and the farther these masses are from the centre of pendulous action, the greater is their power of straining the wheels, and of increasing the labour of keeping the engine to the rails. Thus the proper function of the fore wheels is to guide the engine laterally, and that of the hind wheels is to prevent pitching, vertically.

To meet the third kind of irregular motion, rocking, the springs must be sufficiently stiff to absorb rapidly the rolling motion, and sufficiently apart, transversely, to have the necessary leverage upon, and command of, the rolling load, consistent with their desirable flexibility ; for the wider apart the springs are transversely, the lighter or at least the more flexible they may be.

Such precautionary arrangements are demanded only for high-speed engines, or such as are destined for speeds above 20 to 25 miles ; and under the existing conditions of railway traffic, the great majority of engines must be so designed. For short lines, small branch lines, and mineral lines, inferior speeds are quite suitable.

Experimental Evidence.—The foregoing principles have been abundantly established by experience ; and to illustrate the influence of the disposition of the wheels on stability, we have thrown together, in diagram-plate VI., Parts I. and II., outline elevations of engines which have been and are in actual existence, types of the classes of arrangement to which, as carriages, they belong.

Ordinary Inside-Cylinder Locomotives.—No. 1 is the primitive form of four-wheeled engines, with inside horizontal cylinders, adopted in the Planet by Stephenson, and extensively imitated by other makers. No. 1 was succeeded by No. 4, with an extra pair of wheels behind the firebox, to remove the pitching due to the overhang in the former. The six-wheeled arrangement, thus produced, has not been excelled, as a carriage, by anything that has been turned out since. No. 2 is the four-wheeled engine, with inside horizontal cylinders, and an overhung circular fire-box, introduced originally by Bury; as a carriage, it is inferior to No. 1, for the overhang is greater at both ends, giving rise, at high speeds, to injurious pitching and to sinuous motion. No. 3 is a modification of Bury's engine, used on the Edinburgh and Glasgow railway, in which the boiler is lengthened, and the wheel-base is doubled by the addition of a pair of wheels in front, under the cylinders. This engine we have found, by direct experience on the buffer-beam, to "lead" well, as the wheels are well forward, and laterally it is very steady; but the pitching, by the overhang of the boiler, is still violent. Nos. 5, 6, 7, 8, are amplifications of design No. 4 by different makers. In all of these the firebox, the heaviest part of the boiler, is well supported; the leading wheels are also well forward, except in No. 8, in which the cylinders, with their cranks, are placed widely apart to clear the boiler, and to admit it nearer to the driving axle; the cylinders, therefore, encroach upon the leading wheels, which are thus placed quite in their rear. In this way, the overhang in front is greater than in the other engines, and the leverage of the principal overhung masses, on the leading wheels and guards, is increased by the greater diameter of the driving wheels, which requires higher cylinders. In consequence, this engine, of which an example is to be found on the North British Railway, does not lead well; it sways from side to side, at high speeds, with great power, bending the guard-plates, heating the journals, and wearing down the flanges of the leading wheels, by the severe lateral friction to which they are exposed. With its high wheels and large boiler, it was designed for high-speed trains; but the truth is, that engines by the same makers, with six-feet wheels, and arranged precisely like No. 6, with the same overhang, run much more steadily, with heavier trains, and at higher speeds. The horizontal distance of the mid-length of the cylinder beyond the centre of the leading axle, we find for the four engines, as follow:—

No. 5,	...	...	29 inches.
No. 6,	...	...	29 ,,
No. 7,	...	...	31 ,,
No. 8,	...	...	38 ,,

These measures are expressions of the leverage of the principal overhanging masses, and they show that No. 8 has 7 to 9 inches more leverage than the others, which, with its flexible axleguards, accounts for its inferior stability. The cylinders ought to have been considerably inclined upwards, like those of No. 30, partially to clear the leading wheels, and permit of their being set forward. No. 9 is a modification lately introduced by Stephenson, in which the cylinders are coupled

to an intermediate crank-shaft, from which outside rods are conveyed to the driving wheels placed behind the firebox; this plan is designed to combine the stability of Crampton's engine with the benefit of a separate driving-shaft carried by the frame, and relieved of all engine-weight. There is much difference of opinion as to the propriety of adding to the number of parts for the sake of relieving the crank-shaft.

Light Tank-Locomotives.—Nos. 10, 11, 12, 13, are engines which carry their own coke and water; they are all steadily placed on their wheels, except No. 13, in which the cylinders overhang in the same manner, and for the same reason, as in No. 8. Nos. 10 and 12 are stable machines, with moderate wheel-bases of 10 to 12 feet, suitable for light engines, and qualifying them to pass along curves, and run either end foremost with facility and safety. In No. 11, a 12 ton engine, the wheel-base of 15 feet is extravagant and unsafe; engines of this class, though perfectly steady at all speeds, are liable to leave the rails on quick curves, owing to the long base, the want of flexibility in the axle-guards, and the insufficiency of the weight to keep them down. They must have weight on the driving-wheels, to give the necessary adhesion; but this can only be increased by relieving the other wheels of part of their weight, and reducing their power of keeping the rails. Thus there are two distinct and opposing demands,—for adhesion-weight and leading weight; but, for purposes of stability, the hind wheels do not require above a mere trifle of load, which indeed is rather to keep all their bearings taut; whereas, in this engine, there is some weight unavoidably thrown away on the back wheels, of no use for either adhesion or safety. The engine would, then, be improved by removing the back tank forward, to increase the useful weight; and by shifting the hind wheels two feet forward, to add to the safety by shortening the wheel-base. No. 12 labours under the same disadvantage of an overhanging tank, and accordingly we find the front and hind wheels equally loaded, and out of 14 tons weight, only 7½ tons are available as driving weight. The carriage would be improved, like No. 11, by removing the tank forward. In fact, back loads in light engines like Nos. 11 and 12 are injudiciously placed, for they are not only useless for stability where they stand, but they balance and neutralise a part of the useful weight forward. They are only advisable in engines like No. 13, where the hind wheels are coupled, as all the weight is utilised, and a more convenient distribution of the whole weight may be effected. It is true, when in six-wheel tank engines, the hind wheels are well loaded, the engines may run either end foremost with greater safety; and this is an advantage where means of turning are not provided. Still, an efficient machine is the first thing, even at the cost of a little trouble in turning; and where tank-engines are expected to run either end foremost, the hind wheels, if there be six altogether, ought certainly to be coupled so as to utilise the back loads for driving weight.

Coupled Wheel Locomotives.—Nos. 14—21, are all, except one, examples of coupled engines. No. 14 is very deficient as a carriage. It has a relatively short wheel-base, and is much overhung at both ends. The frame is, however, absolutely inflexible, as it is composed of bar iron 4½ inches wide and 2 inches deep. Nos. 15 and 16 are patterns of steady engines; with No. 15 there is more command of adhesion-weight, but where the trailing-weight is sufficient, No. 16 with the back wheels coupled, is preferable, as the leading wheels are left free for their proper functions. No. 17 is superior to No. 14, as it leads better, and has a longer wheel-base, partly in virtue of its longer boiler; to Nos. 15 and 16, it is inferior, as its overhung firebox is found to pitch heavily at high speeds, for not even its great length of boiler can save it. For the same reason it is inferior to Nos. 18–21, where everything is solidly supported. In Nos. 19, 20, special care is taken to lead the machine well, as the front axle is placed unusually far forward, nearly flush with the front of the cylinders, and the wheels are aided by a second pair immediately behind. In No. 20, the four leading wheels are on a separate frame or "bogie," which swivels on a centre pin under the boiler, and yields to all curvatures of the rails. The superior action of this separate frame system is proved by the superior smoothness of the motion, and the very small wear of the leading wheel-flanges.

Light Outside Cylinder Tank-Locomotives.—Nos. 22–26. No. 22 has the old fault of an overhanging firebox, and is unfitted for running alone and unsupported, with steadiness. It is, however, light, and may be controlled by sufficient coupling to the carriage-tender with which Mr. Adams supplements his light engines. In No. 23, the wheel-base is moderate—only eleven feet, and there is no weight behind the hind-wheels; thus nearly all the load is available for leading and adhesion. The cylinders, being horizontal, completely over-hang the leading wheels; they are, however, from their small size, very light and short, and the wheels being only 3 feet in diameter, the middle of their lengths does not over-hang the leading axle above 31 inches. The engine may therefore lead very well, and for additional steadiness, the leading guardplate should be stiffened by a direct connection with the cylinder, as in No. 25. In No. 24, the general arrangement is the same as that of Adams', No. 22, with the leading wheels in front of the cylinders, and the tank below the barrel; and with a third pair of wheels and a smaller tank behind the firebox, extending the wheel-base to 16 feet nearly. The wheel-base is much too long for such a light engine, and the back tank ought to have found room forward; this would have increased the useful weight, and allowed above 18 inches shorter base. In No. 25, the arrangement is generally good; the cylinder has but a moderate overhang of 29 inches, the leading guardplate is bound to the cylinder, and the wheel-base is limited to 13 feet; still, there should not have been any back tank, and the hind axle might be shifted two feet forward with advantage. In No. 26, on Crampton's system, the wheel-base, 12 feet, is moderate; and as the load is placed equally on the extreme wheels, the engine is well qualified to run either end foremost. There is, however, a deficiency of available load for driving, as the hind wheels do not command above half the whole weight, even were the middle wheels to be removed.

Ordinary Outside-Cylinder Passenger-Locomotives.—Nos. 27–34. When engines of this kind have the cylinders horizontal, as in No. 27, they want the facilities of inside-cylinder engines for setting the leading wheels forward. The cylinders are in the way, and they must be entirely over-hung to clear the leading wheels,—or, in other words, the wheels must clear the cylinders, and be kept quite in their rear; just as in the case of No. 8, with wide-spread inside-cylinders. In No. 27 the middle of the cylinder overhangs the axle 37 inches. Accordingly engines of this kind are essentially severe on the front wheels, and do not lead well, particularly when, as in No. 27, the guards are long and narrow. No. 28, designed by Mr. W. Johnstone, Camden station, is an ingenious adaptation of the marine steeple arrangement, to place the cylinders within the wheel-base, and to reduce the distance of the acting and resisting parts of the frame. No. 29, by Stirling of Dundee, contains a mode of getting the leading wheels forward, by raising and inclining the cylinders, which reduces the horizontal over-hang to 20 inches; the engine should thus be well led, but the inclination of the cylinder, 1 in 4½, is quite too great for general stability. In No. 30, where the cylinder is inclined at 1 in 10½ only, the fair action of a horizontal cylinder is substantially obtained, while the overhang is only 28 inches, or but three-fourths of that in No. 27, with the horizontal cylinder. The outside frame is also rendered inflexible at the front by the completeness with which it is bolted and stayed to the cylinders and inside frame, and by the shortness of the leading guards. These favourable conditions unite in giving the engine great stability as a carriage. No. 31 is perhaps the most imperfect arrangement of all, as the cylinders, which are horizontal, overhang the axle 42 inches, and the firebox is entirely overhung at the other end; in consequence, of this kind are very unsteady, both vertically and laterally, and are liable to heat in the leading journals, while they wear the leading axle-boxes and wheel-flanges rapidly. No. 32 is an improvement upon the other, as the cylinders are withdrawn from the front; still the vertical action remains uncured. In No. 33 an extra pair of wheels is applied behind the firebox, precisely what was done with the very first engine, No. 1, to cure the pitching. The extended wheel-base amounts to 18½ feet; but as the trailing wheels have no flanges, the facility for running on curves remains the same. Crampton's plan, No. 34, undeniably removes every kind of in-stability; but the extensive base, 16 feet, is too great for sound practice. An arrangement like No. 33 is much better.

Outside-Cylinder Locomotives with Coupled Wheels.—Nos. 35–42. Of these engines, Nos. 35, 36, with horizontal overhung cylinders, are subject to the disqualification of leading imperfectly at high speeds, as already pointed out for No. 27; and when the front wheels are coupled, there is still less facility for its removal, as they are larger than single leading wheels would be, and demand a greater inclination of the cylinders. No. 36, a tank-locomotive, is, however, designed for mineral traffic at low speeds, for which it appears well suited; the machinery is entirely on the outside, and an intermediate shaft is employed to receive and transmit the action from the cylinders. No. 37 was designed to run on mineral lines in Wales, at slow speeds with heavy trains. To ease the rails, which are light, the load is distributed upon eight wheels, placed between the smoke and fire-boxes. This engine is of course unsuitable for speeds above 10 or 15 miles, both on account of its small wheels and the confined wheel-base. In No. 38 the cylinders are placed well up over the leading wheels, and the load is sufficiently commanded;

but the inclination is so great as could only be tolerated at low speeds, under 20 miles; while the middle springs, to resist the vertical action of the steam and the reciprocating masses, must be nearly rigid. In No. 39, the cylinders are placed behind the leading wheels, but the inclination can be no less than in No. 38, as the cylinders must stand high enough to clear not only the wheels but also the coupling rods. In No. 40, a bogie with very small wheels is placed right under the cylinders, and thus commands the machine; and in No. 41 a single pair of wheels is placed for the same object. In both of these the inclination of the cylinders is objectionably great, except for low speeds, and the diameter of leading wheels is very small; moreover, in No. 41, a sufficiency of leading weight must be placed upon the front wheels, directly at the expense of the front driving load, and causing a very objectionable inequality of loads on the coupled axles.

It seems, in fine, that when all the wheels are coupled, outside cylinders are quite in the way, and there is no generally good plan for their disposal in high-speed engines. There appears nothing for it but to reduce the leading wheels into ordinary carriers, and to fall back upon the Crewe engine, No. 42, as the most generally suitable arrangement for outside-cylinders goods-engines that can be devised, with ordinary boiler, wheels and machinery. In this, as in the Crewe passenger-engine, No. 30, the cylinders are moderately inclined,—at an angle of 1 in 8¼,—the frame and leading axle-guards are made inflexible, and the leading axle, just 32 inches behind the middle of the cylinder, is sufficiently forward to command the head of the engine.

Arrangement of the Springs.—As the lateral stability is increased by extending the width of the spring or elastic base, or the transverse distance of the springs, it is by so much preferable to place the axleboxes and the springs upon outside bearings, or on journals overhanging the wheels, in place of bearings inside. This arrangement, of course, spreads the machinery, and involves a more elaborate frame than where inside bearings alone are employed; but the smaller diameter of journals, and the extra stability and accommodation obtained, are sufficient inducements for its general adoption. Exclusive inside bearings for all the axles have, to be sure, been constantly advocated and practised by Bury & Co., and one or two others, on the score of durability of axles, as the downward pressure of the load on the journals, acts usefully to counteract the strain on the axle due to side blows on the wheel-flanges. This argument is no doubt of some weight for crank axles, which are of an essentially weak form, as is proved by the superior durability of crank axles with inside bearings only, compared with such as have outside bearings alone or in conjunction with inside ones; but, for straight carrying axles, experience has not shown any superior durability in inside bearings. The best practical arrangement, combining durability and stability, is the employment of inside bearings alone for the driving axle, whether crank or straight, and for other axles coupled to it; and outside bearings for the independent carrying axles.* The engines of Wilson, Kitson, Crampton, and Allan, Nos. 6, 15, 16, 30, 34, are examples of this style of arrangement. Sharp's

engine, No. 5, has extra outside bearings to the driving axle. Bury's, Sharp's, and Gooch's coupled goods-engine, Nos. 14, 17, 21, have exclusively inside bearings, which admit of compact outside couplings close to the wheels; and Sturrock's, No. 18, has outside bearings to all the axles, and overhung couplings. Bury's, Neilson's, and Stephenson's passenger-engines, Nos. 7, 24, 31, 32, have exclusively inside bearings.

The arrangement of bearings we have recommended is specially useful in engines otherwise disposed to be unsteady, whether by want of balance or otherwise. In engines which are otherwise complete, however, it does not appear in practice that outside bearings for the independent wheels materially increase the stability. With Bury's passenger-engine, No. 7, and his six-wheel goods-engine, with four wheels coupled, arranged like No. 15, with inside cylinders, and inside bearings only, we have run at 50 to 60 miles per hour, with perfect steadiness. With outside cylinders, particularly if inclined, as in Nos. 30 and 42, outside bearings are of material benefit.

Besides the position, the flexibility of the springs requires adjustment to the position assigned to them. The better the load is commanded by the wheels, the more flexible may the springs be with safety; and *vice versa*. This has been practically tested by Mr. John Gray, upon some long boiler overhung engines on the South Eastern Railway, like No. 31 of the diagram-plate; he reduced the flexibility of the fore and hind springs by shortening them from 3 to 2 feet span, with the same number and thickness of plates, and he found that the engines pitched less, and kept the rails better.[†]

To perfect the action of the springs, they are in some cases *coupled* by the use of intermediate compensating levers, as in Sturrock's goods-engine, by Wilson, No. 18 (see also Plates); the driving and front springs, A, B, Fig. 223 abut on

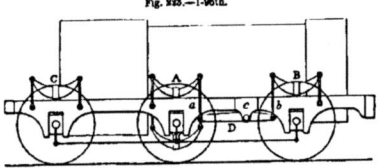

Fig. 223.—1·96th.

Sturrock's Goods Engine.—Coupled Springs.

the axles as usual, and their inner links, *a*, *b*, are produced below the frame and attach to the lever D, swung on the frame at *c*. The fulcrum, *c*, must be placed so as to divide the beam in the inverse ratio of the relative loads on the springs, or such that the arms *ca*, *cb*, are to each other as the load on *b* is to the load on *a*. In this way the loads on the springs are equilibrated, or maintained in a constant ratio to each other, as any deflection in either spring, by failure or inequalities of the road, is taken up by the other; and the suspended mass is better protected from the effects of concussion.

The Americans make use of equilibriating levers for the driving and hind wheels, like Figs. 224 and 225, in the latter of which the bottom of the firebox supplies the

---

* An arrangement patented by Mr. John Gray, in 1839.

† Circular Letter on *Long Boiler Engines*, 1847.

fulcrum, and the elasticity of the hind bearing is derived entirely from the driving spring through the lever. They

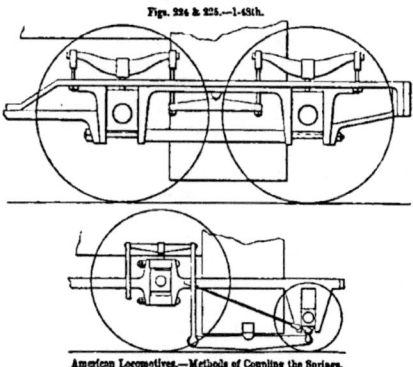

Figs. 224 & 225.—1-48th.

American Locomotives.—Methods of Coupling the Springs.

occasionally employ levers with variable fulcra, to vary the adjustment of the loads as required.*

For moderate spans, 5 feet and under, Mr. D. Gooch employs a single spring on each side of the engine, between two pair of wheels, as in his 8 wheel passenger-engine, and in his tank-engine, for the leading axles. In the latter engine (Plate 7), the spring A, fig. 226, applied in-

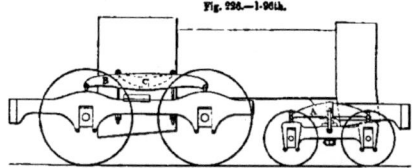

Fig. 226.—1-96th.

D. Gooch's Tank-Locomotive.—Application of Inverted Springs and Compensating Levers.

versely, is 5 feet long, and is linked by the butt to the bogie-frame, the ends bearing on the journals. The spring itself becomes the compensating lever, and the concussions from the wheels enter it, not at the butt, but at the ends. It is, in fact, a part of the suspended mass, and the dead weight between the spring and the journal is reduced to a minimum. This we reckon the most perfect method of employing the agency of a spring. For coupling under one spring the driving and hind axles of the tank-engine, 7 feet 8 inches apart, Mr. Gooch interposes a lever, B, fig. 226, of the same span, the ends of which rest on the journals, and on the middle of which the butt of the spring C, is supported. The ends of the spring are linked to the frame; and the whole system secures constantly equal loads on the axles. But the action would have been improved by inverting the spring as in the bogie, at A, linking the butt to the frame, and the ends to the lever, as the spring would have become part of the suspended mass, and concussive actions would have been received and neutralized nearer to the ends of the lever. This arrangement has lately been employed by Hawthorn, in coupling the three journals on each side with

* *Practical Mechanic's Journal*, vol. ii.

two inverted springs. A, A, fig. 227, are the springs, abutting on the frame, and linked at the ends to the levers, B, B,

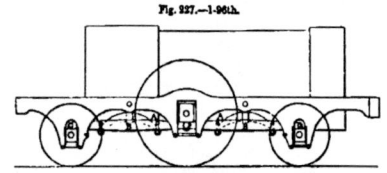

Fig. 227.—1-96th.

Hawthorn's Locomotive.—Combination of Inverted Springs and Compensating Levers.

which are jointed to the axle-boxes. This gives a smooth action, and insures constant loads on all the axles; but it confines the spring-base injuriously to one-half the length of the wheel-base, leaving overhanging masses at both ends.

A single inverted spring is in some cases applied transversely to the hind axle, in place of two separate springs, abutting on the frame at the centre, and spanning the axle-boxes; transverse springs have also been applied to the driving axles of ordinary outside-cylinder engines, and also of Crampton's engine; and, by J. V. Gooch, to the leading axle in conjunction with separate outside springs. Transverse springs alone are not generally advisable, particularly with outside cylinders, as they reduce the general stability of the machine, and its power of resisting internal disturbing causes. The chief design of Mr. Crampton in applying a single spring to the driving axle is to reduce the number of bearings on the elastic base of the machine; by placing only one pair of springs between the leading and middle axles, as in D. Gooch's plan, he reduces the elastic bearings of the machine to three points, and secures constant loads on the springs independent of all inequalities of the machine or the road. In this way the engine No. 9, diagram-plate 6, by Stephenson, is based.

Height of the Centre of Gravity, and the Centre Line of Traction.—Though it is proper to keep down the mass of the machine so far as convenient, the height of the centre of gravity is practically a matter of minor importance. We have found high-pitched engines to run very steadily, showing no peculiar susceptibility to roll, even with inside bearings only: so much depends for stability on other and entirely different conditions. Indentations of the boiler to clear the axles and the machinery, or the removal of the driving axle altogether to the rear, with the object of lowering the boiler, are expedients which we regard with indifference, and they can only be viewed as imperfect remedies for what may otherwise be efficiently prevented. It is supposed, indeed, that the centre of gravity ought to be in or as near as possible to the level of the line of traction, or of the draw-bars. But there is very little relation between them, for the real point is to place the draw-bar, or traction-line, level with the centre of the driving axle, or point of propulsion. If it be above, the pull on the draw-bar tends to rear the engine on its hind wheels, off the leaders; this actually happened to many of the primitive and light engines, particularly Bury's earlier class, causing them to lift in front when starting trains under full pressure, and in quick running, and no doubt having assisted to lift them off the rails on different occasions. In six-wheeled engines a modified action of the same kind takes place from the same cause. A remarkable example occurs in the engine Euclid on the Edinburgh and Glasgow Railway, with a 5¼ feet driving wheel, in which the line of the draw-bar is 10 inches *above* the centre of the axle. This engine is known to *slip the least with the heaviest loads*; that is, the extra pull with the heavier trains brings her more on her haunches, and increases the driving weight.[*]

Facilities for Running on Curves.—It is proved by the extra wear of the leading wheel-flanges of engines, that the labour of guiding the machine falls chiefly upon the leading wheels. In overhung engines like the Sphynx, No. 17 of the diagram-plate, the labour is proved by the sections of tyre, fig. 217, to be excessive; and it is aggravated by the originally less thickness of flange of the driving wheels, as their flanges thereby had no part in guiding the machine, and the duty devolved entirely upon the extreme wheel-flanges. The absence of the strain at the driving flanges, due to their inferior thickness, certainly eased the passage of the engine on curves, considering that the extreme flanges fixed the position of the engine on the rails; but, the longer the guiding *flange*-base of the engine, the greater is the obliquity of the extreme axles, and the constrained angle of wheels with the rails; and in the same degree greater is the labour and friction of the leading flanges. The point is, therefore, to combine a short flange-base with a long wheel-base;—the former, to place the leading wheels parallel, or nearly so, to the rails, that they may roll freely and lead gently; the latter to maintain the general stability. On this principle, the leading and middle flanges should be equally thick, to assume the entire duty of guiding the machine, and the trailing flanges should be removed, or retained merely for security at a reduced thickness. It is amply proved by the worn sections of engine-wheels that their hind flanges, from their generally perfect forms even when the other flanges require renewal, bear little or nothing of the lateral straining of the engine. To carry out the idea, the middle axle should, where advisable, be placed close in front of the firebox, to give a sufficient length of flange-base, and to include the centre of gravity of the machine within this base. Thus the general stability would be secured: the centre of gravity being *before* and also *near* the middle axle, the leading and middle flanges would absorb the entire centrifugal force on curves, of which the middle flange would receive the greater proportion, and would by so much relieve the leaders; whilst, a moderate remainder being reserved to the latter, both the leading and middle flanges would feel the centrifugal force, and be kept taut to the outer rail. Nor is anything to be feared from the want of guiding flanges on the hind wheels, as all the lateral disturbing forces arise and are absorbed in the forward part of the machine; and, moreover, the hind wheels reserve the lateral frictional resistance of the tyres on the rails. Even in cases where the middle axle is placed before the centre of gravity, when the engine might be liable on curves to

heel round to the outer rail, the tendency is a safe one, as it would ease off the leading flange, and turn the head of the engine still more into the track. The reduction of the hind flanges must be adapted to the average of the quickest curves on which the engine is to work. In curves of a ¼ mile radius, than which there are few quicker curves, the versed sine of a 16 feet length of rail, representing a 16 feet base, is ₁₆ inch; and to permit the middle wheel-flange to bear on the outer rail, when of the same thickness as the leading flange, it must be let up to this extent, by reducing the hind flange about double the amount, or ⅛ inch in thickness. The shorter the wheel-base, the nearer the drivers are to the hind wheels, and the flatter the curve, the less is the reduction required. To meet every case, then, we should adopt a fixed difference of ⅛ inch in the thickness of the leading and trailing flanges, and keep up the thickness of the middle flange equal to that of the leaders.

Thus, we believe, may the problem be solved of combining a long wheel-base in engines with fixed wheels and axles running in fixed bearings, with a facility for running on quick curves. In such single engines as Adams' or Crampton's, in which the driving wheels are placed at the ends, with one object amongst others of placing the greatest loads on the extreme wheels, the method is inapplicable. In Adams' four-wheel engine, indeed, the reduction of flange is not wanted, as the wheel-base is moderate; and to the other plan we attach no practical importance, as a heavy-loaded hind wheel is not essential for stability. Loads on the extreme wheels are useful only to correct imperfections which may be otherwise met by a proper distribution of the axles, and the equilibration of internal disturbing forces.

The method of the swivelling bogie-frame, carrying two axles with wheels, under the fore part, is a more perfect and perhaps more durable application for adjusting the position of the leading axles, and guiding the machine. It is, however, a complication, and limits the diameter of the leading wheels; and is not, we believe, expedient except upon railways having their prevailing curvature of less than a quarter-mile radius.

CHAPTER IX.

CONDITIONS OF THE GENERAL ARRANGEMENT (CONTINUED.)—
POSITION OF THE CENTRE OF GRAVITY, AND ARRANGEMENT
OF THE AXLES.

THE influence of the relative disposition of the masses which constitute the weight of the locomotive, on the loads which are to be carried by the different axles, is referrible ultimately to its influence upon the centre of gravity. The position of the centre with respect to the axles, longitudinally, may readily be found in terms of the distance apart of the axles and their respective loads measured at the rails; and, conversely, when the total weight and the positions of the centre and the axles are known, the loads on the wheels may be found.

Definition.—The "load or weight on the wheels or on the axle" is meant not only to express the weight suspended by

---

[*] There is a fallacy in the ordinary mode of representing the level of the centre of gravity, as coinciding with the centre-line of the barrel of the boiler. This is by no means the case, for the centre is usually very little above the upper side of the frame, being, in narrow-gauge engines, generally about four feet above the rails. In fig. 183, the position of the centre of gravity is indicated by the inscribed star.

them, but to include also the weight of the wheels and axles themselves with their appurtenances; or, totally, the weight on the rails.

Relations of the Centre of Gravity and the Loads on the Wheels.—1st. In a four-wheeled engine. Let A B be the frame and C, D the two wheels on one side; draw the line *a b*, parallel to the rails, in which the centre is assumed to lie, and the perpendiculars *a* C, *b* D, through which the loads on each axle are assumed to act on the rails. If the centre

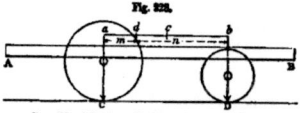

Fig. 228.

Four-Wheel Engine.—Position of Centre of Gravity.

be at *c*, midway between *a* and *b*, the total weight acts on the rails through the equal arms *c a*, *c b*, of the imaginary lever *a b*, and is divided into two equal loads at C and D. If the centre be at *d*, one-fourth of the distance apart of the axles from *a*, it divides the distance *a b* in the ratio of 1 to 3, and the weight is divided in the same ratio inversely, or such that the load at C, through the shorter arm *a d*, is 3 times that at D, through the longer arm. In general, the loads at the wheels are to each other inversely as the horizontal distances of the centre of gravity from the vertical lines through the axles; and the products of the loads by their respective distances from the centre of gravity, are equal.

Putting W for the total weight, and C and D, for the loads at the respective wheels; *s* for the span or length of the wheel-base, and *m*, *n*, for the respective distances of the axles C, D, from the centre; then

$$C \times m = D \times n,$$

or C : D :: *n* : *m*, and C + D, or W : C :: *m* + *n*, or *s* : *n*.

Consequently $n = \dfrac{s \times C}{W}$ ... ... (1.)

and, $C = \dfrac{W \times n}{s}$ ... ... (2.)

which will afterwards be reduced to rules.

2d. In a six-wheeled engine. Let A B, fig. 229, be the frame; C, D, E, the three wheels and axles, and also the loads on them, and *c b*, the horizontal line through the centre of gravity; put W for the total load, *s* for the wheel-base *c b*;

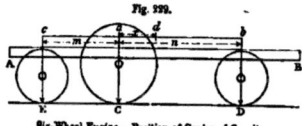

Fig. 229.

Six-Wheel Engine.—Position of Centre of Gravity.

m, *n*, for the distances apart of the axles, *c a*, *a b*; and *x*, for the distance *a d* of the centre *d* from the middle axle. Then the sum of the products of the loads E, C, on one side of the centre, by their distances from it, is equal to the product of the load D on the other side by its distance; or

$$(C \times s) + (E \times (m + s)) = D \times (n - s),$$

and W = C + D + E, whence

$$s = \dfrac{(D \times n) - (E \times m)}{W} \quad ... \quad ... \quad (3.)$$

Conversely, the centre being given, also the positions of the axles, and the total load, the loads on the wheels may be varied; for, unlike the case of four wheels on two axles in which the loads are fixed and unalterable, three axles admit of a variety of loads, but the variation is always such, that the loads on the extreme axles increase and diminish together, though not in the same ratio. If the load on the middle axle be reduced by suitably adjusting the middle springs, the difference is distributed simultaneously between both the end axles; if increased, the increase is withdrawn from both ends. If, again, the load on either of the end axles be increased at the springs, the load on the other end axle is increased simultaneously, and to meet these joint demands the middle axle loses an equivalent of its load; if the load on one end axle be reduced at the springs, that of the other end axle is also reduced, and the two portions thus set free are added to the load at the middle. The relation of the loads is, then, affected in the same manner, whether the fore, the middle, or the hind springs be submitted to adjustment; it is a matter of indifference which, as by an adjustment of any one or other of these pairs of springs, every practicable alteration of relative loads with independent springs can be effected.

As the loads on the axles may be various, they can only be determined by fixing the value of one; when one is fixed, it fixes the two others, and the following is the method of finding them:—

First, when the load C on the middle axle is given. Substitute for E in equation (3), its value (W — C — D), and reduce; then

$$D = \dfrac{W(m + s) - C m}{m + n} \quad ... \quad ... \quad ... \quad (4.)$$

and E = W — C — D.

Second, when the load D on one of the end axles is given.

Invert formula (4), and we have

$$C = \dfrac{W(m + s) - D(m + n)}{m} \quad ... \quad ... \quad (5.)$$

and E = W — C — D.

From the foregoing formulas we deduce the following rules:—

RULE I.—*To find the Position of the Centre of Gravity horizontally, when the loads on the axles and their distances apart are given.*

1st. For engines with four wheels, multiply the load on the driving axle in tons, by the length of wheel-base in feet,—and divide by the total weight in tons. The quotient is the horizontal distance in feet, of the centre of gravity from the other axle. (Formula 1.)

Note.—When the loads on the axles are equal, the centre of gravity lies half-way between them.

2. For engines with six wheels. Multiply the loads on the fore and hind axles, in tons, by their respective distances from the middle axle, in feet,—find the difference of the products so found,—and divide this difference by the total weight in tons. The quotient is the distance in feet, of the centre of gravity from the middle axle, measured towards the axle for which the greatest product was found. (Formula 3.)

Note.—When the products are equal, the centre of gravity lies exactly over the middle axle.

RULE II.—*To find the Loads on the Axles, when the total weight, the distances of the axles, and the position of the centre of gravity, horizontally, are given.*

1st. For engines with four wheels. Multiply the total

weight in tons, by the distance of the centre of gravity from the driving axle,—and divide by the length of wheel-base. The quotient is the load on the other axle, in tons; and the difference of this and the total weight is the load on the driving axle in tons. (Formula 2).

Note.—When the centre of gravity is half-way between the axles, the loads on the axles are equal.

2d. For engines with six wheels. (1.) When the load on the middle axle is given. Multiply the total weight in tons by the distance of the centre of gravity from the hind axle, in feet,—multiply also the load on the middle axle by its distance from the hind axle,—find the difference of these two products,—and divide it by the wheel-base. The quotient is the load in tons upon the front axle; whence the load on the hind axle may also be found. (Formula 4.)

(2.) When the load on one of the end axles is given. Multiply the total weight by the distance of the centre of gravity from the other end axle, on which the load is unknown,—multiply also the given load by the wheel-base,—find the difference of these products,—and divide it by the distance of the middle axle from the aforesaid end axle. The quotient is the load in tons upon the middle axle; whence the remaining load may be found. (Formula 5.)

Note.—Rules might also be given for finding, inversely, the positions of the wheels due to a given centre of gravity. These positions may, however, be found approximately by a few trials with the rules already given.

Examples of the application of the Rules.—To find the centre of gravity of No. 1 four-wheel engine of the diagram-plate 6. The wheel-base is 5 feet, total weight 9 tons, load on driving axle $5\frac{1}{2}$ tons: by Rule I, $5\frac{1}{2} \times 5 \div 9 = 3{\cdot}05$ feet, or $36\frac{5}{8}$ inches, the distance of the centre of gravity from the leading axle, or nearly 2 feet from the drivers, as shown by the vertical dot-line c on the diagram.

To find the centre of gravity of No. 4 six-wheel engine. The total weight is $11\frac{1}{2}$ tons, and the fore and hind axles are $4\frac{1}{2}$ and $4\frac{3}{4}$ feet from the driving axle, with $4\frac{1}{2}$ and 2 tons of load: by Rule I, $4\frac{1}{2} \times 4\frac{1}{2} = 20\frac{1}{4}$ for the fore axle, and $4\frac{3}{4} \times 2 = 9\frac{1}{2}$ for the hind axle; and $20\frac{1}{4} - 9\frac{1}{2} = 10\frac{3}{4}$, the difference in favour of the fore axle. Finally $10\frac{3}{4} \div 11\frac{1}{2} = {\cdot}935$ feet or $11\frac{1}{4}$ inches, the distance of the centre of gravity in front of the driving axle.

To find the centre of gravity of No. 20 eight-wheel engine. The loads on the coupled wheels being equalised by an equilibriating spring, and also those of the bogie wheels, the engine may be estimated as a four-wheeler on a wheel-base of 8 feet + one-half of 7 feet 8 inches, or 11 feet 10 inches. The total weight is 35·8 tons, load on driving wheels 21·3 tons; then $21{\cdot}3 \times 11{\cdot}83 \div 35{\cdot}8 = 7$ feet, the distance of the centre of gravity from the centre of the bogie, or 1 foot in front of the driving axle.

Influence of the Relative Positions of the Centre of Gravity and the Axles, upon the Loads on the Wheels.—The conditions which chiefly control the arrangement of the axles, are that there shall be a sufficiency of weight on the leading wheels for safely guiding the machine, and on the driving wheels for purposes of traction. If the axles be so placed or so loaded that there is too little driving weight, and a surplus of guiding weight, the conditions are imperfectly complied with; and it is important to know not only how to set out an engine from the foundation, but how also to remedy defective arrangements. To illustrate the subject, we have selected the Crewe passenger and goods-locomotives, Nos. 30 and 42, diagram-plate 6, of which the following are the necessary data:—

	Passenger Locomotive.*	Goods Locomotive.
Wheel-base, ...	12 feet	12 feet 8 inches.
Front to middle wheel, ...	5 feet 6 inches	5 ,, 4 ,,
Middle to hind do., ...	6 ,, 6 ,,	7 ,, 4 ,,
Centre of gravity with respect to middle axle, ...	6 inches before.	4 inches behind.
Total weight, ...	19 tons	19 tons 12 cwt.
Load on front axle, ...	5 tons 15 cwt.	5 ,, 16 ,,
Do. middle do., ...	9 ,, 15 ,,	9 ,, 0 ,,
Do. hind do., ...	3 ,, 10 ,,	4 ,, 16 ,,

On these data the Table No. xc. is constructed, to show by example the influence of the position of the centre of gravity, and reciprocally the positions of the axles, upon the loads on the wheels, in which, generally, the results are worked out separately for fixed loads on the driving wheels, and on the leading wheels.

In the first part of the table, the centre of gravity is supposed to range over 4 feet horizontally, or 2 feet before and behind the driving axle, a constant load of $9\frac{1}{2}$ tons being secured to the driving wheels. As it shifts backwards, the front load is reduced from $8\frac{3}{4}$ to 2 tons, from superfluously much to too little; while the hind load increases, and is good for very little. As a front load of 5 tons is considered necessary and sufficient, the centre of gravity should by the table be at least as far forward as the driving axle. But, with only 5 tons in front, and $9\frac{1}{2}$ tons at the middle, there is a balance of $4\frac{1}{2}$ tons not usefully employed, which may be usefully thrown into the driving weight: to show what may be done in this way, in the same part of the table are added the middle and hind weights, with a constant front weight of 5 tons, due to the prescribed positions of the centre of gravity, from which it appears that when the centre is 18 inches before the axle, the whole balance of 14 tons becomes driving weight, leaving nothing for the hind wheels; as the centre shifts backwards, the driving weight falls to 4 tons, leaving 10 tons of trailing weight in the rear. Thus, in either case, the removal of the centre of gravity *from* the front, reduces the useful loads,—those on the front and driving axles,—and throws a surplus upon the hind axle; and the object should be, to select such a position for the centre, over or in front of the middle axle, as shall yield, besides the reserve of 5 tons for the front load, the greatest desirable driving load, leaving a trifle for the hind axle to keep the bearings taut.

But we cannot readily shift the centre of gravity. We may, however, place the driving axle with facility where required; and this is, for present purposes, equivalent to an alteration of the centre, as it yields the means of throwing the centre into the desired position with respect to the middle axle, and of thereby adjusting the loads.

Influence of the Position of the Middle Axle.—The second part of the table shows that in removing the middle axle backwards from under the centre of gravity to 24 inches behind it, the front load is increased, when the driving load

* The particulars of this engine are obtained from No. 13, C.R., one of a number made after the existing Crewe pattern. The weights were taken by one of Pooley's machines.

TABLE, No. XC.—TO SHOW THE INFLUENCE OF THE RELATIVE POSITIONS OF THE AXLES AND THE CENTRE OF GRAVITY UPON THE DISTRIBUTION OF THE LOADS ON THE WHEELS.

Exemplified in the L. & N. W. R. Passenger and Goods Locomotives, arranged by Mr. Allan, Nos. 30 and 42 of the diagram-plate 6.

Passenger-Locomotive, 19 tons total weight in working order.

1st. When the POSITION OF THE CENTRE OF GRAVITY is varied longitudinally. Wheel-base constant, 12 feet.

Position of Centre of Gravity, with respect to the Middle Axle:— + *before* the Axle. − *behind* do.	Loads on the Wheels, due to the Position of the Centre of Gravity.					
	With a Constant Load on the Middle Wheels, of 9½ tons, or half the total Weight.			With a Constant Load on the Front Wheels, of 5 tons.		
	Front.	Middle.	Hind.	Front.	Middle	Hind.
inches.	tons.	tons.	tons.	tons.	tons.	tons.
+ 24	8·25	9·5	1·25	(+18)5	14	0
+ 12	6·75	9·5	2·75	5	12·75	1·25
0	5·15	9·5	4·35	5	9·75	4·25
− 12	3·5	9·5	6·0	5	6·8	7·2
− 24	2·0	9·5	7·5	5	4·0	10·0

2d. When the POSITION OF THE MIDDLE AXLE is varied longitudinally. Wheel-base, 12 feet.

Position of the Middle Axle, with respect to the Centre of Gravity:— + *before* the Centre. − *behind* do.	Loads on the Axles, due to the Position of the Middle Axle.					
	Constant Load on Middle Wheels, 9½ tons.			Constant Load on the Front Wheels, 5 tons.		
	Front.	Middle.	Hind.	Front.	Middle.	Hind.
inches.	tons.	tons.	tons.	tons.	tons.	tons
0	5·5	9·5	4·0	5	10·5	3·5
− 6	6·0	9·5	3·5	5	11·25	2·75
− 12	6·3	9·5	3·2	5	12·25	1·73
− 18	6·75	9·5	2·75	5	13·25	0·75
− 24	7·25	9·5	2·25	5	14·0	0·0

3d. When the POSITION OF THE FRONT AXLE is varied longitudinally. Wheel-base, varying.

Position of the Axle, in advance of the Middle Axle.	Loads on the Axles, due to the Position of the Front Axle.					
	Constant Load on Middle Wheels, 9½ tons.			Constant Load on Front Wheels, 5 tons.		
	Front.	Middle.	Hind.	Front.	Middle.	Hind.
feet.	tons.	tons.	tons.	tons.	tons.	tons.
5 (Wheel-base 11½ ft.)	6·2	9·5	3·3	5	11·6	2·4
5½ (Do. 12 ft.)	6·0	9·5	3·5	5	11·2	2·8
6 (Do. 12½ ft.)	5·7	9·5	3·8	5	10·8	3·2
6½ (Do. 13 ft.)	5·4	9·5	4·1	5	10·5	3·5

4th. When the POSITION OF THE HIND AXLE is varied longitudinally. Wheel-base, varying.

Position of the Axle behind the Middle Axle.	Loads on the Axles, due to the Position of the Hind Axle.					
	Constant Load on Middle Wheels, 9½ tons.			Constant Load on Front Wheels, 5 tons.		
	Front.	Middle.	Hind.	Front.	Middle.	Hind.
feet.	tons.	tons.	tons.	tons.	tons.	tons.
6½ (Wheel-base 12 ft.)	6·0	9·5	3·5	5	11·2	2·8
7 (Do. 12½ ft.)	6·1	9·5	3·4	5	11·4	2·6
7½ (Do. 13 ft.)	6·2	9·5	3·3	5	11·6	2·4
8 (Do. 13½ ft.)	6·3	9·5	3·2	5	11·75	2·25

5th. When the LOAD ON THE MIDDLE AXLE is varied. Wheel-base, 12 feet.

Centre of Gravity 6 inches before Middle Axle, in No. 30, diagram-plate 6.	Loads on the Axles, due to the Reduction of the Load on the Middle Axle.					
	With Axles as arranged in No. 30.			Middle Axle placed 6 inches forward, under the Centre of Gravity.		
	Front.	Middle.	Hind.	Front.	Middle.	Hind.
	tons.	tons.	tons.	tons.	tons.	tons.
	1·75	17·25	0	0	19	0
	3·5	14	1·5	3	14	2
	4·8	12	2·2	4	12	3
	6·0	10	3	5·25	10	3·75
	7·0	8	4	6·4	8	4·6
	8·0	6	5	7·6	6	5·4
	9·0	4	6	9·0	4	6·0
	10·0	2	7	10·0	2	7·0

TABLE, No. XC.—(*Continued.*)

Goods-Locomotive, 19½ tons total weight in working order.

6th. When the POSITION OF THE MIDDLE AXLE is varied longitudinally. Wheel-base, 12 feet 8 inches.

Position of the Middle Axle, with respect to the Centre of Gravity:— + *before* the Centre. − *behind* do.	Loads on the Axles, due to the Position of the Middle Axle.					
	With Constant Load on Front Wheels, 5 tons.			With Equal Loads on the Middle and Hind Axles.		
	Front.	Middle.	Hind.	Front.	Middle.	Hind.
inches.	tons.	tons.	tons.	tons.	tons.	tons
+ 12	5	9·2	5·3	6·75	6·37	6·37
+ 6	5	9·8	4·7	7·1	6·2	6·2
0	5	10·5	4·0	7·5	6·0	6·0
− 6	5	11·3	3·2	7·76	5·87	5·87
− 12	5	12·25	2·25	8·0	5·75	5·75

7th. FRONT AXLE shifted FORWARD 8 inches. POSITION of MIDDLE AXLE varied. Wheel-base, 13 feet 4 inches.

Position of the Middle Axle.	Loads, due to the Position of Middle Axle.					
inches.	tons.	tons.	tons.	tons.	tons.	tons.
+ 18	5	8·25	6·25	5·7	6·9	6·9
+ 12	5	8·75	5·75	6·27	6·62	6·62
+ 6	5	9·3	5·2	6·6	6·45	6·45
0	5	10·0	4·5	6·9	6·3	6·3
− 6	5	10·8	3·7	7·25	5·62	5·62
− 12	5	11·7	2·8	7·5	6·0	6·0

is constant; and that, with a constant front load, the driving load is increased; while, in both cases the hind load is reduced. The effect on the distribution of the load is thus substantially the same, whether the middle axle be removed behind the centre, or the centre removed before the axle: the sum of the working loads on the front and middle axles being increased, and the passive load on the hind axle reduced; and the position of the middle axle may be adjusted to convert anything short of 14 tons into driving weight, with a reserve of 5 tons for leading.

Influence of the Position of the Front and Hind Axles.—The third and fourth parts of the table show that, within practical limits, this influence is small. Such as it is, the farther forward the front wheels are placed, the less is the whole front and middle load and the greater is the hind load; the farther back the hind wheels are placed, the greater is the whole load for the front and middle axles.

Nature of the simultaneous Variations of the Three Loads.—This is illustrated in the fifth part, showing two cases, in which the centre of gravity is 6 inches before the middle axle, and exactly over it. In the first case, it is impossible to deprive the front axle of all its load; in the second, this may be done, and still more readily so, if the centre be *behind* the axle. It is obvious that the front and hind loads rise and fall together, that if the one vary the other must also vary, and that as they rise or fall, the middle load inversely must fall or rise, and *vice versa*.

Variations of the Loads of the Goods-Engine, with Coupled Wheels.—1st. When the hind wheels are coupled to the middle or driving wheels, the hind load becomes useful as driving weight, and it is an object to equalise the loads on the two axles, and that this be done with the least sacrifice of driving load, incurred by superfluously charging the front axle. The sixth part of the table contains the loads due to positions of the driving axle from 12 inches before to 12 inches behind the centre, with a fixed front load of 5 tons, and 14½ tons driving weight on the two other axles. It appears that, in all positions, the middle is greater than the hind load, but that they approach nearer to equality, the farther forward the middle axle is placed. In the same part of the table, the loads for equal middle and hind weights are given; showing that the greatest amount of driving weight, 12¾ tons, is had with the foremost position of the middle axle, leaving 6¾ tons in front, or 1¾ tons more than necessary for leading. Thus, an equality of middle and hind loads can be had only by a partial sacrifice of the total driving weight; and on this ground it is that Mr. Allan has preferred such an excess of load on his driving wheels.

The removal of the front axle forward, assists in equalising and keeping up the amount of driving weight. In the seventh part of table, the front axle is shifted forward 8 inches, which in the Crewe engine would of course demand 8 inches longer boiler. This permits the driving axle 18 inches before the centre, by which the difference of the middle and hind loads, with 5 tons front load, is reduced from 4 to 2 tons; and, by the same part of the table, those loads may be equalised by a sacrifice of only ·7 ton, making a front load of 5·7 tons, and a driving load of 13·8 tons.

2d. When the front wheels are coupled, the conditions are similar to those of a single wheel engine, in so far as the middle axle should be placed well back, to take up the trailing weight, and to throw more upon the leading axle; and for the same reason, the leading wheels should be kept as well back as is consistent with their proper function of leading. In the second part of the table, where the middle axle is loaded to 9½ tons, and placed 24 inches behind the centre, the front load is 7¼ tons, making 16¾ tons of driving weight, and leaving only 2¼ tons behind. When the leading wheels are coupled, the cylinders should be placed inside.

3d. When both the front and hind wheels are coupled, the object is to distribute the weight equally on the three axles; and the conditions are partially the same as those for engines in which the hind wheels alone are coupled, as the same steps must be taken to charge the hind axles,—by setting forward the front and driving axles. In the Crewe goods-engine, if all the wheels were coupled, the middle axle would do well where it is, and, by the table, sixth part, it would do better by being placed at least 6 inches before the centre; and still better if the front axle were removed 8 inches forward. In Nos. 18 and 21, coupled engines, though the leading axles are, by the inside-cylinder arrangement, let better forward than in the Crewe engine, there is still a deficiency of trailing weight, as the centre of gravity is nearer the front than the hind axle, and is also before the middle axle. In both cases, the middle axle ought to be placed before the centre, *or closer to the end axle which is nearest the centre*, to secure an equal distribution of the weight. Accordingly, in No. 21, where the driving axle is better forward than in No. 18, the loads are more nearly equal; and in No. 17, where the hind axle is well forward, the middle axle is placed next to it, because the hind is nearer the centre than the leading wheels, and an equal division of the weight is effected.

Influence of the Position of the Driving Axle in the rear.—When the driving wheel is behind the firebox, (Crampton's system), the removal backward of the driving wheels, cylinders, and gearing, 2 to 3 tons weight, to suit this arrangement, carries with it the centre of gravity so far, and facilitates the adjustment of the driving load on the hind wheels. As the Crewe engine stands, the fifth part of table shows that not materially above 7 tons can be got on the hind wheels, leaving 10 tons on the front; if the gearing were actually removed, these loads would probably be equalised, and in fact, in No. 34 of the diagram-plate, on Crampton's plan, the extreme loads are exactly equal, 11½ tons each. A bare equality of the hind and front loads is, however, all that can be attained, as the centre of gravity, in a superior position though it be, is still as far from the hind as from the front axle: in the example before us, No. 34, it is just equally distant. But, the relative position of the centre of gravity is adjustable also by shifting forward the front axle, which places the centre relatively nearer the hind axle; and, to obtain sufficient driving weight, Crampton's engines are commonly so designed,—with a long wheel-base, amounting in No. 34 to 16 feet. In his tank-engine, No. 26, and in the "Liverpool," (page 19) the front wheels are also placed well forward, not so much to lead well, there being little extreme weight in front, as to discharge the load over to the hind wheels.

It follows that Crampton's are essentially heavy engines, as their front loads must be always at least as great as their driving loads, and therefore superfluously great; and as, consequently, with three axles, of which the middle one claims a load, the driving weight can never amount to even one-half the total weight.

5th. When all the axles, single or coupled, are placed between the smokebox and firebox, (lately Stephenson's system) as in Nos. 31, 32, there is great facility for increasing the driving load,—in No. 31 particularly, where the driving axle is in the middle and nearly under the centre of gravity. This engine is indeed dangerously easy of adjustment, as the centre is *behind* the axle, and the driving spring may be set up sufficiently to take off the entire leading weight. This we have known actually to happen in one case, where the engine ran more than one trip with the leading springs quite relaxed. In No. 32, the driving axle is much more safely placed than in No. 31, as it can only borrow an extra load from the middle wheels; and the more the driving load, the more also is the leading load, while the stability is undiminished.

CHAPTER X.

Summary of the Foregoing Discussions, and Conclusions.—Rules for Practice.

It has been shown that the stability of the locomotive as a carriage depends mainly on the internal arrangement, the balancing of the revolving and reciprocating masses, the disposal of the wheels and axles, and the distribution of the load. Whereas it has usually been held to be a necessary condition of steadiness that the axles should be equally loaded, and that the extreme axles especially should be well loaded; it appears that however beneficial as a corrective, this condition can be viewed only as an expedient, and that though it may lop off some of the grosser forms of instability, it leaves untouched the more deeply seated and equally formidable disturbing causes. Further, it is found that when the internal disturbing causes are balanced, and the extreme axles properly placed fore and aft to control the suspended masses, great and valuable liberties may be taken with the general arrangement, and with the distribution of the weight upon the axles, without damaging the carriage qualifications of the machine :—by a proper attention to detail, outside and inside cylinder engines may be made equally steady, the centre of gravity may be high or low, within practical limits, the driving wheels may be placed anywhere, and the loads on the axles may be proportioned at pleasure, reserving a small proportion for necessary leading weight.

Balance of the Internal Disturbing Forces.—The instability arising from the internal unbalanced action of the machinery is developed in four different forms of oscillation :—sinuous, pitching, rocking, and reciprocating fore-and-aft movements. The first and last are caused by the reciprocating masses of the crank, piston, and connections, and by unequal admissions of steam to the front and back ends of the cylinders; the second and third by the oblique action of the connecting rods on the guidebars, due to the steam-pressure, and by the direct pressure of the steam in inclined cylinders. With outside cylinders the action of these causes is better developed than with inside cylinders. The former irregular motions are removed by the application of counterweights in the wheels, between the spokes, equivalent, with outside cylinders, to the whole revolving and reciprocating weights of the crank, piston, and connections, referred to the crank-pin, and exactly opposed to the crank; and, with cylinders inside, to about three-fourths of this weight, more or less according to the greater or less width apart of the cylinders, not directly opposed to the crank, but diverging to one side towards the counterweight in the neighbouring wheel, when seen in side elevation. The other irregular movements are controlled and rendered harmless by an adjustment of the valve-gear to cut off the steam equally for the front and back strokes, by the use of a sufficiently long connecting rod, at least six times the length of crank, by placing the cylinders horizontally, or nearly so, at an angle not greater than 1 in 10 for high-speed engines, and 1 in 8 for engines running under 30 miles per hour; and by regulating the flexibility of the springs. For all practical purposes, an angle of 1 in 14 is as good as a horizontal position for the cylinders; and for speeds under 20 miles an angle of 1 in 5 may be tolerated.

The advantages of balancing the machinery are, that the motion is steadier, the straining of the engine and the rails is less, there is less tear and wear of everything concerned, there is less resistance to the progressive motion on the rails, with the same power a higher speed is attainable, and the facilities for carrying out the most desirable arrangement of the machine are greatly increased.

Incidental Causes of Instability.—Instability is also occasioned and increased internally by a want of parallelism of the axles, which leads the carriage to run awry, by the play of the axleboxes between their guards, which throws the axles off the square, by the wear of tyres into hollow sections, and by their unequal wear, forming wheels of unequal diameters, both of which results increase the oscillatory movements.

Engines are liable to vertical instability, when the centre of the draw-bar is above the level of the centre of the driving axle, as the tendency of the difference of level is to relieve the leading wheels of their load.

The external causes of instability, in the permanent way, are to be found in the form and clearance of the rails, and in their want of exact gauge. If the rails be flat-headed, either by the original section, by wear, bruising, or otherwise, the wheels find themselves running, in virtue of their conicity, on constantly varying diameters. A rounded head reduces the limits of this variation, and promotes stability. If the clearance of the rails and the wheel-flanges, usually a total of $\frac{1}{2}$ inch, be locally reduced or increased, concussions laterally are increased in the first case, and in the second the rolling diameter of the wheel when going straight ahead, is varied. A want of gauge laterally or vertically is similarly unfavourable.

Arrangement of the Frame, Axle-bearings, and Springs.—In general, outside bearings, springs, and frames, should be employed for the merely carrying axles; and inside bearings alone for the driving and coupled axles. The duplicate frame-plates required on each side for this purpose, when properly united, greatly increase the strength of the frame; and abundance of room is made for the springs and their connections. The lateral spread of bearing is specially useful for outside-cylinder engines. In goods-engines with all the axles coupled, inside bearings alone should be employed. For engines under 12 to 15 tons weight, inside bearings only may be used, for simplicity of framing; and in consideration also of the lighter loads, and the greater space for the stowage of inside springs. The springs may be linked for the sake of compensation in some of the ways already described, particularly in coupled engines.

Arrangement and Number of the Axles.—Stability depends greatly on the arrangement of the axles and the springs; and the necessary conditions are regulated by the speed on the rails. 1st, For high-speed engines, or such as are destined to run above 20 to 25 miles per hour, the machine must be well supported fore and aft: the centre of the leading axle should in all cases be within 12 inches from the smoke-box tube-plate, or from the back of the cylinders when these are in front; or at least not more in any case than 30 inches from the mid-length of the cylinders. The trailing axle should invariably be behind the firebox, as closely as is otherwise desirable, to limit the wheel-base; though this condition may perhaps be relaxed in the case of light engines, under 12 tons, with four wheels. 2d, For low-speed engines, running under 20 miles per hour, the foregoing conditions should be attended to when convenient. One axle may, however, be withdrawn, in engines under 18 tons total weight, leaving only two axles; and the firebox may be overhung without injury to the carriage; the cylinders, whether inside or outside, may also be placed horizontally, and overhung sufficiently to clear the leading wheels, as in Nos. 8, 14, 31, 35, of Diagram-plate 6.

In engines with independent wheels, the axles should be arranged with reference to the loads they require. The leading axle demands weight to keep the wheels to the rails, and the driving axle requires weight for adhesion; the two axles have separate functions, and they should not be identified or combined in one, as in No. 10, Diagram-plate 6. In well-balanced and well-arranged engines, one-fourth of the total weight is, we believe, necessary and sufficient for the leading wheels. The position of the leading axle being fixed as above specified, the best position of the driving axle is in front of the firebox, as there the greatest amount of driving load is available, out of a given total weight of engine. If behind the firebox, it cannot receive above one-half of the whole weight, as it involves an equal and unnecessary outlay of leading weight, and upon the whole a weightier engine for the same driving load. Comparing Nos. 7 and 34, Diagram-plate 6, we have the following total and driving weights:—

	Position of Driving Wheel, as to firebox.	Total Weight.	Driving Weight.
No. 7 (Bury),	In Front	20½ tons	12 tons.
No. 34 (Crampton),	Behind	27 ,,	11½ ,,
	Difference,	6½ tons.	

From this it is apparent that a 20-ton ordinary engine commands as great a driving load as a 27-ton engine with hind drivers; while, if balanced, it runs equally steady.

It follows that if the driving axle should lie in front of the firebox, an extra pair of wheels are required behind; and a six-wheeled engine is the result. The trailing axle does not require above 1 or 2 tons of load, as its function is simply to receive and absorb the pitching of the engine. Thus, the advantage of ordinary four-wheeled engines in securing a large proportion of driving load, may be substantially combined with the utility of an extra axle behind. In six-wheel engines with central drivers, the rails, it is true, are liable, as observed by Mr. W. B. Adams, to deflect under the driving load, if excessive, and to throw it partly on the end wheels, causing the engine to slip; and this is a circumstance which with extreme drivers cannot take place. The true remedy is not, as has been argued by the advocates of four-wheel engines, to remove the trailing wheels, but to stiffen the rails; and, besides, the central springs may be made of great flexibility, to follow up the deflections of the rails without materially reducing the driving load.

Consistently with stability, then, one-fourth at least of the total weight should be placed on the leading axle, and one-twelfth on the trailing axle; and the remainder, or two-thirds, on the driving axle. But 12 tons is the greatest load, with regard to the rails, that ought to be placed on one pair of wheels. Now, 12 tons are two-thirds of 18 tons, therefore 18 tons is the greatest useful weight of single-wheel engines, with respect to their available traction-loads, as the extra weight of heavier engines must be borne entirely on the leading and trailing axles. Accordingly, Sharp's engine, No. 5, of 18 tons, would, were the driving axle nearer the firebox, command as great a traction-load as Bury's, No. 7, of 20½ tons, and Wilson's and Hawthorn's, Nos. 6 and 8, of 27 tons; and the extra weight of these engines is useful only as it represents greater steam-producing power. As a high-speed, steam-producing engine, Crampton's, No. 34, of 27 tons, is on a par with the others, as it is heavy enough to command the practical maximum of driving load; but, for total weights of less than 24, or twice 12 tons, Crampton's arrangement is inferior to the others, as respects the available traction-load.

It follows that passenger-engines above 18 or 20 tons weight should have one of the axles coupled, to admit of the distribution and useful employment of the extra weight; except such as are chiefly employed to run at express speeds, in which the desiderata are great evaporating power and free running, with a moderate driving load.

In coupled engines, the main point in the distribution of the weight is to equalize the load on the coupled axles, without throwing any superfluous load on the disengaged wheels, if there be any. With the hind wheels coupled, a total of 32 tons is required, to yield 24 tons, the maximum of driving weight on two coupled axles, namely, one-fourth or 8 tons leading, 12 tons driving, and 12 tons trailing; with the fore wheels coupled, the total is 26½ tons, namely, 12 tons leading, 12 tons driving, and one-twelfth or 2½ tons trailing; with all the wheels coupled, 24 tons would yield the same traction-load. Thus, to yield the same traction-load, the total weights of the three classes of coupled engines, when their leading and trailing loads are duly attended to, are as 32, 26½, 24, or as 1·33, 1·1, 1, respectively, for coupled hind wheels, coupled fore wheels, and six wheels coupled.

Upon the whole, six-wheeled engines with the hind wheels coupled, appear to be the best arrangement for four coupled-wheel high-speed engines, as the leading wheels, charged with a suitable load, are free for their proper function, and are unburdened with driving weight; with outside cylinders, no other arrangement is properly available, as the leading wheels should be free and of smaller diameter to permit of a suitable adjustment of the cylinder at a moderate inclination. When the hind driving load is materially inferior to the middle load, it may be increased by the application of extra dead weight over the axle, in the form of a heavy foot-plate of cast iron, or otherwise.

The loads on the axles are regulated by their relative distances from the centre of gravity of the whole machine. There is great uniformity in the locality of the centre of gravity, in similarly arranged engines. In engines like Nos. 6, 18, 19, 20, with 10½ to 11 feet barrels, and large fireboxes, the centre lies about 7½ feet from the fore end of the barrel, or 3 feet in front of the firebox-shell. In these cases, the firebox and the trailing wheels appear to balance the greater part of barrel, the cylinders and gearing, and the leading wheels. In other cases, as Nos. 14, 17, and 31, the extra length of barrel is neutralized by the advance of the hind wheels, aided in the first and third cases by the greater overhang of the cylinders, and the centre is, as in the others, about 7½ feet from the front of the barrel. In Nos. 5, 30, and 42, with shorter barrels and shorter fireboxes, and very advanced driving axles, the centre is 12 to 15 inches nearer the front, and is still 3 to 3½ feet before the firebox-shell.

Now, a 10½ feet barrel gives an 11 feet tube nearly, which is a length suitable for every size of boiler; length of boiler, also, in so far as it involves length of carriage, is conducive to stability; besides that, independently of the magnitude of the machine, the length must bear a sufficient ratio to the gauge of the rails; moreover, the driving axle must clear the back of the cylinder sufficiently to make room for connections. The length of barrel, therefore, should not be less than 10 or 10½ feet, and we have the certainty of finding the centre of gravity considerably in advance of the firebox.

The normal arrangement (No. 4) of the locomotive as a carriage, elaborated by Stephenson, appears upon the whole to be the most generally excellent, and will be adhered to as such in the discussions which follow. The general features are:—Cylinders in front, horizontal; six wheels, of which the drivers are in the middle, in front of the firebox, and the trailing wheels behind it; boiler of the usual form, with horizontal tubes.

For passing freely along curves, the leading and driving wheel-flanges should be kept up to the full section, 1¼ inch thick, with ¼ inch clearance on each side, or a total of ½ inch; and the trailing wheels should be formed either plain, or with thinner flanges, according to circumstances. If the driving axle be well up to the firebox, and the hind load under 2 tons, the hind wheels should not be flanged, as, in backing into sidings, &c., they take the lead, and may be insufficient to control the whole mass; and consequently, with flanges, they may over-ride the rails, and lead the engine off the line. If the hind load be materially above 2 tons, the wheels should have thin flanges, ¾ or ⅞ inch thick, with at least ⅜ inch clearance on each side; to allow free running ahead, and to lead the engine in backing. The hind flanges might indeed be removed, even when loaded sufficiently for leading, where the driving wheels are placed well back, as the driving flanges might lead the engine in backing, just as in a four-wheel engine; this is not done, however, with the same facility, because the hind wheels with their loads have a leverage upon the drivers, and offer a resistance to the lateral translation to which they are subjected on curves; this increases the duty of the drivers, and is an extra duty to which they are not subject in four-wheel engines. Hence the propriety of removing the hind flanges when lightly loaded, for safety in backing; and of retaining them when sufficiently loaded, for facility in backing. This is a safe general rule, for when the back loads are light, the driving wheels are necessarily well back and well placed for leading backwards; and when the drivers are too far forward to lead well in backing, the hind wheels are necessarily well loaded, and suitably qualified to lead. Thus, the steadying or wheel base remains unrestricted, while the acting flange-base is suitably limited. On this system, the driving wheel-flanges are designed to take the chief centrifugal strain of the engine, throwing the front wheels free for leading. Upon inside cranks having inside bearings alone, as they ought to have, this strain does not operate injuriously; for concussion, not mere pressure, is what ruins an axle.

When the cylinders are outside and overhung in front, the leading wheels, when free, may be 3½ feet diameter with 6 feet driving wheels, 3 feet 9 inches with 6½ feet wheels, and 4 feet with 7 feet wheels. For inside cylinders, they may be 3½ feet with 5 feet driving wheels, 4½ feet for 6 feet wheels, and 5½ feet for 7 feet wheels. In all cases they should be as large as possible, consistent with the due arrangement of the engine. The hind wheels, when free, may be of the same diameters as those just given for the leaders. It is bad practice to assume, as is commonly done, that, on the score of safety, single leading wheels should not exceed 4 feet. In all cases, the leading axle-guards must be well bound and *practically inflexible*, to discourage oscillation, and keep the head of the engine to the rails. In coupled engines, the leading axle should, when practicable, be left free. When free, it should not be heavily loaded; it should have outside bearings and springs, to increase the stability, and the accommodation for springs, &c. The middle axle-guards, on the system of the reduced flange-base, must also be inflexible, for which their shortness and strength are favourable. The hind axle-guards may and should possess some flexibility, to ease the engine over an occasional hitch.

The buffing springs between engine and tender should be of very moderate strength, equivalent in fact to such as are applied between carriages.

Swivelling bogies at the front of the engine, carrying two pairs of leading wheels, are recommended for lines on which the ruling curves are of a ½ mile radius or less.

Loose wheels on the axles, rolling independently of each other, though undoubtedly of some advantage on curves, have not as yet been made to work well in practice. From what is known of ordinary carriage-wheels, there seems no doubt of the feasibility of loose wheels on railways.

Practical Rules for the Disposition of the Axles, and the Distribution of the Load.—The adjustment of the wheel-loads has been found to depend materially on the positions of the axles, and indirectly on the length of the barrel. The positions of the front and hind axles are, in the four principal classes of high-speed engines, single and coupled,—setting aside tank-engines,—unalterably related to the smokebox and firebox; as the centre of the leading axle ought to be as much as possible within, and at least not more than 12 or 15 inches off the back of the cylinders, which are assumed to be flush with the smokebox tube-plate; and that of the hind axle within 6 inches from the firebox. Adjustment must therefore be effected by operating only upon the position of the middle axle, and on the length of barrel, which takes the leading axle with it, bearing in mind that the driving axle must be at least 7½ to 8 feet clear of the back of the cylinders.

Rules.—*For the Proportional Loads on the Axles of Six-Wheel Engines.*

I. *In single-wheeled engines under* 18 *tons total weight.*—Divide the total weight into 12 parts; and place 3 parts on the leading axle, 8 parts on the driving axle, and 1 part on the trailing axle. In other words, one-fourth, two-thirds, and one-twelfth, respectively.

II. *In single-wheel engines above* 18 *tons total weight.*—Place 12 tons on the driving axle; and distribute the balance between the leading and trailing axles, reserving at least one-fourth of the total weight for the leader.

III. *In coupled-wheel engines.*—Load the free axle, if any, with the weight assigned to it by the first rule, and divide the balance of the weight equally upon the coupled axles. If all the axles are coupled, place one-third of the weight upon each.

Rules.—*For the Disposition of three Axles.*

IV. *Ordinary engines with single wheels.*—Barrel 11 feet long; centre of driving axle between 1 and 2 feet from the firebox-shell.

V. *With the front wheels coupled.*—Barrel 10 feet, centre of driving axle as close as practicable to firebox.

VI. *With the hind wheels coupled.*—Barrel 12 to 13 feet,

varying with the weight, and with the length of firebox-shell between $3\frac{1}{4}$ and 5 feet; driving axle 5 to 4 feet in front of firebox-shell, less as the shell is longer.

VII. *With all six wheels coupled.*—Barrel 12 feet, driving axle 4 to $3\frac{1}{2}$ feet in front of firebox-shell, less as the shell is longer.

VIII. *For tank-engines.* (1.) *Single wheels.* Barrel 12 feet, driving axle in front of firebox, water-tanks also in front, over or under the barrel; cylinders at the smokebox, or behind the leading wheels.

(2.) *Hind wheels coupled.* Barrel 10 feet, driving axle 2 to 3 feet in front of the firebox-shell; water-tanks chiefly behind the boiler; cylinders at the smokebox.

IX. *Tank-engines to run either end foremost.*—(1.) *Single wheels.* Boiler, or firebox-shell and barrel, 13 feet over all; wheel-base 12 feet, driving axle mid-way between end axles; water-tanks in front of firebox; driving load one-half the whole weight.

Or, secondly: boiler 12 feet over all, wheel-base 12 feet, driving axle mid-way; water-tanks chiefly behind firebox; driving load one-half.

Or, thirdly: boiler 12 feet, wheel-base $12\frac{1}{4}$ feet, driving axle behind firebox (Crampton's system), within 6 inches when the tanks are before the firebox, and 18 inches clear when behind.

(2.) *Hind wheels coupled.* Boiler 12 feet, wheel-base 12 feet, driving axle 5 feet behind leading axle; water-tanks chiefly behind firebox; front load one-fourth.

NOTE 1. These rules are expected to yield substantially correct results, fit for ordinary good practice, assuming the mechanism to be duly balanced; where perfect adjustment is contemplated in an original design, the individual weight and centre of gravity of each element must be calculated, in order to deduce the total weight and common centre of gravity of the whole, and thence the axle-loads by the rules in the preceding chapter.

2. Four-wheel engines should never exceed 18 tons weight, and should be employed only for speeds under 20 miles, with the probable exception referred to in next note. If single-wheeled, the firebox should be overhung. If coupled, the hind axle may be behind the firebox, when the barrel should be under 9 or 10 feet long; or, if the hind axle be in front, the firebox should be short, the barrel longer.

3. Four-wheel single engines not exceeding 12 tons, may be employed for high speeds, arranged on Adams' pattern, with an overhung firebox, to secure a sufficiency of driving weight. For such light engines, four wheels are perhaps preferable where a facility of running either end foremost is desirable, as on short lines and branches. They are preferable also for quick-curve lines, where a short wheel-base is conducive to safety. In Adams' design, two-thirds of the whole load are available for driving weight, and one-third for leading.

4. Six-wheel tank-engines with single wheels, designed to run either end foremost, should weigh at least 18 tons, to give a sufficiency of driving weight.

5. Where the weight is deficient in the lighter kinds of engines, for driving or leading, the deficiency may properly be made up by the addition of dead weight.

6. It is assumed that for engines running either end fore-most, all the wheel-flanges are finished to the full thickness, $1\frac{1}{4}$ inch; and that for those which are not so designed, the hind flanges are $\frac{1}{2}$ or $\frac{5}{8}$-inch thinner than the others.

7. When alterations are contemplated in engines already made, with a view to improving the distribution of the load, the following principles should be kept in view:—the longer the barrel, the greater is the facility for the adjustment of the loads; the removal forward of the front, middle, and hind axles, all or any of them, reduces the middle and increases the hind load, when the front load remains constant; and it reduces the front, and increases the hind load, when the middle load is constant; the reverse takes place when any or all of the axles are removed backwards; the shifting of the middle axle affects the distribution of the weight much more than that of the others; finally, the effect of shifting one axle may be neutralised by shifting another the opposite way, so as to leave the separate axle-loads unchanged.

The following Table shows the respective loads on the axles, by Rule I. for uncoupled six-wheel engines, from 9 to 18 tons total weight.

TABLE, No. XCI.—OF THE SUITABLE DISTRIBUTION OF THE TOTAL WEIGHT ON THE AXLES OF UNCOUPLED SIX-WHEEL ENGINES.

FROM 9 TO 18 TONS TOTAL WEIGHT.

Total Weight.	Distribution of the Weight.					
	Leading Axle.		Driving Axle.		Trailing Axle.	
tons	tons.	cwt.	tons	cwt.	tons	cwt.
9	2	5	6	0	0	15
10	2	10	6	13	0	17
11	2	15	7	7	0	18
12	3	0	8	0	1	0
13	3	5	8	13	1	2
14	3	10	9	7	1	3
15	3	15	10	0	1	5
16	4	0	10	13	1	7
17	4	5	11	7	1	8
18	4	10	12	0	1	10

Note. For single engines above 18 tons, as already noted, the distribution of the weight is a matter of indifference, beyond the placing of 12 tons on the driving wheels, and one-fourth of the whole weight upon the leaders.

At this stage of our progress it may be proper to interpolate a few words of explanation. We have passed in review and analysed, we trust to some purpose, the three elements of the locomotive,—the engine, the boiler, and the carriage; and we have, in all important cases, placed before our readers the principles, the facts, and the observations from which our conclusions have been drawn. Before we can be said, however, to have completed this, the physiological discussion of the locomotive, it is incumbent on us to compare and harmonize the three branches of the discussion, by considering the respective claims and necessities of things so very diverse as engines, boilers, and wheeled carriages, and working out for practical use a consistent system of principles approved by the more general laws of matter, and sanctioned by direct experience. But though we have reached a point from which an extensive retrospect may be obtained, it is thought better to defer the consideration of the more general question, until the locomotive shall have been anatomically reviewed; when, at the same time, we shall be in a position to lay before our readers, one compact mass of consistent results, carefully worked out, and reduced into numerous formulas and rules for practice.

SECTION III.—ANATOMY OF LOCOMOTIVES.

Our business is now with the mechanical construction of locomotives, and with the principles which affect their constructive design and arrangement. We shall have, in the first place, to bring forward the existing practice of mechanical engineers, illustrating it with the examples contained in our Plates; secondly, to work out and establish by practical evidence the constructive principles and style of detail which ought to regulate the composition of the locomotive, and the modifications suitable for the different service of railways.

The following literal references to Fairbairn's passenger-engine give the names and designations of the elements of the locomotive; and they will assist the imperfectly initiated in following out the ensuing descriptions both of that and of the other engines which fall under notice.

Literal References to Passenger-Locomotive.—Plates I., II., III.

Boiler.
- A, barrel or cylindrical part of boiler.
  - *a*, firebars, or grate-bars.
  - *b*, roofribs, or roof-stays.
  - *c*, firedoor.
  - *d*, screw plug.
- B, firebox-shell.
  - *e*, steam-dome, or regulator-chamber.
  - *f*, safety-valve.
  - *g*, feed-pump.
  - *h*, heating cock.
  - *i*, blow off cock.
  - *j*, steam-whistle, or alarm-whistle.
- C, firebox.
- D, tubes.
- E, smokebox.
- F, chimney.
- G, ash pan.

Engine.
- H, regulator.
  - *k*, valve of regulator.
- I, steampipe.
- K, valve chest.
- L, cylinders.
- M, exhaust or blastpipe.
- N, piston.
  - *l*, crosshead on piston-rod, slides, and guidebars.
  - *m*, transverse stay-plate, or motion-plate, binding together frame, boiler, and guide-bars.
- O, connecting rod.
- P, crank-axle, or driving axle.
- Q, driving wheel.
- R, valve-gear, comprising eccentrics on driving axle, eccentric-rods, &c.
- S, valve, slide, or slide-valve.
  - *n*, sink.
  - *o*, reversing shaft.
  - *p*, reversing handle.

Frame.
- T, frame.
  - *q*, inside frame-plates.
  - *r*, stays in front, binding together inside and outside frames.
  - *s*, stays, binding firebox shell to frame.
  - *t*, stays, binding inside frame-plates to firebox-shell.
- U, fore wheels, front wheels, or leading wheels.
- V, hind wheels, back wheels, or trailing wheels.
  - *u*, axle-boxes.
  - *v*, side-springs, or bearing springs.
  - *w*, safety-guards.

Locomotives are classified according to the nature of the service and the position of the cylinders. According to the service, they are of three classes. 1st. Passenger-engines, to run with passengers, and to do other work requiring the greatest speed: with large driving wheels, to moderate the rate of reciprocation of the mechanism, and having all the wheels independent. 2d. Goods-engines, to draw heavy loads at moderate speeds; they have small wheels all coupled, and generally long-stroked cylinders. 3d. Mixed engines, an intermediate class, more lately introduced, to work heavy passenger-traffic on steep lines, and moderate goods-traffic. They have six wheels, and only four wheels coupled.

Of late, another class, known as tank-engines, has been employed, of all sizes and weights, but generally lighter than ordinary passenger-engines. They carry a supply of water and coke, and thus dispense with the separate tender; and are designed generally for express trains, and for working short lines.

According to the position of the cylinders, there are two kinds:—inside-cylinder engines, and outside-cylinder engines, which are employed indiscriminately for all kinds of service.

SUB-SECTION I.

EXISTING PRACTICE OF CONSTRUCTION, WITH EXAMPLES. DESCRIPTION OF PLATES.

A series of locomotives has been selected for illustration by engravings to a scale generally of one-sixteenth full size, in Plates I. to XXX. These may be arranged in the following order:—1st. Inside and outside-cylinder passenger-engines; 2d. Inside and outside-cylinder goods-engines; 3d. Outside-cylinder tank-engines for the lighter traffic.

CHAPTER I.

Ordinary Passenger-Locomotives with Inside Cylinders.

I. Passenger-Locomotive with Independent Wheels, by William Fairbairn and Sons, Manchester. Plates I., II., III.

Area of grate, ...	13·9 square feet.
Diameter of cylinder, ...	16 inches.
Stroke of piston, ...	21 "
Diameter of driving wheel, ...	5 feet 8 inches.
Length of wheel-base, ...	14 feet.
Total weight in working order, ...	23 tons.

General Arrangement. Ordinary boiler, with horizontal tubes, cylinders inside and horizontal; six wheels, of which the drivers are in front of the firebox, the leading wheels behind the cylinders, and the trailing wheels behind the firebox.

Boiler. In three parts—1st. The firebox-shell and firebox, B, C; 2d. The barrel and tubes, A, D; 3d. The smokebox and chimney, E, F.

Firebox-shell. Of ⅜ in. plates, 4 ft. 6 in. by 4 ft. 3 in. broad, outside; with an 8 inch necking to carry safety-valves. End plates lap-jointed to sides and top; top and sides joined with 4 in. welts.

Firebox. Of ½ in. copper plates, ¾ in. at tubes, lap-jointed; 3 ft. 10½ in. by 3 ft. 7½ in. broad, and 5 ft. 2 in. high off grate, inside. Joined to shell with 3 in. waterspace angle-iron, and stayed to it with ⅞ in. copper stay-bolts, about 4½ in. pitch. Stiffened by seven roofribs and 1 in. rivetted bolts. Doorway made with wrought iron ring and ⅝ in. rivets. Door of ⅜ in. plate, with ¼ in. shield. Grate-bars of wrought iron, 1½ in. thick, with 1 in. airspaces; placed in wrought iron frame carried by brackets.

Ash-pan. Of $\frac{1}{4}$ in. plate, made with $1\frac{1}{2}$ in. angle-iron, and band on upper edge; joined to firebox with four welts. Door of $\frac{1}{4}$ in. plate, hinged by upper edge, and worked by a lever and rod carried to footplate.

Barrel. Of $\frac{1}{2}$ in. iron plates lap-jointed; 3 ft. 11 in. diameter inside, 10 feet long, with 3 in. angle-iron joints at ends. Dome of $\frac{3}{8}$ in. plate worked in one piece, 23 in. diameter. End plates of boiler stayed with six $\frac{13}{16}$ in., and two 1 in. rods, cottered into blocks rivetted to plates.

Tubes. 202 brass tubes, in 14 rows; 196 are 2 in., and 6 are $1\frac{1}{2}$ in. diameter outside, $\frac{5}{8}$ in. clear, 10 ft. $3\frac{3}{8}$ in. long between plates. Fixed with ferules at both ends.

Smokebox. 2 ft. $4\frac{7}{8}$ in. long, 4 ft. 3 in. broad, outside, flush with frame-plates. Tube-plate $\frac{5}{8}$ in., of iron, other plates $\frac{1}{4}$ in.; joined with $2\frac{1}{2}$ in. angle-iron, and to inside frameplates with welts, completing the enclosure of the cylinders.

Chimney. 15 in. diameter, of $\frac{3}{16}$ in. plate.

Rivets. In firebox, shell, and barrel, $\frac{3}{4}$ in. diameter, $1\frac{3}{4}$ in. pitch. In smokebox, $\frac{1}{2}$ in. diameter, at 2 in. pitch.

Brass Mounting of Boiler.—Safety-valves. Have two $3\frac{1}{2}$ in. conical spindle-valves. Valve-seat in one casting, bolted to necking on firebox-shell. Levers 27 in. long, $3\frac{1}{4}$ in. pivot to valve: leverage 8·3 to 1; with two Salter's balances.

Fig. 230.—Scale 1-4th.

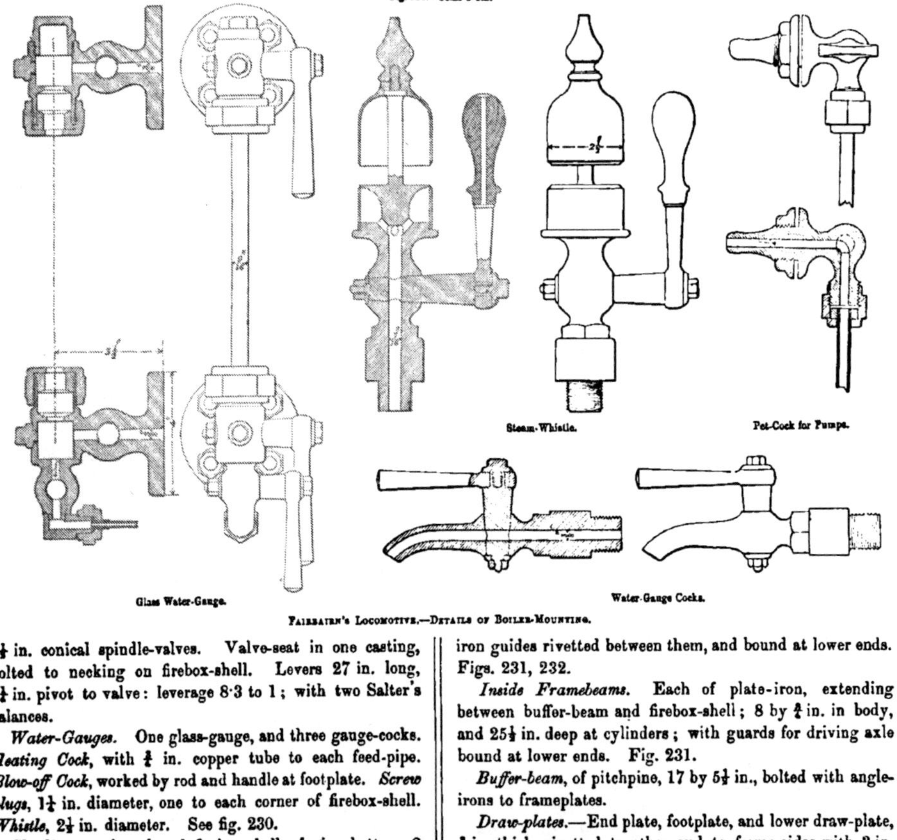

Glass Water-Gauge. Steam-Whistle. Pet-Cock for Pumps. Water-Gauge Cocks.

FAIRBAIRN'S LOCOMOTIVE.—DETAILS OF BOILER-MOUNTING.

Water-Gauges. One glass-gauge, and three gauge-cocks. *Heating Cock*, with $\frac{3}{4}$ in. copper tube to each feed-pipe. *Blow-off Cock*, worked by rod and handle at footplate. *Screw plugs*, $1\frac{1}{2}$ in. diameter, one to each corner of firebox-shell. *Whistle*, $2\frac{1}{2}$ in. diameter. See fig. 230.

Cleading, on barrel and firebox-shell, of pine battens 2 by $\frac{3}{4}$ in., grooved and tongued, covered with $\frac{1}{8}$ in. sheet iron strapped with hoop-iron. Corners of boiler, and dome and safety-valves, covered with burnished and sheet brass $\frac{1}{16}$ in. thick.

FRAME. Composed of two outside and two inside longitudinal beams, with transverse buffer-beam, draw-plates, and stays.

Outside Framebeams. Of pitchpine 3 by $10\frac{1}{2}$ in., with $\frac{7}{16}$ in. iron plate on each side, bound with two rows of $\frac{3}{4}$ in. bolts and nuts. Plates made with axleguards, having cast iron guides rivetted between them, and bound at lower ends. Figs. 231, 232.

Inside Framebeams. Each of plate-iron, extending between buffer-beam and firebox-shell; 8 by $\frac{3}{4}$ in. in body, and $25\frac{1}{2}$ in. deep at cylinders; with guards for driving axle bound at lower ends. Fig. 231.

Buffer-beam, of pitchpine, 17 by $5\frac{1}{2}$ in., bolted with angle-irons to frameplates.

Draw-plates.—End plate, footplate, and lower draw-plate, $\frac{3}{4}$ in. thick, rivetted together and to frame-sides with 3 in. angle-iron. Footplate and draw-plate rivetted together with distance pieces at centre, and have extra thicknesses to receive 2 in. draw-bolt, and two $1\frac{1}{2}$ in. safety-bolts. End plate faced with two $\frac{3}{4}$ in. buffing plates.

Frame-stays.—1st. The cylinders, which are bolted together and to the inside frameplates. In the same locality, the in and outside beams on each side, are bound with a piece of $\frac{1}{2}$ in. plate, rivetted with angle-iron. 2d. The motion-stayplate, $\frac{5}{8}$ in. thick, in four pieces, joined at middle by a bar under valve-gear, welted over inside frameplates, and rivetted with angle-iron to barrel and frame. 3d. Brass brackets rivetted to firebox-shell, with wrought-iron plates bolted to them, to carry ends of inside frameplates, giving

liberty for unequal expansion of boiler and frame. 4th. Boiler-stays, consisting, first, of the tube and front plates of-smokebox, which are extended laterally and joined with

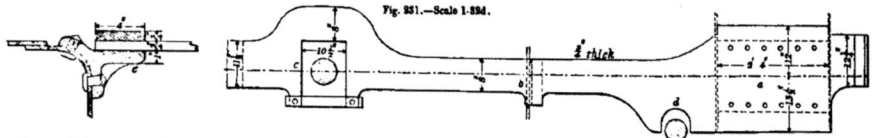

Fig. 231.—Scale 1-33d.

FAIRBAIRN's LOCOMOTIVE.—INSIDE FRAMEPLATE. *a*, Cylinder-platform; *b*, Junction of Motion-plate; *c*, Axleguard and Tie; *d*, Safety-guard for leading axle in case of fracture; *e*, Detail of Junction at Firebox.

angle-irons to outside framebeams; second, firebox-stayplates, on edge, rivetted with flanges to shell, and with angle-iron to frame.

Wheels and Axles.—Of wrought-iron, with cast naves; driving wheels 5 ft. 8 in. diameter, with 18 spokes; smaller wheels 3½ feet, with 12 spokes. Tyres 5 by 2½ in. thick,

fixed to rim with taper bolts and nuts. Driving axle, 6 in. diameter of body, with four bearings.

Axleboxes. Of cast iron, with flanges to embrace guides, brass bushes, and lower bushes of cast iron pinned up. Grease-chamber above, with sheet iron covers. Fig. 232.

Springs. Of steel plates 4 by ⅝ in., except back and short

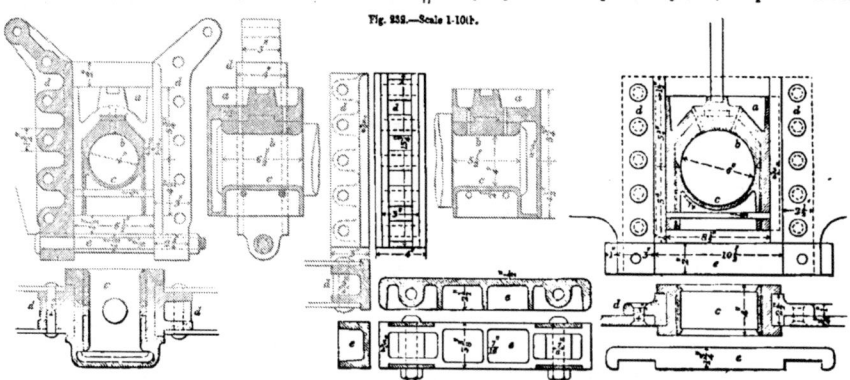

Fig. 232.—Scale 1-10th.

FAIRBAIRN's LOCOMOTIVE.—AXLEBOXES. *a*, Axlebox; *b*, Upper Bush; *c*, Lower Bush; *d*, Guides; *e*, Ties.

plates, ½ in.; span 2 feet 7 in.; 13 plates in leading springs, 12 plates in the others. Round spring-rods let into shackles and top of axleboxes. Spring-ends linked to frame. Links of front and driving springs formed with right and left hand screws to adjust the loads on the axles, and the level of the machine.

ENGINE, consisting of cylinders and valve-chest, pistons, rods, guide-bars, valve-gearing, reversing gear, regulator, steam-pipes, pumps.

Cylinders. Of cast iron, cast with valve-chest in two pieces; bolted together with ⅞ in. bolts and nuts at 4 in. pitch, and to each inside frameplate with twelve 1 in. bolts

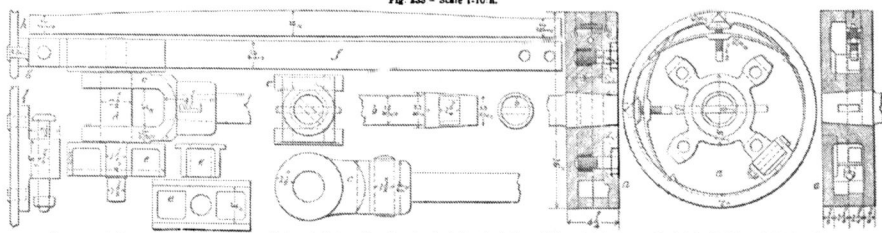

Fig. 233.—Scale 1-10th.

FAIRBAIRN's LOCOMOTIVE.—PISTON, &c. *a*, Piston; *b*, Piston rod; *c*, Crosshead; *d*, Crosshead-pin; *e*, Slides; *f*, Guidebar; *g*, Bracket for Guidebar; *h*, Motion-plate.

and nuts. Diameter 16 in., stroke 21 in., steamports 11 by 1⅜ in., exhaust ports 3 in., lap of valve ¾ in. outside, ₁₆ in. inside, lead ¼ in. full gear, travel 4½ in. Thickness of cylinder, chest, and steamways, ¾ in.; flanges at joints ⅝ in., front and back ⅞ in., at frame 1 in.; covers 1 in. Two

brass water-cocks to each cylinder, worked by rod and handle at footplate.

Pistons of cast iron, 4¼ in. thick; two packing rings of cast iron, 1¼ in. thick; junc-ring fixed with four ½ in. bolts screwed into brass nuts let into body. Rings cut each at one place, fitted with wedge and spring. Wought iron rest pinned to body, to support it on the rings. Fig. 233.

Piston-Rod of wrought iron, 2¾ in. diameter, tapered and cottered into piston and crosshead. Fig. 233.

Crosshead, of wrought iron, with jaws to admit connecting rod, and 2⅞ in. pin. *Slides* of cast iron, two to each cylinder. Fig. 233.

Guide-Bars of steel, 2¼ in. broad; two pairs to each cylinder, bolted to cylinder-covers and to motion-plate. Fig. 233.

Connecting Rod of wrought iron, with single ends, brass and straps; centres 5 ft. 8¼ in. Strap for large butt, bevelled at points to enter and fit recesses formed in butt, and fixed with gibs and cotters. Brass bush fixed with pin and cotter bearing on bush directly. Oil-cup forged on strap; lid screwed in, with ¼ in. hole. One gib and cotter to small end, operating on the strap, which fixes the brass against the butt. Oil-cup of brass screwed into strap. Fig. 234.

Eccentrics, Rods, and Expansion-Link. Eccentrics of

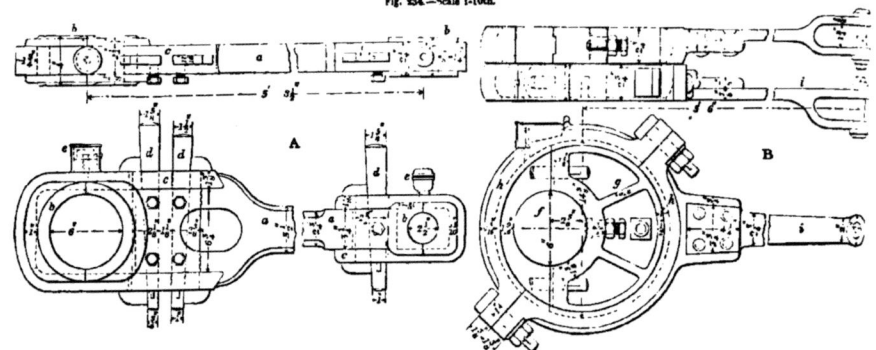

Fig. 234.—Scale 1-10th.

FAIRBAIRN'S LOCOMOTIVE.—CONNECTING ROD (A) and ECCENTRIC ROD (B). *a* Body of Connecting Rod ; *b,* Bushes ; *c,* Straps ; *d,* Cotters and Gibs ; *e,* Oil-cups; *f,* Driving Axle, *g,* Eccentric ; *h,* Strap ; *i,* Rod.

cast iron, 14¾ in. diameter, 2⅛ in. radius, giving 5¼ in. throw; in two pieces grooved and tongued, joined with two 1 in. bolts and cotters; fixed on axle with one key and ¾ in. set-screw working in wrought iron nut let into casting. Strap of brass, in two pieces, joined with palms and 1 in. bolts, nuts, and cotters; with oil-cup and lid. Rods, of

iron, ⅞ in. thick, 5½ ft. centres, each with palm dovetailed into strap, and rivetted to it; forked to join link at 16 in. centres, which is 1¾ in. thick, and curved to a 5½ feet radius. Figs. 234, 235.

Valve and Rods. Valve of brass ½ in. thick in body. (See also *Cylinders.*) Valve-rod 1⅜ in. diameter, with

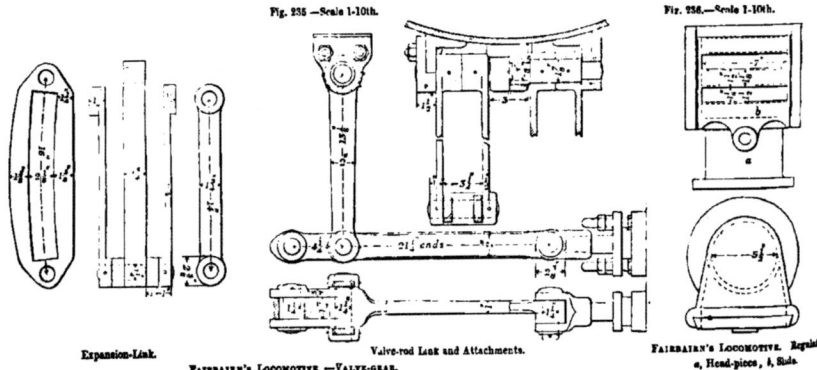

Fig. 235.—Scale 1-10th.　　　　　Fig. 236.—Scale 1-10th.

Expansion-Link.　　FAIRBAIRN'S LOCOMOTIVE.—VALVE-GEAR.　　Valve-rod Link and Attachments.　　FAIRBAIRN'S LOCOMOTIVE. Regulator. *a,* Head-piece ; *b,* Slide.

bearings at both ends of chest, and strap embracing valve ; link pinned to valve-rod, and forked at other end to embrace the link-block, and suspended by links from boiler. Fig. 235.

Reversing Gear. Shaft 2¾ in., in cast iron bearings bolted to inside frameplates. Levers forged solid on shaft, to carry expansion-links and balance-weight, and to take end of reversing rod. Reversing lever works on pin fixed

to firebox-shell, with detent-rod and lever acted on by a helical spring let into body of main lever. Segmental guide in two parts, curved to 12 in. outside radius, and bolted together at the ends; fixed to firebox-shell. Fig. 237.

Valve-gear and reversing gear, of wrought-iron with working surfaces case-hardened.

Regulator and Steam-pipes. Brass face and slide with inlet ports, placed in dome; bolted to 5¼ in. cast iron steam-pipe stayed to boiler, and joined to horizontal copper pipe led to smokebox; cast iron branch pipes in smokebox, leading to valvechest. Slide of regulator linked to and worked by a 2 in. lever on spindle with brass bearing in firebox-shell, and 16 in. handle. *Exhaust pipe*, of copper, 5¼ in. diameter, with orifice flush with bottom of chimney. Fig. 236.

Fig 237.—Scale 1-10th.

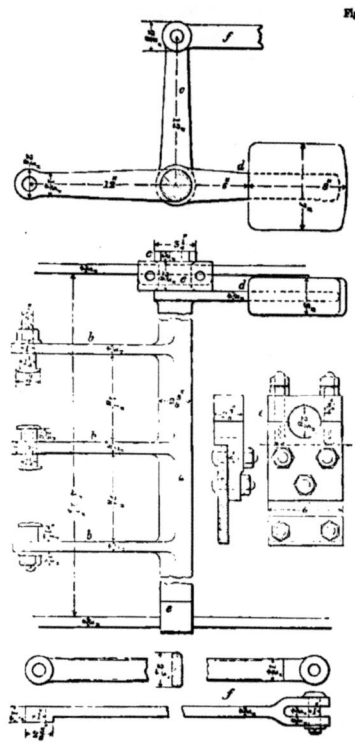

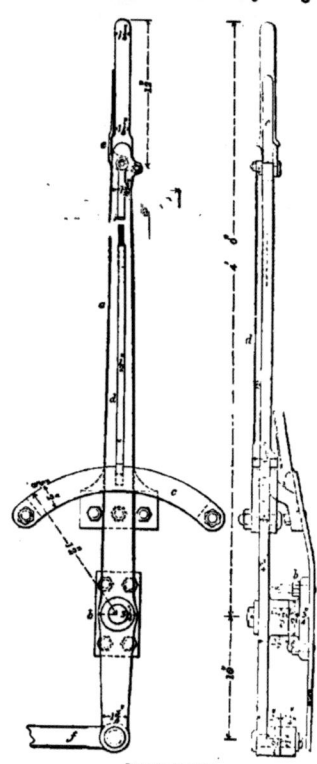

Reversing Shaft, &c.

a, Shaft; *b*, Link levers, *c*, Rod-lever; *d*, Balanceweight and Lever; *e*, Journals and Bearings; *f*, Reversing Rod.

Reversing Lever, &c.

a, Lever; *b*, Fulcrum; *c*, Guide; *d*, Detent-rod; *e*, Detent-lever; *f*, Reversing-rod.

FAIRBAIRN'S LOCOMOTIVE.—REVERSING GEAR.

Feed-pumps. Two, bodies of brass, ⁷⁄₁₆ in. thick; ram of wrought iron, 1¾ in. diameter, with eye fixed on crosshead-pin, and worked by it. Waterways in body 2 in., in valves 1¾ in. Three ball-valves, with 2¼ in. hollow balls, one for suction, and two for delivery. Pumps bolted to inside frameplates. Cock on delivery-pipe, of brass, bolted to barrel. Pipes of ½ in. copper, 2 in. diameter, coupled to tender with double ball-and-socket joint. Petcocks of brass, and copper tubes. Figs. 230, 238.

General Fittings.—Two indiarubber-buffers, with cast iron sockets bolted to buffer-beam; also draw-hook and 1 in. chain. Fence of sheet iron, fixed to footplate and coping with 1 in. angle-iron. Hand-rails of 1¼ in. round iron, along sides and front of boiler. Footsteps of plate iron rivetted to leading and trailing guardplates. Brass oil-cocks fixed to sides of smokebox with tubes to valve-chests.

The foregoing locomotive has been detailed with considerable minuteness, for it may be considered as a leading example of workmanship, combining the matured results of lengthened experience; and the completeness of detail in the first example offers the best means of introducing the cases which succeed it, and admits of greater brevity in the treatment of the latter.

The passenger-locomotive which forms the subject of Plates I.–III., is closely similar to that made by Sharp, Stewart, and Co. (lately Sharp Brothers, and Co.), and is in many respects identical with it. The example before us may therefore be accepted as an embodiment of the latest practice of two of the most conspicuous locomotive-building firms in England. It is in fact the ultimate result of the gradual development of the early six-wheel type of engine produced by Stephenson, in which, while the general design has been substantially adhered to, the details in many important respects have been materially modified and improved; and is probably the best that can be made of the species of single wheel locomotive which it represents, with respect to its details. The employment of four bearings on the driving axle, inside and outside, which constitutes the leading distinction of the species, is, however, in our view radically and essentially defective; in succeeding

2 o

illustrations, it will be shown how simply the number of bearings may be reduced to two, placed exclusively inside the wheels; and in the subsequent discussions on locomotive-framing, it will be fully demonstrated, from experience,

Fig. 238.—Scale 1-10th.

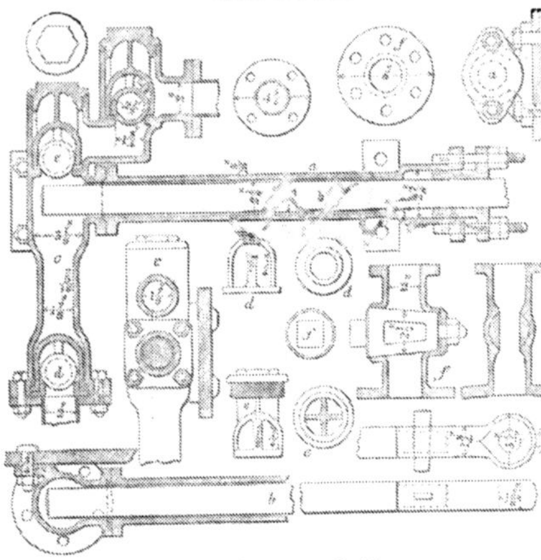

FAIRBAIRN'S LOCOMOTIVE. Feed Pump.
a, Working chamber or barrel; *b*, Plunger or ram; *c*, Valve-chambers; *d*, Suction-valve; *e*, Delivery-valves; *f*, Stopcock at boiler.

that however elaborately and carefully expedients may be employed for neutralizing the inherent defects of an accumulation of bearings on the driving axle, it is practically impossible to prevent the dislocation due to the antagonism of inside and outside bearings.

II. MIXED PASSENGER-LOCOMOTIVE, WITH HIND WHEELS COUPLED, BY KITSON, THOMPSON, AND HEWITSON, LEEDS. PLATES IV. V. VI.

Area of grate, ...	15·5 square feet.
Diameter of cylinder, ...	16 inches.
Stroke of piston, ...	22 do.
Diameter of driving wheels, ...	6 feet.
Length of wheel-base, ...	15 do.
Total weight in working order, ...	about 26 tons.

General Arrangement.—Ordinary boiler, and cylinders horizontal, inside; six wheels, of which the leading wheels are behind the cylinders, and the driving and trailing wheels before and behind the firebox.

BOILER.—Firebox-shell of $\frac{1}{2}$ in. plates, except side plates, $\frac{3}{4}$ in., made with wings to connect to inside frameplates. Firebox of $\frac{1}{2}$ in. copper plates, made $\frac{7}{8}$ in. at tubes; 4 ft. 3 in. by 3 ft. $7\frac{3}{8}$ in. wide, and 4 ft. $9\frac{1}{4}$ in. high above grate, inside; with 3 and 4 in. waterspaces. Ashpan, of $\frac{1}{4}$ in. plate. Barrel, of $\frac{3}{8}$ in. plate, oval in section, being 3 ft. $9\frac{1}{2}$ in. deep, 3 ft. $7\frac{1}{2}$ in. wide, outside, and $10\frac{1}{2}$ ft. long. Inside Boiler-stays:—Firebox stayed to shell with $\frac{7}{8}$ in. copper bolts, 4 to $4\frac{5}{8}$ in. centres; six roofstays to firebox, each of two bars rivetted together. Two $1\frac{1}{4}$ in. tie-rods bind each end plate to barrel, pinned to palms rivetted to plates and crown of barrel. Tubes: 147 brass tubes, $1\frac{7}{8}$ in. diameter outside; thickness tapers from No. 13 gauge at firebox to No. 14 at smokebox; length 10 ft. $10\frac{1}{8}$ in. between plates. Smokebox of same length as cylinders; closed at bottom to exclude cylinders. Tube-plate $\frac{7}{8}$ in. Rivets for steam-joints, $\frac{3}{4}$ in. at $1\frac{7}{8}$ in. pitch.

FRAME.—Composed of two outside longitudinal plates, two inside plates, transverse timber beam at each end, and draw-plates. Outside frameplates, each in one plate 8 by 1 in. thick. Leading axleguards, each of two $\frac{5}{8}$ in. plates, rivetted to frame with wrought-iron guides. Inside Framing:—Two plates 8 by $1\frac{1}{8}$ in., from buffer-beam to firebox, and two extra plates from firebox to hind beam, rivetted and bolted to wings of firebox-shell. Hind and middle axleguards of $\frac{5}{8}$ in. plate, rivetted to framing and firebox. End beams of English oak; buffer-beams 6 by 18 in., hind beams 6 by 16 in. Draw-plates: Two $\frac{7}{8}$ in. plates rivetted to inside framing. Draw-bolt 3 in.

Frame-Stays.—1st, The cylinders, bolted together and to the inside frameplates. 2d, The motion-stayplate, $\frac{3}{4}$ in. thick, in one piece, binding the inside frameplates and the barrel of boiler, with 3 in. angle-iron. 3d, Two box-stays, at motion-plate, one on each side of engine, between in and outside frameplates, composed of two tie-plates rivetted with

Fig. 239.—Scale 1-10th.

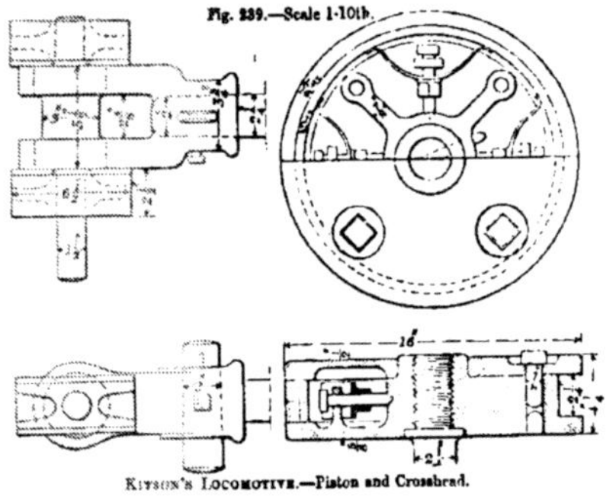

KITSON'S LOCOMOTIVE.—Piston and Crosshead.

3 in. angle-iron. 4th, Boiler-stays; first, smokebox-stays of $\frac{1}{2}$ in. plate on edge, fixed with angle-iron to smokebox

Fig. 240.—Scale 1-10th.

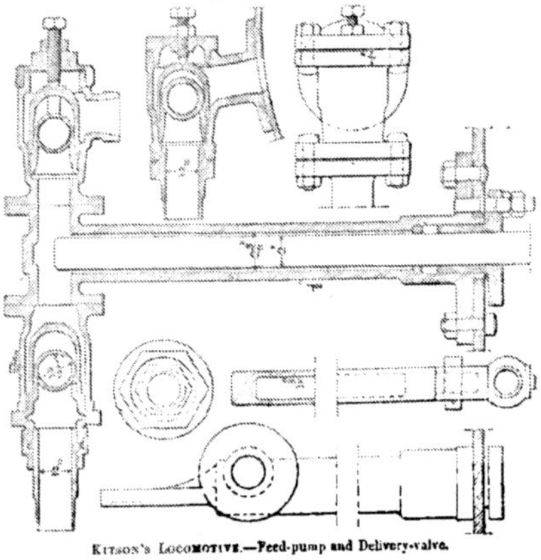

KITSON'S LOCOMOTIVE.—Feed-pump and Delivery-valve.

and to frameplates; second, the barrel-stays of $\frac{3}{8}$ in. plate, in three parts, one to each side, and one reaching below the boiler, lapped and rivetted to the boiler and inside frame-plates; third, the firebox-stays of $\frac{1}{2}$ plate, lapped and rivetted to boiler and outside frameplates.

Wheels and Axles.—Of wrought iron, with cast naves. Large wheels, 6 ft., with 3 in. crankpins. Crank axle $6\frac{1}{4}$ in.,

trailing axle $6\frac{1}{4}$ in. Leading wheels $4\frac{1}{2}$ ft. Axleboxes of cast iron, with brass bushes. Springs, each of 17 plates $3\frac{1}{4}$ by $\frac{5}{8}$ in., 39 in. long.

ENGINE.—Cylinders and valve-chest of cast iron, in two pieces, bolted together and to frame. Cylinder, 16 in. by

Fig. 241.—Scale 1-10th.

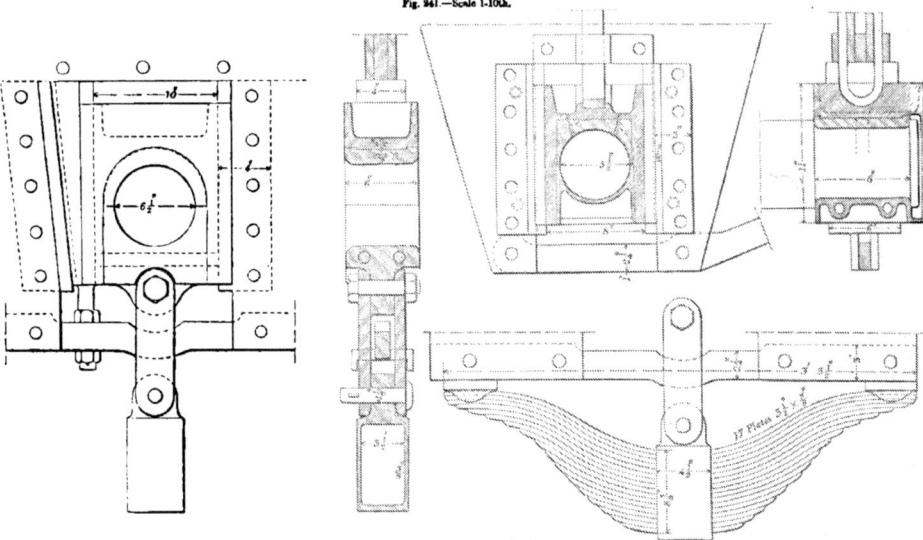

KITSON'S LOCOMOTIVE.—Driving Axlebox. Leading Axlebox. Spring.

22 in. stroke; steam-ports $14\frac{1}{4}$ by $1\frac{1}{4}$ in., exhaust $2\frac{3}{4}$ in.; lap of valve 1 in. outside, $\frac{1}{16}$ in. inside, lead in full gear $\frac{1}{16}$ in., travel $4\frac{1}{2}$ in. Pistons of brass, $4\frac{1}{4}$ in. thick. Rod of iron, $2\frac{1}{4}$ in. diameter, screwed and pinned into piston.

Guide-bars, of wrought iron, $2\frac{1}{4}$ in. broad, two pairs to

each cylinder. Connecting rod, 5 ft. 10 in. centres. Coupling rod, $7\frac{1}{4}$ ft. centres.

Eccentrics of cast iron, giving $4\frac{1}{4}$ in. throw. Straps of brass Rods 4 ft. $4\frac{1}{2}$ in. centres, pinned behind to link, at $9\frac{1}{4}$ in. apart. Link $1\frac{1}{4}$ in. thick. Valve of brass (see

Fig. 242.—Scale 1-10th.

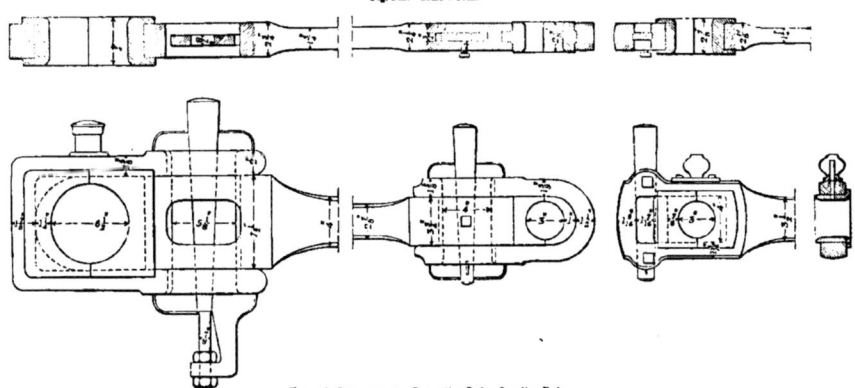

KITSON'S LOCOMOTIVE.—Connecting Rod. Coupling Rod.

Cylinder). Rod $1\frac{1}{4}$ in., cottered into wrought iron slide which carries the sliding block. Slide guided in blocks carried by two pairs of transverse bars fixed to guide-bars. Reversing Gear:—Shaft $2\frac{1}{4}$ in., in wrought iron bearings

bolted to frame, with levers carrying expansion-links and balance-weights; linked to intermediate shaft worked by reversing handle.

Regulator made with $9\frac{1}{4}$ in. circular disc, and rotating brass valve. Steam-pipe of cast iron in dome, of copper in barrel; cast iron branch pipes in smokebox. Blastpipe of copper, with 4⅝ in. orifice.

Feed-pump: Chamber of cast iron, bolted to motion-plate and middle axleguard. Ram 2 in., of wrought iron, worked by crosshead. Water-way 2 in. Feed-pipe of copper, 2 in.

III. Mixed Tank-Locomotive with Hind Wheels coupled, by Daniel Gooch, London. Plates VII. VIII. IX.

Area of grate, ...	19 square feet.
Diameter of cylinder, ...	17 inches.
Stroke of piston, ...	24 „
Diameter of driving wheels, ...	6 feet.
Length of wheel-base, ...	18 feet 2 inches.
Weight on four leading wheels, ...	14¼ tons.
Do. driving and hind wheels, ...	21¼ „
Total weight in working order, ...	35½ tons.

General Arrangement. Boiler of the ordinary form, cylinders inside; eight wheels, of which the drivers are in front of firebox, and coupled to hind wheels behind firebox; four front wheels and two axles placed in a bogie-frame and swivelled to a pivot behind the smokebox. Water-tank placed over the barrel of boiler. Sledge-brake applied between driving and trailing wheels.

Boiler. Firebox-shell of ⅜ in. plates, except lower part of front plate ½ in. Firebox of ½ in. copper plates, ⅞ in. at tubes; 4 ft. 4 in. by 4 ft. 8¾ in. wide, and 4 ft. 4 in. deep above bars at front, 4 ft. 7½ in. back. Waterspace 2½ in. at bottom, 3½ in. at top. Transverse mid-feather with 3 and 4 in. waterspace. Ashpan, of 3/16 in. plate. Barrel 4 ft. 3 in. diameter inside, 10 ft. 6 in. long; upper plates ⅜ in., lower ½ in. full. Ends joined with 3½ in. angle-iron, cut down to 3 in. on upper part of barrel. Inside stays: copper stays of firebox ⅞ in., except round lower part of barrel, and in uppermost row round firebox, and at shell stays, where they are 1 in. Ten roofstays of wrought iron. Eleven 1½ in. tie-rods between extreme plates, and two rods between plates of firebox. Tubes:—219 brass tubes, 2 in. outside; No. 9 gauge at firebox, tapering to No. 12 at 18 in. distance, thence to No. 14 at smokebox; length 10 ft. 9¾ in. between plates. Smokebox made to enclose cylinders. Tubeplate ¾ in., other plates ½ in., except lower part of front plate ⅝ in. Damper in smokebox, formed with "Venetian blinds" of sheet iron worked by handle at footplate. Rivets for steam-joints, ¾ in., at 1¾ in. pitch; except at junction of firebox and shell, ⅞ in. at 1⅞ in. pitch; and in lower halves of angle-iron at ends of barrel, where they are arranged zig-zag.

Fig. 243.—Scale 1-8th.

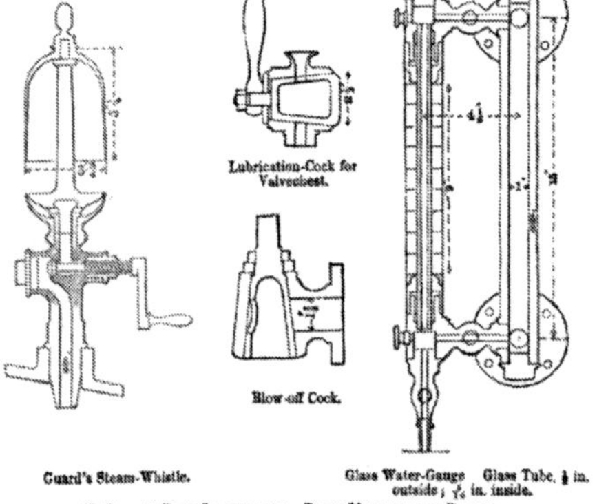
Lubrication-Cock for Valvechest.
Blow-off Cock.

Guard's Steam-Whistle. Glass Water-Gauge. Glass Tube, ⅝ in. outside; 7/16 in. inside.

D. Gooch's Tank-Locomotive.—Brass Mounting of Boiler.

Frame. Sides, of oak 3 by 10½ in. deep, with ½ in. plate on each side, fixed with ⅞ in. bolts and nuts. Guards for driving and hind axles, made with cast iron guides. Buffer-beams of oak 18 by 6 in., front beam bolted to palms turned on ½ in. plates rivetted one on each side of smokebox, and stiffened by wrought iron brackets. Middle Stay for Driving Axle, of two ½ in. plates fixed with angle iron to barrel; with cast iron checks. Frame-Stays: 1st. Two barrel-stays, of ⅝ in. plate; 2d. Two firebox-stays of 1 in. plate, fixed to firebox with eight 1 in. stud-bolts screwed through into firebox, with nuts inside.

Fig. 244.—Scale 1-10th.

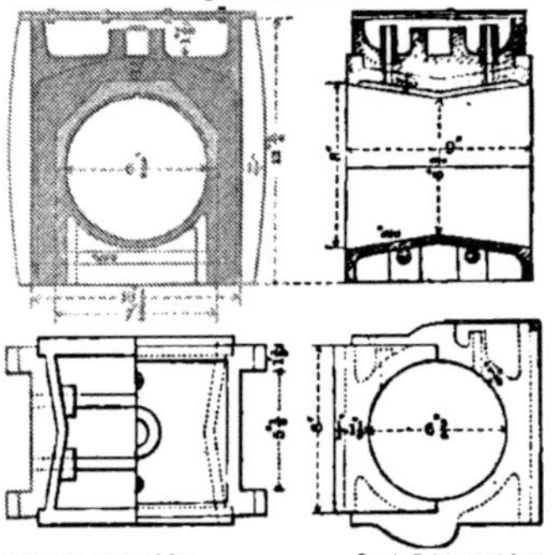

Outside Driving Axlebox. Inside Driving Axlebox.

D. Gooch's Locomotive.—Axleboxes.

Fig. 245.—Scale 1-10th.

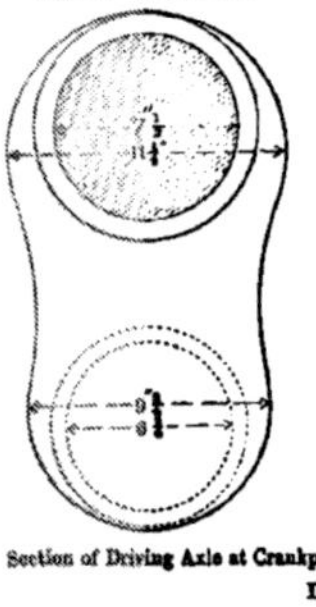

Section of Driving Axle at Crankpin.

Fig. 246.—Scale 1-10th.

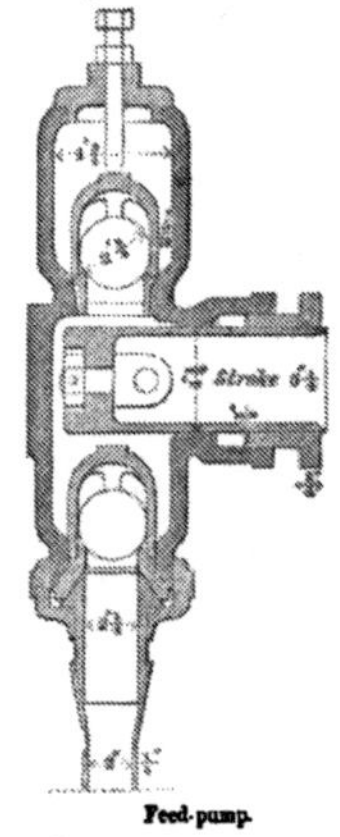
Stroke

Feed-pump.

D. Gooch's Locomotive.

Bogie—Of wrought iron, with four axleguards, and cup to receive pivot. Pivot of wrought iron 3½ in. diameter, with 9 in. spherical bearing, rivetted into double gusset of ⅝ in. plate rivetted into angle of barrel and smokebox.

Draw-plates: Two ⅝ in. plates, rivetted to back of firebox-shell all the width. Draw-bolt 2½ in., bar. 3 in.

Wheels and Axles: Of wrought iron with inside bearings. Large wheels 6 ft., with 3 in. crankpins; bogie-wheels 3½ ft. Tyres faced with steel, fixed on iron with dovetail and zinc joint. Crank-axle 6½ in. in body, and very heavy and rigid at cranks; hind axle 6 in., bogie-axles 5¼ in. Axle boxes of cast iron, with brass bushes lined with white metal. Springs: Driving spring, 14 plates 4 by ½ in., 3½ ft. span, with shackle bearing on seat, with hardened

Fig. 247.—Scale 1-10th.

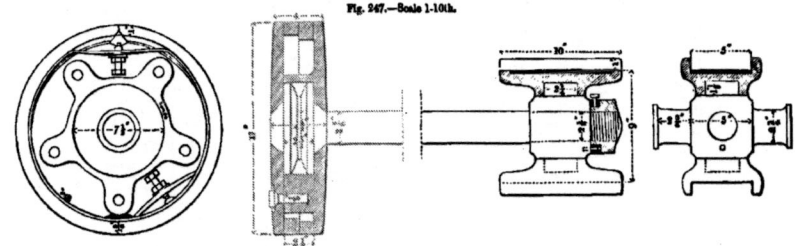

D. GOOCH's LOCOMOTIVE.—Piston, Rod, and Crosshead.

Fig. 248.—Scale 1-10th.

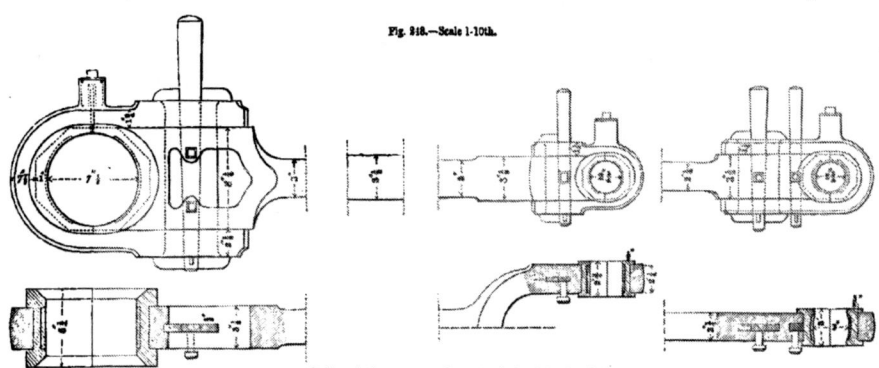

D. GOOCH's LOCOMOTIVE.—Connecting Rod, and Coupling Rod End.

Fig. 249.—Scale 1-10th.

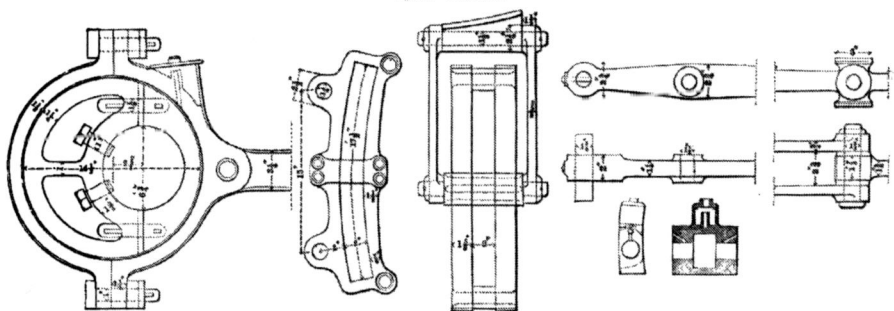

D. GOOCH's LOCOMOTIVE.—Eccentric and Strap. Expansion Link. Valve-Rod Link and Sliding-Block.

steel surfaces; seat rivetted between two ½ in. plates bolted together and forming compensating beam resting at ends on axle-boxes. Bogie springs, 10 plates, 4 by ⅝ in., 5 ft. span; shackle linked to frame, and ends linked to rods bearing on axleboxes.

ENGINE. Cylinders and valve-chest, of cast iron in three pieces bolted together and to front and back-plates of smokebox. Cylinder 17 in., 24 in. stroke; steam-ports 13 by 1¾ in., exhaust-port 3¼ in.; lap of valve 1¼ in. outside, 1/16 in. inside, lead ¼ in., full travel 5 in.*

* The lead and the travel have been altered to the above values since the preparation of the illustrative Plates.

Piston of cast iron, 4¼ in. thick. Rod of wrought iron, 2⅜ in., with two collars embraced between disc of piston and the cover. Crosshead of wrought iron with two 2¼ in. journals forged on it. Two cast iron slides lined with white metal. Guide-bars of wrought iron faced with steel, 5 in. broad; motion-plates ⅞ in. thick, one to each cylinder, rivetted to barrel of boiler.

Connecting Rod of wrought iron, 6¼ feet centres, with butts and straps. Brass bushes lined with white metal.

Coupling Rods of wrought iron, 7 ft. 8 in. centres, with butts and straps. Bushes of brass lined with white metal.

Eccentrics of cast iron, 5¼ in. throw; straps and rods of wrought iron. Link in two parts rivetted together, and pinned behind to rods, suspended from boiler. Valve of brass (see *Cylinder*). Rod 1⅜ in. in two pieces tapped into buckle; finished with slide working in guides cast on valve-chest, and pinned to radius link, which carries sliding block. Reversing Gear:—shaft 3 in., with brass bearings screwed to guide-bars; with two levers to work radius links, and one lever worked by reversing lever at foot-plate.

Regulator: body of cast iron fixed in smokebox, with brass slide, working over two ports. Copper steam-pipe in boiler, whole length, fixed into end-plates with ferules; upper surface pierced with ⁷⁄₁₆ in. holes. Steampipe of copper in smokebox. Blastpipe of ¼ in. charcoal plate iron, with 5⅜ in. orifice.

Feed-pump of cast iron, with 4¼ in. brass ram worked by back eccentrics; 2¼ in. copper pipe to boiler, and 2 in. pipe from tank.

TANK.—Of charcoal plate iron, saddle-form, placed on

barrel; 6 lbs. per foot for top and sides; and ₇⁄₁₆ in. thick for bottom. Stiffened with ties inside. Sides joined w..h 2 in. copper pipe passed below boiler.

BRAKE.—Of wrought iron. Two sledges to slide on rails under the firebox; worked by levers and screw-motion foot-plate.

SAND-BOX fixed on top of tank, with 1¼ in. copper pipe branched to reach the rails on each side.

TABLE OF THE DISTRIBUTION FOR D. GOOCH'S TANK-LOCOMOTIVE. STROKE 24 IN. LAP 1¼ IN OUTSIDE, ₇⁄₁₆ IN. INSIDE. LEAD ¼ IN.

No. of Notch	Travel of Valve.	Valve opens.		Suppression.		Release.		Compress.	
		Front.	Back	Front.	Back.	Front.	Back.	Front	Back
	inches	inches.	inches.	inches.	inches.	inches.	inches	inches.	inches.
1	5	1¹⁄₁₆	1⅝	17⅛	17⅛	22⅛	21⅝	2⅜	3
2	4½	⅞	1¹⁄₁₆	15⅜	15⅛	21⅝	20⅛	2⅜	3½
3	4	⅝	1⅛	13⅛	13⅛	20⅛	20	3½	4⅝
4	3¼	⁷⁄₁₆	1⅛	10	10½	19⅛	18⅛	4¼	5½
5	3⁷⁄₁₆	⅜	⅝	7⅝	8	18⅜	17½	6	7

IV. PASSENGER-LOCOMOTIVE, WITH OUTSIDE VALVE-GEAR, AND INDEPENDENT WHEELS, BY ROBERT STEPHENSON & CO., NEWCASTLE-ON-TYNE. PLATE XV.

Area of grate, ...	13 75 square feet.
Diameter of cylinder, ...	16 inches.
Stroke of piston, ...	20 do.
Diameter of driving wheels, ...	6 feet 7 inches.
Length of wheel-base, ...	14 do. 6 do.
Load on front wheels, ...	8½
Do. driving wheels, ...	11·
Do. hind wheels, ...	6
Total weight in working order, ...	**25½**

Fig. 260.—Scale 1-10th.

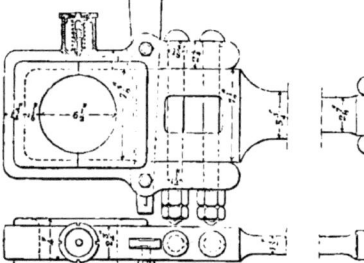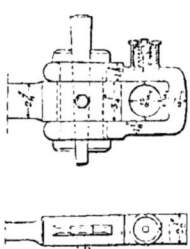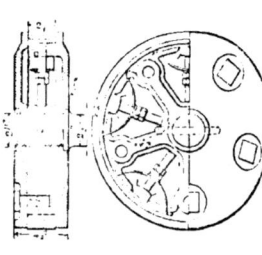

STEPHENSON'S LOCOMOTIVE.—Piston and Connecting rod.

General Arrangement. Ordinary boiler, with horizontal tubes. Cylinders inside and horizontal; valves and gearing outside; six wheels, of which the leading wheels are behind the cylinders, and the driving and hind wheels before and behind the firebox.

BOILER. Firebox-shell of ⁷⁄₁₆ in. plates back and front, ½ in. sides, and ⅜ in. top. Sides made with wings to join drawplate. Firebox of copper, tube plate ¾ in., back plate ⅝ in. round fire-door, and thinned down to ⁷⁄₁₆ in. at outer edges, sides and top ⁷⁄₁₆ in. Inside length 3 ft. 9 in., width 3 ft. 8 in., height of bars 5 ft. 2¼ in. Barrel of ⅜ in. plates, oval in section, 3 ft. 8 in. by 3 ft. 9 in. inside, and 11 ft. long; 174 tubes 1⅝ in. diameter outside, ¼ in. clear,

Nos. 12 and 14 wire-gauge, 11 ft. 3½ in. long. Smoke-box 2 ft. 4½ in. long, tubeplate ¾ in.; sides ¼ in., front plate ½ in.

FRAME. Principal members, two outside and two inside longitudinal plates, with end beams. Outside plates, extending from end to end, 9 in. by 1 in., except at cylinders 9 in. deep; inside plates extending between buffer-beam and firebox, 8 in. by 1 in., except between barrel-stays and firebox 12 in. deep. Carrying axleguards of two ½ in. plates rivetted together and to the frameplates; driving axleguards forged on inside plates. Buffer-beam 24 by 6 in., hind cross beam 9 by 6 in. Two ½ in. drawplates rivetted with angle-iron to back and to side wings of firebox-shell; draw-bolt 2¼ in.

Frame-Stays. 1st, the cylinders, binding together the

four longitudinal plates in front. 2d, the motion-plate, ⅞ in. thick, rivetted to the frameplates and to the barrel, with angle-iron. 3d, Brackets rivetted to front of firebox-shell, with plates to embrace ends of inside frameplates, with liberty for expansion. 4th, The boiler stays, at smokebox, barrel, and firebox, of ⅞ in. plate, 6½ in. broad, with palms rivetted to boiler and to frameplates. 5th, Upper drawplate joined with angle-iron to the end beam, and binding it to the firebox.

Wheels and Axles. Of wrought iron; large wheels 6 ft. 7 in. diameter, crank-axle 6½ in.; small wheels 3 ft. 10 in., with 5 in. axles. Springs 3 ft. span.

ENGINE. Cylinders underhung, castings in two pieces bolted together and to each frameplate with flanges; valve-chests outside the cylinders, exhaust passage between them. Chest covers of wrought iron. Cylinders 16 in. by 20 in. stroke, 29½ in. centres. Steam-ports 13 by 1¼ in., exhaust 2½ in.; lap of valve 1 in., lead 3/16 in., travel 4½ in. Pistons 4½ in. thick, of brass; rod 2⅛ in., screwed into and pinned to piston. Connecting-rod 6 ft. 2 in. centres, with strap at large end fixed with two taper bolts and nuts. Two pairs of guide bars and two slides to each crosshead.

Eccentrics 5½ in. throw, fixed on axle outside the wheels. Rods 5 ft. centres, pinned to ends of link at 18 in. centres; link 1¾ in. thick, shifted by the reversing gear. Valve of brass, rod 1¼ in., made with square end to work in guides, and carry link-block. Reversing shaft 2½ in. at ends, 3 in. at centre, with bearings on outside framing; with levers to carry expansion-links and balanceweights, and with rod and lever at footplate. Regulator placed in dome.

Feed-pump on each side of firebox, bolted to shell. Ram 3½ in., and 5½ in. stroke, worked with link from back eccentric. Copper feed-pipe, 2 in.

V. PASSENGER LOCOMOTIVE "FOLKSTONE" WITH INTERMEDIATE DRIVING SHAFT AND INDEPENDENT WHEELS, BY ROBERT STEPHENSON & CO., NEWCASTLE-ON-TYNE. PLATE XXIX.

Area of grate, ...	14 square feet.
Diameter of cylinder, ...	15 inches.
Stroke of piston, ...	22 do.
Diameter of driving wheel, ...	6 feet.
Length of wheel-base, ...	16 do.
Load on four front wheels, ...	16¼ tons.
Do. driving wheels, ...	10 do.
Total weight in working order,... ...	26¼ tons.

General Arrangement. Ordinary horizontal boiler; cylinders inside and horizontal, valves and gearing inside; intermediate crank shaft in front of firebox, driving wheels and straight axle behind firebox, two pairs of carrying wheels and axles in front.

BOILER. Firebox shell of 7/16 in. plate, except back and front plates ½ in. Firebox of ½ in. copper plate, except tubeplate ⅞ in. at tubes; 4 ft. long, 3½ ft. wide, and 5 ft. 4 in. high, with 3 in. longitudinal midfeather, waterspace 2½ in. round firebox. Barrel in plates ⅜ in. full, 4 ft. 2 in. diameter outside, 10 ft. 8¼ in. long; 184 tubes 2 in. outside, ⅝ in. clear, Nos. 12 and 13 W. G., 10 ft. 11 in. long. Smokebox of 5/16 in. plates, tubeplate ⅝ in.

FRAME. Composed of two longitudinal plates outside, and two inside, extending from end to end, with buffer beam and transverse plates. The two insides are 9 by 1 in. general section, made deeper at the cylinders, and formed with guards for the crank shaft and driving axle. The crank shaft guards are fitted with cast iron guides, and wrought iron adjusting wedges. The axleguards have also cast iron guides, rivetted and fitted to a pair of transverse ½ in. tie-plates, rivetted and bolted to and between the guards. The outside plates are 9 by ½ in., made with guards for the leading and second axles; and stiffened at the guards with a second plate and a thickness of timber between, and with cast iron guides for the axleboxes. Buffer beam 14 by 6, plated at junction with longitudinals for stiffness, and joined with angle-iron. End plate ½ in., rivetted with angle-iron to sides and drawplate. Drawplate ½ in., and footplate ¼ in., rivetted with angle-iron into compartment of frame behind driving axle, and rivetted together with kneed plates forming draw-chamber. Bolt 2½ in.

Frame-stays. 1st, The cylinder-castings between the inside plates. 2d, The motion-plate, ⅝ in. thick, binding the inside plates. 3d, Transverse plate 9 by ½ in., in front of firebox. 4th, Two transverse ½ in. plates behind firebox, binding axleguards. 5th, Drawplate as above described. 6th, Boiler-stays: of which there is, first, the lower part of the smokebox front, of ⅝ in. plate, formed with wings rivetted with angle-iron to the inner and outer framing; second, two pairs of wing-stays of ⅝ in. plate on edge, rivetted to barrel and to frame; third, two pairs of filling-up plates inserted between firebox-shell and inside frameplates, through which the latter are bolted together.

Wheels and Axles. Of solid wrought iron; driving wheels 6 ft., axle 6¼ in.; carrying wheels 3½ ft., axles 5 in.; crank-shaft 5¼ in. Leading axleboxes of cast iron with brass bushes; crank shaft boxes of brass, adjusted laterally; driving axleboxes of brass. Single hindspring applied transversely above footplate and linked to it at middle, to span the axleboxes. Single leading spring on each side to span the fore and middle axleboxes, linked to outside framing.

ENGINE. Cylinder castings in two pieces bolted together and between the inside frameplates. Cylinders 15 by 22 in. stroke, 30 in. centres. Steamports 1¼ in., exhaust 2½ in., lap of valve 1⅛ in., lead 3/16 in., travel 4½ in. Piston of brass, same as for engine previously described, piston-rod 2½ in., connecting rod 6 ft. 4 in. centres, of same form as in last engine.

Eccentrics 6 in. throw, rods 6 ft. centres, expansion-link 1¾ in. thick, 17¼ in. centres, pinned to rods at ends, and sustained at mid-length. Reversing shaft underhung, with bearings on motion-plate, 2¼ in. at ends, 2¾ in. at middle. Valve of brass, rod 1⅝ in. and 1⅝ in. in stuffing-boxes, working also in fixed guide carried by guide-bars.

Regulator placed in smokebox, steam-pipe extended whole length of boiler, and perforated on upper side to collect the steam.

Feed-pump fixed on each side of firebox shell, worked by eccentric on crank shaft. Ram 3½ in.

The detail of this and the foregoing locomotive, such as is not worked out in the engravings, may be supplied generally by reference to the more elaborate representations of other specimens of locomotive work, in the present section.

CHAPTER II.

ORDINARY PASSENGER-LOCOMOTIVES, WITH OUTSIDE CYLINDERS.

I. PASSENGER-LOCOMOTIVE WITH INDEPENDENT WHEELS, BY JOHN V. GOOCH, LONDON. PLATES X., XI., XII.

Area of grate, ...	12·4 square feet.
Diameter of cylinder,...	14¼ inches.
Stroke of piston, ...	21 do.
Diameter of driving wheel, ...	6½ feet.
Wheel-base, ...	12 ft., 8½ inches.
Load on leading wheels, ...	8 tons.
Do. driving wheels, ...	6 ,,
Do. hind wheels, ...	5 ,,
Total weight in working order, ...	... 19 tons.

General Arrangement.—Boiler of the ordinary form, cylinders outside, and inclined to clear the leading wheels ; six wheels, of which the leading wheels are behind the cylinders, and the driving and trailing wheels before and behind the firebox.

BOILER.—Firebox-shell, of ⅜ in. plates. Firebox, of ½ in. copper plates, made ¾ in. at tubes ; 3 ft. 5½ in. by 3 ft. 7¼ in. wide at bottom, and 3 ft. 10 in. mean height, inside, off bars. Waterspace 2 in. at back and sides, widening upwards to 3 in., and 2¼ in. at front. Mid-feather of corrugated plate. Ashpan of ₇⁄₁₆ in. plate. Barrel, 3 ft. 7½ in. outside diameter, 10 ft. long ; of ⅜ in. plates. Inside Stays : Firebox stayed to shell with ⅞ in. iron bolts, 3½ in. to 4 in. pitch. Six roof-stays of rib-iron, linked also to shell. Eight thorough tie-rods, ⅞ in. Tubes : 181 brass tubes, 1¾ in. diameter, except 12 in. at firebox 1½ in. No. 13 gauge at firebox, tapering to No. 14 at smokebox. Smokebox : Tubeplate ½ in., other plates ₇⁄₁₆ in., made to cover cylinders, and rivetted to outside frameplates. Venetian damper at tube-ends.

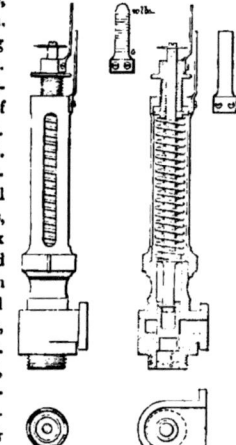

Fig. 251.

J. V. GOOCH'S LOCOMOTIVE.
Safety-Valve and Pressure-Indicator.

Rivets, for steam-joints, ⅞ in. at 1¼ in. pitch ; in smokebox ⅜ in. at 1½ in. pitch.

FRAME.—Composed of outside and inside wrought iron plates, bound with end plates, brackets, and cross stays. Outside plates 9 in. deep, ⅞ in. thick in front of middle cross stay, and ½ in. behind it ; made with an extra ⅜ in. plate at hind wheels, with beam of heart-of-oak. Leading axleguard of ⅞ in. plate bolted to frame ; with angle-iron guides. Trailing axleguard of two ½ in. plates, with cast iron guides. Inside plates 9 in. deep, ¾ in. thick, formed with driving axleguard ; inside leading axleguard of ⅞ in. plate, bolted to it with angle-iron guides. Frame-Stays : 1st, Three transverse angle-iron stays, ⅞ in. thick, joining inside frame-

plates : one at the front, and two before and behind firebox. 2d, a ⅞ in. plate at end, bound with diagonal stays to side plates. 3d, Inside and outside plates joined with knees at ends, with the cylinder-castings, and with two wrought-iron brackets at each side. 4th, Boiler-stays, of which there are two joining barrel to inside plates, and two angle-iron firebox-stays resting on inside plates. Draw-bolt 2 in., let into eyes welded on diagonal stays and rivetted to end plate. Buffer-Beam, 4½ by 15 in., bolted to front plate. Wheels and Axles, of wrought-iron, with steeled tyres. Driving wheels 6 ft. 6½ in., with 3½ in. crankpin. Smaller wheels 4 ft. ⅞ in. Axles hollow at middle ; leading axle has four bearings. Two eccentrics forged solid on driving axle to work pumps. Axleboxes, of cast iron with Fenton's metal bushes. Springs :—plates 4 by ⅜ in., except in outside leading springs ½ in. ; transverse leading spring abutting on barrel of boiler, and linked at ends to axleboxes.

ENGINE.—Cylinders, each with its chest in one piece, fitted between and bolted to frameplates. Cylinder 14¼ in., Steam-ports 13 by 1¾ in., exhaust port 2½ in. Lap of valve 1 in., lead ⅛ in., full travel 4½ in. Piston of brass, with cast-iron cover, 4 in. thick. Rod of iron 2½ in. diameter, fixed with double collar between body and cover of piston. Guide-bars of steel, 4 in. broad, fixed to rib-iron carriers, with ½ in. of hardwood packing. Connecting Rod, 6 feet centres, with white metal bushes. Eccentrics of wrought-iron, 4¾ in. throw ; with brass straps. Fore rod 4 ft. 1½ in. Centres, back rod 4 ft. 3 in. centres, pinned to link behind. Link of wrought-iron sustained by pivot fixed to frame. Valve of brass, with double inlets, and cast iron plate with ports in it, on the back, to admit steam at two points. Rod 1½ in., with slide, pinned to radius link. Reversing Gear : shaft underhung, with levers to work the radius links, and connected to reversing lever. Regulator, of cast iron, in bottom of smokebox, with two brass valves worked by a shaft and levers outside, and lever at footplate. Steampipe of brass, No. 14 Gauge, pierced with ₇⁄₁₆ in. holes on upper part. Blastpipe of copper, with 4½ in. orifice.

Feed-pump of brass, with 4 in. plunger, 3½ in. stroke, attached to hangers from boiler. Feed-pipe of copper, 1½ in. from tender, and 2 in. to boiler.

II. PASSENGER-LOCOMOTIVE WITH INDEPENDENT WHEELS, ON CRAMPTON'S SYSTEM, BY DEROSNE & CAIL, PARIS. PLATES XIII. XIV.

Area of grate, ...	15·4 square feet
Diameter of cylinder, ...	15½ inches.
Stroke of piston, ...	22 do.
Diameter of driving wheel, ...	6 feet 10¾ in.
Wheel-base, ...	16 feet.
Load on leading wheels, ...	11½ tons.
Do. middle do.	4 do.
Do. driving do.	11½ do.
Total weight in working order, ...	... 27 tons.

General Arrangement.—Ordinary boiler, cylinders outside at middle of barrel, and horizontal ; six wheels, of which the driving wheels are behind the firebox, and the leading and middle wheels under the barrel.

BOILER. Firebox-shell and smokebox flush on upper side with barrel ; the barrel being continued into the smokebox. Firebox-shell of ₇⁄₁₆ in. plate, except top ½ in.

Firebox. Of $\frac{1}{16}$ in. copper plates, 4 ft. 6 in. by 3 ft. 5 in. wide at bottom, and 4 ft. 3¾ in. high above grate, inside.

Fig. 252.—Scale 1-10th.

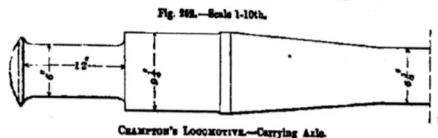

CRAMPTON'S LOCOMOTIVE.—Carrying Axle.

Waterspace 2⅜ in. at bottom. Barrel. 4 ft. diam. outside,

11 ft. 7¾ in. long, of ⅜ in. plates. Inside stays: copper bolts between firebox and shell, at 4 in. centres. Seven roof-stays. Eight thorough 1½ in. tie-rods. Tubes: 177 brass tubes; 173 of 2 in., and 4 of 1¾ in. diam. outside, No. 14½ gauge, 11 ft. 10 in. long between plates. Smokebox, of ⅜ in. plate; tubeplate 1 in.

FRAME.—Composed of two outside and two inside plates, with buffer-beam, end plate, and transverse stays. Outside and inside plates, of iron 8⅜ in. by 1 in. thick, leading and middle axleguards each of one plate rivetted to outside plates,

Fig. 253.—Scale 1-50th.

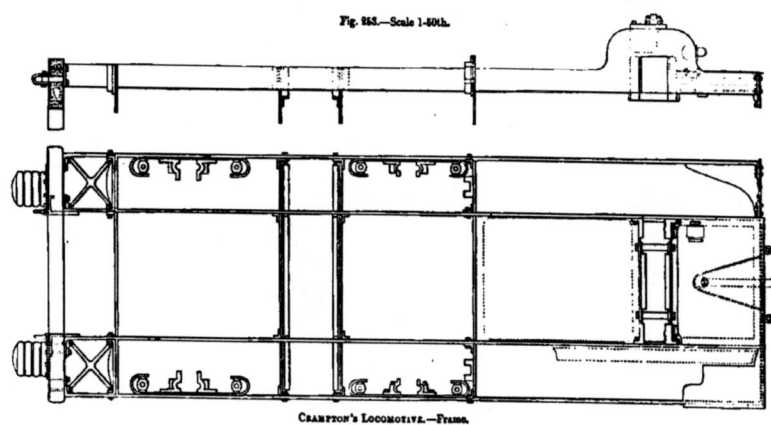

CRAMPTON'S LOCOMOTIVE.—Frame.

and formed with bearings for spring-links, and cast iron guides bolted on inside. Driving axleguards formed on inside plates, with wrought iron guides bolted to inside, and worked upon two transverse plates binding the inside frame-plates.

Fig. 254.—Scale 1-10th.   Fig. 255.—Scale 1-10th.

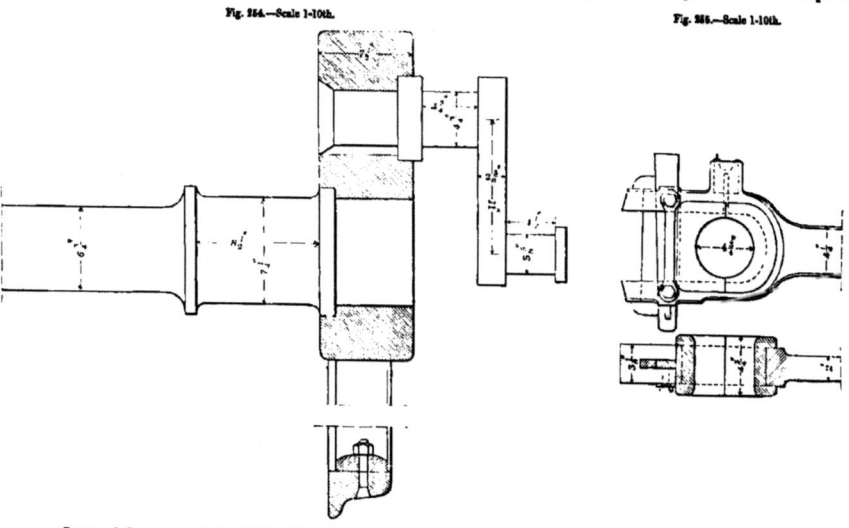

CRAMPTON'S LOCOMOTIVE.—Section of Driving Wheel, showing Axle and Overhung Crank.   CRAMPTON'S LOCOMOTIVE.—Connecting Rod End.

Framestays, &c. 1st. Buffer-beam 6¼ in. thick. 2d. End plate and four transverse stays, ½ in. thick; of which the two middle stays bind the cylinders, and are rivetted to barrel. 3d. Two ¾ in. plates, binding driving axle-guides.

4th. The inside and outside frameplates on each side, are bound with diagonal stays at front end; and with gussets to end plate. 5th. Inside plates bound together, and to end plate and driving axleguard-plates, with footplate and lower draw-plate. 6th. Boilerstays; first, two stays of flat iron rivetted to barrel and smokebox and to inside frameplates; second, two wings of firebox-shell, rivetted to ditto; third, a flat iron stay joining back of firebox-shell to driving axleguard-plate.

Wheels and Axles, of wrought iron; leading, middle,

Fig. 256.—Scale 1-10th.

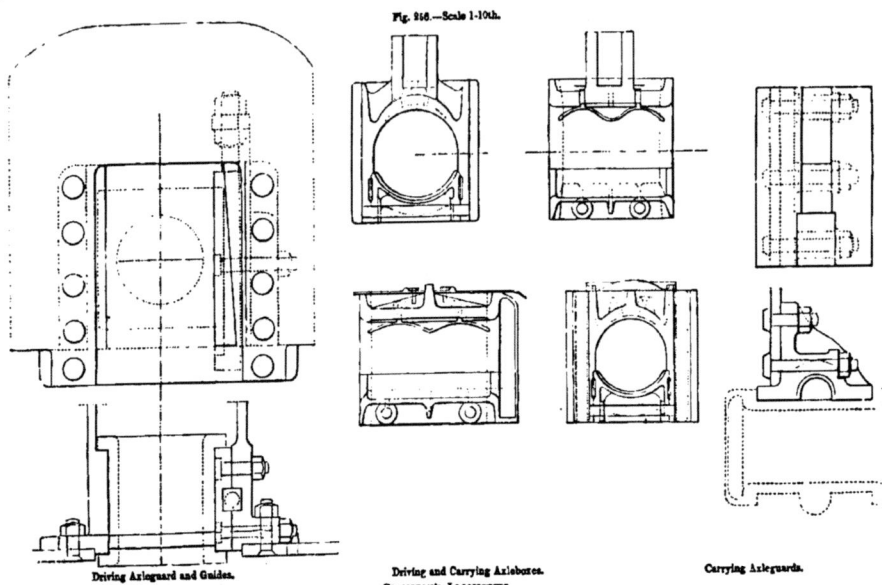

Driving Axleguard and Guides.

Driving and Carrying Axleboxes.
CRAMPTON'S LOCOMOTIVE.

Carrying Axleguards.

and driving, respectively 4 ft. 3 in., 4 ft., and 6 ft. 10½ in. Driving axle has inside bearings; crankpin let into nave, and formed with overhung crank and pin to carry eccentrics. Axleboxes of brass. Springs: all of 3 ft. 3 in. span; leading and driving, 13 plates; middle 10 plates, 4 by 1⅟₁₆ in., except back plates ⅜ in.

ENGINE. Cylinders, each cast in one piece with its valvechest; bolted with flanges between the outside and inside frameplates; 15¾ in. diam., steamports 11 by 2 in., exhaust 3½ in.; lap of valve 1 in. outside, ⅛ in. inside. Piston of cast iron 4⅟₁₆ in. thick, rod 2¾ in., continued through front cover of cylinder to work pump. Connecting rod,

Fig. 257.—Scale 1-10th.

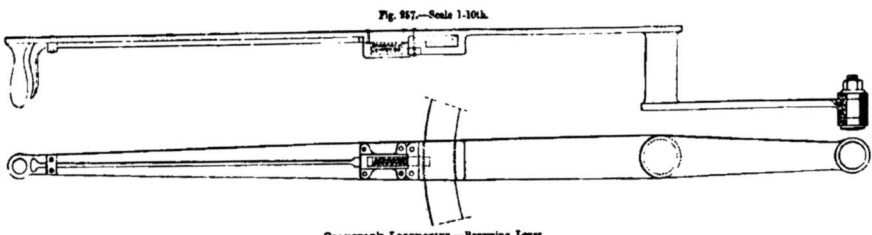

CRAMPTON'S LOCOMOTIVE.—Reversing Lever.

7 ft. 7 in. centres; small end solid, set with an inside wedge; large end forked and closed with gib and cotter. Eccentrics in.one piece keyed on overhung cranks. Straps of brass. Link pinned to rods at ends, carried by reversing gear. Valve-rod 1¼ in., with square guide. Reversing Gear: Shaft has bearings on stay-plate; linked to expansion-link, with balanceweights. Reversing lever made with crank at journal to clear the framing.

Regulator: Of cast iron with brass slide-valve, on crown of barrel; with copper steampipe, all the length of boiler, having narrow slit on upper side, to admit steam. Exhaust pipe of copper, from each cylinder; finished with brass blastpipe, with variable orifice, adjusted by rod and handle at footplate.

Feed pump: Of brass, bolted to front framestay, with ram 2⅟₁₆ in. diam. cottered to piston-rod.

III. Passenger-Locomotive with Independent Wheels, by Alexander Allan, Crewe.—Plate XXIX.

Area of grate, ...	10·5 square feet.
Diameter of cylinder, ...	15 inches.
Stroke of piston, ...	20 do.
Diameter of driving wheel, ...	6 feet.
Wheel-base, ...	13 do.
Load on leading wheels, ...	6 tons 3 cwt.
Do. driving do.	9 ,,
Do. hind do.	3 ,, 2 ,,
Total weight in working order, ...	18¼ tons.

This engine is here referred to as embodying the latest modifications adopted at the Crewe Works. In detail it is generally the same as the goods-engine by Allan; and as this engine is described at length in the succeeding chapter, it is deemed unnecessary to be otherwise specific in our

Fig. 258.—Scale 1-10th.

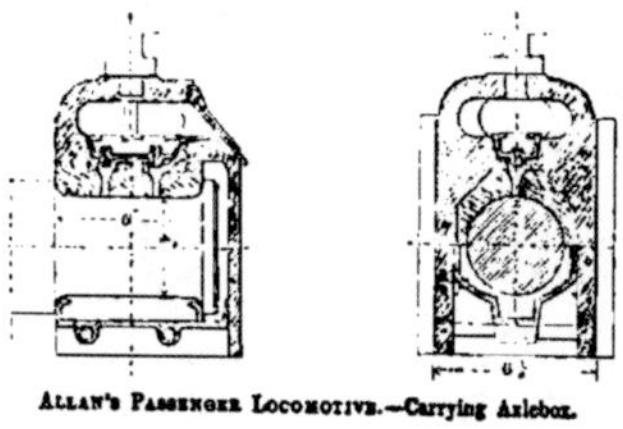

Allan's Passenger Locomotive.—Carrying Axlebox.

notice of the passenger-engine, than in pointing out the characteristic features of the later design, which it embodies.

General Arrangement.—Ordinary boiler, cylinders outside, inclined to clear the leading wheels; six wheels, of which the drivers are in front of the firebox, and the hind wheels behind.

Boiler.—Firebox 3 ft. by 3 ft. 6 in. wide inside. Barrel 3 ft. 6 in. diam., 10 ft. 3 in. long; 158 tubes 1¾ in. out-

Fig. 259.—Scale 1-10th.

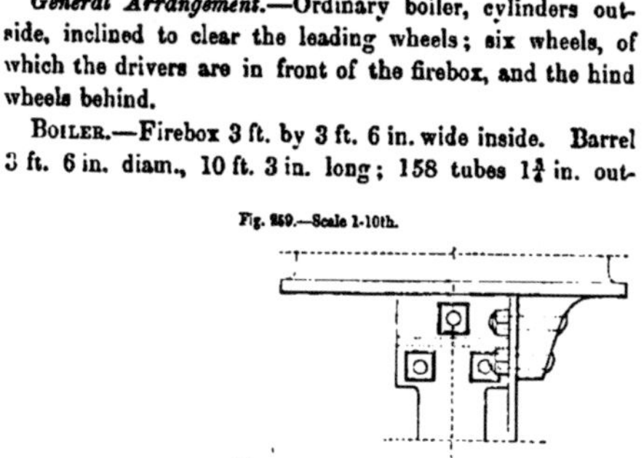

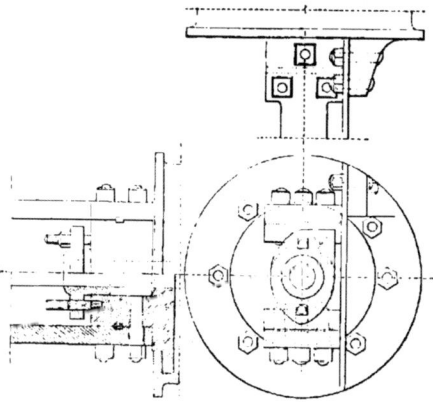

Allan's Passenger Locomotive.—Fixing of Cylinder, Outside Frame, and Guide-bars

side, 10 ft. 6 in. long between plates. Steam-pipe, 4½ in., traversing the whole length of boiler, and fitted with regulator over firebox; two steam-chambers, one over firebox, and one on middle of barrel, each fitted with a diaphragm, boxing off a separating chamber, into which the steam is admitted by one aperture and from which it is withdrawn by another; the steam from the barrel being conveyed by a 3 in. branch-pipe to the regulator.

Frame.—Composed of inside and outside longitudinals, from end to end, with transverse bindings, applied as in the goods-engine, with modifications to suit the single-wheel arrangement.

Engine.—Cylinders 15 by 20 in., laid at an angle of 1 in 12, wheel 6 ft., arranged as in the goods-engine. Valve, 1¼ in. lap, 3/16 in. lead, 4½ in. travel. Blast-orifice 3¾ in.

Feed-pumps bolted to transverse plate in front of driving axle, and worked by rod pinned to back eccentric-strap.

CHAPTER III.

Three-Cylinder Passenger-Locomotive, having Inside and Outside Cylinders combined, by Robert Stephenson & Co., Newcastle-on-Tyne.—Plate XVI.

This class of engine was designed for the obtainment of greater natural stability than was arrived at in other locomotives. It is fitted with three cylinders, two outside and one inside. The crank-pins outside the wheels are placed next the same side of the axle, so that the reciprocations of the two outside pistons exactly coincide; the inside crank is at right angles to the outsides. As the movements of the reciprocating masses acting out of the centre line of the machine, exactly balance each other, the tendency to sinuous action is removed, and fore-and-aft action alone remains to be balanced. This engine, accordingly, runs with very superior steadiness, even when unassisted with balance-weights in the wheels; and from its peculiar arrangement, it is susceptible of a very perfect equilibration. It is found to give unqualified satisfaction on the York, Newcastle, and Berwick Railway, where it is on regular duty.

Area of grate, ...	11·83 square feet.
Diameter of inside cylinder, ...	16½ inches.
Stroke of do., ...	18 do.
Diameter of outside do., ...	10½ do.
Stroke of do., ...	22 do.
Diameter of driving wheel, ...	6 feet 8 inches.
Wheel-base, ...	14 feet.
Load on leading wheels, ...	9 tons.
Do. driving do., ...	12 do.
Do. hind do., ...	6 do.
Total weight in working order, ...	27 tons.

General Arrangement.—Ordinary boiler; three cylinders horizontal, one inside cylinder in centre line of machine, working to inside crank; two outside cylinders, working to outside crankpins; six wheels, of which the drivers are in front of the firebox, and the trailing wheels behind.

Boiler—Firebox-shell of ½ in. plates, except top 7/16 in. full. Firebox of ⅝ in. copper, except at tubes ⅞ in. Water-spaces 2½ in. except midfeather 3½ in. at bottom, and 4 in. at top. Firebox 3 ft. 6¾ in. by 3 ft. 9¼ in. long, and 5 ft. high. Barrel, of plates 7/16 in. full, 3 ft. 8 in. diam., 11 ft. long; 170 brass tubes, 1⅞ in. diam., 11 ft. 3 in. long. Tube-plate ¾ in., smokebox-plates ⅜ in.

Frame.—Four longitudinals 1 in. thick, with axleguards

forged on; bound transversely by end beams, by cylinder-castings, by motion-plate, which is rivetted also to boiler, and by boiler-stays. Two $\frac{5}{8}$ in. draw-plates rivetted to firebox-shell. Axlebox-guides of cast iron rivetted to frame.

Fig. 260.—Scale 1 10th.

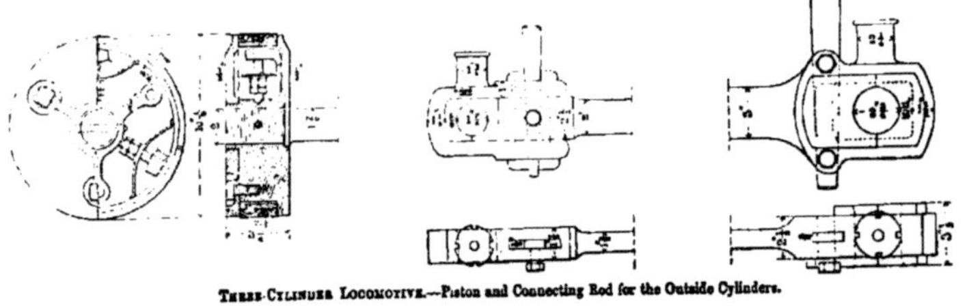

THREE-CYLINDER LOCOMOTIVE.—Piston and Connecting Rod for the Outside Cylinders.

Carrying wheels 3 ft. 9 in., axles $5\frac{3}{4}$ in. at middle, journals double-coned, 5 in. at middle, 12 in. long; driving axle $6\frac{1}{4}$ in.

ENGINE.—Cylinder-castings in three pieces bolted together and to the frameplates, with flanges; two pairs of guidebars to each cylinder, bolted to one motion-plate. Valves worked by shifting links, one for the inside cylinder, and one for the two outsides, the latter working a traverse shaft from which the motion is given to the two valve-spindles. Reversing shaft overhung and worked in the usual manner. Regulator placed in dome over the barrel of boiler. Blast-orifice $4\frac{3}{4}$ in.

Feed-pumps bolted to front of firebox-shell and worked by rods from the back eccentrics, formed with hoops to pass round the axle; plungers 3 in.

CHAPTER IV.

GOODS-LOCOMOTIVES, WITH INSIDE CYLINDERS.

I. GOODS-LOCOMOTIVE WITH SIX WHEELS COUPLED, BY ARCHIBALD STURROCK, DONCASTER; MADE BY E. B. WILSON & CO., LEEDS. PLATE XVII.

Area of grate, ...	14·5 square feet.	
Diameter of cylinder, ...	16 inches.	
Stroke of piston, ...	24 do.	
Diameter of wheels, ...	5 feet.	
Wheel-base, ...	15 ft. 6 in.	
	empty.	charged.
Load or leading wheels, ...	$9\frac{1}{4}$ tons.	$10\frac{1}{2}$ tons.
Do. driving do., ...	$9\frac{3}{4}$ „	$11\frac{1}{2}$ „
Do. trailing do., ...	$6\frac{3}{4}$ „	$7\frac{1}{2}$ „
Total weight, ...	$26\frac{1}{4}$ tons.	$29\frac{1}{2}$ tons.

Fig. 261.—Scale 1-10th.

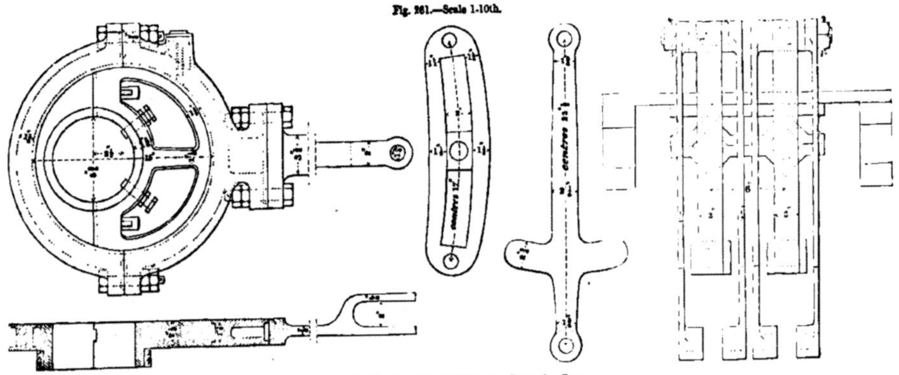

STURROCK'S LOCOMOTIVE, BY WILSON.—Expansion Gear.

General Arrangement. Ordinary boiler; cylinders inside, inclined to clear leading axle; six wheels all coupled, under the barrel and behind the firebox.

BOILER. Firebox-shell, of $\frac{1}{2}$ in. plates. Firebox, of $\frac{1}{2}$ in. copper plates, $\frac{13}{16}$ in. at tubes; with mid-feather; 4 ft. 6 in. by 3 ft. 7 in. wide, and 5 ft. 2 in. high above grate, inside. Waterspace 3 in. Ashpan, of $\frac{1}{4}$ in. plate, with damper. Barrel, of $\frac{7}{16}$ in. plates, oval section 4 ft. 3 in. deep by 4 ft. 1 in. wide, inside, and $10\frac{1}{2}$ ft. long. Inside Stays: Firebox stayed with $\frac{7}{8}$ in. copper bolts, at 4 in. centres, and eight roofstays linked to shell. Eight thorough $1\frac{1}{4}$ in. tie-rods, and three $1\frac{1}{2}$ in. tie-rods from back plate to crown of barrel. Tubes:—187 brass tubes, 2 in. diam., No. 9 gauge at firebox, tapering to No. 12, at 18 in. distance, thence to No. 14 at smokebox; 10 ft. $9\frac{3}{16}$ in. long between plates. Smokebox, of $\frac{5}{16}$ in. plate; tubeplate $\frac{3}{4}$ in.; with Venetian blind damper. Rivets, for joints under steam-pressure, $\frac{3}{4}$ in. at $1\frac{3}{4}$ in. pitch.

FRAME.—Composed of two outside and two inside frame-beams, with buffer and end transverse beams. Outside frame-beams, of sapling ash 10 by $3\frac{5}{8}$ in., with $\frac{7}{16}$ in. plate on each side, made with axleguards and cast iron guides. Inside frameplates, of iron 9 by 1 in., from cylinders to firebox, with guards for driving axle, and wrought iron guides. Buffer-beam of English oak 6 by 16 in., hind beam 6 by 10 in. Two drawplates of ½ in. plate, rivetted to firebox-shell; bolt 2¼ in. Frame-stays:—1st. The cylinders, bolted together and to inside frameplates. 2d. The two motion-plates, ¹¹⁄₁₆ in. thick, one for each cylinder, rivetted to outside and inside beams, and to barrel of boiler. 3d. Two wings from the shell-plates bolted to inside plates. 4th. Boiler-stays: first, smokebox stays of ⅜ in. plate, bolted to outside and inside plates; second, firebox-stays of ⅜ in. plate, fixed to outside framebeam. Wheels and axles, of wrought iron; wheels 5 feet diam., crank axle with four bearings, 6¾ in. between cranks; fore and hind axles, two bearings, 6¼ in. Journals, double-conical. Outside cranks keyed on axles, 14 in. radius, with 3 in. pins. Axleboxes, of cast iron, except inside boxes of brass, with brass bushes. Springs: Of steel plates 3½ by ⅝ in., with ½ in. back plates, all 3 feet span. Fore and hind springs, 18 plates; driving, outside 12 plates, inside 14 plates. Leading and outside driving springs linked by compensating lever.

ENGINE. Cylinders and valvechest, of cast iron in two pieces, bolted together and to inside frameplates. Diameter 16 in., stroke 24 in.; steamports 14 by 1¼ in., exhaust 3½ in.; lap of valve 1¼ in., lead ₁⁄₁₆ in. full gear, travel 4¼ in. Piston of brass, 4⅝ in. thick. Rod, of iron 2⅝ in.

Eccentrics of cast iron, with wrought iron rings shrunk on at sides; Rods, 5 ft. centres. Expansion link 2 in. thick. Valve of brass. Rod 1¼ in., with square slide working in bearing carried by guide-bars. Reversing gear: Shaft 3 in.,

with bearings on the motion-plates; carrying links and balance-weights.

Regulator: Cast iron pipe in dome, with vertical face at upper end, and two ports, and slide-valve. Joined to copper pipe going to smokebox. Blastpipe of cast iron, with copper nozzle; orifice 4½ to 5 in.

Feed-pumps: Of cast iron, bolted to motion-plates and to inside frame-plates. Ram 1⅜ in., worked by crosshead. Feed-pipes 2 in.

II. GOODS-LOCOMOTIVE WITH SIX WHEELS COUPLED, BY SHARP BROTHERS AND CO., MANCHESTER. PLATES XVIII. XIX., XX.

Area of grate,	...	...	...	10·56 square feet.
Diameter of cylinder,		...	...	18 inches.
Stroke of piston,		...	...	24 do.
Diameter of wheels,		...	...	5 feet ½ inch.
Wheel-base,	...	...	...	12 ft., 2 inches.
Load on leading wheels,		...	...	8½ tons.
Do. driving do.,		...	...	9 ,,
Do. trailing do.,		...	...	8¼ ,,
Total weight in working order,		...	...	26¼ tons.

General Arrangement. Ordinary boiler, cylinders inside and inclined; six wheels all coupled, with inside bearings, and axles placed between firebox and smokebox.

BOILER. Firebox-shell, of ₇⁄₁₆ in. plate. Firebox. Of ½ in. copper plates, ⅞ in. at tubes; with mid-feather; 3 ft. 8 in. by 3 ft. 3¼ in. wide, and 4 ft. 7½ in. high above bars, inside. Ashpan of ¼ in. plate, with damper. Barrel of ⅜ in. plates,

Fig 262.—Scale 1-32d.

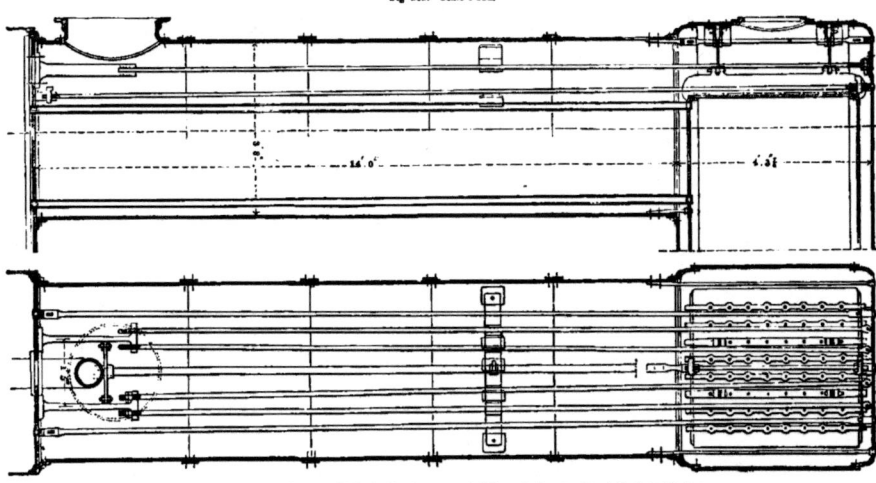

SHARP's LOCOMOTIVE.—Sections of Boiler to show Arrangement of Stay-rods, &c., according to the Latest Designs.

3 ft. 8 in. inside, 14 ft. long. Inside stays:—Firebox stayed to shell with copper bolts 3½ to 4½ in. centres. Eight roofstays, linked also to shell. Eleven thorough ⅞ in. tie-rods, and eleven ⅞ in. tie-rods between back plate of

boiler and end of barrel. 133 brass tubes, 2¼ in., No. 14 gauge, 14 ft. 3¼ in. long between plates. Smokebox—tubeplate ⅝ in. full, front ⅜ in. Rivets in steam-joints ¾ in.; at 1¾ in. pitch.

FRAME. Two inside frameplates 1 in. thick, made with three axleguards, and cast iron guides. Buffer-beam of English elm. End and interior drawplates rivetted to footplate and lower drawplate, and to frameplates. Bolt 2 in.

Fig. 263.—Scale 1-16th.

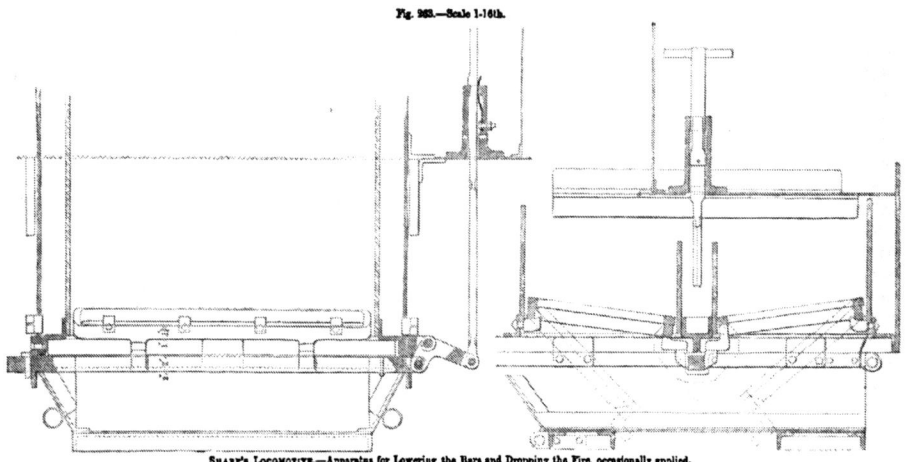

SHARP'S LOCOMOTIVE.—Apparatus for Lowering the Bars and Dropping the Fire, occasionally applied.

Frame-stays. 1st, The cylinders. 2d. Motionplate, 1½ in. thick rivetted to frameplates and to boiler. 3d, Stay-plate 1½ in. thick, between driving and hind axles, fixed to frameplates and to boiler. 4th, Firebox-stays, of angle-iron, one to each side.

Wheels and Axles. Wheels of cast iron, 5 ft. ½ in. diam.

Fig. 264.—Scale 1-10th.

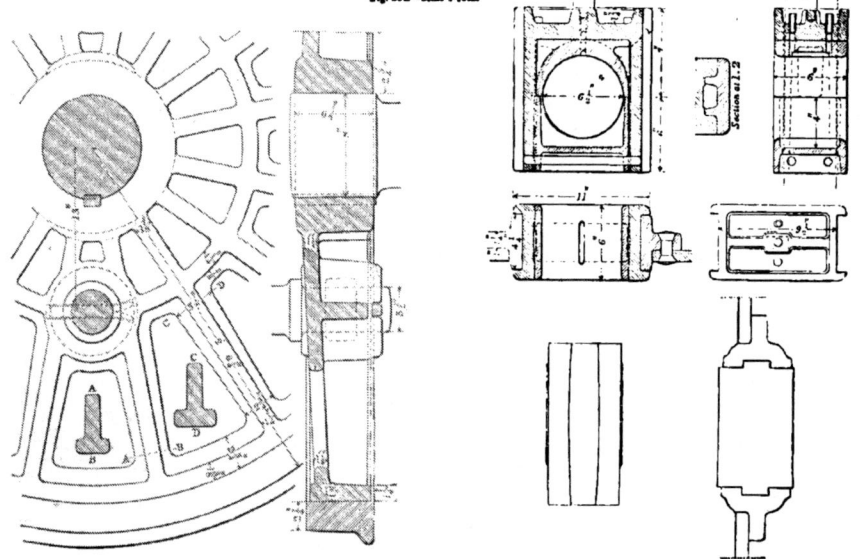

Detail of Cast Iron Wheel.   Detail of Axleboxes and Outline View of Alternative Axlebox and Guides.

SHARP'S LOCOMOTIVE.

Outside crank-pins at 13 in. radius. Crank axle 6½ in. diam., fore and hind axles 6 in. Axleboxes of cast iron, with brass bushes. Springs of steel plates 4 by ⁵⁄₁₆ in., with ⅜ in. back and short plates.

ENGINE. Cylinders and valvechest of cast iron in two pieces, with chest underhung. Bolted together and to frameplates; 18 in. diam. 24 in. stroke; steamports 11 by 1¼ in., exhaust 4½ in.; lap of valve ⅞ in., lead ⅛ in. in full

Fig. 265.—Scale 1-10th.

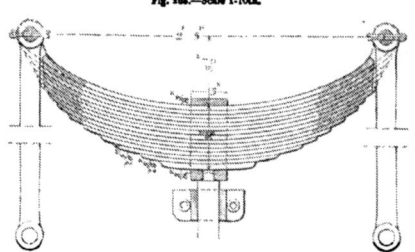

Driving and Leading Springs, when unloaded; 30-inch Span when Loaded.

SHARP's LOCOMOTIVE.

Fig. 266.—Scale 1-10th.

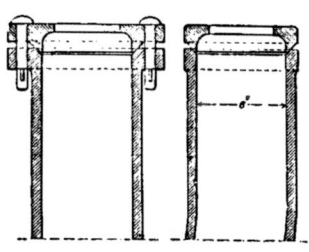

Termination of Blastpipe Applied in Later Examples.

gear, travel 4½⅜ in. Piston of cast iron, 4½ in. thick; rod of iron 2¾ in. Guide-bars of sheer-steel, 3 in. broad. Connecting rod, 5 ft. 4 in. centres.

Eccentrics of cast iron, 5 in. throw; link 2 in. thick. Valve of brass, rod 1¼ in., linked to pendulum lever hung from boiler and carrying sliding block. Reversing shaft

Fig. 267.—Scale 1-10th.

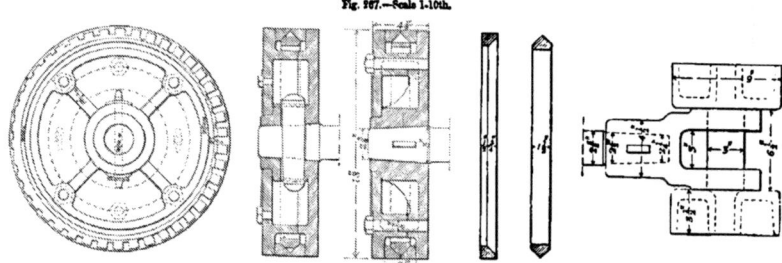

SHARP's LOCOMOTIVE.—Details of Piston, Rod, and Crosshead.

with cast iron bearings on frameplates; with one lever to carry expansion-links.

Regulator: Head piece of brass, with circular disc and valve. Blastpipe of cast iron with nozzle and cone for

Fig. 268.—Scale 1-10th.

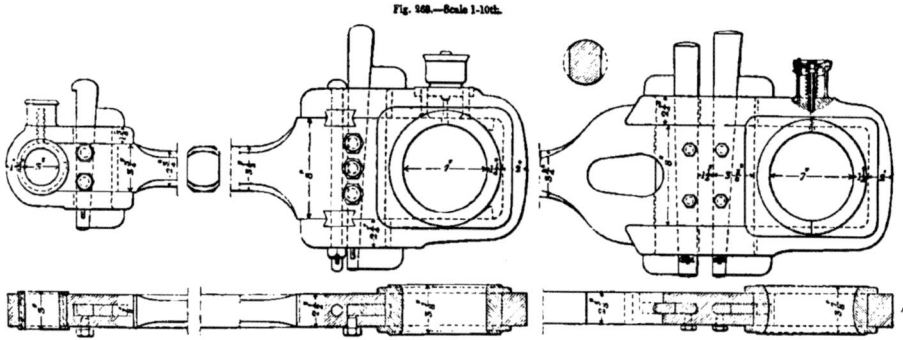

SHARP's LOCOMOTIVE.—Detail of Connecting Rod, with Alternative Design of Crank End, introduced in the later Examples.

regulating area of orifice. Occasionally and more commonly made with a fixed orifice of cast iron, adjusted as in Fig. 266.

Feedpumps: Of brass, with 1¼ in. ram worked by crosshead. Feed-pipe 2¼ in., of copper.

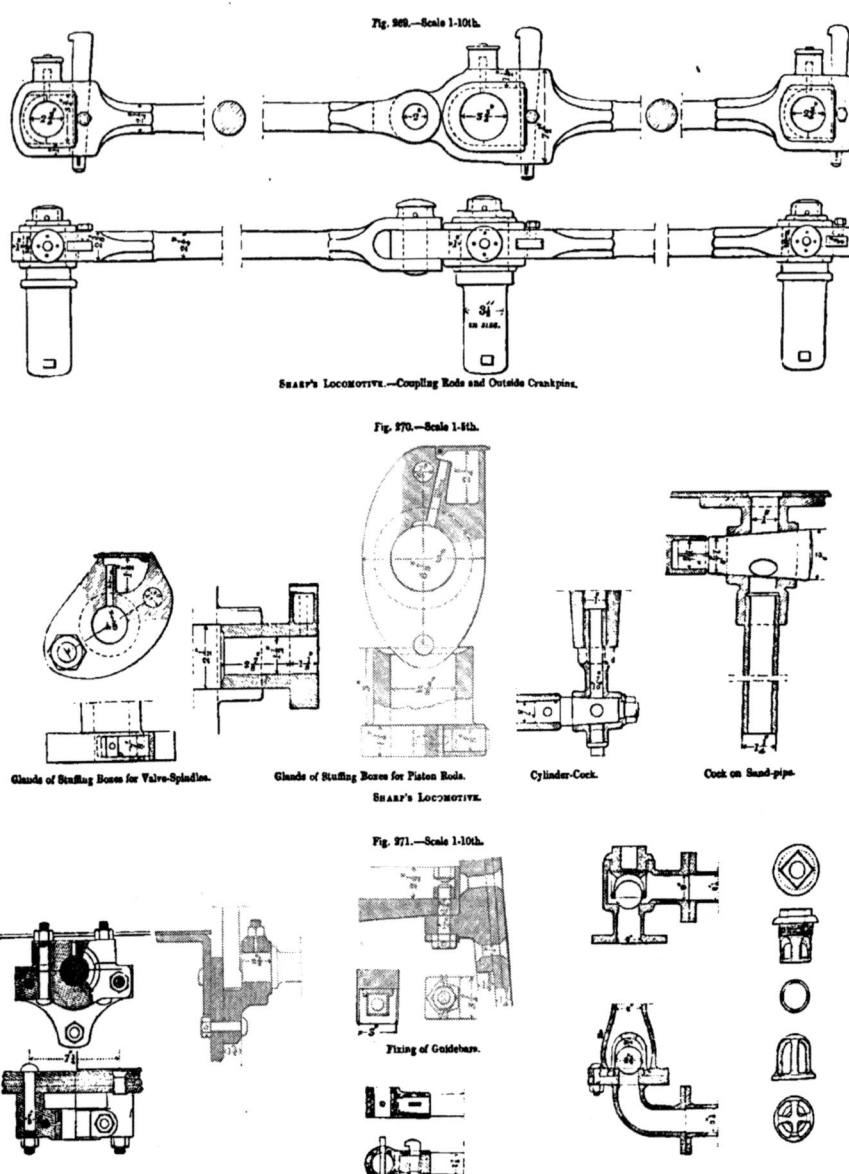

Fig. 269.—Scale 1-10th.

Sharp's Locomotive.—Coupling Rods and Outside Crankpins.

Fig. 270.—Scale 1-8th.

Glands of Stuffing Boxes for Valve-Spindles.   Glands of Stuffing Boxes for Piston Rods.   Cylinder-Cock.   Cock on Sand-pipe.

Sharp's Locomotive.

Fig. 271.—Scale 1-10th.

Fixing of Guidebars.

Cast Iron Bearings for Reversing Shaft.   Pumprod-end.   Pump-Valves and Seats.

CHAPTER V.

GOODS-LOCOMOTIVES WITH OUTSIDE CYLINDERS.

GOODS - LOCOMOTIVE WITH SIX WHEELS, AND FOUR COUPLED, BY ALEXANDER ALLAN, CREWE.—PLATES XXI., XXII., XXIII.

Area of grate, ...	10·5 square feet.	
Diameter of cylinder, ...	15 inches.	
Stroke of piston, ...	20 do.	
Diameter of driving wheels, ...	5 feet.	
Wheel-base, ...	12 ft., 8 inches.	

	Empty.	Charged
Load on leading wheels, ...	5¼ tons.	5¼ tons.
Do. driving do., ...	7¾ ,,	9 ,,
Do. trailing do., ...	4½ ,,	4½ ,,
Total weight, ...	17½ tons.	19¼ tons.

General Arrangement. Ordinary boiler, cylinders outside, and inclined; six wheels, of which the driving and hind wheels are coupled before and behind firebox, and leading wheels behind cylinders.

BOILER. Firebox-shell of ⅜ in. plates. Firebox 3 ft. by 3½ ft. wide, and 3 ft. 10 in. high off grate, inside; of ⅟₁₆ in. copper plate, except tube plate ¾ in. throughout. Door made with shield inclosing space between with an airtight ring; 1½ in. airholes in door, and ⅜ in. holes in shield, to admit air. Ashpan of ⁷⁄₁₆ in. plate, with vertical sliding damper. Barrel of ⅜ in. plates, 3½ ft. by 9 ft. 4¾ in. long. Inside stays: ⅞ in. copper bolts for walls of firebox, 4 in. centres. Eight roofstays. Eleven 1⅛ in. tie-rods through boiler. Tubes: 158 brass tubes, 1¾ in.; No. 10 gauge at firebox, for 12 in. of length; changed to No. 11, and tapered off to No. 14. Lapped over at ends, and expanded at inside of plates, and ferruled at firebox. Smokebox: tubeplate ⅜ in., side plates carried round to inclose cylinders. Front plate bolted on. Rivets for steam-joints, ⅞ in. at 2 in. centres.

FRAME. Composed of two outside and two inside plates, bound with four transverse plates. Outside plates 8 by ½ in.; leading axleguards, ¾ in. thick, bolted to plates, and extended to take spring-brackets. Cast iron guides and spring-brackets bolted on inside. Inside frame-plates ¾ in. from front to motion-plate; 1¼ in. thence to end; with driving and trailing axleguards, and cast iron guides Front plate ⅜ in. End plate, foot-plate, and lower drawplate, ⅜ in., rivetted together and to side plates. Draw-bolt 2 in. Frame-stays: 1st. The cylinders, which bind together the in and outside plates, right and left. 2d. Smokebox tube-plate, made with flanges bolted to inside plates. 3d. Motion-plate, ½ in., in three pieces made with knees and flanges; rivetted to and binding the four frameplates. 4th. Stay of ½ in. plate, in front of firebox, flanged and with knees rivetted to and binding inside frameplates. 5th. Two ⅜ in.

Fig. 272.—Scale 1-10th.

Fig. 273.—Scale 1-10th.

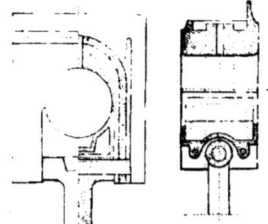 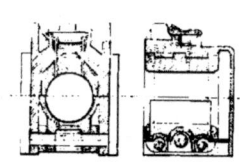

ALLAN'S LOCOMOTIVE.—Driving and Leading Axleboxes.

plates bolted to and binding trailing axleguards, to carry trailing spring. 6th. 2½ in. angle-iron binding, to stiffen

Fig. 274.—Scale 1-10th.

and unite side and end plates. 7th. Firebox-stay of angle-iron on each side. 8th. Barrel-stays, on each side,

Fig. 275.—Scale 1-10th.

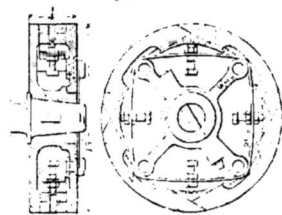 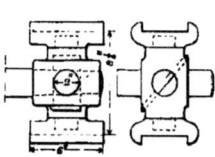

ALLAN'S LOCOMOTIVE.—Piston and Crosshead.

of ½ in. plate, rivetted to barrel, and bolted with flanges to motion-plate.

Wheels and axles of wrought iron, 5 ft. and 3½ ft.

Crankpins outside, at 10 in. radius. Axles 6 and 5 in. diam. Axleboxes of brass, of which the larger are bound with wrought iron straps to connect springs. Springs of steel plates, taper in plan; one trailing spring, applied transversely, shackled to hangers from frame, and linked to axleboxes.

ENGINE. Cylinders and valvechests of cast iron, chest-covers of wrought iron. Bolted with flanges to side plates. Diameter 15 in., stroke 20 in.; lap of valve 1 in., lead in

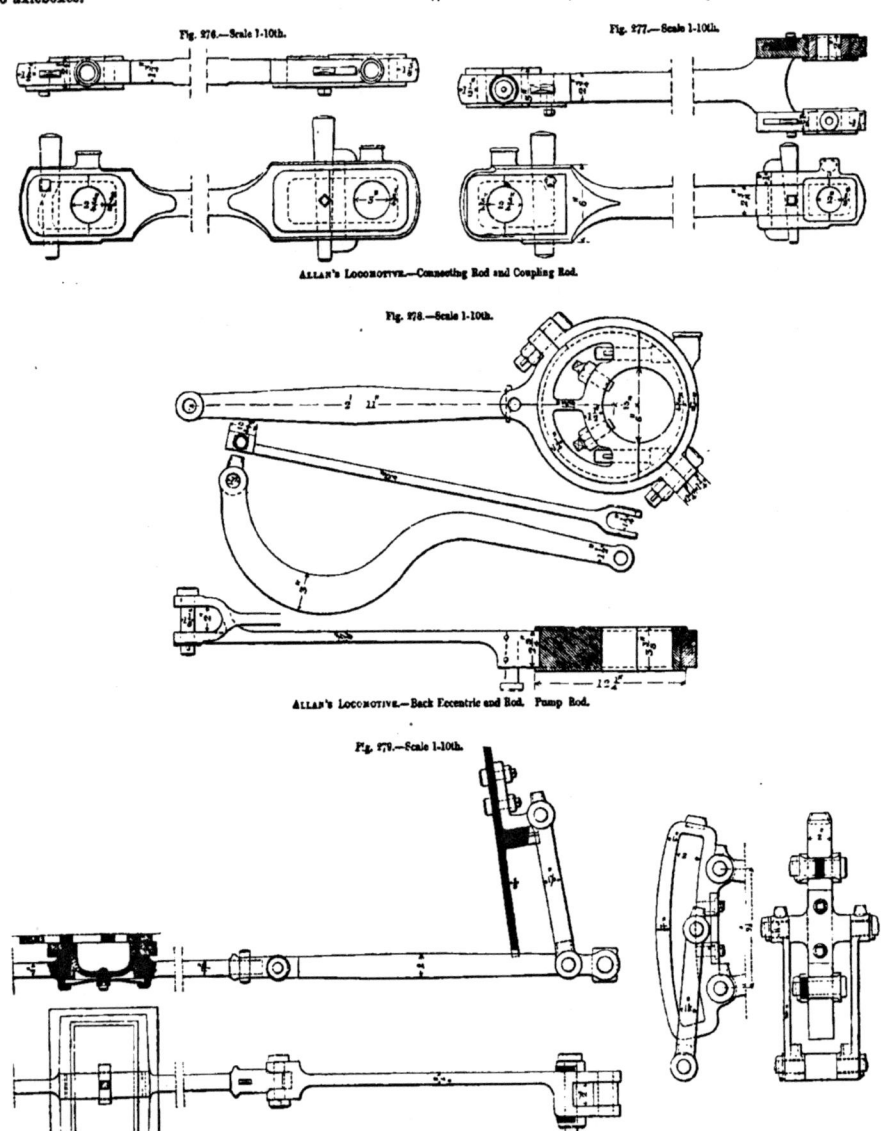

Fig. 276.—Scale 1-10th.

Fig. 277.—Scale 1-10th.

ALLAN's LOCOMOTIVE.—Connecting Rod and Coupling Rod.

Fig. 278.—Scale 1-10th.

ALLAN's LOCOMOTIVE.—Back Eccentric and Rod. Pump Rod.

Fig. 279.—Scale 1-10th.

ALLAN's LOCOMOTIVE.—Valve and Rod. Radius Link. Expansion-Link.

full gear ½ in., travel 4 in., steamports 10 by 1¼ in., exhaust 2½ in. Piston of brass, 4 in. thick, with cast iron packing. Rod 2¼ in. Connecting rod forked at small end, with two bearings, butts and straps; large end solid; centres 5 ft. Coupling rods, solid ends.

Eccentrics of cast iron, with wrought iron, rods and

straps; rods pinned to link behind. Valve of brass, with spring to hold it to face; rod 1¾ in. pinned to link suspended from wings of boiler. Reversing shaft in bearings bolted to side plates, with two levers to carry links.

Fig. 280.—Scale 1-10th.

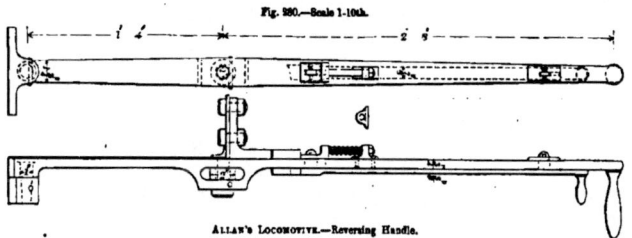

ALLAN'S LOCOMOTIVE.—Reversing Handle.

Regulator, of brass, bolted to back of firebox-shell; cylindrical valve, made to rotate in the chamber of the regulator, with end fitted conically to seat; handle works in skew guides, from which the necessary longitudinal motion of the valve is derived, and the amount of opening regulated. Steam and blast pipes of copper, No. 10, W. G., in the

Fig. 281.—Scale 1-10th.

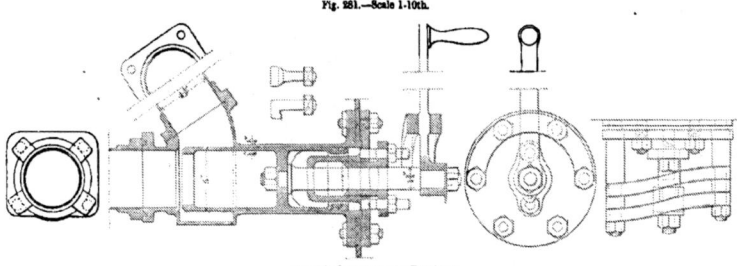

ALLAN'S LOCOMOTIVE.—Regulator.

boiler, and No. 6, W. G., in the smokebox; blast-orifice 3½ in.

Feed-pumps: of brass, with 3¾ in. plungers worked by back eccentric; bolted to frame.

Fig. 282.—Scale 1-10th.

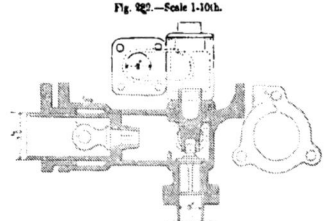

ALLAN'S LOCOMOTIVE.—Feed-pump.

Fig. 283.—Scale 1-10th.

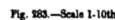
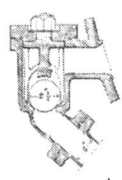

ALLAN'S LOCOMOTIVE.—Delivery Valve on Feed-pipe.

CHAPTER VI.

LIGHT TANK-LOCOMOTIVES.

1. LOCOMOTIVE WITH OUTSIDE CYLINDERS AND SIX INDEPENDENT WHEELS, BY ROBERT SINCLAIR, GLASGOW.—PLATES XXIV., XXV., XXVI.

Area of grate,	8·3 square feet.
Diameter of cylinder,	9 inches.
Stroke of piston,	15 ,,
Diameter of driving wheel,	5 feet 1 inch.
Wheel-base,	13 feet.

General Arrangement. Ordinary boiler, cylinders outside, overhung, and horizontal; six wheels, of which the leaders and drivers are below the barrel, and the hind wheels behind the firebox. Two water-tanks, one below barrel, and one behind firebox. Brake applied to hind wheels.

BOILER. Firebox of ½ in. copper, tube plate ¾ in.; 2 ft. 5¾ in., by 3 ft. 4 in. wide inside, and 3 ft. 3 in. deep. Sides and back of firebox sloped inwards at the rate of 1 in 11. Barrel of ½ in. plate, 2½ ft. by 8 ft. 7½ in. long. Ninety-eight brass tubes 1½ in., No. 9, W. G., 8 ft. 10½ in. long, lapped over and expanded at inside of plates. Rivets ¾ in., zig-zag, 2 in. pitch. Firedoor-ring, of brass. Smokebox-plates ⅜ in., tubeplate ⅝ in.

FRAME. Four longitudinals 6 by 1 in.; outer plates reduced to ½ in. between axleguards. Bound by ½ in. end plates, and by transverse stays and angle-iron binding. Driving wheels 5 ft. 1 in., Carrying wheels 3 ft. 1 in., axles 5½ and 5 in. Springs:—one transverse spring for driving axle, 12 plates 4½ in. by ⅜ in., and ½ in. back plate; carrying springs, plates 3 by ⅜ in.

Engine. Cylinders 9 in. by 15 in. stroke, underhung and bolted to frameplates. Valve, 1 in. lap, $\frac{1}{16}$ in. lead, travel 4 in.; steamport 8 by 1 in. Piston of brass, packing rings of cast iron. Valvechest-cover of wrought iron. Guide-bars of cast iron. Expansion-link stationary, in two pieces bolted together, in box form. Rods forked to take studs on link, and made with bolts and straps; and with double screw joint to adjust length. Valve of brass, rod 1⅛ in., with radius link. Regulator of brass with conical bearing, 3½ in. steampipe; blast-orifice 3 in.

Feed pumps of brass, fixed to outside frameplates; ram 1½ in., worked by crosshead; copper pipe 1½ in. Water-tanks of ¼ in. plate.

Brake: two parallel bars carrying the blocks, worked by levers and screw-motion at footplate.

II. Locomotive with Outside Cylinders and Six Independent Wheels, by John V. Gooch, London.—Plate XXVII.

Area of grate, ...	9·41 square feet.
Diameter of cylinder, ...	12 inches.
Stroke of piston, ...	22 do.
Diameter of driving wheel, ...	6 feet 6 inches.
Wheel-base, ...	14 feet.
Load on leading wheels, ...	8½ tons.
Do. driving do.	9 do.
Do. hind do.	7½ do.
Total weight in working order, ...	24¾ tons.

General Arrangement. Ordinary boiler, cylinders outside, and inclined to overhang and clear the leading wheels; six wheels, of which the drivers are before the firebox; two water-tanks, one under the barrel and one behind the fire-box; coke-box behind. Brakes applied to hind wheels.

Boiler. Firebox 3 ft. 3½ in. by 2 ft. 10½ in. long, and 3 ft. 11 in. deep, with midfeather of ½ in. copper, with ⅞ in. tubeplate. Shell of ⅜ in. plate. Barrel 3 ft. 2 in. by 10 ft. long, of ⅜ in. plates; 127 tubes 1⅞ in. outside, Nos. 12 and 16 W. G., 10 ft. 2¾ in. long, arranged in vertical rows, at 2½ in. centres. Safety-valves: one lever-valve 3½ in. diameter, and one pressure-indicator the same as in J. V. Gooch's ordinary passenger-engine.

Frame. Four longitudinals from end to end, inner plates ½ in., outer plates ¾ in., except between motion-brackets and firebox-brackets, ⅞ in. thick. Stiffened at intervals with angle-iron, and bound transversely by brackets, and by ½ in. end plates.

Engine. Cylinders 12 in. by 22 in. stroke. Valve-face faced with steel. Steam-ports 11 by 1⅜ in. Valves 1 in. lap, $\frac{1}{16}$ in. lead, and 4 in. travel, made with back sliding plate with secondary inlet opening to facilitate the admission of the steam. Stationary link-motion, with slotted link connected behind. Regulator placed in the smokebox, with three-ported sliding valve and face. Steampipe 4½ in. in boiler, extending the whole length and minutely perforated on upper surface to receive the steam. Blast-orifice 4 in.

Feed-pumps fixed on front of firebox, worked by rod from back eccentric-strap. Feed-pipe 1⅞ in. Water-tanks of $\frac{3}{16}$ in. plate. Blast-pipe fitted with valve and copper pipe leading into tank, through which part of exhaust steam may be blown back to heat the feed-water on its way to the pumps.

Brake, composed of two parallel bars carrying blocks to embrace the hind wheels and worked by levers and screw-motion from footplate.

III. Locomotive with Outside Cylinders and Four Independent Wheels, by Robert Stephenson and Co., Newcastle-on-Tyne.—Plate XXVIII.

Area of grate, ...	about 7 square feet.
Diameter of cylinder, ...	11 inches.
Stroke of piston, ...	18 do.
Diameter of driving wheel, ...	5 feet.
Wheel-base, ...	10 feet 4 inches.
Probable weight in working order, ...	13 tons,
(of which two-thirds may be on the driving axle.)	

General Arrangement. Ordinary boiler, cylinders outside, horizontal, and placed behind the leading wheels; four wheels, of which the drivers are in front of firebox, and the leaders under the smokebox.

Boiler. Firebox-shell 2 ft. 11½ in. long, 3 ft. 7½ in. wide, outside. Barrel 3 ft. diam., outside, 11 ft. 4 in. long; 115 tubes 1⅝ in. diam., ⅜ in. clear, about 11 ft. 7 in. long.

Frame; two longitudinals 7 by 1 in. thick, with axle-guards; trussed with bars 3 by 1 in. connecting the ends of frame with the ends of the axleguards. Bound transversely with end beams and boiler-stays. Leading wheels 3 ft. 1 in. diam.

Engine. Cylinders 11 in. by 18 in. stroke, bolted with flanges to the frame-sides and truss bars. Pistons and packing of brass, with two pairs of guidebars to each. Driving wheels 5 ft.

Water-tanks, one under barrel, and one behind firebox. Cokeboxes on footplate at sides of firebox.

Brake applied to driving wheels.

CHAPTER VII.

Sundry Details.

This chapter is to be devoted to the exhibition of details not comprised in the foregoing selection of examples; yet worthy of being placed on record.

Boilers. Stephenson, until lately, made his firebox-

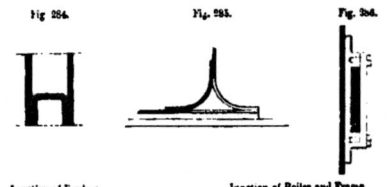

Fig. 284.

Fig. 285.

Fig. 286.

Junction of Firebox. Junction of Boiler and Frame.

shell with a vaulted roof, formed of the four lateral plates continued tapering upwards and closed and seamed together; forming a capacious steam-chamber. See Fig. 19.

Hackworth and Buddicom join the firebox and shell at bottom with a piece of plate doubled up and rivetted to the inner and outer plates separately. Fig. 284.

Allan, at Crewe, has made the roofribs in two pieces, creased to form the eyes for the bolts, and welded together

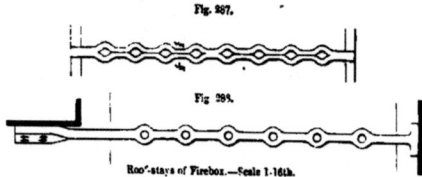

Fig. 287.

Fig. 288.

Roof-stays of Firebox.—Scale 1-16th.

at the middle and the ends, Fig. 287. Robertson, Glasgow, extends the firebox roofribs to the back plate of the shell, to which they are bolted. He also extends the two outer ribs inwardly and rivets them to the barrel, Fig. 288.

Boiler-stays. Stephenson produces the plates of the firebox-shell, laterally, forming wings by which it is bolted to the frameplates and drawplate, Fig. 285.

A simple fixing for flat bar framing, Fig. 286, has been used, in which a plate is rivetted to the firebox-shell, with snugs between which the framebar is fixed by a cover screwed to the plate.

Safety-valves. Derosne and Cail, Paris, make the safety-

valve with a flat seat and narrow bearing, like D. Gooch's. J. F. Ruthven, Edinburgh, rounds the surfaces of contact,

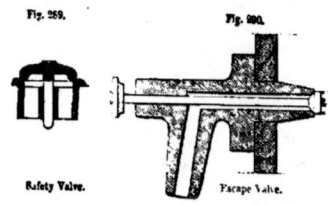

Fig. 289.   Fig. 290.

Safety Valve.   Escape Valve.

and reduces the bearing to a mere line, like the contact of two rings of circular section, Fig. 289.

Water-gauges. J. F. Ruthven uses a ⅜ in. "button-valve," Fig. 290, with spindle and head by which it is opened by hand.

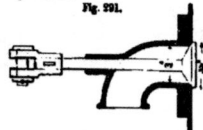

Fig. 291.

Blow - off valves. Ruthven proposes large disc valves, Fig. 291, like inverted safety-valves, in place of the usual cocks, to be opened by a suitable lever, and to give a free and rapid discharge.

Blow-off Valve.

Frame. Bury & Co. have followed out in their latest engines, the style of frame originated by them, composed

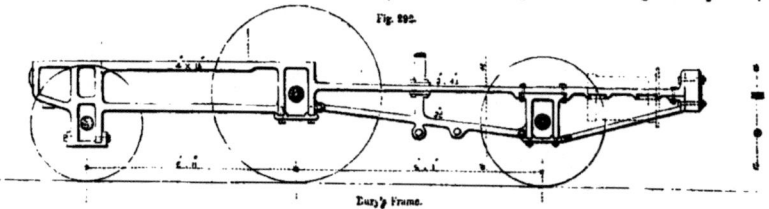

Fig. 292.

Bury's Frame.

of bar iron, flat and round, forged and pinned together, and made with inside bearings for the axles. Fig. 292 is the frame of their latest passenger-engine.

Adams and others use flat plate framing, resembling Bury's in design, in so far as the principal frameplate is strongly trussed by the guardplates, and bound with strong

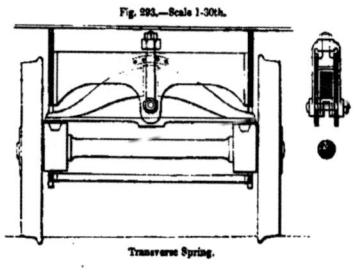

Fig. 293.—Scale 1-30th.

Transverse Spring.

bars joining the extremities, very different from the flimsy rods usually applied: making a compound frame of great strength and depth to comprise all the axle-bearings. Sinclair effects the same object in his goods-engines by making

the side frame of one plate 28 in. deep. See diagram-plate 6, No. 36.

Springs. On the Lyons Railway, the hind axle is fitted with one transverse spring, swivelled by the butt to the frame, and spanning the axleboxes. Fig. 293.

Wheels. Bury, in his earliest engines, and for many years, used a wheel with round spokes and rim of wrought iron, and cast nave. The spokes and nave were turned and bored to fit, and keyed up: the spokes inclining out and in alternately.

Stephenson, some years ago, made his wheels of rib-iron

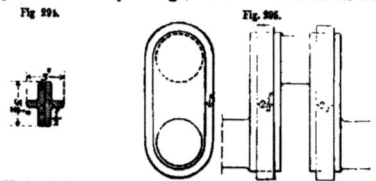

Fig. 294.   Fig. 295.

Wheel-spoke Section.   Straps on Inside Cranks.

bent in segments to form the spokes and the rim, with a cast nave. Fig. 294.

R. Thornton made wrought iron wheels, on the North

British Railway, with flat spokes, placed alternately parallel and at right angles to the plane of the wheel, to render it perfectly rigid under the shrinkage of the tyre.

Crank axles. Hawthorn binds the jaws of inside cranks with wrought iron hoops shrunk on; Fig. 295.

Cylinders. Bury & Co., in their latest designs, bolt the cylinders together and with flanges to the frame, and incline the valve-faces upwards and outwards, to find room for the valves, and to afford convenient access. Fig. 296.

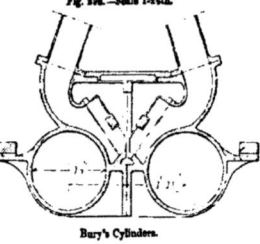

Fig. 296.—Scale 1-24th.

Bury's Cylinders.

Buddicom, Rouen, plants the cylinders on the top of the frame, outside, with snugs fitted between the plates forming

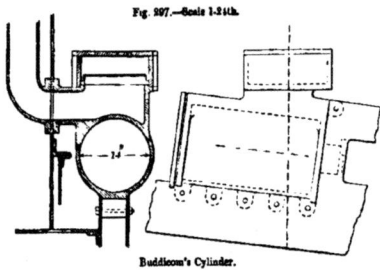

Fig. 297.—Scale 1-24th.

Buddicom's Cylinder.

the outside frameplate, and bolted to them. The valve-chest is on the top of the cylinder. Fig. 297, and No. 22, diagram-plate 7.

Grease-cock, for the cylinders. A convenient form is used by Sinclair, Fig. 298. It is similar to Sharp's.

Pistons. Various plans of packing rings are shown in Figs. 300—302, in all of which the steel spring is carried entirely round the piston. Fig. 299 shows a form of spring formerly used. Helical packing, in one piece coiled four times round the piston, has also been employed, Fig. 303.

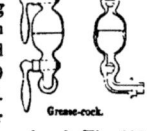

Fig. 298.—Scale 1-10th.

Grease-cock.

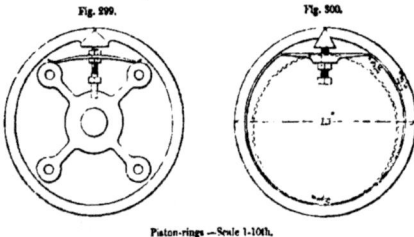

Fig. 299.   Fig. 300.

Piston-rings —Scale 1-10th.

Crossheads. Stephenson has used a simple form, Fig. 304, requiring but one pair of guide-bars, to work with a forked connecting rod. Tulk and Ley, Whitehaven, fit the cross-

head with bush-metal faces, removable when worn, and easily replaced. Hackworth fixes the slides on the cross-head with tapped bolts, Fig. 305.

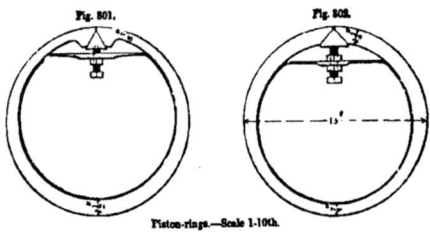

Fig. 301.   Fig. 302.

Piston-rings.—Scale 1-10th.

M. Polonceau, Paris, fixes the bush in the crosshead, and the pin in the connecting-rod end, Fig. 306.

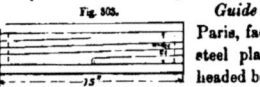

Fig. 303.

Helical Piston-packing.

Guide-bars. M. Barrault, Paris, faces the guide-bars with steel plates, fixed with flush-headed bolts and nuts.

Sinclair makes the guidebars and the slides of cast iron, and fastens the guidebars with clips and set screws to the cylinder-cover, Fig. 307.

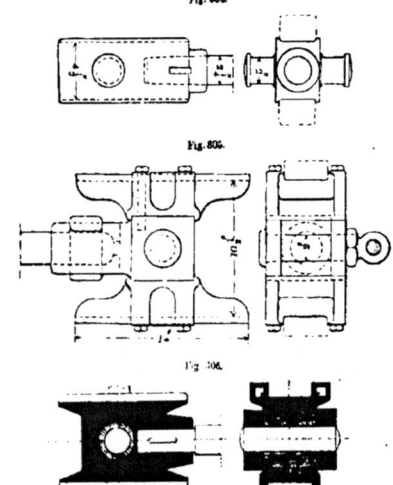

Fig. 304.

Fig. 305.

Fig. 306.

Crossheads and Slides.—Scales 1-10th.

Connecting rods. Various plans have been tried, for removing the cotters from the crank-ends, to reduce the

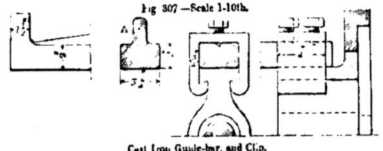

Fig 307 —Scale 1-10th.

Cast Iron Guide-bar, and Clip.

clearance required for inside cranks. Fig. 308 shows the rod used for the crosshead, Fig. 306. Humphreys, Fig. 309, has the strap dowelled and screwed to the butt, and a set screw tapped into the latter, with a capstan-headbearing on a steel plate set into the bush. Hawthorn, Fig. 310, relies upon longitudinal bolts. Sharp, Fig. 311, in his tank-engine

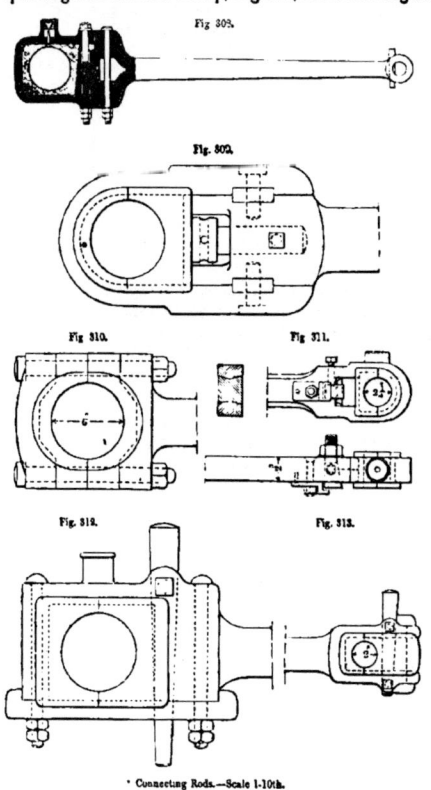

Fig 309.

Fig. 309.

Fig. 310. Fig. 311.

Fig. 312. Fig. 313.

Connecting Rods.—Scale 1-10th.

with outside cylinders applies a wedge transversely in the small end of the connecting rod. E. Reynolds introduced

on the Eastern Counties Railway, a form of large end for inside cranks, Fig. 312, in which the butt embraces the bushes on three sides, leaving the lower side to be closed by a strap

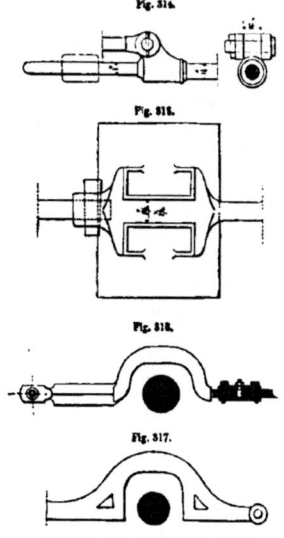

Fig. 314.

Fig. 315.

Fig. 316.

Fig. 317.

Valve-Rods and Eccentric-Rods.—Scale 1-10th.

fixed with bolts and nuts: the special object being to throw the action mainly on one piece of metal. Fig. 313, as a small end, has been much used by Stephenson.

Valve-gear. In the earlier designs of the Crewe engine, the valve-rod link is pinned to an offset eye on the socket of the rod, Fig. 314. Bury & Co. bridle the slide-valves as in Fig. 315, to suit their plan of cylinders. Figs. 316, 317 show modes of clearing the axles when in the way of the gearing. Hackworth uses what he calls a "pass-over" valve, with two bars across the exhaust cavity to work over a double exhaust port, with the view of preventing a premature escape of steam, and also of "passing over" the exhaust steam from one end of the cylinder to the other.

Fig. 318.—Scale 1-8th.

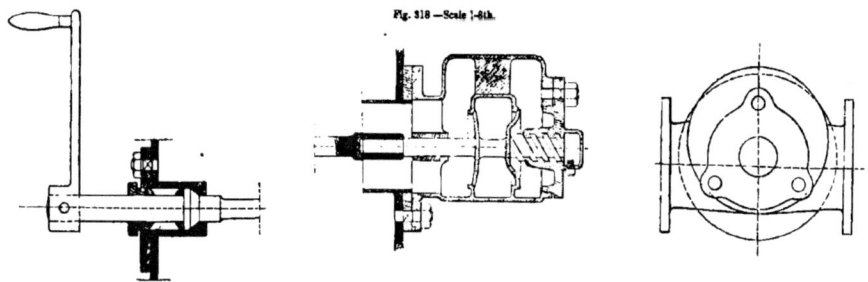

Bury's Regulator.

Regulators. Bury & Co. use a double disc-valve, worked by a screw-motion. Fig. 318.

Pumps. Fig. 320 shows a frequent form of short-stroke plunger. Figs. 321 and 322 are long-stroke pumps by Buddicom, and Flachat, Paris; in the latter of which care is taken to provide a free exit for air in the chamber. Hum-

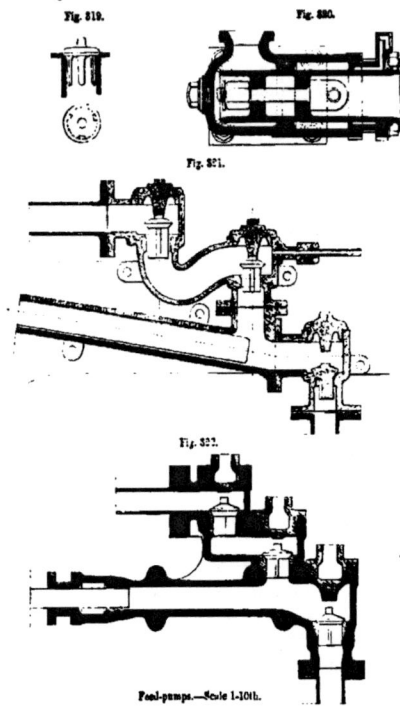

Fig. 319. Fig. 320.

Fig. 321.

Fig. 322.

Feed-pumps.—Scale 1-10th.

phreys employs a three-fanged disc-valve, without webs. Fig. 319.

SUB-SECTION II.

PRINCIPLES OF CONSTRUCTION.

LIGHTNESS, strength, durability, and accessibility, are the leading constructive qualities of well-designed engines. To meet these objects, directness of connection, and simplicity of arrangement and construction, are indispensable. "Next to a good boiler," says Mr. Bury, "which governs the economy of fuel, the most important point in the construction of a locomotive, is to connect all the parts firmly together by a strong and well-arranged framing, so that they shall retain their relative positions when the engine is in motion, and that it shall receive and bear the strain and the concussions to which every part is subject." These just remarks apply with equal force to every detail of the engine. Every strain should be communicated and received directly, by the simplest available means. Simplicity facilitates also the examination of the machine, giving freedom of access to all its parts, and admitting of their ready dismemberment for purposes of repair.

It is of importance, also, that the proper functions of the boiler, the engine, and the carriage, should be clearly distinguished, and that these three elements, though made to fit together with perfect nicety, should be as distinct as possible, and should, in action, be quite independent of each other.

CHAPTER I.

ANATOMY OF THE BOILER.

THE shell of the boiler is usually made of Yorkshire, Staffordshire, or Lowmoor plate. The latter, though the most costly, is the most tenacious and the most easily wrought. The thickness varies from ⅜ in. for the smaller diameters of barrel to ½ in. for the larger, rarely exceeding 4 feet 3 in. inside. Mr. Fairbairn finds that boiler-plate bears a tensile strain of 23 tons per square inch before rupture; which is reduced to 16 tons per inch when double-rivetted joints intervene, and to 13 tons, or about 30,000 lbs. for single-rivetted joints. The bursting strain on a 4 feet barrel under steam of 200 lbs. per inch is 48 times 200 lbs., or 9600 lbs. per inch of length; if the metal be ⅜ in. thick, a length of $8 \div 3 = 2\frac{2}{3}$ in., is necessary to make a square inch of section; on which the pressure is therefore $9600 \times 2\frac{2}{3} = 25,600$ lbs. per square inch. This is not an uncommon pressure in practice, and it approaches the ultimate strength of single-rivetted plates. To increase the resistance to explosion, the plates of the barrel should break joint, and should be made in moderate widths. The plates are equally strong parallel to and across the grain. The joints are either lap- or jump-joints; in the former case the plates lap 2 in. for single rivetting; in the latter case 4 in. welts are applied at the seams, and fixed with two courses of rivets, and the plates are, or ought to be, planed at the edges. The rivetting is usually single; but for strength it should be double, in a zig-zag course, as in D. Gooch's boiler. Rivets are usually ¾ in. diam., and placed at 1⅞ in. pitch; Gooch makes them ⅞ in. at 1¼ in. pitch. The rivet-holes should be slightly widened on both sides, as in Sharp's boiler. The barrel is usually joined with 3 in. angle-iron to the smokebox and firebox; Hackworth turns flanges on the ends of the barrel; but for this there should not in general be any necessity, and it is advisable only when the boiler is converted into a frame, as in D. Gooch's tank-locomotive, and made to pass the strains of the engine through it.

In the firebox-shell, the front and back plates are joined to the others either by 3 in. angle-iron, or by flanges turned on them to a 4 or 5 in. radius; the former is the simpler process, the latter is the more secure, and is the plan most generally followed.

The manholes are made with neckings formed of usually thicker metal than that of the boiler, and flanged to join the boiler; they are planed on the upper flange to receive the cover or the dome. The dome is usually worked out of one sheet with a spherical top; or finished with a dished cover of plate or cast iron, bolted on.

Firebox and Tubes. Fireboxes are almost universally of copper-plates. Iron, though it answers for American wood-burning engines, does not wear well under the intense heat of coke and coal; flaws, though slight, become inflamed; and the metal blisters and burns off. Iron is also more liable than copper to leak at the tubes, to be burned away and ruptured at thick lap-joints: at the joints of midfeathers with the sides, for example, and at places where steam and sediment collect, as its power of conducting heat is inferior to that of copper. Zerah Colburn, America, finds that thin iron is less liable to blister than thick iron: while iron fireboxes of $\frac{3}{8}$ inch plate become badly blistered after a short wear, $\frac{1}{4}$ inch iron, on the same line, wears extremely well. In tubeplates, iron is particularly deficient, as the crowding of tubes, and the small clearance between them, weakens the metal, and, in connection with the upright position of the plate, causes an accumulation of steam in front. Copper does better; and, even with copper, the plates occasionally open across the tube-holes, by violent alternations of heat and cold, when the clearance is less than $\frac{1}{2}$ in. The detention of steam about the tubes is proved by the occasional bulging inwards of the tubeplate just below the tubes, due to overheating and weakening. Mr. Paton, of the Edinburgh and Glasgow Railway, recommends, for economy, tubeplates of copper, and the others of iron. Firebox-plates are made $\frac{7}{16}$ in. to $\frac{1}{2}$ in. thick, and $\frac{3}{4}$ to $\frac{7}{8}$ in. at the tubes; Allan and others make the tubeplate $\frac{3}{4}$ in. thick throughout, to assist in resisting the weakening effect of overheating just mentioned. Flanges are turned nearly square on the front and back plates, and lapped 2 in. under the top and sides; fixed with $\frac{3}{4}$ in. rivets at $1\frac{3}{4}$ in. pitch. The tubes may be of brass or iron, copper is too soft; brass is better than iron, as it conducts the heat better, resists the abrasive action of small coke inside, and the action of impure water outside better, springs more easily under extra expansion by heat than iron, and is not so liable to leak; commercially also, brass tubes are as good as iron, as they fetch half of their original value as old metal, when done with. Tubes are usually fixed in the plates by widening with a mandril to fill the holes completely, turning over their protruding ends upon the plates, and clinching them with ferules or thimbles of steel at the firebox, and iron at the smokebox, $\frac{1}{8}$ to $\frac{3}{16}$ in. thick, and 1 in. long. Steel is too sensitive to heat and cold, and is now nearly disused, as it increases leakage; wrought iron is most common, and, within the last few years, Mr. D. Gooch has used cast-iron ferules with advantage, and continues to use them. Mackie Brothers, Alloa, have used copper ferules in upright tubes successfully, when others failed. Ferules at the smokebox end are frequently omitted, and with benefit; as the tubes do without them, and a free passage is given for small coke and dust into the smokebox. Sturrock tapers the thickness of the firebox ferules inwards; thus all impracticable pieces of coke must stop at the entrance. Ferules are sometimes omitted at the firebox. Allan's method of expanding the tubes just within the plates, as shown in the "Crewe" engine, gives elasticity lengthwise, and is of great benefit. Ferules should be plain cylinders, not flanged, slightly taper, and should, when driven, be left with $\frac{1}{8}$ in. projection into the firebox, so that they may be tightened by a tap from the end of a pinch should the tubes spring a leak on the road. Tubes above 12 feet long are sometimes propped at mid-length with a perforated transverse plate in the barrel; this is unnecessary, as the tubes are stiff enough without it, and are, in fact, floated in the water; the partition, also, is likely to injure the circulation of water, when the water is delivered to the boiler, as it ought to be, in the fore part of the barrel. The thickness of tubes varies between No. 9 and No. 14 Wire Gauge, or fully $\frac{1}{8}$ in. and two-thirds of $\frac{1}{8}$ in. They are either of equal thickness throughout, of No. 13 or 14 W. G., or are of tapering thickness, from No. 9 at the firebox to No. 14 at the smokebox. Tubes wear unequally on the inside, and mostly at the firebox end: in a tube 100 inches long, and originally of equal thickness, the first, second, and last 10-inch lengths weighed, after a period of service, respectively 11·75, 15, and 18·8 ounces, showing that in the first foot of length much the greatest wear takes place. The first foot should therefore, as in Allan's, and in Gooch's boilers, be of No. 9 or No. 10 W. G. in thickness, tapering uniformly to No. 14 at the smokebox. The crown of the firebox should, in all cases, be perfectly flat, and the upper row of tubes should be entered as near the top as possible: they operate as a safety-valve in cases of low water, as they will give way before the firebox, if uncovered. Bury's old fireboxes with vaulted crowns 5 or 6 inches above the tubes, were troublesome in this respect. A fusible plug of lead, or of a compound metal which melts at the same temperature, is usually screwed into the crown of the firebox; so that should the water get too low, and the crown be overheated, the plug will melt out, and give warning by the discharge of steam. Plugs are not to be depended on, as they become incrusted, and don't operate, and tend rather to deceive. The firebox is surrounded by a waterspace on all sides, 2 to $3\frac{1}{2}$ in. wide, and widening upwards, by the slope of the firebox, to 3 or 4 in., for the free disengagement and ascent of steam. Sinclair slopes out the waterspace in his tank-engine from $1\frac{1}{2}$ in. at bottom to 6 or 7 in. at top, at the rate of 1 in 11. In some boilers the walls of the firebox are vertical, and the space uniform. They should in all cases be sloped, and very considerably so, even as much as in Sinclair's boiler, as the loss of heating surface by so doing is trifling, and the gain in free circulation certain; for it is known that under the doorway and the tubes, and at the bend of midfeathers, where the steam is detained, the wear of the firebox is greatest, owing doubtless to overheating and slow combustion of the metal. The space usually allowed is altogether too narrow; it should be, where practicable, 4 in. at bottom, as in the earliest boilers, to allow for the collection of sediment, and experience has proved the superior durability of fireboxes so arranged. Midfeathers should be at least 4 in. wide, with sloping sides; 6 in. would probably be still better, to balance the disadvantage of position. The sides of the firebox at the junction with the midfeather should not be entirely cut through, as they are thus needlessly weakened; but they should be freely pierced, and have numerous openings, as in the Sphynx, and cut away particularly at the extreme top and bottom of the junction, to prevent any lodgment for steam above or sediment below.

The firebox is joined to the shell at the bottom, in various ways. The simplest and most direct method is to insert an iron bar between the plates, made in one frame and well fitted in, and rivetted with $\frac{3}{4}$ in. rivets at $1\frac{3}{4}$ in. pitch. The regular pitch of the rivets, it is plain, cannot be preserved at the corners of the firebox; as in turning the corner the pitch must be increased outside the shell, and reduced inside the firebox. The corners are thus found to be the weakest points, and the most subject to leakage at the rivets; and partially to meet this difficulty, Allan sets out the bottom of the firebox all round, by half-an-inch, reducing the interval from a $2\frac{1}{2}$ inch waterspace to 2 inches; and forms the junction with a 2 inch square bar. With the same object, probably, Bury reduces the space to $1\frac{1}{2}$ inch. By the reduction of the interval, shorter rivets, also, are available; and in all cases, shorter rivets make tighter joints than longer rivets. Occasionally, the firebox is set out to touch the shell, and a plain rivet-joint is made, as in D. Gooch's boiler, and according to old-established practice. This plan no doubt makes the tightest and strongest junction, but it gives a narrow and awkward lodgment for mud, and reduces the useful depth of the firebox, which is objectionable. The advantages of short rivetting, and regular pitching, are also obtained by making a binding of angle-iron, either in two pieces rivetted together and separately to the box and shell, or rolled in one piece of waterspace-angleiron, as employed by Fairbairn and others. But, in these modes, when inside rivet-heads break off, they are difficult to repair; the angleiron frames are also weak at the corners, where the iron is necessarily cut, bent, and subjected to welding: these corners have always proved uncertain. In cases where repairs of the firebox have to be made, requiring access to the waterspace, the removal of part of the angle-iron is rather a serious matter; whereas, when the binding consists of a plain bar, part of the bar may be cut out with great facility, by the aid of the common drill, and replaced by a new piece as in Fig. 323,

Fig 323.

showing the junction in plan. By forming the inserted piece, a, with tongues to let into the adjoining parts of the bar, they may be thoroughly rivetted; and, as the parts are strong, the seams may be easily and securely calked. As respects plan, construction, and repair, then, the plain bar has the advantage of other modes of joining the firebox; and a breadth of 2 inches seems to be the best.

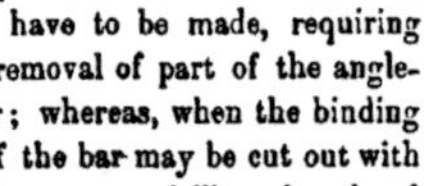

Waterspace-angleirons have been in some cases substituted by castings of brass, in which of course the binding is equally strong at the corners and sides.

The doorway is made with a ring usually of wrought iron, sometimes brass, faced on both sides to fit between the box and the shell, and fixed with rivets. The inside plate is sometimes partially set out to reduce the thickness of ring, but it is better flat, as the steam below escapes more freely. Sinclair uses a brass ring for his tank-engine, with flanges, as the waterspace is very wide.

The firedoor is usually of $\frac{1}{4}$ or $\frac{5}{16}$ in. plate, made to lap $\frac{1}{4}$ in. on the doorway. It is shielded by an inside plate rivetted to it at an inch or two apart. Allan incloses the interval all round, perforates the shield with small holes,

and makes four 1 inch holes in the door, for the admission and distribution of air into the firebox. This plan is useful in burning coal, which requires for its complete combustion an addition of fresh air *above* the grate; but the apertures should be controlled by valves. It seems better to dispense with the air-holes in the door, and to open the door itself more or less, in the customary manner, when fresh air is required. The doorway should be placed low in the firebox, such that the threshold be level, or nearly so, with the upper surface of the fuel when fully charged: 18 to 24 inches above the grate. The air thus admitted at the level of the fuel, mixes most directly and effectually with the combustible gases, and is less likely to flow over into the tubes, and set them leaking; it will also have less effect in reducing the pressure of the steam.

Inside Stays of Boiler. The firebox being flat-sided, is of a weak form, and is stayed or stiffened at all points. The strength of copper, under the circumstances, is not worth considering, and it is best not to depend upon it at all for large surfaces. The walls of the firebox are united to the shell at $3\frac{1}{2}$ to $4\frac{1}{2}$ inch intervals, vertically and horizontally, by rows of $\frac{3}{4}$ to $\frac{7}{8}$ in. copper or iron bolts, screwed into both the box and the shell, and rivetted over on the outside to fix them and give extra hold, with a cup-headed or conical finish. Copper bolts are more easily unscrewed than iron, as iron rusts into iron, and are so far preferable when they require to be taken out for repair. For this object, the lower rows are in some cases formed with square ends projecting into the firebox, which serve also to shield the midfeathers and other parts exposed to the violence of fuel thrown in. D. Gooch screws stud-bolts in addition into the midfeathers for this purpose. Transverse midfeathers are the parts most liable to overheating, as they are in the body of the fuel, and are unfavourably placed for circulation; their stay-bolts should be at shorter intervals than in the walls of the firebox. The crown of the firebox is stiffened by parallel wrought-iron ribs, running fore and aft, about $4\frac{1}{2}$ in. apart centres, and $1\frac{1}{4}$ in. thick by $4\frac{1}{2}$ in. high. This section and distance apart are sufficient for fireboxes $3\frac{1}{2}$ to 4 ft. long, under 150 lbs. steam. D. Gooch makes the ribs 5 in. apart, $6\frac{1}{4}$ in. at middle, tapering to $4\frac{1}{4}$ in. at ends, and 1 in. thick, for a 4 ft. 3 in. firebox. The ribs are, by some, made double, in two thicknesses rivetted together, and sufficiently apart to admit the bolts between them; in these the labour of forming the bolt-eyes is saved. When the ribs are of taper depth, they should be reduced by steps, to give a square bearing for the bolts. They should stand $\frac{1}{4}$ in. clear of the crownplate to let the water below them and prevent overheating, with bearings at the ends which should be well overhung, as in the Sphynx, and nicely fitted to the edges of the plate and to the bends of the front and back plates, to take off the strain upon the corners; neglect of this has led to serious ruptures and explosions. At the bolts, washers or ferules, loose or forged on the bolts or the ribs, are placed between the plate and the ribs, to take up the strain of the bolts. The ribs should be firmly linked at, say, four distant points to the crown of the firebox-shell, as in the Sphynx, to take up part of the downward strain on the lateral fixings of the firebox, and to stiffen the shell at the manhole; the shell should have angle-iron ribs rivetted to it transversely to receive the links, and to distribute the benefit of the connection.

The shell, like the firebox, is not trusted with much of its inherent strength, except at the cylindrical pieces,—the barrel, and the upper part of the firebox-shell as now almost universally made. All the flat parts, not stayed to the firebox, are bound with tie-rods, of which, for barrels above $3\frac{1}{2}$ feet, there are usually about eleven rods binding the extreme end plates, $\frac{7}{8}$ to $1\frac{1}{4}$ in. diam., conveniently and equally spaced out between and over the roofribs, and in some cases additional short tie-rods between the back and front plates of the firebox-shell, or made with a landing on the interior of the barrel. Kitson & Co. have no through tie-rods at all, and have only two shorter rods from the back plate, and two from the front tubeplate, with fixings on the crown of the barrel ; to make amends for which their plates are extra thick,—$\frac{1}{2}$ in. plates for the firebox, and a $\frac{3}{4}$ in. tubeplate. Tie-rods are cottered to studs rivetted to the plates, or pinned to double lines of angle-iron rivetted on ; or finished with screwed ends made up to a greater diameter, passed through the plates and fixed with nuts outside and inside. The second is perhaps the best plan, as it diffuses the strain of the rods over the plates. Bury & Co. introduce a few tie-rods between the two tubeplates, at the sacrifice of a few tubes ; this does not appear necessary, as there is only the pressure due to the interspaces of the tubeplates to be met, and this is efficiently done by the tubes; the tubeplate, it is true, may have occasionally been observed to yield inwards, but this must have arisen from excessive overheating by the lodging of steam in front, which should be altogether prevented by other means.

Grate. The bars are of wrought iron, and are made from $\frac{3}{4}$ to $1\frac{1}{4}$ in. thick on the upper edge, and thinned away below to half the thickness for the freer admission of air. The best thickness is $\frac{1}{2}$ or $\frac{3}{4}$ in., with equal interspaces, as the bar is more easily kept cool than when thicker, and when thinner it is liable to twist. Fire-bars should not be thinned below, as they require their full thickness for strength, and a small chamfer on the lower edge is sufficient. They are made 3 to 4 in. uniform depth, and sometimes deeper, but for spans above 3 feet it is better to make them in two lengths, as in J. V. Gooch's and Bury's engines, or to throw across a bar below them, as in Fairbairn's. They are made with flat ends to rest on the frame, and broad enough when set close, to space them out sufficiently. The bar-frame is generally of bar-iron, about $1 \times 1\frac{1}{2}$ in. deep, with four sides to lie clear of rivet heads, and propped by studs rivetted to the firebox ; or, two angle-iron bearers are screwed to the bottom of the firebox, as in Allan's engine ; and notched to receive the bars, as in J. V. Gooch's. The grate should be closely fitted to the walls of the firebox, particularly at the front, under the tubes, to prevent the influx of cold air unconsumed. When the bars are to be movable, it is better to put the whole grate on hinges, than a few bars, as they glue together with the slag from impure coke; Sharp's method of hinging and dropping the grate is efficient. The bar-surface should be a few inches above the bottom of the waterspace, to leave sediment at rest.

Ash-pan and Damper. The ashpan is of $\frac{1}{4}$ in. plate,

framed with angle-iron, and flat iron round the upper edge. It should be at least 10 in. deep, to admit a sufficiency of air, and to hold a quantity of ashes without choking the draught and burning the bars. It should be closely fitted to the bottom of the firebox, as even a $\frac{1}{4}$ in. chink weakens the draught, and destroys the action of the damper when air is to be excluded. Nevertheless, many engineers are very careless about the ashpan, and lose sight of its most useful function. It is not merely to collect ashes and stray cinders, nor even to concentrate the draught alone, but mainly to supply a means of nicely regulating the supply of air to the furnace, by the aid of the damper. The damper is a flat plate fitted accurately and hinged to the entrance of the pan, and worked by a handle at the footplate ; it is designed to close the ashpan entirely and stop the draught, or to vary the draught by varying the opening, as required. As sufficient air may leak through a very narrow opening to burn and waste the fuel very sensibly when not required, the tightness of the ashpan is essential to the economical consumption of fuel. Allan slides the damper vertically ; this gives a better entrance to the air. The ashpan would be improved by fitting it with a door in the bottom, through which ashes could be cleaned out readily and simply, and by which also the fire might be dropped. The ashpan should be bolted or rivetted to the firebox-shell with straps on the outside or inside, as in D. Gooch's and Fairbairn's engines ; in Kitson's, where it is simply linked, the fastening does not give the desirable stability.

The venetian-damper in the smokebox employed by the Goochs, and already described, operates very well ; especially in conjunction with the ashpan-damper. Indeed, the two dampers ought to be placed upon all locomotive boilers, so as directly and effectually to isolate the boiler at both ends, from the air, when required. A damper, consisting of a short iron disc, is usually applied, when required, to the upper end of the chimney; we should, however, prefer one like Gooch's, applying close to the tube-ends, the more completely to check the circulation of the smoke.

The *smokebox* is usually of $\frac{1}{4}$ inch plate, joined to the tubeplate and frameplates ; and occasionally formed as an entire cylinder, detached from the frame, either as a prolongation of the barrel of the boiler, or made with angle-iron to a larger diameter. The door should be large enough to give free access to all the tubes, and should be carefully mitred into its seat in the front plate ; and it should be slightly dished outwards, to enable it to resist the pressure without against the partial vacuum inside, and to maintain it air-tight. For the same purpose, it should be fastened at four or more points in its periphery, by a number of shot-bolts worked by a handle at the centre, which is perhaps the best way ; or by a series of brass detents outside, as in Sharp's and Gooch's engines. It should also have a shield of $\frac{3}{16}$ or $\frac{1}{4}$ in. plate rivetted on inside.

Every smokebox should be made with a sufficient opening near the crown, fitted with a sliding plate worked from the footplate ; to afford a means of damping the draught by admitting air into the smokebox, instead of damping by the firedoor as is commonly done.

The *Chimney* should be of $\frac{1}{4}$ in. plate, to bear the action of the blast and the rasping of cinders and ashes. It should be flush-jointed outside, with a welt inside; and fixed to the smokebox with bolts and nuts.

Brackets.—The boiler may be said to rest upon the frame, and to be bolted to it. It is, besides, an important source of stiffness to the frame, and is, in some designs, made largely subservient to this object. The union is made permanent and unalterable at the smokebox-end, where the cylinders and their connections are situated; at the firebox allowance is made, either in the elasticity of the brackets, or in the freedom of the bolt-holes, for the varying length of the boiler by heat. The want of this liberty, small but essential, is destructive to the machine, and leads to certain rupture in the seams of the boiler, or in the frame. In ordinary practice, the boiler is supported on each side at three places, the firebox, middle of barrel, and smokebox; the supports are usually made of bar-iron 6 or 7 inches by ⅝ or ⅞ inch thick; formed triangularly with three palms, one to join the frame and two to join the boiler. The boiler-palms should be of good length, 11 to 14 inches, and well rivetted on, to make a rigid bracket, and to insure its sliding with the boiler at the frame-bolts. The barrel-brackets are usually joined by a piece of the same section passed below the barrel and rivetted to it, as in Crampton's and Kitson's engines; thus making a firm junction with the frame. Sharp, and Fairbairn, in their passenger-engines, use plates on edge to connect the boiler with the frame; those at the smokebox being simple extensions laterally of the tubeplate and frontplate. Kitson fits a ½ inch plate on edge, on each side of the smokebox, and between the frameplates, and rivets the whole together with 3 inch angle-iron; and, in some cases, the side plates of the smokebox are joined to the inside frameplates. With outside cylinders, these methods are inadmissible, and the tubeplate, and occasionally also the front plate, are flanged and bolted to the inside frameplates. When the inside frameplates are extended behind the firebox, an excellent bracketting is made of with 3½ inch angle-iron rivetted on each side of the firebox-shell, for its whole length, to rest upon the frame, and bolted to inverted angle-iron rivetted on the outside of the frameplate, as in Sharp's and Allan's engines.

Boiler Mounting. Safety-Valves. There are two in every boiler, as a matter of security, either together or at separate points; at the firebox, or on the barrel, and generally at the summit of the dome, when present. It is better to place the safety-valves apart from the orifice of the steampipe, as they divert the current of steam when blowing off, and reduce the tendency to prime. In the design of the valve, the points are that it shall act readily and rapidly, so as in ordinary circumstances to discharge the steam without permitting the pressure to rise dangerously high. Safety-valves of locomotives are hardly known to gag, being so frequently opened; we should, however, prefer the flat valve of D. Gooch, or Ruthven's "ring valve," with very small contact, to the conical valves in ordinary use, as more free in action, and as offering a wide exit for steam, at a given elevation of the valve; if conical valves be used, the bevel should at least not exceed 30°. One or both of the valves are fitted with levers controlled each by a Salter's balance fitted with a helical spring and graduated to indicate 1 lb., 5 lb., or 10 lb. intervals of pressure, and such that a weight of 1 lb. on the spring-rod with the balance inverted, would raise the index 1 lb. by the scale; but, the intervention of a lever multiplies the power of the balance upon the valve, in the ratio of the leverage, and there must be as many square inches in the lower surface of the valve as the number of times that the whole length of the lever contains the distance of the centre of the valve from the fulcrum; or, in short, as the number expressing the leverage. Thus, to take Allan's safety-valve: it is 2½ in. diam. on the steam-side, and has 5 in. of area; the lever is 17½ in. long, and is 3½ in. from the fulcrum to the valve; the leverage is, therefore, $17\frac{1}{2} \div 3\frac{1}{2} = 5$, that is, the balance has a leverage of 5 to 1 upon the valve, and acts as if the valve, though actually of 5 in. area, were reduced to 1 in. area: the virtue of which coincidence is that, when the steam is just blowing off, the spring balance indicates the pressure in the boiler *per square inch*. Different makers adopt different leverages, and therefore different areas of valve to compensate; Bury & Co. have constantly used a leverage of 5 to 1, and a 2½ in. valve, even for their largest boilers; and this explains, we think, the rapid action of their safety-valves in their early engines, compared with those of other makers, exemplified in the case with which the steam blew off. The majority of other makers extend the leverage to 11 or 12 to 1, and use about 4 inch valves, with 12 in. area, as they presume a larger valve gives a more rapid discharge. This we very much doubt, as the circumference of the valve, which represents the exit for steam increases more slowly than the area, and to cause a given elevation of the valve from its seat, a higher pressure must exist in the boiler, with greater leverage. Altogether, we should prefer the shorter leverage of 5 to 1, with the 2½ in. valve; and the choice appears confirmed by practice, as it has often been found that, even with 4 in. valves, the pressure in the boiler may rise to double that indicated at the balance, through the inability of the valve to let off the steam with sufficient rapidity. Indeed, the principle of more direct action has been boldly carried out by J. V. Gooch, who dismissed the lever entirely, and planted the balance on the top of the valve; the valve which was virtually reduced to 1 in. area by the lever, was now literally so, being but $1\frac{1}{16}$ in. diam.; and it works satisfactorily. The liveliness of a safety-valve is not necessarily in proportion to its size; the question is, what excess of pressure above that to which the balance is adjusted, will give a sufficiency of outlet, with the same balance, and with different sizes of valves and corresponding levers? and if it be agreed, as there can be no doubt, that a smaller valve and shorter lever, or even Gooch's direct connection, opens as fully as a larger valve and lever, under the same pressure, the presumption is in favour of the smaller valves, seeing that the outlet is in any case less than the area of the passage to the valve.

For larger boilers, therefore, larger valves are not so much the object, *as balances on a larger scale*, or such as have more elastic springs, with greater scope, and moving through a greater distance per pound of extra pressure. The graduations for given intervals of pressure being wider, the valve will rise higher, and will give a wider outlet, for a given excess of pressure, and discharge more steam in a given time.

As the area of grate regulates the production of steam, it

should regulate also the scale of the balance. Assuming a 2½ in. valve, and a lever of 5 to 1, for all boilers, it has been found by experience that the ordinary Salter balance, is sufficiently active for Bury's original 9 feet grates; for grates, then, of a different area, the elasticity of the balance should vary proportionally. Salter's ordinary balance acts at the rate of 10 lbs. pressure per inch of elastic action, and as the elastic force of the spring should be inversely as the area of grate, multiply 10 lbs. by 9, giving 90 for a constant quantity, and divide by the given area to find the proper elasticity;—hence the rule:—

RULE. *To find the elasticity of the spring-balance for a 2½ in. valve, and a lever of 5 to 1, due to a given area of grate.* Divide 90 by the area of grate, in square feet. The quotient expresses the elasticity in pounds per inch of action.

Example. For a 12 feet grate; $90 \div 12 = 7½$ lbs. per inch of extension or compression, the required action of the spring-balance.

One of the safety-valves is sometimes loaded by a helical steel spring, directly applied, and inclosed in the dome beyond the control of the driver.

Manometers, or pressure-gauges, indicating the pressure of the steam at all times, are now being introduced and attached to boilers. Of these, Bourdon's is, we think, the most perfect. Pressure-gauges are a luxury rather than a necessity, as, after a little practice, engine-drivers are able, by a touch of the Salter-balance, and the degree of resistance it opposes to the opening of the valve, to judge very nearly of the strength of the steam.

Whistles are usually of hard brass, the bell being 3 in. in diameter, and 2½ in. deep; this size gives the musical note D natural, which is a good pitch for ordinary whistles, and comes well out with 80 lbs. steam; higher pressures produce the harmonic fifth above, a shrill and piercing tone. As the fulness of tone is affected by the pressure in the boiler, the steam should be suitably wiredrawn by the handle. To do so with precision, D. Gooch uses a screw motion and valve. Guard's whistles are made larger, of a decidedly lower tone than the ordinary whistle; a 4 in. bell, 5 in. deep, makes an excellent guard's signal.

Blow-off Cocks and Valves. Fixed to the firebox-shell, at the bottom, to blow off foul water and sediment; usually 1 to 2 in. diameter. This is too small for the most successful action; loose matter is, to be sure, carried off, but a larger vent, say 3 to 4 in. diameter, gives a more rapid discharge, which, apparently by the sudden expansion of nascent steam, causes much of the scale to peel off, and scours much more effectually. Two such large vents may be opened at the same time.

Screw-plugs should be at least 2 in. diameter, with a slight taper; of hard brass, not iron, to prevent rusting in; with large square heads to bear the strain of the screw-key. There should be at least two, at diagonally opposite corners, to give the range of the four sides of the firebox, and two to command the midfeather where this exists. The thread of the screw-plug should be cut to a fine pitch, to give it a good hold in the metal. Allan inserts a lining of plate iron inside at each corner of the firebox-shell, to increase the hold of the plug, and reduce the liability to leakage; as, besides the unfavourable bend of the plate at the corners,

which weakens the hold of the screw, the cleaning rods wear away the sides of the holes, and reduce the hold still more.

Scum-cock, fixed to the back of the firebox, at the ordinary water-level, with 1½ in. copper pipe to draw off the frothy impurities which rise to the surface of the water, and which, while there, conduce greatly to priming.

Water-gauges. To show the level of water in the boiler. At least one glass-gauge with brass fixings is applied, to the back or side of the firebox-shell. The glass tube is commonly of ¼ in. bore, and ⅛ in. thick; it should be well annealed, to prevent fracture by sudden applications of heat, and by external accident; packed with hemp or lint, and left with the ends free for expansion. A visible range of 10 inches is sufficient; and the gauge should be so fixed that the bottom of the visible part of the glass be level with the crown of the firebox,—certainly not lower, as, if so, it is liable to deceive the driver, by the appearance of water in the glass, while there may be none above the firebox. Though the water-level ought to be kept up to 5 or 6 in. over the firebox, for security, practised drivers take liberties occasionally, when they require "all the steam," and exclude the feed-water, thus permitting the water to run low in the glass; and it is proper they should know precisely what depth of water they may depend upon. Openings through which the passages may be probed when stopped up, are made opposite each passage, and stopped by screw-plugs. The passages to the boiler should be ⅝ in. or, better, ½ in. diameter, to reduce the liability to stoppage.

Three gauge-cocks are tapped into the firebox-shell, at three levels: usually *at* the crown of firebox, 3 in. above, and 6 in. above it; to be used in case of failure of the glass-gauge. In some cases, they are screwed into a hollow stem joining the firebox at top and bottom, upon which also the glass-gauge is grafted, as in D. Gooch's gauge. This plan reduces the security, as there is no resource when the passages to the boiler are stopped; indeed it may deceive when the cocks are trusted to, as, should the upper channel be stopped, the cocks would be supplied with water from the lower channel, while the water-level might really be much below them. Accidents have frequently occurred in this way; and it is better that the gauge-cocks should join the boiler independently.

Heating Cock. Fixed to the firebox-shell at or near the crown, or to the dome, with 1 in. copper pipe to one or both feedpipes, and joined with soldered thimbles or with screw couplings. In tank-engines, the pipe is led directly into the tank, and should be laid in two or three feet, with the end plugged, and perforated with small holes to distribute the steam admitted for heating the water.

CHAPTER II.

ANATOMICAL DISCUSSION OF THE CARRIAGE: GENERAL PRINCIPLES OF THE FRAME.

Inside-Cylinder Locomotives.—In the earliest locomotives, no regard was paid to the propriety of classifying and separating the duties of the different parts of the machine. The boiler was the real foundation upon which the engine was erected, and the axle-bearings fastened : the cylinders have been plunged into the boiler, or fixed severally upon the smokebox, the barrel, and the firebox, with intermediate axles hung upon the boiler, and in various attitudes according to the taste of the designer ; the gearing was stuck on anywhere, and the shell of the boiler pierced with numerous bolt-holes ; for what could be stronger than a hollow cylinder of plate iron rivetted into one compact barrel, and what more suitable for strength and rigidity to the mechanism fastened to it ?

Cylindrical surfaces, though strong, were not found convenient for attachments ; so a frame was provided to carry the engine, machinery, wheels, and the boiler itself. The boiler, though relieved considerably by the change, was still charged with the cylinders which were placed below, inside the smokebox, and bolted to the front and tubeplates ; though, immediately on the outside, the smokebox was bound by brackets to the frame, and the strain between the cylinders and driving-axle thereby transmitted, without running through the body of the boiler. See diagram-plate 7, Nos. 1 and 3.

But though some difficulties were thus removed, others supervened. The strain between the cylinders and the axle is no trifle, for it is, in fact, the pressure of the steam in the cylinder ; the pressure acts on the ends of the cylinders alternately, and also on the pistons, from which the strain is transmitted by the connecting rods to the axle. Thus the cylinders and the axle are alternately strained together and strained asunder. To meet this alternate straining, the outside frame was interposed, uniting the cylinders to the axle, through the medium of the smokebox-brackets. The frame thus acted as a strut to prevent compression, and as a tie to prevent elongation ; but imperfectly, *because the connection was not direct ;* it was made laterally through the smokebox-stays, and these stays could not be kept in good order ; they worked loose, and set the whole framing a-twisting. It is true, inside frames were applied, uniting the smokebox to the firebox, and embracing the axle with the object of meeting the horizontal strain upon it ; but these were little better than figments, their capacity was limited, their bearings on the axle narrow, and, though well intended, they readily wore clear of the axle, and left the outside frame to do the greater part of the duty. Bury,—and when we say Bury, we generally mean James Kennedy, his accomplished and responsible partner,—knowing the essential weakness of the outside frame for the required purpose, dismissed it entirely, and gave his engines a pair of broad and responsible bearings upon the axles inside the wheels alone, carrying out the frame inside the wheels, and close outside the smokebox and firebox. But, while he acted thus far on sound principles, and while his frame actually grazed the cylinders, he did not in his first engines seize the opportunity of binding the cylinders at once to the frame : he, like others, bolted the cylinders to the front and back plates of the smokebox, and, removing the smokebox-stays, led the strain circuitously through the boiler and the brackets by which it was bolted to the frame. The real distinction on the question of framing, then, is, that while others had their principal framing outside the wheels, Bury placed his principal and

only frame inside, and by so much shortened and stiffened the lateral connections formed by the boiler-brackets between the cylinders and the driving axle : meriting the opinion of M'Connell, in 1845, that his engine was " a good, strong, compact machine."

In later designs, Bury remedied the fault of his earliest plans, by placing under and fitting to the cylinders two strong transverse bars, passing through the sides of the smokebox, and bolted to the frame and to wings cast upon the cylinders ; this made a very firm and direct connection, relieving the boiler of all straining from the engine.

Sharp, retaining the outside frame as the foundation of his passenger-engine, for the sake of outside axle-bearings and better accommodation between the wheels, and aware of its weakness on the score of indirect connection, resolved to provide for this by uniting all the parts of the machine in one solid mass, which would stand or fall as a whole. He threw out wings from the front and back plates of the smokebox, which rested on and were rivetted to the frame, and inserted filling-up plates between and rivetted to the smokebox, frame, and wings, so as to forbid any play in that quarter ; he bound the firebox to the frame by similar wings consisting of plates on edge, of great strength, flanged and rivetted, and by an extensive footplate and lower drawplate rivetted with lines of angle-iron to the frame and the back and sides of the firebox. The boiler being thus wedged into the frame, and being further bound together by four inside stay-plates between the firebox and smokebox, it was reasonably expected that nothing could give way ; and, in truth, it is to this almost invincible elaboration of framework, that Sharp's engines are known over the world as the most durable of outside-framed engines, as Bury's have been unquestionably the most durable of engines with inside frames.

The durable qualities of Sharp's and Bury's engines are, however, very differently derived. Sharp, by a due accumulation of iron and rivetting, opposed the strength of iron successfully to the disorganizing action of high-pressure steam. Bury went directly to the point : he placed the frame where the frame should be, and conducted the steam-pressure to its destination through a single solid bar. Sharp certainly established a secure, though circuitous, communication with the driving axle ; Bury went straight at it, and caught the axle by the neck. On the principle of direct connection already laid down, we are bound to prefer Bury's general design, without committing ourselves to details ; and a reference to the general plans of Bury's and Sharp's engines, Nos. 2 and 4, diagram-plate 7, of which the latter is a later modification of Sharp, will show the relative simplicity of Bury's design.

Closely allied to the question of direct connection, is the question of inside and outside bearings on the driving-axle. The wheel, the crankpin, and the axle-bearing or journal, on each side of the machine, should be in close juxtaposition ; if it were possible, they should be at the same part of the axle. At each there is something to be done, and transmitted along the axle ; and the closer they are, the more direct is the action of one on the other, and the less their lateral leverage, and the incidental straining to which the axle is subjected. Here again, Bury had the advantage, for, by connecting the cylinder directly with the axle, and inside the wheel, he planted his bearing immediately between the wheel and the crank, and thus compacted the straining within the smallest possible physical limits. This advantage Sharp, even with his rigid frame, could not reach, as his inside bearings were mere auxiliaries to the outsides ; and, in the due course of wear, his axle broke loose from the insides, and depended more and more upon the extreme bearings outside. In this way, the very rigidity of his frame told upon the durability of the axle, as there was no scope for a compromise : the outside frame *would not* work loose, and the axle must therefore yield more and more under the horizontal strain, before obtaining relief from the inside bearings, as the latter wore away, until its horizontal deflection would reach and surpass the limits of natural elasticity, and lead inevitably though gradually to a final rupture.

Of course, the propriety of having the responsible and only bearings of the driving axle inside, between and close to the wheels, on the grounds just stated, does not affect the position of the bearings of the merely carrying axles, as these have nothing to do with the action of the engine. When the bearings are all between the wheels, they fall into a direct line on each side, and demand a simpler frame than when the carrying axles have their bearings outside the wheels; as, in this case, double framing is necessary to embrace the inner and outer bearings. For this reason, and also because the downward pressure of the load on inside bearings, assists the wheels in resisting lateral concussions between their flanges and the rails, Bury has constantly employed inside bearings exclusively for all the axles. To the latter argument we attach no importance, as experience has amply proved that well-formed carrying axles with outside bearings are as durable as any; indeed we should feel, on a first view of the case, rather in favour of outside bearings, as the axle may safely be reduced beyond the wheel, and the journal made of much less diameter than if inside, which both increases the elasticity of the axle,—increasing also its probable durability,—and reduces the journal-friction, this friction being in proportion to diameter and independent of length. The greater simplicity of frame for inside bearings is admitted; at the same time, the most important parts of the framing,—the inside connections of the cylinders and driving axle,—are simplified by being relieved of the provision for other bearings, better accommodation is provided for the springs, and, as already insisted upon in a previous chapter, outside bearings to the carrying axles, increase the stability of the machine. To the argument for simplicity, then, little weight is attached, as the vital parts, those which receive and transmit the action of the steam, are unimpaired by the removal of the inside carrying bearings,—indeed, we think, rather improved.

Stimulated, doubtless by the example of Bury's engines, and by their own experience, the makers of outside-framed engines felt the necessity of adding to the durability of their inside bearings: and they made them longer, to be of equal area with the outsides, or such that the length multiplied by the diameter was the same in the two cases, and in hopes also that by equalizing the wearing surfaces of the

axleboxes between their guides, the boxes on the two sides of the wheel would wear equally, and that the axle would thus work fairly and durably. The axleboxes, however, do *not* wear equally, as the elasticity of the axle is still at work, and as the inner bearing is nearer the crankpin, the origin of the working force, it receives the greater part of the strain, and wears more rapidly than the outer. Thus recurs the evil of a strained axle, with wide points of resistance, only more gradually consummating a fracture than in previous designs.

To bring about equal wear of the outer and inner axleboxes, their wearing surfaces would probably require to be in the inverse ratio of their distances from the crankpin. Taking Sharp's later engine, with which Fairbairn's (Plate I.) is nearly identical, the centres of the journals are $8\frac{1}{4}$ and $20\frac{1}{4}$ in. distant laterally from the centre of the crankpin, or at mean distances as 1 to $2\frac{1}{2}$ nearly : the wearing surface of the inner box should then be $2\frac{1}{2}$ times that of the outer, to wear equally. Were such a ratio to be observed, however, the outer box would necessarily be so reduced as to render it of little service for horizontal action; and it would be preferable either to dismiss it entirely, or to confine its operation to merely sustaining its load, the driving weight being divided equally between the inside and outside boxes. With this view, the outside guides should be retained, merely for steadiment, with sufficient clearance from the box, to prevent horizontal action. In this way the architectural character of such as Sharp's and Fairbairn's engines would be preserved; and we should really regret to find these beautiful models of framing superseded.

As the inside members of double framing rose into importance, a more secure connection with the cylinders became obviously desirable. Bury had again set the example: he had carried out the inside frames to the buffer-beam, and had bound the cylinders to them independently of the smokebox fixings; while, in the double frame, makers had been content to land the insides upon the back of the smokebox, and to bolt them to it, thus interposing the tubeplates, to which the insides and the cylinders were separately attached. This connection was indirect ; the insides were, therefore, extended to the buffer-beam, and lateral flanges were added to the cylinders, by which a broad, secure, and direct connection was effected.

At the same time, as the result of modifications in the valve-gear, by which vertical valve-faces were introduced, placed between the cylinders and facing each other, the two valve-chests, previously separate, were thrown into one, and they formed with the cylinders two large castings, which were bolted together and to the inside frames. Thus was elaborated the system of inside-cylinder connections now generally practised, by which the inside frames and the cylinders became thoroughly bound together into one mass, and gained immensely in strength and power of resistance to shocks of every kind. Bury, dismissing the transverse bars which bound his cylinders, modified his engines in the same way.

But the frame, besides converting the steam-pressure into tractive force, by turning the driving axle, also transmits the tractive force through the draw-gear. This should be done exclusively by the frame, and Bury and Sharp provide for it by suitable connections behind the boiler. In many earlier engines, and in some of the latest, the draw-gear is fixed directly to the back of the firebox, as in Nos. 3 and 5, diagram-plate 7; thus the force comes on the boiler, which of course must receive it from the frame, in violation of the first principle of direct connection. Many makers terminate the inside frame in front of the firebox, and fix it with brackets, to permit of the lateral extension of the firebox to the utmost width permissible between the wheels. This expedient is unnecessary, as fireboxes of sufficient dimensions may be arranged without resorting to it. And really the gain in width is just about 2 inches,—a mere trifle, unworthy of the amount of preparation made for it.

In coupled-wheel engines, every consideration in favour of direct connection is of still greater importance, as the extra straining of coupled axles is to be met, due not only to the additional points of traction, but to the unequal action induced by tear and wear described in a previous chapter. The coupled axles ought to have their bearings all and exclusively inside, and in one continuous frame, as in Bury's and Sharp's engines, Nos. 14, 15, diagram-plate 7; and any attempt to confer outside bearings on the coupled axles, as in Hawthorn's and Sturrock's, Nos. 10, 13, leads to the same evils in an aggravated form, that characterize the single-wheel engine under the like arrangement. The attachment of the drawplates to the boiler in coupled engines, as in Sturrock's, is also particularly inexpedient, as the outside frame receives and transmits almost the whole of the tractive action, which must, of course, have to pass into the boiler through the lateral brackets a, a, and the fixings b, b, of the inside frames. Hawthorn, in No. 10, arranges better; he makes the best of his general design by fixing the drawplates exclusively to the outside framing.

Outside-Cylinder Locomotives. The application of the principles just discussed, to the conditions of outside-cylinder framing, is pretty obvious. The general practice is to use inside frames with inside bearings on the driving axle, and to bolt the cylinders to the same frames. The cylinders are necessarily external to these frames, and are entirely apart; the benefit of the strong union of inside cylinders together and to the frame being thus unavailable, the framing must be stiffened and bound together by other means. Some makers use merely a single inside plate on each side, with inside bearings to all the axles, as in Stephenson's, No. 20; others, as Crampton, and Allan, Nos. 21, 24, add a second plate outside the wheels, with outside bearings for the carrying axles. The double framing is preferable, as it gives outside bearings, which are more important for stability than with inside cylinders; it also strengthens the connection of the cylinders by giving them an additional hold, and it stiffens the whole frame generally. When all the wheels are coupled, an outside frame-plate is not expedient.

Examples of Locomotive-Framing; Discourse on the contents of Diagram-plate 7.—A specific notice of each example will afford scope for the illustration and application of the principles of framing; and, according to Mr. Bourne's favourite method of instruction, we shall show what to avoid, as well as what to imitate.

Inside-Cylinder Framing.—Nos. 1 and 3 are examples of the original compound-framed engine, in which the axle bearings, a, a, were outside the wheels, w, w, and the driving axle, d, had auxiliary bearings, b, b, inside; as the latter bearings gave way, and the axle depended upon the outer bearings alone, it obviously became liable to very unfair straining from the transverse action of the steam-pressure through the connecting rods c, c. The draw-bar was coupled at d, to the frame of No. 1, and to the firebox of No. 3, in the latter of which it is plain that, when the inside bearings fell slack, the labour of traction devolved chiefly upon the outside frame, and acted through the brackets, a, a, upon the boiler, from which it passed off at d. Thus, while the brackets in No. 1, were strained and shaken loose at the outset, and so long as the inside bearings were good, in transmitting the tractive action to the outside frame; those in No. 3 were strained and worked only *after* the inside bearings fell into disorder. So far, the second was an improvement on the first; but either way, the evil of indirect connection was sufficiently experienced.

In No. 2, by Bury, the framing and the axle-bearings a, a, were exclusively inside, and the draw-centre d was sustained by the frame, quite clear of the boiler. Thus, all the action was confined between the wheels, and the driving axle was supported close to the cranks, much to its advantage.

No. 4, (reduced from Plate II.), is the matured plan of framing adopted by Sharp, and by Fairbairn, at the present day, for single engines. The frame-beams, n, o, are carried up to the buffer-beam p, and bolted to it; they are also bound together by the motion-plate m, and by the cylinder-castings q, and the plating r, rivetted with angle-iron. The insides terminate at the firebox, and the outsides are bound behind the boiler, with plates, s, to which is attached the draw-gear. The driving axle has large inside and outside bearings. This style of framing is rigid in its way; yet we have seen cases in which even Sharp's outside frames have broken loose from their fixings to the insides and to the boiler, due to the horizontal wear of the inside axleboxes, their desertion from duty, and the inevitable concentration of the steam-power upon the outside bearings.

No. 5, by Wilson, shows a material deviation from the normal form adhered to by Sharp. The outside framing, n, is entirely relieved of the driving axle and the draw-gear, and carries only the fore and hind axleguards, and is bound by brackets a, a, to the engine and boiler. The inside plates o, exclusively receive the steam-power from the cylinders, q; and they transmit it to the traction-plate s through the firebox, all being rivetted together. This, as already noted, is in bad taste, as though the firebox be a very strongly built structure, and perhaps capable of doing all that is required of it for traction, it should not be seized on all sides in this way; it should be left to its own proper duties, and the inside framing extended independently to the rear, where the fixings for the draw-gear may be directly attached to it. In front, the inside frame-plates terminate flush with the cylinders, and are isolated from the buffer-beam, with the object of saving the engine and gearing from all direct concussion in that quarter. This is, we think, very erroneous practice, as the framing is thereby deprived of the very legitimate accession to its strength in the compact union of the cylinders and inside plates, so fully recognized in No. 4. Cylinders and pistons are no doubt very nice matters; but a shock that would dislocate the cylinder-fixings would smash the outer framing twice over; and it would be better to carry up the insides to the beams, and thus greatly add to the strength of the whole frame, by which collisions, otherwise destructive, might be rendered harmless. If the plan has been found good by Sharp, it cannot be wrong in Wilson's hands.

No. 6, by England, displays much originality and some sound practice. The boiler is totally distinct from the engine, and is at no point in connection with it, except through the steam-pipes; the cylinders are hung between a couple of transverse plates, fixed to the side frames, quite clear of the smokebox, and easily accessible; the frame is further bound by the motion-plate, and by a comprehensive plate *t*, covering the whole area in front of the cylinders, and bolted down. The driving axle is, however, made with outside bearings, and these only; the object being, doubtless, to simplify the framing, by dismissing the usual inside plates; direct connection, certainly, is secured in this way, but the practice of outside bearings for driving axles, and particularly outside bearings alone, is now nearly obsolete, and has been proved by all experience to be unsound, and we need only express surprise at Mr. England ever committing such a blunder. Already, on the Edinburgh and Glasgow Railway, within two years from delivery (1852), this engine is working with its second crank-axle.

No. 7, by Stephenson, is arranged with outside valves and gearing,—that is, outside the wheels. The frame is double, with inside bearings for the driving axles, and outsides to the others; and it is thoroughly bound by the cylinder-castings, which embrace both the inner and outer frame-plates, and, with the buffer-beam fixings, make a very firm connection in front. The insides are bolted to the firebox, which transmit the tractive force to the double drawplates at *s*, rivetted with angle-iron to the whole width of the back of the firebox, and to wings from the side-plates. Here the outside frame is quite clear of the traction, and apart from the impropriety of pulling through the firebox, this frame is of the most solid and durable character. Not so is the frame of No. 8, designed like the other for outside gearing; the inside frames are placed inside, between the cranks and the cylinders, these being widely apart, to clear out for a low boiler; the cylinder-castings are quite separate and are bolted between the outer and inner frame-beams, and these are bound in front only by the buffer-beam, to which they are severally bolted. The driving axle has both outer and inner bearings, the eccentric gear being placed between the wheels and the outer frames. The inside frames are bolted to the front of the firebox, and the drawplate *s*, rivetted to the back; and the end beam of the outside frame is bound to it by the straps, *u, u,* so that the pulls on the outer and inner frames at the driving axle are separately conveyed to the drawplate, as well as through the boiler-stays. As usual, however, the inside bearings wear loose, the pull concentrates in the outer frames, and these, imperfectly trussed as they are, and unprepared for the chances of wear, shake loose from their fixings both with the cylinders and the boiler. The designers, apparently, did not anticipate these consequences, and they seem to have relied solely on the fixings to the inside frames; as

the boiler-brackets do little more than rest upon the outer frames, and are fixed to them by only one bolt each, through the wood. The cylinders, likewise, are fixed to the outer frames with but four bolts each, down through the wood. With these flimsy fastenings, it is plain that the engine could not hold long together; and in the "Queen" on the North British Railway, of this pattern, the outer frame wore loose from the cylinders in the most regular manner, exactly as the play on the inside bearings increased. Smith, of the locomotive department, oblivious of the causes of the dislocation, and therefore unacquainted with the proper remedy, added a few more bolts at the loose points, and merely gave the engine a little more to do before reducing the frame to its wonted condition. And so injuriously do such imperfections operate, that within a year or two of the delivery in June 1849, the driving axle gave way, and was replaced by a new one.

No. 9, by Stephenson, with an intermediate crank shaft, is, in our mind, a practically perfect frame. The inside plates run from end to end, and take the entire straining of the engine. They are firmly united together by the buffer-beam, by the cylinders, and by transverse plates before and behind the firebox, and particularly at the driving axle bearings; also stiffened by a well-considered union with the outer frames. These themselves are made double with timber, at the carrying axle bearings, *a, a.* The drawplates are bound into the rectangular space *s* behind the driving axleguards.

No. 10, by Hawthorn, with the hind wheels coupled, has outside gearing, just inside the wheels; thus the cylinders and cranks are remarkably close. The inside frameplates are, in the primitive style, bolted between the smokebox and firebox, with bearings to the driving axle, and all the axles have bearings in the outer frame. To the outer framing, also, is fixed the drawplate. This is, perhaps, the worst combination we have noticed: the centre lines of the cylinders being so close, the leverage upon the outside bearings and the straining of the axle are unusually severe, and are further increased by the coupling of the wheels, and the facility for applying extra pressure; moreover, the action of the steam must pass wholly through the boiler-stays to the outer frame, and these are all that the frame has to depend upon for stiffness, as the insides are cut short at the smokebox, and have no connection with the cylinders and the buffer-beam. The essential weakness of this framing has been fully experienced in the engines of the North British Railway. The late superintendent on this line, attempted to remedy the defect by taking out the inside bearings altogether (!), when the frames flew to pieces, five crank axles broke in the course of two months, and the destruction was allayed only by replacing the bearings. He also introduced gussets at the smokebox-stays to stiffen them, but, like Smith, he overlooked the radical defects of the engines, which mere tinkering could never amend.

In No. 11, by Kitson and Co., the framing is, upon the whole, very good; the bearings of the coupled axles are inside, the action of the engine is confined to the inside framing, the whole is well and completely bound together. The only objectionable feature is the interpolation of the sides of the firebox in the inside frames; the junctions are made with

2 G

wings on the side plates, which are $\frac{3}{4}$ in. thick, and strongly united to the framing; and make, no doubt, a very durable job.

In No. 12, Mr. Gooch started on the principle that the boiler should be the foundation of the engine, and as the front four wheels are hung in a bogie swivelled to the fore end of the boiler at a, he cut short the ordinary frame at the barrel stays s, probably also to give accommodation for the bogie-springs; he erected a buffer-beam by plates and brackets rivetted to the sides of the smokebox, uses an inside frame for the driving and coupled hind axles, fixes it by two pairs of brackets to the firebox and barrel, and rivets a double drawplate to the back of the firebox. Here, the strain passes from the cylinders, through the boiler and the brackets to the inside frames, and thence through the firebox to the drawplates. We have already expressed our dissent from the system of working through the boiler; the designer has, however, made the best of it by using a $\frac{3}{4}$ in. tubeplate, and $\frac{1}{2}$ in. plates for the lower side of the barrel and the front of the firebox, strongly double-rivetting them together, planting a strong gusset a, in the angle of the smokebox and barrel to carry the pivot, and staying the bottom of the firebox to the gusset with a $1\frac{3}{4}$ in. tie-rod. The difficulties in the way of maturing a first design for high-speed bogie-engines, in this country, sufficiently explain the transitional aspect of this engine; and the success with which engines of this class have been working on the most difficult parts of the South Devon and other railways, will no doubt clear the way for some obvious modifications. It must be added, that the firebox-brackets are so short and form so close a binding that any play between the boiler and the frame is almost inadmissible.

No. 13, by Sturrock, is subject to all the objections to No. 10; and, with three coupled axles, large cylinders, and outside framing, it appears very imperfectly qualified to meet the ordinary working of the engine.

Nos. 14 and 15, by Bury and by Sharp, are excellent designs of framing for goods-engines with all the wheels coupled. The frames are strictly self-contained, simple and direct, and receive and transmit all the straining within themselves. Of the two, Sharp's is preferable, as the cylinders are more thoroughly united to it, the framing itself is simpler, and the two plates are bound together by transverse stays, mutually stiffening each other, and thereby making a lighter frame equally strong with Bury's, of which the two sides are stiff enough to be independent.

Outside-Cylinder Framing.—No. 16, by W. B. Adams, is very simply arranged, and directly connected: two plain bars from end to end constitute the side frames; carrying the cylinders, and with inside bearings for the axles. On the small scale of this engine, less than 12 tons weight, outside bearings for the carrying axle are perhaps not worth providing. To Mr. Adams is due the distinguished merit of having originated the modern light-engine system, so generously and so ably brought forward by Mr. Samuel on the Eastern Counties Railway. In No. 17, by Sinclair, the framing is double, and the cylinders are bolted firmly between the outer and inner plates; these plates are further bound by the smokebox and other transverse plates, which form a complete bond. Outside bearings are given to the carrying axles. No. 18, by Sharp, has plain inside framing, with all

the bearings inside; the frameplates are strongly b between the cylinders with a horizontal plate rivetted angle-iron to the frames and to the smokebox-plate.

No. 19, by Robertson, and No. 20, by Stephenson, inside bearings, are well and simply put together.

No. 21, by Crampton, is an elaborated frame, i respects complete and good. The cylinders are embraced and bolted between the plates, which are widely apart the purpose, and the number and position of transverse confer the most perfect rigidity.

Nos. 22, 23, 24, by Buddicom, J. V. Gooch, and Al are varieties of one general design; outside cylinders in the slightly inclined over the leading wheels; double frame with outside bearings to carrying axles, extended from to end, and independent of the boiler for its action. No is a complicated article, and indicates excessive carefulness in covering weak points, notwithstanding which there is a great defect: the indirect connection of the cylinders with the driving axle; the cylinders are planted over and bound with snugs into the double piece of outside frame n, which leads nowhere, in particular, and which is bound laterally by plates and angle-iron to the inside frame o, carrying the axle. The framing is stiffly bound at, and between the cylinders by the smokebox-plates, and the insides are also stiffened with a thickness of timber and plate, between the firebox and smokebox; the outsides are stiffened in the way over the carrying axles. No. 23, like 22, shows great preparation; it is, however, simpler and is directly connected. The frame is complete at the front, independently of the buffer-beam; the inside plates are single, and are stiffened by a connection with the barrel at mid-length; they are also deflected in front of the firebox to pass clear alongside and are bound at these weak points r r by a transverse plate. These deflections are objectionable, and have been found in working to give way; they are, in short, cases of indirect connection, and the knee brackets at n, n, employed to stiffen the outside frame, might have been applied with more advantage in strengthening the insides. In No. 24 the frame is reduced to the simplest form consistent with outside bearings, everything is direct, and duly stiffened with angle-iron.

Nos. 25, 26, 27, by Sinclair and by Allan, are cases of coupled goods-engines; No. 25, a tank-locomotive, with an intermediate shaft, has a very simple frame and direct connection; the gearing being entirely on the outside, the tanks are ingeniously formed upon the frameplate, to which the bodies are rivetted, thereby stiffening the frame, and superseding the ordinary transverse ties. We should prefer an independent frame, and isolated tanks, as probably less costly, more correct in design, and more readily repaired. No. 26 is a counterpart of Sharp's frame for inside cylinders, No. 15, and is simple and good, as it combines the essentials of a durable and economical frame; the outer angle-iron r, is merely overhung to carry the footplate, and forms no part of the frame proper. No. 27 is a very complete frame, directly and firmly connected, with outside frameplates to take the leading axle journals; these plates are carried out the whole length of frame, and are bound to the cylinders and to the inside framing, with angle-iron. Thus a stiff, light, and durable frame is obtained.

CHAPTER III.

Details of the Frame.

THE longitudinal frame-plates are most commonly of single iron bars, made with the necessary appendages for receiving the cylinders, and forming the axleguards and junctions of the framing. The inside bars are of a rectangular section, varying from 6 by 1 in. thick, for lighter engines of 12 tons and thereabouts, to 8, 9, or 10 in. deep by ¾ to 1¼ in. thick. These sections are observed only where there is no occasion to depart from them: at the cylinders the depth may be increased, and may be more than doubled, where a wide base is required for fixing them, as in Fairbairn's engine, in which the cylinder-flanges cover a depth of 17½ in.; the plate itself is 25½ in. deep to afford a clear conjunction with the side and bottom plates of the smokebox. When the cylinders are outside, an aperture is made through the plate to admit the valve-chest to the interior; or, the plate may be entirely under-cut for the purpose, as in Sinclair's tank-engine. Other makers, as Kitson, make no difference on the frame at this part, and the cylinders are simply suspended from it by flanges. With inside cylinders and outside valve-chests and gearing, this is the most convenient plan, and it also gives freedom for the location of the cylinders, whether the valvechests be in or outside.

Outside cylinders which are inclined upwards to clear the leading wheels, are let into one or both plates of the frame from above, and bolted to it with flanges, the frame being duly depressed to receive them.

The outside longitudinal bars are usually of the same section as the insides; sometimes much thinner, in which case they are stiffened. Allan, and Stephenson, use ½ in. plates, with binding of 2½ and 2 in. angle-iron.

The thickness or the depth of the plates is in some cases increased at parts exposed to the greatest strain. Allan thickens the inside plates from ⅞ to 1¼ inch at the driving axle, for the full length between the neighbouring transverse stays; Stephenson, in his latest plans, makes the depth one-half greater. Buddicom adds a second plate from firebox to smokebox with a ply of wood between.

Some makers adhere to the compound of wood and iron for outside frames with inside cylinders: a beam of oak or pitchpine, usually 3 in. thick, between two 5/16 to ½ in. plates bolted together, as in Fairbairn's and D. Gooch's engine.

The axleguards are either forged upon the frame, and of the same thickness, or are bolted on separately. In single-plate frames, short guards, or such as have the centre of the axle not materially more than 6 in. below the lower side of the frame, may be forged on,—driving axleguards, for example. Where the guards are much longer, as those for carrying axles, with low wheels, they are, with single-plate frames, most commonly made separately, usually in two ½ or ⅝ in. thicknesses, and bolted on together, one on each side of the plate; the two pieces are bound together by the axle-guides and by the foot-tie, and are stiffer than a single piece of their united thickness would be. Hind carrying axleguards, though usually double, may be of a single ⅝ in. plate, as used by Allan. For the short leading guards required in his frames, a single ¾ in. plate is also sufficient, bolted to the outside framing. In double-plated timber frames, all the axleguards are formed in one with the plates; being of thin plate, the long guards should be well stiffened by the axle-guides, which should be carried up between the plates into the timber, and well bolted, as in Fairbairn's engine. Leading guards of thin plates, when not so stiffened, require extra thicknesses rivetted on outside and inside. Without stiffening they always fail; and the longer the guard, and the unsteadier the motion, the more rapidly they do so. A slight increase of thickness gives proportionally a much greater increase of strength and steadiness laterally, as the strength increases as the square of the thickness, and the stiffness as the cube of thickness: an increase from ⅜ to ½ in., for example, nearly doubles the strength; and it much more than doubles the stiffness.

When guards are forged on, the frame, over the slot, should be of the regular depth, at least, and raised if necessary; and the outline above and outside the guards, should be well rounded and gradually filled in. Separate guards bolted on, should also have a wide spread upwards, with a landing of 3 to 3½ feet on the frame, and of its whole depth, and fixed with twelve ¾ in. rivets.

When the cylinders are outside, the leading guards, though carrying, may be forged upon the frame, whether this be inside or out, as in Adams' and Sinclair's tank-engines; for the frame must be deepened to join the cylinders, and may be extended to join the neighbouring guards, which are by so much shortened and stiffened. The same may be done for inside leading guards, with inside cylinders, when the frame is duly deepened.

The inside frameplates should be formed to connect the cylinders and the driving axle as directly as possible, and such that the centre line of action should in side elevation fall within their outline: as in Fairbairn's and Crampton's engines, in which the frame is in this respect perfect; and in Sharp's goods-engine. In Kitson's engine the lines are very much out, and there must be considerable transverse strain on the frame; in Allan's, also, the centre line falls below the frame. As frameplates are in one piece, and are stiffened in various ways, and as the cylinders may be directly and solidly united to them, this objection of indirect action is not felt in practice. When the bearings are all inside, the objections may be removed by binding the lower ends of the guards together; thereby trussing the frame and virtually increasing its depth. To do so efficiently, stiff bars on edge should be applied, checked upon and well fitted and bolted to: as in Sharp's goods-engine, where 2¾ by 1¼ in. bars are used, and in Adams' and Stephenson's tank-engines, in the latter of which 3 by 1 in. bars are applied. In these engines, where the cylinders are outside and behind the leading guards, the bars afford an additional attachment for the cylinders, and greatly add to the general solidity of the structure. Long ago, Bury set an example in the composition of his side frames.

In some engines, as Kitson's, the outside leading guards are tied to the buffer-beams to relieve the frame in resisting concussions; this is particularly useful, where the centre line of the buffers is much below that of the side plates. Outside fore and hind guards are, by some, tied longitudinally; this is not wanted, as their longitudinal strength is abundant. The two feet of each guard should in all cases be tied by plates or castings checked upon and bolted to them; and when the guards are inside, each pair may with great advantage be bound transversely, by rods bolted to the foot ties, as in Sharp's goods-engine, where tie-bars $2\frac{1}{4}$ by 1 in. are applied. Thus the lateral strength of both guards is combined, and this is an advantage unavailable by outside guards, as the wheels are in the way. For the same reason that the inside framing should run by the centre line of the engine, the continuation should comprise the line of traction joining the axle to the drawbar. The traction-line should be parallel to the rail, to maintain unaltered the distribution of the load on the axles.

The longitudinals are bound transversely at several points; particularly at the cylinders, the driving axles, and the draw-gear. Inside cylinders make a first-rate bond for inside plates, as already explained, and, in Stephenson's engine with outside valvechests, the castings are joined also to the outside plates, and firmly unite the whole framing; where this is not done with double framing, efficient junctions at the cylinders should be effected with the outside plates, as in Fairbairn's or Kitson's engine, to fortify the whole structure against concussions. When the cylinders are outside, the inside plates, deprived of their aid, are strongly bound by one or both of the smokebox-plates, as in Sharp's and Buddicom's engines; or, what is better, by the tubeplate and an extra plate at the extreme front, extended to join the outside plates, as in J. V. Gooch's and Allan's. Either way, the frame is completed in that quarter independently of the buffer-beam. Outside plates, when present, are firmly bound to the insides by the cylinders, with flanges. Between the cylinders and the driving axle, about mid-way, the motion-plate, or "belly-stay," is placed, being a transverse plate which, with inside cylinders, carries the guide-bars, and, with outsides, merely binds the frameplates; and is, in the latter case, supplemented by exterior plates to carry the bars, overhung as in Sinclair's goods-engine, or bound to the outer plates when present, as in Allan's. In the former case, where there are outside plates, there are also extra bindings to unite them to the insides. Behind the driving axle, in front of the firebox, another transverse plate unites the inside plates, when these are continued past the firebox; if they terminate there, brackets are rivetted to the firebox to hold them, as in Wilson's engine. Behind the driving wheels, also, outside plates are united to the insides or to the firebox. Lastly, the end-plate binds up the frame behind, and draw-plates are rivetted to it and to the side frames, as in Fairbairn's and Allan's engines; which are in some cases further united by plates on edge, as in Sharp's goods, and Crampton's, boxing off a sort of draw-chamber, and useful for guiding the drawbar when entered for coupling. When the hind axle is coupled, and the inside plates carried out, a preparation for a single transverse spring is made, in Allan's goods, by a couple of transverse plates bolted to the guides, to which spring-suspenders are bolted mid-way.

The foregoing is the average of the best existing practice. The transverse stays located between the firebox and smoke-box, are by some replaced by indirect isolated stays from the boiler, as in J. V. Gooch's and Stephenson's outside cylinder engines; but the direct junction of the frameplates is the first object, while, as an auxiliary stay, they may very pro-

perly be made to embrace the lower part of the barrel, and be rivetted to it,—at least such as are distant from the fire-box, as in Sharp's goods. Or, wings may be thrown out from the barrel resting upon and bolted to the motion-plate, as done by Allan. Direct junctions may be dispensed with in light engines, as Adams' and Stephenson's tank-engine, and fixings to the boiler used.

The transverse plates properly forming the frame, are usually $\frac{3}{8}$ to $\frac{1}{2}$ in. thick, of at least the full depth of the sides, joining them with knees, and formed to suit the situation. Allan increases the front plate from 9 to 13 in. deep between the inside plates. He turns a $2\frac{1}{2}$ in. flange along one edge of the interior transverse plates, and makes them with 9 to 12 in. knees; he stiffens the outer ones with $2\frac{1}{2}$ in. angle-iron; and also runs lines of $2\frac{1}{2}$ in. angle-iron along the upper edges of the side plates when free to receive it, and fixes the angle-iron with $\frac{5}{8}$ in. rivets, 3 to $3\frac{1}{4}$ in. pitch. In Sharp's goods, the two middle transverse plates are $1\frac{1}{4}$ in. thick, equally set off between the axles, and of which the foremost is also the motion-plate; they are both rivetted with angle-irons to the barrel, and joined with solid shoes to the side plates. They are unusually thick, as the span from smoke-box to firebox, 14 feet, is unusually great, and the action of three coupled axles is thrown upon this part of the frame. In Sharp's tank-engine, with a $10\frac{1}{4}$ ft. barrel, there is but one transverse plate, $\frac{3}{4}$ in. thick.

Motion-plates for inside cylinders are $\frac{3}{8}$ to $\frac{1}{2}$ in. thick, rivetted to the side plates their full depth, and to the barrel; the side plates are in some cases deepened at the junction, to lengthen the attachment, as in Fairbairn's engine.

Openings are made in the motion-plate to clear the connecting rods, and the eccentric-gearing, which very much divides the plate at the middle; and, for economy, Fairbairn makes it in two pieces joined at bottom with a bar of iron; D. Gooch and Wilson keep the two sides distinct; Sharp and others make it in one plate. When continuous at bottom, it supports the eccentric-rod ends in case of a break-down. It is simplified by arranging the eccentric-gearing so as to fall short of it, especially if the shifting link-motion, with stationary valve-rod link, is applied; for it may in this case be carried clear over the gearing, as in Allan's engine.

The junctions of outside plates with the insides, are made at the ends, and usually at three convenient intermediate places, as already described. If made with outside bearings for driving or coupled axles, which happens only with inside cylinders, the union must be very strong. Fairbairn, in his passenger-engine, fits a $\frac{1}{2}$ in. plate, 22 in. long, between the outer and inner frameplates, at the cylinders, and rivets them together with two lines of $2\frac{1}{4}$ in. angle-iron. He also, like Sharp, extends the smokebox front and tubeplates to the outsides; adds wings to the motionplate, $\frac{3}{4}$ in. thick, and welted to it; and rivets wings of $\frac{1}{2}$ in. plate on edge, of great depth, to the sides of the firebox; rivetting them all with angle-iron to the top and inner side of the outer framebeams. When the outside beams are free of the driving axle, as they ought to be, the junctions may be efficiently made by simple extensions of the boiler-brackets. Cylinders outside make a thorough junction in front, and dispense with brackets; and their motion-plates do the same towards the middle, as in Allan's engine. At this point, Kitson inserts two short union plates, on edge, ⅜ in. thick, the whole depth of the side plates, 22 in. apart, and framed with 3 in. angle-iron. At the firebox, Allan inserts a short ½ in. union plate, on edge, joining it with angle-iron; in his goods-engine, where the coupling rods must be cleared, he uses only angle-iron binding. The front extremities of the side plates do not, with cylinders inside, require binding, and are severally bolted direct to the buffer-beam, with flanges turned on them, or with 3 in. angle-iron; with outside cylinders, Allan joins the inside plates with flanges and the outer plates with 2½ in. angle-iron, to the front plate, to which also the buffer-beam is bolted; and to confine the direct buffing action within the scope of the inside plates, which are duly stiffened to meet it, as well as to develope the elasticity of the beam, it is bevelled on the inside for a length of 20 inches at each end, to stand clear of the outer framing. Buffer-beams are usually 6 in. thick, 16 to 18 in. deep, and 7½ to 8 feet long; and the inside frameplates are deepened to 12 or 18 in. at the junction with them; they are mostly of English oak; Sharp makes them of English elm, and Fairbairn, of pitchpine. The hind end of the frame is occasionally made with a timber-beam as in front, but mostly with plate rivetted to the side plates. Drawplates are composed of the footplate and a second plate below, or of two distinct plates, suitably apart, ⅜ to ½ in. thick, and 15 to 18 in. wide, or more; they are rivetted to the side plates, with flanges or angle-iron, and made up with extra thicknesses round the drawbolt. When the draw-plates are fixed to the firebox-shell, they should be closely rivetted to it, along its whole width, with flanges or angle-irons, to diffuse the strain by traction. The drawbolt is 2 in. diameter; sometimes 2½ or 3 in., if the plates are widely apart; it should be made with a shallow head, ½ in. thick, and tapered at the point to enter easily; and may be secured with a cotter below. Two safety-bolts, 1½ in. diam., may be entered, one on each side of the drawbolt, to receive the safety-chains.

CHAPTER IV.

Wheels and Axles.

Axles. Axles consist of three distinct parts:—the body, or shaft; the bosses to receive the wheels; and the journals, or bearings. The principles involved in the form and construction of axles, so as to combine lightness, strength, and durability, will be duly considered when we come to the subject of carriages; meantime we have to indicate the usual form and dimensions of axles for locomotives; and to add some remarks on crank anxles.

Ordinary carrying axles are commonly of uniform diameter in the shaft, between the wheels, 4½ to 5½ or 6 inches, according to the weight of the engine, and the load on the wheels:—usually 5 to 5½ inches, for 18 to 20-ton engines. In Bury's 20-ton passenger-engine, the fore and hind axles are 6 and 5 in.: in D. Gooch's tank-engine of 36 tons, the bogie-axles are 5½ inches; in Stephenson's light tank-engine of 13 or 14 tons, the carrying axle is 4½ inches.

Straight driving axles, for outside cylinders, are from 4½ to 6 inches; most commonly 6 inches, for all sizes of engine. Crank axles, for inside cylinders, are 6 to 7 inches between the cranks; usually 6½ inches. Coupled axles are of the same diameter, or a little less than the drivers, usually 6 inches.

The cheeks of crank axles are made as thick as the design of the machine admits of, consistently with the space required for bearings between the wheels. They are usually rectangular in section, 4 to 5 in. thick by 7½ to 9 inches. D. Gooch, in his tank-engine, on the 7 feet gauge, where there is plenty of room, makes the cheeks 6 inches thick, and 9 to 11 inches broad; and slopes them apart from the crank pin towards the axle, making the whole system as nearly rigid as possible. Hawthorn and others shrink on hoops of wrought iron to add to the strength. We have already shown that the comparative weakness of crank axles is to be ascribed to the radical error of imposing four bearings upon them; and we believe that no power on earth would save them under such conditions. The true policy is to confine the number of bearings to two, and to place them just outside the cranks, as adopted originally and adhered to by Bury.

The inside bearings and pins of crank axles are usually of the same diameter as the body of the axle; the bearings, sometimes, a trifle less, the pins a trifle more. As crank axles fail usually at the pins, it is advisable to make the pin of a large diameter. The pins are 4 to 4½ inches long, usually 4 inches; the bearings 6 to 8 inches long, and by D. Gooch 9 inches. Bury attaches great importance to length of bearing, which he succeeds in making 8 inches, by placing his cylinders and cranks as close as possible, and setting out the wheel-naves. Fairbairn, in his passenger-engine, has only 4 inches length of inside bearing, as he sets out the cylinders and cranks as widely as possible, with a view, we presume, of keeping down the height of the boiler; he, however, like Sharp, depends upon his outside bearing also. Sturrock, in his goods-engines, relies almost entirely on the outside bearings of the driving axle.

For outside cylinders, the crankpin should have about half the diameter of the axle, and the length of journal should be a little more than its diameter. It should be made with a very slight taper, and let into a deep and well fortified boss wrought into the spokes of the wheel. It may be keyed or cottered into cast naves, and rivetted over on the end in wrought naves; the boss, when of wrought iron, may be heated to receive the pin, and to shrink upon it. The same sizes of pin may be adopted for coupled wheels, with inside cylinders, and in this case, the radial distance of the pins is commonly an inch or two greater than the half-length of the stroke, to aid in relieving the coupling rods of the fatigue peculiar to their situation, when the coupled wheels are irregularly worn, and baffle each other. When the cylinders are outside, and the wheels coupled, the pin of the driving wheel must be overhung to admit the coupling rod next the wheel, upon a journal a little larger than that of the connecting rod.

The bearings of coupled axles are made to the same size as those of the driving axle. The bearings of simple carrying axles should in general be outside the wheels, as they may be made of a reduced diameter, and are more conveniently placed than when inside. They are 3½ to 5½ inches diameter, usually 4 inches; and 6 to 6½ inches long.

The bosses for the wheels are usually made 1 to 1½ inches larger in diameter than the neighbouring bearings; and at least as large as the body of the axle, usually larger, by ½ inch or more, so as to receive the keys which fix the wheels without weakening the axle. A large boss is advisable, also, because the larger the diameter, the more leverage it obviously has upon the wheel, and the firmer is the connection made by the keys.

Wheels. The wheels consist of the nave, the spokes or arms, the rim or ring, and the tyre or hoop. Wheels are made frequently with wrought iron rim and spokes, and cast iron naves; but most commonly of wrought iron throughout, the central ends of the spokes being welded together to form the nave. The solid wrought iron wheel, though more costly, is now generally preferred to the wheel with cast nave, as it is generally stronger, lighter, and more durable. For driving and leading wheels, which have tough work before them, solid wrought naves and spokes are almost in all cases used. For single hind wheels we believe cast naves sufficiently good. When cast naves are used in front, the spokes are usually found to hammer loose in the nave; though if means be taken to secure a thorough union of the spoke-ends with the material of the nave, by properly dividing them, and cleaning and heating them in the mould, with other precautions, the cast naves will stand well; and if besides the metal be toughened with an infusion of wrought iron prior to being poured into the mould, a wheel judiciously so made will be found practically as good as one of solid wrought iron. Very much is due to quality of manufacture; even "solid" wrought iron wheels are not really solid in the nave, for the shrinkage of the tyre, if considerable, may be observed to reduce the diameter of the eye. Wrought iron binding hoops shrunk on cast naves are beneficial. Solid cast iron wheels are successfully employed by Sharp in his goods-engines; they are never used for high speeds.

The depth of the nave is usually equal to the diameter of the boss on which it fits, or ½ to 1 inch more, where there is room. The thickness round the axle, when the nave is of wrought iron, is about one-half the diameter; when of cast iron, the thickness is equal to the diameter.

The number of spokes should be simply in proportion to the diameter of the wheel, that the ring and the tyre may in all cases be adequately stayed. Three spokes per foot of diameter, is very general practice; and is such that the spokes join the rim at 11 to 12 inch intervals. D. Gooch and Kitson place the spokes at 10 inch intervals. The spokes are usually made of flat bars with 4 to 6 square inches of section at the nave, 1 to 1½ inches thick, and 3½ to 5 inches wide, with a slight taper towards the rim: being heavier for larger wheels. Thick and narrow spokes are stronger than thinner ones of equal section, and they bear the shrink of the tyre better. Thin spokes in large wheels are liable to yield under the pressure of the tyre, and assume a serpentine form. Allan makes the spokes of his 5 feet wheels 3½ by 1½ inch at the nave, and the wheels are found to be of great strength. Kitson uses spokes of a circular section, 2½ inch diameter, only 4 inches area, and inclines them alternately outwards and inwards, in the style of Bury's original wheel. He thus combines lightness and stiffness, and the peculiar form and set of the spokes enables him to plant them in a cast nave, as he obtains a sufficiency of metal round the spoke-ends, and distributes the strain along the breadth of the nave. This plan gives, we believe, the most generally excellent wheel with cast nave.

The rim is usually 1 inch by 4½ to 5 inches broad, slightly rounded off to the edges. Allan makes it 1¼ inch thick

Of cast iron engine-wheels, only one example (Fig. 264) exists in this country, in Sharp's goods-engines. The wheel is 5 ft. in diameter, cast in one piece; it has 12 spokes, at about 10½ inch intervals on the rim, which with the nave and rim are strongly ribbed. The nave is 2¾ in. thick round an 8 inch boss; and the thickness of metal throughout the spokes and rim averages 1¼ inch. It is, upon the whole, a most excellently proportioned wheel: the metal is well and uniformly distributed.

The tyre, which is the wearing part, and is placed over all, is made of Lowmoor iron, to wear equally and well. It is bored out to a slightly smaller diameter than the rim of the wheel, so that when expanded by heat it may be slipped over the rim, and may shrink on tightly when it is cold. The *shrinkage* measured diametrically, should not exceed 1/16 inch per foot diameter of the wheel. Shrinkage is useful for taking up the slackening of the tyre by rolling out, as it wears; but if too much is given, the wheel is unduly strained, and the tyre is liable to snap.

Tyres are, in general, 5 inches broad, 2 inches thick at the middle of their width, and coned on the outside at the rate of 1 in 20 on the radius, or ½ inch for the whole width of five inches. They have, in some cases, been made only 4¾ or 4½ inches broad, as it is found that the direct wear takes place only on the middle of the breadth; the economy of narrowing the tyre is, however, questionable, as the outer part, though not directly worn, is useful for staving in the middle part, and keeping it to its work. Indeed, the rolling out of the tyre laterally is obvious upon worn tyres. Still further to aid in staving in the wearing parts, Sharp and others make their goods-engine tyres 5½ in. broad. Of course, the more heavily the wheel is loaded, the greater is the lateral tendency to spread. The tyre is sometimes made 2¼ inch thick, and even 2½ inch. It is well, of course, to make a tyre to last as long as possible, but the accumulation of metal about the periphery of a wheel, is a matter of very questionable propriety, particularly in high-speed engines, as it adds to the unsuspended and revolving mass of the engine, and must operate prejudicially upon the rails at irregular points. The flange is usually made to project 1¼ inch from the surface of the tyre, sometimes only 1 or 1½ inch, and though the deeper flange is nominally the safer, there appears no ground in practice for preferring it. The root of the flange is the part that guides the wheel; at this part the flange is well rounded in to the form of the rails, so as to act smoothly, and is sloped off to the summit. The thickness at the middle of the height is from 1 to 1¼ inch; the greater thickness is better, as it gives a stiffer flange, and assists in preventing the lateral displacement to which thin flanges are liable.

In six and eight-wheeled engines, the middle wheels are,

in some cases, deprived of their flanges. This we think is a bad practice, for it only diminishes the security without rendering an equivalent.

Steeled tyres had been for some years worked by D. Gooch, and by J. V. Gooch. In durability they are much superior to plain iron tyres; but when they wear down to the quick, where the iron meets the steel, the wear is necessarily irregular and makes an unsteady wheel.

The tyre is secured to the wheel by conical rivets entered from the outside and rivetted inside the ring, or screwed up with a nut. The rivet or bolt should be made with a long taper to retain its hold while the tyre wears down, and should be of iron not harder than the tyre, so as to wear with it; nor much softer, as it staves in, in course of time, and loses its grip. D. Gooch's fastening, by a continuous dovetail joint, ¼ inch deep on each side of the rim, filled in with melted zinc, appears to be preferable to the bolt or rivet. It has been found to work very well, and is shown in the detail of his tank-engine. The coarser the zinc used, the better is the joint.

The wheels are fixed on the axles by steel keys: usually two for each driving wheel, set at right angles, as in D. Gooch's tank-engine, about 1½ by 1 inch thick, let ½ to ¾ inch into the axle, with 1/16 inch of taper. Allan employs four keys 1¼ by ¾ inch; Sharp, only one key, 1⅞ by ⅞ inch for his cast-iron wheels. Simple carrying wheels are usually fixed with one key, a little smaller than those used for driving wheels.

Plate-wheels, or disc-wheels, formed of solid plates, and dispensing with spokes, are stronger than the latter, offer less resistance to the atmosphere, and raise less dust. For engines, the disc-wheel, though at present hardly known in this country, must eventually supersede the spoke-wheel.

Chilled cast-iron tyres are much used in America for goods-engines, on account of their cheapness and durability. They are put on with a slight taper, and fix themselves on the wheels without the aid of bolts or rivets. The process of replacing worn tyres is thus extremely simplified, and is conducted without removing the wheels from under the engine.

CHAPTER V.

Axleboxes and Springs.

Guides for Axleboxes. The guides, or "cheeks," are most commonly of cast-iron, when they may be conveniently made strong enough; they are planed to fit the guards and suit the axleboxes with perfect accuracy, and to have their working faces parallel. They are in all cases checked upon the guards, which directly take up the longitudinal straining, and so far relieve the bolts; they are made with flanges fitting to the insides of the guards, when these are of a single plate, as in Sharp's goods-engine; or between the plates, when the guards are double, as in Fairbairn's engine; for double-plate guards, attached to single-plate framing, as in Kitson's engine, the interspace is so thin as to require guides of wrought-iron, to have fins sufficiently strong. Allan casts the two guides for each driving guard in one piece, joining them at top and well flanged, to stiffen the guard. The working faces are 4 to 6 in. broad, mostly 4½ in.; with inside bearings they cannot conveniently be had wider. They are 2 to 3 in. deeper than the axlebox, to allow for the vertical play of the latter, and the freedom for play should not be interfered with. In good circumstances, the play rarely exceeds ¾ in., and the clearance should be mostly above the axlebox, to meet the setting of springs. The more permanent the spring, the less will do. Sharp allows 1½ in. above, and ¾ in. below; some allow 1¾ in. above, and others only ⅞ in.; the average practice is 1½ in. above, and 1 in. below. The face is 1 in. thick, and the flanges 1¼ to 1½ in., for single-plate guards; for double-plate guards the flange must be thick enough to occupy the interval of the plates, and is lightened out between the bolts. The bolts for the guides are ¾ or ⅞ in. diam., usually flush-headed and counter-sunk into the frame, and rivetted or screwed up with square nuts inside; at 2½ to 3 in. centres, five or six to each guide. Some engineers prefer the guides entirely of wrought-iron.

Axleboxes. Usually of cast-iron, with brass bushes. For driving, they are 11 to 14 in. deep; for carrying, 9 to 11 in. The depth is much a matter of convenience; yet there should be some relation between the area of guiding surface and the horizontal action upon it. For driving axleboxes, the surface is usually 55 to 60 square inches on each face, and D. Gooch makes it about 70 ins. for the wide gauge; for carrying, it is usually 40 to 50 ins. Flanges are cast on each side of the axleboxes, for their whole depth, to bear on the edges of the guides, and steady the machine laterally; they project ¾ to 1½ in., usually 1 in., and are ¾ to 1 in. thick. The working faces of the axlebox, in contact with the guides, are ¾ to 1 in. thick; for driving axleboxes with underhung springs they should be thicker, as the whole load is borne through the sides of the axlebox, which frequently fail with 1 in. of thickness. With underhung springs, driving axleboxes should be entirely of brass, at least 1½ in. thick at the working faces; Allan does so, and further strengthens them with a wrought-iron strap 2 by ⅝ in., bent over the box, with one end passed down through each face, to take the spring-pin. Sinclair has substituted solid wrought-iron axleboxes with some success; they are of course strong, but do not wear well. More lately, he has successfully employed malleable brass, a compound of zinc and copper, known as Muntz's metal. It is probable that Stirling's toughened cast-iron would meet all the requirements of axleboxes.

The bush is semi-cylindrical inside, and is tightly fitted into the upper part of the axlebox, metal to metal on the top and sides; sometimes with fitting strips at the sides. Bushes are 1 to 1½ in. thick at the crown, and should not be less than 1/16 in. at the sides, to be strong enough to resist compression upon the axle when they wear down. They are usually bevelled off on each outer side to 45°, to economize metal, and the box is cast to fit; Sharp in his goods-engine rounds the outer surface eccentrically with the inner, forming the box with an arched roof to fit; and, to fix the bush laterally and longitudinally, wings are thrown out flush with the crown, which enter suitable recesses in the box. Usually, small flanges are thrown up from the crown, as by Allan, to fix the bush; or a short cylindrical stud, as by Fairbairn; or substantial flanges on the outside, as by D. Gooch, where there is plenty of accommodation.

The bush should be bored out to a diameter $\frac{1}{16}$ in. greater than the journal, that it may lie loosely on the journal, and fit itself gradually; there is thus much less liability of new bushes heating than if closely fitted at first. The bush should be just slack on the journal lengthwise, and no play given. For merely carrying axles, the bush may be close-fitted over only one-fourth of the circumference at the crown, the remaining sides being recessed to a larger radius, to clear the journal entirely. This works well and reduces the chance of heating.

The roof of the box is $1\frac{1}{4}$ in. to $1\frac{1}{2}$ in. thick over the bush, which it follows generally in outline. It is formed at the top with a seat for the spring-rod, when the springs are above; the four walls form the grease-chamber above the roof, filled with tallow and oil for lubrication. Two $\frac{1}{4}$ in. or $\frac{3}{8}$ in. oil-holes are made through the roof and the bush, into which short syphon tubes are screwed, to supply oil or grease to the axle by cotton wicks, the capillary action of which insures constant and regular lubrication; small semicircular grooves are run along the surface of the bush from hole to hole, and sometimes diagonally over the journal, with the object of distributing and equalizing the oil. The diagonal courses are useless, indeed hurtful, as they lead off and waste the oil or grease over the sides of the journal. One horizontal channel in the crown of the bush, connecting the two passages from the chamber above, and extending to nearly both ends of the journal, is sufficient, under proper management, for the lubrication of the working parts. The lower part of the box is closed in by a light casting of $\frac{1}{16}$ or $\frac{3}{8}$ in. iron, accurately fitting between the jaws of the axlebox and up to the journal at each end, being slightly recessed along the interior, to permit a flow of loose oil or grease below; and sustained by one or two $\frac{1}{2}$ in. pins passed through its flanges into the jaws. Sharp makes a flat-bottomed recess, $\frac{3}{4}$ in. deep at the lowest point, which becomes a constant reservoir of oil or grease to lave the journal while running. Allan sinks a chamber, $1\frac{1}{2}$ to $2\frac{1}{2}$ in. wide, the full length of the journal, containing a sponge which imbibes and reproduces the precipitated oil, with excellent effect; while he introduces fresh oil above. He also inserts removable brass oil-vessels into the upper side of the carrying axleboxes, to be cleaned when necessary; for the driving axleboxes, he fixes the oil-vessel upon the side of the boiler, for ready access, and leads the oil through a small tube to the axlebox. These arrangements have been (1853) in operation for ten years, and work well and economically.

The upper chamber is covered by a sheet-iron or brass lid, hinged and closed by a spring, as in Allan's plans, or more usually fitted loosely to and checked upon the guides, closing the chamber by its own gravity. D. Gooch uses this plate and rivets to it a thick leather lining, to close better and to soften vibration. When thus lined, the plate may be cut in two across the journal, and the outer part used as a lid.

Springs. A spring should be uniformly flexible throughout its length, or such that it yields equally at every part; for this object the plates of ordinary plate-springs are suc-

cessively shortened towards the butt or centre. Springs, when loaded within the limits of their capacity for burdens, deflect through sensibly equal spaces for equal additions of load, when the span is sensibly constant; when the compass is considerable, the span sensibly increases with the load, owing to the flattening and spreading of the spring, and in so far causes a slight increase of deflection per ton of load, as the total load is increased. The *elastic strength* of a spring is expressible by the load necessary to cause a given deflection, and, conversely, its *elasticity*, or *flexibility* is expressible by the deflection caused by a given load. The *strength*, simply, or the capacity for burden, is expressible by the greatest load which can be borne without giving way; when overloaded, the symptoms presaging rupture, consist in the greater apparent elasticity of the spring, or its greater deflection under a given increase of load, independently of what may be due to an increase of span. Thus the point at which a decided change of elasticity takes place is an index to the strength of a spring.

The following table of observations on one of the front and middle springs of Sharp's goods-engine, illustrates the constancy of the elasticity for sensibly equal spans, and its slight increase as the load is increased, due to the increase of span.

TABLE, No XCII.—OF THE DEFLECTIONS OF ONE OF SHARP'S PLATE SPRINGS, UNDER GIVEN LOADS.

SPAN IN WORKING ORDER 30 INCHES.

16 plates $\left\{ \begin{array}{l} 2 \text{ of } \frac{1}{4} \text{ in. thick} \\ 14 \text{ of } \frac{5}{16} \text{ in. do.} \end{array} \right\}$ 4 in. broad.

Loads.	Compass, Measured to the Centres of the Spring-bolts.	Total Deflection.	Span, Measured to Centres of Spring-bolts.
cwts.	inches.	inches.	inches.
0	$5\frac{1}{4}$ full	0	$28\frac{1}{4}$
35	$5\frac{1}{16}$	$\frac{1}{4}$	$29\frac{1}{16}$
40	$5\frac{1}{16}$	$\frac{7}{16}$	$29\frac{1}{16}$
45	$5\frac{1}{16}$ full	$\frac{3}{8}$ full	$29\frac{1}{4}$
50	5 full	$\frac{1}{2}$ full	$29\frac{1}{16}$
55	$4\frac{7}{8}$	$1\frac{1}{4}$ full	$29\frac{1}{4}$
60	$4\frac{3}{4}$ bare	$\frac{1}{2}$	$29\frac{1}{16}$
65	$4\frac{1}{2}$ full	$\frac{3}{4}$	$29\frac{1}{4}$ bare
70	$4\frac{1}{4}$ full	$\frac{7}{8}$	$29\frac{1}{4}$ full
75	$4\frac{1}{4}$	1 full	$29\frac{1}{4}$
80	$4\frac{1}{16}$ bare	$1\frac{1}{16}$ full	$29\frac{1}{2}$
85	$4\frac{1}{16}$ full	$1\frac{1}{4}$	$29\frac{1}{2}$
90	$4\frac{1}{8}$ full	$1\frac{1}{4}$	30
95	$4\frac{1}{8}$	$1\frac{5}{16}$ full	30 full
100	$4\frac{1}{4}$	$1\frac{1}{2}$	$30\frac{1}{16}$
After shaking lever.........	$4\frac{1}{8}$	$1\frac{1}{2}$ ($\frac{1}{4}$ in. set)	$30\frac{1}{4}$ full

Here, the flexibility increases from $3\frac{1}{2}$-16ths to 5-16ths inch per ton, when the span reaches 30 inches. This is considerable, and the very sensible extension of span by which it is caused, is due to the great compass of the spring. The absolute strength, and the elastic strength of a spring are, then, different things; and the elasticity is distinct from both. The strength varies as the span inversely, as the number of plates directly, as the square of the thickness of plates, and as the breadth of plates; whereas, the elasticity varies as the cube of the span, as the number of plates inversely, as the cube of the thickness of plates inversely, and as the breadth of plates inversely. Thus, the flexibility increases in a very high ratio with the span, much more rapidly than the strength is reduced. To illustrate:—

If the span be increased as, ... 1. 2. 3. 4.
the strength is reduced as, ... 1. $\frac{1}{2}$. $\frac{1}{3}$. $\frac{1}{4}$.
while the flexibility increases as, ... 1, 8, 27, 64;

'so,

If the thickness of plate be reduced as,	1,	$\frac{1}{2}$,	$\frac{1}{3}$,	$\frac{1}{4}$.
the strength is reduced as, ...	1,	$\frac{1}{2}$,	$\frac{1}{3}$,	$\frac{1}{16}$.
while the flexibility increases as, ...	1,	8,	27,	64.

...at is, for example, if the span be doubled, or the thick-...ss halved, the flexibility is multiplied eight times; also ...e strength is reduced, in the first case, just one-half, and in ...e second case, to one-fourth, but in either case much less ...an the flexibility increases.

In practice, the flexibility of engine bearing-springs varies ...om $\frac{1}{4}$ to 1 in. per ton of load; at times as low as $\frac{1}{8}$ in. ...or prompt and rapid action, to promote stability on the ...ails, to save the framing from twisting strains, and to keep ...he bearings fair, the leading springs should in general be ...he least flexible; they have the most laborious duty, as they have the most to do with irregularities of motion due to the machine and to the way. In ordinary single six-wheel engines, the driving springs should have great elasticity, to follow the rails freely and to maintain the tractive-load as equal as possible; this is the more important, as the driving is the heaviest load, and the rails may sink under it and partially elude it, when the hind wheels are in reserve to take it up. The hind springs should also be very flexible, to give way to the driving springs when they sink, and to ease the motion generally; while they retain sufficient elastic strength to steady the engine. When the wheels are well placed, and the engine well-balanced, an elasticity of $\frac{1}{2}$ in. per ton for the leading springs, and 1 in. per ton for the driving and trailing, may be adopted in practice. When the hind wheels are coupled, the middle and hind springs may be made with $\frac{1}{2}$ in. per ton, of elasticity. For engines much overhung either before or behind, not more than $\frac{1}{2}$ in. per ton should be allowed for the extreme springs; if the overhang be behind, it should be reduced to $\frac{1}{3}$ in. per ton. John Gray saved an overhung long-boiler engine by reducing the hind springs, from 3 ft. to 2 ft. long; thereby the flexibility, previously $\frac{1}{2}$ in. per ton, was reduced in the ratio of 3" to 2", or as 27 to 8, to a trifle above $\frac{1}{8}$ in. In six-coupled goods-engines, which run at low speeds, the flexibility need not, and perhaps should not, exceed $\frac{1}{4}$ or $\frac{5}{16}$ in. per ton. The leading and middle springs of Sharp's goods-engine are adjusted to work at $\frac{5}{16}$ in. per ton, and the hind springs to a flexibility of fully $\frac{1}{2}$ in. per ton,—the greater elastic strength of the latter being very suitably adapted to contend with the overhang of the firebox; though the length of spring is also limited by its proximity to the firebox.

Engine bearing-springs have three varieties of form:— 1st. The oldest and most common form, consisting of plates in close contact throughout their length, with wrought-iron eyes welded on the ends of the back, or longest plate, to which the links are pinned; as in Sharp's and Fairbairn's engines. 2d. The form introduced by Stephenson, in which three or more of the longest plates are brought up to one length; and either pierced at the ends to admit the links, or left solid to rest in shoes or stirrups; as in Kitson's engine. 3d. The form, first used on the Great Western Railway, we believe, in which the plates are parted at the hoop by thinner slips of iron, and touch only at the ends; as in Gooch's engine. In the first and second varieties,

$\frac{1}{16}$ in. plates are commonly used for the body or mass of the spring, and two or more $\frac{3}{8}$ in. plates for the "back" and "short" plates, or the longest and the shortest, because these are outside and are least supported by their neighbours; $\frac{1}{2}$ in. plates are sometimes used, and thicker plates should not be put into close-set springs, as their conversion is less perfect. Spring-plates are in general $3\frac{1}{2}$ or 4 in. broad; Allan, and Sinclair, taper the breadth, from 6 or 8 in. at the middle to 4 or $4\frac{1}{2}$ in. at the ends, with $\frac{3}{8}$ and $\frac{1}{2}$ in. plates. In the third variety of spring, with open plates, the plates are unsupported by each other, and depend more on their individual strength; they are made thicker generally than others, from $\frac{3}{8}$ to $\frac{5}{8}$ in., with $\frac{1}{4}$ in. space-plates. This variety is preferable to the close-plate kinds, where they are exposed to continued damp, and are imperfectly ventilated, as in the position of draw-springs; for, when the plates are close, they retain the moisture, become oxidized or, in common language, rusty and stiff, and they lose their temper. For bearing springs, the ordinary close-plate varieties are, we think, preferable; as they are not known to decay when in active use, and attended to, and besides, thinner and more perfect steel may be used. Of the two close-plate varieties, we should prefer the first, with bolt-eyes worked on the back-plate, as it gives a better form of spring. It admits of a single uniform curvature for all the plates, which is more favourable for free action than the other variety, in which the double curvature, besides being necessarily quicker than single curvature, incurs a tendency to set fast the shorter plates on the longer, or at least to increase their sliding friction. The first variety also admits of a better distribution of metal, as less accumulation at the ends is wanted.

Our preference for thin plates, $\frac{1}{16}$ and $\frac{3}{8}$ in., is confined to springs under $3\frac{1}{2}$ ft. span, and this span is more than ample for all the requirements of ordinary bearing springs; for greater spans of $3\frac{1}{2}$ to 5 feet, $\frac{1}{2}$ and $\frac{5}{8}$ in. plates are more suitable, as they keep down the weight of the spring, agreeably to the laws of deflection, by which extra thickness is much more efficient for rigidity than extra number, and is an exact balance to extra span. It is not want of strength but want of rigidity, that is to be feared in long springs. In general, long springs, above $3\frac{1}{2}$ ft., should, as a matter of economy, be avoided; they are advisable chiefly for spanning the bearings of coupled hind axles, or bearings on the same side of the engine, as in bogie-frames, and other situations where accommodation is limited. The loads on contiguous journals, coupled or single, may be equilibrated by means of short springs and compensating levers in any of the ways already described elsewhere.

The ends of each plate in a spring are finished either to the full breadth, and "drawn" or tapered in thickness; or are "spear-pointed," that is, tapered in the width to an angle of 45°, and of the full thickness. The latter is the cheaper, the former possesses the better action. The outer contour of the spring embracing the tips of the plates, should be finished so as to conform as nearly as practicable to a parabolic outline when the spring is flat, to secure uniformity of strength. The outline so determined defines the proper length of each plate. The compass of the spring unloaded is a measure of the curvature of the plates; and well-formed springs work most freely when so loaded as to reduce the back plate nearly straight, as the frictional action of the plates on each other is then least. The compass is frequently so adjusted, as to turn out a nearly flat spring when loaded; but it is most usually made two to four times the deflection due to the anticipated load. Sharp makes the span equal to 5 or 6 times the original compass, or about 7 times the loaded compass; D. Gooch makes the span 13 times the loaded compass, and in many cases much more, when the spring becomes nearly flat. These are the extremes of practice. Springs should be qualified to carry just about twice the load for which they are designed, so that, when weighted, they may be strong enough to bear an occasional increase of load, and also heavily enough loaded to keep them constantly on tension under ordinary fluctuations. If an over-strong spring be lightly loaded, the load merely dances upon the spring, and the result is a disagreeable hard vibration. The greatest average play of axleboxes vertically is 1 inch, or $\frac{1}{2}$ in. up and $\frac{1}{2}$ in. down; all springs should therefore be deflected *at least* $\frac{1}{2}$ inch, whatever more, under their loads.

The plates of springs are kept fair with each other by studs punched up at the ends of each plate entering slots in the contiguous plates; also by the hoop at the centre or butt, which is shrunk on and binds the whole together. The hoop is of wrought-iron 3 to 5 in. broad, $\frac{1}{2}$ to $\frac{3}{4}$ in. thick in the top and sides, and about $\frac{3}{4}$ in. in bottom; as usually applied, it receives the end of the spring-rod, and gives it a bearing. The rod is of round or flat iron according to its position; it is guided in sockets rivetted or let into the frames, and rests upon the axlebox. Sturrock fits a plate iron cover over the whole area of the axlebox, to receive the thrust of the rod. With single-plate framing, the rod is sometimes double, and may be formed either in two pieces with independent bearings, or in one piece doubled up and resting in a semicircular bearing on the axlebox, as in Kitson's engine. The links are pinned with eyes to the spring and the frame with $1\frac{1}{4}$ in. bolts; and are usually either plain or forked, with double-screw and jam-nuts to adjust loads and levels. Kitson makes them stirrup-form to embrace the ends of the springs, leaving these entire without slots or other inroads.

Rules anent Springs. The whole subject of springs is in the hands of empiricists, who work by thumb and by rote. The most important principles concern the relations of the flexibility to the span and the thickness of plates; the others may be safely assumed, and we shall try what can be done in turning the principles to practical account.

First, of the relation of span and flexibility in springs of similar form. The springs of Sharp's goods-engine supply a very good example in point: the middle springs have 16 plates and 30 in. span; the hind ones 12 plates and 22 in. span. The elasticity is proportional to the number of plates inversely, and to the cube of the span; or in the united ratios,

12 to 16

and 30^3 to 22^3, or 27000 to 10648,

which, being multiplied together, give a final ratio of 2 to 1 very nearly. This is the actual ratio of the elasticities, which are $\frac{1}{16}$ and $\frac{1}{32}$ in.

Again, from amongst a number of springs tested on the Great Western Railway, the following cases are selected:—

Span.	No. of Plates.	Section.	Elasticity.
(1.) 2 ft. 11 in.	6	$3 \times \frac{1}{2}$ in.	$\frac{1}{2}$ in. per ton. (mean of two)
(2.) 6 ft. 3 in.	6	$4 \times \frac{1}{2}$,,	$4\frac{1}{4}$,, ,,
(3.) 9 ft. ,,	12	$4 \times \frac{1}{2}$,,	$5\frac{1}{2}$,, ,, (mean of three)

Increasing the elasticity in the 2d and 3d cases, for 3 inch plates, in the proportion of 3 to 4, we have the results in the first row following, for comparison with those in the second row, in which, for the 2d and 3d cases, the elasticity due to the spans and numbers of plates, is deduced from the observed elasticity in the first case, in the ratio of the number of plates simply and the cube of the spans.

	(1.)	(2.)	(3.)
Elasticity reduced for 3 in. broad,...	$\frac{1}{2}$ in.	$5\frac{1}{2}$ in.	7 in.
Do. in terms of span and number of plates, according to the given ratios, ...	$\frac{1}{2}$ in.	5 in.	$7\frac{1}{2}$ in.

These results of calculation so obviously agree with experiment, and in such very extreme cases, that it is deemed unnecessary to adduce further evidence on this head.

Next, as to the relation of the thickness of plates to the elasticity. In the same set of experiments, we find as follows:—

Span.	No. of Plates.	Section.	Elasticity.
(1.) 6 ft. 2 in.	16 $\begin{cases} 2 \\ 14 \end{cases}$	$4 \times \frac{3}{8}$ in. $4 \times \frac{1}{4}$,,	9 in. per ton.
(2.) 6 ft. 3 in.	6	$4 \times \frac{1}{2}$,,	$4\frac{1}{4}$,, ,,

Taking the liberty of exchanging the two $\frac{3}{8}$ in. plates for seven $\frac{1}{4}$ in. plates, as of equal strength according to the law of the cubes; allowing, also, for the difference of span, we find that

	(1.)	(2.)
by experiment the elasticities are ...	9 in.	and $4\frac{1}{4}$ in.,
and by the given ratios, in terms of span and thickness of plates, ...	9 in.	and $4\frac{1}{16}$ in.;

showing that the elasticity varies in practice according to the cube of the thickness of plate.

Having found that the received laws of deflection apply with great exactness to steel-plate springs of good material, a good practical formula may readily be constructed.

Let l = the length or span, in inches, when loaded.
  b = the breadth of plates in inches, supposed uniform.
  t = the thickness of plates in sixteenths of an inch.
  n = the number of plates.
  z = the elasticity in sixteenths of an inch per ton of load.
  m = a constant coefficient.

Then, by the laws of deflection,

$$z = m\,\frac{l^3}{b\,t^3\,n}.$$

To find the value of m, take a known case: the leading and middle springs of Sharp's goods-engine; these have 16 plates, of which two are $\frac{3}{8}$ in., and the others $\frac{5}{16}$ in. The $\frac{3}{8}$ in. plates must be replaced by an equivalent number of $\frac{5}{16}$ in., in the ratio of the cubes of the thicknesses inversely, as 5^3 to 6^3, or 125 to 216; then $2 \times 216 \div 125 = 3\frac{1}{2}$ plates is the number, to be added to 14, and making a total of $17\frac{1}{2}$ plates $\frac{5}{16}$ in. thick, equivalent for deflection to the plates actually used. The plates being thus reduced to one thickness, the formula becomes available; and $l = 30$, $b = 4$, $t = 5$, $n = 17.5$, $z = 5$. Substituting these values we have

$$5 = m\,\frac{30^3}{4 \times 5^3 \times 17.5}, \text{ and } m = \frac{4 \times 5^4 \times 17.5}{30^3};$$

reducing, we find 1·62, or say, as a round number, 1·66, for the value of the coefficient, and we have, finally, the working formula,

$$E = 1{\cdot}66 \frac{l^3}{b\, t^3\, n}, \qquad \ldots \qquad \ldots \quad (1.)$$

by which the elasticity of any given spring may be found; and by inversion, the length, or the number of plates, required for a given elasticity, and size of plate, may also be found. Whence the following rules:—

Rules for the Elasticity of Springs:—

Rule I. *To find the elasticity of a given steel-plate spring.* Multiply the breadth of the plates in inches by the cube of the thickness in sixteenths,—and by the number of plates;—divide the cube of the span in inches by the product so found,—and multiply by 1·66. The result is the elasticity in sixteenths of an inch per ton of load.

Rule II. *To find the span due to a given elasticity, and number and size of plates.* Multiply the elasticity in sixteenths per ton by the breadth of plate in inches,—and by the cube of the thickness in sixteenths,—and by the number of plates;—divide by 1·66,—and find the cube root of the quotient. The result is the span in inches.

Rule III. *To find the number of plates due to a given elasticity, span, and size of plate.* Multiply the cube of the span in inches by 1·66;—multiply the elasticity in sixteenths by the breadth of plate in inches,—and by the cube of the thickness in sixteenths;—divide the former product by the latter. The quotient is the number of plates.

Note 1. The span and elasticity are those due to the spring *when weighted.*

2. When extra thick back and short plates are used, they must be replaced by an equivalent number of the prevailing thickness, prior to the application of the rules; this is found by multiplying the number of extra plates by the cube of their thickness, and dividing by the cube of the ruling thickness. Conversely, the number of plates of the ruling thickness require to be removed to make room for a given number of extra thick plates, may be found in the same way.

3. It is assumed that the springs are similarly and regularly formed, and that the plates are of uniform width, and but slightly tapered at the ends. Also, that the steel is of best quality.

4. Rules might with equal facility have been made for finding the suitable width and thickness of plates; but these data are usually predetermined, and they may be found, if required, by a few trials with the rules given.

Examples. To find the elasticity of the Great Western 35 in. spring, with 6 plates 3 by ⅜ in., already discussed. By Rule I.,

$$\frac{35^3}{3 \times 6^3 \times 6} \times 1{\cdot}66 = 7{\cdot}8 \text{ sixteenths, or } \tfrac{1}{2} \text{ in. very nearly;}$$

which was the elasticity actually observed. Likewise, the elasticities of the 6½ and 9 ft. springs quoted at the same place, are found by the same rule, 3 $\frac{9}{16}$ and 5 $\frac{5}{16}$ in., and they were 4½ and 5½ in. by experiment.

To construct rules for the simple strength of springs, or at least for finding the greatest working loads they should bear in practice, we shall as before take Sharp's spring as a standard. Continuing the same notification, and making s = the working strength or load in tons, we have by the laws of strength,

$$s = m \frac{b\, t^2\, n}{l}.$$

The ⅜ in. plates must be replaced, as before, by an equivalent number of $\frac{5}{16}$ in. plates, in the ratio of the squares of the thicknesses inversely, or as 25 to 36; then 2 × 36 ÷ 25 = 3 plates is the number, to be added to 14, making a total of 17 plates $\frac{5}{16}$ in. thick, of equal strength. The working strength, also, is 5 tons; and by substitution, we have

$$5 = m \frac{4 \times 5^2 \times 17}{30}; \text{ and } m = \frac{5 \times 30}{4 \times 5^2 \times 17} = \frac{1}{11{\cdot}3};$$

and finally the working formula

$$s = \frac{b\, t^2\, n}{11{\cdot}3\, l}, \qquad \ldots \qquad \ldots \quad (2.)$$

from which the following rules are derived:—

Rules for the Working Strength of Springs:—

Rule IV. *To find the working strength of a given steel-plate spring.* Multiply the breadth of plates in inches by the square of the thickness in sixteenths,—and by the number of plates;—multiply, also, the working span in inches by 11·3;—divide the former product by the latter. The result is the working strength in tons burden.

Rule V. *To find the span due to a given strength, and number and size of plate.* Multiply the breadth of plate in inches by the square of the thickness in sixteenths,—and by the number of plates;—multiply, also, the strength in tons by 11·3;—divide the former product by the latter. The result is the working span in inches.

Rule VI. *To find the number of plates due to a given strength, span, and size of plate.* Multiply the strength in tons by the span in inches;—and by 11·3;—multiply, also, the breadth of plate in inches by the square of the thickness in sixteenths;—divide the former product by the latter. The result is the number of plates.

Rule VII. *To find the required original compass of the spring.* Multiply the elasticity in inches per ton by the working strength in tons;—add the product to the desired working compass. The sum is the whole original compass; to which an allowance of ¼ to ⅜ in. should be added for the permanent setting of the spring.

Note 1. The span is that due to the form of the spring when weighted.

2. Extra thick plates must be replaced by an equivalent number of plates of the ruling thickness, before applying the rules. To find this, multiply the number of extra plates by the square of their thickness, and divide by the square of the ruling thickness. Conversely, the number of plates of the ruling thickness to be removed to make room for a given number of extra plates, may be found in the same way.

Example. The hind spring of Sharp's goods-engine has 12 plates, $\frac{5}{16}$ and ⅜ in., by 4 in., and a 22 in. span loaded. What is the working strength? Reducing the ⅜ in. plates, the equivalent number of $\frac{5}{16}$ in. plates is 13. Then, by Rule IV., the strength is

$$\frac{4 \times 5^2 \times 13}{22 \times 11{\cdot}3} = \frac{1300}{248{\cdot}6} = 5 \text{ tons,}$$

which is the same as that of the fore springs.

Springs should be placed over, rather than under the axle-boxes, as they suspend better, and work more freely, above than below. Above, they naturally keep their place, and swing right without any constraint; but below, when suspended as under Allan's driving axleboxes, for example, their tendency is to escape the load and swerve aside, fore or aft. This oblique action strains the connections, and particularly the spring-shackle, occasionally shifting its place on the spring, and driving the end-links out of their just positions. When the end-links are comparatively short, as in the leading spring of Allan's goods-engine, the objectionable tendency is all the greater, and to resist this tendency the shackle requires to be strongly and firmly connected to the axlebox. When the springs are required to be underhung, it is preferable either to dispense with end-links, and to give the spring-ends plain bearings on flat surfaces, as in Kitson's engines; or, what is better, though less simple, to couple the ends with reversed links, in the style of the bogie-springs of D. Gooch's tank-engine, which are found to work beautifully. The object in all cases should be to place the end-links on tension, and not in a state of compression; as the equilibrium in the former case is stable, in the latter unstable.

To adjust the loads on the respective axles, if three in number, the links of at least one pair of springs are usually made with a screw adjustment. If the springs be of good material and properly compassed and tested, the variable links are unnecessary. In six-coupled-wheel engines they are not required. In passenger-engines, there are usually one or two pairs of springs so fitted, to adjust them to the loads and to the weather; two pairs are necessary when the level of the engine requires adjustment.

The whole subject of axleboxes and springs will be revised when we come to the treatment of carriage and waggon-stock.

CHAPTER VI.

ANATOMICAL DISCUSSION OF THE ENGINE:—CYLINDERS AND VALVE-CHESTS.

IN the following discussion of the engine, it is to be observed that the dimensions given and the designs recommended have reference generally to engines with the usual 15 to 18 inch cylinders, except when otherwise stated. No attempt is made to generalise for all classes of engines; particular cases may be worked out according to the discretion of the designer.

The cylinders are universally of cast iron, and should be hard and homogeneous, to wear well and equally. They have, to be sure, been made, in a few instances, of wrought iron; and though lighter than cast iron ones, and perhaps more durable, those of wrought iron are very much costlier, and are not likely to come into general use. D. Gooch employs toughened cast iron for his cylinder-castings—that is, a mixture of wrought and cast iron; this is, we believe, the only proper application of wrought iron for locomotive-cylinders, and it works well.

In setting out cylinders, the chief points to be observed are, to place the cylinders and valve-chests as conveniently as possible clear of the wheels, to bind them well and solidly together and to the frames, to have them easy of access and easy for repairs, to limit the clearance as much as practicable,

and to make the steam-ways wide and easy, having a direct and sufficient exhaust passage.

The conditions for well-placing the cylinders have already been examined in treating of the frame physiologically. The valve-chest is usually cast in one piece with the cylinder, and so placed that the valve works on edge; the valve-face, or table of the cylinder, being vertical, and a simple and direct connection for the valves being obtained. The cylinders are fixed with flanges cast upon them, and extending their entire length, which are well fitted and bolted to the frame-plates. This is done in a great variety of ways, displaying more or less solicitude on the part of the designers to effect a firm and durable union. Inside cylinders may be very completely bound, as they may, from their proximity, be bolted together, throwing the two valvechests into one, and bolted by outer flanges to the frameplates; thus making a very perfect union, the frame and the cylinders binding and stiffening each other. Some makers, as Sharp, and Fairbairn, bolt inside cylinders to the frameplates by flanges above and below, deepening the framing for the purpose. Others, as Kitson, and Wilson, are content with hanging the cylinders from the frame by upper flanges alone; in this way, a simpler frame is used, and, the cylinders being underhung, there is freedom for their lateral adjustment. Stephenson, with his outside valve-gear and underhung cylinders, makes a beautiful and solid bond by throwing up four flanges to join the four inner and outer frameplates, and by joining the cylinders together, enclosing the exhaust passage between them.

Outside cylinders are placed above, below, or against the outside of the framing; in the latter case, of course, the framing being exclusively inside. When inclined upwards, flanges are thrown down to the framing on which they rest, in which case the framing should be double to afford a firmer and more central union by means of two distinct flanges, as done by Allan and by J. V. Gooch. When the cylinders are horizontal, they are either underhung from double framing, as done by Sinclair in his tank-engine, or bolted by upper and lower flanges to the inside frameplate; in both cases, they usefully stiffen the frameplates, and strengthen the leading axleguards. When the cylinders are placed behind the leading wheels, as in the smaller tank-engines by Adams and by Stephenson, they may be very completely fixed at the double points of attachment afforded by the frameplates, and the tie-bars uniting the lower ends of the axleguards.

To add to the security of the cylinder-fastenings, when either underhung, as by Kitson, or overhung, as by Allan, the flanges may be extended along the frame and bolted beyond the cylinders, as done by those makers.

A number of stiffening ribs are inserted transversely, to stiffen and bind the junction-flanges together and to the body of the cylinder.

The cylinders are made open at the ends, and closed by cast iron covers. At each end they should be made a little larger in diameter, just beyond the space traversed by the piston, to receive the debris of grease, priming, &c. that may be pushed over by the piston. The front cover, also, is turned to fit the wider part, and the extra width is supposed to be at least as great as the total allowance for re-boring. The hind end of the cylinder is usually cast with a reduced circular opening 5 or 6 inches less than the diameter of the cylinder, and is fitted with a smaller cover to suit. The reduction, which is equivalent to adding an inside flange to the cylinder, is supposed to add materially to its strength, and it makes a more compact union with the cover, where space is an object. The hind cover is in some cases entered from within, as by Allan; but it should be put on from without like the front cover. J. V. Gooch, in his tank-engine, casts the hind cover, with its stuffing box, in one piece with the cylinder, by which all junctions at that part are dispensed with. The covers should make truly cylindrical joints with the cylinder; the front covers have in some cases, as in J. V. Gooch's early engine, been made with conical joints, the tendency of which was to split the cylinder, when the bolts were screwed up; and it did so frequently.

The clear inside length of the cylinder is necessarily equal to the stroke, plus the thickness of the piston, plus the clearance off the cover at each end. The clearance is from $\frac{1}{4}$ to $\frac{1}{2}$ inch at each end, most commonly $\frac{3}{8}$ inch, and is provided as a safety-space, to allow for variations of the length of the connecting rod and other causes affecting the precise position of the piston in the cylinder; it is useful also as a refuge for mud or other accumulations, and for water in the cylinder, whether by priming or by condensation.

The steam-ways are cast in one with the cylinder, and on one side, terminating in the flat table or valve-face, on which the valve works, and where the distribution is conducted. The sectional area of the steam-way is the chief item of calculation, and it matters little whether the passage be long and narrow, or short and wide: the particular dimensions are matters of convenience. The length of the steam-ports in the valve-face, is usually about two-thirds of the diameter of the cylinder, and the passage is continued of the same section to the cylinder. The face of the table usually projects at least $\frac{1}{4}$ inch above the surrounding level, to keep the surface clear, and to allow depth of metal for wear; and the passages should penetrate the table-surface perpendicularly for at least $\frac{1}{2}$ inch. The steam-passages are usually run partly into the covers at both ends of the cylinders, to reduce the amount by which they would otherwise cut into the body of the cylinder, and consequently also the amount by which the piston would overhang the opening, when at the end of the stroke.

The ports are usually finished with sharp rectangular corners in the valveface. Allan slightly rounds the angles, and this is found to wear better and more evenly with the valve, the sliding surfaces being liable to wear into grooves and ridges, particularly at the angles. Uniformity of wear is promoted by so adjusting the length of the table that the valve may considerably overshoot it at each end of the stroke.

The valvechest, though usually in a piece with the cylinder, is by some makers, as Allan and D. Gooch, bolted to it; the latter bolting the chest between the two inside cylinders. The separate casting permits of a more convenient access to the cylinder-table for planing and dressing. It should be roomy enough to allow the valve full play, and to allow the free circulation of steam round it. It should have deep fitting strips on the sides, by which it may be planed and fitted to the table, and which may also act as guides and sliding-surfaces for the valve, and so far relieve the spindle. The cover required for the valvechests of outside cylinders, is usually of $\frac{1}{2}$ or $\frac{5}{8}$-inch plate-iron, forming the back of the chest, and affording the means of access to the inside. With inside cylinders and valvechests, where the chest is narrow, the cover is applied in front, as the best available point of access; and sometimes also at the back. In the broad-gauge engines, where there is plenty of room, the cover is applied below, and forms the bottom of the chest; entrance being effected through the bottom of the smokebox. In Sharp's goods-engine, where the valves are underhung, and the valve-faces nearly horizontal, the whole bottom and ends of the chest are removable when required. Stephenson's outside valvechest has the cover on the outside, and is certainly in the most accessible of all positions.

The body of the cylinder is usually $\frac{3}{4}$ inch thick, sometimes $\frac{7}{8}$ inch, and even $1\frac{1}{16}$ inch in goods-engines; the steam-passage and valvechest are $\frac{5}{8}$ to $\frac{3}{4}$ inch thick; the flanges and the end covers of the cylinder and the chest, generally $\frac{3}{4}$ to $1\frac{1}{4}$ inch thick; usually 1 inch, though the cylinder-covers and the frame-flanges are sometimes $1\frac{1}{2}$ or $1\frac{3}{4}$ inch, particularly the flanges, when the cylinders are much underhung, as in Kitson's engine.

All the joints about the cylinders are made metal to metal. The covers of the cylinders and valvechest are fixed with stud-bolts and nuts. The bolts in the cylinder-covers are $\frac{3}{4}$ to 1 inch diameter, placed at $5\frac{1}{2}$ to 7 inch centres; in the valvechest-covers they are at 3 to 4 inch centres. Inside cylinders are bolted together at the valvechest-joint, with $\frac{3}{4}$ to 1 inch bolts and nuts, at $3\frac{1}{2}$ to $4\frac{1}{2}$ inch centres. As to the fixings to the frame, when the cylinders are inside and bolted together, and are bolted to the frame-sides both above and below their centre lines, 10 or 12 one-inch bolts and nuts to each cylinder are sufficient; but when either underhung or overhung, laterally or vertically, 16 to 20 bolts and nuts are applied, $\frac{3}{4}$ to 1 inch, usually 1 inch diameter, to withstand the unavoidable leverage of the steam-pressure upon the cylinder-fixings.

The foregoing data apply to ordinary cylinders, 15 to 18 inches diameter. For smaller diameters, of course, less elaborate preparations will suffice. With Bury's exceptional frame, only four holding bolts are applied for each cylinder; wings being thrown out and fitted to the lower sides of the frame-bars, and keyed up between snugs welded upon them. Thus the bolts are relieved by the snugs from the longitudinal straining on the cylinders.

For valvechest-covers, exposed to smoke and dust in the smokebox, brass nuts are preferable to iron, as they slack off more easily; and the depth of the nuts should be greater than the projection of the bolt-ends, for the same reason. In some cases the nuts are capped, and entirely enclose the bolt.

Stuffing-boxes and Glands. The stuffing-boxes are cast in one piece with the hind cylinder-cover and valvechest to which they belong; the former carries also the ears or fixings for the guidebars, thus properly identifying the parallel motion as a continuation of the cylinder. The stuffing-space round the piston-rod is $\frac{1}{4}$ to $\frac{3}{8}$ inch, and the box is deep enough to hold 3 to 5 inches of stuffing; round the valve-rod there is usually a ½ inch space, 2 to 3 or 3½ inches deep. The box is fitted with a short brass necking to guide the piston-rod, and the gland is of brass turned to fit the box exactly. The necking and the gland are hollowed out towards the stuffing, to bring it to bear upon the rod when under pressure. The gland is set up by two stud-bolts tapped into the box, passing through wings cast on the gland, with a nut and jam-nut to each. A small oil-chamber is usually cast on each gland, to oil the rod, fitted with a syphon passage, and hinged cover. The valve-rod is continued for support through the front of the chest, and works in a second stuffing-box and gland. This front gland is, in some cases, finished with a close chamber, as in Allan's engine, in which the valve-rod works; or is made a fixture and screwed in, as in J. V. Gooch's. In these cases, small holes should be drilled for the escape of the leakage. The open stuffing-box appears to be preferable.

Water-cocks are tapped into the cylinder-castings at the lowest points, to draw off the water that accumulates within. There should be one to each end of the cylinder, and one to the valvechest if exposed, or in a low position, as in Sharp's goods-engine. They should have a ¼ or $\frac{5}{16}$ inch bore; not larger, for when the engine runs with them open, there is of course a considerable escape of steam. They should be connected and worked by a handle at the footplate.

Grease-cocks are used for the lubrication of the cylinders and valves, for which melted tallow is employed. There should be one tapped into the front corner of each cylinder, and one let into the side of the smokebox with a tube to each valve; though several makers are content with the cylinder-cocks only, leaving to the exhaust steam the lubrication of the valve with what it can carry off with it. Others use no grease-cock at all, and inject the tallow through the water-cocks at starting. Steam itself is a lubricant, for we know that engines running without steam are liable to heat their pistons if not otherwise lubricated; and, on hilly lines, where the engines have long distances to run without steam, the grease-cocks should be made double, with a reservoir, as used by Sinclair, on the Caledonian Railway, from which tallow may be discharged into the cylinder at the proper points of the road.

CHAPTER VII.

Pistons and Piston-Rods.

Pistons are in three parts: the body, keyed on the rod, the cover or junc-ring, screwed to the body, and the packing rings, between the body and the cover. The body and cover are usually of cast iron or of brass, most commonly the latter; brass is preferable to iron for pistons, not only as it is lighter, but also as it ruptures less readily under the action of priming, slack bolts, and other obstructions, and gives warning of their presence. They have been proposed to be of wrought iron, for the sake of lightness and strength; but a piston may be too strong, for it is better that the piston should yield, than that the cylinder should be fractured. The rings are generally of cast iron, occasionally of brass, and have been proposed of steel; steel is liable to fracture, and to grip and cut the cylinders; brass works sweetly, and acts lightly on the cylinder, but it wears rapidly, and requires frequent inspection; cast iron is generally the best material for packing rings, as it is the most durable, and if properly attended to when newly put in, the rings wear well and smoothly, polish and preserve the cylinder, and require little inspection. When the cylinder is of soft iron, brass is preferable to cast iron for rings, as it does not injure the cylinder. Mr. Allan finds that a mixture of 2½ oz. tin, and ½ oz. zinc, per pound of copper, works best as brass packing. If the metal be much harder, having more tin, it wears rapidly, and requires daily inspection; if softer, the rings jar and work unsteadily, and cut themselves.

The wedges and tongues inserted at openings of the rings, should be of brass; and the setting springs, of steel.

Piston-rods have been made of steel, but they are now preferred of Lowmoor, or the best scrap iron, as they are thus less costly and less liable to snap than steel rods.

As the duty of the packing rings is to follow the inequalities of the cylinder, and make a steamtight piston, they should be free, and easy, and pliable in action. The cylinder wears most rapidly about the middle of its length, under the action of the piston; and during each reciprocation of the piston, the ring expands and contracts accordingly; not quite circularly, it may be, for the cylinder usually wears oval vertically, by the weight of the piston. Now, to meet the oval wear, as well as the merely circular, a ring cut at four points, in four segments, works better than a ring in one piece, cut at only one point, as it deviates more readily from the normal form, and it also expands with less transverse friction at the circumference. For example, if the total alternate action be ½ inch, on the circumference of the ring, it would be distributed over the openings of the ring in four segments, and at no point in the circumference would the transverse travel of the ring on the cylinder exceed ⅛ inch; whereas, in a ring of one piece, the transverse action is necessarily accumulated towards one opening, where it must amount to ½ inch. Thus not only is the whole transverse friction greater with the ring in one piece, but it is unequally distributed, being greatest about the opening, and least at the butt of the ring, or the part diametrically opposite the opening.

The expansive force should be the same at every part of the ring, to equalize the pressure on the surface of the cylinder; and this condition is perfectly complied with by the four-cut ring. In the single-cut ring, the unequal transverse friction destroys the equality of pressure; and it is observed in practice that, whereas the four-cut ring wears equally at all parts of the circumference, the ordinary single-cut ring wears chiefly at the opening, and is not so durable as the other.

Single-cut rings are made to operate partially by their inherent elasticity, and partially by the aid of steel springs when that elasticity is exhausted. They are turned originally to a larger diameter than the cylinder, about ⅜ inch more for a 15-inch piston; a piece is then cut out of each ring, ⅜ to ½ inch, and the ring compressed nearly to that extent, so that its ends nearly meet, when it just fits the cylinder. Operating thus by its own elasticity, the expansive force is uniform throughout the ring, and the ring is then in its best condition. As it wears and expands, the force of the ring becomes less, and is assisted by the internal spring which, acting on a wedge placed in the opening, more or less perfectly supplies the necessary elasticity.

The steel springs were in earlier plans made to abut on the body of the piston, as in Fig. 299, with a set-screw to adjust the pressure on the wedge. Here the action was essentially imperfect, as the outward pressure on the ring was confined entirely to the neighbourhood of the wedge, and consequently also the wear; and though, were the whole action frictionless, the lateral pressure of the wedge would have been duly transmitted throughout the ring, and the imperfection would have been reduced, yet the actual transverse friction between the ends of the ring and the cylinder very much absorbed the action of the spring; and hence the very partial action and wear which really existed. The next step was to transfer the abutment from the body of the piston to the ring itself, by projecting snugs from the inside of the ring, to receive the ends of the spring, as in Fairbairn's piston; thus the reaction of the spring was usefully confined to the body of the ring, and the centrifugal pressure was better distributed. In another way, by continuing the spring round the body of the piston, and abutting it on the opposite side of the ring, as shown in dotting, Fig. 300, the elastic pressure was confined chiefly to the two opposite parts of the ring, and at those points chiefly the wear of the ring took place. To diffuse the pressure, the circular spring was finally modified as in Fig. 300, (in full lining), and formed to bear continuously on the inside of the ring. The circular spring is in some cases cut at the abutment, opposite the opening of the ring, to give it liberty for expansion; but this introduces the element of friction between the spring and the ring, and is besides of no use.

Packing-rings in one piece are either concentric or eccentric,—that is, of uniform or of tapering thickness, as in Figs. 300, 301, and 302. Taper rings are cut at the thinnest or the thickest point, as the fancy may be; some preferring a uniformly elastic ring, others, a more durable ring. When the ring is cut at the thickest point, it wears less unequally, by a balance of imperfections; and, having more stuff for wear about the opening, it lasts longer than when cut at the thinnest point. A concentric ring appears preferable to either, and practically as durable.

The wedge should be made to a moderate angle of about 70° between the working surfaces, to combine proper lateral action on the ring, with free and moderate action radially; and to preserve the cylinder from the injurious action of the wedge. The sharper the wedge, the more powerful is its lateral action; but the more active also it must be in advancing and retiring, and the more liable it is to score the cylinder and to gag the ring. A more obtuse angle, again, gives greater freedom to the wedge and a shorter range, but the lateral thrust is reduced, while the radial thrust is increased, and adds to the friction between the ring and the cylinder. The set-screw may be either screwed into the eye of the spring, or passed through it, and fixed in either case with jam-nuts.

Single-cut rings are used in couples, placed with the openings at right angles, to assist in neutralizing the partial action of one on the cylinder, by that of the other; also to break joint, and to complete a steamtight circuit. With the

same object, a brass tongue is in some cases inserted at the opening of the ring, and let equally into both jaws. For smaller pistons, one ring may suffice, and the joint may be made by fixing a slip of brass half the depth of the ring, flush into one jaw, and made to overlap the other.

Helical packing in one piece, Fig. 303, has been tried, and has utterly failed. It was found to break up when the cylinder got a little worn, as the great transverse friction at the circumference, accumulated upon four coils, deprived it of the power of contracting after it had expanded into the wide part.

In Goodfellow's packing, Fig. 267, employed by Sharp in his goods-engine, single-cut rings are applied in the best manner. A circular steel spring bears uniformly on the entire circumference of the packing rings; thus diffusing the pressure, equalizing the wear of the rings, and increasing their durability; being in fact supplementary to them, and supplying the necessary range of elasticity. The rings are cut obliquely on the face, which removes all liability to wear grooves in the cylinder.

Another system of single-cut ring, with diffused pressure, is employed by Stephenson and others, Figs. 239 and 250, consisting of a pair of ordinary rings, with one interior concentric ring, on which four or five springs are brought to bear, and through which the pressure is diffused. The rings are of brass, with the object, we presume, of reducing their working friction to a minimum, and of economizing the thickness of metal in the rings, as brass wears down to a much less thickness than cast iron, without rupture. These pistons are on a good principle, but rather complicated in detail. Indeed, we might naturally ask what is the use of the inner ring at all! why may not the springs be applied directly to the outer rings!

Of packing-rings in four segments, Allan's, Fig. 274, is, we believe, the best in detail. The springs are in one continuous piece, abutting on the four corners of the body; and should one screw get an extra turn, the extra pressure is partially transmitted to the others, and diffused. There is but one ring, and the segments are half-lapped at the ends, and made steamtight by tongues. The wedges are very obtuse, being formed to an angle of 122°; thus their radial movement is comparatively small, and they never reach the surface of the cylinder; while, by the division of the ring into four parts, their action is free and indeed superior to that of the sharper wedges usually so employed. The wedges in four-cut rings, also, work more truly in following up the wear of the ring than in single-cut rings; because, for a given wear, their radial displacement is less, and they thus differ less from the altered angles of the openings.

Of all the varieties of packing, that which is now most generally employed, is the single-cut cast iron ring, Fig. 302, eccentric and divided at the thickest part, and sprung with a wedge and continuous steel spring.

The piston-rod is usually finished with a taper, entering by the front of the piston, and cottered into the eye. The junction must be exact, to be durable; and the cotter should have a long bearing in the eye, which is thickened or extended for the purpose. A nut is, in some cases, screwed on the end of the rod, as an additional security; but it is not to be depended on, should the cotter slack out.

Stephenson and others dismiss the cotter, and screw the rod through the body of the piston, fixing it with a small round pin passed through the rod and the boss together. The best fixing is that employed by D. Gooch and J. V. Gooch, Fig. 247, who form collars on the rod, with square necks, against which the body and cover are brought up and screwed together. There is no cotter to work loose, nor is there any strain on the bolts; and by only slacking back the bolts, the piston may easily be shifted round on the rod, to change the surfaces and equalize the wear. A wrought iron piston forged solid on the rod would probably, in respect of solidity, be the best for high-speed engines; it would be lightest and most durable, and if the discs forged on buffer-rod ends are worth the workmanship, the solid piston should be at least equally so.

The cover is bored out to fit the ends of the boss, and is screwed to the body with four or five tapped bolts, which are prevented from undoing themselves by a piece of sheet iron indented to clip the bolt-heads, and pinned to the cover. Fairbairn inserts brass nuts into the body of the cast iron piston, Fig. 233, to receive the bolts; when the bolts are tapped into the cast-iron, the thread wears off, and the bolt slackens, and increases the danger of rupture. The bolt-heads are usually let partially or wholly into the cover, to reduce the projection on the piston, and the required clearance. Sharp taps two bolts into the cover, which are removed and replaced by handles when the cover is to be taken off.

The weight of the piston is, in some instances, partially thrown upon the rings, by a simple coupling, as in Fairbairn's piston, Fig 233. The fixing serves also to retain the rings in position; and the two rings may otherwise be coupled by a small pin tapped into one, and let into the other. Circular springs may be screwed to the rings at the butt, as in D. Gooch's piston, Fig. 247; or they may be sufficiently fixed by projecting the head of the set-screw into the boss.

The entire thickness of pistons is usually 4 inches at the circumference, for 15 inch pistons, up to $4\frac{1}{4}$ inches for 18 inch pistons: made up of the disc, the rings, and the cover. The ruling thickness of metal in the body and cover is $\frac{3}{4}$ to $\frac{7}{8}$ inch for cast iron, and $\frac{1}{8}$ to $\frac{1}{6}$ inch for brass, made up at the rim to complete the required thickness of piston. The thickness round the eye, when the piston is cottered or screwed in, is $\frac{3}{4}$ to $1\frac{1}{4}$ inch for brass, and $1\frac{1}{2}$ inch for cast iron; and Allan extends the bearing for the cotter to 3 inches on each side. Cotters are $\frac{5}{8}$ inch thick, by $1\frac{1}{4}$ to $1\frac{3}{4}$ inch broad, with a taper of 1 in 32, or $\frac{3}{8}$ inch per foot; occasionally split, or fixed by a small split cotter. The screw-bolts for the cover are $\frac{3}{4}$ to 1 inch diameter. The packing-rings are $1\frac{1}{4}$ to $1\frac{1}{2}$ inch broad, and $\frac{3}{8}$ to $\frac{7}{8}$ inch mean thickness for 15 inch pistons; but Stephenson's outer packing rings are $\frac{5}{8}$ inch uniform thickness, the inner ring $\frac{3}{4}$ inch. The circular steel-springs for single-cut rings may be $\frac{3}{8}$ inch thick for a short length at the set-screw, $\frac{3}{4}$ inch next it, tapered to $\frac{5}{16}$ inch at its point of contact with the ring, and to $\frac{1}{4}$ inch at the butt; their breadth is the same as that of the rings, or nearly so. In Allan's four-cut ring, the spring is 2 inches broad, nearly $\frac{5}{16}$ inch thick at the screws, tapered to $\frac{1}{8}$ inch at the abutments. The piston-rod is $2\frac{1}{4}$ to $2\frac{5}{8}$ inch

diameter for 15 to 18 inch pistons, or one-sixth to one-seventh of the piston; with a taper in the piston of 1 in 7, to 1 in 8 or 9, or usually $\frac{1}{4}$ inch for a piston 4 inches thick.

CHAPTER VIII.

CROSSHEADS AND GUIDEBARS.

CROSSHEADS are of wrought iron, made with a socket to receive the piston-rod, with one or two journals for the connecting rod, and with slides to work on the guidebars. They are arranged in two ways:—with lateral slides and two pairs of guidebars, and with slides placed vertically and one pair of guidebars. The former is generally the best arrangement, though involving two pairs of bars, as it gives the best action, and admits of a single-ended connecting rod. The latter gives a longer connecting rod, and is on that account sometimes advisable, as in Allan's engine. Some crossheads with vertical slides, are made with overhung jaws, so as to receive a single end; but they are essentially bad, as, while they considerably shorten the connecting rod, the slides do not fairly receive the strain of the connecting rod, and wear mostly in front, while the oblique strain is partially transmitted to the piston-rod. The pin of the crosshead should be centrally placed, lengthwise, with respect to the slides.

The piston-rod is usually finished and cottered into the crosshead with a taper of $\frac{1}{4}$ inch on $4\frac{1}{2}$ to 5 inches long, at a rate of about 1 in 20; Allan makes it 1 in 30. Cotters are about 2 by $\frac{1}{2}$ inch, tapered 1 in 25 to 30. Allan allows no taper in the cotter at all, nor draw on the rod, but makes an entirely solid fit; others cotter up the end of the rod against a shoulder in the crosshead, as in Kitson's engine, without depending on the taper of the rod. D. Gooch uses no cotter, but screws up with a nut, which, in his case, is more conveniently applied. Cotters in general hold better than screws; they should be rounded on the edges, as done by Kitson, as it diminishes the chance of fracture, and should be fixed with a set-screw or a split cotter through the end. The socket should be $\frac{3}{4}$ to 1 inch thick round the rod. The journals may be 3 by $2\frac{1}{4}$ to 3 inches when single, and 2 by 2, to $2\frac{1}{4}$ by $2\frac{1}{4}$ inches when double; when single, they are inserted as pins into the jaws of the crosshead, and extended, at $1\frac{1}{2}$ to $1\frac{3}{4}$ inch diameter, to carry the slides; when double, they are forged on. For double journals, the fork of the connecting rod should be just so long as to clear the crosshead, and the guidebars must be wide enough apart to clear the connecting rod. The slides are usually of cast iron, which works well with any metal that may be opposed to it; steeled or casehardened wrought iron faces are uncertain, they are liable to cut up the guidebars; brass or white metal facings work well. The slides are 6 to 10 inches long, with lateral flanges to work on the guidebars, and lightened out. Hackworth, Fig. 305, makes them 14 inches long, and screws them to the crosshead; this is too long, for it makes them heavy, and the mode of fixing is too elaborate and is unnecessary. They should be simply bored out to fit the working pin, if lateral; or to fit upon cylindrical studs on the crossheads, if vertical. Either way, they work steadily and are easily replaced. Stephenson has used a simple crosshead, with double journals, Fig. 304, in one piece, but, from its small depth, $4\frac{1}{2}$ inches between the bars, the connecting rod requires a very long fork to clear the whole length of guidebar.

Guidebars are $2\frac{1}{4}$ to 3 inches broad, if lateral; and 4 to 5 inches, if vertical; 2 inches thick at the middle, tapered to $1\frac{1}{4}$ to $1\frac{1}{2}$ inches at the ends. They are generally bolted or screwed to seats cast on the hind cylinder-cover, and to blocks or brackets rivetted or bolted to the motion-plate. The clips, Fig. 307, for joining to cover are expensive. Bars are usually of scrap iron casehardened, or steeled; sometimes of solid shear steel, or of cast iron. Cast iron bars and slides work very well together, if properly attended to; Sinclair uses no other metal.

CHAPTER IX.

Connecting Rods, and Coupling Rods.

Connecting and coupling rods are of scrap iron, with brass bushes and steel cotters. Connecting rods with single ends are preferable to forked rods; when forked, the branches should be as short as practicable, as long forks are weak and liable to give way, when the small bushes are unequally adjusted or wear unequally; and they also cause extra wear of the slides laterally. They should be at least six times the length of the crank; never shorter than five times. For inside cranks, each end is composed of a butt and a strap cottered together, with the bushes between them; the large butt and strap should be united into one mass; and the draw should be confined to the strap of the small end. Thus, a strong union is made, and the length of the rod is less affected by the wear and the cottering up of the bushes than when the large strap is movable on the butt, like the small one. Sharp fixed the large strap by dovetails, Fig. 268, let into both the strap and butt, and a bolt down through the whole; this plan was rather delicate, and when the strap worked at all loose, it was liable to fracture at the dovetail. Sharp now disuses the dovetail and bolt; he bevils the ends of the strap and cotters them up into recesses formed on the butt; making a perfect and durable union, Fig. 268. Stephenson fixes the strap by a couple of bolts and nuts. E. Reynolds' butt, Fig. 312, made to surround the journal on three sides and strapped only below, receives on one piece of metal all the longitudinal strain; it is a good idea. Others remove the strap, and fork the rod to embrace the journal, as in Figs. 255 and 313, depending entirely on the cotter; in which the cotter is too much exposed and unsupported. Some makers adhere to the movable strap; it is generally durable and simple. Others, to save head-room, use bolts and set-screws, as in Figs. 310 and 311; of which the former is too loose, and the latter has too many small pieces for high-speed engines.

The butts should be square-ended, to have a flat bearing on the bush; the straps, also, should be flat inside at the end, and rounded only on the outside, for the same purpose, and because they are stiffer than when circled or made semi-octagonal as in D. Gooch's rod. In the latter case, the bush, when worn down, is liable to yield and to be compressed over the journal by the alteration and elongation of the strap. For small ends, the form of the bearing surface is less important.

Outside connecting rods should have the crank-ends in one forging; thus made, they are simple and durable, and require simply a cotter. Stephenson's, Fig. 260, is neat and light.

The bushes at the large end have 1 to $1\frac{1}{4}$ inch clear thickness on the centre line, and $\frac{3}{8}$ to $\frac{1}{2}$ inch at the sides; with $\frac{3}{8}$ to $\frac{1}{2}$ inch flanges. At the small end, they are $\frac{3}{4}$ or 1 inch on the centre line, and $\frac{5}{8}$ inch at the side. The butts are $2\frac{1}{4}$ to $2\frac{3}{4}$ inches thick, as the length of journal may regulate; the straps $1\frac{1}{4}$ to $1\frac{3}{4}$ inch thick at the large end, 1 to $1\frac{3}{8}$ inch at the small end, thickened up to receive cotters or bolts. The gibs and cotters are $\frac{5}{8}$ to $\frac{3}{4}$ inch thick, and should be rounded on the outer edges. The cotters for bushes should taper about 1 in 16, the fixed cotters 1 in 32; pinched each with two set-screws, and detained for further security with a small split cotter passed through the end. The body of the rod may be flat or round, or nearly circular in section, wanting only two small lateral segments, as in Sharp's engine, Fig. 268; the last of which appears the best. When not circular, the depth is usually increased towards the large end, where the swing and fatigue by torsion on the journal are greater. The area of section next the small butt should be one-third more than that of the piston-rod for inside cylinders, with large crankpins; for outside cylinders it may be just equal. In round rods, the diameter at both ends is the same, with a swell at the middle.

Coupling rods should be made with the ends forged in one piece, and with the cotters driven off the same side of the crankpins, to preserve the length constant under the wear of the bushes. When two pairs of wheels are coupled to the drivers, the rods are in two parts on each side, pinned together at the middle journal, to permit them to yield vertically with the wheels. When round, the coupling rods are made $\frac{1}{2}$ or $\frac{3}{4}$ inch less in diameter at the necks, than the piston-rod; when flat, they are of at least equal section; and in all cases they are swelled towards the middle.

The "ends" of connecting and coupling rods, are made with oil-cups forged on, with syphon tubes, and brass covers screwed in. Some are made to work with the aid of a capillary thread, of which one end is turned into the tube, and the other end is immersed in the oil; these are in action whether the engine be in motion or at rest. The wick appears to be of little moment, for there are cups of a kind first used by Sharp, (Fig. 268, section) having no wick, and acting only when the engine is at work, the swing of the connecting rod throwing up the oil into the central tube. J. V. Gooch dispenses with oil-cups, and lubricates with a sponge let into a recess cut in the upper part of the bush; there is the rather serious disadvantage in this arrangement, that the best bearing part of the bush is cut away.

Hardened steel ferules are, by some, inserted into the small ends of outside connecting rods, which are forged solid for the purpose; they supersede the use of a cotter, wear well, and are easily replaced when worn. Sinclair employs them successfully.

CHAPTER X.

VALVE-GEAR AND REVERSING GEAR.

SLIDE-VALVES are usually of brass, sometimes cast iron; both metals work well, and cast iron wears less than brass, but the valve-face of the cylinder wears less with brass than with iron valves. The exhaust cavity should be rounded, and should be deep enough to give free exit to the steam, and no more; 2¼ to 2½ inches depth is enough. The body should be ⅜ to ½ inch thick; the face should be 1 inch thick to allow for wear. J. V. Gooch's double valve, with a superposed plate and steamways, to give a double entrance for the steam, and facilitate its admission, is not in practice superior to the simple valve with one entrance; it has, besides, two friction-surfaces, and the extra wear due to this valve has led to the steeling of the cylinder-table. The proper course of improvement is to balance the valves, and render them frictionless. Hackworth's "passover" valve, (referred to, page 223) is a mischievous absurdity; a free and untrammelled exhaust is indispensable.

The valve-rod should be forged in one piece, and framed to embrace the back of the valve, which is squared for the purpose, with a large surface of contact, to reduce the tendency to wear loose; the valve is at liberty to wear up to the cylinder-face. The valve should be embraced close to the back of the flange, and the rod adjusted to do so, with a steel spring to keep the valve to the face. The rod should be 1¼ to 1½ inch diameter throughout, and prolonged to work, for steadiness, through the front of the valvechest. When worked by a stationary expansion-link, the valve-rod is coupled by a radius link, ¾ to 1¼ inch thick according to the length, which carries the expansion-block; and the rod usually works in square guides or round bushes to resist the angular action of the radius-link; D. Gooch projects cast iron guides from the valvechest for this purpose. With a shifting expansion-link, the valve-rod is usually coupled by a link suspended from the boiler or overhung from a pivot or shaft fixed to the frame below, and no extra guide is wanted; or it is finished with a square end working in a frame fixed to the guidebars, as in Kitson's engine. The shifting link-motion is most commonly preferred to the stationary; as, though the distribution afforded by the latter is, perhaps, more correct, the former works more sweetly and less angularly, and is less severe upon the connections.

To clear an axle, the couplings of the valve-rod may be bent or doubled, as in Figs. 316 and 317; and where the valve-rod does not tend to the centre of the axle, the angle may be rectified by the use of an intermediate lever, as in Sharp's goods. Indirect couplings of the valve-rod, as in Fig. 314, and in Plate V., are always weak and uncertain.

The eccentrics are of cast iron, in two pieces joined over the axle with two 1 to 1½ inch bolts cottered or screwed into the smaller piece and cottered into the larger. The halves are groove-and-tongued together, and the eccentric is fixed on the axle by one or two ¾ or 1 inch steel set-screws. The smaller piece is occasionally of wrought iron. Eccentrics must be large enough to surround the axle, and to have at least ¾ inch thickness at the thinnest place if of wrought iron, and 1½ to 2 inches if of cast iron, or less if the iron

be toughened; they are 2¼ to 3 inches broad. The strap is usually of brass, sometimes wrought iron, put on in two halves bolted together with palms and 1 inch bolts and nuts, and small safety-cotters. It is usually 1¼ inch thick, and equal in breadth to the eccentric, and converts the whole width into wearing surface. To keep the eccentric and the strap together laterally, the former is rounded on the rim to fit a recess in the latter; or, more frequently the strap is made with a square recess ¼ inch deep, with ⅛ inch ledges, to fit the rebated surface of the eccentric. Where there is plenty of breadth, the eccentric may be recessed, and the strap let into it clear of the ledges.

The eccentric-rods are of wrought iron, usually ¾ inch thick, welded to the straps if of wrought iron. To brass straps they are rivetted with palms dovetailed into suitable expansions on the straps, as in Fig. 234; or most commonly bolted with square jointed palms, as in Fig. 261. This plan admits of a ready adjustment of the length of the rod. The rod is, in some cases, in two pieces, joined and adjustable by a right and left screw thimble; but the joint is found troublesome to keep in perfect order. The fore eccentric should be exactly in line with the link, so as to obtain a straight fore rod, and to throw the necessary obliquity entirely upon the back rod. The rods are forked at the ends to join the link.

The most common form of expansion-link is that originally adopted by Stephenson:—the slot link, as in Fig. 235, all in one forging, to which the eccentric-rods are pinned at the ends in the centre-line of the slot. It works well and durably. The back-coupled slot-link, Fig. 249, is less steady in its movements, but it has the advantage of commanding the full throw of the eccentrics. The box-link, detailed in Plate XXIV., partially combines the advantages of the others, but it is more complex. The slot-link in either form is, upon the whole, more eligible than the box-link. The slot-link is usually in one single piece, 2 inches broad uniformly, 2 or 2¼ inches width of slot. D. Gooch divides the link in two halves vertically, each 1¾ inch broad, rivetted together at the ends, and receiving the eccentric-rod ends and radius-link between them. The eccentric-rods should be attached to the link at a distance between centres 2½ to 3 times the throw of the eccentrics, when coupled behind or on the sides; and 3 to 4 times, when coupled on end. The farther apart the centres, the less is the oblique working of the link; and, in the latter case, the more nearly may the greatest available travel of the valve be equal to the throw of the eccentrics. The expansion-block is of wrought iron, the full breadth of the slot-link, 2½ to 3 inches long, and well-fitting the slot. For the box link, it is in two pieces, one to each side. D. Gooch works an oil-cup on the block; he has used some blocks of cast iron.

To prevent inside valve-gear from jarring, as the links reciprocate past each other, in near neighbourhood, Sharp fences the links with small discs pinned upon the centre pivot; for the same purpose, under a different arrangement, Wilson forges guides upon the sustaining links, Fig. 261.

The reversing shaft is of wrought iron, usually 2½ inches diameter, in some cases swelled to 2¾ or 3 inches at the middle. It works in bearings of cast or wrought iron bolted to the framing. The levers are usually ¾ inch thick, or thicker where they have double duty; they should be forged on the rod; they are coupled to the expansion-links or the radius-links, as required, and in the former case are counterweighted to balance the load.

The reversing lever is centred on the frame, at the footplate; it works in the sector-frame which is notched to receive the detent, usually at equal intervals. The notches should, however, be more closely placed towards the centre or mid-gear, so as to cut off the steam at equal intervals of the stroke, as judiciously practised by D. Gooch. The sector should be made to as large a radius as convenient, 2 or 3 feet, the better to control the valve-gear; with this view, the fulcrum should be at the end of the lever, as in Gooch's, Sturrock's, and Kitson's engines, where the idea is well worked out. Both sides of the sector should be notched and the detent made sufficiently broad to embrace them. The reversing rod, from the lever to the other gearing, should, if possible, be straight; bends or twists greatly reduce its stiffness and increase vibration.

The working pins of the valve-gear are $1\frac{1}{4}$ to $1\frac{1}{2}$ inch diameter, for such as are directly exposed to the working strain; those employed merely for suspension and reversing are usually a little smaller; the pin of the expansion-block is a little larger. The width of bearing in each piece is equal to the diameter of the pin, or a little more, when unaffected by other circumstances.

The valve-gear and reversing gear, with the exceptions already stated, are of wrought iron, steeled or hardened, or casehardened, on the working surfaces of the expansion-link and block, and the pins and eyes; the detent and the notches in the sector should also be casehardened, as practised by D. Gooch. Allan and others line the eyes of the expansion-link and the other parts most liable to wear, with steel ferules, which, when worn, may readily be replaced by others. Sinclair uses white metal ferules.

Allan applies small oil-cups to all the vibrating bearings of the valve-gear, forged upon the eyes of the links; and also one on the top of the expansion-link, and one on the block. They are each occupied by a piece of sponge saturated with oil.

The proper proportions of the valves and steamports, and the principles on which link-motions should be arranged, to yield the best practical results, have already been amply discussed in our physiological section.

CHAPTER XI.

STEAMPIPES AND REGULATOR.

STEAMPIPES are usually of copper, about $\frac{1}{8}$ in. thick, or No. 9 or 10 wire-gauge, within the boiler; they are $\frac{5}{16}$ in. or No. 6 gauge in the smokebox, being of a greater thickness to allow for wear by the action of smoke and cinders. The upright piece in the steam-dome is of cast iron, $\frac{1}{2}$ or $\frac{3}{8}$ inch thick; the steampipe in the smokebox is also occasionally of cast iron, $\frac{3}{8}$ inch thick; but cast iron quickly corrodes.

The blastpipe is of cast iron, copper, or charcoal plate; most usually of copper, No. 10 or 11 gauge; Allan makes it No. 6 gauge.

Copper pipes have brass flanges soldered to them, to make the joints. Allan makes the joints with circular grooves and fillets turned on the flanges. The inside pipes are stayed from the crown of the boiler, when necessary.

The steampipe should be of uniform diameter throughout, between one-third and one-fourth of that of the piston; say two-sevenths, giving a sectional area of one-twelfth. This we have found (page 108) sufficient for the free passage of the steam to the cylinder.

The regulator is of brass, and may be placed at the entrance to the steampipe, or at some other convenient point. Regulators are variously made:—circular discs with apertures, to rotate on a flat surface, as in Sharp's engine, placed in the dome, and worked by levers and links from the spindle; or as a common flat valve to slide over ports, applied either in the dome, as in Fairbairn's engine, or in the smokebox, as in Gooch's; or as a conical valve fitting a conical seat, as in Allan's engine.

Bury, in his latest engines, makes the valve of a double-beat form, Fig. 318, and works it by a small double-thread screw. Allan's regulator is, in our mind, the best; as it is very simple, extremely durable, easily worked, and certain in action. With the others, there is more or less wear of the regulating surfaces; in Allan's, the wear is almost nominal, and gives no trouble. J. V. Gooch, and some others, place the regulator close to the cylinders, thus placing the steampipes in the smokebox under a constant pressure of steam, and adding to the number of points at which leakage of steam may take place.

The regulator-spindle is brought through a stuffing-box to the back of the firebox-shell, and mounted with a handle of 18 to 24 inch radius; Kitson's swan-neck lever is of the best form for easy handling. Allan works the handle between two helical guides, segments of screws, by which the opening of the regulator is adjusted. Gooch and others employ a lever to communicate the longitudinal movement of the slide-valve regulators; in which case the leverage should be at least 8 to 1, and double this leverage is better.

The maximum useful opening of the regulator, and area of entrance to the steampipe, for the free passage of steam, we have already found to be not greater than one-twentieth of the area of piston.

CHAPTER XII.

FEED-PUMPS.

FEED-PUMPS are of two classes:—long stroke and short stroke, worked respectively by the crossheads, having a stroke equal to that of the piston; and by the back eccentrics, or by separate eccentrics on the driving axle, having a stroke equal to the throw of the eccentric. The selection of the class of pump is very much a question of convenience:—for inside cylinders, the long stroke is generally used, and the pump may be worked by an extension of the crosshead-pin; for outside cylinders, the short stroke is the more expedient, as an outside position in connection with the crosshead is exposed, and in frosty weather the pumps are liable to freezing up and to ruptures in consequence; whereas, with the short-stroke, the pumps may be got inside, and, with outside cylinders, there is plenty of room for them.

The pumps should be bolted to the frame, entirely clear of the boiler, as the working strain is considerable, particularly by short-stroke pumps, which must have larger diameters of plungers than long-stroke pumps. Nevertheless, it is the practice of some engineers to bolt the pumps to the boiler; and Wilson has even gone so far out of the way as to apply short-stroke pumps to inside-cylinder engines, and to bolt them to the outer sides of the firebox-shell, working them by eccentric pins in the ends of the driving axle. In one case, the short-stroke pumps were bolted to the middle transverse plate; but, the plate having proved too weak, two struts were carried from it to the back of the smokebox, and the result was that the seams of the boiler, under the strain of the pumps, sprung a leak at the junction of the barrel with the smokebox, which was only remedied by the insertion of extra securities. There is a false simplicity in such random connections: the entire independence of the boiler, with respect to the direct working strains of the mechanism, should be invariably maintained.

The delivery-pipe from the pump should join the boiler at the smokebox end. This is better than at the firebox, because, first, the joints of the feedpipe are not affected by the variable length of the boiler, the boiler being, in judiciously arranged engines, unalterably fixed to the frame at the fore end; feedpipes are a constant source of trouble when they are strained by the alternate expansion and contraction of the boiler; at least unless, as in Sharp's goods-engine, provision be made in the pipe, by doubling it or otherwise, for the required elasticity. Secondly, at the smokebox-end, the water is delivered at the least warm part of the boiler, and is less likely to cause leakage by its sudden cooling action on the heated surfaces on which it impinges, and their sudden and unequal contraction in consequence. We have known some remarkable examples of the sensitiveness of the firebox and tubes to the introduction of cold feed-water at the firebox-end: the tubes regularly springing a leak when the feed was set on, and closing when it was cut off. Engineers are well aware of the unfavourable influences above described, and the general practice now is to deliver the water near the smokebox. J. V. Gooch, in his tank-engine, disposes the tubes considerably clear of the sides of the barrel, in the latitude of the delivery-orifices, that the feed-water may be dispersed and diluted with hotter water, before it reaches the tubes.

Pumps should be formed to command the best possible vacuum, so as to insure a certain supply of water: the volume of clear space in the chamber of the pump, around the plunger, and of the interval between the supply-valve and the first delivery-valve, should be reduced to the smallest possible limits. Also, this clear space should be so formed as to facilitate the discharge of air or steam that may be lodged there; a lodgment for air operates as an air-vessel within the chamber of the pump, and either diminishes or entirely suspends the delivery of water. In inclined long-stroke pumps, the upper part of the chamber forms a lodgment for air; and in cases where such pumps have been uncertain, the partial slackening of the stuffing-box gland, to afford an escape for the confined air, has improved their

action. All water contains air in suspension, and the churning of the water by the pump-plunger naturally separates the air in the chamber, which should be removed as it is separated.

The supply and delivery valves should be placed at the far end of the pump, as in Kitson's and Allan's pumps, for thereby the clearance round the plunger may be reduced to a minimum, and the action of the pump is the simplest. Sharp, in the inclined pump applied to his goods-engine, places the water-passages and valves at the neck of the chamber, and gives a clearance of nearly $\frac{3}{4}$ inch to make a passage for the water flowing into and out of the barrel, round the plunger. In this plan, the entrance of the water is resisted by double friction,—on the plunger and on the chamber; and the action is less perfect than when the valves are placed at the other extremity, when there is only the friction upon the interior of the chamber to retard the entrance of the water.

There are three valves to each pump, one on the suction-pipe, and two on the delivery-pipe, for security against leakage of back steam; of which last one valve is placed close to the chamber, and one at the entrance to the boiler. These valves are of two kinds: ordinary disc-valves, with conical bearings on their seats, guided by three feathers; and ball-valves working in cages. Both kinds have been applied in various ways; but the plan adopted by Allan, of having two disc-valves next the pump, and one ball-valve at the boiler, Figs. 282, 283, appears the most suitable. Valves, of either form, should have very narrow bearings on their seats, not more than $\frac{1}{16}$ inch broad. This secures light and ready action, and prevents the concussive action of valves with broad seats, whether of the ball or disc form.[*] A two-inch water-way is sufficiently wide, and the lift of the valve should not in any case exceed $\frac{5}{16}$ inch. In light express work, the lift may even be confined to $\frac{1}{4}$ inch, and with benefit, as it improves and "sweetens" the action of the pump. All the valves should be freely accessible, and should have independent covers, that they may readily be examined when necessary. Some engineers apply a stop cock at the entrance to the boiler, and have but one delivery-valve; the cock is about the most useless as well as the most dangerous thing that could be applied, and, with it, we lose the security of a second valve.

The body of the pump may be of toughened cast iron, $\frac{1}{2}$ inch thick, or of tough brass $\frac{5}{16}$ inch thick, with $\frac{1}{4}$ inch clearance round the plunger. The plunger is of solid or tubular wrought iron for long strokes, and of tough brass for short strokes. Each pump should be capable singly of feeding the boiler; two pumps being applied as a security, should one be disabled. The capacity of the pump is made larger than would inject the necessary supply were it fully charged each stroke; because a full charge is not to be expected, owing to imperfect vacuum, excessive speed, and other causes; and also because the feed is, on irregular lines, supplied at intervals, not continuously, and must be sufficient to fill up the boiler when required, as well as to replace the current consumption of steam. The capacity of

* Mr. W. G. Armstrong read a paper lately, on the "Concussion of Pump-valves," at the Institution of Civil Engineers (1852-3), to which we may refer those who wish to investigate the subject further.

the pump,—that is, the area of the plunger multiplied by the stroke,—averages in practice 1-80th of that of the cylinder; and if we suppose the cylinders to be filled with 100 lbs. steam in full gear, for three-fourths of the stroke, four times in each revolution, and consequently for one discharge of the pump, the volume of water thus consumed as steam, will be

$$\frac{1}{259 \text{ (rel. vol. of 100 lbs. steam)} + 4 \times \frac{1}{4}} = \frac{1}{87} \text{th of the capacity of the cylinder.}$$

Now, the capacity of one pump is 1-80th of that of the cylinder, and is thus sufficient to supply the demand. For higher pressures under 150 lbs. per inch, we should recommend a capacity of 1-70th of the cylinder, which would give, for long-stroke pumps, a diameter of plunger about 1-8th of the diameter of piston. In short-stroke pumps, the diameter is regulated by the throw of the eccentric, which gives the stroke of the pump; and is found by dividing the capacity of the cylinder by the throw of the eccentric, and by 70; and taking four-fifths of the square root of the quotient.

A short-stroke pump should be worked by rods pinned to the back eccentric-rods or straps, at least five times the length of stroke. When the pumps are placed close behind the driving axle, it is necessary to connect the pump-rods in front of it, to obtain a sufficient length; bending them to clear the axle, as in Allan's engine, Fig. 278.

Feed-pipes are of copper, 2 inches diameter inside, $\frac{1}{8}$ inch thick or No. 11 gauge. Quick curves or angular bends are to be avoided in feed-pipes, as they interrupt the flow, and cause violent straining and leakage, particularly if on the delivery side of the pump. A small air-vessel on the suction-pipe, just behind the supply-valve, and one on the delivery-pipe, between the valves, would soften the straining.

The pet-cock is connected by a copper tube, and is designed to draw off air or steam lodging in the chamber of the pump, and also to test the action. It should be at least $\frac{1}{4}$ inch diameter inside, to let off the confined air, and to give the fang quickly. The tube should be entered at the highest point of the interior of the chamber.

Auxiliary Feed-Pumps. An assistant pump should be placed on the engine or tender, with connections for being worked by the steam from the boiler, and forcing the feed-water into it while the engine may be at rest. It is serviceable on all engines, but especially on goods-engines, as these are subject to frequent and long detention at stations. It is useful while the engine is running, when one or both pumps is out of order, or when the engine is worked at very high speeds, and has small driving wheels, as in light tank-engines. In the latter case the reciprocations of the ordinary pumps are necessarily rapid, and unfavourably so for the best action; whereas the separate pump may be worked at a speed of its own, independently of the speed of the engine.

Auxiliary pumps, to be wrought by hand, have been for several years applied to the engines of the Great Western Railway; but experience has shown that hand-pumps are inconvenient, and fail of their object, as it is less troublesome to set the engine a-running on the rails than to work the pump. The best remedy is to drive the pumps

with steam from the boiler, which only requires of the attendants to open and close a cock.

The auxiliary steam-pump, Fig. 324, patented and made by Carrett, Marshall, & Co., Leeds, is simple, compact,

Fig. 324.—Scale, 1-12th.

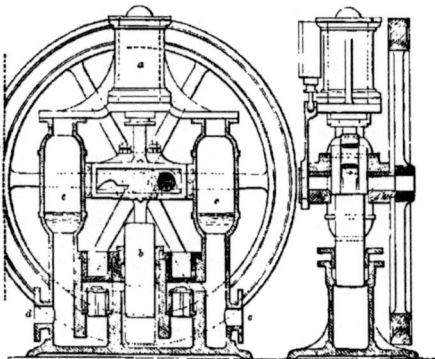

W. B. Carrett's Auxiliary Feed-Pump.
a, steam-cylinder; *b*, pump-plunger; *c*, outlet-passage; *d*, inlet-passage; *e, e*, air-vessels.

and efficient. The presence of the air-vessels, in connection with the suction and force pipes, greatly improves and equalises the flow of the water.

CHAPTER XIII.

RIGGING AND FINISHING.

Cleading. The boiler should be completely enveloped, at all approachable points, in a non-conducting garment, consisting of several plies of felt, covered with $\frac{3}{4}$ inch pine battens grooved and tongued, and finished with sheet iron, No. 17 wire gauge, strapped well down.

For the chimney, Mr. Adams proposes a double structure, containing an air-interspace to preserve the steam from condensation during its ascent, and maintain the full power of the blast. The air in the chamber, though perfect as a non-conductor, would circulate and thus cool the steam in another way; and perhaps the best way would be to fill the interspace with some solid non-conductor,—ash or brick-dust.

The cylinders and valve-chests should be thoroughly clad, like the boiler. A steam-jacket would also be of great utility in working the steam expansively with economy.

Footplates, Fences, and Hand-rails. The footplate should be of ribbed plate iron, to give foothold. It may be $\frac{1}{4}$ inch thick round the machine, and $\frac{3}{8}$ inch thick behind the fire-box, where it is subject to wear, and is also made to do duty as part of the frame. It is supported by and rivetted to the frame with angle-iron; or overhung by knees bolted to the frame, and edged with angle-iron, as in Sharp's goods-engine, where there are no outside frameplates. Footplates should be carried uninterruptedly round the engine.

The area behind and round the firebox should be fenced

with thin sheet iron, properly bound with pillars and hand-rails, and closed upon the firebox-shell. There should also be a sufficient fence-plate erected over and at the back of the firebox, to protect the engine-men. It is abominable policy to expose them, in the absurd hope of their doing their duty better. In stormy districts, indeed everywhere, the American "cab" should be built upon the platform of the engine, so as effectually to house the functionaries. Hand-rails of round iron should be placed entirely along the front and sides of the machine, fixed by standards rivetted to the boiler. Two iron steps should be bolted to the frame at each side of the platform, and placed so as to descend towards the front of the engine. A step may also be fixed on each side, near the fore-end, to give ready access to the machinery.

There should not be any brass ornamental work about locomotives; as, to appear well, it requires continual cleaning.

Buffers are frequently of curled horse-hair sewed into leather cases, hooped and fixed to blocks bolted to the front beam. A volute spring, consisting of a steel plate coiled into a spiral form, and placed in a cast or wrought iron box with telescope end faced with wood, is, we believe, the best form of engine-buffer. It also works well as a buffing spring between engine and tender.

Rail-guards. Sharp's is the best form of guard, solidly bolted to the frame. Guards should clear the rails at least 1 inch. Brooms are usually bound to the side of the guards to sweep the rails in snowy weather; but they wear, and require frequent re-setting. It would be better to have sheet iron scrapers, supported by the guards, and acted on by springs, to descend to the rails. If snow is not cleared off the rails, the leading wheels mount it and compress it; and, while partially relieving the drivers of their load, they also prepare a slippery surface for them.

Sand-boxes. One sand-box should be placed on each side of the engine, before the driving wheel, with a tube to descend with a curve towards the rail, so as to drop the sand gently before the wheel, and reduce the liability to roll off. The sand should be clean and sharp.

CHAPTER XIV.

Materials and Workmanship used in the Construction of Locomotives.

In this chapter, we have thrown together some remarks on materials and workmanship, which did not find their place in the foregoing chapters, or were but passingly alluded to.

Materials. — To combine lightness with strength and durability, locomotives should be made of the best materials suited for the different parts.

Wrought Iron and Steel. Every part of the shell of the boiler under steam-pressure, — the firebox-shell, the barrel, and the smokebox-tubeplate, — should be of the first quality of iron, of Lowmoor, or iron equally good, when the steam is worked at pressures of 90 lbs. and upwards. For lower pressures, the barrel may be of the best Staffordshire or the best Scotch plate; and also the firebox-shell, where the front and back plates are finished flat and joined with angle-iron to the crown and side plates. The steam-chambers and

their covers, which are severely treated, must be of Lowmoor quality.

For the smokebox, chimney, brackets, and other parts of the boiler, the metal may be of good medium quality.

The principal longitudinal frame-plates should be of hammered scrap iron. The other parts of the frame, if well bound together, may be of the best Staffordshire plate. End plates liable to buckling from collisions, should be of Lowmoor, to facilitate their re-adjustment when damaged.

The whole of the wheels should be of scrap iron; except the tyres, which must be of Lowmoor quality, to wear well. The axles should be very carefully wrought in faggots, repeatedly piled and drawn to give the peculiar power of resistance by torsion, required in axles.

All the wrought iron work of the mechanism should be of scrap iron, finished with working parts of Lowmoor iron, or of Lowmoor scraps wrought up; except the piston-rod, which should be of Lowmoor iron throughout, or solid steel; the expansion-link should also be entirely of Lowmoor iron. The guide-bars are occasionally of shear steel, with hardened faces.

The springs are of steel prepared for the purpose; and they should have Lowmoor shackles and links.

Cast Iron. All the iron castings should be toughened with an infusion of wrought iron, on Stirling's plan.

Brass, &c. The most suitable composition of brass varies with the situation. After very varied trials, Mr. Allan has found the following mixtures the most suitable for the respective purposes:—

	Copper. oz.	Tin. oz.	Zinc. oz.	Lead. oz.
Axle-bearings,	16	3	¼	
Slide-valves,	16	2½	¼	
Piston-rings,	16	2½	¼	
Bushes of connecting rods,	16	2¼	¼	
Glands,	16	2¼	¼	
Pump-rams,	16	2¼	¼	
Body of pumps,	16	1¾	¼	
Clack-boxes,	16	1¾	¼	
Safety-valve pillars, to polish,	16	1½	½	
Cocks,	16	1	½	½
Plugs for cocks,	16	1½	½	½
Yellow brass, which will not braze,	16	0	8	½
Yellow brass, to braze with other work,	16	0	8	

For piston-rings, Allan tried mixtures having from 4 oz. to 1 oz. of tin per pound of copper, varying from extreme hardness to extreme softness: the mixture above given is found to wear best, as brass; though, for piston rings, cast iron is preferred before any composition. For pistons and their covers, he uses ordinary yellow brass, which is less brittle than the harder brasses.

Mr. John Sked, of Dunbar, an engineer of much experience and keen observation, uses the following mixtures. For bearings in pillow-blocks, and other situations, where they are well-supported,

Copper 16 oz. Tin 3¼ oz. Zinc ¼ oz.

For eccentric-straps, glands, and other parts subject to severe strains,

Copper 16 oz. Tin 2 oz. Zinc ½ oz.

For footsteps, very hard,

Copper 16 oz. Tin 3½ oz. Zinc ¼ oz.

Mr. J. F. Ruthven, Edinburgh, uses one mixture for all varieties of brass bearings; as follows:—

Copper 16 oz. Tin 1½ oz. Lead ½ or ¼ oz.

To this may be added 1 or 2 oz. of fine brass, which, he says, makes the metal flow better, and produces a tougher and more solid casting. For yellow brass, he mixes

Copper 16 oz. Zinc 7 oz.

Dr. Alban's composition for slide-valves, is

Copper 16 oz. Tin 2¼ oz.

The recipes of the three last-named engineers, are specially suited for stationary-engine bearings, where the speeds are less than in locomotives. The tin element confers hardness, and ultimately brittleness if in excess. The copper confers toughness. The zinc is added to improve the flow of the melted metal, and the temper of the alloy. Where two brasses work together, as cocks and plugs, they must be of different mixtures, to prevent cutting.

"White metal" is applied only as a lining to bushes and axlebearings, as it is too soft to remain unsupported; it is composed of the same materials as brass, but in reverse proportions. Sinclair uses the following mixture with advantage:—

Copper 1 oz. Tin 4 oz. Zinc 13 oz.

"Babbitt metal" is also used as a lining for bearings. It is commonly mixed as follows:—

Copper 1 oz. Tin 20 oz. Antimony 2 oz.

For driving axleboxes, Sinclair uses the following composition:—

Copper 16 oz. Zinc 10½ oz.

White metal wears well, in fact, too well, for it is found to wear down the bearings much more rapidly than hard brass. Brass, though it has been partially eclipsed by white metal, still holds its place, and will no doubt continue to do so.

WORKMANSHIP.—The plates of the boiler are usually shaped and finished by the hammer and mallet. Sharp and others plane the edges of the plates which make jump joints. When the joints are lapped, they do not require planed edges. The rivet-holes should be bored, not punched, and the rivets should be clenched by machine, where practicable. The joints should be caulked by pressure, if possible, instead of by hammer.

The inside longitudinal frameplates should be planed throughout on both sides, and in the axleguards, to afford a perfectly true platform for junctions and fixings. Outside frameplates should be planed on the inside. The junctions of transverse frameplates with the sides should also be planed, to have complete and solid joinings.

The entire bearing and working surfaces of the cylinder and axlebox castings, should be planed, turned, or bored, as required, to afford in all cases perfect forms and complete metallic contact. The cylinder and valve-chest ends and covers should be finished bright where exposed. The slide-valves and valvefaces are commonly scraped to make a dead contact. It is better to put them together off the planing tool, and allow them to wear up to a solid contact. But the cylinder-joints, under steam-pressure, should be scraped.

The whole surface of the reciprocating mechanism should be turned or planed and polished:—in other words, finished bright. Nothing but dead fits will do in locomotive machinery; besides, a cleanly engine is of great importance to the durability of the working surfaces, in the prevention of grit, and the brightness of the work secures for it greater attention in cleaning, as it is more easily cleaned, and shows soiling more readily than black or painted surfaces. The working surfaces of the guidebars and slides, and of the axleboxes and guides, are usually, like the valvefaces, scraped to a dead flatness; but it is better, as in these cases, to leave the tool-marks on the sliding surfaces, as they form very small grooves, which retain oil between the wearing surfaces, and work down into hard, polished, and durable flats. The whole surface of an inside crank-axle should be polished, to allow of its being well and easily cleaned, particularly as, by its revolving motion, it is likely to receive and accumulate a large share of dirt. Straight axles need not be turned on the open surfaces.

The whole of the reversing mechanism should also be finished bright; and all the brass mounting of the boiler.

The unpolished exposed surfaces should be sufficiently painted with a mixture of red and white lead, before receiving the colour paint; and they should be finished with varnish.

The tires of the wheels are turned and bored on the whole surface. The rims are turned where they touch the tire. The naves are bored out, and the key-seats are slotted.

SECTION IV.—TENDERS.

THE tender, as the name indicates, is the vehicle which accompanies the locomotive, and carries stores of fuel and water, and other articles necessary to meet the wants of the leading machine. It is also employed as the principal brake of the train. In general design, the tender is very simple: it has wheels, axles, axleboxes, guards, and springs, fitted and mounted like those of the engine.

The water-tank is the only superstructure, and it is usually worked into a horse-shoe form, so as to inclose, on three sides, a compartment for fuel; the fourth side being open

towards the engine, and free access to the fuel afforded to the stoker.

The brake is a screw and lever apparatus, fitted with wood blocks formed to embrace the wheels on one or both sides of the tender. Willow is the best timber for brake-blocks, as it grips well and is noiseless.

Two feed-pipes, one on each side, are carried from the bottom of the tank, and coupled to the feed-pipes carried by the engine. They are fitted with valves or plugs to regulate the supply of water to the engine.

The draw gear and buffing gear are variously designed. Sharp applies a transverse spring at each end, for both drawing and buffing. The pull between engine and tender should, as has already been argued, be solid and inelastic, and buffer springs should be placed between engine and tender only as auxiliaries to reduce unsteadiness.

The leverage necessary for efficiently controlling the wheels of ordinary tenders by the brake, is about 500 to 1; that is, the velocity of the hand, which applies the moving power, at the handle or hand-wheel, is reduced 500 times by the brake-gearing, and the blocks move up to the wheels with only 1-500th of the speed of the hand. The braking force is thus multiplied 500 times. If the leverage be materially greater, the frame is liable to be wrenched, while it adds nothing to the efficiency; as a leverage of 500 to 1 is sufficiently powerful to chock the wheels of a 10 or 12 ton tender; indeed, it is thought that the best action is obtained when the wheels are just permitted to revolve. As the requisite leverage varies with the whole load to be braked, let us assume a standard leverage of 500 to 1, for a weight of 12 tons. This would give a leverage of, say, 40 to 1, per ton of weight; and the required leverage for any weight may be simply computed by multiplying the weight in tons by 40. In employing leverages greater than 500 to 1, the frame must be specially fortified against the deranging action of the brake. To distribute the strain of the brake, and prevent its undue concentration on particular parts of the frame, the reduction of the motion should be thrown as much as may be into the system of levers beyond the screw; for this purpose, the screw should be of a wide pitch, and the lever to which the action of the screw is conveyed, should be long in respect of the shorter levers which act on the brake-blocks. To compare, for example, Sharp's brake applied to the tender of his passenger-engine, with Allan's brake applied to the Crewe tenders, we have as follows:—

	SHARP. 12 inches.	ALLAN. 7 inches.
Radius of hand-lever or wheel,	12 inches.	7 inches.
Pitch of screw on which hand-lever is fixed,	¼ ,,	¼ ,,
Length of lever on transverse shaft, linked to nut of screw,	12 ,,	39 ,,
Length of levers on transverse shaft, linked to brake-blocks,	6 ,,	7 ,,

In these brakes, the power is doubly concentrated, first, by the hand-lever and screw; secondly, by the unequal levers on the transverse shaft. The first reduction is represented by the ratio of the path described by the handle in one turn, to the pitch of the screw; and the second, by the ratio of the longer to the shorter levers, all of the latter being presumed to be of equal lengths. Premising that the path of the handle is, in fact, the circumference of the circle described by the length of the hand-lever as a radius, the successive reductions are as follow:—

SHARP. { (1st.) 75 to ⅓, or 225 to 1 by screw.
{ (2d.) 12 to 6, or 2 to 1 by levers.
{ Total reduction, 450 to 1.

ALLAN. { (1st.) 44 to ½, or 88 to 1 by screw.
{ (2d.) 39 to 7, or 5·6 to 1 by levers.
{ Total reduction, 493 to 1.

It thus appears that while Sharp at once reduces the motion, or concentrates the power, 225 times, by the use of a long hand-lever and a finely pitched screw, Allan reduces it only 88 times, using a shorter handle, and a more widely pitched screw; and accordingly Sharp only doubles the power in the second conversion, while Allan, reserving a greater proportion of the duty for the last, reduces the motion, or increases the power, nearly 6 times. It is clear that Sharp, by the very violent concentration of power in the first stage, necessarily strains the framing much more severely than Allan, who divides it more equally; at the same time, the final power obtained by Allan is also greater, being nearly 500 times the pressure at the handle; while Sharp obtains only 450 times the pressure.

It is advisable, therefore, to relieve the screw-motion, and to concentrate the power, as much as may be, by the succeeding levers. For this purpose, the hand-lever should be short, and the screw should be widely pitched, double or triple-threaded if necessary; the first lever on the transverse shaft should be long, and the levers bearing on the blocks should be short. These conditions should in all cases be observed, so far as circumstances may permit.

With respect to the sledge-brake, of which an example occurs in D. Gooch's tank-engine, and which applies the braking force to the rails direct, it is no doubt the most correct form of brake; but it wants maturing, and, in all applications of the sledge-brake, it ought to be so arranged as not to incur any risk of the wheels leaving the rails.

The number of wheels placed under the tender is usually six, sometimes four. Four wheels have been proved sufficient in practice; and are therefore preferable to six.

The capacity of the tank for water, should be, for ordinary passenger-engines, and for the lighter class of goods-engines, about 900 to 1000 gallons, or about 150 to 160 cubic feet. For the heaviest goods-engines, it may be 1500 gallons, or about 240 cubic feet. For light tank-engines, it may be 500 to 600 gallons, or about 80 to 100 cubic feet. But water is heavy, 36 cubic feet weighing a ton; and, therefore, to carry out the light-engine principle, the tank should be only as large as will supply, say, a 30-mile stage; for which the capacity, at 2 cubic feet per mile, would amount to 60 cubic feet.

The tank should be of best plate, ¼ inch thick to allow for wear by the action of water, which is often considerable, and should be well stayed, to prevent alteration of form and the consequent probability of leakage. When the water-supply is impure, a sieve or drainer should be placed at the entrance to the tank, to detain gross impurities. But the prevailing practice of first admitting impure water to the tank, and then introducing chemical agents to purify it, is absurd. The water should be purified in the reservoir, before reaching the tender; thus the duration of both the tank and the boiler would be prolonged.

Our business is next with the carriage and waggon stock, and afterwards with the rails. Then will be treated the subjects of train-resistance and performance of engines; to be followed up with a digest of all the evidence, and conclusions founded thereupon, that shall have been brought forward in these pages.

PART SECOND.—CARRIAGES AND WAGGONS.

SECTION I.—PHYSIOLOGICAL PRINCIPLES.*

In making a railway there is usually a datum-line by which the levels are regulated. It would seem that there should also be a datum-line for the purposes to which it is to be applied:—the transit of passengers and goods. Goods may, in some cases, be divisible into such packages as may be easily stowed in any kind of waggon, without considering its form too curiously. But passengers are a standard commodity; they cannot conveniently be made to fit the carriages, and therefore the carriages must be adapted to them with more or less accuracy.

This may vary with a long or a short journey, for a man may put up with an inconvenient posture for an hour, which would be intolerable for half a day. For a long journey, change of posture from sitting to standing is essential. The sitting posture, too long continued, compresses the channels of the blood, impedes circulation, and induces cold feet and other evils. Hence the desire felt by passengers on long journeys, to get out of the carriage when the train stops, for the sake of temporary exercise. Therefore, the standard height of man is the natural datum for the inside height of passenger-carriages on railways.

From the height of the carriage, say six feet, the breadth of it may be estimated. It should at least be one-half more, in order to keep the centre of gravity low, and to prevent the tendency to oscillation while running. This would give nine feet; but it would be advantageous to have even ten feet, supposing that the bridges, platforms, stations, and interspaces between the rails would permit it.

The length may be at least four times the breadth, say forty feet, in order to prevent any forward pitching motion, and particularly the disagreeable diagonal pitching combined with lateral oscillation, so common in short carriages on four wheels.

The great width of ten feet, now contemplated, would of course overhang the rails considerably, on the 4 feet 8½ inch gauge; and it would be expedient only in connection with great length. There are, however, two bases to a carriage: the fixed or wheel-base on the rails, and the elastic or spring-base on the axle-bearings. The latter is practically independent of the former, and may be extended to any width; though the so-called fixed base is sometimes rather shaky, owing to bad joints of rails, weak rails, or infirm foundations.

The force of this objection to wide carriages is met by the superior facilities afforded by great length, for reducing unsteadiness, by adding to the number of wheels and axles, and extending the wheel-base longitudinally.

In comparison with carriages of the ordinary length and width, 18 feet by 7 feet 4 inches, the larger carriage has a greater cubical content under a given external surface, and consequently economizes passenger accommodation. It also shortens the total length of train, in virtue of its greater width and the reduced number of buffer-spaces; and, as it reduces the number of gaps in the train, as well as the lateral outside surface, the atmospheric resistance which, at high speeds, becomes an important element, is likewise reduced.

Safety to passengers in cases of collision is greater in the longer carriages, as these remain on the rails, while the shorter carriages mount one upon another, and get crushed; and the compressed buffer-springs, thus suddenly released, project the buffers into the neighbouring carriages.

With respect to the internal resistance to traction, apart from that of the atmosphere, already mentioned, it may be resolved into axle-friction, and rolling friction:—friction of the journals in their bearings, and the friction of the wheels on the rails; both increasing in proportion to the bad condition of the wheel-tires and the rail-surfaces, and to the imperfect state of the lubrication; all augmented by the want of sufficiently flexible springs. Upon the state of the wheels and the rails depends the amount of resistance to traction, and of the engine-power required. If, by good and well fixed rails, and well arranged carriages, the resistance of the train could be reduced one-half, engines of one-half the power, with one-half the coke, oil, grease, and water, and with a greatly reduced maintenance of way, would suffice to draw them.

The friction of the axle, supposing it to be rightly made and lubricated, is in proportion to the load on the axle, with an allowance for concussion superadded.

The friction of the peripheries of the wheels on the rails arises, for the most part, from the same causes which give rise to unsteadiness of motion. These have already been discussed in a preceding chapter, with reference to wheels fixed on their axles, and formed conically on the tire, according to the prevailing practice, and may here be briefly recapitulated. Wheels run with friction when,

1st, The tread on the rails is irregular,

2d, The axles are not parallel to each other,

3d, The wheels are not in the same plane,

4th, The axles are not at right angles with the line of traction,

5th, The rolling diameters are not equal to each other. To which may be added,

6th, When the wheels are impeded from moving freely to right and left to suit irregularities.

The frequent irregular movement of the waggons in a goods-train while running, is caused by the wheels being

*For the line of argument pursued in this introductory section, and for the substance of the reasonings and deductions, the author is indebted to Mr. W. B. Adams; than whom few men have done more for the advancement of railway transit. The author has also largely availed himself, by direct quotations, of unpublished MSS. kindly placed at his disposal by Mr. Adams.

2 x

fixed in a parallel plane, to the carriage-sides, without power of lateral movement independently of the waggon, in their efforts to compensate for the irregularities of the rails. Where the wheel goes, the waggon must follow; and, upon an irregular line, the erratic movement from side to side, is rather a sign of good waggon-construction, than the contrary, as it indicates that the waggon is not biassed towards one side, by inclined axles or unequal wheels. In passenger-trains this irregular movement is so annoying, by lateral oscillation, that means are taken to convert the whole train into a single carriage by close coupling with right and left hand screws. By this process the wheels are prevented from following their mechanical bias, and become more or less sledges, adding greatly to the resistance to traction. The smooth burnish so commonly seen upon rails,—a burnish not produced by a rolling movement,—may be accounted for in this way.

Supposing the wheels be truly formed with sufficient length and play of cone,—an expedient which we have already described as a means of compensating for the difference of path on the outer and inner rails of curved lines; the question arises, How long will they remain so ! It is found in practice that the tires wear down to a cylindrical form and ultimately into a groove, when of course their power of self-adjustment is destroyed; and that they require frequent re-turning. They are accordingly made 1¾ inch to 2 inches thick to allow for wear, and another evil is introduced,—overweighting of the peripheries and converting them into fly-wheels. Again, when the wheels are in the best order, their power of adjustment to irregularities of the rails is fully available only at slow speeds, as they must have time to move from side to side.

When a coupled train has run for some time, the wheels acquire end-play, due to the wearing of the bushes endwise by the collars of the axle, unless some process of adjustment be employed; the buffers then, by alternate elastic action, on either side, keep up a lateral movement like that due to the alternation of the wheel-cones.

The remedy proposed by Mr. W. B. Adams for these evils, is to permit the wheels to revolve on the axle independently of each other; without, however, interfering with the free revolution of the axle in its bearings. In this case, each wheel would traverse the greater or less path of the outer or inner rail, and accommodate itself by more or less revolutions. Thus there would be a fair rolling movement on the periphery, there would be no torsion on the axle, and the tread of the wheel might be cylindrical and over a greater breadth of rail, inducing greater durability. Moreover, there would no longer be the necessity to make the wheels with the same external accuracy as to diameter. They would, in short, be independent wheels as in highway carriages, but with a revolving axle superadded; so that, if one of the wheels or the axle stuck fast, there would still be free revolution, and the danger of hot bearings removed.

The manufacture of such wheels properly, would require a centre or nave, at least equal in length to the semi-diameter of the wheel, to counteract the flange-leverage at the periphery, and so hardened as not to wear, or provided with some cheap and simple means of repair when worn. These wheels would cost more money at the outset, but they would be durable, would diminish the chances of accident, and would lessen resistance to traction.

As to the structure of wheels, the first consideration is that they be true circles, and next that no blows on the tire should be able to disturb its circular form while running. In most railway wheels the tire constitutes the felly, or external framing, or nearly so; the frame proper being so thin as to form flat sides when the tire is shrunk on hot. The wheel, subsequently put in the lathe, is reduced to a true circle externally, but the tire is left of unequal thickness and the balance of the wheel is lost, while its strength is materially impaired by the irregularities of the blows whilst running, and considerable resistance to traction and unsteadiness of movement is generated.

If therefore the tire be not strong enough in itself to maintain its true circular form while putting on and while running, till it is worn out, provision must be made for it in the framing of the wheel. The object of the spokes is to provide a strut or bearing from the centre of the wheel to the periphery; if the spokes be few, they must be very strong, and the felly or rim also; but it is found in practice that, the more spokes, the truer and better is the wheel, and this brings us to a solid centre as the best of all. Cast iron wheels, if they do not break on account of flaws, are, therefore, so far, a very desirable wheel.

A solid wrought iron wheel has lately obtained much favour, that is, a wheel in which the centre, the spokes, and the periphery or tire, are all welded together, looking like a common spoke wheel. There is an advantage in this, that all the materials are in a state of rest; but, when the periphery is worn down, it must be replaced by an ordinary tire. There is another disadvantage, common to all spoke wheels, that they act as fanners, producing resistance to traction, proportional to their speed; and they, moreover, raise a quantity of dust, to the annoyance of passengers, and the damage of machinery. The disc-wheel possesses, again, a lateral resiliency which does not belong to a spoke wheel, as in the latter, the spokes present their edges to the side blows between the rails and the wheel-flanges. Lastly, the disc form admits of the tire being put on without shrinkage, and of its being worn thinner than with the spoke form, before requiring to be replaced. For these reasons, the disc-form or solid centre, seems the best adapted for wheels on railways. Disc wheels have been made in two modes;—with radial pieces of timber, put together and forming a solid body, with cast iron boss in two pieces, and tires variously applied; and, secondly, with discs of boiler-plate or of cast-iron to form the body, instead of wood.

The proper diameter of the wheels is regulated by the speeds, and by the character of the road. If the speeds be high, or the road be weak or rough, the wheels should be large, say, 3 feet 6 inches diameter, or 4 feet where there is accommodation; but for low speeds, or good roads, 3 feet may suffice. The larger the wheel, the easier is the motion, and the less is the traction per ton; but, a larger wheel entails a greater weight and greater outlay.

The axlebox, as it has commonly been constructed, has a bush of gun-metal which bears on the upper part of the axle-journal. The bush is pierced with one or two holes immediately over the journal, which open into a grease-hopper, whence a supply of the lubricating material is supposed to pass through these holes as through the hopper of a mill, and, as by a mill process, the used grease drops away below the axle, from the open bottom of the box. But it sometimes happens that grit and other foreign substances stop the feed-holes, and in such a case the lubrication ceases, and the bearings heat; and though the holes be cleaned out, free lubrication cannot be obtained till the surfaces be separated by lifting, and the lubricating matter be interposed between them.

The principle of a lubricating substance is, the interposing between the two bearing surfaces a fluid body forming a universal cushion, keeping apart the salient and re-entrant angles of which the surfaces are microscopically composed, and serving as a series of infinitesimally small rollers analogous to a bedding of small shot, thus preventing the interlocking of the angles. If the lubricating material be removed, the angles interlock, and heating is induced by the process of forcibly tearing away portions of metal.

In proportion as the bearing surfaces are fine, hard, and polished, the more fluid may be the lubricating material. Thus fine oil may be used instead of soap. But the finer, or less viscid, the lubricating material, proportionately larger must be the size of the bearing; the bearing should also be in proportion to the superincumbent load, and to the amount and intensity of concussion between them; and thus, on a railway in bad order, the axle-bearings will be more likely to heat than when the railway is in good order. It is probable, that concussion was originally the inducement to use soap as a lubrication on railways, apart from the difficulty of preventing oil from being wasted.

The defects of the common axlebox are, then, chiefly, the uncertain lubrication, the accumulation of grit under the journal, the waste of grease, and the want of sufficient surface to resist end-wear. The remedies are obvious, at least now that we have been told what to do: the axlebox should be made grease-tight, by suitable appliances at the back; and an end-wearing piece, independent of the bush, should be applied to the end of the journal, and renewable at pleasure. Mr. Adams foresaw and provided for these objects in his patents of 1846–47, and the importance of such provisions is now generally appreciated. By retaining the grease below the journal, the journal is constantly bathed at its under side while running, thus rendering it practically independent of the upper feed-holes, and at the same time preventing any entrance of dirt; and, whereas, in the mode of lubricating from above, all dirt in the grease is carried to the axle, in the mode of lubricating from below, the grease deposits its dirt in the magazine, and only the clean portion touches the bearing.

• " After the question of wheels, the next consideration is that of bearing springs. By the interposition of bearing springs, rapid transit on wheels becomes both agreeable and economical; without them, our travelling machinery would be rapidly destroyed, and travelling by land, as we now understand it, would be impracticable. Bearing springs not merely ease the locomotion, but they serve to keep the wheels always pressing on the rails without blows or jolting, if rightly constructed, and by avoiding concussion they facilitate draught, converting what would be concussion into simple increase of pressure. In Morin's experiments on

traction, it is stated that ' at a speed of nine miles per hour, springs diminish the resistance by one-half;' and that ' experiments made upon two waggons exactly similar in all other respects, but one with and one without springs, showed that the wear of the roads, as well as the increase of traction, was sensibly the same after the passage of 4577 tons over the same track, for the carriage without springs going at a walk of from 2·237 to 2·684 miles per hour, and for that with springs going at a trot of from 7·158 to 8·053 miles per hour.'

" These experiments do not, however, state the quality of the springs used, or the difference between springs as perfect as they can be made, and those which are very imperfect. It must be clear that a spring, to be useful in the highest degree, should develop its elastic action in every direction from which concussion may take place between the wheel and road or rail.

" In the usual application of railway bearing springs upon an axlebox which can only slide up and down vertically, it is evident that only vertical concussion is provided for. Impressed with this objection, Mr. Adams, many years back, devised the bowspring, which fulfilled the condition of universal yielding, and being composed only of single plates instead of laminæ, was capable of being hermetically sealed against rust, while the frictional surfaces were confined to simple axis movements capable of lubrication. Whether the blow on the wheel were vertically, laterally, longitudinally, or diagonally, the elastic action was available to intercept it, and instantaneously. The first trial of these springs gave great satisfaction, and a considerable number were made and supplied.

" But the maximum speed on railways was then under 20 miles per hour. When it increased to 30 miles and upwards, the defective proportions of the carriage frames and bodies, formerly pointed out, began to demonstrate that the centre of gravity was not well placed, and the oscillation was so great that it stopped the use of bowsprings in England, but not so on the Continent. The engineer of the Hamburg and Bergedorf Railway, Mr. William Lindley, determined to use six-wheel carriages for the narrow gauge, and those carriages thirty feet in length. The result proved that the oscillation disappeared, while the smoothness of motion and greatly increased facility of traction remained. In consequence, at this time the bowspring is almost universally used in Germany, while here it is now scarcely known.

" In using the bowspring, Mr. Adams abandoned the use of axle guards or forks, which are made to answer a similar purpose in railway carriages that rowlocks serve in a boat. He allowed the spring to draw the axle and wheels, as is common on highways; sometimes guards were applied, though not as guides laterally, but to keep the axles square.

" In order to insure the rolling of wheels on a railway with the minimum of friction, the true plan is to leave them to themselves, when they will infallibly find the path they prefer, that is, to leave them free lateral motion to accommodate themselves to curves and irregularities of the rails.

" Subsequently to the bowspring, a spring was introduced, called the ' tension-spring.' It was formed by drawing the spring tight between brackets or scroll-irons. It was analogous, in short, to a ' tight-rope.' Whatever spring was in it must have been obtained by bending the carriage-frame. The extreme of its deflection was about half an inch, and, consequently, every violent blow of the wheel was felt as a jerk. It was said to answer in first-class carriages, but this was scarcely a proof of efficiency, as the load of 18 passengers in a vehicle weighing upwards of four tons produced but little displacement, and spring cushions and soft stuffing would neutralize much hardness.

" In most railway carriages and waggons a practice prevails of tying the carriages and waggon frames down upon the wheels with a force equivalent to the load. Consequently, when there is no load, they can scarcely be considered spring carriages, and on an uneven line the wheels may be very apt to get off the rail, as they are prevented from pressing under all circumstances, such, for example, as a sunken rail. If the bodies hang loosely and flexibly on the springs, the wheels will always press on the rails; but in such case a short four-wheel waggon or carriage will infallibly oscillate from want of a sufficiently stable centre of gravity.

" A four-wheel waggon in running strikes the leading wheels alternately to right and left against the rails. The effect of the blow is converted into a vertical increase of pressure on the spring, possibly acting on it with three-fourths of the weight of the total load, and with a great chance of breaking it. To prevent this, each spring is made to carry three times as much load as it would carry supposing there were no oscillation. Consequently, the springs are not springs at all save when the waggon is oscillating, and the result must be great injury to the road and the goods, and great resistance to traction.

" Length and numerous wheels to support it is the only remedy for this. If the waggon were on eight wheels and eight springs, it is obvious that there could be no pitching, and, therefore, each spring might be made flexible, and just strong enough to carry its own load, and no more. Moreover, the waggon of double length may be constructed of greater width, and thus eight wheels to one waggon may carry a much more voluminous load than eight wheels to two separate waggons.

" But it will be argued, and with reason, that large waggons and carriages involve many other considerations; difficulty of moving to and from workshops, and difficulty of dealing with in case of their getting off the line of rails.

" This difficulty is very easily remedied. The waggons and carriages may be built as four-wheeled carriages, and then arranged to bolt together, so as to form a single frame easily unbolted when required. The wheels may be arranged to traverse by means of long spring links four inches either way, so that a double carriage of forty feet in length may pass freely round a curve of 300 feet radius.

" As the springs in ordinary use are formed of several laminæ, they become less flexible on account of the rust which accumulates between the plates. It is therefore desirable that some means should be found of preventing rust and increasing flexibility. Mr. Adams has suggested and employed the process of tinning. He also rolls the steel to a peculiar form; alternate ribs and hollows fit one another at the centre of the plate, which thus dispense with the mischievous and tedious process of the slots and studs used to keep the plates parallel, while the edges are kept thin;

by the peculiar section, the strength of the steel is considerably greater than in the ordinary form with the same weight.

" In making up trains with such long carriages and waggons, there is no necessity for tight coupling for the purpose of steady running. Each carriage maintains itself steady by its own form, and only requires coupling by a loose chain. The number of the wheels and flexibility of the springs renders it very difficult to get off the rails. Were it practicable on account of curves, it would be desirable that the carriages and waggons in a train should mutually support each other, and equalize the horizontal bearing on the springs.

" In order to facilitate the running of ordinary carriages, upon the same principle of converting two into one, Mr. Adams has devised a simple and more secure kind of coupling. The two buffer-heads are connected by a double iron link of an I form, with two bolts to each. Thus the buffers are kept to the same horizontal level, and the carriages are prevented from pitching, while the connecting links act as coupling chains, and the buffer rods may serve as traction rods. Volute or spiral springs being applied on the buffer rods, both elastic traction and propulsion are insured, and the coupling can be effected without going between the carriages. If the buffer-heads were secured tightly together, so as not to slide laterally, considerable flange friction would take place, unless the wheels were permitted lateral action; but, as the double connection will permit some lateral movement, the same freedom will exist as with ordinary coupling, although the pitching will be prevented. Of the extent of the irregularity of movement in four-wheel railway carriages, some idea may be formed by the grinding process on the buffer heads, both vertically and laterally, where they come in contact.

" Apart from the general destruction in the running mechanism of railway carriages and highway carriages, there is another element,—the provision for longitudinal shocks. In the early, and, in many existing waggons, the traction is performed by a solid bar without elastic yielding, and propulsion or stoppages are produced by the medium of what are called bumpers—that is, the solid ends of the lower longitudinal side timbers, or by blocks of solid wood. Now, it is evident that a sudden snatch by the engine at a very heavy train is very liable to break the connection, unless a traction-spring be applied to each waggon or carriage of the train; this, by moderating the jerk, saves breakage.

" In some cases the traction-springs are arranged so that the traction rod elongates with the action of the spring. This may answer well enough for a single carriage; but it is obvious that with a train of carriages and increased resistance, the spring would be overpowered, and the traction-rod would become rigid.

" The true mode, therefore, of applying traction-springs, is to keep the traction-rod solid, and not elongated, and so to apply the springs that each carriage may be, as it were, elastically strung upon it, with just spring power enough for its own weight acting in either direction. If then the various carriages be connected by slightly loose links, each may be started in succession without a jerk on any of them, and without undue stress on the springs. It is a most important thing that all engines should be provided with traction-springs, for otherwise enormously heavy traction-ironwork is required, and even then it is very liable to be broken, or to break the frame.

"The 'bumpers,' or solid blocks of the earlier carriages, having been found very annoying to passengers, by the frequent concussions, they were made movable by being attached to rods or pistons, the ends of which abutted on a spring, and they then took the name of buffers, a corruption probably from the word 'rebuff.' But the use of the buffer-spring is important not merely for passenger-carriages, but for goods-waggons also, to avoid destruction. If, for example, a waggon be forcibly struck on one corner while standing on a curve, if it has no buffer-spring, it will be driven out of the square, and the axles being no longer at a right angle with the line of traction, the machine will become a sledge, and will be very likely to run off the rails. If the blow be struck on a sufficient buffer-spring, the blow will not damage the waggon.

"Buffer-springs serve also another purpose. If an engine be standing on the line with a long train behind it, and a second engine runs into the train, each carriage has the power of collapsing, or shortening, by the driving in of the buffer-rods, while it furnishes its quota of resistance to the shock, and so far reduces it. Should the engine at the head of the train remain immovable, while the engine behind presses on, the very strength of the buffer-springs would be an evil; for although they act something like the hands when drawing back to catch a cricket ball, yet they will not remain quiet, but will, if they can, recoil in some mode or other, and will seek to displace the carriages. They cannot move sideways or downwards, and therefore they spring upwards off the rails. As one pair of buffers escapes over the upper edge of the adjoining pair, they are shot out by the spring like the action of a cannon ball, and frequently break the legs of the passengers in the corner seats. The carriages thus mount one on another, and are thrown in a heap.

"It would be desirable, therefore, that, if possible, buffer-springs should have no recoil. The large laminated springs commonly used, when they get rusty between the plates, take a considerable extra force to compress them, but they are unpleasant to passengers by reason of their grating noise. The same process prevents their recoiling very rapidly. But the springs in such a condition are very liable to breakage. Volute and spiral springs are now commonly used both for buffing and traction, but they have the disadvantage of quick action, though economical and convenient for arrangement.

"Impressed with these disadvantages in ordinary buffer-springs, Mr. Adams devised a non-recoiling spring. An air-barrel of metal was provided, and the internal end of the buffer-rod was formed into a piston with a length of stroke equivalent to the stroke of the buffer-rod. A number of light springs kept the piston to the upper end of the barrel; at the opposite end was a hole for the entrance and exit of air, to which might be applied a regulating adjustment. A violent blow on the buffer would act elastically on the air in the barrel, which would be driven through the hole with more or less violence according to the strength of the blow and the size of the hole. When driven home the

piston would not recoil violently, but would be gently driven back by the action of the springs regulated by the entrance of the air. It was found a practical difficulty to get a barrel large enough to arrange inside a carriage framing, and the plan was laid aside for the time, but it might be applied externally with advantage, and moreover it would be one of the most efficient self-acting station-buffers that could well be applied.

"The spring-buffers in common use may be divided into two kinds, the long laminated plate-springs and the spirals; the former are chiefly used with rods within the framings; the latter are mostly used externally, though occasionally applied with rods internally.

"In constructing railway-carriages, especial care must be taken so to form the frames that they will bear the strain of traction and buffing. If the traction apparatus be so contrived that the rod is continuous, and that the haulage on each carriage be only so much as is due to its own weight, not much calculation is required. But to bear the compression of buffing, very great strength is needed, and it is a moot point which is mechanically the best material, iron or timber. It is quite clear that, for a tensile strain, iron is the best; but for a thrust, with a given weight of material, timber is the stiffest, unless the iron be made tubular, or of some form approaching to it. But this is not the whole consideration. Timber is apt to warp and twist. It is mechanically strongest when wet, and apt to rend and split when thoroughly dry. Iron is apt to rust, but timber is apt to rot; and, if the iron be hermetically sealed in paint, it may be made very durable. If the wood be chemically treated to prevent rot, it becomes brittle; if it be hermetically sealed in paint before it is quite dry, the dry rot supervenes, and the best mode of treatment, injection with oily or resinous fluids, renders it difficult to work and of unpleasant odour. Again, it is very difficult to prevent the timber from hogging or bending over the supports on the springs, a defect to which most wooden carriage-frames are subject. Upon the whole, it appears that a proper combination of iron and wood in the under-frames would be most advantageous. The principle of making a rivetted frame does not seem advisable, for in case of a blow which destroys its correct form, a heavy amount of labour in taking the whole to pieces to repair, is requisite.

"It is worthy of remark that the earliest carriage-frames on the Greenwich Railway were of iron, and that the use of them was abandoned for that of timber, which has since continued on all the southern and most other lines.

"In regard to waggon-bodies, iron does not seem a good material. If strong enough not to dint with goods or packages, it is heavy; and rust where the paint is rubbed off, is mischievous. In this, as in other cases, the combination of iron and wood is best and strongest.

"With regard to passenger-carriages, bodies formed of iron rivetted together, if made so strong as not to collapse in a collision, may be very safe; but if they did collapse, and wounded passengers were crushed within them, it would be a fearful process while unrivetting, to extricate them.

"It is undoubtedly practicable to make bodies of wood so strong and heavy, and so softly lined, that passengers might be as safe in them in a collision as in a cotton bale, provided the passengers be few ; but this is expensive, and would preclude travelling to the many. Upon the whole, it is desirable to make the under-frames sufficiently strong to bear the shock, and to make the bodies very slight, so that there may be little material to inflict damage by splinters.

"Exposed as railway-carriages are to heat and cold, to sun and rain, there is much difficulty in getting panelling to withstand the variations without cracking. Honduras mahogany is the material commonly used, but the hurry with which carriages are usually built, renders it difficult to insure that they be of the exact degree of dryness required. For this reason *papier maché* has been tried to some extent, but this also has its disadvantages if wet gets in at the edges. Another material is thin corrugated iron, either galvanized or painted, or covered with a thin surface of glass; it is found to answer well, being strong and light, and serving to stiffen the framing.

"Apart from the question of carriage structure and the considerations of traction and propulsion, there is yet one other, that of retardation. To get a train into motion requires the expenditure of a certain amount of power to overcome the vis inertia, proportional to the weight and resistance of the train. If there be no retarding causes, this amount of power will continue in the train during the whole run as momentum, while a comparatively small force would keep up the speed. But if any circumstance happens suddenly to check the train, such as the engine getting off the line, the momentum will expend itself in destruction by one carriage running into another. When it is required to stop, as at a station, and not to lose time, mechanical means are resorted to, to impede the free run of the wheels, and bring the train to a stand. This might be accomplished by putting the station on a rising ground or elevation, in which case the momentum would be expended by the action of gravitation in ascending, to stop, and the same gravitation would be useful to start down the descent. But such an arrangement would suppose trains all nearly of one length. Were a railway to be so worked, it would be requisite to make the main line level between the stations and the elevating sidings going behind the stations, placing each station as it were in an island, and the two stations communicating by a bridge across the main line.

"In the absence of any such arrangement, the usual plan of retardation is to apply the friction of blocks of wood to the periphery of the wheels by machinery acted on by hand. Some of these breaks are on the tender of the engine, some on a break-van containing luggage behind the engine, and some on a break-van at the back of the train. Formerly, it was the custom to apply the breaks to first-class carriages only, because of their greater weight ; as the action of the breaks, in most cases, varies with the load on the wheels ; and the second-class, depending on the number of passengers who happen to be in the carriage, is a more varying load. Subsequently, the breaks were applied to second-class of larger size, and ultimately to break-vans, which could be made artificially heavy if required.

"If a train could be stopped suddenly from a great speed, it would, of course, fly to pieces, as it does when the engine gets off the rails; but it is a desirable thing to stop as quickly as possible without damage. The best place to apply the retarding power is the last carriage, because it holds the train back as an Irishman does a pig—by the tail, and prevents one carriage over-running another. But one carriage could do little to stop the engine, being a proportion of four to five tons tonnage to thirty or forty, engine and tender. The best way to stop quickly is to apply breaks to every vehicle, supposing a very heavy train ; but this would involve a guard to every vehicle, and therefore many propositions have been made to make breaks self-acting ; that is, the momentum of the train, when the engine slacks, causing a collapse of the buffer-rods, and a corresponding movement of the break-blocks.

"But there is a serious defect in the whole system of breaks as applied to the wheels. In the ordinary mode of breaks suspended by hangers from the carriage-frame, when the breaks are applied the action of the springs is stopped, and there is some chance of the wheels getting off the rails. In the other mode, of what are called sliding breaks, a broad bar is affixed to the two axleboxes on each side ; along these bars slide the break-blocks, put in motion by the machinery. As the pressure continues the wheels are stopped, and the bearings are, in the process, forced partly out of the brasses. When the wheels are stopped they become a kind of sledge, acting against the rails upon a very small surface, and abrading them, breaking the chairs, and forcing the joints apart; while the peripheries of the wheels themselves are ground into flat surfaces, increasing in number with the number of the stoppages. All breaks acting only on the wheels produce more or less of this mischief ; and it has been publicly stated that the annual cost of replacing the tires only on a break-van in constant use is upwards of twenty-two pounds, without reckoning breakblocks and other portions of the machinery.

"The remedy for this evil is not difficult to be found. What is required is, to convert the carriage or van into a sledge bearing on the rails, and the surest mode of doing this is to make the wheels the sledge-runners. Friction on the rails, and not on the wheels, is required ; and although it is true that the amount of friction is as the weight, without regard to the surface generally, it does not hold good in this instance. A broad bearing surface is better than the narrow, in this instance, by reason of the dirt and sand. Therefore, the sledge-break, independent of the wheels, is better than the wheel-break; and the greater the surface the better.

"Several kinds of sledge-breaks have been proposed, and some tried, similar to the drag-shoes of the highway. This kind is objectionable, by reason of the jerk in putting on." Mr. Adams' design appears the most feasible, and will be afterwards described.

"Having come to the conclusion that long and wide carriages, upon eight wheels, laterally movable, and with very flexible springs, are the most desirable both for the conveyance of passengers and of goods, the writer proposes to discuss the question of inside fittings with reference to that form. Ten feet would be the desirable width for the narrow, twelve for the broad gauge, and the only objection can be in the want of space. If the railways have been set out too narrow for the most efficient stock as regards economy of stowage and free running, their owners must be content with what they can get : 9 feet, or 8 feet 6 inches.

"If we take one of the commonest articles carried on railways—coal, it must be quite clear that it is essential for it to be carried on elastic springs, at least for domestic use, for it is very likely to be pulverized in rough waggons, and, as much deterioration mightthus be induced as thewholefreight would come to, for it is not what is put into the waggon at the colliery, but what is available on its arrival at the point of consumption, that is the question at issue, and it were better to bring a smaller waggon-load on good springs that delivered it undamaged, than a larger load of which a portion was wasted. And there is an infallible rule, that the same process that damages the load damages the road also.

"In the structure of waggons, it is clearly desirable that all, with the exception of timber waggons, should be covered from the wet. As a matter of durability of the waggon itself, keeping out wet is a matter of primary importance, for the covered waggon will last at least twice as long as the uncovered. In carrying coal, the soakage of water from rain adds considerably to the weight. In carrying coke, the same objection occurs, with the addition that it takes much longer to dry, and wet coke, especially for a locomotive engine, is the most wasteful of all fuel. Quick-lime would be spoiled in an open waggon; and every common brick will soak up nearly a pint of water. Thus, a waggon of bricks might carry upwards of two tons of useless load. Sand, cinders, &c., are loads of similar kind. For goods of more value the advantage of covered waggons must be obvious, against fire as well as wet; and the drawing daily of tons of useless lumber very soon runs up a cost that would pay for covering the waggons.

"The proportion between the weights of the waggons and the load actually borne as paying weight, is yet far from being reduced to the maximum of economy. It is probable that if the waggons were brought down to something near the same proportion as road waggons, and all extraneous loads, such as rain water, were avoided, and the waggons full stowed, as ships commonly are, the saving of coke in the year's haulage of goods would be nearer a half than a third.

"In the construction of the internal parts of railway-carriages, there are many points to consider. First, the position of the seats:—

"Passengers may be divided into two kinds—the isolated and the gregarious—those who like to think, and those who like to talk; or, putting it in another way, those who like themselves, and those who like their neighbours. The isolated are probably not above one-sixth of the whole, and occasionally a first-class traveller, dissatisfied with his own society, will get into a second-class, not to be alone.

"The first-class passenger likes an arm-chair, in which he is separated from others, either face or back to the engine. But he occasionally pays a penalty for this, by a longitudinal shock, which drives him into his neighbour's face, or his neighbour into his, to the crushing of a nose or the loss of some teeth. And the more roomy the body the more mischievous is the result. The second-class body, with less space, projects its passengers with less momentum. But even risk is a matter of calculation against inconvenience.

"Although the separate bodies transverse to the carriage have their convenience in easy exit and entrance, they are far from the safest mode of sitting.' The omnibus mode of sitting sideways, or shoulder to shoulder, is much safer. Seats might be provided with elbows in that mode as well as in the other, and the chief objection would be its interfering with the view from the windows; but, for night-travelling, the side seats would be the safest. Act of Parliament has assigned sixteen inches as the width requisite for an average omnibus or stage-coach passenger. Four feet three inches to four feet six inches is the space accorded by railway authorities for second-class railway bodies, with the passengers face to face. Therefore, a carriage measuring nine feet six inches in width, would admit four rows of benches longitudinally. The measure of a man's thigh, averaging to the knees about two feet, thus leaves about nine inches space. If the longitudinal measurement of a double carriage were made 44 feet, it would carry, on four longitudinal benches, 128 passengers. But, supposing the doors to be at the sides, as usual, the benches must be made folding on the doorways, which might involve a slight inconvenience, unless they were reserved for passengers who preferred standing. The Americans, who use railway-carriages upwards of forty feet in length, dispense with side doors, and provide only a kind of gallery platform for entrance at either end. But they carry few passengers in proportion to their space.

"If, instead of longitudinal benches, the seats were arranged transversely in separate bodies, as usual, the same carriage would carry 140 passengers; but they would have only a space of 4 feet 3 inches between the opposite passengers, instead of 4 feet 9 inches.

"In referring to the American carriages, commonly called bogey carriages on eight wheels, it may be as well to explain their construction. The Americans, at the outset of their railways, were wise enough to reflect, that if railways did not come to and through their cities, the cities would ultimately have to go to them. For this reason, so runs the tale, Mr. Robert Stephenson, the English engineer, who built their first locomotive, was instructed so to arrange it that it would go round street corners. Consequently, the engine was made two-wheeled, and a small truck on four low wheels supported the front end, being swivelled to it by a centre pin, or what the highroad people call a perch-bolt. This kind of truck, known in many places as a lorry, a trolly, and many other names, was, it appears, called in Newcastle a bogey, and the engine was therefore shipped as a bogey engine. It became the pattern or type for American locomotives. In the construction of the carriages, forty, and occasionally sixty feet in length, the same principle was resorted to, only using two bogeys or four-wheel trucks, instead of one, and swivelled merely at the extremities. Thus these carriages are made to pass round the corners of wide streets and through the towns. At first it was the practice to take off the locomotive, and draw the train through the towns by horses; then the locomotive was allowed to take it slowly; then a self-acting bell was made for the locomotive to ring, and painted over it, ' Look out for the locomotive when the bell rings.' The locomotive then slackens its pace, the women and children run out of the way of the rails, and the train passes. And, in truth, there is less of risk than from a number of omnibuses passing, for with the omnibuses there is the risk of uncertain paths, bad driving, and wilful horses; whereas the train is confined to the rails, from which every one knows how to escape.

" But, although apparently well fitted to deal with curves, these 'bogey carriages' are, in reality, very heavy of draught, and especially on curves. All the evils before described, as pertaining to the system of wheels, are multiplied by the shortness and unsteadiness of the four-wheel truck. On curves, the leading truck has the tendency to get its axles radiating in the wrong direction, giving it the character of a sledge. Again, in case of collision, the upper frame is apt to be driven off the trucks, and there is no efficient spring arrangement to take off shocks, while the frame, being unsteadily supported on the trucks, has an uncomfortable rolling motion. What with the bad construction of the carriages, and the usually slight and inferior character of the roads, it would seem that the Americans get a far less result out of the consumption of a given quantity of fuel, in the shape of passengers or goods, than we do in England, to set against which they profess to have less to pay for interest of money. But, on the whole, there is no doubt that a railway, like a manufactory, with sufficient work to do, will pay best with the best tools. By the American mode of structure, it would be difficult to construct the carriages in two parts, as one end would be heavier than the other when separated. And to construct such very long carriages in single frames, would be objectionable in many ways.

" In using wide carriages open throughout, there is the advantage that the guards may traverse the whole length of the train inside—an important matter in case of accidents to the machinery, and also in case of sudden illness to passengers, or violence, or quarrelling. And this mode would afford the facility of inclosing separate cabins for ladies, individuals, or parties, as in steam-vessels on rivers or at sea.

" There is yet another consideration. For long journeys it is essential to avoid stoppages; yet it is essential to obtain refreshment. To devour refreshment hurriedly, as is now done at stopping stations, is not to be refreshed, but to be made ill. A free passage through the train would facilitate all this.

" As regards the upholstery arrangements, it would be a great advantage to make them all movable. The ordinary mode of trimming with cloth and wool, and other similar substances, involves a large crop of moths, and is moreover a recipient for nuisance from the breaths of closely shut up passengers, which is not easily got rid of. Moreover, the seats and stuffing which are agreeable in the winter are uncomfortable in the summer, and vice versa. The railway carriage in its structure should be regarded as an unfurnished apartment, and the furniture should be separate, and put in as required.

" The windows are made for ventilation as well as light, and it is important to be able to open them more or less at pleasure, as we do the windows of houses. The common plan has been to pull them up and down by means of a strap running over a roller; but of late the practice of counterbalancing them, like house windows, is on the increase.

In all cases it is cheaper to use plate glass, on account of its durability.

" But with regard to rising and falling windows, there is one very important consideration. People's tastes vary about the admission of air when that air comes in the form of a draught. For this reason custom gives the control of the window to the person exposed to the draught. In long carriages open all through, it is a serious evil if one person at the front part of the carriage persists in opening a window that exposes all the other passengers to cold; and yet he himself may be suffocating. The true object therefore to aim at is, to procure efficient ventilation without any draught.

" If, along the centre of the roof of each carriage longitudinally a large trough be fixed, with the front and back open, the air will rush through it with a rapidity proportioned to the speed of the train. Into this trough, then, there should be openings along the roof of the carriage, to cover with sliding panels at pleasure. Thus the heated air would ascend into the trough, and be carried off by the longitudinal current. This would be found ample for the purposes of ventilation, though not for the purposes of coolness in hot weather. Additional openings should be provided in the ends of the carriage, at a lower level, to accomplish this. As perfect a result might thus be attained as with the ventilation by windsails at sea.

" The last point is the warming railway passenger-carriages in the winter. On the Continent this is partly accomplished by sheet iron cases, filled with warm water, beneath the feet. In the United States a stove is used, with a funnel, as on shipboard. For large carriages, probably the best arrangement would be a water stove, with a circulation of hot water below the seats, or an ordinary stove of firebrick, with a chimney for burning coke.

RECAPITULATION.—" 1. Such length and breadth of carriages and waggons should be employed as will, by a proper disposition of the centre of gravity, maintain constant steadiness while running.

" 2. Such a mechanical arrangement of the wheels and axles, as to permit them free compensating movement on the irregular portions of the road.

" 3. Such an arrangement of the axleboxes, or main revolving surfaces, as to insure a free lubrication.

" 4. That the wheels be constructed with solid centres; that is, without open spokes, to prevent any mischievous fanning action serving to raise dust and to retard movement; that the metal in the wheel tires should be in a state of rest, and not of tension, and that the axles should not be exposed to a torsion strain.

" 5. That the bearing springs should be perfectly elastic and flexible, with one to every wheel of an eight-wheel carriage, so that no single spring can be unduly loaded, as is the case with four-wheel carriages.

" 6. That all carriages and waggons should be provided with efficient traction-springs, the springs taking no other strain than the weight of their own carriage.

" 7. That buffer-springs should be made non-recoiling, yet with self-acting arrangement to prepare for another shock.

" 8. That the framings of railway-carriages, to preserve from and withstand shocks, should be made of compound timber and iron, bolted, not rivetted together, with a view to easy repairs.

9. "That metallic panels are more advisable than timber.

10. "That breaks should be made, if possible, self-acting, and to act on the rails by making the carriage into a sledge, without damaging the wheels.

11. "That it is desirable to make all engines and carriages covered, to keep out wet and fire.

12. "That the engines should be made as light as strength will permit.

13. "That side-seats in carriages are far safer to passengers, than front or back to the engine.

14. "That the best constructed machinery is really the cheapest in railways as in manufactories.

15. "That it is desirable to have all the upholstery work movable.

16. "That ventilation should be performed by the roof with a thorough current, independent of the carriage windows.

17. "That warming the carriages should be contrived either by a water-stove or a fire-brick stove."

SECTION II.—ANATOMY OF THE CARRYING-STOCK.

CHAPTER I.

CLASSIFICATION OF CARRIAGES AND WAGGONS.

THE carriage-stock comprises all vehicles concerned in the conveyance of passengers and their luggage, and of private carriages and horses, the vehicles to carry the latter being usually attached to, and run as part of, the passenger-train, in which their owners are conveyed. The carriage-stock may be otherwise designated as the "passenger-train stock."

The waggon-stock comprises the vehicles employed in the conveyance of goods or merchandise, as distinct from passengers and their luggage. This stock may be otherwise designated as the "goods-train stock."

The carrying-stock may, of course, be as various as the purposes for which it may be designed. The usual kinds are as follow:—

Passenger-train stock :—

   First-class carriage.
   Second-class carriage.
   Third-class carriage.
   Composite, or hermaphrodite, carriage.
   Luggage-van.
   Horse-box.
   Carriage-truck.

Goods-train stock :—

   Platform waggon.
   Open box waggon.
   High-sided round-end waggon.
   Covered goods waggon.
   Cattle waggon.
   Sheep waggon.
   Coal waggon.
   Coke waggon.
   Brake-van or waggon.

Composite carriages, as their name implies, combine compartments of different classes in one carriage, usually first and second class. Composites occasionally combine a second or third-class, and a luggage compartment with the guard's brake. Fourth class carriages are still in use on some lines.

Besides the varieties of goods-waggon, above-named, others are specially designed for special traffic, as gunpowder, salt, and lime-waggons. Ballast-waggons are also made, but they are not properly goods-waggons; they are private stock.

Passenger-Train Stock. Carriages.—The classification of carriages is designed to meet the various requirements of the travelling public;—some preferring seclusion, ease, luxury, high speed; others preferring society, if tolerable, and economy, with moderate comfort and moderate speed; others, economy simply, irrespective of other considerations. For the sake of uniformity externally, and in many of the details, carriages are usually made of the same external length, width, and height; and suitably arranged in the interior. The underframes may thus be identical in their construction and their mounting; and a uniformity of working and wearing parts is thus secured, promoting economy of maintenance.

Goods-Train Stock.—The waggon-stock should be as uniform as possible; uniformity of waggons is more important than that of carriages, as their total number and cost are much greater, and the supervision with which they are favoured is less minute; besides, the cost of maintenance is less than where many kinds of waggons exist on the same line. But, whatever may be the upper-works, the underframes of the whole waggon-stock, like those of the carriages, should be entirely uniform.

Waggons are of two general classes:—first, for the conveyance of packed or heaped goods; and, secondly, for conveying live goods, as cattle and sheep, in which ventilation and cleanliness must be specially provided for. Of the first class, there may be many varieties, but there are two kinds of very general utility: the covered waggons, for fine goods, and generally all goods requiring care and protection; and the open box waggon, for rough goods, as minerals, heavy castings, rails, which may be exposed without injury, and may be carried in less costly and lighter waggons. On lines which deal extensively with particular kinds of goods, as the Great Northern, with its coal traffic, the waggons are specifically adapted to the work; and many varieties may thus be created to meet particular traffic and ways of working.

CHAPTER II.

UNDERFRAMES.

THE underframe is the foundation of the vehicle, as the frame is that of the locomotive; it should be simple, durable, and strong, to be easily repaired, to be easily maintained, and to carry the load and resist concussions, without injury or alteration of form. The alterations of form to which underframes are most liable, are, hogging, or drooping at the ends, rising at the middle like the back of a hog; and going out of square, horizontally, so that the frame ceases to be rectangular. Both of these affections are injurious, the first, chiefly because it strains the body, or upper works, loosening the joints, splitting the panels, and jamming the doors; the second, because it also strains the body, and, besides, deranges the wheels and axles, causing irregular movements on the rails. Hogging is partially caused by the frame being unequally supported by the springs: as, for example, when the centres of the axles are too near, leaving the ends insufficiently supported; the tension-plate, that has been much in vogue, increases the hogging action. Hogging is partially checked by placing the heart of the side-soles uppermost, and by placing the wheel-centres sufficiently apart, at a little over half the whole length of the underframes. It may, indeed, be entirely prevented by stiffening the frame with iron plates, or otherwise with trusses.

The horizontal derangement of the frame is prevented by a suitable use of diagonal timbers, and a firm union of the parts.

It is now generally agreed that every railway carriage and waggon should have buffing and draw-springs; as the durability of the vehicle is thus very much increased, as compared with a vehicle without springs, and the ultimate economy is greater.

Carriage-builders, in this country, have fallen very much into one style and scantling of underframe for passenger-carriages on the 4 feet 8½ inch gauge, typified in Brown, Marshall, and Co.'s carriages, Plates XXXIX. and XL. In these the frame is 17 feet 11 inches long, or 1 inch shorter than the body, and 6 feet 8 inches wide outside, giving 6 feet 4 inches centres of journals; sides and ends 11 inches deep by 4 inches thick, two middle transoms 11 inches by 3 inches, intermediate transoms 9 inches by 3 inches, diagonals 4 inches by 3 inches, and cradle between the two middle transoms to carry the buffing-springs, with central-struts 4 inches by 3 inches from the middle transoms to the end-bars. The frame is bound transversely with ¾ inch round tie-rods and strap-bolts to each middle transom, a strap-bolt to each end of the intermediate transoms, and wrought-iron knees or knee-plates at the extreme corners, joining the side and end-soles. Further, the diagonals and struts are bound to the middle transoms with wrought-iron plates applied below, suitably branched, and with bolts and nuts; the struts are bound in the same way to the end-beams. The buffer-springs, which are also the draw-springs, are two in number, laminated, sufficiently long to span the buffer-rods, and placed together in the central compartment of the under-frame. They are confined to the cradle by bar-iron guides, between which the shackles are free to slide; and the ends bear upon cast-iron shoes cottered to the ends of the buffer-

rods. The buffer-rods work through cast-iron slides bolted to the end bars, and have 12 inches of action. The draw-rods are pinned to the spring-shackles, and are finished with hooks on the outside, where they are carried by cast-iron plates bolted on the end bars. In the clear intervals between the transoms, the axleguards are bolted to the insides of the side-soles, which have, or ought to have, washer-plates on the outsides, against which the nuts may be firmly screwed up. Washer-plates should also be placed outside, for the nuts of the transverse tie-rods and strap-bolts.

The objections to this system of underframe are, that there are too many pieces in it; there are many separate forgings, which are expensive, and are not likely to be so efficient as fewer and more direct attachments would be; the draw-rod is not continuous, and the traction-strain is transmitted through the springs and thrown entirely upon the frame, so that the framing of every carriage must be made strong enough to pull after it the heaviest train that may ever be required. These objections have been partially met by Mr. Williams, who links together the shackles of the two draw-springs, thus making the draw-rod continuous, and relieving the frame of all extra traction-strain above what is necessary for the traction of the carriage to which it belongs; he thus reserves the springs for buffing alone.

To resist the hogging action upon the underframe, Williams applies a flat bar of wrought iron to each side-sole, as exemplified in the horse-box, Plate XLI., 3¼ inches by ¼ or ⅝ inch thick, set in the middle, with the ends inclining upwards, and let flush into the timber and screwed to it. These bars are effective, but they cut into the wood, and are not available for giving bearings to the bolts and nuts for the guard-irons and tie-rods. Separate forgings are required for these; whereas it would be well to take advantage of the stiffening plates for the purpose.

Wood underframes have been otherwise stiffened by tension rods from the middle to the ends; also, by timber struts applied below.

The carriage-underframes of the Great Western Railway, illustrated by Plates XXXI.—XXXVI., are entirely of wrought iron, in plates, and angle-iron rivetted together.

The underframes of waggons are variously designed. Those of Henson's waggons, Plates XLIII.—XLVII., are favourable specimens of what are in common use. The frame is well bound; the longitudinal tie-rods are in three pieces, so as to turn to account the stiffness of all the parts of the transverse framing, under the action of the draw-bars. The draw-bars are not continuous, and each waggon in a train must be submitted to the entire strain due to the traction of all the waggons which follow it.

The conditions of a strong, simple, and durable underframe, are, that it should be simple in its arrangement, few in its parts, direct in its connections, and completely defended by springs. The author believes he has to some extent been successful in conforming to these conditions in the design of the carriages prepared by him for the Great North of Scotland Railway, of which the underframe is shown in Plate XLII. The frame is 17 feet 11 inches long, and 6 feet 11 inches wide on the side soles, giving a length between centres of journals, of 6 feet 8 inches. These are the usual sides, a, 11 inches by 3¼ inches thick; the ends, b, 11 inches by

4 inches; the middle transoms, c, 11 inches by 3 inches; the intermediate transoms, d, 9 inches by 3 inches; and the diagonals, e, 5 inches by 3½ inches. The side soles are plated on the outside with sheet iron, No. 9 wire-gauge, for their whole length and depth, screwed on; these plates are finished at the ends with angle-irons rivetted to them, by which the side soles are bolted to the end soles, forming a solid and durable union. The extremities of the end bars are bound with flat iron straps, to prevent any tendency to rupture. The frame is also bound transversely with two ⅝ inch tie-rods at each transom or cross bar; and longitudinally by one continuous tie-rod, ¾ inch diameter, towards each side, next the landing of the diagonals on the end bars. On this plan, there is a general substitution of rolled iron for forgings, as no knees are required, no strap-bolts, no branched plates for the joints of the inside timbers, no washerplates and straps on the outside of the side soles to give a bearing for the bolt-heads and nuts of the tie-rods and guard irons; all the joints are acted on and brought home by the outside plates and the tie-rods.

The ordinary laminated buffing springs are dismissed, and the cradle is replaced by the struts, f, to complete the diagonal circuit. The drawrod g is continuous, being made in two pieces cottered together into the ferrule, h. The buffing and draw springs, i, k, consist of compact volutes, threaded by the buffer rods, l, and the draw-rods, and are entirely independent in action. The continuity of the draw-rod, and the isolation of the springs for buffing and drawing, are most important elements, as they relieve the frame, and admit of its being made light and simple in construction. The middle transoms are strutted by two pieces, m, screwed to the side soles, to relieve the tenons from the buffing strain. The buffer-rods are finished on the inner ends with cast iron blocks, n, cottered upon them, to check the recoil of the rods, and have discs welded on their outer ends to carry the hardwood buffer-heads, o, screwed on. The buffer-rods are turned to 2¼ inches diameter at the outer ends, and worked down to 1¾ inch square for the rest of their length; they work in cast-iron guides bored and squared out, and bolted to the frame-timbers, and thus they are prevented from turning round. A collar is forged on each buffer-rod to shoulder the springs, and these have their bearings on iron plates bolted to the transoms. Each buffer-spring consists of a pair of volutes, with a cast iron plate between the coils, made to slide loosely on the rod, and to sustain the coils in their concentric positions. The coils are made right and left hand, so that in compressing they may revolve on their axis in the same direction without friction; for all such springs naturally revolve in some degree when they suffer compression or elongation, and the want of liberty to do so is a cause of breakage, sometimes attributed unfairly to the quality of the material. Each coil has 4½ inches of action, making 9 inches together; the buffer is permanently compressed 1 inch, to keep its bearings taut, and the difference, 8 inches, is the free range of the buffer, which is enough for all ordinary action. The draw-springs have each 3½ inches of range, of which ½ inch is permanently compressed, 1½ inches are set up, and 1½ inches remain; thus the draw-rod has a total play of 3 inches, and the draw operates only through the springs, upon the middle transoms alone, the hooks being made to clear the end soles. The two springs bear upon cast iron plates bolted to the middle transoms, and are set up by a cast iron ferrule cottered on the rod between them. The rod works through a cast iron plate at each end, in which it has 2 inches of liberty laterally, to radiate to curves.

The safety chains, p, are hung on staples near the longitudinal tie-rods, and passed through the same washer-plate. Thus the chains, when brought into action, draw almost directly from the tie-rods, and the frame does not suffer; and the action of the chains is softened by the interposition of 6 lbs. volutes, q.

For waggon-underframes, the same principles of construction apply as for carriages, with little variation; as in the underframe of the open-box waggon, plate 42. Here, the system of buffers is simpler than in the carriage, as only 3 inches play of buffer is required, and a single volute, 25 lbs. weight, is placed in a cast iron case, with wrought iron flange, bolted upon the end soles at each corner. Where, as in cattlewaggons, a longer stroke of, say 6 inches, is required, a system of buffer-rods and double volutes, should be adopted, as in the carriages; for it is lighter, better distributed, and less costly than the long-stroke plunger-buffer.

It may be added, finally, that the great width of the underframes above described, gives them three advantages over those of the ordinary width, 6 feet 7½ inches or 6 feet 8 inches outside. First, that they provide for longer axles, and a greater transverse distance between centres of journals and springs, or 6 feet 8 inch centres, instead of 6 feet 4 inches. Second, that they give more room for internal arrangements. Third, that they simplify the construction of the bodies of waggons, as less overhang is needed for given widths of body, and the attachments may be more directly effected.

CHAPTER III.

WHEELS AND AXLES.

MANY observations and experiments have been made upon wheels and axles, to determine the best forms and proportions; and the results appear to be as follow:—

That the body of the wheel should be independent of the tyre, for its form and strength, so as to remain unalterable whatever may be the condition of the tyre.

That, for this object, spoke-wheels should have the spokes sufficiently numerous to maintain the rim inflexible—say, eight spokes for a 3 feet wheel, landing upon the rim at about 2 inch intervals.

That disc wheels are preferable to spoke wheels, as they may be more simply made, and afford a continuous bearing to the tyre.

That the tyre, or wearing part, should be quite distinct from the body of the wheel, so as to be readily renewable; but secured to it continuously, and not at wide intervals.

That the tyre should, so far as practicable, be made a rigid ring, and should preserve its form even after it is well worn.

That the body of the wheel should have some amount of

elasticity, to cushion the blows radially, and to resile from lateral concussions.

That the necessary variations in the diameter of the axle be made gradually, not suddenly: as by a series of swells or undulations, not steps, so that the elasticity of the axle may be uniform, and the pulsations by concussion uninterrupted. This condition promotes the durability of the axle. A square neck or shoulder is an incipient fracture, it is the beginning of a break.

The foregoing remarks have reference directly to existing practice. In a perfect system, the wheels must be loose on the axles.

A selection of wheels and axles that have been tried on the London and North Western and other railways, is given in Diagram-plate 8; the illustrations will afford some idea of the course of invention and experience in wheels and axles for carriages and waggons. The cast iron wheels are good in form, but are unsafe at high speeds and in frosty weather. In the wrought iron spoke-wheels, the provision for resisting the shrinkage of the tyre, and alterations of form by the concussions on the rails, are generally insufficient. In Haddan's wheel, the wood segments inserted between the spoke-irons are liable to shrink, loosen, and drop out. In Wharton's "cheese-wheel," made of wooden circular blocks, like cheeses, built round a cast iron nave, with cast iron wedges to tighten up, there are too many pieces. Smith's solid wrought iron disc-wheel, is carried quite to the other extreme. It is too rigid and inflexible, and the wearing part, the tyre, is in one piece with the body. The tread will, moreover, wear much more rapidly than on ordinary wheels, on account of the absolute rigidity of the wheel. Mansell's wood disc-wheel has been found to work very well, but there is too much workmanship about it. It will afterwards be more particularly described. Adams' wood-disc wheel is put together simply and efficiently; it has not yet been tried, but it appears superior to Mansell's. A flange is rolled on the tyre, by which it is bedded on the disc, and simply fastened to it. There are no bolts through the tyre, and it may be worn down nearly to the wood. Adams' iron disc-wheel, with a chilled cast iron tyre, is also remarkable for its simplicity. The nave and the tyre are cast upon the disc, which is of wrought iron, and is continuously perforated at the interior and exterior rims, so as intimately to unite the disc and the castings. This wheel, if properly worked out, will make a durable and simple wheel. The nave is shown as loose on the axle, and the length is made equal to half the diameter of the wheel, to insure steady and durable working. The wheel is free to turn on the axle, and the axle is free to turn in the axleboxes.

Of the axles, separately illustrated, the first example represents an axle that was extensively used by Mr. Bury on the London and Birmingham Railway; many axles on this plan failed while at work, giving way generally behind the nave of one of the wheels, just at the shoulders. In the second example, the shoulder still exists, but is bevelled down at a slope of 45°, to join the boss, or part within the nave. This was found an advantageous modification, and was applied in some of Henson's patent waggons. The third example represents the form of axle designed by Mr. Henson, to replace Bury's original axles, and which is now the standard axle for the waggon-stock of the London and Birmingham Railway. In this axle, Mr. Henson has virtually removed the shoulder behind the nave, and swelled the axle from 4½ inches in the nave to 4¾ inches behind it, giving ¼ inch excess of diameter, on a conical surface ½ inch long, or a slope of 1 in 8. He has tapered the axle uniformly from 4¾ inches diameter at the nave to 3¾ inches at the middle, in conformity with old and good practice, and thus lightens the axle without affecting the working strength, and infuses into it a measure of elasticity to distribute the effects of concussion. This is a practically perfect axle, and in working has given proofs of its great durability. To Mr. Henson, who is waggon-superintendent on the London and Birmingham Railway, much credit is due for the good sense and judgment he has shown in the investigation of the troublesome question of railway axles, and in the simple remedies he has applied for the prevention of fracture. In this respect, his labours have been fully as satisfactory as those of some industrious experimentalists, who have tested axles in all sorts of ways, more or less irrelevant; and, whatever may be the process of conversion to which the material of badly formed axles may be subject in the course of working, Mr. Henson has, apart from the general question, successfully applied a specific remedy for a specific complaint.

In the form of the journals, Mr. Henson has not made any material variation. He simply turns down the axle to a cylindrical form, 3 inches diameter by 6 inches long, with a collar on the end, 4 inches diameter, forming a ½ inch ledge, the angles being rounded. To provide against the end wear of the bearings, and the consequent lateral play on the journals, Mr. Brunel coned the journal at both ends, as shown in the Great Western axle, Plates XXXI. &c., in hopes that the bearing would wear down like a wedge upon the journal, and remain tight. This proving insufficient, he extended the bases of the cones towards the middle of the journal, leaving only 1 inch of the length cylindrical, as in the Bristol and Exeter axle, making what is known as the "double-cone" journal. This form of journal has received its latest development from Mr. Sturrock, in the Great Northern axle, as shown in the Diagram-plate.

For carriages and waggons, the double-cone journal is, we believe, a failure; as it does not prevent lateral oscillation, the slope of the cone being much too gentle. It is also more liable to heat than a cylindrical journal, on account of original misfitting of bearing, and the tendency to jam in the bearing when swayed laterally. On the Bristol and Exeter Railway, where both double-cone and cylindrical journals are at work, by far the greater proportion of hot boxes occurs with double-cone journals, and Mr. Bridges, the carriage-superintendent, finds it much to his advantage to turn down the journals to the cylindrical form. W. A. Adams, after much experience, finds that the cylindrical is the best form of journal. He applies a ⅜ inch ledge and shoulder at the ends of the journal, which he finds much superior to ¼ inch surfaces in moderating end wear.

The dimensions of cylindrical journals have been increased from 5 inches by 2¼ inches, to 8 or 9 inches by 3 inches diameter, in consideration of the heavier loads placed on them. For journals as long as 8 inches, a diameter of

3¼ inches is, perhaps, more suitable than 3 inches. W. B. Adams was the first to depart from the old established dimensions, 5 by 2¾ inches; he adopted a journal 6 by 3 inches, which, though at first repudiated by the authorities, has since been extensively employed.

Hollow axles have long been contemplated and occasionally used for railway rolling stock; they have of late been extensively manufactured by the Patent-Shaft and Axletree Company, on a very efficient system of piling and welding designed and perfected by their managing partner. The axle is shown in section in the Diagram-plate, with double-cone journals, for which it is perhaps better adapted than for cylindrical journals. It weighs only two-thirds of an ordinary solid axle, and is said to be as strong. For resisting the torsional strain to which axles with fixed wheels are subject, the hollow axle is no doubt better qualified than a solid axle of equal weight. The use of the hollow axle is, however, in our mind, only provisional. We must, one day, arrive at loose wheels turning independently on axles; and then there will be no more torsion, when there will cease to be any practical advantage in the hollow over the solid axle.

The wheels and axles adopted by the author, after much consideration, for the carrying stock of the Great North of Scotland Railway, remain to be described. The axle is shown in the Diagram-plate 8, and is employed under both the carriages and the waggons. The form and dimensions of the axle within and between the wheel-naves, are borrowed from Mr. Henson. The journals are 8 inches by 3¼ inches diameter, and are placed some inches further apart on the axle than is customary in narrow-gauge stock, after the practice of Mr. W. B. Adams; they measure 6 feet 8 inches apart between centres, or 6 feet between the shoulders. This extra length admits of the wheel-naves being properly formed and placed fair with the tyres; it gives additional overhang beyond the naves, which is favourable for elastic action and is conducive to durability; and it affords room for the fittings of the axlebox. Outside the naves, the axle is turned down with a slope to a diameter ¼ inch less than in the nave, to clear the key-seat and to give an unbroken bearing for the grit-shield. The extreme ends of the axle are turned and finished flat and smooth, without centre-marks, to receive the end bearing of the axlebox. This axle is designed to carry a maximum gross load of 10 tons per pair of axles, above the springs; or 2½ tons per journal.

The waggon-wheel, shown, with the axle, in Plate XLII., is 3 feet diameter, with eight wrought iron spokes, and a cast iron nave. The spokes are of bar iron, 3 inches broad by ¾ inch thick, bent into segments placed together so as to form both the rim and the spokes. Thus arranged, they are placed in a mould, and have the naves cast upon their central ends, uniting the whole into one body. The vacant angles at the rim, formed by the contiguous segments, are filled up with wedges of wrought iron welded in, and forming a solid continuous ring. The two parts of each spoke are slightly convex towards each other, the better to resist the shrinkage of the tyre, though, if the ring be well united, it should of itself possess sufficient stiffness and resistance. The rim is turned on the outer surface and inner edge to fit the tyre; the tyre being turned to the proper section, and bored out to fit the body with a slight shrinkage, having an inside fillet or flange, ¼ inch deep, to bear upon the rim, and to take the lateral strain off the uniting bolts. There are four ¾ inch taper-headed bolts and nuts to bind each tyre to the rim. The tyres of each pair of wheels are gauged to stand 4 feet 5½ inches apart between backs, when fixed; and, the flanges having 1¼ inch of working thickness at the base, a clearance of ¼ inch at each wheel, or ½ inch in all, is left as play between the wheels and the rails. The tyre is 5 inches broad; at the tread it is turned cylindrical, 1⅝ inch thick, and the outer half width is coned down ⅛ inch on the thickness. The nave is plain, and free from the petty mouldings which usually grace the conceptions of professionals; it is 7 inches deep, and 11 inches diameter, and bored out to fit the axle. The wheel is fixed on the axle with one steel key ¾ inch by ⅝ inch thick, let ⅜ inch into the axle.

For waggons, as for carriages, wood-disc wheels properly constructed would be preferable. Something simpler, however, than what are now used as wood wheels, requires to be introduced, to command a preference.

For the carriage-stock, the wheel employed is the wooden disc wheel on Mansell's patent, shown in Plate XLII. The body is built in segments, of seasoned hardwood or red pine, placed with the grain radially, and compressed into the tyre with a pressure of 80 to 100 tons on one side. It is bored out to receive the nave, and turned on the two faces. The nave is of cast iron bored to fit the axle, and made with a fast and a loose flange, between which the body is bolted firmly. The body is turned conically on the rim, and the tyre is bored out to fit, and is otherwise turned and grooved to receive the "retaining rings." These rings are of wrought iron, turned with fillets to enter the grooves in the sides of the tyre, and they are bolted to the body. Thus the whole wheel is bound together, and there are no bolt-holes through the tyre. The tyre wears much longer, and can be worn much thinner, than the tyres of ordinary spoke-wheels. The wheel is gauged and fixed on the axle with one steel key, in the usual way.

CHAPTER IV.

Axleboxes and Springs.

Axleboxes are in good working order when the lubrication is free and constant, when there is no heating, when there is no waste of grease, when the external dust or grit is excluded, when there is no lurching fore and aft, and no injurious end play. To promote the fulfilment of these conditions, the bush should fit easily upon the journal, and should be tight nowhere, the grease-chamber should be capacious and kept full of grease, the grease-holes should be wide, and should be occasionally probed to clear the passages, the axlebox should be entirely closed upon the journal, and there should be provision for readily compensating the end wear.

A selection of axleboxes is given in Diagram-plate 9 for comparison. The first axleboxes, No. 1., used under coal-waggons, without springs, were of the simplest kind: they were not axleboxes, in fact, but were semi-circular bearings of cast-iron, called pedestals, bolted to the waggon-framing, with sides or jaws passing down and joined under the axle by a plate or a bolt to prevent the axle from dropping out.

Subsequently, springs were interposed between the axleboxes and the frame, and bolted down by the middle to the axleboxes, as indicated in No. 2. Grease-chambers or hoppers were added, brass bearings were also inserted, to take the wear, and an under cover was applied to the axlebox, to shield the axle from grit, and to reduce the waste of grease. Nos. 2 and 3 indicate the successive and obvious improvements made in the details of axleboxes.

Further, in other cases, interlocking discs and grooves were applied, as in No. 4, not in frictional contact, but so close as to diminish the circulation of air and dust into the axlebox. For the same object, the projection of the journals from the wheel-naves was limited, and the axleboxes were carried close up to the wheel-naves, and occasionally finished with a plain circular expansion, as in No. 3, flanged towards the naves. Williams, by the way, casts alternating circular flanges, No. 11, on the back of the axlebox and the wheel-nave.

But, end-wear of bearings was unprovided against; and the entire exclusion of grit, a fertile cause of hot boxes, was not accomplished. In 1846-7, W. B. Adams patented his grease-tight axlebox, No. 5, having a leather collar on the axle, screwed up to the back of the axlebox, with a plate over it. To correct the imperfect lubrication from the upper side of the journal, he converted the lower part of the box into a bath of oil or grease, feeding it from above with floating wooden rollers, so as to lave the journal from below; and he introduced a piece of hardwood or metal between the front of the axlebox, which was movable, and the end of the journal, to check the end-wear of the bearings; the end bearing being renewable when the end play became excessive.

In 1848, W. J. Normanville, No. 8, patented a grease-tight axlebox, in which he applied a ring of india rubber, or other elastic substance, between the wheel-nave and the axlebox, revolving with the wheel, and faced with brass to wear against the box. He hoped that the elastic ring would make a constant tight joint at the back of the box, as it would suit itself to the lateral play of the bearing. The india rubber did not give satisfaction, for want of durability, being liable to heat and inflame, and to decompose by the action of the lubricant. It has been given up for some time, and Normanville recurred to Adams' plan of the leather collar, embracing the axle, and bolted to the back of the axlebox, with provision for shifting it upwards with the vertical wear of the bearings. Subsequently, in 1848, he cast a groove in the back of the axlebox, No. 9, to receive the leather loosely, and to admit of its working up with the wear. Henson's edition of the grease-tight box, applied to waggons, is shown at No. 10.

In his patents of 1846-7, Adams provided for the self-adjustment of the collar to the wear of the bearing. He proposed to insert a conical metal spring in a circular groove at the back of the box, No. 6, expanding upon a strip of leather lining the groove, and embracing a leather collar on the axle; the ends of the spring overlap. In another plan, No. 7, he used a conical pipe of blocked leather, the edges

of which were secured by elastic rings, like key-rings. (In this plan is shown also Adams' mode of applying movable journals to old or new axles). The spring cone and the leather cone at the back of the box would by their free action suit themselves to every movement of the box.

To supply a readily adjustable appliance for checking end play, Joseph Barrans patented in 1849, the use of an adjustment, No. 12, applied at the end of the journal. A cylindrical pin, sliding in a cylindrical opening through the front of the box, is made with a series of notches spirally arranged; the set-screw enters one of the notches, and fixes the slide opposite the end of the journal within $\frac{1}{16}$ inch of the required clearance. In some cases, Barrans applied screws and wedges for adjusting the slide. To lubricate the slide, a small opening from the grease-chamber was made directly over it. A grease-drawer was fitted into the lower part of the box, to collect the drippings from the journal. This was found useful as an economiser, but, apparently from the trouble attending its use, it was discontinued in subsequent axleboxes.

The adjustable end-bearing piece was an improvement upon Adams' fixed pieces of wood; but the means of setting it up were objectionable, as it might be jammed against the axle-end, and would cause heating and other bad results. To reduce this liability, Barrans made a plain rectangular slide, No. 13, grooved it transversely on the upper side, with notches $\frac{1}{8}$ inch pitch, and inserted a die, similarly grooved, through the upper side of the slide-rest, to engage with the slide. A bolt was passed through the whole, and secured it with a nut on the upper side. The slide was pointed with a gun-metal wearing piece rivetted to it. This plan has been found, so far as it has been tried, to work uniformly well and satisfactorily. The engines and carriages in which it has been applied, on the South Eastern and Brighton Railways, are sensibly steadier in running, and on this plan there has not been one instance of a hot box.

Still, the notching is an imperfection; for at $\frac{1}{8}$ inch pitch, a lateral play of $\frac{1}{8}$ inch totally on the two ends of the axle is possible, and there must in practice be a general average of $\frac{1}{16}$ inch play when the slides are newly adjusted. The author, therefore, conceives it would be better to omit the notches, leaving the surfaces flat, as the slide would then be adjustable with perfect nicety, and would, there is no doubt, remain in its place, as the lateral blows on the axle, tending to start it, are comparatively insignificant. To reduce the projection of the external appliances, the sectional area of the slide may be increased and its length shortened. With these modifications, the author has adopted Barrans' axlebox, as in No. 14, and in Plate XLII., for the whole of the rolling stock of the Great North of Scotland Railway.

At the back of his original axlebox, No. 12, Barrans applied interlocking rings sufficiently clear to allow for wear, to shield the entrance, without aspiring to grease-tightness. He subsequently adopted, as a simpler and more efficient grit-shield, a plain diaphragm of lime tree, in No. 13, with a circular hole to fit the axle, placed in a groove in the axlebox, and sliding freely upward in this groove as the bearing wears down. As a shield, wood is superior to leather, for it is stiffer and offers a more durable wearing surface; and, in the case before us, the diaphragm, while sufficiently tight prevent leakage, yields vertically with facility, and incurs little liability to wear wide on the axle. This appears to be the simplest and best of all the means that have been tried for making a grease-tight axlebox; it is adopted in No. 14. R. C. Mansell, No. 15, provides in another way, against end play, by extending the journal through the face of the axlebox, of a smaller diameter, and taking up the play by an adjustable nut. He also relieves the axlebox of all but its own weight, by placing the load directly upon the bush, through the cover; the bush is thus free to work down as it wears, while the axlebox rests independently on the axle, and it is hoped that the wear of the box upon the journal will be so little that it will remain practically grease and oil-tight.

The idea of lubricating the journal from below as well as above, has been worked out variously. Allan, in his engine axlebox, No. 16 (and Fig. 258, page 211), places a sponge in a longitudinal trough below the journal, which retains the oil that works round from above, and continuously lubricates the journal. With oil, the sponge works well. P. R. Hodge has lately reproduced an American axlebox, No. 17, stuffed full of cotton waste, which entirely envelopes the lower part and the end of the journal. It is lubricated with oil, which is poured in by the plug-hole, until no more is received by the waste; the waste distributes the oil over the whole surface of the journal, and continues to do so while there is oil to be disposed of, and while the interstices of the waste remain unobstructed. The used oil drips into a chamber below, whence it is tapped for other uses. The box is closed behind with a leather diaphragm bound with a plate, and working in a grooved iron collar shrunk on the axle. This axlebox is said to be extensively used in America, and to be working well and economically in England.

But, in a grease-tight axlebox, special provision for lubrication below seems unnecessary, at least where grease is used; for the grease deposited below accumulates about the journal, and it forms a shell into which the accessions of melted grease from above must continuously flow. A natural bath is thus worked out of the grease, and it has been proved by Barrans' experiments to be efficient in keeping the journal in good order.

Axleboxes should be of toughened cast-iron; they may be in one main casting, two castings, or three. The fewer the pieces, the less is the probability of loose working and noisiness; but the less is the convenience also, for by casting the cover and the bottom separately from the body of the box, they may be removed at any time, and the interior freely inspected and cleaned out. By properly fitting and fixing the castings together, the cover being held down simply by the spring, and the bottom fixed up by two bolts and cotters, with a thin packing of leather or hemp to take off the concussions, a practically tight and solid box is obtained.

The lid, formerly of sheet iron or sheet brass, is now usually of cast iron, hinged to the upper part, and made to close the opening of the grease-chamber with a fin all round to overlap and exclude grit and water. It should be kept shut with a stiff spring, to prevent loose play.

If of simple cast iron, the ruling thickness of axleboxes should be not less than $\frac{3}{8}$ inch; if of toughened iron, they may be $\frac{1}{16}$ inch to $\frac{1}{4}$ inch. They should be at least $\frac{1}{2}$ inch to $\frac{5}{8}$-inch thick over the bush, and the same thickness in the top or cover, to carry the load. The bush should be $1\frac{1}{4}$ inch thick at the crown, to allow for wear, and to obviate the frequency of renewal; but this must be in conjunction with end bearing pieces, to prevent end wear, otherwise, extra thickness is of no use, as ordinary bushes are renewed not usually on account of vertical, but of end wear, and accordingly their ordinary thickness, when new, is only $\frac{1}{2}$ inch to $\frac{3}{4}$ inch in the crown. The bearing surface of the bush, transversely to the axles, should be about three-fourths of the diameter of the journal, not more; if broader, so as to lap over the journal, it interferes with free lubrication. Craven allows a width of only two-thirds, or 2 inches out of 3 inches, which is the diameter of the journal. By thus narrowing the bearing, it becomes so shallow as to embrace vertically only one-fourth of the diameter, when measuring three-fourths transversely; yet, the axles keep their bearings satisfactorily, under ordinary circumstances. Lateral checks are, however, simply provided by adding wings to the bearings; and they may be necessary under brake-vans, when the brake-blocks act on only one side of the wheels. The outer contour of the bush, is usually semi-octagonal; to combine economy of material and fixity of position. But, when bearings of this form wear down, they are liable to turn with the axle out of their seats. A square outline is better, and perhaps the form of bush proposed by Mr. Barrans, No. 13, which is solidly bedded, and in which material is economised, is the most generally suitable. Even when the bearing wears down sharp at the edges, it may, on account of its limited width, be harmless in stripping the journal of the lubricant; and may, in consequence, not require lifting and examination until worn out. Barrans has observed that the limited width of bearing, 2 inches upon a 3 inch journal, adopted by him, is sufficient for steady running; and he has never found that the journal, by leaving the bearing, had touched the walls of the axlebox, or at least had made any impression upon them. This result is probable enough, when the vehicle is fitted with bearing, drawing, and buffing-springs; but, in the absence of spring-buffers, W. A. Adams, No. 18, has found it necessary, with bearings $2\frac{1}{2}$ inches wide, on 3 inch journals, to limit the lateral play of the journal to $\frac{1}{4}$ inch off each side of the box, in order to prevent damage to the bearing. The simple expedient of so limiting the play may in all cases be employed, and the author has, in his modifications of Barrans' box, allowed just $\frac{1}{16}$ inch play on each side.

Area of bearing surface on the journal has usually been thought a primary consideration in axleboxes. It is in reality only secondary, as is clearly proved by the superior results obtained from narrow bearings, and it is over-ruled by the considerations of free lubrication, and steadiness in virtue of length of journal. When these are realized, there is no want of bearing surface; accordingly, Henson and others adhere to the 6 by 3 inch journal for their heaviest waggons. But, of course, the shorter the journal the greater care must be bestowed upon the fittings of the axlebox and the spring to insure steadiness. Our preference is for 8 inches of length, and 3 or $3\frac{1}{2}$ inches diameter. This will amply suffice to carry a gross superincumbent load of 10 tons on two axles, or 2½ tons per journal; which gives 2 cwt. per square inch of horizontal area of journal measured by the product of the length by the diameter, and 3 cwt. per square inch of the surface in actual contact, allowing a contact of 2 inches wide, and the whole length of the journal.

As the mere extent of surface in contact is a secondary consideration, the position of the holes through the bearing for lubrication, is not of much importance; the grease-holes do abstract a part of the bearing-surface of the bush, but the area so deducted is small, and materially insignificant. The best place for the entrance for the lubricant is precisely over the crown of the journal. The holes may be ⅜ inch diameter and hopper-mouthed towards the grease-chamber; two ruts may be cut in the bearing, extending one from each hole diagonally along the surface of contact, to equalize the lubrication.

The guiding-grooves on the outsides of the axlebox should be of the full depth of the box, to insure steadiness, particularly if the spring be not bolted to the box. They should be just slack between the horns of the guard, longitudinally, to keep the axles square; and, for high speeds, they should be only ⅛ inch wider than the thickness of the guard, laterally; but, for low speeds, under 20 miles an hour, they may be ¼ inch wider, as the lateral freedom eases the motion, and reduces the tractive power required.

The spring should not be bolted rigidly to the axlebox, as is commonly practised; but should be simply placed upon it, to promote free action, and sufficiently checked to prevent lateral displacement. Williams, and W. A. Adams have adopted this system with advantage; the author casts a rectangular socket on the cover, to receive the spring-hoop, a flat piece of wood being interposed to cushion the spring. Between the socket and the spring-shoes, or the scroll irons, the spring is sufficiently stayed, and its action is free.

The following results of the extensive experience of W. A. Adams, Birmingham, in rolling stock, are communicated by himself. They refer to the springs, journals, and axleboxes of waggons designed to carry a load of 6 tons 6 cwt., let out and maintained by him. They are employed chiefly in the coal trade, and run at moderate speeds:—

"The bearing-springs weigh 52½ lbs. each, and the four springs deflect 1¾ inches with a load of 6 tons 6 cwt., and the waggon-body. The spring-plates are coated with hot tar separately to prevent oxidation.

"The form of journal should be cylindrical, and nearly square at the angles, rounded, say, to $\frac{1}{16}$ inch radius, as, in practice, it is found that the full rounded angles allow the bearings to wear endwise to a very injurious extent. The shoulder and collar of the journal should be not less than ⅜ inch deep.

"*Note.*—That in nine cases out of ten, the end wear of bearing is at the shoulder, and not at the button or collar.

"The axlebox [No.18 Diagram-plate 9], has a grease and water-tight cover, forming a seat or cradle for the spring.

"The wearing surface of the brass should not exceed one-third of the diameter of the journal, measured vertically; otherwise it tends to strip the journal of the lubricating medium.

"Care must be taken that the side-cheeks of the bearing, A, A, be of sufficient depth, otherwise, when the brass wears down, it will turn round in the seat.

"The cheeks of the axlebox at B, must not be more than ⅛ inch clear of the journal, otherwise in shunting, the bearing is driven over the journal, and the bearing surface is damaged by again falling into its place.

"For the same reason, excessive jumping of the waggon is prevented; the clearance at D between the journal and the under-cap is limited to ⅜ inch.

"The journal is 3 inches diameter by 6 inches long; the bush is 1 inch thick, and 5⅞ inches long when new, or ⅛ inch shorter than the journal; and the under-cap is made 5 $\frac{9}{16}$ inches long under the journal, or $\frac{5}{16}$ inch shorter than the bearing, so that when the brass has worn much endwise, the under-cap receives the ends of the journal and checks the play.

"When the springs are not bolted firmly to the axlebox, it is necessary that the guiding grooves of the box be not less than 9 inches deep, and that they should truly fit the guard longitudinally."

There is sound doctrine here, but the provision against end-wear of the bearings is altogether insufficient except for very moderate speeds. It is remarkable that the end-wear, according to Mr. W. A. Adams, takes place chiefly next the shoulder, at the open end of the box. This is doubtless due to the action of grit, and proves the advantage of closing the box at the back. Even in the closely and carefully fitted carrying axleboxes of the Crewe engines, with sponges to wipe the journals, Mr. Allan found that the grit penetrated ½ to ¾ inch from the shoulder.

Bearing Springs.—For narrow-gauge carriages the bearing or side springs are of steel plates 3 inches broad, and $\frac{5}{16}$ inch thick, except two of them, the back and short plates, which are ⅜ inch thick. These are thicker because they are outside plates, and partially unsupported. Ordinary first-class carriages, with four wheels, have nine plates in the side springs; second and third class have ten plates; passenger luggage-vans have nine ⅜ inch plates. The springs have, in addition, a tension-plate of wrought iron ½ inch thick, placed upon the back plate. This tension-plate has eyes worked on the ends to take the suspending links, which are pinned to them, and to what are, by courtesy, called scroll irons, these being only plain wrought iron brackets bolted to the underframe. The springs, when weighted, are 5 feet 3 inches long, the tension-plates 5 feet 6 inches to the centres, the scroll irons 6 feet apart centres.

For horseboxes and carriage-trucks, the springs should have six plates, and may be 3 feet 9 inches, or 4 feet long.

Waggon-springs vary much in all respects. But a flexibility of 1 inch per ton of load appears to be the most suitable. The plates may be 3 or 3½ inches broad, and ⅜ inch thick. The span should be not less than 2 feet 6 inches for slow running waggons, and should be 3 to 3½ feet for regular waggons. For a load of 6 tons 6 cwt., and the waggon-body extra, say 8 tons in all, W. A. Adams uses, as we have seen, four springs of 52½ lbs. of steel each, under this load, which gives 2 tons per spring, and a flexibility of ⅞ inch per ton. For waggons designed to carry heavier loads of, say 8 tons, making about 10 tons total, the springs should have 70 lbs. of steel. In these cases ⅜ inch plates are contemplated; if thinner plates be used, much more steel is necessary. Some thin-plate springs weigh 112 lbs.

For an investigation of the properties of laminated springs, we may refer to a previous chapter, page 239.

CHAPTER V.

AXLEGUARDS.

AXLEGUARDS, or hornplates, are of wrought iron plate $\frac{5}{8}$ inch to $\frac{3}{4}$ inch thick, bolted to the inside of the side soles; they are of various forms, as shown by the illustrative plates. The most common form has been that of a five-sided figure in outline, with a peak at the upper end, to embrace a sufficient depth of the under frame, tapering below, and slotted out to form the "horns," and to receive the axle-box. There are two objections to this plan; it is costly in the manufacture, and is deficient in spread. Timber requires to be widely embraced, to give a proper hold for iron fixings, especially when it is exposed to leverage or wrenching action, as in axleguards. Guards are now usually made as in Plate XLII., of bar iron 3 inches broad, doubled up at the forge to form the guides or horns, and with wings of bar iron, $2\frac{1}{2}$ or 3 inches broad, welded to the guides near their lower ends, and carried up with a spread to join the side soles. The guards are $\frac{3}{4}$ inch thick, and are secured to the side soles with $\frac{3}{4}$ inch bolts and nuts, three in the bend, and two in each wing, making seven in all; the extreme bolts in each guard may be as much as 3 feet asunder, the farther apart the more command they have longitudinally over the wheels and axles. Laterally, their stiffness depends on the depth of their hold upon the side soles, and they should be applied for the whole depth, or as much of it as may be convenient.

Besides the spread, the solidity of the bolt-fastenings is to be regarded. If the bolt-heads, outside, be received merely on washers, they are likely to work loose in the timber, which wants firmness to resist the tendency of the bolt-holes to wear ovally. The bolt-heads should be received upon large washer-plates, $\frac{1}{4}$ inch thick, counterparts, in fact, of the bearing surface of the guard inside. The washer-plates, embracing a large surface of timber, bear solidly and firmly, and keep the bolts tight. For simplicity, and for still greater firmness, the whole area of the side sole at each guard should be covered with one iron sheet of the full depth. But, where the side soles are plated over their whole length and depth, for the general purposes of strength and simplicity, as in the Great North of Scotland under-frames, no washer-plates are required at all, and the best possible surface is afforded for bolt-hold. Thomas Forsyth, now of Wolverton, appreciated the advantage of fortifying the frame at the axleguards: in some waggons he designed for the Edinburgh and Glasgow Railway, he sunk a $\frac{3}{8}$ inch iron plate flush into the wood, on the inside, of the full depth of the side sole, and as wide as the guard; it was separately bolted with 8 or 10 flush headed bolts to the sole, and over and through it the guard was bolted with other 8 or 10 bolts. By this plan, the sole was riddled with bolts, but the guard was thoroughly secured, as the plate clipped the

guard-bolts; and, accordingly, in the late accident at the foot of Cowlairs incline, when a train of loaded waggons ran into the station, the guards of some waggons on this construction were found, amongst the debris, to be sheared off flush with the lower side of the side soles, while the upper parts of the guards remained intact.

Mr. W. B. Adams proposes the use of angle-iron for axleguards, as it would be lighter and stiffer than the flat bars, and would offer a broader surface on edge to the axle-box. It is doubtful if the rigidity of angle-iron is advisable; some lateral elasticity like that which accompanies the flat bar is desirable.

The ends of each guard are tied together by a strap bolted to them, and it is common also to connect the two guards on each side of the vehicle with a $1\frac{1}{4}$ inch round tie rod, either in one forging with the straps, or separately bolted, to stiffen the guards and assist the frame. The separate attachment is better than the continuous forging, as the straps may in the former case be more conveniently removed when the wheels and axles have to be taken out; besides, when the continuous forging is removed, the under frame obeys its natural tendency to collapse, or hog, and it is troublesome to replace the tie. Some makers carry up tie-rods at each end from the guards to the buffer-beams, thus completely trussing the under-frame. But the whole thing is too fine; the guards, if well made, do not require trussing, and the frame should be stiffened by the plates already described.

CHAPTER VI.

BUFFING AND DRAW SPRINGS.

To what has already been said of the buffing and draw-springs of the carrying stock, it may be added that many kinds of springs have been thus employed. India-rubber springs are much used, formed of circular discs of that substance strung upon the buffing and draw-rods. Also, helical and spiral springs, formed of a rod of steel twisted into a coil or volute; of which the section has usually been circular, but is now made oval, on John Brown's system, and with advantage. The "volute" proper, as made by Spencer, is made of a plate of steel twisted into a coil, and has already been referred to. Cork and other materials have been used for buffers; but they are now set aside, and the forms and materials above enumerated are those now principally in use.

CHAPTER VII.

BODIES:—CARRIAGE-BODIES.

THE bodies of carriages and waggons are usually of wood; they consist generally of framings, or skeletons, clothed with lining, and sometimes also with outside panelling. Panelling is employed only in passenger-train stock, as the framing consists of many pieces of small scantling, and requires the protection afforded by panels against the weather.

2 M

The inferior classes of carriages, and the luggage-vans, are occasionally open-framed; but it appears consistent with common sense that, in a variable climate like that of Great Britain, the framing should be covered in, to exclude water, and promote the comfort of passengers, the security of luggage, and the durability of the vehicle. In waggons, the framing is in fewer pieces, and of larger scantling; and if well put together, it does not require the protection of panelling. In some waggons, framing is almost entirely dispensed with, and the lining does double duty; for which purpose it is made thicker than when placed on framing. Where this style of construction can be conveniently and simply carried out, it appears preferable to lined framing; in construction it is simple, and it is uniformly strong and elastic.

Diagonals have been much used in the body-framing of waggons, and occasionally in that of carriages; but the propriety of diagonals is questionable. Perfect rigidity is not wanted in bodies; John Ross, of Birmingham, remarks that they should elastically resemble wicker-work. We have never observed that diagonals, as such, are of the slightest use, except to patch up framing otherwise defective; they also add much to the workmanship, and it is certain that, in all cases, the same quantity of timber may be superiorly arranged, and will do more duty, in simple rectangular framing, than in a compound of rectangular and diagonal framing. Besides, the lining and, in carriages, the panelling, aid materially to strengthen the framing.

Carriage-bodies.—These are made very much on one general plan for the narrow gauge, represented by the examples in Plates XXXIX., XL., for the respective classes of carriage, which are fully detailed. The bodies are 18 feet long outside, and 7 feet 4 inches wide; and as the underframe is usually only 6 feet 8 inches wide over the soles, or 8 inches less than the body, the latter is usually turned under, to reduce the overhang; but, in all cases, the body should overhang the underframe by at least ½ inch, at the sides and ends, to throw off water. But the turn-under is a mere prejudice; it is borrowed from the old practice of private carriage-building. A flat side is simpler and cheaper, and is at least as strong. The clear height of the body from the floor to the roof at the centre is about 6 feet, with 4 to 5 inches of a fall towards the sides.

Adams' large eight-wheel carriages, Plates XXXVII., XXXVIII., are in two 20-feet lengths, 40 feet in all, and 9 feet wide. The Great Western carriages, Plates XXXI.—XXXVI., are 24 to 27 feet long, and 9 feet wide.

The framing of carriage-bodies is simply designed; the principal members being the upper and lower side and end rails, connected by the corner and intermediate side pillars. The side pillars are placed at the partitions and at both sides of the doorways, and also, if necessary, at more frequent intervals for the required strength of the body. The side framing is bound by intermediate rails fitted between the pillars, so placed as to receive the joints of the panelling and to stiffen it, and to carry the quarter-lights. The end of the body, being flat and unbroken, is framed with upright and transverse battens lapped into each other, and mortised into or lapped upon the corner pillars; the uprights being sufficiently numerous to stay the panelling.

The roof is framed with ribs placed transversely, to span the upper side rails; and the ribs are arched to afford headroom inside, and to throw off rain water.

The sides and ends of unstuffed carriage-bodies are made up 3 inches thick, with ½ inch or ¾ inch lining, and ⅜ inch to ½ inch panelling. The panel-boards are blocked to the framing with canvass and glue; they are grooved into the lower side and end rails, and the corner and door pillars; they are jump-jointed over the battens, and the joints covered with beads. The edges of the beads, and in general all projecting edges, are rounded off to dislodge dust and water. In first class carriages stuffing is substituted for wood lining.

The floor-boards are checked into the lower side-rails from the under side and screwed to them. They are usually in two ¾ inch thicknesses, laid diagonally to cross each other, or longitudinally and transversely, and screwed together.

The roof-boards are ¾ to 1 inch thick, and laid longitudinally and screwed upon the ribs; they are grooved and iron-tongued. The boards should project over the upper rails, to throw off water; and a light moulding may be placed in the angle. This is better than the more usual plan, of finishing the boarding flush with the upper rails, and adding a cornice moulding to project, as this gives a joint for the retention of water, which rots the upper rails. The roof is covered with ox-hides stretched tightly over it, or stout canvass, well saturated with white lead; ox-hide is superior to canvass when luggage is to be carried on the roof. The covering is turned over at the edges of the roofing and fastened under the cornice mouldings.

The Great Western carriage-bodies, of the third class, are made of sheet iron, No. 11, wire gauge, framed with angle iron, as shown in Plate XXXIV.

Fourth class carriages are made so much in the style of open waggons, that it is needless formally to describe them in detail. They are merely high-sided waggons, with a few partition-rails inside, and bordered with a fence rail to keep the passengers from falling out. In this country, and with the present railway speeds, open uncovered carriages are barbarous, and are barely fit for the lowest classes of passengers.

As to interior arrangement, the first class body is usually divided into three compartments, measuring each 6 feet long on the outside; with double rows of seats transversely, partitioned off with elbow-rests for three persons abreast, and receiving in all 18 passengers. Second class bodies are divided into four compartments, of which the alternate partitions are in some cases carried up only to the level of the shoulders. The seats are disposed transversely, two in each compartment, and they receive 4 persons to each seat, or 32 passengers in all.

Third class bodies are arranged variously, usually in one apartment with seats arranged along the sides and ends, and a double seat down the middle. On this plan, the body should be 8 feet wide. Allowing at least 16 inches width of seat per passenger, which is the smallest width allowed by law, this plan of third class receives 44 persons; and, if the body be made 6 inches longer, or 18 feet 6 inches in all, it would hold 48 persons. But it is desirable to have all the classes of carriages of uniform width, say 7 feet 4 inches outside ; under this limitation the interior may be arranged in two compartments, with transverse seats, as in plate 40, to hold 36 persons ; or, the second class arrangement may be adopted, with four doors in each side ; each seat would hold 5 persons, giving a total of 40 passengers.

Saloon carriages may, of course, be planned variously, as in Adams' long carriage, Plate XXXVII., and otherwise. The business public appear generally to prefer the ordinary partitioned carriage.

Travelling post-offices are set out to meet the requirements of the department to which they belong.

The lining and seat cushions of first class carriages are of cloth, and are stuffed with curled horse hair. The cushions are, in some instances, placed upon a number of small spiral steel springs, to improve and increase their action. The glass-frames in the doors are commonly stayed by steel springs, to prevent their pattering in the door-styles. The best application of the spring for this purpose appears to be Slater's plan, in which a bar of zinc is interposed between the springs and the glass-frames, acting as a slide upon the frame, and taking off the sharp friction of the tips of the springs.*

In first class carriages, the floors are carpeted in summer, and are usually laid with woollen rugs in winter. Hat suspenders are fixed inside the roof, and receptacles for umbrellas, &c., made of nets hung upon rods, are fixed to the upper part of the partitions, above the elbow-rests.

Roof lamps should be placed in all carriages, to light them up in tunnels and at night. They are, in some cases, denied to third class passengers, on the vulgar and inhumane principle adopted by some railway companies, that the lower priced conveyance should be made sufficiently uncomfortable to drive those who can pay into a superior class of carriage; those who remain through inability to pay more in money, being made to pay in inconvenience and suffering. Roof-lamp protectors of sheet iron, outside lamp-irons, iron steps to the roof, and other furnishings, are applied as may be required for the purposes of the traffic.

Horseboxes are made with stalls to receive three horses. Their length is regulated by that of a horse, and it is supplemented with two dog-boxes, one at each end, useful for carrying dogs and harness. The full length so obtained makes a reasonably long underframe, with wheels properly apart for steady running. It so happens, inconveniently in this respect, that horseboxes, to be readily uncoupled at the proper stations, are in general placed at the end of the train, where there is most liberty for unsteady carriages ; thus, a proper length of wheel-base is indispensable for horseboxes.

The same remark is applicable to carriage-trucks, not only on account of their position, but also because they are light in themselves, and their burdens are light.

Horseboxes should be padded inside the stalls, and free from angularities, to prevent damage to the animals should they be restive, or in other ways be knocked about. Padding is applied at the sides, the back, the front, and at the roof above the horse's head.

Carriage-trucks are laid for their whole length with two tram-ways of iron plate, to receive the wheels of the vehicle. The vehicle is locked by two bars laid across and pinned down to the upper edges of the sides, made with forks to take one of the fore and the hind wheels. The wheels are also strapped to the sides, the pull of the straps being outwards so as to slack the wheels off the axles, and prevent the heating of the axles by the constant vibration from the motion of the train.

CHAPTER VIII.

BODIES OF WAGGONS.

THE bodies of narrow gauge waggons are made from 13 feet 6 inches to 17 feet long, according to the load which they are designed to carry. Six tons per waggon is an ordinary regulation-load, for which the length is 13 feet 6 inches. But, as the dead weight of the waggon increases much more slowly than the capacity for goods, it is thought advisable to have them of a greater length, 16 feet, to carry 8 tons. The width is determined by the mode of construction of the sides, and is generally about 7 feet 6 inches to 7 feet 8 inches. Bodies are made both of wood and of sheet iron. If of wood, framed, the lining is usually 1¼ inch thick ; if built, it is in battens 2¼ to 2½ inch thick, or even 3 inches. Sheet iron lining, on a wood framing, may be No. 12 wire-gauge, or nearly ⅛ inch thick ; when built up with rivetted joints and overings, it is ⅟₁₆ inch to ¼ inch thick, in which case the joints should be welted, to stiffen them. W. B. Adams, and Henson, employ corrugated sheet iron, and require less framing with it ; but they differ in their mode of using it, Henson using corrugations 4 inches pitch, and Adams preferring narrow corrugations less than 1 inch pitch.

Various modes of waggon-construction are shown in Plates XLII.—XLVII., and the drawings are in such complete detail as to render unnecessary any systematic enumeration of their contents.

Open box waggons have plain sides and ends, usually about 2 feet deep ; made with or without doors in the sides, as the nature of the traffic may require. Doorways and doors should be avoided as much as may be, as they add to the workmanship, and weaken the waggon. They should never be made in the ends, as a solid end is essential for properly withstanding the violence due to suddenly stopping and starting, by the concussion or pressure of goods. Two examples of box-waggons occur in Plates XLII., XLIII., with and without doors. In the first example, pillars, 4 inches square, are applied and bolted to the underframe for its whole depth, to stiffen the ends and the side at the doorway. External fastening in this way is stronger and otherwise better than mortising, for the principal upright members, as the timbers are less cut up, water is less liable to lodge, and the chance of decay is less. Each pillar is fixed to the underframe with a wrought iron staple embracing it, with wings for two bolts through the frame; and at the lower ends with one bolt, passed through a large cast iron washer-plate, of a kind first

* To diminish the friction of the springs upon the door-styles, above referred to, Wright used to mount them with small friction-rollers. The men forgot to oil them, and the rollers chirruped in the performance of their duty ; hence the name of "Cheeping birds" by which these springs have been known.

used by W. B. Adams, with fins to clip the sides of the pillars and check the tendency to split. The corners of the body are covered with one plate, ½ inch thick, for the whole depth. This is better than any number of isolated straps, as it binds the body into one piece, and the corner joints can not work loose or abraid. Corner-plates were first applied in this way by H. H. Henson, as in Plate XLIII. The overing consists of angle iron 2¼ inch × 2¼ inch × ½ inch, which protects the timber, and considerably stiffens the body. Henson's overing is a flat bar 2 inches by ¾ inch.

The cattle-waggon, Plate XLII., exemplifies what may be called the perpendicular style of waggon-architecture. Diagonals are abandoned, and the pillars are firmly attached to the under-frame, as already described in the open box waggon, same plate, and bound together by rails at the middle and the top. They are further strutted at the lower end, by battens well fitted between them and bolted to the under-frame, which absolutely prevent any looseness there. These struts supersede the staples applied for the same purpose in the open waggon. The pillars being thus firmly bound at the bottom, they are incapable of displacement unless they break across; and this firm binding supersedes diagonals for stiffening. Simple corner straps of iron 2 inches by ¾ inch, are applied at the upper and middle rails, and at the lower ends; the middle corner straps at each end of the body, are joined by a strap ¼ inch thick, passed along the middle end rail, and binding the end framing. To increase its power of resistance to the thrusts endwise, by the swaying of cattle or other movable goods in the waggon, the middle end rail is bulked out horizontally towards the middle, to a flat-segmental form. The middle end pillars are mortised into the upper end rails. Upon the whole, it is apparent that the end framing of these waggons is suitably designed to receive and resist the longitudinal strains to which they are exposed. The side pillars are only mortised into the upper side-rails, as the lateral action upon them is not great.

The flooring of waggons is of battens 2½ or 3 inches thick; it should be laid longitudinally, and should be let in flush with the side and end bars of the under-frame, having its bearing upon the interior members of the frame, and upon rebates formed on the inner edges of the end bars. In this way, the flooring materially stiffens the under-frame. In covered waggons, the flooring is laid close and iron-tongued. In open waggons, and others, as cattle waggons, requiring to be drained, some of the floor battens are laid ½ inch apart, to pass the water. The better way is to pack them close, and iron-tongue them, to secure the stiffness thus obtained; and to bore drain-holes at suitable intervals, and fit them with cast-iron ferrules having a waterway about 1 inch diameter, flush with the upper side of the floor and projecting below the under side to draw the water clear off. The drainage is thus more complete, as the water is not permitted to loiter about the under side of the floor-boards.

In the designing of the open box and cattle waggons, Plate XLII., it has been studied to dispense with hammered iron work as much as seemed practicable; and to insure the necessary strength, by simple and direct combinations, and the free use of rolled iron.

The principles observed in the construction of the waggons which have just been discussed are of general application to all varieties of waggons. It may only now be added that the exposed surfaces, or angles of timber, subject to wear, abrasion, or violence, should be protected by iron straps or by angle iron, as may be most suitable; as at door-ways and on the upper edges of open waggons. Mortises and tenons should be machine-made to make a perfect fit, and should be put together with white lead and iron-pinned. No nails should be used in any part of the framing of a carriage or waggon; screws alone should be used, for they hold better and do not split the wood.

CHAPTER IX.

BRAKES.[*]

To put a railway train into motion, requires the expenditure of a considerably greater force than is required to keep up the motion while running: that is, supposing the line to be a level plane without irregular surface. But circumstances might exist in which the force of starting might be less than that required in running. For example, the train might start down an incline, and continue to run up an incline, or along a very rough and uneven road, in which case the initial force might be less than the constant force. Up a steep incline or over a very bad road, it might happen that no initial force or momentum existed in the train, which would be constantly, in horse-phrase, "at the collar:" that is, the moment the engine ceased to pull, the train would cease to move.

But a train in very rapid motion presupposes a tolerably good road, in which the initial momentum is not materially absorbed. Where frequent stoppages are required, it is desirable to use considerable speed, in order to make up for the stoppages, and, therefore, considerable momentum has to be absorbed at each stoppage, or previous to the stoppage. To expend the momentum at the stoppage suddenly, would be equivalent to a violent blow, and therefore a retarding process must be resorted to, to expend the momentum gradually previous to the stoppage.

There is one obviously simple means of absorbing the momentum—making the train run up an incline previous to stopping, causing the gravity of the train gradually to expend the momentum, as a runaway horse is stopped by expending his power in running up hill.

But there are many cases in which this would be inconvenient or impracticable, and therefore the practice has obtained of absorbing the momentum by friction. The prevalent rule has been to apply the friction apparently to the wheels, but in reality to cause friction to take place between the wheels and rails. The brakes, first retarding and then stopping the wheels, convert them into a bad kind of sledge with a very small surface, the result being to grind flat places on the surface of the wheels, to drive the rails forward out of their chairs, and to cut away the surfaces of the rails and work out hollows at the rail joints. An examination of the rails near stopping stations, will show the much more rapid wear existing there than on other portions of the line.

[*] The author is indebted for this chapter to Mr. W. B. Adams.

The earliest wheel brakes used on railways were probably f a very simple kind—a piece of timber put through the pokes of the wheels to arrest their revolution, and still used, if the writer be correctly informed, on the Lickey in-line, as an impromptu resource when a waggon without a brake happens to be in the train. This is analogous to the process of tying a rope to the spoke of the wheel of a high-way vehicle when the dragshoe is missing. But as loose pieces of timber are awkward and not always at hand, the next step in progress was attained, viz., fastening a heavy iron lever to the side of the waggon, moving on a centre and with a wood block fastened to the short end to press on the wheel, when the long end was relieved from its supporting hook, and the weight made to press downwards. This kind of brake may in one sense be said to be self-acting, in so far that when once applied, it has no tendency to relieve the pres-sure on the wheel till the brake block be worn out, unless the wheel be stopped. It is the form of brake almost exclu-sively applied to waggons. [See Plates XLIII.—XLVII.]

The next kind of brake is, in its principle, the same as the foregoing, viz., pressing a block of wood against the wheels, though not in its application. Four wood blocks are suspended by iron hangers from the frame of the carriage, by a transverse shaft connected to thrusting rods, and which revolves by means of a lever at right angles, and a bell-crank connected with a vertical screw turned by the guard of the train, the four blocks are forced against the wheels, and if the action of the screw were continued, the blocks might be worn out if the revolution of the wheel were not stopped.

Apart from the evil of grinding flat places on the wheels by stopping them, this brake has another disadvantage. It makes the frame and the wheel a rigid connection, and stops the action of the springs. But this kind of brake has been more used than any other. The means of mechani-cally applying it have been various.

On the Great Western Railway, where the wheels of some of the six-wheel carriages were very close together, a very simple mode of application was used. A pair of thrusting bars, one connected to each block, were attached by their centres at an angle of about 45 degrees. A ver-tical screw worked immediately above by the guard of the train within the carriage, drew the thrusting bars to a more obtuse angle, and thus forced the blocks against the wheels. The mechanical action thus obtained was more powerful, but the defect of the connection between the wheels and frame preventing the action of the springs, remained the same as in the former example,

There is a considerable disadvantage in the action of all these brakes, inasmuch as the strain of the resistance to the pressure is thrown upon the axle-bearings, and may tend to force the journal against the cast-iron, and supposing this objection removed, there is a tendency to strain the axle guards. This probably gave rise to the brakes nipping both sides of the wheel, sometimes called the tender-brake. This is acted on by rods passing over both sides of the wheels, and pulling the blocks against them at each side of the periphery. [Plate XXXV.] This brake, like the foregoing, impedes the action of the springs.

With a view to ameliorate the jarring action produced by the application of wood-blocks to the wheels, Mr. Joseph Beattie, about the year 1840, applied a peculiar brake-block, formed of a piece of elastic steel, armed with a surface of platted hemp, which taking a gradual bearing, prevented the sudden snatch sometimes taking place with the common wood blocks.

As the friction of a carriage-brake for the purpose of re-tarding a train depends materially on the weight of the carriage, it was the custom to apply the brakes for the guards of the trains to the first-class carriages, because they were the heaviest. When the elastic action of the springs was stopped by the application of the usual hanging brakes, and the jar was thus communicated to the body, it was of course very annoying to the passengers, and it may be added, that the safety of the wheels on the rails was also lessened by the practice. For this reason Mr. Nathaniel Worsdell, about the year 1838, turned his attention to the practicability of applying brakes to the wheels without direct contact with the body. The result of this was the brake known as the "slide brake," consisting of a straight flat bar on each side of the carriage, spanning the axleboxes, and carrying a pair of wood-blocks, with iron-brackets to slide on the bar. The blocks were operated upon by the screw and lever motion in the usual manner. This brake fulfils the conditions of removing the jar from the body, and also prevents the strain on the axle-guards, but it leaves un-touched the difficulty arising from forcing the journals against the bearings, and also that of damaging the tyres by grinding flat places on them.

If we advert to the practice of retarding on highways, we rarely find the practice obtain of converting the wheel itself into a sledge by preventing its revolution. The usual plan is to put a shoe or sledge beneath the wheel, which holds it down, and the friction is thus transferred to the sledge, and the tyre is saved from damage.

A perception of the advantages thus obtained on high-ways, led to various attempts to imitate the shoe on railways. Mr. Lee obtained a patent for a brake of this kind in the year 1842, consisting of an iron-block fixed to a lever with its fulcrum on the axle, so as to bring the block under the wheel as required.

It is clear that if this brake were used in front of the wheel, and touching it, the tendency would be for the wheel to run on it if it had space. If it were behind the wheel, a con-stant pressure must be kept up by the guard. But there would be a considerable disadvantage if used in front. If it descended between the rail and wheel, the effect would be that of a sudden jerk, always dangerous at high speeds on railways. On the highway, the carriage stops to have the drag-shoe put on, and also to have it taken off, but it would not be convenient to stop a railway train to put on or take off brakes.

The principle evidently aimed at in this brake is, by means of an eccentric movement on the axle-box, to cause a large shoe to approach to or recede from the wheel and rail, or both. But the application at the end of a lever is disadvantageous.

A variety of this brake, known as Handley's brake, with double blocks and levers, has been used to some extent.

In the year 1842, Mr. Bodmer patented a brake to bear against the wheels and rails, particularly adapted to a tender, but which, instead of being suspended to the axles, as in the cases of Lee's and Handley's brakes, are suspended from the body of the tender, which is six-wheeled, a sledge being placed between each pair of wheels. The sledges, four in number, are provided with flanges similar to those of the wheels, and are some inches shorter than the distance between the wheels. Knuckle-jointed levers were applied between the frame and the sledges, similarly to Gooch's brake [Plate VIII.], and by straightening these levers by the screw-motion, the sledges are forced down on the rails. There is a mechanical objection to this brake, that it acts by raising the body off the wheels at the same time that it scotches them.

In Gooch's mode of making the body rest on the sledges without the intervention of springs, mischief is done both to the machinery and roadway, and a less steady and less safe friction is induced.

Dissatisfied with all the brakes he had seen, as not fulfilling the whole of the requisite conditions, viz.:—first, to convert the carriage into a sledge from a rolling body; secondly, not in any way to interfere with the action of the springs; thirdly, to get the whole of the insistent weight to bear on the sledges; fourthly, not to interfere with the action of the wheels, or in any way to rub the surface of the tyres; and, fifthly, to work in either direction; the writer set himself to work in 1846 to produce a brake corresponding to these requisites. The result was as follows:— The two axle-boxes were connected together on each side by a powerful horizontal bar. The sledges flanged at the lower side were connected to the bar by jointed bars, like a parallel ruler. One of these bars is prolonged upwards, and serves for a lever acted on by the rod and bell-crank, being prevented by a stop from working too far.

This brake fulfilled all the requisite conditions, but it fulfilled the last one—working in either direction—imperfectly. Running in one direction, the action on the rail would tend to keep the sledges up to their work without much strain on the crank. But in working the reverse way, there would be a constant action tending to lift the sledges from the rail.

To remedy this difficulty, the writer, in the year 1851, devised two other plans, both independent of the body, and both calculated for running in either direction. In one plan a bar connects the axle-boxes on each side of the carriage. To this bar are hinged the sledges, eight in number. Each pair of sledges is connected by a cross bar by an axis at the end, the bars being very strong and increasing to the centre, where a revolving nut is attached to each. Through these nuts are inserted a longitudinal bar, with screw-thrusts on its right and left. As the rod is turned in one direction by means of the ordinary guard's tackle, the sledges approach each other in pairs, and descend upon the rail with more or less pressure, as may be desired. When the bar is turned in the opposite direction the sledges rise.

This arrangement fulfils all the conditions required. It does not in any way interfere with the action of the springs, for the body can rise and fall on the vertical shaft worked by the guard, the wheel-tyres are not touched, the whole of the insistent weight is on the sledges. Under-bearings are provided to the boxes to take the upward pressure when the

sledges lift the wheels, and the sledges may either have flanges to them, or stops may be placed to limit the rise.

The other variety of sledge brake [Plates XL. and XLI.] produces a similar result, but is various in its action. The two axle-boxes are connected together by a horizontal bar similarly to the ordinary slide-brake. But the bar is formed into an angle-frame by the descending portions. On these descending portions slide the sledges. When sliding in the downward direction they approach the rail, and in the upward direction they recede from the rail. Two levers are attached by centres to the horizontal bar. The lower ends of these levers are attached to the sledges by slotted forks, working on pins to prevent the rise and fall. The upper ends of the levers are connected to tension-rods, which, when acted on by the lever and screw motion, set the sledges on to the rail. The opposite action lifts the sledges upwards. The levers and the sledges are connected to those on the opposite side by cross bars, and thus all act in unison.

It will be seen that this brake acts with the carriage running in either direction. There is a tendency in the friction on the rail to lift the two forward sledges, but there is a counteracting tendency to keep the two hinder ones to their work, so that the action is balanced. The sledges are not intended to touch the wheels, but they may if preferred; but it would be a disadvantage.

Apart from the question of obtaining retarding friction between the wheel and rail, or sledge and rail, there is another consideration as to the best mode of applying the friction, whether by the agency of the human hand, or by the force of the momentum. If applied by hand, it is essential, at least with passenger trains, that there should be a separate brakesman to every brake. This would involve expense; and for this and other reasons it has often been proposed to make brakes self-acting, and more than once experimentally practised. It is usually accomplished by means of the buffer-rods. When the speed of the engine is checked, the train collapses in length by the sliding in of the buffer-rods. To the ends of the buffer-rods are attached levers which act on the brakes, and bring them in contact with the wheels. But if this be done by rigid movement, without elastic compensation, the result will be a jumping action, endangering breakage and getting off the line.

Now, it is clear that on the self-acting principle the action of the brakes must depend on the stroke of the buffer-rod; but as this varies with the momentum and weight of the different parts of the train, to get a good adjustment the springs which provide the elastic compensation ought to vary in strength—strongest next the engine, and lessening towards the tail of the train. But it is evident that the practical making up of railway trains will permit of no such nicety.

Supposing that the brakes were only made self-acting with the extreme stroke of the buffer-rod, that could only take place by the sudden retardation of the engine. In such case there does not appear any advantage in self-acting brakes. If the engine had power enough to arrest itself, and cause all the buffer-rods to strike home, the train could not well overrun it, and would not need brakes.

Supposing the springs were made to put the brakes on at

the half-stroke of the buffer-rods, there would be the disadvantage of retardation of the train frequently when not required.

It appears, therefore, that the notion of stopping a train rapidly by any self-acting process, is not founded on any sound mechanical principle; and, in case of collision, there would be no advantage in so doing.

CHAPTER X.

MATERIALS.

THE underframes of carriages and waggons are usually of oak. Carriage-bodies are usually framed of ash, or the pillars may be of oak; and waggon-bodies, when framed, are usually framed of oak. The roof-ribs of carriages are of ash. The lining, roofing, and flooring of carriages, and waggons, are of yellow or red deals. The panelling of carriages is of mahogany. Step-boards are of birch.

Teak has been extensively employed by Williams, and by other makers, in the construction of rolling stock. Sabecu has also been employed for underframes. But, for framework, English oak appears to give the most general satisfaction.

The whole of the small iron work should be of best Staffordshire. The axles should be of Patent Shaft make, and the tyres of Patent Shaft or Yorkshire iron.

Painting. The painting of carriages externally is an elaborate process. The following is the process followed by Brown, Marshall, & Co.:—1st, The panelling is cleaned off smooth by the body-maker, ready for the painter. 2d, It then receives four coats of priming, composed of white-lead, lamp-black, linseed oil, and turpentine. 3d, It is filled up with five coats, composed of ochre, white lead, turpentine, and varnish. 4th, It is rubbed down with pumice-stone to make a clear surface. 5th, Receives two coats of lead colour. 6th, Is faced, or prepared to receive the ground colour. 7th, Receives the ground colour, the colouring matter of which is earthy. 8th, The ground colour is finished with lake prepared from cochineal. 9th, Receives three coats of copal varnish. 10th, Receives other three coats of copal varnish, and flatted after each course. 11th, Receives nine more coats of varnish

Williams, and some others, do not apply so elaborate a course of painting to teak-built carriages, but content themselves with applying a few coats of gold size and varnish.

Waggons should be painted with two or three coats of a mixture of red and white lead, and finished with one of lead colour. The iron work and springs should be japanned.

PART THIRD.—PERMANENT WAY.

THE consideration of the Permanent Way necessarily follows that of the rolling stock which it carries; as the two are inseparable, and their interests are identical, and so much is their identity appreciated, that the rails and the wheels are often compared to man and wife. We feel happy in being able to refer to, and to make the freest use of, Mr. W. B. Adams' paper on Permanent Way, read before the Institution of Civil Engineers, February 10, 1852, through the kindness of the Secretary, who has, in the most liberal manner, placed the entire paper, with the illustrations, at our disposal. The value of the favour is much enhanced by the circumstance that this paper contains, so far as we know, the only systematic investigation of the important question of rails; and that it is written by one who has made himself master of the subject, and who has the qualifications necessary for giving a reason for the faith that he holds.

"In examining the 'permanent way' of various kinds, used up to the present period, it is necessary," says Mr. Adams, "first to settle the exact meaning of the term. In its simple sense, it would imply a way of great durability; but that it does not satisfactorily fulfil this condition, may be assumed from the numerous changes and attempts at improvement it is constantly undergoing.

"It must therefore be understood," he proceeds, "that the term 'permanent way' means some kind of way left by the contractor, when he has removed his temporary way,

and which may be of greater, or less, durability, or permanence, according to its structure, but which must, in most cases, be governed by the quality of the material that can be most easily procured. Where timber is plentiful, it is largely used for the substructure; if it is scarce, stone is substituted; and if the capital is restricted, the iron is pinched too closely, as on the early railways in the United States. Whilst the ballast also varies according to locality, from broken stone, and burnt clay, to sand and gravel.

"The principal requirements of 'permanent way' are; that it be well drained, and especially in contiguity to the substructure. That the weight and damaging power of the engines and rollingstock, should be considered as the datum for calculation. That the strength, hardness, and tenacity of the rails, and the immobility of the substructure, should be adapted for the hardest work to which the railway is to be subjected. That the substructure should have an amount of bearing surface, proportioned to the load to be borne, and the nature of the soil, or ballast; and a sufficiently firm hold in the ground, to prevent looseness, or lateral movement, from the side lurches of the engines, or trains. That the rails should possess so much vertical and lateral stiffness, either in themselves, or by their fastenings, as to prevent all deflection, and have sufficient hardness of surface not to laminate, or to disintegrate, beneath the rolling loads; and have sufficient breadth, or tread-surface, to diminish the effect of the crushing power of the wheels. They should be as smooth as possible on the running surface, to prevent concussion; and be laid at the proper angle, and the curves regularly bent, so as to insure the accurate tread of the wheels: whilst the joints should be so made, that the rails may, practically, become continuous bars, yet with freedom to expand and contract without being too loose. And with all this, there should be interposed, between the rails and the solid ground, some medium, sufficiently elastic to absorb the effect of the blows of the wheels, without being crushed, or forced down into the ballast, and yet stiff enough to keep the upper surface of the rails in a uniform plane.

" If these conditions are fulfilled, the railway will be a ' permanent way' in the full sense of the term.

" The ballast may be considered the foundation of the railway; and the depth of it must vary with the structure. If sleepers are used in the ordinary manner, they should be sunk into the ballast, and yet have a sufficient quantity below, to prevent them from gradually sinking. Therefore, the thicker and more efficient the sleeper, the greater must be the depth of the ballast; and this makes the choice of the sleeper an important consideration; which again, is regulated by the kind of rail intended to be used.

" The earliest, cheapest, or rather lowest priced and worst form, of wrought-iron rails, is the flat tire-bar rail, spiked down on a longitudinal balk. This was adopted on most of the American railways at the outset, but is now abandoned, on account of the enormous wear and tear, and the great danger to passengers, as the ends curled up, and occasionally killed a passenger, through the bottom of the carriage.

" A variation of this kind of way, with the bars edgewise, has been for many years in use in quarries and other places where only a slow motion of the trains is required.

" The next in order is the single T fish-bellied rail, ranging from 28 lbs. to 35 lbs. per yard. It was originally patented by Mr. Birkinshaw, in the year 1820, and was first employed to any considerable extent, by Mr. G. Stephenson, on the Liverpool and Manchester Railway (1829-30); but is now no longer manufactured. This rail is a remarkable instance of correct reasoning from unproved data, for though all chair-rails are practically girders, the chairs being the supporting piers, yet in a rail 15 feet long, when the chairs yielded, that reduced portion of the rail which was supported by them, would also yield and bend; so that instead of making the rail a succession of fish-bellies, it ought rather to have been one single curved line at the bottom, as in the case of the cast-iron fish-bellied rail.

" The next is the single T parallel rail used with a cast-iron chair: this form, which was first extensively used by Mr. Vignoles, about the year 1833, is a valuable rail, under some special applications, hereafter to be noticed.

" The next is the double I parallel rail, generally used with chairs: this is a convenient, as well as a very strong mechanical form, and is well adapted for traffic. This double table-rail was first practically adopted on the Grand Junction Railway, by Mr. Locke, M.P., V.P., under whose directions the precise form was carried out by Mr. C. Manby (now Secretary of the Institution of Civil Engineers), to whom the order was given for manufacturing the first quantity, at the Ebbw Vale Ironworks, South Wales, early in the year 1835, when a very elaborate series of investigations was made by Mr. Locke, on the various forms of rails, and chairs, the material for, and the distances between the sleepers, &c. The rail was 4½ inches deep, with a flat bearing-surface of 2¼ inches wide on the top and bottom tables, which were precisely similar, and the weight was about 62 lbs. per yard. The chairs were of cast-iron, and were originally intended to have in each a metal filling-in piece, with a round oak trenail, or plug, between it and the face of the jaw of the chair, in order to force it against the web of the rail: this plan was, however, after a very short trial, abandoned, and solid plugs of oak were substituted for the iron filling-in piece and oak trenail. These oak plugs, or keys, were compressed into iron moulds, under hydraulic presses, by Mr. Beattie, at the Crown Street works, Liverpool, where, under Mr. Locke's directions, the same process had been in operation for two years previously, and the compressed plugs were first tried on the Liverpool and Manchester Railway.

" The foot-rail, a single (reversed) ⊥ section, with a broad foot, or base, to stand on longitudinal timbers, or on cross sleepers, to which it was bolted down, through holes in the foot, was generally known as the 'Stephenson and Vignoles rail.' It is now commonly used by contractors for a temporary way, with transverse sleepers, to which it is attached by dogs, or spikes, and it was, at one period, extensively used in the United States for permanent way, but being sometimes insufficiently fastened down by spikes, it not unfrequently caused accidents.

" Then comes the well-known bridge-rail, first used by Mr. Brunel on the Great Western Railway in 1838, and subsequently, on many other lines.

" Split rails, or rails rolled in two pieces, both in the form of the half of a double I, and also as a foot-rail, with a vertical joint between them, and put together so as to ' break joint,' are extensively used in America, being manufactured under a patent in England. The object of this form of rail is, in fact, to give a longitudinal scarf through the whole length, so as to prevent bad joints.

" Barlow's 'saddle-back rail' is the latest great innovation; it is used without sleepers; or, in the words of the patentee, 'is a trough rail, bearing on the ballast, and riveted to bearers.'

" Two general systems, known as the transverse and the longitudinal methods, have been adopted, for securing rails upon timber sleepers, and sometimes the two have been combined. But the desirability of adopting a material chemically durable, originally induced the use of stone blocks; and as these have been almost altogether abandoned, it will be well to inquire, why this has taken place, and if for sufficient reasons.

" The blocks were usually about 2 feet square, by 1 foot in depth, containing 4 cubic feet of stone. They were of various qualities according to the localities, and were placed, sometimes rectangularly in line, with intervals between them, and at others diagonally, nearly touching at the corners, and forming a continuous foundation, or substructure; in some instances they were laid in ballast, and in others only in the natural soil.

" To insure solidity, which was the object then aimed at, the cast-iron chairs were fitted accurately to the stones, and fastened to them by a pair of iron spikes, each driven into an oak trenail, bedded about 6 inches deep, in a hole bored in the stone block. It was soon found, however, that the chairs worked loose and cut into the stones; and to remedy this, a layer of felt, an eighth of an inch in thickness, was placed between the chair and the stone. but the felt being crushed by the heavy weights, the chairs became looser than before. The most probable solution of the defect is this :—the stone blocks partially subsided, irregularly deflecting the rails, which were held down by the spikes, until the elasticity of the rail, in seeking to regain its form, gradually drew the fastenings, and then an incessant hammering ensued between the chair and the stone, on the passage of trains, gradually cutting into the surface of the stone a recess of the form of the chair. To pack the stone blocks, or to restore them to their proper position, at so great a depth, involved a costly operation. Moreover, the noise in travelling was a nuisance to the passengers, and the hardness was found to be very destructive to the rolling stock, and therefore the use of stone blocks was discontinued, and in many cases they were removed from existing lines, and were replaced by transverse timber-sleepers, previously only used in embankments of new construction, being in fact merely "contractors' way," but of larger scantling and materials.

"Before the question was finally disposed of, an experiment was made on a portion of the Leeds and Manchester line, by levelling the solid rock, in which there could be no subsidence, and fastening the chairs to it, exactly as they had previously been attached to the stone blocks. The result, it is said, was to produce a road so hard and rigid, that it was impossible to continue the use of it, and this was considered to have definitely settled the question. If, however, instead of discarding the stone blocks, they had been used as foundations for supporting the timber sleepers, to which the rails could have been attached, it is probable that a much more really permanent way would have resulted."

On the Manchester and Bury line, Mr. Jesse Hartley laid some part of the line upon continuous walls of masonry, which were soon knocked up from the rigidity. In placing the stone blocks under the sleepers, Mr. Adams supposes them to be placed in rows, in close and continuous contact; so that the foundation would be practically permanent and undisturbed, as more particularly described by him further on.

"The mechanical change that was effected, by the substitution of timber for stone, was comparative freedom from noise, which [the noise] was undoubtedly an indication of a deflecting rail, rising and falling with the chairs on the blocks.

"The same rail, transferred to the transverse sleepers, would also rise and fall, but without noise. And that they do deflect is proved by the oozing of watery mud from beneath the sleepers, in wet weather; by the quantity of dust, in dry weather, and by the necessity for continually packing the sleepers, which latter forms a large item in the cost of "maintenance of way."

"Supposing the rails to be integrally strong enough to prevent deflection, when supported at their two ends, the seat of the rail in the chairs requires to be of sufficient area

to prevent that indentation both of rail and chair, which may be occasionally seen to the depth of a quarter, or even three-eighths of an inch.

"The last consideration is, the bearing surface of the sleepers themselves on the ballast. There are generally under each parallel pair of rails, of 15 feet in length, six sleepers of about 9 feet in length, by 10 inches in width, and 5 inches in thickness."

Three or four sleepers, seldom five, per rail of 15 feet length, used to be thought sufficient, and this was the common practice. Sleepers are now placed more closely: the Great Northern line has a sleeper per yard, and one extra for the joint, many if not most of the rails being 18 feet long. Rails of 21 feet long are finding their way into use.

"The rail," it is continued, "thus becomes a girder-bridge supported on piers, and when the rail deflects, the sleepers are forced into the ballast in detail.

"To overcome this depression of the sleepers, either their number must be extended, if needful, till they touch each other, like the corduroy, or plank roads of America, or else the depth and strength of the rails must be increased, so as to prevent all deflection.

"In the longitudinal system of timber-sleepers, as used on the Great Western and other lines, with bridge-rails, having a continuous bearing on the timber, the bearing surface of the rails on the timber is about 6 inches in width, and that of the sleepers on the ballast is about 13 inches. The depth of the rail being about $3\frac{1}{2}$ inches, and the depth of the timber 6 inches." These dimensions have been increased since Mr. Adams' paper was written

"The quantity of timber used in the transverse system, with four intermediate sleepers to each length of rail, is rather less than 16 cubic feet, and on the longitudinal system it is rather more than 16 cubic feet; or, with about the same quantity of timber, the bearing surface on the transverse plan will be about 12 inches in width; and on the longitudinal plan, about 13 inches, giving an advantage of 1 inch in width to each rail, or 2 inches to the pair of rails, in the longitudinal plan; but, as in the latter plan, the sleepers are 1 inch deeper over the whole surface, the effective quantity of timber is nearly 3 cubic feet more. In comparing the expense of the two systems, the cost of the fastening of the rails may be assumed to be equal in both cases; and, as the quantity of timber has been shown to be about equal, and the quality ought to be the same, the cost should be alike. For a long period the transverse timber system was considered the cheapest, but the reason was, that on many lines, the sleepers were very small, and of inferior quality, while in the case of the longitudinal system, it was essential always to have good timber. In addition to the increase of bearing surface in the longitudinal system, the broad base of the bridge-rail makes it much stiffer laterally, than the double $\mathbf{I}$ rail, and its smaller depth offers less opportunity of accident, from sudden lurches of the engine. But, on the other hand, the bridge-rail being only $3\frac{1}{2}$ inches in depth, is liable to deflect under loads, by which the double $\mathbf{I}$ rail, 5 inches in depth, would not be affected.

"Though the longitudinal timber tends to stiffen the bridge-rail vertically, the real effect depends entirely on the fastenings. The rail has two lateral flanches about 1¾ inch wide by ⅛ inch in thickness, through which holes are pierced at intervals of 3 feet.

" In the earlier examples these rails were fastened down by screws ; but as the rails and the timber deflected, a sliding movement took place between them, similar to that between the plates of a carriage-spring ; the screws were loosened, drawn out, or broken, and the timber was crushed in detail. To remedy this, in some cases the timber was cross-boarded, with manifest advantage ; and, in most cases, bolts with nuts passing through the rail-flanches and the timber, were substituted for the screw bolts ; subsequently, plates were introduced under the rail-ends, and also below the timber, and the bolts passed through all. But the author is not aware of any fastening yet being found quite effectual in preventing deflection, or the working movement between the rails and the timbers, or the loosening of the bolt-heads.

" On the old Croydon line, where the longitudinal system was used, with very light bridge-rails, it was not uncommon to find rails broken into two or more lengths, by constant deflection, and they were repaired by placing a plate beneath the fractured ends.

" With regard to the cost of repairs, the mere packing of the sleepers, under equal weights, should be less in the longitudinal system, because there is more bearing surface ; but to set against that, the wood is more crushed than in the transverse system with chairs, and the access to the bolts is very troublesome, while the fastening of the double ⊥ rails in the chairs, by wooden keys, is very simple, though in the joint chair, it is insecure, and the rising of the ends is a common cause of accident. The author, therefore, in the year 1848, suggested a new variation, combining the use of the double ⊥ rail with the longitudinal sleeper, so as to avoid deflection and to obtain the continuous bearing. Dividing the half balk of timber, about 7 inches by 14 inches, into two parts, the double ⊥ rail was half-grooved into each, and bolts being passed through below the rail, it was held as in a continuous wooden vice, embedded to the upper lip, the flanch of the engine-wheels being cleared by a shallow groove. Four lengths of this were laid down [by Mr. Samuel, the engineer] on the Eastern Counties' line, where it appeared to answer well, and is still in good order." Since the foregoing was written, the trial line was taken up, in 1853, in consequence, it is said, of the timber having failed, and broken up in the due course of tear and wear.

" With respect to the durability of timber-sleepers there appears to be some difference of opinion, arising, probably, from the various descriptions of timber employed. There have been two principal systems employed, for rendering timber artificially durable. The one was by saturation with certain chemical solutions, or mineral salts, which act chiefly on the albumen, producing a kind of tanning effect, but by which the mechanical strength of the timber is stated to be impaired ; moreover, the salt being soluble in water, is apt to be washed out again. The other system, now very generally employed, is by ' creosoting,' or injecting coal-oil, under pressure, by which both mechanical toughness and chemical durability are produced."

It is now generally believed that the strength of the

timber is not increased by the creosoting process. The chemical durability is fully established.

" Engineers have recently shown a disposition to resort to other materials, and it has been considered, whether it would not be possible to employ stone, which is chemically and mechanically the most durable material, and would afford a perfect foundation, provided the rails could be properly attached to the blocks.

" If the thickness of these blocks was reduced from 12 inches to 6 inches, the superficies remaining the same, and they were laid beneath each line of rails, nearly touching each other, and so as to support longitudinal sleepers, 8 inches by 6 inches deep, with bridge-rails, bolted down between every joint of the stones, through rails and timber to a small block below, a continuous bearing would be formed of chemically durable sleepers, equal to 60 feet of surface beneath two rails, whilst a sufficient amount of elasticity would be given. At the same time, it is probable that no other ballast would be required, as the extended bearing surface would prevent displacement, and a true permanent way, when once settled and undisturbed by the rolling loads, would thus be formed.

" Of course, the question of the cost of stone must depend chiefly on locality. In some districts it might be desirable to use cast-iron, or slate-flags, or the slag of the iron furnaces might be run into moulds. On this plan any kind of rail might be used ; for instance, a deep foot-rail, with a half-foot angle-plate, bolted laterally to its break-joint, to save timber, or a girder-rail between timbers, or probably the double ⊥ rail bedded between two timbers, as before described.

" The objections to the use of timber-sleepers, rendered very prominent by the inferior wood used in transverse structures, induced Mr. Reynolds, in 1836, to propose inverted troughs of cast-iron, lined with wood.[*]

" Subsequently, in 1846, Mr. Greaves, of Manchester, introduced a new metal sleeper, possessing several useful properties. (Figs. 325, 326, 327.) This sleeper is a semi-spheroidal bowl of cast-iron, having the chair, of any form, cast upon its apex, and is connected firmly with the opposite sleeper, at intervals, by a transverse bar, which preserves the gauge and retains the travelling table of the rail at the

Fig. 325.

Greaves' and Douglas' fish-joint Chair and Sleeper.

Fig. 326.

Greaves' surface-packed Sleepers, with Douglas' fish-joint Chairs.

proper angle. The joint sleeper has Douglas' fish-chair applied to it ; this is a double-headed chair, with loose fishing

---

[*] Vide Trans. Inst. C.E., vol. ii., 1838, page 73.

's of cast or wrought iron, attached to the rails by split keys.

There are several advantages in this system; the form he sleeper is strong—it holds well in the ground—the r is not liable to be detached—the whole bearing sur is directly beneath the load—the ballast is always kept and elastic—and there is an extremely ingenious con ance for packing it through two holes, with a pointed mer, from the surface, so that the sleeper and rail can forced upwards, without disturbing the general bed of last, or they may be lowered by taking out a portion from interior. The danger of admitting water, by opening ground, is thus obviated, and in certain situations this of great importance."

On the Egyptian Railway, where Greaves' sleepers have en laid down, it is found that the soft soil on which they st, is pumped up through the packing holes. This is an

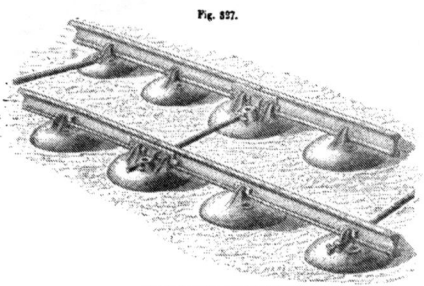

Fig. 327.

Greaves' Surface-packed Sleepers.

objection which requires to be met, before the sleepers can be generally employed.

" The next kind of cast-iron sleeper was that introduced by Mr. Peter W. Barlow, M. Inst. C. E., in the year 1849, on the South-Eastern Railway. (Figs. 328, 329.) Each sleeper is in two pieces, and consists of a plate 3 feet long by 7 inches wide, with two half-chair heads cast upon it,

except that for the joint-chair, which has three half-chair heads on it; these are made to grip the lower half of the rail tightly, by means of screw-bolts passing through the chair-heads below the rails, and holding them as in a vice. The casting of these plates so as to fit the rail perfectly, and to preserve all the metal in a state of rest, is a work of some nicety.

" Another cast-iron sleeper, figs. 330, 331, was brought forward by Mr. William H. Barlow, M. Inst. C. E.: it was very similar to the former, except that it was cast in

Fig. 328.

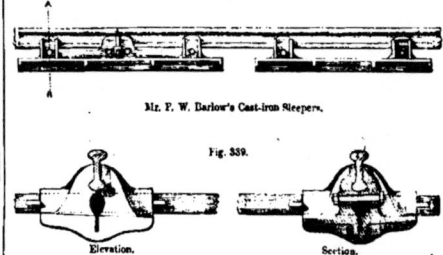

Mr. P. W. Barlow's Cast-iron Sleepers.

Fig. 329.

Elevation.   Section.

Fig. 330.

Mr. W. H. Barlow's Cast-iron fish-joint Sleeper, as used on the Midland Railway.

Fig. 331.

Elevation.

one piece, the rails being fixed in the chairs by keys, in the usual manner, or by resting the rail on a wooden block, keyed in below it."

" The cast-iron sleeper, Figs. 332, 333, introduced by Mr. Samuel, M. Inst. C. E., is a wedge-shaped trough, deep

Fig. 332.—Scale 1-48th.

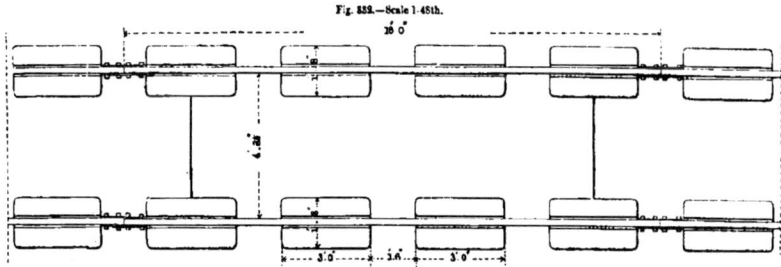

Samuel's Cast-iron Timber-bedded Permanent Way, with Fish-joints.

Fig. 333.—Scale 1-12th.

Detail of Sleeper.

enough to take the total depth of the rail, with two inclined side wings, at the upper part, to bear on the ballast. The rail is grooved into two pieces of timber, which clip it at the bottom and the sides, and being forced into the trough, the wood is compressed. The troughs are, however, not continuous bearings, and therefore the rail must be strong enough not to deflect."

This appears, mechanically, the best arrangement of cast-iron sleepers hitherto examined. It has depth of keel, to prevent lee-way, and has deep transverse flanges, which hold deep in the ballast, and prevent longitudinal motion. It supplies an elastic cushion between the rail and the sleeper; the rail is suspended out of contact with iron, and consequently remains uninjured on the lower side; by the system of cushioning, there is no nice fitting of the chair to the rail required, as the wooden blocks supply the adjustment; and, for the same reason, the same casting is applicable to various rails with similar sections.

"Cast-iron may be used, efficiently, for railway sleepers, but the masses must be larger than have hitherto been applied, and the form must be continuous; or, if detached, the sleepers should only serve as piers, or points of support, in which case the rail must be non-deflecting.

"Having examined the different kinds of sleepers, with reference to the vertical and lateral support they afford to the rails, the next question is that of the various modes of attaching the rails to the sleepers, in order to prevent the jolting and unsteadiness usually experienced on ordinary railways.

"About the year 1832, or 1833, a reward of £100 sterling was offered by a railway company, for the best mode of securing rails to chairs. Many plans were sent in, but none were integrally adopted. It was said, that an amalgamation was effected between three of the competitors, and the reward was divided.

"The fastening so rewarded was not successful, and it was soon found that the wooden key was the only arrangement that did not rapidly get loose. Many of these, however, were too small; the rails were loosened laterally, and a creeping motion was induced by the action of the brakes on the wheels, not unfrequently causing accidents."

Mr. Locke is understood to be the inventor of the wooden key. It is very questionable if the travelling of the rails is owing to any great extent to the action of the brakes, except perhaps on inclines, and at stations, as it takes place on the line where the brakes are seldom used. The travelling is probably due very much to the unevenness of the rail ends at the joints, as described further on; so that the wheels strike the elevated ends of the rails and drive them forward.

"The mode of fastening the chairs to the sleepers, by means of iron spikes, was insufficient. Rust got in between; the two irons were then rapidly worn away, and all became loose. This gave rise to the improved chairs of Messrs. Ransomes and May, with large-sized compressed trenails of oak, to attach them to the sleepers." (Figs. 334—339.)*

The oak trenails are stated to be in actual use on between two and three thousand miles of railway, and are being applied on the Indian lines by Mr. Rendel. The chairs are cast in iron moulds, to unite facility in moulding, with

---

* *Vide* Minutes of Proceedings Inst. C.E., 1842, vol. ii., page 72.

accuracy of form, good fitting, and correct in the rail.

Fig. 334.

Elevation of Chair, showing the inclination of the Rail.

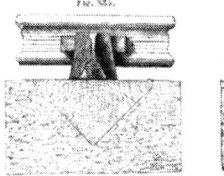

Fig. 335.　　　　　　　　Fig. 336.

Joint Chair.—End View.　　　Intermediate Chair.—End

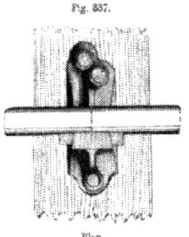
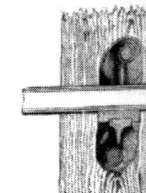

Fig. 337.　　　　　　　　Fig. 338.

Plan.　　　　　　　　　Plan.

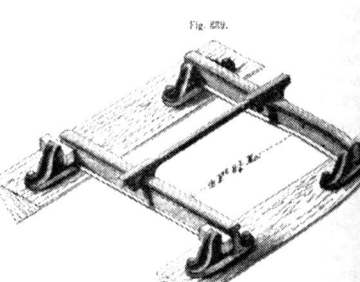

Fig. 339.

Rails, Chairs, and Sleepers, with the "cramp-gauge" affixed.

Ransomes and May's Chairs and compressed Wedges and Trenails.

Mr. Adams proposes the use of square, or rather ob trenails, instead of round ones, to facilitate the proc boring the trenail holes, and to prevent the sp d tro sleepers, which sometimes happens with the rou when the holes are not very accurately bored. oblong section, the proposed trenail would drive very in the direction of the grain of the sleeper, and we the greatest amount of resistance in the direction lurch of the engines; while it could not split the sle it would be of less width than the hole across the g

" The wood keys should also have ample bearing surface, so as not to be crushed with the side-lurch of the engine.

" Apart from the question of securing the rails to the sleepers, is that of the best mode of securing the ends of the rails to each other, so as to approximate to a continuous bar.

" One of the earliest attempts to obviate the evils arising from insufficient connection at the rail-joints, was on the Blackwall Railway.

" In that case the rail-ends were connected together by a scarf-joint, about 6 inches in length, with the points dovetailed, and the whole wedged into the chair. As these rails were only used with rope-traction, and were not tested by locomotive work, for which they were not intended, no deduction can be drawn from them; but they were weakened by the scarf, and were expensive in manufacture.

" On examining the joints of a railway out of order, it will be found that the forward end of each rail, in the direction of the traffic, stands, apparently, slightly higher than the hinder end of the rail in front of it (Fig. 340). When the weight comes on it, so as to press it down to the chair, it becomes the lowest, as the under part has been hammered in the chair, and the rail is reduced in depth. When once

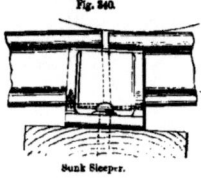

Fig. 340.

Sunk Sleeper.

rails are thus hammered, it becomes impracticable to secure them firmly in the chairs, except by cutting off their ends.

" The joints of the rails are evidently the weakest parts of the line of way; therefore the great object is how to strengthen them; and this cannot be done by taking away metal from the already too weak part. Supporting the joint by extra sleepers appears a simple remedy, but the sleepers are not practically supports, as they only bear on loose ballast, and not on any continuous surface. It becomes necessary, then, to join the rails firmly together. The operation of 'fishing,' by the addition of pieces of metal to each side, then presents itself; but to secure these 'fishes,' becomes the next question. The simplest mode is to take the rail-joint wholly out of the chair, and to place a sleeper, with a chair on it, on each side of the joint, thus suspending the joint between the two chairs. The 'fishes' being then driven in on each side of the rails, the rails and chairs are connected together. This was practised by the author in 1847.

" The damaged rails were thus supported by the chairs in the undamaged part, and they were made practically continuous, while permitting expansion and contraction, by the sliding of the 'fishes.' But putting the 'fishes' into the chairs involved the necessity for fresh castings, and it was found a simpler operation to punch holes in the rails, and connect the 'fishes' together by four bolts passing through all— the holes in the rails being larger than the holes in the 'fishes,' to permit of expansion and contraction. The first 'fishes' tried were of cast-iron, and they answered very well; but subsequently wrought-iron was substituted—the edges of the 'fishes' bearing against the top and bottom of the web of the rail, leaving the middle untouched, so that the bolts were held as it were in spring tension endways, and therefore did

not work loose. So perfect was this arrangement, that old rails, which had become useless, when battered at the ends, so that one end projected nearly a quarter of an inch above the other, when once firmly connected by the 'fishes,' gradually rolled, under the working of the trains, to a perfectly level surface."

" The application of the 'fishing-plates' to ordinary rails is very simply and rapidly effected, and the results are very satisfactory." (Figs. 341, 342).

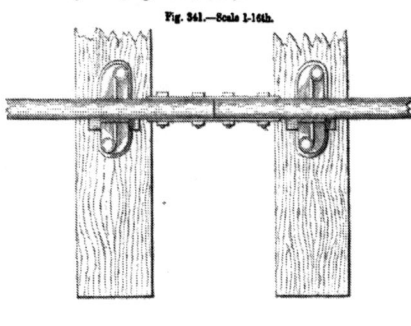

Fig. 341.—Scale 1-16th.

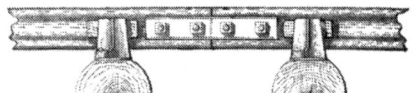

Fishing-plates applied to ordinary Rails.

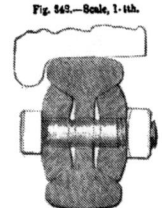

Fig. 342.—Scale, 1-4th.

Enlarged Section of Rail and Fishing-plates.

" The next proposition for improving joints was by Professor Gordon. It was to make a horizontal lap, by cutting away 3 inches from the top of one rail, and 3 inches from the bottom of its neighbour, to half the depth of each, and then lapping them together and securing them in the chair. It was expected that the hinder rail in the line of progress, thus lapping over the forward one, would keep both down together. But whether from bad iron, or from the diminished strength of the parts, it was found that the ends broke off, and the plan was abandoned.

" At length, in the year 1849, the authorities on the Eastern Counties Railway resolved to try the experiment of the 'fish-joint.' Some half-dozen rails were jointed with cast-iron 'fishes,' and they were found to answer.

" Many persons went to examine them, yet though all appeared satisfied, the railway companies and the engineers exercised a wise discretion in waiting till experiment had become experience. Progress under such circumstances is slow; and, moreover, as the trial seemed to throw a new light on the question of good joints, many new experiments were made."

The fish-joint is now in extended use on many principal lines; particularly, the London and North-Western Railway, the Midland, and the Eastern Counties.

There is an advantage arising from the use of cast-iron fishes instead of wrought. An unwise economy has in some cases led to such a diminution of the weight of the wrought fishes that they acquire a permanent set under the weight of the engines. The tendency of the rails under the rolling of the wheels is to arch upwards, precisely as if a series of wedges had been driven into their upper surface. Strong and powerful fishes counteract this; weak ones subside into a hole. In some cases where fishes are applied, the joint sleeper, for the sake of economy, is wholly taken away; thus putting an extra strain on the fishes both vertically and laterally, in which direction the rail is weakest, and the rails may be forced outwards, and the bolts broken. The iron being tough, the setting of the fishes is not noticed. But if cast-iron is used, the breakage tells the tale; and it is needful to renew them till sufficient strength be attained.

"Mr. J. Fowler, M. Inst. C. E., produced a joint-chair (Fig. 343), formed of three pairs of jaws cast together upon a sole-plate, the two extremities resting upon two sleepers

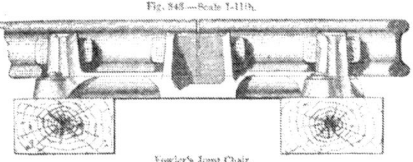

Fig. 343.—Scale 1-11th.

Fowler's Joint Chair.

below: it is said to answer well on the East Lincolnshire line, and has been in use there since 1849. Various other plans also were tried or suggested."

Mr. James Bell, of Edinburgh, patented, in 1851 or 1852, a joint chair of cast-iron having a sole 2 to 3 feet long, with two jaws cast to the exact form of the web and lower table of the rail, just sufficiently slack to be driven upon the rails endwise, and to hold them as in a vice. Two wooden keys were driven into the chair, one at each end, to bring up the bearings. This plan has given much satisfaction.

Mr. R. S. Norris, of Warrington, introduced a new joint chair, in 1852, which he casts in its place, from a portable cupola; it embraces the bottom and sides of the two ends of the rails at the joint, and being about 12 inches long, it firmly unites the rails into one practically continuous girder. It works most satisfactorily.

"In applying the 'fish-joint' to the repair of rails on lines, when funds had grown scarce, an objection arose to the cost of an extra sleeper and chair, in addition to the 'fishes.' To meet this objection, Mr. Samuel contrived a modification of the 'fish.' (Fig. 344.) A chair was cast with only one jaw, made to fit against one side of the rails, a wrought-iron 'fish' being placed against the other side, and all bolted together through the rails and 'fishes.'" This plan required only one sleeper at the joint, and its peculiar value consisted in substituting a secure for an insecure

joint, without interfering with the sleepers ab re-spacing them.

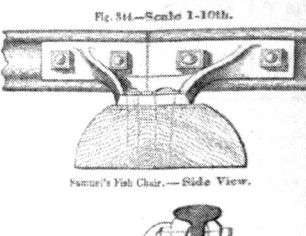

Fig. 344.—Scale 1-10th.

Samuel's Fish Chair. — Side View.

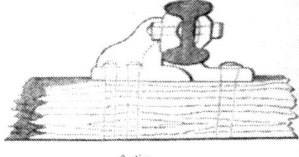

Section.

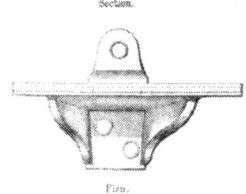

Plan.

With the same object, Mr. Adams has lately 1854) proposed a new plan, whereby, in securing t

Fig. 345.—Scale 1-8th.

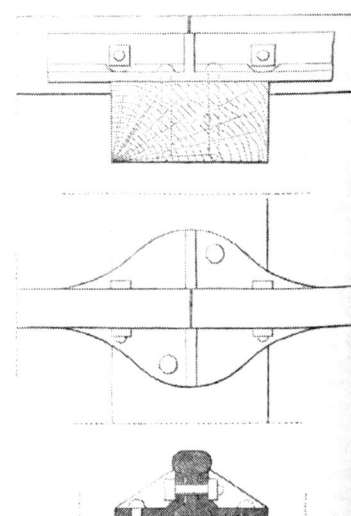

W. B. Adams' Cast-iron Bracket-joint, without wood keys.

of an existing line, the existing joint-sleeper may remain; and the removal of the inefficient joint-chair may make way for an efficient iron-bracket joint without wood-keys, or with wood-brackets for those who prefer it. Fig. 345 shows this in plan, side view, and cross section. A pair of cast-iron brackets are bolted to the rails in the side channels by two bolts, instead of four, as in the case of the 'fish-joint.' Each of the brackets has a broad foot which bears on the sleeper, and is spiked down to it: the lower table of the rail projecting below the feet, and, being grooved into the sleeper, keeps the gauge without strain on the spikes, and in this mode the bolts through the rails are sufficient. This plan appears the simplest of any of the modes of securing the joints of double ⊥ rails, and would be effective in stiffening the rails laterally as well as vertically.

A simple method, planned by Mr. Adams, of avoiding the use of cast-iron chairs, and at the same time of firmly attaching the rails to the sleepers, is shown in Fig. 346, in

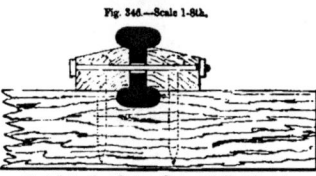

Fig. 346.—Scale 1-8th.

Adam's Rail without Cast-iron Chairs, with Wood Brackets.

which the double-headed rail in common use, is entirely bedded with timber side brackets on the timber sleeper, and is free from concussion and noise. The following is Mr. Adams' statement of the advantages derivable from the use of the timber brackets, as shown:—"In the ordinary mode of using this rail, a cast-iron chair or shoe is spiked down to a transverse sleeper of wood. In this chair of iron the rail is fixed by a lateral wedge of wood, and when so fixed, the top of the rail is raised seven inches above the top of the sleeper. But, in the mode of fixing the rail with timber brackets, the iron chair is dispensed with, the lower table of the rail is sunk an inch into the sleeper, and thus the total height of the rail above the sleeper is only four inches, instead of seven, as when used with iron chairs. It is obvious that the more the rail is elevated, the more difficult it is to keep it firm against the lateral blows of the engine and carriage wheels. The advantage, therefore, of the improved mode in lowering the rail, nearly one-half, must be clear.

"In using cast chairs, which are spiked down to the sleepers, the spikes alone have to sustain all the lateral shocks. In the improved mode, the rail being grooved into the sleepers, takes the lateral resistance directly, and the only use of the spikes is to hold down vertically. This is a source of great safety.

"Again, the grooves for the two rails being cut by machinery, an accurate gauge is obtained and maintained, independently of skilled labour in laying down.

"Again, the double-headed rail was originally designed for the purpose of reversing, so that, the upper side being too much worn, or proving unsound, the lower side might be turned upwards. Practically, it has not served the former purpose, because it is so battered and crushed in the cast-

iron chairs, as mostly to be useless for any firm fixing in that mode. But in many cases, these damaged rails, unfitted for cast chairs, may be turned to account by securing them with the wood brackets. The side channels of the rails are generally unaltered in form, and to them the brackets can at any time be fastened, and the grooves in the sleepers may be cut to any form the table of the rail has taken. In this mode, several years' further work might be taken out of the rails, and the value of the old chairs might help to pay for the improvement.

"By using the rail only with timber fastenings, as shown in the diagram, the rail is in no way damaged, and may be effectually reversed. In the mode of using these rails with iron chairs, and wood keys, the height and unsteadiness of the rail rapidly crushes and loosens the key, so that it is continually falling out. And this occurring at the joint, is a source of great danger, independently of the occasional fracture of the cast-iron chairs.

"The two pieces of hardwood are about 9 inches in length, and 3¼ inches in width and thickness, and are bolted by a single bolt through the rail, one in each channel, the lower rib of the rail resting on a cross channel of the transverse sleeper. Spikes are driven through the pieces of oak into the sleeper, and the whole is secure. If the timber shrinks, the bolt is tightened in its dry condition, and will ever after remain tight. At the joints, plates of iron are placed in the rail channels, between the timber brackets and the rail, the same bolts securing the whole. In some cases, in laying new rails in perfect condition, and with hardwood brackets, the joint plates might be dispensed with. If preferred, the brackets, instead of being in short lengths, might be continuous with the rails.

"In addition to the mechanical advantages, there is a considerable economical saving in maintenance to calculate on from the reduced height and better bedding of the rail. And by reason of the reduced height, a saving in ballast may be effected, and upon the general outlay, taking waste into consideration by breakage of chairs, the saving in laying down a line may be considered as equivalent to the whole value of the cast-iron chairs."

"Occasional breakages of cast-iron sleepers," it is continued in the paper already quoted from, "owing to the desire to lessen the first cost of material, and thus unduly reducing its proportions, caused attention to be turned to the capabilities of wrought-iron.

"The saddle-back rail of Mr. W. H. Barlow, previously alluded to, was the first result. This rail, Fig. 347, is

Fig. 347.—Scale 1-8th.

Mr. W. H. Barlow's Saddle-back Rail.

usually 13 inches in width, and 5¾ inches deep, and weighs 126 lbs. to the yard.* It is stated, that 'it will bear a

* The weight now generally used [1854] is 90 lbs. to 94 lbs. per yard. —See. Inst. C.E.

pressure of 40 tons without spreading out in width, and of 27 tons between bearings, 4 feet 4 inches apart, without its elasticity being injured; the stiffness of the rail virtually increases its bearing surface, for if a weight be placed over the centre sleeper of a length, and the rail be flexible, the whole of that weight will be borne by the sleeper, whereas, if the rail be rigid, the weight will be equally distributed over the adjoining sleepers.'

" If this rail be as rigid as it is described to be, with a proper extent of bearing surface, and is sufficiently heavy to remain quiescent under the rolling loads, there ought to be no cost of 'maintenance of way,' but only the expense of renewal from time to time. But, upon examination it appears, that though the rail is 13 inches wide, this is not all true bearing surface. If the trough, or hollow, were filled with adhesive ballast, that could not leave it, the whole width would be bearing surface, but it appears to lie on the ballast as a saddle lies on a horse's back. It is stated, that considerable noise is experienced in running over this rail. If so, this would indicate a hollowness. In dry sandy ballast, however well the hollow of the rail might be packed, it must always be falling away from the upper part of the trough. Then again, the side surface to resist displacement, by the lurch of the engine, is but 4 inches, in a wedge form, tapering down to a sharp edge, like the form of a plough-share. This want of hold must render the process of packing very difficult.

" It is stated, that ' in this wrought-iron rail, there is a sensation of hardness, which appears to result from the rails having been laid down a short time, and not having been worn to sufficient evenness on the upper surface.' There can be no doubt, that the mere roughness, from the rolls, on the surface of rails, is sufficient to produce positive blows at high speeds, and were it practicable to produce a smooth surface on them, there would be a great advantage in it, not merely by the even face, but by hardening. But assuming the saddle-back rail to be a rigid girder, another consideration ensues. It is stated, by experimenters, that the limit of weight which can be borne by the best wrought-iron, before it begins to be crushed, is 11 tons to the square inch. Rail-iron has been stated to be only equivalent to 8 tons per square inch. But the impact of a driving-wheel with 7 tons weight on it, is only on a point, and under favourable circumstances a line, unless the rail deflects and partly laps round the wheels. If this be correct, it follows, that a rail ought to laminate and roll out under heavy engines, as has actually occurred in many instances. Though it must be stated, on the other side, that there are many rails which have been down for years under heavy engines, and are still not injured, probably escaping lamination by elastic deflection.

" If it be resolved to continue the use of inflexible girder rails, one of two methods must be resorted to. The first is, to make the rail of steel, or to steel the surfaces; and the other is, to increase the width. As the weight on the engine is greater than that on the train-carriages, or waggons, it might be desirable to construct the rails with two surfaces, the double surface for the engines, and the single surface for the train, with a channel rolled between the two for the holding-down bolts, which will be presently alluded to.

" Reasoning on the absolute necessity, in regard to economy of 'maintenance of way,' of obtaining an inflexible rail, that will not crush either the ballast, or the sleepers in detail, the question changes from Mr. Barlow's rail to his mode of connecting his rail-ends together; for if the connection does not produce equal strength with the other portions of the rail, mischievous results ought to ensue, unless the middle of the rail be three times the breaking, or deflecting strength, and the joint only twice, and then there is a waste of one-third of the strength of the rail.

" The mode used, is to place below the two rail-ends a saddle of wrought-iron, about 2 feet in length fitting the trough. To this saddle the two rail-ends are rivetted firmly at the outer edges, without any provision for expansion or contraction. The upper portions of the rails abut closely together, and thus the lower part is in tension, and the upper part in compression, and the two together form a beam, the strength of which must depend on the power of the rivets to resist being sheared off."

The joint plates are now [1854] made about 2 feet 6 inches long, and additional rivets are found desirable.

" Supposing the upper, or abutting portion to be removed, the lower portion with the rivets would be apt to bend under a load, consequently the strength of the joint must depend on the abutting ends and the strength of the rivets. If, therefore, there be any expansion, the rails must elongate through the whole length, and slide over the surface, or they will buckle upwards or sideways. But it is said there is no expansion; and if so, it is possible that the contact of the earth carries off the heat as it is generated, just as water carries off the heat applied to the bottom of a boiler.

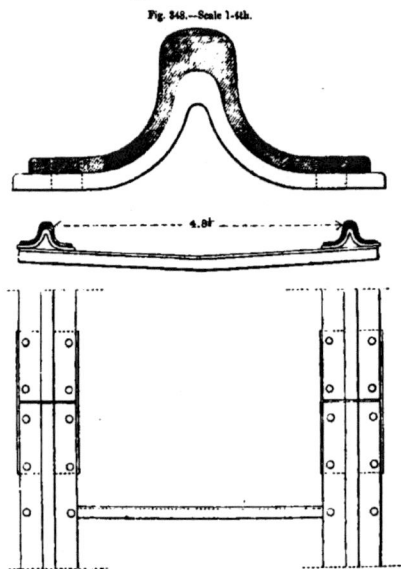

Fig. 248.—Scale 1-4th.

W. H. Barlow's Saddle-back Rail, latest Section.—Scale 1-84th.

" It would appear clear, that when the upper portion of this rail is worn by the traffic, a very large quantity of iron will have to be removed, and renewed. This, of course, is a matter for commercial consideration on one side, and of mechanical convenience on the other."

Of late, the form of the saddle-back rail has been modified; and the rail is now (March, 1854) recommended and applied by the Permanent Way Company, of the form shown in Fig. 348, in which the ploughshare-action, alluded to by Mr. Adams, is much reduced, if not quite removed, as the rails lie more flatly upon the ballast. This section, 92 lbs. per yard, is employed by Mr. Brunel on the West Cornwall Railway.

"Assuming that, for certain purposes, the solid rail might be desirable, it remains to be proved that the saddle-back is the best form, either for strength or for packing. Lateral and vertical stiffness, with large bearing surface vertically, and security against lateral shifting, are the objects sought for; and with these points in view, the T-form section, Fig. 349,

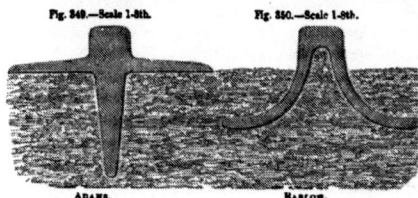

Fig. 349.—Scale 1-8th.   Fig. 350.—Scale 1-8th.

ADAMS.   BARLOW.

Comparative views of Barlow's Saddle-back Rail, and Girder Rail proposed by W. B. Adams.

with the rail, or rib, on the upper surface, appears to be well adapted for general use. In this form there is a bearing surface horizontally of 14 inches in width, the total depth is 9 inches, and the depth below the horizontal surface is 6¼ inches, giving great vertical stiffness, and serving as a keel to prevent lateral movement in the ground, the rail being used without any sleepers. To form the joints, two cheek-plates, about 2 feet in length, must be bolted to the vertical and horizontal portion, with allowance for expansion and contraction in the holes through the rails, which are made larger than in the cheek-plates. This rail would lie very firmly in the ballast, and the packing from the surface would be very easy, the vertical web forming a solid back to ram the ballast against. If it were required to key more firmly in the ground, a timber might be bolted to the lower edge. It might be objected that there would be a difficulty in rolling this rail, but practice decreases those objections daily; in fact, there is, practically, no mechanical difficulty to large demands. It might be objected to this rail that it might be noisy, but probably it would be less so than a trough-form rail.

"If a quiet rail be required, without vertical deflection, it may be produced by rolling an upper table with a deep thin vertical web, and bolting it laterally between two timbers. To secure adhesion between the timbers, the sides may be rolled to the form of the planking of a clincher-built ship, multiplying in that mode horizontal bearing surface on the timber, or a T-formed rail may be used."

Fig. 352 is a girder-rail proposed by Mr. Adams, so as to employ the smallest number of parts together with the maximum of vertical and lateral stiffness. "It may be considered," he says, in his description of it, "as a single-headed

form, with a pair of lateral supporting wings superadded at the position of the neutral axis; or it may be considered as a foot-rail on the American plan, with a lower vertical rib

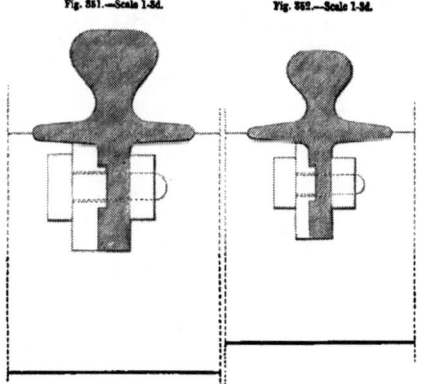

Fig. 351.—Scale 1-3d.   Fig. 352.—Scale 1-3d.

Girder Rails by W. B. Adams.

superadded to give vertical stiffness, and keep the gauge without straining the holding-down spikes by the blows of the wheels. Two varieties are shown, one 4½ inches in depth by 3½ inches in width, weighing 42 lbs. to the yard. A joint plate 1 foot 6 inches in length, 2½ inches wide, and ½ inch thick is secured to the rail-ends by two bolts. The rails are in 18-feet lengths. The rails are fixed in cross-sleepers accurately cut or grooved by a machine. The head of the rail appears small, but it is amply sufficient for the tread of the wheel. The height above the sleeper is only 2½ inches, though the total depth is 4½ inches, or ½ inch deeper than the deepest American rail.

"The other variety (Fig. 351) is of a similar form, weighing 65 lbs. per yard, and is 5½ inches in depth, and 4 inches in width across the supporting wings. The joint-plates are 1 foot 6 inches in length, 2½ inches deep, and ⅝ inch thick. The head, or wearing table of this rail, is 2½ inches, which is amply sufficient for wheel-tread, unless under enormous and unprofitable weights. Rails were originally 1¾ inch wide, and they were gradually widened to 2½ inches; but this required much more metal, because, as the rails wore down flat, the edges cut away when not supported by a sufficient depth of metal. In the last variety shown, the head is sufficiently wide to prevent vertical cutting of the edges, and the two lateral wings give great strength against side shocks. With the double T-rail, or with the American foot-rail, the tread requires greater width than the girder-rail to preserve lateral stiffness.

"For countries where skilled labour is dear, this girder-rail is especially valuable. The sleepers cut by machines render accuracy of gauge certain, though the commonest labourers be employed to lay down the line and keep it in repair. The ordinary American rail, as now constructed, is 4 inches in height and 4 inches in width, and it is simply fastened down by spikes driven on either side the foot. The rail is therefore subject to constant displacement by the blows of the wheels and the loosening of the spikes, involving great risk of the engine getting off the line. Moreover, the flat plate beneath the joints bolted down to the wood does not efficiently keep the rails secure.

"The most common defect in rails is the want of vertical depth. They have usually been made shallow to prevent them from rocking, and the result is, that the rails deflect vertically, and the wheels are constantly running up hill and wasting steam-power."

Fig. 353 shows a "channel"-rail, designed by W. B. Adams, especially adapted for level crossings, and for street or highway lines where other vehicles are intended to run. It is shown as intended to reverse. The form is that of the

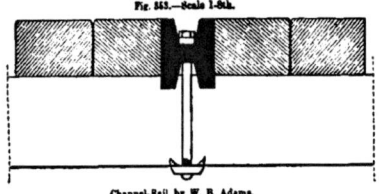

Fig. 353.—Scale 1-8th.

Channel-Rail, by W. B. Adams.

letter H. The horizontal web which connects the two vertical sides together is formed with holes, through which pass bolts or screws to fasten it to the transverse, or horizontal sleeper, into which it is slightly grooved to secure the gauge. For street and road work it is required that the paving should come close up to the rail to secure it, and preserve the level. Consequently, the flange of the wheel must run between, and it can be either a central or side flange, according as the wheel may be required to sustain a heavier or lighter load. This rail may be made with a single channel if preferred, but with a double channel it is capable of four reversals if used with light loads. Made with a single channel it would be about 65 lbs. per yard; double, it would be about 90 lbs. per yard. It must be borne in mind that rails exposed to be run over by heavy road-carts and waggons would require to be more firmly fixed than such as are protected from lateral blows. The joints are made by an iron casting, or a piece of the same rail, bolted beneath or laterally. Instead of timber-sleepers, stone may be used, and the sleepers may be either transverse or longitudinal. If stone-sleepers be used, elastic material should be placed beneath the rails.

"There is another subject in railway maintenance," proceeds Mr. Adams, in his published paper, "which appears to have been overlooked. Provision has been made for drainage, but not for drainage in immediate contact with the rail. It is known by experience, that the vibration of passing trains commonly opens a thinner, or thicker air-space, between the vertical edges of the sleepers and the ballast, when the weather is dry, and that into these portions of the way rain finds its way as to a drain. The sleeper, being absolutely loose from all lateral adhesion, springs up and down beneath the trains, and packing is required. The oozing of the fine-washed sand from the sides of the sleepers, points this out to the way-men. Moreover, even in continuous rainy weather, the ballast being an absorbent material, or sponge, and the sleeper non-absorbent,

the greater mass of water will be found at the point of contact, precisely as the water of gravel-beds is intercepted by a clay stratum.

"Impressed with this defect, the author was led to consider the practicability of getting the drains close to the sleeper, and the most obvious mode was, to make the sleeper itself the drain, by constructing it of perforated iron, or supposing iron-rails to be used without sleepers, to make the rail itself the sleeper. The plan proposed to accomplish this, is to roll a rail with a deep thin vertical web; two angle-pieces of cast, or of sheet iron, bent to the requisite form are bolted to the rail above and below, breaking-joint; these angle-plates are perforated, and the water will find its way through the perforations, precisely as it does in ordinary clay drain-pipes, and may be led away to the exterior at convenient intervals."

We have thus endeavoured, to the best of our ability, to place before our readers a complete and connected account of the plans of permanent way now before the public; and we have to acknowledge, in addition to the courtesy of Mr. Charles Manby, the Secretary of the Institution of Civil Engineers, the valuable assistance we have derived from Mr. Charles May, and Mr. James Samuel, of the Permanent Way Company, both of them engineers of large and varied experience. We have also to acknowledge the valuable aid of Mr. W. B. Adams, who has given us the benefit of his mature experience and observation, and has enabled us to make some important additions to the stock of information contained in his paper already published and referred to. This paper, it must be observed, was written early in 1852, and, on the more changeable and progressive topics for consideration, it has now, we hope, been duly supplemented, up till the present time [March, 1854].

Before leaving the subject, we must add a few remarks on the question of progress, which is occasionally designated as "speculation." It is quite clear that "permanent way" is not yet finally permanent, by any known processes, and if new processes are not to be proved there can be no chance of improvement. All probable plans should therefore be tried and compared, not in the costly and unwise course frequently resorted to under the pressure of a difficulty, making a wide change without previous trial, but having constantly on trial everything appearing theoretically right, and that cannot theoretically be demonstrated to be wrong. If such experiments were systematically pursued on a small scale with every variety of fixed and movable plant, on any one railway, or under the inspection of the Board of Trade, the result in saving of maintenance would now be demonstrated. To illustrate what we mean, we may refer to the fish-joint, which laid for a long time in abeyance after its first production. It is clear that the principle was as sound the day it left the inventor's brain, as it is, now that so many railway companies have adopted it, and that the probabilities were all in its favour theoretically. But it was a "speculation;" it had not been tried—an objection applying equally well at the outset to the whole railway system—and therefore it was neglected, and the saving of scores of pounds per mile per annum in maintenance was protracted and left to the chapter of accidents.

PART FOURTH.—RESISTANCES OF ENGINES AND TRAINS.

CHAPTER I.

HISTORICAL SKETCH.

THE doctrine of engine and train-resistances has not yet (1854) been placed on a satisfactory basis; and much experiment is wanting for the obtainment of sufficient data, and the development of correct principles. The circumstances affecting the resistance of railway trains in motion, are so various and so involved, that nothing short of a Government Commission, or a combination among railway authorities, on a large scale, would suffice for the discussion of the subject on the scale demanded by its importance. Be it our duty to do what we can for the promotion of the inquiry, and to submit the results of our own experience and investigation.

The late Mr. Stephenson and Mr. Nicholas Wood made some experiments, in 1818, with the coal waggons on the Killingworth Railway, to ascertain their tractive resistance at slow walking speeds. The experiments were made by means of a pendulum dynamometer, carefully constructed, and accurately graduated, and they were conducted with much care and success. The waggons had four cast-iron wheels, 34 inches in diameter, with flanges $\frac{3}{4}$ inch high, fixed on wrought-iron axles which were 4 feet apart, with inside journals, $2\frac{3}{4}$ inches diameter. The rails were of cast-iron, in lengths of 3 feet $9\frac{1}{2}$ inches. The resistance to traction on a level, varied from 10 lbs. to 20 lbs. per ton of the total weight of the waggons, with their loads. The variation was due to the state of the wheels and the bearings. The traction was least with casehardened wheels and brass bearings; with soft or unhardened wheels, and cast-iron bearings, it was greater; and it was greatest of all, with soft and worn wheels, and wrought-iron bearings off the hammer.

Many other experiments on the resistance of trains have since been made, with various loads and speeds. But they are, most of them at least, open to the objection of not being applicable under the actual conditions of trains drawn by engines and tenders. Such are all those that have been made by the force of gravity on inclined planes. Mr. Wyndham Harding read a paper on the "Resistances to Railway Trains at different Velocities," in 1846, before the Institution of Civil Engineers. His conclusions were based principally upon experiments made on the 4 feet 8½ inch gauge, by gravity on inclined planes, and by the Atmospheric Railway apparatus. The formula embodying his results, and constructed by Mr. J. Scott Russell, was adopted by him simply as an empirical formula. It recognizes three elements: first, friction, constant at all velocities; second, frontage resistance, increasing as the square of the speed; third, resistance from concussion and vibration, held to vary simply as the velocity. Let 6 lbs. per ton represent the friction, T = the total weight of the train in tons, V = the velocity in miles per hour, ·0025 lbs. = the wind resistance per square foot of frontage, $\frac{V}{3}$ = the concussion resistance

at and above 10 miles per hour, N = the frontage of the train in square feet. Then the formula is

$$6 + \frac{V}{3} + \frac{V^2 \times \cdot 0025 \times N}{T} = \text{Total resistance in pounds per ton.}$$

The conditions under which the formula is expected to apply, are, an uniform speed maintained in calm weather, an uniform inclination upon a line free from sharp curves, and the rails and carriages in good working order. The following selection of examples from Mr. Harding's table illustrates the application of the formula:—

TABLE NO. XCIII.—RESISTANCE OF TRAINS ON THE 4 FEET 8½ INCH GAUGE. SELECTION FROM WYNDHAM HARDING'S TABLE OF RESULTS.

Number of Carriages.	Speed.	Weight of Train.	Resistance.		Wind.
			Observed.	By Formula.	
Number.	Miles per hour.	Tons.	lbs. per ton.	lbs. per ton.	
2	14	9·0	12·6	13·9	Favourable.
4	16	20·5	8·5	13·2	do.
8	20	40·75	8·5	14·1	do.
4	21	18·0	12·6	16·7	do.
*8	26	40·75	12·6	17·1	do.
8	27	40·75	12·6	17·7	do.
4	32	14·5	22·5	27·2	Calm.
6	34	30·4	25·0	23·1	Nearly calm.
4	37	20·4	25·0	28·4	Favourable.
3	47	31·75	33·7	33·1	Light, against.
6	50	30·0	32·9	35·3	Calm.
5	55	26·0	36·0	43·5	Light, against.
4	61	21·5	52·6	54·8	Calm.

* Spaces between carriages made up with stretched canvas.

The formula, it will be seen, gives generally approximate values for the resistance. Still, in some cases, it is widely amiss. It is not, we conceive, comprehensive enough, nor is it founded on correct principles; because, first, the frontage only is taken as the measure of wind resistance, whereas, even in calm weather, the sides, top, and bottom of the carriages, must offer resistance to the atmosphere. A formula specifically recognizing atmospheric resistance, should include, as an element, the length of the train, as well as its height and width. Secondly, all the variable resistances must vary as the square of the speed, in compliance with the universal laws of impulse and vibration, and it is therefore incorrect to introduce any element of variable resistance, regulated by the velocity simply.

Mr. Daniel Gooch is the only experimentalist whose results are worthy of implicit confidence, for he operated with the trains precisely under the conditions of ordinary practice. His experiments were made in 1847, on the Bristol and Exeter Railway, 7 feet gauge, in connection with the gauge question then agitated, and were published in 1848.* It is our conviction that they were conducted in a spirit of the strictest impartiality; and as the experimental apparatus was elaborated with the utmost care and consideration, worthy of the high character of Mr. Gooch as an experimentalist and observer, we shall have pleasure in investigating the results of his experiments, as we hope

* Report of the Commissioners of Railways respecting Railway Communication between London and Birmingham; together with an Appendix, 1848.

to educe some principles of general value, and to construct some useful formulas.

CHAPTER II.

RESISTANCES OF TRAINS ON THE SEVEN FEET GAUGE.

IN a paper " On the Resistance to Railway Trains at different Velocities," read by Mr. Gooch before the Institution of Civil Engineers, April 18, 1848, he embodied the results of his experiments, and he showed in what respects the experiments of his predecessors were deficient. With respect to experiments made by the force of gravity on descending planes, he truly says that " the resistance may be made to vary with every change in the position and weights of the carriages in the train. A heavy carriage, for instance, placed between some light ones, will show a greater resistance for that train than if it was placed in the front; and so in proportion as the carriages are pushed, instead of being pulled down the incline, will the resistance increase.

" The first carriage," he proceeds, " whether heavy or light, if not preceded by a locomotive engine, must, with a head wind, get the whole resistance due to the frontage." " This retarding force has to be overcome by the gravity of the various carriages in the train pushing at the first one, and consequently pushing each other, and increasing many of the sources of resistance; in fact, exactly reversing the practical working of a railway train. The resistances measured by this method must, therefore, be very uncertain, and will, I think, in all cases, exceed the amount due to the same train worked in the usual manner."

In the same paper, Mr. Gooch subsequently describes the dynamometer-carriage made by him at Swindon, and employed in the experiments:—" All the results required are registered upon a large scale, opposite each other, on the same roll of paper. The results that are thus obtained are brought together in the manner shown in the details of the experiments accompanying this paper; and, first, as to the tractive power exerted. This is shown by a slightly-undulating line, each undulation corresponding with a revolution of the driving-wheel. The cause of these regular undulations appears to be the slight variation in the power of the engine, arising from the angle of the rods causing a little more power to be admitted on one side of the piston than the other, and this happens to both cranks on the same side of the centre. I found no difficulty, however, in producing a straight traction-line by the use of a pair of small close-ended cylinders with loose fitting pistons attached to the dynamometer spring, and filled with oil. These cylinders have the effect of averaging any rapid or sudden impulses, such as the unequal pulling of the engine upon the spring, from the oil not being able to pass the piston quick enough to allow of the variation of power in each impulse being registered. But not seeing any disadvantages in the undulating traction-line, I considered it better, in making these experiments, not to use the oil-cylinders, so that I might avoid any doubts or questions being raised as to the effect they might have upon the accuracy of the experiments. I have, however, on several occasions tried the effect of the oil-cylinders, by suddenly driving out the key holding the

piston, and found the straight line changed into one undulating equally above and below it. The traction-spring used was 7 feet 6 inches long, consisting of five plates, carefully tapered, and kept at a distance of ½ inch apart in the middle, and the distance pieces at the ends were made to act as rollers. The whole was very carefully fitted, and made to work free from friction. A pencil is carried from this spring to a table above, upon which a roll of paper is moved by a measuring wheel upon the rail, and which measures and registers upon the paper every 1/50th of a mile travelled over. In connection with these distances, a time-piece is used to register the time every ¼th of a second.

" It is only necessary, therefore, to count the number of seconds or fractions of a second in one or more of the distance divisions, or in a portion of one of these divisions, and the speed is very accurately ascertained. This I consider a very important part of any dynamometer, as a very small increase or diminution in the velocity of the train during a short experiment has a very great effect upon the amount of power required, which is clearly proved in many of the experiments I have made; and it must not be forgotten that it is not merely the acceleration of velocity due to the mass of the train that we have to contend with, but each wheel and axle in the train has its rotation accelerated. The resistance from this cause amounts in the aggregate to much more than, I think, has generally been calculated upon, and, it appears to me, may account for some of those discrepancies that are found in experiments on railway resistances when the speeds have been taken by a watch, and averaged over a quarter of a mile, or more frequently a longer distance. There is another important element affecting the resistance of railway trains, which I endeavoured to register, viz., the force and direction of the wind. The knowledge of its force is useful in a comparison of the several experiments, and the *direction* has a very important bearing upon the resistance to be overcome. For instance, a wind directly ahead has only the direct frontage of the train to act upon, but a wind striking the train at an angle converts the whole side of the train more or less into frontage, according to the amount of such angle, and this is a frontage of a very objectionable character, as the effect of it is to throw all the flaunches or cones of the wheels hard against the side of the opposite rail, thereby causing a serious increase in the rolling friction. To register the force and direction of the wind, a wind-gauge was placed 5 feet above the top of the dynamometer-carriage, having the necessary connections brought down to pencils on the table, so that if a line is ruled directly across the paper all the various results are obtained at a corresponding period of time.

" It was important in making this inquiry to have all the check possible upon the accuracy of the results, and I therefore applied a steam-indicator to the cylinder of the engine, and accurately measured the power of steam used in it. These cards I endeavoured to take at four points in each experiment, and succeeded in doing so in most cases, the chief exceptions being at the very high velocities, where the sudden starting of the instrument occasionally caused either the paper or card to fail. The difficulty in taking steam-cards at 60 miles per hour will be readily understood when it is considered that it is necessary to sit on the front buffer beam of the engine, and in this windy position take four sets of cards in three quarters of a minute; an occasional failure might, therefore, be expected. Having now endeavoured to explain the nature of the instruments employed, I will proceed to the experiments themselves.

" I selected a mile of line perfectly straight and level, and nearly on the surface of the ground, a plan and section of which accompanies these experiments, and upon which the height of the hedges, trees, &c., are marked as affecting the action of the force of the wind upon the train. To judge of the force of the wind during each experiment, as distinct from that registered by the dynamometer, I noticed the effect it had upon some willows growing on the side of the line, as explained in the sheet containing the diagram of the experiments.

" It was my intention, on commencing the experiments, to make four with 100 tons each, at speeds of 20, 40, and 60 miles per hour, and the same number with 50 tons. The experimental train consisted of first and second class carriages, on six wheels 4 feet in diameter, taken indiscriminately from the working stock of the company, and loaded with iron to represent a fair load of passengers; this gives an average gross weight for each coach of 10 tons. The weather during the four days was not very favourable, there being a great deal of wind and rain. All these particulars were, however, very carefully noted, and will have to be taken into consideration in determining the correct resistance in each experiment. It was also found impossible to obtain exactly the speed required, or yet to get the speed perfectly *uniform* over the *trial* mile, and for a short distance before coming to it, allowance will, therefore, also have to be made for any acceleration or diminution of velocity during the experiments, which I, however, fear is a very difficult amount to estimate. In the tables accompanying this paper, [and in Report] the various experiments are arranged in series, according to the weight of the train and the speed." A series of experiments were also made on Brimscombe incline, with various trains and speeds, and the results are added to the tables above referred to.

From Mr. Gooch's extensive tables, the primary results are condensed and arranged in Table No. 94; namely, the weights and composition of the engines and trains, the observed speeds, the observed resistances, and the observed weather and state of rails. As the observed speeds were seldom uniform, but were generally increasing or decreasing, it appeared desirable to correct the resistances due to varying velocities, for uniform average speeds; and by estimating the corrections on proper principles, all of the experiments would be made available for the determination of the laws of resistance, without risk of error by forming empirical estimates, or altogether neglecting the corrections.

Our first object, then, was to find the extra tractive force required for an observed acceleration of the speed, above that required for the uniform average speed; or, inversely, the diminution of tractive force due to an observed retardation of the speed. As the observed variations of speed were comparatively small, and as the recorded tractions and speeds were actual averages, it may be assumed, without material error, that the differences of the observed traction, and the traction due to the uniform average speed, was due simply to the acceleration or retardation of the mass of the train,

as a moving body in motion. Now, by the law of bodies in motion, the height through which a heavy body must fall from a state of rest to acquire a given velocity by gravitation, multiplied by the weight of the body, will express the work accumulated in the moving body. Consequently, the difference of the heights due to the observed speeds of the train at the beginning and end respectively of a given distance run, multiplied by the weight of the train, will express the work consumed in its acceleration or retardation. Finally, the work so found, divided by the distance over which the observation extends, will express the tractive force applied in doing this work. For example, let the observed distance run be 1 mile, or 5280 feet; and the speeds at the beginning and end of the distance, 60 miles and 61 miles per hour respectively, or 88 and 89·466 feet per second. The heights due to these speeds are found by means of the usual expression, $v = 8\sqrt{h}$, in which v is the velocity in feet per second, and h the height in feet. They are,

For 60 miles per hour, $\dfrac{88^2}{64} = 121$ feet;

For 61 miles per hour, $\dfrac{89\cdot466^2}{64} = 125$ feet;

and the difference is 4 feet. Thus, the work done upon 1 ton, or 2240 lbs., in acceleration, is $2240 \times 4 = 8960$; and $8960 \div 5280 = 1\cdot7$ lbs., is the accelerating tractive force per ton, employed in raising the speed from 60 miles to 61 miles per hour upon 1 mile run. Inversely, if the speed be retarded from 61 miles to 60 miles per hour, 1·7 lbs. would express the retarding force per ton, exerted in reducing the speed. To reduce this operation to the simplest terms, let x be the accelerating or retarding force per ton; d, the space over which the variation of speed takes place, v and v' the initial and final velocities, and h and h' the heights due to these velocities—

Then $h = \dfrac{v^2}{64}$, and $h' = \dfrac{v'^2}{64}$;

also, $x = 2240\,\dfrac{h - h'}{d} = 2240\,\dfrac{v^2 - v'^2}{64\,d}$, or

$$x = 35\,\frac{v^2 - v'^2}{d} \quad\quad\dotfill(1.)$$

To express, for simplicity, the speeds in miles per hour (v and v′), and the distance in miles (D), in this formula; substitute for v and v', the values of v and v′ multiplied by 1·466, seeing that 1 mile per hour is equal to 1·466 feet per second; also, for d, substitute D $\times$ 5280 feet in one mile. We have, then,

$$x = 35\,\frac{(v^2 - v'^2) \times 1\cdot466}{D \times 5280}, \text{ or}$$

$$x = \frac{v^2 - v'^2}{70\,D} \quad\quad\dotfill(2.)$$

Whence the following rule:—

RULE.—*To find the accelerating or retarding force due to a given variation of the speed of the train, over a given distance.* Square the observed speeds, in miles per hour, at the beginning and the end of the given distance,—find the difference of the squares;—divide the difference so found by the distance in miles,—and by 70. The quotient is the force of traction in pounds per ton of the train, expressing the accelerating force if the final speed be the greater, or the retarding force if the final speed be the less.

TABLE NO. XCIV.—RESULTS OF EXPERIMENTS ON THE RESISTANCES OF ENGINES AND TRAINS, MADE ON THE BRISTOL AND EXETER RAILWAY, BY MR. DANIEL GOOCH, IN 1847. GAUGE OF RAILS, 7 FEET. CYLINDERS OF ENGINE, 18 INCHES DIAMETER, 24 INCHES STROKE. WHEEL, 8 FEET. [1854.]

100 Tons Train, over the Measured Mile of Straight and Level Railway.—September, 1847.

No.	Composition of Train	Engine and Tender (Tons)	Train (Tons)	Engine, Tender, and Train (Tons)	Initial Speed	Final Speed	Difference of Initial and Final Speeds	Miles per hour	Average speed	Angle of Deviation	Resist. of Wind	Of Engine and Tender, by diff. of areas of In-dia. and Dynamometer	Of Train above, by Dynamometer	Of Engine, Tender, and Train, by Engine Indicator	Of Engine and Tender	Of Train above	Of Engine, Tender, and Train	Obs.	Observations on the Weather, the State of the Rails, &c.
1	10 carriages	50·7	100	150·7	14·0	12·6	1·4 decreasing	13·1	16	1·5	12·38	7·56	9·04	12·91	8·09	9·57	1	Fine. Slight side-wind. Rails dry. First trial after the train had stood all night.
2	do.	51·6	100	151·6	18·4	20·0	1·6 increasing	19·4	16	1·3	17·6	8·43	11·8	16·74	7·87	10·94	11	Very bright and clear. Slight wind. Rails dry and bright.
3	do.	50·8	100	150·8	19·5	20·6	1·1 do.	19·8	23	5·4	14·1	9·01	10·65	13·74	8·65	10·29	14	Fine. Moderate side-wind. Rails dry and bright.
4	do.	49·0	100	149·0	19·2	20·8	1·6 do.	19·8	18	1·8	16·7	9·09	11·4	15·79	8·18	10·49	18	Fine. Very strong side-wind. Rails dry and bright. Engine primed a little.
5	do.	50·2	100	150·2	19·3	21·0	1·7 do.	20·2	19·7	1·8	19·0	8·19	12·2	18·02	7·21	11·22	17	Fine. Moderate side-wind. Rails dry and bright. Engine primed at starting.
6	do.	50·8	100	150·8	21·4	21·4	uniform.	21·1	8	3·3	15·2	8·43	10·4	15·20	8·43	10·40	2	Fine. Moderate side-wind. Rails dry and bright.
7	do.	52·2	100	152·2	42·4	45·9	3·5 increasing	44·1	1·2	8·9	34·0	21·10	25·5	29·49	16·89	21·09	3	Fine. Strong side-wind. Rails dry and clean.
8	do.	48·2	100	148·2	45·9	44·1	1·8 decreasing.	45·3	12	9	27·7	13·18	21·6	30·01	15·49	24·11	16	Fine. Strong side-wind. Rails dry. Engine primed.
9	do.	50·0	100	150·0	45·0	45·0	uniform.	45·6	8	8·7	30·7	13·77	21·9	30·70	13·77	21·90	12	Fine. Slight side-wind. Rails dry and bright.
10	do.	49·2	100	149·2	56·2	56·2	do.	56·6	0·3	..	49·1	21·80	31·0	49·10	21·80	31·0	4	Fine. Very strong side-wind. Rails dry and clean.
11	do.	49·0	100	149·0	57·6	56·2	1·4 decreasing.	57·4	8·3	12	35·5	17·81	23·6	37·80	20·11	26·1	23	Fine. Strong side-wind. Rails dry and clean.
12	do.	50·2	100	150·2	57·6	59·2	1·6 increasing.	58·1	9·5	12·3	21·63	..	..	19·16	..	..	22	Fine. Strong side-wind. Rails dry and clean.
13	do.	45·8	100	145·8	59·2	60·8	1·6 do.	59·4	13	8·4	24·38	..	..	21·84	..	..	15	Fine. Very strong side-wind. Rails dry and clean.
14	do.	49·5	100	149·5	60·8	60·8	uniform.	61·3	8·6	..	19·80	..	..	19·80	..	..	13	Fine. Perfectly calm. Rails dry and bright.

50 Tons Train, over the Measured Mile of Straight and Level Railway.—September, 1847.

No.	Composition of Train	Engine and Tender (Tons)	Train (Tons)	Engine, Tender, and Train (Tons)	Initial Speed	Final Speed	Difference of Initial and Final Speeds	Miles per hour	Average speed	Angle of Deviation	Resist. of Wind	Of Engine and Tender	Of Train above	Of Engine, Tender, and Train	Of Engine and Tender	Of Train above	Of Engine, Tender, and Train	Obs.	Observations on the Weather, the State of the Rails, &c.
15	5 carriages.	51·3	50	101·3	19·3	20·4	1·1 increasing.	19·8	19·1	2·2	18·5	8·86	13·6	17·88	8·24	13·18	8	Fine. Slight side-wind. Rails wet and clean. First trial after the train had stood all night.
16	do.	48·5	50	98·5	21·8	21·8	uniform.	21·8	15·1	1·6	21·7	9·28	17·4	21·7	9·28	17·4	26	Fine. Moderate side-wind. Rails dry and clean.
17	do.	50·0	50	100·0	23·9	25·2	1·3 increasing.	24·7	8·3	3·9	17·6	10·42	14·1	16·89	9·51	13·19	5	Cloudy. Strong side-wind. Rails spotted with rain.
18	do.	51·7	50	101·7	36·3	44·1	7·8 do.	40·1	1·1	4·5	38·2	23·88	30·9	29·24	14·92	21·94	19	Dull. Calm. Rails dirty and wet by dew over-night. Engine slipping very much, with 12 tons driving-weight.
19	do.	49·6	50	99·6	42·4	42·4	uniform.	42·3	10·8	8	23·6	13·8	19·9	23·6	13·6	19·3	9	Fine. Slight side-wind. Rails nearly dry, and clean.
20	do.	49·5	50	99·5	44·1	44·1	do.	43·9	12·2	9·1	27·4	14·48	21·1	27·4	14·48	21·1	25	Fine. Strong side-wind. Rails dry and clean.
21	do.	50·8	50	100·8	45·0	42·0	3·0 decreasing.	44·0	5	9·6	24·0	15·72	19·7	27·73	19·45	23·43	6	Very wet. Stormy. Rails very dirty and wet. Engine slipped very much before reaching the measured mile.
22	do.	50·1	50	100·1	51·5	51·1	0·4 do.	51·2	4·1	..	33·4	17·08	27·0	33·96	17·56	27·58	7	Very wet. Stormy and strong wind. Rails wet and dirty. Engine slipped very much.
23	do.	50·7	50	100·7	57·6	59·2	1·4 increasing.	58·0	3·1	..	40·5	22·22	31·8	38·16	19·88	28·96	20	Dull. Calm. Rails very dirty and wet. Engine slipped very much, with 15 tons driving-weight.
24	do.	50·2	50	100·2	57·6	60·8	3·2 do.	59·2	8	12·3	39·8	24·18	32·6	33·89	20·77	27·19	10	Fine. Moderate side-wind. Rails dry and clean.
25	do.	49·4	50	99·4	57·6	60·8	3·2 do.	59·2	11·3	13	49·9	30·78	37·4	44·49	25·37	31·99	24	Fine. Very strong side-wind. Rails dry and clean.
26	do.	50·4	50	100·4	62·5	61·8	0·7 decreasing.	62·4	ahead	..	29·8	16·38	23·6	31·04	17·62	24·84	21	Dull. Quite calm. Rails dry and clean.

80 Tons Train, over Measured Miles, partially Level and partially Inclined.—September, 1847.

No.	Composition of Train	Engine and Tender (Tons)	Train (Tons)	Engine, Tender, and Train (Tons)	Initial Speed	Final Speed	Difference of Initial and Final Speeds	Miles per hour	Average speed	Angle of Deviation	Resist. of Wind	Of Engine and Tender	Of Train above	Of Engine, Tender, and Train	Of Engine and Tender	Of Train above	Of Engine, Tender, and Train	Obs.	Observations on the Weather, the State of the Rails, &c.
27	8 carriages.	50	80	130	45·9	41·3	4·6 decreasing.	43·2	9·5	..	..	6·62	..	..	12·35	..	30	Fine. Calm. Rails dry. Up incline 1 in 352, for which a deduction of 6·3 lbs. per ton is made.
28	do.	50	80	130	47·6	45·9	1·9 do.	47·0	7	..	..	10·45	..	..	12·99	..	30	Fine. Calm. Rails dry.
29	do.	50	80	130	46·8	50·5	3·7 increasing.	48·5	4·8	6·9	..	22·15	..	..	17·01	..	27	Fine. Calm. Rails dry.
30	do.	50	80	130	54·4	49·4	5·0 decreasing.	51·9	3	9·2	..	7·9	..	..	16·8	..	29	Fine. Calm. Rails dry.
31	do.	50	80	130	56·2	57·6	1·4 increasing.	56·8	4·6	11	..	19·4	..	..	17·1	..	28	Fine. Calm. Rails dry.

Trains of various Weights, on Brinscombe Incline, over Average Gradients, varying from 1 in 72 to 1 in 86, Corrected for a Level Railway.—April, 1847.

No.	Composition of Train	Train (Tons)	Initial Speed	Final Speed	Difference of Initial and Final Speeds	Miles per hour	Of Engine, Tender, and Train	Of Engine, Tender, and Train (corrected)	Obs.	Observations on the Weather, the State of the Rails, &c.
32	1 car., 10 wag.	118	16·7	17·7	1·0 increasing	18·3	7·8	6·31	31	Fine. Calm. Rails dry.
33	1 car., 12 wag.	140	17·7	17·7	uniform.	19·2	9·0	9·0	32	Fine. Calm. Rails dry.
34	1 car., 6 wag.	74	22·2	22·0	0·2 decreasing.	26·0	9·3	9·43	33	Fine. Calm. Rails dry.
35	10 car., 1 wag.	110	23·0	23·0	uniform.	26·0	10·2	10·2	34	Fine. Calm. Rails dry.
36	1 car., 6 wag.	71	20·9	20·7	0·2 decreasing.	27·1	9·4	9·52	35	Fine. Calm. Rails dry.
37	9 car., 1 wag.	100	23·2	23·1	0·1 do.	27·6	8·50	8·62	36	Fine. Calm. Rails dry.
38	2 car., 5 wag.	69	22·5	22·9	0·4 increasing	27·9	9·8	8·54	37	Fine. Calm. Rails dry.
39	6 carriages.	59	29·2	29·7	0·5 do.	30·5	9·7	8·28	38	Fine. Calm. Rails dry.
40	1 car., 1½ wag.	60	28·8	28·8	uniform.	32·2	11·2	11·2	39	Fine. Calm. Rails dry.
41	1 car., 8 wag.	101	30·0	30·0	do.	32·9	11·7	11·7	40	Rainy. Calm.
42	6 carriages.	59	30·0	30·0	do.	34·5	10·5	10·5	41	Fine. Calm. Rails dry.
43	10 carriages.	99	33·5	33·0	0·5 decreasing.	34·7	10·0	10·47	42	Calm. Rails wet.
44	6 carriages.	60	36·9	36·2	0·7 do.	37·4	11·0	11·73	43	Fine. Calm. Rails dry.

TABLE NO. XCIV.—RESULTS OF EXPERIMENTS ON THE RESISTANCES OF ENGINES AND TRAINS, MADE ON THE CALEDONIAN AND EDINBURGH AND GLASGOW RAILWAYS, BY D. K. CLARK, IN 1850. GAUGE OF RAILS, 4 FEET 8½ INCHES. [1854.]

No. of Observation or Experiments	Date of Trial	Name of Railway	Name or Number of Engine and Tender	Cylinder Diam.	Cylinder Stroke	Diameter of Driving Wheel	Number of Vehicles in the Train	Weight of Engine and Tender	Weight of Train	Gross Weight of Engine, Tender, and Train	Number of Miles run during the Trial	Average Gradient	Observed Average Speed	Resistance per Ton	Observations on the Locality, Weather, &c.
No.	Date.	Name.	Name.	Inches.	Inches.	Feet.	Number.	Tons.	Tons.	Tons.	Miles.	Gradient.	Miles per Hour.	Lbs. per Ton.	
1	1850. Mar. 27.	Caledonian.	No. 48, back coupled.	15	20	6	5 goods wags.	30	40·25	70·25	10 / 10	1 in 76 up.	20	16 / (train alone) 11·28	Beattock Incline, full of curves. Side wind ahead, and sleet. Resistance of train alone, estimated by subtracting engine and tender resistance at same speed; including extra engine friction.
2	July 22.	Greenock.	..	..	..	..	19 goods wags. 32 goods wags. 35 goods wags.	.. .. ..	82·5 157·5 167·65	.. .. ..	1 5 5 5	1 in 2000 dn. to 1 in 400 dn.	12 24 21 32	7·66 9·67 7·8 12·3	Very slight side wind. Fair. Rails dry. Resistance observed by traction spring, composed of Salter's balances, between the tender and the train.
3	July 3.	Caledonian.	No. 127, coupled.	17	24	4' 7"	28 coal waggons.	35	182	217	34	1 in 330 up.	17	25	Gariongill to Beattock Summit. Calm and dry.
4	July 4.	Do.	Do.	17 17 17	24 24 24	4' 7" 4' 7"	25 coal waggons. 23 coal waggons. 23 coal waggons.	35 35 35	162·5 149·5 149·5	197·5 184·5 184·5	2 1·75 5	1 in 80 up. 1 in 80 up. 1 in 75 up.	6·7 10 10·5	26·5 26·87 24·5	Beattock Incline. Weather dry and calm.
5	July 29.	Do.	Do.	17	24	4' 7"	44 coal waggons.	35	198	233	4·5 7·5	1 in 126 up. 1 in 211 up.	12·3 14	18·5 18·2	Wishaw Incline. Weather calm, dry, warm. Auchengray Incline. Weather calm, dry, warm.
6	June 18.	Do.	No. 102, coupled.	16	18	4' 6"	20 goods wag. 22 goods wag.	28 28	91 99	119 127	2 1·5 1	1 in 115 up. 1 in 120 up. 1 in 100 up. level.	28 19 22 28	22 26·3 28·7 27	Goods train; Edinburgh to Carstairs. Weather calm and fair.
7		Ed. & Glasg.	No. 61, coupled.	15	22	4' 6"	34 goods wag.	18	170	188	10	1 in 1159 up.	10	13	Cowlairs to Croy. Weather damp, calm, mild.
8	Aug. 29.	Caledonian.	No. 42.	15	20	6	8 carriages. 7 carriages.	28 28	44 38	72 66	9 23 10 21	1 in 116 up. 1 in 322 up. 1 in 1000 dn. 1 in 503 dn.	32·7 33 45 45	25 28·5 28 34·3	Results of one trip with express train from Glasgow to Carlisle, taken on four successive stages, averaged over long distances, and selected when the train was at working speed. Stiff side wind all the way.
9	Aug. 29.	Do.	Do.	15	20	6	6 carriages.	28	33	61	9	1 in 75 up.	28	24	Return express train. Beattock Incline. Stiff side wind.
10	Oct. 9.	Ed. & Glasg.	Nile.	16	18	6	5 carriages. 10 carriages, 2 horseboxes. 13 carriages.	35 35 35	275 63 71	62·5 98 106	10 10 2	1 in 1440 up. 1 in 1853 dn. 1 in 1056 up.	37·5 40 32	32 25·4 25·6	Express train from Edinburgh to Glasgow. Breeze ahead. Weather dry.
11	Sept. 2.	Do.	America.	16	18	6	17 carriages, 1 horsebox, 1 car. truck.	35	101	136	1	1 in 1159 dn.	33	24	Ordinary train. Strong head-wind.
12 13	1851. July 15. July 11.	Do.	England.	9	12	4' 6"	7 carriages. 7 carriages.	12 12	38 38	50 50	4 8	1 in 1159 up. level.	37 35	27 23	Express. Slight wind, favourable. Express. Smart wind, favourable.
14	Mar. 4.	Caledonian.	No 33.	15	20	6	7 carriages. 6 carriages. 7 carriages. 7 carriages. 7 carriages. 7 carriages.	28 28 28 28 28 28	38 33 38 38 38 35	66 61 66 66 66 63	1 1 1 1 1 1	1 in 75 up. 1 in 100 up. 1 in 100 up. 1 in 150 up. 1 in 200 up. 1 in 300 up.	20·5 18 17 20·6 11·6 23	22 19 22 23·2 26·5 24·4	Parliamentary train. Calm and dry.
15	Mar. 6.	Do.	Do.	15	20	6	6 carriages.	28	33	61	1 1	1 in 200 up. 1 in 200 up. 1 in 75 up.	20·6 26 20·5	26·5 30 29·3	Mail train. Dry; strong side and head wind.
16	Mar. 8.	Do.	Do.	15	20	6	4 carriages.	28	22	50	1	1 in 330 dn.	44	38·6	Express train. Perfectly calm
17	Mar. 1.	Do.	Do.	15	20	6	12 carriages.	28	60	88	5 2	1 in 200 up and down. 1 in 1056 up and down.	35 30	23 24·6	Mail train. Wind ahead.

ENGINE AND TENDER ALONE.

		Name	No.	Cyl. Diam.	Stroke	Wheel		Weight				Gradient	Speed	Resist.	Observations
Outside Cylinders.		Caledonian.	No. 13.	15	20	6	..	..	28	..	..	up and down, slight incline.	very slow.	7·37	In good free working order. On straight line.
		Do.	No. 14.	15	20	6	..	..	28	..	..	level.	do.	15·6	Working loosely; much out of repair. On straight line.
		Do.	No. 33.	15	20	6	..	..	28	..	..	up and down, slight incline.	do.	8·64	In good free working order. On straight line.
		Do.	No. 41.	15	20	6	..	..	28	..	..	level.	do.	22·34	Engine stiff; just out of repairing shop. On straight line.
		Do.	No. 42.	15	20	6	..	..	28	..	..	1 in 144 up.	do.	13·5	In good working order. Straight line.
		Do.	No. 102, coupled.	16	18	4' 6"	..	..	28	..	..	to and fro.	do.	23·4	Rather out of repair. On sharp curve.
		Do.	No. 125.	17	24	4' 7"	..	..	35	..	..	do.	do.	9·75 / 10·4	In good free working order. Straight line.
		Do.	No. 127.	17	24	4' 7"	..	..	35	..	..	1 in 144 up.	do.	15	In good working order. Lately turned out new.
Inside Cylinders.		Greenock.	No. 73, C. R.	13	18	5	..	..	22	..	..	level.	do.	11	In free working order. Old 6-wheel class.
		Ed. & Glasg.	Jupiter.	15	20	5' 6"	..	..	28	..	..	up and down, incline.	do.	22	In good working order. New 6-wheel class, by Sharp Brothers.
		Do.	Pallas.	15	20	6	..	..	35	..	..	do.	do.	22	In good working order. Heavy 6-wheel class.
		Do.	England.	9	12	4' 6"	..	..	12	..	..	incline. do.	14 28	12·8 20·6	In good working order. Light tank engine, by England. Stiff side-wind.

By this rule, the observed resistances in columns 10, 11, 12, of the annexed table, No. XCIV., are corrected for uniform average speeds, and the corrected values are placed in columns 13, 14, 15. These resistances clearly increase with the speed; and, to find the mean rate of increase by graphic representation, draw base-lines, Diagram-plate 10, one to each group of observations, to represent the speeds in miles per hour; on these lines, set off from one end, the distances representing the speeds contained in column 9, and draw verticals from the points so set off, equal in length by convenient scales to the observed resistances in columns 13, 14, 15, and terminate them by stars. Through the several groups of results thus depicted, draw mean curve lines, to show the average relations of the resistances and the speeds. Experiments 14 and 26 are omitted, as they are exceptional cases of perfect calmness and bright rails. In all these diagrams, it will be found, the resistances are divisible into two parts: the constant and the variable resistance, of which the latter varies as the square of the speed, starting from nothing when the train is just in motion. The constant resistance is due to the internal friction of wheels, axles, and machinery; the variable resistance is due to the atmosphere, to lateral oscillation and concussion, to vertical oscillations and concussion between the wheels and the rails, due to imperfections of the permanent way, to the coning of the wheels, and their consequent sledging on the rails at high speeds, and to other cognizable causes. All these varying resistances ought, we believe, to vary as the square of the speed, as we find in fact that they do, and not as the speed simply.

For facility of reference, the following statement is given, showing the resistances at extreme speeds,—when the engine or train is just in motion, and at 60 miles per hour: the former being the constant resistance, which must be met before any motion at all can be produced; and the latter, comprising the constant and the variable resistances.

1st, Engine and Tender alone:—

		At 60 miles per hour.
With 100 tons train,	12½ lbs. per ton, constant.	44 lbs. per ton.
With 50 do.	14½ lbs. do. do.	40 lbs. do.

2d, Train only:—

100 tons train;	6¼ lbs. per ton, constant.	21½ lbs. per ton.
50 do.	8 lbs. do. do.	23 lbs. do.

3d, Engine, Tender, and Train, total:—

With 100 tons train,	8 lbs. per ton, constant.	31 lbs. per ton.
With 50 do.	10 lbs. do. do.	32 lbs. do.

It is observable that, in each case, the constant resistance with the 50 tons train is about 2 lbs. per ton more than with the 100 tons train. This excess is due to the state of the rails, which were, with the 100 tons train, in all cases dry and clean; but with the 50 tons train, were dirty and wet in seven cases out of twelve. But, though the constant resistance was thus raised, the state of the rails did not affect the variable resistance; because the variable resistance per ton at 60 miles per hour, is virtually the same for both trains; being

for the 100 tons train, 21½ — 6¼ = 15¼ lbs. per ton.
,, 50 do. 23 — 8 = 15 lbs. do.

There is no doubt that, had the rails been in equally good order, the constant resistances also would have been the same.

As, then, an addition to train-weight made no difference on the tonnage-resistance of the train, as carriages; the addition of the train to the engine and tender, could not have affected the tonnage-resistance of the latter, as carriages. Therefore, any extra variable resistance of engine and tender with the 100 tons train, as compared with the 50 tons train, must be due to the friction of the engine-machinery; and it is, at 60 miles per hour, as follows:—

With 100 tons train, 44 — 12½ = 31½ lbs. per ton variable resistance.
,, 50 do. 40 — 14½ = 25½ lbs. do. do.

Difference.............. 6 lbs. per ton;

that is, the extra friction of the engine-machinery, due to the increase of the train from 50 tons to 100 tons, amounts to 6 lbs. per ton of engine and tender at 60 miles per hour.

The friction of the engine-machinery due to the first 50 tons must, therefore, also be 6 lbs. per ton of engine and tender, at 60 miles per hour; and this leaves 31½ — 12 = 19½ lbs. as the variable resistance of the engine and tender per ton, at 60 miles per hour. To illustrate our meaning, the diagram of resistance of engine and tender, with 100 tons train is repeated in diagram-plate 10, with a horizontal line setting off the constant resistance; and two curves are interpolated to show the variable resistances of the engine and tender per ton, when running alone, and running with trains of 50 tons and 100 tons.

The variable resistance of the engine and tender alone, at 60 miles per hour, is 19½ lbs. per ton, and this represents their resistance as carriages, and the friction of the machinery on their own account. Now, the friction of machinery due to engine and tender, should bear the same ratio to their resistance per ton as carriages, that the friction of machinery due to a 50 tons train bears to its resistance per ton. We say, a 50 tons train, as the engine and tender together weigh 50 tons. The variable machinery-friction for a 50 tons train, has already been found to be 6 lbs. per ton of engine and tender; and its variable resistance per ton, 15 lbs.; both at 60 miles per hour. Divide 19½ lbs. in the ratio of 6 to 15, thus:—

(6 + 15) is to 19½, as 6 is to 5½;

that is, the variable machinery-friction due to the traction of the engine and tender, is 5½ lbs. per ton; leaving 19½–5½, or 14 lbs. per ton, for their variable resistance as carriages; both at 60 miles per hour. From these data, a third curve may be interpolated, in the diagram of engine-resistance, to separate the variable resistance of the engine and tender as carriages, from the machinery-friction expended in their personal traction. And here it may be noted how nearly equal the variable resistance of the engine and tender as carriages, is to that of the train; they are respectively 14 lbs. and 15 lbs. per ton, at 60 miles per hour. The former is, in fact, less than the latter, showing that the extra resistance of the engine and tender as carriages, due to the more concentrated loads on individual wheels, is more than compensated by the reduction of wind-resistance, due to their superior compactness per ton of weight. The variable machinery-friction also, is nearly the same for the engine and tender, and the carriages; being respectively 5½ lbs. and 6 lbs. per ton of engine and tender at 60 miles per hour. We may thus, for simplicity, and without material error, adopt the same variable resistances for both the engine and train, averaged so :—

Variable Resistances in
pounds per ton, at
60 miles per hour.

15 lbs. per ton of Engine, Tender, and Train ; as carriages.
6 lbs. per ton of Engine, Tender, and Train ; machinery-friction.

21 lbs. per ton, total variable resistance, at 60 miles per hour.

Now, to analyze the constant resistances of the engine and tender. These were found to be, totally, $12\frac{1}{4}$ lbs. per ton of engine and tender, with a train of 100 tons attached, and upon clean and dry rails. It is reasonable that the resistance of the engine and tender as carriages, when just in motion, should be the same as that of the train, $6\frac{1}{4}$ lbs. per ton; and the balance, $6\frac{1}{4}$ lbs., would be the whole machinery-friction per ton of engine and tender, due to the traction of the total weight of engine, tender, and train, 150 tons. Dividing $6\frac{1}{4}$ lbs. into three equal parts, we have, say, 2 lbs. per ton of engine and tender, for constant machinery-friction due to the 50 tons of engine and tender, and the same due to each 50 tons of train. We may, therefore, finally, adopt the following values for the elements of the engine and tender resistance, avoiding fractions :—

Constant Resistance in
pounds per ton of
engine and tender.

6 lbs. for Engine and Tender alone, as carriages, without machinery-friction.
8 lbs. for Engine and Tender alone, including machinery-friction.
10 lbs. for Engine and Tender, and 50 tons Train.
12 lbs. for Engine and Tender, and 100 tons Train.

Lines representing these constant resistances, are added to the diagram, in diagram-plate 10.

The allowance of machinery-friction for the train per ton, is the same as that for the engine and tender. The constant resistance of the train as carriages, is also the same as that taken for the engine and tender. We have, then, for the average constant resistances:—

Average Constant Resistances,
in pounds per ton.

6 lbs. per ton of Engine, Tender, and Train: as carriages.
2 lbs. per ton of Engine, Tender, and Train; machinery-friction.

8 lbs. per ton, total constant resistance.

The resistances thus analyzed and valued, are based ultimately on the experimental results with the 100 tons train: upon a straight and level railway, with fair weather, with constant side winds, varying in strength from slight to very strong, and with dry and clean rails, and with the road, the engine, and the train, in ordinary good order. The influence of some of these circumstances upon the resistance is illustrated in the table. Thus, in experiments 14 and 26, the weather was perfectly calm, and the train moved at a mean speed of 62 miles per hour; with the usual side wind, the resistance at that speed, would have averaged, according to the curve of resistance, 22 lbs. per ton, whereas the mean observed resistance was 18·71 lbs., being fully $3\frac{1}{4}$ lbs. or 15 per cent. less. Again, the dirty state of the rails with the 50 tons train, added 2 lbs. per ton to the constant resistance due to clean rails.

Turning to the trials with the 80 tons train, with dry rails and calm weather; the resistance, by the curve for 80 tons, in the diagram-plate, was 15 lbs. per ton at 50 miles per hour. Now, with the 100 tons train, and side winds, it amounted, by the curve, to 16·4 lbs. per ton, which was 1·4 lbs., or 9·33 per cent. more. The probable occurrence of curves in the parts of the line run over by the 80 tons train, would add to the resistance which would have been due upon a straight line, and therefore the resistance due to side winds in the case before us, is really greater than 9·33 per cent.

Then, with the trains on the Brimscombe incline, with uniformly dry and calm weather and clean rails, the resistance, reduced for a level, was, by the curve, 13 lbs. per ton at 40 miles per hour. Whereas, with the 100 tons train, the resistance at the same speed was only 12·66 lbs. per ton, or ·33 lbs. less. Mr. Gooch ascribes the excessive resistance on the incline to the circumstance that the waggons in the trains were four-wheeled, while the carriages composing the 100 tons train had six wheels. This we doubt much, and we believe the excess to be due simply to the curves on the incline, in passing which the trains must have bound hard, on so steep an incline. From the other examples, we should infer that about $1\frac{1}{4}$ lb. per ton was thus lost by binding on curves, or 10 to $1\frac{1}{2}$ per cent.

It seems utterly useless to attempt any more minute analysis of the resistances of trains, from the data before us; as any such analysis, to be useful, must be founded on a much greater variety of results than have been supplied in the experiments under consideration. The separate resistances from wind, oscillation, imperfections of way, wear of wheels, &c., are no doubt worth determining. Meantime, we must be content with finding the resistances in the mass, and must take trains as they are. When we shall have examined some further results on the 4 feet $8\frac{1}{2}$ inch gauge, some useful comparisons may be made.

Formulas for resistance at various speeds may be readily constructed from the data worked out, on the principle that all the variable resistances vary as the square of the speed. First, for the Total Resistance of the engine, tender, and train. Let v be the given speed; and R, the total resistance per ton. Then, as 21 lbs. per ton is the total variable resistance at 60 miles per hour, that due to the speed v is found by the proportion

$$60^2 : v^2 :: 21 : \frac{21 v^2}{60^2},$$

making, by reduction, $\frac{v^2}{171\cdot4}$, or, say $\frac{v^2}{171}$;

and, adding the total constant resistance, 8 lbs. per ton, we have the formula

$$R = 8 + \frac{v^2}{171} \quad \text{............................(1.)}$$

Secondly, for the resistance (R') of the train alone. The variable resistance per ton of train alone is 15 lbs. at 60 miles per hour, and by proportion, for any other speed v,

$$60^2 : v^2 :: 15 : \frac{15 v^2}{60^2} = \frac{v^2}{240}.$$

Adding 6 lbs. per ton, for constant resistance, we have

$$R' = 6 + \frac{v^2}{240} \quad \text{............................(2.)}$$

Thirdly, for the resistance (R) of the engine and tender alone, including machinery-friction. Let $w =$ the weight

2 P

of the engine and tender, and $w =$ the weight of the train. The resistance of the engine and tender as carriages, is found by the preceding formula for the train. The total variable machinery-friction at 60 miles per hour, is 6 lbs. per ton of engine, tender, and train; and for any other speed v, it will be, per ton,

$$\frac{6 \times v^2}{60^2} = \frac{v^2}{600};$$

or, for the whole weight of train,

$$(\mathbf{w} + w) \times \frac{v^2}{600};$$

and per ton of engine and tender alone, it is

$$\frac{\mathbf{w} + w}{\mathbf{w}} \cdot \frac{v^2}{600}.$$

The total constant machinery-friction is 2 lbs. per ton of engine, tender, and train, or $(\mathbf{w} + w) \times 2$; and, per ton of engine, tender, and train alone, it is

$$\frac{\mathbf{w} + w}{\mathbf{w}} \times 2.$$

Adding the two parts, we have, for the whole machinery-friction,

$$\left(\frac{\mathbf{w} + w}{\mathbf{w}}\right) \times \left(2 + \frac{v^2}{600}\right).$$

Making a further addition of the resistance of the engine and tender as carriages, we have finally

$$\mathbf{r} = 6 + \frac{v^2}{240} + \left(\left(2 + \frac{v^2}{600}\right) \times \left(\frac{\mathbf{w} + w}{\mathbf{w}}\right)\right)\ldots\ldots\ldots\ldots(3.)$$

The last, which is the most complex, is also the most useless formula of the lot. The three formulas are reduced to rules as follows :—

RULES FOR THE RESISTANCE OF ENGINES AND TRAINS ON THE 7 FEET GAUGE:—

RULE I. *To find the total resistance of the Engine, Tender, and Train, at a given speed.* Square the speed in miles per hour,—divide it by 171,—and add 8 to the quotient. The result is the total resistance at the rails in pounds per ton weight.

RULE II. *To find the resistance of the Train alone, at a given speed.* Square the speed in miles per hour,—divide it by 240,—and add 6 to the quotient. The result is the resistance at the rails in pounds per ton weight.

RULE III. *To find the whole resistance of the Engine and Tender alone, with a given train, at a given speed.*

1st, Find the resistance as carriages by Rule II.

2d, Square the speed,—and divide it by 600,—and add 2 to the quotient ;—multiply the sum thus found by the total weight of engine, tender, and train,—and divide by the weight of the engine and tender. The quotient expresses the total machinery-friction.

3d, Add together the two results thus obtained. The sum is the whole resistance, at the rails, in pounds per ton weight.[*]

---

[*] Mr. John Sewell has discussed Mr. Gooch's experiments at some length, in the last edition of Tredgold on the Steam Engine (1850). He has constructed a formula of considerable dimensions ; proceeding, like Harding, on the principles, that the oscillatory resistance of the engine, tender, and train, varies with the velocity simply ; that the atmospheric resistance is the only element varying as the square of the velocity ; and that there is a constant train-resistance by friction,

CHAPTER III.

RESISTANCES ON THE 4 FEET 8½ INCH GAUGE.

THE author made numerous experiments on the resistance of trains on the Caledonian and Edinburgh and Glasgow Railways, by the use of M'Naught's steam-indicator already described. Obtained from the front end of one cylinder, the diagram was assumed to represent the force exerted during each stroke of each cylinder. The results so estimated must be in excess of the real power, as the steam was, in most cases, by the motion of the valve-gear, admitted for a greater part of the front stroke than of the back stroke. The excess is not, however, for our present purposes, material, and certainly does not exceed 5 per cent. of the actual power. We have, moreover, selected the results of the most equally working engines, for the measurement of tractive force.

From the large number of observations so made, the author has selected some of the best ascertained and most useful of them, and placed them in Table No. XCIV., page 295. The circumstances of engine, train, loads, gradients, speeds, and weather are detailed for each experiment, and the resistances per ton gross, are reduced from the indicator-diagrams, to the equivalent traction at the rails.

The speeds, as observed, were in many cases uniform. In other cases they varied, and the resistances have been reduced for the observed average speeds, taken as uniform, by the formula already explained. But, in all cases, the allowances so estimated were very small, generally a fraction of a pound per ton. The acceleration or retardation was estimated simply from the difference of the initial and final

of 6 lbs. per ton. He assumes, also, that the atmospheric resistance of the train varies with its bulk, or cubic content. The elements of the formula are as follows :—Let τ be the weight of the train in tons, 6 lbs. the friction of the train per ton, $\mathbf{B}$ the bulk of the train in cubic feet, $\mathbf{R}$ the weight of the engine and tender in tons, $\mathbf{v}$ the velocity. Then

$$\mathbf{R} \times \left[\left((\mathbf{v} \times \cdot 5) + 5\right) + \left(\mathbf{v}^2 \times \tau \times \cdot 00004\right)\right] = \begin{cases} \text{engine and tender} \\ \text{resistance.} \end{cases}$$

$$\mathbf{v}^2 \times \mathbf{B} \times \cdot 00002 \ldots\ldots\ldots\ldots\ldots\ldots\ldots\ldots = \begin{cases} \text{atmospheric re-} \\ \text{sistance of train.} \end{cases}$$

$$\frac{\mathbf{v} \times \tau}{15} \ldots\ldots\ldots\ldots\ldots\ldots\ldots\ldots\ldots = \begin{cases} \text{oscillatory resist-} \\ \text{ance.} \end{cases}$$

$$\tau \times 6 \ldots\ldots\ldots\ldots\ldots\ldots\ldots\ldots\ldots = \begin{cases} \text{friction resist-} \\ \text{ance.} \end{cases}$$

Putting these together in juxtaposition, for they will not amalgamate, and dividing the sum total by the weight of the engine, tender, and train ; the formula would, as Mr. Sewell naively states, " briefly " stand thus :—

$$\frac{\mathbf{R} \times \left[\left((\mathbf{v} \times 5) + 5\right) + \left(\mathbf{v}^2 \times \tau \times \cdot 00004\right)\right] + \left(\mathbf{v}^2 \times \mathbf{B} \times \cdot 00002\right)\ \frac{\mathbf{v} \times \tau}{15} + (\tau \times 6)}{\mathbf{R} + \tau}$$

resistance per ton.

This does not look like the right formula. It is wrong in principle, on two important points, first as to the rate of variation of the oscillatory resistances, which he assumes to be in the ratio of the speed simply, instead of the square of the speed, which it undoubtedly follows. Secondly, the atmospheric resistance is assumed to vary with the bulk of the train, which is manifestly an erroneous assumption, as that resistance is entirely superficial, and must be regulated by the superficial area of the train, not by the cubic contents. A formula for resistance should either comprise every element of resistance, or should be confined to two terms, expressing, comprehensively, the constant resistance, and the variable resistance, as exemplified in the text.

s observed, without regarding the intermediate fluctua-
of speed that may have taken place, as that difference
ctly expresses the average variation.

ie Table is in three parts : showing, first, the resistance
ods-trains ; secondly, the resistance of passenger-trains;
ly, the resistance of engine and tender alone.

ie first experiment was made with 5 ordinary goods wag-
, with outside bearings, loaded with coke, and was satis-
rily worked out. The second, showing the resistance of
s-waggons alone, was made with a rudely planned
ion-spring ; and though probably near the truth, it
iot be implicitly received. In the third and fourth, the
e-gear worked very truly, and the results may be im-
itly accepted ; the waggons had 3 feet wheels, with inside
rings. The fifth, likewise ; the wheels averaged 2 feet
iches diameter, with inside bearings, and half inch end
v. The sixth and seventh are also reliable ; they were
de with ordinary waggons having outside bearings.

The eighth experiment comprises the results of one train
r long distances, averaged from indicator-diagrams taken
intervals of 2 miles. The ninth gives one result from the
urn train. The tenth and eleventh were made with two
gines of the same class, and with various sizes of train ;
d the results are averaged from indicator-diagrams taken
1 mile intervals. The twelfth and thirteenth were made
th one of England's light tank-engines. The remaining
sults, with trains, are reduced from isolated observations
ith No. 33, C. R. engine, while at uniform speeds on the
veral inclines specified.

Then follow the results of some observations upon engines
nd tenders alone, showing their personal resistance as
arriages and machines, measured in traction at the rails.

CHAPTER IV.

RESISTANCES OF ENGINE AND TENDER.

The personal resistances of engines and tenders are shown
, by the last part of the table to be extremely diverse;
they range from 7 lbs. to 23 lbs. per ton. The causes of
the diversity, briefly noted in the columns of observations,
are to be found in the comparative state of repair of the
engines, and their general working order. Of the outside
cylinder engines, with single wheels, the mean resistance of
Nos. 13 and 33, C.R., moving slowly, was 8 lbs. per ton ;
these engines were in free working order at the time of the
observations, and as the results are averaged from the indicated resistance in both directions over the same ground,
they are put forward as perfectly reliable data, showing that
the constant resistance of outside-cylinder single-wheel
engines, in good and free working order, amounts to 8 lbs.
per ton of engine and tender, on a level. The case of
No. 41, C. R., with 22·34 lbs. per ton resistance, shows that
the stiffness of the working parts nearly triples the amount
of resistance due to the most favourable conditions. No. 14,
C. R., with 15½ lbs. per ton resistance, and working abundantly easily, shows how disrepair may double the resistance.
Of the coupled engines, No. 125 C. R., with six coupled

wheels, and in free working order, shows a mean of 10 lbs.
per ton resistance. No. 127 C. R., of the same class, then
lately turned out new, showed 15 lbs. per ton, or one-half
more resistance. No. 102, C. R., with six wheels, half
coupled, in free working order, shows how a sharp curve adds
to the resistance, making it 23½ lbs. per ton, more than
twice the resistance of a six coupled engine and tender on a
straight line.

The inside-cylinder engines which were proved, had six
single wheels ; all of them with crank-axles placed in four
bearings, except the England, which had only two bearings.
Of these, the England shows the most favourably, having
about 13 lbs. per ton resistance at 14 miles per hour, which
would probably be reduced to less than that of No. 73, C. R.,
11 lbs. per ton, when moving very slowly. The superiority
of the England is probably due to the simplicity of the
crank-axle bearings. To compare the average resistances
from outside and inside-cylinder engines, the means of all
the resistances are as follow :—

Outside-cylinder Engines and Tenders, 14 lbs. per ton.
Inside-cylinder, do. do. 17 lbs. per ton.

Showing that, upon the whole, outside-cylinder engines present less resistance to traction than inside-cylinder engines.

CHAPTER V.

RESISTANCE OF ENGINES, TENDERS, AND TRAINS.

To begin with the experiments with coal trains, Nos. 3, 4, 5 ;
the waggons used in No. 5 experiment offered much less resistance than those in Nos. 3 and 4. The averages were,

For Nos. 3 and 4, at 11 miles per hour, 27 lbs. per ton.
For No. 5, at 13 do. do. 18 lbs. per ton.

of which the latter is only two-thirds of the former. The
advantage is due, we believe, chiefly to the lateral play of
the journals in the bearings, in the latter case, which enabled
the wheels to adjust themselves without effort to the rails,
swaying towards either side, as the conical tyres and unlevel
rails might bias them. In the former case, the want of end
play prevented the wheels so adjusting themselves laterally
without carrying with them the superincumbent loads. For
the moderate speeds at which these trains were run, some
lateral play at the bearings is undoubtedly beneficial. At
high speeds, lateral play becomes dangerous and is inadmissible ; which leads to the only general solution of the
difficulty, the use of loose wheels and axles, incessantly in-
culcated by Mr. Adams.

The experiments with ordinary goods-waggons, Nos.
1, 2, 6, 7, show an extraordinary diversity of resistance per
ton ; varying from 7½ lbs. per ton with the train alone, and
13 lbs. per ton, including the engine, to 29 lbs. per ton of
engine, tender, and train, at speeds under 30 miles per hour.
This extreme diversity is no doubt due to the state of repair
of the waggons, and of the way, the state of lubrication, and
the curves on the line. The more the end play of the bearings, the less is the resistance, at low speeds under 15 to
20 miles per hour ; and so far, therefore, the disrepair of
the waggons is favourable to free running.

With the passenger-trains, the resistances vary between 20 lbs. and 30 lbs. per ton of engine, tender, and train, at speeds of 20 to 40 miles per hour.

CHAPTER VI.

INFLUENCE OF INDIVIDUAL CAUSES ON TRAIN RESISTANCE.

Curves.—In No. 8 experiment, with No. 42 C. R., the results are worthy of study, as the trials were made in one continuous run on varying gradients, and with various curves. To find from these results, the influence of curves on the resistance, the following data are given, showing the positions and lengths of the different parts of the line on which the given results were obtained, in the order of the table, and the number of curves, under 1 mile radius, which occur in them.

Mile-posts.	Distance.	Number of Curves of 1 mile Radius, and under.	Average number of Miles to each Curve.
(1.) 88th to 79th,	9 miles.	5	1·8 miles.
(2.) 73d to 50th,	23 do.	10	2·3 do.
(3.) 37th to 27th,	10 do.	none	—
(4.) 23d to 2d,	21 do.	8	2·62 do.

Comparing, now, the speeds and resistances with the curves, we have

Average Speed.	Resistance.	Average Number of Miles to each Curve.
(1.) 32·7 miles per hour,	25 lbs. per ton,	1·8 miles.
(2.) 38 do.	28·5 lbs. do.	2·3 do.
(3.) 45 do.	28 lbs. do.	—
(4.) 45 do.	34·3 lbs. do.	2·62 do.

It appears that, though the average speeds were 38 miles and 45 miles per hour in the second and third observations, the resistances were the same, 28 lbs. per ton. And that conversely, in the third and fourth results, while the speeds were the same, the resistance rose from 28 lbs. to 34·3 lbs. per ton. These variations are explained by the condition of the line as to curves; for, whereas, during the second and fourth trials, there was one curve under 1 mile radius for every 2·3 and 2·6 miles run, there were no curves during the third trial, and in this case the line was practically straight. It happened that the extra resistance due to the increase of speed from 38 to 45 miles per hour, was balanced by the transition from a curved part of the line (2) to a straight part (3), and the total resistance remained the same; and that, on the contrary, the transition from the straight part of the line (3) to a curved part (4), raised the resistance from 28 lbs. to 34·3 lbs., while the speed remained the same. In this case, the excess is 6·3 lbs., due to curves, and is above 20 per cent. of the resistance on the straight part of the line.

Wind.—The results are not sufficiently numerous fully to show the influence of wind. But, taking an average of the cases most nearly alike in speed, in Nos. 14 and 15 experiments, with No. 33, C. R., we have the following resistances :—

At 20 miles per hour, 22 lbs. per ton, calm and dry ;
At 22   ,,   28·6 lbs. do. strong side and head winds ;
showing a difference of 6·6 lbs. per ton due to side and head winds, or 30 per cent. of excess over the resistance in calm weather.

It is known that a train may be stopt by a heavy side wind, which acts both by offering direct resistance to the motion of the train ; and by pressing the wheel-flanges against the rails. With a combination of heavy side winds and quick curves, the engine-power is severely tried, and the resistance may be one-half more than with a straight line and calm weather, and in some cases doubled.

Inclines.—It does not appear from the experiments that inclines possess any influence over the amount of resistance, beyond what is due to the action of gravity. For example, in No. 14 experiment, the results obtained upon inclines varying from 1 in 75 to 1 in 300, give sensibly the same resistance per ton, reduced to a level, at the same speed.

Weight of Engine and Tender.—This appears to be altogether a matter of indifference, as affects the resistance per ton. For example, the total tonnage-resistances with the Caledonian engines and tenders, weighing 28 tons, are fully as great as those with the Edinburgh and Glasgow engines and tenders of 35 tons ; and, moreover, with the England tank-engine, weighing 12 tons, the resistances are fully as great per ton, as with the heavier engines preceding it, allowing for the state of the wind. Thus,

Average with nine heavy } 37 miles per hour, 27·4 lbs. per ton. Side
  Engines and Tenders. }   and head winds.
With England .... { 36 miles per hour, 25·0 lbs. per ton.
                { Favourable winds.

This would show that the advantage of light engines in the question of traction, consists simply in their superior lightness.

CHAPTER VII.

COMPARISON OF TRAIN RESISTANCES ON THE BROAD AND NARROW GAUGES, 7 FEET, AND 4 FEET 8½ INCHES.

FROM the foregoing discussion, it is plain that the tonnage-resistances on the 7 feet gauge are decidedly less than on the 4 feet 8½ inches gauge. There are, probably, several causes for the difference, but the principal one is, in our mind, the superior permanent way employed on the Bristol and Exeter Railway, compared with that of the Caledonian, and Edinburgh and Glasgow lines : — continuous longitudinal bearing versus interrupted transverse-sleeper bearing ; also, the more perfect joints of the rails in contrast with the broken and yielding joints of the narrow-gauge rails. Then, the narrow-gauge trials were made over lines with curves, whilst those of the broad-gauge were made on a straight line ; and some allowance is to be made for this in a general comparison. Let us, however, take the third run with No. 42, C. R., No. 8 experiment, Table No. xciv., over a distance of 10 miles on a part of the line which is practically straight. The resistance was found to be 28 lbs. per ton of engine, tender, and train, at 45 miles per hour, with a stiff side wind. The circumstances of weather are the same as those of the Exeter experiments, and, from the formula derived from these, we find that the resistance at that speed is 20 lbs. per ton. The result of the Caledonian experiment, which we believe to be an average one, is, then, 8 lbs. in excess of that due by our broad-gauge formula, amounting to 40 per cent. We are disposed to convert this particular result into a general conclusion, and to infer, generally, that the tonnage-resistance on the narrow-gauge, under the circumstances of our trials, was 40 per cent. in excess of that on the broad-gauge.

The excess is, probably, not exclusively due to the condition of the permanent way, but also, to a small extent, to the greater superficies of the train per ton exposed to atmospheric resistance; and to the smaller wheels of the rolling stock. But the greater part of the excess is unquestionably due to the inferiority of the road. On a good road, the size of the wheels is not likely to influence materially the resistance, as larger wheels imply greater weights to be moved; and, what is worse, greater weights beneath the springs, in hard contact with the rails. It appears, therefore, inexpedient to use inconveniently large wheels upon good roads; they are advisable only on inferior roads, such as ought not to exist.

The results of experiment do not now enable us to push the inquiry much further; but enough has been done to show in what direction the improvement of railways, and the diminution of resistance are to be effected. The grand element for improvement is the permanent way; and it appears almost ridiculous that such infinite pains should have been bestowed upon the rolling stock, for its improvement, whilst the road, an equally important element, should have been comparatively neglected. Expensive economy in the permanent way has been practised, which with railway companies, of all companies, is least pardonable. But the necessities of the way are now better understood, and more durable constructions are employed, in pursuance of a system of wise economy, to the decided advantage of the railway companies.

CHAPTER VIII.

CONCLUSIONS.

THERE is no doubt that formulas of resistance for the narrow-gauge should have the same construction as those already given for the broad-gauge; and, as our data are insufficient for the construction of narrow-gauge formulas, we shall meantime adopt our broad-gauge formulas as standard ones, and as representing the resistances independent of gauge, under the circumstances of Mr. Gooch's experiments. The circumstances were—

First, A permanent way in good order at the time of the trials: smooth, continuous, and unyielding.

Second, An engine, tender, and train in good order.

Third, A straight line of rails.

Fourth, Fair weather, and dry and clean rails.

Fifth, An average side wind, of average strength, varying in the experiments from *slight* to VERY *strong*.

Any deviation from these conditions affects the resistance. An imperfect road has been estimated, from the experiments detailed, to have added about 40 per cent. to the resistance on a good, sound road.

A curved line has been estimated to have added 10 to 12 per cent. to the resistance, in the case of Brimscombe Incline, on the broad-gauge, the curvature being undetermined. On the narrow-gauge (Caledonian), it was estimated that a curvy line, having one curve under 1 mile radius for every 2½ miles incurred an excess of resistance equal to 20 per cent. of that due to a line practically straight. The quantity of curvature thus expressed, represents a high average for curved lines.

The state of the rails, as to dryness or wetness, does not greatly affect the total resistance; it was estimated to have added 2 lbs. per ton to the constant resistance.

The influence of strong side winds has been estimated to have added above 9·33 per cent. in the broad-gauge trials, to the resistance due to a calm; and 30 per cent., in the narrow-gauge trials.

It so happens, in this comparison, that the influence of curves and side winds in increasing the resistance, has been greater on the narrow than on the broad-gauge. How much of the difference may be in the causes, how much in the state of the way, and how much in the gauge, we cannot say. It is our impression that much, if not most, of it, is due to the respective conditions of the permanent way. However, if we sum up the extra resistances due to the causes named, we have as follows:—

By an imperfect road.................................40 per cent.
By curve lines, narrow gauge.........................20   „
By strong side winds (excess of narrow-gauge
    over broad-gauge).................................20   „

          Total extra resistance....................80 per cent.

Leaving open the question of the influence of gauge upon the resistance, it seems clear that, one way and another, 80 per cent. has been added by the circumstances of the narrow-gauge experiments, to the resistance found in the broad-gauge experiments. Out of the first item above charged, we shall be safe in deducting 30 per cent., from the whole 40 per cent., as an excess due directly to inferiority of way; and deducting that from the total excess, 80 per cent., we have a balance of 50 per cent., to represent the excess of resistance due to curves and strong side winds on the narrow-gauge, above what was found on the broad-gauge with a straight line and an average side wind. The greater part of this 50 per cent. of excess, would no doubt be experienced on the broad-gauge also, with sharp curves and high winds; and, therefore, finally, we shall adopt the three formulas already worked out, page 298, for the resistances on both the broad and the narrow-gauges, under the conditions there particularized, of a good, sound road, a straight road, an average side-wind, and engine and train in good order; and shall add 50 per cent., or one-half more, to meet the extreme conditions of frequent sharp curves, and strong side and head winds: the supposition of an inferior road being altogether eliminated from the question.

Of the influence of inclines we have said nothing, because that is simply estimated when the gradient is given, and it has been shown that inclines do not sensibly affect the resistance, otherwise than by introducing the element of gravity.

In a succeeding chapter, a Table of Resistances will be given, for practical use.

PART FIFTH.—GENERAL CONCLUSIONS AND PRACTICAL RULES.

SECTION I.—SUMMARY OF THE PHYSIOLOGICAL PRINCIPLES OF THE LOCOMOTIVE.

WE have now briefly to review the result of the evidence adduced with respect to the working of the locomotive; to harmonize the requirements of the engine, the boiler, and the carriage; and to work out some practical rules for setting out locomotives, and proportioning them to the work for which they are designed.

CHAPTER I.

EVIDENCE AS TO THE ENGINE.

IT is premised that, unless otherwise stated, the cylinders, valve-chests, and passages, are well protected, so that there is no condensation of steam by exposure.

The link-motion may in all cases be usefully employed for the distribution of the steam in the cylinders, for working the steam with variable expansion, and for reversing the engine. For all these purposes, the link-motion is well adapted, and, in connection with a single slide-valve, it may be made practically perfect in its action. The steam may be freely admitted to the cylinder, fully expanded, and fully exhausted; so that there may be no injurious wiredrawing by the valve; no material loss by premature exhaustion, or by imperfect exhaustion; and no injurious back pressure by compression.

The cylinders may be arranged to co-operate with the valve-gear, and to meet these conditions.

So also may the details of the smokebox, the chimney, and the blast-pipe.

More particularly, it was found that with valve-gear of desirable proportions, the steam may, under full gear, be admitted to the cylinder during three-fourths, or 75 per cent., of the stroke, which is a good working maximum; and may be cut off as early as at 17 per cent., or one-sixth, of the stroke, with shifting links, and at 12 per cent., or one-eighth, with stationary links. These ratios obtain when the lap is 22 per cent. of the travel of valve in full gear, and the lead 7 per cent.—or when the travel is $4\frac{1}{2}$ inches, for example, the lap is 1 inch, and the lead is $\frac{7}{10}$ inch. Pages 29–59.

For the best action of steam, the cylinders must be well heated and protected externally, to prevent the condensation of the steam. When the cylinders are imperfectly protected, as in ordinary outside-cylinder engines, the condensation of steam increases with the degree of expansion, until, when the steam is cut off at one-third of the stroke, the proportion of steam condensed is indicated to be about

one-fifth; and when cut off at one-fifth, the indicated condensation amounts to one-third.

The wiredrawing of steam while admitted to the cylinder, increases with the speed. There is no material wiredrawing, in full gear, when the speed of piston is under 600 feet per minute. For shorter admissions, the proportion of wiredrawing is greater. Long lap and wide ports are favourable for the prevention of wiredrawing. Pages 69–85.

The exhaust back pressure increases with the density of the steam to be exhausted, and with the speed. It is less, also, as the area of the blast-orifice is greater, that area being assumed to be the smallest section of the exhaust passage, and assuming the steam-passage to be at least as large in section as the blast-orifice. When the area of the blast-orifice is $\frac{1}{11}$th of that of the piston, the back exhaust pressure, at speeds of piston of 800 to 900 feet per minute, or about 60 miles per hour on the rails, is about 10 per cent. of the mean positive pressure in full gear; and falls to about 2 per cent. in cutting off at one-third of the stroke. Pages 85–98.

In the working of ordinary locomotives, the pressure in the cylinder, while the steam is admitted, is, in general, considerably less than that in the boiler. The fall of pressure is due to wiredrawing by the regulator, and by lateral friction, bends, and strictures in the steam-passages. It increases with the speed; and it is greatly increased by the presence of water in the steam, due to priming or condensation. The fall of pressure in the cylinder-passages, with dry steam, and when the ports are so large as one-tenth of the piston in area, never exceeds 9 per cent., even at the highest speeds. In steam-pipes not less than one-tenth of the piston in area, the fall of pressure, with ordinary steam, is practically nothing; when the steam is highly dried, steam-pipes one-thirteenth of the piston, pass the steam without any fall of pressure. The greatest useful opening of the regulator does not, in any case, exceed one-twentieth of the area of the piston. Pages 103–108.

With respect to the ultimate practical efficiency of the steam in the cylinders of the locomotive, worked expansively by the link-motion, the following results were obtained with well-protected cylinders and passages; with steam-ports, blast-orifice, and inside lead, respectively $\frac{1}{11}$th, $\frac{1}{11}$th, and $\frac{1}{13}$th of the area of the piston.

First, the loss of power by back exhaust pressure, at 60 miles per hour, or 800 to 900 feet of piston per minute, is one-tenth of the whole power in full gear. It falls as the admission is reduced; and is only one-fiftieth of the whole power, when the admission is 20 per cent. of the stroke. At 30 miles per hour, or 400 to 500 feet of piston per minute, the loss is about one-fortieth, in full gear.

Second, the resistance by compression rises slowly with the speed, and also with the degree of expansive working; but compression is not reckoned as loss of power.

Third, the whole drawback by the united back pressure of exhaust and compression, is nearly the same for all degrees of expansion, at high speeds.

Fourth, the greatest useful admission of steam, at high speeds, with heavy loads, is at least 75 per cent. of the stroke.

Fifth, the effective mean pressure in the cylinder varies with the period of admission: for admissions varying from three-fourths to one-sixth of the stroke, the effective mean pressure varies from 90 per cent. to 25 per cent. of the maximum pressure during admission.

Sixth, the consumption of water, as steam, per horse-power per hour, is practically the same for all speeds, when the period of admission is the same.

Seventh, the efficiency of steam worked expansively, increases uniformly as the period of admission is shortened; until, for 10 per cent. admission, it is about double the efficiency of steam under ordinary full gear, with 75 per cent. admission. That is, the steam, when urged to the utmost degree of expansion by the link-motion, is capable of doing about twice as much work per pound weight, as when under full gear.

Eighth, the steam, or water as steam, consumed per horse-power per hour, varies, accordingly, from 30½ lbs. in full gear, to 16 lbs., with an admission of 10 per cent.

Ninth, the consumption of coke, allowing 1 lb. for 8 lbs. of water evaporated, varies from 3·8 lbs. to 2 lbs. per horse-power per hour. If 1 lb. of coke evaporate 10 lbs. of water, the consumption would vary from 3 lbs. to 1·6 lbs. per horse-power per hour.

Tenth, the foregoing conclusions also hold good, at speeds under 30 to 40 miles per hour, or about 500 feet of piston per minute, when the ports are not more than $\frac{1}{12}$th of the piston, and the blast-orifice at least $\frac{1}{12}$th.

Eleventh, the foregoing conclusions apply to all dimensions of cylinders, when the mechanism is in good order.

Twelfth, in all locomotives, the efficiency of the steam can only be thoroughly developed by well protecting and well heating the cylinders and steam-passages, by providing wide and easy steam-passages, by maintaining the valve-gear in the best order, by adopting the smallest practicable clearance at the ends of the cylinders, and by adopting a sufficiently high pressure in the boiler. Pages 109–120.

CHAPTER II.

EVIDENCE AS TO THE BOILER.

THE blast-pipe may, in all well arranged boilers, be usefully and economically employed for the creation of the draft, and the generation of steam; in so far as the action of the blast may be made sufficiently powerful without injuriously contracting the blast-orifice against the pistons. The area of blast-orifice is regulated mainly by the following elements of the boiler, in the order of their importance:—

the grate-area, the sectional areas of flue-way through the tube-ferules at the firebox, and through the tubes themselves, and the air-space of grate. It is regulated very much by the sectional area of chimney, and also by the capacity of smokebox. The smaller the grate and the flue-ways, the smaller also must be the blast-orifice. The most favourable proportion of chimney, giving the widest blast-pipe, is that of which the sectional area is one-fifteenth of the grate-area; and the capacity of the smokebox should be about three cubic feet per foot of grate-area. The blast-orifice should terminate considerably below the bottom of the chimney, at a difference of level equal to the diameter of the chimney, or nearly so, according to the form of the entrance. The blast-area is practically independent of the dimensions of the cylinder. In ordinary boilers, of which the sectional ferule-area at firebox is about one-fifth of the grate-area, and the tube-area about one-fourth, the blast-area may be made as wide as one-sixty-sixth of the grate-area, by suitably arranging the details of the boiler and the blast-pipe. Pages 128–140.

For the prevention of priming, the steam-space in the barrel should average, in depth, at least one-fourth of the diameter; the capacity of steam-space in the firebox-shell should be equal to that in the barrel; the steam should be withdrawn at a sufficient elevation above the water-level,—equal to the diameter of the barrel, if taken at one point, or at the crown of the barrel, if taken off by Hawthorn's perforated tube; the water in the boiler must be perfectly clean. If the water be foul, or muddy, it is sure to prime, and no practical amount of steam-room can prevent its doing so. But priming may be separated from the current of steam by the use of separating pipes. Pages 142–153.

The evaporation of 9 lbs. of water per pound of coke, is adopted as the economical standard in average practice. The rate of evaporation per pound of fuel, or the poundage of water, is regulated by the grate-area, the heating surface, and the rate of evaporation per hour. In general, the smaller the firegrate, or the greater the heating surface, or the less the hourly evaporation, within practical limits, the greater is the poundage of water. The evaporative power per hour, allowing 9 lbs. of water per pound of coke, increases, within practical limits, as the grate-area is reduced, while the heating surface remains the same; and it increases as the square of the heating surface, while the grate remains the same. The grate, therefore, should be made as small as is consistent with the demands for steam, and the greatest useful rate of combustion. The maximum rate of combustion recommended, is 112 lbs., or 1 cwt., of coke per square foot of grate per hour; and, at the rate of 9 lbs. water per pound of coke, this gives an evaporation of 16 cubic feet of water per square foot of grate per hour. These rates of consumption require a heating surface of 85 square feet for each square foot of grate. The evaporative power of locomotive-boilers is the same at all speeds. The evaporative efficiency of coal, in terms of the relative weight of water evaporable by it, is, in ordinary practice, about two-thirds of that of coke. The clearance between the tubes should be proportioned to their number; and the foregoing deductions are based upon an allowance of clearance at the rate of ⅛th inch for every thirty tubes. Pages 154–165.

CHAPTER III.

EVIDENCE AS TO THE LOCOMOTIVE AS A CARRIAGE.

THE requirements of the locomotive as a carriage are that it should be heavy enough to give sufficient adhesion on the rails, for traction, and that it should run steadily at all speeds. The causes of unsteadiness arise from the reciprocating motion of the machinery, the mal-arrangement and disrepair of the vehicle, and imperfections of the permanent way. These causes may all be neutralized or removed, and a steady-going carriage obtained.

The reciprocating mechanism may be balanced by counterweights in the driving wheels, equivalent, when reduced to the length of crank, to the whole weight of the revolving and reciprocating masses requiring to be balanced. Counterweights thus estimated, and properly applied, totally prevent unsteadiness from that cause; and they go far to mitigate the instability due to disrepair of the working parts. But, of course, when the machine is in disrepair, the best way to remove instability, on that score, is to repair it. Pages 165–183.

In so far as stability depends upon the general arrangement of the machine, it depends chiefly on the positions of the axles, and the loads upon them. They should be placed well forward, to lead well, and steady the machine laterally; and well backward, to steady it vertically. The length of the barrel of boiler should not in any case be shorter than 10 feet; and it should in some cases be longer, to facilitate the proper arrangement of the axles. The distribution of the load upon the axles, may be conveniently adapted to the requirements of the driving wheels for adhesion-weight, consistently with the principal condition that at least one-fourth of the total weight should be placed upon the front axle, as leading weight, necessary for steady running at high speeds. Pages 183–196.

The position of the cylinders, outside or inside, is another element which may affect the stability of the machine. But, practically, this element does not necessarily affect the stability, if the reciprocating parts be duly balanced. The complete and efficient balancing of the mechanism is the one great and indispensable condition of general stability. It is the condition, also, of running at high speeds, as an unstable locomotive cannot attain so high speeds as a well-balanced one, and can only be moved at the same speed by a greater expenditure of power.

CHAPTER IV.

MUTUAL ADAPTATION OF THE ENGINE, THE BOILER, AND THE CARRIAGE.

BETWEEN the engine and the boiler, the only point at issue is the size of the blast-orifice. To suit the engine, it must be large enough to admit of a free exhaust, without back pressure. To suit the boiler, it must be small enough to create the necessary draft for combustion. Now, an orifice having 1-10th the area of piston, is abundantly large for the engine; and an orifice having 1-66th of the grate-area is sufficiently small for boilers of ordinary proportions, when rightly detailed. But, for margin, allow for the greatest area of blast-orifice, only 1-80th of the grate. The orifice must, then, be not less than 1-10th of the piston, and not more than 1-80th of the grate; and, to reconcile these conditions, the piston should be not more than 1-8th of the grate, because $\frac{1}{10} \times \frac{1}{8} = \frac{1}{80}$. It will be shown that these are most liberal conditions: that the engine and the boiler need no longer exist in a state of antagonism, as there is enough in the blast-pipe to meet the requirements of both.

With respect to the department of the carriage, the only point in which it bears upon the engine, is in the placing of the driving axle, when the hind axle is coupled to it; because, in this case, the driving axle should be set well forward, to throw adhesive-weight upon the hind axle; but it should, on the contrary, be set well backward, to give sufficient length of connecting rod, without unduly extending the wheel-base; for the leading wheels, we have seen, to command the cylinders, must be well up to them, if in front. A compromise may, in general, be effected, without material disadvantage.

Between the carriage and the boiler, the antagonism is of another kind, inasmuch as, when the front wheels only are coupled, the barrel of the boiler should be short, say 10 feet; for the leading wheels should be set backwards, towards the centre of gravity, to take an equal share of the load with the drivers, and the boilers should be correspondingly limited in length forward.

In fine, there does not appear to exist any substantial difficulty in working out the diverse requirements of the locomotive, and in so adjusting the necessities of the different sections, as to produce one harmonious whole.

SECTION II.—RULES FOR PROPORTIONING LOCOMOTIVES.

CHAPTER I.

PRELIMINARY CONSIDERATIONS.

THE circumstances by which the proportions and dimensions of locomotives are regulated, are variously estimated by different makers; and hence the infinite variety of locomotive machines in existence in this country. If all the makers be right, they should employ substantially the same plan of locomotive, to do the same work, when the conditions are the same. But, as, in fact, they differ considerably and essentially, not only in matters of construction, but also in vital questions of proportion, it is clear they cannot all be right, and most of them must be wrong. The simplest plan of procedure will, therefore, be, to begin at the beginning, and to expiscate, with a mixture of reason and experience, the conditions which must necessarily be observed, for the correct adaptation of the moving power to the work to be done.

The first consideration is, that the dimensions of the engine, and the dimensions of the boiler, are regulated by different sets of circumstances; and that there is no fixed relation between them. The dimensions of the engine, namely, the diameter and stroke of the pistons, and the diameter of the driving wheels, depend upon the maximum tractive force required to be exerted; those of the boiler depend upon the maximum tractive power required to be expended. By *tractive force*, is meant the pressure of the steam on the pistons reduced through the cranks and the wheels, to the equivalent pressure at the rails; this equivalent pressure acts through the wheels upon the rails, in the direction of the motion of the train, and is the force applied to overcome the train-resistance. The *tractive power* is an expression of the work done in drawing the train, and is composed of two elements: the tractive force, and the speed, which being multiplied together, express the power. The tractive power, then, varies with the speed, even while the tractive force may remain constant. The tractive force may, or may not, increase as the speed accelerates; and the same cylinders which would suffice to start the train, or to draw it at a low speed on a steep incline, working under full gear, and receiving upon the pistons the full boiler-pressure, when the tractive force is at its maximum, are capable also of drawing the train at a high speed, with absolutely less pressure on the pistons than is exerted at starting in getting up the speed, or on a steep incline. But, though the cylinder-pressure may be no greater at high speeds than at starting, and though the weight of steam expended for each stroke of the piston may be even less; yet the cylinders are filled and refilled in more rapid succession, and there may, therefore, be a much greater consumption of steam in a given time. It is the function of the boiler to supply the steam thus consumed, and it follows that, in general, while the greatest tractive force of the engine is demanded at low speeds, and is ruled by the load, the greatest development of power, and in consequence the most rapid consumption of steam from the boiler, is demanded at high speeds, and is ruled by the load and the speed conjointly. This consideration leads to the following distinctive conclusions :—

That, in general, the dimensions of the engine must be adapted to the maximum load.

And that the dimensions of the boiler must be adapted to the maximum speed, conjointly with the maximum load.

The load is, of course, virtually increased on ascending inclines, in so far as the gravitation of the load on inclines, or the tendency downwards, acts in conjunction with the proper resistance on a level, to increase the work to be done. It may, therefore, happen that the duty of the boiler on ascending inclines, at low speeds, may be as great as on a level, at high speeds; and it will now be shown how far this is likely to occur in practice, within the usual limits of speed.

For passenger-trains, let the inferior limit of actual speed be 20 miles per hour on ascending inclines; and the superior limit, 60 miles per hour on a level. For goods-trains, let the inferior and superior limits of speed be 10 miles and 30 miles per hour respectively, on ascending inclines and on levels.

With respect to passenger-trains, the resistances on a level, by the first part of Table, No. 98, p. 310, are

For 20 miles per hour, 10·3 lbs. per ton.
For 60 do. 29 lbs. do.

The consumption of steam in a given time, on a level, must be in the compound ratio of the resistance per ton, and the speed. The speeds being as 1 to 3, the consumptions will be as 10·3 lbs. to 29 lbs. × 3; or in the ratio of 10·3 lbs. to 87 lbs., at 20 miles and 60 miles per hour respectively; and the steam used at 60 miles will draw the train, at 20 miles, up an incline steep enough to raise the resistance from 10·3 lbs., due to a level, to 87 lbs. per ton. By Table, No. 98, the resistance at 20 miles per hour, amounts to 85 lbs. per ton, a trifle less than the allowance, on an incline of 1 in 30; and it follows, finally, that the consumption of steam due to a speed of 60 miles per hour on a level, is sufficient to draw the same train at 20 miles per hour up an incline of 1 in 30.

Similarly, with respect to goods-trains, the resistances on a level, being

For 10 miles per hour, 8·6 lbs. per ton.
For 30 do. 13·2 lbs. do.

and the speeds being as 1 to 3, the consumptions of steam will be as 8·6 lbs. to 13·2 lbs. × 3, or as 8·6 lbs. to 39·6 lbs. at the respective speeds. The incline which, at 10 miles per hour, would raise the resistance from 8·6 lbs. on a level, to 39·6 lbs. per ton, is 1 in 70, by Table No. 98.

It appears, then, that the consumption of steam which would take a passenger-train at 60 miles per hour on a level, would take it at 20 miles per hour up an incline of 1 in 30; and that the steam which would draw a goods-train at 30 miles per hour on a level, would draw it at 10 miles per hour up an incline of 1 in 70. These cases have been worked out to show that when the speed is provided for in the boiler, there should be, in general, abundance of steam for inclines. Inclines steeper than 1 in 70 are rarely to be encountered; but when they are, of course the boiler-power for goods-trains must be adapted to them; or, the speed may be less. With respect to passenger-trains, it is shown that if 60 miles per hour on a level is provided for, there is a great surplus of boiler-power for inclines; if 45 miles per hour on a level be secured, the same boiler-power will draw the train up an incline of 1 in 60 at 20 miles per hour.

The above comparative results are based upon the first part of the Table of Resistances, No. 98. The second part of the Table is more suited for general practice, as it allows for quick curves and strong winds; and the allowances so made, which are very considerable at the higher speeds, provide for still better performances at lower speeds on inclines, than are found by the first part of the Table. Thus, the boiler-power which would, by the second part of the Table, draw a train at 45 miles per hour on a level, would take it up an incline of 1 in 45 at 20 miles per hour.

With respect to the capabilities of the engine, or the cylinder-capacity, as it may be called for obvious distinction, it is clear that, in the cases above specified, the cylinder-capacity would be in excess at the high speeds on the level; and would, on the contrary, be most fully taxed at the lower speeds on the inclines.

The ruling data, concerned in the designing of locomo-

2 Q

tives, appear, then, to be, first, the maximum gross weight of engine, tender, and train; second, the maximum uniform speed on a level; thirdly, the steepest incline which the engine, tender, and train are to ascend without assistance.

The inquiry naturally divides itself into two:—First, the design of the engine; secondly, the design of the boiler.

CHAPTER II.

CONSIDERATIONS AFFECTING THE DIMENSIONS OF THE ENGINE.

IN setting out the engine, by which is now meant the cylinders and driving-wheels, there are three things to be determined:—the diameter of the cylinder, the stroke of the piston, and the diameter of the driving-wheels; and these must be assigned with relation to the gross tractive force required, the maximum pressure in the boiler, and the maximum speed. It is desirable to limit the diameter of piston, and consequently the area, in order to prevent an excessive concentration of steam-pressure on the bearings. It is desirable also to limit the speed of piston, in order to moderate the number and violence of the reciprocations. The area and the maximum speed of the piston, therefore, must be adapted to each other, so that the conditions due to the extremes of speed may be satisfied; as they are, in conjunction with the steam-pressure, the elements of the engine-power. Upon the whole, it is preferable that the maximum speed of piston should be estimated rather high, within the limits of employing a suitably long stroke, and a wheel of moderated diameter; the area of piston being proportionally moderated. Consequently, for low speeds and heavy loads, a long stroke and small wheels should be adopted; for higher speeds and lighter loads, there must be a shorter stroke and a larger wheel.

But, the area of the piston should be suitably related to the boiler-pressure; or such, that the full pressure in the boiler may be made available in the cylinders during admission, in ordinary working, without wiredrawing by the regulator, and by the use of the variable expansion-gear, the piston being large enough to develop the greatest tractive force required, under full steam, and so adjusted in area, that the required variations of tractive force should be effected by varying the period of admission, with the steam from the boilers turned constantly full on to the cylinders. In short, the tractive power should be varied exclusively by the use of the expansion-gear, without any material wiredrawing by the regulator; the regulator ceasing to be a regulator, and virtually a mere steam-cock.

CHAPTER III.

CONSIDERATIONS AFFECTING THE DIMENSIONS OF THE BOILER.

WITH respect to the boiler, the leading values to be assigned are, the area of the grate, and the total heating surface: to be determined with relation to the maximum rate of the consumption of steam in the cylinders, and the maximum rate of combustion of fuel per square foot of grate per hour. The boiler should be light, powerful, and economical; and these conditions are promoted by a quick, intense combustion of the fuel, which adds to the efficiency of the heating surface, and requires less area of grate. The practical limit to the intensity of combustion is imposed by the contingent force of the draft, which must necessarily be rapid to insure intense combustion, while it should not be so active as to lift and carry off the fuel through the tubes. The limit thus imposed, varies, of course, with the quality of the fuel.

CHAPTER IV.

GENERAL DATA REGULATING THE PROPORTIONS OF THE ENGINE AND THE BOILER.

Maximum Speed of Piston.—A speed of piston, of about 600 feet per minute, for a speed of 40 miles per hour on the rails, may be adopted as a standard ratio for all speeds of 40 miles per hour and upwards; that is, more simply, 15 feet of piston per minute for each mile per hour on the rails. In this ratio, the speed of piston would amount to 900 feet per minute, at 60 miles per hour.

For maximum speeds on the rails, less than 40 miles per hour, the maximum speed of piston should be as great as may be found consistent with good proportion.

But, though positive limits to the speed of piston are thus suggested, it must be added that, so long as a locomotive runs steadily, there does not seem to be any limit to the speed, indicated in practical working, with respect to the usage of the mechanical organs; the limit grows out of the necessity for quickly exhausting the steam, to prevent injurious loss of power by back pressure.

Maximum Pressure in the Boiler.—Considerations of economy and convenience, point to the advantage of a high working pressure, not less than 100 lbs. per square inch. It should, probably, not be greater than about 150 lbs. per inch.

Ratio of the Diameter to the Stroke of Piston.—The orthodox ratio is 3 to 4; thus, for 15 inches diameter, the stroke is 20 inches. But any ratio may be adopted to suit circumstances. In general, a moderate diameter and a lengthened stroke, are preferable to the reverse design. The stroke may be, in all cases, at least 2 inches greater than the diameter; and it may not in any case exceed twice the diameter.

Ratio of the Stroke of Piston to the Diameter of Driving-wheel.—The ratio is affected by several circumstances. For 600 feet of piston per minute, at 40 miles per hour, the ratio is about 1 to 3½, and a ratio of from 1 to 3½, to 1 to 4, works well for high speeds on the rails. For lower maximum speeds, the ratio should be greater as the speed is less, but it should in no case, perhaps, exceed 1 to 2, when the length of stroke becomes half the diameter of the wheel.

Degree of Expansion Working.—This is necessarily a very varying quantity, and must be regulated by convenience. It may, however, be stated generally, that an engine working on a level, at a uniform speed, and with its regulation-load, should cut off not later than at half-stroke; cutting off sooner on a descending gradient, and later on an ascending gradient; and cutting off sooner, also, with a smaller load. This order of working may be as favourable as could be expected with heavy goods-trains; but with lighter trains, and with passenger-trains, expansive-working should, as a general rule, be more fully carried out. Indeed, there appear to be no limits but those assigned by the capabilities of expansion-gear, the strength of materials, the ability of the wearing parts to work under high temperatures and pressures, and the efficiency of the protection of the cylinders.

Maximum Rate of Combustion of Fuel.—This may be taken at 112 lbs., or 1 cwt., of good coke or coal per square foot of grate per hour. For fuel of mixed quality, say 100 lbs. per square foot per hour. No allowance need be made for small boilers, if constructed with a proper amount of water-room, as an internal reservoir of heat, to meet irregularities of firing and feeding.

Maximum Rate of Evaporation.—Allowing 9 lbs. of water per pound of coke, it would amount to 16 cubic feet of water per square foot of grate per hour, for 1 cwt. of coke consumed per foot per hour; and to about 14 cubic feet of water per foot per hour, for 100 lbs. of coke.

CHAPTER V.

PRACTICAL RULES.

THE simplest way to deal with the problem of the locomotive, is, first, to assume given dimensions of cylinder and driving-wheel, a given steam-pressure in the boiler, and a given period of admission; and to find from these the tractive force at the rails. Secondly, to assume a given speed, and to find the grate-area and heating surface of boiler due to the given speed, the given period of admission, and the tractive force at the rails as found. Thirdly, to find the total load that can be drawn, at the given speed, and with the tractive force at the rails as found.

First, for the tractive force at the rails. Assuming the maximum initial pressure in the cylinder to be equal to that in the boiler, find by Rule 7, page 116, the effective mean pressure in the cylinder, due to the given period of admission; multiply by the area of piston, and by four times the stroke, to represent the duplicate action of two cylinders; and divide by the circumference of the driving-wheel. The result is the tractive force at the rails.

Secondly, for the grate-area and the heating surface. Find, by Rule 8, page 116, either the consumption of water, or the consumption of coke, per horse-power per hour due to the given period of admission; find the horse-power required to draw the train, in terms of the tractive force at the rails and the speed; multiply together the two values thus found, to give the consumption per hour; and divide the product by the assumed maximum rate of combustion, or of evaporation, per foot of grate; the result is the re-

quired area of grate. The necessary heating surface may be found, in terms of the consumption of water and the area of grate, by Rule 4, page 159.

Thirdly, for the total load that can be drawn. Find, by the aid of Rule 1, page 298, the resistance per ton on the given incline or level, at the given speed; and divide the total tractive force by the resistance per ton thus found; the quotient is the total load that can be drawn. Tables Nos. 98, 99, are constructed by means of the above-named Rule, and will facilitate calculations.

Expressing the diameter and stroke of piston in inches, the diameter of wheel in feet, the steam-pressure in pounds per square inch, and the period of admission in hundredth parts of the stroke; and following the process above indicated for finding the tractive force at the rails, the tractive force is expressed by

$$\frac{\text{diar. piston}^2 \times \cdot7854 \times \text{stroke} \times 4 \times (13\cdot3 \sqrt{\text{admission}} - 28) \times \tfrac{1}{100}\text{ pressure in boiler.}}{\text{diameter of wheel} \times 3\cdot1416 \times 12}$$

which, being reduced to the simplest form, becomes

$$\frac{(\cdot01125 \sqrt{\text{admission}} - \cdot0233) \times \text{diar. piston}^2 \times \text{stroke} \times \text{pressure}}{\text{diameter of wheel}} \quad \dots\dots(1)$$

Expressing the grate-area and the heating surface in square feet, and the speed in miles per hour; and assuming the maximum rate of combustion of coke to be 100 lbs. per square foot of grate per hour, the area of grate is expressed by

$$\frac{((\cdot0275 \times \text{admission}) + 1\cdot75) \times \left(\dfrac{\text{tractive force} \times \text{speed} \times 88}{33,000}\right)}{100}$$

which, by reduction, becomes

$$\frac{((\cdot0275 \times \text{admission}) + 1\cdot75) \times \text{tractive force} \times \text{speed})}{37,500}$$

But, this formula is based on an allowance of 8 lbs. of water evaporated per pound of coke. Whereas, we have now to assume, as the standard, for working, an evaporation of 9 lbs. of water per pound of coke. The required area of grate is, therefore, to be taken as less than that signified by the above formula, in the ratio of 9 to 8, and multiplying the formula by 8, and dividing by 9, we have, as the final working formula,

$$\frac{((\cdot0275 \times \text{admission}) + 1\cdot75) \times \text{tractive force} \times \text{speed}}{42,187} \quad (2)$$

The heating surface is expressed by

$$\text{area of grate} \times 80 \quad \dots\dots\dots(3)$$

The total load in tons is expressed by

$$\frac{\text{tractive force}}{\text{resistance per ton.}} \quad \dots\dots\dots(4)$$

These formulas are expressed by the following rules:—

RULE I.—*To find the Tractive Force at the Rails, due to given Dimensions of Engine, and Boiler-pressure.* Find the square root of the period of admission in hundredths of the stroke,—multiply it by ·01125,—and subtract ·0233 from the product.—Multiply the remainder by the square of the diameter of piston in inches.—and by the stroke in inches,—and by the pressure in the boiler in pounds per square inch.

TABLE NO. XCVL.—OF TRACTIVE FORCES DUE TO GIVEN PERIODS OF ADMISSION. AND GIVEN DIMENSIONS OF ENGINE.
INITIAL PRESSURE OF STEAM IN THE CYLINDER, 100 LBS. PER SQUARE INCH.

Dimensions of Engine.			Periods of Admission of Steam to the Cylinders, in parts of the Stroke.											Speed in Miles per Hour on the Rails.					
Cylinder.		Diameter of Driving Wheel.	10 p. cent.	12½ p. cent.	15 p. cent.	17½ p. cent.	20 p. cent.	30 p. cent.	40 p. cent.	50 p. cent.	60 p. cent.	70 p. cent.	75 p. cent.	80 p. cent	10 miles.	20 miles.	30 miles.	40 miles.	50 miles.	60 miles.
Diameter.	Stroke.		TOTAL TRACTIVE FORCE AT THE RAILS, in pounds, due to the annexed Dimensions of Engine, the above Periods of Admission, and an Initial Pressure in the Cylinder of 100 lbs. per square inch.												SPEED OF PISTON, in feet per minute, due to the annexed Dimensions of Engine, and the above Speeds on the Rails.					
inches.	inches.	feet.	lbs.	lbs.	lbs.	lbs.	lbs.	lbs.	lbs.	lbs.	lbs.	lbs.	lbs.	lbs.	feet.	feet.	feet.	feet.	feet.	feet.
8	12	4	252	316	389	456	541	788	919	1,080	1,226	1,360	1,410	1,484	140	280	420	560	700	840
	14	"	294	368	454	532	631	861	1,071	1,260	1,430	1,586	1,645	1,732	165	330	495	660	825	980
	16	"	336	422	519	608	721	984	1,225	1,440	1,634	1,813	1,881	1,979	186	372	560	746	933	1,120
9	12	"	318	400	492	577	685	934	1,163	1,367	1,551	1,721	1,801	1,878	140	280	420	560	700	840
	14	"	372	467	574	674	799	1,069	1,357	1,595	1,810	2,008	2,102	2,191	165	330	495	660	825	980
	16	"	425	534	656	770	913	1,245	1,550	1,822	2,068	2,294	2,402	2,503	186	372	560	746	933	1,120
	18	"	478	600	738	866	1,027	1,400	1,744	2,050	2,327	2,581	2,702	2,818	210	420	630	840	1,050	1,260
10	12	"	393	494	606	713	854	1,153	1,436	1,688	1,915	2,125	2,224	2,319	140	280	420	560	700	840
	14	"	459	577	709	832	986	1,345	1,675	1,969	2,234	2,474	2,594	2,705	165	330	495	660	825	980
	16	"	524	659	810	950	1,125	1,537	1,914	2,250	2,553	2,828	2,965	3,092	186	372	560	746	933	1,120
	18	"	590	741	912	1,069	1,268	1,729	2,153	2,532	2,872	3,172	3,335	3,478	210	420	630	840	1,050	1,260
	20	"	655	824	1,013	1,188	1,409	1,921	2,392	2,813	3,191	3,521	3,706	3,865	233	467	700	933	1,166	1,400
11	14	"	555	698	856	1,006	1,193	1,627	2,026	2,382	2,703	2,999	3,139	3,289	165	330	495	660	825	980
	16	"	634	797	978	1,150	1,364	1,860	2,316	2,722	3,089	3,427	3,587	3,753	186	372	560	746	933	1,120
	18	"	713	897	1,101	1,294	1,535	2,092	2,605	3,062	3,475	3,856	4,036	4,216	210	420	630	840	1,050	1,260
	20	"	792	997	1,223	1,437	1,705	2,324	2,995	3,403	3,862	4,284	4,484	4,680	233	467	700	933	1,166	1,400
	22	"	872	1,096	1,345	1,581	1,875	2,557	3,184	3,743	4,248	4,713	4,933	5,144	257	513	770	1,026	1,283	1,540
12	14	"	660	830	1,021	1,196	1,420	1,936	2,412	2,569	3,217	3,569	3,736	3,914	165	330	495	660	825	980
	16	"	755	949	1,167	1,369	1,623	2,213	2,756	3,237	3,677	4,079	4,074	9,447	186	372	560	746	933	1,120
	18	"	849	1,067	1,313	1,540	1,826	2,490	3,101	4,085	4,136	4,589	4,412	5,020	210	420	630	840	1,050	1,260
	20	"	943	1,186	1,459	1,711	2,029	2,766	3,445	4,344	4,596	5,099	4,750	5,573	233	467	700	933	1,166	1,400
	22	"	1,037	1,304	1,604	1,882	2,232	3,043	3,790	4,602	5,055	5,609	5,088	6,126	257	513	770	1,026	1,283	1,540
	24	"	1,132	1,423	1,750	2,053	2,435	3,319	4,134	4,860	5,515	6,119	5,426	6,679	280	560	840	1,120	1,400	1,680
13	15	"	830	1,044	1,284	1,506	1,786	2,435	3,033	3,565	4,045	4,486	4,698	4,899	175	350	525	700	875	1,050
	16	"	886	1,113	1,370	1,606	1,905	2,597	3,235	4,787	4,315	4,787	5,011	5,225	186	372	560	746	933	1,120
	18	"	996	1,252	1,541	1,807	2,143	2,922	3,639	5,016	4,854	5,385	5,637	5,878	210	420	630	840	1,050	1,260
	20	"	1,107	1,392	1,712	2,008	2,381	3,247	4,043	5,245	5,393	5,984	6,264	6,531	233	467	700	933	1,166	1,400
	22	"	1,228	1,531	1,883	2,209	2,619	3,571	4,448	5,475	5,933	6,582	6,890	7,185	257	513	770	1,026	1,283	1,540
	24	"	1,328	1,670	2,054	2,409	2,857	3,896	4,852	5,704	6,472	7,181	7,517	7,838	280	560	840	1,120	1,400	1,680
14	16	"	1,034	1,292	1,588	1,863	2,219	2,692	3,751	4,410	5,004	5,552	5,812	6,116	186	372	560	746	933	1,120
	18	"	1,153	1,453	1,787	2,096	2,485	2,916	4,221	4,961	5,630	6,246	6,788	6,821	210	420	630	840	1,050	1,260
	20	"	1,281	1,618	1,985	2,319	2,761	3,141	4,689	5,512	6,225	6,940	7,765	7,645	233	467	700	933	1,166	1,400
	22	"	1,409	1,776	2,184	2,561	3,048	3,365	5,156	6,064	6,880	7,634	8,741	8,410	257	513	770	1,026	1,283	1,540
	24	"	1,537	1,937	2,383	2,794	3,360	3,589	5,627	6,615	7,506	8,328	9,718	9,175	280	560	840	1,120	1,400	1,680
15	18	"	1,326	1,688	2,051	2,406	2,853	3,890	4,846	5,696	6,463	7,171	7,506	7,825	210	420	630	840	1,050	1,260
	20	"	1,474	1,853	2,279	2,673	3,170	4,322	5,383	6,328	7,181	7,968	8,340	8,695	233	467	700	933	1,166	1,400
	22	"	1,621	2,038	2,507	2,940	3,487	4,755	5,922	6,961	7,899	8,764	9,174	9,563	257	513	770	1,026	1,283	1,540
	24	"	1,768	2,223	2,735	3,208	3,804	5,187	6,480	7,594	8,617	9,561	10,008	10,435	280	560	840	1,120	1,400	1,680
16	18	"	1,509	1,897	2,334	2,737	3,246	4,426	5,512	6,480	7,353	8,159	8,540	8,905	210	420	630	840	1,050	1,260
	20	"	1,677	2,108	2,593	3,041	3,607	4,918	6,125	7,200	8,170	9,063	9,489	9,894	233	467	700	933	1,166	1,400
	22	"	1,844	2,319	2,853	3,345	3,968	5,409	6,736	7,920	8,987	9,971	10,437	10,883	257	513	770	1,026	1,283	1,540
	24	"	2,012	2,530	3,112	3,650	4,329	5,901	7,350	8,640	9,804	10,877	11,386	11,873	280	560	840	1,120	1,400	1,680
17	20	"	1,893	2,380	2,928	3,433	4,072	5,552	6,914	8,128	9,223	10,233	10,711	11,168	233	467	700	933	1,166	1,400
	22	"	2,082	2,618	3,295	3,777	4,480	6,107	7,605	8,941	10,145	11,256	11,782	12,286	257	513	770	1,026	1,283	1,540
	24	"	2,272	2,856	3,513	4,120	4,886	6,662	8,297	9,754	11,064	12,280	12,854	13,403	280	560	840	1,120	1,400	1,680
18	20	"	2,122	2,693	3,312	3,921	4,607	6,283	7,823	9,197	10,437	11,578	12,120	12,638	233	467	700	933	1,166	1,400
	22	"	2,334	2,962	3,644	4,313	5,068	6,911	8,606	10,116	11,479	12,736	13,332	13,902	257	513	770	1,026	1,283	1,540
	24	"	2,547	3,231	3,975	4,705	5,529	7,540	9,388	11,036	12,523	13,894	14,544	15,166	280	560	840	1,120	1,400	1,680

NOTE 1.—The Tractive Force due to any other Diameter of Driving Wheel than that named in the Table, namely 4 feet, is inversely proportional to the diameters, other circumstances being the same; and is found by multiplying the Tractive Force shown in the Table by 4, and dividing the product by the given diameter of the wheel in feet.

[2.—The Tractive Force due to any other Boiler-pressure than 100 lbs. per square inch, which is assumed as a constant in the Table, is found by multiplying the Tractive Force given in the Table by 100, and dividing by the required Boiler-pressure in pounds per square inch. This method applies with sufficient exactness to boiler-pressures ranging from 80 lbs. to 150 lbs. per inch.

3.—The columns of Speeds of Piston are added as a check in working out the dimensions and proportions of the Engines; and the Speed of piston due to any other diameter of Driving Wheel than 4 feet, is estimated in precisely the same way as the Tractive Force, Note 1

—Divide the product by the diameter of the wheel in feet. The result is the tractive force at the rails in pounds.

RULE II.—*To find the Area of Grate due to given Dimensions of Engine, Boiler-pressure, and Speed.* Multiply the period of admission in hundredths of the stroke, by ·0275, —and add 4·75 to the product.—Multiply the sum by the tractive force due to the given dimensions of engine, found by Rule I.,—and by the speed in miles per hour.—Divide the product by 42,187. The result is the area of grate in square feet.

RULE III.—*To find the Heating Surface due to a given Area of Grate, consuming 100 lbs. of coke per foot of grate per hour.* Multiply the area of grate in square feet by 80. The product is the heating surface in square feet.

RULE IV.—*To find the Total Load due to given Dimensions of Engine, and given Speeds.* Divide the tractive force, found by Rule I., by the resistance in pounds per ton, found by Rule I., page 298. The quotient is the total load in tons, comprising engine, tender, and train.

By the aid of these rules, the Tables, Nos. 96 and 97, are

TABLE NO. XCVII.—OF GRATE-AREAS AND HEATING SURFACES, REQUIRED FOR GIVEN SPEEDS, TRACTIVE FORCES, AND PERIODS OF ADMISSION.

Total Tractive Force at Rails.	Period of Admission of Steam to Cylinders, in parts of the Stroke.	Speeds, in miles per hour, on the Rails. GRATE-AREAS AND HEATING SURFACES, in square feet, due to the annexed Tractive Force and Period of Admission, and the above Speeds on the Rails.													
		10		20		30		40		50		60		70	
		Area of Grate.	Heating Surface.	Area of Grate.	Heating Surface.	Area of Grate.	Heating Surface.	Area of Grate.	Heating Surface.	Area of Grate.	Heating Surface.	Area of Grate.	Heating Surface.	Area of Grate.	Heating Surface.
lbs.	percentage.	square feet.	square feet.	square feet.	square feet.	square feet.	square feet.	square feet.	square feet.	square feet.	square feet.	square feet.	square feet.	square feet.	square feet.
1,000	50	..	..	..	..	..	..	..	..	3·7	296	4·5	356	5·3	415
1,500	"	..	..	..	..	3·3	265	4·5	356	5·6	444	6·7	533	7·8	623
2,000	"	..	..	..	..	4·5	355	6·0	474	7·4	592	8·9	710	10·4	830
2,500	"	..	..	3·7	296	5·6	444	7·4	592	9·3	740	11·1	889	13·0	1037
3,000	"	..	..	4·5	355	6·7	534	8·9	710	11·1	889	13·3	1067	15·6	1245
3,500	"	..	..	5·2	415	7·8	623	10·4	830	13·0	1037	15·6	1244	18·2	1451
4,000	"	..	..	6·0	474	8·9	711	11·9	948	14·8	1185	17·6	1421	20·8	1658
4,500	"	3·3	266	6·7	531	10·0	800	13·4	1067	16·7	1333	20·0	1599	22·3	1865
5,000	"	3·7	296	7·4	592	11·1	889	14·8	1185	18·5	1481	22·2	1777	25·9	2077
5,500	"	4·1	326	8·2	652	12·2	978	16·3	1308	20·4	1637	24·4	1954	28·5	2280
6,000	"	4·5	355	8·9	710	13·3	1066	17·8	1422	22·2	1776	26·7	2132	..	..
6,500	"	4·8	385	9·6	770	14·5	1155	19·3	1540	24·0	1926	29·0	2310	..	..
7,000	"	5·2	414	10·4	830	15·6	1244	20·6	1658	26·0	2074	..	..	..	..
7,500	"	5·6	444	11·1	888	16·7	1332	22·2	1776	27·8	2222	..	..	..	..
8,000	"	6·0	474	11·9	947	17·6	1422	23·7	1896	29·6	2368	..	..	..	..
8,500	"	6·3	503	12·6	1006	18·9	1510	25·2	2014	..	..	..	..	..	..
9,000	"	6·7	531	13·3	1066	20·0	1599	26·7	2133	..	..	..	..	..	..
9,500	"	7·0	563	14·0	1125	21·0	1689	28·2	2251	..	..	..	..	..	..
10,000	"	7·4	593	14·8	1184	22·2	1777	29·6	2386	..	..	..	..	..	..
10,500	"	7·6	622	15·5	1243	23·3	1866	..	..	..	..	..	..	..	..
11,000	"	8·2	651	16·3	1302	24·4	1954	..	..	..	..	..	..	..	..
11,500	"	8·5	681	17·2	1370	25·6	2044	..	..	..	..	..	..	..	..
12,000	"	8·9	710	17·8	1421	26·7	2183	..	..	..	..	..	..	..	..
12,500	"	9·3	740	18·5	1480	27·8	2222	..	..	..	..	..	..	..	..
13,000	"	9·6	770	19·2	1539	29·0	2310	..	..	..	..	..	..	..	..
13,500	"	10·0	799	20·0	1596	30·0	2399	..	..	..	..	..	..	..	..
14,000	"	10·4	830	20·6	1648	..	..	..	..	..	..	..	..	..	..
14,500	"	10·7	858	21·5	1717	..	..	..	..	..	..	..	..	..	..
15,000	"	11·1	889	22·2	1778	..	..	..	..	..	..	..	..	..	..
16,000	"	12·0	948	23·6	1894	..	..	..	..	..	..	..	..	..	..
18,000	"	13·4	1062	26·6	2132	..	..	..	..	..	..	..	..	..	..
20,000	"	14·8	1186	29·6	2368	..	..	..	..	..	..	..	..	..	..

NOTE 1.—The smallest Area of Grate recognised in this Table as useful for practical purposes, is 4 square feet; and the largest area of grate is 30 square feet.

NOTE 2.—To find the Grate-Areas and Heating Surfaces due to any other period of Admission, multiply the quantities given in the Table for an admission of 50 per cent., by the multipliers annexed to the given period of admission in the following table: This table is constructed from table No. LVI., page 117.

Periods of Admission, in hundredth parts of the Stroke.	10	12½	15	17½	20	30	40	50	60	70	75	80
Multipliers.	·65	·67	·69	·71	·74	·82	·91	1·0	1·1	1·2	1·22	1·23

drawn up. The first Table, No. 96, contains the tractive force at the rails, by Rule I. above, due to given dimensions of engine, and given periods of admission; the boiler-pressure has been taken throughout at 100 lbs. per square inch, and the diameter of wheel at 4 feet, as the table would otherwise have been expanded to inconvenient dimensions. The relative speeds of piston are also given, and are found by Rule IV., page 110. The second Table, No. 97, contains the grate-areas and heating surfaces of boiler, due to given tractive forces, given periods of admission, and given speeds.

The next in order is a table of resistances for various speeds and gradients. Table, No. 98, has been formed by the aid of Rule I., page 298, showing the resistances per ton of gross load of engine, tender, and train; at speeds of 10 to 70 miles per hour; on a level, and on ascending gradients of 1 in 20 to 1 in 1000. The resistances are estimated according to the conditions explained in the Table. Tables of the resistance of engines and trains separately, might be constructed with the aid of the other rules given. But they would be of little practical use, as engines and trains work in conjunction, not separately.

There remains to be constructed a table showing the load that can be drawn with a given tractive force, at a given speed, on a given gradient. Table No. 99 is formed on this plan, and shows the total load in tons of engine, tender, and train, that can be drawn with a tractive force of 1000 lbs. at the rails, at various speeds, and on various gradients. The total loads are found by dividing 1000 lbs. by the resistances per ton contained in Table No. 98, due to given speeds and gradients.

These Tables will very much facilitate the application of the foregoing rules in calculations respecting engine-power and boiler-power, and performance.

In the next part, it is proposed to close the investigation of the Locomotive with some accounts of its actual performance during the last few years; which will serve to show what can be done with it in its present state of advancement, and as data for comparison with future results.

TABLE NO. XCVIII.—OF THE RESISTANCES PER TON OF ENGINE, TENDER, AND TRAIN, AT VARIOUS UNIFORM SPEEDS, AND ON VARIOUS ASCENDING GRADIENTS.

Measured by Tractive Force at the Rails.

First Part. Conditions:— A good sound road. A straight road. An average side-wind. Engine, Tender, and Train, in good working order.

Second Part. Conditions:— A good sound road. Frequent sharp curves under 1 mile radius. Strong side and head winds. Engine, Tender, and Train, in good working order.

Total Resistance in pounds per ton, due to the above Speeds and the annexed Ascending Gradients. Constant, 8 lbs. (First Part); Constant, 12 lbs. (Second Part).

Ascending Gradients	First Part — Speeds in Miles per hour													Second Part — Speeds in Miles per hour													Ascending Gradients
	10	15	20	25	30	35	40	45	50	55	60	65	70	10	15	20	25	30	35	40	45	50	55	60	65	70	
Level	8·6	9·3	10·3	11·6	13·2	15·0	17·3	19·8	22·6	25·7	29	32·7	36·6	13	14	15·5	17·5	20	22·6	26	30	34	38·6	43·5	49	55	Level
1 in 20	120	121	122	124	125	127	129	132	135	138	141	145	149	125	126	128	130	132	135	138	142	146	151	156	161	167	1 in 20
1 in 25	98	99	100	101	103	105	107	109	112	115	119	122	126	103	104	105	107	110	112	116	120	124	129	133	139	145	1 in 25
1 in 30	83	84	86	86	88	90	92	94	97	100	104	107	111	88	89	90	92	95	97	101	105	109	113	118	124	130	1 in 30
1 in 40	64	65	66	68	69	71	73	76	79	82	85	89	93	69	70	71	73	76	78	82	86	90	94	99	105	111	1 in 40
1 in 50	53	54	55	56	58	60	62	64	67	70	74	77	81	58	59	60	62	65	67	71	75	79	83	88	94	100	1 in 50
1 in 60	46	47	48	49	50	52	55	57	60	63	66	70	74	50	51	53	55	57	60	63	67	71	76	81	86	92	1 in 60
1 in 70	40	41	42	44	45	47	49	52	55	58	61	65	69	43	46	47	49	52	54	58	62	66	70	75	81	87	1 in 70
1 in 80	36	37	38	40	41	43	45	48	51	54	57	61	65	41	42	43	45	48	50	54	58	62	66	71	77	83	1 in 80
1 in 90	33	34	35	37	38	40	42	45	48	51	54	58	62	38	39	40	42	45	47	51	55	59	63	68	74	80	1 in 90
1 in 100	31	32	33	34	36	37	40	42	45	48	51	55	59	35	36	38	40	43	45	48	52	56	61	66	71	77	1 in 100
1 in 110	29	30	31	32	33	35	38	40	43	46	49	53	57	33	34	36	38	40	43	46	50	54	59	64	69	75	1 in 110
1 in 120	27	28	29	30	32	34	36	38	41	44	48	51	55	32	33	34	36	39	41	45	49	53	57	62	68	74	1 in 120
1 in 130	26	27	28	29	30	32	35	38	40	43	46	50	54	30	31	33	36	37	40	43	47	51	56	61	66	72	1 in 130
1 in 140	25	26	27	28	29	31	33	36	39	42	45	49	52	29	30	31	33	35	38	42	46	50	54	59	65	71	1 in 140
1 in 150	24	25	26	27	28	30	32	35	38	41	45	49	51	28	29	30	32	35	37	41	45	49	53	58	64	70	1 in 150
1 in 160	23	24	25	26	27	29	31	34	37	40	43	47	50	27	28	29	31	34	36	40	44	48	52	57	63	69	1 in 160
1 in 180	22	23	24	25	26	27	30	33	36	39	43	47	51	26	27	28	30	33	35	39	43	47	51	56	62	68	1 in 180
1 in 200	20	21	22	23	25	26	29	31	34	37	40	44	48	24	25	27	29	31	34	37	41	45	50	55	60	66	1 in 200
1 in 250	18	19	20	21	22	24	26	29	32	35	38	42	46	22	23	25	27	29	32	35	39	43	48	53	58	64	1 in 250
1 in 300	16	17	18	19	21	23	25	27	30	33	36	40	44	20	21	23	25	27	30	33	37	41	46	51	56	62	1 in 300
1 in 350	15	16	17	18	20	22	24	26	29	32	35	39	43	19	20	22	24	26	29	32	36	40	45	50	55	61	1 in 350
1 in 400	14	15	16	17	19	21	23	25	28	31	34	38	42	18	19	21	23	25	28	31	35	39	44	49	54	60	1 in 400
1 in 500	13	14	15	16	18	20	22	24	27	30	33	37	41	17	18	19	22	24	27	30	34	38	43	48	53	59	1 in 500
1 in 600	12	13	14	15	17	19	21	23	26	29	32	35	39	16	17	18	20	23	25	29	33	37	41	46	52	58	1 in 600
1 in 800	11	12	13	14	16	18	20	22	25	28	32	35	39	16	17	18	20	23	25	29	33	37	41	46	52	58	1 in 800
1 in 1000	11	11·5	12	14	15	17	19	22	25	28	30	35	39	15	16	18	20	22	25	28	32	36	41	46	51	57	1 in 1000
Level	8·6	9·3	10·3	11·6	13·2	15	17·3	19·8	22·6	25·7	29	32·7	36·6	13	14	15·5	17·5	20	22·6	26	30	34	38·6	43·5	49	55	Level

TABLE NO. XCIX.—OF THE TOTAL LOADS THAT CAN BE DRAWN WITH A TRACTIVE FORCE AT THE RAILS, OF 1000 lbs.; AT VARIOUS UNIFORM SPEEDS, AND ON VARIOUS ASCENDING GRADIENTS.

Measured in Tons Weight of Engine, Tender, and Train.

First Part. Conditions:— A good sound road. A straight road. An average side-wind. Engine, Tender, and Train, in good working order.

Second Part. Conditions:— A good sound road. Frequent sharp curves, under 1 mile radius. Strong side and head winds. Engine, Tender, and Train, in good working order.

Total Load, in tons, of Engine, Tender, and Train, due to the above Speeds and the annexed Ascending Gradients, and to a Tractive Force of 1000 lbs.

Ascending Gradients	First Part — Speeds in Miles per hour													Second Part — Speeds in Miles per hour													Ascending Gradients
	10	15	20	25	30	35	40	45	50	55	60	65	70	10	15	20	25	30	35	40	45	50	55	60	65	70	
Level	116	108	97	80	76	67	58	50	44	39	34	30	27	77	71	64	57	50	44	38	33	29	26	23	20	18	Level
1 in 20	8	8	8	8	8	8	8	8	7	7	7	7	7	8	8	8	8	8	7	7	7	7	7	6	6	6	1 in 20
1 in 25	10	10	10	10	10	9	9	9	9	8	8	8	8	10	10	9	9	9	8	8	8	8	7	7	7	7	1 in 25
1 in 30	12	12	12	12	11	11	11	11	10	10	10	9	9	11	11	11	11	10	10	10	10	9	9	8	8	8	1 in 30
1 in 40	17	15	15	15	14	14	14	13	13	12	12	11	11	14	14	14	14	13	13	12	12	11	11	10	10	10	1 in 40
1 in 50	19	18	18	18	17	17	16	16	15	14	14	13	12	17	17	17	16	15	15	14	13	13	12	11	11	10	1 in 50
1 in 60	22	21	21	20	19	19	18	18	16	16	15	14	13	20	20	19	18	18	17	16	15	14	13	12	12	11	1 in 60
1 in 70	25	24	24	23	22	21	20	19	18	17	16	15	14	22	22	21	20	19	18	17	16	15	14	13	12	11	1 in 70
1 in 80	28	27	26	25	24	23	22	21	20	18	17	16	15	24	24	23	22	21	20	19	17	16	15	14	13	12	1 in 80
1 in 90	30	29	29	27	25	24	22	21	20	18	17	16	15	26	26	25	24	22	21	20	18	17	16	15	14	13	1 in 90
1 in 100	32	31	30	29	28	27	25	24	22	21	20	18	17	28	28	26	25	24	22	21	19	18	16	15	14	13	1 in 100
1 in 120	37	36	34	33	31	29	28	26	24	22	20	19	18	33	32	30	28	26	24	22	20	18	17	16	15		1 in 120
1 in 130	38	37	36	34	33	31	29	27	25	23	22	20	18	33	32	30	29	27	25	23	21	20	18	16	15	14	1 in 130
1 in 140	40	38	37	36	34	32	30	28	26	24	22	20	19	34	33	32	30	28	26	24	22	20	18	17	15	14	1 in 140
1 in 150	42	40	38	37	36	33	31	29	26	24	21	20	18	36	34	32	31	29	27	25	22	20	18	17	16	14	1 in 150
1 in 160	43	42	40	38	37	34	32	29	27	25	23	21	20	37	35	34	32	29	28	25	23	21	19	17	16	14	1 in 160
1 in 180	45	44	42	40	38	37	33	30	28	26	24	22	20	38	37	36	33	30	28	26	23	21	20	18	16	15	1 in 180
1 in 200	50	48	45	43	40	38	34	32	29	27	25	23	21	42	40	37	34	32	29	27	24	22	20	18	17	16	1 in 200
1 in 250	55	53	50	48	45	42	38	34	31	29	25	23	21	45	43	40	37	33	30	27	24	22	20	19	17	16	1 in 250
1 in 300	63	59	56	53	48	43	40	37	33	30	28	25	23	50	48	43	40	37	33	30	27	24	22	20	18	16	1 in 300
1 in 400	71	67	62	59	53	48	42	40	36	32	29	26	24	56	53	48	43	40	36	32	29	26	23	20	18	17	1 in 400
1 in 600	83	77	71	67	59	53	48	42	38	34	31	29	26	58	56	53	48	43	38	33	30	26	24	21	19	17	1 in 600
1 in 1000	91	87	83	71	67	59	53	45	40	36	33	29	26	67	62	56	50	45	40	36	31	28	24	22	20	18	1 in 1000
Level	116	108	97	80	76	67	58	50	44	39	34	30	27	77	71	64	57	50	44	38	33	29	26	23	20	18	Level

Note.—To find the Total Load that can be drawn due to any other given Tractive Force, multiply the Load in the Table due to the given Speed and Gradient, by the given Tractive Force, in pounds, and divide by 1000.

PART SIXTH.—PERFORMANCES OF LOCOMOTIVES.

Our business is now to illustrate the performance and duty of existing locomotives, at their regular duty, and under ordinary circumstances. Care has been exercised, in the selection of examples, to produce such only as are genuine and have been well authenticated, ignoring the random statements of sanguine projectors and interested partizans.

The performance of some early engines on the 4 feet 8½ inch gauge, observed during the year 1829–38, have already been tabulated at pages 7 and 11 of this work.

Performances of some of the early passenger-engines of the Great Western Railway, 7 feet guage, in 1842, are given in Table No. 100; and, with the others which follow, are abstracted from some very elaborate tables of the performance of engines on that line, placed at the author's service by Mr. Daniel Gooch.

TABLE NO. C. — OF PERFORMANCES OF THE EARLY LOCOMOTIVES OF THE GREAT WESTERN RAILWAY. JANUARY TO MAY, 1842. BETWEEN PADDINGTON AND SWINDON, 77 MILES.

Name of Engine	Boiler-Surfaces.		Weights.		Speed.		Consumption of Coke.		Consumption of Water.					Remarks.
	Area of Grate.	Total Heating Surface, measured on the outside.	Weight of Engine and Tender.	Weight of Train.	Excluding Stops.	Including Stops.	Used while in Motion.	Total average per mile run.	While in Motion.	While at Rest.	Temperature in Tender.	Per lb. of Coke.	Per hour in Motion.	
	square feet.	square feet.	tons.	tons.	miles per hour.	miles per hour.	lbs. per mile.	lbs. per mile.	cubic ft.	cubic ft.	Fahr.	lbs.	cubic ft.	
Mentor....... } Cyclops....... }	13·6	699	31	65	30·5	27·5	31	38	262	20	100°	7·25	109	Average of 27 trips. Slight wind.
Giraffe...........	12·5	608	32·5	75	31·2	26·2	31·5	37	280	16·6	92°	7·2	111	Average of 10 trips. Weather various.
Hesperus........	12·4	804	32	54	31	28	26	30	287	21·4	62°	10·3	124	Average of 4 trips. Strong wind.
Royal Star.....	11·7	822	35	89	29	25·6	37·5	42	343	19	65°	7·4	127	Average of 10 trips. Strong wind.
Etna .... } Capricornus.. }	11·4	467	31	146	22·4	13	52	56	703	...	55°	6·9	122	Average of 4 trips. Calm.

NOTE.—1. The boiler-tubes were 2 inches diameter outside. The Hesperus had Hawthorn's return-tubes.
2. The cylinders had 14 to 15½ inches diameter, and 18 inches stroke. Driving-wheels 6 to 7 feet diameter.

The next table, No. 101, contains the results of performances of more recently built passenger-engines of the Great Western Railway, in 1847; showing that much higher speeds were attained by the later engines, with much greater total loads, for about the same consumption of coke per mile.

TABLE NO. CI.—OF RESULTS OF PERFORMANCES OF EIGHT-WHEELED PASSENGER-ENGINES ON THE GREAT WESTERN RAILWAY, IN AUGUST AND SEPTEMBER, 1847, WITH EXPRESS TRAINS BETWEEN PADDINGTON AND SWINDON.

Name of Engine	Consumption of Water and Coke.					Speed and Weight.			Remarks.
	Water per mile in Motion.	Water per hour in Motion.	Temperature of Water in Tender.	Total Water per lb. of Coke.	Average Coke per Mile.	Time in Motion.	Average Speed.	Average Weight of Engine, Tender, and Train.	
	cubic ft.	cubic ft.	Fahr.	lbs.	lbs.	minutes.	miles per hour.	tons.	
Great Britain..	4·2	200	100°	8·4	34·3	192	48·2	107	Dry down and up. Detained 22½ minutes.
	4·5	233	109°	8·3	36·9	184	50·0	105	Wet down and up. Strong S.W. wind.
	4·5	244	109°	8·4	36·1	170	54·5	103	Dry. West wind down and up.
	4·8	232	114°	8·5	34·5	180	51·2	105	Fine down and up. Strong side-wind.
	3·7	196	103°	8·4	30·8	180	51·3	100·4	Fine and dry.
	3·5	181	116°	7·4	33·8	186	49·6	101·4	Fine and dry.
Iron Duke......	4·9	261	94°	8	37·9	167	55·3	101·6	Rain. Strong N.E. wind.
	4·7	170	126°	9·4	32·6	252	40·3	100	Dry. Time up, 3 hours 45 minutes.
	4·7	266	121°	8·4	37·8	166	55·6	106	Wet down. Fine up.
	4·5	264	117°	8·4	37·4	164	56	99	Dry and fine.
	4·2	242	95°	8	35·3	163	56·7	100·5	Dry and fine.
	4·7	288	96°	8·2	39	165	56	120	Dry and fine.
Great Western	3·7	187	146°	7	36	174	53·1	105	Dry and fine.
	3·6	190	155°	7·6	32·2	180	56·3	105	Dry down and up. Stormy west wind.
	3·8	209	152°	6·9	37	174	53·1	104	Dry and fine. West wind.
	4·4	244	132°	7·5	39·7	170	54·5	105	Dry. Strong west wind.
	4·2	227	140°	7·8	35	173	53·5	104·5	Wet. Strong west wind.
	3·9	217	143°	7·5	37·3	171	54	107	Dry all day.
TOTAL AVERAGES.									
Great Britain..	4·2	215	109°	8·23	34·4	180	51	103·5	
Iron Duke......	4·6	245	91°	8·4	36·6	166	53·4	105	
Great Western	4·0	212	144°	7·4	36·2	170	53	106	

NOTE 1. The distance travelled each day, from Paddington to Swindon and back, was 154 miles.
2. The weight of Engine and Tender was 50 tons.

TABLE NO. CII.—OF RESULTS OF PERFORMANCES OF EIGHT-WHEELED PASSENGER-ENGINES, ON THE GREAT WESTERN RAILWAY, IN MARCH AND APRIL, 1849, WITH EXPRESS TRAINS, BETWEEN PADDINGTON AND BRISTOL.

Description of Coke.	Name of Engine.	Consumption of Water and Coke.			Speed and Weight.			Estimate of Tractive Force.			Tractive Force at the Rails.		Weather.
		Water per hour.	Water per pound of Coke.	Coke per mile.	Time in Motion.	Average Speed.	Average Weight of Engine, Tender, and Train.	Average Forced of Admission.	Average Initial Pressure of Steam, in the cylinders.	Effective mean Pressure in the cylinders.	Total.	Per Ton of Engine, Tender, and Train, including friction of Engine.	
		cubic ft.	lbs.	lbs.	minutes.	miles per hour.	tons.	inches of stroke.	lbs. per sq. inch.	lbs. per sq. inch	lbs.	lbs.	
No. 1	Wizard	219·4	7·04	38·51	283·5	50·19	106·7	14·1	49·16	39·33	3185·7	29·3	Dry, with N. wind
"	Dragon	190·5	7·37	31·1	276	51·5	104·2	12·5	42·89	34·32	2778·3	26·6	Dry. Wind from N.W. down. S.E. up.
"	Hirondelle	202·0	6·8	35·4	276	51·5	101·0	10·6	54·50	43·0	3531·6	34·9	Strong side-wind, with rain.
No. 1, 58 Best, 21	Tartar	189·9	6·28	37·3	283·5	50·19	100·7	13·12	42·55	34·04	2757·2	27·3	Dry. Wind. S.W. down; E., up. Stopped at Twyford on down trip to leave a carriage with broken wheel, and at Reading to take a carriage on.
No. 1	Lightning	214·5	7·65	34·58	283	50·28	101·0	13·6	49·11	39·29	3183·3	31·5	Dry down. Wet up. Light W. wind.
"	Rougemont	168·4	7·55	31·07	319	44·54	101·0	11·95	46·79	37·44	3032·0	30·0	Strong wind from S E. Wet part of trip
No. 1, 55 2, 25¼	Emperor	232·7	7·36	38·16	277	51·33	104·2	13·08	55·24	44·20	3580·2	34·3	Wet, with strong side-wind.
No. 2	Pasha	247·2	8·1	37·7	286·5	49·6	101·0						Dry. Strong side-wind from S. Detained at Wallingford, tracks off line
"	Courier	209·4	7·55	34·26	283·5	50·19	106·0	12·62	51·25	41·0	3321·0	31·3	Dry down. Strong S. and E. wind. Wet part of up trip.
"	Wizard	213·2	7·2	34·4	267·5	53·1	101·0	12·2	50·18	40·15	3248·1	32·1	Dry, with strong side-wind.
"	Warlock	212·8	8·04	32·1	278·5	51·0	101·0	12·2	52·63	42·1	3410·1	33·7	Dry, with strong side-wind.
"	Dragon	187·8	7·8	29·4	282·5	50·3	101·0	11·66	46·56	37·25	3013·2	29·8	Wet, rain and hail greater part of trip S. wind.
No. 3	Emperor	226·6	7·28	39·0	288	49·37	109·2	12·08	60·93	48·75	3946·3	36·1	Wet, from Farringdon Road to Bristol and back to Swindon. Side-wind.
"	Sultan	219·0	7·8	34·4	283·5	50·1	104·2	12·9	53·36	42·7	3458·7	33·1	Dry, with heavy side-wind.
"	Lightning	234·7	7·68	36·1	271·5	52·3	104·7	13·4	53·29	42·6	3261·0	31·1	Fine. Strong N.E wind
"	Pasha	221·8	6·9	38·7	279	50·9	106·0						N E. and S.W. winds. Fine weather.
"	Rougemont	208·8	7·2	34·3	273·5	51·9	101·0	10·9	54·05	44·0	3564·0	35·2	Wet; with snow. Strong side-wind down, from S.W.
"	Courier	210·1	6·64	38·16	276·5	51·4	104·2	11·91	51·83	41·67	3375·2	32·3	Wet, with snow, part of trip Wind S.W.

No. 1. Coke. Old oven coke under the shed—Burnt 48 hours.—Yield 12·71 cwts. per ton.
No. 2. " New round ovens " 72 " " 12·00 " "
No. 3. Cox's coke. Burnt in his large ovens " 48 " " 11·74 " "

NOTE 1.—The distance travelled each day, from Paddington to Bristol and back, was 237 miles.
2.—Average Weight of Engine and Tender, 50 tons.

Table No. 102 contains some performances, in 1849, of the latest class of passenger-engines on the Great Western Railway, the engines being selected indiscriminately from the two varieties represented by the Great Britain and the Courier. The difference of these varieties consists in the fire-box of the latter being a little longer, and the tubes a little shorter, than those of the former; which gave the following areas of surface respectively:—

	Great Britain variety.	Courier variety.
Area of grate	21 sq. ft.	23·62 sq. ft.
Fire-box surface (outside measure)	142 do.	149·75 do.
Tube-surface do. do.	1627 do.	1590 do.
Total heating-surface	1769 do.	1730·75 do.

The cylinders are, for both varieties, 18 inches by 24 inches, and the driving wheels 8 feet diameter. The engines pertaining to each variety are as follow:—

First variety:—Great Britain.	Second variety:—Courier.
" Iron Duke.	" Wizard.
" Emperor.	" Dragon.
" Pasha.	" Hirondelle.
" Sultan.	" Tartar.
" Lightning.	" Rougemont.
	" Warlock.
Number of Engines, 6	7

And their performances, with respects to evaporative power, and evaporative economy, may be averaged and classified as follow:—

Quality of Coke.	Consumption of Water.			
	First Variety.		Second Variety.	
	Total per hour.	Per pound of Coke.	Total per hour.	Per pound of Coke.
	cubic feet.	lbs.	cubic feet.	lbs.
No. 1 coke	223·6	7·5	194·2	7·01
No. 2 coke	247·2	8·1	205·8	7·65
No. 3 coke	225·5	7·41	209·45	6·92
Means	232·1	7·67	203·15	7·19

These abstracts contain a remarkable confirmation of the author's doctrine of a limited fire-grate, no larger than necessary for the proper combustion of the fuel, and extended heating-surface. The second variety, having a larger grate than the first variety, and sensibly the same heating-surface, is shown to be inferior to the first variety in the evaporative power of the fuel, successively with each of the three kinds of coke, and in the mean ratio of 7·19 lbs. of water per pound of coke to 7·67 lbs.; notwithstanding that, in the former case, the total evaporation per hour is more moderate than in the latter case, in the mean ratio of 203 cubic feet of water to 232 cubic feet.

Table, No. 103, shows the performance of the latest goods-engines of the Great Western Railway. The length of time standing at stations, is unfavourable for economy, and should always be noted in such experiments.

TABLE NO. CIII.—OF RESULTS OF PERFORMANCES OF SIX COUPLED WHEEL GOODS-ENGINES ON THE GREAT WESTERN RAILWAY, IN 1848, WORKED FROM PADDINGTON.

Name of Engine	Miles run	Average Number of Waggons exclusive of Train	Average Weight of Train, exclusive of Engine and Tender	Time In Motion	Time Stopped at Stations	Mean Speed	Coke consumed Per mile	Coke consumed Per ton of Train per mile	Water consumed per pound of Coke	Remarks
	Miles.	Waggons.	tons.	h. m.	h. m.	miles per hour	lbs.	lbs.	lbs.	
Pyracmon	154			6 34	12 26	23·4	51·4	·152	8·4	Dry up and down. Paddington Pilot to Didcot.
	83			3 26	6 31	24·1	36·4	·251	6·6	Showery down. Wind dry up.
	154			7 59	11 6	19·2	61·8	·180	7·7	Dry up. Showery down. Slippery, and strong side wind.
	154			6 41	9 32	23·04	49·09	·201	7·6	Dry up and down. Strong side wind down.
	157			6 13	17 31	25·2	47·7	·287	7·1	Dry up and down. Bank engine from Box to top of Tunnel.
	83			3 34	6 33	23·2	43·8	·221	7·4	Dry down and up. Bank engine from Box to top of Wotton-Basset Incline.
	785			34 27		23·01	49·0	·209	7·6	Assisted by Pilot and Bank Engine.
Mammoth	154		320	8 13	7 34	18·6	54·85	·168	8·4	Wet up. Dry down. Wind.
	154		300	8 14	4 42	18·7	57·3	·191	8·7	Fine and Dry. Piston blowing.
	169		210	7 3	4 19	23·8	54·2	·258	7·2	Piston blowing badly.
	154		460	7 59	6 21	10·8	75·6	·173	7·9	Fine and dry.
	169		150	8 3	3 36	20·8	45·7	·285	6·5	Boiler very dirty. Fine and dry.
	83		280	3 4	3 35	23·1	45·9	·156	8·1	Pilot Engine 3 miles up Bank.
	853		288	42 36		20·0	58·1	·201	7·7	Pilot 23 miles.
Caliban	154	31·4		7 30	4 53	20·5	59·07	·187	8·03	Wet and slippery up. Dry down.
	183	24·0		3 27	2 8	24·05	50·2	·209	7·5	Dry down and up.
	154	18·7		6 28	6 38	23·81	56·3	·301	7·8	Wet part of up. Dry down. Detained 1 hour 40 min.
	83	21·08		4 8	1 54	20·08	48·5	·230	7·5	Wet part of down trip. Dry up. Assisted 11 miles up.
	154	23·4		6 43	2 37	22·9	45·8	·195	7·5	Dry up and down. Strong wind up.
	83	22·8		4 5	1 32	20·3	40·4	·177	8·8	Dry down and up.
	154	27 2		6 18	2 40	24·4	49·2	·180	7·8	Dry up and down.
	86	24·5		3 59	2 36	21·8	54·6	·222	7·4	Wet part of up trip. Strong head wind. Dry down.
	154	25·9		6 23	2 4	24·1	56·7	·218	7·4	Dry up and down.
	86	12·9		3 47	2 6	22·7	50·1	·388	7·1	Dry down and up. Strong head wind up.
	83	13·9		3 19	2 34	25·02	39·1	·280	7·3	Dry down and up.
	154	29·0		6 27	1 53	23·8	51·2	·176	7·6	Dry down and up. Strong head wind up.
	1423	22·8		62 34		22·75	51·04	·224	7·6	

NOTE.—These Engines have a grate-area of 18½ square feet, a heating-surface of 1363 square feet, measured on the outside; cylinders 16 inches diameter, 24 inches stroke; and driving-wheels 5 feet.

The engines of the London and South-Western Railway, Snake class, have been experimented upon in various ways by Mr. J. V. Gooch, and subsequently by Mr. Beattie and others. The following are the results of trials of the Snake, with weighted trains, made by Mr. Gooch, in September 1848:—

Length of double trip, with trains, ...	156 miles.
Time of running, ...	3 hours 27 minutes.
Time of standing unattached to trains,	3 „ 25 „
Time of steam being up, ...	9 „ 15 „
Number of stoppages, ...	4
Time of ditto, ...	23 „
Average speed, including stoppages,	41·4 miles p. hour.
Do., excluding do., ...	51·25 do.
Consumption of coke per mile, ...	23·2 lbs.
Do. of water per pound of coke.	8·9 lbs.
Average number of carriages in train, ...	10½ carriages.
Average weight of train, ...	77½ tons.
Average period of admission in parts of stroke,	40 per cent.
Steam-pressure in boiler, ...	75 lbs. to 80 lbs.

Cylinder 14½ by 21 inches, wheel 6½ feet, grate-area 12·4 feet, heating-surface 898·5 feet.

Some of the engines on the same line, on the same general plan as the Snake, have lately been fitted with Mr. Beattie's double fire-box, one box, burning coal, being placed behind the other box, burning coke; so that the smoke of the coal is passed over the incandescent coke before entering the tubes, to insure its complete combustion. An apparatus, by Mr. Beattie, for heating the feed-water by the waste steam, is applied in the same engines. The results of the working of one of the engines, the Britannia, between London and Southampton, observed by Mr. Edward Woods and Mr. W. P. Marshall, in 1853-4,* are contained in Table No. 104.

TABLE NO. CIV — PERFORMANCE OF THE BRITANNIA, L. & S.W.R., WITH BEATTIE'S DOUBLE FIRE-BOX.

	1853 Oct. 26.	1854 Jan. 17.
Length of double trip, with train.......miles	157½	157½
Do. do. with engine ...... do.	161½	161½
Down trip, average train..............cars.	12·8	11·2
Do., average speed running...miles per hour	31·4	28·3
Do., number of stoppages......	8	8
Up trip, average train...............cars.	18·5	19·3
Do., average speed running.....miles per hour	29·4	27·5
Do., number of stoppages......	7	7
Total consumption of coke............cwts.	16	18
Do. coal............cwts.	8	8½
Do. per mile of train........lbs.	17·1	18·6
Do. do. engine........lbs.	16·7	18·2
Water evaporated per pound of fuel........lbs.	8·3	8·1
Average pressure of steam, down.........lbs.	...	105
Do. do. up........lbs.	...	100
Greatest pressure ....lbs.	...	128
Least do. (omitting last 10 miles).......lbs	...	82
Average do. in up trip over 17 miles, rising 1 in 250.	...	122

The cylinders are 15 by 21 inches, wheels 7 feet; area of grate, for coke 14½ feet, for coal 2½ feet; heating-surface, 930 feet.

* Proceedings of the Institution of Mechanical Engineers, January, 1854.

The averages for the week ending 26th October, 1853, were found, from the Engineman's Diary, to be:—Total miles run, 807½; average load, 14 carriages; consumption of fuel per mile, 16·3 lbs., one-fifth of which was coal. The author obtained the following results of one day's trip to Southampton and back, on the 9th January, 1854:—Average train, 11 carriages; fuel per mile, 16 lbs.; strong side-wind, coal of inferior quality. The economy of fuel apparent in the above results is due, probably, for the greater part, to the feed-water heating apparatus.

On the Eastern Counties Railway, No. 24 Tank Locomotive, illustrated in our plates, and designed by Mr. J. V. Gooch, performed as recorded in Table No. 105.

On the Manchester, Sheffield, and Lincolnshire Railway, some comparative trials of speed, with given trains, were made in 1848, by Mr. Peacock, with engines of different proportions, on the first 18¼ miles out of Manchester, which rises continuously, on an average gradient of 1 in 136 for that distance.

TABLE NO. CV.—PERFORMANCE OF J. V. GOOCH'S TANK LOCOMOTIVE, E. C. R., 1853.

	June 22.	June 24.	July 26.	July 28.
Miles run, London to Norwich and back ... miles	259	259	259	259
Weight of train, excluding engine, tons	45·6	45·6	68	68
Number of stoppages ...	7	9	8	6
Time of do. ... minutes	45	63	61	44
Mean speed, including stoppages ... miles per hour	37	37·5	39	38·6
Do., excluding do., do. ...	41·4	44·2	46	43·3
Coke consumed per mile ... lbs.	15·1	15·5	15·5	15·1
Water consumed per lb. of coke ... lbs.	8·3	9·7*	8·5	8·5
Average steam-pressure in boiler ... lbs. per inch	83	84	105	100

* Excess of water due to leakages.

TABLE NO. CVI.—RESULTS OF COMPARATIVE TRIALS OF LOCOMOTIVES ON THE MANCHESTER, SHEFFIELD, AND LINCOLNSHIRE RAILWAY, BY RICHARD PEACOCK, 1848.

Date of trial ... Name of engine ... Name of maker ...	May 21. Ixion. Sharp.	May 21. Jenny Sharp. Sharp.	July 2. Jenny Lind. Wilson.	July 2. Jenny Sharp. Sharp.	July 2. Lablache. Wilson.
Diameter and stroke of cylinders ... inches	15 × 20	16 × 20	15 × 20	16 × 20	16 21
Diameter of driving wheels ... feet	5	5½	6	5½	7
Length of grate ... feet, inches	3 0	3 2	3 6	3 2	5 2
Breadth of do. ... do. do.	3 6⅛	3 7¼	3 6	3 7½	3 6
Number of tubes ...	178	161	124	161	166
Length of do. ... feet	10¾	10	11	10	13
Outside diameter of do. ... inches	1⅝	2	2	2	2
Inside diameter of ferules at fire-box ... do.	1	$1\frac{7}{16}$	1⅝	$1\frac{7}{16}$	1½
Area of grate ... square feet	10·5	11·4	12·25	11·4	18
Heating-surface of fire-box ... do.	55·3	89	81	89	101
Do. of tubes ... do.	776	843	708	843	1122
Do. total ... do.	831	952	789	932	1223
Sectional area of flue-way in tubes ... square inches	142	262	311	262	430
Weight of train ... tons	50	50	70	70	70
Mean pressure in the boiler ... lbs.	67	73	78	79	97
Average speed ... miles per hour	35	41	34	39	34

The results, in Table No. 106, are remarkable, and a comparison will show the benefit of a liberal sectional area of flue-way, and the fallacy of very large boilers, and large wheels, as opposed to moderate dimensions and compact proportions.

On the London and North-Western Railway, a series of experiments was made in 1853, by Messrs. Edward Woods and William P. Marshall, on the performances of locomotives between London and Birmingham.* The Southern Division engines selected, were No. 291, as the type of the most approved class of engines then running, and No. 300, a new engine on M'Connell's patent. The Northern Division engines selected, were the Heron, Prince of Wales, and Rocket. The two former are of the general class of engines used on the Northern Division; the latter is one of a new class. The leading particulars of the engines are given in Table No. 107.

The novelty of No. 300 consists in the boiler, which was designed to promote evaporative economy:—First, by extending the fire-box into the barrel of the boiler, and setting the tubes thus far forward, to form a combustion-chamber, in which the carbonic oxide, if any, arising from the fuel, may be consumed, by mixture with jets of air introduced from below. Second, by the use of a superheating vessel in the smoke-box, through which the steam and priming water pass on the way to the cylinders.

* For the particulars of these experiments, the author is indebted to the Report of the experimentalists to the General Locomotive Committee, dated April 5, 1853.

TABLE NO. CVII.—PARTICULARS OF ENGINES, ON THE LONDON AND NORTH-WESTERN RAILWAY, TRIED BY MESSRS WOODS AND MARSHALL, IN 1853.

Name of Engine ...	Rocket	Heron.	Prince of Wales	No. 291.	No. 300.
Cylinders, diameter ... inches	16	15·08	16	16	18
Do., stroke ... inches	20	20	20	22	24
Driving Wheels diameter ... feet	7	6	6	7	7½
Heating-Surface, Fire-box ... square feet	56	51	51	165	260
Do., Tubes,* .. do.	658	658	658	1166	903
Do., Total ... do	718	709	709	1331	1163
Grate, length ... feet, inches	3 0	3 0	3 0	5 1½	5 8½
Do., breadth ... do.	3 6	3 6	3 6	3 8½	3 10½
Do., area ... square feet	10·5	10·5	10·5	19	22
Air-passage through Grate ... do.	5·5	5·5	5·5	6·25	8·6 Ex. No 9, 12·3
Weights in working order, Engine .. tons	20	18	18	30	31
Do. do., Tender .. do	10	10	10	16	17

* Internal Tube-surface taken.

The trains represented were as follows:—

	Number of Carriages.	Train Weight.	Running Speed.	Number of Stoppages.
		tons.	miles p. hour.	
1st. Express ...	9	46	42	3
2d. Day Mail ...	13	66	38	5
3d. Night Mail ...	17	86	34	7
4th. Stopping Train ...	21	106	31	9
5th. Heavy Stopping Train	25	126	28	11

TABLE No. ...

AND BITUMINOUS, ...

	PASSENGER ENGINES.												GOODS ENGINES.		

Number of Experiment, Date of Experiment.	1 Feb. 24.	2 Feb. 25.	3 Feb. 26.	4 Feb. 28.	5 March 1.	6 March 4.	7 March 5.	8 March 7.	9 March 8.	10 March 18.	11 March 19.
Name or Number of Engine,	N. 291 Rocket.	N. 291 Rocket.	N. 291 Heron.	N. 291 Heron.	N. 291 Heron.	N. 300 Heron.	N. 300 Heron.	N. 300 N. 291	N. 291 N. 300	N. 227	N. 2
Division, South or North, Mr. Marshall or Mr Woods,	N. M. S. W.	N. M. S. W.	N. M. S. W.	N. M. S. W.	N. M. S. W.	N. M. S. W.	N. M. S. W.	N. M. S. W.	N. M. S. W.	S. Holt. Hector and Powis	S. Edit Hector and Powis
Distance run, miles,										Rugby to London	Rugby to London
Number of Stoppages,											
Wind,	Calm.	Strong side-wind.	Strong side-wind.	Strong side-wind.	Mode-rate side-wind.	Strong head-wind.	Mode-rate wind behind.	Calm.	Calm.	Side-wind.	Little side-wind.
Weather,	Fair. Frosty.	Fair.	Fair.	Fair.	Scarce shower.	Fair.	Mist.	Rain.	Fair.	Scarce shower.	Fair. Frosty.

The total coke used throughout the day, in lighting the fire, raising steam, and working the engine, is included in the tabulated consumption, allowance being made for coke remaining unconsumed in the fire-box at the end of each day's work. The coke was the best Pease's West. The results of the experiments are given in Table No. 108.

From the light trains of nine carriages to the heavy trains of twenty-five carriages, the consumption of coke, in round numbers, ranges from 20 lbs. to 30 lbs. per mile, the speeds ranging from 42 to 29 miles per hour. The corrected weights of trains due to the difference of tenders, is estimated by adding to the trains of the Southern Division engines, the excess weight of tender above 10 tons, so as to match with the performance of the Northern Division engines.

The consumption of coke per square foot of grate was as follows:—

No. 300, mean of three trips.....................47 lbs. per foot per hour.
No. 291, mean of six trips.....................52 lbs.   do.
Heron, mean of five trips.....................84 lbs.   do.
No. 300, with contracted blast-pipe, and } 67 lbs.   do.
enlarged air-spaces in grate.................

In economy of evaporation, the engines rank as follows:—

No. 300. .... 8·13 lbs. water per pound of coke.
Heron.............................. 7·69 lbs.   do.
Rocket. .... 7·31 lbs.   do.
No. 291............................ 6·81 lbs.   do.
No. 300, with altered blast-pipe } 7·99 lbs.   do.
and fire-bars......................

With the same train as No. 300 had in the last case, the Heron and Prince of Wales evaporated respectively 8·29 lbs. and 8·39 lbs. per pound of coke.

The weights on the driving wheels of the engines were:—

12 tons for the Southern Division.
9 tons for the Northern Division.

Practically, there was no slipping of the wheels during the experiments.

The results do not show that the patent boiler possessed any apparent advantages. Experiments lately made confirm our deductions from indirect experiment, detailed in another part of this work, that, in ordinary working, there is no disengagement of free carbonic oxide in the locomotive furnace; the driver of No. 300 seems to have held the same opinion, as he worked with the air-holes closed. The great extension of fire-box surface, also, arrived at in the patent boiler, by the aid of large dimensions and numerous modifications, is founded in what we have proved in another place to be a fallacy, namely, that there is some peculiar advantage in fire-box surface over tube surface.[*]

The results of subsequent experiments made by Messrs. Woods and Marshall, with Nos. 291 and 300, on the comparative mechanical values of coke and coal in the evaporation of water, confirm the results of the author's experiments on the same subject, already announced:—that, with equal weights of coke and coal, the coke is capable of evaporating 50 per cent. more water than the coal, their mechanical values being in the ratio of 2 to 3.

It is usual to express the work of an engine in terms of the fuel consumed per mile per ton of the gross weight of the train. Several examples of this form of expression occur in the tables of performance, and viewed commercially it is no doubt the correct form; but, mechanically, the duty should be represented in terms of the fuel per mile per ton of the gross total weight of engine, tender, and train. The former varies much with the weight of the train, being less as the train is greater; the latter varies also, but in a less degree than the other, and ranges from $\frac{1}{4}$ lb. to $\frac{1}{2}$ lb. per mile per ton gross, with ordinary passenger trains. With heavy trains, passenger or goods, the consumption falls as low as $\frac{1}{4}$ lb. to $\frac{1}{10}$ lb. per mile per ton gross total. The greater economy with the heavier loads is due to the higher steam-pressure required in the cylinders, and the relatively smaller loss by atmospheric resistance, which takes place under the ordinary circumstances of engines. But it ought not so to be, for the lighter the load, the more expansively and the more economically should the steam be worked, the initial pressure of the steam in the cylinders remaining the same. There is much scope for improvement in the locomotive, if not anatomically, at least physiologically; and there is much to be anticipated from the honourable rivalry of the regular steam-engineers who desire to retain the essential features of the steam-engine proper; and those who, with Siemens and with Rankine in the van, devote their efforts to "regenerative" means of exhausting the force of steam and of air under elevated temperatures.

---

[*] Locomotive-boilers have already been treated at considerable length by the author in this work, and also in a paper on "Locomotive-Boilers," read by him at the Institution of Civil Engineers, March 8. 1853.

DIVISION II.—FIXED OR STATIONARY PLANT.

PART FIRST.—APPARATUS FOR SHIFTING AND TURNING ROLLING STOCK AND GOODS.

SECTION I.—SWITCHES AND CROSSINGS.

SWITCHES and crossings are usually constructed from the rails in common use on the railway for which they are made. They are carried in cast-iron chairs spiked down to sleepers. The switches consist of moveable rails, and are worked by rods connected to handles to which heavy weights are attached, the function of the weights being to retain the points in one position, and to act as a self-acting adjustment in restoring them to it, after they are shifted for the passage of a train.

Crossings, also, are usually made from the rails used in the permanent way, and suitably put together, seated in chairs, and put down permanently as fixtures.

Switches are made either double or single,—with one moveable rail, or two moveable rails. The latter plan is generally used for main-line sidings, as it throws the rails less out of gauge than the former, and disturbs to a less extent the continuity of the bearing surface of the rails.

CHAPTER I.

GENERAL DESCRIPTION OF SWITCHES AND CROSSINGS.

THE best detailed system of switches and crossings, made from ordinary rails, is, in our mind, that employed by Mr. James Bell, resident engineer of the North British Railway, shown in Plate 48. His switches and crossings are the result of long and intelligent experience.

Double Switches.—Bell's double switch consists of two sliding tongues or points, two stock or main rails, and one guard-rail for the long tongue, carried in chairs suitably formed. The points are worked by rods and weighted levers, inclosed in a cast-iron box; which, with the chairs, are shown in full detail. The points are tapered towards their extremities, and move horizontally and radially upon their butts or " heels." The chairs are lettered for distinction. The switches are pinned into heel chairs K, L; and slide in others chairs A, made with sliding surfaces, and having the jaws sufficiently apart to allow the required travel of the switch, while they act as checks to define the travel, and to support the points. The weight commands

both points through the medium of the switch-rod; and, acting constantly in one direction, it maintains the points open to the main line, as shown in the plan. The position of the points when shifted and opened to the siding, is shown by dot-lining; the long tongue is supported by the main rail, and its duty is to turn out the train upon the siding. The guard-rail guides the train, by engaging the left hand wheels and holding them up to the siding rail, and so carrying the right hand wheel-flanges clear of the tip of the long tongue. The guard-rail also protects the check in the main rail from wheel-flanges, which might otherwise foul the return or shoulder of the check, in front of the long tongue. Similarly, the long tongue protects the short tongue, when open to the siding. A train entering the main line from the siding, will of itself open the points to the siding, by wedging them open, and when it has passed, the points are returned by the weight to their permanent position, upon the main line.

Single Switches.—Single switches, as arranged by Mr. Bell, Plate 48, consist of a tongue, a fixed point, two fixed main and siding rails, and a guard-rail. The switch is commanded by a weight, and held open to the main line. The guard-rail protects the tongue; and it is carried up alongside the fixed point, and keeps the wheels on the rails while passing the gap fronting the point. When a train is to enter the siding, the switch is hauled up to the main rail, and the wheels on entering, are first caught by the guard-rail, and conducted clear of the tongue. As the wheels advance, the guard ceases to act on them laterally, they get into contact with the closed tongue, and are pressed well up to the siding rail till they clear the fixed point. Again, when the switch is open to the main line, a train advancing against the points, will pass clear of the tongue; and, further on, the tongue will take the flanges of the near wheels and hold them up to the main rail, and thus enable the off-wheels to clear the fixed point. Thus, it appears, the switch guards the fixed point, both for the main line and for the siding.

Crossings.—The crossing, Plate 48, consists of the point, formed by the junction of the siding and the main-line rails; two wing rails, main line and siding; and the guard-rails. The guard-rails confine and guide the wheels when running against the point, that the flanges may clear; whilst the wing-rails hold the wheels well up, and secure to them all the available bearing while passing the gap in front of the point.

CHAPTER II.

PHYSIOLOGY AND ANATOMY OF SWITCHES AND CROSSINGS.

Preliminary.—The gauging of the points, and the travel necessary to be given them, are regulated by the thickness of the wheel-flanges, and the gauge of the wheels. Allowance is also to be made for lateral wear of the flanges, which increases the play of the wheels. The thickness of flanges, when new, varies from $1\frac{1}{8}$ inch to $1\frac{1}{4}$ inch; and the gauge of the wheels, or distance between the backs of the tyres, is from 4 feet $5\frac{1}{4}$ inches to 4 feet 6 inches. Thus, the lateral play of the wheels, when new, varies from $\frac{1}{4}$ inch to $\frac{1}{2}$ inch, on a railway of 4 feet $8\frac{1}{2}$ inches gauge. Locomotive wheels are not usually allowed to wear to less than $\frac{3}{4}$ inch thick in the flange; nor carriages and waggons to less than $\frac{1}{2}$ inch thick. A pair of wheels gauged to 4 feet $5\frac{1}{4}$ inches, with $\frac{3}{4}$ inch thick flanges, measures 4 feet $6\frac{3}{4}$ inches including flanges; it has 2 inches play between the rails, and either wheel may overhang the rail $2\frac{1}{4}$ inches, on the inside, measured from the inside of the rail to the back of the flange. Allowing $\frac{1}{4}$ inch more for occasional deviation of gauge, the extreme overhang of a wheel may be 3 inches; and the throw of the switch should be sufficient to clear the wheel in such a case, that there may be no risk of the wheels tripping on the points.

The setting of the guard-rails, also, depends on the gauge of the wheels. When they occur in pairs, as at crossings, they should not be set wider apart than the gauge of the wheels, that they may not be wedged between the backs of the tyres, and that they may not strike the wheels with greater force than is necessary in the business of guiding them through the points. If the guard-rails be gauged to 4 feet $5\frac{1}{4}$ inches between the outer sides, they stand 3 inches short of the inside gauge of the ordinary rails; and this leaves $1\frac{1}{2}$ inch on each side, as clearance between the main and guard-rails, which is sufficient to pass any wheel-flange.

It is, then, the general practice to place guard-rails, double or single, $1\frac{1}{2}$ inches clear of the main rails; and Mr. Bell gives the long tongues about 4 inches throw at the tip, leaving a passage, $3\frac{1}{2}$ or $3\frac{3}{4}$ inches wide, clear of the main rail.

To obtain an easy entrance, the tongues and the fixed rails should be fitted to each other, that the inner edges of the tongues, when closed, may run evenly into those of the rails.

The tongues are made unequal in length, in order that one of them, the longer tongue, with the check in the main rail, may be protected by the guard next the siding-rail.

Bell's Double Switches.—The tongues are made out of rails respectively 12 and 10 feet long, of which the longer tongue is laid in the outer rail of the siding, forming part of the siding, whilst the short tongue forms part of the main line; accordingly, the 'main rail' keeps its due course, and the 'main and siding rail' is set out just in front of the short tongue.

The tongues are tapered on the upper side for part of their lengths, as shown, and finish $\frac{1}{4}$ inch thick at the tips. The fixed or stock-rails are notched to receive the tongues, $\frac{1}{4}$ inch deep, and the outer sides of the tongues are bevelled off on the upper edge to $\frac{1}{8}$ inch thick so as to sweep flush with the rails. They are also rounded on the outer edges. The taper of the tongue-rails being executed on both sides, towards the web, the angle formed by the taper is extinguished on the inner or working edge, and the entrance improved, by setting the rail laterally, to bring the whole length of the edge into a straight line. The under tables of the tongue-rails are planed off on the sides adjoining the stock-rails, like the upper tables; but the outer sides are left whole, to retain so much of the stiffness of the rails, and of their lower bearing surface. The upper surface of the tongues is steeled, owing to the narrowness of bearing, for a length of 12 or 15 inches from the tips, and $\frac{1}{4}$ to $\frac{1}{2}$ inch deep.

The guard-rail consists of a half-length rail, 8 feet long. The overhang of the rail beyond the chair at each end, should be considerable, to admit of some elasticity and ease of action, and for the same reason the splay should be moderate, just sufficient to clear approaching wheel-flanges. Mr. Bell splays to 3 inches clear of the stock-rail, and he overhangs 21 inches next the tongue, which is as much as he can command.

The stock-rails are of the ordinary full-length rails in use on the line, in our example, 16 feet; and, as the joints of the stock-rails and tongues, in the heel-chairs, are all in a straight line transversely, it is clear that a set of double switches may be conveniently laid down at any part of the line by lifting up a couple of the permanent rails.

The gauge of the switches, when open to the main line, is sensibly correct all the way; when open to the siding, it is reduced $\frac{3}{4}$ inch, to 4 feet $7\frac{3}{4}$ inches, just in front of the short tongue, owing to the divergence of the long tongue, from the working edge of which the gauge is measured. This tightness of gauge is useful in driving the wheels over to the siding rail, and thus guarding the short tongue; and the tightness regularly diminishes beyond the tip of the tongue, and vanishes at the heel-chairs, where the correct gauge is resumed.

The switches are worked by rods, set with adjusting screws, to gauge the tongues; a weight of 100 lbs. is attached to the fulcrum of the switch-handle, and, by a leverage of $5\frac{1}{2}$ to 4, acts with a horizontal force of about 140 lbs. on the tongues. It is found that a weight thus powerful is necessary to control the points under the exigencies of their situation, and to insure their self-action in all ordinary cases. In this respect, the short switches of 10 and 12 feet, employed by Mr. Bell, have the advantage of the long ones of 16 feet, previously in vogue. The switch-rod No. 2, is used for passing under lines of rail intervening between the switch-box and the switches.

Single Switches.—The tongue-rail is 12 feet long, and is laid down on the outside of the curve of the siding. It is tapered like the tongues of the double switches, and finishes $\frac{3}{4}$ inch thick; and is placed in chairs like the others. It has a throw of 4 inches at the tip. The fixed tongue-rail is 16 feet long, and is tapered to $\frac{3}{4}$ inch thick, the taper being suited to the angle of the siding rail. The siding-rail is 16 feet long, and is set to a uniform curve, diverging regularly till it runs out parallel to the outer side of the fixed tongue-rail, with a clearance of 1½ inches. The guard-rail is 16 feet long, straight, and parallel to the main rail and to the inner side of the tongue-rail, with a clearance of 1½ inches, and the ends overhanging with the usual splay.

The use of the guard-rail is to defend the tongue when open to the main line, and also to keep the wheels well over upon the siding-rail, so as to insure to them all the available breadth of bearing in passing along the gap which extends in front of the fixed tongue for the whole length of the sliding tongue. The sliding tongue is, at the same time, useful, when open to the main line, in checking the excessive lateral movement of the wheels over to the siding rail, and thus also guards the fixed point. When the switch is open to the siding, the gauge of the siding is reduced by the sliding tongue, to 4 feet 7¾ inches in front of the fixed point, and thus again the sliding tongue guards the fixed tongue for entering trains.

This is a simple switch, and is preferable to the double switch for sidings clear of the main line. The greatly reduced bearing surface on the siding rail, when open to the main line, is the chief objection to the single switch.

Both tongues should be steeled on their upper surfaces. The siding-rail should also be steeled in the neighbourhood of the end of the fixed point; for a width of 1¼ inch. If not steeled, these surfaces wear down very quickly.

Crossing.—An ordinary crossing is made to an angle of 1 in 10, and is formed of two 16 feet rails, set together and bolted as shown. The wing-rails are of different lengths, 16 and 14 feet long, to break joint; and the guard-rails are half-lengths, 8 feet long.

The end of the crossing-point is steeled; also the upper surfaces of the wing-rails, from the neighbourhood of the point to the elbows, that they may be strengthened where there is a deficiency of bearing surface.

CHAPTER III.

WILD AND PARSONS' SWITCHES AND CROSSINGS.

Ordinary Double Switch.—Wild's switches, Plate 49, are extensively used. Their chief peculiarity consists in such a formation of the ends of the tongues, as to leave the stock-rails entire and uncut. The tongue is so tapered that the end of it is housed beneath the upper table of the fixed rail,

when closed; towards the heel, the switch is gradually developed, passing from under the rail, and acquiring a surface of its own to carry the wheels, as illustrated by contour sections in the Plate. By so forming the tongue, a wheel, moving into the siding, passes a considerable distance beyond the commencement of the tongue, before it bears vertically on it, and it does so only after the tongue acquires sufficient stiffness to carry a load, whilst it is instrumental from the extremity onwards in shifting the course of the wheel by lateral action on the flange.

In his ordinary double switch, Wild makes the tongues 15 and 10 feet long. The difference of length, 5 feet, gives rise to an increase of gauge of the main line to nearly 4 feet 10 inches at the tip of the short tongue, due to the divergence of the siding rail. The extra gauge is excessive, and is required in order that the short tongue may be out of reach of wheel-flanges, when the switch is open to the main line; the short tongue is guarded by the long tongue, and the shorter it is, the better is it guarded.

Three-Throw Switch.—In Plate 49, Wild's plan of three-throw switch, or double turn-out, working into two sidings off the main line, is arranged in the usual manner.

Wild and Parsons' Switch is formed with shallow stock and tongue rails having wide bases; the stock-rails are rivetted to wrought-iron plates for their whole length; and the same plates carry slides to support the tongues. The tongues, being shallow, and broad at the base, slide with steadiness, and are very stiff laterally. This is an expensive form of switch; and, more lately, the designers have substituted ordinary sleepers, stock-rails, and chairs, retaining the principle of the shallow tongue, for which dwarf rails are employed.

Wild and Parsons' Crossing is formed of dwarf rails, combined and rivetted together, on a cast-iron sole. But this crossing, which is costly, is now superseded by a simple arrangement in which the wearing parts—the end of the tongue and the elbows of the wings—are formed separately, and let in and bolted to the fixed rails, to be readily renewable when worn.

Mr. Baines, of Birmingham, has invented a switch, having the tongue-rails deeper than the stock-rails, but of a similar section, with upper and lower tables; so that the lower table of the tongue slides beneath that of the stock-rail, and clears away mud and other accumulations from between them. The sliding surface of the slide-chairs, is of an ogee form, so as to offer a precipice for the dirt to fall clear out of the way. This switch has given satisfaction.

SECTION II.—TURNTABLES AND TRAVERSERS.

TURNTABLES are of two classes:—for turning carriages and waggons, and for turning engines and tenders together. They differ chiefly in dimensions, and necessarily also in detail; the former are manipulated by the direct application of manual force, and the latter generally by the intervention of gearing.

CHAPTER I.

TURNTABLES FOR CARRIAGES AND WAGGONS.

TURNTABLES for the carrying stock are usually 12 to 14 feet in diameter, sufficiently large to receive conveniently vehicles of which the axle centres are 8 to 10 feet apart. Ordinary tables are composed of four distinct parts:—the floor, which carries the rails; the pivot and the system of rollers, which carry respectively the centre and the circumference of the floor; the sole, which receives the total load, and upon which the pivot and the rollers travel; and the curb, for inclosing the working parts, stiffening the structure, and affording fixed points for maintaining the floor in position. The best detailed table of this character, is, in our mind, that produced by Charles Heard Wild, and detailed in Plate 50. Mr. Wild thus describes the design of his turntable:—

Wild's Turntable.—" In designing this turntable an endeavour has been made to supply the following desiderata, partly by a revival of old arrangements, partly by the invention of new :—Strength; steadiness under a passing load; reduction of friction in turning; an avoidance, as far as possible, of dependence upon foundations.

" The first and second requirements are nearly allied, and, being obtained, insure durability. To secure them, the top plate has been made much stronger than is usual, and its bearing upon the friction-rollers is as near as possible to its periphery; so that, in some positions of the rollers, the points of support are further out than the ends of the rails upon which the passing wheel impinges, and are never within them.

" The rollers have bearings equal in length to their own diameter, and have massive axles capable of maintaining the necessary radial direction of the axes of the rollers. They are also inclined so that their upper bearing-surfaces are in a plane, to which form the bearing-surface of the top plate is also turned; the object of this peculiarity being to permit the inevitable lateral motion of the top plate, caused by the passage of trains, to take place without interfering with its equal bearing upon all the rollers; whereas, in ordinary turntables, where this bearing-surface is of a conical form, the slightest departure from concentricity causes the weight to be thrown upon three only of the rollers.

" The segments of the lower roller-path and the curbs are cast together, and are perfectly jointed throughout their depth prior to the path being faced, which by these means forming a part of so substantial a circular girder, is more certain to retain its true form than are the shallow, flimsy castings ordinarily employed for this purpose, which, possessing no strength in themselves, rely entirely for their truth on the smoothness and uniformity of their foundations.

" In tables of moderate diameter, for instance up to 13 feet, no weight is taken by the centre pin, the correctness of the work and the perfect radiality of the axes of the rollers sufficiently reducing the friction of turning; but in larger sizes, particularly in those intended for six-wheeled carriages, an additional apparatus has been introduced for this purpose, consisting of weighted levers pressing upwards against the centre pin, with a force somewhat less than the weight of the top plate. The friction due to moving a body on rollers, though small, is far in excess of that due to its revolving upon a centre pin; but the latter description of support is inadmissible in stations, owing to its instability. By merely counterbalancing the weight of the

top plate in the way described, the weight so counterbalanced is turning on a pivot, sufficient pressure is left upon the rollers to insure contact and to prevent blows, and only that part of the top plate uncounterbalanced, and the carriage which is being turned upon the rollers (together amounting to about one-third of the gross moving weight)."

Dunn's Turntable.—This table, Plate 50, is formed chiefly of wrought-iron, is very shallow, and depends entirely upon the goodness of the foundation for its good working. There are two races, an inner one of cast-iron in one piece with the socket for the pivot; and an outer one formed of ordinary 60 lbs. rails, carried in cast-iron chairs spiked down to sleepers. The floor is formed of two bridge-rails, rivetted to a plate-frame, planked between the rails. The rollers are hung in cast-iron bearings bolted to the floor.

Goods-Shed Turntable.—This table, Plate 50, is shallow, only 6 inches deep, and is suitable for laying into shed floors, for turning waggons. It is all of cast-iron.

Parsons' Turntable.—This table, Plate 52, is made with a wrought-iron floor. It is recommended by Mr. Parsons as being lighter, stronger, more durable, and cheaper than those made of cast-iron. The rollers are fixed in the curb, which is of cast-iron; and the curb and the pedestal carrying the pivot, are independent castings; leaving the table to depend for stiffness on the foundation.

Woods' Turntable.—The floor of this table, Plate 52, is constructed of wrought-iron rails framed together with a cast-iron centre piece. The race is also of rails laid in chairs. The centre is of cast-iron, and is laid independently of the race. The floor is covered with battens, and moves on live rollers.

Woods' Self-Foundation Turntable.—The floor, Plate 52, is constructed entirely of rails, with a cast-iron socket to carry the pivot, and is covered with battens. The sole and the curb are cast together, in two semicircular castings bolted together, to form the self-foundation, so as to render the table to a great extent independent of the foundation proper.

Hancock's Turntable.—Hancock has widely diverged from the ordinary plan of table, by making the pivot the most important feature. He swings the table entirely on the pivot, which is made of considerable length, and props the circumference from the base of the pivot or pillar, as in an ordinary wharf-crane, working with rollers bearing round the pillar. The load of a waggon resting on the table, is thus, when fairly balanced, entirely borne by the pillar, the function of the bearing-surfaces, at the base of the pillar, being to meet unbalanced pressure. This table, when in good order, works with ease, as the resistance of friction is in all parts reduced to a minimum. But it is expensive in construction, in the foundation it wants firmness and base, it is essentially top-heavy, and experience has proved the difficulty of maintaining it in good order.

Ellis's Turntable.—Ellis's table, like Hancock's, is hung on a central spindle, which is, unlike Hancock's, carried in a foot-step suspended from above by tension-rods going to the curb-ring at the surface. In the foundation, Ellis's is better and more simply devised than the other, as he throws the load entirely upon the upper surface of the curb-masonry. Yet, the method of suspension is wanting in rigidity, and Ellis uses guide rollers at the circumference of the floor to steady its motion. The necessity for guide-rollers in this, as in Hancock's table, leads us to the general practical conclusion, that a wide foundation, and widely-placed bearings, are both the most convenient, and the most conducive to durability.

It seems, then, essential to a carriage or waggon turntable, good for general purposes, that the parts of the table be few and simple; that there be little framework about it, in order to insure stiffness; that, for the same reason, it should be compact and self-contained; that the strain be conveyed directly to the points of resistance, through the fewest points of contact,—a condition necessary for withstanding the variety of concussions to which the table is exposed; that the base should be co-extensive with the floor, the supports being liberally and widely distributed; and that the table should not require more than ordinary attention.

CHAPTER II.

ENGINE-AND-TENDER TURNTABLES.

TURNTABLES for engine-and-tender are usually on the following plan:—a circular pit is sunk of the required diameter; two parallel baulks of timber occupying one line of rails, framed together and filled in with cast-iron footplates, constitute the floor or wearing part; being supported by a pair of rollers at each end, running on a circular rail, and by a small ordinary turnplate, with six rollers about the centre. The table is turned by gearing attached to one or more of the outer rollers. In some cases, though not usually, the segmental vacancy at each side of the floor is covered with a light deck supported by rollers on the outer rail. This is more finished looking, but it adds to the weight to be moved.

Fox, Henderson, & Co's. table, Plate 51, is an example of the ordinary kind of table. John Winder's is of a plainer construction, mostly of timber; the gearing is simple, and the table is very easily worked. In Yule & Wilkie's table, the two rollers diametrically opposed, which are in other tables turned by independent gearing, are worked from one pair of winch-handles, to which the manual force is applied. This arrangement increases the quantity of gearing to some extent, and of course the driving power required. The longitudinal beams in the floor, under the

rails, are in four parts, swivelled upon the central girder, to allow the end-rollers to follow any irregularities of the foundation, and thus maintain their adhesion for driving. Lloyds, Foster, & Co's. table, Plate 52, is simple and good.

The main condition of success about a large turntable, is a perfectly unyielding foundation. It is indispensable for proper action; as a want of rigidity about the foundation very greatly increases the labour of working the table. For large areas of 30 to 40 feet in diameter, it is impracticable to make the floor of the table itself sufficiently rigid, independently of the foundation, without incurring an unwarrantable expenditure; and the proper course, where the soil is not reliable, is to lay a thick bed of concrete over the whole area, 2 feet deep or thereby, well cemented, and closed with iron borings rusted into the upper surface. An excellent example of this kind of foundation exists at the Berwick station of the North British Railway, applied by Mr. Bell, the resident engineer. In addition to the concrete bed, he lays a foundation of half-baulks of timber, laid radially under the arms of the sole of the table, and polygonally under the race, bedded flush with the concrete.

Allan's floating table, Plate 52, is an ingenious application of hydrostatic principles. The table consists of a watertight wooden float, resting on a water-surface, in a watertight pit. It is thus free to move with a slight exertion of force, whether loaded or unloaded. The level of the table is not materially affected by the load placed upon it; as the slightest depression of the table is accompanied by a great rise of water around it, and by a relative accession of hydrostatic pressure to buoy up the load. Results of trials have shown that this table works with very great ease; and it possesses the advantage of being independent of the quality of the foundation, as the water-medium of support adapts itself to every irregularity of surface.

CHAPTER III.

TRAVERSERS.

THE traverser, Plate 50, is a convenient substitute for turntables. It runs on rails laid transversely to the parallel lines of rails at stations, and at the same level, so as not to require pits or trenches. The traversers made by Dunn, Hattersley, & Co., are much used, and work successfully. They are made of either cast or wrought iron. The wheels on which they are carried are placed in pairs, as shown, to pass the gaps in the transverse rails without shock.

SECTION III.—WAGGON-HOISTS.

HOISTS and drops are interposed at what may be called breaks of the line, at railway stations, to raise or lower goods, as the case may be, between one line of rails and another, or between the rails and the common road, or the road and the platform. They are used for shifting loaded

waggons, in the goods department; and passengers' luggage, in the passenger department.

Waggon-hoists consist generally of a platform sufficiently large to carry a railway waggon, suspended between four posts at the corners, which guide the platform and carry the

2 s

balance-weights, and in some cases they carry also the elevating gear.

On the Manchester and Leeds Railway, the platform is raised by four flat ropes passed over pulleys at the top of the four pillars. On the Eastern Counties Railway, the platform of the earlier hoists is lifted by a water-press, of which the ram is applied directly to the centre of the platform, and has a stroke equal to the required lift. On the Glasgow and South Western Railway, a hoist was erected, in 1840, at the Glasgow terminus, having 20 feet lift, from the floor of the warehouse to the level of the rails. The machine is supported, at the corners, by four cast-iron columns, bound together by girders at the top. The driving machinery is all placed below the level of the warehouse-floor. There are four upright revolving shafts, one at each corner, the whole depth of the machine; they carry each a sliding screw having a feather which fits a slot in the shaft, so that the screw turns with the shaft, and is free to slide vertically. Each screw supports a bracket embracing the shaft and bolted to a corner of the platform, and thus the platform is carried by the four corners. The screws gear into four cylindrical racks, parallel to and behind the shafts, placed in bearings at their upper and lower ends, and capable of revolving with the screws, in order to avoid the friction incurred by the contact of the screws with fixed racks. The upright shafts are turned simultaneously by suitable gearing below, carrying the screws round with them; and, when turned in one direction, the platform is raised; in the other direction, it is lowered. The platform is balanced by counter-weights hung within the corner columns, by chains over pulleys at the top. The machine is worked by a "six-horse" engine, and lifts from 8 to 9 tons, in about one minute. It works well and economically.

The Ten-ton Waggon-hoist, planned by Mr. Peter Ashcroft, made for the Eastern Counties Railway, in 1852, and illustrated in Plate 56, is worked on the same principle as the one just described. It is framed of timber; the circular racks have been discarded, as the friction of the screws has been found to be so small that the racks

do not at all times turn with them; fixed segmental racks, bolted to the corner pillars, are applied instead; they are simpler, and more solidly erected than the revolving racks, and they offer a greater area of bearing surface to the screws. The wood work is of pitch pine; the corner posts and lintels are 14 inches square; the platform is 21 feet by 10 feet, having four longitudinal pieces, two of them 14 by 12 inches, to carry the rails, and the other two, at the sides, 14 by 7 inches. They are floored with 3 inch planks, and are trussed with 1½ inch iron rods, and are carried on a pair of cast-iron beams, each with two eyes at the ends bored out to embrace and slide upon the four upright shafts. These shafts are 4 inches diameter, and they carry each a screw of between five and six turns, made of wrought-iron, 15 inches diameter, 3 inches pitch. The screws are made right and left-handed, in pairs, to counteract each other laterally, in the tendency to wind the platform; and wrought-iron nuts are interposed between them and the beam-ends, made with snugs to take into the beams, and prevent their turning with the screws. The upright shafts are driven by means of a system of horizontal shafts and mitre gearing, having teeth of 2 inches pitch, and 5 inches breadth, worked by a twenty-horse steam-engine. The racks are cast in lengths, fitted together, and to the pillars; and have snugs or joggles cast on the back, which are let into the pillars, and take much of the strain off the bolts. The balance weights, one at each corner, are of cast-iron, and work within enclosures formed by sheet-iron sheaths bolted to the pillars. The weights are connected by ⅝ inch chains, passing over covered pulleys at the top, to the cast-iron beams carrying the platform. Reversing gear is applied between the engine and the machine, that the platform may be raised or lowered as required. Brakes are not required. The hoist works very well.

Waggon-hoists are, at best, disconveniences; their merit lies in their compactness, and they are not used where they can be avoided. At the Birmingham station of the Midland Railway, the hoist originally placed at the goods terminus, has been superseded by an inclined plane.

SECTION IV.—LUGGAGE SLIDES AND LORRIES.

PASSENGERS' luggage is required to be transmitted from the landing of the booking office, to the railway-platform opposite the luggage-van. When the levels are the same, the luggage is at once placed on lorries and wheeled to the train. When the road-level is above that of the rails, the luggage is, in some places, slid down an inclined plane to the platform, as at the old Haymarket station for passengers, on the Edinburgh and Glasgow Railway; and, in others, where the difference of level is considerable, it is sent down a vertical shaft, as at the Waverley station of the same railway, in Edinburgh. The upright shaft, with the cradle and gearing connected with it, is called a Luggage Slide.

CHAPTER I.

LUGGAGE SLIDES.

THE only vertical luggage slides which, so far as the author is aware, are at work in this country, are the two erected in 1847, at the Waverley station, Edinburgh, designed by the author for John Miller, Esq., C.E.; and illustrated by Plate 57. The shaft is 4 feet 9 inches square, and 30 feet high. The cradle is made to fit the shaft, with a platform of wood, and framed of wrought-iron, and hung with guide-rollers working on two light rails fixed in two corners of the shaft diagonally. It is hung by a chain over a pulley above the shaft, and is balanced by a counter-weight working in a compartment boxed off at one side, with guide-rollers working on rails. Two separate chains are attached to the lower sides of the cradle and the counter-weight, which descend and pass under pulleys below the level of the platform, and terminate upon the barrel of a friction-brake conveniently placed at one side. Thus the connection is continuous, and the brakesman controls the machine in every position. The pulleys are 32 inches in diameter, the barrel 12 inches, and the brake-wheel 30 inches. Spur gearing is applied to the brakes, to be used for raising loads, when required. The cradle rests upon a raised seat at the bottom of the shaft; at the top, it is prevented from rising too far, by stops fixed into the floor, and it is fixed there by detents, aided by the extra security of the brake. A small winding handle is applied to the roller-shaft, to enable the brakesman to raise the cradle speedily, as, without loading the counter-weight to an inconvenient extent, it could not be made to ascend of its own accord. Once started, the cradle ascends easily. The brakesman can let down with safety 8 cwt. of luggage.

It would be an improvement to increase the braking power of this apparatus, not so much for the transmission of greater loads, as to improve the control of the brakesman. The brake-wheel should be 3 feet in diameter, and the strap should be lined with saugh to increase the grip. The roller should be large in diameter, to moderate the number of turns of the chains, and the angularity of the chains with respect to the pulleys.

CHAPTER II.

LUGGAGE-LORRIES.

LUGGAGE-LORRIES are used to convey luggage and parcels along the platform. Two of the most common varieties are shown in Plate 57. The Great Northern lorry has only a floor and two ends, wanting sides entirely. This plan affords great convenience for loading and unloading baggage, and works well. The floor of the lorry, also, stands low, only 10 inches from the ground. It runs on three wheels, tyred with india rubber, of which the single wheel is hung in a swivel, and is manœuvred with great facility.

The other, the Liverpool and Manchester lorry, is not so convenient as the Great Northern. It stands higher, the side being 21 inches above the floor; and is placed on four wheels, of which one pair with their axle, are swivelled under one end of the body; requiring, of course, a draw-handle to steer them. The Great Northern is, we should say, the best lorry going.

SECTION V.—INCLINE GEARING.

TRAINS are drawn up steep inclines, by locomotive power, or by stationary power, as may be found necessary or expedient. The line of demarcation between the useful employment of the one and that of the other, varies with the situation, the length of the gradient, and the state of perfection of the power.

Gradients now present fewer difficulties in ascending them by locomotive power than they did at earlier periods, as locomotives are now not only heavier than before, but are also more powerful, and the application of their power is better understood. An incline of 1 in 46 on the Manchester and Leeds Railway, is worked by locomotives; also 1 in 40 on the East Lancashire Railway, and 1 in 37 on the Birmingham and Gloucester Railway. When inclines are distant from terminal stations, it is expedient that the locomotive should be independent of stationary power; but when they occur at terminal stations, as at Liverpool, and at Glasgow on the Edinburgh and Glasgow Railway, stationary power has found a preference. The engines and gearing used first and last in working the latter incline, 1 in 42, 1¼ miles long, between Glasgow and Cowlairs Stations, have been described in two engineering periodicals of the time,* and we are indebted to these journals for the following account of the Cowlairs engines and machinery, with their performances.

---

* *Practical Mechanic and Engineer's Magazine*, vol. iii.; 1844 — *Practical Mechanic's Journal*, vol. i.; 1848-49.

The stationary system of working the incline, by engines stationed at the summit, was adopted at the opening of the line; but, from the deficiency of the power of the engines, and other defects in their arrangement, and more particularly from the objectionable working of the hemp rope then employed, the system was discontinued in 1844, and replaced by locomotive power until the end of 1847. Early in 1848, the stationary engines were reverted to, as the powerful locomotives made by Mr. Paton, the superintendent, to work the incline, were attended with two disadvantages—the slipping of the wheels, and the nuisance of steam and smoke, in the long tunnel through which the incline is made.

The stationary engines, as originally constructed, were non-condensing, and had two cylinders 28 inches diameter, 6 feet stroke, coupled to one crank shaft, making 19 revolutions per minute. The boilers, eight in number, were cylindrical, 5 feet diameter, 30 feet long, having each one flue 20¼ inches diameter; regulation pressure 40 lbs. A spur-wheel was placed on the crank shaft, 12 feet diameter, working a front or first-motion pinion of 6 feet 7 inches diameter, and a back or second-motion pinion, same size. The shafts of these two pinions were connected by two pinions, 8 feet and 5 feet diameter, to yield two speeds of the traction-rope; and by placing the shafts on sliding pillow-blocks, the one or the other could be geared with the wheel. In practice, the first-motion was never applied, for want of power. The rope traversing the incline was continuous, and passed from the up line over the main pulley at the head of the incline, 18 feet diameter, with three grooves in its circumference. From this pulley the rope passed over a 15 feet double-grooved pulley, so that the rope lapped the larger pulley three times, and the smaller pulley twice. Thence, it passed to the bogie or tension-pulley, 11 feet diameter, with two grooves, placed on a carriage on rails; the carriage had a run of 60 feet, and the tension on the rope was produced by a weight of 4 tons, suspended in a well by a chain passing over a guide-pulley, and attached to the carriage. From the tension-pulley, the rope passed round a 7 feet pulley, and returned over the tension-pulley; so that the action of the tension weight was doubled. The rope then departed from the tension-pulley, and finally passed round a vertical pulley, 10 feet diameter, to the down line of rails. On the up and down lines the rope was carried by small grooved pulleys, laid in the centre of the tracks, at about 18 feet distances apart; and it returned over a horizontal pulley, 11 feet diameter, placed below the rails at the foot of the incline. The rope was of hemp, 7 inches circumference; it was peculiarly liable to breakage, from its great friction on the pulleys, and its exposure to moisture. This objection, together with the deficiency of engine power, led to the abandonment of the rope-system in 1844.

On the resumption of the rope-system, in 1848, several alterations for the better were made. The original boilers were retained, but were re-set, with narrower and deeper flues. The furnace bars were reduced in thickness from 1¼ to ⅞ inch. The sectional area of the chimney was increased, from 9 feet to 25 feet, and the draft, formerly insufficient, is now so good as to permit of the exclusive use of culm as fuel. The cylinders were enlarged to 36 inches diameter, and the waste steam was directed into a water-tank forming the roof of the house, to heat the water for the supply of the locomotives. An auxiliary engine is employed in pumping water into the boilers during the intervals of rest. The gearing now consists of a 9½ feet spur-wheel on the crank shaft, working into another wheel of the same size on the main pulley shaft, without any other intermediate gearing. Two friction-wheels are applied, one on each side of the second spur-wheel, and are operated upon through levers attached to the piston-rods of two small cylinders. The main pulley, 18 feet diameter, has the rim of cast-iron, put on in two halves, and turned in the grooves; the unturned grooves of the original wheels having caused the rope frequently to leave the pulley. The rope is now passed but once over the tension-pulley, the intermediate 7 feet pulley having been dispensed with. The new rope is of wire, by Newall, 4¼ inches in circumference, weighing 19 tons; it is composed of six strands, each of six wires twisted round a light strand of hemp, which adds to the flexibility; it is carried upon 18 inch grooved pulleys placed in the lines of the rails at 30 feet distances.

Previous to the departure of each train from Glasgow, the locomotive intended for its conveyance is sent down the incline, from Cowlairs Station, and attached to it; and, at the same time, to the wire rope. The signal to start is then given by telegraph, to the engineman at Cowlairs;

and, after the train is set in motion, the locomotive-driver partially turns on his steam, to aid the stationary engine and increase the speed up the incline. The stationary engineman watches the approach of the train, and shuts off the steam and applies the brake shortly before the train arrives at the termination of the rope. At the same time, the locomotive-driver lets on full steam; and, as the speed of the rope becomes less than that of the train, the latter detaches itself and continues on the journey.

The action of the messenger-rope is simple and efficient. The rope is of hemp, a few feet in length, and is attached to the wire rope by means of a few loose strands lashed about it. It is finished with an iron ring, which is hung on an inverted draw-hook, with an inclined entrance, fixed to the bufferbeam of the engine. So long as the strain from the traction-rope continues, the rope retains its hold upon the engine draw-hook; but, immediately that the brake of the stationary engine is applied, the speed of the rope relaxes, and it slips off the hook, leaving the engine and train to proceed alone. The messenger-rope is afterwards detached from the main rope, and returned to the foot of the incline for further duty. As a precautionary measure, two brake-waggons, each with a brakesman, are hooked on behind, and sent up with every train; and the leading brakesman uncouples the waggons, on reaching the summit of the incline. Two or more brake-waggons are sent down the incline in front of every arriving train, to regulate the speed of descent and control the train. One waggon weighs 9 tons; two of them can take down 16 loaded carriages at 20 miles per hour, and pull up at 50 yards distance when the rails are in good order.

The time occupied by a train in ascending the incline 1½ mile long, is from 4 to 5 minutes, according to weight; or at a speed of 15 to 20 miles per hour.

It has been found from experiments made with a M'Naught's indicator, that the power consumed in driving the several parts of the engine and gearing is as follows:—

Engine driving the gearing and wire rope only:—Effective mean pressure on each piston, 9·23 lbs. per square inch; deducting 2 lbs. per inch for resistance of engine, there remains 7·23 lbs. for the resistance of the gearing and the rope, which gives 126 horse-power as the power required to drive the gearing and rope alone. A pressure of 3¼ lbs. per inch is required for driving the engine and gearing alone, exclusive of the rope; and deducting 2 lbs. per inch for friction of engine, there remains 1¼ lb. per inch for resistance of main gearing.

With the hemp rope, the resistance of engine, gearing, and rope was found to be measured by 112 horse-power at 19 turns of the crank shaft per minute; and, at 25 turns per minute, it would be 147 horse-power. This shows a considerable excess of power consumed upon the hemp rope, though it weighed only 11 tons, whilst the wire rope weighed 19 tons.

Engine drawing up a train of ten carriages:—Effective mean pressure, 20·43 lbs. per inch of piston; which, at 25 turns per minute, gives 320 horse-power required to move the gearing, rope, and train, deducting 2 lbs. per inch for resistance of engine, and 5 per cent. of the whole power for labouring friction, due to the increased pressure of the working parts in moving the train.

Engine drawing up a train of thirteen waggons:—Effective mean pressure, 28·71 lbs. per inch of piston, giving 464 horse-power, at 25 revolutions of the crank shaft per minute.

The Cowlairs Engine and gearing form an excellent example of the old school of construction:—ponderous engines, low speed of piston, and intermediate gearing to bring up the speed. The incline engines and gearing of Edinburgh, Leith and Granton Railway, at Edinburgh Station, are examples of a more advanced school, where the gearing is simple and the engines act directly upon it, with a high speed of piston. The engines consist of two horizontal cylinders, coupled to a crank shaft, as in a locomotive, and the main pulley shaft is a continuation of the crank shaft.

PART SECOND.—SUNDRY APPARATUS.

CHAPTER I.

WATER-TANKS.

WATER-TANKS are erected, to afford reservoirs of water for the supply of engines at different stations on the line, as required. They are carried on stone walls, or pillars, and are placed at some height above the rails, 12 to 15 feet, to afford a head of pressure sufficient to fill the tender in the course of a few minutes, so as to prevent delay on the journey.

Tanks may be of any form and size. They are usually rectangular, from 4 to 5 feet deep, formed of cast-iron plates 4 feet square, ¼ inch thick, with flange-joints made with rust or india rubber, and bolted together; and otherwise detailed as shown in Plates 53, 54. The bottom of the tank is supported on a row of cast-iron beams, one under every joint in the plate. Carrett's tank, Plate 53, is hexagonal, to suit the design of the building which carries it.

Water-tanks are filled either by gravitation, or by pumping from a lower level; and, in the latter case, the pump, and the engine and boiler if any, are usually erected within the building, as exemplified in Plate 53.

A level-gauge should be applied to the tank, to show at all times the depth of the water it contains, without. A good and simple gauge is made by bringing down a small tube from the bottom of the tank, next the wall, and terminating it with a ½ inch glass tube, of which the length is equal to the depth of the tank, fixed in a frame against the wall. Within the tube depends a wire attached to a float at the surface of the water, and terminated with a small solid body as a mark, say a piece of red sealing-wax, which has the range of the glass tube. The mark rises and falls with the float, and indicates, upon a scale of inches placed behind the tube, the level of the water. A cock should be adapted to the lower end of the glass tube, to let off water, and scour the tube.

A pipe of 9 or 12 inches diameter is led from the bottom of the tank to the watercranes or columns from which the tenders are filled. If for the supply of one crane only, 6 inches diameter is sufficient. The flow through the main pipe is regulated by a sluice-valve, or by a conical plug, over the entrance, as done by Carrett. In some cases, the tank is placed just where the supply is wanted; and a short nozzle is fixed to the side of the tank, next the bottom, fitted with a shut-off valve; and with a leather hose well bound to it, which depends from it when not in use, and is lifted up, and placed with its lower end into the entrance of the tank to be filled.

In frosty weather, the water must be heated to prevent its freezing. When the pumping engine is under or near the tank, the exhaust steam may be sent through the water, and the boiler chimney may also be taken through the tank, as done by Carrett, Plate 53; or, in absence of such means, heating apparatus may be applied, similar to what is commonly used for heating conservatories by the circulation of hot water. Fox, Henderson, and Co. apply a simple apparatus, Plate 54, consisting of a cast-iron firebox and shell, from the inner of which proceeds a 6 inch cast-iron flue right up through the tank, and from the outer shell proceeds a 12 inch pipe enveloping the flue, carried up to the bottom of the tank, and open to it, admitting of a free circulation of water about the firebox and the flue.

CHAPTER II.

WATER-PUMPS.

DIRECT action pumps are cheapest, best, and most compact; and, probably, Carrett's style of pump, Plates 53, 54, is best suited for railway purposes. In Plate 53, his pump, engine, and boiler, are placed all on one foundation, and are said to be capable of raising 22,000 gallons, 50 feet high, in 10 hours. They are built over the well from which the water is drawn, or if necessary at a convenient distance.

Carrett's larger pump, Plate 54, is said to be able to lift 30,000 gallons, 50 feet high, in 10 hours. The cylinder is 7¼ inches diameter, with 10 inch stroke; the pump ram is 6¼ inches diameter; and, being connected direct with the piston, has also 10 inch stroke. The crank-shaft is prolonged to carry a belt-pulley or pinion, from which a motion may be derived for driving the machinery of a small repair-shop. The larger sizes of pump to raise 75,000 gallons and 100,000 gallons in 10 hours are of a similar construction proportionate; but in cases where the water-line in well exceeds 20 to 25 feet in depth, a " Deep-water Lift " arrangement is applied in which the pump is put down in the well.

CHAPTER III.

WATER-CRANES.

WATER-CRANES are erected in connection with water-tanks, or other sources of water-supply; and they are posted in such situations, at a distance from the tanks, as are convenient for the delivery of water to the engine-tenders. They are made under a variety of forms, reducible to two classes: swing-cranes, and water-columns simply, as exemplified in Plate 55. The mode of operation is simple:—the swing-cranes are turned round, so that the leather hose with which they are furnished, may drop into the opening of the tank to be filled; and, in the case of the column water-crane, from which a long hose depends, the hose is lifted up over the side of the tender, and the end laid into the opening. In Ransomes & Sims' crane, a roller is hung to the side of the swing pipe, at its entrance into the column, and rolls on an inclined path formed circularly round the top of the column; the object being to facilitate the return of the crane to its position of rest, after the tender has got its supply of water.

CHAPTER IV.

COKING APPARATUS.

THE engine-tender is supplied with coke and coal in measured loads, from platforms elevated above the rails. Basket measures, holding 1 cwt. of coke, are commonly used; but 5 cwt. measures are preferable, as, when properly handled, they expedite the coking process. The coke and coal being stored on a floor above the level of the top of the tender, it may, by a suitable contrivance, be quickly discharged into the tender.

An arrangement of this kind is shown in Plate 58, and is employed on the London and North Western Railway, Northern Division. A moveable platform is hung by one end upon the edge of the coke floor, and is balanced by a counterweight, so that it may readily be hauled up out of the way when not in use; and let down to a level with the floor, partly overhanging the tender, when the load of fuel is to be discharged. The coke is made up in 5 cwt. quantities, filled into a small iron waggon of suitable capacity, as shown; and is hauled to the extremity of the overhung platform. By a simple movement, the front side of the waggon is loosed, and, being hinged by the upper edge, it is forced open by the pressure of the coke within, and the fuel discharges itself into the tender. To empty the waggon entirely, it is tilted upon its wheels by the handle attached to the back. It is then replaced on its hind wheels, and drawn aside to make way for another loaded waggon. The small waggons weigh 3½ cwt. each.

An efficient and compact coking-machine has been erected by Mr. Ramsbottom, at the London Road Station, Manchester, where want of room was much felt. He erected a central shaft inclined from the vertical, and rigged it with suspenders all round, like the ribs of an umbrella, 20 in number, united by a ring at the extremities, 20 feet in diameter. Each suspender carries a wrought-iron cylindrical coke-box, 2 feet 6 inches diameter, and 2 feet 8 inches deep, linked to it with a bow handle and swivel, so as to be readily turned over when the load is to be discharged; and capable of holding 3 cwt. of coke. As the boxes revolve about the central shaft, they dip towards the coke-waggon, from which they can be filled directly; and they rise through a vertical height of 6 feet, towards the upper side of the tender, into which they are emptied. In this way, a stock of coke may be loaded ready for immediate delivery from consecutive boxes; and the operation of discharging 21 cwt. of coke does not exceed two minutes. The machine is revolved by hand, by means of intermediate gearing.*

CHAPTER V.

SIGNALS.

A SYSTEM of signals is indispensable on all lines, for the safe and efficient working of traffic. Signals are of various forms; the main signals, erected at stations, are mounted on pillars planted in the ground, and raised to a considerable altitude, regulated by the necessities of each case, so as to insure the signals being visible to enginemen at sufficient distances along the line. The signals are made by revolving discs, or by radiating arms, known as semaphores; the latter form is now generally preferred, as it is capable of indicating the different degrees of safety with greater distinctness and precision than the former. Some of the usual forms and arrangements of semaphores are shown in Plate 59; and, in connection with each semaphore, a lamp is shown attached to the pillar, to signal at night, and is worked in concert with the semaphore. The lamps are fitted with glasses to show three colours, red, green, and white; either fixed into and forming part of each lamp, or placed in a separate frame. In the first case, the lamp revolves on an axis, to show the red, green, or white light as required; in the second case, the lamp is made a fixture, and the frame of tricoloured glass, is shifted either with a simply vertical movement; or, radially, with a couple of glasses like spectacle-eyes, red and green, to rise before the lamp and convert what is technically a white light, into a red or a green one.

The signals in regular use are of three kinds, namely:—Semaphores, and flags, by day; and lamps by night. Flags and lamps are distinguished by colours, as follows:—

White ....*All right*—Go on.
Green........................*Caution*—Proceed slowly.
Red............................*Danger*—Stop.

---

* This notice of Ramsbottom's machine is derived from the *Proceedings of the Institution of Mechanical Engineers*, October, 1853.

Signals by semaphore are made as follow :—The signal, *All right*, is given by the arm being lowered into the sheath out of sight, as observed from an engine or train approaching the station.

The signal, *Caution*, is given by the arm being raised on the left hand side of the post, half way to the horizontal position.

The signal, *Danger*, is given by the arm being raised on the left hand side of the post, to the horizontal position. It signifies that the engine must not pass the signal-post, so long as the arm is so raised.

The semaphore lamps are lighted, to give signals, at night, by white, green, and red lights as required. Distant-signals, or such as are placed at a distance from a station, are worked from the station by means of a wire-connection, sufficiently loaded at the signal-post, to keep the wire on constant tension, and to take down the signal-arm when released.

Self-acting signals have been frequently tried, and have not, as yet, succeeded. One must draw the line somewhere, between automatic perfection, and human superintendence.

CHAPTER VI.

WEIGHBRIDGES.

WEIGHBRIDGES for railway purposes, are of various classes :—for waggons and their loads, for separate merchandise, for passengers' luggage, and so on. As they may all be constructed on the same principles, whether large or small, and really are done so by each maker, on his own system, the selection of a 25 ton weighbridge for waggons may suffice for present purposes of illustration.

The example selected, Plate 60, is that patented by Henry Pooley and Son, Liverpool, who have been long and justly famous for the excellence of their designs and the quality of their workmanship. They have studied to combine simplicity, ready means of adjustment, and relief from strain or wear of the working parts. In comparison with the earlier, or common machine, Pooley's is much in advance, in these three important points. The former contains three levers under the platform, the latter contains but two; it may be said indeed to have but one principal lever below, reaching to the foot of the pillar, as the other is properly an auxiliary, placed there to transmit the load from the other end of the platform to the main beam.

It appears, further, that, in this machine, the knife-edged bearings and fulcra are hung in swinging links, suspended within frames, so as to admit of perfect freedom of action, and to insure the clear and free suspension of the platform, which naturally, when thus suspended, seeks the lowest situation, and remains in one position. The platform, thus hung, is free from the liability of rubbing against the kerbs; and the principal and auxiliary levers preserve their proper relative positions.

By this disposition of the levers, also, all the knife-edges about the machine, are arranged in parallel planes; and, in action, their oscillations are consequently in the same direction, so as to banish the crossing or locking of the working centres, to which the older machines are liable, and which give rise to considerable inaccuracy.

The suspension of the working parts by links, further, promotes the durability of the knife-edges, as the transverse straining and friction, to which they would otherwise be exposed, is almost entirely removed; and the knife-edges of the under levers are made 6 inches long, to insure their durability.

The end centres of the under levers are ranged in the same plane horizontally, as indicated in the longitudinal section, and the material of the beams is thrown under that level, that they may rest with stability on their own centres.

The fulcrum-frames, on which the load is ultimately received, are made in separate castings, with a large square base, well bedded, and secured by holding-down bolts to the foundation.

The foundation is, in the plan of this machine, made to carry the whole load, and must be perfectly sound and unyielding; as the action of the machine is entirely dependent upon the goodness of the substructure. Our remarks on the foundations of turntables are equally applicable to those of weighbridges. The building is bound on the upper edges by a cast-iron kerb, enclosing the table, with ½-inch clearance, and made with a flange lapping the masonwork at each end, to enable it to receive and check the oscillation of the table. In certain cases, where masonry has been expensive, the fulcra of the levers have been suspended from the kerb, which has been strengthened for the purpose; and, thereby, the fulcrum-frames and the stone-foundations have been dispensed with altogether.

The under levers are surmounted by two parallel cast-iron beams, constituting the rails of the table, and of sufficient strength for that purpose; they are of the full length of the table, and are made with bearing-brackets bolted to them, having steel faces resting upon knife-edged "verges" let into the levers. The rail-beams are framed together with transoms bolted to them, and are laid with a floor of cast-iron plates, bolted to their inner flanges, covering in the whole area of the pit, and ribbed and studded on the upper surface for the convenience of horse-traffic.

The balance-lever, or steelyard, is suspended in a cast-iron frame, and is linked with its short end vertically over the extremity of the principal lever. The longer arm is graduated to a scale, indicating tons, hundredweights, or pounds, as the nature of the duty may demand, and is adjusted to any required length. The equilibrium of the machine when unloaded, is adjusted by the counterbalance appended to the steelyard. A poise, moveable along the lever, indicates the weight of any load placed on the platform of the weighbridge, until it reaches the limit of the scale; after which, loose weights are placed on the counterbalance appended, and the excess weight taken by sliding the poise on the steelyard as before.

The steelyard is formed with a chamber within the longer arm, to contain a compensating weight, which is made with a rack and pinion connection, adjustable for the purpose of maintaining the equilibrium of the machine when affected by changes of weather, or other causes. The weight carries a toothed rack in its lower side, geared into by a pinion working in bearings in the lever. A keyhole is formed within the point of the pinion, for which the key is kept by the person in charge; and by an application of the key, by the equilibrium may readily be restored. By this arrangement it is out of the power of any one to tamper with the balance, or to alter it without the consent of the properly authorized person.

The method of relieving the mechanism from strain or tear and wear, except whilst in actual use, is as follows:— The fulcrum of the steelyard is suspended by a flat-link chain, passing over a pulley on the head of the pillar, within which the fulcra of the steelyard are lodged; and thence over a quadrant, which is turned by a hand lever keyed upon the same pivot with it. When the machine is to be put in gear, for weighing, the handle is turned down to the horizontal position, and fixed by a catch on the frame; the steelyard is thereby raised into position by the chain-connection, and also, in direct connection with it, the system of levers under the platform, as well as the platform itself. The whole is then in a state of free suspension, and ready for use. To relieve the machine, the hand-lever is raised to the upright position, the chain relaxed, the steelyard let down, the under levers lowered out of contact with the platform, and the platform, with the beams sustaining it, deposited solidly upon the upper ends of the fulcrum-frames, on seats prepared for them. To facilitate the use of the relieving mechanism, the suspended parts are balanced by a counterweight, hung by a chain over a quadrant upon the hand lever, and loaded to produce a correct balance.

The leading dimensions and proportions of the weigh-bridge are as follow:—Table, 19 feet long, by 8 feet 1 inch broad; gauge of rails, 7 feet.

Under levers:—horizontal distance from the fulcra to the verges, 7$\frac{7}{16}$ inches; perpendicular distance from fulcra of main under lever to its extreme end centre, 15 feet 3$\frac{1}{4}$ inches.

Steelyard:—length of short end, from fulcrum to end centre, 1$\frac{13}{16}$ inches; length of long end, from fulcrum to end centre, 40$\frac{1}{4}$ inches; distance from fulcrum to commencement of scale, 3$\frac{3}{4}$ inches; and to end of scale, 35$\frac{1}{16}$ inches; length of scale, 31$\frac{1}{16}$ inches.

From these dimensions, the following leverages are obtained:—

inches.   inches.

For under levers, as 7$\frac{7}{16}$ to 183$\frac{1}{4}$, or as 1 to 25·3
For steelyard, as 1$\frac{13}{16}$ to 40$\frac{1}{4}$, or as 1 to 22·14

Total leverage, for the loose poises, 1 to 560

The next question is, the mutual adjustment of the permanent counterweight at the end of the steelyard, the sliding poise, and the steelyard. The principle of the machine being such that equilibrium should exist when the table is free of load, and the sliding poise is placed at the commencement of the scale, it is obvious that the dead weight of the table and under levers is to be balanced jointly by the steelyard, the permanent counterweight, and the sliding poise; and it is plain that these three may be variously apportioned, provided the condition of equilibrium

be observed. The heavier the sliding poise, the less range does it require for the balancing of given loads, and the shorter may be the steelyard; in a double proportion, also, is the permanent counterweight affected. But, though three unknown quantities are thus presented for treatment, the solution of the problem is practically controlled by convenience and by circumstances of construction: a given length and range of steelyard being adopted, the sliding poise is adjusted to the range, and to the position of the commencement of the scale with respect to the fulcrum; and the counterweight is so loaded as duly to supplement the steelyard and the poise. In the example before us, the sliding poise weighs 10 lbs. 3 ounces, and the scale commences at 3$\frac{3}{4}$ inches from the fulcrum. The total initial leverage of the poise, then, with respect to the table, is deduced as follows:—

For under levers, already found,   as 1 to 25·3
For steelyard, at commencement of scale, as 1$\frac{13}{16}$ to 3$\frac{3}{4}$, or as 1 to 2·035

Total initial leverage of poise,   1 to 51·49

The poise, therefore, at the commencement of the scale, balances an equivalent at the table, of 51·49 times its own weight, or 10 lbs. 3 oz. × 51·49 = 524·55 lbs. The range of the scale is designed to embrace a maximum of 2 tons as the load that can be weighed by the sliding poise, and the required length of the scale may be found either by direct trial, or it may be deduced from the leverage at which the poise can balance the weight. In estimating this leverage, it should be noted that the load to be balanced by the sliding poise is not only the maximum load placed on the table—2 tons; but, besides that, the equivalent load, referred to the table, 524·55 lbs., which was found to be balanced by the poise when at the commencement of the scale, and which of course requires to be balanced, or allowed for, otherwise, when the poise is removed. The total maximum load to be balanced by the poise is, then, 2 tons or 4480 lbs., added to 524·55 lbs., or, in all, 5004·55 lbs.; and the total leverage of the poise must be as its weight, 10 lbs. 3 oz., to 5004·55 lbs., or as 1 to 491·23. Dividing this ratio by the leverage of the under lever, 1 to 25·3, the result is the ratio 1 to 19·416, being the required leverage on the steelyard, to balance the maximum load; and, 1$\frac{13}{16}$ × 19·416 = 35$\frac{1}{16}$ inches, is the distance of the end of the scale from the fulcrum.

Having so determined the length of the scale, it may be graduated into equal intervals, as required for indicating hundredweights and quarters. In the example before us, the number of graduations is 160, showing intervals to measure quarters, or 28 lbs.

The range of the poise on the scale commands a measurement of 2 tons, and the loose poises placed on the seat at the end of the steelyard, are adjusted to balance 2 tons on the table; being 8 lbs. weight acting through a leverage of 1 to 560. Thus, by depositing a sufficient number of loose poises, and supplementing them with the sliding poise, any load up to the capacity of the machine, in this case 25 tons, may be weighed.

THE END.

INDEX.

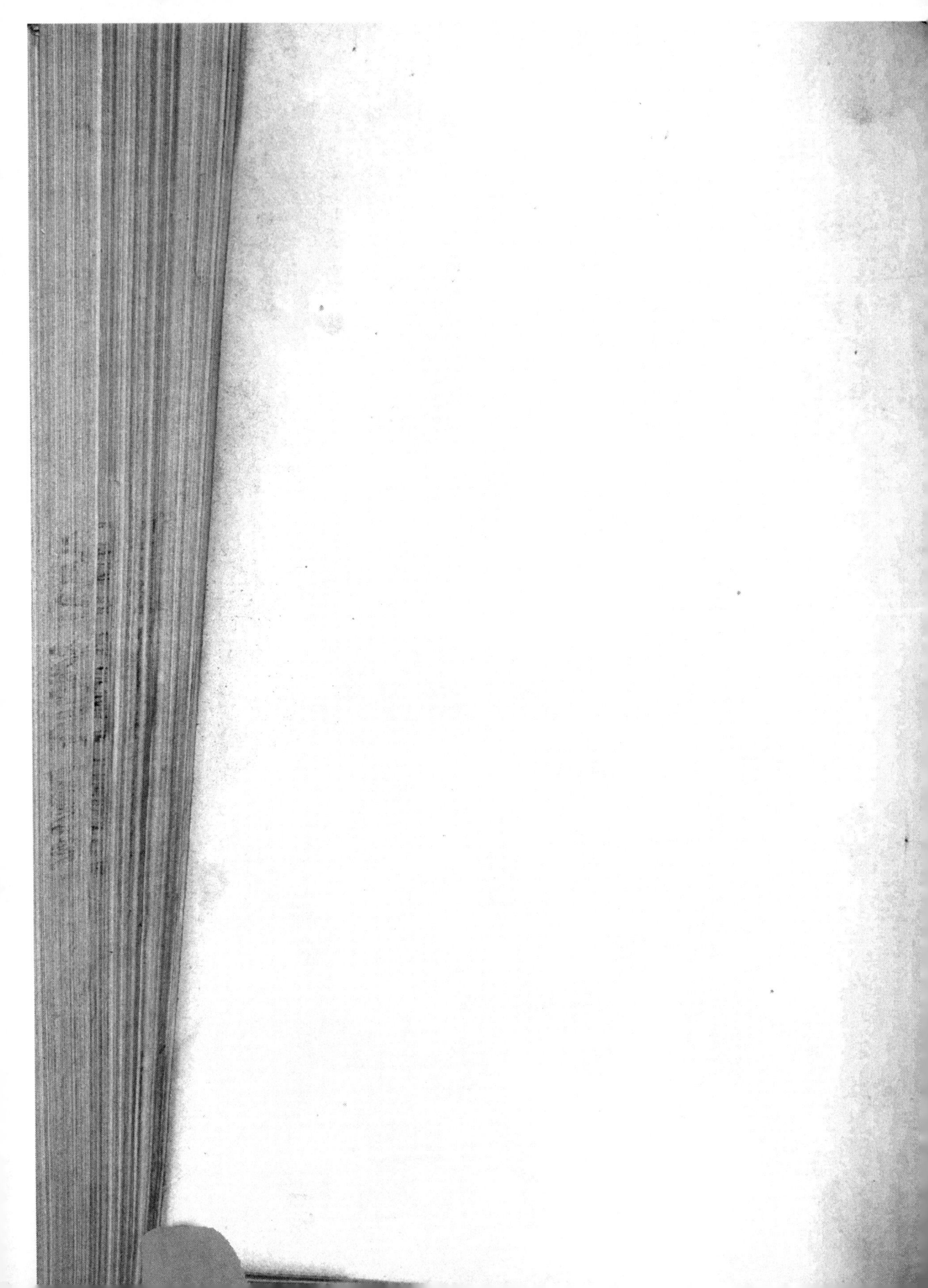

CPSIA information can be obtained at www.ICGtesting.com
Printed in the USA
BVOW051140170112

280756BV00003B/5/P